CASES AND MATERIALS ON CIVIL PROCEDURE

FIFTH EDITION

LexisNexis®

LexisNexis Law School Publishing Advisory Board

CASES AND MATERIALS ON CIVIL PROCEDURE

FIFTH EDITION

David Crump
John B. Neibel Professor of Law
University of Houston

William V. Dorsaneo, III
Chief Justice John and Lena Hickman Distinguished Faculty Fellow
and Professor of Law
Southern Methodist University

Rex R. Perschbacher
Dean and Professor of Law
University of California at Davis

Debra Lyn Bassett
Professor of Law and Judge Frank M. Johnson, Jr., Scholar
University of Alabama

2008

ISBN#: 978-1-4224-2564-0

Editorial Offices
744 Broad Street, Newark, NJ 07102 (973) 820-2000
201 Mission St., San Francisco, CA 94105-1831 (415) 908-3200
701 East Water Street, Charlottesville, VA 22902-7587 (434) 972-7600
www.lexis.com

(Pub.061)

PREFACE TO THE FIFTH EDITION

Organization and Methodology. As with the earlier editions, the Fifth Edition is organized in a traditional manner. The Fifth Edition begins with an introductory chapter that contains an overview of the litigation process and the entire subject. Subsequent chapters cover personal jurisdiction, *forum non conveniens*, subject matter jurisdiction, the *Erie* doctrine and choice of law, pleadings, discovery, summary judgment, trial practice, post-trial motions, appellate practice and procedure, preclusion doctrines, provisional remedies, enforcement of judgments, and alternative dispute resolution. Although each chapter contains one or more problems or exercises, the Fifth Edition primarily uses the case method of instruction, supplemented with copious notes and questions. Law professors will recognize most of the "old favorite" cases, including *International Shoe Co. v. Washington*, *Erie Railroad v. Tompkins*, and *Hickman v. Taylor*; modern classics such as *Burger King Corp. v. Rudzewicz* and *Reeves v. Sanderson Plumbing Co.*, and many others. Careful and rigorous editing of the cases throughout the book makes coverage of a wide variety of issues possible.

Major Revisions and Additions. Building on the foundation established in earlier editions, the Fifth Edition contains the following major revisions and additions:

- Comprehensive coverage of supplemental jurisdiction, including the incorporation of *Exxon Mobil Corp. v. Allapattah* and detailed explanatory notes.

- Expanded coverage of arising-under jurisdiction covering *Grable & Sons Metal Products, Inc. v. Darue Engineering & Manufacturing*.

- Recent Supreme Court decisions addressing pleading requirements, incorporating *Bell Atlantic v. Twombly* and other recent decisions.

- Coverage of the Class Action Fairness Act of 2005.

- Detailed coverage of e-discovery rules and e-discovery practice.

- Extensive coverage of the judge-jury relationship and the role of reviewing courts in evaluating the sufficiency of the evidence supporting the jury's verdict.

- Coverage of postjudgment motion practice and appellate complaint preservation requirements, incorporating *Unitherm Food Systems, Inc. v. Swift-Eckrich, Inc.*

In addition, amendments made to the Federal Rules of Civil Procedure and the Federal Rules of Appellate Procedure that became effective after the publication of the Fourth Edition and the proposed "restyling" amendments expected to become effective in December 2007 have also been incorporated into the Fifth Edition.

Special Features. The Fifth Edition also includes the following special features:

- *An Introduction to the Practice of Civil Litigation through Actual Litigation Documents.* Unlike most Civil Procedure books, the Fifth Edition includes documents from actual cases. Complaints and answers, motions, briefs, orders, and in the discovery chapter, a short deposition, are all excerpted for the student to review and study. A set of self-initiated disclosures adapted from a real case is also included. In some instances, a series of related papers paints a more complete picture. For example, Chapter 2 ends with an appendix containing all of the major pleadings, motions and briefs generated in a typical forum contest. Likewise, Chapter 9 contains the documents presented by both sides in an actual summary judgment proceeding, as well as President Clinton's successful motion for summary judgment in *Jones v. Clinton*. Similarly, Chapter 10 contains fascinating excerpts from the jury selection, court's charge, and final arguments in *Pennzoil Co. v. Texaco Inc.* — the case that produced the largest jury verdict in history. These unique "real world" materials help students to understand both the theory and practice of civil litigation.

- *Problems, Including "Chapter Summary Problems."* Most of the chapters contain "Chapter Summary Problems." These comprehensive problems call for application of the students' composite knowledge of the difficult parts of each chapter, requiring students to "put the chapter together" and to apply what they have learned. These problems are placed early in the chapter, encouraging the student to think about the issues beforehand, but they can be answered only after the student has studied the materials in the chapter.

- *"Improving the System."* We have included sections at the end of most chapters entitled "Improving the System." These sections are designed to help students think critically about current practice. A significant pedagogical benefit can be derived from the consideration of current problems and proposed improvements. Our experience has been that this method encourages critical thought about the purposes of procedural rules and statutes. Such critical analysis not only facilitates mastery of the materials, but also tends to more fully engage the students.

- *Supplementation of Traditional Federal Materials Though/By Comparison With State Practices; Use of California, New York, and Texas as "Benchmark" States.* It is traditional to concentrate or emphasize the federal system in first-year Civil Procedure courses. Although the Fifth Edition provides thorough and detailed coverage of federal practice and procedure, we have supplemented the federal material with a comparative explanation of analogous material taken from three benchmark states: California, New York, and Texas. We selected these states because of their size and because their procedural systems are well developed. In every chapter, the treatment of state practice is brief and is designed to enhance comprehension of the subjects covered without detracting from the book's major federal theme.

• *A "User Friendly" Book.* The Fifth Edition is also designed to be user friendly. Although Civil Procedure may be the most difficult course in the first-year curriculum, we have done our best to make fundamental concepts easier for students to comprehend. For example, we have selected cases with interesting and amusing fact patterns and particularly difficult cases are preceded by notes pointing the students in the right direction. The cases are also edited with student comprehension in mind, but without oversimplification. Our philosophy is that it is best for the student to come to class with a basic comprehension of the material in the book, so that the professor can cover more sophisticated issues during class.

• *Appendix Concerning the Quality of Life for a Litigation Lawyer.* In recent years, litigators have encountered increasing difficulty in combining a good quality of life with a professional practice in the adversary system. For this reason, the Fifth Edition contains a unique Appendix that deals with whether and how an ethical and competent litigator can live a full life and happy life. The Appendix is designed to help students avoid, or at least minimize, some of the more negative aspects of real-world litigation.

We hope and expect that you and your students will enjoy using the Fifth Edition. We know that they will find it interesting, challenging and entertaining.

DAVID CRUMP
WILLIAM V. DORSANEO III
REX R. PERSCHBACHER
DEBRA LYN BASSETT
October 2007

TABLE OF CONTENTS

Page

Page

Page

Page

Chapter 11
Post-Trial Motions

CHAPTER 1

AN OVERVIEW OF THE PROCEDURAL SYSTEM

§ 1.01 What a Civil Procedure Course Is About

A course in civil procedure concerns itself principally with the way in which people litigate in the civil courts. In the federal courts, this process is governed mainly by a set of rules called the "Federal Rules of Civil Procedure." These rules traditionally are a major component of the civil procedure course. In a larger sense, the course may be about various processes through which civil disputes are resolved, including such mechanisms as negotiation and arbitration.

There are several objectives to such a course. First, and most obviously, the course can help you to begin learning how to handle litigation. To do that, you must understand the purpose of each procedural device and the way it fits into the overall scheme of dispute resolution. Secondly, you need a knowledge of civil procedure to understand the subjects taught in your other courses. If a case in your contracts or torts casebook has been decided as it has because the complaint was inadequate or because the evidence does not support the verdict, you can understand the case better by understanding the underlying procedure.

Finally, a procedure course should make you aware of ways in which our system of justice can be improved. Just how should the jurisdiction of various different kinds of courts be defined? How strict, or how flexible, should be our standards for the sufficiency of papers filed with a court? Questions like these involve deeper issues, and the people best equipped to answer them are those who are thoroughly familiar with our procedural system.

§ 1.02 The Stages in a Civil Suit: An Introduction

Let us use a simple hypothetical dispute as the basis for an outline of litigation in a civil suit. Imagine that Priscilla Nongrata is alleged to have punched Hart Hertz in the nose in Las Vegas, Nevada. Hart Hertz suffered a (fortunately) non-fatal heart malfunction, and he is considering suit against Priscilla.

Priscilla lives in San Francisco, California (in precise legal terms, let us say that she is a "citizen" of California, residing in San Francisco). At the time of the incident, she owned a chain of restaurants, and she wanted to expand her operations. One of the restaurants she owned was in Dallas, and she wanted to open another in Houston. She telephoned Hart, a citizen of Texas residing in Houston, in an effort to undertake the venture cooperatively with him. Priscilla suggested to Hart that they both fly to Las Vegas and meet at the Starlight Hotel. While the two tycoons were meeting, they had a disagreement, and that is when Priscilla allegedly assaulted Hart.

The following discussion uses this dispute as an example. The discussion is sprinkled with various problems, each of which is designed to give you a simple situation to which you can apply the material that precedes it. At the end of this section, you will find a brief explanation for each problem.

[A] The Pre-Litigation Phase of a Civil Dispute

A great deal can happen *before* Hart files his lawsuit. In a procedure course, which is likely to focus on court decisions, there may be little that directly concerns this first stage of dispute resolution, simply because it is rarely memorialized in a reproducible form. You should be aware, however, that actions taken at this stage can affect outcomes.

Before suit, Hart Hertz must have recognized that a potential dispute has arisen and decided that its resolution calls for the mechanisms of the law. Ordinarily, he will have consulted an attorney, a process that creates an attorney-client relationship. The characterization of the dispute — is it a contract claim, or a tort, or some kind of statutory violation? — is a sophisticated undertaking in some cases. At least some investigation must precede the filing of a suit. Finally, many disputes, probably the vast majority, are settled without suit, because of the expense, delay and uncertainty of litigation. In fact, it might be said that settlement is an integral part of our civil procedure, or even that settlement is the norm and that the small percentage of cases that are judicially resolved are the exception.

[B] What Court Can Hear the Suit, and Where?: "Jurisdiction" and "Venue"

Subject-Matter Jurisdiction. One of the first questions that will face Hart Hertz's lawyer is, "What kind of court (if any) can hear this type of case?" We say that a court having power to decide a particular type of dispute has "subject-matter jurisdiction" over it.

Subject-Matter Jurisdiction in State and Federal Courts. There are state court systems, and there is a system of federal courts. Much of what each court system does is similar to what the other does. In fact, it is not unusual for *both* the federal and the state courts to have potential jurisdiction over the subject-matter of a particular dispute. In that event, the claimant has a choice. One kind of case that is within the jurisdiction of both federal courts and state courts is "diversity" cases, as they are called: cases in which the parties are citizens of different states, and in which more than $75,000 is in controversy. If Hart's suit is for more than $75,000, as is likely, his lawyer will have this option, since the parties are citizens of different states. Thus, Hart's suit may be filed in either a state court or a federal court.

Trial Courts and Appellate Courts. Within a given court system, there are different kinds of courts. For example, there are "trial" courts and "appellate" courts. The trial courts are the "intake" point. There, complaints and answers are filed, witnesses are heard, and juries render verdicts. A record is made of the proceedings, and the function of the appellate court is to review that record. In addition to this trial-appellate distinction, there are specialized courts, such as probate courts, domestic relations courts, or other particularized courts in given states, whose jurisdiction is defined.

A Diagram of the Court System. Figure 1A shows a bird's-eye view of our court system. At the top is the United States Supreme Court, which can review federal issues decided by state courts as well as judgments of lower federal courts. On the right side is the federal court system. On the left side is a prototypical state court system, with trial courts at the bottom, intermediate appellate courts, and a state supreme court.

FIGURE 1A

A SIMPLIFIED DIAGRAM OF THE SYSTEM OF STATE AND FEDERAL COURTS

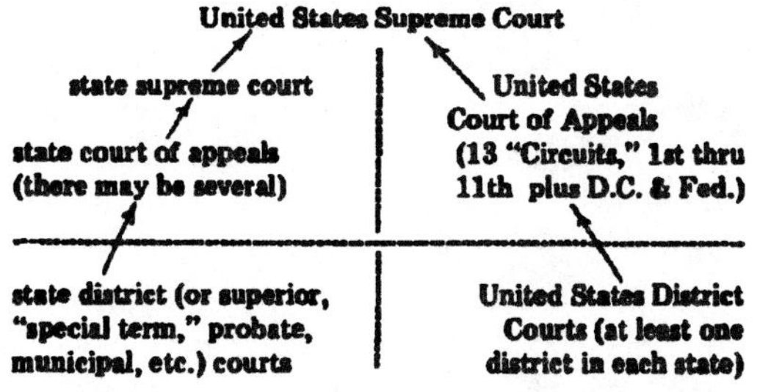

Different State Court Systems: Three States as Examples. There are many variations upon this model. In New York, for example, the "Supreme Court" (which is not supreme at all) is the general trial court; the "Appellate Division" is an intermediate court; and the "New York Court of Appeals" is the court of last resort, analogous to a state supreme court. In California, the "superior court" is the general trial court, several "district courts of appeal" comprise the intermediate level, and the California Supreme Court is at the top. In Texas, state "district" courts render judgments that are appealed to courts of appeals, and from there, a civil case can sometimes go to the Texas Supreme Court. Although each of these states has different names for its courts, the three systems are structurally similar.

A Second Jurisdictional Requirement: Jurisdiction Over the Person of the Defendant. In addition to jurisdiction over the subject-matter, the court must have jurisdiction over the person of the defendant. While subject-matter jurisdiction means power to decide this type of dispute, jurisdiction over the person means power to render a decree enforceable against this individual defendant. One of the concerns inherent in personal jurisdiction is distant forum abuse. A person who has had no contact with another state, for example, cannot properly be sued in the state courts there. If, for example, Priscilla has never had any dealings with anyone in Massachusetts, and has never been there, Hart could not file his suit there and force Priscilla to answer. In that event, the Massachusetts court might have jurisdiction over the subject-matter of the dispute, but it would not have "jurisdiction over the person" of defendant Priscilla. However, there are several proper choices open to Hart. He might, for example, prefer having the "home court advantage"; if so, he would file suit in Texas. He could file the suit either in a district court of the State of Texas, or, as we have already seen, in a federal court located in Texas; in either case, he would base jurisdiction over Priscilla's person upon the contacts she has had with Texas, including the Dallas restaurant that she owns. If he wished, Hart could probably also file suit in Nevada or California.

Serving the Papers on the Defendant. Hart must "serve" the defendant, Priscilla, with "process" (*i.e.*, with the suit papers) in a manner that conforms to law. The method varies with the situation; the traditional method is for a sheriff, marshal or other appropriate person to hand-deliver a copy of the suit papers to the defendant. This step, which gives the defendant notice of the litigation, is also necessary to the court's jurisdiction over the person of the defendant.

Venue. There may be many courts in different places with potential jurisdiction over a given dispute. Within the states of California, Texas and Nevada, for example, there would be many courts that could acquire both subject-matter and personal jurisdiction over Hart's and Priscilla's dispute. Some of them might be inconveniently located. Venue statutes provide a series of rules for determining which, among these courts, would be the most appropriate.

Forum Contests: The Motion to Dismiss. It sometimes happens that a plaintiff files suit in a given court, but the defendant does not agree that this court is a proper forum for the dispute. In that situation, the defendant may wish to file what is called a "motion to dismiss" or, in appropriate circumstances, a "motion to transfer." The plaintiff, of course, can dispute these initiatives by the defendant. A "forum contest" results. The choice of forum is important because some courts may have more advantageous rules for one side or the other, may be inconveniently distant from one party, or may have a jury pool that is likely to result in higher damages. It occasionally happens, in fact, that after a forum contest is resolved, the parties know what their lawsuit is "worth," and they promptly settle.

PROBLEM A

Amanda sues Barney for $1,000,000 in a small claims court. It should be obvious to you that there is something inappropriate about this choice of forum. What is the technical name of the concept that tells you so (*i.e.*, what is it that the court lacks)? What can Barney do about the plaintiff's choice of forum, and what will be the court's probable response? What can Amanda then do, if she wants to continue with the suit?

PROBLEM B

In Rochester, New York, Chauncey was driving a car manufactured by United Motors when he was seriously injured because of its allegedly defective design. United Motors is one of the nation's largest manufacturers of automobiles, selling many thousands of vehicles annually in every state. United is a citizen of Michigan with its principal place of business in Detroit, and Chauncey is a citizen of New York, residing in Rochester. In what court(s) could Chauncey properly sue United Motors?

A federal district court in Detroit?

A state trial court in Rochester?

A state trial court in Buffalo?

[*A possible outcome:* Chauncey will file suit in a state trial court in Rochester (not Detroit, because he wants it in his home court). United may prefer federal procedures and, if so, will "remove" the case to federal court. United may also move for a transfer of venue to Detroit, but the Rochester federal judge will probably not grant it.]

PROBLEM C

A state court of appeals "reverses" a decision by a trial court and "remands" the case to that court for a new trial. The state supreme court refuses to grant a writ of error, thereby declining to review the case. What does all of this jargon mean?

[C] The "Size" of the Lawsuit: Multiple Parties and Claims

The Simplest Situation: One "Plaintiff" Sues One "Defendant." On appeal, the appealing party (that is, the loser at trial) becomes the "Appellant." The other party is the "Appellee."

Multiple Parties in One Case. It is also possible for there to be more than one plaintiff in a case, or for the plaintiff(s) to sue more than one defendant. If, for example, Hart thinks that the Starlight Hotel was at fault in furnishing inadequate security (so that his injuries at Priscilla's hands were more serious than they otherwise might have been), he can claim against both Priscilla and the Hotel Corporation. If Hart's wife, Sarah, has a valid claim for the loss of his companionship, she may join as a plaintiff. The lawsuit would then be *Hart and Sarah Hertz, Plaintiffs, v. Priscilla Nongrata and Starlight Hotel Corporation, Defendants.* (Lawyers usually state only the names of the first plaintiff and first defendant: *Hertz v. Nongrata.*)

Multiple Claims in One Case. Sometimes a lawsuit may contain different kinds of claims. For example, if Priscilla contends that Hart assaulted her (rather than the other way around), she may file a "counterclaim." If Priscilla believes that a co-defendant is really at fault, she may file a "cross claim" (against the Starlight Hotel, for example). If she believes that a third person who is not a party to the suit should be liable, she can bring that person into the dispute by filing a "third party claim." If there is someone left out of the suit who wants to join it (example: Hart's wife, Sarah), that person may be able to "intervene." In summary, the plaintiff is not always the only party who wants to make a claim, and the rules accommodate others' doing so.

"Compulsory" Joinder. It sometimes happens that a person left out of a suit has such an important interest in it, or will be so affected by it, that it would be unfair for the suit to proceed without him or her. This is one of the circumstances in which the omitted person would be a "person[] required to be joined if feasible," in the terminology of the Federal Rules. The court then has the authority to force the parties to include him or, in unusual cases, to abort the proceedings if he cannot be included.

Complex Devices. There are other procedures designed to handle cases with very large numbers of parties or cases in which multiple inconsistent claims are asserted. The "class action," involving claimants too numerous to be brought into court individually, is perhaps the best known of these devices.

PROBLEM D

Harriet and Ida were injured in a three-car collision when Harriet's car came into contact with cars driven by Jim and Ken, respectively. Harriet and Ida think that Jim, Ken, or both, were negligent; Jim, who was also injured, thinks that the other two drivers were negligent. What is likely to happen (that is, what claims will be brought)?

[D] The "Suit Papers": Pleadings and Motions

The Complaint. Hart Hertz would commence his action against Priscilla by filing what is called a "complaint." In some states, this document is called a "petition." It sets forth in general terms the contentions upon which the plaintiff bases his legal theory, and it also states what the plaintiff wants ("a demand for the relief sought").

The Answer: The Defendant's Response to the Plaintiff's Suit. The defendant responds with an "answer" (or, in some circumstances, a motion or other procedural device), which may raise several different kinds of issues. For example, it may allege that there were procedural deficiencies in the way the action was brought, such as a lack of jurisdiction. Alternatively, it may attack the sufficiency of the complaint (different states have various names for this kind of attack, calling it respectively a "motion to dismiss for failure to state a claim," or a "special exception," or a "demurrer").

Answers "On the Merits": Admissions, Denials, and Affirmative Defenses. Finally, the defendant may attack the validity of the plaintiff's claim itself. This last kind of answer is described as an answer "on the merits." There are two basic kinds of answers on the merits: first, admissions and denials, which agree with or rebut facts claimed by the plaintiff; and secondly, affirmative defenses, which say that even if the plaintiff can prove the elements of the claim, there is an external reason why the plaintiff should not recover. Contributory negligence and the statute of limitations are examples of affirmative defenses. In Hart and Priscilla's case, for instance, Priscilla might file an answer admitting her presence with Hart at the Starlight Hotel, but denying the alleged assault (if those were the facts as she claimed them). She might also plead the affirmative defense of self-defense, if she contended that Hart had started the fight. If she believed that the court lacked jurisdiction, or that the complaint was insufficient, she might file a motion to dismiss for lack of jurisdiction or a motion to dismiss for failure to state a claim upon which relief could be granted.

Motions. A "motion" is simply an application to the court for an order of a particular kind. We say that a lawyer "files a motion" for, or "moves" for, a given kind of action by the court. The motions to dismiss discussed above are examples, and there are also other common motions. For example, if Priscilla fails to file an answer, Hart can file a "motion for default judgment," which is the kind of judgment that is available in that situation. If Priscilla answers by admitting all of Hart's allegations, the pleadings themselves might be an adequate basis for resolving the dispute. Hart then might file what is called a "motion for judgment on the pleadings." There are many other kinds of orders (in fact, an infinite variety) that a court could be asked, by motion, to grant.

Motion for Summary Judgment. If the undisputed facts developed before trial show that one side or the other is clearly entitled to judgment, a "motion for summary judgment" may be filed and granted. "Summary judgment" disposes of the case without a trial. It is available, however, *only* when there is no reasonable way in which the opposing party could prevail. For example, if Priscilla were to stipulate to the amount of Hart's damages and also were to testify in a pretrial deposition to facts unambiguously admitting that she did assault Hart and cause his injuries, Hart might be able to obtain a summary judgment.

PROBLEM E

[Taken from a tragic case, reported in the newspapers:] Larry has a terminal disease, and the only apparent way to preserve his life is a transplant of bone marrow from his relative, Marty. But Marty refuses to consent to the operation that would take the bone marrow from him. Larry therefore sues Marty. He sets out these facts in his complaint and requests that the court issue an order requiring Marty to submit to the operation. Assume that there is no legal principle enabling a person to invade the body of another for these purposes. The complaint thus cannot be the basis of any relief, even if entirely true. What procedural step is defendant Marty likely to take?

PROBLEM F

Natalie files suit against Philip, alleging that Philip's negligence in stopping his car on a public road caused Natalie certain injuries. The court has jurisdiction and the complaint is pleaded sufficiently, but Philip's position is that the facts are not as Natalie alleges them. Specifically, although Philip agrees that he did stop on a public road, he contends that he was not negligent in stopping. Further, Philip believes that Natalie herself was negligent and caused her own injuries. What pleading(s) does Philip file to get these positions considered by the court?

PROBLEM G

After the pleadings are all complete in the case of *Natalie v. Philip*, Natalie testifies in a pretrial deposition that she was traveling in her automobile at 100 miles per hour on the occasion in question and that she ran into Philip from behind while he was stopped at a stop sign. What should Philip do and what is the likely result?

[E] Discovery, Disclosures, Investigation, and Pretrial Conferences

Discovery. The term "discovery" refers to pretrial procedures by which a litigant may obtain information from opponents and witnesses. Some basic information, called "initial disclosures," must be provided by one litigant to the other without awaiting a discovery request. Other discovery methods are also available. In the case of *Hertz v. Nongrata*, for example, it is likely that each party would want to take the "oral deposition" of the other. This procedure allows an attorney to question a party or witness in the presence of a court reporter, who records the questions and answers. Depositions usually take place not in the court-room, but in a private setting such as a lawyer's office. Another discovery device, called written interrogatories, consists of written questions directed to an opponent. Priscilla might want to direct written interrogatories to Hart, asking for such information as the identities of physicians he has consulted. Still another device, called a request for production or inspection, allows a party to obtain documents or tangible items. Priscilla might use this device to obtain medical records in Hart's possession or control. A request for admissions requires the opponent to admit or deny facts and is useful for establishing undisputed matters; for example, Hart might ask Priscilla to admit that she was present at the Starlight Hotel on the day in question.

The Scope of Discovery. The rules of discovery allow for broader inquiry than the evidence that will be admissible at trial. After all, discovery is part of the investigative stage of the proceeding. Even if a particular piece of information is inadmissible, it may help to find other information that can be admitted at trial. In general, discovery extends to information that is "reasonably calculated to lead to the discovery of admissible evidence." For instance, Hart can inquire in a deposition whether Priscilla was arrested or interrogated by the police concerning this incident, even though the fact of arrest may not be admissible in evidence at trial.

Investigation. A lawyer usually does a large part of the investigation in a lawsuit on his or her own, rather than through discovery. For example, one does not usually depose a friendly witness, because that procedure would be tantamount to cross-examining him in front of the adversary. Instead, it may be better simply to interview the witness or to take a written statement from him. (There is a degree of risk in this method, however, because the written statement will probably be inadmissible at trial. If there is danger that the witness may be unavailable, taking his deposition would be better.)

Pretrial Conference. In many jurisdictions, the judge meets with the lawyers informally to discuss the way the trial is to be conducted, to explore and encourage settlement, or to rule on pretrial matters such as discovery disputes. There may be a single conference held just before the trial itself, or there may be a series of conferences, particularly in a complex case. In *Hertz v. Nongrata,* the court might very well hold a pretrial conference to discuss what the identities and order of witnesses would be, what documents might be offered by both parties at trial, how the jury might be instructed, and like matters.

PROBLEM H

While taking Priscilla's deposition, Hart's lawyer asks her what, if anything, she has heard other people say about the alleged assault that is the focus of the suit. Priscilla's lawyer correctly interjects that the question calls for hearsay. Hart's lawyer, in response, points out that although the answer might not be admissible at trial, it might allow him to find and interview useful witnesses. Is the question properly within the scope of discovery? Why or why not?

PROBLEM I

What would be the best method(s) to obtain information from the following persons?

a. Information about how an automobile accident happened from the opposing party in the suit, who is expected to be evasive in answering questions.

b. Information as to what doctors the opposing party consulted, and what charges he paid for what services.

c. Information from the physician your own client consulted (the physician is forthcoming with answers and will be available for trial).

d. The exact appearance and condition of the vehicle that was involved in the accident, which is in the control of the opposing party.

e. Verification that the defendant was indeed the person driving the accident vehicle.

[F] The Trial Itself

Functions of the Judge and of the Jury. The judge presides over the trial and decides questions of law. The proper definition of an assault and the admissibility or exclusion of evidence are examples of questions of law that might come up in *Hertz v. Nongrata.* The jury, on the other hand, decides disputed questions of fact. Whether Priscilla's conduct amounted to an assault as defined, and whether her representations of self-defense are credible, are examples of factual issues that the jury might resolve. Sometimes, a trial may be held before the judge sitting without a jury (a "non-jury trial" or "bench trial"), and in that event, the judge decides both the facts and the law.

Jury Selection. Potential jurors are summoned at random to create an array or panel. These potential jurors, or "venire members," are subject to examination by the judge (or by the lawyers, or by both) to determine their fitness to serve. The attorneys can "challenge" any juror they believe is disqualified (for example, one who has an unacceptable bias against a party). The number of challenges for this reason, called "challenges for cause," is unlimited. In addition, the attorneys have a specified number of "peremptory" challenges, by which they may remove a certain number of venire members without stating any reason. In the trial of *Hertz v. Nongrata,* for instance, if a potential juror said she disliked Priscilla so much that she could not judge the case fairly, Priscilla's lawyer would exercise a challenge for cause to remove her. If Hart's lawyer senses that a particular venire member is unlikely to award damages in a significant amount, he can use a peremptory challenge to remove this individual.

Opening Statements and Presentation of the Case. After the jury is empanelled and sworn, the lawyers make opening statements, explaining to the jurors the testimony they expect to offer. The plaintiff, Hart, would then present his witnesses and evidence, followed by Priscilla. Both sides may offer rebuttal or surrebuttal evidence.

Rules of Evidence. Not every sort of information may be heard by the jury. For example, with certain exceptions, hearsay is excluded. Thus if Hart were to offer to testify that other individuals had made informal statements to him about the alleged assault, Priscilla's lawyer could object to and exclude this testimony.

Burden of Proof. Hart Hertz would have the "burden of proving" the elements of his assault and battery claim. This burden of proof, in turn, implies two different kinds of obligations. First, Hart must introduce evidence that is at least minimally sufficient to support a finding by the jury. If he produces no evidence, he loses. Thus we say that Hart has the "burden of producing evidence" or the "burden of production." Furthermore, Hart has the burden of persuading the jury that his claim is probably correct. This "burden of persuasion" is by the "preponderance of the evidence"; in other words, the jury must be satisfied by the preponderance, or the greater weight, of the credible evidence that Hart's claim is correct. (Notice that civil cases do not require proof "beyond a reasonable doubt"; that more stringent standard applies to criminal cases.) What about Priscilla's affirmative defense of self-defense? In most jurisdictions, Priscilla, as defendant, would have the burden of proof on this issue; she would therefore have the burden of producing evidence sufficient to authorize a jury finding and the burden of actually persuading the jury by the preponderance of the evidence, on her affirmative defense.

Motion for Judgment as a Matter of Law. If Hart Hertz were to testify that he could not remember the incident because it all happened very quickly, and if he were to rest his case without producing any other evidence about the event, he would not have carried his burden of production. The jury could not reasonably make a finding by the preponderance of the evidence in his favor. In this situation, defendant Priscilla could move for, and the court could grant, a "judgment as a matter of law" (formerly called a "directed verdict," sometimes called an "instructed verdict"). This procedure aborts the trial and prevents a party from having his or her claim or defense decided by the jury. The standard for this procedure, understandably, is stringent: the judge must be satisfied that there is no reasonable way for the jury to decide in Hart's favor. In that circumstance, we say that the movant is entitled to judgment "as a matter of law," and the judge decides it.

Jury Arguments, the Court's Charge, and the Verdict. After all of the evidence has been presented, the parties' attorneys may make arguments to the jury. They tell the jury what they think the evidence shows and explain how they think their factual inferences fit with the law that will be given by the judge. The judge then "charges" the jury, giving it definitions of necessary terms and legal propositions essential to the decision. The jury deliberates; it returns an answer (or answers) called its "verdict."

PROBLEM J

In a case tried before a jury, the plaintiff has introduced some evidence that a person could within reason believe, covering each issue required to be proved by the plaintiff.

However, the judge believes that the preponderance of the evidence favors the defendant — that is, the defendant would win if the judge were hearing the case in a non-jury trial. If the defendant files a motion for judgment as a matter of law, how should the court rule on it, and why?

PROBLEM K

Quentin was killed in an automobile accident. His heirs have brought suit against the estate of the other driver, who was also killed. Robert was a passenger in Quentin's car and was the only witness who survived. Robert made a detailed oral statement to the investigating officer, Officer Smith, showing that the other driver was grossly negligent and caused Quentin's death. But three months later, witness Robert unexpectedly dropped dead of a heart attack. At the trial, Quentin's heirs plan to offer the testimony of Officer Smith as to what Robert told him about the accident. What will happen if they do so? What ruling is the court likely to make if the defendant's lawyer objects? If Quentin's heirs have no other evidence, what motion will the defendant's lawyer make, and what will be the probable ruling?

[G] The Post-Trial Stage

Post-Trial Motions: Renewing the Judgment as a Matter of Law. If the verdict loser believes that the verdict is unsupported by the evidence, she may renew her "motion for judgment as a matter of law" (formerly called a "motion for judgment notwithstanding the verdict" when requested post-verdict). This procedural device is closely similar to the motion for judgment as a matter of law requested before the jury leaves the courtroom: it can be granted only if there is no reasonable way to infer support in the evidence for the jury's decision, so that the moving party is entitled to judgment as a matter of law. For example, if the jury finds for Hart after he has rested his case in *Hertz v. Nongrata* without offering evidence other than his own testimony that he cannot remember the event, judgment as a matter of law can properly be granted in Priscilla's favor.

Motion for New Trial. In the alternative, the verdict loser may make a "motion for new trial." The function of this procedure is quite different from that of the post-trial motion for judgment as a matter of law; it seeks relief from trial errors or other procedural miscarriages. For example, if the jury has found in Hart's favor, but Priscilla persuades the judge that he gave the jury an erroneous charge, the court may be able to grant her a new trial.

Judgments and Remedies. The court will, in the final analysis, issue a "judgment" (either based on the verdict or contrary to it) stating what relief is granted or refused. The relief may be money damages ordered to be paid, or an injunction, or a "declaratory judgment" that states what the legal rights of the parties are — or it may be a judgment for defendant, stating that plaintiff shall "take nothing."

Enforcement of Judgment. The issuance of a judgment does not always result in its satisfaction. If the defendant fails to pay, the court may issue a "writ of execution," ordering an officer to seize and sell his non-exempt assets, if any. There are enforcement procedures in addition to execution, such as post-judgment "garnishment," which is a means of obtaining property due the defendant but held by third persons.

The Binding Effect of Judgments: Res Judicata. A judgment, once entered and final, can be asserted as a bar to a later suit raising the same claim. This doctrine is called "res judicata," which is Latin for "the thing has been adjudicated."

PROBLEM L

The jury has found defendant Tom negligent and has also found that his negligence proximately caused $50,000 in damages to Ursula. Tom finds an opinion of the state supreme court disapproving the definition of negligence that the judge used in his instructions to the jury. Does this mean that Tom is entitled to a judgment as a matter of law? Why or why not? If not, what should Tom do to assert his rights? Assuming that the trial judge concludes that this case is distinguishable from the state supreme court case Tom relies on, and that the definition was correct, what will happen next? What if Tom has no unusual assets, but has a house and a car (both of which are exempt from execution under controlling law) and a bank account containing $2,000? If, after the judgment becomes final, Ursula brings another suit on the same claim because she thinks she should have recovered a larger amount, what can Tom do?

[H] A Side Issue: One Jurisdiction Applies Another's Law

The Law Binding a Court. A state trial court is bound by statutes passed by the state legislature, by the ruling of appellate courts over it, and by the state constitution. All courts are bound by federal law, including the United States Constitution. (In fact, there is nothing anomalous about a state court's deciding a claim that is based upon federal law; that happens frequently.) But by the same token, courts in one state are not generally bound by the rulings of courts in another state. If, in one of your casebooks, there appears an opinion of the California Supreme Court alongside an opinion of the New York Court of Appeals that reaches the opposite conclusion, this does not mean something is wrong; the law of the two states on this issue is merely different.

Conflict of Laws (or "Choice" of Law). Sometimes courts apply the law of another state in deciding a case. For example, if Hart's suit against Priscilla is heard in a Texas state court, it might be appropriate for that court to apply the law of Nevada in defining assault and battery or self-defense. The parties were in Nevada when the conduct at issue took place. They would be likely to expect Nevada law to govern, and Nevada has the most direct interest in regulating their conduct.

State Law in the Federal Courts (and Vice Versa). As we have seen, Hart's suit could have been brought in either a state or a federal court. But there is no federal law prohibiting this alleged assault and battery; the law governing a garden-variety brawl in Nevada (or any other state) is state law. Accordingly, a federal court would use state law in these matters. If, for example, Hart's suit were brought in a federal court located in Texas, that court would try to decide it the way a Texas state court would. (The Texas court might follow Nevada law, and if so, the federal court would too.)

PROBLEM M

Arnold, a citizen of Massachusetts, and Billy, a citizen of New York, drove to Florida. While in Florida, they had an accident in which Billy was injured and which he attributes to Arnold's negligence. Billy later files suit for $500,000 against Arnold in a Massachusetts state court. Incidental question: Does the Massachusetts state court have jurisdiction? Principal question: What state's legal principles should the Massachusetts state court use to decide whether Arnold should pay Billy? What would be the answer if the case were brought in a federal court located in Massachusetts?

[I] Appeals

The Functions of an Appellate Court. An appellate court does not normally hear evidence or decide disputed questions of fact. It has two functions: to decide whether the case was tried in accordance with the law and to determine whether the evidence in the record supports the verdict according to legal standards.

An Appellate Court's Review of the Evidence. In reviewing the evidence, moreover, the appellate court cannot reverse merely because it disagrees with the jury. It must determine that the evidence is not reasonably capable of interpretation so as to support the verdict under the applicable law. Thus, when an appellate court speaks of "the facts" in the case, it may be speaking only about the set of inferences that best support the verdict. The court may eliminate the bulk of the evidentiary disputes in describing what happened in the lower court, and a case that took weeks to try may emerge in the opinion as a short, simple narrative.

The Documents and Record Before the Appellate Court. The appellate court considers only the briefs of the parties, the record (consisting of the evidence and papers filed in the case), the arguments of counsel (if any), and the law.

PROBLEM N

George has lost a jury trial in which all of the issues were hotly disputed in the evidence. George believes that the opponent's witnesses did not tell the truth, that the jury was hoodwinked, and that the opposing lawyer thus obtained a verdict that does not conform to the true facts. Can he use these arguments to obtain a reversal on appeal?

BRIEF ANSWERS TO PROBLEMS IN THIS SECTION

A. The small claims court lacks subject-matter jurisdiction. Barney can make a motion to dismiss, which the court should grant. Amanda can then file suit in the proper court.

B. A federal court in Detroit has both personal jurisdiction (United obviously has sufficient contacts there) and subject-matter jurisdiction (there is diversity of citizenship, and the "serious injury" will exceed $75,000). The state court in Rochester also has both kinds of jurisdiction (United sells automobiles there). So, probably, does the state court in Buffalo; venue rules may, however, enable United to challenge this forum.

C. This jargon means that the court of appeals has nullified the trial court's judgment, it is sending the case back for retrial, and the state supreme court has refused to consider reversing the reversal.

D. Harriet and Ida can join their claims against Jim and Ken. Jim can counterclaim against Harriet and cross-claim against Ken. (In fact, given human nature, everybody may wind up claiming against everybody else.)

E. Marty can file a motion to dismiss for failure to state a claim upon which relief can be granted.

F. Philip would file an answer denying negligence and causation (and, if required in this jurisdiction, admitting other facts claimed by Natalie that he believes are true). He should also include the affirmative defense of contributory negligence in his answer.

G. Philip should move for summary judgment, because the only reasonable interpretation of the undisputed evidence is that he was not causally negligent as Natalie alleged.

H. Priscilla's answer to this question is discoverable because the information, although it is hearsay, is reasonably calculated to lead to the discovery of admissible evidence.

I. (a) Oral depositions are the superior means of obtaining controversial information from an opponent. (b) Interrogatories are useful for obtaining this sort of specific information. (c) It may be best first to interview this cooperative witness rather than depose him. (d) A request for production and inspection obtains access to the vehicle in the opponent's possession. (e) A request for admissions efficiently establishes non-controversial facts.

J. The court cannot grant judgment as a matter of law because the standard for this procedure is that there must be no way a reasonable juror could find for the opponent. (The judge's inferences about the preponderance of the evidence are irrelevant here; that's the jury's job.)

K. Officer Smith's repetition of Robert's statements is inadmissible hearsay, and the defendant should be successful in moving for judgment as a matter of law if there is no other evidence.

L. Tom is not entitled to judgment as a matter of law. He would have to show that he is entitled to judgment as a matter of law (meaning that no reasonable person could find for Ursula on the evidence). Tom may succeed, however, in a motion for new trial. If there was no error, the judge would grant judgment in accordance with the jury's verdict. Tom's exempt assets cannot be executed upon, but a writ of garnishment may be used with respect to the bank account. Tom should plead res judicata to bar Ursula's assertion of the same claim after final judgment.

M. The Massachusetts state court would have jurisdiction. It *might* very well apply Florida law in deciding the merits; it is impossible, however, to provide a definitive answer. A *federal* court located in Massachusetts would apply whatever state's law a Massachusetts *state* court would apply — including Florida law, if that were the case.

N. In most jurisdictions, an appellate court has no authority to consider the factual disputes George seeks to raise.

§ 1.03 Jurisdiction: The Court's Power to Act

HOW TO READ THE CASE OF *STRAWBRIDGE v. CURTISS*

As you read the case that follows, you should take care to understand its procedural history. In what court was the suit filed? Where did it go from that court? What is the procedural issue that controls the disposition of the case? How does the court decide that issue? What are the sources of the law that the court uses to decide it, and how is its reasoning explained? (Specifically, is it an interpretation of the Constitution, of a rule of court, of a statute, or of that court-generated body of principles that we refer to as the "common law"?)

The case concerns the scope of diversity jurisdiction. If a plaintiff who is a citizen of one state sues a defendant who is a citizen of another state, the problem is straightforward. But what is to be done if a plaintiff sues one defendant of diverse citizenship and, in the same suit, also sues another who is of the same citizenship as the plaintiff? The Constitution is the ultimate source of diversity jurisdiction, but it does not provide much guidance in this case. It simply says that the "judicial power shall extend . . . to Controversies . . . between citizens of Different States." U.S. Const. art. III, § 2. This constitutional provision is implemented by a statute passed by Congress, which (in its present form) says that the federal district courts have jurisdiction over "all civil actions where the matter in controversy exceeds the sum or value of $75,000, . . . and is between . . . Citizens of different States." 28 U.S.C. § 1332. The dispute in *Strawbridge v. Curtiss* is controlled by an earlier version of this statute, but the outcome does not depend on that difference. (Incidentally, the "circuit" court at that time was the federal trial court.)

Strawbridge v. Curtiss is a venerable case, decided by one of this nation's most famous chief justices, and the principle that it enunciates is still good law today.

Read 28 U.S.C. § 1332 (the diversity statute) and U.S. Const. art. III, § 2 (the constitutional diversity provision).

STRAWBRIDGE v. CURTISS
7 U.S. (3 Cranch) 267 (1806)

THIS was an appeal from a decree of the circuit court, for the district of Massachusetts, which dismissed the complainants' bill in chancery, for want of jurisdiction.

Some of the complainants were alleged to be citizens of the state of Massachusetts. The defendants were also stated to be citizens of the same state, excepting Curtiss, who was averred to be a citizen of the state of Vermont, and upon whom the *subpoena* was served in that state. . . .

MARSHALL, CH. J. delivered the opinion of the court.

The court has considered this case, and is of opinion that the jurisdiction cannot be supported.

The words of the act of congress are, "where an alien is a party; or the suit is between a citizen of a state where the suit is brought, and a citizen of another state."

The court understands these expressions to mean, that each distinct interest should be represented by persons, all of whom are entitled to sue, or may be sued, in the federal courts. That is, that where the interest is joint, each of the persons concerned in that interest must be competent to sue, or liable to be sued, in those courts. . . .

Decree affirmed.

NOTES AND QUESTIONS

(1) *What Kind of Jurisdiction?* This case concerns a jurisdictional issue, as you can infer from its placement in this book. But what kind of jurisdiction is at issue — subject-matter jurisdiction or jurisdiction over the person of the defendant? [Note: Don't be confused by the fact that diversity jurisdiction has something to do with the state affiliations of the parties. Subject-matter jurisdiction is power to decide the generic type of dispute, while personal jurisdiction concerns the court's power to bind a particular defendant.]

(2) *Constitutional Versus Statutory Interpretation.* Is this decision an interpretation of the Constitution or of the diversity statute passed by the Congress? What difference would it make? [Note: If it is a Constitutional decision, could Congress *ever* provide for jurisdiction in this situation? If it is not based on the Constitution, couldn't Congress do so simply by rewriting the statute?]

(3) *Who "Won"?* What does this decision mean to the parties? Who has "won," and what does it mean to say that the party has "won"? What can the plaintiff do now?

HOW TO BRIEF THE CASE OF *STRAWBRIDGE v. CURTISS*

Within your first week in law school, you will probably be introduced to the concept of "briefing" a case. A case brief is just a set of notes about the case, abstracting its important elements, which usually include such aspects as the parties, the issues, the court's holding and the reason for the court's decision. There are an infinite variety of ways to go about briefing, and you should use the method that your instructor prefers. (For example, if he or she suggests that you note the holding of each court that has had anything to do with the case, do so.) In the alternative, you should use the method that you find most useful. Briefing is a means of forcing yourself to undertake systematic analysis of the case and of providing yourself with a convenient way to remember it, and the best way for you may be different from that for your neighbor.

With these qualifications in mind, you should consider Figure 1B. It contains a brief of *Strawbridge v. Curtiss*, done in one of the many possible ways that it could be done. Having seen this sample, you should brief the next case yourself.

FIGURE 1B

Strawbridge v. Curtiss (S. Ct. 1806)

I. Facts: citizens of Massachusetts sued citizens of Vermont and Massachusetts in a "circuit" court (then the federal trial court). That court dismissed for lack of jurisdiction; appeal to S. Ct.

II. Issue: Must all parties be of diverse citizenship from all adverse parties for diversity jurisdiction to exist in the federal courts?

III. Narrow holding: Dismissal affirmed. No jurisdiction.

IV. Broad holding: The diversity statute as passed by Congress required complete diversity among all adverse parties.

V. Reasoning: The Act of Congress conferring jurisdiction said that a diversity suit could be brought "between a citizen of a state . . . and a citizen of another state." The Court interpreted this language to mean that all claimants must be qualified to sue all defendants.

HOW TO READ THE CASE OF *WYMAN v. NEWHOUSE*

Remember that the plaintiff must have the suit papers "served" upon the defendant. Remember, too, that the defendant must have some kind of relationship to the court, such as contacts with the state in which it is located. Another way for jurisdiction to attach is for the plaintiff to have the defendant served *while he is within* the state.

In essence, that is what *Wyman v. Newhouse* is about. But it is about a great deal more: the foulest of treachery, the mystery of intrigue, and the triumph of justice through good legal advice to the defendant, all combine to make this a wonderful case. As you read it, ask yourself: Why did Ms. Wyman engage in the treachery that so unfortunately characterized her actions? What advantage did she hope to gain?

WYMAN v. NEWHOUSE
93 F.2d 313 (2d Cir. 1937)

[Sarah Wyman sued Edgar Newhouse in a Florida state court. Her complaint included claims for "money loaned, money advanced . . . , and for seduction under promise of marriage." Following his lawyer's advice, Newhouse did not answer the suit, and a default judgment was entered against him.

[Because Newhouse had no assets in Florida, the Florida judgment was itself of no value to Wyman. However, she filed an "action on the judgment" in a federal District Court in New York. An action on the judgment is a suit of a peculiar kind: it pleads that the plaintiff has a judgment from another state, and it asks the court to enter a judgment enforceable within its jurisdiction.

[The Full Faith and Credit Clause of the Constitution requires courts to honor "the public Acts, Records, and Judicial Proceedings of every other State." U.S. Const. art. IV, § 1. This clause is implemented by a Congressional Act requiring that duly authenticated judicial proceedings "shall have the same full faith and credit in every court within the United States and its Territories and Possessions as they have by law or usage in the courts of such State, Territory or Possession from which they are taken." 28 U.S.C. § 1738. Thus, if the Florida judgment would be enforceable in Florida, the New York federal court was required to enforce it in New York. However, the court dismissed Wyman's action, agreeing with Newhouse that the Florida judgment was unenforceable. Wyman appealed.

[The Court of Appeals therefore considers the validity of the Florida judgment. Its validity depends upon the effectiveness of the service of process on Newhouse in Florida. He claims it was ineffective because Wyman had fraudulently enticed him into Florida for the sole purpose of serving him with process.]

Appellant and appellee were both married, but before this suit appellant's husband died. They had known each other for some years and had engaged in meretricious relations.

The affidavits submitted by the appellee . . . established that he was a resident of New York and never lived in Florida. On October 25, 1935, while appellee was in Salt Lake City, Utah, he received a telegram from the appellant, which read: "Account illness home planning leaving. Please come on way back. Must see you." Upon appellee's return to New York he received a letter from appellant stating that her mother was dying in Ireland; that she was leaving the United States for good to go to her mother; that she could not go without seeing the appellee once more; and that she wanted to discuss her affairs with him before she left. Shortly after the receipt of this letter, they spoke to each other on the telephone, whereupon the appellant repeated, in a hysterical and distressed voice, the substance of her letter. Appellee promised to go to Florida in a week or ten days and agreed to notify her when he would arrive. This he did, but before leaving

New York by plane he received a letter couched in endearing terms and expressing love and affection for him, as well as her delight at his coming. Before leaving New York, appellee telegraphed appellant, suggesting arrangements for their accommodations together while in Miami, Fla. She telegraphed him at a hotel in Washington, D.C., where he was to stop en route, advising him that the arrangements requested had been made. Appellee arrived at 6 o'clock in the morning at the Miami Airport and saw the appellant standing with her sister some 75 feet distant. He was met by a deputy sheriff who, upon identifying appellee, served him with process in a suit for $500,000. A photographer was present who attempted to take his picture. Thereupon a stranger introduced himself and offered to take appellee to his home, stating that he knew a lawyer who was acquainted with the appellant's attorney. The attorney whom appellee was advised to consult came to the stranger's home and seemed to know about the case. The attorney invited appellee to his office, and upon his arrival he found one of the lawyers for the appellant there. Appellee did not retain the Florida attorney to represent him. He returned to New York by plane that evening and consulted his New York counsel, who advised him to ignore the summons served in Florida. He did so, and judgment was entered by default. . . .

These facts and reasonable deductions therefrom convincingly establish that the appellee was induced to enter the jurisdiction of the state of Florida by a fraud perpetrated upon him by the appellant in falsely representing her mother's illness, her intention to leave the United States, and her love and affection for him, when her sole purpose and apparent thought was to induce him to come within the Florida jurisdiction so as to serve him in an action for damages. . . .

. . . A judgment procured fraudulently [in Florida], as here, lacks jurisdiction and is null and void [citing Florida decisions]. A fraud affecting the jurisdiction is equivalent to a lack of jurisdiction [citing Florida decisions]. . . . The appellee was not required to proceed against the judgment in Florida. . . .

Judgment [dismissing Wyman's action] affirmed.

NOTES AND QUESTIONS

(1) *Non-Fraudulent Contact or Injury.* How would the result differ if Wyman's entreaties and professions of affection for Newhouse had been genuine? Imagine that he came to Florida and stayed for several pleasant days until a disagreement erupted, and Wyman filed suit and had him served before he left Florida. What result? Alternatively, imagine that during this pleasant visit, a disagreement occurred and resulted in Newhouse's injuring Wyman — he struck her and broke her nose, for example — and he left Florida before she could sue. Is Wyman required to go to New York to file suit for this injury inflicted by Newhouse in Florida?

(2) *The Claimed Basis for Jurisdiction.* Why, then, did Wyman lure Newhouse to Florida? If she were to attempt to explain why she thought the Florida court had power to act, what would she give as the general principle on which that power could be based?

(3) *Where Can Wyman Properly Bring Suit?* Is there anywhere that Wyman can properly sue Newhouse now, if she believes her claim is valid? What were the reasons she didn't sue there in the first place?

§ 1.04 Pleadings: The Complaint and Answer

Read Rule 8(a), (e) of the Federal Rules of Civil Procedure.

NOTE: THE FEDERAL RULES OF CIVIL PROCEDURE AND THEIR EFFECTS ON PLEADINGS

The Federal Rules of Civil Procedure govern many procedural matters in federal court (although, as you have seen, there are also matters that are governed directly by the Constitution or by statutes). Typically, rule changes originate in an Advisory Committee to the Supreme Court and are promulgated by that Court to govern the district courts.

Rules of Pleading. The cases in this section deal with the question: just what does a plaintiff have to say in a complaint in order to have it survive the first wave of attack by the defendant? The most relevant provisions are contained in Rule 8: The complaint "must contain . . . a short and plain statement of the claim showing that the pleader is entitled to relief," "[n]o technical form is required," and pleadings "must be construed so as to do justice." But these general provisions beg the question, to some degree, and they result in differing views of the problem.

Conley v. Gibson, which follows next, represents a liberal view. The Court says that a pleading will not be dismissed for failure to state a claim upon which relief can be granted, unless it appears "beyond doubt" that the plaintiff "can prove no set of facts" that would entitle him to relief under his claim. The complaint need not be specific; it need only give "notice" to the defendant. It should be apparent to you that *Conley* sets a stringent standard for dismissal. However, the note case that follows *Conley, Thomas v. Torres*, shows the other side of the picture: a dismissal for failure to state a claim, pursuant to Rule 12(b)(6), can indeed be granted. You should concentrate upon the standards by which the complaint is judged and try to determine why the two cases are decided differently.

CONLEY v. GIBSON
355 U.S. 41 (1957)

MR. JUSTICE BLACK delivered the opinion of the Court.

Once again Negro employees are here under the Railway Labor Act asking that their collective bargaining agent be compelled to represent them fairly. In a series of cases beginning with *Steele v. Louisville & Nashville R. Co.*, 323 U.S. 192, this Court has emphatically and repeatedly ruled that an exclusive bargaining agent under the Railway Labor Act is obligated to represent all employees in the bargaining unit fairly and without discrimination because of race and has held that the courts have power to protect employees against such invidious discrimination.

This class suit was brought in a Federal District Court in Texas by certain Negro members of the Brotherhood of Railway and Steamship Clerks, petitioners here, on behalf of themselves and other Negro employees similarly situated against the Brotherhood, its Local Union No. 28 and certain officers of both. In summary, the complaint made the following allegations relevant to our decision: Petitioners were employees of the Texas and New Orleans Railroad at its Houston Freight House. Local 28 of the Brotherhood was the designated bargaining agent under the Railway Labor Act for the bargaining unit to which petitioners belonged. A contract existed between the Union and the Railroad which gave the employees in the bargaining unit certain protection from discharge and loss of seniority. In May 1954, the Railroad purported to abolish 45 jobs held by petitioners or other Negroes all of whom were either discharged or demoted. In truth the 45 jobs were not abolished at all but instead filled by whites as the Negroes were ousted, except for a few instances where Negroes were rehired to fill their old jobs but with loss of seniority. Despite repeated pleas by petitioners, the Union, acting according to plan, did nothing to protect them against these discriminatory discharges and refused to give them protection comparable to that given white employees. The complaint then went on to allege that the Union had failed in general to represent Negro employees equally and in good faith. It charged that such discrimination constituted a violation of petitioners' rights under the Railway Labor Act to fair representation from their bargaining agent. And it concluded by asking for relief in the nature of declaratory judgment, injunction and damages.

The respondents appeared and moved to dismiss the complaint on several grounds: (1) the National Railroad Adjustment Board had exclusive jurisdiction over the controversy; (2) the Texas and New Orleans Railroad, which had not been joined, was an indispensable party defendant; and (3) the complaint failed to state a claim upon which relief could be given. The District Court granted the motion to dismiss holding that Congress had given the Adjustment Board exclusive jurisdiction over the controversy. The Court of Appeals for the Fifth Circuit, apparently relying on the same ground, affirmed. . . . Since the case raised an important question concerning the protection of employee rights under the Railway Labor Act we granted certiorari. . . .

[The court considers the first ground of dismissal. It holds that the National Railroad Adjustment Board does not have exclusive jurisdiction. Therefore, the District Court erred in dismissing for lack of jurisdiction.]

Although the District Court did not pass on the other reasons advanced for dismissal of the complaint we think it timely and proper for us to consider them here. They have been briefed and argued by both parties and respondents urge that the decision below be upheld, if necessary, on these other grounds.

As in the courts below, respondents contend that the Texas and New Orleans Railroad Company is an indispensable party which the petitioners have failed to join as a defendant. On the basis of the allegations made in the complaint and the relief demanded by petitioners we believe that contention is unjustifiable. We cannot see how the Railroad's rights or interests will be affected by this action to enforce the duty of the bargaining representative to represent petitioners fairly. This is not a suit, directly or indirectly, against the Railroad. No relief is asked from it and there is no prospect that any will or can be granted which will bind it. If an issue does develop which necessitates joining the Railroad either it or the respondents will then have an adequate opportunity to request joinder.

Turning to respondents' final ground, we hold that under the general principles laid down in the *Steele* [and other] cases the complaint adequately set forth a claim upon which relief could be granted. In appraising the sufficiency of the complaint we follow, of course, the accepted rule that a complaint should not be dismissed for failure to state a claim unless it appears beyond doubt that the plaintiff can prove no set of facts in support of his claim which would entitle him to relief. Here, the complaint alleged, in part, that petitioners were discharged wrongfully by the Railroad and that the Union, acting according to plan, refused to protect their jobs as it did those of white employees or to help them with their grievances all because they were Negroes. If these allegations are proven there has been a manifest breach of the Union's statutory duty to represent fairly and without hostile discrimination all of the employees in the bargaining unit. This Court squarely held in *Steele* and subsequent cases that discrimination in representation because of race is prohibited by the Railway Labor Act. . . .

The respondents also argue that the complaint failed to set forth specific facts to support its general allegations of discrimination and that its dismissal is therefore proper. The decisive answer to this is that the Federal Rules of Civil Procedure do not require a claimant to set out in detail the facts upon which he bases his claim. To the contrary, all the Rules require is "a short and plain statement of the claim" that will give the defendant fair notice of what the plaintiff's claim is and the grounds upon which it rests. The illustrative forms appended to the Rules plainly demonstrate this. Such simplified "notice pleading" is made possible by the liberal opportunity for discovery and the other pretrial procedures established by the Rules to disclose more precisely the basis of both claim and defense and to define more narrowly the disputed facts and issues. Following the simple guide of Rule 8(f) that "all pleadings shall be so construed as to do substantial justice" [now Rule 8(e), which states "Pleadings must be construed so as to do justice." —Eds.], we have no doubt that petitioners' complaint adequately set forth a claim and gave the respondents fair notice of its basis. . . .

The judgment is reversed and the cause is remanded to the District Court for further proceedings not inconsistent with this opinion.

THOMAS v. TORRES, 717 F.2d 248 (5th Cir. 1983). Plaintiff Thomas, an inmate of the Texas Department of Corrections, appealed the dismissal under Rule 12(b)(6) of his complaint by the district court for failure to state a claim upon which relief could be granted. Thomas alleged that the Texas Board of Pardons and Paroles had denied him due process by failing adequately to consider the merits of his case for parole, by denying him parole on the basis of an "outspoken attitude," and by considering the seriousness of his offenses in making its decision. Later, Thomas filed a supplemental complaint alleging that the Board had failed to find him a job and housing and had failed properly to consider his good time credit. The Court of Appeals, in a per curiam opinion, upheld the dismissal. It began by stating that no civil rights relief could be had in the absence of an allegation that the plaintiff had been deprived of some right secured to him by the United States Constitution or laws. It quoted the Supreme Court: "There is no constitutional or inherent right of a convicted person to be conditionally released before the expiration of a valid sentence." *Greenholtz v. Inmates of the Nebraska Penal and Correctional Complex*, 442 U.S. 1 (1979). The "sensitive choices" presented by the administrative decision to grant parole did not "automatically invoke due process protection." *Id.* Because the Texas parole system did not create any legally cognizable "expectancy" of release, and the complaint did not allege the deprivation of any right secured under the Constitution or laws, the dismissal was proper.

NOTES AND QUESTIONS

(1) *The Consequences of Upholding the Complaint.* In *Conley*, the plaintiffs "won" in the Supreme Court in the sense that the dismissal of their complaint was reversed.

But what is it that they have "won"? Do they now get the injunction, damages and declaratory relief they want? In that regard, notice that the Court recites what appear to be the "facts" underlying the dispute. What is the source from which the Court takes the facts that it states, and does that mean they have been firmly established (are these "facts" really facts)? Given that the dismissal of a complaint is undertaken without an examination to determine what the "true facts" are, doesn't it make sense that the standard for dismissal is difficult for the defendant to meet? As we will see in Chapter 5, some have wondered if a recent Supreme Court decision might have changed the *Conley v. Gibson* pleading standard to one that is less favorable to plaintiffs. What are the benefits, and the detriments, of the *Conley* standard?

(2) *When Can a Complaint Be Dismissed?* State, in a single sentence, the conditions under which, according to *Conley*, it would be appropriate for a District Court to dismiss a complaint. Can the dismissal in *Thomas v. Torres* be supported under this standard? Isn't there at least a bare possibility that Thomas could produce proof in support of his allegations that would entitle him to *some* relief — for example, what if the Parole Board's consideration of his "outspoken attitude" was such that it denied him the freedom of speech? What, then, is the difference between *Conley* and *Thomas v. Torres*?

(3) *Prisoner Litigation Inarticulately Alleging Civil Rights Violations: An "Acid Test" for Liberal Pleading Rules.* Dismissal of invalid claims is of considerable importance to state officials, who may reasonably see themselves as hampered in essential duties by a blizzard of complaints drafted by inmates *pro se* in their spare time. Many of these complaints display no awareness of either substantive law or procedure, and many are inarticulate or even unintelligible. But the discovery and other procedures necessary for dealing with even an unfounded complaint, entail significant additional expense and time away from other duties. On the other hand, a *pro se* inmate sometimes has a real gripe (or even a valid claim) that is masked by his draftsmanship, and presumably it is preferable for him to air even an invalid dispute in the courts than to seek redress by extrajudicial means. Consider the following excerpts from Stancill, *Inmate Lawsuits Mushroom: Court Costs Whopping $630,000 in 12-Month Period*, Houston Chronicle (1985):*

> The winter doldrums must have hit TDC prisoner Joseph Anthony Parker particularly hard.
>
> From December through February, Parker, an inmate at the Darrington unit of the Texas Department of Corrections, stayed busy by filing 21 federal lawsuits alleging that prison officials and others violated his civil rights.
>
> Parker, in handwritten complaints from his Rosharon cell, contended that TDC officials were responsible for defective snacks and provisions he bought from a prison store, such as stale corn chips and bitter coffee that gave him "sinus headaches, stomach and chest pains."
>
> W.C. Davis, an inmate at the Harris County rehabilitation center, filed only one federal lawsuit in February but it was a memorable one.
>
> Davis claims he is wrongfully imprisoned because a key witness in his trial "had sex with me while I was asleep and she lied to cover up her transgressions."
>
> Other complaints are equally as bizarre. One inmate claimed TDC has "tortured me on a psychotic drug" while another sued Mayor Kathy Whitmire, claiming she sent a rapist murderer to his family's house equipped with recording devices to entrap him. . . .

> Taxpayers spent a whopping $630,000 to cover court costs of handling inmate lawsuits filed in federal district court in Houston and Galveston over the past 12 months ending in February, says Max Brown, a management analyst in U.S. District Court Clerk Jesse Clark's office.
>
> Brown says the $630,000 figure, which includes percentages of salaries of magistrates, law clerks and clerical personnel as well as travel and administrative expenses, is "a fairly conservative estimate." . . .
>
> "I think the inmates probably file them because they are unhappy," says Clark. "Maybe they wouldn't file so many if they had some better way to express themselves or be heard. Out in the free world, we can be heard in other ways, by going to City Council meetings, or the polls or writing to newspaper editors." . . .
>
> U.S. Magistrate H. Lingo Platter, who says he now spends nearly all of his time on prisoner cases, says magistrates "have got to go to their friends" to find an attorney willing to volunteer time to represent prisoners in civil rights cases. The laws currently do not provide for paying attorneys to handle prisoner civil rights matters, he says, and few lawyers relish working with prisoners, who are often difficult and sometimes sue their legal counsel. . . .
>
> Platter's most immediate example of a case without merit is a case filed by a prisoner who alleged civil rights violations because he was served three meatballs in the lunch line while other inmates got four.
>
> But he also points out he has seen cases that should be aired, such as prisoner beatings and other mistreatment. One such case that recently ended in a settlement, he says, was one by two men who were bitten severely when they served as "dog boys" to help train prison dogs.
>
> "Prisoners file the lawsuits for several reasons," Platter says. "Sometimes it is retaliation against prison officials and the judicial system, fighting back at society which put them there."

The judges in this district have considered involuntary appointment of attorneys without fee to such cases, using the court's authority over admission of attorneys to practice before it as a means of enforcement. Is this solution appropriate (if appointed, how would you counsel your client in the "meatballs" case)? Should taxpayer dollars be used for the payment of attorneys who take such cases voluntarily? Or should such suits be more readily subject to dismissal?

After enduring this phenomenon for many years, Congress passed the Prisoner Litigation Reform Act in 1996. The Act requires that prisoners exhaust all administrative remedies available to them before suing, authorizes judges to screen all suits before ordering a hearing, allows revocation of good time credits for frivolous suits, and provides that inmates must pay substantial filing fees (in the past, filing for indigents was free). *See Prison Suits Drop Under New Federal Restrictions*, S.F. Daily Journal, June 19, 1997, at 1 (reporting 25% decrease in some locations).

§ 1.04 Appendix Pleadings and Decision in *Wytinger v. Two Unknown Police Officers*

HOW TO READ THE PLEADINGS IN *WYTINGER v. TWO UNKNOWN POLICE OFFICERS*

On February 20, 1980, William David Wytinger committed suicide by hanging himself in the London City jail in the State of West York (a hypothetical city in a typical state of the United States). Shortly thereafter, Wytinger's surviving parents brought a civil rights suit, naming as defendants two police officers and the City of London. The underlying claim is based on 42 U.S.C. § 1983, often referred to by lawyers as "1983 " or "the civil rights statute."

Section 1983 gives redress for deprivation of constitutional rights under color of state law, such as the right to due process under the Fourteenth Amendment and the right to not be subjected to cruel and unusual punishment under the Eighth Amendment. Very often, as shown here, plaintiffs bring Section 1983 actions when seeking compensation for the alleged wrongful conduct of police, prison guards, or other government agents. Because such conduct usually involves a brief, one-time-only encounter, a plaintiff is often unable to learn the identity of an individual defendant until after he or she files the action and obtains this information through discovery. By temporarily allowing "John Doe" as an initial named defendant, Section 1983 prevents the original complaint from being dismissed prior to discovery and, as a result, allows the plaintiff an opportunity to identify the actual defendant. *See Maclin v. Paulson*, 627 F.2d 83 (7th Cir. 1980) (ruling prisoner's pleading in civil rights case did not require arresting officers' actual names until their identity could be learned through discovery).

Section 1983 liability may be imposed in cases involving prisoners or pretrial detainees if the individual officers acted with deliberate indifference to the person's serious medical needs. *Estelle v. Gamble*, 429 U.S. 97, 104-05 (1976). Proof of an official city policy or a persistent widespread municipal custom is required to hold a municipality accountable for the decedent's injuries and death. *Monell v. Department of Social Services*, 436 U.S. 658, 690-91 (1978). Hence, the plaintiff must allege acts or omissions sufficiently harmful to evidence a deliberate indifference to serious medical needs, and in order to state a claim against the City of London, the plaintiff must allege that the City caused the decedent's injury through an official policy or pursuant to a widespread custom that is so well-settled that, though not officially adopted, it can be said to fairly represent municipal policy. As you read the following materials, you should keep these legal standards in mind, together with the standard for dismissal of a complaint set forth in *Conley v. Gibson.*

These documents are taken from a real case. The "business" parts of the documents are closely similar to the original ones in the real case, but they have been edited and the names are changed.

THE COMPLAINT

IN THE UNITED STATES DISTRICT COURT
FOR THE MIDDLE DISTRICT OF WEST YORK
LONDON DIVISION

BARRY WYTINGER and PAULA WYTINGER, Plaintiffs v. TWO UNKNOWN POLICE OFFICERS and the CITY OF LONDON, WEST YORK, Defendants.	CIVIL ACTION NO. _______ COMPLAINT FOR DAMAGES JURY DEMAND

PLAINTIFFS' ORIGINAL COMPLAINT

Come now BARRY WYTINGER and PAULA WYTINGER, Plaintiffs, complaining of TWO UNKNOWN POLICE OFFICERS and THE CITY OF LONDON, WEST YORK, and would show as follows:

PARTIES, JURISDICTION, AND VENUE

1. Plaintiffs are the surviving parents of WILLIAM DAVID WYTINGER, deceased. Decedent died intestate in, and while a resident of, the County of Manero, State of West York. During all times mentioned in this complaint, Plaintiffs were, and still are, citizens of the United States, and they resided, and still reside, in London, Manero County, West York. Plaintiffs are the sole heirs at law of decedent WILLIAM DAVID WYTINGER.

2. Defendant UNKNOWN POLICE OFFICERS were, at all times material to this complaint, duly appointed, employed, and acting police officers of the Defendant CITY OF LONDON, and were acting under color of the statutes and ordinances of the City of London and the State of West York. Though the identity of Defendant UNKNOWN OFFICERS is unavailable to Plaintiffs at this time, Plaintiffs will request discovery of their names from Defendant CITY OF LONDON. Plaintiff alleges that the deprivation of Decedent's rights, as hereinafter detailed, was part of a deliberate pattern of conduct or policy of the Defendant CITY OF LONDON.

3. This is an action at law to redress the deprivation under color of statute, ordinance, regulation, custom, or usage, of rights, privileges, and immunities secured to Decedent and Plaintiffs by the Constitution of the United States and by federal law, particularly the Civil Rights Act, 42 U.S.C. section 1983.

4. The action arises under said Section 1983; under the Fourth, Fifth, Eighth and Fourteenth Amendments to the Constitution of the United States; and under other provisions of federal law. This Court has jurisdiction under and by virtue of 28 U.S.C. section 1331 (the General Federal Question Statute) and 28 U.S.C. section 1343 (the Civil Rights Jurisdiction Statute). All defendants reside, and the claim arose, in the Middle District of West York, London Division.

CLAIM PURSUANT TO 42 U.S.C. SECTION 1983

5. On or about the 21st day of February, 1980, in the early afternoon, Plaintiffs' decedent, WILLIAM DAVID WYTINGER, was accosted by two unidentified London Police Officers. Decedent was a 20 year old man, afflicted with minimal brain damage and heart disease. He was under the almost constant supervision of his mother, Plaintiff PAULA WYTINGER, as his physical and emotional state required constant attention and care. Plaintiffs' decedent had also been under the treatment of a psychiatrist.

6. Defendant UNKNOWN OFFICERS began to question decedent about a burglary which had occurred in the area. Decedent, due to his fragile emotional disposition, became hysterical. On the scene were various neighbors, and Decedent's father, Plaintiff BARRY WYTINGER.

7. The Defendant OFFICERS asked Plaintiff BARRY WYTINGER if Decedent was "all right," and more specifically, whether Decedent had ever "had any sort of nervous breakdown." Decedent's father, pleading that his son not be jailed, answered in the affirmative, and directed the OFFICERS' attention to two bracelets Decedent wore around his wrist. The bracelets read: "MEDICAL WARNING. SEE WALLET CARD." and "HEART PATIENT." Again, Plaintiff BARRY WYTINGER asked that his son not be jailed.

8. Defendant OFFICERS removed the two bracelets and dangled them in front of Decedent's father, telling him that if he would obtain a letter from the boy's psychiatrist, attesting to the boy's condition and to the danger of his being confined, that the boy would in all likelihood be released. Defendant OFFICERS then proceeded to force the hysterical WILLIAM DAVID WYTINGER into their squad car.

9. About an hour later, Plaintiff PAULA WYTINGER spoke to her son over the phone. Decedent was highly distraught at the prospect of confinement in the city jail.

10. Around midnight, PAULA WYTINGER received word that her son had been found hanging from the bars of his jail cell, an apparent suicide.

11. Decedent's death was proximately caused by the acts or omissions of both the TWO UNKNOWN OFFICERS and by the custom or policy in effect at the CITY OF LONDON through its police department. Defendant OFFICERS should have known, in light of Decedent's warning bracelets, his hysterical behavior, and his father's admonitions not to jail him, that to proceed with Decedent's confinement would likely result in some harm or even death to Decedent. Indeed, Plaintiffs allege that Decedent was known at the police department to be a mental patient, by indications on his arrest record.

12. CITY OF LONDON and its police department caused Decedent's death in either or both of the following respects:

a. By allowing a known mental patient, obviously distraught and under unusual stress, to be confined despite exhortations not to by Decedent's father; and

b. By failing to make adequate routine checks of Decedent's cell, which failure of supervision tragically resulted in Decedent's suicide.

13. As a direct and proximate result of the above-detailed conduct of Defendant UNKNOWN POLICE OFFICERS and of Defendant CITY OF LONDON, Plaintiffs and their decedent were deprived of the following rights, privileges, and immunities secured to them by the Constitution of the United States:

a. The right of Decedent to be secure in his person and effects against unreasonable search and seizure under the Fourth and Fourteenth Amendments to the Constitution of the United States;

b. The right of Decedent not to be deprived of life, liberty, or property without due process of law, and the right to equal protection of the laws secured by the Fourteenth Amendment to the Constitution of the United States; and

c. The right to freedom from physical abuse, coercion, and intimidation and from cruel and unusual punishment.

These rights were secured by the provisions of the due process clause of the Fifth and Fourteenth Amendments to the Constitution of the United States, by the Fourth Amendment, by the Eighth Amendment, and by Title 42, United States Code, Section 1983.

14. The acts of Defendants, as described above, were done with callous and reckless indifference to and disregard of Decedent's safety and continued life by reason of which Decedent was, in his lifetime, entitled, by virtue of the West York Wrongful Death statutes, to compensatory damages in the sum of TWENTY THOUSAND and NO/100 ($20,000.00) DOLLARS, and to punitive damages in the sum of ONE HUNDRED THOUSAND and NO/100 ($100,000.00) DOLLARS, and his heirs are now entitled, by virtue of such statute, to an award of such compensatory and punitive damages.

15. Plaintiffs are also entitled to the costs of funeral expenses incurred by their son's death, in the amount of ONE THOUSAND and NO/100 ($1,000.00) DOLLARS, which sum is reasonable and necessary for such costs in Manero County, West York.

16. At the time of his death, Decedent was 20 years of age. By reason of Decedent's wrongful death and the loss to his parents, Plaintiffs BARRY WYTINGER and PAULA WYTINGER, of the aid, association, support, protection, comfort, care and society of the Decedent, and the loss of their respective shares in such estate as the Decedent might reasonably have accumulated in his natural life expectancy, Plaintiffs BARRY WYTINGER and PAULA WYTINGER, as the sole surviving heirs of Decedent, have been damaged in the sum of TWENTY THOUSAND and NO/100 ($20,000.00) DOLLARS.

PRAYER

WHEREFORE, Plaintiffs demand judgment: (a) Awarding Plaintiffs compensatory damages of $ 20,000; (b) Awarding Plaintiffs punitive damages of $100,000; (c) Awarding Plaintiffs funeral expenses of $1,000; (d) Awarding Plaintiffs loss of future support of $20,000; (e) Awarding Plaintiffs the reasonable costs and expenses of this action, and such other and further relief as may be just.

JURY DEMAND

Plaintiffs respectfully demand trial by jury on all issues so triable.

Respectfully submitted,

DONALD A. PETERS
2200 Linden Avenue, Suite 100
London, West York 77006
(713) 555-6060

THE MOTION TO DISMISS

IN THE UNITED STATES DISTRICT COURT
FOR THE MIDDLE DISTRICT OF WEST YORK
LONDON DIVISION

BARRY WYTINGER and PAULA WYTINGER, Plaintiffs v. TWO UNKNOWN POLICE OFFICERS and the CITY OF LONDON, WEST YORK, Defendants.	CIVIL ACTION NO. CIV-80-2346-G

DEFENDANT CITY OF LONDON'S MOTION TO DISMISS

COMES NOW the CITY OF LONDON, named as a defendant in the above styled and numbered action, and would move the Court to dismiss the complaint as to it, and would show as follows:

1. The complaint herein fails to state a claim upon which relief can be granted against this defendant, in that it asserts no facts whatsoever upon which any theory could support a judgment or expose this defendant to liability under 42 U.S.C. Section 1983. *Estelle v. Gamble*, 429 U.S. 97 (1976) (complaint for inadequate medical attention does not state a claim under 1983 unless it alleges "acts or omissions sufficiently harmful to evidence a deliberate indifference to serious medical needs").

2. Further, the complaint fails to state a claim upon which relief can be granted in that it seeks to hold the CITY OF LONDON liable on the theory that it employed individuals who performed the acts complained of. This theory, known in the law as *respondent superior*, is not a theory under which a plaintiff may recover in a suit under 42 U.S.C. section 1983. *Monell v. Department of Social Services*, 436 U.S. 658 (1978) (requiring causation by city's own "official" custom or policy); *Baskin v. Parker*, 602 F.2d 1205 (5th Cir. 1979) (same); *Perry v. Jones*, 506 F.2d 778 (5th Cir. 1975) (same); *Ford v. Byrd*, 544 F.2d 194 (5th Cir. 1976) (same).

WHEREFORE, PREMISES CONSIDERED, the CITY OF LONDON prays that plaintiffs' complaint be dismissed and that it be awarded costs of court.

Respectfully submitted,

J.D. THOMAS, JR.
City Attorney
By: __________
RANDALL PARKS
Assistant City Attorney
P.O. Box 8127
London, West York, 77002
(713) 555-6021

NOTE ON OTHER PLEADINGS, AMENDED COMPLAINT, AND BRIEFS

Amended Complaint. After the defendants moved to dismiss the complaint, the plaintiffs filed an amended complaint. The amended complaint alleged more detailed acts and omissions by specifically identified police officers. It also alleged that the plaintiffs "will show that the Defendants . . . engaged in a deliberate pattern of conduct which constituted the policy of the [City of London's] jail policy for the handling of detained citizens which policy was familiar to the City of [London]." In addition, specific deficiencies in municipal policy or practice were identified, including: "Failure to adequately train the jail personnel to handle arrested citizens with known mental problems." The plaintiffs also added a negligence claim under state law.

Additional Motions, Briefs and Ruling. The individual defendants also filed motions to dismiss. Both sides also filed briefs discussing the *Gamble* and *Monell* decisions, as well as other cases. The court later ruled on the motions to dismiss by issuing the following order.

THE COURT'S ORDER OF DISMISSAL

IN THE UNITED STATES DISTRICT COURT
FOR THE MIDDLE DISTRICT OF WEST YORK
LONDON DIVISION

BARRY WYTINGER and PAULA WYTINGER, Plaintiffs, v. TWO UNKNOWN POLICE OFFICERS and the CITY OF LONDON, WEST YORK, Defendants.	CIVIL ACTION NO. CIV-80-2346-G

ORDER

Pending before the court is Defendants' Motion to Dismiss Plaintiffs' claim under 42 U.S.C. § 1983 (1976) for failure to state a claim upon which relief may be granted pursuant to Rule 12(b)(6), Fed. R. Civ. P. . . .

Upon review of the record, Defendants' motion to dismiss, and Plaintiffs' response, it is the opinion of the Court that Plaintiffs' 1983 action is insufficient to state a claim for relief in light of *Estelle v. Gamble*, 429 U.S. 97 (1976) where the Supreme Court concluded that "[i]n order to constitute a cognizable claim, a prisoner must allege acts or omissions sufficiently harmful to evidence deliberate indifference to serious medical needs. . . ."

The allegations in Plaintiffs' complaint, liberally construed and accepted as true, are that decedent was arrested for suspicion of burglary and theft, that he had been diagnosed as suffering from restlessness and anxiety as a result of chronic mild organic brain syndrome, that upon arrest his hysterical and agitated behavior — specifically, striking his head against the windshield and divided glass — alerted Defendants to decedent's condition, that Defendants were aware that decedent was under the care of a psychologist, that the medical-alert bracelets on decedent's wrists and the psychologist's note in his wallet alerted the officers to decedent's condition, and that the conditions of his confinement aggravated his medical needs and led to his suicide.

. . . In light of considerations established by the Court of Appeals for the Fifth Circuit in *Woodall v. Foti*, 648 F.2d 268 (5th Cir. 1981), to determine whether the alleged denial amounts to deliberate indifference to the decedent's medical needs, it is the opinion of the Court that the Plaintiffs' claim is insufficient to state a claim for relief under 42 U.S.C. § 1983 (1976).

Since the Court is of the opinion that Plaintiffs' federal claims are insufficient to state a claim, the Court declines [supplemental] jurisdiction over Plaintiffs' state claims. . . . It is, therefore,

ORDERED that Defendants' motion to dismiss is granted. It is further ordered that Plaintiffs' complaint is dismissed without prejudice. . . .

Signed this _____ day of September, 1983.

GEORGE GILLIAM, JR.
United States District Judge

NOTES AND QUESTIONS

(1) *The Substantive Standard: What Must Plaintiffs Plead and Prove?* Make sure that you understand the required allegations and proof for a prisoner or detainee to prevail on the claim at issue: There must be acts or omissions evidencing (1) "deliberate indifference" to (2) "serious medical needs," and for the city to be liable, they must be caused by (3) an "official custom or policy." This is the required minimum for the civil rights claim asserted here (of course, a separate negligence claim under state law, if available against the city and its officers, would involve a lesser standard of proof). Do you agree with this substantive law standard?

(2) *Evaluating the Dismissal of the Complaint.* Given the substantive legal standard (whether you agree with it or not), do you think the dismissal is correct? You should compare the allegations of the complaint to the required elements of the claim. Also, you should remember the standard for dismissing a complaint.

(3) *Would You Appeal?* The attorneys in a case of this nature typically would operate on a contingent fee basis (*i.e.*, they receive no fee unless there is a plaintiff's recovery). Would you have accepted employment in the case on this basis? Would you be willing to represent the client upon appeal, knowing that you must expend more effort and funds for the appeal and will not recover unless you ultimately prevail?

(4) *The Appeal of the Dismissal: A Cliffhanger.* Plaintiffs' counsel did appeal. Initially, a panel of the court of appeals held for plaintiffs and reversed the dismissal, with one judge dissenting. *Partridge v. Two Unknown Police Officers*, 751 F.2d 1448 (5th Cir. 1985). However, Defendants filed a motion for rehearing. The court then took the unusual step of withdrawing its published opinion, stating that "a new decision and judgment will be entered in due course." 755 F.2d 1126 (5th Cir. 1985). More than six years after plaintiffs' decedent's death, the Fifth Circuit issued another opinion, reversing the dismissal, again with one judge dissenting, 791 F.2d 1182 (5th Cir. 1986); *see also* § 5.03[B] of Chapter 5, below (in which the opinion is summarized). Why do you think this case is such a cliffhanger?

§ 1.05 Multiple Parties and Claims

CONLEY v. GIBSON, 355 U.S. 41 (1957). This case appears in § 1.04, above. Reconsider the defendant Union's argument that the suit should have been dismissed because the Railroad Company was required to be included in the suit (*i.e.*, as a "person[] required to be joined if feasible," in the current terminology of Fed. R. Civ. P. 19). The Court concluded that the contention was "unjustifiable": "We cannot see how the Railroad's rights or interests will be affected by this action to enforce the duty of the bargaining representative to represent petitioners fairly. This is not a suit, directly or indirectly, against the Railroad. No relief is asked from it. . . . If an issue does develop which necessitates joining the Railroad either it or the [Union] will then have an adequate opportunity to request joinder."

NOTES AND QUESTIONS

(1) *The Standard for Required Joinder of a Party.* Is the court saying that the performance of the Union really can have no actual effect on the Railroad? Or is it saying that the Railroad has no enforceable legal rights or obligations at issue in the matter? Which approach would make more sense? [Note: Many suits may have indirect effects on nonparties — *e.g.*, relatives of a personal injury plaintiff — but would it make sense to require that everyone indirectly affected in any degree be included?]

(2) *Permissive Joinder.* Could the plaintiffs have joined the Railroad as an additional defendant if they had thought they had a claim against it for, say, conspiring with the Union to deny equal employment opportunities to them? Rule 20 states that joinder is permissible, but not required, when a right to relief is asserted "jointly, severally or in the alternative," arising from the "same . . . series of transactions or occurrences," if "any question of law or fact common to all defendants will arise in the action."

§ 1.06 Discovery

Read Rule 26(b)(1)-(2) of the Federal Rules of Civil Procedure.

NOTE ON THE FEDERAL RULES GOVERNING DISCOVERY

Remember what discovery is: a procedure for obtaining information from opposing parties or non-party witnesses. Discovery is really an aspect of the attorney's investigation. Federal Rule 26(b) defines the scope of discovery as extending to information that is "relevant to any party's claim or defense" and "not privileged."

"Relevant to Any Party's Claim or Defense" and "Not Privileged." But what does "relevant to any party's claim or defense" and "not privileged" mean? First, as for "relevance," the Rule says that discovery includes even matters that will be inadmissible at trial, if they are "reasonably calculated to lead to the discovery of admissible evidence." This standard is broad. For example, your opponent's lawyer may be entitled to copy a large number of sensitive documents that your client would rather not show to anybody. Such broad discovery is appropriate because it is difficult to know at the investigative stage what information might be useful. On the other hand, "privileged" information is exempted from discovery. But this exemption is narrow; it covers only the kinds of confidences protected by the attorney-client privilege, patient-physician privilege,

(sometimes) privileges for government secrets, and similar legal principles. Your client (who is unlikely to be pleased with the breadth of discovery unless it is aimed at the opponent) cannot successfully resist disclosure merely by the claim that the requested information is confidential or sensitive.

Protective Orders. A "protective order" may be useful to your client in this situation, however. Rule 26(c) says that the court has authority to limit disclosure to protect against embarrassment, oppression, or other disadvantages. But since the authority to grant a protective order is discretionary, the judge decides in each case where to draw the line.

The Proper Balance? In the following case, prison-inmate plaintiffs seek discovery of parole personnel files and other sensitive information. Notice the broad nature of the inferences the court is willing to make in analyzing the "relevance" issue. Notice, also, the court's treatment of several different "privilege" arguments. The trial court granted a "protective order," which this appellate court upholds, but the defendant clearly is not satisfied by it. At the same time, however, one might ask whether the plaintiffs will be able to prove a possibly meritorious claim without the discovery they seek. Do the courts strike the proper balance in this case between the need for information and the burdens of the discovery request?

KERR v. UNITED STATES DISTRICT COURT
511 F.2d 192 (9th Cir.), aff'd, 426 U.S. 394 (1976)

[Seven California prison inmates brought a civil rights class action seeking an injunction requiring the Adult Authority (California's parole agency) to recognize certain claimed procedural rights in parole revocation proceedings. After taking depositions, the plaintiffs served interrogatories and requests for production upon the Adult Authority defendants. The defendants objected to several interrogatories and to document requests numbered "7", "15", "18", "20", "21" and "22".

[These requests sought: "7. All files, including all personnel files . . . with respect to each member, each hearing representative, and the Executive Officer of the Adult Authority"; "14. Each report submitted by any [official or employee] . . ."; "15. All written statements written or delivered by any [official or employee . . . during the past 5 years favoring, opposing or in any way commenting upon bills or other legislation . . ."; "18. All written proposals for any change whatsoever in . . . substantive criteria or procedures . . . [in parole proceedings]"; "20. All memoranda written by the Chairman of the Adult Authority, no matter to whom sent . . ."; "21. All documents in effect on November 15, 1972 which pertain to any Policy Statement or Resolution . . . and all such documents . . . issued subsequent to that date"; and "22. All documents, however formal or informal, issued during the past calendar year, which concern the Adult Authority's adoption of new policies. . . ."

[The District Court overruled all objections to these requests and granted the inmates' motion to compel production. It granted protective orders, however, concerning certain of the document requests. For example, with reference to request number 7 (pertaining to "files, including . . . personnel files"), the court ordered "that no . . . file of any plaintiffs . . . and no personnel file . . . shall be shown to any person except counsel of record for the plaintiffs and no more than a total of two investigators designated by such counsel. . . ."

[The Adult Authority defendants brought these issues before the Court of Appeals by a petition for a writ of prohibition or mandamus that would vacate the trial judge's orders.

The Court of Appeals first pointed out that mandamus or prohibition during a pending case is an extraordinary remedy, subject to more difficult requirements than an ordinary appeal from a final judgment. It then analyzed the discovery requests, as follows:]

Petitioners first direct their attention to the documents described in request number seven. . . . These documents consist of the personnel files maintained by petitioners pertaining to each member of the Adult Authority, each hearing representative, and the Executive Officer of the Adult Authority. On the merits of the district court order, petitioners argue that the contents of these personnel files have no relevance to the subject matter of the civil rights action, and for this reason alone, the district court discovery order should be vacated with regard to request number seven.

One of the plaintiffs' allegations in their civil rights complaint is that members and executive personnel of the Adult Authority have "no expertise in arriving at fair decisions" because of their narrow partisan backgrounds, their bias against prisoners, their inexperience, and their failure to reflect a representative cross section of the population of California. As indicated by the earlier review of the relief sought in the civil rights suit, plaintiffs do not attack the qualifications of petitioners with an expectation of obtaining a judicial determination that an Adult Authority so constituted cannot accord due process to prisoners who come before them. Instead, they expect that, by proving such an allegation, they will demonstrate the need of imposing stringent procedural requirements governing the functioning of the Adult Authority.

Since this would appear to be a proper line of attack for plaintiffs, the district court's holding of the personnel files relevant for discovery purposes is not so questionable as to invoke mandamus. For the question of relevancy "is to be more loosely construed at the discovery stage than at the trial." 8 Wright & Miller, *Federal Practice and Procedure*, § 2008 at 41 (1970). Thus under Fed. R. Civ. P. 26(b)(1), it is no ground for objection that information sought in pretrial discovery would not be admissible at trial, " 'if the testimony sought appears reasonably calculated to lead to the discovery of admissible evidence.' . . ." *Olympic Refining Company v. Carter*, 332 F.2d 260, 266 (9th Cir. 1964). In addition to discovering information pertaining to a party's case in chief, it is entirely proper to obtain information for other purposes such as cross-examination of adverse witnesses. . . .

Because the issue of relevancy in discovery matters is subject to such a broad standard, a district court's decision will rarely be overturned by a petition for mandamus. . . .

Petitioners further argue, however, that [three] established principles of California law and federal law create an absolute or qualified privilege for the personnel files [and certain other documents], and for this reason discovery should not have been ordered. In the alternative, petitioners argue that, at the very least, the district court should have required *in camera* inspection to ascertain relevancy and judge the need to maintain the confidentiality of the Authority's files.

The claim of privilege under California law is based upon California Evidence Code § 1040, and California Government Code §§ 6250-6260 and 6254(f) (Supp. 1974). However, the civil rights action was instituted in federal court under a federal statute, 42 U.S.C. § 1983, which was enacted particularly to vindicate federal rights against deprivation by state action. . . . As this court recently pointed out in *Heathman v. United States District Court*, 503 F.2d at 1034: "[I]n federal question cases the clear weight of authority and logic supports reference to federal law on the issue of the existence and scope of an asserted privilege." [California privilege law therefore is inapplicable.]

[Second, Petitioners also argue that the documents are privileged under the federal Freedom of Information Act. That Act does create certain exemptions from disclosure, but the court rejects petitioners' arguments because (1) the Act applies only to federal information and (2) it does not apply to discovery proceedings in any event.]

[Third,] Petitioners also contend that the common law governmental privilege (encompassing and referred to sometimes as the official or state secret privilege) covers the requested documents. . . .

These cases, however, indicate that this is only a qualified privilege, contingent upon the competing interests of the requesting litigant and subject to disclosure especially where protective measures are taken, as in this case. But we do not have to reach the question of whether this privilege extends to these documents or if a further protective order in the nature of *in camera* inspection was necessary before allowing disclosure. The governmental privilege must be formally asserted and delineated in order to be raised properly. *United States v. Reynolds*, 345 U.S. 1, 7-8, 10-11, 73 S. Ct. 528, 97 L. Ed. 727 (1953). . . .

The claiming official must " 'have seen and considered the contents of the documents and himself have formed the view that on grounds of public interest they ought not to be produced' " and state with specificity the rationale of the claimed privilege. . . . In the civil rights suit, petitioners' counsel merely raised a blanket objection covering any and all documents in request numbers 7, 14, 15, 18, 20, 21 and 22. Formally claiming a privilege should involve specifying which documents or class of documents are privileged and for what reasons, especially where the nature of the requested documents does not reveal an obviously privileged matter. *See Pleasant Hill Bank v. United States*, 58 F.R.D. at 101. Since there may be information in the requested documents which should be protected, the petitioners may assert a privilege to a particular document or class of documents, and perhaps seek *in camera* inspection, at the time the documents are discovered in the district court. *See United States v. Reynolds*, 345 U.S. at 10-11, 73 S. Ct. 528.

In sum, the petition fails to show such an usurpation by the district court that warrants the extraordinary remedy of writ of mandamus. In promulgating the discovery order the district court did enter some protective measures. The granting of mandamus as to discovery orders is limited, and this case does not appear to present exceptional circumstances.

The stay of this court is vacated, and the petition for mandamus or prohibition is denied.

KERR v. UNITED STATES DISTRICT COURT, 426 U.S. 394 (1976), *aff'g* 511 F.2d 192 (9th Cir. 1975). The Supreme Court granted review in *Kerr.* It affirmed the court of appeals' denial of mandamus. In doing so, however, it recognized that the claim of government privilege might rest upon concerns for preventing "substantial injury." Disclosure of some of the requested information could "chill" the exchange of information between personnel, "dry . . . up confidential sources," and "compromise" the Authority's records. Since the weight of these considerations would vary with each document, *in camera* review was "eminently worthwhile." The Court of Appeals' decision had not foreclosed *in camera* review. If a proper official personally asserted the government privilege as to specific documents, said the Supreme Court, *in camera* review could still be available when the proceedings were resumed in the District Court.

NOTES AND QUESTIONS

(1) *Scope of Discovery: "Relevance."* Try to state, in a single sentence, why the Court of Appeals decided that the personnel files contained or were "reasonably calculated to lead to the discovery of admissible evidence."

(2) *"Privilege."* If a document is privileged, it cannot be discovered by any means, no matter how relevant. The Adult Authority defendants argued three different kinds of privileges here. Does the court's rejection of these privileges seem logically reasoned? Is there good reason for restricting the scope of a privilege?

(3) *Protective Order.* The Federal Rules do not set specific standards for the scope of a protective order, which instead is left to the discretion of the district judge. Could the judge in *Kerr* properly have issued a protective order that simply denied discovery as to *all* of the contested documents?

(4) *The Realities of Discovery.* Discovery is extremely important to a litigator. In fact, discovery is the activity in which most litigators spend most of their time. In a complex case, documents produced in discovery can easily number in the millions. On the one hand, discovery is the litigant's means of finding "smoking gun" evidence in the opponent's possession. On the other hand, it can have the effect of harassment, and in the real world, litigants sometimes employ it for that purpose.

§ 1.07 Disposition Without Trial: Summary Judgment

Read Rule 56(c) of the Federal Rules of Civil Procedure.

NOTE ON THE STANDARDS FOR SUMMARY JUDGMENT

Fed. R. Civ. P. 56(c) says that a summary judgment "should be rendered if the pleadings, the discovery and disclosure materials on file, and any affidavits show that there is no genuine issue as to any material fact and that the movant is entitled to judgment as a matter of law." Because this procedure dispenses with the need for a trial, the moving party bears a heavy burden. It is not enough for the moving party to show that she is likely to win at trial; she must demonstrate that there are not even any controversies about the facts that could make any difference in the result.

WARREN v. MEDLEY

521 S.W.2d 137 (Tex. Civ. App.— Beaumont 1975, writ ref'd n.r.e.)

KEITH, JUSTICE.

Plaintiffs appeal from a take nothing judgment entered after defendant's motion for summary judgment had been sustained by the court, and we will designate the parties as they appeared below.

On the evening of the incident in question, plaintiffs were accompanied by a friend to a restaurant where the parties dined. They then went to a nightclub in Dallas where, according to our record, the principal form of entertainment was furnished by bare-breasted female "go-go" dancers who performed upon some type of plexiglass covered platform in the club. Having been so entertained, the parties returned to plaintiffs' home but remained there only a very short time. They then went next door to defendant's home where he and his wife were entertaining another couple, Mr. and Mrs. John Reynolds,

III. Plaintiffs' arrival interrupted the poker game then in progress and soon the conversation drifted to an account of the performance of the go-go girls at the nightclub. There is a slight but unimportant difference in the testimony of the parties as to exactly what happened next. Defendant and Reynolds said that Mrs. Warren demonstrated the dance which she had seen at the club but this was denied by Mrs. Warren.

Reynolds urged Mrs. Warren to repeat her exhibition but she declined. Reynolds then grabbed her around the waist and placed her upon the top of the table where the poker game had been conducted. This was a glass-topped table with a wrought iron frame and legs with the glass resting entirely within the framework of the table without center support. Defendant knew it would not support the weight of an adult.

A few seconds after being placed on the table and before she had begun any dancing, instead while pleading to be helped down, the glass top broke. Mrs. Warren fell through the broken top and sustained injury to her leg from the broken shards. Plaintiffs sued defendant and Reynolds. The trial court sustained defendant's motion for summary judgment; and plaintiffs, after settling their suit against Reynolds, now appeal from the take nothing judgment. We affirm.

After a careful review of the deposition testimony forming a part of the summary judgment record, we are of the opinion that the defendant successfully negated plaintiffs' right to recover. In arriving at this conclusion we have borne in mind the rules enunciated by our Supreme Court, including, *inter alia*, the following:

> 1. Defendant labored under the burden of establishing as a matter of law that he is not liable under any theory fairly presented by the allegations of plaintiffs' petition. *Kelsey-Seybold Clinic v. Maclay*, 466 S.W.2d 716, 720 (Tex. 1971).
>
> 2. If reasonable minds could differ as to the conclusions to be drawn from the summary judgment facts, the defendant did not discharge the burden placed upon him. *Adam Dante Corporation v. Sharpe*, 483 S.W.2d 452, 455 (Tex. 1972). . . .

Our decision is simplified somewhat by the agreement of the parties that plaintiffs occupied the status of licensees at the time Mrs. Warren received her injuries. Admittedly, the plaintiffs were social guests in defendant's home; and, as such, were licensees. *Weekes v. Kelley*, 433 S.W.2d 769, 771 (Tex. Civ. App.-Eastland 1968, writ ref'd n.r.e.). . . .

The duty owed to a licensee by the owner or licensor has been restated by our Supreme Court in *State v. Tennison*, 509 S.W.2d 560, 562 (Tex. 1974), in these words:

> It is well settled in this State that if the person injured was on the premises as a licensee, the duty that the proprietor or licensor owed him was not to injure him by willful, wanton or gross negligence.

In *McPhearson v. Sullivan*, 463 S.W.2d 174 (Tex. 1971), the Court reaffirmed the earlier definition of gross negligence:

> Gross negligence is "that entire want of care which would raise the belief that the act or omission complained of was the result of a conscious indifference to the right or welfare of the person or persons to be affected by it."

Plaintiffs, citing several out of state cases, argue that the duty of a host to a social guest is in a process of change from the willful and wanton conduct or gross negligence test [as set out in *Tennison, supra*] to one which requires that the host exercise reasonable care to refrain from injuring the guest by "active" negligence.

As an intermediate appellate court, it is our duty to follow the clear decisions of our Supreme Court as to the substantive law when it can be ascertained with certainty.

Tennison, supra, is clear as to the duty owed by a host-licensor to his guest-licensee. If there is to be relaxation of the rule, it should come from our court of last resort. We will continue to follow *Tennison* until otherwise notified by the Supreme Court.

In the clearest possible language, Mrs. Warren testified that defendant did not suggest that she be placed on the table and that he "expressed surprise" at seeing her there. Finally, it was her testimony that "t[h]e [defendant] couldn't have prevented it." From our careful review of the deposition testimony of Mrs. Warren, we conclude that reasonable minds could not differ as to the sequence of events leading up to the accident. It was Reynolds' act in placing her on top of the table — an act in which defendant did not participate — which brought about her injuries.

Defendant has successfully discharged his onerous burden of showing that he was not guilty of any willful or wanton conduct or gross negligence toward Mrs. Warren on the occasion in question. Moreover, he has negated both proximate cause and cause in fact as a matter of law. . . .

The judgment of the trial court is affirmed.

NOTES AND QUESTIONS

(1) *Relationship Between Summary Judgment and the Substantive Law.* In some states (California, for example), distinctions depending upon an injured person's status as a social guest or "licensee" are not controlling in a suit of this kind. In these states, a host may be liable upon a standard of "simple" negligence, rather than the gross negligence standard applied in *Warren v. Medley. E.g., Rowland v. Christian*, 69 Cal. 2d 108, 443 P.2d 561, 70 Cal. Rptr. 97 (1968). If this case had arisen and been heard in California, would the result be different? [Note: Doesn't the summary judgment evidence here negate the contention that the incident was caused by simple negligence on defendant's part?]

(2) *Denial of Jury Trial as a Consequence of Summary Judgment.* The federal Constitution guarantees a right to jury trial in federal courts (and the constitutions of most states do likewise in their courts). Ms. Warren obviously has not been afforded a jury trial on her claim. How can the granting of summary judgment be considered constitutional? [Note: What kinds of decisions is a jury supposed to make, and would a jury have had any function to fulfill in this case?]

(3) *Settlement with One Defendant.* Note that the plaintiff, by settlement, has received some compensation from one defendant (the one who seems most clearly to have been causally negligent). This case should remind you of the prevalence of settlement as a means of resolving disputes. The subject of settlement sometimes raises knotty questions. For example, should a claimant be permitted to compromise her claim with the "most guilty" defendant in order to obtain a "war chest" with which to seek a recovery based upon proof of full damages against a "slightly guilty" defendant?

§ 1.08 Trial: Functions of the Judge and Jury

[A] Jury Selection, Evidence, Verdict, and Judgment

FEIN v. PERMANENTE MEDICAL GROUP
38 Cal. 3d 137, 695 P.2d 665, 211 Cal. Rptr. 368 (1985)

KAUS, JUSTICE.

In this medical malpractice action, both parties appeal from a judgment awarding plaintiff about $1 million in damages. Defendant claims that the trial court committed reversible error during the selection of the jury, in instructions on liability as well as damages, and in failing to order that the bulk of plaintiff's award be paid periodically rather than in a lump sum. Plaintiff defends the judgment against defendant's attacks, but maintains that the trial court, in fixing damages, should not have applied two provisions of the Medical Injury Compensation Reform Act of 1975 (MICRA): Civil Code section 3333.2, which limits non-economic damages in medical malpractice cases to $250,000, and Civil Code section 3333.1, which modifies the traditional "collateral source" rule in such litigation. Plaintiff's claims are based on a constitutional challenge similar to the challenges to other provisions of MICRA that we recently addressed and rejected in *American Bank & Trust Co. v. Community Hospital* (1984) 36 Cal. 3d 359. . . . We conclude that the judgment should be affirmed in all respects.

I

[Plaintiff Lawrence Fein, an attorney, felt chest pains while exercising. He was unable to see his regular physician at Permanente Medical Group, an affiliate of the Kaiser Health Foundation. However, he obtained a "short appointment" the afternoon he called. He was examined by Cheryl Welch, whom he knew to be a nurse practitioner, and who worked under the supervision of Dr. Wintrop Franz. After consulting Dr. Franz, Nurse Welch advised Fein that she and Dr. Franz believed he had suffered a muscle spasm, and she gave him Dr. Franz's prescription for Valium.

[That night, Fein had severe chest pains, went to the Kaiser emergency room, and was X-rayed by Dr. Lowell Redding, who also diagnosed muscle spasms and administered pain medication. Later, after further pain, Fein returned again, and Dr. Donald Oliver directed an electrocardiogram (EKG). The EKG showed that Fein was suffering a heart attack (acute myocardial infarction). He was transferred to the cardiac care unit and treated without surgery. By the time of trial, he had been permitted to return to virtually all of his prior recreational activities, including jogging, swimming, bicycling, and skiing.

[Fein sued Permanente on the claim that his condition should have been diagnosed earlier and treated to prevent the heart attack or reduce its residual effects.]

At trial, Dr. Harold Swan, the head of cardiology at the Cedars-Sinai Medical Center in Los Angeles, was the principal witness for plaintiff. Dr. Swan testified that an important signal that a heart attack may be imminent is chest pain which can radiate to other parts of the body. Such pain is not relieved by rest or pain medication. He stated that if the condition is properly diagnosed, a patient can be given Inderal to stabilize his condition, and that continued medication or surgery may relieve the condition.

Dr. Swan further testified that in his opinion any patient who appears with chest pains should be given an EKG to rule out the worst possibility, a heart problem. He stated that the symptoms that plaintiff had described to Nurse Welch at the 4 p.m. examination on Thursday, February 26, should have indicated to her that an EKG was in order. He also stated that when plaintiff returned to Kaiser late that same night with his chest pain unrelieved by the medication he had been given, Dr. Redding should also have ordered an EKG. According to Dr. Swan, if an EKG had been ordered at those times it could have revealed plaintiff's imminent heart attack, and treatment could have been administered which might have prevented or minimized the attack.

Dr. Swan also testified to the damage caused by the attack. He stated that as a result of the attack a large portion of the plaintiff's heart muscle had died, reducing plaintiff's future life expectancy by about one-half, to about 16 or 17 years. Although Dr. Swan acknowledged that some of plaintiff's other coronary arteries also suffer from disease, he felt that if plaintiff had been properly treated his future life expectancy would be decreased by only 10 to 15 percent, rather than half.

Nurse Welch and Dr. Redding testified on behalf of the defense, indicating that the symptoms that plaintiff had reported to them at the time of the examinations were not the same symptoms he had described at trial. Defendant also introduced a number of expert witnesses — not employed by Kaiser — who stated that on the basis of the symptoms reported and observed before the heart attack, the medical personnel could not reasonably have determined that a heart attack was imminent. Additional defense evidence indicated (1) that an EKG would not have shown that a heart attack was imminent, (2) that because of the severe disease in the coronary arteries which caused plaintiff's heart attack, the attack could not have been prevented even had it been known that it was about to occur, and finally (3) that, given the deterioration in plaintiff's other coronary arteries, the heart attack had not affected plaintiff's life expectancy to the degree suggested by Dr. Swan.

In the face of this sharply conflicting evidence, the jury found in favor of plaintiff on the issue of liability and, pursuant to the trial court's instructions, returned special verdicts itemizing various elements of damages. The jury awarded $24,733 for wages lost by plaintiff to the time of trial, $63,000 for future medical expenses, and $700,000 for wages lost in the future as a result of the reduction in plaintiff's life expectancy. Finally, the jury awarded $500,000 for "noneconomic damages," to compensate for pain, suffering, inconvenience, physical impairment and other intangible damages sustained by plaintiff from the time of the injury until his death.

After the verdict was returned, defendant requested the court to modify the award and enter a judgment pursuant to three separate provisions of MICRA: (1) Civil Code section 3333.2 — which places a $250,000 limit on noneconomic damages, [and two other Civil Code sections]. The trial court, which had rejected plaintiff's constitutional challenge . . . in a pretrial ruling, reduced the noneconomic damages to $250,000 [and made other adjustments that he thought were required by the Civil Code. Thus, the jury's $500,000 award for noneconomic damages translated into only a $250,000 recovery because of the $250,000 "cap" in the Civil Code].

As noted, both parties have appealed from the judgment. Defendant maintains that the trial court committed reversible error in (1) excusing all Kaiser members from the jury, (2) instructing on the duty of care of a nurse practitioner, (3) instructing on causation, (4) permitting plaintiff to recover wages lost because of his diminished life expectancy, and (5) refusing to order the periodic payment of all future damages. Plaintiff argues that the judgment in his favor should be affirmed, but asserts that the court erred in upholding the MICRA provisions at issue here [*i.e.*, the $250,000 "cap"]. Since defendant's claims go to the basic validity of the judgment in favor of plaintiff, we turn first to its contentions.

II

At the outset of the empanelment of the jury, the court indicated that it would excuse from the jury those prospective jurors who would refuse to go to Kaiser for treatment under any circumstances and also those prospective jurors who were members of the Kaiser medical plan. When defendant noted its objection to the court's exclusion of the Kaiser members without conducting individual voir dire examinations, the court explained to the jury panel: "I am going to excuse you at this time because we've found that we can prolong the jury selection by just such a very long time by going through each and every juror under these circumstances. I'm not suggesting that . . . everyone who goes to Kaiser could not fairly and with an open mind resolve the issues in this case, but we may be here for four weeks trying to get a jury under the circumstances. [¶] I hope you can appreciate that. Probably some of you have sat in on situations where we've tried to get jurors in cases and it just goes on and on and on and on because you'll be questioned in great detail." On inquiry, it turned out that 24 of the 60 persons on the initial jury panel were members of Kaiser. They were excused. Voir dire then proceeded in the ordinary fashion, with each party questioning the remaining jurors and exercising challenges for cause and peremptory challenges.

Although defendant does not contend that any of the jurors who ultimately served on the jury and decided the case were biased against it, it nonetheless asserts that the discharge of the Kaiser members was improper and warrants reversal. In support of its contention, it argues that a potential juror's mere membership in Kaiser does not provide a basis for a challenge for cause under the applicable California statute, Code of Civil Procedure section 602.

Past decisions do not provide a clear-cut answer to the question whether a potential juror's membership in Kaiser would itself render the juror subject to a statutory challenge for cause. Section 602 does not define with precision the degree of "interest" or connection with a party that will support a challenge for cause, and courts in other states have come to different conclusions with respect to the eligibility of potential jurors whose relationship to one of the parties is similar to Kaiser members' relationship to defendant. Some cases have found error when a trial court has failed to excuse such persons for cause (*see, e.g., M & A Electric Power Cooperative v. Georger* (Mo. 1972) 480 S.W.2d 868, 871-874 [members of "consumer" electrical cooperative . . .]). In *McKernan v. Los Angeles Gas etc. Co.* (1911) 16 Cal. App. 280, 283, 116 P. 677 — perhaps the closest California case in point — the court indicated that the mere fact that some of the jurors were customers of the defendant utility company would not, in itself, mandate their excusal for cause.

But whether or not under California law membership in Kaiser rendered the prospective jurors excludable for cause under section 602, we believe that it is clear that the trial court's discharge of such members provides no basis for reversing the judgment in this case. To begin with, even if membership in Kaiser is not itself disqualifying, it is not apparent that the trial court abused the broad discretion it retains over the jury selection process (*see, e.g., Rousseau v. West Coast House Movers* (1967) 256 Cal. App. 2d 878, 883-886, 64 Cal. Rptr. 655) by excusing the members in this case. As its comments to the jury suggest, the court had apparently discovered through past experience that in this situation the individual voir dire procedure would prove very time-consuming and unproductive, with a substantial proportion of the Kaiser members ultimately being subject to challenge by one party or the other. Furthermore, the trial court may reasonably have felt that the process of conducting an extensive voir dire of all Kaiser members might itself prejudice prospective jurors who did not belong to Kaiser. From experience, it may have foreseen that such questioning would invariably involve the recounting of specific, potentially prejudicial incidents concerning the prospective jurors and Kaiser, as well as the exploration of the relative satisfaction or dissatisfaction with Kaiser of the particular jurors on this venire. Such matters would, of course, not be admissible in the actual trial of the case, and the court may have feared that such revelations on voir dire might "taint" all of the other prospective jurors in the courtroom. Under these circumstances, it cannot be said that the trial court abused its discretion in excusing the Kaiser members without individual examination.

Further, even if the trial court did err in this regard, the error clearly would not warrant reversal. This follows from the general rule that an erroneous exclusion of a juror for cause provides no basis for overturning a judgment. . . . As the court explained in *Dragovich v. Slosson* (1952) 110 Cal. App. 2d 370, 371, 242 P.2d 945: " 'Since a defendant or a party is not entitled to a jury composed of any particular jurors, the court may of its own motion discharge a qualified juror without committing any error, provided there is finally selected a jury composed of qualified and competent persons.' " Although defendant attempts to fit this case within the proviso of the above rule — on the theory that the removal of the Kaiser members rendered the jury panel unconstitutionally nonrepresentative (*cf. Thiel v. Southern Pacific Co.* (1946) 328 U.S. 217, 66 S. Ct. 984, 90 L. Ed. 1181 [exclusion of daily wage earners]) — defendant points to no authority which even remotely supports its claim that Kaiser members are a "cognizable class," and the record in this case provides no evidence to suggest that this group has the kind of shared experiences, ideology or background that have been identified as the *sine qua non* of such a class. . . . On this record, we cannot find that the jury that tried this matter was any less a cross-section of the community than it would have been had Kaiser members not been excused.

Accordingly, the manner in which the jury was selected provides no basis for reversing the judgment.

[Other parts of the court's opinion appear in section [B], below.]

NOTES AND QUESTIONS

(1) *Selecting the Jury.* In jury selection, both sides have an opportunity to ask (or have the judge ask) questions. From the answers, each side may challenge (*i.e.*, remove) a certain number of persons without assigning any reason, as well as an unlimited number of persons "for cause" (such as demonstrable bias or "interest" in the outcome). Could the Kaiser plan members have been properly excluded for "interest"? If not, what kinds of questions would the parties probably want to ask these prospective jurors, and what characteristics might they have that would affect their jury service? Why did the trial judge adopt the solution of excusing them as a group?

(2) *Composition of the Jury Venire.* The court's ruling excused 24 of 60 jurors (or 40 percent of the entire panel). As a matter of trial strategy, why were the defendants dissatisfied with this ruling (how did the initial panel differ in bias or lack thereof from the group that remained?). The court holds, however, that the final group was not "any less a cross-section of the community than it would have been had Kaiser members not been excused." Is this statement true? Can the case be distinguished from such decisions as *Thiel v. Southern Pacific Co.*, cited in the opinion, in which the trial judge declined to summon any laborers who were paid by the day, on the ground that jury service would be a hardship to them? In that case, the Supreme Court held that the excusal of this "cognizable group" was improper.

(3) *The Jury's Function.* Remember that the jury is to decide the contested facts, while the judge is to decide matters of law. The evidence in this case was "sharply conflicting." What kinds of issues of fact was the jury responsible for deciding? For example, should the jury have been limited to deciding questions of "fact" such as whether Fein or the defense witness were telling the truth about the symptoms he had reported? Or should

the jury be allowed to decide such "facts" as whether the diagnosis was "negligently" made?

(4) *The Judge's Function with Respect to the Verdict.* Notice that the judge did not award judgment for the full amount of damages found by the jury. The jury's verdict may or may not specify who wins, and in fact it may or may not even control who wins. Remember, disputed facts are for the jury to decide, while law is for the judge. What is the function of the judge with respect to the jury's verdict?

[B] Instructing the Jury

FEIN v. PERMANENTE MEDICAL GROUP
38 Cal. 3d 137, 695 P.2d 665, 211 Cal. Rptr. 368 (1985)

[The facts and holding in this case are given in the preceding section. Briefly, Fein sued Permanente for negligent diagnosis and treatment. The evidence showed relevant actions by both a nurse and a physician employed by Permanente. The facts were hotly contested. The jury found Permanente liable and, by special verdicts, apportioned damages to lost wages, medical expenses, reduced life expectancy, and "noneconomic damages." The judge granted judgment for plaintiff Fein, but he "capped" the noneconomic damages at $250,000 in accordance with a controversial California statute. In this excerpt of the opinion, the court discusses defendant's attacks on the court's instructions to the jury.] . . .

III

Defendant next contends that the trial court misinstructed the jury on the standard of care by which Nurse Welch's conduct should be judged. In addition to the general BAJI instruction on the duty of care of a graduate nurse, the court told the jury that "the standard of care required of a nurse practitioner is that of a physician and surgeon . . . when the nurse practitioner is examining a patient or making a diagnosis."

We agree with defendant that this instruction is inconsistent with recent legislation setting forth general guidelines for the services that may properly be performed by registered nurses in this state. Section 2725 of the Business and Professions Code, as amended in 1974, explicitly declares a legislative intent "to recognize the existence of overlapping functions between physicians and registered nurses and to permit additional sharing of functions within organized health care systems which provide for collaboration between physicians and registered nurses." Section 2725 also includes, among the functions that properly fall within "the practice of nursing" in California, the "[o]bservation of signs and symptoms of illness, reactions to treatment, general behavior, or general physical condition, and . . . determination of whether such signs, symptoms, reactions, behavior or general appearance exhibit abnormal characteristics. . . ." In light of these provisions, the "examination" or "diagnosis" of a patient cannot in all circumstances be said — as a matter of law — to be a function reserved to physicians, rather than registered nurses or nurse practitioners. Although plaintiff was certainly entitled to have the jury determine (1) whether defendant medical center was negligent in permitting a nurse practitioner to see a patient who exhibited the symptoms of which plaintiff complained and (2) whether Nurse Welch met the standard of care of a reasonably prudent nurse practitioner in conducting the examination and prescribing treatment in conjunction with her supervising physician, the court should not have told the jury that the nurse's conduct in this case must — as a matter of law — be measured by the standard of care of a physician or surgeon.

But while the instruction was erroneous, it is not reasonably probable that the error affected the judgment in this case. . . . As noted, several hours after Nurse Welch examined plaintiff and gave him the Valium that her supervising doctor had prescribed, plaintiff returned to the medical center with similar complaints and was examined by a physician, Dr. Redding. Although there was considerable expert testimony that the failure of the medication to provide relief and the continued chest pain rendered the diagnosis of muscle spasm more questionable, Dr. Redding — like Nurse Welch — failed to order an EKG. Given these facts, the jury could not reasonably have found Nurse Welch negligent under the physician standard of care without also finding Dr. Redding — who had more information and to whom the physician standard of care was properly applicable — similarly negligent. . . . Accordingly, the erroneous instruction on the standard of care of a nurse practitioner does not warrant reversal.

[The court rejected all other contentions of both plaintiff and defendant and upheld the judgment. Defendant argued, for example, that the trial court's instructions on causation required reversal; the court held, however, that the instructions were not erroneous. Defendant also argued that damages for "lost years" — *i.e.*, reduced life expectancy — were not recoverable as a separate item of damages, but were redundant of noneconomic damages; in a lengthy section of its opinion, the court held that these damages were properly awarded. Finally, in the most significant portion of its opinion, the court upheld the controversial California Medical Injury Compensation Reform Act (MICRA), which had been the subject of several constitutional attacks in both this and earlier cases. Three members of the court, led by Chief Justice Bird, dissented from this holding, which resulted in the capping of the $500,000 noneconomic award at $250,000.]

NOTES AND QUESTIONS

(1) *The Judge's Function in Instructing the Jury.* When the jury decides a "fact" such as whether a defendant was "negligent," is it really deciding a question of "fact," a question of "law," or both mixed together? How does the jury find out what the law is? If a relevant principle of law is not given to the jury during jury instructions, or if it is given to the jury erroneously, how might the decision of the case be affected?

(2) *"Harmless" Error.* Notice that the court forthrightly agrees with defendant that the instructions were wrong, but it refuses to reverse. Why (and do you agree with the court)?

(3) *The Use of "Special Verdicts."* The opinion says that the trial judge obtained "special verdicts" from the jury. What that means is that the judge asked the jury separate questions about the different kinds of damages — lost wages, medical expenses, reduced life expectancy, and "noneconomic damages" — rather than lumping them all together and asking for a "general" verdict on damages. Why did the judge do it this way?

§ 1.09 Taking the Case Away From the Jury: Motion for Judgment as a Matter of Law or New Trial

NOTE ON STANDARDS AND PROCEDURES FOR TAKING THE CASE AWAY FROM THE JURY

The jury, as you recall, decides factual disputes. But if, after presentation of the plaintiff's proof, there is no reasonable way that the facts can be construed in the plaintiff's favor, the law controls the case. The judge then has authority to decide the case without the intervention of the jury. (It is usually the defendant who moves for judgment as a matter of law, although this is not always the case.)

Judgment as a Matter of Law. There are two different but very similar procedures for accomplishing this result. During trial, after the opponent has rested his or her case, a party may move for "judgment as a matter of law" (formerly called a "directed verdict"). The court may grant the motion if indeed the moving party is entitled to judgment as a matter of law (or, in other words, if there are no factual issues in the evidence that could make a difference). In the alternative, after the jury has rendered its verdict, the court may grant a renewed motion for judgment as a matter of law (formerly called a "motion for judgment notwithstanding the verdict"), so long as the moving party filed the same motion pre-verdict. The standard is essentially the same, except that it takes place after the trial is over and the jury discharged.

Motion for New Trial. A "motion for new trial" is a broader device. It seeks to have the court remedy injustices on grounds that may range from trial errors to newly discovered evidence to a verdict against the great weight of the evidence. This procedure, however, does not result in the grant of judgment for the moving party; it merely results in a new trial. A losing party may make both a post-verdict motion for judgment as a matter of law and an alternative motion for new trial.

NOTE ON HOW TO READ THE CASE OF *WILCOX DEVELOPMENT CO. v. FIRST INTERSTATE BANK OF OREGON* THE "PRIME RATE ANTITRUST CASES"

A number of suits have been brought against banking corporations on a "prime rate antitrust" theory. The Sherman Antitrust Act provides that a "contract, combination or conspiracy in restraint of trade" is illegal. A contract, combination or conspiracy to fix prices is *per se* considered an illegal restraint of trade.

Because lending agreements are often long-term propositions, commercial parties may be able to strike a mutually acceptable bargain by using an index as the basis of the interest rate. (The same idea is used in some consumer loans; for example, a homeowner's adjustable rate mortgage usually incorporates Treasury bill rates as an index and may enable the lender to set the rate lower than if it were fixed.) In commercial transactions, the lender may use some index such as the rates charged by other banks. The antitrust theory advanced by dissatisfied borrowers in that situation is that the lender has thereby "contracted, combined or conspired" with others to fix the rate.

To use this theory, however, the plaintiff must submit evidence showing not merely that an individual lender used such an index as a consequence of its own business judgment, but that there is a basis for inferring an agreement among lenders. The agreement need not be formal or even express, and it may be shown by conduct. But lenders in this situation would promptly point out that they are forced by inexorable laws of economics to respond to the market. If they act independently but reach parallel behavior as a result of market forces, there is no antitrust violation. Thus, proof may depend upon the plaintiff's ability to prove not just parallel behavior, but some "plus factor" showing that the parallelism is the result of tacit agreement.

In some of these cases, verdicts have been returned in favor of the lenders. In the case that follows, *Wilcox Development Co. v. First Interstate Bank of Oregon*, the jury decided that there had been an antitrust violation, and its verdict would in the normal course of events be the basis of a judgment for damages for the plaintiff. The defendant, however, filed a motion for judgment as a matter of law and an alternative motion for new trial. (In fact, the defendant called the motion for judgment as a matter of law a "motion for judgment notwithstanding the verdict," or a "judgment n.o.v.," because that was the language used to described these motions at the time they were made.)

POST-TRIAL MOTIONS IN *WILCOX DEVELOPMENT CO. v. FIRST INTERSTATE BANK OF OREGON*

Civil No. 81-1127-RE (D. Ore. Jan. 7, 1985)

IN THE UNITED STATES DISTRICT COURT
FOR THE DISTRICT OF OREGON

WILCOX DEVELOPMENT CO. v. FIRST INTERSTATE BANK OF OREGON	Civil No. 82-754-RE

MOTION FOR JUDGMENT [AS A MATTER OF LAW] OR IN THE ALTERNATIVE FOR A NEW TRIAL

1. Defendants having at the close of all the evidence moved for a [judgment as a matter of law], which motion was denied, and the jury having returned a verdict for plaintiffs, defendants move pursuant to Rule 50(b) Fed. R. Civ. P. for an order setting the verdict aside and entering judgment in favor of each defendant in accordance with said motion, on the ground asserted in support thereof that the evidence was insufficient for the jury to find a conspiracy on the part of either defendant in restraint of trade in violation of § 1 of the Sherman Act.

2. If the foregoing motion is denied, defendants move pursuant to Rule 59(a) Fed. R. Civ. P. for an order setting aside the verdict thereon and granting each defendant a new trial, on the following grounds:

a. The court erred in submitting to the jury the issue of a conspiracy between [the defendant banks].

b. The court erred in its instructions to the jury on parallel business conduct and in refusing to give defendants' requested or the court's proposed instruction on that subject.

c. The verdict is contrary to law and against the weight of the evidence.

SPEARS, LUBERSKY,
CAMPBELL, BLEDSOE,
ANDERSON & YOUNG
James H. Clarke

WILCOX DEVELOPMENT CO. v. FIRST INTERSTATE BANK OF OREGON
605 F. Supp. 592 (D. Ore. 1985)

REDDEN, JUDGE:

These four cases were consolidated for trial on plaintiffs' allegations of defendants' violation of 15 U.S.C. § 1, the Sherman Antitrust Act. Plaintiffs asserted some twenty other claims in these four cases, all of which were decided in favor of defendants in subsequent trials, or upon summary judgment.

In the antitrust claim, plaintiffs alleged that defendants had agreed with other banks to raise, fix and maintain the "prime" interest rate at an artificial and anticompetitive level. . . .

The cases were tried to a jury in April and May and resulted in a verdict for plaintiffs. Defendants now move the court for an order granting them a judgment [as a matter of law], or in the alternative, for a new trial. For the reasons set forth below, I grant defendants' motion for judgment [as a matter of law].

DISCUSSION

I. *Standard for Judgment [as a Matter of Law]*

In considering a motion for judgment [as a matter of law], the court must give appropriate deference to the jury's verdict. Such a motion should only be granted if, without accounting for the credibility of the witnesses, the evidence and all its inferences, considered in the light most favorable to the non-moving party, can support only one conclusion: that the moving party is entitled to judgment. *William Inglis and Sons v. ITT Continental Baking Co.*, 668 F.2d 1014, 1026 (9th Cir. 1981). The verdict of the jury must stand if it is supported by substantial evidence. . . . Substantial evidence is such relevant evidence as a reasonable mind might accept as adequate to support a conclusion. . . .

II. *What Constitutes a Violation of 15 U.S.C. § 1*

To be successful in a cause of action alleging a violation of 15 U.S.C. § 1, plaintiffs must establish: 1) an agreement among two or more persons or distinct business entities, which is 2) intended to harm or unreasonably restrain competition, and 3) which actually causes harm to competition. *Rosebrough Monument Co. v. Memorial Park Cemetery*, 666 F.2d 1130, 1138 (8th Cir.), *cert. denied*, 457 U.S. 1111 (1981). . . .

In the absence of an express agreement, courts often consider the existence of parallel business behavior when inferring an agreement. However, parallel action alone will never be enough to establish an agreement for purposes of showing a conspiracy in violation of 15 U.S.C. § 1. *Granddad Bread, Inc. v. Continental Baking Co.*, 612 F.2d 1105 (9th Cir.), *cert. denied*, 449 U.S. 1076 (1979). Conscious parallel conduct will be regarded as evidence of an agreement only in those situations in which the similarity of behavior can only be attributed to a tacit agreement, and the parties are acting in a manner against their own individual business interest, or there is motivation to enter into an agreement requiring parallel behavior. . . . Additionally, evidence of lawful business reasons for parallel conduct will dispel any inference of a conspiracy. . . .

There are a series of "plus factors" to be considered by the court when inferring an agreement for purposes of 15 U.S.C. § 1. *C-O Two Fire Equipment Co. v. United States*, 197 F.2d 489 (9th Cir. 1952). In addition to parallel conduct (expressed as price and product uniformity), the court should look for exchanges of price information among alleged conspirators, and meetings affording them an opportunity to form industry-wide policies. . . .

III. *Evidence Presented at Trial*

Plaintiffs argue that the virtual identity of prime rates among defendants and seven other major west coast banks, in and of itself, establishes the conscious parallel conduct needed to infer an agreement. . . .

There was ample testimony from all expert witnesses at trial that defendants' "prime rate" is a national prime rate imposed by national economic conditions. The testimony of the experts clearly established that the prime rates used by banks are set to reflect market demands and individual self-interest in attracting new and retaining old customers.

Dr. Horvitz, plaintiffs' principal expert witness, testified that although there are noncompetitive factors which influence an individual bank's prime rate, all banks will use essentially the same rate, even without any agreement or collusion among the banks. Dr. Fischer testified that any divergence from the national prime rate by a bank would be "foolishness." Dr. Eisenbeis stated that all banks use substantially the same rate because the market so demands, and that in order for a bank to be competitive in the market, it must adhere to the uniform prime rate.

There was also extensive testimony to the effect that defendants could not maintain their prime rate at a level different from other large commercial banks. If defendants maintained their rates higher than that of other banks, their customers would take their business elsewhere. Likewise, if defendants were to set their prime rate lower than other banks, they would lose revenues on existing prime-based loans and dangerously reduce their profit margin. . . .

In setting its prime rate [defendant] FIOR uses what it calls a "count to four" method. FIOR will change its prime rate when four of seven specific major west coast banks change theirs. These banks adjust their prime rate to reflect the rates set by the nation's largest banks. Plaintiffs contend that this practice infers an agreement because the changes are not tied to FIOR's cost of funds. Thus, plaintiffs argue, no good faith business judgment sparks FIOR's decision to change its prime rate. This argument fails because it was established that changes in the national prime rate reflect changes in the cost of money. It was also established that FIOR's "count to four" method was instituted unilaterally, and that none of the other banks used this method in adjusting their prime rates.

It is not unlawful for a business enterprise to take the prices charged by its competitors into account when setting its own prices, or to follow or copy the prices of a competitor, if the decision to do so is the result of unilateral business judgment, and not the result of a collusive agreement. *United States v. International Harvester Co.*, 274 U.S. 693 (1927). . . .

I find the existence of a near universal prime rate does not support an inference of an agreement among defendants and other banks to "fix the prime rate." FIOR adjusts its prime rate, up or down, in response to changes by four named west coast banks. Those banks, in turn, respond to eastern pacesetters. Invariably the rate adjustments start with the larger east coast banks early in the banking day. The adjustments roll across the country as does the sun, and virtually every bank in the nation responds. . . . The evidence supports the conclusion that FIOR exercises its independent business judgment in order to maintain its ability to compete. This response to competition is not illegal.

Plaintiffs note that it is a common practice of businesses and financial institutions to subscribe to wire services that quickly transmit changes in the prime rates across the country. This practice, plaintiffs argue, constitutes an "exchange of prices" among the banks. Plaintiffs further state that this "plus factor," coupled with the uniform prime rate charged by banks, creates the necessary inference of an agreement. In support of the argument plaintiffs cite *United States v. Container Corporation of America*, 393 U.S. 333 (1969). Plaintiffs' reliance on this case is misplaced. . . .

Here, plaintiffs contend that public information which is regularly disseminated to all types of businesses including financial institutions and the media should be considered in the same light as the private and specific price information in *Container*. I do not agree. . . .

Plaintiffs also point to various industry-wide conventions which provided other banks with an opportunity to conspire with Bancorp and its subsidiaries to fix the prime rate. These facts, plaintiffs argue, supply yet another "plus factor" and substantiate their claims of a violation of § 1 of the Sherman Antitrust Act. . . .

As for plaintiffs' notation regarding the conventions, there was no direct evidence of collusion, or even a discussion among the bankers at conventions to fix the level of the prime rate. Absent any evidence, I decline to infer the existence of any such agreement on the basis of the fact that bankers were gathered together in one central location at a given point in time. . . .

[The court also held that the verdict could not be upheld by other factual and legal arguments presented in the case.]

CONCLUSION

After a review of the evidence presented at trial, and all reasonable inferences drawn therefrom and considered in the light most favorable to plaintiffs, I find only one conclusion can be supported; that FIOR is entitled to judgment [as a matter of law]. I also find that the verdict of the jury was not supported by substantial evidence.

[After granting judgment as a matter of law, the judge was required by Fed. R. Civ. P. 50 to rule conditionally on defendant's Motion for New Trial. The court ordered that, if the judgment as a matter of law were to be reversed on appeal, the verdict would be set aside and a new trial granted.]

Dated this _____ day of January, 1985.

James A. Redden
United States District Judge

NOTES AND QUESTIONS

(1) *The Standard for Decision.* Does the court grant judgment as a matter of law because the judge disagrees with the jury on the evidence? If not, just what is the judge saying about the relationship between the evidence and the jury's verdict?

(2) *The Correctness of the Judge's Decision Here.* The judge makes a point of reference to the jury's verdict. Do you believe that the judge has correctly applied the standard for judgment as a matter of law here? Is the judge saying that he declines to infer a conspiracy, or is he saying that no reasonable person could make the inference under the governing law?

(3) *Grant of Post-Verdict Judgment as a Matter of Law After Denial of Both Summary Judgment and a Pre-Verdict Motion for Judgment as a Matter of Law.* The court had

earlier denied summary judgment in this case. *See Wilcox Development Co. v. First Interstate Bank of Oregon*, 590 F. Supp. 445 (D. Ore. 1984). Actually, it is perfectly consistent to deny summary judgment and then grant a post-verdict judgment as a matter of law because of the different contexts of the two procedures. Can you explain why? Furthermore, it is sensible for the trial judge to deny an initial motion for judgment as a matter of law (also called a "directed verdict") and later grant a renewed motion for judgment as a matter of law (also called a "judgment notwithstanding the verdict"), even though the standards for these procedures are closely similar. Can you explain why?

(4) *New Trial.* The judge has broad discretion in granting a new trial on the basis of trial errors even if they would not suffice for appellate reversal, or on the basis of a verdict that he or she considers against the great weight of the evidence even if a judgment as a matter of law could not be granted. The grant of a new trial is not reviewable by an appellate court except on abuse of discretion grounds. Does this procedure give excessive power to the trial judge? (Actually, experienced trial lawyers will tell you that judges use the power to grant new trials sparingly. Can you guess why?)

§ 1.10 Appeal

NOTE ABOUT THE FUNCTION OF AN APPELLATE COURT

A common misconception is that appellate courts decide cases on a clean slate. On the contrary, appellate courts do not have authority to change most of the actions taken in most trials. The appellate courts decide only questions of law, and then they may reverse only in the event that an error has occurred that has harmed the substantial rights of the complaining party, *if* that party has taken the proper steps to present the issue to both the trial and the appellate courts. It may be helpful to regard the process as resembling an upside-down funnel: At the trial level, issues are diffuse and fact-oriented, but they become more focused and law-oriented in the appeals process.

The funnel image is also useful in visualizing the frequency of appeals as a means of dispute resolution. Most disputes do not result in suits, most suits do not result in trials, and most trials do not result in appeals. The cases that you read in casebooks should not convey the misleading impression that appeal is the norm. Appellate decisions are important because they set standards for trials, but they represent only a small percentage of cases actually litigated.

FEIN v. PERMANENTE MEDICAL GROUP, 38 Cal. 3d 137, 695 P.2d 665, 211 Cal. Rptr. 368 (1985). Reconsider this case, which appears in § 1.08, above. Fein sued Permanente for negligent diagnosis and treatment. The evidence was hotly contested. The jury found Permanente liable and rendered special verdicts on various damage items. The judge granted judgment for Fein but "capped" noneconomic damages at $250,000 in accordance with a California statute. Both sides appealed. The California Supreme Court first considered defendant's contention that the trial judge had erred in excusing 40 percent of the panel who were members of the Kaiser plan; without deciding whether these venire members were excludable on grounds of "interest," the court upheld the "broad discretion" of the trial judge in jury selection. The court rejected defendant's attack on the jury instructions because although they were erroneous, it was "not reasonably probable that the instructional error affected the judgment." The court rejected plaintiff's attack on the "capped" judgment because a four-to-three majority concluded that the California statute limiting noneconomic recoveries was constitutional.

NOTES AND QUESTIONS

(1) *Appellate Review of Trial Court Discretion.* Appellate review spreads responsibility among several judges, and our system includes appeals so that a single judge cannot make unexplained decisions on major issues affecting parties' rights. Why, then, did the California Supreme Court uphold the excusing of 40 percent of the panel by deferring to the "broad discretion" of the trial judge? Does the court's decision mean that trial judges can make no errors in excusing groups of jurors (and if not, at what point does a trial judge transgress a limit that can result in appellate reversal)?

(2) *Appellate Decision of Questions of Law: The Constitutional Issue.* Why didn't the court uphold "capping" of the verdict by just deferring to the trial court's discretion?

(3) *Error That Did Not Have a "Reasonably Probable" Effect.* Should the appellate court refuse to reverse when it does not see a "reasonable probability" that an admitted error affected the judgment? This approach is sometimes called the "harmless error" doctrine. Would it be better to reverse whenever there is any possibility that the error tainted the result? [Note: What is the likelihood of an error-free trial in a case such as *Fein v. Permanente*?]

(4) *Deference to the Jury's Verdict.* Notice that the appellate court simply states the evidence and the jury's holding, without weighing the evidence or commenting on whether the jury was correct. Why? Could the court reverse if it disagreed with the jury? If it disagreed very strongly? If it concluded that there was no reasonable way to justify the jury's verdict based on the evidence?

CHAPTER 2

THE COURT'S POWER OVER PERSONS AND PROPERTY

§ 2.01 The Concerns Underlying Personal Jurisdiction and Venue

Your client brings you a copy of a judgment taken against her in a distant state, one where she has never done any business or even visited. She expresses surprise about the judgment and tells you that she thinks its entry is abusive to her. In addition, she tells you that she never was informed that any suit had been filed against her, and the judgment was obtained without her knowledge.

The Distant Forum Concern. If you were the client, you would consider this suit abusive because, in the first place, it was brought in a place distant from your home, governed by laws with which you have no connection. This concern for preventing distant forum abuse will be one of the major issues we will consider in this chapter.

The Notice Concern. In the second place, you would be concerned about the absence of notice about the suit. You might have been able to defend against it if you had known about it. This notice concern is also one of the major themes underlying this chapter.

State Laws and the Due Process Clause of the Fourteenth Amendment. Until the adoption of the Fourteenth Amendment, these forum abuse and notice issues were addressed primarily by state law. Now, the Fourteenth Amendment provides that "No State shall . . . deprive any person of life, liberty, or property without due process of law." This concise Due Process Clause is the source of a wide variety of rights and limits on government. In this chapter, we will consider due process as a limit on distant forum abuse and as a requirement for notice. State laws also are still applicable in these areas, and a litigant may be provided with protections against distant forum abuse and lack of notice both by state law and by the Due Process Clause.

A Little History: Territoriality and the Physical Power Concept. Many years ago, civil actions were commenced by seizure of the person or property of the defendant within the territory of the forum. The court obtained jurisdiction by the exercise of raw physical power over persons or property within its territory. This "physical power" method of determining jurisdiction had certain advantages: There were few questions of distant forum abuse, few questions of notice, and few infringements by one sovereign of the rights of another. But seizure also raised obvious fairness problems. The method of having a sheriff or other officer walk up to the defendant and hand him a set of papers commanding the defendant to answer is a more modern invention, signifying that physical power could be asserted, but avoiding the unnecessary use of force. However, this history is still relevant today because the "physical power" notion has influenced the way our jurisdictional concepts have developed.

PROBLEM A: CHAPTER 2 SUMMARY PROBLEM

VANDIVER v. SMALL ELECTRONICS, INC. (A HYPOTHETICAL CASE OF NATIONWIDE "STREAM OF COMMERCE"). This problem implicates many of the materials in this chapter and should be "solved" at the end of the chapter (or used as your instructor directs).

Small Electronics, Inc. is a New York corporation that manufactures and sells components to General Systems Corporation, all within New York State. General Systems Corporation, in turn, uses the components to manufacture goods that it sells throughout the entire nation. The result is that these nationwide sales indirectly bring hundreds of thousands of dollars annually to Small Electronics, even though it has no direct dealings elsewhere than in New York. Paula Vandiver is a Florida resident who happened to be on vacation in Las Vegas, Nevada. While there, she was injured by a product manufactured by General Systems. An investigation has produced indications that the cause of the injuries was a defect in the components manufactured by Small Electronics.

Vandiver, seeking to sue Small Electronics, consults a Florida lawyer. She would like to file suit in Florida (her residence), where many of General System's products incorporating the Small Electronics components are sold annually, rather than Nevada (even though the accident happened there) or New York. If you were the Florida lawyer, would you take the case on a contingent fee basis? [Adapted from a real case in which one of the authors advised the attorneys for "Vandiver."] You should answer the following questions in this connection:

1. Is it likely that a Florida court would have potential personal jurisdiction over Small Electronics?
2. How can Vandiver have process (*i.e.*, the litigation papers) served upon Small?
3. What result would you expect if Small moves to transfer the suit to Nevada (or to New York)?

§ 2.02 Jurisdiction Over Persons and Property

[A] The Development of Our Concept of Jurisdiction

[1] Territoriality

HOW TO READ AND UNDERSTAND *PENNOYER v. NEFF*

The case that follows, *Pennoyer v. Neff*, is a venerable landmark. For insight into the characters and the story behind the case, *see* Perdue, *Sin, Scandal and Substantive Due Process: Personal Jurisdiction and* Pennoyer *Reconsidered*, 62 Wash. L. Rev. 479, 480-96 (1987). Some of what the case says is no longer the law today. It would be unthinkable, however, not to include it in this book, because it provides such wonderful insight into the basis of our jurisdictional concepts. In reading this case, you should be alert for several broad themes.

Territoriality and Sovereignty. Each state, according to this case, is a separate entity and is sovereign within its territory. Therefore, the service of process (*i.e.*, of suit papers) is heavily affected by territorial boundaries. If it were not, the states allegedly would infringe each other's sovereignty. According to the Court, there would be no way to afford full faith and credit to sister state judgments without conflict if state territorial boundaries were not honored. [These are among the propositions in *Pennoyer* that no longer are controlling.]

The Effect of Service of Process Within the Territory. The same notions of territoriality support the exercise of jurisdiction whenever a defendant is physically served with process inside the state. Even if he is present only briefly and for an unrelated purpose, the state obtains power over him, if it can serve him inside its borders, according to this reasoning.

"In Rem" Jurisdiction: Power Over Property Within the Territory. A state also may exercise what is known as "*in rem*" jurisdiction. "*In rem*" is Latin for "against the thing." If the object of adjudication is a "thing" within the territory of the state, the state has power over it in the same way that it has power over persons served with process inside the state. For example, if there is an issue of title to land located within the state, the state can adjudicate this issue even though it might not be able to obtain personal jurisdiction over the claimants, because it has power over the property in question. "*Quasi in rem*" actions are not "pure" *in rem* actions because, like actions *in personam*, they bind only certain named defendants and because, in one type of "*quasi in rem*" action, the defendant's property is seized to give the court jurisdiction to adjudicate disputes not otherwise related to the property.

Jurisdiction of Persons Outside the State. The "flip side" of this notion of territoriality is that the state has little, if any, power over persons located outside the state. The state can, as is indicated above, affect those persons' rights by *in rem* actions against property within the state. But if a nonresident comes into a state and causes a tortious injury, and leaves the state before being served with process, according to *Pennoyer*, the state has no power to render an in personam judgment against the nonresident.

> Read U.S. Const. amend. XIV § 1 cl. 3 (the Fourteenth Amendment Due Process Clause).

PENNOYER v. NEFF
95 U.S. 714 (1877)

[Neff had originally owned a tract of land in Oregon. However, Neff had a contract with one J.H. Mitchell to pay for Mitchell's services as an attorney. When Neff allegedly did not pay, Mitchell sued Neff in an Oregon state court for his fee. Because Neff was a nonresident of Oregon, Mitchell had Neff served with process "by publication": That is, in accordance with governing Oregon statutes, Mitchell published an advertisement in an Oregon newspaper for six successive weeks, containing information about the suit. Neff failed to appear, and Mitchell took a default judgment. Neff's tract of land was sold in a sheriff's sale to satisfy the judgment. Pennoyer acquired title derived from the sheriff's sale.

[When Neff learned of these events, he sued Pennoyer in a federal trial court for the District of Oregon (then called a "Circuit Court") to recover the land. The trial court held for Neff, and Pennoyer took the case to the Supreme Court. But the issue in *Pennoyer v. Neff* really depends upon the earlier suit by Mitchell against Neff. If the court had jurisdiction in *Mitchell v. Neff*, the sheriff's sale was valid, and Pennoyer keeps the land. If it did not have jurisdiction, the sheriff's sale was invalid, and Neff recovers the land. The issue thus depends upon whether the service by publication was effective to give Oregon jurisdiction over the nonresident Neff; the Supreme Court here holds that it was not.]

MR. JUSTICE FIELD delivered the opinion of the Court:

. . . [Plaintiff Neff contends] that the judgment in the State court against the plaintiff was void for want of personal service of process on him, or of his appearance in the action in which it was rendered, and that the premises in controversy could not be subjected to the payment of the demand of a resident creditor except by a proceeding *in rem*; that is, by a direct proceeding against the property for that purpose. If these positions are sound, the ruling of the Circuit Court as to the invalidity of that judgment must be sustained. . . . And that they are sound would seem to follow from two well-established principles of public law respecting the jurisdiction of an independent State over persons and property. . . . [First], except as restrained and limited by [the Constitution, the states] possess and exercise the authority of independent States, and the principles of public law to which we have referred are applicable to them. One of these principles is that every State possesses exclusive jurisdiction and sovereignty over persons and property within its territory. . . . The other principle of public law referred to follows from the one mentioned; that is, that no State can exercise direct jurisdiction and authority over persons or property without its territory. Story, *Confl. Laws*, c.2. . . . The several States are of equal dignity and authority, and the independence of one implies the exclusion of power from all others. And so it is laid down by jurists, as an elementary principle, that the laws of one State have no operation outside of its territory, except so far as is allowed by comity; and that no tribunal established by it can extend its process beyond that territory so as to subject either persons or property to its decisions. "Any exertion of authority of this sort beyond this limit," says Story, "is a mere nullity, and incapable of binding such persons or property in any other tribunals." Story, *Confl. Laws*, sect. 539.

So the State, through its tribunals, may subject property situated within its limits owned by non-residents to the payment of the demand of its own citizens against them; and the exercise of this jurisdiction in no respect infringes upon the sovereignty of the State where the owners are domiciled. Every State owes protection to its own citizens; and, when non-residents deal with them, it is a legitimate and just exercise of authority to hold and appropriate any property owned by such non-residents to satisfy the claims of its citizens. It is in virtue of the State's jurisdiction over the property of the non-resident situated within its limits that its tribunals can inquire into that non-resident's obligations to its own citizens, and the inquiry can then be carried only to the extent necessary to control the disposition of the property. If the non-resident has no property in the State, there is nothing upon which the tribunals can adjudicate.

Substituted service by publication, or in any other authorized form, may be sufficient to inform parties of the object of proceedings taken where property is once brought under the control of the court by seizure or some equivalent act. The law assumes that property is always in the possession of its owner, in person or by agent; and it proceeds upon the theory that its seizure will inform him, not only that it is taken into the custody of the court, but that he must look to any proceedings authorized by law upon such seizure for its condemnation and sale. Such service may also be sufficient in cases where the object of the action is to reach and dispose of property in the State, or of some interest therein, by enforcing a contract or a lien respecting the same, or to partition it among different owners, or, when the public is a party, to condemn and appropriate it for a public purpose. In other words, such service may answer in all actions which are substantially proceedings *in rem*. But where the entire object of the action is to determine the personal rights and obligations of the defendants, that is, where the suit is merely *in personam*, constructive service in this form upon a non-resident is ineffectual for any purpose. Process from the tribunals of one State cannot run into another State, and summon parties there domiciled to leave its territory and respond to proceedings against them. Publication of process or notice within the State where the tribunal sits cannot create any greater obligation upon the non-resident to appear. Process sent to him out of the State, and process published within it, are equally unavailing in proceedings to establish his personal liability.

The want of authority of the tribunals of a State to adjudicate upon the obligations of non-residents, where they have no property within its limits, is not denied . . . : but the position is assumed, that, where they have property within the State, it is immaterial whether the property is in the first instance brought under the control of the court by attachment or some other equivalent act, and afterwards applied by its judgment to the satisfaction of demands against its owner; or such demands be first established in a personal action, and the property of the non-resident be afterwards seized and sold on execution. But the answer to this position has already been given in the statement, that the jurisdiction of the court to inquire into and determine his obligations at all is only incidental to its jurisdiction over the property. Its jurisdiction in that respect cannot be made to depend upon facts to be ascertained after it has tried the cause and rendered the judgment. If the judgment be previously void, it will not become valid by the subsequent discovery of property of the defendant, or by his subsequent acquisition of it. The judgment, if void when rendered, will always remain void: it cannot occupy the doubtful position of being valid if property be found, and void if there be none. . . .

The force and effect of judgments rendered against non-residents without personal service of process upon them, or their voluntary appearance, have been the subject of frequent consideration in the courts of the United States and of the several States, as attempts have been made to enforce such judgments in States other than those in which they were rendered, under the provision of the Constitution requiring that "full faith and credit shall be given in each State to the public acts, records, and judicial proceedings of every other State" . . . .

Be that as it may, the courts of the United States are not required to give effect to judgments of this character when any right is claimed under them. Whilst they are not foreign tribunals in their relations to the State courts, they are tribunals of a different sovereignty, exercising a distinct and independent jurisdiction, and are bound to give to the judgments of the State courts only the same faith and credit which the courts of another State are bound to give to them.

Since the adoption of the Fourteenth Amendment to the Federal Constitution, the validity of such judgments may be directly questioned, and their enforcement in the State resisted on the ground that proceedings in a court of justice to determine the personal rights and obligations of parties over whom that court has no jurisdiction do not constitute due process of law. . . . To give such proceedings any validity, there must be a tribunal competent by its constitution — that is, by the law of its creation — to pass upon the subject-matter of the suit; and, if that involves merely a determination of the personal liability of the defendant, he must be brought within its jurisdiction by service of process within the State, or his voluntary appearance. . . .

It follows from the views expressed that the personal judgment recovered in the State court of Oregon against the plaintiff herein, then a non-resident of the State, was without any validity, and did not authorize a sale of the property in controversy.

To prevent any misapplication of the views expressed in this opinion, it is proper to observe that we do not mean to assert, by any thing we have said, that a State may not authorize proceedings to determine the *status* of one of its citizens towards a non-resident, which would be binding within the State, though made without service of process or personal notice to the non-resident. The jurisdiction which every State possesses to determine the civil *status* and capacities of all its inhabitants involves authority to prescribe the conditions on which proceedings affecting them may be commenced and carried on within its territory. The State, for example, has absolute right to prescribe the conditions upon which the marriage relation between its own citizens shall be created, and the causes for which it may be dissolved. One of the parties guilty of acts for which, by the law of the State, a dissolution may be granted, may have removed to a State where no dissolution is permitted. The complaining party would, therefore, fail if a divorce were sought in the State of the defendant; and if application could not be made to the tribunals of the complainant's domicile in such case, and proceedings be there instituted without personal service of process or personal notice to the offending party, the injured citizen would be without redress. . . .

Neither do we mean to assert that a State may not require a non-resident entering into a partnership or association within its limits, or making contracts enforceable there, to appoint an agent or representative in the State to receive service of process and notice in legal proceedings instituted with respect to such partnership, association, or contracts, or to designate a place where such service may be made and notice given, and provide, upon their failure, to make such appointment or to designate such place that service may be made upon a public officer designated for that purpose, or in some other prescribed way, and that judgments rendered upon such service may not be binding upon the non-residents both within and without the State. . . .

Judgment [restoring the property to Neff] affirmed.

NOTES AND QUESTIONS

(1) *Reconsidering Wyman v. Newhouse, supra.* Reconsider *Wyman v. Newhouse*, which appears above in § 1.03. In that case, Wyman lured Newhouse to Florida, a state to which he had no connection, with false messages about her affection for him. When he came, a sheriff was waiting at the airport to serve him with process. In a later action on the resulting default judgment, a court in New York held that Florida had not obtained jurisdiction even though the defendant was served inside the state, because the service was obtained by fraud. Is it clear, now, why Ms. Wyman engaged in her treachery, and what she hoped to gain from it? Is the decision in *Wyman v. Newhouse* consistent with *Pennoyer* (or is it an exception with which *Pennoyer* simply does not deal)?

(2) *"Consent" by Appearance.* Imagine that a nonresident defendant is served with defective process. However, she comes to the forum and makes an appearance in the case. In fact, she files an answer, litigates the case through trial, and loses, without ever raising any question of jurisdiction. After losing, however, she objects on the ground that the court lacks power over her. What result, according to *Pennoyer*?

(3) *"Consent" by Required Appointment of an Agent.* The Court says that a state can condition permission to do business upon a nonresident's appointment of an agent for receipt of service within the state. Explain how this result follows from territorial sovereignty notions. What should happen if a nonresident does business in the state without appointing an agent? Can the state then appoint one for him, or provide by statute that doing business without a local agent automatically results in the appointment by

operation of law of somebody (such as the state's Secretary of State) as the nonresident's "agent"?

(4) *"In Rem" Jurisdiction.* Territoriality and sovereignty notions provide strong support for the concept of *in rem* jurisdiction. Remember that "*in rem*" proceedings are proceedings "against a thing." The thing need not be a corporeal object; in fact, it can be something like a debt or an inheritance right under a will. If a decedent is domiciled in a given state, that state may be able to probate the will notwithstanding the claims of nonresidents under or against the will. Is this result sound? [Note: If not, would there be any state that would be able to probate the will?] On the other hand, is it appropriate for a court to obtain jurisdiction by seizure of property and to use that jurisdiction to adjudicate an issue completely unrelated to the property? [Although *Pennoyer* allows this result, doesn't it amount to using the property as a hostage to make the owner submit to jurisdiction?]

(5) *Actual In-Hand Service on a Person Traveling Through the State.* Imagine that a citizen of California is driving to New York, and while he is on an interstate highway in Nebraska, a sheriff stops his car to serve him with summons in a suit in that state. If this defendant has never been to Nebraska and is just passing through, is it fair for the service to result in jurisdiction? In any event, whether "fair" or not, would the service be upheld under the reasoning in *Pennoyer v. Neff*? The governing principle under *Pennoyer* seems to be that, subject to rare exceptions (such as fraudulent enticement as in *Wyman v. Newhouse*), service within the state creates jurisdiction no matter how briefly the defendant is present in the state and no matter for what purpose. Consider the following case.

GRACE v. MACARTHUR, 170 F. Supp. 442 (E.D. Ark. 1959). Defendant was served with process in a suit in a federal District Court in Arkansas. The service was accomplished while defendant was a passenger over Arkansas airspace on a nonstop flight between Memphis and Dallas on a commercial airliner. (As the court put it, defendant was "physically above the City of Pine Bluff in the Eastern District of Arkansas.") Defendant attacked the service as invalid. The court upheld the service and jurisdiction on the ground that it had taken place while defendant was within the "territorial limits" of the State of Arkansas. [*See also State ex rel. Sivnksty v. Duffield*, 137 W. Va. 112, 71 S.E.2d 113 (1952) (non-resident validly served with process while in jail); *Darrah v. Watson*, 36 Iowa 116 (1872) (non-resident served while in jurisdiction for a few hours); *Peabody v. Hamilton*, 106 Mass. 217 (1870) (non-resident served while on a British ship in Boston harbor).] Interestingly, the judge in *Grace v. MacArthur* speculated that "a time may come . . . when commercial aircraft will fly at altitudes so high that it would be unrealistic to consider them as being within the territorial limits . . . of any particular State while flying at such altitudes," but concluded that "no such situation is here presented" because defendant was in "an ordinary commercial aircraft." Is this reasoning sound?

[2] Implied Consent

HESS v. PAWLOSKI, 274 U.S. 352 (1927). Pawloski sued Hess in a Massachusetts state court for personal injuries received in an automobile accident that occurred in

Massachusetts. The defendant was not personally served with process, nor was his property attached; instead, he was served under the terms of a Massachusetts statute that provided as follows:

> The acceptance by a nonresident of the rights and privileges . . . [of] operating a motor vehicle on a public way in the commonwealth . . . shall be deemed equivalent to an appointment by such nonresident of the registrar or his successor in office, to be his . . . [agent for receipt of service of process in any action] growing out of any accident or collision in which said nonresident may be involved while operating a motor vehicle on such a way. . . . Service of process shall be made by leaving a copy of the process with a fee of two dollars in the hands of the registrar . . . ; provided, that notice of such service and a copy of the process are forthwith sent by registered mail by the plaintiff to the defendant, and the defendant's return receipt and the plaintiff's affidavit of compliance herewith are appended to the writ. . . .

The defendant received the required copy of the process sent him by mail. He appeared specially to contest the jurisdiction of the court by filing a motion to dismiss, arguing that the method of service deprived him of due process. The Massachusetts courts upheld the service, and so did the United States Supreme Court. The Court reasoned as follows:

> The process of a court of one State cannot run into another and summon a party there domiciled. . . . *Pennoyer v. Neff* . . . . There must be actual service within the State of notice upon him or upon someone authorized to accept service for him. . . . The power of a State to exclude foreign corporations . . . is the ground upon which [their consent is implied to the appointment of such an agent].
>
> Motor vehicles are dangerous machines; and, even when they are skillfully and carefully operated, their use is attended by serious dangers to persons and property. In the public interest, the State may make and enforce regulations reasonably calculated to promote care on the part of all, residents and non-residents alike, who use its highways. The measure in question operates to require a non-resident to answer for his conduct in the State where arise causes of action alleged against him, as well as to provide for a claimant a convenient method by which he may sue to enforce his rights. . . . [I]n advance of the operation of a motor vehicle on its highways by a non-resident, the State may require him to appoint one of its officials as his agent on whom process may be served in proceedings growing out of such use. *Kane v. New Jersey*, 242 U.S. 160, 167. That case recognizes the power of the State to exclude a non-resident until the formal appointment is made. And, having power so to exclude, the State may declare that the use of the highway by the non-resident is the equivalent of the appointment of the registrar as agent on whom process may be served. . . .

Judgment affirmed.

NOTES AND QUESTIONS

(1) *Implied (Fictitious?) Consent.* The effect of the Massachusetts statute was that defendant Hess "consented" to the appointment of the registrar as his agent for service. What act of his was it that resulted in this consent? Did he even know he was consenting at the time? Isn't the consent fictitious?

(2) *The Influence of Pennoyer.* Explain why the statute employs this mechanism of consent. Notice that the Court commences its discussion by citing *Pennoyer*. How does the implication of consent to the appointment of the registrar bring the statute into compliance with *Pennoyer*?

(3) *Criticizing the Reasoning in Hess v. Pawloski.* At least in theory, the law should produce uniform decisions resulting from rules of general applicability. This opinion may not be advantageous from that standpoint. What if the defendant had injured the plaintiff in Massachusetts, but on a private driveway as opposed to a "public way"? What if defendant had injured plaintiff with an airplane, a boat, a gun, or a can opener, used within the State of Massachusetts? Does Massachusetts need to pass a statute covering every possible dangerous instrumentality that could be used within its borders to injure its citizens?

(4) *A Better Way.* The Court gives a glimpse of a better rule when it says that the Massachusetts statute "operates to require a non-resident to answer for his conduct in the State wherein arise causes of action alleged against him, as well as to provide for a claimant a convenient method by which he may sue to enforce his rights." See whether you can use this language to articulate a different and better approach that would cover injuries (by guns, boats, can openers or anything else) that should fairly give rise to suit in Massachusetts. *See International Shoe Co. v. Washington,* in the next section.

[B] The Modern "Minimum Contacts" Doctrine

[1] The *International Shoe* Decision

NOTE ON THE DEVELOPMENT OF LONG-ARM JURISDICTION FROM *PENNOYER* TO *INTERNATIONAL SHOE*

Early Rules Against Jurisdiction. The early decisions about jurisdiction focused primarily on corporations. These decisions indicated that a corporation, as an incorporeal entity, had no existence separate from the jurisdiction that had created it, and it was implied that there could not exist authority to sue it elsewhere. As the Supreme Court put it, "a corporation can have no legal existence out of the boundaries of the sovereignty by which it was created." *Bank of Augusta v. Earle,* 38 U.S. (13 Pet.) 519, 588 (1839). Individuals, of course, were not subject to extraterritorial jurisdiction, as recognized in *Pennoyer.*

"Consent" Implied from "Doing Business." Later, the authority of a state to exclude a corporate business was recognized in a number of decisions, including *Pennoyer,* as a basis for requiring a corporation to designate an agent for service of process. This theory faltered in *Flexner v. Farson,* 248 U.S. 289 (1919), in which the Supreme Court refused to allow implication of consent under a state statute by a partnership that had done business within the state. *Hess v. Pawloski, supra,* revived the implied consent theory, as did *Henry L. Doherty & Co. v. Goodman,* 294 U.S. 623 (1935), which upheld jurisdiction over an individual who had "consented" by the act of selling securities in the state. But the implied consent rationale continued to have its ups and downs, primarily because of holdings that a state could not exclude a person or entity from conducting interstate activities without violating the Fourteenth Amendment's proscription against discrimination.

"Presence" Implied from "Doing Business." At the same time, a line of cases held that a defendant could be subjected to process if it was "doing business" sufficiently so that it could be said to be "present" in the state. *E.g., Philadelphia & Reading R.R. v. McKibbin,* 243 U.S. 264 (1917). Some of the decisions made relatively sophisticated balances between the convenience of the defendant in defending in plaintiff's chosen forum, versus the plaintiff's inconvenience in going to defendant's chosen forum, by

evaluating the extent of the defendant's "presence" within the forum state. *E.g.*, *Hutchinson v. Chase & Gilbert*, 45 F.2d 139, 141-42 (2d Cir. 1930) ("We are to inquire whether the extent and continuity of what it has done in the state in question makes it reasonable to bring it before one of its courts."). Nevertheless, the jurisdictional concept of "doing business" had no clear definition and produced inconsistent results.

The International Shoe Holding. The decision that follows, *International Shoe Co. v. Washington*, was the landmark case that rationalized these differing approaches and established the foundations of modern jurisdictional concepts. As you read it, try to concentrate on this question: What is the test that governs whether a state's exercise of jurisdiction over a nonresident is consistent with the Due Process Clause?

INTERNATIONAL SHOE CO. v. WASHINGTON
326 U.S. 310 (1945)

MR. CHIEF JUSTICE STONE delivered the opinion of the Court.

The questions for decision are (1) whether, within the limitations of the due process clause of the Fourteenth Amendment, appellant, a Delaware corporation, has by its activities in the State of Washington rendered itself amenable to proceedings in the courts of that state to recover unpaid contributions to the state unemployment compensation fund exacted by state statutes, . . . and (2) whether the state can exact those contributions consistently with the due process clause of the Fourteenth Amendment.

The statutes in question set up a comprehensive scheme of unemployment compensation, the costs of which are defrayed by contributions required to be made by employers to a state unemployment compensation fund. . . . Section 14 (c) of the Act (Wash. Rev. Stat., 1941 Supp., § 9998-114c) authorizes appellee Commissioner to issue an order and notice of assessment of delinquent contributions upon prescribed personal service of the notice upon the employer if found within the state, or, if not so found, by mailing the notice to the employer by registered mail at his last known address. . . .

In this case notice of assessment for the years in question was personally served upon a sales solicitor employed by appellant in the State of Washington, and a copy of the notice was mailed by registered mail to appellant at its address in St. Louis, Missouri. Appellant appeared specially before the office of unemployment and moved to set aside the order and notice of assessment. . . .

The motion was heard on evidence and a stipulation of facts by the appeal tribunal which denied the motion and ruled that appellee Commissioner was entitled to recover the unpaid contributions. That action was affirmed by the Commissioner; both the Superior Court and the [Washington] Supreme Court affirmed. . . . Appellant in each of these courts assailed the statute as applied, as a violation of the due process clause of the Fourteenth Amendment, and as imposing a constitutionally prohibited burden on interstate commerce. . . .

The facts as found by the appeal tribunal and accepted by the state Superior Court and Supreme Court, are not in dispute. Appellant is a Delaware corporation, having its principal place of business in St. Louis, Missouri, and is engaged in the manufacture and sale of shoes and other footwear. It maintains places of business in several states, other than Washington, at which its manufacturing is carried on and from which its merchandise is distributed interstate through several sales units or branches located outside the State of Washington.

Appellant has no office in Washington and makes no contracts either for sale or purchase of merchandise there. It maintains no stock of merchandise in that state and makes there no deliveries of goods in intrastate commerce. During the years from 1937 to 1940, now in question, appellant employed eleven to thirteen salesmen under direct supervision and control of sales managers located in St. Louis. These salesmen resided in Washington; their principal activities were confined to that state; and they were compensated by commissions based upon the amount of their sales. The commissions for each year totaled more than $31,000. Appellant supplies its salesmen with a line of samples, each consisting of one shoe of a pair, which they display to prospective purchasers. On occasion they rent permanent sample rooms, for exhibiting samples, in business buildings, or rent rooms in hotels or business buildings temporarily for that purpose. The cost of such rentals is reimbursed by appellant.

The authority of the salesmen is limited to exhibiting their samples and soliciting orders from prospective buyers, at prices and on terms fixed by appellant. The salesmen transmit the orders to appellant's office in St. Louis for acceptance or rejection, and when accepted the merchandise for filling the orders is shipped f.o.b. from points outside Washington to the purchasers within the state. All the merchandise shipped into Washington is invoiced at the place of shipment from which collections are made. No salesman has authority to enter into contracts or to make collections. . . .

Appellant . . . insists that its activities within the state were not sufficient to manifest its "presence" there and that in its absence the state courts were without jurisdiction, that consequently it was a denial of due process for the state to subject appellant to suit. It refers to those cases in which it was said that the mere solicitation of orders for the purchase of goods within a state, to be accepted without the state and filled by shipment of the purchased goods interstate, does not render the corporation seller amenable to suit within the state. *See Green v. Chicago, B. & Q. R. Co.*, 205 U.S. 530, 533. . . .

Historically the jurisdiction of courts to render judgment *in personam* is grounded on their *de facto* power over the defendant's person. Hence his presence within the territorial jurisdiction of a court was prerequisite to its rendition of a judgment personally binding him. *Pennoyer v. Neff*, 95 U.S. 714, 733. But now that the *capias ad respondendum* has given way to personal service of summons or other form of notice, due process requires only that in order to subject a defendant to a judgment *in personam*, if he be not present within the territory of the forum, he have certain minimum contacts with it such that the maintenance of the suit does not offend "traditional notions of fair play and substantial justice." *Milliken v. Meyer*, 311 U.S. 457, 463. *See* Holmes, J., in *McDonald v. Mabee*, 243 U.S. 90, 91. . . .

. . . To say that the corporation is so far "present" there as to satisfy due process requirements, for purposes of taxation or the maintenance of suits against it in the courts of the state, is to beg the question to be decided. For the terms "present" or "presence" are used merely to symbolize those activities of the corporation's agent within the state which courts will deem to be sufficient to satisfy the demands of due process. L. Hand, J., in *Hutchinson v. Chase & Gilbert*, 45 F.2d 139, 141. Those demands may be met by such contacts of the corporation with the state of the forum as make it reasonable, in the context of our federal system of government, to require the corporation to defend the particular suit which is brought there. An "estimate of the inconveniences" which would result to the corporation from a trial away from its "home" or principal place of business is relevant in this connection. *Hutchinson v. Chase & Gilbert, supra*, 141.

"Presence" in the state in this sense has never been doubted when the activities of the corporation there have not only been continuous and systematic, but also give rise to the liabilities sued on, even though no consent to be sued or authorization to an agent to accept service of process has been given. *St. Clair v. Cox*, 106 U.S. 350, 355. . . . Conversely it has been generally recognized that the casual presence of the corporate agent or even his conduct of single or isolated [a]ctivities in a state in the corporation's behalf are not enough to subject it to suit on causes of action unconnected with the activities there. *St. Clair v. Cox, supra*, 359, 360. . . .

Finally, although the commission of some single or occasional acts of the corporate agent in a state sufficient to impose an obligation or liability on the corporation has not been thought to confer upon the state authority to enforce it, *Rosenberg Bros. & Co. v. Curtis Brown Co.*, 260 U.S. 516, other such acts, because of their nature and quality and the circumstances of their commission, may be deemed sufficient to render the corporation liable to suit. *Cf. Kane v. New Jersey*, 242 U.S. 160; *Hess v. Pawloski, supra*; *Young v. Masci, supra*. . . .

It is evident that the criteria by which we mark the boundary line between those activities which justify the subjection of a corporation to suit, and those which do not, cannot be simply mechanical or quantitative. The test is not merely, as has sometimes been suggested, whether the activity, which the corporation has seen fit to procure through its agents in another state, is a little more or a little less. . . . Whether due process is satisfied must depend rather upon the quality and nature of the activity in relation to the fair and orderly administration of the laws which it was the purpose of the due process clause to insure. That clause does not contemplate that a state may make binding a judgment *in personam* against an individual or corporate defendant with which the state has no contacts, ties, or relations. *Cf. Pennoyer v. Neff, supra; Minnesota Commercial Men's Assn. v. Benn*, 261 U.S. 140.

But to the extent that a corporation exercises the privilege of conducting activities within a state, it enjoys the benefits and protection of the laws of that state. The exercise of that privilege may give rise to obligations, and, so far as those obligations arise out of or are connected with the activities within the state, a procedure which requires the corporation to respond to a suit brought to enforce them can, in most instances, hardly be said to be undue. . . .

Applying these standards, the activities carried on in behalf of appellant in the State of Washington were neither irregular nor casual. They were systematic and continuous throughout the years in question. They resulted in a large volume of interstate business, in the course of which appellant received the benefits and protection of the laws of the state, including the right to resort to the courts for the enforcement of its rights. The obligation which is here sued upon arose out of those very activities. It is evident that these operations establish sufficient contacts or ties with the state of the forum to make it reasonable and just, according to our traditional conception of fair play and substantial justice, to permit the state to enforce the obligations which appellant has incurred there. . . .

[The Court also holds, on the merits, that the state has constitutional power to impose and collect the tax.] Affirmed.

MR. JUSTICE BLACK delivered the following opinion.

The criteria adopted insofar as they can be identified read as follows: Due Process does permit State courts to "enforce the obligations which appellant has incurred" if it be found "reasonable and just according to our traditional conception of fair play and substantial justice." . . .

I believe that the Federal Constitution leaves to each State, without any "ifs" or "buts," a power to tax and to open the doors of its courts for its citizens to sue corporations whose agents do business in those States. Believing that the Constitution gave the States that power, I think it a judicial deprivation to condition its exercise upon this Court's notion of "fair play," however appealing that term may be. Nor can I stretch the meaning of due process so far as to authorize this Court to deprive a State of the right to afford judicial protection to its citizens on the ground that it would be more "convenient" for the corporation to be sued somewhere else.

There is a strong emotional appeal in the words "fair play," "justice," and "reasonableness." But they were not chosen by those who wrote the original Constitution or the Fourteenth Amendment as a measuring rod for this Court to use in invalidating State or Federal laws passed by elected legislative representatives. . . . For application of this natural law concept, whether under the terms "reasonableness," "justice," or "fair play," makes judges the supreme arbiters of the country's laws and practices. . . .

NOTES AND QUESTIONS

(1) *The International Shoe Test.* In a single sentence, try to articulate the *"International Shoe* test" for the exercise of jurisdiction over a nonresident consistently with due process. The test is not the same as the older notions of "consent," "doing business," or "presence," although it is related to those concepts. As a shorthand rendition, the modern standard is called the "minimum contacts" test.

(2) *"Minimum Contacts."* Almost any relationship of the defendant with a state or with persons inside it can be a contact, including sales to persons in the state, employees in the state, correspondence, contracts, torts, ownership or rental of property, visits to the state, etc. However, a particular contact may or may not make a significant contribution to the court's jurisdiction.

(3) *Justice Black's Criticism; Vagueness.* Justice Black criticizes the Court on the grounds that the standard it creates is not in the Constitution and is so vague that it will make the Justices "supreme arbiters" of state power. Do you agree? In particular, what are the harmful results of a test that is excessively vague? Will a vague test contribute to more litigation, or less? Will it enable individuals and corporations to plan their obligations with confidence? Will it contribute to uniform adjudication, or to inconsistency? On the other hand, the Constitution doesn't say exactly when distant forum abuse violates due process. Does "due process" have any real meaning in this context if it is not translated into usable standards by court interpretation? And isn't it preferable to have a flexible test, rather than to have one that produces inconsistency — as did the approaches before *International Shoe*? *See* Lewis, *A Brave New World for Personal Jurisdiction: Flexible Tests under Uniform Standards*, 37 Vand. L. Rev. 1 (1984); Waits, *Values, Intuitions, and Opinion Writing: The Judicial Process and State Court Jurisdiction*, 1983 U. Ill. L. Rev. 917. For an excellent treatment of the application of this flexible-but-vague test, *see* Abramson, *Clarifying "Fair Play and Substantial Justice": How the Courts Apply the Supreme Court Standard for Personal Jurisdiction*, 18 Hastings Const. L.Q. 441 (1991).

[2] "General" and "Specific" Jurisdiction

NOTE: "GENERAL" JURISDICTION VERSUS "SPECIFIC" JURISDICTION

In *International Shoe*, the Court noted that the claim asserted by the State of Washington was closely related to the contacts on which the exercise of jurisdiction was based. In fact, Washington's claim for taxes arose out of the same contacts that created jurisdiction. In such a case, the maintenance of a suit might reasonably be deemed fair with fewer contacts than would be required if the contacts were unrelated to the claim. This situation, in which the claim arises out of or is related to the contacts, is called "specific jurisdiction." The situation in which the claim has arisen in another place, and is unrelated to the contacts with the forum, is referred to as "general jurisdiction." Systematic and continuous contacts are required in a case of general jurisdiction. Consider the following cases.

McGEE v. INTERNATIONAL LIFE INS. CO., 355 U.S. 220 (1957). Petitioner Lulu B. McGee claimed the proceeds of a life insurance policy purchased by her deceased son, Lowell Franklin. Franklin had initially purchased the policy from an Arizona corporation called Empire Mutual, but International Life took over Empire's business. It offered to extend insurance to Franklin by sending him a reinsurance certificate by mail to his home in California. He accepted, and from that date until his death, he sent the required premiums to International Life's office in Texas. When he died, McGee made proof of loss, but International Life refused to pay, stating that Franklin had committed suicide. McGee then filed suit in a California court and had International Life served under a California statute applicable to nonresident insurers. International Life declined to appear, and McGcc obtained a default judgment in the California court. She next brought an action on the judgment in Texas, but the Texas courts refused to enforce the judgment on the ground that California's assertion of jurisdiction violated the Fourteenth Amendment.

International Life had no office, agents, employees, or other business in California. In fact, the striking aspect of the case was that the record showed *no* contact other than the *single* policy of insurance International Life had with McGee's decedent. As the Court put it, "so far as the record before us shows, respondent has never done any insurance business in California apart from the policy involved here."

However, the Court upheld California's exercise of jurisdiction and ordered the Texas courts to extend full faith and credit to the judgment, reasoning as follows:

> . . . [I]n *International Shoe Co. v. Washington* . . . , the Court decided that "due process requires only that in order to subject a defendant to a judgment *in personam*, if he be not present in the territory of the forum, he have certain minimum contacts with it such that the maintenance of the suit does not offend 'traditional notions of fair play and substantial justice.' " . . .
>
> Turning to this case, we think it apparent that the Due Process Clause did not preclude the California court from entering a judgment binding on respondent. It is sufficient for purposes of due process that the suit was based on a contract that had substantial connection with that State. . . . The contract was delivered in California, the premiums were paid from there and the insured was a resident of that State when he died. It cannot be denied that California has a manifest interest in providing effective means of redress to its residents when their insurers refuse to pay claims. These

residents would be at a severe disadvantage if they were forced to follow the insurance company to a distant State in order to hold it legally accountable. . . .

PERKINS v. BENGUET CONSOLIDATED MINING CO., 342 U.S. 437 (1952). Plaintiff Perkins filed suit against the Defendant Benguet in a state court in Clermont County, Ohio. Her claim, however, had nothing to do with Ohio; it had arisen in the Philippines, where the company (which was a Philippines corporation) had operated profitable gold and silver mines. The Philippine Islands were occupied by the Japanese during World War II, and operations were halted. The president of the company (who was also its general manager and principal stockholder) then established an office in Clermont County, where he resided. He maintained bank accounts there, and he carried on correspondence, drew salary checks, and supervised the rehabilitation of the company's properties from that location. The Ohio courts held that the exercise of jurisdiction was improper. The Supreme Court disagreed, and it upheld the jurisdiction:

> The essence of the issue here, at the constitutional level, is . . . one of general fairness to the corporation. Appropriate tests for that are discussed in *International Shoe Co. v. Washington*. . . . [I]f the . . . corporation carries on other continuous and systematic corporate activities as it did here — consisting of directors' meetings, business correspondence, banking, stock transfers, payment of salaries, purchasing of machinery, etc. — those activities are enough. . . .
>
> The instant case takes us one step further to a proceeding *in personam* to enforce a cause of action not arising out of the corporation's activities in the state of the forum. Using the tests mentioned above we find no requirement of federal due process that either *prohibits* Ohio from opening its courts to the cause of action here presented or *compels* Ohio to do so. . . .

NOTES AND QUESTIONS

(1) *General and Specific Jurisdiction.* Remember that "specific" jurisdiction means that the claim is related to the contacts; "general" jurisdiction means that it is not. Is *McGee* a case of specific or general jurisdiction? What about *Perkins*? What difference does it make (for example, if the claim in *McGee* had been unrelated to the insurance policy purchased by McGee's decedent, would the jurisdiction have been upheld)?

(2) *Breadth of the Minimum Contacts Test.* Students are sometimes surprised by the development of personal jurisdiction after *International Shoe*. Is the test too broad, as it is applied in such cases as *McGee* and *Perkins*? Does it need to be restricted?

[3] "Long-Arm" Statutes: State Law Restrictions on Jurisdiction

NOTE ON STATE "LONG-ARM" STATUTES

Remember that the extent of a state's jurisdiction is actually subject to two different kinds of restrictions. First, it must comply with due process. The basic test for this requirement is the minimum contacts test. Secondly, it must comply with *state* law. Each state has one or more "long arm" statutes. The reach of long arm jurisdiction depends upon the traditions and values of the people of the state, as expressed by its legislature in its long-arm statute.

There are several different models for long-arm statutes. For example, a state might simply incorporate the due process test in its statute, thereby reaching every defendant it can constitutionally reach. A fundamentally different approach is that of the "laundry list" statute. This type of statute lists the circumstances in which defendants can be subjected to long-arm jurisdiction. The Illinois statute, which has served as the prototype for statutes in several other states, is an example.

A "LAUNDRY LIST" LONG-ARM STATUTE

Ill. Rev. Stat. ch. 110, § 2–209 (1983)

§ 2-209. Act submitting to jurisdiction — Process.

(a) Any person, whether or not a citizen or resident of this State, who in person or through an agent does any of the acts hereinafter enumerated, thereby submits such person, and, if an individual, his or her personal representative, to the jurisdiction of the courts of this State as to any cause of action arising from the doing of any of such acts:

(1) The transaction of any business within this State;

(2) The commission of a tortious act within this State;

(3) The ownership, use, or possession of any real estate situated in this State;

(4) Contracting to insure any person, property or risk located within this State at the time of contracting;

(5) With respect to actions of dissolution of marriage and legal separation, the maintenance in this State of a matrimonial domicile at the time this cause of action arose or the commission in this State of any act giving rise to the cause of action.

(b) Service of process upon any person who is subject to the jurisdiction of the courts of this State, as provided in this Section, may be made by personally serving the summons upon the defendant outside this State, as provided in this Act, with the same force and effect as though summons had been personally served within this State. . . .

GRAY v. AMERICAN RADIATOR & STANDARD SANITARY CORP.

22 Ill. 2d 432, 176 N.E.2d 761 (1961)

KLINGBIEL, JUSTICE.

Phyllis Gray appeals from a judgment of the circuit court of Cook County dismissing her action for damages. The issues are concerned with the construction and validity of our statute providing for substituted service of process on nonresidents. Since a constitutional question is involved, the appeal is direct to this court.

The suit was brought against the Titan Valve Manufacturing Company and others, on the ground that a certain water heater had exploded and injured the plaintiff. The complaint charges, *inter alia*, that the Titan company, a foreign corporation, had negligently constructed the safety valve; and that the injuries were suffered as a proximate result thereof. Summons issued and was duly served on Titan's registered agent in Cleveland, Ohio. The corporation appeared specially, filing a motion to quash on the ground that it had not committed a tortious act in Illinois. Its affidavit stated that it does no business here; that it has no agent physically present in Illinois; and that it sells the completed valves to defendant American Radiator & Standard Sanitary Corporation, outside Illinois. The American Radiator & Standard Sanitary Corporation (also made a defendant) filed an answer in which it set up a crossclaim against Titan, alleging that Titan made certain warranties to American Radiator, and that if the latter is held liable to the plaintiff it should be indemnified and held harmless by Titan. The court granted Titan's motion, dismissing both the complaint and the crossclaim.

Section 16 of the Civil Practice Act provides that summons may be personally served upon any party outside the State; and that as to nonresidents who have submitted to the jurisdiction of our courts, such service has the force and effect of personal service within Illinois. (Ill. Rev. Stat. 1959, chap. 110, par. 16.) Under section 17(1)(b) a nonresident who, either in person or through an agent, commits a tortious act within this State submits to jurisdiction. (Ill. Rev. Stat. 1959, chap. 110, par. 17.) The questions in this case are (1) whether a tortious act was committed here, within the meaning of the statute, despite the fact that the Titan corporation had no agent in Illinois; and (2) whether the statute, if so construed, violates due process of law.

The first aspect to which we must direct our attention is one of statutory construction. Under section 17(1)(b) jurisdiction is predicated on the committing of a tortious act in this State. It is not disputed, for the purpose of this appeal, that a tortious act was committed. The issue depends on whether it was committed in Illinois, so as to warrant the assertion of personal jurisdiction by service of summons in Ohio.

The wrong in the case at bar did not originate in the conduct of a servant physically present here, but arose instead from acts performed at the place of manufacture. Only the consequences occurred in Illinois. It is well established, however, that in law the place of a wrong is where the last event takes place which is necessary to render the actor liable. Restatement, Conflict of Laws, sec. 377. A second indication that the place of injury is the determining factor is found in rules governing the time within which an action must be brought. In applying statutes of limitation our court has computed the period from the time when the injury is done.

We think it is clear that the alleged negligence in manufacturing the valve cannot be separated from the resulting injury; and that for present purposes, like those of liability and limitations, the tort was committed in Illinois.

Titan seeks to avoid this result by arguing that instead of using the word "tort," the legislature employed the term "tortious act"; and that the latter refers only to the act or conduct, separate and apart from any consequences thereof. We cannot accept the argument. To be tortious an act must cause injury. The concept of injury is an inseparable part of the phrase. In determining legislative intention courts will read words in their ordinary and popularly understood sense. . . . We think the intent should be determined less from technicalities of definition than from considerations of general purpose and effect. To adopt the criteria urged by defendant would tend to promote litigation over extraneous issues concerning the elements of a tort and the territorial incidence of each, whereas the test should be concerned more with those substantial elements of convenience and justice presumably contemplated by the legislature. As we observed in *Nelson v. Miller*, 11 Ill. 2d 378, 143 N.E.2d 673, the statute contemplates the exertion of jurisdiction over nonresident defendants to the extent permitted by the due-process clause.

The Titan company contends that if the statute is applied so as to confer jurisdiction in this case it violates the requirement of due process of law. The precise constitutional question thus presented has not heretofore been considered by this court. . . .

Under modern doctrine the power of a State court to enter a binding judgment against one not served with process within the State depends upon two questions: first, whether he has certain minimum contacts with the State (*see International Shoe Co. v. State of Washington*, 326 U.S. 310, 316, 66 S. Ct. 154, 90 L. Ed. 95, 102), and second whether there has been a reasonable method of notification. *See International Shoe Co. v. State of Washington*, 326 U.S. 310, 320. . . .

A proper determination of the question presented requires analysis of those cases which have dealt with the quantum of contact sufficient to warrant jurisdiction. Since the decision in *Pennoyer v. Neff*, 95 U.S. 714, 24 L. Ed. 565, the power of a State to exert jurisdiction over nonresidents has been greatly expanded, particularly with respect to foreign corporations. . . .

Where the business done by a foreign corporation in the State of the forum is of a sufficiently substantial nature, it has been held permissible for the State to entertain a suit against it even though the cause of action arose from activities entirely distinct from its conduct within the State. *Perkins v. Benguet Consolidated Mining Co.*, 342 U.S. 437. . . .

In *McGee v. International Life Insurance Co.*, 355 U.S. 220, 78 S. Ct. 199, 201, 2 L. Ed. 2d 223, suit was brought in California against a foreign insurance company on a policy issued to a resident of California. The defendant was not served with process in that State but was notified by registered mail at its place of business in Texas, pursuant to a statute permitting such service in suits on insurance contracts. The contract in question was delivered in California, the premiums were mailed from there and the insured was a resident of the State when he died, but defendant had no office or agent in California nor did it solicit any business there apart from the policy sued on. After referring briefly to the *International Shoe* case the court held that "it is sufficient for purposes of due process that the suit was based on *a contract* which had substantial connection" with California. (Emphasis supplied.)

In *Nelson v. Miller*, 11 Ill. 2d 378, 143 N.E.2d 673, the commission of a single tort within this State was held sufficient to sustain jurisdiction under the present statute. The defendant in that case, a resident of Wisconsin, was engaged in the business of selling appliances. It was alleged that in the process of delivering a stove in Illinois, an employee of the defendant negligently caused injury to the plaintiff. . . .

In the case at bar defendant does not claim that the present use of its product in Illinois is an isolated instance. While the record does not disclose the volume of Titan's business or the territory in which appliances incorporating its valves are marketed, it is a reasonable inference that its commercial transactions, like those of other manufacturers, result in substantial use and consumption in this State. To the extent that its business may be directly affected by transactions occurring here it enjoys benefits from the laws of this State, and it has undoubtedly benefitted, to a degree, from the protection which our law has given to the marketing of hot water heaters containing its valves. Where the alleged liability arises, as in this case, from the manufacture of products presumably sold in contemplation of use here, it should not matter that the purchase was made from an independent middleman or that someone other than the defendant shipped the product into this State. . . .

We construe section 17(1)(b) [now codified as § 2–209(a)(2), *see* statute preceding this case] as providing for jurisdiction under the circumstances shown in this case, and we hold that as so construed the statute does not violate due process of law.

Reversed and remanded, with directions.

FIGURE 2A
HOW LONG IS THE LONG ARM?

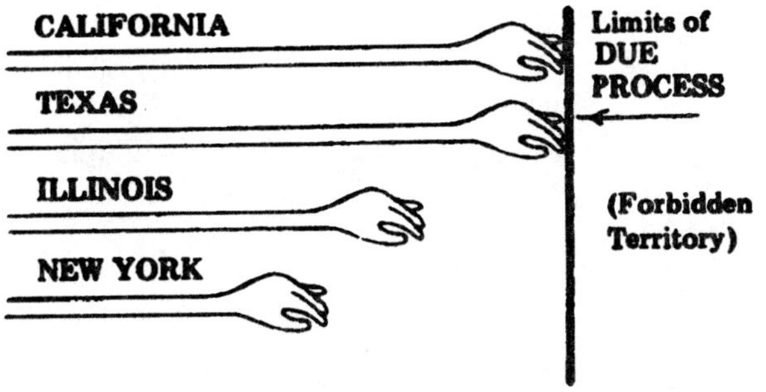

NOTES AND QUESTIONS

(1) *The Two Issues in Gray.* The first step in understanding *Gray* is to formulate the two questions that the court analyzes. One is a question of state law, the other of federal law. Be sure that you can identify the two questions and explain the holding on each. See Figure 2A for a graphic depiction of the two issues, considering the statutes of four different states.

(2) *"Tortious Act."* In the *Nelson* case analyzed in *Gray*, the defendant's employees actually came into Illinois and caused damage by an act done while they were physically inside the state. Isn't this situation factually distinguishable from *Gray*? Had the defendant, Titan, done any "act" in Illinois? Notice, however, that the court, in *Gray*, reaches its result by reading the words "tortious act" to mean "tort." Is this interpretation consistent with the language of the Illinois law (or does it result in the elimination of the requirement of an "act" from the statute)?

(3) *Statutory Construction.* There are many ways to interpret statutes. One is to look to definitions of key terms that would have been available to the legislature (the court in *Gray* does this by considering conflict-of-laws usages and statutes of limitations). Another is to consider legislative intent, which is discerned by such indications as legislative history or policy considerations (the court in *Gray* infers a legislative intent to reach to the "extent permitted by due process"). Another interpretive approach is to give emphasis to the actual words of the enactment, particularly if they have a "plain" meaning. What would be the result if that approach were adopted in a case like *Gray*? Consider the decision below.

(4) *Illinois Lengthens Its Long Arm by Amendment — and Eliminates the Problem Illustrated in Gray.* Following the *Gray* decision, Illinois amended its long arm statute to add the following provision, among others: "A court may also exercise jurisdiction on any other basis now or hereafter permitted by the Illinois Constitution and the

Constitution of the United States." Why do you think Illinois adopted this amendment? What effect does it have?

FEATHERS v. McLUCAS, 15 N.Y.2d 443, 209 N.E.2d 68 (1965). The Featherses were seriously injured by the explosion of a truck-driven propane tank on a public highway near their home in Berlin, New York. They sued the manufacturer of the tank in a New York trial court on negligence and breach of warranty theories. The New York long-arm statute was closely similar to the Illinois statute at issue in *Gray*; in relevant part, it provided: "A court may exercise personal jurisdiction over any nondomiciliary . . . if, in person or through an agent, he . . . commits a tortious act within the state . . ." The manufacturer moved to dismiss, on the ground that it carried on all its business from a factory in Kansas City, Kansas, and had never had any agents in New York or transacted any business there. The trial court granted the motion to dismiss. The Appellate Division reversed on the ground that the manufacturer had "knowledge" that the tank was designed for a Pennsylvania trucking company, could "foresee" its use in New York, and therefore had the requisite "minimum contacts" with that state.

Speaking through its renowned Judge Fuld, the New York Court of Appeals reversed the Appellate Division and reinstated the dismissal, holding that the New York long-arm statute required a tortious "act" in the state, even if due process did not and even if the Illinois courts did not.

> [T]he question presented is not — as the Appellate Division indicated it was by its reference to minimum contacts — whether the Legislature *could* constitutionally have enacted legislation expanding the jurisdiction of our courts to the extent determined by the Appellate Division or whether, indeed, the Legislature *should* have done so in light of the pertinent policy considerations. . . .
>
> The language of [the statute] — conferring personal jurisdiction over a nondomiciliary "if, in person or through an agent, he . . . commits a tortious act *within* the state" is too plain and precise to permit it to be read, as has the Appellate Division, as if it were synonymous with "committing a tortious act *without* the state which causes injury within the state" . . . .
>
> Our attention is directed to the broad interpretation accorded in *Gray v. American Radiator & Sanitary Corp.* . . .
>
> We find [*Gray*] unconvincing. It certainly does not follow that, if the "place of the wrong" for purposes of conflict of laws is a particular state, the "place of commission of a tortious act" is also that same state for purposes of interpreting a statute conferring jurisdiction. . . . Moreover, the place of the "tort" is not necessarily the same as the place of the defendant's commission of the "tortious act." In our view, then, the interpretation accorded the statute by the Illinois courts disregards its plain language and exceeds the bounds of sound statutory construction. . . .

MARKHAM v. ANDERSON, 531 F.2d 634 (2d Cir. 1976). After *Feathers v. McLucas, supra*, the New York Legislature took a hint from Justice Fuld's opinion and amended the New York long-arm statute. It added another provision to the statute, covering a person who

> . . . commits a tortious act without the state causing injury to person or property within the state, . . . if he

(i) regularly does or solicits business, or engages in any other persistent course of conduct, or derives substantial revenue from goods used or consumed or services rendered, in the state, or

(ii) expects or should reasonably expect the act to have consequences in the state and derives substantial revenue from interstate or international commerce . . . .

Dr. Anderson examined a truck driver in Pennsylvania and certified that he was qualified under federal regulations to operate a commercial truck. The truck driver, who was a diabetic, was driving through New York when insulin deprivation caused him to lapse into semi-consciousness, whereupon he struck a toll booth and seriously injured plaintiff Markham. Markham sued Dr. Anderson for negligence and served him with process under the New York long-arm statute quoted above. The Court of Appeals held that jurisdiction could not be exercised, because although there had been injury inside New York, Dr. Anderson's practice did not constitute "regular" or "continuous" business in New York and did not result in his deriving "substantial" revenue from interstate commerce.

NOTES AND QUESTIONS

(1) *Construing New York's Statutes.* Notice that the amendment of New York's statute considerably broadened the tortious act provision. What would have been the result in *Feathers v. McLucas* if it had occurred after this broadening statutory amendment?

(2) *Other Provisions in New York's Long-Arm Statute, Including the Transacting of Business in the State: George Reiner & Co. v. Schwartz, 41 N.Y.2d 648, 394 N.Y.S.2d 844, 363 N.E.2d 551 (1977).* The New York statute contains several other provisions. *See generally* O. Chase, 1 *Weinstein, Korn & Miller CPLR Manual* §§ 3.05-3.06 (1997). The most important of these provisions covers a person who "transacts any business within the state or contracts anywhere to supply goods or services in the state." *George Reiner & Co. v. Schwartz,* for example, was a suit against a sales agent for breach of contract. Although the agent's performance of his duties had taken place entirely outside New York, the contract had been negotiated and agreed to in a single afternoon in New York. The Court of Appeals held that the exercise of long-arm jurisdiction was properly based on the defendant's transaction of business in the state, based upon this contract.

THE "LIMITS-OF-DUE-PROCESS" LONG-ARM MODEL
Cal. Code Civ. Proc. § 410.10

A different kind of statutory model simply adopts the limits of due process as the limits of the long arm. By enacting this kind of statute, a legislature authorizes the state courts to exercise jurisdiction over any claim that they can reach under the Constitution. The California statute provides as follows:

§ 410.10 Basis [of Jurisdiction]

A court of this state may exercise jurisdiction on any basis not inconsistent with the Constitution of this state or of the United States.

See also R.I. Gen. Laws § 9-5-33 (1985) (which provides, "Every foreign corporation, [individual, or entity] . . . that shall have the necessary minimum contacts with the state of Rhode Island, shall be subject to the jurisdiction of the state . . .").

"INTERMEDIATE" LONG-ARM MODELS

Some states adopt neither the "laundry list" nor the "limits of due process" model. For example, the provision of the former Texas statute construed in the case that follows provided that a nonresident doing business within the state was subject to process "in any action . . . *arising out of such business done in this State."* Former Tex. Rev. Civ. Stat. Ann. art. 2031b (emphasis added). Read literally, this statute would seem to have covered only cases of specific jurisdiction. General jurisdiction cases, such as *Perkins v. Benguet, supra,* would not "arise out of . . . business done in" the state.

However, every state's statutes are subject to interpretation by the courts of that state. The Texas Supreme Court construed that state's long-arm provision in the following case. What did the court do to the statute?

HALL v. HELICOPTEROS NACIONALES DE COLOMBIA, S.A., 638 S.W.2d 870 (Tex. 1982), *rev'd on other grounds,* 466 U.S. 408 (1984). Plaintiffs' decedents were killed in Peru by the crash of a helicopter operated by the defendant. Defendant was a Colombian entity that maintained no office in Texas, though it had purchased helicopters and supplies extensively in that state. The Texas Supreme Court recognized that the claim did not "arise out of" the defendant's "business done in this State," as the literal terms of the statute seemed to require. Nevertheless, a five-member majority of the court, speaking through Justice Wallace, upheld the exercise of jurisdiction. The majority reasoned that the "arising out of" requirement

> . . . is useful in any fact situation in which a jurisdiction question exists; and it is a necessary requirement where the nonresident defendant only maintained single or few contacts with the forum. However, [it] is unnecessary when the nonresident defendant's presence in the forum through numerous contacts is of such a nature, as in this case, so as to satisfy the demands of the ultimate test of due process. Accordingly, through the statutory authority of Art. 2031b . . . , there remains a single inquiry: is the exercise of jurisdiction consistent with the requirements of due process of law under the United States Constitution?

Texas' Chief Justice Pope, joined by three other members of the court, dissented on the grounds that both the Texas statute and due process prohibited jurisdiction:

> Article 2031b expressly requires a *nexus* between the helicopter crash and the contacts relied on to justify jurisdiction. The nexus requirement is found in the clear wording of the statute itself. . . .
>
> . . . While the reach of a particular statute could always be coextensive with constitutional confines outlined by the Supreme Court, states were not compelled to assert jurisdiction that far. . . .

The United States Supreme Court later reversed on due process grounds (see the report of its decision in the next section), but its decision left in place the Texas court's construction of the Texas statute, over which the United States Supreme Court had no jurisdiction. However, the Texas Supreme Court subsequently withdrew its opinion in *Hall* (677 S.W.2d 19 (Tex. 1984)), leaving the scope of the statute in controversy.

NOTES AND QUESTIONS

(1) *The Effect of the Texas Court's Interpretation.* What has the Texas court done to the Texas statute? Is the majority's interpretation persuasive, or is Chief Justice Pope's dissent correct? *See* Richardson, *Hall v. Helicopteros: Clarifying the Limits of Personal Jurisdiction,* 48 Tex. B.J. 651 (1985).

(2) *Amendment of the Texas Statute.* The Texas legislature recodified the Texas statute after *Helicopteros v. Hall.* Tex. Civ. Prac. & Rem. Code § 17.044(a)(1) now provides that anyone who "engages in business" in the state is subject to process. Doing business is defined broadly; it includes not only "business" in the conventional sense, but also any contacts, including torts committed in whole or in part in the state. However, in distinct contrast, § 17.044(b) contains a nexus requirement ("aris[ing] out of the business done in this state").

(3) *Choosing Between Long-Arm Models.* If you were a legislator in the newly created hypothetical state of "West York," and you were given the responsibility to draft your state's first long-arm statute, which model would you select — the narrower "laundry list" type, or the broader "limits-of-due process" version? [Note: Which model would give more rights to the constituents who voted for your election? Does this reasoning explain the construction given the statute in Texas, where judges are elected?] On the other hand, which kind of statute is "better" philosophically? Can it be argued that the limits-of-due-process approach abdicates the responsibility of the state to set standards for the protection of defendants (or would a narrower approach provide inadequate forum availability for plaintiffs, who might have to go to distant forums for injuries suffered at home)? Auerbach, *General Jurisdiction of Courts — A Critique of the Maryland Law,* 40 Md. L. Rev. 485, 506-07 (1981); Strachan, *In Personam Jurisdiction in Utah,* 1977 Utah L. Rev. 235.

[C] Modern Expansions and Contractions of the Minimum Contacts Doctrine

[1] Commercial Defendants: "Purposeful Availing," "Reasonable Anticipation," and "Convenience"

HANSON v. DENCKLA
357 U.S. 235 (1958)

Dora Donner set up a trust in Delaware and named a Delaware bank as trustee. In the trust instrument, she reserved a life estate (*i.e.*, she was entitled to the income for life), and she also reserved a "power of appointment" (which gave her the authority to designate to whom the trust property would pass upon her death). Ms. Donner later moved to Florida. There, she received income from the Delaware trustee, communicated regularly with the trustee regarding trust business, and did "several bits of trust administration." Before her death in Florida, she exercised the power of appointment, providing that the trust assets would pass to Hanson and others. She also executed a will that gave the residue of her property to Denckla and others. In this litigation, the Denckla group sought to invalidate the trust, so that the trust assets would pass to them under the will. The Hanson group, of course, sought to uphold the trust so as to receive under the power of appointment.

Two different suits were commenced. One, in Florida, resulted in a holding that the trust was invalid, that the appointment was ineffective, and that the trust assets passed to the Denckla group under the will. The other, in Delaware, came to the opposite result. The Delaware courts refused to give full faith and credit to the Florida judgment and upheld the trust, so that interests in the trust passed by virtue of the power of appointment to the Hanson group. The Supreme Court granted certiorari to resolve the underlying jurisdictional questions.

The key to the case was whether Florida had been justified in exercising jurisdiction over the Delaware trustee, which did not appear, but which Florida considered an indispensable party. The trustee had no offices, property or business in Florida and had no dealings with that state other than its connection with Ms. Donner. The Supreme Court upheld the judgment of the Delaware court and held that the Florida courts had no jurisdiction over the Delaware trustee.

The Court first rejected *in rem* jurisdiction as a basis for Florida's claimed power over the trustee. Florida had *in rem* jurisdiction over assets admittedly passing under a local will, but the situs of the trust was Delaware, not Florida. The Court then stated that a "stronger argument" supported the claim of *in personam* jurisdiction, but it went on to reject that basis as well. The *International Shoe* test was not satisfied because the absent trustee did not have the requisite *kind* of contacts. The Court recognized the trend toward expansion of jurisdiction under such decisions as *McGee v. International Life Ins. Co.*, but it said:

> . . . [I]t is a mistake to assume that this trend heralds the eventual demise of all restrictions on the personal jurisdiction of state courts. . . . Those restrictions are more than a guarantee of immunity from inconvenient or distant litigation. They are a consequence of territorial limitations on the power of the respective States [citing *International Shoe* and, earlier in the same paragraph, *Pennoyer*]. . . .
>
> The cause of action in this case is not one that arises out of an act done or transaction consummated in the forum State. In that respect, it differs from [*McGee*] . . . . [T]he record discloses no instance in which the *trustee* performed any acts in Florida that bear the same relationship to the [trust] agreement as the solicitation in *McGee* . . . .
>
> . . . The unilateral activity of those who claim some relationship with a nonresident defendant cannot satisfy the requirement of contact with the forum State. . . . [I]t is essential in each case that there be some act by which the defendant purposefully avails itself of the privilege of conducting activities within the forum State, thus invoking the benefits and protections of its laws [citing *International Shoe*]. [Mrs. Donner's] execution in Florida of her power of appointment cannot remedy the absence of such an act in this case. . . .

Four Justices dissented from this holding. "[T]here is nothing in the Due Process Clause which denied Florida [jurisdiction]," said Justice Black for three of the dissenters. "Florida had a strong interest in marshalling assets of its domiciliary, distributing them, and winding up her estate." Justice Black concluded,

> It seems to me that where a transaction has as much relationship to a State as Mrs. Donner's appointment had to Florida its courts ought to have power to adjudicate controversies arising out of that transaction, unless litigation there would impose such a heavy and disproportionate burden on a nonresident that it would offend what this Court has referred to as "traditional notions of fair play and substantial justice." . . . Florida . . . was a reasonably convenient forum for all. Certainly there is nothing fundamentally unfair in subjecting the corporate trustee to the jurisdiction of the Florida courts. It chose to maintain business relations with Mrs. Donner in that State for eight years, regularly communicating with her with respect to the business of the trust, including the very appointment at issue. . . .

WORLD-WIDE VOLKSWAGEN CORP. v. WOODSON

444 U.S. 286 (1980)

MR. JUSTICE WHITE delivered the opinion of the Court.

The issue before us is whether, consistently with the due process clause of the fourteenth amendment, an Oklahoma court may exercise *in personam* jurisdiction over a non-resident automobile retailer and its wholesale distributor in a products-liability action, when the defendants' only connection with Oklahoma is the fact that an automobile sold in New York to New York residents became involved in an accident in Oklahoma.

I.

[Plaintiffs were traveling from New York, where they had purchased the automobile, to a new home in Arizona. As they passed through Oklahoma, another car struck their vehicle in the rear, causing a fire and severely injuring the wife and her two children. Plaintiffs brought a products liability action in an Oklahoma state court, claiming that their injuries resulted from defective design and placement of the vehicle's gas tank and fuel system. They joined four defendants: the automobile's European manufacturer (Audi); its importer (Volkswagen of America, Inc.); its regional distributor (World-Wide Volkswagen Corp.); and its retail dealer (Seaway). The retailer and distributor entered special appearances, claiming that the exercise of jurisdiction over them by Oklahoma would violate the Due Process Clause. World-Wide was a New York corporation with a contract to distribute in New York, New Jersey and Connecticut. The retailer was a New York corporation, with operations entirely in New York. Neither had done any business in Oklahoma, and there was no showing that any automobile sold by either had ever entered Oklahoma with the single exception of the vehicle involved in the present case.

[The Oklahoma trial court held that it had jurisdiction under an Oklahoma statute that supported suit if a defendant caused "tortious injury in this state by an act or omission outside this state if he regularly does or solicits business or engages in any other persistent course of conduct, or derives substantial revenue from . . . this state . . . ." The Oklahoma Supreme Court upheld the trial court. The United States Supreme Court reversed, holding that there was no jurisdiction over the retailer and distributor.]

II.

. . . As has long been settled, and as we reaffirm today, a state court may exercise personal jurisdiction over a nonresident defendant only so long as there exist "minimum contacts" between the defendant and the forum state. *International Shoe Co. v. Washington*. The concept of minimum contacts, in turn, can be seen to perform two related, but distinguishable functions. It protects the defendants against the burdens of litigating in a distant or inconvenient forum. And it acts to insure that the states, through their courts, do not reach out beyond the limits imposed upon them by their status as coequal sovereigns in a federal system.

The protection against inconvenient litigation is typically described in terms of "reasonableness" or "fairness." We have said that the defendants' contacts with the forum state must be such that maintenance of the suit "does not offend 'traditional notions of fair play and substantial justice.' " *International Shoe Co. v. Washington*, . . . The relationship between the defendant and the forum must be such that it is "reasonable

. . . to require the corporation to defend the particular suit which is brought there." . . . Implicit in this emphasis on reasonableness is the understanding that the burden on the defendant, while always a primary concern, will in an appropriate case be considered in light of other relevant factors, including the forum state's interest in adjudicating the dispute, *see McGee v. International Life Ins. Co.*; the plaintiff's interest in obtaining convenient and effective relief. . . , at least when that interest is not adequately protected by the plaintiff's power to choose the forum, . . . ; the interstate judicial system's interest in obtaining the most efficient resolution of the controversy; and the shared interest of the several States in furthering fundamental substantive social policies. . . . Nevertheless, we have never accepted the proposition that state lines are irrelevant for jurisdictional purposes. . . . Even if the defendant would suffer minimal or no inconvenience from being forced to litigate before the tribunals of another state; even if the forum state has a strong interest in applying its law to the controversy; even if the forum state is the most convenient location for litigation, the Due Process Clause, acting as an instrument of interstate federalism, may sometimes act to divest the state of its power to render a valid judgment. *Hanson v. Denckla*. . . .

III.

Applying these principles to the case at hand, we find in the record before us a total absence of those affiliating circumstances that are a necessary predicate to any exercise of state-court jurisdiction. Petitioners carry on no activity whatsoever in Oklahoma. They close no sales and perform no services there. . . . In short, respondents seek to base jurisdiction on . . . the fortuitous circumstances that a single Audi automobile, sold in New York to New York residents, happened to suffer an accident while passing through Oklahoma.

It is argued, however, that because an automobile is mobile by its very design and purpose it was "foreseeable that the [vehicle] would cause injury in Oklahoma." Yet "foreseeability" alone has never been a sufficient benchmark for personal jurisdiction under the Due Process Clause. In *Hanson v. Denckla*, . . . it was no doubt foreseeable that the settlor of a Delaware trust would subsequently move to Florida and seek to exercise a power of appointment there; yet we held that Florida courts could not constitutionally exercise jurisdiction over a Delaware trustee that had no other contacts with the forum state. . . .

This is not to say, of course, that foreseeability is wholly irrelevant. But the foreseeability that is critical to due process analysis is not the mere likelihood that a product will find its way into the forum state. Rather, it is that the defendant's conduct and connection with the forum state are such that he should reasonably anticipate being haled into court there. [Citations omitted.] The Due Process Clause, by insuring the "orderly administration of the laws," *International Shoe Co. v. Washington* . . . , gives a degree of predictability to the legal system that allows potential defendants to structure their primary conduct with some minimum assurance as to where that conduct will and will not render them liable to suit.

When a corporation "purposefully avails itself of the privileges of conducting activities within the forum State," *Hanson v. Denckla*, it has clear notice that it is subject to suit there, and can act to alleviate the risk of burdensome litigation by procuring insurance, passing the expected costs on to consumers, or, if the risks are too great, severing its connection with the State. Hence if the sale of a product of a manufacturer or distributor . . . is not simply an isolated occurrence, but arises from the efforts of the manufacturer or the distributor to serve, directly or indirectly, the market for its product in other states, it is not unreasonable to subject it to suit in one of those states if its allegedly defective merchandise has been the source of injury to its owner or to others. The forum state does not exceed its powers under the due process clause if it asserts personal jurisdiction over a corporation that delivers its products into the stream of commerce with the expectation that they will be purchased by consumers in the forum state. *Compare Gray v. American Radiator & Standard Sanitary Corp.* . . .

. . . In our view, whatever marginal revenues petitioners may have received by virtue of the fact that their products are capable of use in Oklahoma is far too attenuated a contact to justify that State's exercise of *in personam* jurisdiction over them. . . . Reversed.

MR. JUSTICE BRENNAN, dissenting. . . .

I.

The Court's opinions focus tightly on the existence of contacts between the forum and the defendant. In so doing, they accord too little weight to the strength of the forum state's interest in the case and fail to explore whether there would be any actual inconvenience to the defendant. . . .

. . . Because lesser burdens reduce the unfairness to the defendant, jurisdiction may be justified despite less significant contacts. . . . Due process limits on jurisdiction do not protect a defendant from all inconvenience of travel, *McGee*, . . . and it would not be sensible to make the constitutional rule turn solely on the number of miles the defendant must travel to the courtroom. Instead, the constitutionally significant "burden" to be analyzed relates to the mobility of the defendant's defense. For instance, if having to travel to a foreign forum would hamper the defense because witnesses or evidence or the defendant himself were immobile, or if there were a disproportionately large number of witnesses or amount of evidence that would have to be transported at the defendant's expense, or if being away from home for the duration of the trial would work some special hardship on the defendant, then the Constitution would require special consideration for the defendant's interests. . . .

. . . [T]he interest of the forum state and its connection to the litigation is strong. The automobile accident underlying the litigation occurred in Oklahoma. The plaintiffs were hospitalized in Oklahoma when they brought suit. Essential witnesses and evidence were in Oklahoma. The state has a legitimate interest in enforcing its laws designed to keep its highway system safe, and the trial can proceed at least as efficiently in Oklahoma as anywhere else.

The petitioners are not unconnected with the forum. Although both sell automobiles within limited sales territories, each sold the automobile which in fact was driven to Oklahoma where it was involved in an accident. [Defendants' intentions, if any, to limit jurisdiction over them to certain states] were unrealistic hopes that cannot be treated as an automatic constitutional shield.

An automobile simply is not a stationary item or one designed to be used in one place. An automobile is *intended* to be moved around. . . .

. . . Commercial activity is more likely to cause effects in a larger sphere, and the actor derives an economic benefit from the activity that makes it fair to require him to answer for his conduct where its effects are felt. The profits may be used to pay the cost of suit, and knowing that the activity is likely to have effects on other states the defendant can readily insure against the costs of those effects, thereby sparing himself much of the inconvenience of defending in a distant forum.

. . . I believe [sufficient] contacts are to be found here and that, considering all of the interests and policies at stake, requiring petitioners to defend this action in Oklahoma is not beyond the bounds of the Constitution. Accordingly, I dissent.

[The dissenting opinion of MR. JUSTICE BLACKMUN is omitted.]

HELICOPTEROS NACIONALES DE COLOMBIA, S.A. v. HALL, 466 U.S. 408 (1984). Plaintiffs' decedents were killed in Peru in the crash of a helicopter operated by the defendant. Defendant was a Colombian corporation that maintained no office in Texas, although it had purchased helicopters and supplies extensively in Texas. It had also sent pilots to Texas for training, accepted a check drawn on a Texas bank, and sent its president to Texas to negotiate and sign the contract for helicopter service. The Texas Supreme Court held that the defendant was within the scope of the Texas long-arm statute and that the exercise of jurisdiction was consistent with due process [the Texas Supreme Court's opinion is summarized in the preceding section]. The United States Supreme Court reversed on due process grounds.

The Court first distinguished between "specific" jurisdiction, in which the claim arises out of or is related to the contacts, and "general" jurisdiction, in which the claim and the contacts are not related. It characterized this case as one of general jurisdiction. Therefore, it concluded, jurisdiction could be supported only by "continuous and systematic" contacts. Defendant's acceptance of a Texas check was of "little significance" in meeting this standard, and its president's single trip to Texas "cannot be described as a contact of a 'continuous and systematic' nature." Finally, purchases from Texas, even if frequent, could not fulfill the requirement of continuous and systematic business:

> . . . *Rosenberg Bros. & Co. v. Curtis Brown Co.*, 260 U.S. 516 . . . makes clear that purchases and related trips, standing alone, are not a sufficient basis for a State's assertion of jurisdiction.
>
> The defendant in *Rosenberg* was a small retailer in Tulsa, Oklahoma, who dealt in men's clothing and furnishings. . . . Its only connection with New York was that it purchased from New York wholesalers a large portion of its merchandise sold in its Tulsa store. . . . The Court concluded: "Visits on such business, even if occurring at regular intervals, would not warrant the inference that the corporation was present within the jurisdiction of [New York]."

The Court observed that it was not required to decide whether purchases could be the basis of specific jurisdiction. Thus it left open the question of jurisdiction in a suit for payment based directly on a purchase contract signed by a nonresident.

Justice Brennan dissented. Helicopteros "obtained numerous benefits from the transaction of business in Texas," and it was "eminently fair and reasonable to expect [it] to face the obligations that attach to its participation in such commercial transactions." Furthermore, Justice Brennan questioned the conclusion that the case was one of general jurisdiction, which he saw as overly dependent upon the vagaries of the pleading of the claim. For example, the complaint had alleged pilot error; if it had instead alleged negligence in the training of the pilot in Texas, it would then "arise out of" or be "related to" the contacts, and "presumably the Court would concede that the specific jurisdiction of the Texas courts was applicable."

BURGER KING CORP. v. RUDZEWICZ

471 U.S. 462 (1985)

JUSTICE BRENNAN delivered the opinion of the Court.

The State of Florida's long-arm statute extends jurisdiction to "[a]ny person, whether or not a citizen or resident of this state," who, *inter alia*, "[b]reach[es] a contract in this state by failing to perform acts required by the contract to be performed in this state," so long as the cause of action arises from the alleged contractual breach. Fla. Stat. § 48.193(1)(g) (Supp. 1984). The United States District Court for the Southern District of Florida, sitting in diversity, relied on this provision in exercising personal jurisdiction over a Michigan resident who allegedly had breached a franchise agreement with a Florida corporation by failing to make required payments in Florida. The question presented is whether this exercise of long-arm jurisdiction offended "traditional conception[s] of fair play and substantial justice" embodied in the Due Process Clause of the Fourteenth Amendment. *International Shoe Co. v. Washington*. . . .

I

A

Burger King Corporation is a Florida corporation whose principal offices are in Miami. It is one of the world's largest restaurant organizations, with over 3,000 outlets in the 50 states, the Commonwealth of Puerto Rico, and 8 foreign nations. Burger King conducts approximately 80% of its business through a franchise operation that the company styles the "Burger King System" — "a comprehensive restaurant format and operating system for the sale of uniform and quality food products." . . . Burger King licenses its franchisees to use its trademarks and service marks for a period of 20 years and leases standardized restaurant facilities to them for the same term. In addition, franchisees acquire a variety of proprietary information concerning the "standards, specifications, procedures and methods for operating a Burger King Restaurant." . . . They also receive market research and advertising assistance; ongoing training in restaurant management; and accounting, cost-control, and inventory-control guidance. By permitting franchisees to tap into Burger King's established national reputation and to benefit from proven procedures for dispensing standardized fare, this system enables them to go into the restaurant business with significantly lowered barriers to entry.

Rudzewicz and MacShara jointly applied for a franchise to Burger King's Birmingham, Michigan district office in the autumn of 1978. Their application was forwarded to Burger King's Miami headquarters, which entered into a preliminary agreement with them in February 1979. During the ensuing four months it was agreed that Rudzewicz and MacShara would assume operation of an existing facility in Drayton Plains, Michigan. MacShara attended the prescribed management courses in Miami during this period, . . . and the franchisees purchased $165,000 worth of restaurant equipment from Burger King's Davmor Industries division in Miami. Even before the final agreements were signed, however, the parties began to disagree over site-development fees, building design, computation of monthly rent, and whether the franchisees would be able to assign their liabilities to a corporation they had formed. During these disputes Rudzewicz and MacShara negotiated both with the Birmingham district office and with the Miami headquarters. With some misgivings, Rudzewicz and MacShara finally obtained limited concessions from the Miami headquarters, signed the final agreements, and commenced operations in June 1979. By signing the final agreements, Rudzewicz obligated himself personally to payments exceeding $1 million over the 20-year franchise relationship.

The Drayton Plains facility apparently enjoyed steady business during the summer of 1979, but patronage declined after a recession began later that year. Rudzewicz and MacShara soon fell far behind in their monthly payments to Miami. Headquarters sent notices of default, and an extended period of negotiations began among the franchisees, the Birmingham district office, and the Miami headquarters. After several Burger King officials in Miami had engaged in prolonged but ultimately unsuccessful negotiations with the franchisees by mail and by telephone, headquarters terminated the franchise and ordered Rudzewicz and MacShara to vacate the premises. They refused and continued to occupy and operate the facility as a Burger King restaurant.

B

Burger King commenced the instant action in the United States District Court for the Southern District of Florida in May 1981, invoking that court's diversity jurisdiction pursuant to 28 U.S.C. § 1332(a) and its original jurisdiction over federal trademark disputes pursuant to § 1338(a). Burger King alleged that Rudzewicz and MacShara had breached their franchise obligations "within [the jurisdiction of] this district court" by failing to make the required payments "at plaintiff's place of business in Miami, Dade County, Florida" . . . and also charged that they were tortiously infringing its trademarks and service marks through their continued unauthorized operation as a Burger King restaurant. . . . Burger King sought damages, injunctive relief, and costs and attorney's fees. Rudzewicz and MacShara entered special appearances, and argued *inter alia*, that because they were Michigan residents and because Burger King's claim did not "arise" within the Southern District of Florida, the District Court lacked personal jurisdiction over them. The District Court denied their motions after a hearing, holding that, pursuant to Florida's long-arm statute, "a non-resident Burger King franchisee is subject to the personal jurisdiction of this Court in actions arising out of its franchise agreements." . . .

After a 3-day bench trial, the court again concluded that it had "jurisdiction over the subject matter and the parties to this cause." . . . Finding that Rudzewicz and MacShara had breached their franchise agreements with Burger King and had infringed Burger King's trademarks and service marks, the court entered judgment against them, jointly and severally, for $228,875 in contract damages. The court also ordered them "to immediately close Burger King Restaurant Number 775 from continued operation or to immediately give the keys and possession of said restaurant to Burger King Corporation," *id.*, at 163, found that they had failed to prove any of the required elements of their counterclaim, and awarded costs and attorney's fees to Burger King.

Rudzewicz appealed to the Court of Appeals for the Eleventh Circuit. A divided panel of that Circuit reversed the judgment, concluding that the District Court could not properly exercise personal jurisdiction over Rudzewicz pursuant to Fla. Stat. § 48.193(1)(g) (Supp. 1984) because "the circumstances of the Drayton Plains franchise and the negotiations which led to it left Rudzewicz bereft of reasonable notice and financially unprepared for the prospect of franchise litigation in Florida." *Burger King Corp. v. MacShara*, 724 F.2d 1505, 1513 (1984). Accordingly, the panel majority concluded that "[j]urisdiction under these circumstances would offend the fundamental fairness which is the touchstone of due process." *Ibid.*

. . . Treating the jurisdictional statement as a petition for a writ of certiorari, . . . we grant the petition and now reverse.

II

A

The Due Process Clause protects an individual's liberty interest in not being subject to the binding judgments of a forum with which he has established no meaningful "contacts, ties, or relations." *International Shoe Co. v. Washington.* . . . By requiring that individuals have "fair warning that a particular activity may subject [them] to the jurisdiction of a foreign sovereign," . . . the Due Process Clause "gives a degree of predictability to the legal system that allows potential defendants to structure their primary conduct with some minimum assurance as to where that conduct will and will not render them liable to suit," *World-Wide Volkswagen Corp. v. Woodson.* . . .

Where a forum seeks to assert specific jurisdiction over an out-of-state defendant, who has not consented to suit there,[14] this "fair warning" requirement is satisfied if the defendant has "purposefully directed" his activities at residents of the forum, . . . and the litigation results from alleged injuries that "arise out of or relate to" those activities, *Helicopteros Nacionales de Colombia, S.A. v. Hall* . . . .[15] Thus "[t]he forum State does not exceed its powers under the Due Process Clause if it asserts personal jurisdiction over a corporation that delivers its products into the stream of commerce with the expectation that they will be purchased by consumers in the forum State" and those products subsequently injure forum consumers. *World-Wide Volkswagen Corp. v. Woodson, supra,* 444 U.S., at 297-298, 100 S. Ct., at 567-568. Similarly, a publisher who distributes magazines in a distant State may fairly be held accountable in that forum for damages resulting there from an allegedly defamatory story. *Keeton v. Hustler Magazine, Inc., supra; see also Calder v. Jones,* 465 U.S. 783, 104 S. Ct. 1482, 79 L. Ed. 2d 804 (1984) (suit against author and editor). And with respect to interstate contractual obligations, we have emphasized that parties who "reach out beyond one state and create continuing relationships and obligations with citizens of another state" are subject to regulation and sanctions in the other State for the consequences of their activities. *Travelers Health Assn. v. Virginia,* 339 U.S. 643, 647, 70 S. Ct. 927, 929, 94 L. Ed. 1154 (1950). *See also McGee v. International Life Insurance Co.* . . .

[T]he constitutional touchstone remains whether the defendant purposefully established "minimum contacts" in the forum State. *International Shoe Co. v. Washington.* . . . Although it has been argued that foreseeability of causing *injury* in another State should be sufficient to establish such contacts there when policy considerations so require, the

[14] We have noted that, because the personal jurisdiction requirement is a waivable right, there are a "variety of legal arrangements" by which a litigant may give "express or implied consent to the personal jurisdiction of the court." *Insurance Corp. of Ireland, Ltd. v. Compagnie des Bauxites de Guinee, supra,* at 703, 102 S. Ct., at 2105. For example, particularly in the commercial context, parties frequently stipulate in advance to submit their controversies for resolution within a particular jurisdiction. *See National Equipment Rental, Ltd. v. Szukhent,* 375 U.S. 311, 84 S. Ct. 411, 11 L. Ed. 2d 354 (1964). Where such forum-selection provisions have been obtained through "freely negotiated" agreements and are not "unreasonable and unjust," *The Bremen v. Zapata Off-Shore Co.,* 407 U.S. 1, 15, 92 S. Ct. 1907, 1916, 32 L. Ed. 2d 513 (1972), their enforcement does not offend due process.

[15] "Specific" jurisdiction contrasts with "general" jurisdiction, pursuant to which "a State exercises personal jurisdiction over a defendant in a suit not arising out of or related to the defendant's contacts with the forum." *Helicopteros Nacionales de Colombia, S.A. v. Hall,* 466 U.S. 408, 414, n. 9, 104 S. Ct. 1868, 1872, n. 9, 80 L. Ed.2d 404 (1984); *see also Perkins v. Benguet Consolidated Mining Co.,* 342 U.S. 437, 72 S. Ct. 413, 96 L. Ed. 485 (1952).

Court has consistently held that this kind of foreseeability is not a "sufficient benchmark" for exercising personal jurisdiction. *World-Wide Volkswagen Corp. v. Woodson*. . . . Instead, "the foreseeability that is critical to due process analysis . . . is that the defendant's conduct and connection with the forum State are such that he should reasonably anticipate being haled into court there." *Id.*, at 297, 100 S. Ct., at 567. In defining when it is that a potential defendant should "reasonably anticipate" out-of-state litigation, the Court frequently has drawn from the reasoning of *Hanson v. Denckla* . . . :

> The unilateral activity of those who claim some relationship with a nonresident defendant cannot satisfy the requirement of contact with the forum State. The application of that rule will vary with the quality and nature of the defendant's activity, but it is essential in each case that there be some act by which the defendant purposefully avails itself of the privilege of conducting activities within the forum State, thus invoking the benefits and protections of its laws.

This "purposeful availment" requirement ensures that a defendant will not be haled into a jurisdiction solely as a result of "random," "fortuitous," or "attenuated" contacts, . . . *World-Wide Volkswagen Corp. v. Woodson*, 444 U.S., at 299, 100 S. Ct., at 568, or of the "unilateral activity of another party or a third person," *Helicopteros Nacionales de Colombia, S.A. v. Hall, supra*, 466 U.S., at 417, 104 S. Ct., at 1873. Jurisdiction is proper, however, where the contacts proximately result from actions by the defendant *himself* that create a "substantial connection" with the forum State. *McGee v. International Life Insurance Co., supra*, 355 U.S., at 223, 78 S. Ct., at 201; *see also Kulko v. California Superior Court, supra*, 436 U.S., at 94, n. 7, 98 S. Ct., at 1698, n. 7. Thus where the defendant "deliberately" has engaged in significant activities within a State, *Keeton v. Hustler Magazine, Inc.*, 465 U.S., at 781, 104 S. Ct., at 1481, or has created "continuing obligations" between himself and residents of the forum, *Travelers Health Assn. v. Virginia*, 339 U.S., at 648, 70 S. Ct., at 929, he manifestly has availed himself of the privilege of conducting business there, and because his activities are shielded by "the benefits and protections" of the forum's laws it is presumptively not unreasonable to require him to submit to the burdens of litigation in that forum as well.

Jurisdiction in these circumstances may not be avoided merely because the defendant did not *physically* enter the forum State. Although territorial presence frequently will enhance a potential defendant's affiliation with a State and reinforce the reasonable foreseeability of suit there, it is an inescapable fact of modern commercial life that a substantial amount of business is transacted solely by mail and wire communications across state lines, thus obviating the need for physical presence within a State in which business is conducted. So long as a commercial actor's efforts are "purposefully directed" toward residents of another State, we have consistently rejected the notion that an absence of physical contacts can defeat personal jurisdiction there. . . .

Once it has been decided that a defendant purposefully established minimum contacts within the forum State, these contacts may be considered in light of other factors to determine whether the assertion of personal jurisdiction would comport with "fair play and substantial justice." *International Shoe Co. v. Washington*, 326 U.S., at 320, 66 S. Ct., at 160. Thus courts in "appropriate case[s]" may evaluate "the burden on the defendant," "the forum State's interest in adjudicating the dispute," "the plaintiff's interest in obtaining convenient and effective relief," "the interstate judicial system's interest in obtaining the most efficient resolution of controversies," and the "shared interest of the several States in furthering fundamental substantive social policies." *World-Wide*

Volkswagen Corp. v. Woodson, supra. . . . These considerations sometimes serve to establish the reasonableness of jurisdiction upon a lesser showing of minimum contacts than would otherwise be required. *See, e.g.*, . . . *McGee v. International Life Insurance Co., supra*, 355 U.S., at 223-224, 78 S. Ct., at 201-202. On the other hand, where a defendant who purposefully has directed his activities at forum residents seeks to defeat jurisdiction, he must present a compelling case that the presence of some other considerations would render jurisdiction unreasonable. Most such considerations usually may be accommodated through means short of finding jurisdiction unconstitutional. For example, the potential clash of the forum's law with the "fundamental substantive social policies" of another State may be accommodated through application of the forum's choice-of-law rules. Similarly, a defendant claiming substantial inconvenience may seek a change of venue. . . .

B

(1)

Applying these principles to the case at hand, we believe there is substantial record evidence supporting the District Court's conclusion that the assertion of personal jurisdiction over Rudzewicz in Florida for the alleged breach of his franchise agreement did not offend due process. At the outset, we note a continued division among lower courts respecting whether and to what extent a contract can constitute a "contact" for purposes of due process analysis. If the question is whether an individual's contract with an out-of-state party *alone* can automatically establish sufficient minimum contacts in the other party's home forum, we believe the answer clearly is that it cannot. The Court long ago rejected the notion that personal jurisdiction might turn on "mechanical" tests, *International Shoe Co. v. Washington*, . . . or on "conceptualistic . . . theories of the place of contracting or of performance" . . . . Instead, we have emphasized the need for a "highly realistic" approach that recognizes that a "contract" is "ordinarily but an intermediate step serving to tie up prior business negotiations with future consequences which themselves are the real object of the business transaction." . . .

In this case, no physical ties to Florida can be attributed to Rudzewicz other than MacShara's brief training course in Miami. Rudzewicz did not maintain offices in Florida and, for all that appears from the record, has never even visited there. Yet this franchise dispute grew directly out of "a contract which had a *substantial* connection with that State." *McGee v. International Life Insurance Co.*, . . . (emphasis added). Eschewing the option of operating an independent local enterprise, Rudzewicz deliberately "reach[ed] out beyond" Michigan and negotiated with a Florida corporation for the purchase of a long-term franchise and the manifold benefits that would derive from affiliation with a nationwide organization. *Travelers Health Assn. v. Virginia*, 339 U.S., at 647, 70 S. Ct., at 929. Upon approval, he entered into a carefully structured 20-year relationship that envisioned continuing and wide-reaching contacts with Burger King in Florida. In light of Rudzewicz's voluntary acceptance of the long-term and exacting regulation of his business from Burger King's Miami headquarters, the "quality and nature" of his relationship to the company in Florida can in no sense be viewed as "random," "fortuitous," or "attenuated." *Hanson v. Denckla*, 357 U.S., at 253, 78 S. Ct., at 1239; . . . *World-Wide Volkswagen Corp. v. Woodson*, 444 U.S., at 299, 100 S. Ct., at 568. Rudzewicz's refusal to make the contractually required payments in Miami, and his continued use of Burger King's trademarks and confidential business information after his termination, caused foreseeable injuries to the corporation in Florida. For these reasons it was, at the very least, presumptively reasonable for Rudzewicz to be called to account there for such injuries.

[The Court rejects the lower court's conclusion that Rudzewicz had no "reason to anticipate a Burger King suit outside of Michigan." The contract documents emphasized the location of the headquarters, required notices and payments there, and specified that agreements were made and enforced from Miami. The course of dealings of the parties emphasized that decision-making authority for Burger King was in Miami.

[Further, the contract contained an express provision that Florida law would govern the contract. The lower court pointed out that jurisdiction and choice of law are different issues. Nevertheless, an express choice of law provision agreed to by a party is to be considered in determining whether a party has invoked the protections of the laws of the forum.]

(2)

Nor has Rudzewicz pointed to other factors that can be said persuasively to outweigh the considerations discussed above and to establish the *unconstitutionality* of Florida's assertion of jurisdiction. We cannot conclude that Florida had no "legitimate interest in holding [Rudzewicz] answerable on a claim related to" the contacts he had established in that State.

The Court of Appeals also concluded, however, that the parties' dealings involved "a characteristic disparity of bargaining power" and "elements of surprise," and that Rudzewicz "lacked fair notice" of the potential for litigation in Florida because the contractual provisions suggesting to the contrary were merely "boilerplate declarations in a lengthy printed contract." . . . To the contrary, Rudzewicz was represented by counsel throughout these complex transactions and, as Judge Johnson observed in dissent below, was himself an experienced accountant "who for five months conducted negotiations with Burger King over the terms of the franchise and lease agreements, and who obligated himself personally to contracts requiring over time payments that exceeded $1 million." . . . Rudzewicz was able to secure a modest reduction in rent and other concessions from Miami headquarters . . . ; moreover, to the extent that Burger King's terms were inflexible, Rudzewicz presumably decided that the advantages of affiliating with a national organization provided sufficient commercial benefits as to offset the detriments.

III

Notwithstanding these considerations, the Court of Appeals apparently believed that it was necessary to reject jurisdiction in this case as a prophylactic measure, reasoning that an affirmance of the District Court's judgment would result in the exercise of jurisdiction over "out-of-state consumers to collect payments due on modest personal purchases" and would "sow the seeds of default judgments against franchisees owing smaller debts." . . . We share the Court of Appeals' broader concerns and therefore reject any talismanic jurisdictional formulas; "the facts of each case must [always] be weighed" in determining whether personal jurisdiction would comport with "fair play and substantial justice." *Kulko v. California Superior Court*, 436 U.S., at 92, 98 S. Ct., at 1696-1697. The "quality and nature" of an interstate transaction may sometimes be so "random," "fortuitous," or "attenuated" that it cannot fairly be said that the potential defendant "should reasonably anticipate being haled into court" in another jurisdiction. *World-Wide Volkswagen Corp. v. Woodson*, 444 U.S., at 297, 100 S. Ct., at 567 . . . . We also have emphasized that jurisdiction may not be grounded on a contract whose terms have been obtained through "fraud, undue influence, or overweening bargaining power" and whose application would render litigation "so gravely difficult and inconvenient that [a party] will for all practical purposes be deprived of his day in court." . . .

For the reasons set forth above, however, these dangers are not present in the instant case. Because Rudzewicz established a substantial and continuing relationship with Burger King's Miami headquarters, received fair notice from the contract documents and the course of dealing that he might be subject to suit in Florida, and has failed to demonstrate how jurisdiction in that forum would otherwise be fundamentally unfair, we conclude that the District Court's exercise of jurisdiction pursuant to Florida Stat. § 48.193(1)(g) (Supp. 1984) did not offend due process. The judgment of the Court of Appeals is accordingly reversed, and the case is remanded for further proceedings consistent with this opinion.

Justice Stevens, with whom Justice White joins, dissenting.

In my opinion there is a significant element of unfairness in requiring a franchisee to defend a case of this kind in the forum chosen by the franchisor. It is undisputed that respondent maintained no place of business in Florida, that he had no employees in that State, and that he was not licensed to do business there. Respondent did not prepare his french fries, shakes, and hamburgers in Michigan, and then deliver them into the stream of commerce "with the expectation that they [would] be purchased by consumers in" Florida. . . . To the contrary, respondent did business only in Michigan, his business, property, and payroll taxes were payable in that state, and he sold all of his products there.

Throughout the business relationship, respondent's principal contacts with petitioner were with its Michigan office. Notwithstanding its disclaimer, . . . , the Court seems ultimately to rely on nothing more than standard boilerplate language contained in various documents, . . . to establish that respondent " 'purposefully availed himself of the benefits and protections of Florida's laws.' " . . . Such superficial analysis creates a potential for unfairness not only in negotiations between franchisors and their franchisees but, more significantly, in the resolution of the disputes that inevitably arise from time to time in such relationships.

Accordingly, I respectfully dissent.

NOTES AND QUESTIONS

(1) *Justice Brennan's View Prevails.* The *Burger King* decision might appropriately be called "Justice Brennan's Triumph." *See* Perschbacher, *Minimum Contacts Reapplied: Mr. Justice Brennan Has It His Way, in Burger King Corp. v. Rudzewicz*, 1986 Ariz. St. L.J. 585. After dissenting in *Hanson v. Denckla, World-Wide Volkswagen*, and *Helicopteros* (as well as *Kulko v. Superior Court*, which you will encounter in the next section), he is in the majority and writes the opinion in *Burger King*. Notice that he retains the concept of "purposefully availing," and emphasizes that Rudzewicz purposely established a "long term franchise," *i.e.*, commercial relationship "that envisioned continuing and wide-reaching contacts with Burger King in Florida." In this situation, the scales are tipped against Rudzewicz, who could not make a "compelling" showing that other factors rendered jurisdiction unreasonable.

(2) *Literature.* There is a substantial literature on the expansions and contractions of the minimum contacts doctrine. For an analysis of pre-*Helicopteros* cases, *see* Kamp, *Beyond Minimum Contacts: The Supreme Court's New Jurisdictional Theory*, 15 Ga.

L. Rev. 19 (1980). *See also* Knudsen, *Keeton, Calder, Helicopteros, and Burger King — International Shoe's Most Recent Progeny*, 39 U. Miami L. Rev. 809 (1985); Sonenshein, *The Error of a Balancing Approach to Due Process Jurisdiction Over the Person*, 59 Temp. L.Q. 47 (1986).

(3) *Is There a Commercial-Noncommercial Distinction?* Is it appropriate to treat a "commercial" defendant differently from a "noncommercial" one? Consider the case of a small business, such as the Oklahoma haberdashery in the *Rosenberg* case (cited in *Helicopteros*, above). Should this sort of defendant be more (or less) amenable to jurisdiction than, say, a nonresident spouse who is being sued for child or spousal support?

(4) *The Relatedness Requirement for Specific Jurisdiction.* The Court notes that specific jurisdiction requires the suit must "arise out of" or be "related to the defendant's contacts with the forum." But what kind of nexus is required under these terms? Does a product liability action for personal injury damages sustained in State X "arise out of" the sale of the same product lines in States Y and Z? If not, is the products liability action brought in State X based on a purchase in State Y "related to" the sale of the same product in State X to other buyers? What if Audi and Volkswagen of America had challenged jurisdiction in Oklahoma? Could they have been subject to specific jurisdiction in *World-Wide Volkswagen* based on the sale of the vehicle in New York if they directly or indirectly sold a lot of cars in Oklahoma?

In trying to define what is "related," some courts have used a "but-for" test that is jurisdictionally expansive because it embraces every event in every jurisdiction that hindsight can logically identify in the causative chain. Others have adopted a restrictive relatedness test requiring the nonresident's contacts to be relevant to an element of the plaintiff's claim, and some have applied a sliding scale of relatedness. Another possible approach is a "similarity" standard that would allow specific jurisdiction principles to be applied in every state where the nonresident engaged in similar activities. *See generally* Maloney, *Specific Jurisdiction and the "Arise From or Relate to" Requirement . . . What Does It Mean?*, 50 Wash. & Lee L. Rev. 1265, 2176–86, 1299 (1993).

Try to make the best jurisdictional arguments you can for dismissal of the suit brought in State X, (1) alleging injuries [where were the injuries suffered?] from the sale of defective goods in State Y in an action in which the defendant has sold other similar goods in State X or (2) alleging injuries arising from a car accident that occurred in State Y in an action in which the defendant traveled from State X to State Y causing the accident there.

(5) *Extent of Contacts Needed for General Jurisdiction.* How extensive do contacts need to be for general jurisdiction? If Audi and Volkswagen of America could not be subject to specific jurisdiction in Oklahoma in the *World-Wide Volkswagen* case, could they be haled into an Oklahoma court under principles of general jurisdiction? The courts and commentators have suggested that their contacts with Oklahoma would need to be fairly substantial. *See* Brilmayer, *A General Look at General Jurisdiction*, 66 Tex. L. Rev. 723, 742 (1988) ("The basic inquiry must be whether the defendant's level of activity rises to the level of activity of an insider, so that relegating the defendant to the political processes is fair."); *cf.* Twitchell, *The Myth of General Jurisdiction*, 101 Harv. L. Rev. 610, 635 (1988) ("traditional indicia" of general jurisdiction are "a home base, an agent for service of process, a local office, or the pursuance of business from a tangible locale within the state"). Could Rudzewicz have been subject to general jurisdiction in Florida? Could International Shoe have been subjected to general jurisdiction (under present day jurisdictional standards) in Washington?

(6) *Another Remedy: Forum Non Conveniens.* Another doctrine, *forum non conveniens*, may provide another way to resolve these issues. *See, e.g., Direct Color Services, Inc. v. Eastman Kodak Co.*, 929 S.W.2d 558 (Tex. App. Tyler 1996, pet. denied) — dismissal based on common law doctrine of *forum non conveniens*. *See* § 2.05, *infra*.

NOTE ON LONG-ARMING THE PRESS: *CALDER v. JONES* AND *KEETON v. HUSTLER MAGAZINE, INC.*

Should the First Amendment affect the scope of the long arm? When a reporter writes a story that is printed and distributed in a magazine or newspaper nationwide, is the reporter then subject to suit for defamation or invasion of privacy in any and every court in the nation? The First Amendment limits the conditions under which a plaintiff may recover for defamation. In the past, there have been some decisions that seemed to indicate that it might limit the extent to which media defendants could be long-armed, too.

In *Calder v. Jones*, 465 U.S. 783 (1984), the Supreme Court rejected this reasoning. The *National Enquirer* published a story reporting that Actress Shirley Jones drank so heavily as to prevent her from fulfilling her professional obligations. She sued the *Enquirer*, its editor, and its reporter for defamation. The *Enquirer* had a circulation of approximately 600,000 in California, where Jones sued; thus the defendants' "intentional, and allegedly tortious, actions were expressly aimed at California." The defendants, including the reporter, knew that the story would have a "devastating effect" on the plaintiff, "the brunt of [which] would be felt" in California. Therefore, they could "reasonably anticipate being haled into court there." The Court rejected the defendant's First Amendment arguments with the observation that "the potential chill on protected First Amendment activity . . . is already taken into account in the constitutional limitations on the substantive law governing such suits . . . . To reintroduce those concerns at the jurisdictional stage would be a form of double counting."

In *Keeton v. Hustler Magazine, Inc.*, 465 U.S. 770 (1984), plaintiff sued in New Hampshire, where between 10,000 and 15,000 copies of a national magazine were distributed monthly. The apparent purpose of the choice of forum was New Hampshire's unusually long statute of limitations (six years in libel cases); an earlier suit in Ohio had been dismissed on limitations grounds. The Supreme Court held that the plaintiff could thus choose the forum: "Petitioner's successful search for a State with a lengthy statute of limitations is no different from the litigation strategy of countless plaintiffs who seek a forum with favorable substantive or procedural rules or sympathetic local populations." The plaintiff was not required to have "minimum contacts" with the forum (by filing suit, the plaintiff had consented to jurisdiction over her). As for the defendant, the Court rejected the argument that "invisible radiations from the First Amendment" limited New Hampshire's long arm. While it was "undoubtedly true that the bulk of the harm done to petitioners occurred outside New Hampshire," that would be true in almost every libel suit brought outside plaintiff's domicile; the defendants had "continuously and deliberately exploited the New Hampshire market," produced a "national publication" of which a "substantial number of copies" regularly were sold there, and could "reasonably anticipate being haled into court there."

PROBLEM B

CONNOLLY v. BURT, *cert. granted but dismissed as moot*, 475 U.S. 1063 (1986). Defendant in this case was a professor at the University of Nebraska. He received a private inquiry from a hospital located in Colorado concerning the performance of the plaintiff, one of his former students, who was seeking an orthopedic residency. He responded to the request by a written communication to the Colorado hospital. Plaintiff later sued him in Colorado, alleging defamation. The Colorado Supreme Court held that, under *Calder v. Jones* and *Keeton v. Hustler Magazine*, this single communication was sufficient to support jurisdiction. The Supreme Court of the United States granted certiorari; however, it later ordered the case dismissed as moot (generally, such a dismissal occurs when the dispute has been settled by the parties or otherwise resolved). The question is: If the case had not become moot, how should the Supreme Court have decided it? Note: You should notice the relevance of *Hanson v. Denckla*; the professor perhaps is like the trustee in *Hanson*, who simply corresponded with Ms. Donner in Florida because she happened to be there, not because he had "purposefully availed" himself of opportunities in the forum. On the other hand, *Connolly v. Burt* clearly is a specific jurisdiction case; moreover, the Colorado court's citation of *Keeton* and *Calder* seems on point. Is the professor engaged in a commercial activity like the defendant Rudzewicz in *Burger King*? Finally, does this case call for recognition that the professor is a "little guy" in some sense? The authors had predicted reversal by the Supreme Court — but very tentatively.

ASAHI METAL INDUSTRY CO. v. SUPERIOR COURT

480 U.S. 102 (1987)

JUSTICE O'CONNOR announced the judgment of the Court and delivered the unanimous opinion of the Court with respect to Part I, the opinion of the Court with respect to Part II-B, in which THE CHIEF JUSTICE, JUSTICE BRENNAN, JUSTICE WHITE, JUSTICE MARSHALL, JUSTICE BLACKMUN, JUSTICE POWELL, and JUSTICE STEVENS join, and an opinion with respect to Parts II-A and III, in which THE CHIEF JUSTICE, JUSTICE POWELL, and JUSTICE SCALIA join.

[Zurcher was injured when his motorcycle went out of control and collided with a tractor. He sued Cheng Shin Rubber Industrial Company, Ltd. (Cheng Shin), a Taiwanese corporation, in California Superior Court for Solano County, claiming that the accident was caused in part by a defective tube it manufactured.] Cheng Shin in turn filed a cross-complaint seeking indemnification from . . . petitioner, Asahi Metal Industry Co., Ltd. (Asahi), the manufacturer of the tube's valve assembly. Zurcher's claims against Cheng Shin and the other defendants were eventually settled and dismissed, leaving only Cheng Shin's indemnity action against Asahi. . . .

Asahi moved to quash Cheng Shin's service of summons arguing the State could not exert jurisdiction over it, consistent with the Due Process Clause of the Fourteenth Amendment.

[The following information was submitted by Asahi and Cheng Shin: Asahi is a Japanese corporation. It manufactures tire valve assemblies in Japan and sells the assemblies to Cheng Shin, and to several other tire manufacturers, for use as components in finished tire tubes. Asahi's sales to Cheng Shin took place in Taiwan. The shipments from Asahi to Cheng Shin were sent from Japan to Taiwan. Cheng Shin bought and incorporated into its tire tubes 150,000 Asahi valve assemblies in 1978; 500,000 in 1979; 500,000 in 1980; 100,000 in 1981; and 100,000 in 1982. Sales to Cheng Shin accounted for 1.24 percent of Asahi's income in 1981 and 0.44 percent in 1982. Cheng Shin alleged that approximately 20 percent of its sales in the United States are in California. Cheng Shin purchases valve assemblies from other suppliers as well, and sells finished tubes throughout the world.]

[T]he Superior Court denied the motion to quash. . . . The [California] Supreme Court . . . found the exercise of jurisdiction over Asahi to be consistent with the Due Process Clause. . . .

We . . . reverse.

II

A

[After reviewing the basic decisional law of minimum contacts, the Court turned specifically to *World-Wide Volkswagen.*]

Since *World-Wide Volkswagen*, lower courts have been confronted with cases in which the defendant acted by placing a product in the stream of commerce, and the stream eventually swept defendant's product into the forum State, but the defendant did nothing else to purposefully avail itself of the market in the forum state. Some courts have understood the Due Process Clause, as interpreted in *World-Wide Volkswagen*, to allow an exercise of personal jurisdiction to be based on no more than the defendant's act of placing the product in the stream of commerce. Other courts have understood the Due Process Clause and . . . *World-Wide Volkswagen* to require the action of the defendant to be more purposefully directed at the forum State than the mere act of placing a product in the stream of commerce.

We [adopt the] latter position. . . . The "substantial connection," . . . between the defendant and the forum State necessary for a finding of minimum contacts must come about by *an action of the defendant purposefully directed toward the forum State* (citations omitted). The placement of a product into the stream of commerce, without more, is not an act of the defendant purposefully directed toward the forum State. Additional conduct of the defendant may indicate an intent or purpose to serve the market in the forum State, for example, designing the product for the market in the forum State, advertising in the forum State, establishing channels for providing regular advice to customers in the forum State, or marketing the product through a distributor who has agreed to serve as the sales agent in the forum State. But a defendant's awareness that the stream of commerce may or will sweep the product into the forum State does not convert the mere act of placing the product into the stream into an act purposefully directed toward the forum State.

[R]espondents have not demonstrated any action by Asahi to purposefully avail itself of the California market. Asahi does not do business in California. It has no office, agents, employees, or property in California. It does not advertise or otherwise solicit business in California. It did not create, control, or employ the distribution system that brought its valves to California. . . . There is no evidence that Asahi designed its product in anticipation of sales in California. . . . On the basis of these facts, the exertion of personal jurisdiction over Asahi by the Superior Court of California exceeds the limits of due process.

B

The strictures of the Due Process Clause forbid a state court from exercising personal jurisdiction over Asahi under circumstances that would offend "traditional notions of fair play and substantial justice" (citations omitted).

We have previously explained that the determination of the reasonableness of the exercise of jurisdiction in each case will depend on an evaluation of several factors. . . .

A consideration of these factors in the present case clearly reveals the unreasonableness of the assertion of jurisdiction over Asahi, even apart from the question of the placement of goods in the stream of commerce.

Certainly the burden on the defendant in this case is severe. Asahi has been commanded by the Supreme Court of California not only to traverse the distance between Asahi's headquarters in Japan and the Superior Court of California in and for the County of Solano, but also to submit its dispute with Cheng Shin to a foreign nation's judicial system. The unique burdens placed upon one who must defend oneself in a foreign legal system should have significant weight in assessing the reasonableness of stretching the long arm of personal jurisdiction over national borders.

When minimum contacts have been established, often the interests of the plaintiff and the forum in the exercise of jurisdiction will justify even the serious burdens placed on the alien defendant. In the present case, however, the interests of the plaintiff and the forum in California's assertion of jurisdiction over Asahi are slight. All that remains is a claim for indemnification asserted by Cheng Shin, a Taiwanese corporation, against Asahi. The transaction on which the indemnification claim is based took place in Taiwan; Asahi's components were shipped from Japan to Taiwan. Cheng Shin has not demonstrated that it is more convenient for it to litigate its indemnification claim against Asahi in California rather than in Taiwan or Japan.

Because the plaintiff is not a California resident, California's legitimate interests in the dispute have considerably diminished. The Supreme Court of California argued that the State had an interest in "protecting its consumers by ensuring that foreign manufacturers comply with the state's safety standards. . . ." The State Supreme Court's definition of California's interest, however, was overly broad. The dispute between Cheng Shin and Asahi is primarily about indemnification rather than safety standards. . . .

World-Wide Volkswagen also admonished courts to take into consideration the interests of the "several States," in addition to the forum state, in the efficient judicial resolution of the dispute and the advancement of substantive policies. In the present case, this advice calls for a court to consider the procedural and substantive policies of other *nations* whose interests are affected by the assertion of jurisdiction by the California court. The procedural and substantive interests of other nations in a state court's assertion of jurisdiction over an alien defendant will differ from case to case. In every case, however, those interests, as well as the Federal interest in its foreign relations policies, will be best served by a careful inquiry into the reasonableness of the assertion of jurisdiction in the particular case, and an unwillingness to find the serious burdens on an alien defendant outweighed by minimal interests on the part of the plaintiff or the forum State. "Great care and reserve should be exercised when extending our notions of personal jurisdiction into the international field." [Citations omitted.]

Considering the international context, the heavy burden on the alien defendant, and the slight interests of the plaintiff and the forum State, the exercise of personal jurisdiction by a California court over Asahi in this instance would be unreasonable and unfair.

III

Because the facts of this case do not establish minimum contacts such that the exercise of personal jurisdiction is consistent with fair play and substantial justice, the judgment of [the] Supreme Court of California is reversed, and the case is remanded for further proceedings not inconsistent with this opinion. . . .

JUSTICE BRENNAN, with whom JUSTICES WHITE, MARSHALL, and BLACKMUN join, concurring in part and in the judgment.

I do not agree with the plurality's interpretation of the stream-of-commerce theory, nor with its conclusion that Asahi did not "purposefully avail itself of the California market. . . ." I do agree, however, with the Court's conclusion in Part II-B that the exercise of personal jurisdiction over Asahi in this case would not comport with "fair play and substantial justice," [citation omitted]. This is one of those rare cases in which "minimum requirements inherent in the concept of 'fair play and substantial justice' . . . defeat the reasonableness of jurisdiction even [though] the defendant has purposefully engaged in forum activities" (citation omitted). I therefore join Parts I and II-B of the Court's opinion, and write separately to explain my disagreement with Part II-A. . . .

The stream of commerce refers not to unpredictable currents or eddies, but to the regular and anticipated flow of products from manufacture to distribution to retail sale. As long as a participant in this process is aware that the final product is being marketed in the forum State, the possibility of a lawsuit there cannot come as a surprise. Nor will the litigation present a burden for which there is no corresponding benefit. . . .

[A]ccordingly, I cannot join the plurality's determination that Asahi's regular and extensive sales of component parts to a manufacturer it knew was making regular sales of the final product in California is insufficient to establish minimum contacts with California.

JUSTICE STEVENS, with whom JUSTICE WHITE and JUSTICE BLACKMUN join, concurring in part and concurring in the judgment.

The judgment of the Supreme Court of California should be reversed for the reasons stated in Part II-B of the Court's opinion. While I join Parts I and II-B, I do not join Part II-A for two reasons. First, it is not necessary to the Court's decision. An examination of minimum contacts is not always necessary to determine whether a state court's assertion of personal jurisdiction is constitutional. [Citation omitted.] Part II-B establishes, after considering the factors set forth in *World-Wide Volkswagen Corp. v. Woodson*, . . . that California's exercise of jurisdiction over Asahi in this case would be "unreasonable and unfair. . . ." This finding alone requires reversal. . . .

Second, even assuming that the test ought to be formulated here, Part II-A misapplies it to the facts of this case. The Court seems to assume that an unwavering line can be drawn between "mere awareness" that a component will find its way into the forum State and "purposeful availment" of the forum's market. . . . Over the course of its dealings with Cheng Shin, Asahi has arguably engaged in a higher quantum of conduct than "[t]he placement of a product into the stream of commerce, without more. . . ." Whether or not this conduct rises to the level of purposeful availment requires a constitutional determination that is affected by the volume, the value, and the hazardous character of the components. In most circumstances I would be inclined to conclude that a regular course of dealing that results in deliveries of over 100,000 units annually over a period of several years would constitute "purposeful availment" even though the item delivered to the forum State was a standard product marketed throughout the world.

NOTES AND QUESTIONS

(1) *Sorting Out the Justices' Opinions.* Justices O'Connor, Brennan and Stevens each wrote opinions in *Asahi*. Three different groupings of Justices joined in parts of O'Connor's opinion. Try your hand at lining up the Justices and the views they endorsed.

(2) *A New Direction for the Court?* The only thing the Justices fully agreed on was the statement of the facts, and that, under these facts, the exercise of jurisdiction over Asahi was "unreasonable and unfair." Given the unusual set of facts — with the California plaintiff out of the case, the California court had two alien corporations left before it that were fighting over indemnity (secondary liability) only — just how significant is this case for the future?

(3) *Supplemental Personal Jurisdiction.* If a majority of the Court would have upheld jurisdiction over Zurcher's initial claim against Cheng Shin (certainly a possibility), does that mean the case would have been decided differently if the plaintiff's claim had not been settled and dismissed? Should it have been decided differently? In actions with multiple claims and parties, do we need a doctrine of supplemental personal jurisdiction (akin to supplemental subject matter jurisdiction, *see* §§ 3.03[C][1] & [2]) to allow the court to determine all parts of a complex dispute in a single proceeding?

(4) *Commentary. Asahi* has provoked considerable scholarly commentary. *See Symposium: Asahi Metal Industry Co. v. Superior Court and the Future of Personal Jurisdiction*, 39 S.C. L. Rev. 729 (1988).

[2] Non-Commercial Defendants

KULKO v. SUPERIOR COURT, 436 U.S. 84 (1978). Ezra and Sharon Kulko were married in 1959 during Ezra's three-day stopover in California en route from a military base in Texas to a tour of duty in Korea. Both Ezra and Sharon were residents of New York. Sharon returned to New York immediately after the marriage, and Ezra returned, with another stop in California, after his tour of duty. The Kulkos had two children in New York. Later, after thirteen years of marriage, they signed a separation agreement in New York, providing for the children to remain with Ezra during the school year and to spend vacations with Sharon. After a divorce from Ezra in Haiti, Sharon remarried in California.

A year later, the oldest child told Ezra she wanted to live with Sharon, and he bought her a one-way airplane ticket to California. Three years later, Sharon surreptitiously sent a ticket to the younger child, who flew to California to take up residence with her. Less than a month later, Sharon sued Ezra in a California superior court to establish the Haitian decree as a California judgment, to obtain full custody, and to increase Ezra's child-support obligations. Ezra appeared specially to question the jurisdiction of the California courts, which ruled against him.

The Supreme Court reversed, holding that California could not constitutionally exercise jurisdiction over Ezra. If jurisdiction had been based on the marriage ceremony in California thirteen years earlier, said the Court, it would "make a mockery of" the Fourteenth Amendment. Nor could jurisdiction be based on Ezra's cooperation in the oldest child's move, as the California Supreme Court had held. "A father who agrees, in the interests of family harmony and his children's preferences, to allow them to spend more time in California than was required under a separation agreement, can hardly be said to have 'purposefully availed himself' of the 'benefits and protections' of California's laws."

NOTE ON INTERSTATE JURISDICTION IN FAMILY LAW CASES

Jurisdiction, Full Faith and Credit, and Interstate Conflicts. The "flip side" of *Kulko* is the historical lack of finality in family law judgments. A spouse may obtain a judicial decree in one state only to have it frustrated by the other spouse's act of physically taking the children to another state and there obtaining a different decree. The Supreme Court's decision in *May v. Anderson*, 345 U.S. 528 (1953), provided indirect support for this conduct by confusing the extent to which full faith and credit would apply. The forum's authority to modify existing decrees even to the extent they were binding, and to enter emergency orders (such as those pursuant to *habeas corpus* jurisdiction over a child), exacerbated the resulting conflicts and encouraged child snatching.

The UCCJEA and the PKPA. The Uniform Child Custody Jurisdiction and Enforcement Act (a uniform state law commonly called the "UCCJEA") and the Parental Kidnapping Prevention Act (a federal law codified principally in 28 U.S.C. § 1738A and referred to as the "PKPA") constitute an effort to respond to this problem. For example, the UCCJEA creates a preference in child custody cases for jurisdiction in the child's "home state," which generally is the state in which the child has resided for at least six months. The UCCJEA has been adopted, now, in almost all of the states.

Support. The Uniform Interstate Family Support Act ("UIFSA") provides ways for interstate enforcement of child support orders. In fact, in *Kulko, supra*, the Supreme Court concluded that any interest California had in the support of the Kulko children residing in California was "already being served" by UIFSA's statutory predecessor. UIFSA contains a broad long-arm statute and authorizes proceedings involving two or more states, if personal jurisdiction cannot be obtained over a nonresident parent.

Jurisdiction over Property. A court that has jurisdiction over the parties to the marriage often assumes jurisdiction to divide the property, wherever situated. The court may not consider that it has direct authority to alter titles to property such as real estate with clear situs in another state; nevertheless, in such a situation, the court may be able to achieve the same result by the expedient of ordering a *party* subject to its jurisdiction to execute a conveyance. Conflicts between courts with power over the persons and those with power over the property sometimes arise (see the subsection [D], below), but property jurisdiction creates fewer difficulties than child custody and support jurisdiction.

Family Law Long-Arm Statutes. In *Kulko*, the Supreme Court also supported its result by pointing out that California could have asserted a particularized state interest by enacting a long-arm statute providing for jurisdiction based on specific kinds of contacts, but it had not done so. Should a state (such as California) that has a general, limits-of-due-process long-arm statute also pass particularized statutes directed to frequently recurring relationships?

A Poor Fit? Family law may have suffered from the application of ill-fitting jurisdictional doctrines that have developed mainly in a commercial context. Students who wish to contribute to legal doctrine that touches the lives of many could do so by thoughtfully researching and writing on these issues.

[3] Keystroke Contacts: The Internet and Other Electronic Media

COMPUSERVE, INC. v. PATTERSON
89 F.3d 1257 (6th Cir. 1996)

[In this case, the court upheld jurisdiction based on computer keystrokes. Patterson, located in Texas, entered into a "shareware" arrangement with CompuServe, located in Ohio, which then was the second largest provider of computing and information services on the Internet. The shareware contract enabled CompuServe to market software owned by Patterson to end users. CompuServe charged a 15 percent fee and remitted the rest to Patterson. The arrangement was formalized in a "Shareware Registration Agreement," which incorporated a "Service Agreement." Both of these documents, standardized by Compuserve, provided that they were entered into in Ohio, and the Service Agreement was to be "governed by and construed in accordance with" Ohio law. Patterson signified his acceptance of these documents by typing the word "AGREE" at various points on the documents in his own computer in Texas, and transmitting the documents back to Ohio.

[Later, CompuServe generated its own programs that competed with Patterson's and marketed them on its networks. Patterson e-mailed to CompuServe allegations that CompuServe's actions violated his trademarks. CompuServe then filed an action in a federal court in Ohio, seeking a declaratory judgment that it was not guilty of infringement. The District Court granted Patterson's motion to dismiss for lack of personal jurisdiction, The Court of Appeals, however, here reversed and held that the contacts are sufficient to support jurisdiction, for the following reasons.]

This case presents a novel question of first impression: Did CompuServe make a prima facie showing that Patterson's contacts with Ohio, which have been almost entirely electronic in nature, are sufficient, under the Due Process Clause, to support the district court's exercise of personal jurisdiction over him?

The Supreme Court has noted, on more than one occasion, the confluence of the "increasing nationalization of commerce" and "modern transportation and communication," and the resulting relaxation of the limits that the Due Process Clause imposes on courts' jurisdiction. *E.g., World-Wide Volkswagen Corp. v. Woodson.* Simply stated, there is less perceived need today for the federal constitution to protect defendants from "inconvenient litigation," because all but the most remote forums are easily accessible for the pursuit of both business and litigation. *Id.* The Court has also, however, reminded us that the due process rights of a defendant should be the courts' primary concern where personal jurisdiction is at issue.

The Internet represents perhaps the latest and greatest manifestation of these historical, globe-shrinking trends. It enables anyone with the right equipment and knowledge — that is, people like Patterson — to operate an international business cheaply, and from a desktop. That business operator, however, remains entitled to the protection of the Due Process Clause, which mandates that potential defendants be able "to structure their primary conduct with some minimum assurance as to where the conduct will and will not render them liable to suit." *World-Wide Volkswagen.* Thus, this case presents a situation where we must reconsider the scope of our jurisdictional reach.

As always in this context, the crucial federal constitutional inquiry is whether, given the facts of the case, the nonresident defendant has sufficient contacts with the forum state that the district court's exercise of jurisdiction would comport with "traditional notions of fair play and substantial justice." *International Shoe Co. v. Washington* . . . .

We conclude that Patterson has knowingly made an effort — and, in fact, purposefully contracted — to market a product in other states, with Ohio-based CompuServe operating, in effect, as his distribution center. Thus, it is reasonable to subject Patterson to suit in Ohio, the state which is home to the computer network service he chose to employ.

The real question is whether these connections with Ohio are "substantial" enough that Patterson should reasonably have anticipated being haled into an Ohio court. The district court did not think so. It looked to "cases involving interstate business negotiations and relationships" and held that the relationship between CompuServe and Patterson, because it was marked by a "minimal course of dealing," was insufficient to satisfy the purposeful availment test. . . .

In fact, it is Patterson's relationship with CompuServe as a software provider and marketer that is crucial to this case. The district court's analysis misses the mark because it disregards the most salient facts of that relationship: that Patterson chose to transmit his software from Texas to CompuServe's system in Ohio, that myriad others gained access to Patterson's software via that system, and that Patterson advertised and sold his product through that system. Though all this happened with a distinct paucity of tangible, physical evidence, there can be no doubt that Patterson purposefully transacted business in Ohio. . . . [Next, the court concluded that this was a case of specific jurisdiction, reasoning as follows.]

If a defendant's contacts with the forum state are related to the operative facts of the controversy, then an action will be deemed to have arisen from those contacts.

The district court viewed the presence of Patterson's software on the CompuServe system in Ohio as "entirely incidental to the alleged dispute between the parties." In the district court's opinion, Patterson could have claimed trademark or trade name protection for his software against CompuServe even if he had placed his software on another computer network altogether, or in a retail store. . . .

Again, we must disagree with the district court's holding. The cause of action in the instant case concerns allegations of trademark or trade name infringement and unfair competition. Patterson's contacts with Ohio are certainly related to the operative facts of that controversy. He placed his software on CompuServe's Ohio-based system. He used that system to advertise his software and sell it. The proceeds of those sales flowed to him through Ohio. According to CompuServe's allegations, Patterson has marketed his product exclusively on their system.

As the district court points out, Patterson could have placed his software anywhere and had the same result. Nevertheless, it is uncontroverted that Patterson placed, marketed, and sold his software only on Ohio-based CompuServe. Thus, any common law trademark or trade name which Patterson might have in his product would arguably have been created in Ohio, and any violation of those alleged trademarks or trade names by CompuServe would have occurred, at least in part, in Ohio. . . .

Moreover, as noted heretofore with regard to the purposeful availment test, CompuServe's declaratory judgment action arose in part because Patterson threatened, via regular and electronic mail, to seek an injunction against CompuServe's sales of its software product, or to seek damages at law if CompuServe did not pay to settle his purported claim. Thus, Patterson's threats — which were contacts with Ohio — gave rise to the case before us . . . .

The district court analogized the instant case to a standard consumer suit in which CompuServe might have brought suit in Ohio "to collect a small amount of user fees from a Texas resident who, while seated at his computer terminal, became a member of the CompuServe network."

That is not, however, the case at bar. Here, we have an entrepreneur who purposefully employed CompuServe to market his computer software product. It may be burdensome for Patterson to defend a suit in Ohio, but he knew when he entered into the Shareware Registration Agreement with CompuServe that he was making a connection with Ohio, and presumably he hoped that connection would work to his benefit. Further, Ohio has a strong interest in resolving a dispute involving an Ohio company, which will involve the Ohio law on common law trademarks and trade names. CompuServe alleges that more than $10 million could be at stake in this case . . . .

Finally, because of the unique nature of this case, we deem it important to note what we do not hold. We need not and do not hold that Patterson would be subject to suit in any state where his software was purchased or used; that is not the case before us. *See World-Wide Volkswagen* (rejecting the idea that a seller of chattels could "appoint the chattel his agent for service of process"). We also do not have before us an attempt by another party from a third state to sue Patterson in Ohio for, say, a "computer virus" caused by his software, and thus we need not address whether personal jurisdiction could be found on those facts. Finally, we need not and do not hold that CompuServe may, as the district court posited, sue any regular subscriber to its service for nonpayment in Ohio, even if the subscriber is a native Alaskan who has never left home. Each of those cases may well arise someday, but they are not before us now. . . .

[W]e believe that Patterson had sufficient contacts with Ohio to support the exercise of personal jurisdiction over him. . . .

NOTES AND QUESTIONS

(1) *Is It Possible that Patterson "Got Hometowned"?* Consider whether the court may have been too eager to protect a local business, particularly in light of the following: (a) its emphasis that an Ohio company had more than $10 million at stake. (By this reasoning, wouldn't it equally follow that Patterson's claims should be heard in Texas where Patterson equally probably suffered an unlawful economic loss?) (b) its conclusion that the case was one of specific jurisdiction. (Was it really the contracts, or was it CompuServe's worldwide marketing of products using trademarks that Patterson claimed were his, that gave rise to the case?) (c) its conclusion that "Patterson's threats" of litigation "gave rise to the case before us." (If this were true, wouldn't all claimants who contact out-of-staters, and ask them to desist from injuring them, submit to jurisdiction if the out-of-staters then race to the local courthouse first?) (d) its reasoning that today, there is "less perceived need . . . to protect defendants from 'inconvenient litigation.' " (Is this conclusion justified by the fact that this is an Internet case? If so, how does it square with the court's conclusion that the forum "may be burdensome" for Patterson, who will need to employ counsel and follow the same litigation steps as a non-Internet litigant?)

(2) *Are the Contacts Sufficient for General Jurisdiction?* The court also makes the point that Patterson's contacts with Ohio were purposeful and repeated. Perhaps one can argue that the contacts support general jurisdiction, even if specific jurisdiction is lacking. Is this a better basis for the holding? (Elsewhere in the opinion, however, the court quotes Patterson's affidavit to the effect that he had only twelve Ohio customers and received only $650 worth of business from them.)

(3) *Does the Existence of the Internet Really Call for a Court to "Reconsider the Scope of [Its] Jurisdictional Reach"?* The court refers to this as "a case of first impression." It perceives less need to protect defendants from distant forum abuse in light of modern communication and transportation, in which the "greatest" change, it says, has come from the Internet. Consider whether this reasoning means that there is a new jurisdictional standard today. If so, does this lesser due process protection apply just to Internet cases, or does the Internet allegedly reduce forum abuse in all types of cases?

(4) *An Electronic Contacts Case That Comes to a Conclusion Opposite from CompuServe: Future Technology Today, Inc. v. OSF Healthcare Systems, 218 F.3d 1247 (11th Cir. 2000).* A Florida corporation contracted with an Illinois corporation to perform remedial services on the latter's computer equipment. The work was to be done by the Florida corporation at its Florida offices, with large quantities of data transmitted back and forth between Florida and Illinois. The Illinois corporation ultimately declared the Florida servicer in default, and its employees visited Florida for three days to inspect the work. At that time, the Florida servicer charged that the Illinois corporation had converted its trade secrets. Later, the Florida servicer filed suit in Florida against the Illinois customer for contract damages that it claimed exceeded $4 million, as well as for the alleged conversion.

The District Court dismissed for want of personal jurisdiction, and the Court of Appeals affirmed the dismissal. It reasoned that the Illinois defendant would suffer a "great" burden in defending in Florida, and that it held that there was not any "strong state interest in haling people into Florida courts from all over the country for entering into one service arrangement, . . . without ever setting foot in Florida." But Patterson also entered into "one service arrangement" with CompuServe, "without ever setting foot in [Ohio]." Are the cases inconsistent, and if so, which is correct?

(5) *The Distinction Between "Interactivity," "Passivity," and Mere Posting.* In *Gorman d/b/a Cashbackrealty.com v. Ameritrade Holding Corp.*, 293 F.3d 506 (D.C. Cir. 2002), the D.C. Circuit held that an interactive website enabling residents of the forum to engage in the trading of securities constituted "continuous and systematic" contact with the forum sufficient to support the exercise of personal jurisdiction over the foreign website operator. Noting that "'Cyberspace' . . . is not some mystical incantation capable of warding off the jurisdiction of courts built from bricks and mortar," the court distinguished an "essentially passive" website merely accessed for information from the website in this case. *Id.* at 510. "[A]meritrade concedes that District residents use its website to engage in electronic transactions with the firm. . . . As a result of their electronic interactions, Ameritrade and its District of Columbia customers enter into binding contracts, the customers become the owners of valuable securities, and Ameritrade obtains valuable revenue." *Id.* at 512-13. Moreover, because such transactions can occur 24 hours a day, the defendant had continuous and systematic contacts "to a degree that traditional foreign corporations can never even approach." *Id.* at 513.

Meanwhile, the Fourth Circuit, in *ALS Scan, Inc. v. Digital Service Consultants, Inc.*, 293 F.3d 707 (4th Cir. 2002), held that merely providing Internet service constitutes passive activity rather than purposeful availment, and thus is insufficient to support the exercise of personal jurisdiction over the nonresident Internet service provider. In this case, a website owner, whose Internet access was provided by Digital Service Consultants, Inc. of Georgia, allegedly posted copyright-protected photographs on his website. ALS Scan, Inc., the copyright holder, sued Digital Service (in addition to the website owner), alleging that Digital enabled the copyright infringement. The Fourth Circuit found that Digital's electronic transmissions were "at most passive," and that Digital did not purposefully avail itself of the privilege of operating within the forum state of Maryland.

An often-cited district court decision, *Zippo Manufacturing Co. v. Zippo Dot Com, Inc.*, 952 F. Supp. 1119 (W.D. Pa. 1997), noted that Internet contacts can be evaluated on a "sliding scale," ranging from defendants who enter "into contracts with residents of a foreign jurisdiction that involve the knowing and repeated transmission of computer files over the Internet," and for which the assertion of personal jurisdiction is proper, to "situations where a defendant has simply posted information on an Internet Web site which is accessible to users in foreign jurisdictions. A passive Web site that does little more than make information available to those who are interested in it is not grounds for the exercise of personal jurisdiction." *Id.* at 1124. The court continued, "The middle ground is occupied by interactive Web sites where a user can exchange information with the host computer. In these cases, the exercise of jurisdiction is determined by examining the level of interactivity and commercial nature of the exchange of information that occurs on the Web site." *Id.*

[D] *In Rem* Jurisdiction: Power Over Property

LEGITIMATE USES OF POWER OVER PROPERTY

Title and Related Issues. The classic *in rem* case is one involving title to land in the forum. A state has a universally recognized interest in clear titles to land within its borders. Even if claimants to a particular parcel may be scattered among the other forty-nine states and foreign countries, few would disagree with the holding in *Pennoyer v. Neff* affording adjudicatory power to the state where the land is located. Similar issues arise in cases of forfeiture. Thus, one sees case styles such as *State v. One 1969 Chevrolet Automobile* when a vehicle that allegedly has been used to transport contraband is found within the territory. Another example is probate jurisdiction; the forum has a strong interest in promptly and definitively distributing the estates of its domiciliaries.

Satisfaction of Judgments and Provisional Remedies: "Garnishment," "Attachment," and "Sequestration." A fundamentally different (but equally legitimate) exercise of *in rem* jurisdiction is in securing and enforcing judgments. If the defendant has a debtor in another state, such as a bank in which he has deposited money, this obligation should not be exempt from the satisfaction of a judgment taken against him. The judgment creditor can file an application for a *writ of garnishment* in these circumstances. The application seeks to force the garnishee (*i.e.*, the judgment debtor's debtor) to pay the funds to the judgment creditor. Different issues are presented by "provisional" remedies, which seek to secure property before liability is litigated. For example, *attachment* is a writ used to seize property of a debtor prior to judgment when it may otherwise be wasted, concealed or lost, and *sequestration* is a similar but slightly different procedure; garnishment, too, can sometimes be used as a provisional remedy. The terminology varies from state to state, but most jurisdictions recognize these procedures, or variants upon them, as methods of preserving property before judgment.

ABUSES OF *IN REM* JURISDICTION: *HARRIS v. BALK* AND *SEIDER v. ROTH*

Every "Property" Interest Is Held by a Person. The trouble with power over property is that it is really equivalent to power to adjudicate the interests of *persons* in the property. Such an exercise of power is not troublesome if the property interests are really the issue at stake. The difficulty arises when the presence of property is used as a justification for deciding issues *unrelated* to the property. For example, in *Pennoyer v. Neff*, the Supreme Court said that Mitchell could have commenced his Oregon action by seizing Neff's property in that state. The Court did not acknowledge the unfairness of this procedure if, for example, the claim had nothing to do with Oregon or with the land. Unfortunately, this holding gave rise to several cases in which the incidental presence of property was used to justify unrelated (and oppressive) adjudications against persons. The two cases that follow, *Harris v. Balk* and *Seider v. Roth*, are examples.

HARRIS v. BALK, 198 U.S. 215 (1905). Epstein, a resident of Maryland, claimed that Balk, a resident of North Carolina, owed him $300. Balk, in turn, had a claim against Harris (who was also a North Carolina resident) for $180. One day, while Harris was visiting Maryland, Epstein obtained a writ of attachment and had it served on Harris in Maryland, thereby "seizing" the debt that Harris owed Balk. Epstein simultaneously commenced a garnishment action that sought to order Harris to pay the $180 to Epstein, in partial satisfaction of his claim against Balk. Harris did not contest these proceedings, paid the resulting Maryland judgment to Epstein, and later set up the judgment and its satisfaction as a defense when Balk sued him in North Carolina for the $180. Balk objected that the Maryland court had not had jurisdiction to extinguish the debt owed him by Harris, on the theory that its situs was in North Carolina. Balk also pointed out that the Maryland court obviously could not have acquired jurisdiction over him personally. Notwithstanding these arguments, the Supreme Court held that the Maryland court had acquired jurisdiction. This holding required North Carolina to give the Maryland judgment full faith and credit, extinguishing Balk's claim. "The obligation of a debtor to pay his debt clings to him and accompanies him wherever he goes," said the Court. "In such a case the situs is unimportant. . . . We can see no reason why the attachment could not thus be laid, provided the creditor . . . could himself sue in that state. . . ." The Supreme Court's holding thus enabled the Maryland courts to extinguish Balk's claim even though Balk had no contact with Maryland — and neither did the debt, other than by the temporary presence of Harris, the debtor. Balk had obtained notice of the proceedings, said the Court, and he could have appeared in Maryland to claim against Harris and defend against Epstein.

SEIDER v. ROTH, 17 N.Y.2d 111, 216 N.E.2d 312 (1966). Plaintiffs, who were New York residents, were injured in an automobile accident in Vermont. Unable to obtain jurisdiction over the other driver in New York, plaintiffs obtained and served a writ of attachment on the other driver's liability insurer to seize the obligations of that driver's insurance company, which did business in New York. The New York Court of Appeals upheld the attachment on the theory that the insurance policy, which imposed on the insurer a contractual duty to defend and indemnify the driver, created a "debt." The "debtor" insurance company's presence in New York brought the case within the rule of *Harris v. Balk.* Hence, by "seizing" the alleged "debt" created by the insurance policy, plaintiffs were able to sue in a forum to which neither the defendant driver nor the accident had any relationship.

Criticizing Harris v. Balk and Seider v. Roth. Balk's claim was extinguished in a distant forum to which neither he nor Epstein's claim against him had any apparent connection. In fact, the debt was subject to attachment by Epstein (or another of Balk's claimed creditors) in any foreign place that Harris happened to visit. This exercise of jurisdiction seems inconsistent with the fairness theme of *International Shoe.* In *Seider v. Roth,* the insurer was present in New York, but the insured driver was not, and he could be faced with expensive obligations in appearing to defend. Further, the insurer was forced to litigate in a forum distant from the witnesses and events that gave rise to the suit. These questionable rules were accepted as law until 1977, when *Shaffer v. Heitner* was decided.

SHAFFER v. HEITNER
433 U.S. 186 (1977)

[Plaintiff Heitner brought suit in a Delaware court against Greyhound Corporation, a Delaware corporation, one of its subsidiaries, and 28 present or former officers or directors. Heitner owned one share of Greyhound stock, and his action was a "shareholder's derivative suit," meaning that it sought to force the individuals to pay to the corporation damages they had allegedly caused it. Greyhound's corporate headquarters were in Arizona. The allegedly wrongful actions had occurred in Oregon. Simultaneously with the suit, Heitner filed a motion for an order of "sequestration," which the court granted. This Delaware procedure allowed for the seizure of a defendant's property. In this case, the sequestration order was directed to holdings of stock and related corporate rights held by the individual defendants, and it was carried out by the use of "stop transfer orders" placed on the company's books, which had an effect similar to seizure of the stock. So far as the record showed, none of the stock certificates was present in Delaware, but the situs of the stock under Delaware law was deemed to be in Delaware because Greyhound was a Delaware corporation.

[Defendant Shaffer was a nonresident of Delaware. Together with other individual defendants, he appeared specially for the purpose of moving to quash service and to vacate the sequestration order. The Delaware trial court rejected the defendants' arguments that the sequestration violated due process. It said,

> The primary purpose of "sequestration" . . . is not to secure possession of property pending a trial. . . . On the contrary, as here employed, "sequestration" is a process used to compel the personal appearance of a nonresident. . . . If the defendant enters a general appearance, the sequestered property is routinely released. . . .

The Delaware Supreme Court affirmed. The United States Supreme Court then accepted the case for review. It reversed, for the following reasons.]

MR. JUSTICE MARSHALL delivered the opinion of the Court.

. . . .

II

The Delaware courts rejected appellants' jurisdictional challenge by noting that this suit was brought as a *quasi in rem* proceeding. Since *quasi in rem* jurisdiction is traditionally based on attachment or seizure of property present in the jurisdiction, not on contacts between the defendant and the State, the courts considered appellants' claimed lack of contacts with Delaware to be unimportant. This categorical analysis assumes the continued soundness of the conceptual structure founded on the century-old case of *Pennoyer v. Neff*, 95 U.S. 714, 24 L. Ed. 565 (1878).

[The Court described the holdings and reasoning of *Pennoyer*.]

From our perspective, the importance of *Pennoyer* is not its result, but the fact that its principles and corollaries derived from them became the basic elements of the constitutional doctrine governing state court jurisdiction. . . . As we have noted, under *Pennoyer* state authority to adjudicate was based on the jurisdiction's power over either persons or property. This fundamental concept is embodied in the very vocabulary which we use to describe judgments. If a court's jurisdiction is based on its authority over the defendant's person, the action and judgment are denominated "*in personam*" and can impose a personal obligation on the defendant in favor of the plaintiff. If jurisdiction is based on the court's power over property within its territory, the action is called "*in rem*" or "*quasi in rem*." The effect of a judgment in such a case is limited to the property that supports jurisdiction and does not impose a personal liability on the property owner, since he is not before the court.[17] In *Pennoyer*'s terms, the owner is affected only "indirectly" by an *in rem* judgment adverse to his interest in the property subject to the court's disposition.

By concluding that "[t]he authority of every tribunal is necessarily restricted by the territorial limits of the State in which it is established," . . . *Pennoyer* sharply limited the availability of *in personam* jurisdiction over defendants not resident in the forum State. If a nonresident defendant could not be found in a State, he could not be sued there. On the other hand, since the State in which property was located was considered to have exclusive sovereignty over that property, *in rem* actions could proceed regardless of the owner's location. Indeed, since a State's process could not reach beyond its borders, this Court held after *Pennoyer* that due process did not require any effort to give a property owner personal notice that his property was involved in an *in rem* proceeding. . . .

The *Pennoyer* rules generally favored nonresident defendants by making them harder to sue. This advantage was reduced, however, by the ability of a resident plaintiff to satisfy a claim against a nonresident defendant by bringing into court any property of the defendant located in the plaintiff's State. . . . For example, in the well-known case of *Harris v. Balk*, . . . Epstein, a resident of Maryland, had a claim against Balk, a resident of North Carolina. Harris, another North Carolina resident, owed money to Balk. When Harris happened to visit Maryland. Epstein garnished his debt to Balk. Harris did not contest the debt to Balk and paid it to Epstein's North Carolina attorney. When Balk later sued Harris in North Carolina, this Court held that the Full Faith and Credit Clause, U.S. Const, Art IV, § 1, required that Harris' payment to Epstein be treated as a discharge of his debt to Balk. This Court reasoned that the debt Harris owed Balk was an intangible form of property belonging to Balk, and that the location of that property traveled with the debtor. By obtaining personal jurisdiction over Harris, Epstein had "arrested" his debt to Balk, . . . and brought it into the Maryland court. Under the structure established by *Pennoyer*, Epstein was then entitled to proceed against that debt to vindicate his claim against Balk, even though Balk himself was not subject to the jurisdiction of a Maryland tribunal. . . .

[The Court reviewed the expansion of personal jurisdiction after *Pennoyer* and *Harris v. Balk*, including such decisions as *Hess v. Pawloski* and *International Shoe Co. v. Washington*.]

The question in *International Shoe* was whether the corporation was subject to the judicial and taxing jurisdiction of Washington. Mr. Chief Justice Stone's opinion for the Court began its analysis of that question by noting that the historical basis of *in personam* jurisdiction was a court's power over the defendant's person. That power, however, was no longer the central concern:

> But now that the *capias ad respondendum* has given way to personal service of summons or other form of notice, due process requires only that in order to subject a defendant to a judgment *in personam*, if he be not present within the territory of

---

[17] "A judgment *in rem* affects the interests of all persons in designated property. A judgment *quasi in rem* affects the interests of particular persons in designated property. The latter is of two types. In one the plaintiff is seeking to secure a pre-existing claim in the subject property and to extinguish or establish the nonexistence of similar interests of particular persons. In the other the plaintiff seeks to apply what he concedes to be the property of the defendant to the satisfaction of a claim against him. Restatement, Judgments, 5-9." *Hanson v. Denckla*. . . . As did the Court in *Hanson*, we will for convenience generally use the term "*in rem*" in place of "*in rem* and *quasi in rem*."

> the forum, he have certain minimum contacts with it such that the maintenance of the suit does not offend "traditional notions of fair play and substantial justice." . . .

Mechanical or quantitative evaluations of the defendant's activities in the forum could not resolve the question of reasonableness:

> Whether due process is satisfied must depend rather upon the quality and nature of the activity in relation to the fair and orderly administration of the laws which it was the purpose of the due process clause to insure. That clause does not contemplate that a state may make binding a judgment in personam against an individual or corporate defendant with which the state has no contacts, ties, or relations. . . .

Thus, the relationship among the defendant, the forum, and the litigation, rather than the mutually exclusive sovereignty of the States on which the rules of *Pennoyer* rest, became the central concern of the inquiry into personal jurisdiction. The immediate effect of this departure from *Pennoyer*'s conceptual apparatus was to increase the ability of the state courts to obtain personal jurisdiction over nonresident defendants. . . .

No equally dramatic change has occurred in the law governing jurisdiction *in rem*. There have, however, been intimations that the collapse of the *in personam* wing of *Pennoyer* has not left that decision unweakened as a foundation for *in rem* jurisdiction. Well-reasoned lower court opinions have questioned the proposition that the presence of property in a State gives that State jurisdiction to adjudicate rights to the property regardless of the relationship of the underlying dispute and the property owner to the forum. . . . The overwhelming majority of commentators have also rejected *Pennoyer*'s premise that a proceeding "against" property is not a proceeding against the owners of that property. . . .

It is clear, therefore, that the law of state-court jurisdiction no longer stands securely on the foundation established in *Pennoyer*. We think that the time is ripe to consider whether the standard of fairness and substantial justice set forth in *International Shoe* should be held to govern actions *in rem* as well as *in personam*.

III

The case for applying to jurisdiction *in rem* the same test of "fair play and substantial justice" as governs assertions of jurisdiction *in personam* is simple and straightforward. It is premised on recognition that "[t]he phrase, 'judicial jurisdiction over a thing,' is a customary elliptical way of referring to jurisdiction over the interests of persons in a thing." Restatement (Second) of Conflict of Laws § 56, Introductory Note (1971) (hereafter Restatement). This recognition leads to the conclusion that in order to justify an exercise of jurisdiction *in rem*, the basis for jurisdiction must be sufficient to justify exercising "jurisdiction over the interests of persons in a thing." The standard for determining whether an exercise of jurisdiction over the interests of persons is consistent with the Due Process Clause is the minimum-contacts standard elucidated in *International Shoe*.

This argument, of course, does not ignore the fact that the presence of property in a State may bear on the existence of jurisdiction by providing contacts among the forum State, the defendant, and the litigation. For example, when claims to the property itself are the source of the underlying controversy between the plaintiff and the defendant, it would be unusual for the State where the property is located not to have jurisdiction.In such cases, the defendant's claim to property located in the State would normally[25] indicate that he expected to benefit from the State's protection of his interest. The State's strong interests in assuring the marketability of property within its borders and in providing a procedure for peaceful resolution of disputes about the possession of that property would also support jurisdiction, as would the likelihood that important records and witnesses will be found in the State. The presence of property may also favor jurisdiction in cases, such as suits for injury suffered on the land of an absentee owner, where the defendant's ownership of the property is conceded but the cause of action is otherwise related to rights and duties growing out of that ownership.

It appears, therefore, that jurisdiction over many types of actions which now are or might be brought *in rem* would not be affected by a holding that any assertion of state-court jurisdiction must satisfy the *International Shoe* standard.[30] For the type of *quasi in rem* action typified by *Harris v. Balk* and the present case, however, accepting the proposed analysis would result in significant change. These are cases where the property which now serves as the basis for state-court jurisdiction is completely unrelated to the plaintiff's cause of action. Thus, although the presence of the defendant's property in a State might suggest the existence of other ties among the defendant, the State, and the litigation, the presence of the property alone would not support the State's jurisdiction. . . .

Since acceptance of the *International Shoe* test would most affect this class of cases, we examine the arguments against adopting that standard as they relate to this category of litigation. Before doing so, however, we note that this type of case also presents the clearest illustration of the argument in favor of assessing assertions of jurisdiction by a single standard. For in cases such as *Harris* and this one, the only role played by the property is to provide the basis for bringing the defendant into court. Indeed, the express purpose of the Delaware sequestration procedure is to compel the defendant to enter a personal appearance. In such cases, if a direct assertion of personal jurisdiction over the defendant would violate the Constitution, it would seem that an indirect assertion of that jurisdiction should be equally impermissible.

The primary rationale for treating the presence of property as a sufficient basis for jurisdiction to adjudicate claims over which the State would not have jurisdiction if *International Shoe* applied is that a wrongdoer

> should not be able to avoid payment of his obligations by the expedient of removing his assets to a place where he is not subject to an *in personam* suit.

Restatement § 66, Comment a. . . . This justification, however, does not explain why jurisdiction should be recognized without regard to whether the property is present in the State because of an effort to avoid the owner's obligations. Nor does it support jurisdiction to adjudicate the underlying claim. At most, it suggests that a State in which property is located should have jurisdiction to attach that property, by use of proper procedures, as security for a judgment being sought in a forum where the litigation can be maintained consistently with *International Shoe*. . . . Moreover, we know of nothing

---

[25] In some circumstances the presence of property in the forum State will not support the inference suggested in text. *Cf., e.g.*, Restatement § 60, Comments c, d; . . . Note, *The Power of a State to Affect Title in a Chattel Atypically Removed to It*, 47 Colum. L. Rev. 767 (1947).

[30] . . . We do not suggest that jurisdictional doctrines other than those discussed in text, such as the particularized rules governing adjudications of status, are inconsistent with the standard of fairness. . . .

to justify the assumption that a debtor can avoid paying his obligations by removing his property to a State in which his creditor cannot obtain personal jurisdiction over him. The Full Faith and Credit Clause, after all, makes the valid *in personam* judgment of one State enforceable in all other States.[36] . . .

We therefore conclude that all assertions of state-court jurisdiction must be evaluated according to the standards set forth in *International Shoe* and its progeny.[39]

IV

. . . Appellee Heitner did not allege and does not now claim that appellants have ever set foot in Delaware. Nor does he identify any act related to his cause of action as having taken place in Delaware. Nevertheless, he contends that appellants' positions as directors and officers of a corporation chartered in Delaware provide sufficient "contacts, ties, or relations" . . . with that State to give its courts jurisdiction over appellants in this stockholder's derivative action. This argument is based primarily on what Heitner asserts to be the strong interest of Delaware in supervising the management of a Delaware corporation. . . . In order to protect this interest, appellee concludes, Delaware's courts must have jurisdiction over corporate fiduciaries such as appellants.

This argument is undercut by the failure of the Delaware Legislature to assert the state interest appellee finds so compelling. Delaware law bases jurisdiction, not on appellants' status as corporate fiduciaries, but rather on the presence of their property in the State. . . . If Delaware perceived its interest in securing jurisdiction over corporate fiduciaries . . . to be as great as Heitner suggests, we would expect it to have enacted a statute more clearly designed to protect that interest.

Moreover, even if Heitner's assessment of the importance of Delaware's interest is accepted, his argument fails to demonstrate that Delaware is a fair forum for this litigation. The interest appellee has identified may support the application of Delaware law to resolve any controversy over appellants' actions in their capacities as officers and directors. But we have rejected the argument that if a State's law can properly be applied to a dispute, its courts necessarily have jurisdiction over the parties to that dispute.

Appellee suggests that by accepting positions as officers or directors of a Delaware corporation, appellants performed the acts required by *Hanson v. Denckla*. He notes that Delaware law provides substantial benefits to corporate officers and directors, and that these benefits were at least in part the incentive for appellants to assume their positions. It is, he says, "only fair and just" to require appellants, in return for these benefits, to respond in the State of Delaware when they are accused of misusing their power. . . .

But like Heitner's first argument, this line of reasoning establishes only that it is appropriate for Delaware law to govern the obligations of appellants to Greyhound and its stockholders. It does not demonstrate that appellants have "purposefully avail[ed themselves] of the privilege of conducting activities within the forum State," *Hanson*

---

[36] Once it has been determined by a court of competent jurisdiction that the defendant is a debtor of the plaintiff, there would seem to be no unfairness in allowing an action to realize on that debt in a State where the defendant has property, whether or not that State would have jurisdiction to determine the existence of the debt as an original matter. . . .

[39] It would not be fruitful for us to reexamine the facts of cases decided on the rationales of *Pennoyer* and *Harris* to determine whether jurisdiction might have been sustained under the standard we adopt today. To the extent that prior decisions are inconsistent with this standard, they are overruled.

v. Denckla, . . . in a way that would justify bringing them before a Delaware tribunal. Appellants have simply had nothing to do with the State of Delaware. Moreover, appellants had no reason to expect to be haled before a Delaware court. Delaware, unlike some States, has not enacted a statute that treats acceptance of a directorship as consent to jurisdiction in the State. And "[i]t strains reason . . . to suggest that anyone buying securities in a corporation formed in Delaware 'impliedly consents' to subject himself to Delaware's . . . jurisdiction on any cause of action." . . . Appellants, who were not required to acquire interests in Greyhound in order to hold their positions, did not by acquiring those interests surrender their right to be brought to judgment only in States with which they had had "minimum contacts." . . . Delaware's assertion of jurisdiction over appellants in this case is inconsistent with that constitutional limitation on state power. The judgment of the Delaware Supreme Court must, therefore, be reversed.

MR. JUSTICE POWELL, concurring.

. . .

I would explicitly reserve judgment . . . on whether the ownership of some forms of property whose situs is indisputably and permanently located within a State may, without more, provide the contacts necessary to subject a defendant to jurisdiction within the State to the extent of the value of the property. In the case of real property, in particular, preservation of the common-law concept of *quasi in rem* jurisdiction arguably would avoid the uncertainty of the general *International Shoe* standard without significant cost to " 'traditional notions of fair play and substantial justice.' " . . .

Subject to the foregoing reservation, I join the opinion of the Court.

MR. JUSTICE STEVENS, concurring in the judgment.

One who purchases shares of stock on the open market can hardly be expected to know that he has thereby become subject to suit in a forum remote from his residence and unrelated to the transaction. As a practical matter, the Delaware sequestration statute creates an unacceptable risk of judgment without notice. . . . I therefore agree with the Court that on the record before us no adequate basis for jurisdiction exists and that the Delaware statute is unconstitutional on its face.

How the Court's opinion may be applied in other contexts is not entirely clear to me. I agree with Mr. Justice Powell that it should not be read to invalidate *in rem* jurisdiction where real estate is involved. I would also not read it as invalidating other long-accepted methods of acquiring jurisdiction over persons with adequate notice of both the particular controversy and the fact that their local activities might subject them to suit. My uncertainty as to the reach of the opinion, and my fear that it purports to decide a great deal more than is necessary to dispose of this case, persuade me merely to concur in the judgment.

MR. JUSTICE BRENNAN, concurring in part and dissenting in part.

I join Parts I-III of the Court's opinion. I fully agree that the minimum-contacts analysis developed in *International Shoe Co. v. Washington*, . . . represents a far more sensible construct for the exercise of state-court jurisdiction than the patchwork of legal and factual fictions that has been generated from the decision in *Pennoyer v. Neff*. . . . It is precisely because the inquiry into minimum contacts is now of such overriding importance, however, that I must respectfully dissent from Part IV of the Court's opinion.

I

. . . [T]he Court in Part IV reaches the minimum-contacts question and finds such contacts lacking as applied to appellants. Succinctly stated, once having properly and persuasively decided that the *quasi in rem* statute that Delaware admits to having enacted is invalid, the Court then proceeds to find that a minimum-contacts law that Delaware expressly *denies* having enacted also could not be constitutionally applied in this case.

In my view, a purer example of an advisory opinion is not to be found. . . .

II

Nonetheless, because the Court rules on the minimum-contacts question, I feel impelled to express my view. . . . I am convinced that as a general rule a state forum has jurisdiction to adjudicate a shareholder derivative action centering on the conduct and policies of the directors and officers of a corporation chartered by that State. Unlike the Court, I therefore would not foreclose Delaware from asserting jurisdiction over appellants were it persuaded to do so on the basis of minimum contacts. . . .

I, therefore, would approach the minimum-contacts analysis differently than does the Court. Crucial to me is the fact that appellants voluntarily associated themselves with the State of Delaware, "invoking the benefits and protections of its laws," *Hanson v. Denckla* . . . . I thus do not believe that it is unfair to insist that appellants make themselves available to suit in a competent forum that Delaware might create for vindication of its important public policies directly pertaining to appellants' fiduciary associations with the State.

NOTES AND QUESTIONS

(1) *Understanding Shaffer: The "Three-Way Relationship" and the "Fairness" Test.* Before you continue reading, make sure that you understand the essential holding in *Shaffer*. It depends upon a "three-way relationship" among the defendant, the forum, and the litigation. The relationship must be sufficient to comply with the "fairness" test.

(2) *Legitimate Uses of In Rem Jurisdiction After Shaffer.* Even after *Shaffer*, a state should have authority to probate wills, to determine real property titles, or to enforce forfeitures, notwithstanding the claims of nonresidents. In fact, these legitimate exercises of state authority are perfectly consistent with *Shaffer*. Can you explain why? [If a state is determining a non-resident's title to property located inside its borders, aren't the requisite "ties among the [person], the state and the litigation" present? And isn't the exercise of jurisdiction consistent with "fair play and substantial justice" precisely because the object of the suit is to determine claims to property located within the forum state?]

(3) *Harris v. Balk and Seider v. Roth After Shaffer.* It is reasonably clear that *Shaffer* overrules *Harris v. Balk*. There were no "ties among" Balk, the State of Maryland, and the litigation that would have satisfied the "fairness" test. But what about *Seider v. Roth*? That case is arguably different, in that the insurer was the "real" target of the suit, and it had clear ties to New York since it did extensive business there. *See* Comment, *The Constitutionality of Seider v. Roth After Shaffer v. Heitner*, 78 Colum. L. Rev. 409 (1978).

(4) *Rush v. Savchuk, 444 U.S. 320 (1980).* In this case, the Supreme Court overruled *Seider v. Roth* and held that attachment of an insurance policy as a means of obtaining jurisdiction to adjudicate a nonresident's liability was unconstitutional. The Court emphasized that the named defendant was the nonresident driver, who had no contact with the forum. (Is this reasoning persuasive?) *See* Comment, *Seider v. Roth Jurisdiction: A Durable Rule Dies a Slow Death with the Advent of Rush v. Savchuk*, 16 New Eng. L. Rev. (1981). But the New York Court of Appeals has held that quasi-in-rem jurisdiction still survives these decisions in certain circumstances. *Banco Ambrosiano, S.P.A. v. Artoc*

Bank & Trust Ltd., 62 N.Y.2d 65, 476 N.Y.S.2d 64, 464 N.E.2d 432 (1984). A centuries-old concept is hard to subject completely to a "slow death!"

(5) *Enforcement of Judgments After Shaffer.* Assume that plaintiff has a judgment against defendant. Both reside in Pennsylvania, which is also the state where the claim arose and where the judgment was taken. But defendant's only asset is a large bank account in Arizona, a state to which he has no other connections. May plaintiff apply for a writ of garnishment in Arizona as a means of subjecting the Arizona bank account to the satisfaction of his Pennsylvania judgment? [Note: *See* Footnote 36 of *Shaffer*, which supports this jurisdiction. Since the garnishment of defendant's account is the sole issue, isn't the requisite three-way relationship among the defendant, the state and the litigation present?] The result might be different, however, if plaintiff had sought to bring his initial action to determine defendant's liability in Arizona, rather than Pennsylvania. Can you explain why?

(6) *"Atypically Removed" Property After Shaffer.* What should happen if one spouse transfers all of the parties' bank accounts to another state, sues for divorce there, and seeks division of the bank accounts as an incident of the divorce? Or what if title to an expensive airplane is in issue, and one claimant surreptitiously flies it to his home jurisdiction before filing suit there? In both cases, there is a three-way relationship between the absent defendant (who claims an interest in the property), the state (where the property is now located), and the litigation (which seeks to obtain the property). Does jurisdiction exist? [Note: Footnote 25 of *Shaffer* distinguishes property "atypically removed to" the forum, since its presence cannot support the inference that the absent defendant expected to benefit from the forum's protection of his interest. The "relationship" must not only exist, but must satisfy the "fairness" test.]

(7) *Is In Rem Jurisdiction Abolished After Shaffer?* Since jurisdiction now depends upon the relationship of the defendant to the forum and the litigation, and since the relationship must satisfy the fairness test, doesn't *Shaffer* abolish *in rem* jurisdiction as a distinct basis of adjudicatory power? What, if anything, is the difference between *in rem* and *in personam* jurisdiction after *Shaffer*?

(8) *Can Plaintiff Still Validly Serve, In-Hand, a Defendant Travelling through the State?* Reconsider *Grace v. MacArthur, supra*, § 2.02 (in-hand service valid when made upon defendant in commercial airliner overflying state). Is the holding still viable after *Shaffer* (is the three-way relationship sufficient to satisfy the fairness test?) *Cf. Humphrey v. Langford*, 246 Ga. 732, 273 S.E.2d 22 (1980) (post-*Shaffer* service upheld in analogous situation). Consider the case that follows, in which the Supreme Court revisited this question and decided in favor of very broad jurisdiction.

[E] "Tag" Jurisdiction or In-State Service on a Foreign Defendant: Does "Fairness" Control or Does "Tradition" Control?

BURNHAM v. SUPERIOR COURT
495 U.S. 604 (1990)

JUSTICE SCALIA announced the judgment of the Court and delivered an opinion in which THE CHIEF JUSTICE and JUSTICE KENNEDY join, and in which JUSTICE WHITE joins with respect to Parts I, II-A, II-B, and II-C.

The question presented is whether the Due Process Clause of the Fourteenth Amendment denies California courts jurisdiction over a nonresident, who was personally served with process while temporarily in that State, in a suit unrelated to his activities in the State.

I

[The Burnhams were married in West Virginia in 1976. In 1977, they moved to New Jersey, where their two children were born. In July 1987, the Burnhams decided to separate. They agreed that Mrs. Burnham, who intended to move to California, would take custody of the children. Mrs. Burnham brought suit for divorce in California state court in early January 1988. In late January, petitioner visited southern California on business, after which he went north to visit his children in the San Francisco Bay area, where he was served with a California court summons and a copy of Mrs. Burnham's divorce petition. He then returned to New Jersey.]

Later that year, petitioner made a special appearance in the California Superior Court, moving to quash the service of process on the ground that the court lacked personal jurisdiction over him because his only contacts with California were a few short visits to the State for the purposes of conducting business and visiting his children. The Superior Court denied the motion, and the California Court of Appeal denied mandamus relief, rejecting petitioner's contention that the Due Process Clause prohibited California courts from asserting jurisdiction over him because he lacked "minimum contacts" with the State. The court held it to be "a valid jurisdictional predicate for *in personam* jurisdiction" that the "defendant [was] present in the forum state and personally served with process." [Note: this doctrine is sometimes called "tag" jurisdiction. Can you see why?]

II

A

To determine whether the assertion of personal jurisdiction is consistent with due process, we have long relied on the principles traditionally followed by American courts in marking out the territorial limits of each State's authority. That criterion was first announced in *Pennoyer v. Neff*. . . . Since *International Shoe*, we have only been called upon to decide whether these "traditional notions" permit States to exercise jurisdiction over absent defendants in a manner that deviates from the rules of jurisdiction applied in the 19th century. We have held such deviations permissible, but only with respect to suits arising out of the absent defendant's contact with the State. . . . The question we must decide today is whether due process requires a similar connection between the litigation and the defendant's contacts with the State in cases where the defendant is physically present in the State at the time process is served upon him.

B

Among the most firmly established principles of personal jurisdiction in American tradition is that the courts of a State have jurisdiction over nonresidents who are physically present in the State. The view developed early that each State had the power to hale before its courts any individual who could be found within its borders, and that once having acquired jurisdiction over such a person by properly serving him with process, the State could retain jurisdiction to enter judgment against him, no matter how fleeting his visit.

[P]articularly striking is the fact that, as far as we have been able to determine, *not one* American case from the period (or for that matter, not one American case until 1978) held, or even suggested, that in-state personal service on an individual was insufficient to confer personal jurisdiction. . . .

This American jurisdictional practice is, moreover, not merely old; it is continuing. It remains the practice of, not only a substantial number of the States, but as far as we are aware *all* the States and the federal government. . . . We do not know of a single State or federal statute, or a single judicial decision resting upon State law, that has abandoned in-State service as a basis of jurisdiction . . . .

C

Despite this formidable body of precedent, petitioner contends, in reliance on our decisions applying the *International Shoe* standard, that in the absence of "continuous and systematic" contacts with the forum . . . a nonresident defendant can be subjected to judgment only as to matters that arise out of or relate to his contacts with the forum. This argument rests on a thorough misunderstanding of our cases. . . .

. . . The short of the matter is that jurisdiction based on physical presence alone constitutes due process because it is one of the continuing traditions of our legal system that define the due process standard of "traditional notions of fair play and substantial justice." That standard was developed by *analogy* to "physical presence," and it would be perverse to say it could now be turned against that touchstone of jurisdiction.

D

Petitioner's strongest argument, though we ultimately reject it, relies upon our decision in *Shaffer v. Heitner*, 433 U.S. 186 (1977). . . . *Shaffer*, like *International Shoe*, involved jurisdiction over an *absent defendant*, and it stands for nothing more than the proposition that when the "minimum contact" that is a substitute for physical presence consists of property ownership it must, like other minimum contacts, be related to the litigation. Petitioner wrenches out of its context our statement in *Shaffer* that "all assertions of state-court jurisdiction must be evaluated according to the standards set forth in *International Shoe* and its progeny," 433 U.S., at 212 . . . . The logic of *Shaffer*'s holding — which places all suits against absent nonresidents on the same constitutional footing, regardless of whether a separate Latin label is attached to one particular basis of contact — does not compel the conclusion that physically present defendants must be treated identically to absent ones . . . .

It is fair to say, however, that while our holding today does not contradict *Shaffer*, our basic approach to the due process question is different. We have conducted no independent inquiry into the desirability or fairness of the prevailing in-state service rule, leaving that judgment to the legislatures that are free to amend it; for our purposes, its validation is its pedigree, as the phrase "*traditional notions* of fair play and substantial justice" makes clear. *Shaffer* did conduct such an independent inquiry, asserting that "traditional notions of fair play and substantial justice can be as readily offended by the perpetuation of ancient forms that are no longer justified as by the adoption of new procedures that are inconsistent with the basic values of our constitutional heritage. . . . " Where, however, as in the present case, a jurisdictional principle is both firmly approved by tradition and still favored, it is impossible to imagine what standard we could appeal to for the judgment that it is "no longer justified." While in no way receding from or casting doubt upon the holding of *Shaffer* or any other case, we reaffirm today our time-honored approach. . . . For new procedures, hitherto unknown, the Due Process clause requires analysis to determine whether "traditional notions of fair play and substantial justice" have been offended . . . . But a doctrine of personal jurisdiction that dates back to the adoption of the Fourteenth Amendment and is still generally observed unquestionably meets that standard.

III

A few words in response to Justice Brennan's concurrence: It insists that we apply "contemporary notions of due process" to determine the constitutionality of California's assertion of jurisdiction. . . . The "contemporary notions of due process" applicable to personal jurisdiction are the enduring "*traditional* notions of fair play and substantial justice" established as the test by *International Shoe*. By its very language, that test is satisfied if a state court adheres to jurisdictional rules that are generally applied and have always been applied in the United States.

But the concurrence's proposed standard of "contemporary notions of due process" requires more: it measures state-court jurisdiction not only against traditional doctrines in this country, including current state-court practice, but against each Justice's subjective assessment of what is fair and just. Authority for that seductive standard is not to be found in any of our personal jurisdiction cases. It is, indeed, an outright break with the test of "traditional notions of fair play and substantial justice," which would have to be reformulated "*our* notions of fair play and substantial justice. . . ."

. . . .

Because the Due Process Clause does not prohibit the California courts from exercising jurisdiction over petitioner based on the fact of in-state service of process, the judgment is

Affirmed.

JUSTICE WHITE, concurring in part and concurring in the judgment.

I join Part I and Parts II-A, II-B, and II-C of Justice Scalia's opinion and concur in the judgment of affirmance. [A]lthough the Court has the authority under the [Fourteenth] Amendment to examine even traditionally accepted procedures and declare them invalid, . . . there has been no showing here or elsewhere that as a general proposition the [rule in question] is so arbitrary and lacking in common sense in so many instances that it should be held violative of Due Process in every case. . . .

JUSTICE BRENNAN, with whom JUSTICE MARSHALL, JUSTICE BLACKMUN, and JUSTICE O'CONNOR join, concurring in the judgment.

I agree with Justice Scalia that the Due Process Clause of the Fourteenth Amendment generally permits a state court to exercise jurisdiction over a defendant if he is served with process while voluntarily present in the forum State. I do not perceive the need, however, to decide that a jurisdictional rule that "has been immemorially the actual law of the land," . . . automatically comports with due process simply by virtue of its "pedigree." Although I agree that history is an important factor in establishing whether a jurisdictional rule satisfied due process requirements, I cannot agree that it is the *only* factor such that all traditional rules of jurisdiction are, *ipso facto*, forever constitutional. Unlike Justice Scalia, I would undertake an "independent inquiry into the . . . fairness of the prevailing in-state service rule. . . ." I therefore concur [only] in the judgment.

I

I believe that the approach adopted by Justice Scalia's opinion today — reliance solely on historical pedigree — is foreclosed by our decisions in *International Shoe Co. v. Washington* . . . and *Shaffer v. Heitner* . . . .

In *Shaffer*, we stated that "*all* assertions of state-court jurisdiction must be evaluated according to the standards set forth in *International Shoe* and its progeny. . . ." The critical insight of *Shaffer* is that all rules of jurisdiction, even ancient ones, must satisfy contemporary notions of due process. . . .

While our *holding* in *Shaffer* may have been limited to *quasi in rem* jurisdiction, our mode of analysis was not. Indeed, that we were willing in *Shaffer* to examine anew the appropriateness of the *quasi in rem* rule — until that time dutifully accepted by American courts for at least a century — demonstrates that we did not believe that the "pedigree" of a jurisdictional practice was dispositive in deciding whether it was consistent with due process. . . . Notwithstanding the nimble gymnastics of Justice Scalia's opinion today, it is not faithful to our decision in *Shaffer*.

II

Tradition, though alone not dispositive, is of course *relevant* to the question whether the rule of transient jurisdiction is consistent with due process. Tradition is salient not in the sense that practices of the past are automatically reasonable today. . . .

Rather, I find the historical background relevant because, [t]he fact that American courts have announced the rule for perhaps a century [p]rovides a defendant voluntarily present in a particular State *today* "clear notice that [he] is subject to suit" in the forum. . . .

[O]ur common understanding *now*, fortified by a century of judicial practice, is that jurisdiction is often a function of geography. . . .

By visiting the forum State, a transient defendant actually "avail[s]" himself, . . . of significant benefits provided by the State. His health and safety are guaranteed by the State's police, fire, and emergency medical services; he is free to travel on the State's roads and waterways; he likely enjoys the fruits of the State's economy as well. . . .

The potential burdens on a transient defendant are slight. [T]hat the defendant has already journeyed at least once before to the forum — as evidenced by the fact that he was served with process there — is an indication that suit in the forum likely would not be prohibitively inconvenient. Finally, any burdens that do arise can be ameliorated by a variety of procedural devices. For these reasons, as a rule the exercise of personal jurisdiction over a defendant based on his voluntary presence in the forum will satisfy the requirements of due process. . . .

[The concurring opinion of JUSTICE STEVENS is omitted.]

NOTES AND QUESTIONS

(1) *Still a Fragmented Court.* Note that, as in *Asahi, supra*, there is no majority opinion for a unanimous Court. Thus, the specific issue — the continuing viability of transient jurisdiction — is resolved, but an articulated basis for the decision is absent.

(2) *Is the Court's Due Process Analysis Obsolete*? What is the status of the "minimum contacts" test, today? For 40 years, the court struggled to bring all issues of personal

jurisdiction within a coherent body of rules. But today's Court sees restrictions on the usefulness of the minimum contacts test. What is there in the *Burnham* opinions that could replace minimum contacts? Without a settled doctrine, personal jurisdiction cases will have to be decided on an *ad hoc*, case-by-case basis. One commentator has suggested that the Court should abandon due process as a basis for regulating personal jurisdiction and let the states and Congress provide legislative direction. *See* Borchers, *The Death of the Constitutional Law of Personal Jurisdiction: From Pennoyer to Burnham and Back Again*, 24 U.C. Davis L. Rev. 19 (1990).

(3) *Maybe Tag Jurisdiction Simply Is a Different Matter From Long-Arm Jurisdiction (but Should it Be, in a General Jurisdiction Case)?* The plurality opinion of Justice Scalia advances the argument that "tag" jurisdiction (when the defendant is served personally while present inside the State's borders) does not require a review of all of the defendant's contacts with the State; it just has to fit within the tradition of what has been accepted. And traditionally, tag jurisdiction has been upheld in nearly all kinds of cases, with few exceptions. Maybe this simple difference distinguishes this tag case from all of the long-arm cases, as Justice Scalia argues. Is this all there is to this case? Or should it make a difference if the case involves general jurisdiction — if the defendant's presence is unrelated to the suit?

[F] Special Bases of Jurisdiction: "Implied Consent," "Contract," "Necessity," and "Nationwide Contacts"

[1] Implied Consent

HESS v. PAWLOSKI

[Reconsider this case, which appears in § 2.02[A][2] above.]

NOTES AND QUESTIONS

(1) *Consent Before Suit.* The most common situations in which prior consent is required or implied involve (1) corporations doing business within the state, which are typically required to appoint a resident as agent for receipt of service, and (2) implied consent statutes covering nonresident motorists, as in *Hess*. Are there situations in which a state should not be allowed to condition the doing of business on consent to suit in the state? (What about a statute providing that "any person ordering any goods by mail from this State consents to the appointment of the Secretary of State as agent for service of process on any claim against that person"?)

(2) *Using Implied Consent to Make Directors Amenable to Jurisdiction in the State of Incorporation After Shaffer v. Heitner, supra.* "[A]ppellants had no reason to expect to be haled before a Delaware court," said the majority in *Shaffer v. Heitner*. "Delaware, unlike some States, has not enacted a statute that treats acceptance of a directorship as consent to jurisdiction in the State." Delaware acted promptly to remedy this oversight: it adopted a new long-arm statute providing that anyone serving as a corporate director "shall . . . be deemed thereby to have consented to the appointment of the registered agent of such corporation" as his agent for service of process. In *Armstrong v. Pomerance*, 423 A.2d 174 (Del. 1980), neither the corporation nor the directors had done any business in Delaware other than the minimum necessary to maintain Delaware corporate status; nevertheless, the Delaware Supreme Court upheld the exercise of jurisdiction over directors served under this new long-arm provision in a fiduciary duty suit similar to

Shaffer. The court reasoned that the directors "had purposefully avail[ed] themselves of the privilege of becoming directors of a Delaware corporation," that they had received "benefits and protection" under Delaware law, that they had consented to jurisdiction pursuant to express statutory notice, and that Delaware had "substantial interest" in overseeing the fiduciary duties of directors of its corporations. Is this result correct, given that it historically has been common for entrepreneurs to choose Delaware as the state of incorporation for businesses located entirely in other states, simply because the Delaware law of corporations is well developed?

(3) *Consent by Raising the Jurisdictional Issue, Then Failing to Follow the Court's Orders: Insurance Corp. of Ireland v. Compagnie des Bauxites de Guinee, 456 U.S. 694 (1982).* Defendant was a foreign corporation, and it objected to jurisdiction by a properly filed motion to dismiss. The plaintiff then attempted to use discovery to find evidence of the defendant's contacts. Defendant refused to give discovery and disobeyed court orders requiring it to furnish information. The District Court responded to this disobedience by simply holding that jurisdiction existed, under the authority of rules allowing the trial judge to sanction parties disobeying discovery orders. The Supreme Court affirmed. It noted that its decisions repeatedly had upheld jurisdiction by "constructive consent," and it said: "Because the requirement of personal jurisdiction represents first of all an individual right, it can, like other such rights, be waived."

(4) *Consent by "General" (as opposed to "Special") Appearance.* In virtually all common law jurisdictions, a nonresident consents to jurisdiction if he appears in the action to defend it, even if he has no connection with the forum. Is this rule fair? [If a defendant participates in the trial, loses, and only then raises the jurisdictional issue, is it fair *not* to consider his appearance as consent?] Fed. R. Civ. P. 12(h)(1) embodies an analogous approach; if the defendant files an answer, but does not raise the jurisdictional issue within the time for amendment by right, he "waives" the issue (*i.e.*, he has consented). An appearance in a common-law court solely to raise the jurisdictional issue is called a "special" appearance; any other appearance is a "general" appearance. Consider the following case.

GONZALEZ v. GONZALEZ, 484 S.W.2d 611 (Tex. Civ. App. 1972, writ ref'd n.r.e.). Defendant was not served with process in this divorce case, and he filed no written answer or appearance. The only indication of any action by the defendant in the record was the signature of the defendant's attorney on the judgment of divorce and property division, in a blank below the words: "Approved as to Form." The appellate court held that this action constituted a general appearance sufficient to confer jurisdiction on the trial court.

[2] Private Contracts Fixing Jurisdiction

CARNIVAL CRUISE LINES, INC. v. SHUTE, 499 U.S. 585 (1991). The Shutes, residents of Washington State, purchased passage on a Carnival Cruise Lines ship through their local travel agent. Their tickets, paid for through the agent, each contained a notice generally advising them that the ticket was subject to terms and conditions recited upon the ticket in small print. Among the terms and conditions was a pre-printed agreement that "all disputes and matters whatsoever arising under, in connection with or incident to this Contract shall be litigated, if at all, in and before a Court located in the State of Florida, U.S.A., to the exclusion of the Courts of any other state or country." The

Shutes boarded Carnival's ship in Los Angeles. While cruising in international waters off Mexico, Mrs. Shute was injured when she slipped on a deck mat during a guided tour of the ship's galley. The Shutes sued Carnival for the injuries in U.S. District Court in Washington. The District Court dismissed their action on the ground that Carnival had insufficient contacts with Washington to support the exercise of personal jurisdiction. The Court of Appeals reversed, finding sufficient contacts based on Carnival's solicitation of business in Washington, and refused to enforce the forum-selection clause because it was "not freely bargained for" and because there was evidence that the Shutes would be "physically and financially incapable of pursuing [the] litigation in Florida."

The Supreme Court, in an opinion by Justice Blackmun, reversed. The Court decided the case solely on the basis of the forum-selection clause. If they are reasonable, even non-negotiated clauses in a form contract are enforceable under some circumstances. Here the cruise line had a special interest in limiting the fora in which it would be subject to litigation; this clause eliminated any confusion over where such suits could be brought, saving litigants and the courts time and expense and likely passing on reduced fares to the passengers. The Court found an insufficient basis in the record to support a claim that the Shutes could not pursue the case in Florida, and found that even great inconvenience to them would not deny enforcement of the clause when they had sufficient notice. The Court emphasized that form contract clauses are subject to scrutiny for "fundamental fairness," but found no evidence of fraud or overreaching by Carnival.

Justices Stevens and Marshall would have limited enforcement of forum-selection clauses under *The Bremen* holding to commercial arrangements between parties with equal bargaining power. They also disputed the Court's claim that the Shutes were fully and fairly notified of the choice of forum clause through the fine print on the back of the ticket by appending a facsimile of the ticket to the opinion. *See* 111 S. Ct. at 1534-38.

NOTES AND QUESTIONS

(1) *Validity of Jurisdictional Contracts: The Bremen v. Zapata Off-Shore Co., 407 U.S. 1 (1972).* In some jurisdictions, forum selection agreements are not enforceable on public policy grounds. Is this approach appropriate? [Consider the negotiations between two large corporations, one of which would loan the other badly needed funds if it could be assured that suit upon default could be brought in a convenient forum. Should the borrower corporation then be able to consent? *Cf. The Bremen v. Zapata Off-Shore Co.*, above, in which the court enforced such an agreement in the commercial context, as "freely negotiated" and not "unreasonable or unjust." *See also National Equipment Rental, Ltd. v. Szukhent*, 375 U.S. 311 (1964) (enforcing farm equipment lease containing appointment of agent for receipt of service in creditor's chosen state).]

(2) *Invalidity Because of Oppression. Szukhent* was a five-to-four decision. Justice Black's dissent argued that creditors would routinely insert "boiler-plate" requiring individuals to defend themselves in distant forums. Consider the following possibilities, and analyze whether they would make a difference in the result in *Szukhent.* (1) The consent to jurisdiction is written in print so fine and language so complicated that an intelligent consumer could not be expected to comprehend it. [Note: Even if contractual provisions are generally enforceable, might a given provision be unenforceable either because it was not agreed to or because the circumstances of its adoption contravene public policy?] (2) Jurisdiction is fixed in a place that could only have been selected to make defense difficult (*e.g.*, in a state that has no relationship to defendant, plaintiff, or the transaction). (3) Defendant signs a "cognovit" note, consenting not only to waiver

of service but also to *confession of judgment* against him in his absence, by an agent chosen by plaintiff. [In *D.H. Overmyer Co. v. Frick Co.*, 405 U.S. 174 (1972), the Supreme Court held that a cognovit note was valid and enforceable, although it might not be if tainted by inequality of bargaining power, etc.]

(3) *Oppression as a Result of the Carnival Cruise Case?* Does applying the forum selection clause in *Carnival* also create jurisdiction where it would not otherwise exist? Would Carnival have been able to sue the Shutes in Florida had they negligently damaged the cruise ship? [Maybe. Remember *Burger King Corp. v. Rudzewicz*, § [2.02[C][1], *supra.*]

(4) *Strong Support for Forum Clauses.* Taken together, *Carnival Cruise Lines, The Bremen*, and *Szukhent*, reflect the Court's willingness to enforce forum-selection clauses in an exceptionally wide range of circumstances. The clauses need not be negotiated — they may be inserted in form contracts. They may be enforced in favor of commercial entities against consumers. Only exceptional circumstances — fraud or requiring litigation in a forum chosen specifically to disadvantage one party — seem likely to trigger the "fundamental fairness" limitation. Although the buyer should beware, what can she do to avoid such a clause?

[3] Necessity, Rule 4(k) and "Nationwide Contacts"

NOTE ON "JURISDICTION BY NECESSITY"

There may be unusual cases in which a forum lacking consent or relationship to the claimants may be justified in exercising jurisdiction simply because there is no more appropriate forum to adjudicate a question that requires resolution. This elusive concept is called "jurisdiction by necessity." The Supreme Court never has expressly approved the doctrine as such.

In *Mullane v. Central Hanover Bank & Trust Co.*, 339 U.S. 306 (1950) [which is also reproduced below, in § 2.03(A)], in connection with notice issues], the common trustee of more than 100 small trusts petitioned for approval of its accounts. This procedure would cut off claims of beneficiaries against the trustee. The beneficiaries were scattered through various states, and some were impossible to identify or locate. The trustee argued that the court had power to adjudicate because the situs of the trust was within the territory of the state, so that *in rem* jurisdiction attached. Certain objecting beneficiaries argued that the suit was *in personam*, so that personal jurisdiction over all beneficiaries was required. The Supreme Court upheld the jurisdiction of the New York courts to approve the accounts, but it refused to rest its decision upon distinctions between *in rem* or *in personam* jurisdiction. The Court said, "It is not readily apparent how the courts of New York did or would classify the present proceeding, which has some characteristics and is wanting in some features of proceedings both *in rem* and *in personam*. . . . It is sufficient to observe that, whatever the technical definition of its chosen procedure, the interest of each state in providing means to close trusts that exist by the grace of its laws and are administered under the supervision of its courts is so insistent and rooted in custom as to establish beyond doubt the right of its courts to determine the interests of all claimants, resident or nonresident, provided its procedure accords full opportunity to appear and be heard." [Question: Is *Mullane* a case of jurisdiction by necessity?]

In *Helicopteros Nacionales de Colombia, S.A. v. Hall* [which appears in § 2.02[C][1], *supra*], the Court held that defendant's purchases of helicopters from the forum were insufficient to confer jurisdiction. As an alternative ground, plaintiffs argued that they would be unable to sue the Colombian, Peruvian, and United States defendants together in any single forum unless jurisdiction by necessity in Texas was upheld. The Court rejected this argument because plaintiffs had not demonstrated that all defendants could not be sued together in Colombia or Peru. The Court added, "We decline to consider adoption of a doctrine of jurisdiction by necessity — a potentially far-reaching modification of existing law — in the absence of a complete record."

NOTE ON RULE 4(k) AND ON CONGRESSIONAL PROVISIONS FOR NATIONWIDE SERVICE

Rule 4(k) provides that service of a summons or filing a waiver of service is effective to establish personal jurisdiction over a defendant "who is subject to the jurisdiction of a court of general jurisdiction in the state where the district court is located" or "when authorized by a federal statute." Fed. R. Civ. P. 4(k)(1)(A) and (C).

Congress has provided for nationwide service of process in a few federal statutes. These provisions cover actions seeking mandamus against federal officials, enforcement suits under the Federal Trade Commission Act, and suits under the securities laws, among other situations. Congress has the apparent power to determine, for example, that when a person issues or sells federally regulated securities, it may be appropriate to dispense with the limitations of state boundaries and to conclude that he has undertaken a nationwide activity that should be subject to nationwide process.

The Courts have generally upheld these provisions. Thus, in *United States v. Union Pacific Railroad*, 98 U.S. 569, 603-04 (1879), the Supreme Court said:

> The jurisdiction of the Supreme Court and the Court of Claims is not confined by geographical boundaries. . . .
>
> There is . . . nothing in the Constitution which forbids Congress to enact that any [federal] court . . . shall, by process served anywhere in the United States, have the power to bring before it all the parties necessary to its decision.

See also Federal Trade Commission v. Jim Walter Corp., 651 F.2d 251 (5th Cir. 1981) (upholding subpoena issued in Texas under FTC Act directed to corporation having all its employees in Florida). It might seem (although the Fourteenth Amendment Due Process Clause is inapplicable to the federal government), at some point the Fifth Amendment Due Process Clause must impose limits upon congressionally sanctioned distant forum abuse. *See* Abraham, *Constitutional Limitations Upon the Territorial Reach of Federal Process*, 8 Vill. L. Rev. 520, 535 (1963) (Fifth Amendment may imply requirement of relationship between action and forum). But at least one case suggests that there are no such limits. *Busch v. Buchman, Buchman & O'Brien*, 11 F.3d 1255 (5th Cir. 1994) (for New York law firm sued in Texas federal court under Securities Exchange Act, Fifth Amendment due process clause was satisfied by defendant law firm's nationwide contacts with, and residence in, United States as a whole, irrespective of contacts or lack of contacts with district of suit).

Rule 4(k)(2) also provides further that "[f]or a claim that arises under federal law, serving a summons or filing a waiver of service establishes personal jurisdiction over a defendant if . . . the defendant is not subject to jurisdiction in any state's courts of general jurisdiction; and . . . exercising jurisdiction is consistent with the United States Constitution and laws." Fed. R. Civ. P. 4(k)(2). This paragraph, which operates as a separate federal long-arm provision, allows jurisdiction to be obtained over a person when the claim against that person: (1) arises under federal law, (2) personal jurisdiction is not available in any state or under a situation-specific federal statute, and (3) the person's contacts with the nation as a whole as enough to satisfy applicable constitutional requirements. *See United States v. Swiss Am. Bank Ltd.*, 191 F.3d 30, 39-40 (1st Cir. 1999).

[G] Challenging Personal Jurisdiction

Read Fed. R. Civ. P. 12(b), 12(g), and 12(h)(1).

[1] By Default Followed by Collateral Attack

WYMAN v. NEWHOUSE

[Reconsider this case, which appears in § 1.03 above.]

[2] By Special Appearance or Analogous Procedures

NOTE ON SPECIAL APPEARANCE AND ITS FEDERAL ANALOGUE

Collateral Attack Distinguished. The plaintiff is the party who commences the action, and she may select a forum favorable to her. She does this simply by filing suit and having the papers served on the defendant. The defendant may not agree, however, that the forum has jurisdiction, and if he wants to raise the issue, he has two choices. First, he may simply refuse to appear, as in *Wyman v. Newhouse*. If he follows this course, he may later attack the jurisdiction in his home state when an action on the default judgment is brought against him. This attack, made in a court other than the one that rendered judgment, is called a "collateral" attack. Since the default judgment generally cannot be invalidated on any basis other than lack of jurisdiction, a collateral attack is risky. It forecloses the defendant from offering any defenses on the merits. Therefore, default followed by collateral attack is not advisable except in clear-cut cases such as *Wyman*.

Special Appearance, Motion to Dismiss, or Analogous Procedures. Another means of challenging jurisdiction is by "special appearance." A special appearance is made in the court whose jurisdiction is challenged, and it is made solely for the purpose of asserting the challenge. If properly made, it does not subject the defendant to the power of the court. Some states require the defendant to avoid litigating the merits until the jurisdictional issue is resolved. The Federal Rules are more liberal; instead of requiring a strict special appearance, they permit the defendant to assert the issue by motion to dismiss under Rule 12(b) or to include it in the answer. If the defendant makes a Rule 12(b) *motion*, it must include a Rule 12(b)(2) motion to dismiss for lack of personal jurisdiction. Otherwise, the defense is waived. If the defendant responds by filing an *answer*, the answer should include the same defense, but the answer may be amended as permitted by Rule 15(a) within 20 days after service on the plaintiff, assuming the case has not been calendared for trial.

Limits on the Special Appearance. There are a few qualifications to this description of the special appearance, however. First, if the appearance is not properly made — for example, if made late in the case, long after an answer has been filed — the answer will be treated as a general appearance and is a consent to the jurisdiction of the court. Secondly, the special appearance *does consent* to the jurisdiction of the court *for the limited purpose of adjudicating its jurisdiction*. The defendant will be bound by the result. In most jurisdictions, he can defend the case on the merits if he loses the jurisdictional issue, and he then may appeal both the merits and the jurisdictional holding of the trial court. But he is generally foreclosed from collaterally attacking the judgment in another state. In summary, the defendant gets "one bite at the apple": he may either default and collaterally attack the judgment, or he may appear specially and litigate jurisdiction in the trial court chosen by the plaintiff and on appeal, but he cannot do both.

HARKNESS v. HYDE

98 U.S. 476 (1878)

MR. JUSTICE FIELD delivered the opinion of the court.

This was an action . . . brought in September, 1873, in a District Court of the Territory of Idaho for the county of Oneida. The summons, with a copy of the complaint, was soon afterwards served by the sheriff of the county on the defendant, at his place of residence, which was on the Indian reservation, known as the Shoshonee reservation.

The defendant thereupon appeared specially by counsel appointed for the purpose, and moved the court to dismiss the action, on the ground that the service thus made upon him on the Indian reservation was outside of the bailiwick of the sheriff, and without the jurisdiction of the court. Upon stipulation of the parties, the motion was adjourned to the Supreme Court of the Territory, and was there overruled. To the decision an exception was taken. The case was then remanded to the District Court, and the defendant filed an answer to the complaint. Upon the trial which followed, the plaintiff obtained a verdict for $3,500. Upon a motion for a new trial, the amount was reduced to $2,500; for which judgment was entered. On appeal in the Supreme Court of the Territory, the judgment was affirmed. The defendant thereupon brought the case here, and now seeks a reversal of the judgment, for the alleged error of the court in refusing to dismiss the action for want of jurisdiction over him.

The act of Congress of March 3, 1863, organizing the Territory of Idaho, provides that it shall not embrace within its limits or jurisdiction any territory of an Indian tribe without the latter's assent, but that "all such territory shall be excepted out of the boundaries, and constitute no part of the Territory of Idaho," until the tribe shall signify its assent to the President to be included within the Territory. . . . The territory reserved, therefore, was as much beyond the jurisdiction, legislative or judicial, of the government of Idaho, as if it had been set apart within the limits of another country, or of a foreign State. Its lines marked the bounds of that government. . . .

The service was an unlawful act of the sheriff. The court below should, therefore, have set it aside on its attention being called to the fact that it was made upon the defendant on the reservation.

The right of the defendant to insist upon the objection to the illegality of the service was not waived by the special appearance of counsel for him to move the dismissal of the action on that ground, or what we consider as intended, that the service be set aside; nor, when that motion was overruled, by their answering for him to the merits of the action. Illegality in a proceeding by which jurisdiction is to be obtained is in no case waived by the appearance of the defendant for the purpose of calling the attention of the court to such irregularity; nor is the objection waived when being urged it is overruled, and the defendant is thereby compelled to answer. He is not considered as abandoning his objection because he does not submit to further proceedings without contestation.

It is only where he pleads to the merits in the first instance, without insisting upon the illegality, that the objection is deemed to be waived.

The judgment of the Supreme Court of the Territory, therefore, must be reversed, and the case remanded with directions to reverse the judgment of the District Court for Oneida County, and to direct that court to set aside the service made upon the defendant; and it is so ordered.

BALDWIN v. IOWA STATE TRAVELING MEN'S ASSOCIATION, 283 U.S. 522 (1931). Plaintiff sued defendant in a Missouri court. Defendant appeared specially and moved to dismiss. After hearing the evidence about the defendant's contacts with the forum, the court denied the motion and ordered the defendant to answer on the merits within thirty days. When the defendant failed to answer, the Missouri court granted judgment against the defendant. The plaintiff then filed an action on the judgment in Iowa, where the defendant was incorporated. The defendant again moved to dismiss, claiming that the judgment had been rendered by a court lacking jurisdiction over it. The plaintiff objected to the raising of this issue on the ground that it "constituted a collateral attack and a retrial of an issue settled in the first suit." The Supreme Court agreed, and it held that the judgment must be enforced:

> . . . the special appearance gives point to the fact that the respondent entered the Missouri court for the very purpose of litigating the question of jurisdiction. It had the election not to appear at all. . . . It also had the right to appeal from the decision of the Missouri district court. It elected to follow neither of those courses. . . .
>
> Public policy dictates that there be an end of litigation. . . . We see no reason why this doctrine should not apply in every case where one voluntarily appears, presents his case, and is fully heard, or why he should not, in the absence of fraud, be concluded by the judgment of the tribunal to which he has submitted his cause. . . .

§ 2.03 Notice Requirements and Service of Process

[A] Due Process Notice Standards

MULLANE v. CENTRAL HANOVER BANK & TRUST CO.
339 U.S. 306 (1950)

[A New York statute permitted trust companies to pool small trusts into a common fund for more efficient administration. The statute also permitted a trust company to petition for judicial approval of its accounts. This procedure had the effect of cutting off potential claims, if any, that beneficiaries of the trusts might have against the trust company. The statute provided that notice to beneficiaries in such a proceeding would be sufficient if given by newspaper advertisement stating merely the name and address of the trust company, the date of establishment of the common trust, and a list of participating estates, trusts, or funds.

[In this portion of its opinion, the Supreme Court interpreted the Due Process Clause as setting minimum standards for notice in legal proceedings.]

. . . Many controversies have raged about the cryptic and abstract words of the Due Process Clause but there can be no doubt that at a minimum they require that deprivation of life, liberty or property by adjudication be preceded by notice and opportunity for hearing appropriate to the nature of the case. . . .

Personal service of written notice within the jurisdiction is the classic form of notice always adequate in any type of proceeding. But the vital interest of the State in bringing any issues as to its fiduciaries to a final settlement can be served only if interests or claims of individuals who are outside of the State can somehow be determined. A construction of the Due Process Clause which would place impossible or impractical obstacles in the way could not be justified.

Against this interest of the State we must balance the individual interest sought to be protected by the Fourteenth Amendment. This is defined by our holding that "The fundamental requisite of due process of law is the opportunity to be heard." *Grannis v. Ordean*, 234 U.S. 385, 394. This right to be heard has little reality or worth unless one is informed that the matter is pending and can choose for himself whether to appear or default, acquiesce or contest.

The Court has not committed itself to any formula achieving a balance between these interests in a particular proceeding or determining when constructive notice may be utilized or what test it must meet. . . . But a few general principles stand out in the books.

An elementary and fundamental requirement of due process in any proceeding which is to be accorded finality is notice reasonably calculated, under all the circumstances, to apprise interested parties of the pendency of the action and afford them an opportunity to present their objections. . . . The notice must be of such nature as reasonably to convey the required information, . . . and it must afford a reasonable time for those interested to make their appearance . . . . But if with due regard for the practicalities and peculiarities of the case these conditions are reasonably met, the constitutional requirements are satisfied.

. . . The means employed must be such as one desirous of actually informing the absentee might reasonably adopt to accomplish it. The reasonableness and hence the constitutional validity of any chosen method may be defended on the ground that it is in itself reasonably certain to inform those affected . . ., or, where conditions do not permit such notice, that the form chosen is not substantially less likely to bring home notice than other of the feasible and customary substitutes.

It would be idle to pretend that publication alone, as prescribed here, is a reliable means of acquainting interested parties of the fact that their rights are before the courts. . . . The chance of actual notice is further reduced when, as here, the notice required does not even name those whose attention it is supposed to attract, and does not inform acquaintances who might call it to attention. In weighing its sufficiency on the basis of equivalence with actual notice, we are unable to regard this as more than a feint.

Nor is publication here reinforced by steps likely to attract the parties' attention to the proceeding. It is true that publication traditionally has been acceptable as notification supplemental to other action which in itself may reasonably be expected to convey a warning. The ways of an owner with tangible property are such that he usually arranges means to learn of any direct attack upon his possessory or proprietary rights . . . . When the state within which the owner has located such property seizes it for some reason, publication or posting affords an additional measure of notification. A state may indulge the assumption that one who has left tangible property in the state either has abandoned it, in which case proceedings against it deprive him of nothing, . . . or that he has left some caretaker under a duty to let him know that it is being jeopardized. . . .

In the case before us there is, of course, no abandonment. On the other hand these beneficiaries do have a resident fiduciary as caretaker of their interest in this property. But it is their caretaker who in the accounting becomes their adversary. Their trustee is released from giving notice of jeopardy, and no one else is expected to do so. . . .

This Court has not hesitated to approve of resort to publication as a customary substitute in another class of cases where it is not reasonably possible or practicable to give more adequate warning. Thus it has been recognized that, in the case of persons missing or unknown, employment of an indirect and even a probably futile means of notification is all that the situation permits and creates no constitutional bar to a final decree foreclosing their rights. . . .

Those beneficiaries represented by appellant whose interests or whereabouts could not with due diligence be ascertained come clearly within this category. As to them the statutory notice is sufficient. However great the odds that publication will never reach the eyes of such unknown parties, it is not in the typical case much more likely to fail than any of the choices open to legislators endeavoring to prescribe the best notice practicable.

Nor do we consider it unreasonable for the State to dispense with more certain notice to those beneficiaries whose interests are either conjectural or future or, although they could be discovered upon investigation, do not in due course of business come to knowledge of the common trustee. . . .

Accordingly we overrule appellant's constitutional objections to published notice insofar as they are urged on behalf of any beneficiaries whose interests or addresses are unknown to the trustee.

As to known present beneficiaries of known place of residence, however, notice by publication stands on a different footing. . . . Where the names and post-office addresses of those affected by a proceeding are at hand, the reasons disappear for resort to means less likely than the mails to apprise them of its pendency.

The trustee has on its books the names and addresses of the income beneficiaries represented by appellant, and we find no tenable ground for dispensing with a serious effort to inform them personally of the accounting, at least by ordinary mail to the record addresses . . . . The trustee periodically remits their income to them, and we think that they might reasonably expect that with or apart from their remittances word might come to them personally that steps were being taken affecting their interests.

. . . This type of trust presupposes a large number of small interests. The individual interest does not stand alone but is identical with that of a class. The rights of each in the integrity of the fund and the fidelity of the trustee are shared by many other beneficiaries. Therefore notice reasonably certain to reach most of those interested in objecting is likely to safeguard the interests of all, since any objection sustained would inure to the benefit of all. We think that under such circumstances reasonable risks that notice might not actually reach every beneficiary are justifiable . . .

The statutory notice to known beneficiaries is inadequate, not because in fact it fails to reach everyone, but because under the circumstances it is not reasonably calculated to reach those who could easily be informed by other means at hand. . . . [T]he fact that the trust company has been able to give mailed notice to known beneficiaries at the time the common trust fund was established is persuasive that postal notification at the time of the accounting would not seriously burden the plan.

In some situation the law requires greater precautions in its proceedings than the business world accepts for its own purposes. In few, if any, will it be satisfied with less. Certainly it is instructive, in determining the reasonableness of the impersonal broadcast notification here used, to ask whether it would satisfy a prudent man of business, counting his pennies but finding it in his interest to convey information to many persons whose names and addresses are in his files. We are not satisfied that it would. Publication may theoretically be available for all the world to see, but it is too much in our day to suppose that each or any individual beneficiary does or could examine all that is published to see if something may be tucked away in it that affects his property interests. . . .

We hold that the notice of judicial settlement of accounts required by the New York Banking Law . . . is incompatible with the requirements of the Fourteenth Amendment as a basis for adjudication depriving known persons whose whereabouts are also known of substantial property rights. Accordingly the judgment is reversed and the cause remanded for further proceedings not inconsistent with this opinion.

[MR. JUSTICE BURTON's dissenting opinion is omitted.]

AGUCHAK v. MONTGOMERY WARD CO., 520 P.2d 1352 (Alaska 1974). Montgomery Ward sold a snowmobile and freezer to the Aguchaks in Anchorage. They took these items to their home in remote Scammon Bay, Alaska, which had a population of 166 persons and was accessible to Anchorage only by air at a fare of $186 with at least one overnight stopover. When the Aguchaks allegedly did not pay, Montgomery Ward sued in a District Court in Anchorage and obtained judgment by default for $988.28 plus costs. On appeal, the Supreme Court of Alaska held that the default should have been set aside because "the form of summons served upon [the Aguchaks] so inadequately informed them of their rights and obligations in small claims proceedings that they were deprived of due process of law." The court based its decision on the due process clause of the Alaska Constitution, but because that clause was identical to the federal clause, the court used the *Mullane* test: the notice must be "reasonably calculated, under all the circumstances, to apprise interested parties . . . and afford them an opportunity to present their objections . . . . The notice must be of such nature as reasonably to convey the required information. . . ."

The summons informed the defendants only that they were "required to appear . . . [on a date certain] and answer and present any defense you might have to [Montgomery Ward's complaint, which was served with the summons]" and that if they did not, "a judgment by default will be given." The notice did not inform the Aguchaks that they could properly appear by a written pleading. Furthermore, the Aguchaks had the right to request a change of venue, and, according to the court, "one would expect venue would have been transferred" given the circumstances. However, the summons failed to advise them of this venue right.

The court recognized that it would be inappropriate to adopt procedures that would make suit excessively costly, because "[u]ndue expenses of collection will be passed on to the consumer through scarce and expensive credit." Nevertheless, said the court, "The specific remedy we fashion here — correction of a defective summons — only enforces a preexisting right to change the venue of this action or defend it by filing written materials." The court ordered that, until a final rule of court could be promulgated, the summons in small claims cases must include the following:

> If . . . the court where you have been ordered to appear is too far from where you live for you to go to a hearing there, you should WRITE TO THE COURT and ask to have the case moved to the Alaska District Court closest to where you live. You may also ask to have the case moved near where you work, if that is more convenient. . . . YOUR LETTER MUST EXPLAIN SOME FACTS TO SHOW YOU CAN DEFEND AGAINST THE CLAIM; otherwise the judge will not move the case

for you. YOU SHOULD MAIL YOUR LETTER AT LEAST THREE DAYS BEFORE THE DAY THIS SUMMONS ORDERS YOU TO BE IN COURT. If you do not, the court may enter a final judgment against you, and your wages and property can be taken to pay the judgment.

MIEDREICH v. LAUENSTEIN, 232 U.S. 236 (1914). The officer serving process in this case made a "false return of a pretended summons," saying that he had served the defendant when in fact he had not. The defendant never received notice, and plaintiff took a default judgment. A sale pursuant to mortgage foreclosure resulted. In a subsequent proceeding, the former defendant sued to set aside the foreclosure. The Supreme Court, however, upheld the judgment, observing that state law allowed the defendant to recover against the sheriff's bond. Although the amount of the bond might be small in relation to the defendant's loss, "We are of the opinion that this system of jurisprudence, with its provisions for safeguarding the rights of litigants, is due process of law." The original plaintiff was free of fraud or collusion with the sheriff and "did all that the law required in the issue of and attempt to serve process." And if the rule were otherwise, said the Court, there would be "no protection to parties who have relied on judicial proceedings importing veracity," including plaintiffs, purchasers at foreclosure sales, and people who rely upon real property title records.

Updating this Decision: Peralta v. Heights Medical Center, Inc., 485 U.S. 80 (1988). Peralta was not properly served. The state courts nevertheless upheld a final judgment against him because he could not show a "meritorious defense." The Supreme Court reversed and said, "[U]nder our cases, a judgment entered without notice or service is constitutionally infirm." Perhaps this decision overrules *Miedreich,* above (but one can argue that it is distinguishable because it did not involve property records).

NOTES AND QUESTIONS

(1) *Notice That Is Never Received: Can It Comply With Due Process?* Remember that the *Mullane* test requires only a method of service that is "reasonably calculated" to fulfill its constitutional purposes. It does not require that the notice actually be received. In fact, the *Mullane* court explicitly recognized that there were "risks" that individual beneficiaries might not receive the notice mailed to them, but it held that the settlement of their accounts would nevertheless be valid. Given that holding, is *Miedreich v. Lauenstein* consistent with *Mullane*?

(2) *Procedures for Reopening Judgments Taken Without Notice.* Even though due process may not so require, many jurisdictions do provide procedures by which judgments taken without actual notice may be reopened after they have become final. *Cf.* Fed. R. Civ. P. 60 (judgment taken by fraud or mistake, etc.). *Texas Industries, Inc. v. Sanchez,* 521 S.W.2d 133, *aff'd per curiam,* 525 S.W.2d 870 (1975), is a striking factual situation: the sheriff set the process on a table near the defendant, a state legislator, who was accompanied by two reporters and talking on the telephone in the press room at the courthouse; he testified that he was unaware anyone had attempted to serve him with process and had no recollection of the event. The appellate court held that he could use a common law procedure called a "bill of review" to set aside the resulting default judgment on the ground that he had not been served. California provides an analogous procedure by statute; *see* CCP § 473.5 (court may set default or default judgment aside on timely motion and on whatever terms "may be just," whenever service of a summons has not resulted in actual notice to a party in time to defend the action).

(3) *"Sewer" Service.* In some jurisdictions, at some times, there have been widespread instances of false returns by process servers who have not served the defendants in question. *Cf.* Comment, *Abuse of Process: "Sewer" Service*, 3 Colum. J.L. & Soc. Prob. 17 (1967) (reporting study showing suspiciously large number of daily summonses served by individual process servers). Ironically, one cause of sewer service is overly stringent requirements that the process server serve the defendant individually, in hand, personally. Should process service that might be slightly less certain to reach the defendant — such as process left with a co-resident of defendant's abode, or service by certified mail, with return receipt, restricted to the addressee only — be permitted, as a means of reducing the cost to the plaintiff and reducing the incentive toward sewer service?

(4) *"Posted" Service: Greene v. Lindsey, 456 U.S. 444 (1982).* This case concerned a Kentucky law that allowed process to be posted on the tenant's door in eviction proceedings, in which prompt service is particularly desirable. The tenants in a public housing project claimed not to have received process. Justice Brennan, for a majority of the Supreme Court, observed that posting would be not only constitutionally permissible but "singularly appropriate" in most residential tenancy situations, because the tenant is highly likely to receive it if in residence and unlikely to suffer injury if not. Nevertheless, in this public housing setting, where notices were "not infrequently" removed by children, posting was insufficient unless accompanied by mailed service. Justice O'Connor, in dissent, argued that mailboxes too were subject to tampering, and concluded that the Court was not in a position "to evaluate the risks . . . of loss, misdelivery, lengthy delay, or theft" that may be greater as a result of mailed notice rather than posted notice. [Question: Was the Court "legislating" in *Greene*, or was it simply applying the *Mullane* criteria to particularized facts?]

(5) *Balancing the Cost of Service Against the Risk of Loss to Defendant.* There are instances in which service may be inappropriately costly. Consider the case of *Butler v. Butler*, in subsection [B][2], *infra*. Also, in *Boddie v. Connecticut*, 401 U.S. 371 (1971), the Court held unconstitutional a system that required an average fee of $60, including service, to bring a divorce action, as applied to an indigent (unless the state pays). Won't the cost of mailing notice, to every individual who can be reasonably identified, add to the cost of administering trusts after *Mullane*, reducing the interest or other income enjoyed by beneficiaries? Would it be better, given that few will have sufficient stake to hire counsel individually and all have identical interests, to allow notice to the largest beneficiaries plus a random sample of smaller ones? In *Aguchak*, although the court recognizes that costs of collection are directly related to costs of credit, doesn't its opinion increase both? [The cost may be influenced more by the apparent requirement that Montgomery Ward send counsel to Scammon Bay to sue for goods sold in Anchorage; *see* the venue materials in § 2.05 below.]

(6) *Is Easily Understandable Notice Required?* After *Aguchak*, does a plaintiff have a general obligation to notify the defendant of all procedural or substantive defenses that may be available, or is Alaska venue in a special category? Does a plaintiff need to provide notice that can be understood by the particular defendant in his particular circumstances (*e.g.*, in the language customarily spoken by defendant, or by a means taking account of defendant's mental abilities)? *Cf. Covey v. Town of Somers*, 351 U.S. 141 (1956) (mailed notice, though normally sufficient, held insufficient as applied to person known to be insane and under care of guardian). California requires several notices in a summons, including a suggestion that the recipient seek the advice of an attorney, and a boldface warning, in both English and Spanish: "Notice! You have been sued. The

court may decide against you without your being heard unless you respond within 30 days. Read information below." Counties may designate additional languages. *See* C.C.P. § 412.20.

(7) *Service by Publication: When and How?* When is service by publication valid? *Mullane* makes it a last resort but clearly indicates that it is then valid. Can the imperfections of publication be ameliorated by allowance of a lengthy period of time during which defendant has a right to set aside any resulting default judgment? *Cf.* Tex. R. Civ. P. 109, 329, 819 (authorizing publication only when other means are impractical; requiring appointment of attorney *ad litem* to represent absent defendant; prohibiting default judgment, and requiring actual trial; allowing two years after judgment for motion for new trial); *see also* C.C.P. §§ 415.50, 585(c) (special California provisions for default judgments after service by publication). In this view, judgment based on citation by publication merely starts a time period running after which the judgment is valid against attack. As applied to (for example) the claimants in *Mullane* or absent potential claimants of real estate, should this solution be considered constitutionally acceptable?

[B] The Ceremony of Service: Complying With The Rules

[1] Serving Individuals and Corporations: Rule 4(e) and 4(h)

Read Fed. R. Civ. P. 4, with special attention to subdivisions 4(d)(2), (3) (waiver), 4(e) (service on individuals), 4(h) (service on corporations), 4(k) (territorial limits), and 4(m) (time limits). Also, read Rule 5(a), (b), (d).

LEIGH v. LYNTON

9 F.R.D. 28 (E.D.N.Y. 1949)

[Plaintiff Leigh leased a rent-controlled apartment from Defendant Lynton. He claimed that Lynton had conditioned the lease upon Leigh's purchase of furniture for $5,500, which included disguised rent, and he sued for treble damages under applicable statutes.

[Defendant Lynton was a native of England. During the time of the transaction with Leigh, Lynton resided in the United States, but shortly thereafter, he returned to England and remained there. Lynton's wife, meanwhile, rented an apartment at the Hotel Wyndham in New York City. Leigh had process served upon Lynton by having the deputy marshal leave it with his wife at her apartment in the Hotel Wyndham. Lynton filed a motion to dismiss "or, in lieu thereof, to quash the return of the summons," contending that this service was inadequate under the Federal Rules. The court began by setting forth the relevant provisions of the governing Rule, which is now numbered Rule 4(e)(2), allowing service "[u]pon an individual . . . by delivering a copy of the summons and of the complaint to him personally or by leaving copies thereof at his dwelling house or usual place of abode with some person of suitable age and discretion then residing therein. . . ."]

Bouvier defines abode as the place in which a person dwells. *Earle v. McVeigh*, 91 U.S. 503, page 508, 23 L. Ed. 398, in defining usual place of abode held:

> . . . the intention evidently is that the person against whom the notice is directed should then be living or have his home in the said house. . . .

In support of the service of process, two cases have been cited, *Rovinski v. Rowe*, 6 Cir., 131 F.2d 687; and *Skidmore v. Green*, D.C.S.D.N.Y., 33 F. Supp. 529, 530. In both cases, service pursuant to [the Rule] had been upheld. They are clearly distinguishable.

In the *Rovinski* case, service of process was effected by delivery to defendant's mother at a house in Menominee, Michigan, and the defendant testified that he always considered and held that place out as his home, that he kept some odds and ends there, and that there was always a bedroom ready for his occupancy when he returned home, and that he invariably occupied it.

In the *Skidmore* case, the facts indicate that the defendant was a retired New York policeman who spent most of his time traveling about the country in an automobile and trailer. The summons and complaint had been delivered to a sister-in-law at the home of defendant's brother in Kingston, New York, which in the application for his New York automobile license, the defendant gave as his address, indicating that this was his home. The court made this comment: ". . . so far as the migratory nature of his life permits of any place of abode or dwelling house, it is the house in Kingston, New York."

As to the defendant, Phillip Lynton, the Hotel Wyndham was not his usual place of abode or dwelling as contemplated in . . . the Federal Rules of Civil Procedure.

Service of the summons and complaint must, therefore, be quashed.

NATIONAL DEVELOPMENT COMPANY v. TRIAD HOLDING CORPORATION, 930 F.2d 253 (2d Cir. 1991). This case involved a motion filed by wealthy, globetrotting Saudi businessman Adnan Khashoggi, to set aside a default judgment for allegedly improper service. The District Court held an evidentiary hearing, which showed that the papers had been served on one Aurora DaSilva, the housekeeper residing at a $20-25 million condominium apartment owned by Khashoggi in the Olympic Towers on Fifth Avenue in New York City. Khashoggi claimed he did not get notice until after rendition of the judgment (although the court cited some contrary evidence). He said that he considered his domicile to be a ten-acre compound in Riyadh, Saudi Arabia. The Court of Appeals noted that the cases construing Rule 4 "do not produce consistent results"; some courts, for example, require that "the defendant sought to be served be actually living in the residence at the time service is effected," while others do not. The District Court upheld the service and the default judgment, and the Court of Appeals affirmed:

> There is no dispute that Mrs. DaSilva, with whom the papers were left, is a "person of suitable age and discretion then residing" at the Olympic Tower apartment. We are called upon only to determine whether the Olympic Tower apartment was Khashoggi's "dwelling house or usual place of abode," terms that thus far have eluded "any hard and fast definition." [I]ndeed these quaint terms are now archaic and survive only in religious hymns, romantic sonnets and, unhappily, in jurisdictional statutes. . . .
>
> [K]hashoggi testified that the Olympic Tower apartment was only one of twelve locations around the world where he spends his time, including a "home" which he owns in Marabella, Spain, and "houses" in Rome, Paris and Monte Carlo. . . .
>
> There is nothing startling in the conclusion that a person can have two or more "dwelling houses or usual places of abode," provided each contains sufficient indicia of permanence . . . .
>
> It cannot seriously be disputed that the Olympic Tower apartment has sufficient indicia of permanence. Khashoggi owned and furnished the apartment and spent a considerable amount of money remodelling it to fit his lifestyle. [S]ince Khashoggi

was actually living in the Olympic Tower apartment on December 22, 1986, service there on that day was, if not the most likely method of ensuring that he received the summons and complaint, reasonably calculated to provide actual notice of the action. *See Mullane v. Central Hanover Bank & Trust Co.*, [above]. [S]urely with so itinerant a defendant as Khashoggi, plaintiff should not be expected to do more.

[W]e express no opinion upon the validity of service had Khashoggi not been actually living at the Olympic Tower apartment when service was effected.

MORTON v. F.H. PASCHEN, INC., No. 96-7179, 1997 U.S. Dist. LEXIS 9181 (E.D. Pa. June 27, 1997). Plaintiff Morton alleged that defendant F.H. Paschen, Inc. ("Paschen") had discriminated against him in employment on account of his race. He filed his suit in a federal court in Pennsylvania. He served process on Paschen, which was an out-of-state corporation, by sending the complaint and summons by certified mail, return receipt requested, to Paschen's out-of-state address. Plaintiff's Motion argued that this method complied with Federal Rule 4(h) because it complied with the Pennsylvania rules for long-arm service. Defendant Paschen, however, filed a motion to dismiss for insufficient service, arguing that only in-hand service would comply with Pennsylvania law.

The court upheld the service as valid. It began its analysis by quoting Federal Rule 4(h), which allows for two distinct methods of service on a "domestic or foreign corporation." First, the rule allows service by personal delivery to "an officer, a managing or general agent, or any other agent authorized by appointment or by law to receive service of process." Service by mail is not personal delivery. Second, however, Rule 4(h) also provides for service "in the manner prescribed by Rule 4(e)(1) for serving an individual," which allows service not only by personal delivery, but also service that "follow[s] state law for serving a summons in an action brought in courts of general jurisdiction in the state where the district court is located or where service is made." The court concluded: "Therefore, a plaintiff may serve a summons and complaint [on] a [foreign] corporation by mail if state law permits service in that manner."

Next, to resolve the parties' agreements, the court had to consider three Pennsylvania Rules of Civil Procedure: Rule 424, Rule 404, and Rule 403, to see whether they authorized mailed service to an out-of-state corporation. Rule 424 provided that service "upon a corporation or similar entity shall be made by handing a copy to" any one of various specified agents, including an officer, a manager, or a person in charge of a regular place of business. Paschen argued that this rule meant that only in-hand service, not mail, was authorized, because the rule used the mandatory word "shall." But Morton directed the court's attention to Pennsylvania Rule 404, which provided that:

> Original process shall be served outside the Commonwealth . . . by any competent adult by mail in the manner provided by Rule 403. . . .

Rule 403, in turn, provided that service by mail could be done through "any form of mail requiring a receipt signed by the defendant or his authorized agent."

The dispute thus boiled down to whether Pennsylvania Rule 424, which provided that service "shall" be done by in-hand delivery, was the exclusive and mandatory method, or whether Rule 404, which authorized out-of-state service by mail, provided an additional means of service on a non-Pennsylvania corporation. If the state rule authorized service, so did Federal Rule 4, since it incorporates state-law methods. The court agreed with the plaintiff, mainly by examining the case authority:

. . . Plaintiff notes that the Pennsylvania Superior Court has explicitly held that a plaintiff may serve a foreign corporation by mail. *See Reichert v. TRW, Inc. Cutting Tools Div.*, 385 Pa.Super. 416, 561 A.2d 745, 753 (Pa.Super.Ct.1989) ("[S]ervice by regular mail continues to be a viable method of service upon corporations pursuant to [R]ule 404(2)."), *rev'd on other grounds*, 531 Pa. 193, 611 A.2d 1191 (Pa.1992). . . .

A review of the relevant case law reveals that few courts have addressed the issue of whether a Pennsylvania plaintiff may serve a foreign corporation by mail. *See City of Allentown v. O'Brien & Gere Eng'r*, No. CIV.A.94-2384 (E.D.Pa. June 26, 1995); *Trzcinski v. Prudential Property & Casualty Insurance Co.*, 409 Pa.Super. 114, 597 A.2d 687 (Pa.Super.Ct.1991); *Reichert*, 561 A.2d at 753. Although the Supreme Court of Pennsylvania has not examined this particular issue, . . . [i]n *City of Allentown*, a similar case, a defendant attempted to dismiss a plaintiff's complaint by arguing that the plaintiff could only effect service of the complaint and summons by hand delivery. *Id.* Relying on the decisions of the Pennsylvania Superior Court, Judge Troutman declined to dismiss the complaint, concluding that "the Pennsylvania Supreme Court would . . . reach the same result if it were to consider whether Rule 404(2) permits service of process by mail on foreign corporations despite the apparently conflicting provisions of [R]ule 424." *Id.*

The court also considered the purposes of Pennsylvania Rule 404. In concluded that Paschen's interpretation would place "such a narrow restriction on service of original process on foreign corporations," that it would "adversely affect the legislature's efforts to facilitate actions by Pennsylvania residents to recover for harm caused to them by foreign corporations."

NOTES AND QUESTIONS

(1) *Changing the Facts in Leigh v. Lynton.* Would the service on Lynton's wife be valid if he had a tacit or express understanding with her that she would handle all his business in the United States during his absence (would she then be an agent authorized "by appointment"?) What if the couple intended that Lynton would stay at the Wyndham apartment if ever he came to New York? What if he had visited on two or three occasions and kept a change of clothes there? *See Rovinski v. Rowe*, 131 F.2d 687 (6th Cir. 1942) (rule should be "liberally" construed, in favor of upholding service).

(2) *Valid Service in Lynton?* How could Leigh have procured a valid service upon Lynton under the circumstances? [Note: Lynton is in England; consider Rule 4(f), which provides for "Service Upon Individuals in a Foreign Country." *See* Weintraub, *The Fifth Circuit Wrestles With the Texas Long Arm*, 14 Texas Tech. L. Rev. 1 (1983).]

(3) *What To Do About Motions to Quash Service.* In *Leigh v. Lynton*, the defendant appeared in court with the papers literally in his possession and moved to dismiss the actions on the ground that process was insufficient. If the purpose of service of process is to give the defendant notice (which this defendant obviously received), what purpose is served by dismissal? Some jurisdictions refuse to dismiss in this situation and merely give the defendant an extension of time to answer. *Cf. Butler v. Butler*, in the next section. Isn't this solution better? (In fact, doesn't dismissal hold the legal system up to possible ridicule?)

(4) *Rule Requirements as Opposed to Minimum Due Process Notice Requirements.* These cases should correct a common misconception about service. It is not enough for

plaintiff to adopt *some* method of communicating to defendant that might satisfy constitutional notice requirements. Due process sets a minimum standard, and the forum is free to specify better means of service. For example, if the rules of the forum insist on nothing less than actual in-hand service, plaintiff would not accomplish valid service by mailing process to the defendant. The method of service must comply not only with due process, but also with the governing statute or rule, which courts occasionally construe rigorously, as though correct service of process were a ceremony imbued with a kind of magic. (But perhaps ceremonial treatment is justifiable in that commencement of the suit in a manner that drives home clearcut notice to the defendant is highly desirable.)

(5) *Service on an Agent Authorized by Appointment or by Law.* Both Rule 4(e), pertaining to individuals, and Rule 4(h), pertaining to business organizations, allow service upon an agent authorized by appointment or by law. For an example of an appointed agent, consider *National Equipment Rental, Ltd. v. Szukhent,* discussed above in § 2.02[F][2] (defendant signed promissory note appointing agent within the forum). For an example of an agent authorized by law, consider *Hess v. Pawloski,* in § 2.02[A][2] (state registrar designated by law as agent of nonresident motorist).

(6) *Electronic Service.* Federal Rules 5(d)(3) and 6(d) authorize electronic service of post-complaint filings under certain circumstances, and additional time is given to respond to such filings. Courts are also authorized to institute local rules to "allow" or, under some circumstances, to "require" electronic filing.

[2] The Defendant Who Evades Process: "Substituted Service"

BUTLER v. BUTLER
577 S.W.2d 501 (Tex. Civ. App. 1978)

RAY, JUSTICE.

This is a divorce case. . . .

Appellant and appellee were married on December 30, 1961. Two children, Billy Joe Butler and Cynthia Kay Butler, were born in Texas during the marriage. . . . On August 12, 1975, Wylie Neal Butler left his wife and moved to Louisiana. Mrs. Butler filed her petition for divorce in Dallas County on August 22, 1975.

When Wylie Neal Butler left, he took his minor daughter, Cynthia Kay, with him. Appellant never told his wife his new location or communicated any information to her concerning the well-being of Cynthia. Appellee was never able to obtain personal service upon her husband, who always eluded service. She enlisted the services of the sheriff's departments of four different counties and parishes and hired a private investigator to locate her husband and daughter. In addition, Mrs. Butler used the Parent Locator Service of the Texas Department of Welfare to try to locate appellant. It was not until she was served with process in a lawsuit instituted by Wylie Neal Butler in Bossier Parish, Louisiana, seeking separation from bed and board and custody of their minor daughter, that Nancy Kay Butler learned the location of her husband and daughter. She obtained a Texas temporary restraining order, hired another private investigator, and went to Louisiana to get temporary custody of her daughter. She was successful in gaining possession of Cynthia Kay while in Louisiana and has retained possession since that time.

On June 24, 1977, the trial court authorized substituted service of citation upon Wylie Neal Butler by delivering the citation to James B. Wells, his attorney of record in the

Louisiana divorce proceeding by certified mail, return receipt requested. Service was had on June 27, 1977, and the return was filed with the district clerk of Dallas County on July 1, 1977. . . .

Appellant Butler filed a special appearance in the Texas divorce proceeding on July 1, 1977, asserting that he was not amenable to process issued by the courts of this State. . . . [At the hearing,] [n]o evidence was offered that appellant was not amenable to the jurisdiction of the Texas court. By only raising the issue of defective service, appellant waived his special appearance. On the same day, the trial court . . . entered a decree of divorce, made Nancy Kay the managing conservator of the minor children, ordered child support, and entered a decree for attorney's fees in favor of appellee.

Appellant's main contentions are: (1) that the trial court did not have *in personam* jurisdiction over him; (2) that the manner of substituted service on his attorney of record in the Louisiana proceeding was improper; and (3) that the trial court could not immediately proceed to enter judgment against him. . . .

[The court overruled Wylie Neal's argument that he was not within the scope of the long-arm statute or due process limits. For example, the relevant custody statute allowed service upon a person who had "resided with the child in this state" or in cases in which the child had been "conceived in this state" under certain circumstances. Furthermore, the court pointed out that Wylie Neal had moved to dismiss on jurisdictional grounds, but he had asserted only matters pertaining to the adequacy of service, and those issues, in this jurisdiction, must be raised if at all by a motion to quash the service. If granted, such a motion has only the effect of delaying the deadline for defendant's answer; in this state, it does not invalidate the service or result in dismissal as it would in some jurisdictions. Thus Wylie Neal's purported "special" appearance was, in actuality, a *general* appearance — and a consent to the jurisdiction of the court(!).]

Appellant [also] contends that the substituted service of process, executed by sending the citation by certified mail, return receipt requested, to his attorney of record in the Louisiana proceeding, was not reasonably calculated to give him notice of the suit. He does not contend that he failed to receive actual notice of the suit.

. . . Tex. R. Civ. P. 106 (Supp. 1978) . . . provides that where it is impractical to secure personal service, then the court, upon motion [supported by sworn evidence], may authorize service in any other manner which will be reasonably effective to give the defendant notice of the suit. In the present case, a hearing was held, and an order was entered directing that service upon Wylie Neal Butler be had by delivering citation to his Louisiana attorney by certified mail, return receipt requested. . . .

. . . Appellant relies upon *Sindorf v. Cen-Tex Supply Co.*, 172 S.W.2d 775 . . . , for the point that personal service can never be effected by service upon a person's attorney. In *Sindorf*, citation was made on Kenneth Slack by delivering a copy . . . to T.F. Slack, "his attorney." [No hearing was held or order sought showing that normal service was impractical in *Sindorf;* the plaintiff simply served the defendant's alleged attorney outright.] *Sindorf* is not a substituted service case under Rule 106 . . . and is not applicable to the present case. [The court proceeded to hold that substituted service upon Wylie Neal Butler, under the special court order allowing service on his attorney after service on him was shown impractical, complied with both due process and with the state rule governing substituted service.]

. . . [I]t was not error for the trial court to immediately proceed to trial in the absence of an answer having been filed by appellant.

. . . The fact that appellant turned his special appearance into a general appearance in this case does not afford appellant additional time in which to file an answer. Appellant could have filed his answer along with this sworn special appearance . . . and have forestalled the default judgment which was taken by appellee. Since the court had jurisdiction [and the method of service was proper under both the Constitution and the governing rules], the trial court was authorized to proceed to judgment because no answer had been filed by appellant and the required time for answering had elapsed . . . .

The judgment of the trial court is affirmed.

HUNSINGER v. GATEWAY MANAGEMENT CORP., 169 F.R.D. 152 (D. Kan. 1996). Before suit, the parties conducted a mediation in which defendant Gateway was represented by a San Francisco law firm. The mediation was unsuccessful in producing a settlement. Plaintiff's counsel then filed this action in a Kansas federal court. Instead of actual service, he sent a request for waiver of service pursuant to Rule 4(d) to the San Francisco attorney who had represented the defendant in the mediation. Later, once 120 days had passed without actual service, defendant Gateway refused to waive service, and represented now by different counsel, moved for dismissal pursuant to Rule 4(m). This Rule provides that the court "must dismiss" if service has not been effected within 120 days. (The opinion does not indicate whether the requested dismissal would have taken effect after the running of the statute of limitations, but these types of dismissals have occurred, with the result of barring the litigation.)

Plaintiff's counsel countered by relying on the provision in Rule 4(m) that allows an extension of time for "good cause." As basis for a finding of good cause, plaintiff's counsel offered an affidavit stating that the San Francisco lawyer had said he was "considering" the 4(d) waiver request, that there was no reason to believe he lacked authority to waive service, and that actual service now was imminent. Gateway vehemently responded that these assertions were "factual misrepresentations in a desperate attempt to avoid the consequences of [plaintiff's] blatant disregard for proper service procedure in federal court litigation," and it attached an affidavit from the San Francisco lawyer categorically denying the alleged remark about "consideration" of a waiver.

The District Judge denied the motion to dismiss. Rather than infer false representations from either affidavit, the court preferred to "attribute this conflict of recollections to a misunderstanding between counsel." It was clear, nevertheless, that the 4(d) request for waiver had been received by counsel who previously had represented the defendant in this same matter. He did not refuse to waive service until more than 120 days already had passed. Even if these facts did not constitute good cause, Rule 4(m) allows the court, as an alternative to dismissal, to "order that service be made within a specified time," which this court interpreted as granting the judge discretion to allow service after the 120 day limit.

NOTES AND QUESTIONS

(1) *What Should Be Done About the Defendant Who Evades Process?* The defendant who deliberately frustrates efforts to serve him is not, unfortunately, uncommon. For an interesting example in addition to *Butler v. Butler*, consider *International Controls Corp. v. Vesco*, 593 F.2d 166 (2d Cir. 1979). After Bahamian counsel was unable to serve the fugitive financier Robert Vesco, the plaintiff obtained an order appointing a process server

who was met at the bolted gate by guards who denied entry; she attempted unsuccessfully to serve the guards, then she threw the papers at a young man who identified Vesco as "my father," but he threw the papers back at her. She then telephoned the judge, who authorized further substituted efforts, and effected service by throwing the papers, bound with a blue ribbon, over the fence and onto the lawn, where she photographed them. After accomplishing these acts, she was threatened by armed guards who attempted to enter and then followed her cab. In accordance with the judge's order, the process server also mailed a copy of the summons and complaint to Vesco by ordinary first-class mail (not certified mail, which Vesco could have simply refused). The court later upheld this "blue ribbon" service (but later, a Vesco bodyguard successfully frustrated service of an amended complaint by picking it up from the ground and putting it in the process server's car).

What should be the response of the law to such conduct? Would it be wise or constitutional for the courts to treat evasion as equivalent to notice? To make the defendant liable for expenses of service (or for significant penalties or punitive damages)? To grant default judgment, subject to setting aside on a showing by defendant that he did not know of or deliberately elude service? To enact disciplinary rules sanctioning attorneys who assist in willful evasion? To allow liberal service by mail (including service by plain first-class mail if the defendant refuses to accept certified mail, as often happens)?

(2) *Service by Mail.* Many states allow service by certified mail. Under most state rules, the delivery must be restricted to the addressee only, and the receipt must be filed as part of the return. Federal service may be accomplished by this means if the court is located in one of these states (because Rule 4 adopts state-law means of service). *See* Siegel, *Changes in Federal Summons Service Under Amended Rule 4 of the Federal Rules of Civil Procedure*, 96 F.R.D. 81 (1983). A similar procedure has been suggested as part of the Federal Rules themselves. Should this proposal be adopted? Or is mailed service significantly less likely to communicate to defendants the seriousness of the papers and more subject to fraud than in-hand service?

(3) *The Waiver-of-Service Provision and 120-Day Time Limit as in the Hunsinger Case.* The waiver procedure avoids cost and delay in some instances. If the defendant refuses waiver, however, plaintiffs may suffer disastrous results owing to the 120-day limit and applicable statutes of limitation. It is best to use the waiver procedure early in the 120-day period, if one uses it at all, and then to document one's action, and to act promptly if the defendant is nonresponsive.

§ 2.04 Service of Process in International Litigation

"Letters Rogatory," Rule 4(f) and the Hague Convention. International litigation today is more prevalent than ever before. The Hague Convention on the Service Abroad of Judicial and Extrajudicial Documents in Civil or Commercial Matters, 20 U.S.T. 361, T.I.A.S. 6638, is a treaty ratified by 32 nations, providing for means of service with certain reservations by participating nations. Rule 4(f) says that if there is an "internationally agreed" method of service such as the Hague Convention, the service must follow this method. If there is no internationally agreed method, the Rule provides alternative methods, including service "prescribed by the law of the foreign country" or "as directed by the foreign authority in response to a letter rogatory or letter of request." A letter of request is explained in the discovery chapter, below. A letter rogatory is "the medium, in effect, whereby one country, speaking through one of its courts, requests another country, acting through its own courts, . . . to assist the administration of justice in the

foreign country . . . ." *The Signe*, 37 F. Supp. 819, 820 (E.D. La. 1941). The Hague Convention provides for flexible means of service — but it is limited by the parties' reservations. It also provides for a model certificate of service (equivalent to a return) and for the enforcement and setting aside of default judgments. Service by a court in the United States upon a person in France or Germany, for example, must be perfected in accordance with the Convention. A litigant may experience serious difficulties if the rules under which she is operating are not compatible with it. *See* Jones, *International Service of Process Requirements in U.S. District Court*, 26 N.H.B.J. 39 (1984).

An Example: Low v. Bayerische Motoren Werke, A.G., 88 A.D.2d 504, 449 N.Y.S.2d 733 (1st Dep't 1982). Low purchased a BMW in Germany. Although he had acted through its subsidiary to initiate the purchase, his first direct contact with the defendant was in Germany. While driving the car in Germany, he was injured. Later, he brought a personal injury action against the defendant in a New York state court. Pursuant to the New York statute, he served the secretary of state and mailed a copy of the summons and complaint to the defendant in Germany. The Appellate Division held this service ineffective. Although article 10 of the Hague Convention allows service by mail, the article is subject to reservation. In its ratification, the Federal Republic of Germany objected to article 10 and declared that such service should not be effective. The treaty and reservation made under it were held to prevail over the state statute. Plaintiff Low could have obtained service by letter rogatory or by other means provided by the Convention.

Service a Foreign Subject Inside the United States. In *Volkswagenwerk Aktiengesellschaft v. Schlunk*, 486 U.S. 694 (1988), the Supreme Court interpreted the Hague Service Convention as not applying when process is served on a foreign corporation by serving its domestic subsidiary which, under state law, is the corporation's involuntary agent for service of process.

"Where service on a domestic agent is valid and complete under both state law and the Due Process Clause, our inquiry ends and the Convention has no further implications. . . . The only transmittal to which the Convention applies is a transmittal abroad that is required as a necessary part of service." 486 U.S. at 707.

NOTES AND QUESTIONS

(1) *Is E-Mail Service Among the Available Methods of International Service Under Rule 4(f)?* Rule 4(f) contains a "catch-all" provision allowing service upon individuals outside the United States "by other means not prohibited by international agreement as may be directed by the court." In *Rio Properties, Inc. v. Rio International Interlink*, 284 F.3d 1007 (9th Cir. 2002), the Ninth Circuit had to consider whether a U.S. plaintiff could use e-mail under Rule 4(f)(3) to serve a Costa Rican business entity that was not subject to service in the United States and appeared to be evading the more usual means of service of process. Federal Rule 5(b)(2)(D) authorizes the use of e-mail to serve papers other than the summons and complaint, but there is no explicit authority for the use of e-mail to serve a summons and complaint either within or without the territory of the United States. Nevertheless, the Ninth Circuit approved the use of e-mail service in this case. The court concluded that Rule 4(f)(3) required only that service be directed by the court and not be prohibited by international agreement, even if the method was in contravention of the laws of the foreign country where service was made. The court also rejected an interpretation that Rule 4(f) creates a "hierarchy of preferred methods of service of process," and that service under Rule 4(f)(3) must be a "last resort" to be used only when diplomatic channels or letters rogatory have been tried and failed. Instead,

"Rule 4(f)(3) is an equal means of effectuating service of process under the Federal Rules of Civil Procedure, and we commit to the sound discretion of the district court the task of determining when the particularities and necessities of a given case require alternate service of process under Rule 4(f)(3)." 284 F.3d at 1016. Given the Ninth Circuit's grant of broad authority to the district courts, is it not likely that domestic plaintiffs will in fact prefer using alternatives to traditional service methods rather than employing the less familiar but more traditional letters rogatory and formal diplomatic methods under the Hague Convention?

(2) *Service by Regular Mail to Post Office Box?* After initially upholding service of process upon an English defendant by regular mail to a post office box in England, the Ninth Circuit panel changed its mind. In *Brockmeyer v. May*, 383 F.3d 798 (9th Cir. 2004), in a substituted opinion, the Ninth Circuit panel found such service unauthorized. International service of process by regular mail is authorized by Article 10(a) of the Hague Convention when the law of the forum state authorizes such service and the state of destination does not object. Here, however, "the law of the forum state" did not authorize such service because the plaintiffs did not obtain a waiver of service under Fed. R. Civ. P. 4(d) nor comply with any of the provisions of Rule 4(f).

§ 2.05 Venue and *Forum Non Conveniens*

[A] *Forum Non Conveniens*

NOTE ON THE DOCTRINE OF *FORUM NON CONVENIENS*

Sometimes, a distant and inconvenient forum may have personal jurisdiction over a defendant, because personal jurisdiction is broadly defined. But the mere existence of raw adjudicatory power does not mean that the court should always exercise it. There is a common law doctrine, called *"forum non conveniens,"* that allows the court to dismiss so that the action can be brought in another, more appropriate forum. *Forum non conveniens* is Latin for "inconvenient forum," and application of the doctrine is discretionary with the court. The case that follows is an example.

PIPER AIRCRAFT CO. v. REYNO

454 U.S. 235 (1982)

[Five Scottish subjects were killed in the crash of a small aircraft in the Scottish highlands during a charter flight from Blackpool to Perth. A preliminary British Department of Trade report suggested propeller defects as the cause of the crash. A government hearing, however, found no evidence of defective equipment, and the final investigative report concluded that the inexperienced pilot had caused the accident by pilot error.

[The decedent's survivors employed counsel in California, whose legal secretary, Reyno, qualified as administrator of the decedents' estates. Reyno then commenced wrongful death actions in California state court against Piper, the manufacturer of the aircraft, and Hartzell Propeller, Inc., the manufacturer of the propellers. The United Kingdom companies that owned, maintained and operated the charter flight were not within the jurisdiction of the court and were not included in the suit. After removal of the case to federal court, and transfer to Pennsylvania, Piper and Hartzell moved for dismissal on the ground of *forum non conveniens*, a discretionary common law doctrine that enables a District Court having jurisdiction to dismiss in deference to a more convenient forum.

[The District Court granted the motion and dismissed. It applied a balancing test set out in *Gulf Oil Corp. v. Gilbert,* 330 U.S. 501 (1947), which required *forum non conveniens* motions to be decided by the weighing of such factors as the availability of proof, compulsory process, and jury view of premises; practical problems of inexpensive and expeditious trial; public interest considerations; and the interest of the plaintiff in his choice of forum. The District Court noted that Piper and Hartzell had agreed to submit to jurisdiction in the Scottish courts, and they had waived any statute of limitations defenses that might be applicable, so that plaintiffs were assured of a Scottish forum. On the other hand, Reyno was a representative of foreign citizens who candidly sought a forum that would apply more favorable substantive tort law to them. Scottish law did not recognize strict liability in tort, permitted only relatives to sue for wrongful death, and limited damages to "loss of support and society." The District Court observed that a plaintiff's choice of forum was usually entitled to substantial deference but concluded that it should be given little weight in this case because it was motivated by efforts to obtain favorable substantive law.

[The District Court also found "overwhelming" support in the *Gilbert* balancing test for considering Scotland the appropriate forum. The wreckage was there; witnesses to the crash were there and could not be reached in the United States by compulsory process; the charter and maintenance companies could not be made third party defendants in the United States but could only be sued for indemnity later in the United Kingdom, with a "serious risk of inconsistent verdicts"; trial in the United States would require instructing the jury partly in Scottish and partly in American law, creating confusion; and the District Court was unfamiliar with Scottish law and would need to rely upon experts.

[The Court of Appeals reversed. It held that dismissal was "never appropriate when the law of the alternative forum is less favorable to the plaintiff." It considered the plaintiff's forum choice to be "burdensome" but not "unfair" to the defendants. It also rejected the District Court's "public interest" analysis, holding that American law could be applied and that the States where the propellers and aircraft had been manufactured had greater interest in the suit than did Scotland.

[The Supreme Court granted certiorari, reversed the decision of the Court of Appeals, and reinstated the trial court's dismissal, for the following reasons.]

II

JUSTICE MARSHALL delivered the opinion of the Court.

. . . .

The Court of Appeals erred in holding that plaintiffs may defeat a motion to dismiss on the ground of *forum non conveniens* merely by showing that the substantive law that would be applied in the alternative forum is less favorable to the plaintiffs than that of the present forum. The possibility of a change in substantive law should ordinarily not be given conclusive or even substantial weight in the *forum non conveniens* inquiry.

The Court of Appeals' decision is inconsistent with this Court's earlier *forum non conveniens* decisions in another respect. Those decisions have repeatedly emphasized the need to retain flexibility. . . .

In fact, if conclusive or substantial weight were given to the possibility of a change in law, the *forum non conveniens* doctrine would become virtually useless. Jurisdiction and venue requirements are often easily satisfied. As a result, many plaintiffs are able to choose from among several forums. Ordinarily, these plaintiffs will select that forum whose choice-of-law rules are most advantageous. Thus, if the possibility of an unfavorable change in substantive law is given substantial weight in the *forum non conveniens* inquiry, dismissal would rarely be proper. . . .

The Court of Appeals' approach is not only inconsistent with the purpose of the *forum non conveniens* doctrine, but also poses substantial practical problems. If the possibility of a change in law were given substantial weight, deciding motions to dismiss on the ground of *forum non conveniens* would become quite difficult. Choice-of-law analysis would become extremely important, and the courts would frequently be required to interpret the law of foreign jurisdictions. . . . The doctrine of *forum non conveniens*, however, is designed in part to help courts avoid conducting complex exercises in comparative law. As we stated in *Gilbert*, the public interest factors point towards dismissal where the court would be required to "untangle problems in conflict of laws, and in law foreign to itself." . . .

Upholding the decision of the Court of Appeals would result in other practical problems. At least where the foreign plaintiff named an American manufacturer as defendant, a court could not dismiss the case on grounds of *forum non conveniens* where dismissal might lead to an unfavorable change in law. The American courts, which are already extremely attractive to foreign plaintiffs, would become even more attractive. The flow of litigation into the United States would increase and further congest already crowded courts.

We do not hold that the possibility of an unfavorable change in law should *never* be a relevant consideration in a *forum non conveniens* inquiry. Of course, if the remedy provided by the alternative forum is so clearly inadequate or unsatisfactory that it is no remedy at all, the unfavorable change in law may be given substantial weight; the District Court may conclude that dismissal would not be in the interests of justice. In these cases, however, the remedies that would be provided by the Scottish courts do not fall within this category. Although the relatives of the decedents may not be able to rely on a strict liability theory, and although their potential damages award may be smaller, there is no danger that they will be deprived of any remedy or treated unfairly.

III

The Court of Appeals also erred in rejecting the District Court's *Gilbert* analysis. . . .

A

The District Court acknowledged that there is ordinarily a strong presumption in favor of the plaintiff's choice of forum, which may be overcome only when the private and public interest factors clearly point towards trial in the alternative forum. It held, however, that the presumption applies with less force when the plaintiff or real parties in interest are foreign.

The District Court's distinction between resident or citizen plaintiffs and foreign plaintiffs is fully justified. . . . When the home forum has been chosen, it is reasonable to assume that this choice is convenient. When the plaintiff is foreign, however, this assumption is much less reasonable. Because the central purpose of any *forum non conveniens* inquiry is to ensure that the trial is convenient, a foreign plaintiff's choice deserves less deference.

B

The *forum non conveniens* determination is committed to the sound discretion of the trial court. . . . In examining the District Court's analysis of the public and private interests, however, the Court of Appeals seems to have lost sight of this rule, and substituted its own judgment for that of the District Court.

(1)

In analyzing the private interest factors, the District Court stated that the connections with Scotland are "overwhelming." . . . This characterization may be somewhat exaggerated. Particularly with respect to the question of relative ease of access to sources of proof, the private interests point in both directions. As respondent emphasizes, records concerning the design, manufacture, and testing of the propeller and plane are located in the United States. She would have greater access to sources of proof relevant to her strict liability and negligence theories if trial were held here. However, the District Court did not act unreasonably in concluding that fewer evidentiary problems would be posed if the trial were held in Scotland. A large proportion of the relevant evidence is located in Great Britain. . . .

The District Court correctly concluded that the problems posed by the inability to implead potential third-party defendants clearly supported holding the trial in Scotland. . . . The Court of Appeals rejected this argument. Forcing petitioners to rely on actions for indemnity or contribution would be "burdensome" but not "unfair." . . . Finding that trial in the plaintiff's chosen forum would be burdensome, however, is sufficient to support dismissal on grounds of *forum non conveniens.*

(2)

The District Court's review of the factors relating to the public interest was also reasonable. . . .

Scotland has a very strong interest in this litigation. The accident occurred in its airspace. All of the decedents were Scottish. Apart from Piper and Hartzell, all potential plaintiffs and defendants are either Scottish or English. As we stated in *Gilbert,* there is "a local interest in having localized controversies decided at home." . . . Respondent argues that American citizens have an interest in ensuring that American manufacturers are deterred from producing defective products, and that additional deterrence might be obtained if Piper and Hartzell were tried in the United States, where they could be sued on the basis of both negligence and strict liability. However, the incremental deterrence that would be gained if this trial were held in an American court is likely to be insignificant. The American interest in this accident is simply not sufficient to justify the enormous commitment of judicial time and resources that would inevitably be required if the case were to be tried here.

IV

. . . [The District Court] did not act unreasonably in deciding that the private interests pointed towards trial in Scotland. Nor did it act unreasonably in deciding that the public interests favored trial in Scotland. Thus, the judgment of the Court of Appeals is reversed.

NOTES AND QUESTIONS

(1) *Examining the Factors Underlying Piper Aircraft v. Reyno.* How would the result in *Piper Aircraft v. Reyno* have been influenced if the decedents' survivors had been

American citizens rather than Scots? What if the remedy for wrongful death in the alternative forum was limited by a ceiling of $1,000 or was barred by a non-waivable statute of limitations? What if all of the world's expert witnesses knowledgeable about the propellers resided in the United States? *See* Abbott, *The Emerging Doctrine of Forum Non Conveniens: A Comparison of the English, Scottish, and United States Applications*, 18 Vand. J. Transnat'l L. 111 (1985).

(2) *Dismissal or Stay? California's and New York's Statutes.* CCP § 410.30(a) empowers a California court to stay the litigation — *i.e.*, to cease all proceedings but leave the case pending — in lieu of dismissing. Would this alternative be useful? New York also allows this alternative in CPLR 327.

For a striking example of California doctrine, see *Stangvik v. Shiley, Inc.*, 54 Cal. 3d 744, 819 P.2d 14, 1 Cal. Rptr. 2d 556 (1991). There, Norwegian and Swedish plaintiffs sued a heart valve manufacturer for claimed defects. Even though the defendant itself was located in California, the trial court entered a stay under the *forum non conveniens* doctrine — and the state supreme court upheld it. Citing *Piper Aircraft v. Reyno*, the court emphasized that Norway and Sweden would provide adequate remedies, and it concluded that a nonresident alien is not entitled to deference in forum selection. (But is this reasoning persuasive when the defendant is a forum resident?)

(3) *The Relationship Between Forum Non Conveniens and Venue. Forum non conveniens* preceded modern venue provisions containing more structured means of designating convenient places for trial. Within the federal system, there is also a discretionary venue transfer provision (discussed in § 2.04[B][2], below) that derives from *forum non conveniens* notions, but does not require dismissal; accordingly, the *forum non conveniens* doctrine is superseded insofar as deference by one federal forum to another is concerned. *Forum non conveniens* is, however, still the tool for deference by the courts of one state to another — *e.g.*, a Nebraska court might dismiss so that suit could be brought in Maine — or, as in *Piper Aircraft v. Reyno*, by the federal courts to foreign courts.

[B] Venue

[1] The Federal Venue Statutes

Read 28 U.S.C. §§ 1391-1392 (general venue provisions); 1400(b) (patent venue); 1404(a) (change of venue); 1406 (cure or waiver of defects).

PROBLEM C

APPLYING THE FEDERAL VENUE STATUTES. Plaintiff A, a resident of San Francisco (in the Northern District of California), has been injured in an automobile collision occurring in Los Angeles (within the Central District of California), as a result of the careless operation of a car driven by Defendant B, a resident of the Boston Division of the District of Massachusetts. The following questions ask you to identify places of proper venue, to discuss tools that parties may use to alter or attack venue, and to analyze their strategies. Figure 2B is a graphic depiction of these problems.

FIGURE 2B
ILLUSTRATION OF VENUE PROBLEM (NO. 2C)

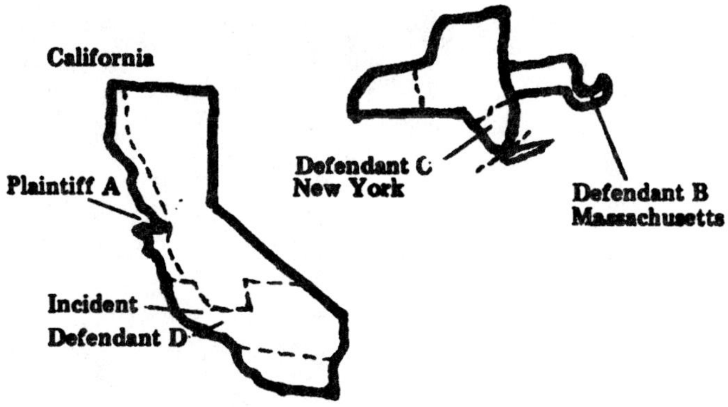

(1) *Venue in Diversity Cases.* Identify the places of proper venue for a diversity action by A against B. [Note: § 1391(a) of the venue provisions governs.]

(2) *Multiple Defendants in Different States.* What difference would it make if Plaintiff were to join a second defendant, C, who resides in the Southern District of New York? [Note: § 1391(a) provides that defendants residing in different districts may be sued in either district — but *only* if the two districts are in the same state; and there is now no place where "all" defendants reside. What places are left under the analysis in question 1?]

(3) *Improper Venue.* Imagine that plaintiff files suit only against B — but he files it in a federal court in the Northern District of Illinois, which is no one's residence and is not where any of the "events or omissions giving rise to the claim occurred." If defendant B is dissatisfied with this location and is convinced venue is improper, is there anything he can do? [*See* § 1406: dismissal or transfer in the event of improperly laid venue. Note that if defendant defaults, the resulting default judgment may be valid if personal jurisdiction can be established, because venue rights, unlike lack of jurisdiction, can be waived by nonappearance.]

(4) *Corporations.* Now, imagine that B is a corporation (whose employee carelessly operated B's car) that is incorporated under Massachusetts law with its headquarters in Syracuse, New York (Northern District of New York). B Corporation is licensed to transact business in New York, and has an agent for service of process and a registered office in New York City (Southern District of New York). B Corporation has factories and distribution centers in Houston, Texas (Southern District of Texas) and in San Diego, California (Southern District of California). What are the places of proper venue now? [*See* § 1391(c).]

(5) *Forum Shopping and Venue Choices.* If Plaintiff has many venue choices (as in the case of the suit against the corporation in question 4, above), how is he likely to go about deciding where to sue? [What kinds of considerations influence how one goes about "forum shopping"?]

(6) *Proper But Inconvenient Venue; Transfer.* What is the defendant corporation's remedy if a forum-shopping plaintiff files suit in a district where venue is proper, but one having nothing to do with the parties or the litigation, and distant from all witnesses? [Note: § 1404(a) allows discretionary transfer for the "convenience of parties and witnesses, in the interest of justice."]

(7) *Venue in Federal Question Claims.* Now, imagine that Plaintiff A sues Defendant D, asserting a federal civil rights claim. Defendant D is a citizen of California, as is Plaintiff A. Defendant D resides in, and the claim arose in, the Los Angeles Division of the Central District of California. Now, where is the only proper place of venue? [Note: § 1391(b) controls.]

(8) *Limits on the Transfer Provision.* Imagine that Defendant D moves to transfer the civil rights suit, hypothesized in question 7, to San Francisco (A's residence). Notice that this district is *not* one of the places of proper venue provided by § 1391(b) for this suit. Can the transfer lawfully be made? [Note: Section 1404(a) allows transfer only to a district and division where the suit "might have been brought." Consider *Hoffman v. Blaski,* which follows.]

[2] Transfer of Venue

HOFFMAN v. BLASKI
363 U.S. 335 (1960)

[Blaski brought a patent infringement suit against one Howell and a Texas corporation controlled by him. A special statute provides for venue in a patent case at defendant's residence or where defendant has infringed and has a regular established place of business. 28 U.S.C. § 1400(b). Therefore, the suit was brought in the Northern District of Texas, where the defendants resided, were allegedly infringing the patents, and were amenable to service of process. The defendants moved to transfer venue to the Northern District of Illinois, where Plaintiff Blaski resided. The opinion does not explain why defendants sought transfer away from their own district and into the district where plaintiffs resided, but evidently defendants perceived some tactical advantage in such a transfer. They relied upon 28 U.S.C. § 1404(a), which provides: "For the convenience of parties and witnesses, in the interest of justice, a District Court may transfer any civil action to any other district or division *where it might have been brought"* (emphasis added).

[Plaintiff Blaski objected that neither jurisdiction nor venue would be proper in Illinois because defendants did not reside there, were not infringing the patent there, and could not be served in a suit filed there, and Illinois therefore was not a place where the action "might have been brought." The District Court, however, granted the transfer. The Fifth Circuit upheld this action, saying: "[T]he purposes for which the § 1404(a) transfer provision was enacted would be unduly circumscribed if a transfer could not be made 'in the interest of justice' to a district where the defendants not only waive venue but to which they seek the transfer."

[In the Northern District of Illinois, Blaski promptly moved to remand the case to Texas. Judge Hoffman expressed doubt about the Texas court's power to make the transfer, but given the Fifth Circuit's holding, he declined to send the case back. The Seventh Circuit reversed Judge Hoffman and squarely disagreed with the Fifth Circuit. It granted a writ of mandamus, ordering Judge Hoffman to remand the case to Texas, on the ground that Illinois was not a place where it "might have been brought." Defendant Howell successfully petitioned the Supreme Court to review the case, with Judge Hoffman as the nominal party. The Supreme Court held that the transfer was improper, for the following reasons.]

MR. JUSTICE WHITTAKER delivered the opinion of the Court.

. . . .

Petitioners' "thesis" and sole claim is that § 1404(a), being remedial, . . . should be broadly construed, and, when so construed, the phrase "where it might have been brought" should be held to relate not only to the time of the bringing of the action, but also to the time of the transfer; and that "if at such time the transferee forum has the power to adjudicate the issues of the action, it is a forum in which the action might *then* have been brought." (Emphasis added.)

. . . .

We do not agree. We do not think the § 1404(a) phrase "where it might have been brought" can be interpreted to mean, as petitioners' theory would require, "where it may now be rebrought, with defendants' consent." This Court has said, in a different context, that § 1404(a) is "unambiguous, direct [and] clear," . . . and that "the unequivocal words of § 1404(a) and the legislative history . . . establish that Congress indeed meant what it said." . . . Of course, venue, like jurisdiction over the person, may be waived. A defendant, properly served with process by a court having subject matter jurisdiction, waives venue by failing seasonably to assert it, or even simply by making default. . . . But the power of a District Court under § 1404(a) to transfer an action to another district is made to depend not upon the wish or waiver of the defendant but, rather, upon whether the transferee district was one in which the action "might have been brought" by the plaintiff.

The thesis urged by petitioners would not only do violence to the plain words of § 1404(a), but would also inject gross discrimination. That thesis, if adopted, would empower a District Court, upon a finding of convenience, to transfer an action to any district desired by the *defendants* and in which they were willing to waive their statutory defenses as to venue and jurisdiction over their persons, regardless of the fact that such transferee district was not one in which the action "might have been brought" by the plaintiff. Conversely, that thesis would not permit the court, upon motion of the *plaintiffs* and a like showing of convenience, to transfer the action to the same district, without the consent and waiver of venue and personal jurisdiction defenses by the defendants. Nothing in § 1404(a), or in its legislative history, suggests such a unilateral objective and we should not, under the guise of interpretation, ascribe to Congress any such discriminatory purpose. . . . Affirmed.

MR. JUSTICE FRANKFURTER, whom MR. JUSTICE HARLAN and MR. JUSTICE BRENNAN join, dissenting.[a]

The problem in this case is of important concern to the effective administration of justice in the federal courts. At issue is the scope of 28 U.S.C. § 1404(a), providing for the transfer of litigation from one Federal District Court to another. The main federal venue statutes necessarily deal with classes of cases, without regard to the occasional situation in which a normally appropriate venue may operate vexatiously. Section 1404(a) was devised to avoid needless hardship and even miscarriage of justice by empowering district judges to recognize special circumstances calling for special relief.

[a] [This dissenting opinion applied to a companion case, which involved related issues. The dissenting Justices also dissented in *Hoffman v. Blaski*, but on jurisdictional grounds. — Eds.]

. . . .

One would have to be singularly unmindful of the treachery and versatility of our language to deny that as a mere matter of English the words "where it might have been brought" may carry more than one meaning. . . . As a matter of English alone, the phrase might just as well be thought to refer either to those places where the defendant "might have been" served with process, or to those places where the action "might have been brought" in light of the applicable venue provision, for those provisions speak generally of where actions "may be brought." Or the phrase may be thought as a matter of English alone to refer to those places where the action "might have been brought" in light of the applicable statute of limitations, or other provisions preventing a court from reaching the merits of the litigation. On the face of its words alone, the phrase may refer to any one of these considerations, *i.e.*, venue, amenability to service, or period of limitations, to all of them or to none of them, or to others as well . . . .

I submit that it is not clear from the words themselves, and the experience in the lower courts gives compelling proof of it. At least 28 District Courts, located in all parts of the Nation, have had to give concrete meaning to the set of words in controversy. These are the judges who are, to use a familiar but appropriate phrase, on the firing line, who are in much more intimate, continuous touch with the needs for the effective functioning of the federal judicial system at the trial level than is this Court. They have not found the last phrase of § 1404(a) unambiguous. There has been anything but the substantial uniformity of views to be expected in the application of a clear and unambiguous direction. . . .

The experience in the Courts of Appeals is also revealing. Of the six cases where defendants have moved for transfer, in only two has it been held that the defendant's consent to the transfer is not relevant in determining whether the place to which transfer is proposed is a place where the action "might have been brought," and these are the two decisions of the Seventh Circuit now before us. . . .

The relevant legislative history of § 1404(a) is found in the statement in the Reviser's Notes, accompanying the 1948 Judicial Code, that § 1404(a) "was drafted in accordance with the doctrine of *forum non conveniens*." Under the doctrine, the remedy for an inconvenient forum was not to transfer the action, but to dismiss it. In *Gulf Oil Corp. v. Gilbert*, . . . we held that "[i]n all cases in which the doctrine of *forum non conveniens* comes into play, it presupposes at least two forums in which the defendant is amenable to process; the doctrine furnishes criteria for choice between them." It is entirely "in accordance" with this view of the doctrine of *forum non conveniens* to hold that transfer may be made at the instance of the defendant, regardless of the plaintiff's right as an original matter to sue him in the transferee court, so long as the defendant stipulates to going forward with the litigation there. Indeed, to hold otherwise as the Court does is to limit § 1404(a) to a much narrower operation than the nonstatutory doctrine of *forum non conveniens*. Investigation has disclosed several *forum non conveniens* cases, one of them in this Court, where dismissal of the action on the defendant's motion was made upon the condition of the defendant's voluntary submission to the jurisdiction of another more convenient forum when that forum was not available to the plaintiff as of right over the defendant's objection. . . .

The only consideration of the Court not resting on the "plain meaning" of § 1404(a) is that it would constitute "gross discrimination" to permit transfer to be made with the defendant's consent and over the plaintiff's objection to a district to which the plaintiff could not similarly obtain transfer over the defendant's objection. To speak of such a situation as regards this statute as "discrimination" is a sterile use of the concept. . . . Transfer cannot be made under this statute unless it is found to be in the interest of "convenience" and in the interest of "justice." . . . If the interest of justice is being served, as it must be for a transfer to be made, how can it be said that there is "discrimination" in any meaningful sense? Moreover, the transfer provision cannot be viewed in isolation in finding "discrimination." It, after all, operates to temper only to a slight degree the enormous "discrimination" inherent in our system of litigation, whereby the sole choice of forum, from among those where service is possible and venue unobjectionable, is placed with the plaintiff. The plaintiff may choose from among these forums at will; under § 1404(a) the defendant must satisfy a very substantial burden of demonstrating where "justice" and "convenience" lie, in order to have his objection to a forum of hardship, in the particular situation, respected. . . .

NOTES AND QUESTIONS

(1) *Is Hoffman v. Blaski Correctly Decided?* Notice that, as the dissent points out, the lower courts had found § 1404(a) anything but "unambiguous." Furthermore, the transfer provision was based upon experience with *forum non conveniens*; as the dissent points out, that doctrine did allow the action to be recommenced in a place where it could not initially have been brought, if defendant consented. Given these points, is *Hoffman v. Blaski* correctly decided?

(2) *What Law Applies After Transfer? Van Dusen v. Barrack, 376 U.S. 612 (1964).* If the case is transferred, should the new court follow the law applicable in its jurisdiction — or should it follow the same law as the transferring court? If there were a change of law, the court's willingness to allow transfer might be inhibited, and forum shopping would increase. Therefore, the basic principle is that the transfer should bring about only a change of courtrooms, and not a change in the governing law. What problems can you see in the implementation of this rule? (For example, if the case is transferred from a court within the Second Circuit to a court within the Ninth, and the two Circuits follow different rules on a given point, will the transferee court be comfortable in expecting that the Ninth will not reverse if it follows the Second Circuit rule?) *See* Marcus, *Conflicts Among Circuits and Transfers Within the Federal Judicial System*, 93 Yale L.J. 677 (1984).

(3) *Gamesmanship in Venue Transfers and Choice of Law: Ferens v. John Deere Co., 494 U.S. 516 (1990).* In this case, the Supreme Court allowed the plaintiff to avoid the Pennsylvania statute of limitations bar through use of § 1404(a) and *Van Dusen*'s choice of law rules. Ferens, a Pennsylvanian injured in an accident in Pennsylvania with a Deere combine, waited too long to file personal injury claims under Pennsylvania's two-year statute of limitations. He did file timely warranty claims against Deere in Pennsylvania federal court. Ferens then filed the personal injury claims against Deere in Mississippi federal court where he could obtain jurisdiction and venue was proper. Mississippi had a six-year statute of limitations, and, under Mississippi choice of law rules, which the federal court was required to honor under *Erie* principles, its six-year statute applied to Ferens' claim. Ferens then took this forum shopping one step further by moving to transfer the Mississippi federal court action to Pennsylvania under § 1404(a) for consolidation with his action against Deere there.

Ferens argued that the Pennsylvania federal court had to apply the law of the transferor court under *Van Dusen*, but the District Court refused to apply the Mississippi statute of limitations and dismissed the personal injury claims as untimely. The Supreme Court reversed. It found *Van Dusen* should apply to plaintiff-initiated as well as defendant-initiated transfers and that the defendant was no worse off than if transfer had not occurred. This holding also allows the transfer decision to rest solely on convenience factors and avoids burdening federal courts with elaborate choice of law analysis. (But doesn't it also allow plaintiffs to engage in a lot of gamesmanship?)

(4) *Transfer When Venue or Jurisdiction Is Improper: Goldlawr v. Heiman, 369 U.S. 463 (1962).* The general rule is that a court lacking jurisdiction should dismiss. However, 28 U.S.C. § 1406 gives federal District Courts authority to dismiss *or transfer* when venue is improper. In *Goldlawr v. Heiman*, the Supreme Court upheld the authority of the court to transfer when personal jurisdiction is lacking. Is this result appropriate? Shouldn't the Court have held that a court lacking jurisdiction has no authority to do anything to affect the action? On the other hand, isn't transfer to an appropriate forum fairer, simpler, and more expeditious than dismissal (particularly if, say, the statute of limitations has run after the action has been pending for some time)?

(5) *Use of the Transfer Provision in Forum Contests.* The transfer provision may be useful to a defendant who contests jurisdiction. In almost every instance, the defendant should make a motion for transfer in the alternative. In a close case, the court may well resolve its dilemma by granting transfer. However, defendants sometimes overlook the transfer provision in this situation.

(6) *Transfer of Venue and Forum Selection Clauses.* In *Stewart Organization, Inc. v. Ricoh Corp.*, 487 U.S. 22 (1988), the Supreme Court held that a forum selection clause was among the factors a district court should consider in deciding whether to transfer an action under § 1404(a). But such a clause might not be dispositive of the transfer motion. *See* § 2.02[F][2], *supra.*

[C] Venue in State Courts

In this section, we examine the venue systems of three "benchmark states": California, Texas, and New York. As we have previously explained in the Preface, we refer to these three states throughout the book, because their systems are well developed, and they provide points of contrast that will enhance your understanding of the federal procedures that are our principal focus.

[1] The California Venue System

California classifies actions as "local" or "transitory" for venue purposes. If the main relief sought relates to real property in certain ways, the action is local and must be brought in the county where the property is located. CCP § 392. All other actions are transitory. For transitory actions, the basic California venue statute is Code of Civil Procedure § 395(a), which provides: "Except as otherwise provided by law and subject to the power of the court to transfer actions or proceedings as provided in this title, the superior court in the county where the defendants or some of them reside at the commencement of the action is the proper court for the trial of the action . . . ." In summary, the California system is organized on a county-by-county basis, and it creates a preference for venue at the defendant's residence. As is implied by the statute, if there are multiple defendants all of whom have been properly joined, venue generally will be proper in the county of residence of any of them. (This latter provision has sometimes led to efforts to join marginal defendants. CCP § 395(a) therefore provides that if a defendant has been improperly joined or joined "solely" for the purpose of supporting venue, "his or her residence shall not be considered.")

There are many exceptions to the rule of venue at defendant's residence. Some of the exceptions depend upon the type of party that is a defendant. For example, a corporation may be sued "where the contract is made or is to be performed, or where the obligation or liability arises, or the breach occurs; or in the county where the principal place of business of such corporation is situated. . . ." CCP § 395.5. There also are exceptions that depend upon the type of action. For example, a contract (other than with a consumer) to perform an obligation in a particular county may be tried in the county in which the obligation is to be performed, or in which the contract was in fact entered into, or in which the defendant resides. CCP § 395(a). Personal injury tort actions based on negligence are triable either in the county in which any defendant resides or the county where the injury occurred. CCP § 395(a).

A defendant may challenge the plaintiff's selection by moving for a change of venue. CCP §§ 396b, 397. The most common grounds are (1) that the court designated in the complaint is not a court of proper venue and (2) that the convenience of witnesses and the ends of justice would be promoted by a change. The propriety of the venue is determined, in general, from the face of the complaint; for example, the nature of the action is determined by the nature of the claims pleaded. There are, however, instances in which the court must be provided with factual information outside the pleadings — *e.g.*, the actual location of a defendant's residence — and these kinds of facts are shown by affidavit. Also, when the motion is based on the convenience of the witnesses, it typically is supported by affidavits or declarations showing the facts bearing on convenience. The motion for change of venue must be timely filed (a "wrong court" motion must be made within the time allowed for the defendant to answer or demur, CCP § 396b, or the objection is waived and the action may be tried where commenced. *See generally* R. Weil & I. Brown, *California Practice Guide: Civil Procedure Before Trial* ¶¶ 3:450–3:606 (The Rutter Group 2000).

CARRUTH v. SUPERIOR COURT, 80 Cal. App. 3d 215, 145 Cal. Rptr. 344 (1978). Plaintiff filed suit against both an individual defendant and a corporate defendant. The suit was filed in a county that was not the residence of either defendant, although it was one of the places in which a corporation or association could properly be sued under CCP § 395.5. The individual defendant filed a motion for change of venue. The court held that, in such a situation, the individual defendant may obtain a change of venue to the county where he or she resides.

WATHEN v. SUPERIOR COURT, 212 Cal. App. 2d 125, 27 Cal. Rptr. 840 (1963). In a contract action, plaintiff filed suit in the alleged county of performance (Santa Clara), which was different both from the county where the contract was made and from defendant's residence. Plaintiff relied on the venue provisions of CCP § 395(a), allowing venue where the obligation was to be performed. Defendant moved for a change of venue, however, because § 395(a) also specifies that the county in which the contract is made is considered the county in which it is to be performed "unless there is a special contract in writing to the contrary." The contract was written on plaintiff's letterhead, and it simply specified performance at plaintiff's place of business without mentioning a county. Nevertheless, because the letterhead showed that plaintiff's office was in Santa Clara County, the court held that the contract was sufficient to support venue in that county.

[2] The Texas Venue System

In conception, the Texas venue scheme is similar to the California scheme. Under the general rule, venue is proper in the county or counties in which all or a substantial party of the events or omissions giving rise to the claim occurred, in the county of a defendant's residence if the defendant is a natural person, and in the county of the defendant's principal office in Texas if the defendant is not a natural person. Tex. Civ. Prac. & Rem. Code § 15.002. As in California, there are additional "permissive" venue provisions covering written contracts specifying a place of performance (except consumer contracts), corporations, and other special kinds of defendants or actions. Texas law provides for "mandatory" venue in a number of situations, including suits for defamation and for title to land. This type of venue is similar to California's concept of "local" actions. A venue contest is raised by a motion to transfer venue, which must be filed prior to or concurrently with any other plea (except a special appearance), and which is determined on the basis of the pleadings plus affidavits and discovery products (although the entire record is considered on appeal). *See* Tex. Civ. Prac. & Rem. Code §§ 15.001 *et seq.* Texas venue law also provides that a court may transfer an action from a county of proper venue to any other county of proper venue "for the convenience of the parties and witnesses and in the interest of justice." *See* Tex. Civ. Prac. & Rem. Code § 15.002(b). W. Dorsaneo, D. Crump, E. Carlson & E. Thornburg, *Texas Civil Procedure: Pretrial Litigation*, Ch. 6 (2007–08 ed.).

[3] The New York Venue System

Venue in the Supreme Court in New York is similar in some respects to the California scheme, although it is simpler and exhibits some important differences. Local actions, as in California, are those in which a single place of proper venue is fixed independently of the parties' residences. In New York, local actions include, among others, those for title or possession of real property, and venue is based upon its location. Other actions, as in California, are called transitory actions.

The general venue rule in transitory actions is that the suit is to be brought where either any defendant resides or where any plaintiff resides at the time the action is commenced. This allowance of suit where the plaintiff resides is different from the California scheme, and it often results in a choice by the plaintiff that is inconvenient to a distant defendant. The court has discretionary authority to change venue for the convenience of witnesses. In addition, the New York scheme provides several exceptions that resemble some of California's provisions. For example, a corporation may be sued not only at its residence (which is defined as the place of its office listed in the official records of the Secretary of State), but also at its principal place of business. However, New York's allowance of suit at the plaintiff's residence probably eliminates the need for giving the plaintiff extensive other venue choices, which are needed in Texas and California because their rules are more favorable to defendants than New York's. *See* Consol. Laws of N.Y. CPLR §§ 501-513 (2006); *see generally* O. Chase, 1 *Weinstein, Korn & Miller CPLR Manual,* Ch. 5 (1997).

KATZ v. SIROTY, 62 A.D.2d 1011, 403 N.Y.S.2d 770 (1978). Plaintiff, an attorney, filed an action in Kings County for the value of legal services rendered. Defendant invoked procedures for change of venue on the ground that venue was improper and sought transfer to Westchester County, which he alleged was plaintiff's true residence.

The court, while recognizing that a party can have more than one residence, held that the plaintiff's occasional use of a bedroom in his sister's home in Kings County when he transacted business in New York City was insufficient to establish that county as his residence, and it granted the transfer to Westchester county, where plaintiff and his wife owned a home.

BURCH v. PHILLIPS, 88 A.D.2d 896, 450 N.Y.S.2d 600 (1982). In a multiple party action, filed at the residence of one of the defendants, other defendants moved for a discretionary change of venue. Plaintiff filed a cross-motion, which the trial court granted, transferring the action to the county where the plaintiff had taken up residence after the suit. While recognizing that a transfer for the convenience of witnesses and the ends of justice is discretionary and will not be reversed except for abuse, the appellate court noted that the place of the events giving rise to suit should be preferred. Since that county was also the residence of several defendants, was where some witnesses resided or practiced, and was where the plaintiff was hospitalized and resided for a period of time after the accident, the Appellate Division reversed and ordered transfer to the county where the accident had occurred, in accordance with the defendant's motion.

§ 2.06 Improving Our System of Personal Jurisdiction and Venue: Notes and Questions

(1) *Characteristics of a Good System for Service of Process.* An ideal system for service of process would have the following characteristics. First, it would be simple, expeditious, and inexpensive to use. That is to say, it would allow the plaintiff to obtain quick results, without the expenditure of large amounts of attorney or support personnel time. Secondly, it would allow means for service upon the evasive defendant, also as cheaply and easily as possible. Third, it would guarantee a high probability that the defendants would actually receive notice. Finally, it would have a high probability of communicating to the defendant in a clearcut way the importance of the process, so that the defendant, even if unsophisticated, would be likely to engage counsel and file an answer rather than default.

It should be apparent that these goals are inconsistent. For example, relatively inexpensive service methods might not be the best means for ensuring that defendant is likely to receive the process or to recognize its importance.

(2) *Toward a Better System for Service of Process.* With these goals in mind (and perhaps with others that might occur to you), you should evaluate the following proposals. Which ones are reasonable? Which involve disadvantages that outweigh the advantages?

(a) *Proposal for a Variety of Service Methods, Including Mailed Service.* Each jurisdiction should allow alternative methods that include in-hand service, leave-with service, service on an agent authorized by appointment or by law, and mailed service. So that service by mail does not fail to communicate the relevant information, it should be required to be done by registered or certified mail, restricted to the defendant as addressee. Further, mailed service should be accompanied by a summons advising the defendant that he should consult an attorney and must file an answer by a date certain or judgment will be taken against him. The governing rule should set out the language for this summons and prescribe the use of bold type.

(b) *Proposal for a Waiver-of-Service Procedure.* Each jurisdiction should adopt a waiver procedure, and the defendant should be under an obligation to execute and return the waiver. A defendant who does not do so should be liable for expenses of service. In addition, a defendant who willfully, and with understanding of its character, fails to return the executed acknowledgment should be subject to sanctions (including default judgment in extreme cases) upon his being properly served, even if he thereafter files an answer.

(c) *Proposal for Substituted Service and Sanctions Against Evasive Defendants.* The court should have broad authority to authorize substituted service by any "reasonably calculated" means upon a showing that the traditional methods of service appear impractical. Proof of impracticality by written affidavit should be authorized, and actual live testimony should not be required. Upon the defendant's appearance, a showing that he has willfully evaded service of process should subject him to sanctions, including default judgment in extreme cases.

(d) *Proposal for Liberal Relief from Default Judgments.* There should be liberal allowance of relief from a default judgment for a relatively long period (*e.g.*, six months or a year) if the defendant has an arguable defense and did not consciously neglect or evade service.

(3) *Characteristics of a Good System of Forum Selection.* A good system of interstate jurisdiction and venue would provide means by which the defendant sued in an inconvenient forum could obtain dismissal or transfer. However, it would also provide a convenient forum to the plaintiff (or at least one as convenient as is consistent with the defendant's rights). It would provide clearcut and predictable rules so that forum contests were minimized. (This objective may be in competition with the objective of convenience to both parties.) Finally, a good system would minimize forum shopping and distant forum abuse.

(4) *Toward a Better System for Resolving Forum Contests.* Evaluate the following proposals with respect to these objectives:

(a) *Proposal for More Congressional Authorizations of Nationwide Service.* Congress should make more use of its authority to allow nationwide service. A defendant carrying on a large nationwide business should be subject to service in any federal court. The circumstances of this kind of service could be defined by the type of business — *e.g.*, an intercity airline — or its size — any business with assets placing it within the Fortune 500. Provisions for change of venue should then be used to minimize forum shopping or distant forum abuse.

(b) *Proposal for "Laundry List" Statutes Supplemented by a Limited "Catchall" Provision.* Long-arm statutes should conform to the "laundry list" model. This model appears to give greater certainty. There should be a supplementary provision allowing the exercise of jurisdiction under the "limits of due process" model, so that plaintiffs will not be unnecessarily deprived of a convenient forum. However, this "catchall" provision should be subject to invocation only on a showing that the forum is not inconvenient to the defendant and has not been chosen as the result of forum shopping.

(c) *Proposal for Reform of the Venue Transfer Procedure.* Transfer of venue should be more liberally granted. The result in *Hoffman v. Blaski, supra,* should be legislatively reversed. The principle that the court should allow great deference to the plaintiff's choice of forum should be legislatively reversed, and the court should be able to consider the balance of convenience without preference for either party. This approach would decrease the success with which plaintiffs could forum-shop or subject defendants to distant forum abuse.

(d) *Burden of Proof; Attorneys' Fees and Expenses.* The defendant should have the burden of disproving the existence of minimum contacts. This rule is followed in some state courts; *e.g., Hoppenfeld v. Crook,* 498 S.W.2d 52 (Tex. Civ. App.-Austin 1973, writ ref'd n.r.e.).

The rule is based on conclusions that (1) information about the contacts is most readily available to the defendant and (2) an unacceptable percentage of special appearances are brought to impel plaintiffs to make their proof. In addition, the winner of a special appearance should be able to recover reasonable attorneys' fees and expenses from the adversary, whether plaintiff or defendant.

(5) *The Special Problem of Dispersed Defendants.* One problem with the current system of jurisdiction is that it effectively requires the plaintiff to fragment her suit if the defendants she wishes to sue out of a common occurrence are dispersed. For example, in *World-Wide Volkswagen v. Woodson, supra,* if the plaintiffs had wished to sue the local Oklahoma defendant who collided with them in that state, and also to sue World-Wide, they would have found it necessary to file two different suits, one in Oklahoma and one in New York. Shouldn't there be some means of providing a single forum for suits arising out of a common occurrence?

The American Law Institute has proposed a solution. The solution is complicated and requires an understanding of federal subject matter jurisdiction, which you will study in the next chapter. However, the basic outlines of the proposal can be sketched simply:

(a) *Proposal for Congressional Creation of Jurisdiction in Federal Courts When Defendants Are Dispersed.* The proposal would create federal jurisdiction over cases involving dispersed defendants under certain circumstances, even if the jurisdiction could not otherwise exist.

(b) *Related Proposal for Congressional Creation of Nationwide Service of Process to Bring the Dispersed Defendants to a Single Forum.* It would then authorize nationwide service of process upon the defendants, so that they could be compelled to answer in a single forum (such as Oklahoma, in *World-Wide Volkswagen,* § 2.02[C][1], *supra*).

For an excellent discussion of the proposal, *see* Kamp, *The Shrinking Forum: The Supreme Court's Limitation of Jurisdiction — An Argument for a Federal Forum in Multi-Party, Multi-State Litigation,* 21 Wm. & Mary L. Rev. 161 (1979). The original proposal is set forth in ALI, *Study of the Division of Jurisdiction Between State and Federal Courts* 3-4 (1969).

The problem with such a proposal is that one may question the feasibility of reversing *World-Wide Volkswagen.* The Supreme Court reasoned that Oklahoma could not constitutionally exercise jurisdiction over World-Wide. Is the ALI proposal less subject to claims of forum abuse because the court in Oklahoma that would exercise jurisdiction would be a federal court rather than a state one? Furthermore, it is difficult to draft such a proposal without also making it possible for the plaintiffs to sue all the defendants in New York. Would it be fair for the local Oklahoma defendants to be subjected to suit in New York for an Oklahoma occurrence merely because New York is the residence of the distributor and retailer of the car with which they collided?

APPENDIX TO CHAPTER 2

THE ANATOMY OF A FORUM CONTEST: LITIGATION DOCUMENTS IN *GEORGE MILLER CO. v. COMPUDATA, INC.*

§ A BACKGROUND ON THE DISPUTE

On May 1, 2002, George Miller Company contracted with Compudata, Inc., to become a sales representative for Compudata in certain states, including the (imaginary) State of West York. George Miller Company was a West York corporation having its principal place of business in West York, and its activities consisted mainly of soliciting sales for a number of national companies there. Compudata was a manufacturer of disc memory systems for data processing and computing, and it was a corporation created under the laws of, and having its principal place of business in, the "State" of Texafornia.

The sales representation contract provided for a system of commissions to be paid to George Miller Company. It further provided for annual renewal of its terms unless the parties agreed otherwise. It had certain provisions governing termination, including continuation of commissions on a specified basis following notice of termination.

Compudata sent George Miller Company notice of termination on May 22, 2006. Miller later disagreed with Compudata as to (1) the amount of commissions to be paid during the termination notice period and (2) the amount of commission paid during earlier years.

These materials are based upon a real case. The names, dates, places, and events are changed, and the documents are edited or altered for pedagogical purposes. However, the "business" parts of the documents remain close to the originals.

§ B THE PRE-LITIGATION PHASE

DEMAND LETTER

To: Compudata Incorporated
6108 Eureka Avenue
Ann Arbor, Texafornia 94304

Dear Sir or Madam:

After your termination of the agreement between Compudata and George Miller Company ("Miller"), Miller undertook to review that agreement to see exactly what rights it had. It found that Compudata owes Miller more commissions than are currently being paid. Also, Miller discovered for the first time that Compudata owes it commissions due in past years but never paid. We believe that you will agree when you consider the following.

First. The contract provides, on page 6, that Compudata will pay an additional amount equal to half of earned commissions for sales made during the termination notice period. "For sales made within the territory covered by this Agreement during the termination notice period, the Company will afford the Representative an additional protection of one-half the regular payable earned commissions to compensate for sales effort during the period of representation." Thus the contract makes it clear that sales during the termination notice period are to be assigned an *additional* half of earned commissions, and there is no reasonable way to interpret the language to make the half commission serve in lieu of regular commissions. However, Miller has been receiving only half of the regular commission on sales made during the termination notice period, and therefore Compudata owes Miller a further full commission on these sales. Our computations show that the amount thus owed is $26,611.95.

Second. In addition to the problem described above, we find that in years past the commissions paid Miller do not conform to what we consider to be the only reasonable interpretation of the contract. The contract, of course, provides on page 3 for a regressive schedule of commissions, ranging downward from 10%, so that as sales increase, Miller's commission on each successive unit decreases. But this is not the whole story. On page 7, the Agreement further provides that:

> The terms of this Agreement are in effect for one (1) year from the date of signing this Agreement. At the end of each anniversary year, the terms and conditions of this Agreement will be reviewed by the Company and the Representative.
>
> This Agreement shall automatically renew for an additional year on each anniversary date so long as no changes or negotiations take place.

Thus the schedule of commissions was to be renewed each successive twelve-month period, and the first $15,000 of sales for *each* such twelve-month period was to be commissioned at 10%, the next $30,000 at 8% and so forth.

The problem is that commissions paid Miller by Compudata were not computed this way. You did not give the commission schedule renewed effect each year. You simply reduced the commissions percentage to the minimum after the first $225,000 worth of goods were sold and continued to pay at that rate without regard to the lapse of several year periods. According to our computations, Compudata owes Miller a total of $37,020.28 for commissions thus unpaid over the period from May 1, 2003, to the present. Our computations are set forth on papers enclosed with this letter.

This letter constitutes a request for full payment. We are, of course, prepared to listen reasonably to any opinions you may have to the contrary. We request that you contact us promptly to resolve these matters; otherwise, Miller will pursue its legal remedies without further notice.

Very truly yours,
McINTOSH & WALKER
by *David Stone*

RESPONSE TO DEMAND

To: David Stone
McIntosh & Walker
2500 Westar Tower
London, West York 75201

Dear Mr. Stone:

This letter is in response to your letter of November 10, 2006, wherein you made demand upon Compudata, Inc. to pay the George Miller Company certain commissions which you allege are due under a contract dated May 1, 2002.

In the second paragraph of your letter you assert that Miller is entitled to 150 percent of the normal commissions for sales made during the "termination notification period" as provided for in the Contract.

We do not agree with your interpretation of the terms of the Contract governing termination. The text of the relevant provisions is as follows:

> Commissions of orders already on the books . . . are payable in full to the Representative under the terms and conditions of this Agreement upon receipt of payment from the customer.
>
> For sales made within the territory covered by this Agreement during the termination notice period, the Company will forward an additional protection of 1/2 the regular payable earned commissions to compensate for sales effort during the period of representation.

The words "additional protection," when read in context, indicate that the one-half commission rate is in addition to the rights granted under the first paragraph of the above-quoted portion of the Contract; namely, the rights of the Representative to receive full commissions on orders booked as of the date of the termination notice, subject to the other provisions of the Contract governing the payment of commissions. Since the servicing of these orders would occur after termination, the intent of the parties was to reduce the commission. Indeed, it would be ironic to provide for an increase in the commission rate upon notice of termination.

In the second portion of your letter you claim that the Contract should be interpreted so as to renew the schedule of commissions at the beginning of each successive twelve-month period during the term of the Contract. Again, we disagree with your interpretation. The effect of the renewal provisions of the Contract is to renew the obligations of the parties *as they existed* at the end of the preceding year for a renewal term of one year. If the understanding of the parties were otherwise, the bonus provisions contained on page 5 of the contract would not make sense. Furthermore, the conduct of the parties during three renewal years has clearly shown that our interpretation is the correct one.

We hope that our response contained in this letter will persuade you and your client that Compudata has in fact performed all of its obligations to Miller under the Contract. If you feel it will be helpful, we will be happy to discuss this matter with you further. Please be advised, however, that Compudata hereby refuses to comply with your demand for payment.

Very truly yours,
O'HARA, PHILLIPS & STEIN
By *Sarah A. Porter*

NOTES AND QUESTIONS ON THE DEMAND LETTER AND RESPONSE

(1) *The Substantive Law: Who Is "Right"?* Each party has traditional maxims of contract interpretation to use in its favor. Compudata relies on the principle that the contract is to be construed as an entire instrument; that the course of dealings between the parties can be used in its interpretation; and that the intent of the parties governs if ascertainable. Miller uses a "plain language" approach, and it has at least one powerful string in its bow: the maxim of "*interpretatio contra proferentem*," or "the language is to be construed against the party who proposed it" (the contract was written entirely by Compudata). Who, then, do you think is "right"? [Note: You will probably have to guess.

It is unlikely that there is a reported case directly on point, and the court will be faced with uncertainty in deciding the issue.]

(2) *Characteristics of a Good Demand Letter.* The letter sent by Miller's lawyer is known as a "demand letter" (can you see why it is called that?). What are the characteristics of a good demand letter? (Should it be conciliatory, evenhanded, and candid about any weaknesses in the case, or should it be direct, positive, and confident?) The purpose of such a letter, of course, is to precipitate settlement negotiations. It also may have an important function as a "malpractice preventive." Can you see why?

(3) *Should the Dispute be Settled?* Is this a dispute that "ought" to be settled early? For what amount, and why?

§ C COMPLAINT, SERVICE, AND 12(b) MOTIONS

PLAINTIFF FILES SUIT: THE COMPLAINT

IN THE UNITED STATES DISTRICT COURT
FOR THE MIDDLE DISTRICT OF WEST YORK
LONDON DIVISION

GEORGE MILLER COMPANY v. COMPUDATA, INCORPORATED	CIVIL ACTION NO. _______

COMPLAINT

COMES NOW, GEORGE MILLER COMPANY, hereinafter referred to as Plaintiff, complaining of COMPUDATA, INCORPORATED, hereinafter referred to as Defendant, and would show the following:

JURISDICTION, PARTIES AND VENUE

1. Plaintiff is a corporation duly incorporated under the laws of the State of West York and having its principal place of business in Manero County, West York. Defendant is a corporation, incorporated under the laws of, and having its principal place of business in, a State other than the State of West York. The matter in controversy herein, exclusive of interest and costs, exceeds the sum of Seventy-Five Thousand Dollars.

2. Defendant, whose address is 6108 Eureka Avenue, Ann Arbor, Texafornia, 94304, is not registered to do business within the State of West York, but it has caused its merchandise to be sold pursuant to the terms of a sales contract with Plaintiff performable within the State, which conduct constitutes doing business in the State according to West York Civ. Prac. & Rem. C. § 17.042 (the West York long-arm statute). Defendant does not maintain a registered agent or a person at a regular place of business upon whom service of process can be had in this State, and therefore service may be had upon Defendant in accordance with Rule 4, Fed. R. Civ. P. and West York Civ. Prac. & Rem. C. § 17.044, by serving the Secretary of State of the State of West York as Defendant's agent.

3. A substantial part of the events or omissions giving rise to the claim occurred in, and the defendant is subject to personal jurisdiction in, this district and division.

FIRST CLAIM

4. On or about May 1, 2002, Plaintiff contracted to become a sales representative of Defendant. The contract was executed on a form written by Defendant in language chosen by Defendant. The contract is attached hereto and incorporated herein for all purposes as Exhibit "A."

5. The contract was renewed annually according to its terms until Defendant sent Plaintiff notice of termination on May 22, 2006. According to the contract, this notice meant that termination would occur seventy-five (75) days thereafter.

6. The contract provides a schedule of sales commissions and further provides, that in the event of termination, "For sales made within the territory covered by this Agreement during the termination notice period, the Company will afford an additional protection of one-half the regular payable earned commissions to compensate for sales effort during the period of representation." The meaning of this contract language is that Defendant agreed to pay its regular commission to Plaintiff *plus* an additional one-half commission during the termination period.

7. Notwithstanding this language, and in breach of it, Defendant paid only one-half, rather than one and one-half, of regular commissions accrued during the termination notice period. Although Plaintiff has demanded, in addition, payment of the regular commission, which is just, due and owing in the amount of $26,611.95, Defendant has failed and refused, and does fail and refuse, to pay that sum.

8. Further, the commission schedule provided by the contract is based upon the dollar volume of sales to each customer, as follows: "First $15,000 — 10%; Next $30,000 — 8%; Next $60,000 — 6%; Next $120,000 — 4%; and Over $225,000 — A negotiated percent (Rough Guide: 3% down to 1.5% minimum)." The commission thus declined in percentage with increasing dollar volume sold to each customer. However, the contract further provided as follows:

> The terms of this Agreement are in effect for one (1) year from the date of signing this Agreement. At the end of each anniversary year, the terms and conditions of this Agreement will be reviewed by the Company and the Representative.
>
> This Agreement shall automatically renew for an additional year on each anniversary date so long as no changes or negotiations take place.

The meaning of this language was that commissions were to be recomputed separately according to the declining schedule for *each* year period of the existence of the contract.

9. Defendant has failed and refused, and does fail and refuse, to pay Plaintiff's commissions by applying the declining schedule independently to each successive year period. Instead, Defendant has computed and paid commissions by aggregating sales over the entire period of Plaintiff's representation of Defendant, a method resulting in substantially lower commissions. Although Plaintiff has demanded payment of amounts just, due and owing in the sum of $37,020.28, Defendant has failed and refused, and does fail and refuse to pay that sum.

10. The failure and refusal of Defendant to compute commissions properly during the termination notice period, and the failure and refusal of Defendant to make payment according to the declining schedule of commissions applied separately to each successive

year period, constitute breach by Defendant of the contract, all to Plaintiff's damage in the amount of $63,632.23. Further, by reason of Defendant's failure to pay this sum, Plaintiff has been required to put the matter in the hands of the undersigned attorneys for collection, and Defendant is thus liable to Plaintiff for a reasonable attorney's fee. Plaintiff would show that a reasonable attorney's fee would be in the amount of $20,000.

SECOND CLAIM

11. Plaintiff incorporates by reference all allegations contained in Paragraphs 1 through 10 above and realleges those allegations as though fully set out at this point.

12. The contract between Plaintiff and Defendant provided expressly that Defendant had the duty to receive purchase money from customers both on its own and on Plaintiff's behalf, to compute commissions, to deduct numerous kinds of charges from said commissions, to divide certain commissions in a discretionary manner "as the Company considers equitable," and to forward monthly and annual statements to Plaintiff justifying its commission computations. By these undertakings, Defendant assumed the duties of a fiduciary toward Plaintiff with respect to the trust fund consisting of monies collected from customers in Plaintiff's area. Plaintiff relied upon proper computation by Defendant.

13. Defendant, without notice to Plaintiff, ignored contract language in failing to pay monies justly due and owing to Plaintiff, and retained said sums instead. Defendant thus breached its fiduciary duties of care and loyalty to Plaintiff. Further, Defendant's failure to render correct monthly and annual statements to Plaintiff constituted a breach of its duty to account and of its duty to identify and segregate Plaintiff's monies. Further, in addition to express contract language creating trust, Plaintiff would show that Defendant's breach of contract and breach of trust caused monies owing to Plaintiff to become impressed with a constructive trust.

14. By reason of these breaches of trust, Defendant has caused damage to Plaintiff in the amount of $63,632.23. Defendant is further liable for exemplary damages in an amount to be set by the court.

WHEREFORE, Plaintiff prays that this Court render judgment for Plaintiff against Defendant for its damages in the amount of $63,632.23, for exemplary damages, for its attorney's fees and costs, and for any other relief to which it may prove itself justly entitled.

Respectfully submitted,
McINTOSH & WALKER
By *David Stone*

NOTE ON SERVICE OF COMPLAINT AND SUMMONS

David Stone tendered the complaint at the clerk's office, where it was date-stamped and assigned a cause number. The clerk prepared a summons, which contained instructions requiring the defendant to respond.

Stone employed a private process service company which, for a fee, served the summons and complaint on the West York Secretary of State as defendant's agent (paying his fee also). The process server made a return of the service upon the Secretary, which Stone filed among the papers of the case. The Secretary sent the complaint and summons by registered mail, return receipt requested, to the Defendant at the address listed in the complaint, with the following cover letter:

Compudata, Inc.
6108 Eureka
Ann Arbor, Texafornia 94304

Dear Sir or Madam:

Pursuant to the Laws of West York, I forward herewith by Certified Mail, Return Receipt Requested, a copy of process served on the Secretary of State on January 26, 2007.

Very truly yours,
BILL LAFAYETTE
West York Secretary of State
By *Cyrus Vance*
Deputy Secretary

Upon receiving the postal receipt (which was in the form of a green postcard containing the signature of the recipient at Compudata), the Secretary of State prepared a certificate to which the receipt was affixed, to show performance of the Secretary's statutory obligation and receipt by the defendant. Stone then filed this certificate and the receipt. A few days later, the defendant filed the following motion.

DEFENDANT OBJECTS TO JURISDICTION: DEFENDANT'S RULE 12(b) MOTION

IN THE UNITED STATES DISTRICT COURT
FOR THE MIDDLE DISTRICT OF WEST YORK
LONDON DIVISION

GEORGE MILLER COMPANY v. COMPUDATA, INCORPORATED	CIVIL ACTION NO. CA-3-5463-C

DEFENDANT'S MOTION TO DISMISS FOR LACK OF JURISDICTION, TO QUASH SERVICE, AND TO DISMISS FOR IMPROPER VENUE

Pursuant to Fed. R. Civ. P. 12(b), defendant moves the Court as follows:

1. To dismiss the action for lack of jurisdiction of the person of Defendant or, in lieu thereof, to quash the return of service of summons, on the ground that service of a copy of the summons and complaint on the Secretary of State of the State of West York as recited in the return of summons herein is not effective service upon Defendant for the following reasons:

a) Defendant is a corporation organized under the laws of, and having its principal place of business in, the State of Texafornia, and the Secretary of State of West York is not an agent of the defendant authorized by appointment or by law to receive service of process.

b) At the time of the purported service of process and, indeed, at all times prior thereto, Defendant did not maintain any office or warehouse or other place of business in West York, had no bank account in West York, was not listed in any West York telephone directory, was not licensed to do business in West York, did not maintain a registered agent in West York, did not have any directors' or shareholders' meetings in West York, and did not engage in any conduct which constituted doing business in West York.

2. To dismiss the action on the ground that venue is improper, for the reasons stated above.

Respectfully submitted,
WILLIAMS, BEELER & GERSHON
By *Arnold A. Gershon*

NOTES AND QUESTIONS ON PLEADINGS AND SERVICE

(1) *The Complaint.* Identify the parts of the complaint that show jurisdiction of the subject-matter, jurisdiction of the person, and venue. Recall the standard for sufficiency of the complaint to state a claim as against a motion to dismiss and analyze whether the complaint meets that standard.

(2) *Service.* Why is the West York long-arm statute used in this federal complaint? Why is the process "served" on the West York Secretary?

(3) *The Rule 12(b) Motion.* From what you know of the underlying facts at this point, do you think the motion is meritorious? Can Defendant even assert it in good faith?

§ D DISCOVERY AND FACT DEVELOPMENT

PLAINTIFF'S REQUEST FOR ADMISSIONS AND DEFENDANT'S ANSWERS

IN THE UNITED STATES DISTRICT COURT
FOR THE MIDDLE DISTRICT OF WEST YORK
LONDON DIVISION

GEORGE MILLER COMPANY
v.
COMPUDATA, INCORPORATED

CIVIL ACTION NO. CA-3-5463-C

PLAINTIFF'S REQUEST FOR ADMISSIONS

Plaintiff requests that the Defendant admit, for the purpose of this action only and subject to all pertinent objections to admissibility which may be interposed at trial or hearing, the truth of the following facts.

Therefore, you are hereby requested, in accordance with Rule 36 of the Federal Rules of Civil Procedure, to admit the truth of each and all of the following matters, or to deny same, or set forth in detail the reason why you cannot truthfully admit or deny them, within thirty (30) days from the date of receipt hereof; otherwise, they will be taken as admitted. You are further notified that in accordance with Rule 37 of the Federal Rules of Civil Procedure, if these matters are not admitted and the truth of these facts is proved by Plaintiff, Plaintiff will apply to the Court for an order requiring Defendant to pay Plaintiff the reasonable expenses incurred in making proof, including attorney's fees.

1. That Compudata entered into a written contract with George Miller Company on or about May 1, 2002.

RESPONSE: Admitted

2. That this contract was renewed annually until termination in 2006.

RESPONSE: Admitted.

3. That a true copy of this contract is attached to plaintiff's complaint.

RESPONSE: Admitted.

. . .

6. That George Miller Company, during the period May 1, 2002, to a date in 2006, or about that period, actively solicited sales orders for goods to be sold by Compudata within the State of West York, with the knowledge and consent of Compudata.

RESPONSE: Defendant objects to Request No. 6 on the ground that the matter set forth therein is not relevant to the subject matter of the pending action, namely the interpretation of the language of certain portions of the contract. Defendant further objects to Request No. 6 on the grounds that the matters therein set forth are not within the personal knowledge of defendant and that said request assumes a conclusion of law, namely that goods of Compudata were sold within the State of West York.

7. That during the period May 1, 2002, to a date in 2006, or about that period, Compudata sold many thousands of dollars worth of goods to buyers within the State of West York.

RESPONSE: Defendant denies that it sold any goods within the State of West York. Defendant admits that it made deliveries, f.o.b. its plant in Texafornia, of many thousands of dollars worth of goods pursuant to purchase orders sent to it by purchasers giving West York addresses and bearing addresses for shipment within West York.

. . .

9. That during the period May 1, 2002, to a date in 2006, or about that period, Compudata paid many thousands of dollars worth of commissions to George Miller Company.

RESPONSE: Admitted.

10. That such commission payments were made for the purpose of compensating George Miller Company for its performance of the said contract, and for its solicitation of buyers, in whole or in part within the State of West York.

RESPONSE: Defendant cannot truthfully admit or deny the matters set forth in Request No. 10, but defendant must qualify its response and admit that said commissions were paid in part to compensate George Miller Company for soliciting orders prior to May 22, 2006, for Compudata products from organizations located within the State of West York and that said soliciting was done pursuant to said contract.

. . .

12. That Compudata is as of this date still selling thousands of dollars worth of goods to buyers within the State of West York annually.

RESPONSE: Defendant denies that any of its goods are being sold within the State of West York and admits that it is receiving purchase orders from persons giving a West York address for products worth thousands of dollars annually.

13. That Compudata was doing business within the State of West York during the period May 1, 2002, to the present.

RESPONSE: Defendant objects to Request No. 13 on the grounds that it is ambiguous and has no clear meaning which informs the defendant of that to which it is to respond and on the further grounds that it calls for a conclusion of law and that it presents a genuine issue for determination by the trier of fact.

Respectfully submitted,
McINTOSH & WALKER
By: *David Stone . . .*
COMPUDATA, INC.
By: *Andrea G. Dysart,*
Vice President . . .

[The jurat, by which Andrea G. Dysart swore to the answers on behalf of the Defendant before a notary, is omitted here.]

PLAINTIFF'S INTERROGATORIES AND DEFENDANT'S ANSWERS

IN THE UNITED STATES DISTRICT COURT
FOR THE MIDDLE DISTRICT OF WEST YORK
LONDON DIVISION

GEORGE MILLER COMPANY v. COMPUDATA, INCORPORATED	CIVIL ACTION NO. CA-3-5463-C

PLAINTIFF'S INTERROGATORIES TO DEFENDANT

Plaintiff requests the Defendant, by officers or agents thereof, to answer under oath in accordance with Rule 33 of the Federal Rules of Civil Procedure, the following interrogatories as they apply to the Defendant.

These interrogatories are to be deemed continuing interrogatories and the Defendant shall promptly supply, by way of supplemental or amended answer any additional responsive information that may become known to it prior to the trial of this action.

1. State the first date within your knowledge upon which goods of Compudata were sold to any buyer within the State of West York.

ANSWER: All sales of goods of Compudata are consummated within the State of Texafornia pursuant to purchase orders received at its principal office. Deliveries are, and always have been, f.o.b. its plant in Texafornia. Compudata first received a purchase order bearing an address for shipment in West York on or about September 30, 2002.

. . .

4. As to each sale within the past six years of goods of Compudata to any buyer within the State of West York, state the following:

(a) a description of the goods sold.

(b) the quantity of goods sold.

(c) the purchaser.

(d) the location of the purchaser.

(e) the means whereby the purchaser was induced to purchase.

(f) the method of delivery.

(g) the place of delivery.

(h) the date of delivery.

(i) the price of each item sold.

(j) the method of payment.

ANSWER: All sales of goods of Compudata are, and always have been, consummated in the State of Texafornia as described in the answer to Interrogatory No. 1. Purchase orders have been received at Compudata's office in Texafornia from the following organizations showing shipment addresses in West York on their face:

Name	Symbol	Location
Scientific Control Corporation	(SCC)	*Carrollton*
West York Instruments	(WI)	*West City*
University of West York	(UW)	*London*
Tracor	(TRA)	*London*
Space Craft, Int.	(SCI)	*London*
Shell Development Company	(SDC)	*London*
Mobile Research	(MOB)	*West City*
Philco-Ford	(PF)	*London*
NASA	(NAS)	*London*
Camco	(CAM)	*London*
General Computer Systems	(GCS)	*West City*
General Electric	(GE)	*London*
General Electrodynamics Corporation	(GEC)	*Garland*
Infotronics	(INF)	*London*
Ling Temco Vought	(LTV)	*West City*

The goods ordered by such purchasers can be described and identified as follows:

F6, F7 5)
7200 Series) Disc Memory Systems
1737 — Disc Memory System plus controller
FPD — "X" — Video Disc Recorder
Video Disc Systems
Spare parts

Data concerning such purchase orders, and the shipments thereunder, as regards interrogatories 4(a), (b), (c), (d), (e), (f), (g), (h), (i), and (j) can be compiled from the information set forth above in this answer and the data contained on the shipment records of Compudata, copies of which are attached and labeled as Exhibit A. In this connection, Defendant relies on Fed. R. Civ. P. 33(d), which provides the "option to produce business records" in response to interrogatories.

5. State whether Compudata has, within the past six years, entered into any contract performable in whole or in part within the State of West York.

ANSWER: Defendant objects to this interrogatory on the grounds that it is ambiguous, that it does not inform the defendant of that to which it is to respond or of the facts sought by plaintiff, and it asks for a legal conclusion.

6. With reference to such contracts, please state:

(a) the duration of contractual relationships;

(b) any and all modifications;

(c) the dates of each performance within West York;

(d) the purchaser upon each such date;

(e) the dollar amount of each such sale;

(f) the amount of any commission paid.

ANSWER: Defendant objects to this interrogatory, which is a continuation of interrogatory number 5, on the same grounds of objection relied on in objecting to said interrogatory number 5.

7. State whether, during the past six years, Compudata has had any salesmen, sales representatives, manufacturer representatives, or agents within the State of West York, whether by independent contract or by employment. Identify such person or persons if any.

ANSWER: Prior to service of the complaint in this action,

(1) George Miller Company — sales representative

(2) Montgomery Industries, Inc. — sales representative — 6601 Hillcraft Blvd., London, W.Y.

. . .

11. Please give the dates and contents of any and all written correspondence during the past six years sent by Compudata to any person located within the State of West York concerning any business of Compudata or concerning any contract or sale.

ANSWER: Defendant has had written correspondence with the persons identified in the answer to interrogatory number 4 above, as well as with those sales representatives identified in the answer to interrogatory number 7 above. Such correspondence is voluminous and may be inspected by plaintiff, except insofar as it pertains to defendant's trade secrets or other proprietary information, in any manner which is reasonable. Defendant relies on Fed. R. Civ. P. 33(d), which provides the "option to produce business records."

12. State the approximate dates, costs and purpose of any long distance calls made by Compudata or its officers, employees or agents to any person within the State of West York during the past six years.

ANSWER: Defendant acknowledges that some such calls have been made. However, defendant has not kept records of such calls and cannot reasonably provide the detailed facts sought by this interrogatory.

16. Please give the dates of any presence within the State of West York of any officer, director or employee of Compudata within the past six years, identifying the officer, director or agent and stating the purpose of his presence.

ANSWER: Defendant has attached as Exhibit F, various documents indicating the presence of employees of Compudata in West York prior to the service of the complaint.

The trips indicated in this exhibit were made to lend sales support to plaintiff or to conduct sales effort directly. The present and former employees of Compudata who have visited West York at least once in the six years prior to the date of service of the instant complaint are listed on Exhibit G hereto. These temporary visits were either to conduct sales calls, to demonstrate equipment or to repair or maintain products. At no time during this period was any officer or employee resident in West York. Since approximately July, 2004, Mr. Donald Gaines, who is a resident of West York, has been a director of Compudata. Specific details of activities or trips which may have involved officers, employees or directors being present in West York may be ascertainable from the correspondence made available to plaintiff in the answer to interrogatory number 11.

. . .

[Signature blanks omitted.]

PLAINTIFF'S MOTION TO COMPEL ANSWERS AND IMPOSE SANCTIONS

IN THE UNITED STATES DISTRICT COURT
FOR THE MIDDLE DISTRICT OF WEST YORK
LONDON DIVISION

GEORGE MILLER COMPANY v. COMPUDATA, INCORPORATED	CIVIL ACTION NO. CA-3-5463-C

PLAINTIFF'S MOTION FOR RELIEF UNDER RULES 26(g) AND 37

Comes now GEORGE MILLER COMPANY, Plaintiff in the above entitled and numbered cause, and moves that relief under Rules 26(g) and 37 be granted it as against Defendant COMPUDATA, INCORPORATED, and would show the Court as follows:

1. Plaintiff heretofore submitted to Compudata sixteen (16) requests for admissions. Defendant Compudata refused without good reason to answer fully seven (7) of these requests for admissions. The unanswered requests for admissions included the following subjects: That the contract between George Miller Company and Compudata was performable in whole or in part within the State of West York; that George Miller Company solicited sales orders for goods to be sold by Compudata within the State of West York with the knowledge and consent of Compudata; that Compudata was doing business within the State of West York; and that Compudata took purposeful advantage of markets within the State of West York.

2. Compudata had no good reason to object to these requests for admissions and its objections amount to a refusal to answer. As to some such requests, Defendant Compudata objected on the ground that it had no personal knowledge (which is not a permissible reason for refusing to admit). In other cases, Defendant simultaneously objected on the ground that various requests "call for a conclusion of law" and also "present a genuine issue for determination by the trier of fact." These objections are ineffective, because it is permissible to request admission of a fact which the jury might otherwise try, and

it is expressly permissible under Rule 36 to request an admission which requires application of a legal standard.

3. Since these requests are not objectionable pursuant to Rule 36(a), the admissions sought were of substantial importance, Defendant Compudata had no reasonable grounds to believe that it might prevail on the matter, and there was no other good reason for the failure to admit, Rule 37(c) provides that the Court "shall" require the opposing party to pay the reasonable expenses incurred in making proof of the matters requested to be admitted, including reasonable attorneys' fees.

4. By virtue of Defendant's conduct, Plaintiff has been required to incur substantial additional expense, in amount equal to at least $5,000.

5. Plaintiff would further show that Defendant refused to answer its interrogatories No. 5, 6, 9 and 19. Defendant's objections were to the effect that Plaintiff's interrogatories were "ambiguous" or "sought a legal conclusion." Such interrogatories are not ambiguous and the objection of "legal conclusion" is invalid under Rule 33(b) as applied to these interrogatories.

WHEREFORE, Plaintiff moves: (1) that requested admissions which Defendant Compudata refused either to admit or deny be taken as admitted; (2) that Plaintiff recover of Defendant Compudata the reasonable expenses incurred in proving the matters sought to be admitted, including reasonable attorneys' fees, in an amount of at least $1,000; and (3) that Defendant Compudata be ordered to answer Plaintiff's interrogatories numbered above.

Respectfully submitted,
McINTOSH & WALKER
By *David Stone*

NOTE ON FACT DEVELOPMENT BY STIPULATION AND AFFIDAVIT

In addition to these discovery materials, David Stone filed *affidavits* from officers of his client, George Miller Company. These affidavits detailed the contractual relationship between the parties, defendant's sales, the visits by defendant's officers to the State, trade shows in West York, and like matters.

Stone also was informed by his client that Compudata had employed a direct employee in the State of West York since the filing of the suit, who maintained a telephone in the name of Compudata in the City of West City, West York. Stone contacted the opposing lawyer, and in lieu of submitting additional interrogatories, negotiated a *stipulation* to the facts about the employee and telephone. A stipulation is an agreement of counsel that certain facts are to be taken as true for purposes of the proceeding.

NOTES AND QUESTIONS ON DISCOVERY AND FACT DEVELOPMENT

(1) *Nature of the Facts to Be Gathered.* How has plaintiff determined what facts to seek to prove — *i.e.*, what cases guided plaintiff's lawyer in deciding what to ask in his request for admissions and interrogatories?

(2) *How Should the Jurisdictional Issue be Decided?* Explain how you think the District Court should rule, and why. Is the answer doubtful? Or is it clearcut?

(3) *Is Defendant in Compliance With Rules 11 and 26?* Rule 11 provides that when an attorney files a pleading (such as this defendant's motion to dismiss), the attorney's

signature constitutes a certification that, to the best of the attorney's "knowledge, information, and belief, formed after an inquiry reasonable under the circumstances," (1) it is not being presented for an improper purpose, such as harassment or delay, (2) the legal claims are warranted by existing law or by a nonfrivolous argument for a change in the law, and (3) the factual claims have evidentiary support or are likely to have evidentiary support after further investigation and discovery. Could defendant's attorney certify properly and in good faith to these matters in the Rule 12 motion? Also, Rule 26 provides an analogous certification for discovery requests or answers. Can the objections and answers of defendant comply with these certifications? (Rules 11 and 26 provide for sanctions in the event of violations, and these issues are further considered in later chapters.)

(4) *Strategy in Drafting and Answering Discovery Requests.* What strategies can you identify with respect to the drafting of the discovery request and answers? (For example, what are the disadvantages of drafting an interrogatory that is very broad and general? One that is very narrow and specific?)

§ E RESOLUTION OF THE FORUM CONTEST

COURT'S ORDER SETTING PRETRIAL HEARING

To: All counsel in No. *CA-3-5463, Geo. Miller Co. v. Compudata*

You are hereby notified that the above titled and numbered cause is set for a pretrial hearing at 9:00 a.m. on May 9, 2007. Attendance of all counsel is mandatory. NONCOMPLIANCE WILL SUBJECT PARTIES AND COUNSEL TO SANCTIONS PROVIDED BY THE FEDERAL RULES OF CIVIL PROCEDURE.

G.R. McKay, United States District Judge . . .

NOTE ON FILING OF PLAINTIFF'S BRIEF

Upon receiving the above order, plaintiff's attorney prepared and filed the brief that follows. While the order did not require a brief (and defendant did not file one), plaintiff concluded that it would be wise to file one.

PLAINTIFF'S BRIEF ON THE JURISDICTIONAL ISSUE

IN THE UNITED STATES DISTRICT COURT
FOR THE MIDDLE DISTRICT OF WEST YORK
LONDON DIVISION

GEORGE MILLER COMPANY v. COMPUDATA, INCORPORATED	CIVIL ACTION NO. CA-3-5463–C

PLAINTIFF'S BRIEF IN OPPOSITION TO MOTION TO DISMISS

Defendant has filed a motion to dismiss and for other relief, alleging that at the time of service Defendant did no business in the State of West York. The Defendant's motion is unfounded. Actually, Plaintiff's claim is for payments due on a contract arising out of Defendant's activities in the forum State, making the case one of specific jurisdiction. Under the constitutional decisions as well as decisions interpreting the West York Long-Arm Statute, Defendant is clearly amenable to service.

I. FACTS CONCERNING JURISDICTION

A. FACTS ADMITTED BY DEFENDANT

Defendant admits that it sold and shipped to purchasers located in West York well in excess of three million dollars worth of goods during the period of the contract between the parties. (The figure is determined from shipping records of Compudata attached to its answer to interrogatory 4.) Further, Compudata currently has a salaried employee, Will Montgomery, in West City. In addition, before service of the complaint, it has had permanent sales representatives located in West York. (Stipulation between counsel; answer to interrogatory 7.)

Defendant also admits that it entered into a contract with Plaintiff and that the attachment to Plaintiff's Complaint is a true copy of this contract (admissions 1-3). This written contract, by its Appendix A, expressly states that Plaintiff is to be the sales representative of Defendant Compudata in West York. The contract refers to Compudata's "products being sold within the confines of the territory outlined in Appendix A" that is, West York and contiguous states (P. 1), "sales within the territory covered by this agreement" (P. 6), and "company products sold in the territory" (P. 7). Thus, the contract forthrightly states that Compudata was selling and intended to sell its goods in West York, and the shipping records show the same thing. The Complaint is for payment under the same Contract, so that the case is one of specific jurisdiction. Complaint, paragraphs 4–14.

Defendant admits that its officers, employees and agents made numerous trips to West York "to conduct sales calls, to demonstrate equipment or to repair or maintain Compudata products" (answer to interrogatory 16). Defendant Compudata has identified 17 of its employees who visited West York during the last six years (attachments to interrogatory 17). Defendant Compudata failed to identify correspondence concerning business with persons located in West York in response to Plaintiff's interrogatories, on the ground that "such correspondence is voluminous." (Answer to interrogatory 11.)

B. PLAINTIFF'S AFFIDAVITS

The affidavits of Bob Wylie and Evans Pitofsky, who are officers of Plaintiff, indicate the vigorous sales efforts that Plaintiff expended on Defendant's behalf and indicate that the sales to West York purchasers were in excess of three million dollars during the period. Furthermore, Bob Wylie's affidavit indicates that Defendant approached Plaintiff at its office in West York, that the contract was negotiated in West York, and that it was signed in West York. They also show that the claims (see Complaint paragraphs 4-14) arise out of the Defendant's contacts with the forum state. (*See* Affidavit of Bob Wylie; Affidavit of Evans Pitofsky.)

C. STIPULATION CONCERNING DEFENDANT'S EMPLOYEE IN WEST YORK

Defendant Compudata has a permanent employee engaged in selling its goods in West York. This employee is permanently residing in West York, works out of an office located in his home, and answers the phone in the name of Defendant. (*See* Stipulation Between Counsel; answer to interrogatory 7.)

II. COMPUDATA IS AMENABLE TO SERVICE IN WEST YORK BECAUSE OF ITS THREE MILLION DOLLARS WORTH OF BUSINESS DONE IN WEST YORK

A. DUE PROCESS REQUIREMENTS ARE CLEARLY MET

These acts of Defendant establish that Defendant has "minimum contacts" with the forum satisfying "traditional notions of fair play and substantial justice." *International Shoe Co. v. Washington,* 326 U.S. 310 (1945). Furthermore, there has been "some act by which the Defendant purposefully avail[ed] itself of the privilege of conducting activities within the forum state" and it could "reasonably anticipate" suit in this forum. *Hanson v. Denckla,* 357 U.S. 235 (1958); *World-Wide Volkswagen Corp. v. Woodson,* 444 U.S. 286 (1980). The case at bar should also be compared to *McGee v. International Life Ins. Co.,* 355 U.S. 220 (1957), in which the Supreme Court held that a single sale of a policy of life insurance made the insurance company amenable to service in a suit brought by the insured in the state where the policy was sold, even though the Defendant insurance company had no other contacts with that forum. This case, like that one, involves specific jurisdiction because the claims and contacts are related, although the contacts here are far more substantial. The case resembles *Burger King Corp. v. Rudzewicz,* 471 U.S. 462 (1985) (upholding jurisdiction in contract case based on contacts less significant than those in this case). This court's jurisdiction is, therefore, consistent with due process.

B. THE WEST YORK LONG-ARM STATUTE AUTHORIZES SERVICE

The West York statute reaches to the limits of due process. *See* West York Civ. Prac. & Rem. C. § 17.041 et seq. Several decisions of the Court of Appeals (following West York state court opinions) have held out-of-state defendants answerable to process served under the West York long-arm statute in fact situations not nearly so strong as those here. One of the more often cited opinions is that by Chief Judge Brown in *Atwood Hatcheries v. Heisdorf & Nelson Farms,* 357 F.2d 847 (5th Cir. 1966). The court unhesitatingly declared that "the legislative purpose [in enacting the long-arm statute] was to exploit to the maximum the fullest permissible reach under Federal Constitutional restraints." 357 F.2d 847 at 852. *See also Eyerly Aircraft Co. v. Killian,* 414 F.2d 591 (5th Cir. 1969); *Coulter v. Sears, Roebuck and Co.,* 426 F.2d 1315 (5th Cir. 1970); *Jim Fox Enterprises, Inc. v. Air France,* 664 F.2d 63 (5th Cir. 1981).

III. CONCLUSION

Defendant's Motion to Dismiss should be overruled.

Respectfully submitted,
McINTOSH & WALKER
By: *David Stone*

NOTE ON COURT'S RULING ON THE FORUM CONTEST

At the pretrial hearing, after short remarks by both counsel, Judge McKay orally overruled the Motion to Dismiss. (As sometimes happens, this ruling was never memorialized in any written document.) Plaintiff's attorney then sent the following letter to his client:

Bob Wylie
Evans Pitofsky
George Miller Company
2018 Kennedy Parkway, Suite 706
London, West York 75260

Re: *George Miller Company v. Compudata, Incorporated*

Dear Bob and Evans:

The Motion of Compudata to dismiss this case on grounds of lack of jurisdiction was overruled today. We will be able to proceed with the case in West York. The judge has set the case for trial in September. I'll keep you posted.

We now have a great deal of work to do. The case has only started. We need to go through all of our records carefully, obtain Compudata's records, take depositions of a number of Compudata personnel, and prepare our case for trial. As I have explained to you, prevailing on the merits of our case will be much more difficult, in this particular instance, than the jurisdictional issue.

Best regards to both of you.

Sincerely yours,
David Stone

NOTES AND QUESTIONS ON THE FORUM CONTEST

(1) *The 28 U.S.C. § 1404(a) Transfer Provision: A Better Argument?* Might defendant have done better by moving for transfer of venue to Texafornia under 28 U.S.C. § 1404(a)? For example, defendant could have filed a motion reading, in pertinent part, as follows:

. . . MOTION FOR TRANSFER PURSUANT TO 1404(a)

Defendant moves the court to transfer this action to the District of Texafornia, for the convenience of parties and witnesses, for the following reasons:

1. At trial, defendant will be required to call numerous witnesses and introduce numerous documents that are located in the State of Texafornia to show the course of dealings between the parties.

2. Defendant will be required to call witnesses affiliated with other representatives in other States to show how the Agreement has been customarily interpreted. All representatives have close contact with the Texafornia headquarters of Defendant, but few if any have any connection with West York . . . .

Defendants making special appearances sometimes neglect the transfer provision. It should be an alternative argument in most forum contests. Would it have been a better argument here?

(2) *Plaintiff's Brief: Identification of the Issue; Governing Legal Principles; Analysis of the Facts; Conclusion.* Good legal argument (at least when the law is reasonably well established) often begins with the identification of the issue and statement of the legal rule(s) that govern. Analysis of the facts is next, followed by a conclusion. Indeed, this issue-rule-analysis-conclusion methodology is often advocated as a means of answering law school exam questions. Notice that plaintiff's brief contains these elements, but it puts the facts before the law. Why? [Note: Are the facts particularly persuasive?]

§ F THE MERITS: ANSWER AND SETTLEMENT

DEFENDANT'S ANSWER ON THE MERITS

IN THE UNITED STATES DISTRICT COURT
FOR THE MIDDLE DISTRICT OF WEST YORK
LONDON DIVISION

GEORGE MILLER COMPANY v. COMPUDATA, INCORPORATED	CIVIL ACTION NO. CA-3-5463-C

ANSWER

Defendant Compudata Incorporated, for reply to Complaint filed by plaintiff, George Miller Company, says:

FIRST DEFENSE

1. Defendant is without knowledge or information sufficient to form a belief as to whether plaintiff is incorporated under the laws of the State of West York and has its principal place of business in Manero County, West York. Defendant admits that it is a corporation incorporated under the laws of, and having its principal place of business in, a State other than the State of West York. Defendant admits that the amount in controversy exceeds the sum of seventy-five thousand dollars.

2. Defendant admits that it is not registered to do business within the State of West York and that its address is 6108 Eureka, Ann Arbor, Texafornia 94304. Defendant denies the remaining allegations contained in paragraph 2 of the Complaint.

3. Defendant is without knowledge or information sufficient to form a belief as to whether all plaintiffs reside in this district. Defendant denies all other allegations of paragraph 3 of the Complaint.

4. Defendant admits that on or about May 1, 2002, plaintiff and defendant entered into a written contract, a copy of which is attached to the Complaint labeled Exhibit "A." Defendant denies all the remaining allegations of paragraph 4 of the Complaint.

5. Defendant denies the allegations contained in paragraph 5 of the Complaint.

6. Defendant admits the allegations contained in the first sentence of paragraph 6 of the Complaint. Defendant denies all the remaining allegations contained in paragraph 6 of the Complaint.

7. Defendant admits that it has failed and refused, and does fail and refuse, to pay any sums which may be claimed by plaintiff to be due and owing as commissions, in excess of payments actually made by defendant. Defendant denies all the remaining allegations in paragraph 7 of the Complaint.

8. Defendant denies the allegations contained in the last sentence of paragraph 8 of the Complaint, and admits the balance of the allegations contained in paragraph 8 of the Complaint.

9. Defendant admits that it has refused to pay plaintiff commissions by applying the declining schedule independently to each successive one-year period, and that it has computed and paid commissions by aggregating sales to each individual customer account over the entire period of plaintiff's representation of defendant and then applying the declining commission schedule cumulatively to the resulting aggregate. Defendant denies the remaining allegations contained in paragraph 9 of the Complaint.

10. Defendant denies the allegations contained in paragraph 10 of the Complaint.

11. For reply to the allegations contained in paragraph 11 of the Complaint, defendant hereby incorporates by reference each and every denial and statement contained in paragraphs 1 through 10 hereof, and realleges same as though fully set out at this point.

12. Defendant denies the allegations contained in paragraph 12 of the Complaint.

13. Defendant denies the allegations contained in paragraph 13 of the Complaint.

14. Defendant denies the allegations contained in paragraph 14 of the Complaint.

SECOND DEFENSE

15. As another and further defense, Defendant asserts the applicable statutes of limitations as to any payments alleged by Plaintiff to be due it from Defendant and allegedly accruing more than two years, or, in the alternative, more than four years, before the date of commencement of this action.

WHEREFORE, defendant prays that plaintiff take nothing against it and that defendant have judgment for its costs.

Respectfully submitted,
WILLIAMS, BEELER & GERSHON
By: *Arnold A. Gershon*

SETTLEMENT: RELEASE AND AGREEMENT

KNOW ALL PERSONS BY THESE PRESENTS:

1. *Consideration and Mutual General Release.* That for and in consideration of the sum of fifteen thousand dollars ($15,000.00) cash paid by Compudata, Inc., the receipt and sufficiency of which is hereby acknowledged and agreed to, and for and in consideration of the dismissal with prejudice by George Miller Company hereinafter referred to, George Miller Company and Compudata, Inc., do hereby compromise, settle and fully release and forever discharge each other and each other's successors and assigns, and each other's related corporations, partnerships, or business entities, through or with which each, respectively, does business, and also all of each other's present and past officers, directors, employees, representatives, and agents, of and from any and all claims, demands, controversies, contracts, actions or causes of action which either has held or may now or in the future own or hold, or which the heirs, executors, assigns, successors or administrators of either hereafter can, shall or may have, own or hold, for or by any reason for any matter, cause or thing whatsoever occurring or existing prior to the date of this agreement, whether or not now known, including but not limited to any and all claims, demands, controversies, contracts, actions or causes of action alleged in Civil Action No. 3-5463-C, styled *George Miller Company v. Compudata, Inc.*, filed in the United States District Court of the Middle District of West York, or which could have been asserted therein by amendment, counterclaim or other addition.

2. *Agreed Dismissal With Prejudice.* For the aforesaid consideration, George Miller Company agrees to entry of an order in the above-numbered civil action, styled as set forth above, dismissing with prejudice all of the claims, rights and causes of action therein asserted.

3. *No Admission of Liability; Contract, Not Recitals.* It is understood that this settlement agreement is a compromise of a doubtful and disputed claim, and that the payment is not to be construed as an admission of liability on the part of the parties hereby released, by each of whom liability is expressly denied. It is further understood that the terms of this release are contractual and not mere recitals.

4. *No Reliance on Released Parties; Acknowledgement.* In making this agreement and granting this release, the parties hereto acknowledge that they have not relied upon any statement or representation pertaining to this matter made by the parties who are hereby released, or by any person or persons representing them. The signatories further acknowledge that they have carefully read the foregoing release, have consulted with their attorneys concerning the same, know the contents thereof and have signed the same as their own free acts.

WITNESS OUR HANDS THIS 4th day of December, 2007.

GEORGE MILLER COMPANY
By: *Robert E. Wylie*
COMPUDATA, INC.
By: *Andrea G. Dysart*

[The release also contained (1) notarized acknowledgements of the signatures of the parties and (2) signatures of both parties' lawyers approving the release.]

CHAPTER 3

SUBJECT-MATTER JURISDICTION: POWER OVER THE GENERIC TYPE OF DISPUTE

§ 3.01 The Concept of Subject-Matter Jurisdiction

Imagine that you have just been served as defendant in a suit in small claims court. The summons has been properly served, and the complaint has been drafted according to the rules. But when you look at the amount of damages demanded, you notice to your surprise that it exceeds one million dollars.

A Suit for $1 Million in Small Claims Court? In addition to your dismay at being sued in the first place, you legitimately may have strong feelings against being sued for this amount in this particular court. A small claims court has streamlined procedures for pleading, discovery, and trial. It is not equipped to handle large or sophisticated disputes. The state simply has not authorized small claims courts to make binding orders in million-dollar suits. This is the concept of "subject-matter jurisdiction."

The Different Determinants of Subject-Matter Jurisdiction. Briefly defined, subject-matter jurisdiction is the court's power to act with respect to the generic type of dispute before the court in the posture in which it has been filed. The amount in controversy is a typical determinant of subject-matter jurisdiction, but there are many others. For example, a federal court has jurisdiction to hear claims arising under federal law. (Usually these claims may also be brought in state court: the courts have "concurrent" subject-matter jurisdiction.) Or subject-matter jurisdiction may be based upon the relationship between the parties, such as the federal courts' jurisdiction over diversity cases. In this chapter, we will address these concepts. Because the state courts have wider jurisdiction than do federal courts, it is with the state courts that we begin, and, as examples, we describe, very briefly, the court systems of California, Texas and New York, with a case about each. First, however, we offer the following "Chapter Summary Problem," which you may read now, but answer at the end of the chapter (or, you should treat it as your instructor tells you).

PROBLEM A:
CHAPTER 3 SUMMARY PROBLEM

SMITH v. HERALD NEWSPAPER COMPANY: A PROBLEM IMPLICATING DIVERSITY, FEDERAL QUESTION, SUPPLEMENTAL AND REMOVAL JURISDICTION. John Smith was a candidate for the West York State legislature. He submitted an advertisement to the Herald Newspaper, advising voters that he was "*not* in favor of increasing the state income tax." Unfortunately, the Herald inadvertently omitted the word "not," so that the advertisement boldly proclaimed that Smith *was* "in favor of increasing the state income tax."

Smith therefore has filed an action in state court against the Herald Newspaper Company. He has stated one claim, for common law libel. The potential application of this claim is affected by the federal Constitution. *See, e.g., New York Times Co. v. Sullivan*, 376 U.S. 254 (1964) (U.S. Const. Amend. I requires a "federal rule that prohibits a public [figure] from recovering damages for defamatory falsehood [u]nless he proves" defendant's knowledge or reckless disregard of falsity). The complaint therefore contains the following allegations, among others:

> In order to comply with the First Amendment to the United States Constitution, plaintiff is required by federal decisions to prove, and plaintiff hereby does allege, that defendant acted with knowledge of the falsity of the publication, or with reckless disregard of whether it was true or false.

Plaintiff Smith is a citizen of West York. Defendant Newspaper Company is a corporation incorporated in Delaware; it owns and operates newspaper businesses throughout the nation, the largest being in West York, and it has its headquarters in California. The newspaper company has concluded that Smith's claim is unmeritorious because Smith actually approved the advertisement copy (apparently he did not notice the error either), and it plans to counterclaim for the unpaid price of the advertisement in the amount of $10,251.57.

The Newspaper Company wishes to remove the action from state to federal court. Consider the following questions:

1. Does diversity jurisdiction provide a basis?
2. Does federal question jurisdiction provide a basis?
3. Is there a basis for jurisdiction of the counterclaim?
4. Can defendant properly remove?

§ 3.02 State Courts' Subject-Matter Jurisdiction

[A] The Allocation of Jurisdiction Within State Court Systems

NOTE ON THE CALIFORNIA TRIAL COURT SYSTEM

California has achieved a system of trial court unification that leaves only a single trial court (the superior court) with full subject-matter jurisdiction.

California's Trial Courts: The Superior Courts. Before 1998 California had a two-tier trial court system. Each county had a superior court with at least one judge and broad subject matter jurisdiction; and each county had at least one municipal court with limited subject matter jurisdiction. Sometimes jurisdiction was unclear, and sometimes counsel made errors by filing in the wrong courts, and there was a body of decisions that considered these issues. The result was wasteful use of judicial resources. In 1998 California's voters approved a state constitutional amendment that authorized the superior and municipal court judges of each county to unify the trial courts on a county-by-county basis. The legislature added financial incentives to promote unification. As a result, each county's judges have approved trial court unification.

Trial court unification eliminates the municipal courts as separate bodies; each county has or will have only a single unified superior court as the trial court. Nevertheless, many of the distinctive features of the limited jurisdiction municipal courts remain. Cases reflecting the broad jurisdiction of the superior courts are referred to as "unlimited civil cases." Cal. Code Civ. Pro. § 88. Cases previously assigned to the municipal courts — primarily those in which the amount in controversy is $25,000 or less — are now referred to as "limited civil cases." Cal. Code Civ. Pro. § 86. Special discovery rules and rules of court previously governing municipal court cases now govern "limited civil cases." Cal. Rules Ct., Rule 709.

Specialized subject-matter: Different Departments or Divisions of the Unified Superior Court. References to a California "family law court," "probate court," "juvenile court," or the like do not indicate an additional set of trial courts. They merely refer to departments of the superior court that hear cases in these areas for administrative convenience. Superior court judges typically rotate through these departments for limited periods of time. Likewise, "small claims courts" are simply specialized divisions of the municipal courts. Cal. Code Civ. Pro. § 87(a). They operate with simplified procedures, including no representation by counsel, no juries, and no discovery. The maximum amount in controversy is limited to $5,000. *Id.* § 116.220(a)(1).

But the Size of the Case Still Matters: Different Procedures Apply to "Limited" (Small) Civil Cases. Under the unified superior court system, all civil cases not within the exclusive jurisdiction of the federal courts or other non-judicial tribunals are brought in superior court. However, it still matters whether the case is classified as a limited civil case or not. The caption must state that the case is a limited civil case. Cal. Code Civ. Pro. § 422.30(b). Different filing fees may apply; different discovery and trial testimony rules may be invoked; and a different appeals system applies to limited civil cases. The remedy for misclassifying an action as a limited civil case is a motion for reclassification by the opposing party (or the court on its own motion) and payment of new fees (if higher). Cal. Code Civ. Pro. §§ 403.010–403.090.

LEKSE v. MUNICIPAL COURT, 138 Cal. App. 3d 188, 187 Cal. Rptr. 698 (1982). A landlord filed two separate actions against a tenant for unpaid past due rent, covering two separate months. The actions were both filed in the Small Claims Department. Each of the actions, taken separately, was for an amount within the Small Claims jurisdiction, but if the amounts had been claimed in a single suit, they would have exceeded its jurisdiction. The tenant made no appearance, and the court granted default judgment in both suits. The tenant then retained counsel, who moved to quash efforts to enforce the judgments on the ground that the amount in controversy exceeded the jurisdictional limits of the small claims department. The court denied the motion. Ultimately, the Court of Appeal reversed and held that the Small Claims procedure did not apply.

The landlord contended that it was within the discretion of the court not to consolidate the two claims and that the tenant had waived any error in their separation by failing to appear or object. The court disagreed:

> Our Supreme Court has explained that "[t]he theory behind [the Small Claims Department's] organization is that only by escaping from the complexity and delay of the normal course of litigation could anything be gained in a legal proceeding which may involve a small sum. . . . The chief characteristics of its proceedings are that there are no attorneys, no pleadings and no legal rules of evidence" [citing *Sanderson v. Niemann*, 17 Cal. 2d 563, 110 P.2d 1025 (1941)]. . . .

> . . . [A] lay litigant should not have been expected to move the Municipal Court to consolidate the two separate complaints. . . .

The Court then concluded that the two amounts must be added together to determine the amount in controversy. The amount in controversy thus exceeded the power of the Small Claims Department; the consolidated action should have proceeded in the proper system.

NOTE ON THE TEXAS COURT SYSTEM

District, County Level, and Justice Courts. The District Courts are the primary Texas trial courts, and are constitutional courts of general jurisdiction. Tex. Const. Art. 5, § 8; *see also* Tex. Gov. Code §§ 24.007, 24.008, 24.011. As a result of a complex statutory scheme, district courts generally have original civil jurisdiction of cases of divorce, suits for title to land or enforcement of liens on land, election contests, defamation suits, and all civil matters when the amount in controversy is in excess of $500. District Courts share probate and eminent domain jurisdiction with County Level Courts on a county-by-county basis. The County Level Courts are intermediate trial courts which have civil jurisdiction when the amount in controversy exceeds $200 and does not exceed an upper jurisdictional limit provided by statute. This limit is not uniform for County Level Courts and it may vary from five thousand dollars up to $100,000, or more, depending upon the county. Justice Courts have exclusive jurisdiction of civil cases when the amount in controversy does not exceed $200 and concurrent jurisdiction with County Level and District Courts through $10,000. (Notice that this jurisdictional scheme means that in some cases, two courts have concurrent jurisdiction; in fact, in some cases all three do.) The Justice courts also function as Small Claims courts. Appeals from these courts are by trial *de novo* in the County Level courts and in some counties in the District Courts. Appeals from District and County Level Courts are to the Courts of Appeals. The state's highest civil court is the Texas Supreme Court. *See* Dorsaneo, Crump, Carlson & Thornburg, *Texas Civil Procedure: Pre-Trial Litigation*, Ch. 3 (2007–08 ed.).

CONTINENTAL COFFEE PRODUCTS CO. v. CASAREZ, 937 S.W.2d 444 (Tex. 1996). The plaintiff sued her former employer in a county-court-at-law, which had a jurisdictional limit of $100,000. The plaintiff's original petition sought actual damages of $100,000, but seven months after she filed her original petition, the plaintiff amended her pleadings and claimed actual damages of $250,000, which had accumulated since filing. The defendants filed a plea to the court's subject matter jurisdiction, which the trial court denied. Both the court of appeals and the Texas Supreme Court affirmed the trial court's judgment awarding the plaintiff $150,000 in actual damages. The Texas Supreme Court ruled that the trial court had jurisdiction to render judgment for an amount in excess of the court's jurisdictional limits, and did not err in overruling the plea to the jurisdiction, under the principle that "[i]f a plaintiff's original petition is properly brought in a particular court, but an amendment increases the amount in controversy above the court's jurisdictional limits, the court will continue to have jurisdiction if the additional damages accrued because of the passage of time." At the hearing on the plea to the jurisdiction plaintiff testified regarding her state of mind and the way she felt about the defendants, as follows: "[i]t's getting worser [sic], every day."

NOTES AND QUESTIONS

(1) *Figuring the Amount in Controversy.* In state courts, the most frequent determinant of subject-matter jurisdiction is the amount in controversy. Ordinarily the amount is not

difficult to compute, although there can be some ambiguous cases. For example, what if the plaintiff actually recovers less than he pleaded for and less than the jurisdictional limit of the court? If he has made his claim in good faith, most jurisdictions accept this figure; it is the amount "in controversy" that controls. *See, e.g., Rodley v. Curry*, 120 Cal. 541, 543, 52 P. 999, 1000 (1898). What about a non-monetary suit, such as one for an injunction? In that event, valuing the amount in controversy is more complicated. *See* § 3.03[B][3], below.

(2) *The Policy Issue in State Court Jurisdiction: How to Allocate by Amount in Controversy.* Cases depending on jurisdictional issues are, in a sense, illustrations of judicial waste. And while specialization for big cases and little cases may be advantageous, it becomes disadvantageous if it causes waste. Should there, perhaps, be only one trial court, with the authority to invoke different rules for different kinds of cases? If there are to be "superior" and "inferior" courts, might it not make sense to have more substantial limits than $10,000 (such as $100,000 or even more, *cf.* Texas' limits for some county courts) in the intermediate courts? Consider the following description of the New York court system and the case following it.

NOTE ON THE NEW YORK COURT SYSTEM

The Trial and Appellate Courts in New York. The general trial court in New York is the Supreme Court (which is not "supreme" at all, but is below two levels of appellate courts). N.Y. Const. art. VI. The state has conferred jurisdiction over all types of actions upon this court, with only a few exceptions. *See generally* Chase, 1 *Weinstein, Korn, and Miller, CPLR Manual* § 1.04 (1997); *see also* Siegel, *New York Practice* ch. 2 (2d ed. 1991). The next lowest court is the "County" Court, which has jurisdiction of most claims at law not exceeding $25,000, as well as certain other claims. The County Court does not have jurisdiction over most equitable actions (including most actions for injunctions or declaratory relief). In New York City, there is no County Court; the analogue is the Civil Court of the City of New York, which has divisions in each of the city's five counties and is "one of the largest [courts] in the world." Siegel, *supra*, at 20. There are several specialized courts, including Surrogate's Court (probate jurisdiction), Family Court (jurisdiction over juvenile delinquency, adoption, and support proceedings, but ironically, not matrimonial actions, which must be brought in the Supreme Court), and the Court of Claims (which hears civil actions by or against the state). Finally, there are District, City, Town, Village, and Justice Courts, which have varying civil jurisdiction ranging from a few thousand dollars to as much as $15,000, and some of which have small claims jurisdiction up to $3,000. Appeal from some lower courts is to the Supreme Court. From the Supreme Court, appeal can be taken to the Appellate Division. The state's highest court is the New York Court of Appeals.

Concurrent Jurisdiction and the "Transfer" Procedure. Because (at least in theory) almost every case in New York can be heard by the Supreme Court, there typically is concurrent jurisdiction over smaller claims. However, the state has a strong policy in favor of having a case heard in the lowest court with jurisdiction. This policy is carried out by "removal" or "transfer"; generally, the Supreme Court will "transfer down" a case within the jurisdiction of the county court. Furthermore, N.Y. Const. art. VI § 19 authorizes the legislature to apply the higher court's monetary limits in transferred-down cases. The legislature has implemented this authority in CPLR 325(d), which authorizes the lower court to award relief in a transferred case even if it exceeds by many times its normal jurisdictional limits. Siegel, *supra*, at 26. In some parts of the state, this provision has effectively removed the upper limits of the County (or New York City Civil) Courts. Consider the following case.

DENNER v. KATZ, 347 N.Y.S.2d 365, 75 Misc. 2d 51 (N.Y.C. Civ. Ct. 1973). The plaintiff sued on two claims based on a separation agreement. One claim prayed for a decree requiring the defendant to "specifically perform" his contractual obligation to provide plaintiff with a $50,000 insurance policy on his life. The other claim sought monetary relief in the form of attorney's fees expended in enforcing the agreement. Because the specific performance claim was classified as a suit for equitable relief, it was within the jurisdiction only of the Supreme Court, and the plaintiff filed suit there. The parties waived a jury, and the Supreme Court judge ordered a non-jury trial; however, he later struck the case from the trial calendar and transferred it down to the Civil Court of the City of New York. The defendant then moved (1) for a transfer of the action back up to the Supreme Court or (2) in the alternative, for a trial by jury.

The defendant first argued that since the complaint had sought equitable relief, which the lower court lacked jurisdiction to grant, the case should be transferred up. The judge noted, however, that the insurance policy had been delivered to the plaintiff; the claim for performance of that obligation was now moot, and since the only remaining claim was for monetary relief, the civil court could grant it (and indeed could do so today even if it exceeded its ordinary jurisdictional limits). The defendant pointed out, however, that the second claim sought attorney's fees allegedly incurred in bringing the equitable claim, and therefore he argued that it too was "equitable" in nature and outside the court's jurisdiction. The court rejected this argument: "[S]o long as the final judgment requested is for money damages only, I am of the opinion that this Court has complete jurisdiction over the transferred action."

The court also denied the motion to allow a jury trial. "The waiver in this case was specifically made in connection with the transfer of the action, and I feel bound by the 'Order of Transfer' signed by [the Supreme Court judge] which states the action was to be placed on this Court's calendar for trial without a jury."

The court then addressed what it saw as the disadvantages of a fragmented system of court organization:

> I am sure this motion is but a forerunner of many like applications that will be made to this Court requiring the use of precious time needed so urgently on other matters. [T]he transfer of approximately two hundred cases weekly from the Supreme Court to the Civil Court and the necessary clerical help and paper work required to effect such transfers, point up quietly but dramatically the need for the creation of one unified trial court with unlimited general and equitable jurisdiction.
>
> The wholly artificial and arbitrary division of our court system into upper courts of general jurisdiction and lower courts of limited jurisdiction is archaic and defies every principle of efficient court management. The waste of non-judicial personnel is appalling. . . . The use of judicial manpower is at best uneven with many judges overburdened and many others underutilized. . . . Under one Court the simple assignment of judges by the Administrator to those areas and parts where and when needed would eliminate the costly and wasteful procedures now being employed.
>
> In 1971 the National Conference on the Judiciary in its Consensus Statement said,
>
>> There should be only one level of trial court, divided into districts of manageable size. It should possess general jurisdiction, but be organized into specialized

departments for the handling of particular kinds of litigation. Separate specialized courts should be abolished.

. . . [E]quity and efficient management demand such action by the legislature which will in one stroke truly effect reform in our much libeled court system.

NOTES AND QUESTIONS

(1) *"Unified" or "Specialized" Courts?* Is the Civil Court judge right? Should we abolish Probate Courts, Justice Courts, Small Claims Courts, Family Courts, Superior Courts, and Municipal Courts, and have a single court to which judges could be flexibly assigned? A given court could be designated, say, to give preference to probate matters, but it would not lack jurisdiction over any case properly within the judicial power. Or is it better to have distinct courts to ensure (for example) that small claims procedures are not abusively followed in a bigger case?

(2) *The Impact of Jurisdiction and Transfer on Other Procedures.* Another, more subtle, issue is presented here. The lower court judge feels bound by an order entered by the judge of the Supreme Court, although if the Supreme Court judge himself had been confronted with the question, he might have granted the jury trial request by modifying his earlier order. The movant thus may have been deprived of an opportunity to have this order reconsidered. Transfer of a case sometimes creates confusion, conflict, or other side effects of this kind.

(3) *New York's Court Unification Amendment.* In 1986, the New York Legislature voted favorably on a proposed amendment to the State Constitution that would merge all of the trial courts into the Supreme Court (except the Town, Village and Justice Courts, to which the Legislature could grant jurisdiction over actions seeking up to $15,000 as well as some miscellaneous proceedings such as evictions). However, because this proposal requires amendment of the State Constitution, it must be adopted in two successive legislative sessions and ratified by a referendum, in accordance with the procedure for amending the New York Constitution. The measure died when the Legislature failed to pass it for a second time.

[B] Federal Claims and Defenses in State Courts

INTRODUCTORY NOTE

Concurrent State and Federal Jurisdiction. Students occasionally assume, erroneously, that the existence of federal jurisdiction means that state courts are ousted of jurisdiction. On the contrary, there is concurrent state jurisdiction of most federal claims. For example, if the parties are of diverse citizenship and the amount in controversy exceeds $75,000, a suit ordinarily can be brought in either state or federal court. A suit under the federal civil rights laws can generally be brought in federal court, but there is no reason why it cannot instead be brought in state court if the plaintiff chooses. *See* Gordon, *Justiciability of Federal Claims in State Court*, 59 Notre Dame L. Rev. 1145 (1985).

State Judges' Ability and Duty to Apply Federal Law. The truth of the matter is that it is commonplace for state judges to decide federal questions. It is sometimes assumed that a state judge will be less likely than her federal counterpart to enforce federal law accurately, but whatever the merits of this proposition as a generalization about state and federal courts, it is unwarranted to assume that any individual state judge will not accurately enforce federal law. State judges have had legal educations similar to those of their federal counterparts. Likewise, most federal and state judges have had law practices exposing them to both federal and state law. In fact, might not there be some state trial judges who would read federal law more expansively than some federal judges? Consider the following case.

TESTA v. KATT
330 U.S. 386 (1947)

MR. JUSTICE BLACK delivered the opinion of the Court.

Section 205(e) of the Emergency Price Control Act provides that a buyer of goods at above the prescribed ceiling price may sue the seller "in any court of competent jurisdiction" for not more than three times the amount of the overcharge plus costs and a reasonable attorney's fee. Section 205(c) provides that federal district courts shall have jurisdiction of such suits "concurrently with State and Territorial courts." . . .

The respondent was in the automobile business in Providence, Providence County, Rhode Island. In 1944 he sold an automobile to petitioner Testa, who also resides in Providence, for $1,100, $210 above the ceiling price. The petitioner later filed this suit against respondent in the State District Court in Providence. Recovery was sought under § 205(e). The court awarded a judgment of treble damages and costs to petitioner. On appeal to the State Superior Court, where the trial was *de novo*, the petitioner was again awarded judgment, but only for the amount of the overcharge plus attorney's fees. . . . On appeal, the State Supreme Court reversed, 71 R.I. 472, 47 A.2d 312. It interpreted § 205(e) to be "a penal statute in the international sense." [Eds. Note: A "penal" statute is one that provides a "penalty," unlike a private cause of action; foreign courts often refuse to enforce such laws.] It held that an action for violation of § 205(e) could not be maintained in the courts of that State. . . .

For the purposes of this case, we assume, without deciding, that § 205(e) is a penal statute in the "public international," "private international," or any other sense. So far as the question of whether the Rhode Island courts properly declined to try this action, it makes no difference into which of these categories the Rhode Island court chose to place the statute which Congress has passed. For we cannot accept the basic premise on which the Rhode Island Supreme Court held that it has no more obligation to enforce a valid penal law of the United States than it has to enforce a penal law of another state or a foreign country. Such a broad assumption flies in the face of the fact that the States of the Union constitute a nation. It disregards the purpose and effect of Article VI of the Constitution which provides: "This Constitution, and the Laws of the United States which shall be made in Pursuance thereof; and all Treaties made, or which shall be made, under the Authority of the United States, shall be the supreme Law of the Land; and the Judges in every State shall be bound thereby, any Thing in the Constitution or Laws of any State to the Contrary notwithstanding."

It cannot be assumed, the supremacy clause considered, that the responsibilities of a state to enforce the laws of a sister state are identical with its responsibilities to enforce federal laws. . . . The first Congress that convened after the Constitution was adopted conferred jurisdiction upon the state courts to enforce important federal civil laws, and succeeding Congresses conferred on the states jurisdiction over federal crimes and actions for penalties and forfeitures.

Enforcement of federal laws by state courts did not go unchallenged. Violent public controversies existed throughout the first part of the Nineteenth Century until the 1860's concerning the extent of the constitutional supremacy of the Federal Government. . . . But after the fundamental issues over the extent of federal supremacy had been resolved by war, this Court took occasion in 1876 to review the phase of the controversy concerning the relationship of state courts to the Federal Government. *Claflin v. Houseman*, 93 U.S. 130. The opinion of a unanimous court in that case was strongly buttressed by historic references and persuasive reasoning. . . . And the Court stated that "If an act of Congress gives a penalty to a party aggrieved, without specifying a remedy for its enforcement, there is no reason why it should not be enforced, if not provided otherwise by some act of Congress, by a proper action in a State court." . . .

Reversed.

NOTES AND QUESTIONS

(1) *Plaintiff's and Defendant's Choice in Testa v. Katt.* If the plaintiff, Testa, had wanted to, he could have filed his suit in a federal court. His lawyer apparently felt the state court would more likely view his claim with favor, or preferred state procedures, or had some other reason. Likewise, the defendant, Katt, could have removed the case to federal court but did not do so. State courts are frequently the choice of both parties.

(2) *Exclusive Federal Jurisdiction.* There are some kinds of claims for which Congress has provided that the federal courts' jurisdiction is exclusive. For example, actions brought under the federal patent or copyright laws must be brought in the federal courts. 28 U.S.C. § 1338(a) (exclusive jurisdiction). Other examples include actions under the federal bankruptcy laws, actions against consuls of foreign states, and actions to enforce fines, penalties or forfeitures under the laws of the United States.

(3) *Exclusive State Jurisdiction Over Federal Issues.* It may surprise you to learn that when the federal Constitution is invoked as a defense to a state-law claim between citizens of the same state, there is no federal jurisdiction. The state court is the exclusive forum. Consider the following section.

§ 3.03 Federal Subject-Matter Jurisdiction

[A] Federal Question ("Arising Under") Jurisdiction

Read 28 U.S.C. § 1331 (the "arising under" jurisdiction statute); also, read U.S. Const. art. III, § 2 (the constitutional "arising under" provision).

BELL v. HOOD, 327 U.S. 678 (1946). The plaintiffs alleged that agents of the Federal Bureau of Investigation had wrongfully imprisoned them and subjected them to unreasonable searches and seizures. They asserted claims for damages under the Fourth and Fifth Amendments to the federal Constitution. There was no Supreme Court authority recognizing this type of claim for damages. The district court dismissed for lack of jurisdiction, holding that the claim was not one "arising under" federal law as the jurisdictional statute required.

The Supreme Court reversed, holding that the district court must decide the case on the merits. "[P]etitioners seek recovery squarely on the ground that respondents violated the Fourth and Fifth Amendments. . . . It cannot be doubted that it was the pleaders' purpose to make violation of these Constitutional provisions the basis of suit." Whether petitioners might ultimately recover was a separate question: "If the court does later exercise its jurisdiction to determine that the allegations in the complaint do not state a ground for relief, then dismissal would be on the merits, not for want of jurisdiction." Federal jurisdiction existed because the claim was not frivolous, and "the right of the petitioners to recover under their complaint will be sustained if the Constitution. . . . [is] given one construction and will be defeated if it is given another."

HOW TO READ THE CASE OF *LOUISVILLE & NASHVILLE RR. v. MOTTLEY*

Jurisdiction Requires a Claim Arising Under Federal Law (Not a Federal Defense). The jurisdictional statute at issue, which is now 28 U.S.C. § 1331, provides that federal District Courts have jurisdiction of "all civil actions arising under the Constitution, laws, or treaties of the United States." This deceptively simple language has been interpreted to mean that the plaintiff's claim (and not the defendant's defense) must "arise under" federal law. One classic statement of the law is set out in *Gully v. First National Bank in Meridian*, 299 U.S. 109, 112-13 (1936): "To bring a case within the statute, a right or immunity created by the Constitution or laws of the United States must be an element, and an essential one, of the plaintiff's cause of action." Another, slightly different way of putting it is to require "either that federal law creates the cause of action or that the plaintiff's right to relief necessarily depends on resolution of a substantial question of federal law." *Franchise Tax Board v. Construction Laborers Vacation Trust*, 463 U.S. 1 (1983). In the words of an influential commentator, the plaintiff's claim must be "founded 'directly' on federal law." Mishkin, *The Federal "Question" in the District Courts*, 53 Colum. L. Rev. 157, 168 (1953).

"Federal Question Jurisdiction" Is a Misleading Name. The jurisdiction created by section 1331 is commonly called "federal question" jurisdiction. But this label is a misnomer. It might be better to use the term "arising under" jurisdiction, as some have advocated. The mere presence of a federal question somewhere in a case does not create federal jurisdiction; it must be in the claim. For example, if the plaintiff sues on a contract under state law, and the defendant defends with a federal law defense, there is no federal jurisdiction even though there is an issue of federal law in the case. (Students often find this distinction irrational, and in fact there have been many proposals for change.)

"Anticipation" of a Federal Defense by the Plaintiff Also Does Not Create Federal Jurisdiction. Imagine that a plaintiff includes a paragraph in his complaint anticipating the federal defense: "I realize that defendant is going to say that the federal statutes destroy my state-law claim, but I don't agree with that interpretation of the federal law." Does this artful pleading confer jurisdiction on the federal courts? The answer is "No": Neither the defendant's defense, nor the plaintiff's anticipation of that defense, changes the nature of plaintiff's claim, which still arises under state law. In a nutshell, that is the situation the Supreme Court faced in *Louisville & Nashville RR. v. Mottley.*

PROBLEM B

"ARISING UNDER" JURISDICTION PROBLEMS, IN PREPARATION FOR READING THE MOTTLEY CASE. In each of the following situations, you are required to answer "Yes" or "No" to the question, "Does federal jurisdiction exist?" (Assume that there is no diversity of citizenship.)

(a) *A Contract Claim Under State Law.* Acme Bank sues Joe Blow, alleging that he has failed to pay a promissory note, which he signed upon receiving a loan from the Bank. Does federal jurisdiction exist? [Note: There is nothing in the federal

Constitution, laws, or treaties that says a person has to pay a promissory note. The note is a contract, governed by state law.]

(b) *A Federal Defense to the Contract Claim.* In the same suit by Acme Bank, Defendant Joe Blow files an answer alleging as a defense that he is exonerated from having to pay the promissory note because the loan transaction violated the federal banking laws. Now, is there federal jurisdiction?

(c) *An Initial Complaint That Pleads Federal Law to Avoid the Defense.* Now, imagine that Acme Bank knew about Joe's intended defense when it drew up its complaint. It has included in its initial complaint a paragraph alleging, "Any potential defense by Defendant, relying upon the federal banking laws, is inapplicable to this case." Does this pleading create federal jurisdiction?

(d) *A Complaint for Damages Arising Under Federal Law.* Finally, imagine that instead of the Bank suing Joe, Joe sues the Bank. He claims damages because the Bank allegedly violated the federal banking laws in the loan transaction. Do the federal courts have jurisdiction over Joe's claim?

[*The Answers Are:* a. No; b. No; c. No; and d. Yes. Each of the first three situations involves a state-law claim, and neither the defendant's defense nor the plaintiff's anticipation of that defense can create federal jurisdiction. In the final situation, the plaintiff's claim arises directly under federal law. If you do not understand these answers, reread the text that precedes these problems; if you do understand them, proceed to read *Mottley*.]

LOUISVILLE & NASHVILLE RAILROAD v. MOTTLEY
211 U.S. 149 (1908)

The appellees (husband and wife), being residents and citizens of Kentucky, brought this suit in equity in the Circuit Court of the United States for the Western District of Kentucky against the appellant, a railroad company and a citizen of the same State. The object of the suit was to compel the specific performance of the following contract:

Louisville, Ky., Oct. 2nd, 1871.

> The Louisville & Nashville Railroad Company in consideration that E.L. Mottley and wife, Annie E. Mottley, have this day released Company from all damages or claims for damages for injuries received by them on the 7th of September, 1871, in consequence of a collision of trains on the railroad . . ., hereby agrees to issue free passes on said Railroad . . ., to said E.L. & Annie E. Mottley for the remainder of the present year, and thereafter, to renew said passes annually during the lives of said Mottley and wife or either of them.

The [complaint] alleged that in September, 1871, plaintiffs, while passengers upon the defendant railroad, were injured by the defendant's negligence, and released their respective claims for damages in consideration of the agreement for transportation during their lives, expressed in the contract. It is alleged that the contract was performed by the defendant up to January 1, 1907, when the defendant declined to renew the passes. The [complaint] then alleges that the refusal to comply with the contract was based solely upon that part of the act of Congress of June 29, 1906, 34 Stat. 584, which forbids the giving of free passes or free transportation. The bill further alleges: First, that the act of Congress referred to does not prohibit the giving of passes under the circumstances of this case; and, second, that if the law is to be construed as prohibiting such passes, it is in conflict with the Fifth Amendment of the Constitution, because it deprives the plaintiffs of their property without due process of law. The defendant demurred [i.e., it asserted that plaintiffs could not recover on the complaint under the law.] The judge of the Circuit Court overruled the demurrer, entered a decree for the relief prayed for, and the defendant appealed directly to this court.

MR. JUSTICE MOODY, after making the foregoing statement, delivered the opinion of the court.

Two questions of law were raised by the demurrer. . . . They are, first, whether . . . the act of Congress . . . makes it unlawful to perform a contract for transportation of persons, who in good faith, before the passage of the act, had accepted such contract in satisfaction of a valid cause of action against the railroad; and, second, whether the statute, if it should be construed to render such a contract unlawful, is in violation of the Fifth Amendment of the Constitution of the United States. We do not deem it necessary, however, to consider either of these questions, because, in our opinion, the court below was without jurisdiction of the cause. Neither party has questioned that jurisdiction, but it is the duty of this court to see to it that the jurisdiction of the Circuit Court, which is defined and limited by statute, is not exceeded. This duty we have frequently performed of our own motion. . . .

There was no diversity of citizenship and it is not and cannot be suggested that there was any ground of jurisdiction, except that the case was a "suit . . . arising under the Constitution and laws of the United States." It is the settled interpretation of these words, as used in this statute, conferring jurisdiction, that a suit arises under the Constitution and laws of the United States only when the plaintiff's statement of his own cause of action shows that it is based upon those laws or that Constitution. It is not enough that the plaintiff alleges some anticipated defense to his cause of action and asserts that the defense is invalidated by some provision of the Constitution of the United States. Although such allegations show that very likely, in the course of the litigation, a question under the Constitution would arise, they do not show that the suit, that is, the plaintiff's original cause of action, arises under the Constitution. In *Tennessee v. Union & Planters' Bank*, 152 U.S. 454, the plaintiff, the State of Tennessee, brought suit in the Circuit Court of the United States to recover from the defendant certain taxes alleged to be due under the laws of the State. The plaintiff alleged that the defendant claimed an immunity from the taxation by virtue of its charter, and that therefore the tax was void, because in violation of the provision of the Constitution of the United States, which forbids any State from passing a law impairing the obligation of contracts. The cause was held to be beyond the jurisdiction of the Circuit Court, the court saying, by Mr. Justice Gray, "a suggestion of one party, that the other will or may set up a [defense] under the Constitution or laws of the United States, does not make the suit one arising under that Constitution or those laws." Again, in *Boston & Montana Consolidated Copper & Silver Mining Company v. Montana Ore Purchasing Company*, 188 U.S. 632, the plaintiff brought suit in the Circuit Court of the United States for the conversion of copper ore and for an injunction against its continuance. The plaintiff then alleged, for the purpose of showing jurisdiction, in substance, that the defendant would set up in defense certain laws of the United States. The cause was held to be beyond the jurisdiction of the Circuit Court, the court saying, by Mr. Justice Peckham:

> It would be wholly unnecessary and improper in order to prove complainant's cause of action to go into any matters of defence which the defendants might possibly set up and then attempt to reply to such defence, and thus, if possible, to show that a Federal question might or probably would arise in the course of the trial of the case. . . .

> Conforming itself to that rule the complainant would not, in the assertion or proof of its cause of action, bring up a single Federal question. The presentation of its cause of action would not show that it was one arising under the Constitution or laws of the United States.
>
> . . . The application of this rule to the case at bar is decisive against the jurisdiction of the Circuit Court.

It is ordered that the judgment be reversed and the case remitted to the Circuit Court with instructions to dismiss the suit for want of jurisdiction.

NOTES AND QUESTIONS

(1) *What Happens Next in the Mottleys' Dispute with the Railroad?* The Supreme Court's decision did not extinguish the Mottleys' claim. After dismissal of their federal suit, the Mottleys brought suit in a Kentucky state court. As could be expected, the Railroad asserted its defense based on the federal statute. The state trial court held for the Mottleys. The Kentucky Supreme Court affirmed. But then the United States Supreme Court accepted the case for review a second time — and held for the Railroad. The Mottleys recovered nothing. *Louisville & Nashville RR. v. Mottley*, 219 U.S. 467 (1911).

(2) *The "Well Pleaded Complaint" Rule: "Claim" or "Defense"?* The *Mottley* case is said to exemplify the "well pleaded complaint" rule: the claim asserted in the plaintiff's well pleaded complaint (meaning a complaint pleaded without anticipation of purely defensive matter) must be founded in federal law.

(3) *Ambiguity in the Jurisdictional Rules: "Claim" or "Defense"?* The trouble is that sometimes the law does not fit into these neat compartments; it may be that a principle of law has a recognized impact upon the claim but has not been clearly categorized as part of the claim or as part of the defense. Furthermore, there can be instances in which federal legislation affecting a state-law claim is not merely a defense, but is so pervasive that the entire area of law is inherently "federalized" — and then, federal question jurisdiction may be applicable. *E.g., Avco Corp. v. Aero Lodge No. 735*, 390 U.S. 557 (1968) (state court action to enforce labor contract removable because federal labor laws pervade field so completely as to federalize state contract law); *Metropolitan Life Insurance Co. v. Taylor*, 481 U.S. 58 (1987) (extending *Avco* rule to common law contract and tort claims seeking recovery of benefits under an employee benefit plan regulated by the Employee Retirement Income Security Act of 1974 [ERISA]). *Cf.* Hirshman, *Whose Law Is It, Anyway? A Reconsideration of Federal Question Jurisdiction Over Cases of Mixed State and Federal Law*, 60 Ind. L.J. 17 (1985).

(4) *Different Tests for a Federal "Claim": Franchise Tax Bd. v. Construction Laborers Vacation Trust, 463 U.S. 1 (1983).* In this case, the Court articulated two tests for "arising under" jurisdiction: "Either that federal law creates the cause of action [sometimes called the 'creation' test] or that the plaintiff's right to relief necessarily depends upon resolution of a substantial issue of federal law [the 'dependency test']." It has also been suggested that the cases in this area, although confusing, can be reconciled by the following test: "In short, there is federal question jurisdiction if a proposition of federal law is inherent in plaintiff's claim." *Wheeldin v. Wheeler,* 373 U.S. 647 (1963) (Brennan, J., dissenting). Are these tests useful?

(5) *Declaratory Judgments: Skelly Oil Co. v. Phillips Petroleum Co., 339 U.S. 667 (1950).* Would arising-under jurisdiction have existed if the Railroad in the *Mottley* case had filed a preemptive action for a declaration that it was not obligated to issue the railroad

passes to the Mottleys due to the new federal law? In *Skelly Oil*, Phillips sued in federal court under the federal Declaratory Judgment Act, 28 U.S.C. § 2201, which empowers a court to "declare the rights and other legal relations of any interested party." Specifically, Phillips sought a declaration that certain contracts were in existence and had not been terminated. The validity of an attempted termination by the defendant depended, in turn, upon whether the actions of the Federal Power Commission amounted to issuance of a certificate of public convenience and necessity under federal law. The Court held that there was no jurisdiction. The Declaratory Judgment Act did not create jurisdiction but merely authorized a remedy, and Phillips' claimed rights in the contract were a creature of state law. Whatever federal arguments Phillips might be able to urge based upon the FPC's actions "would in any event be injected into the case only in anticipation of a defense." In a sense, an action seeking a declaratory judgment of non-liability reverses the parties and transforms a "defense" into a "claim." Pursuant to *Skelly Oil*, and reaffirmed in *Franchise Tax Board* in Note 4 above, one of the tests for jurisdiction in an action for federal declaratory relief is examined under a "reciprocal coercive action" test — jurisdiction exists if the declaratory judgment plaintiff seeks to determine its potential liability to a declaratory judgment defendant whose potential claim for coercive relief against the declaratory judgment plaintiff would qualify for arising-under jurisdiction. Accordingly, if the Railroad in *Mottley* had filed a preemptive declaratory judgment action, the jurisdictional outcome would have remained the same.

(6) *Policy: Should the Test for Jurisdiction Be Ambiguous? Should It Be Expanded to Authorize Federal Jurisdiction Based Upon Defenses?* It has been suggested that ambiguity in the definition of federal jurisdiction actually may be advantageous(!), because it allows the courts to consider such policy questions as the workload of the federal courts, the likelihood of disposition on state-law questions, and the need for a federal forum to vindicate the rights at issue. Cohen, *The Broken Compass: The Requirement That a Case Arise "Directly" Under Federal Law*, 115 U. Pa. L. Rev. 890, 916 (1967); *see also Gully v. First National Bank*, 299 U.S. 109 (1936). But shouldn't jurisdictional statutes, like rules of the road, be clear? The waste inherent in ambiguity is illustrated by the two trips the Mottleys made to the Supreme Court.

Another policy issue is whether the denial of jurisdiction to federal defenses is appropriate. A federal law asserted as a defense is presumably of equal dignity, and as much a reflection of federal policy, as a federal law-based claim. Thus the American Law Institute proposed federal jurisdiction over cases involving federal defenses or counterclaims. ALI, *Study of the Division of Jurisdiction Between State and Federal Courts* 178-80 (1969). [But might it make sense to argue that federal claims present a higher likelihood of resolution on federal, rather than state, law grounds since a federal defense becomes relevant only if the state law claim succeeds?]

(7) *Implied Rights of Action.* Another problem stems from federal laws that purport to govern conduct but do not mention claims. In that case, a court may be faced with the question whether an "implied" claim creates federal jurisdiction.

(8) *Implied Claims Under the Constitution: Bivens v. Six Unknown Agents of the Federal Bureau of Narcotics, 403 U.S. 388 (1971).* This case illustrates the interplay between jurisdictional issues and implied rights of action. Justice Brennan's opinion begins:

> . . . Petitioner's complaint alleged that . . . agents of the Federal Bureau of Narcotics . . . entered his apartment and arrested him for alleged narcotics violations. The agents manacled petitioner in front of his wife and children, and threatened to

> arrest the entire family. They searched the apartment from stem to stern. Thereafter, petitioner was . . . interrogated, booked, and subjected to a visual strip search.
>
> . . . [P]etitioner brought suit in Federal District Court. [H]is complaint asserted that the arrest and search were effected without a warrant, and that unreasonable force was employed in making the arrest; fairly read, it alleges as well that the arrest was made without probable cause. [Petitioner sought damages for violation of the Fourth Amendment to the Constitution.]. . . . The District Court, on respondents' motion, dismissed the complaint on the ground [that it failed to state a claim]. . . .

Before confronting the merits, the Supreme Court considered whether federal question jurisdiction existed over this claim. The defendants argued that the allegations gave rise only to state-law claims, such as trespass and invasion of privacy; that federal law giving them powers of arrest as officers of the FBN would provide them with a defense; and that the sole relevance of federal constitutional law was that it limited the extent of their federal defense. This combination of a state claim, a federal defense, and a federal restriction on the defense would be similar to the situation in *Louisville & Nashville RR. v. Mottley*; in fact, the defendants argued that the claim should be dismissed for want of jurisdiction precisely because it was the equivalent of *Mottley* in civil rights form. The Supreme Court disagreed. It went on to hold, on the merits, that the Fourth Amendment to the Constitution does imply a right to recover damages for its violation. Justice Brennan reasoned that state laws did not have the same purpose or scope as the Fourth Amendment.

Three Justices dissented. Justice Black pointed out that Congress had created a damages remedy against state officials but had declined to create one against federal officials. There had been "a growing number of frivolous lawsuits, particularly actions for damages against law enforcement officers." The judicial system was "accused by some of nearing the point of collapse." "If I were a legislator I might well find these and other needs so pressing as to make me believe that the resources of lawyers and judges should be devoted to them rather than to civil damage actions against officers who generally strive to perform within constitutional bounds."

MERRELL DOW PHARMACEUTICALS, INC. v. THOMPSON, 478 U.S. 804 (1986). Plaintiffs claimed to have been injured by the drug Bendectin. They sued the manufacturer, an Ohio corporation, in an Ohio state court on theories of negligence, strict liability, and other claims arising under Ohio law. They also alleged that the defendant had "misbranded" the drug in violation of the federal Food, Drug and Cosmetic Act. Plaintiffs further alleged that under Ohio law, this federal violation created a "rebuttable presumption" of negligence. Because of this last allegation, the defendant asserted that the plaintiff's claim was "founded, in part, on an alleged claim arising under the laws of the United States," and the defendant therefore removed the case to federal court under the authority of § 1331 (the general federal question statute). By a five-to-four majority, however, the Supreme Court held that the claim did not "arise under" federal law, and therefore there was no federal jurisdiction.

The claim arose under Ohio law. It was Ohio law, too, that created the "rebuttable presumption" of negligence. The federal Act in question did not itself give rise to the claim; in fact, Congress had clearly indicated that the federal Act did not create a private cause of action. The majority of the Court emphasized "the need for careful judgments about the exercise of federal judicial power in an area of uncertain jurisdiction." In most instances, said the Court, a case arises under federal law if federal law creates the claim. Therefore, the significance of the nonexistence of a private cause of action under the Food, Drug and Cosmetic Act "cannot be overstated." It would flout congressional intent to conclude that the federal courts "might nevertheless exercise federal jurisdiction. . . ."

The Supreme Court discussed its *Merrell Dow* decision at some length in *Grable & Sons Metal Products, Inc. v. Darue Engineering & Manufacturing*, 545 U.S. 308 (2005). In *Grable*, the Supreme Court, resolving a split in the circuits, concluded that *Merrell Dow* did not always require a federal cause of action as a prerequisite for arising-under jurisdiction.

GRABLE & SONS METAL PRODUCTS, INC. v. DARUE ENGINEERING & MANUFACTURING
545 U.S. 308 (2005)

JUSTICE SOUTER delivered the opinion of the Court.

The question is whether want of a federal cause of action to try claims of title to land obtained at a federal tax sale precludes removal to federal court of a state action with non-diverse parties raising a disputed issue of federal title law. We answer no, and hold that the national interest in providing a federal forum for federal tax litigation is sufficiently substantial to support the exercise of federal question jurisdiction over the disputed issue on removal, which would not distort any division of labor between the state and federal courts, provided or assumed by Congress.

I

In 1994, the Internal Revenue Service seized Michigan real property belonging to petitioner Grable & Sons Metal Products, Inc., to satisfy Grable's federal tax delinquency. Title 26 U.S.C. § 6335 required the IRS to give notice of the seizure, and there is no dispute that Grable received actual notice by certified mail before the IRS sold the property to respondent Darue Engineering & Manufacturing. Although Grable also received notice of the sale itself, it did not exercise its statutory right to redeem the property within 180 days of the sale, § 6337(b)(1), and after that period had passed, the Government gave Darue a quitclaim deed. § 6339.

Five years later, Grable brought a quiet title action in state court, claiming that Darue's record title was invalid because the IRS had failed to notify Grable of its seizure of the property in the exact manner required by § 6335(a), which provides that written notice must be "given by the Secretary to the owner of the property [or] left at his usual place of abode or business." Grable said that the statute required personal service, not service by certified mail.

Darue removed the case to Federal District Court as presenting a federal question, because the claim of title depended on the interpretation of the notice statute in the federal tax law. The District Court declined to remand the case at Grable's behest after finding that the "claim does pose a significant question of federal law," . . . and ruling that Grable's lack of a federal right of action to enforce its claim against Darue did not bar the exercise of federal jurisdiction. On the merits, the court granted summary judgment to Darue, holding that although § 6335 by its terms required personal service, substantial compliance with the statute was enough. 207 F. Supp. 2d 694 (W.D. Mich. 2002).

The Court of Appeals for the Sixth Circuit affirmed. 377 F.3d 592 (2004). On the jurisdictional question, the panel thought it sufficed that the title claim raised an issue of federal law that had to be resolved, and implicated a substantial federal interest (in construing federal tax law). The court went on to affirm the District Court's judgment on the merits. We granted certiorari on the jurisdictional question alone . . . to resolve a split within the Courts of Appeals on whether *Merrell Dow Pharmaceuticals, Inc. v. Thompson*, 478 U.S. 804 (1986), always requires a federal cause of action as a condition for exercising federal-question jurisdiction. We now affirm.

II

Darue was entitled to remove the quiet title action if Grable could have brought it in federal district court originally, 28 U.S.C. § 1441(a), as a civil action "arising under the Constitution, laws, or treaties of the United States," § 1331. This provision for federal-question jurisdiction is invoked by and large by plaintiffs pleading a cause of action created by federal law (e.g., claims under 42 U.S.C. § 1983). There is, however, another longstanding, if less frequently encountered, variety of federal "arising under" jurisdiction, this Court having recognized for nearly 100 years that in certain cases federal question jurisdiction will lie over state-law claims that implicate significant federal issues. *E.g., Hopkins v. Walker*, 244 U.S. 486, 490-491 (1917). The doctrine captures the commonsense notion that a federal court ought to be able to hear claims recognized under state law that nonetheless turn on substantial questions of federal law, and thus justify resort to the experience, solicitude, and hope of uniformity that a federal forum offers on federal issues, *see* ALI, Study of the Division of Jurisdiction Between State and Federal Courts 164-166 (1968). . . .

As early as 1912, this Court had confined federal-question jurisdiction over state-law claims to those that "really and substantially involv[e] a dispute or controversy respecting the validity, construction or effect of [federal] law." *Shulthis v. McDougal*, 225 U.S. 561 (1912). . . .

But even when the state action discloses a contested and substantial federal question, the exercise of federal jurisdiction is subject to a possible veto. For the federal issue will ultimately qualify for a federal forum only if federal jurisdiction is consistent with congressional judgment about the sound division of labor between state and federal courts governing the application of § 1331. . . . Because arising-under jurisdiction to hear a state-law claim always raises the possibility of upsetting the state-federal line drawn (or at least assumed) by Congress, the presence of a disputed federal issue and the ostensible importance of a federal forum are never necessarily dispositive; there must always be an assessment of any disruptive portent in exercising federal jurisdiction. *See also Merrell Dow, supra*, at 810.

These considerations have kept us from stating a "single, precise, all-embracing" test for jurisdiction over federal issues embedded in state-law claims between nondiverse parties. *Christianson v. Colt Industries Operating Corp.*, 486 U.S. 800, 821 (1988) (Stevens, J., concurring). We have not kept them out simply because they appeared in state raiment, as Justice Holmes would have done, *see Smith* [*v. Kansas City Title & Trust Co.*, 255 U.S. 180,] 214 [(1921) (dissenting opinion)], but neither have we treated "federal issue" as a password opening federal courts to any state action embracing a point of federal law. Instead, the question is, does a state-law claim necessarily raise a stated federal issue, actually disputed and substantial, which a federal forum may entertain without disturbing any congressionally approved balance of federal and state judicial responsibilities.

III

A

This case warrants federal jurisdiction. Grable's state complaint must specify "the facts establishing the superiority of [its] claim," Mich. Ct. Rule 3.411(B)(2)(c) (2005), and Grable has premised its superior title claim on a failure by the IRS to give it adequate notice, as defined by federal law. Whether Grable was given notice within the meaning of the federal statute is thus an essential element of its quiet title claim, and the meaning of the federal statute is actually in dispute; it appears to be the only legal or factual issue contested in the case. The meaning of the federal tax provision is an important issue of federal law that sensibly belongs in a federal court. The Government has a strong interest in the "prompt and certain collection of delinquent taxes," *United States v. Rodgers*, 461 U.S. 677, 709 (1983), and the ability of the IRS to satisfy its claims from the property of delinquents requires clear terms of notice to allow buyers like Darue to satisfy themselves that the Service has touched the bases necessary for good title. The Government thus has a direct interest in the availability of a federal forum to vindicate its own administrative action, and buyers (as well as tax delinquents) may find it valuable to come before judges used to federal tax matters. Finally, because it will be the rare state title case that raises a contested matter of federal law, federal jurisdiction to resolve genuine disagreement over federal tax title provisions will portend only a microscopic effect on the federal-state division of labor. . . .

B

Merrell Dow Pharmaceuticals, Inc. v. Thompson, 478 U.S. 804 (1986), on which Grable rests its position, is not to the contrary. *Merrell Dow* considered a state tort claim resting in part on the allegation that the defendant drug company had violated a federal misbranding prohibition, and was thus presumptively negligent under Ohio law. *Id.*, at 806. The Court assumed that federal law would have to be applied to resolve the claim, but after closely examining the strength of the federal interest at stake and the implications of opening the federal forum, held federal jurisdiction unavailable. Congress had not provided a private federal cause of action for violation of the federal branding requirement, and the Court found "it would . . . flout, or at least undermine, congressional intent to conclude that federal courts might nevertheless exercise federal-question jurisdiction and provide remedies for violations of that federal statute solely because the violation . . . is said to be a 'proximate cause' under state law." *Id.*, at 812.

Because federal law provides for no quiet title action that could be brought against Darue, Grable argues that there can be no federal jurisdiction here, stressing some broad language in *Merrell Dow* (including the passage just quoted) that on its face supports Grable's position . . . . But an opinion is to be read as a whole, and *Merrell Dow* cannot be read whole as overturning decades of precedent . . . .

Accordingly, *Merrell Dow* should be read in its entirety as treating the absence of a federal private right of action as evidence relevant to, but not dispositive of, the "sensitive judgments about congressional intent" that § 1331 requires. The absence of any federal cause of action affected *Merrell Dow*'s result in two ways. The Court saw the fact as worth some consideration in the assessment of substantiality. But its primary importance emerged when the Court treated the combination of no federal cause of action and no preemption of state remedies for misbranding as an important clue to Congress's conception of the scope of jurisdiction to be exercised under § 1331. The Court saw the missing cause of action not as a missing federal door key, always required, but as a missing welcome mat, required in the circumstances, when exercising federal jurisdiction over a state misbranding action would have attracted a horde of original filings and removal cases raising other state claims with embedded federal issues. For if the federal labeling standard without a federal cause of action could get a state claim into federal court, so could any other federal standard without a federal cause of action. And that would have meant a tremendous number of cases. . . .

Merrell Dow's analysis thus fits within the framework of examining the importance of having a federal forum for the issue, and the consistency of such a forum with Congress's intended division of labor between state and federal courts.

As already indicated, however, a comparable analysis yields a different jurisdictional conclusion in this case. Although Congress also indicated ambivalence in this case by providing no private right of action to Grable, it is the rare state quiet title action that involves contested issues of federal law . . . . Consequently, jurisdiction over actions like Grable's would not materially affect, or threaten to affect, the normal currents of litigation. Given the absence of threatening structural consequences and the clear interest the Government, its buyers, and its delinquents have in the availability of a federal forum, there is no good reason to shirk from federal jurisdiction over the dispositive and contested federal issue at the heart of the state-law title claim.

IV

The judgment of the Court of Appeals, upholding federal jurisdiction over Grable's quiet title action, is affirmed.

[The concurring opinion of Justice Thomas is omitted.]

Read 28 U.S.C. §§ 1330, 1603, 1605(a) (Foreign Sovereign Immunities Act).

NOTE ON THE CONSTITUTIONAL BASIS OF "ARISING UNDER" JURISDICTION: THE EXAMPLE OF THE FOREIGN SOVEREIGN IMMUNITIES ACT

The Breadth of the Constitutional "Arising Under" Provision. The Constitution authorizes federal jurisdiction over actions "arising under" federal law, in language similar to that of § 1331. However, the constitutional provision consistently has been interpreted more broadly than the statute. *See* Chadbourne & Levin, *Original Jurisdiction of Federal Questions*, 90 U. Pa. L. Rev. 639 (1940). That is to say, Congress has considerable leeway in defining the scope of jurisdiction, and the constitutional provision has been interpreted to uphold several other jurisdictional statutes, in addition to § 1331. Thus in *Osborne v. Bank of the United States*, 9 Wheat. 738, 6 L. Ed. 204 (1824), Chief Justice Marshall's opinion upheld a statute allowing the Bank of the United States to sue in federal court, even if the claim was based upon state law.

The Foreign Sovereign Immunities Act. In 1976, Congress passed the Foreign Sovereign Immunities Act, which allows foreign nations or their departments or instrumentalities to be sued in federal courts. Before that time, foreign nations had varying kinds of sovereign immunity from suit; the Act codified a narrow version of this immunity, making foreign nations subject to suit on state or federal claims to the extent this immunity did not apply. It also provides that federal District Courts "have original jurisdiction . . . of any nonjury civil action against a foreign state . . . ." 28 U.S.C. § 1330. *See* Note, *Suits by Foreigners Against Foreign States in United States Courts: A Selective Expansion of Jurisdiction*, 90 Yale L.J. 1861 (1981).

Verlinden B.V. v. Central Bank of Nigeria, 461 U.S. 480 (1983), was the case that tested the constitutionality of the Foreign Sovereign Immunities Act. Verlinden, a Dutch corporation, contracted to deliver 240,000 metric tons of cement to the Federal Republic of Nigeria and sued Nigeria's instrumentality, the Central Bank of Nigeria, when it breached the contract. The claim was controlled by Dutch law. Verlinden sued in the United States District Court for the Southern District of New York. The Bank of Nigeria, in addition to defending on the merits, alleged that the grant of jurisdiction in the Foreign Sovereign Immunities Act was unconstitutional. Citing *Osborne*, the Supreme Court upheld the grant of jurisdiction and said: "Congress may confer on the federal courts jurisdiction over any case or controversy that might call for the application of federal law." The District Court necessarily would have to determine whether sovereign immunity existed under the Foreign Sovereign Immunities Act in that particular case — *i.e.*, apply the Act — but the Act itself was constitutional. Although this application of federal law, since it did not govern the claim itself, would not be sufficient for jurisdiction under the general federal question statute (§ 1331), it was sufficient to bring the Foreign Sovereign Immunities Act within the broader scope of the constitutional "arising under" provision. As the Supreme Court put it, "[T]he many limitations which have been placed on jurisdiction under § 1331 are not limitations on the constitutional power of Congress to confer jurisdiction on the federal courts."

Appendix to § 3.03[A]: "Arising Under" Jurisdiction In Practice

COMPLAINT IN *WYTINGER v. TWO UNKNOWN POLICE OFFICERS*

[Reproduced above in Appendix to § 1.04]

For a concrete example of "arising under" jurisdiction, read (or re-read) the complaint in *Wytinger v. Two Unknown Police Officers*. Identify the parts of the complaint that purport to show jurisdiction. Is jurisdiction proper under the "arising under" statute?

[B] Diversity Jurisdiction

[1] The Requirement of Complete Diversity

Read 28 U.S.C. § 1332 (the diversity statute); also, reconsider U.S. Const. art. III, § 2 (the constitutional diversity provision).

STRAWBRIDGE v. CURTISS, 7 U.S. (3 Cranch) 267 (1806). The text of this opinion appears above at § 1.03 and should be read (or re-read) at this point. In essence, Chief Justice Marshall's decision interpreted the diversity statute to require "complete" diversity: "That is, . . . each of the [parties] must be competent to sue, or liable to be sued" by each other party.

MAS v. PERRY
489 F.2d 1396 (5th Cir. 1974)

AINSWORTH, CIRCUIT JUDGE:

This case presents questions pertaining to federal diversity jurisdiction under 28 U.S.C. § 1332, which, pursuant to article III, section 2 of the Constitution, provides for original jurisdiction in federal district courts of all civil actions that are between, *inter alia*, citizens of different States or citizens of a State and citizens of foreign states and in which the amount in controversy is more than $10,000. [Eds. Note: The $10,000 figure, which was then in effect, later was changed to $75,000.]

Appellees Jean Paul Mas, a citizen of France, and Judy Mas were married at her home in Jackson, Mississippi. Prior to their marriage, the couple were graduate assistants, pursuing coursework as well as performing teaching duties, for approximately nine months and one year, respectively, at Louisiana State University in Baton Rouge, Louisiana. Shortly after their marriage, they returned to Baton Rouge to resume their duties as graduate assistants at LSU. They remained in Baton Rouge for approximately two more years, after which they moved to Park Ridge, Illinois. At the time of the trial in this case, it was their intention to return to Baton Rouge while Mr. Mas finished his studies for the degree of Doctor of Philosophy. Mr. and Mrs. Mas were undecided as to where they would reside after that.

Upon their return to Baton Rouge after their marriage, appellees rented an apartment from appellant Oliver H. Perry, a citizen of Louisiana. This appeal arises from a final judgment entered on a jury verdict awarding $5,000 to Mr. Mas and $15,000 to Mrs. Mas for damages incurred by them as a result of the discovery that their bedroom and bathroom contained "two-way" mirrors and that they had been watched through them by the appellant during three of the first four months of their marriage.

At the close of the appellees' case at trial, appellant made an oral motion to dismiss for lack of jurisdiction. The motion was denied by the District Court. Before this Court, appellant challenges the final judgment below solely on jurisdictional grounds, contending that appellees failed to prove diversity of citizenship among the parties and that the requisite jurisdictional amount is lacking with respect to Mr. Mas. Finding no merit to these contentions, we affirm. Under section 1332(a)(2), the federal judicial power extends to the claim of Mr. Mas, a citizen of France, against the appellant, a citizen of Louisiana. [Eds. Note: At the time, the diversity statute made no distinction pertaining to permanent resident aliens; notice that they now are treated as citizens of their states of domicile. How would this provision affect Mr. Mas today if he were a permanent resident alien?] Since we conclude that Mrs. Mas is a citizen of Mississippi for diversity purposes, the District Court also properly had jurisdiction under § 1332(a)(1) of her claim.

It has long been the general rule that complete diversity of parties is required in order that diversity jurisdiction obtain; that is, no party on one side may be a citizen of the same State as any party on the other side. *Strawbridge v. Curtiss*. . . . As is the case in other areas of federal jurisdiction, the diverse citizenship among adverse parties must be present at the time the complaint is filed. . . . Jurisdiction is unaffected by subsequent changes in the citizenship of the parties. . . . The burden of pleading the diverse citizenship is upon the party invoking federal jurisdiction, . . . and if the diversity jurisdiction is properly challenged, that party also bears the burden of proof. . . .

To be a citizen of a State within the meaning of § 1332, a natural person must be both a citizen of the United States . . . and a domiciliary of that State. . . . For diversity purposes, citizenship means domicile; mere residence in the State is not sufficient. . . .

A person's domicile is the place of "his true, fixed, and permanent home and principal establishment, and to which he has the intention of returning whenever he is absent therefrom. . . ." *Stine v. Moore*, 5 Cir., 1954, 213 F.2d 446, 448. A change of domicile may be effected only by a combination of two elements: (a) taking up residence in a different domicile with (b) the intention to remain there. . . .

It is clear that at the time of her marriage, Mrs. Mas was a domiciliary of the State of Mississippi. . . .[2]

Mrs. Mas's Mississippi domicile was disturbed neither by her year in Louisiana prior to her marriage nor as a result of the time she and her husband spent at LSU after their marriage, since for both periods she was a graduate assistant at LSU. . . . Though she testified that after her marriage she had no intention of returning to her parents' home in Mississippi, Mrs. Mas did not effect a change of domicile since she and Mr. Mas were in Louisiana only as students and lacked the requisite intention to remain there. . . . Until she acquires a new domicile, she remains a domiciliary, and thus a citizen, of Mississippi. . . .

Appellant also contends that Mr. Mas's claim should have been dismissed for failure to establish the requisite jurisdictional amount for diversity cases of more than $10,000 [now $75,000]. In their complaint Mr. and Mrs. Mas alleged that they had each been damaged in the amount of $100,000. As we have noted, Mr. Mas ultimately recovered $5,000.

It is well settled that the amount in controversy is determined by the amount claimed by the plaintiff in good faith. . . . Federal jurisdiction is not lost because a judgment of less than the jurisdictional amount is awarded. . . . That Mr. Mas recovered only $5,000 is, therefore, not compelling. As the Supreme Court stated in *St. Paul Mercury Indemnity Co. v. Red Cab Co.*, 303 U.S. 283, 288-290 . . . :

> [T]he sum claimed by the plaintiff controls if the claim is apparently made in good faith.
>
> It must appear to a legal certainty that the claim is really for less than the jurisdictional amount to justify dismissal. The inability of the plaintiff to recover an amount adequate to give the court jurisdiction does not show his bad faith or oust the jurisdiction. . . .

Thus the power of the federal district court to entertain the claims of appellees in this case stands on two separate legs of diversity jurisdiction: a claim by an alien against a State citizen; and an action between citizens of different States.

Affirmed.

NOTE ON THE POLICY BASIS FOR DIVERSITY JURISDICTION

The reasons for the diversity provision in the Constitution (and for the initial grant by the first Congress) are shrouded in mystery. There is no indication of the underlying

---

[2] The original complaint in this case was filed within several days of Mr. and Mrs. Mas's realization that they had been watched through the mirrors, quite some time before they moved to Park Ridge, Illinois. Because the district court's jurisdiction is not affected by actions of the parties subsequent to the commencement of the suit, *see* C. Wright, Federal Courts 93 (1970), . . . the testimony concerning Mr. and Mrs. Mas's moves after that time is not determinative of the issue of diverse citizenship, though it is of interest insofar as it supports their lack of intent to remain permanently in Louisiana.

policy in the debates on the Constitution, and the legislative history of the early enactment is of little help. But many commentators infer that the concern is about local prejudice. Consider the following:

> However true the fact may be, that the tribunals of the states will administer justice as impartially as [the federal courts], . . . the Constitution itself either entertains apprehensions on this subject, or views with such indulgence the possible fears and apprehensions of suitors, that it has established . . . national tribunals for the decision of controversies . . . between citizens of different states.

Bank of the United States v. Deveaux, 9 U.S. (5 Cranch) 61, 87 (1809) (Marshall, Ch. J.).

> Many legal scholars who have researched this issue have concluded that [diversity jurisdiction] was based on a fear that State courts would be biased or prejudiced against those from out of State. A minority view is that the Nation's early lawmakers shared misgivings as to whether at least some of the State courts would be fair to the interests of creditors, out-of-staters or in-staters. Another position is that, the Federal courts being better than the State, it was preferable to route as many cases into the former as possible.

Abolition of Diversity of Citizenship Jurisdiction, H.R. Rep. No. 95-893, 95th Cong., 2d Sess. 2 (1978). For a detailed history, see generally D. Bassett, *The Hidden Bias in Diversity Jurisdiction*, 81 Wash. U. L.Q. 119 (2003).

NOTES AND QUESTIONS

(1) *The "Local Prejudice" Rationale: Is It Valid?* As these excerpts indicate, a concern about the possibility of local prejudice is the most commonly asserted justification for diversity jurisdiction. But there is some question today about this theory. Transportation and communication have made the nation more unified than ever before. A Californian and a Nebraskan, for example, may have more in common with each other than they have with other individuals from their respective states. Furthermore, there is room for doubt whether the addition of federal courts solves the problem of local prejudice, even assuming it exists. If a case is tried in North Carolina, in a federal court, from what state will the federal District judge come? [He or she is likely to have been chosen by one of North Carolina's senators!] From what state will the jurors be summoned? [Obviously, North Carolina!] Therefore, regardless of whether the sign over the courthouse door says "federal" or "state," isn't the case going to be tried by similar kinds of people under closely analogous procedures?

(2) *Is the "Complete Diversity" Requirement Consistent with the "Local Prejudice" Rationale?* If a North Carolinian brings a state-law claim against two defendants — one a fellow North Carolinian, the other a New Yorker — the suit must be in state court, because diversity is destroyed. But isn't the New Yorker just as much in danger of local prejudice as he would be if sued alone? In fact, since he now may have the fingers of both the North Carolina plaintiff and his North Carolina co-defendant pointed at him before a jury of North Carolinians, doesn't the New Yorker need a federal forum even more than if sued alone? This example suggests that the rationale of local prejudice is inconsistent with the requirement of complete diversity. [For an even more convincing example, consider a suit against a person who is a United States citizen but not domiciled in any state. *Cf. Twentieth Century-Fox Film Corp. v. Taylor*, 239 F. Supp. 913 (S.D.N.Y. 1965) (inclusion of film star Elizabeth Taylor as defendant destroyed diversity because she was domiciled abroad and therefore was not a citizen of any state).]

(3) *Permanent Resident Aliens.* Notice that today, if Mr. Mas happened to be a permanent resident alien, he would be treated as a citizen of the state in which he was domiciled. Is this result consistent with the local prejudice rationale (or does an alien suffer such prejudice even if he is a permanent resident)?

(4) *Defeating or Preserving Diversity: Games Lawyers Play.* Imagine an influential attorney whose client has a claim against a national corporation, based upon dealings with a local agent. This attorney may be able to choose either to create or to defeat federal jurisdiction. If he prefers a state forum (and attorneys have been known to prefer a given court because of personal relationships with the judge, or even because of having assisted in obtaining the judge's election or appointment), he can sue the corporation and join its local agent, who presumably is of the same citizenship as the local plaintiff. This strategy destroys diversity. On the other hand, if the influential attorney likes the federal court better (perhaps for similar kinds of reasons), he would sue the out-of-state corporation alone in federal court. The law facilitates these "games that lawyers play." But should it?

(5) *The Costs of Diversity; Possible Reforms.* Unless diversity is beneficial, it should be abolished, because it has substantial costs: wasteful forum contests, federal-state conflicts, gamesmanship, and impact on the workload of courts that should be hearing federal claims. There have been many proposals for alteration of diversity jurisdiction — or for its outright abolition. *See, e.g.*, Rowe, *Abolishing Diversity Jurisdiction: Positive Side Effects and Potential for Further Reform*, 92 Harv. L. Rev. 963 (1979). We take up some of these arguments at the end of this chapter.

NOTE ON CITIZENSHIPS OF CORPORATIONS OR ASSOCIATIONS

Corporations: Two Kinds of Citizenships. The diversity statute provides that a corporation may have multiple citizenships, including any state in which it is incorporated and the state of its "principal place of business." Although this provision means that a corporation, like an individual, is a citizen for diversity purposes, it also means that it destroys diversity more easily.

"Principal Place of Business." It can sometimes be difficult to determine the principal place of business of a corporation with far-flung operations. One approach is to consider where the "nerve center" of the corporation is. *Scot Typewriter Co. v. Underwood Corp.*, 170 F. Supp. 862 (S.D.N.Y. 1959) ("home office" or "nerve center from which it radiates out to its constituent parts and from which its officers direct, control and coordinate all activities without regard to locale, in the furtherance of the corporate objective"). But as applied to, say, U.S. Steel Corporation, the nerve center concept may be no more than "a pleasant and alluring figure of speech." *Kelly v. U.S. Steel Corp.*, 284 F.2d 850, 853 (3d Cir. 1960) (U.S. Steel "has literally dozens of important places of business, one of which we must pick out as the principal one because the statute says so"). The other major approach is to determine where the bulk of the corporation's activities takes place. The modern view appears to be that the bulk-of-the-activity test controls unless the activities are thoroughly dispersed, in which event the nerve center test controls. *Toms v. Country Quality Meats, Inc.*, 610 F.2d 313 (5th Cir. 1980).

Partnerships, Associations, and Other Entities. Unincorporated entities do not have a citizenship apart from the citizenship(s) of their members. *United Steelworkers of America v. R.H. Bouligny, Inc.*, 382 U.S. 145 (1965) (Court looked to citizenships of all members of labor union); *cf. Navarro Savings Ass'n v. Lee*, 446 U.S. 458 (1980) (Court looked to citizenship of trustees of business trust, rejecting argument for citizenships of all beneficiaries). [Should this approach be changed by Congress? Does it make sense that a corporation has a distinct citizenship but a partnership does not?] *See also Carden v. Arkoma Associates,* 494 U.S 185 (1990) (Court refused to treat limited partnership as corporation, and instead used citizenships of all partners, in spite of policy arguments that included state's formation and treatment of entity in manner analogous to corporation).

Hybrid Entities. Some entities resemble both corporations and partnerships. "Professional corporations," for example, may resemble a partnership or professional association. For diversity purposes, However, the Seventh Circuit held, in *Hoaglund ex rel. Midwest Transit, Inc. v. Sandberg, Phoenix & von Gontard, P.C.*, 385 F.3d 737 (2004), that an entity designated a "professional corporation" under state law is a "corporation" within the meaning of the diversity jurisdiction statute, no matter how much the entity may resemble a partnership or other entity. Accordingly, the citizenship of a "professional corporation" will be the place of its incorporation and principal place of business; the citizenship of its shareholder-members is irrelevant.

PROBLEM C

PAYNE v. UNITED MOTORS CORP. Plaintiff Paul Payne, a citizen of Michigan, has an alleged wrongful discharge claim for more than $100,000 against United Motors, arising under state law. United Motors is a corporation incorporated under the laws of Delaware. Its corporate headquarters are located in an office building in Detroit, Michigan, but virtually all of its manufacturing operations take place just across the state line, in Ohio. You represent Paul Payne. You would like to have the case heard in a federal court if you can; however, you would like to be certain of the basis for jurisdiction if you obtain a judgment, and you would like to avoid prolonged litigation about the issue at the beginning of the case. Question 1: Should you file suit in a federal court? Question 2: How would your answer be affected if you planned to join the United Automobile Workers international union as a second defendant?

Appendix to § 3.03[B][1]: Diversity Jurisdiction in Practice

COMPLAINT IN *GEORGE MILLER CO. v. COMPUDATA, INC.*

[Reproduced above in subsection B of the Appendix to Chapter 2.]

For a concrete example of diversity jurisdiction, read (or re-read) the complaint in *George Miller Co. v. Compudata, Inc.*, which appears above in the Appendix to Chapter 2. Identify the parts of the complaint that purport to show diversity jurisdiction. Is jurisdiction proper?

[2] Parties "Improperly or Collusively Made"

Read 28 U.S.C. § 1359 (the "collusive parties" statute).

KRAMER v. CARIBBEAN MILLS, INC., 394 U.S. 823 (1969). The Panama and Venezuela Finance Company ("Panama"), a Panamanian Corporation, assigned to Kramer a claim it had against Caribbean Mills, a Haitian corporation. Panama would not have been able to sue Caribbean in the federal courts because neither was a citizen of a state, but Kramer (the assignee) was an attorney practicing in Wichita Falls and was a citizen of Texas. Kramer therefore filed an action against Caribbean in a United States District

Court. Caribbean moved to dismiss for lack of jurisdiction, arguing that Kramer was "improperly or collusively made" a party for the purpose of creating diversity in violation of 28 U.S.C. § 1359. The Supreme Court agreed, and it upheld the reversal of a judgment for Kramer.

The stated consideration paid by Kramer was one dollar, in exchange for a claim for $165,000 allegedly owed by Caribbean to Panama. Furthermore, by an instrument executed the same day, Kramer had agreed to pay back to Panama 95% of any net recovery on the assigned claim. "When the assignment to Kramer is considered together with his total lack of previous connection with the matter and his simultaneous reassignment of a 95% interest back to Panama, there can be little doubt that the assignment was for purposes of collection, with Kramer to retain 5% of the net proceeds 'for the use of his name and his trouble in collecting,' " said the Court. The conclusion that the assignment was " 'improperly or collusively made' within the meaning of § 1359" was supported, said the Court, "not only by precedent but also by consideration of the statute's purpose. If federal jurisdiction could be created by assignments of this kind, . . . then a vast quantity of ordinary contract and tort litigation could be channeled into the federal courts at the will of one of the parties."

NOTES AND QUESTIONS

(1) *Changing the Facts in Kramer: Assignment for Business Reasons.* What if Panama were dissolved by its shareholders and its assets transferred to a New Jersey corporation for independent business and tax reasons, unrelated to the ability to sue in federal court? The courts have sometimes regarded transfer to controlled corporations as "presumptively" ineffective to create diversity, *cf. Prudential Oil Corp. v. Phillips Petroleum Co.*, 546 F.2d 469 (2d Cir. 1976). But wouldn't genuine business reasons make a difference?

(2) *Can the Plaintiff's Own Change of Citizenship Create Diversity?* In *Baker v. Keck*, 13 F. Supp. 486 (1936), the plaintiff was originally a citizen of Illinois — as was the defendant he wanted to sue. Plaintiff moved to Oklahoma, taking his family and almost all his possessions, produced food crops there, rented property, and registered to vote. The court concluded that one of plaintiff's motives was "to create diversity of citizenship so that he might maintain a suit in the United States courts." However, said the court, "One may change his citizenship for the purpose of enabling himself to maintain a suit in the federal court, but the change must be an actual legal change made with the intention of bringing about actual citizenship. . . ." Since the court credited plaintiff's testimony that his intention was to make Oklahoma his home, it upheld the jurisdiction. Defense witnesses testified that plaintiff had said he was going to move back to Illinois after he got his case settled, but the court said that "a floating intention to return at some indefinite future period" did not affect citizenship. Is *Keck* consistent with *Kramer*?

[3] Amount in Controversy

NOTE ON ASCERTAINING THE AMOUNT IN CONTROVERSY

Monetary Claims: The Good Faith Complaint. Reconsider *Mas v. Perry*, above. Even though Mr. Mas recovered only $5,000, the amount in controversy was the $100,000 he had prayed for. "It is well settled that the amount in controversy is determined by the amount claimed by the plaintiff in good faith," said the court.

Non-Monetary Claims: The "Value of the Object" and Other Tests. But what if the prayer is not for monetary relief? What if it instead requests an injunction or a declaratory judgment? In that event, the most common test is the so-called "value of the object": The court looks to the value of whatever plaintiff hopes to gain from the suit. Consider the following case.

WILLIAMS v. KLEPPE
539 F.2d 803 (1st Cir. 1976)

The site of this controversy is a beach known as Brush Hollow on the Atlantic shore of Cape Cod, a three mile expanse between two conventionally operated beaches. For some forty or fifty years this spot, hidden behind some of the highest sand dunes on the Cape, had been used by individuals, couples, and small groups for skinny dipping. . . .

As the popularity of Brush Hollow built up, so did the concern of the owners of residential property [n]ear points of access to the beach. [The concerns included "demonstrable damage to the environment, increasing attendance despite attempts of enforcement, record traffic congestion, litter, and trespassing."] . . .

[The government], after considering the alternatives, [a]dopted the regulation at issue, which bars public nude bathing within the seashore to all persons over ten years of age. Suit was brought [by plaintiffs, apparently for a declaration of invalidity of the regulation and for an injunction against responsible government officials' enforcement of it] and hearing was had at which affidavits were accepted and evidence taken. The District Court, although finding that "nude bathing at Brush Hollow is entitled to some constitutional protection," held that the regulation [was valid]. . . .

[Before considering the merits, the Court of Appeals considered whether federal jurisdiction existed to adjudicate the claimed "right" to "skinny dip." Then-existing statutes required an amount in controversy exceeding $10,000, both for diversity and, at that time, for some federal claims. To determine whether the amount exceeded this threshold, the court applied a version of the value of the object test as well as an alternate test, as follows:]

. . . The jurisdictional amount was alleged and has not been made an issue. Applying conventional analysis, we are unwilling to say on this record that the claimed interest of one or more plaintiffs, some being residents of the Seashore area, may not exceed the jurisdictional amount. Perhaps more realistically, we can rely upon the extent of the claimed pecuniary burden on defendants were plaintiffs to prevail. . . .

[On the merits, the court compared the claimed interest to another "protectible, if minor interest, one's desire to wear his hair as he chooses." To the probable disappointment of some readers, the court then proceeded to decide that this "minor" interest in "skinny dipping" was overcome by the "real and substantial interests" supporting the regulation, which it upheld as valid.]

NOTES AND QUESTIONS

(1) *Did the Value of the Object of Plaintiffs' "Minor" Interest Really Exceed the Threshold? The "Legal Certainty" Test.* If the interest truly is "minor," could the government have developed evidence to defeat jurisdiction at the evidentiary hearing? Maybe a "minor" legal interest could have a very high subjective value to a given individual; is this subjective value, rather than the low ranking of the legal interest, the proper focus? Furthermore, remember that the allegation of the jurisdictional amount in good faith is subject to being defeated only if it is shown "to a legal certainty" that plaintiff

never had any prospect of recovering any relief in an amount exceeding the threshold. *Cf. Mas v. Perry, supra.* Another technical consideration is that plaintiffs each must individually meet the threshold and may not aggregate the values of their claims to reach it (see below). Did the court "fudge" this aspect of the case?

(2) *The "Value of the Object" Test: Hunt v. Washington State Apple Advertising Comm'n, 432 U.S. 333 (1977).* In this case, the plaintiff sought an injunction because it claimed that the defendant was illegally enforcing a North Carolina statute that discriminated against Washington apple growers and dealers. Plaintiff was a Washington state agency, and although it had suffered no direct injury itself, the Court held that it could assert the injury incurred by growers and dealers. Furthermore, "[T]he amount in controversy is established by the value of the object of the litigation. . . . Here, that object is the right of the individual Washington apple growers and dealers to conduct their business affairs . . . free from the interference of the challenged statute. The value of the right is measured by the losses that will follow from the statute's enforcement." Since there were at least some apple growers or dealers who would expend more than the jurisdictional amount to comply with the North Carolina statute, the Court upheld the jurisdiction.

(3) *The "Loss to the Defendant" Test; Other Approaches.* What if the plaintiff seeks an injunction to protect a right of little monetary value, and so he alleges an amount less than the jurisdictional amount — but the injunction would result in shutting down the defendant's business? In that event, an alternate test considering the defendant's loss may be appropriate. *American Smelting & Refining Co. v. Godfrey*, 158 F. 225 (8th Cir. 1907) (suit for injunction against nuisance); *cf. Oklahoma Retail Grocers Ass'n v. Wal-Mart Stores, Inc.*, 605 F.2d 1155 (10th Cir. 1979) (where suit by association was for injunction to force compliance with statute, it was proper to accept the defendant's allegation that its costs would exceed the jurisdictional amount).

(4) *The "Aggregation" Problem.* What about multiple claims, none of which exceeds the jurisdictional amount if taken by itself, but which do exceed $75,000 in the aggregate? The federal courts allow distinct claims by a single party to be aggregated. Thus, if a plaintiff sues a defendant for two different breaches of contract, causing different injuries and damages, one for $50,000 and the other for $25,001, the amount in controversy exceeds $75,000. But if two alternative claims are made for the same injuries and damages (*e.g.*, negligence and breach of warranty), the alternative claims are not added together. Claims by different plaintiffs also are not added, unless the claims are legally united and indivisible because they involve the enforcement of a joint right by joint obligees. Finally, the claims of a single plaintiff against multiple defendants are also not aggregated, unless the defendants are both jointly and severally liable for the entire amount. In *Zahn v. International Paper Co.*, 414 U.S. 291 (1973), the Supreme Court applied the multiple plaintiffs-nonaggregation rule to a diversity class action. *Zahn* meant that the federal courts were foreclosed to most consumer class actions based on state law grounds. However, as explained later in this Chapter, the supplemental jurisdiction statute changes this result.

[C] Supplemental Jurisdiction and Exceptions to the Exercise of Jurisdiction

Read 28 U.S.C. § 1367 (supplemental jurisdiction).

INTRODUCTORY NOTE

The Need for Supplemental Jurisdiction. Often, real-world disputes involve multiple parties and multiple claims that are partly within a federal court's jurisdiction and partly outside of it. Thus, a plaintiff suing in federal court on a federal claim may want to add closely related state-law claims to the complaint, all in the same suit. The defendant, in turn, may want to place blame upon a third party against whom he asserts a state-law claim, also related to the plaintiff's suit. But a problem arises: unless the plaintiff's state-law claim and the defendant's third party claim have some basis for federal jurisdiction, they will need to be brought in state court, separately from the federal suit. This result would be wasteful if all of the claims are closely related and involve overlapping evidence.

How Supplemental Jurisdiction Solves These Problems. Congress passed 28 U.S.C. § 1367 (the supplemental jurisdiction statute) to govern this problem. The statute says that, with certain exceptions in diversity cases, the federal court may hear state law claims if they are "so related to claims in the action within [the court's] original jurisdiction that they form part of the same case or controversy under Article III of the Constitution." This broad principle sweeps in a variety of claims that the court otherwise would be required, wastefully, to dismiss. (The statute also permits the court to decline to hear the extra claims in certain circumstances when it would be wasteful to hear them.)

The Relationship of Supplemental Jurisdiction to Two Older Concepts Called "Pendent" and "Ancillary" Jurisdiction. Before Congress passed the supplemental jurisdiction statute, federal judges themselves had invented a solution to the multiple-claim problem. They had created two doctrines called "pendent jurisdiction" and "ancillary jurisdiction." Today, those two doctrines have been replaced by the supplemental jurisdiction statute; you will need to learn about them, however, so that you can understand the present law. *See also* Mengler, Burbank & Rowe, *Congress Accepts Supreme Court's Invitation to Codify Supplemental Jurisdiction*, 74 Judicature 213 (1991). For a comprehensive treatment of 1988-90 changes in venue, diversity, supplemental jurisdiction and removal, see Oakley, *Recent Statutory Changes in the Law of Federal Jurisdiction and Venue: The Judicial Improvements Acts of 1988 and 1990*, 24 U.C. Davis L. Rev. 735 (1991).

[1] Supplemental Jurisdiction of the Kind Formerly Called "Pendent Jurisdiction": Joining State and Federal Claims

NOTE ON THE *GIBBS* CASE: THE EARLIER DOCTRINE OF PENDENT JURISDICTION

Parallel State and Federal Claims. Imagine that you have two closely related claims, one based on federal law and the other based on state law. You want to assert the federal claim in federal court, and you have a right to do so. But you also want to assert the state-law claim in the same suit, and it lacks an independent basis for federal jurisdiction. Unless there is some legal doctrine allowing you to join the nonjurisdictional claim in federal court with the jurisdictional one, you will have to give up the federal forum you want, or else you will need to bring two suits.

Pendent Jurisdiction in the Case of United Mine Workers v. Gibbs, below. This two-claim situation occurred in the Gibbs case. The plaintiff asserted a federal claim arising under the federal labor laws, and he joined it with a claim, arising under state law, for tortious interference with contract. The Supreme Court applied a judge-created doctrine called "pendent jurisdiction" to allow both claims to be brought together. The word "pendent" comes from a Latin word meaning "to hang"; the state-law claim comes within federal jurisdiction because it piggybacks or figuratively "hangs" on the federal claim. Without this type of doctrine, the plaintiff who chose a federal forum for his or her federal claim would be penalized by having to file the state-law claim in another suit, and there would be unnecessary duplication of judicial effort.

Supplemental Jurisdiction Replaces the Older Doctrine of Pendent Jurisdiction. Today, pendent jurisdiction has been replaced by the supplemental jurisdiction statute. The *Gibbs* case was decided under the doctrine of pendent jurisdiction, but it is included here because it is an excellent introduction to the supplemental jurisdiction statute.

UNITED MINE WORKERS v. GIBBS, 383 U.S. 715 (1966). The United Mine Workers opposed the opening of a new coal mine operated by workers in a rival union. Violent activities by local individuals delayed the opening of the new mine, and then the United Mine Workers picketed the location and undertook other union actions in opposition. As a result, the company made no further efforts to open the mine. Gibbs had a contract to be superintendent of the new mine and to haul the coal, and he lost these rights because of the Mine Workers' actions.

Gibbs filed suit in a federal court, asserting two distinct but related claims against the Mine Workers Union. The first was based on section 303 of the federal Labor Management Relations Act, which prohibits secondary boycotts. (A "secondary boycott" is an effort to coerce persons with whom the union does not have a labor dispute, in order to force them to withdraw their dealings with someone else.) The second claim, involving the same course of conduct by the union, was based on state law: Gibbs alleged that the union had tortiously interfered with his contract in violation of the common law of Tennessee.

The trial court asserted jurisdiction over both claims. The tortious interference claim had no federal ingredient, and there was no diversity, and so jurisdiction over this claim was based on what now would be called supplemental jurisdiction (then called pendent jurisdiction). After a jury trial of the overlapping evidence relevant to both claims, the trial judge refused to grant judgment on the federal claim because the union's actions did not amount to a prohibited secondary boycott under section 303. This holding, however, was not dispositive of the tortious interference claim, and the trial court entered a judgment on the jury's verdict against the union.

Ultimately, the Supreme Court reversed the judgment on the merits. The federal labor legislation permitted the union's picketing and other labor activities, and the Supreme Court concluded that it also had the effect of nullifying Gibbs's tortious interference claim that would limit the union's activities. (In technical language, the federal Labor Management Relations Act "preempted" Gibbs's state common-law claim for tortious interference.)

In the course of reaching this conclusion on the merits, however, the Court necessarily had to address the jurisdictional issue. It upheld the trial court's exercise of jurisdiction:

Pendent jurisdiction, in the sense of judicial *power*, exists whenever there is a claim 'arising under [the] Constitution, the Laws of the United States, and Treaties made, or which shall be made, under their Authority . . . ,' U.S. Const., Art. III, § 2, and the relationship between that claim and the state claim permits the conclusion that the entire action before the court comprises but one constitutional "case." The federal claim must have substance sufficient to confer subject-matter jurisdiction on the court. The state and federal claims must derive from a common nucleus of operative fact. But if, considered without regard to their federal or state character, a plaintiff's claims are such that he would ordinarily be expected to try them all in one judicial proceeding, then, assuming substantiality of the federal issues, there is *power* in federal courts to hear the whole.

That power need not be exercised in every case in which it is found to exist. It has consistently been recognized that pendent jurisdiction is a doctrine of discretion, not of plaintiff's right. Its justification lies in considerations of judicial economy, convenience and fairness to litigants; if these are not present a federal court should hesitate to exercise jurisdiction over state claims, even though bound to apply state law to them. . . . Certainly, if the federal claims are dismissed before trial, even though not insubstantial in a jurisdictional sense, the state claims should be dismissed as well. Similarly, if it appears that the state issues substantially predominate, whether in terms of proof, of the scope of the issues raised, or of the comprehensiveness of the remedy sought, the state claims may be dismissed without prejudice and left for resolution to state tribunals. There may, on the other hand, be situations in which the state claim is so closely tied to questions of federal policy that the argument for exercise of pendent jurisdiction is particularly strong. In the present case, for example, the allowable scope of the state claim implicates the federal doctrine of pre-emption; while this interrelationship does not create statutory federal question jurisdiction, *Louisville & N.R. Co. v. Mottley*, 211 U.S. 149, its existence [strengthens the argument for trying both cases together].

It is true that the § 303 claims ultimately failed and that the only recovery allowed respondent was on the state claim. We cannot confidently say, however, that the federal issues were so remote or played such a minor role at the trial that in effect the state claim only was tried. . . . [The circumstances show] no error in [the trial court's exercise of jurisdiction over the state-law claim].

NOTES AND QUESTIONS

(1) *Supplemental Jurisdiction Would Produce the Same Result Today in a Gibbs-Type Situation.* The result would be the same in a *Gibbs*-type case today, under section 1367(a) of the supplemental jurisdiction statute. There are subtle differences between the statute and the older doctrine, but they are closely similar.

(2) *Changing the Facts in UMW v. Gibbs and Applying Supplemental Jurisdiction.* What (if any) difference should it make in *UMW v. Gibbs*, if the following events occurred and if the supplemental jurisdiction statute were applied?

(a) *Early Dismissal of the Federal Claim:* What if the District Court had decided early in the case to dismiss the federal claim, on the theory that it failed to state a basis upon which relief could be granted? [Would the court then have had potential jurisdiction over the state claim, and if so, should it be exercised?]

(b) *Strong State Governmental Interests; Ambiguous State Law:* What if the state-law claim had been based on an elaborate state statute, recently enacted by the state legislature and never construed by the state courts?

(c) *Unrelated State and Federal Claims:* What if the state law claim was not related to Gibbs' loss of the employment and haulage contracts that were the basis of the federal claim, but was instead an effort to collect on a promissory note given by the UMW to Gibbs in an unrelated transaction? [Would jurisdiction even exist in this situation?]

(3) *The Supplemental Jurisdiction Statute Allows the Addition of New Parties.* What happens if a pendent claim involves the addition of new and different parties? Answer: The last sentence of section 1367(a) expressly permits this addition. Earlier, this question had been controversial. *See Aldinger v. Howard,* 513 F.2d 1257 (9th Cir. 1975) (plaintiff brought civil rights suit against state officials for wrongfully discharging her from a county job, but was disallowed from adding a pendent claim against a different defendant, the county itself). *See also Finley v. United States*, 490 U.S. 545 (1989). Today, the supplemental jurisdiction statute departs from the *Aldinger* reasoning to promote greater judicial economy by bringing all related parties into one suit.

Appendix to § 3.03[C][1]: Supplemental Jurisdiction in Practice

ORDER OF DISMISSAL IN *WYTINGER v. TWO UNKNOWN POLICE OFFICERS*

[Reproduced above in Appendix to § 1.04]

For a concrete example of supplemental jurisdiction, read (or re-read) the Order of Dismissal in *Wytinger v. Two Unknown Police Officers*, which appears above in the Appendix to Section 1.04. The Amended Complaint attempted to assert a claim under the federal civil rights statute for the plaintiffs' decedent's suicide, and it added a negligence claim arising under state law. The allegation of jurisdiction would have been amended to include an assertion of supplemental jurisdiction over this state-law claim, as follows:

> 4. The action arises under said [federal] section 1983; . . . AND UNDER THE LAW OF THE STATE OF WEST YORK. This Court has jurisdiction under and by virtue of . . . the General Federal Question Statute . . . AND UNDER 28 U.S.C. § 1367, the Supplemental Jurisdiction Statute.

Note that the court's Order dismisses the federal portion of the complaint for failure to state a claim. The Order also says, "the Court declines jurisdiction over Plaintiffs' state claims under *United Mine Workers v. Gibbs*. . . ." Did supplemental jurisdiction exist? Why or why not? Is the refusal to exercise jurisdiction over the state-law claims appropriate? Why or why not?

[2] Supplemental Jurisdiction of the Kind Formerly Called "Ancillary Jurisdiction": Counterclaims, Third-Party Claims, etc.

NOTE ON THE EARLIER DOCTRINE OF ANCILLARY JURISDICTION

An Example. Imagine that the plaintiff and the defendant have both suffered injuries from a collision between automobiles they were driving. The plaintiff sues the defendant in federal court, basing jurisdiction on diversity of citizenship and claiming damages of

$150,000. The defendant thinks that the accident was actually the plaintiff's fault, and he would like to counterclaim. But he can claim only $40,000 in damages. The defendant therefore is lacking an independent basis for federal jurisdiction over his counterclaim, but it would not be appropriate to disallow him from asserting this claim from the same accident in the same suit.

"Ancillary Jurisdiction" was the judge-created answer to this problem. It allows the court to hear counterclaims, third-party claims, cross-claims, or other added claims that lack an independent jurisdictional basis but that should be heard in the same suit as the principal claim. As with pendent jurisdiction, the purpose of ancillary jurisdiction was to promote efficient and consistent resolution of the entire controversy.

The Relationship Between Ancillary Jurisdiction, Pendent Jurisdiction, and Supplemental Jurisdiction. Originally, ancillary and pendent jurisdiction were separate doctrines. The development of the two doctrines brought them closer together, and they appear to have coalesced in the Supreme Court's opinion in *Owen Equipment & Erection Co. v. Kroger*, 437 U.S. 365 (1978). *See* Miller, *Ancillary and Pendent Jurisdiction*, 26 So. Tex. L. Rev. 1 (1985); Matasar, *A Pendent and Ancillary Jurisdiction Primer: The Scope and Limits of Supplemental Jurisdiction*, 17 U.C.D. L. Rev. 103 (1983). And today, the supplemental jurisdiction statute has replaced both ancillary and pendent jurisdiction — although they still are useful concepts for understanding current law.

NOTES AND QUESTIONS

(1) *The Traditional Uses of Ancillary Jurisdiction.* The most frequent uses of ancillary jurisdiction historically were in situations involving defendants' assertions of third-party claims (also called "impleader"), cross-claims, and counterclaims. Today the supplemental jurisdiction statute governs all of these situations.

(2) *The Exception in Section 1367(b): Prohibiting Certain Uses of Supplemental Jurisdiction by Plaintiffs.* Section 1367(b) disallows supplemental jurisdiction "over claims by plaintiffs against persons made parties under Rule 14 [*i.e.*, third-party defendants]," as well as certain other claims. In other words, the plaintiff cannot assert a state-law claim in federal court against a co-citizen merely because that party has been brought into the case by the defendant. This provision codifies holdings under the earlier doctrine of ancillary jurisdiction.

Owen Equipment & Erection Co. v. Kroger, 437 U.S. 365 (1978), illustrates an important exception to ancillary jurisdiction. In that case, Kroger's husband walked next to a steel crane that came too close to electric lines and died by electrocution. She sued the local power company. Since she was a citizen of Iowa, and the power company was a citizen of Nebraska, Kroger filed her state-law wrongful death claim as a diversity action in federal court. But the defendant filed a third-party action against the crane operator, Owen, alleging that Owen was solely responsible. Kroger realized that if the power company was correct, her only claim might be against Owen, and she therefore amended her complaint to add a claim directly against Owen. She alleged that Owen was a citizen of Nebraska and therefore diverse from her, and Owen admitted this allegation in its answer.

The trial resulted in a verdict for Kroger, but it also revealed that as a result of an avulsion of the Missouri River, Owen's jurisdictional admission was mistaken(!) Owen actually was a citizen of Iowa, the same state as Kroger. Unless ancillary jurisdiction existed, it appeared that Kroger's hard-won verdict would be wiped out.

The Court held that ancillary jurisdiction (or what now would be supplemental jurisdiction) was improper. The doctrine of complete diversity meant that jurisdiction under the diversity statute "does not exist unless each defendant is a citizen of a different State from each plaintiff." The federal courts are courts of limited jurisdiction, and the limits "must be neither disregarded nor evaded." If ancillary jurisdiction were to be recognized here, a plaintiff could exploit it "by the simple expedient of suing only those defendants who were of diverse citizenship and waiting for them to implead nondiverse defendants." Such a claim is "simply not ancillary." The plaintiff could have achieved the goal of unitary litigation in the state courts but instead "voluntarily chose to bring suit upon a state-law claim in a federal court."

The majority's holding resulted because the Court decided to expand the complete diversity doctrine and to confine the ancillary jurisdiction doctrine narrowly. In dissent, Justice White saw "no justification" for this preference. Kroger had filed suit in accordance with a jurisdictional statute and added a claim against Owen only after Owen had been brought in by the independent action of the power company. This use of ancillary jurisdiction did not "flout the congressional command" in the absence of collusion by plaintiff and defendant, "of which there is absolutely no indication here." In case of collusion, the district court had authority to dismiss under 28 U.S.C. § 1359 (*See* § 3.03[B][2], above).

Notice that the prohibition in section 1367(b) would produce the same result if *Owen Equipment v. Kroger* were to arise today. The holding there seems harsh, even tragic, in light of Owen's admission of the jurisdictional facts and Kroger's unquestioned good faith. Justice White points out that Kroger could succeed in a new suit in state court only "if the Iowa statute of limitations will still permit such a suit." Is this complex exception to supplemental jurisdiction in 1367(b) worth the damage it causes? (On the other hand, note that mistaken admissions of jurisdictional facts probably are rare, and they could be remedied by the usual rule that good faith stipulations to such facts are binding. Perhaps the Supreme Court could have preserved its holding and still avoided a strikingly unjust result by applying this binding-stipulation rule against Owen.)

There were a few other situations in which ancillary jurisdiction had been recognized, including intervention of right. *Freeman v. Howe*, 65 U.S. (24 How.) 450 (1860). *Freeman* actually was the case from which ancillary jurisdiction originally derived. The Court there said that when a federal court "effectively controls the property or fund under dispute, other claimants thereto should be allowed to intervene in order to protect their interests, without regard to jurisdiction." Does the supplemental jurisdiction statute reverse the decision in *Freeman*?

(3) *Situations in Which the Court May Decline Jurisdiction.* As noted above, section 1367(c) of the supplemental jurisdiction statute also provides that the court may decline to exercise jurisdiction in certain situations, such as supplemental claims that "predominate."

[3] The Supplemental Jurisdiction Statute

The supplemental jurisdiction statute has been criticized as being poorly drafted and ambiguous. *See, e.g.*, Thomas Arthur & Richard Freer, *Close Enough for Government Work: What Happens When Congress Doesn't Do Its Job*, 40 Emory L.J. 1007 (1991). The drafters of the statute have answered these critics, arguing that the statute satisfactorily responds to the concern, as expressed in the House Report on the bill, that plaintiffs should not be allowed to evade the jurisdictional requirements of 28 U.S.C. § 1332 "by the simple expedient of naming initially only those defendants whose joinder satisfies section 1332's requirements and later adding claims not within federal jurisdiction against other defendants who have intervened or been joined on a supplemental basis." They contend that the statute is clear that cross-claims among defendants, compulsory counterclaims by defendants, and impleader claims are expressly authorized by subsection (a) and not prohibited by subsection (b). Claims by a third-party defendant are treated in the same manner. The result does not depend on whether the case is a diversity or federal question case. The drafters also assert that it provides clear guidance in almost all other situations, contending that the statute clearly prohibits supplemental jurisdiction in the *Kroger* situation (a state-law claim initiated by a diversity plaintiff against a nondiverse third-party defendant), and also prohibits supplemental jurisdiction over claims by plaintiffs against nondiverse defendants who are joined pursuant to Rules 19 and 20. *See* Thomas Rowe, Jr., Stephen Burbank & Thomas Mengler, *A Coda on Supplemental Jurisdiction*, 40 Emory L.J. 993, 995-96 (1991). The following case explains how to interpret subsections 1367(a) and (b).

EXXON MOBIL CORP. v. ALLAPATTAH SERVICES, INC.

547 U.S. —, 125 S. Ct. 2611 (2005)

KENNEDY, J., delivered the opinion of the Court, in which REHNQUIST, C.J., and SCALIA, SOUTER, and THOMAS, JJ., joined. STEVENS, J., filed a dissenting opinion, in which BREYER, J., joined. GINSBURG, J., filed a dissenting opinion, in which STEVENS, O'CONNOR, and BREYER, JJ., joined.

JUSTICE KENNEDY delivered the opinion of the Court.

These consolidated cases present the question whether a federal court in a diversity action may exercise supplemental jurisdiction over additional plaintiffs whose claims do not satisfy the minimum amount-in-controversy requirement, provided the claims are part of the same case or controversy as the claims of plaintiffs who do allege a sufficient amount in controversy. Our decision turns on the correct interpretation of 28 U.S.C. § 1367. The question has divided the Courts of Appeals, and we granted certiorari to resolve the conflict. . . .

We hold that, where the other elements of jurisdiction are present and at least one named plaintiff in the action satisfies the amount-in-controversy requirement, § 1367 does authorize supplemental jurisdiction over the claims of other plaintiffs in the same Article III case or controversy, even if those claims are for less than the jurisdictional amount specified in the statute setting forth the requirements for diversity jurisdiction. We affirm the judgment of the Court of Appeals for the Eleventh Circuit in No. 04-70, and we reverse the judgment of the Court of Appeals for the First Circuit in No. 04-79.

I

In 1991, about 10,000 Exxon dealers filed a class-action suit against the Exxon Corporation in the United States District Court for the Northern District of Florida. The dealers alleged an intentional and systematic scheme by Exxon under which they were overcharged for fuel purchased from Exxon. The plaintiffs invoked the District Court's § 1332(a) diversity jurisdiction. After a unanimous jury verdict in favor of the plaintiffs, the District Court certified the case for interlocutory review, asking whether it had properly exercised § 1367 supplemental jurisdiction over the claims of class members who did not meet the jurisdictional minimum amount in controversy.

The Court of Appeals for the Eleventh Circuit upheld the District Court's extension of supplemental jurisdiction to these class members. *Allapattah Services, Inc. v. Exxon Corp.*, 333 F.3d 1248 (2003). "[W]e find," the court held, "that § 1367 clearly and unambiguously provides district courts with the authority in diversity class actions to exercise supplemental jurisdiction over the claims of class members who do not meet the minimum amount in controversy as long as the district court has original jurisdiction over the claims of at least one of the class representatives." *Id.*, at 1256. This decision accords with the views of the Courts of Appeals for the Fourth, Sixth, and Seventh Circuits. *See Rosmer v. Pfizer, Inc.*, 263 F.3d 110 (4th Cir. 2001); *Olden v. LaFarge Corp.*, 383 F.3d 495 (6th Cir. 2004); *Stromberg Metal Works, Inc. v. Press Mechanical, Inc.*, 77 F.3d 928 (7th Cir. 1996); *In re Brand Name Prescription Drugs Antitrust Litigation*, 123 F.3d 599 (7th Cir. 1997). The Courts of Appeals for the Fifth and Ninth Circuits, adopting a similar analysis of the statute, have held that in a diversity class action the unnamed class members need not meet the amount-in-controversy requirement, provided the named class members do. These decisions, however, are unclear on whether all the named plaintiffs must satisfy this requirement. *In re Abbott Labs.*, 51 F.3d 524 (5th Cir. 1995); *Gibson v. Chrysler Corp.*, 261 F.3d 927 (9th Cir. 2001).

In the other case now before us the Court of Appeals for the First Circuit took a different position on the meaning of § 1367(a). 370 F.3d 124 (2004). In that case, a 9-year-old girl sued Star-Kist in a diversity action in the United States District Court for the District of Puerto Rico, seeking damages for unusually severe injuries she received when she sliced her finger on a tuna can. Her family joined in the suit, seeking damages for emotional distress and certain medical expenses. The District Court granted summary judgment to Star-Kist, finding that none of the plaintiffs met the minimum amount-in-controversy requirement. The Court of Appeals for the First Circuit, however, ruled that the injured girl, but not her family members, had made allegations of damages in the requisite amount.

The Court of Appeals then addressed whether, in light of the fact that one plaintiff met the requirements for original jurisdiction, supplemental jurisdiction over the remaining plaintiffs' claims was proper under § 1367. The court held that § 1367 authorizes supplemental jurisdiction only when the district court has original jurisdiction over the action, and that in a diversity case original jurisdiction is lacking if one plaintiff fails to satisfy the amount-in-controversy requirement. Although the Court of Appeals claimed to "express no view" on whether the result would be the same in a class action, *id.*, at 143, n.19, its analysis is inconsistent with that of the Court of Appeals for the Eleventh Circuit. The Court of Appeals for the First Circuit's view of § 1367 is, however, shared by the Courts of Appeals for the Third, Eighth, and Tenth Circuits, and the latter two Courts of Appeals have expressly applied this rule to class actions. *See Meritcare, Inc. v. St. Paul Mercury Ins. Co.*, 166 F.3d 214 (3d Cir. 1999); *Trimble v. Asarco, Inc.*, 232 F.3d 946 (8th Cir. 2000); *Leonhardt v. Western Sugar Co.*, 160 F.3d 631 (10th Cir. 1998).

II

A

The district courts of the United States, as we have said many times, are "courts of limited jurisdiction. They possess only that power authorized by Constitution and statute," *Kokkonen v. Guardian Life Ins. Co. of America*, 511 U.S. 375, 377, 114 S.Ct. 1673, 128 L.Ed.2d 391 (1994). . . .

Although the district courts may not exercise jurisdiction absent a statutory basis, it is well established — in certain classes of cases — that, once a court has original jurisdiction over some claims in the action, it may exercise supplemental jurisdiction over additional claims that are part of the same case or controversy. The leading modern case for this principle is *United Mine Workers v. Gibbs*, 383 U.S. 715, 86 S.Ct. 1130, 16 L.Ed.2d 218 (1966). . . .

As we later noted, the decision allowing jurisdiction over pendent state claims in *Gibbs* did not mention, let alone come to grips with, the text of the jurisdictional statutes and the bedrock principle that federal courts have no jurisdiction without statutory authorization. *Finley v. United States*, 490 U.S. 545, 548, 109 S.Ct. 2003, 104 L.Ed.2d 593 (1989). In *Finley*, we nonetheless reaffirmed and rationalized *Gibbs* and its progeny by inferring from it the interpretive principle that, in cases involving supplemental jurisdiction over additional claims between parties properly in federal court, the jurisdictional statutes should be read broadly, on the assumption that in this context Congress intended to authorize courts to exercise their full Article III power to dispose of an "entire action before the court [which] comprises but one constitutional 'case.'" 490 U.S., at 549, 109 S.Ct. 2003 (quoting *Gibbs*, *supra*, at 725, 86 S.Ct. 1130).

We have not, however, applied *Gibbs*' expansive interpretive approach to other aspects of the jurisdictional statutes. For instance, we have consistently interpreted § 1332 as requiring complete diversity: In a case with multiple plaintiffs and multiple defendants, the presence in the action of a single plaintiff from the same State as a single defendant deprives the district court of original diversity jurisdiction over the entire action. *Strawbridge v. Curtiss*, 7 U.S. 267, 3 Cranch 267, 2 L.Ed. 435 (1806); *Owen Equipment & Erection Co. v. Kroger*, 437 U.S. 365, 375, 57 L.Ed.2d 274, 98 S.Ct. 2396 (1978). The complete diversity requirement is not mandated by the Constitution, *State Farm Fire & Casualty Co. v. Tashire*, 386 U.S. 523, 530-531, 18 L.Ed.2d 270, 87 S.Ct. 1199 (1967), or by the plain text of § 1332(a). The Court, nonetheless, has adhered to the complete diversity rule in light of the purpose of the diversity requirement, which is to provide a federal forum for important disputes where state courts might favor, or be perceived as favoring, home-state litigants. The presence of parties from the same State on both sides of a case dispels this concern, eliminating a principal reason for conferring § 1332 jurisdiction over any of the claims in the action. *See Wisconsin Dept. of Corrections v. Schacht*, 524 U.S. 381, 389, 141 L.Ed.2d 364, 118 S.Ct. 2047 (1998); *Newman-Green, Inc. v. Alfonzo-Larrain*, 490 U.S. 826, 829, 104 L.Ed.2d 893, 109 S.Ct. 2218 (1989). The specific purpose of the complete diversity rule explains both why we have not adopted *Gibbs*' expansive interpretive approach to this aspect of the jurisdictional statute and why *Gibbs* does not undermine the complete diversity rule. In order for a federal court to invoke supplemental jurisdiction under *Gibbs*, it must first have original jurisdiction over at least one claim in the action. Incomplete diversity destroys original jurisdiction with respect to all claims, so there is nothing to which supplemental jurisdiction can adhere.

In contrast to the diversity requirement, most of the other statutory prerequisites for federal jurisdiction, including the federal-question and amount-in-controversy requirements, can be analyzed claim by claim. True, it does not follow by necessity from this that a district court has authority to exercise supplemental jurisdiction over all claims provided there is original jurisdiction over just one. Before the enactment of § 1367, the Court declined in contexts other than the pendent-claim instance to follow *Gibbs*' expansive approach to interpretation of the jurisdictional statutes. The Court took a more restrictive view of the proper interpretation of these statutes in so-called pendent-party cases involving supplemental jurisdiction over claims involving additional parties — plaintiffs or defendants — where the district courts would lack original jurisdiction over claims by each of the parties standing alone.

. . . .

B

In *Finley* we emphasized that "[w]hatever we say regarding the scope of jurisdiction conferred by a particular statute can of course be changed by Congress." 490 U.S., at 556, 109 S.Ct. 2003. In 1990, Congress accepted the invitation. It passed the Judicial Improvements Act, 104 Stat. 5089, which enacted § 1367, the provision which controls these cases. . . .

Section 1367(a) is a broad grant of supplemental jurisdiction over other claims within the same case or controversy, as long as the action is one in which the district courts would have original jurisdiction. The last sentence of § 1367(a) makes it clear that the grant of supplemental jurisdiction extends to claims involving joinder or intervention of additional parties. The single question before us, therefore, is whether a diversity case in which the claims of some plaintiffs satisfy the amount-in-controversy requirement, but the claims of other plaintiffs do not, presents a "civil action of which the district courts have original jurisdiction." If the answer is yes, § 1367(a) confers supplemental jurisdiction over all claims, including those that do not independently satisfy the amount-in-controversy requirement, if the claims are part of the same Article III case or controversy. If the answer is no, § 1367(a) is inapplicable and, in light of our holdings in *Clark* and *Zahn*, the district court has no statutory basis for exercising supplemental jurisdiction over the additional claims.

We now conclude the answer must be yes. When the well-pleaded complaint contains at least one claim that satisfies the amount-in-controversy requirement, and there are no other relevant jurisdictional defects, the district court, beyond all question, has original jurisdiction over that claim. The presence of other claims in the complaint, over which the district court may lack original jurisdiction, is of no moment. If the court has original jurisdiction over a single claim in the complaint, it has original jurisdiction over a "civil action" within the meaning of § 1367(a), even if the civil action over which it has jurisdiction comprises fewer claims than were included in the complaint. Once the court determines it has original jurisdiction over the civil action, it can turn to the question whether it has a constitutional and statutory basis for exercising supplemental jurisdiction over the other claims in the action.

Section 1367(a) commences with the direction that §§ 1367(b) and (c), or other relevant statutes, may provide specific exceptions, but otherwise § 1367(a) is a broad jurisdictional grant, with no distinction drawn between pendent-claim and pendent-party cases. In fact, the last sentence of § 1367(a) makes clear that the provision grants supplemental jurisdiction over claims involving joinder or intervention of additional parties. . . .

If § 1367(a) were the sum total of the relevant statutory language, our holding would rest on that language alone. The statute, of course, instructs us to examine § 1367(b) to determine if any of its exceptions apply, so we proceed to that section. While § 1367(b) qualifies the broad rule of § 1367(a), it does not withdraw supplemental jurisdiction over the claims of the additional parties at issue here. The specific exceptions to § 1367(a) contained in § 1367(b), moreover, provide additional support for our conclusion that

§ 1367(a) confers supplemental jurisdiction over these claims. Section 1367(b), which applies only to diversity cases, withholds supplemental jurisdiction over the claims of plaintiffs proposed to be joined as indispensable parties under Federal Rule of Civil Procedure 19, or who seek to intervene pursuant to Rule 24. Nothing in the text of § 1367(b), however, withholds supplemental jurisdiction over the claims of plaintiffs permissively joined under Rule 20 (like the additional plaintiffs in No. 04-79) or certified as class-action members pursuant to Rule 23 (like the additional plaintiffs in No. 04-70). The natural, indeed the necessary, inference is that § 1367 confers supplemental jurisdiction over claims by Rule 20 and Rule 23 plaintiffs. This inference, at least with respect to Rule 20 plaintiffs, is strengthened by the fact that § 1367(b) explicitly excludes supplemental jurisdiction over claims against defendants joined under Rule 20.

We cannot accept the view, urged by some of the parties, commentators, and Courts of Appeals, that a district court lacks original jurisdiction over a civil action unless the court has original jurisdiction over every claim in the complaint. As we understand this position, it requires assuming either that all claims in the complaint must stand or fall as a single, indivisible "civil action" as a matter of definitional necessity — what we will refer to as the "indivisibility theory" — or else that the inclusion of a claim or party falling outside the district court's original jurisdiction somehow contaminates every other claim in the complaint, depriving the court of original jurisdiction over any of these claims — what we will refer to as the "contamination theory."

The indivisibility theory is easily dismissed, as it is inconsistent with the whole notion of supplemental jurisdiction. If a district court must have original jurisdiction over every claim in the complaint in order to have "original jurisdiction" over a "civil action," then in *Gibbs* there was no civil action of which the district court could assume original jurisdiction under § 1331, and so no basis for exercising supplemental jurisdiction over any of the claims. The indivisibility theory is further belied by our practice — in both federal-question and diversity cases — of allowing federal courts to cure jurisdictional defects by dismissing the offending parties rather than dismissing the entire action. . . .

The contamination theory, as we have noted, can make some sense in the special context of the complete diversity requirement because the presence of nondiverse parties on both sides of a lawsuit eliminates the justification for providing a federal forum. The theory, however, makes little sense with respect to the amount-in-controversy requirement, which is meant to ensure that a dispute is sufficiently important to warrant federal-court attention. The presence of a single nondiverse party may eliminate the fear of bias with respect to all claims, but the presence of a claim that falls short of the minimum amount in controversy does nothing to reduce the importance of the claims that do meet this requirement.

It is fallacious to suppose, simply from the proposition that § 1332 imposes both the diversity requirement and the amount-in-controversy requirement, that the contamination theory germane to the former is also relevant to the latter. There is no inherent logical connection between the amount-in-controversy requirement and § 1332 diversity jurisdiction. After all, federal-question jurisdiction once had an amount-in-controversy requirement as well. If such a requirement were revived under § 1331, it is clear beyond peradventure that § 1367(a) provides supplemental jurisdiction over federal-question cases where some, but not all, of the federal-law claims involve a sufficient amount in controversy. . . .

. . . .

And so we circle back to the original question. When the well-pleaded complaint in district court includes multiple claims, all part of the same case or controversy, and some, but not all, of the claims are within the court's original jurisdiction, does the court have before it "any civil action of which the district courts have original jurisdiction"? It does. Under § 1367, the court has original jurisdiction over the civil action comprising the claims for which there is no jurisdictional defect. No other reading of § 1367 is plausible in light of the text and structure of the jurisdictional statute. Though the special nature and purpose of the diversity requirement mean that a single nondiverse party can contaminate every other claim in the lawsuit, the contamination does not occur with respect to jurisdictional defects that go only to the substantive importance of individual claims.

It follows from this conclusion that the threshold requirement of § 1367(a) is satisfied in cases, like those now before us, where some, but not all, of the plaintiffs in a diversity action allege a sufficient amount in controversy. We hold that § 1367 by its plain text overruled *Clark* and *Zahn* and authorized supplemental jurisdiction over all claims by diverse parties arising out of the same Article III case or controversy, subject only to enumerated exceptions not applicable in the cases now before us.

C

The proponents of the alternative view of § 1367 insist that the statute is at least ambiguous and that we should look to other interpretive tools, including the legislative history of § 1367, which supposedly demonstrate Congress did not intend § 1367 to overrule *Zahn*. We can reject this argument at the very outset simply because § 1367 is not ambiguous. . . . Even if we were to stipulate . . . that the reading these proponents urge upon us is textually plausible, the legislative history cited to support it would not alter our view as to the best interpretation of § 1367. . . .

[T]he legislative history of § 1367 is far murkier than selective quotation from the House Report would suggest. . . .

D

Finally, we note that the Class Action Fairness Act (CAFA), Pub.L. 109-2, 119 Stat. 4, enacted this year, has no bearing on our analysis of these cases. . . .

The judgment of the Court of Appeals for the Eleventh Circuit is affirmed. The judgment of the Court of Appeals for the First Circuit is reversed, and the case is remanded for proceedings consistent with this opinion.

It is so ordered.

JUSTICE STEVENS, with whom JUSTICE BREYER joins, dissenting.

[A]fter nearly 20 pages of complicated analysis, which explores subtle doctrinal nuances and coins various neologisms, the Court announces that § 1367 could not reasonably be read another way. . . . That conclusion is difficult to accept. Given Justice Ginsburg's persuasive account of the statutory text and its jurisprudential backdrop, and given the uncommonly clear legislative history, I am confident that the majority's interpretation of § 1367 is mistaken. I respectfully dissent.

JUSTICE GINSBURG, with whom JUSTICE STEVENS, JUSTICE O'CONNOR, and JUSTICE BREYER join, dissenting.

[S]ection 1367, all agree, was designed to overturn this Court's decision in *Finley v. United States*, 490 U.S. 545, 109 S.Ct. 2003, 104 L.Ed.2d 593 (1989). *Finley* concerned not diversity-of-citizenship jurisdiction (28 U.S.C. § 1332), but . . . arising under . . . (28 U.S.C. § 1331). The plaintiff in *Finley* sued the United States under the Federal Tort Claims Act (FTCA), 28 U.S.C. § 1346(b), to recover for the death of her husband and children in an airplane crash. She alleged that the Federal Aviation Administration's negligence contributed to the fatal accident. She later amended her complaint to add state-law tort claims against two other defendants, a municipality and a utility company. 490 U.S., at 546-547, 109 S.Ct. 2003. No independent basis for federal subject-matter jurisdiction existed over the state-law claims. The plaintiff could not have brought her entire action in state court, because federal jurisdiction in FTCA actions is exclusive. § 1346(b). Hence, absent federal jurisdiction embracing the state-law claims, she would be obliged to pursue two discrete actions, one in federal court, the other in state court. This Court held, nevertheless, that the District Court lacked jurisdiction over the "pendent-party" state-law claims. *Id.*, at 555-556, 109 S.Ct. 2003. Congress could reverse the result in *Finley*, and permit pendent jurisdiction over state-law claims against additional defendants, if it so chose. *Id.*, at 556, 109 S.Ct. 2003. Congress did so in § 1367.

What more § 1367 wrought is an issue on which courts of appeals have sharply divided. . . .

. . . .

II

A

Section 1367, by its terms, operates only in civil actions "of which the district courts have original jurisdiction." The "original jurisdiction" relevant here is diversity-of-citizenship jurisdiction, conferred by § 1332. The character of that jurisdiction is the essential backdrop for comprehension of § 1367. . . .

[T]his Court has long held that, in determining whether the amount-in-controversy requirement has been satisfied, a single plaintiff may aggregate two or more claims against a single defendant, even if the claims are unrelated. . . . But in multiparty cases, including class actions, we have unyieldingly adhered to the nonaggregation rule stated in *Troy Bank*. . . . The rule that each plaintiff must independently satisfy the amount-in-controversy requirement, unless Congress expressly orders otherwise, was thus the solidly established reading of § 1332 when Congress enacted the Judicial Improvements Act of 1990, which added § 1367 to Title 28.

B

[Section] 1367(a) addresses "civil action[s] of which the district courts have original jurisdiction," a formulation that, in diversity cases, is sensibly read to incorporate the rules on joinder and aggregation tightly tied to § 1332 at the time of § 1367's enactment. On this reading, a complaint must first meet that "original jurisdiction" measurement. If it does not, no supplemental jurisdiction is authorized. If it does, § 1367(a) authorizes "supplemental jurisdiction" over related claims. In other words, § 1367(a) would preserve undiminished, as part and parcel of § 1332 "original jurisdiction" determinations, both the "complete diversity" rule and the decisions restricting aggregation to arrive at the amount in controversy.[9] . . . In contrast to the Court's construction of § 1367, which

---

[9] On this reading of § 1367(a), it is immaterial that § 1367(b) "does not withdraw supplemental jurisdiction over the claims of the additional parties at issue here." . . . Because those claims would not come within § 1367(a) in the first place, Congress would have had no reason to list them in § 1367(b). . . .

draws a sharp line between the diversity and amount-in-controversy components of § 1332, . . . the interpretation presented here does not sever the two jurisdictional requirements.

The more restrained reading of § 1367 just outlined would yield affirmance of the First Circuit's judgment in *Ortega*, and reversal of the Eleventh Circuit's judgment in *Exxon*. It would not discard entirely, as the Court does, the judicially developed doctrines of pendent and ancillary jurisdiction as they existed when *Finley* was decided. Instead, it would recognize § 1367 essentially as a codification of those doctrines, placing them under a single heading, but largely retaining their substance, with overriding *Finley* the only basic change: Supplemental jurisdiction, once the district court has original jurisdiction, would now include "claims that involve the joinder or intervention of additional parties." § 1367(a). . . .

While § 1367's enigmatic text[12] defies flawless interpretation . . .,[13] the precedent-preservative reading, I am persuaded, better accords with the historical and legal context of Congress' enactment of the supplemental jurisdiction statute, . . . and the established limits on pendent and ancillary jurisdiction . . . .

For the reasons stated, I would hold that § 1367 does not overrule *Clark* and *Zahn*. I would therefore affirm the judgment of the Court of Appeals for the First Circuit and reverse the judgment of the Court of Appeals for the Eleventh Circuit.

NOTE ON UNDERSTANDING SUPPLEMENTAL JURISDICTION

The following paragraphs illustrate the proper interpretation of the supplemental jurisdiction statute after the Supreme Court's decision in *Exxon Mobil Corp. v. Allapattah Services, Inc.*, 544 U.S. —, 125 S. Ct. 2611 (2005).

(1) *Codification of Gibbs doctrine in Section 1367(a).* If A sues B and asserts a federal question claim coupled with a state law claim based on the same facts, does the statute provide a basis for supplemental jurisdiction? [Yes, section 1367(a) creates jurisdiction over the related state claims even if A and B are residents of the same state.] It also

---

[12] The Court notes the passage this year of the Class Action Fairness Act (CAFA), . . . only to dismiss that legislation as irrelevant. Subject to several exceptions and qualifications, CAFA provides for federal-court adjudication of state-law-based class actions in which diversity is "minimal" (one plaintiff's diversity from one defendant suffices), and the "matter in controversy" is an aggregate amount in excess of $5,000,000. Significant here, CAFA's enlargement of federal-court diversity jurisdiction was accomplished, "clearly and conspicuously," by amending § 1332. *Cf. Rosario Ortega*, 370 F.3d 124, 142 (1st Cir. 2004).

[13] If § 1367(a) itself renders unnecessary the listing of Rule 20 plaintiffs and Rule 23 class actions in § 1367(b), . . . then it is similarly unnecessary to refer, as § 1367(b) does, to "persons proposed to be joined as plaintiffs under Rule 19." On one account, Congress bracketed such persons with persons "seeking to intervene as plaintiffs under Rule 24" to modify pre-§ 1367 practice. Before enactment of § 1367, courts entertained, under the heading ancillary jurisdiction, claims of Rule 24(a) intervenors "of right," *see Owen Equipment & Erection Co. v. Kroger*, 437 U.S. 365, 375, n. 18, 98 S.Ct. 2396, 57 L.Ed.2d 274 (1978), but denied ancillary jurisdiction over claims of "necessary" Rule 19 plaintiffs, *see* 13 Wright & Miller § 3523, p. 127 (2d ed. Supp. 2005). Congress may have sought simply to underscore that those seeking to join as plaintiffs, whether under Rule 19 or Rule 24, should be treated alike, *i.e.*, denied joinder when "inconsistent with the jurisdictional requirements of section 1332." *See Ortega*, 370 F.3d, at 140, and n. 15 (internal quotation marks omitted); H.R. Rep., at 29 ("Subsection (b) makes one small change in pre-*Finley* practice," *i.e.*, it eliminates the Rule 19/Rule 24 anomaly).

allows supplemental jurisdiction for compulsory counterclaims under Fed. R. Civ. P. 13(a) and cross-claims under Fed. R. Civ. P. 13(g) because the "same transaction or occurrence" requirement for these claims is the functional equivalent of Section 1367(a)'s "same case or controversy under Article III of the United States Constitution."

(2) *Repeal of Finley's Pendent Party Exception by Section 1367(a).* Section 1367(a)'s last sentence reverses *Finley v. United States*, 490 U.S. 545 (1989). If A has a federal question claim against B as well as a state law claim against C, does the statute provide a basis for supplemental jurisdiction over A's claim against C? [Yes, section 1367(a) creates jurisdiction over the related state claims and the last sentence of section 1367(a) extends this approach to additional parties.]

(3) *The Adoption of a "Contamination Theory" for Section 1367(a).* Assume that A has a solid diversity claim (including the amount in controversy requirement) against Big Corporation. Assume that B has a closely similar claim against Big Corporation, B and Big Corporation are of diverse citizenship, but B's claim does not satisfy the amount in controversy requirement. Is there supplemental jurisdiction over B's claim? [Yes, section 1367(a) creates supplemental jurisdiction, and nothing in section 1367(b) precludes supplemental jurisdiction in this situation.] But what if there is no diversity between B and Big Corporation? Under these circumstances, complete diversity does not exist for the entire case of A and B versus Big Corporation. Does the statute also provide for supplemental jurisdiction of B's claim against Big Corporation? [No, as interpreted in *Allapattah Services*, the statute does not go that far. "In order for a federal court to invoke supplemental jurisdiction under *Gibbs*, it must first have original jurisdiction over at least one claim in the action. Incomplete diversity destroys original jurisdiction with respect to all claims, so there is nothing to which supplemental jurisdiction can adhere." 125 S. Ct. at 2618. But "[i]t is fallacious to suppose, simply from the proposition that § 1332 imposes both the diversity requirement and the amount in controversy requirement, that the contamination theory germane to the former is also relevant to the latter." 125 S. Ct. at 2622.]

(4) *Section 1367(b)'s Necessary Party Exception.* Assume the same facts as in the preceding hypothetical. What if B's interest is such that B is a person needed for just adjudication under Fed. R. Civ. P. 19? [Perversely, section 1367(b) prohibits supplemental jurisdiction in this situation.]

(5) *Codification of Kroger in Section 1367(b).* Section 1367(b) codifies *Owen Equipment & Erection Co. v. Kroger*, 437 U.S. 365 (1978). Thus, if A sues B in a diversity case and B brings a third-party action against C, there is supplemental jurisdiction over the third-party claim against C even though the third-party claim does not satisfy the statutory amount in controversy requirement. But what if the third-party plaintiff (B) and the third-party defendant (C) are citizens of the same state? Further, if A sues C, is there supplemental jurisdiction over that claim if they are citizens of the same state? [Section 1367(b) does not prohibit the third-party claim, but precludes the plaintiff from using supplemental jurisdiction to sue C.]

(6) *Reversal of Zahn's Amount in Controversy Requirements.* In *Zahn v. International Paper Co.*, 414 U.S. 291 (1973), the Supreme Court held that even though only the citizenship of the class representatives and the defendant or defendants is considered in deciding whether the complete diversity requirement has been satisfied, every class member's claim must satisfy the amount in controversy requirement. Prior to *Allapattah Services*, several courts of appeals considered whether the supplemental jurisdiction statute reversed *Zahn*. *See, e.g.*, *In re Abbott Laboratories*, 51 F.3d 524 (5th Cir. 1995)

(holding that supplemental jurisdiction covered class claims if the class representative claims satisfied diversity and amount in controversy requirements), *aff'd by an equally divided Court*, 120 S. Ct. 1578 (2000). In *Allapattah Services*, the Court held that the statute reverses *Zahn*. If A has a diversity claim under Fed. R. Civ. P. 23 against B, which satisfies the requirements of complete diversity and the amount in controversy, if A brings a class action against B on behalf of a class of 1,000 similarly situated claims, is there supplemental jurisdiction over the class claims? [Yes, section 1367(a) creates supplemental jurisdiction and nothing in section 1367(b) limits its application to class actions under Fed. R. Civ. P. 23.]

(7) *Reversal of Freeman v. Howe by Section 1367(b).* Another interesting application of the supplemental jurisdiction statute involves the reversal of *Freeman v. Howe*, 65 U.S. (24 How.) 450 (1860). In that case, the Court ruled that an intervenor who claimed an interest in the property that was the subject matter of the action could intervene under principles of ancillary jurisdiction in order to protect the intervenor's interest. Does section 1367(b) preclude the use of supplemental jurisdiction by such an intervenor? [Yes, section 1367(b) specifically provides that supplemental jurisdiction is prohibited under these circumstances.] Does it permit or prohibit the use of supplemental jurisdiction by a permissive intervenor? [Section 1367(a) probably does not permit it, so the fact that section 1367(b) prohibits it, too, is immaterial.]

ACRI v. VARIAN ASSOCIATES, INC.

114 F.3d 999 (9th Cir. 1997)

RYMER, CIRCUIT JUDGE:

George Acri sued his former employer, Varian Associates, Inc., in California Superior Court, alleging age discrimination claims under both federal and California law, as well as contract claims under California law. The parties are non-diverse, but Varian removed the action to federal court on the basis of Acri's claim under the [federal] Age Discrimination in Employment Act. The district court granted summary judgment on the supplemental state law claims as well as the federal age discrimination claim. Acri appealed only the dismissal of his state law claims.

Neither Acri nor Varian, nor the district court, questioned whether supplemental jurisdiction over the state law claims should be declined pursuant to 28 U.S.C. § 1367(c) [containing the discretionary grounds for dismissal]. Under these circumstances, before enactment of the [supplemental jurisdiction statute], we saw no need to consider sua sponte whether the district court should have declined to retain jurisdiction to resolve the state law claims. However, two recent opinions can be read to suggest otherwise: *Reynolds v. County of San Diego,* 84 F.3d 1162, 1171 (9th Cir. 1996) (apparently considering the question without invitation and directing the district court to dismiss state claims left pending after summary judgment on federal claims), and *Allen v. City of Los Angeles,* 92 F.3d 842, 845 (9th Cir. 1996) (stating that . . . "although neither party raised a jurisdictional issue, we examine jurisdiction sua sponte").

We have therefore taken this case en banc [i.e., to be decided by all eleven judges of the court] to consider the extent to which a federal court is obliged to make a § 1367(c) analysis when no one has asked it to do so. We hold that when there is power to hear the case under § 1367(a) [which defines supplemental jurisdiction], the district court may exercise supplemental jurisdiction over state law claims without sua sponte addressing whether it should be declined under § 1367(c). Likewise, we are not required, sua sponte, to decide whether the district court abused its discretion under § 1367(c) when neither party has raised the issue.

This is because a federal district court with power to hear state law claims has discretion to keep, or decline to keep, them under the conditions set out in § 1367(c) — as it has always had under *United Mine Workers v. Gibbs*. That state law claims "should" be dismissed if federal claims are dismissed before trial, as *Gibbs* instructs, has never meant that they must be dismissed. Even more clearly under the statutory scheme, while courts "shall" have supplemental jurisdiction under § 1367(a), they "may" decline to exercise it under § 1367(c). Thus, while a district court must be sure that it has federal jurisdiction under § 1367(a), once it is satisfied that the power to resolve state law claims exists, the court is not required to make a § 1367(c) analysis unless asked to do so by a party. . . .

Having said that, we emphasize that actually exercising discretion and deciding whether to decline, or to retain, supplemental jurisdiction over state law claims when any factor in subdivision (c) is implicated is a responsibility that district courts are duty-bound to take seriously. The Supreme Court has stated, and we have often repeated, that "in the usual case in which all federal-law claims are eliminated before trial, the balance of factors . . . will point toward declining to exercise jurisdiction over the remaining state-law claims." While discretion to decline to exercise supplemental jurisdiction over state law claims is triggered by the presence of one of the conditions in § 1367(c), it is informed by the *Gibbs* values "of economy, convenience, fairness, and comity." . . .

No matter how much we might have preferred a reasoned consideration of the § 1367(c) factors in this case (as in all cases), the district court here was not without jurisdiction over the state law claims and was not required to consider sua sponte whether to decline to continue to exercise that jurisdiction. . . . We overrule suggestions to the contrary in *Reynolds* and *Allen.*

We therefore decline to consider sua sponte whether the district court prudently exercised supplemental jurisdiction in this case, and return [the merits of Acri's appeal] to the panel.

O'Scannlain, Circuit Judge, dissenting: . . .

The majority essentially ignores what the Supreme Court has long required of federal courts exercising supplemental jurisdiction — that the court consider the prudential factors discussed in *Gibbs* . . . . In my view, principles of comity and federalism demand consideration of these factors each time a district court confronts claims brought under its supplemental jurisdiction. The federal nature of our Union, and the commands of [the Supreme Court], matter no less when the parties, for whatever self-serving reasons, fail to object to the exercise of supplemental jurisdiction. . . .

Because sensitive issues of federalism are involved, and because there are strong reasons to discourage the exercise of supplemental jurisdiction when one of the conditions of § 1367(c) is met, district courts should consider sua sponte whether to exercise supplemental jurisdiction. Likewise, when the district court fails to address whether a claim should be in the federal courts at all, the appellate court should raise the question on its own. . . .

I fear that the majority's opinion may incite increasing numbers of litigants to file their state claims in federal court (along with a marginal federal claim) with the hope that their opponents will not object. The resulting burden on the already overloaded dockets of our federal district courts, to say nothing of the heightened tension in federal-state relations, is too high a price to pay for the bright line rule we create today. . . .

NOTES AND QUESTIONS

(1) *Would the Result Have Been Different if Plaintiff Acri Had Made a Timely Objection to Jurisdiction?* If Acri had filed a motion to dismiss or remand the state law claims at the first opportunity, it seems likely that this court would have reached a different result. Can you explain why?

(2) *What if the District Judge Wishes to Decline Jurisdiction for a Reason Not Set Out in the Statute?* Subsection (c) sets out four reasons for declining supplemental jurisdiction. Is this list exclusive, or may the district judge decline jurisdiction for a reason not listed (*e.g.*, desire to lighten a heavy docket)? Notice that the fourth factor is a catchall, allowing jurisdiction to be declined for "compelling" reasons in "extraordinary" cases, but note also that section 1367(a) says that the courts "shall" have jurisdiction under the defined circumstances.

[4] Refusal to Exercise Jurisdiction

[a] The Abstention Doctrines

Justifications for Abstention. In certain circumstances, the federal courts will decline to exercise the jurisdiction given them under the Constitution and statutes. *See generally* Field, *The Abstention Doctrine Today*, 125 U. Pa. L. Rev. 590 (1977). There are at least four situations in which these "abstention doctrines" may apply: (1) when the decision of a constitutional question might be avoided by interpretation of state law; (2) when a federal decision might unnecessarily conflict with a state's governmental affairs; (3) when a significant issue of state law is unsettled; and (4) when there are parallel state and federal proceedings and abstention will reduce the federal workload. *Cf.* C. Wright, *The Law of Federal Courts* 303 (4th ed. 1983).

Abstention Because of Constitutional Issues Involving Pervasive or Ambiguous State Law. Two common abstention doctrines are named after the Supreme Court cases first recognizing them — *Railroad Commission v. Pullman Co.*, 312 U.S. 496 (1941) ("Pullman" abstention), and *Burford v. Sun Oil Co.*, 319 U.S. 315 (1943) ("Burford" abstention). In *Pullman*, the Pullman Company sought to enjoin the enforcement of a state Railroad Commission order. The Supreme Court ordered the trial court to abstain from deciding the case but to retain jurisdiction until a state court decision was obtained on the state issues involved. The Supreme Court reasoned that, in this manner, federal courts could avoid deciding a federal constitutional question prematurely or unnecessarily. In *Burford*, Sun Oil Company attacked the validity of Burford's permit to drill wells in an oil field. The oil field was located in Texas, which had a complicated system for industry regulation. The Supreme Court dismissed the federal proceedings, reasoning that needless conflict with a state's administration of its own affairs should be avoided. Thus, *Burford* abstention avoids the adjudication, by federal courts, of difficult state law questions that threaten to disrupt state policy.

Certification: A Procedure for Federal Courts to Send Difficult Issues of State Law to State Courts. In response to federal abstention, some states have created "certification" procedures. *See* Titze, *Giving Deference to State Law: New South Dakota Certification Statutes Enable Federal Courts to Defer to Supreme Court*, 30 S.D. L. Rev. 299 (1984). In these states, a federal court seeking guidance on a state law question can "certify" the state law question to that state's courts for an answer before proceeding further in the case before it. *Cf. Lehman Bros. v. Schein*, 416 U.S. 386 (1974) (vacating decision of Second Circuit in New York federal diversity action so that court could certify to Florida Supreme Court certain determinative questions of Florida law).

Other Abstention Situations. The Supreme Court also has developed restrictions of the federal courts' authority to enjoin state criminal proceedings. The demands of "our federalism" sometimes require federal courts to refrain from interfering in such an important part of the states' governmental functions even when federally ensured rights may be threatened. *See Younger v. Harris*, 401 U.S. 37 (1971). A more controversial question is whether a federal court should stay its proceedings when a parallel state court action involving the same parties is also underway. *Compare Will v. Calvert Fire Ins. Co.*, 437 U.S. 655 (1978) (deferral to state court proceedings is within the District Court's discretion), *with Moses H. Cone Mem. Hosp. v. Mercury Constr. Corp.*, 460 U.S. 1 (1983) (federal courts have an "obligation" to hear properly brought cases and should defer only in "exceptional circumstances").

[b] The Domestic Relations and Probate Exceptions

The Domestic Relations Exception. If husband and wife are of diverse citizenship, there is no obvious reason why their divorce action cannot be heard by a federal court — but still, it cannot be. There is a judge-created exception to diversity jurisdiction for "domestic relations" cases. The policy underlying this exception is unclear, since it dates from the decision in *Barber v. Barber*, 62 U.S. (21 How.) 582 (1859), in which the Court did uphold federal enforcement of a divorce decree entered in another state but added, in dictum: "We disclaim altogether any jurisdiction in the courts of the United States upon the subject of divorce, or the allowance of alimony, either as an original proceeding or as incident to a divorce. . . ." The exception was later explained by reference to traditional abstention policies and by the special argument that state child welfare, adoption, or custody agencies do not have established relationships with federal courts. Understandably, the scope of the exception is uncertain. *See* Atwood, *Domestic Relations Cases in Federal Court: Toward a Principled Exercise of Jurisdiction*, 35 Hastings L.J. 571 (1984). For example, the federal courts will not exercise jurisdiction to determine alimony — but they usually are able to enforce a contract providing for alimony. The variety of issues appears to be endless; for example, one federal court has written an opinion holding that "palimony" between cohabiting couples is based in contract and is not within the domestic relations exception. *Anastasi v. Anastasi*, 532 F. Supp. 720 (D.N.J. 1982). Unfortunately, the suspicion arises that these jurisdictional ambiguities may, by their possible facilitation of waste and duplication and, thus, harassment, provide an advantage to the party with deeper pockets or more sophistication than his or her spouse. For an analysis, see Baron, *The Evolution of Domestic Relations Cases in Our Federal Courts*, 1985 So. Ill. U. L.J. 353.

The Probate Exception. A federal court may not probate a will or administer an estate, although it can maintain creditors' actions against executors or administrators so long as it does not interfere with the exercise of probate jurisdiction or with control of property by a state court. *See generally* Wright & Kane, *The Law of Federal Courts* 162 (6th ed. 2002). Determination of the extent of jurisdiction, depending as it does on the existence of interference, is sometimes difficult. Furthermore, even if jurisdiction exists, the federal court cannot grant a distribution of the property or order execution to enforce its judgment, but merely decides the claim in a way that can then be enforced in the state probate proceeding. As in the case of the domestic relations exception, the policy basis of this doctrine is unclear (except that it diminishes the workload of the federal courts), and it also can lead to wasteful litigation.

[D] Removal: Defendant's Key to the Federal Courthouse

Read 28 U.S.C. §§ 1441(a), (b), and (c); 1445; 1446; 1447 (the basic removal statutes).

PROBLEM D

APPLYING THE STATUTES DEFINING FEDERAL REMOVAL JURISDICTION. After reading the federal removal jurisdiction statute, 28 U.S.C. § 1441(a)-(c), consider the following cases. All claims are pending in state courts, and all seek damages in excess of $75,000. In each case, answer the question: "Can the defendant remove to federal court?"

(a) *The Straightforward Diversity Situation.* The plaintiff, a citizen of New York, sues defendant, a citizen of Florida, in a New York state trial court, asserting a claim based on state law. [Note: *See* § 1441(a). This one is easy; it boils down to whether the claim is within the federal diversity jurisdiction.]

(b) *A Diversity Case With a Local Defendant.* Now, imagine that the court and suit are the same, but the parties are reversed. That is, the plaintiff is a citizen of Florida, defendant a citizen of New York, and the suit is in a New York State court on state law grounds. [This situation does not call for the same analysis as the first problem! *See* the second sentence of § 1441(b). A local citizen lacks the "local prejudice" argument that is the most frequently stated basis for diversity jurisdiction, and Congress wrote § 1441(b) accordingly.]

(c) *The Federal Question Situation.* Next, imagine the same parties in the same court — but this time, the claim arises under federal law. The Florida citizen sues the New York citizen in a New York state court under the federal civil rights statute, 42 U.S.C. § 1983. [Local prejudice is no longer the relevant consideration. The defendant's interest in having a federal court determine a federal claim is the real issue. Therefore, citizenship is irrelevant. *See* § 1441(b) (first sentence).]

(d) *Two Interconnected Claims, One Otherwise Removable and One Not.* The plaintiff, a citizen of New York, sues a Florida citizen on a federal civil rights claim and a New York citizen on a state-law negligence claim, both for a single injury, allegedly due to the concurrent actions of both. Suit is in a New York state court. [Sections 1441(a) and (b) do not authorize diversity-type removal because diversity is not complete. Section 1441(c) does not authorize removal because the claims are not "separate and independent." Does federal question jurisdiction, together with supplemental jurisdiction, allow removal under § 1441(a) and (b)?]

(e) *"Separate and Independent" Claims, One Removable and One Not.* Finally, imagine that the plaintiff in (d) above alleges that the defendants acted separately and caused different injuries. (The Florida citizen was a police officer who beat him and hurt his head, and then the New York citizen was a doctor who committed malpractice while treating his head, injuring his neck.) Now, the claims are separate and independent, in that they allege different injuries from two different incidents. [§ 1441(c) authorizes removal based upon the existence of federal question jurisdiction over one among several claims.]

Suggested answers: (a) removable; (b) not removable; (c) removable; (d) not removable; (e) removable.

NOTE ON REMOVAL JURISDICTION, PROCEDURE, AND POLICY

The Scope of Removal Jurisdiction. As the problem above demonstrates, the basic thrust of § 1441 is to allow the defendant to remove the case to federal court if it would be suitable for filing there by the plaintiff. However, the statute is slightly more restrictive of removal by defendants than of initial filing by plaintiffs, in that it disallows the use of diversity jurisdiction as a basis for removal by a local defendant. The policy reason is evidently that this defendant can make no argument of local prejudice. The destruction of diversity ordinarily prevents removal, just as it prevents initial filing in federal court by a plaintiff. Notice that this principle enables a plaintiff to structure the suit so that diversity-based removal is prevented, by the expedient of joining a local defendant. However, there should be a limit to this tactic, and § 1441(c) prevents a plaintiff from frustrating removal if the joined claims are not closely related (*i.e.*, if they are "separate and independent") and if an otherwise removable federal claim is included.

Procedure for Removal or Remand. Removal procedure is governed by § 1446. The defendant is required to remove within thirty days of receiving the pleading or other papers upon which removal is based. The statute limits removal in diversity cases to one year after commencement of the action. This statutory provision carries out a policy in favor of prompt determination of which court system is to hear the case. The defendant is required to file a notice of removal in the federal court, stating the grounds. If there are multiple defendants, all must join in the petition, except those who have not been served. All adverse parties must be promptly given written notice and a copy of the notice of removal must be filed with the state court. The reason for these requirements is that the state court is disempowered from further action during the period of removal, even if it later turns out to be improper. Plaintiff can test the propriety of the removal by a "motion to remand," which is governed by § 1447. As a consequence of the policy in favor of expeditious determination of jurisdiction, § 1447(d) provides that a remand order is not reviewable "by appeal or otherwise." *See* Maginess, *Removing a Case to Federal Court*, 12 Colo. Law. 1639 (1983). Consider the following case.

CATERPILLAR INC. v. LEWIS
519 U.S. 61 (1996)

Justice Ginsburg delivered the opinion of the Court.

This case, commenced in a state court, involves personal injury claims arising under state law. The case was removed to a federal court at a time when, the Court of Appeals concluded, complete diversity of citizenship did not exist among the parties. Promptly after the removal, the plaintiff moved to remand the case to the state court, but the District Court denied that motion. Before trial of the case, however, all claims involving the nondiverse defendant were settled, and that defendant was dismissed as a party to the action. Complete diversity thereafter existed. The case proceeded to trial, jury verdict, and judgment for the removing defendant. The Court of Appeals vacated the judgment, concluding that, absent complete diversity at the time of removal, the District Court lacked subject-matter jurisdiction.

The question presented is whether the absence of complete diversity at the time of removal is fatal to federal court adjudication. We hold that a district court's error in failing to remand a case improperly removed is not fatal to the ensuing adjudication if federal jurisdictional requirements are met at the time judgment is entered.

I

[Plaintiff Lewis was injured while operating a bulldozer. He was a citizen of Kentucky, and he filed a Kentucky state court suit for negligence and product defect against two defendants: Whayne Supply Corporation, a Kentucky corporation that had serviced the bulldozer, and Caterpillar, a Delaware corporation, which had manufactured it. Liberty Mutual Insurance Company, a Massachusetts corporation, intervened as a plaintiff to assert what is known as a "subrogation" claim against Whayne and Caterpillar. It had paid workers' compensation benefits to Lewis and was entitled under the law to recover the same amount from the defendants if they were liable. With the suit in this posture, there was no diversity jurisdiction, since Plaintiff Lewis and Defendant Whayne were both citizens of Kentucky.

[A few months later, Lewis settled with Whayne, the Kentucky service company. Caterpillar filed a notice of removal to the federal District Court shortly after learning of the settlement. Caterpillar filed its removal papers less than 30 days after receiving notice of the settlement, and it satisfied, with only one day to spare, the statutory requirement that the removal take place within one year of commencement of the suit. Lewis promptly filed a motion to remand, arguing that Liberty Mutual's claim against Whayne remained in the suit and defeated complete diversity. The District Court denied the motion. The judge evidently reasoned that diversity in Lewis's claim against Caterpillar was sufficient to support jurisdiction.

[Then, shortly before trial, Liberty Mutual also settled with Whayne, so that at last it was clear that diversity was complete. With Caterpillar as the sole defendant adverse to Lewis, the case went to trial in federal court and resulted in a verdict for Caterpillar. The trial judge entered a judgment for the defendant.

[The Court of Appeals accepted Lewis's jurisdictional argument and vacated the judgment. Even though the settlement between Liberty Mutual and Whayne had created complete diversity before entry of judgment, the Court of Appeals concluded that Whayne's continued presence in the case up to that point meant that diversity was not complete at the time of removal. Therefore, denial of Lewis's motion to remand was error. The Supreme Court granted certiorari and here reverses, effectively reinstating the trial court's judgment for the defendant.]

II

. . . .

When a plaintiff files in state court a civil action over which the federal district courts would have original jurisdiction based on diversity of citizenship, the defendant or defendants may remove the action to federal court, 28 U.S.C. § 1441(a), provided that no defendant "is a citizen of the State in which such action is brought," § 1441(b). In a case not originally removable, a defendant who receives a pleading or other paper indicating the post-commencement satisfaction of federal jurisdictional requirements — for example, by reason of the dismissal of a nondiverse party—may remove the case to federal court within 30 days of receiving such information. § 1446(b). No case, however, may be removed from state to federal court based on diversity of citizenship "more than 1 year after commencement of the action."

Once a defendant has filed a notice of removal in the federal district court, a plaintiff objecting to removal "on the basis of any defect in removal procedure" may, within 30 days, file a motion asking the district court to remand the case to state court. § 1447(c). This 30-day limit does not apply, however, to jurisdictional defects: "If at any time before final judgment it appears that the district court lacks subject matter jurisdiction, the case shall be remanded."

III

We note, initially, two "givens" in this case as we have accepted it for review. First, the District Court, in its decision denying Lewis' timely motion to remand, incorrectly treated Whayne Supply, the nondiverse defendant, as effectively dropped from the case prior to removal. Second, the Sixth Circuit correctly determined that the complete diversity requirement was not satisfied at the time of removal.[7] We accordingly home in on this question: Does the District Court's initial misjudgment still burden and run with the case, or is it overcome by the eventual dismissal of the nondiverse defendant?

Petitioner Caterpillar relies heavily on our decisions in *American Fire & Casualty Co. v. Finn*, 341 U.S. 6 (1951), and *Grubbs v. General Elec. Credit Corp.*, 405 U.S. 699 (1972), urging that these decisions "long ago settled the proposition that remand to the state court is unnecessary even if jurisdiction did not exist at the time of removal, so long as the district court had subject matter jurisdiction at the time of judgment." Caterpillar is right that *Finn* and *Grubbs* are key cases in point and tend in Caterpillar's favor. Each suggests that the existence of subject-matter jurisdiction at time of judgment may shield a judgment against later jurisdictional attack. But neither decision resolves dispositively a controversy of the kind we face, for neither involved a plaintiff who moved promptly, but unsuccessfully, to remand a case improperly removed from state court to federal court, and then challenged on appeal a judgment entered by the federal court. . . .

Beyond question, as Lewis acknowledges, there was in this case complete diversity, and therefore federal subject-matter jurisdiction, at the time of trial and judgment. The case had by then become, essentially, a two-party lawsuit: Lewis, a citizen of Kentucky, was the sole plaintiff; Caterpillar, incorporated in Delaware with its principal place of business in Illinois, was the sole defendant Lewis confronted. Caterpillar maintains that this change cured the threshold statutory misstep, i.e., the removal of a case when diversity was incomplete.

Caterpillar moves too quickly over the terrain we must cover. The jurisdictional defect was cured, i.e., complete diversity was established before the trial commenced. Therefore, the Sixth Circuit erred in resting its decision on the absence of subject-matter jurisdiction. But a statutory flaw — Caterpillar's failure to meet the § 1441(a) requirement that the case be fit for federal adjudication at the time the removal petition is filed — remained in the unerasable history of the case.

And Lewis, by timely moving for remand, did all that was required to preserve his objection to removal. An order denying a motion to remand, "standing alone," is "[o]bviously . . . not final and [immediately] appealable" as of right. Nor is a plaintiff

[7] Caterpillar's petition for certiorari raised the question whether the subrogation claim asserted by Liberty Mutual, and thus the citizenship of Whayne Supply, should be disregarded for purposes of determining diversity of citizenship, in view of the settlement agreed upon between Lewis and Whayne Supply. Our order granting review did not encompass that question, and we express no opinion on it.

required to seek permission to take an interlocutory appeal . . . in order to avoid waiving whatever ultimate appeal right he may have. . . .

Having preserved his objection to an improper removal, Lewis urges that an "all's well that ends well" approach is inappropriate here. . . . The course Caterpillar advocates, Lewis observes, would disfavor diligent plaintiffs who timely, but unsuccessfully, move to check improper removals in district court. Further, that course would allow improperly removing defendants to profit from their disregard of Congress' instructions, and their ability to lead district judges into error.

Concretely, in this very case, Lewis emphasizes, adherence to the rules Congress prescribed for removal would have kept the case in state court. Only by removing prematurely was Caterpillar able to get to federal court inside the 1-year limitation set in § 1446(b).[12] Had Caterpillar waited until the case was ripe for removal, i.e., until Whayne Supply was dismissed as a defendant, the 1-year limitation would have barred the way, and plaintiff's choice of forum would have been preserved.[14]

These arguments are hardly meritless, but they run up against an overriding consideration. Once a diversity case has been tried in federal court, . . . considerations of finality, efficiency, and economy become overwhelming. . . .

Our view is in harmony with a main theme of the removal scheme Congress devised. Congress ordered a procedure calling for expeditious superintendence by district courts. The lawmakers specified a short time, 30 days, for motions to remand for defects in removal procedure, and district court orders remanding cases to state courts generally are "not reviewable on appeal or otherwise," § 1447(d). . . . Despite a federal trial court's threshold denial of a motion to remand, if, at the end of the day and case, a jurisdictional defect remains uncured, the judgment must be vacated. In this case, however, no jurisdictional defect lingered through judgment in the District Court. To wipe out the adjudication post-judgment . . . would impose an exorbitant cost on our dual court system, a cost incompatible with the fair and unprotracted administration of justice.

Lewis ultimately argues that, if the final judgment against him is allowed to stand, "all of the various procedural requirements for removal will become unenforceable"; therefore, "defendants will have an enormous incentive to attempt wrongful removals." In particular, Lewis suggests that defendants will remove prematurely "in the hope that some subsequent developments, such as the eventual dismissal of nondiverse defendants, will permit th[e] case to be kept in federal court." We do not anticipate the dire consequences Lewis forecasts.

. . . Lewis' prediction . . . rests on an assumption we do not indulge — that district courts generally will not comprehend, or will balk at applying, the rules on removal Congress has prescribed. The prediction furthermore assumes defendants' readiness to gamble that any jurisdictional defect, for example, the absence of complete diversity, will first escape detection, then disappear prior to judgment. The well-advised defendant, we are satisfied, will foresee the likely outcome of an unwarranted removal — a swift, and nonreviewable remand order, attended by the displeasure of a district court whose authority has been improperly invoked. The odds against any gain from a wrongful

---

[12] Congress amended § 1446(b) in 1988 to include the 1-year limitation in order to "reduc[e] the opportunity for removal after substantial progress has been made in state court."

[14] Lewis preferred state court to federal court based on differences he perceived in, inter alia, the state and federal jury systems and rules of evidence.

removal, in sum, render improbable Lewis' projection of increased resort to the maneuver. . . .

For the reasons stated, the judgment of the Court of Appeals is reversed, and the case is remanded for proceedings consistent with this opinion.

NOTES AND QUESTIONS

(1) *How Broad Is the Caterpillar Ruling?* The Supreme Court addressed this issue in *Grupo Dataflux v. Atlas Global Group, L.P.*, 541 U.S. 567 (2004), in which the Court declined to extend the *Caterpillar* exception. In *Dataflux*, after the jury's verdict but before entry of judgment, Dataflux filed a motion to dismiss for lack of subject-matter jurisdiction because the parties were not diverse at the time the complaint was filed. Atlas, a partnership, urged the district court to disregard the lack of diversity at the time of filing because the non-diverse partners left Atlas before the trial began, and thus diversity existed at the time of trial. Relying on *Caterpillar*, the Fifth Circuit upheld the verdict, noting that the jurisdictional error had been cured before trial. The Supreme Court reversed, holding that a party's post-filing change in citizenship cannot cure a lack of subject-matter jurisdiction existing at the time of filing. The Court distinguished *Caterpillar* as involving a dismissal of a party who had destroyed diversity, whereas here there was no change of party. Accordingly, the Court observed, "jurisdiction depending on the condition of a party is governed by that condition, as it was at the commencement of the suit."

(2) *The 30-Day and One-Year Limits on Removal.* Notice what would have happened if Caterpillar had not removed within the 30-day window (after receiving notice of removability) or within the one-year limit (after commencement of suit). The suit then would have been subject to remand. In fact, Lewis argues that the suit really did not become even arguably removable until Whayne's dismissal (as opposed to the private agreement of the parties to settle), and since this dismissal itself occurred more than a year after commencement, Lewis argued that the suit was nonremovable at the time Caterpillar removed, even under Caterpillar's own arguments. Even so, the Supreme Court's holding preserves the judgment. The defendant's time to remove the case to federal court is triggered by simultaneous service of the summons and complaint on the defendant, or by receipt of the complaint by the defendant through service or otherwise, after and apart from service of the summons, but not by receipt of a "courtesy copy" of the complaint without formal service. *Murphy Bros. v. Michetti Pipe Stringing, Inc.*, 526 U.S. 344 (1999).

(3) *The Motion to Remand and the 30-Day Limit for "Procedural" Defects.* The plaintiff must file a motion to remand within 30 days to avoid waiving procedural defects in the removal. What would have happened, then, if Lewis had not made a timely motion to remand? The answer is that he probably would have given up any right to complain about such issues as the one-year limit. But if diversity had not existed at the time of judgment, even the failure to move for remand would not have prevented the plaintiff from raising the issue later. Explain why this is so.

(4) *Adverse and Non-Adverse Parties: Should the Claim by Liberty Mutual Against Whayne Have Been Disregarded for Diversity and Removal Purposes?* Liberty Mutual's subrogation claim was a peculiar kind of claim against Whayne, and in fact it really could be considered, in practical effect, as a claim against the Plaintiff, Lewis. Whayne's potential liability on the subrogation claim would have extended only to one satisfaction of the damages to Lewis, and if Liberty Mutual prevailed against Whayne, it was entitled

to recover the amount it had paid Lewis, whose recovery would be reduced by the same amount. Liberty Mutual's recovery, in other words, came off the top of Lewis's recovery. Caterpillar's argument, then, was that Liberty Mutual's claim against Whayne did not mean that the two co-citizens, Lewis and Whayne, were adverse, especially since they already had settled. Arguably, therefore, the continued presence of Whayne in the suit did not destroy complete diversity, since no co-citizens were truly diverse(?!) Notice how complex the jurisdictional arguments can become when a case is removed. Consider whether the avoidance of these kinds of ethereal (if not unanswerable) questions indirectly supports the "all's well that ends well" principle created here by the Supreme Court.

(5) *What if a Plaintiff Fraudulently Joins a Nondiverse Party Who Cannot Possibly Be Liable, Merely to Defeat Removal? In re Shell Oil Co., 932 F.2d 1518 (5th Cir. 1991).* The flip side of the adverse-or-nonadverse-party question raised above arises when the plaintiff, eager to prevent removal, adds a local defendant against whom the plaintiff cannot possibly hope to prove a claim. This situation is said to involve "fraudulent joinder," and the fictitious defendant may be disregarded for jurisdictional purposes so that the removal may be allowed. *Cf.* § 3.03[B][2] above (parties "improperly or collusively" joined). But the proof threshold for the removing defendant is high, and any arguable claim by the plaintiff will defeat it. The removing defendant must show, to a legal certainty, that the plaintiff never had any possibility of recovery against the fraudulently-joined defendant.

In the *Shell Oil* case, above, the defendants removed despite the presence of local citizens, asserting that all were fraudulently joined. The plaintiffs moved to remand but waited until the 34th day after removal to do so. The court held that this untimeliness was a waiver of "defects in removal procedure," which it interpreted to include the removal of a case with a local citizen defendant. It therefore upheld the removal without considering whether the defendants were correct in asserting fraudulent joinder. Is it correct to characterize a possible failure to demonstrate fraudulent joinder as a defect in "procedure," or does the defect really destroy the court's jurisdictional basis instead?

(6) *The Tendencies of Plaintiffs to Prefer State Court and of Defendants to Prefer Removal.* In a footnote, the *Caterpillar* Court explained that Plaintiff Lewis preferred state court because of evidentiary and procedural advantages he perceived. Although it is difficult to generalize, target defendants in personal injury cases often prefer to remove, and plaintiffs fight to stay in state court. Plaintiffs sometimes join impecunious local individuals even when the noncitizen target corporation is more clearly liable, and sometimes they include express disclaimers of reliance on federal law ("all of the claims herein arise solely under state law"). See whether you can describe some of the differences between state and federal courts that might lead to these strategies by plaintiffs and defendants.

NOTES AND QUESTIONS ON REMOVAL PROCEDURE

(1) *Counterclaims: Shamrock Oil & Gas Corp. v. Sheets, 313 U.S. 100 (1941).* As we have already seen, a defendant's answer asserting a federal defense cannot create federal jurisdiction — and it does not allow the defendant to remove. But what if the defendant asserts a federal counter-claim? In this case (*Shamrock Oil & Gas Corp. v. Sheets*), the Supreme Court held that removal was not authorized. Should it be? For another interesting jurisdictional issue, involving changes in the parties after removal that affect complete diversity, see Steinman, *Postremoval Changes in the Party Structure of Diversity Cases: The Old Law, the New Law, and Rule 19*, 38 Kan. L. Rev. 863 (1990).

In a case dealing with the appellate jurisdiction of the Court of Appeals for the Federal Circuit, the Supreme Court reaffirmed both the well-pleaded complaint rule and the rule that a counterclaim cannot serve as a basis for federal arising-under jurisdiction. *See The Holmes Group, Inc. v. Vornado Air Circulation Systems, Inc.*, 535 U.S. 826 (2002). The Court observed that "allowing responsive pleadings by the defendant to establish 'arising under' jurisdiction would undermine the clarity and ease of administration of the well-pleaded-complaint doctrine, which serves as a 'quick rule of thumb' for resolving jurisdictional conflicts." *Id.* at 832.

(2) *The Supreme Court Emphasizes the Statutory Nature of Removal: Syngenta Crop Protection, Inc. v. Henson, 537 U.S. 28 (2002).* In *Syngenta*, a state-court products liability action against a chemical manufacturer was removed to federal court. The petitioners asserted federal subject-matter jurisdiction under the All Writs Act (28 U.S.C. § 1651) and the supplemental jurisdiction statute (28 U.S.C. § 1367). The Supreme Court emphasized that "[t]he right of removal is entirely a creature of statute," *id.* at 369, and noted that the removal statute, by its terms, authorizes removal only of those actions over which the district courts have original jurisdiction. The All Writs Act does not provide any federal subject-matter jurisdiction in its own right, and the supplemental jurisdiction statute requires an initial claim over which the court already has subject-matter jurisdiction. Accordingly, neither provided the "original jurisdiction" required for removal under section 1441.

(3) *Claims That Are Non-Removable by Statute.* There are certain kinds of claims that are not removable because Congress has expressly provided by statute that they may not be removed. For example, actions under the Federal Employers Liability Act (providing for claims by injured railroad and sea workers) and actions under worker's compensation laws may be filed in federal court if the plaintiff chooses, but if plaintiff files in state court, the defendant may not remove. 28 U.S.C. §§ 1445(a), (c). These enactments are apparently traceable to a policy of preserving choice of forum for certain favored claimants.

(4) *Claims Involving Concurrent Jurisdiction.* Resolving a split in the circuit courts, the Supreme Court held that the Fair Labor Standards Act, which gives plaintiffs the right to sue in either federal court or state court, may, if filed in state court, be removed to federal court. *Breuer v. Jim's Concrete of Brevard, Inc.*, 538 U.S. 691 (2003). The unanimous Court stated that any exception to the federal removal statute must contain unequivocal, express language, and no such language appears in the FLSA.

(5) *Removal Procedure: The Twilight Zone Between State and Federal Jurisdiction.* Section 1446 imposes a number of requirements for successful removal. What is the status of the jurisdiction when the defendant has filed the removal notice, but has not accomplished the other steps, such as providing written notice to adverse parties or filing the notice with the state court? Unfortunately, the authorities are divided, with some cases holding that the federal court ousts the state court of power when the notice is filed and others holding that the state court remains in control until all steps have been taken. *Compare, e.g., First National Bank in Little Rock v. Johnson & Johnson*, 455 F. Supp. 361 (E.D. Ark. 1978) (effective on filing of petition), *with Beleos v. Life & Cas. Ins. Co. of Tennessee*, 161 F. Supp. 627 (E.D.S.C. 1956) (effective only after later steps). In addition, *Berberian v. Gibney*, 514 F.2d 790 (1st Cir. 1975), holds that both courts (!) have jurisdiction in this "twilight zone." The confusion is compounded by holdings that a plaintiff may waive defective removal and that a defendant can later cure improper procedures. The most serious problems arise when the state court has entered an order

during the twilight period, which the parties then cannot be certain is either valid or invalid. The authorities generally agree that completion of the required steps vests sole jurisdiction in the federal court unless and until that court remands — and this is so even if the removal was done without proper jurisdictional grounds.

(6) *Remand Procedure and Appellate Review: Thermtron Prods., Inc. v. Hermansdorfer, 423 U.S. 336 (1976).* Section 1447 provides for remand only if the case was improperly removed. What happens if the federal court remands simply because it wants to reduce its overloaded docket? In *Thermtron*, the District Court expressly remanded for that reason. The Supreme Court held that the usual rule prohibiting review of remand orders does not apply to an order entered on grounds other than the propriety of the removal, and it reversed. But the trial court has authority to make findings about the propriety of the removal, and if it remands on that ground (even if it is subtly affected by docket pressures and even if it is wrong), its order is not reviewable.

(7) *Determination of Requisites for Removal; Proof.* In general, the plaintiff's pleading in the state court is the determinant of matters such as the nature of the claim. There are some statements in the cases to the effect that plaintiff's pleading is the only permissible source of removal facts; however, this principle would produce absurd results. For example, most state courts do not require allegations of citizenship; some state rules do not require specification of an amount in controversy. In that event, plaintiff's pleading will not show diversity, and defendant then must plead the jurisdictional basis in the notice of removal and make proof of these extrinsic facts. The usual medium of proof is affidavits, although the court may hear testimony.

(8) *Equitable Exception to One-Year Limit on Removal: Telford v. Warner-Lambert Co., 327 U.S. 423 (5th Cir. 2003).* In *Telford*, the Fifth Circuit issued the first federal appellate opinion regarding an equitable exception to section 1446(b)'s one-year time limit in which to remove cases in which subject-matter jurisdiction is based on diversity. Noting that the federal district courts had reached conflicting conclusions as to whether the removal deadline could be subject to an equitable exception, the Fifth Circuit concluded that "the conduct of the parties may affect whether it is equitable to strictly apply the one-year limit."

(9) *What Happens When the Party Seeking to Remove is a Third-Party Defendant?* There is a split of authority when the party seeking to remove the action under section 1441(a) or 1441(c) is a third-party defendant. However, the majority view is that third-party defendants generally are not "defendants" for purposes of section 1441. *See First National Bank of Pulaski v. Curry*, 301 F.3d 456, 461-62 (6th Cir. 2002). An exception is set forth in section 1441(d), relating to suits against "foreign states."

§ 3.04 Improving Our Jurisdictional Systems

[A] State Court Reorganization: Notes and Questions

(1) *Goals of a Good Jurisdictional System.* What are the characteristics of good court organization? Consider the following factors, together with others you might think of:

(a) *Clear Rules for Determining Jurisdiction.* Litigation about where litigation will take place is wasteful. A good court system is like a good traffic code: We should know which side of the road to drive on, and a lawyer ought not to have to guess which court has power to hear his or her suit.

(b) *Specialization.* There should be courts specializing in small disputes with rules that differ from those for million-dollar disputes. There should be courts with domestic relations and probate expertise.

(c) *Avoidance of Overspecialization.* An excess of specialization may lead to narrowness of view and overcomplex jurisprudence. A small specialized bar becomes accustomed to arcane rules that general litigators cannot follow. It is debatable, for example, whether there should be "housing" courts (as there are in some jurisdictions).

(d) *Flexibility.* Docket pressures change faster than the court system can. Rapid development in one county may create sudden demand for more courts. It should be easy to assign underworked judges to help handle the dockets of overworked ones.

(e) *Remedies Against Inappropriate Exercise of Court Authority.* If small claims procedures are used in a case in which they are not authorized, clear means of redress should be readily available.

(f) *Judicial Qualifications Suited to the Jurisdiction.* A judge who is suited to a domestic relations bench may or may not be qualified for another bench. A Small Claims judge arguably must have certain personal qualifications that might not be necessary in a Superior Court judge, and vice versa.

(2) *The Move Toward "Unified" and "Uniform" Court Systems.* These goals have prompted most reformers to call for "unified" or "uniform" systems. Roscoe Pound is generally credited with initiating this movement. He advocated one "great court" with three branches: a "county" court with jurisdiction over smaller claims, a "district" court with general jurisdiction, and a "court of appeal." The key to the proposal was that all judges would be judges of the whole court, and they would be assigned by an administrator to various departments as needed. *See* Guittard, *Court Reform, Texas Style*, 21 Sw. L.J. 451 (1967). New Jersey made a pioneer effort toward this model in 1947, and there since have been various degrees of unification in Alaska, Arizona, California, Colorado, Hawaii, Illinois, and North Carolina. The American Bar Association later made a similar proposal, as follows:

> 1.10 Unified Court System: General Principle. The aims of court organization can be most fully realized in a court system that is unified in its structure and administration. . . .
>
> The structure of the court system should be simple, preferably consisting of a trial court and an appellate court, each having divisions or departments as needed. The trial court should have jurisdiction of all cases and proceedings. It should have specialized procedures and divisions to accommodate the various types of criminal and civil matters within its jurisdiction. The judicial functions of the trial court should be performed by a single class of judges, assisted by legally trained judicial officers (commissioners . . . and similar officials) assigned to such matters as preliminary hearings, non-criminal traffic cases, [and] small claims. . . .

ABA, Commission on Standards of Judicial Administration 2-3 (tent. draft 1973). What do you think would be the advantages and disadvantages of this proposal? If you had a small-claims, probate, or divorce case in a state using this "unified" system, how would the court that would handle it differ from those in Texas or New York?

[B] Reform of Federal Jurisdiction

[1] Should Congress Abolish Diversity Jurisdiction?

ABOLITION OF DIVERSITY OF CITIZENSHIP JURISDICTION
H.R. Rep. No. 95-893, 95th Cong. 2d Sess. (1978)

[House Bill 9622, in 1978, would have abolished diversity jurisdiction between citizens of different states. It would have kept "alienage" jurisdiction (between citizens of states and citizens of foreign countries). It also removed a then-existing requirement in some federal question cases that the amount in controversy exceed $10,000.]

PURPOSE OF THE BILL

. . . Eighteen years ago, in 1959, Chief Justice Earl Warren, in an address to the American Law Institute, observed: "It is essential that we achieve a proper jurisdictional balance between the Federal and State court systems, in the light of the basic principles of federalism." The proposed legislation achieves that goal. As a general proposition, it provides the Federal law questions are to be adjudicated in the Federal courts, regardless of the amount in controversy; and diversity cases, which involve questions of State law, are to be resolved in the State courts. . . .

. . . The Constitution . . . clearly grants [Congress] power to decide whether, and to what extent, there should be diversity jurisdiction. . . .

NEED FOR THE LEGISLATION

. . . [T]he abolition of diversity jurisdiction is an important step in reducing endemic court congestion and its insidious effects on litigants. During the 1977 judicial year, 31,678 diversity cases were filed in the Federal district courts. These filings comprised almost a quarter of the civil caseload at the trial court level. . . .

The diverting of diversity cases from the Federal courts to the State courts will not impose too great a burden on the latter. Essentially, 32,000 cases pending before 400 Federal district judges will cause few problems when allocated among 6,000 State judges of general jurisdiction. . . . The Conference of State Chief Justices in its Resolution of August 3, 1977, observed that the State courts were "able and willing" to assume all or part of the Federal diversity jurisdiction.

It is the view of the committee that the original reasons for diversity jurisdiction have long since disappeared. At present, there is little evidence that the State courts are less qualified or, due to latent prejudice against out-of-staters, unable to render fair and impartial justice in these cases. Since Federal juries are now drawn from the same registration or voter lists as State jurors, although from a larger area within the State, arguments that Federal juries are less biased than their State counterparts are insubstantial. . . .

Today, the United States is a more mobile society than that of the First Congress or even the 80th Congress. People travel often . . . ; communications are made easy by telephone, telegraph and television. Technological change [and] education . . . [have reduced] the risk of prejudice against out-of-staters . . . .

In conclusion, the proposed legislation recognizes that diversity is an idea whose time has passed. The Federal courts are a scarce resource and should be treated as such. . . . [T]here should be only one court per customer — the choice of forum is a luxury that our judicial system can no longer afford. . . . [T]he Federal courts must be freed from the shackles of congestion to do the job they do best — that of adjudicating disputes in traditional Federal subject-matter areas. . . . In addition, the State court systems must be accorded a respected role in the American judicial systems. . . .

NOTE ON THE DEFEAT OF THE DIVERSITY ABOLITION BILL

Passage by the House. The 1978 diversity abolition bill, described above, easily passed the House of Representatives. The Committee vote recommending that it "do pass" actually was unanimous. The House Report chronicled hearings in which professors, lawyers, judges, citizens, and consumer advocates presented testimony. "[T]he vast majority . . . supported abolition of diversity jurisdiction."

The Political Opposition Mobilizes in the Senate. The Senate hearings were different. One of the most effective witnesses was the late Phoenix attorney John P. Frank, who said, "The proposal to abolish the diversity jurisdiction is, from the standpoint of the bar, approximately as popular as tuberculosis in a hospital." Mr. Frank continued:

> These proposals . . . are opposed by the appropriate governing bodies of the State Bars of Arizona, Arkansas, California, Florida, Hawaii, Illinois, Iowa, Kansas, Kentucky, Louisiana, Maine, Michigan, Missouri, New Mexico, New York (Committee on Federal Courts), Ohio, Oregon, Pennsylvania, South Dakota, Texas, Utah, Vermont, West Virginia and Wisconsin . . . ; [they are] supported by not one single state bar. . . .

The Merits of the Opposition. Mr. Frank went on to give three basic reasons for retaining diversity: (1) the disposition of 30,000 cases annually to the general satisfaction of litigants; (2) interaction between the systems with a single, unified bar; and (3) the value of lawyers having a choice:

> The first great value of diversity is its disposition of something on the order of almost 30,000 disputes a year to the general satisfaction of those who need their disposition. . . .
>
> . . . [T]he litigant who loses rarely feels with much conviction that he would have been better off in a different system.
>
> The second great plus is the educational value of having two systems in interaction. . . . The success of the federal rules has led to their widespread emulation in the states. . . .
>
> Those who would drastically cut the diversity jurisdiction . . . think . . . merely that there would be enough federal business left to permit the same effect. . . . I can only say that I do not myself think so. . . . The Federal question cases are more likely to be for specialists in antitrust or FELA or taxes. The inclusion of the full gamut of commercial and tort cases puts the whole litigation bar into federal courts.
>
> Finally, there are elements of prejudice and competence deserving to be taken into account. . . . There are other prejudices than the merely regional, and a litigant may believe that he escapes some of them in federal court. The suggestion has been made that the litigant, if dissatisfied with his state justice, should improve it, not escape it; but this is visionary. . . .
>
> Moreover, interstate prejudice is not dead. . . .
>
> The fact of the matter is that the existence of the option is advantageous to counsel and to litigants wherever it may exist. . . .

> [D]uring the period of Judge Ritter's life, lawyers in Salt Lake City tended to move toward the State side where they could to avoid the problems of dealing with Judge Ritter. . . .
>
> . . . The fact is that since Senator Percy had taken over and improved merit selection in Chicago, . . . [t]he Federal district courts in Chicago have been vastly improved. The lawyers want the option, where possible, in getting before those admirable high-quality judges where they can. . . .

Responsive Arguments Favoring Abolition. Professor Charles Alan Wright was one of the principal speakers in response to Mr. Frank's arguments. He explained that his opposition to an earlier abolition bill had been overtaken by events:

> I think the world has changed since 1963. I did support diversity in 1963. I favor its abolition now. . . .
>
> Mr. Frank, if I understood him . . . seemed to put his greatest emphasis on the concept of one bar and that we need diversity in order to have lawyers who will be going back and forth between State and Federal courts. . . .
>
> I agree with him. I do not want a Federal bar of specialists or an elitist bar. I do not think that is any longer a problem. I think it may very well have been a problem in 1963. . . .
>
> Mr. Frank talked about people. His concern is with the person who . . . will have to wait a long time if the choice is not available. . . .
>
> I am concerned about people also. I am concerned with people who want to take advantage of laws that Congress has passed in the last 15 years, giving rights that did not exist. . . . I want them to be able to get to trial. . . .
>
> Mr. Frank remembers only one case in his own practice in which there was any serious question about whether there was diversity. But his practice surely must be unique. . . .
>
> I know, as a person who has to read all the cases every year and write about them, that litigants are making mistakes repeatedly on whether or not there is Federal jurisdiction. Even when it turns out there has not been a mistake, judges are having to take the time to [decide] . . . whether diversity exists. . . .
>
> Counsel said that we would be reducing the time spent in a civil procedure course. I had two [law students] sitting next to me who are taking a civil procedure course this year here in Washington — and who hope you will pass the bill before the final examination — who said that it gets to the heart of the matter. [Laughter.]

The Senate did not pass the relevant legislation. Since 1978, no bill for the reform or abolition of diversity has passed either House.

[2] Reforming Diversity: Notes and Questions

(1) *"Reform" Rather Than Abolition?* Congress could reduce diversity jurisdiction without abolishing it. *See* Baker, *The History and Tradition of the Amount in Controversy Requirement: A Proposal to Up the Ante in Diversity Jurisdiction*, 102 F.R.D. 299 (1984). One way would be to increase the amount in controversy. This change has a sound historical basis: The original diversity statute required no amount in controversy; later, more than $3,000 was required, then $10,000, then $50,000; and today, the amount is $75,000, although it will be eroded by inflation over the years. Would there be advantages in an increase in the amount in controversy to $100,000 or even $250,000?

(2) *Multi-Party, Multi-State Litigation.* There have been numerous proposals for the creation of a new kind of federal jurisdiction in complex litigation involving multiple litigants scattered throughout the United States or foreign countries. Congress could authorize multi-state, multi-party federal jurisdiction with minimal diversity, perhaps with a significant amount-in-controversy requirement, and provide for nationwide service to avoid fragmented litigation. *See generally* American Law Institute, *Study of the Division of Jurisdiction Between State and Federal Courts* (1969) [hereinafter cited as ALI] for this and other proposals discussed here. [This proposal really addresses problems of personal jurisdiction, and it therefore is discussed in § 2.05 above. But it should be reconsidered here, since it concerns the reform of diversity jurisdiction.]

(3) *Disenabling Local Plaintiffs From Using Diversity.* A local defendant is prohibited from removing because the policy of preventing local prejudice does not apply to him. Should Congress extend the same rule to original filings, by providing that a local plaintiff may not file a diversity suit in a state of which he is a citizen? The ALI has proposed this change.

[C] Reform of "Arising Under" Jurisdiction, Supplemental Jurisdiction, and Removal: Notes and Questions

(1) *Extending "Arising Under" Jurisdiction to Defenses and Counterclaims.* The ALI also has proposed that removal be authorized on the basis of a federal defense or counterclaim. Does this proposal have merit? What are its disadvantages?

(2) *Abolishing § 1441(c); Authorizing Removal by any Non-Local Diverse Defendant.* Section 1441(c), which provides for removal of the entire case if a "separate and independent" federal claim would be removable alone, is widely criticized for creating confusion disproportionate to its limited benefits. Should it be abolished? At the opposite end of the spectrum from abolition, there is the ALI proposal: Any non-local, diverse defendant should be able to remove, even if there are other defendants who destroy complete diversity. What advantages and disadvantages would this proposal have?

(3) *Reforming Supplemental Jurisdiction by Legislative Reversal of the Result in Owen Equipment & Erection Co. v. Kroger.* Recall that, in *Owen*, the plaintiff asserted a claim against a third-party defendant that all parties believed was diverse. Later, the surprise revelation that it was not diverse led to the reversal of an otherwise legitimate judgment for plaintiff — and to possible destruction of the claim by limitations. Should Congress legislatively reverse the result in *Owen*? (Note that, in § 1367(b), Congress actually carried forward and preserved the *Owen* result.)

CHAPTER 4

THE *ERIE* DOCTRINE

§ 4.01 State Law in the Federal Courts: The *Erie* Doctrine

[A] State Substantive Law

NOTE ON HOW TO READ THE *ERIE* CASE

The Erie Question. When a federal court hears a diversity case, the claim actually arises under state law. How should a federal court go about deciding a state law claim? Should it follow the decisions of the supreme court of that state? Or should it try to follow the majority rule among the states, or infer the proper rule from principles of federal law? The differences could be significant.

Background: The Rules of Decision Act and the Older Case of Swift v. Tyson, 41 U.S. (16 Pet.) 1 (1842). The first Congress passed the Rules of Decision Act as part of the Judiciary Act of 1789, which provided that "the laws of the several states" would provide the rules of decision except when federal law required otherwise. It might seem that this enactment would solve the problem. But it did not. In *Swift v. Tyson*, the Supreme Court held that state "laws" did not include all of what we today think of as laws. In particular, the decisions of state courts were not "laws." As the Court put it, court decisions "are, at most, only evidence of what the laws are, and are not of themselves laws. . . . The laws of a state are more usually understood to mean the rules or enactments promulgated by the legislative authority thereof," or laws affecting purely local matters such as property titles. And what was to be the rule of decision in other matters? "General" law, said the Court — meaning that a federal judge would determine what he thought state common law was or should be, by looking to the decisions nationwide.

Tompkins' Suit Against the Erie Railroad. Erie R.R. v. Tompkins, 304 U.S. 64 (1938), which overruled *Swift v. Tyson*, is by far the most celebrated American choice-of-law case. The *Erie* case began sometime after two o'clock in the morning in Hughestown, Pennsylvania, when William Colwell heard a voice shouting that there had been an accident. The story is wonderfully told by Irving Younger, in Younger, *What Happened in Erie*, 56 Texas L. Rev. 1011 (1978):*

> "Don't go," said his wife. "Them fellows are crazy." But William Colwell went. He found a man crumpled against the outside rail [of the Erie line]. Between the rails lay the man's severed arm. The man was his neighbor, Harry James Tompkins. . . .

> An ambulance soon arrived and took Tompkins to the hospital. The stump of his arm was amputated. . . . After leaving the hospital, he went in search of a lawyer.

The lawyer Tompkins hired was Bernard Nemeroff, of New York City, whose father had recommended him to Tompkins. Nemeroff learned that Tompkins had been hit by something protruding from a train — "a black object that looked like a door," as Tompkins would later testify at trial — while walking a path that ran parallel to the tracks. Younger continues the story:

> Nemeroff and his colleagues reasoned that it was not enough to prove that the railroad carelessly had permitted a door to swing loose on a moving freight car. The real question was whether the railroad owed a duty to guard against that specific kind of carelessness. Nemeroff's research disclosed that, under the Pennsylvania cases, a traveler, like Tompkins, on a parallel (or "longitudinal") path is regarded as a trespasser, to whom the railroad owes a duty merely to avoid wanton negligence. Since Tompkins could not prove wanton negligence, to sue in the Pennsylvania courts was to invite disaster. Happily, there were alternatives.
>
> Tompkins was a citizen of Pennsylvania. The Erie Railroad was a New York Corporation. . . . [T]he case would lie in a United States district court. . . . More research. More time in the library. More No. 2 pencils worn to a stub on yellow pads. And they found what they were looking for. . . .
>
> "[G]eneral" law supplied the rule of decision in a federal diversity case [according to the then-controlling rule of *Swift v. Tyson*]. And "general" law, Nemeroff and his colleagues found, in the sense of the "majority" rule, was contrary to the rule in Pennsylvania. A railroad, held most cases outside Pennsylvania, owed a duty of ordinary care to a traveler, like Tompkins, on a parallel or "longitudinal" footpath.
>
> Then into a federal court! . . .

Tompkins' lawyers did, indeed, file suit in a federal District Court. At trial, the railroad's lawyer was Theodore Kiendl, of New York's Davis, Polk, Wardwell, Gardiner & Reed. He moved to dismiss after the plaintiff's proof on the ground that "this permissive pathway doctrine is not applicable in this case under the decisions of the highest courts of Pennsylvania." The judge refused. Following "general" law, over Kiendl's objection, he instead instructed the jury that the railroad had a duty to use reasonable care. The jury returned a verdict for Tompkins, finding $30,000 in damages. The Court of Appeals affirmed. Kiendl petitioned for certiorari. Because the Supreme Court takes only a small percentage of cases presented to it (very few of which are negligence cases), it must have been surprising to all concerned when the Court accepted *Erie v. Tompkins* for review.

Erie in the Supreme Court. In his brief in the Supreme Court, Kiendl avoided making a direct attack on *Swift v. Tyson.* It seemed better to argue that *Swift* had been misapplied than to ask the Court to overrule a case that it had reaffirmed repeatedly for almost a century. But the oral argument showed that some members of the Court were considering a change. The rule of *Swift v. Tyson* had a number of disadvantages. First, *Swift v. Tyson* made differences in result depend, unfairly, on whether the parties had diverse citizenship. Secondly, it encouraged people in Tompkins' position to go to extraordinary lengths to shop for forums. And third, it meant that federal decisions unnecessarily frustrated the deliberately chosen policies of the states. These considerations helped to shape the Court's opinion in *Erie.*

Read 28 U.S.C. § 1652 (the Rules of Decision Act).

ERIE RAILROAD v. TOMPKINS
304 U.S. 64 (1938)

MR. JUSTICE BRANDEIS delivered the opinion of the Court.

The question for decision is whether the oft-challenged doctrine of *Swift v. Tyson* shall now be disapproved.

Tompkins, a citizen of Pennsylvania, was injured on a dark night by a passing freight train of the Erie Railroad Company while walking along its right of way at Hughestown in that State. He claimed that the accident occurred through negligence in the operation, or maintenance, of the train; that he was rightfully on the premises as licensee because on a commonly used beaten footpath which ran for a short distance alongside the tracks; and that he was struck by something which looked like a door projecting from one of the moving cars. To enforce that claim he brought an action in the federal court for southern New York, which had jurisdiction because the company is a corporation of that State. It denied liability; and the case was tried by a jury.

The Erie insisted that its duty to Tompkins was no greater than that owed to a trespasser. It contended, among other things, that its duty to Tompkins, and hence its liability, should be determined in accordance with the Pennsylvania law; that under the law of Pennsylvania, as declared by its highest court, persons who use pathways along the railroad right of way — that is a longitudinal pathway as distinguished from a crossing — are to be deemed trespassers; and that the railroad is not liable for injuries to undiscovered trespassers resulting from its negligence, unless it be wanton or willful. Tompkins denied that any such rule had been established by the decisions of the Pennsylvania courts; and contended that, since there was no statute of the State on the subject, the railroad's duty and liability is to be determined in federal courts as a matter of general law.

The trial judge refused to rule that the applicable law precluded recovery. The jury brought in a verdict of $30,000; and the judgment entered thereon was affirmed by the Circuit Court of Appeals, which held that it was unnecessary to consider whether the law of Pennsylvania was [as] contended, because the question was one not of local, but of general, law and that "upon questions of general law the federal courts are free, in the absence of a local statute, to exercise their independent judgment as to what the law is. . . ."

The Erie had contended that application of the Pennsylvania rule was required, among other things, by [the Rules of Decision Act], which provides:

> The laws of the several States, except where the Constitution, treaties, or statutes of the United States otherwise require or provide, shall be regarded as rules of decision in trials at common law, in the courts of the United States, in cases where they apply.
>
> . . .

First. Swift v. Tyson, 16 Pet. 1, 18, held that federal courts exercising jurisdiction on the ground of diversity of citizenship need not, in matters of general jurisprudence, apply the unwritten law of the State as declared by its highest court; that they are free to exercise an independent judgment as to what the common law of the State is — or should be. . . .

The Court in applying the [Rules of Decision Act] in *Mason v. United States*, 260 U.S. 545, 559, said: "The statute, however, is merely declarative of the rule which would exist in the absence of the statute." The federal courts assumed, in the broad field of "general law," the power to declare rules of decision which Congress was confessedly without power to enact as statutes. Doubt was repeatedly expressed as to the correctness of the construction given [the Act] and as to the soundness of the rule which it introduced. But it was the more recent research of a competent scholar, who examined the original document, which established that the construction given to it by the Court was erroneous; and that the purpose of the section was merely to make certain that, in all matters except those in which some federal law is controlling, the federal courts exercising jurisdiction in diversity of citizenship cases would apply as their rules of decision the law of the State, unwritten as well as written.[5]

Criticism of the doctrine became widespread after the decision of *Black & White Taxicab Co. v. Brown & Yellow Taxicab Co.*, 276 U.S. 518. There, Brown and Yellow, a Kentucky corporation owned by Kentuckians, and the Louisville and Nashville Railroad, also a Kentucky corporation, wished that the former should have the exclusive privilege of soliciting passenger and baggage transportation at the Bowling Green, Kentucky, railroad station; and that the Black and White, a competing Kentucky corporation, should be prevented from interfering with that privilege. Knowing that such a contract would be void under the common law of Kentucky, it was arranged that the Brown and Yellow reincorporate under the law of Tennessee, and that the contract with the railroad should be executed there. The suit was then brought by the Tennessee corporation in the federal court for western Kentucky to enjoin competition by the Black and White; an injunction issued by the District Court was sustained by the Court of Appeals; and this Court, citing many decisions in which the doctrine of *Swift v. Tyson* had been applied, affirmed the decree.

Second. Experience in applying the doctrine of *Swift v. Tyson*, had revealed its defects, political and social; and the benefits expected to flow from the rule did not accrue. Persistence of state courts in their own opinions on questions of common law prevented uniformity; and the impossibility of discovering a satisfactory line of demarcation between the province of general law and that of local law developed a new well of uncertainties.

On the other hand, the mischievous results of the doctrine had become apparent. Diversity of citizenship jurisdiction was conferred in order to prevent apprehended discrimination in state courts against those not citizens of the State. *Swift v. Tyson* introduced grave discrimination by non-citizens against citizens. It made rights enjoyed under the unwritten "general law" vary according to whether enforcement was sought in the state or in the federal court; and the privilege of selecting the court in which the right should be determined was conferred upon the non-citizen. Thus, the doctrine rendered impossible equal protection of the law. In attempting to promote uniformity of law throughout the United States, the doctrine had prevented uniformity in the administration of the law of the State. . . .

In part the discrimination resulted from the wide range of persons held entitled to avail themselves of the federal rule by resort to the diversity of citizenship jurisdiction. Through this jurisdiction individual citizens willing to remove from their own State and become citizens of another might avail themselves of the federal rule. And, without even change of residence, a corporate citizen of the State could avail itself of the federal rule by re-incorporating under the laws of another State, as was done in the *Taxicab* case.

---

[5] Charles Warren, *New Light on the History of the Federal Judiciary Act of 1789* (1923) 37 Harv. L. Rev. 49, 51-52, 81-88, 108.

The injustice and confusion incident to the doctrine of *Swift v. Tyson* have been repeatedly urged as reasons for abolishing or limiting diversity of citizenship jurisdiction. Other legislative relief has been proposed. If only a question of statutory construction were involved, we should not be prepared to abandon a doctrine so widely applied throughout nearly a century. But the unconstitutionality of the course pursued has now been made clear and compels us to do so.

Third. Except in matters governed by the Federal Constitution or by Acts of Congress, the law to be applied in any case is the law of the State. And whether the law of the State shall be declared by its Legislature in a statute or by its highest court in a decision is not a matter of federal concern. There is no federal general common law. Congress has no power to declare substantive rules of common law applicable in a State whether they be local in their nature or "general," be they commercial law or a part of the law of torts. And no clause in the Constitution purports to confer such a power upon the federal courts. . . .

The fallacy underlying the rule declared in *Swift v. Tyson* is made clear by Mr. Justice Holmes.. . . Thus the doctrine of *Swift v. Tyson* is, as Mr. Justice Holmes said, "an unconstitutional assumption of powers by courts of the United States which no lapse of time or respectable array of opinion should make us hesitate to correct." In disapproving that doctrine we do not hold unconstitutional [the Rules of Decision Act] or any other Act of Congress. We merely declare that in applying the doctrine this Court and the lower courts have invaded rights which in our opinion are reserved by the Constitution to the several States.

Fourth. . . . The Circuit Court of Appeals ruled that the question of liability is one of general law; and on that ground declined to decide the issue of state law. As we hold this was error, the judgment is reversed and the case remanded to it for further proceedings in conformity with our opinion.

MR. JUSTICE BUTLER.

. . . .

Defendant's petition for writ of certiorari presented two questions: Whether its duty toward plaintiff should have been determined in accordance with the law as found by the highest court of Pennsylvania, and whether the evidence conclusively showed plaintiff guilty of contributory negligence. . . .

No constitutional question was suggested or argued below or here. And as a general rule, this Court will not consider any question not raised below and presented by the petition. . . . Here it does not decide either of the questions presented but, changing the rule of decision in force since the foundation of the Government, remands the case to be adjudged according to a standard never before deemed permissible. . . .

The doctrine of [*Swift v. Tyson*] has been followed by this Court in an unbroken line of decisions. So far as appears, it was not questioned until more than 50 years later, and then by a single judge. *Baltimore & Ohio R. Co. v. Baugh*, 149 U.S. 368, 390. . . .

The course pursued by the Court in this case is repugnant to the Act of Congress of August 24, 1937, 50 Stat. 751. It declares:

> That whenever the constitutionality of any Act of Congress affecting the public interest is drawn in question in any court of the United States . . . , the court having jurisdiction of the suit or proceeding shall certify such fact to the Attorney General. In any such case the court shall permit the United States to intervene and become a party. . . .

If defendant had applied for and obtained the writ of certiorari upon the claim that, as now held, Congress has no power to prescribe the rule of decision, it would have been the duty of this Court to issue the prescribed certificate to the Attorney General in order that the United States might intervene and be heard on the constitutional question. . . .

I am of opinion that the constitutional validity of the rule need not be considered, because under the law, as found by the courts of Pennsylvania and generally throughout the country, it is plain that the evidence required a finding that plaintiff was guilty of negligence that contributed to cause his injuries and that the judgment below should be reversed upon that ground.

MR. JUSTICE MCREYNOLDS concurs in this opinion.

MR. JUSTICE REED.

I concur in the conclusion reached in this case, in the disapproval of the doctrine of *Swift v. Tyson*, and in the reasoning of the majority opinion except in so far as it relies upon the unconstitutionality of the "course pursued" by the federal courts.

To decide the case now before us and to "disapprove" the doctrine of *Swift v. Tyson* requires only that we say that the words "the laws" include in their meaning the decisions of the local tribunals. As the majority opinion shows, by its reference to Mr. Warren's researches and the first quotation from Mr. Justice Holmes, that this Court is now of the view that "laws" includes "decisions," it is unnecessary to go further and declare that the "course pursued" was "unconstitutional," instead of merely erroneous.

The "unconstitutional" course referred to in the majority opinion is apparently the ruling in *Swift v. Tyson* that the supposed omission of Congress to legislate as to the effect of decisions leaves federal courts free to interpret general law for themselves. I am not at all sure whether, in the absence of federal statutory direction, federal courts would be compelled to follow state decisions. There was sufficient doubt about the matter in 1789 to induce the first Congress to legislate. No former opinions of this Court have passed upon it. . . . If the opinion commits this Court to the position that the Congress is without power to declare what rules of substantive law shall govern the federal courts, that conclusion also seems questionable. The line between procedural and substantive law is hazy but no one doubts federal power over procedure. *Wayman v. Southard*, 10 Wheat. 1. The Judiciary Article and the "necessary and proper" clause of Article One may fully authorize legislation, such as this section of the Judiciary Act. . . .

NOTES AND QUESTIONS

(1) *The Basis of the Erie Decision: The Constitution(?)* Notice that Justice Brandeis purports to base the decision on the Constitution: "[T]he [federal] courts have invaded rights which in our opinion are reserved by the Constitution to the several states." This passage seems to base the decision on the Tenth Amendment, which says that undelegated powers are reserved to the states or to the people. But elsewhere Brandeis says that "Congress has no power to declare substantive rules of common law applicable in a state. . . . And no clause in the Constitution purports to confer such a power upon the federal courts." This language seems to rest the decision on Articles I and III, which create the powers of Congress and of the judiciary. The lack of a citation to the Constitution may reveal a weakness in the opinion. In fact, the constitutional reasoning has been attacked as "dictum" or even "hyperbole." C. Wright & M. Kane, *The Law of Federal Courts* 382-84 (6th ed. 2002) (quoting sources). Note that Justice Reed concurred in the holding but refused to accept its constitutional basis, saying that the Necessary and Proper Clause

of Article I would authorize Congress to provide substantive rules in diversity cases. Is Justice Reed correct?

(2) *The Constitutional Basis: What Difference Does It Make?* Might there be instances in which it would be desirable for Congress to specify rules other than state law as rules of decision in diversity cases? In that event, a constitutional holding could prevent necessary action by Congress. (Of course, that is the purpose of a constitution, but it is also the reason why constitutions should not be read too expansively.) If you have difficulty seeing what problems the constitutional language might cause, see *Sibbach v. Wilson & Co.* and *Hanna v. Plumer*, which appear later in this chapter. *See also* Hill, *The Erie Doctrine and the Constitution*, 53 Nw. U. L. Rev. 427 (1958).

(3) *The Aftermath of Erie: Irving Younger's History.* In *What Happened in Erie*, 56 Texas L. Rev. 1011 (1978), Irving Younger continues his story:*

> . . . Chief Justice Hughes[, during the Court's conference after argument,] opened discussion with the comment, "If we wish to overrule *Swift v. Tyson*, here is our opportunity." It quickly appeared that all but Butler and McReynolds agreed the time had come. . . .

[Justices Butler and McReynolds, were too well known in history to need introduction by Younger, but we should add a word about them here. They were two of the "Four Horsemen," so called because of their votes against New Deal legislation. Several of the Horsemen were former railroad lawyers, and it is wonderfully ironic to see two of their number passionately arguing that a railroad should be held negligent. They asserted (as Wright puts it, "with what must have been glee") that the Court's decision was illegal, since it was made without notice to the Attorney General. Ironically, the notice was required, in all cases challenging the constitutionality of a federal statute, by one of the few provisions of President Roosevelt's "Court-packing" proposal that actually passed Congress. C. Wright, *The Law of Federal Courts* 354-55 (4th ed. 1983). Younger's narrative continues:]

> . . . [F]or a time after the Supreme Court's decision on April 25, it seemed that no one outside the profession would ever hear of [*Erie v. Tompkins*]. . . . [N]o general newspaper mentioned it. On Wednesday, April 27, Felix Frankfurter wrote to President Roosevelt:
>
>> I certainly didn't expect to live to see the day when the Court would announce, as they did on Monday, that it itself has usurped power for nearly a hundred years. And think of not a single New York paper . . . having a nose for the significance of the decision.
>
> The silence persisted. On May 2, 1938, Justice Stone wrote privately to Arthur Krock of the New York Times. . . . On May 3, Krock devoted his column to *Erie v. Tompkins*, heading it "A Momentous Decision of the Supreme Court." . . . The dam had broken, and the flood has yet to recede. . . .
>
> [Later, it was discovered that the district judge, Judge Samuel Mandelbaum, whose first case on the trial bench had been *Erie v. Tompkins*, had written a marginal note in his copy of volume 304 of the United States reports, adjacent to Justice Brandeis's discussion of the trial court's ruling.] There, . . . in his own unique syntax, Samuel Mandelbaum wrote as follows: "Because the *Swift Tyson* case although before this I never knew of its existence to be truthful and for the confusion the decision brought about, it might have been better to leave it alone and stand by good old Swifty."

See also Note, *Swift v. Tyson Exhumed,* 79 Yale L.J. 284 (1969).

(4) *Why Law Professors Love Erie.* The "confusion" part of Judge Mandelbaum's statement is accurate, as you will see in the next few sections of this chapter. But it is hard to agree with his sentiment for keeping *Swift v. Tyson.* The *Erie* decision, for all its faults, has seemed clearly right to generations of lawyers. It is a case, like *International Shoe,* that you will remember the rest of your life; and it is a case to be savored and enjoyed. Wright & Kane (*supra,* at 378), says that "there has hardly been a civil case since *Erie* was decided that has not felt the effect of that decision." Readers may disagree about whether that overstates the case, but they must concur that *Erie* is important.

(5) *What Erie Decided.* The *Erie* holding is deceptively simple. In a diversity case, the District Court follows state substantive law. But several problems are concealed in this formulation of the holding, and they are taken up in the sections of this chapter. In this regard, we offer the following "Chapter Summary Problem," which you may read now but should answer at the end of the chapter (or, as always, you should use it as your instructor directs).

PROBLEM A: CHAPTER 4 SUMMARY PROBLEM

AN ARGUABLE CONFLICT BETWEEN THE FEDERAL RULES OF CIVIL PROCEDURE AND A STATE MEDICAL MALPRACTICE STATUTE. John Payne sued his physician, Dr. Thomas Manson, for personal injury and medical malpractice in a state court of the (hypothetical) State of West York. Manson removed the case to federal court. The State of West York has enacted statutes concerning malpractice suits against health care professionals, ostensibly aimed at "curtailing the filing of frivolous lawsuits against health care professionals and thereby curtailing rising medical costs related to malpractice insurance and litigation." One of these provisions requires: "(A) If a claim against a health professional is asserted in a civil action, the claimant shall certify in a written statement that is filed and served with the claim, whether or not expert testimony is necessary to prove the health care professional's standard of care or liability for the claim. (B) If the claimant certifies that expert opinion testimony is necessary, the claimant shall serve a preliminary expert opinion affidavit with the initial disclosures that are required by the State of West York Rules of Civil Procedure." Under West York law, the preliminary expert opinion affidavit must contain the following information: "(1) The expert's qualifications to express an opinion on the health care professional's standard of care or liability for the claim; (2) The factual basis for each claim against a health care professional; (3) The health care professional's acts, errors, or omissions that the expert considers to be a violation of the applicable standard of care resulting in liability; (4) The manner in which the health care professional's acts, errors, or omissions caused or contributed to the damages or other relief sought by the claimant." West York law further provides that: "The court, on its own motion or the motion of the health care professional, shall dismiss the claim against the health care professional without prejudice if the claimant fails to file and serve a preliminary expert opinion affidavit after the claimant has certified that an affidavit is necessary or the court has ordered the claimant to file and serve an affidavit."

Defendant Manson filed a motion to dismiss the complaint because Plaintiff Payne did not comply with the above West York provisions requiring all plaintiffs filing claims against health care professionals to file a preliminary expert opinion affidavit. Defendant Manson argues that under the *Erie* doctrine, the federal court, sitting in diversity, must apply state substantive law and federal procedural law. Plaintiff Payne argues that the

West York statutes requiring this affidavit do not apply because they are procedural provisions that conflict with federal discovery rules of procedure, specifically Federal Rule of Civil Procedure 26. Fed. R. Civ. P. 26 guides pretrial discovery information gathering. Subdivision (a)(1) requires a party, without making a discovery request, to make initial disclosures of their own supporting evidence. Subsection (a)(2) provides for disclosures of expert testimony. In particular, Rule 26(a)(2) provides that at least 90 days before trial, or when otherwise directed by the court, each party must disclose their expert witnesses who are retained to present expert testimony in the case, accompanied by a written report prepared and signed by the witness containing a complete statement of all opinions to be expressed and the basis and reasons therefor; the data or other information considered by the witness in forming the opinions; any exhibits to be used as a summary of or support for the opinions; the qualifications of the witness, including a list of all publications authored by the witness within the preceding ten years; the compensation to be paid for the study and testimony; and a listing of all other cases in which the witness has testified as an expert at trial or by deposition within the preceding four years.

How should the court rule on Defendant Manson's motion to dismiss? In answering this question, you might consider the following issues:

1. Does state law, or federal law, control the question?
2. How is the answer affected by the existence of Federal Rule of Civil Procedure 26?
3. Is there any incentive for a plaintiff to file in federal court and thereby escape the preliminary expert opinion affidavit that would be required in state court?
4. In the actual case upon which this Summary Problem is based, the court held that the administration of state medical malpractice claims should be the same in both federal and state courts, and therefore in both courts a defendant could bring a motion to dismiss the claim as frivolous based on the failure of the plaintiff to file a preliminary expert opinion affidavit. How could the court justify this conclusion in light of *Hanna v. Plumer*?

[B] Federal Procedural Law

Read 28 U.S.C. §§ 2071, 2072-2074 (the Rules Enabling Act and local rules provision).

NOTE ON THE FEDERAL RULES: THEIR SOURCE AND LEGITIMACY

Federal Procedures: The Federal Rules and the Rules Enabling Act. The Rules Enabling Act, 28 U.S.C. § 2072, provides that the Supreme Court "shall have the power to prescribe general rules of practice and procedure . . . for cases in the [federal courts]." The Act also states, however, that the rules "shall not abridge, enlarge or modify any substantive right." The Supreme Court must transmit proposed rules to Congress by May 1 to allow Congress to act on them, if it chooses, before they take effect, no earlier than December 1 of that year. It is by this process that the Federal Rules of Civil Procedure were adopted in 1938 and are amended.

The Permissible Scope of Federal Procedural Rules: Sibbach v. Wilson & Co., 312 U.S. 1 (1941). The *Erie* doctrine, the Rules Enabling Act, and the substance-procedure distinction all came together shortly after *Erie*, in *Sibbach v. Wilson & Co.* Plaintiff Sibbach brought a diversity suit for personal injuries in a federal court in Illinois. The District Court ordered Sibbach to submit to a medical examination. Although Fed. R. Civ. P. 35 expressly authorized the District Court to make this order, Sibbach refused to comply and pointed out that Illinois state courts had a policy against requiring examinations. She argued that the Rules Enabling Act meant that the court could not change any "substantial" or "important" right that state law gave her, including the right under Illinois law to refuse medical examination. The Supreme Court disagreed: "The asserted right . . . is no more important than many other [procedural] rights. . . . If we should adopt the suggested criterion of the importance of the alleged right, we should invite endless litigation and confusion worse confounded. The test must be whether a rule really regulates procedure. . . ." Four Justices dissented in an opinion written by Justice Frankfurter. The Federal Rule, he said, affected the "inviolability of a person" and was a "drastic change" from previous policy. As such, it should "require explicit legislation" by Congress. [But if the effect was "substantive," would even Congress have the power after the "constitutional" holding in *Erie* to allow federal courts to deviate from state rules?]

§ 4.02 The Substance-Procedure Distinction

NOTE ON THE SUPREME COURT'S VARYING APPROACHES TO THE SUBSTANCE-PROCEDURE PROBLEM

A Confusing Area of Civil Procedure. The deceptive simplicity of the *Erie* holding contrasts sharply with the confusion in the cases that interpret it. Remember: The court follows state substantive law and federal procedural law. The confusion has arisen primarily when the Supreme Court has tried to tell the difference. The distinction is almost metaphysical, and the Court has contributed to the difficulty by inventing new tests without overruling old ones.

The Approaches. It may be a good idea to sketch some of the approaches in advance, together with the cases in which you will see them at work.

(1) *Outcome Determination:* One early test was based upon whether a given rule was "outcome determinative." If it was likely to make a difference in the result, a rule was probably "substantive" — even if it "looked like" a procedural rule. (This famous test comes from *Guaranty Trust Co. v. York*, which is the next case you will read.)

(2) *"Absolute" Outcome Determination:* A later case confined the outcome determination test to rules that had a "strong" likelihood or even a "certainty" of affecting the outcome (*Byrd v. Blue Ridge Rural Elec. Cooperative Inc.*).

(3) *The Interest Balancing Approach:* Several cases classify substance and procedure by the strength of the competing state and federal policies underlying the different rules in question (*Byrd v. Blue Ridge; Walker v. Armco Steel Corp.*). For instance, if the state's policy is definite and important, and the federal interest is slight, this approach would lead to enforcement of the state rule.

(4) *Deference to a Controlling Federal Rule:* Certain other cases say that when the substance-procedure distinction is ambiguous, there should be deference to controlling provisions in the Federal Rules (*Hanna v. Plumer*).

(5) *The Policies-of-Erie Approach:* Finally, some cases indicate that the ultimate test really lies in the policies of *Erie*. Thus, if the application of federal law would

produce irrational differences in results and encourage forum shopping, the matter is substantive; if not, it is procedural (*Hanna v. Plumer*).

None of these approaches has been clearly overruled. There can be no pretense that the decisions are fully consistent or predictable.

An Analogy. The will-o'-the-wisp distinction between substance and procedure calls for an analogy. In an elementary physics class, students would be introduced to two apparently inconsistent theories about the phenomenon that we know as "light." The "particle" theory describes light as particles called photons. This theory is useful to describe some characteristics of light. The "wave" theory instead sees light as electromagnetic waves, and it is useful in describing other phenomena (*e.g.*, color). Which theory is the "correct" one? The answer is that both of them are, and yet neither is. In an attempt to describe a unique property of the universe, the physicists have invented crude models. It is not surprising that no single model fits all cases. And so it is with the substance-procedure distinction. The *Erie* doctrine is a complex idea, and it cannot be fully described by any single formula.

[A] The "Outcome Determinative" Test

GUARANTY TRUST CO. v. YORK
326 U.S. 99 (1945)

[Guaranty was trustee for certain noteholders of Van Swearingen Corporation, including York. In a diversity action brought in a federal court in New York, York sued Guaranty, claiming that Guaranty had breached its fiduciary duties to the noteholders, including York, by cooperating in a plan to rehabilitate the financially troubled Van Swearingen Corporation by permitting the purchase of the notes for 50% of their face value and shares of stock in the Van Swearingen Corporation. The trial court granted summary judgment in favor of Guaranty. On appeal, the Second Circuit Court of Appeals held that the trial court was not required to apply the New York statute of limitations that would govern breach of fiduciary duty cases filed in New York State courts, because the suit was on the "equity side" of the federal district court even though the exclusive basis of federal jurisdiction was diversity of citizenship. The Supreme Court granted certiorari to determine whether the New York statute governed the time for bringing the breach of trust claim, rather than general principles of equity jurisprudence.]

MR. JUSTICE FRANKFURTER delivered the opinion of the Court.

. . . .

Our starting point must be the policy of federal jurisdiction which *Erie R. Co. v. Tompkins*, 304 U.S. 64, embodies. In overruling *Swift v. Tyson*, 16 Pet. 1, *Erie R. Co. v. Tompkins* did not merely overrule a venerable case. It overruled a particular way of looking at law which dominated the judicial process long after its inadequacies had been laid bare. . . . Law was conceived as a "brooding omnipresence" of Reason, of which decisions were merely evidence and not themselves the controlling formulations. Accordingly, federal courts deemed themselves free to ascertain what Reason, and therefore Law, required wholly independent of authoritatively declared State law, even in cases where a legal right as the basis for relief was created by State authority. . . .

In exercising their jurisdiction on the ground of diversity of citizenship, the federal courts, in the long course of their history, have not differentiated in their regard for State law between actions at law and suits in equity. . . .

Partly because the States in the early days varied greatly in the manner in which equitable relief was afforded and in the extent to which it was available, . . . Congress provided that "the forms and modes of proceeding in suits . . . of equity" would conform to the settled uses of courts of equity. § 2, 1 Stat. 275, 276, 28 U.S.C. § 723. But this enactment gave the federal courts no power that they would not have had in any event when courts were given "cognizance," by the first Judiciary Act, of suits "in equity.". . . [C]ongress never gave, nor did the federal courts ever claim, the power to deny substantive rights created by State law or to create substantive rights denied by State law.

This does not mean that whatever equitable remedy is available in a State court must be available in a diversity suit in a federal court, or conversely, that a federal court may not afford an equitable remedy not available in a State court. Equitable relief in a federal court is of course subject to restrictions. . . . State law cannot define the remedies which a federal court must give simply because a federal court in diversity jurisdiction is available as an alternative tribunal to the State's courts. Contrariwise, a federal court may afford an equitable remedy for a substantive right recognized by a State even though a State court cannot give it. . . . [But] the body of adjudications concerning equitable relief in diversity cases leaves no doubt that the federal courts enforced State-created substantive rights if the mode of proceeding and remedy were consonant with the traditional body of equitable remedies, practice and procedure, and in so doing they were enforcing rights created by the States and not arising under any inherent or statutory federal law. . . .

And so this case reduces itself to the narrow question whether, when no recovery could be had in a State court because the action is barred by the statute of limitations, a federal court in equity can take cognizance of the suit because there is diversity of citizenship between the parties. Is the outlawry, according to State law, of a claim created by the States a matter of "substantive rights" to be respected by a federal court of equity when that court's jurisdiction is dependent on the fact that there is a State-created right, or is such statute of "a mere remedial character," . . . which a federal court may disregard?

Matters of "substance" and matters of "procedure" are much talked about in the books as though they defined a great divide cutting across the whole domain of law. But, of course, "substance" and "procedure" are the same keywords to very different problems. Neither "substance" nor "procedure" represents the same invariants. Each implies different variables depending upon the particular problem for which it is used. . . .

And so the question is not whether a statute of limitations is deemed a matter of "procedure" in some sense. The question is whether such a statute concerns merely the manner and the means by which a right to recover, as recognized by the State, is enforced, or whether such statutory limitation is a matter of substance in the aspect that alone is relevant to our problem, namely, does it significantly affect the result of a litigation for a federal court to disregard a law of a State that would be controlling in an action upon the same claim by the same parties in a State court?

It is therefore immaterial whether statutes of limitation are characterized either as "substantive" or "procedural" in State court opinions in any use of those terms unrelated to the specific issue before us. *Erie R. Co. v. Tompkins* was not an endeavor to formulate scientific legal terminology. It expressed a policy that touches vitally the proper distribution of judicial power between State and federal courts. In essence, the intent of that decision was to insure that, in all cases where a federal court is exercising jurisdiction solely because of the diversity of citizenship of the parties, the outcome of the litigation in the federal court should be substantially the same, so far as legal rules determine the outcome of a litigation, as it would be if tried in a State court. The nub of the policy that underlies *Erie R. Co. v. Tompkins* is that for the same transaction the accident of a suit by a non-resident litigant in a federal court instead of in a State court a block away should not lead to a substantially different result. . . .

Plainly enough, a statute that would completely bar recovery in a suit if brought in a State court bears on a State-created right vitally and not merely formally or negligibly. As to consequences that so intimately affect recovery or non-recovery a federal court in a diversity case should follow State law. . . . [I]f a plea of the statute of limitations would bar recovery in a State court, a federal court ought not to afford recovery.

Diversity jurisdiction is founded on assurance to non-resident litigants of courts free from susceptibility to potential local bias. The Framers of the Constitution, according to Marshall, entertained "apprehensions" lest distant suitors be subjected to local bias in State courts, or, at least, viewed with "indulgence the possible fears and apprehensions" of such suitors. *Bank of the United States v. Deveaux*, 5 Cranch 61, 87. And so Congress afforded out-of-State litigants another tribunal, not another body of law. . . .

The judgment is reversed and the case is remanded for proceedings not inconsistent with this opinion.

MR. JUSTICE ROBERTS and MR. JUSTICE DOUGLAS took no part in the consideration or decision of this case.

[The dissenting opinion of Mr. Justice Rutlege is omitted.]

NOTES AND QUESTIONS

(1) *The Fundamental Flaw in the "Outcome Determinative" Test.* There is a fundamental flaw in testing the extent of the *Erie* doctrine by whether the rule in question is "outcome determinative." Can you see what the flaw is? [Note: Doesn't it destroy the possibility of meaningful rules of "procedure"? By definition, if a procedure ever makes a difference — why, then, it ceases to be procedural!] In *Byrd v. Blue Ridge*, which appears in the next section, you will see the Supreme Court refine the test.

(2) *Frankfurter's "Remedy" Distinction.* Justice Frankfurter attempts to prevent this catastrophe in his reasoning by reserving the power for federal courts to order different remedies than state courts. But isn't the remedy just as "substantive" as the underlying "claim"? For instance, imagine that state law provides that, under certain facts, no injunctions can be issued. If a federal court in a diversity case issues an injunction on those facts, hasn't it made as important a difference in outcome as if it had changed the underlying claim?

(3) *Does York Overrule Sibbach?* In *Sibbach v. Wilson & Co.*, discussed in the preceding section, the Court held that a federal judge could order a medical examination even if a state judge could not. Is this difference between state and federal rules a difference in "outcome"? Isn't it sure to change the amount of recovery? Does *York*, then, overrule *Sibbach*? Consider the next series of cases.

[B] Balancing State and Federal Interests

RAGAN v. MERCHANTS' TRANSFER & WAREHOUSE CO., 337 U.S. 530 (1949). Ragan filed a diversity action on September 4, 1945, in a federal court in Kansas, but did not serve the complaint on the defendant until December 28 of that year. The vehicular accident that gave rise to the suit had occurred on October 1, 1943, and since the Kansas two-year statute of limitations provided that suit was not deemed commenced until service was accomplished, Ragan's claim would have been barred if brought in the state courts. Fed. R. Civ. P. 3, however, provides: "A civil action is commenced by filing a complaint with the court." If this Rule, rather than the Kansas provision, was controlling, Ragan's suit would have been timely commenced. The Supreme Court, by an 8 to 1 vote, held that Kansas law was applicable and that Ragan's claim was barred. The Court reasoned that the definition of commencement was "an integral part" of the Kansas statute and therefore should be given effect.

NOTES AND QUESTIONS

(1) *"Outcome Determination," or State-Federal "Interest Balancing"?* It is possible to argue that the Kansas rule in *Ragan* controlled because it expressed a strong state interest in forcing diligent notification of defendants. This state policy was clearly articulated by the Kansas legislature as an "integral part" of the statute of limitations. The federal rule, by contrast, did not clearly advance any distinctly federal interests contrary to the Kansas rule. *See* Leathers, *Erie and Its Progeny as Choice of Law Cases*, 11 Hous. L. Rev. 791 (1974). This reading of *Ragan* may be supported by the Court's later decision in *Walker v. Armco Steel Corp.*, which appears below. On the other hand, there were two companion decisions to *Ragan*, and they strengthened the perception that the outcome-determinative test was controlling.

(2) *Woods v. Interstate Realty Co.*, 337 U.S. 535 (1949). In this companion case to *Ragan*, the plaintiff had not qualified to do business in Mississippi (a requirement that included appointing an agent for service of process). A Mississippi statute provided that a foreign corporation that had not qualified "shall not be permitted to bring or maintain any action or suit in any of the courts of this state." Relying on *York*, the Supreme Court held that this law was substantive, and a foreign corporation that was not qualified could not bring a diversity action in a Mississippi federal court either. On the same day, the Court also decided *Cohen v. Beneficial Loan Corp.*, 337 U.S. 541 (1949). There, it held that a New Jersey statute requiring the plaintiff to post bond as security for costs must be applied in a federal action in New Jersey even though the parallel federal rule contained no such requirement.

(3) *The Impact of* Ragan, *Woods, and Cohen.* After these decisions, the principal drafter of the Federal Rules wrote that "hardly one" of the Rules could be considered safe from attack. "Many observers believed . . . that there was no longer much, if any room for independent federal regulation of procedure." C. Wright & M. Kane, *The Law of Federal Courts* 403 (6th ed. 2002). But the signals were mixed. The opinions did not articulate a consistent reason for the results. Five members of the Court dissented in at least one of the three cases. And later, in *Byrd v. Blue Ridge Rural Elec. Cooperative, Inc.*, the Court took a different approach.

BYRD v. BLUE RIDGE RURAL ELECTRIC COOPERATIVE, INC.

356 U.S. 525 (1958)

[The plaintiff brought a diversity suit in a federal court in South Carolina for injuries sustained in the course of his employment. The defendant pleaded, as a defense, that it was to be deemed the plaintiff's "statutory employer" for purposes of the South Carolina Workers' Compensation Act. This argument, if accepted, would entitle the plaintiff to workers' compensation benefits but would give the employer immunity from suit for negligence. Under the state law, which was established by the decisions of the South Carolina Supreme Court, this immunity issue was to be decided by the judge alone, without the intervention of a jury, because it was a jurisdictional requirement for the administrative agency that decided compensation claims. The United States Supreme Court first decided that it should remand Byrd's suit to enable him to develop evidence rebutting immunity. It then considered whether the immunity issue should be decided on remand in the federal court by the judge alone (as it would be in the state courts), or by a jury.]

MR. JUSTICE BRENNAN delivered the opinion of the Court.

. . . .

First. It was decided in *Erie R. Co. v. Tompkins* that the federal courts in diversity cases must respect the definition of state-created rights and obligations by the state courts. . . . A State may, of course, distribute the functions of its judicial machinery as it sees fit. The [South Carolina state] decisions relied upon, however, furnish no reason for selecting the judge rather than the jury to decide this single affirmative defense in the negligence action. They simply reflect a policy . . . that administrative determination of "jurisdictional facts" should not be final but subject to judicial review. The conclusion is inescapable that the [state] holding is grounded in the practical consideration that the question had theretofore come before the South Carolina courts from the Industrial Commission and the courts had become accustomed to deciding the factual issue of immunity without the aid of juries. We find nothing to suggest that this rule was announced as an integral part of the special relationship created by the statute. Thus the requirement appears to be merely a form and mode of enforcing the immunity, *Guaranty Trust Co. v. York*, 326 U.S. 99, 108, and not a rule intended to be bound up with the definition of the rights and obligations of the parties. . . .

Second. But cases following *Erie* have evinced a broader policy to the effect that the federal courts should conform as near as may be — in the absence of other considerations — to state rules even of form and mode where the state rules may bear substantially on the question whether the litigation would come out one way in the federal court and another way in the state court if the federal court failed to apply a particular local rule. *E.g., Guaranty Trust Co. v. York, supra; Bernhardt v. Polygraphic Co.*, 350 U.S. 198. Concededly the nature of the tribunal which tries issues may be important in the enforcement of the parcel of rights making up a cause of action or defense, and bear significantly upon achievement of uniform enforcement of the right. It may well be that in the instant personal-injury case the outcome would be substantially affected by whether the issue of immunity is decided by a judge or a jury. Therefore, were "outcome" the only consideration, a strong case might appear for saying that the federal court should follow the state practice.

But there are affirmative countervailing considerations at work here. The federal system is an independent system for administering justice to litigants who properly invoke its jurisdiction. An essential characteristic of that system is the manner in which, in civil common-law actions, it distributes trial functions between judge and jury and, under the influence — if not the command — of the Seventh Amendment, assigns the decisions of disputed questions of fact to the jury. . . . The policy of uniform enforcement of state-created rights and obligations, *see e.g., Guaranty Trust Co. v. York, supra*, cannot in every case exact compliance with a state rule — not bound up with rights and obligations — which disrupts the federal system of allocating functions between judge and jury. *Herron v. Southern Pacific Co.*, 283 U.S. 91. Thus the inquiry here is whether the federal policy favoring jury decisions of disputed fact questions should yield to the state rule in the interest of furthering the objective that the litigation should not come out one way in the federal court and another way in the state court.

We think that in the circumstances of this case the federal court should not follow the state rule. It cannot be gainsaid that there is a strong federal policy against allowing state rules to disrupt the judge-jury relationship in the federal courts. In *Herron v. Southern Pacific Co., supra*, the trial judge in a personal-injury negligence action brought in the District Court for Arizona on diversity grounds directed a verdict for the defendant when it appeared as a matter of law that the plaintiff was guilty of contributory negligence. The federal judge refused to be bound by a provision of the Arizona Constitution which made the jury the sole arbiter of the question of contributory negligence. This Court sustained the action of the trial judge, holding that "state laws cannot alter the essential character or function of a federal court" because that function "is not in any sense a local matter, and state statutes which would interfere with the appropriate performance of that function are not binding upon the federal court under either the Conformity Act or the 'Rules of Decision' Act." *Id.*, at 94. Perhaps even more clearly in light of the influence of the Seventh Amendment, the function assigned to the jury "is an essential factor in the process for which the Federal Constitution provides." . . .

Third. We have discussed the problem upon the assumption that the outcome of the litigation may be substantially affected by whether the issue of immunity is decided by a judge or a jury. But clearly there is not present here the certainty that a different result would follow, *cf. Guaranty Trust Co. v. York, supra*, or even the strong possibility that this would be the case, *cf. Bernhardt v. Polygraphic Co., supra.* There are factors present here which might reduce that possibility. The trial judge in the federal system has powers denied the judges of many States to comment on the weight of evidence and credibility of witnesses, and discretion to grant a new trial if the verdict appears to him to be against the weight of the evidence. We do not think the likelihood of a different result is so strong as to require the federal practice of jury determination of disputed factual issues to yield to the state rule in the interest of uniformity of outcome.

Reversed and remanded.

[The dissenting opinions of Justices Whittaker and Frankfurter are omitted.]

NOTES AND QUESTIONS

(1) *The Interest-Balancing Test: How Does It Work?* There are several hidden problems in a test distinguishing substance and procedure by balancing state and federal interests. *See* Smith, *Blue Ridge and Beyond: A Byrd's Eye View of Federalism in Diversity Litigation*, 36 Tul. L. Rev. 443 (1962). First, it may be difficult to identify all of the relevant state and federal policies, particularly if they must be derived from a few words in a statute. Also, it may be impossible to compare the competing policies except in a subjective manner. To see why, you might try applying an interest-balancing test to the decisions in *Ragan, Woods*, and *Cohen*, and ask yourself whether the results would change. *Cf. Szantay v. Beech Aircraft Corp.*, 349 F.2d 60 (4th Cir. 1965) (state statute closing courts to non-qualified foreign corporations, of the type applied in *Woods*, held inapplicable after *Byrd* because it would advance no significant state interest and would interfere with the federal policy in favor of efficient multi-party joinder).

(2) *Has the Outcome-Determinative Test Become a Requirement That the Law in Question Be "Definitively" Outcome Determinative?* The Court in *Byrd* says that the

substitution of a judge for a jury does not create a "certainty" of a different outcome. Elsewhere it puts the issue in terms of whether "the likelihood of a different result . . . is strong." Has the Court reformulated the outcome determinative test to require that the state rule affect the outcome in a "definitive" way? *Cf. Boggs v. Blue Diamond Coal Co.*, 497 F. Supp. 1105, 1120 (E.D. Ky. 1980) (a substantive state rule is one "which, if all the facts were stipulated, would be meaningful in analyzing the rights and liabilities of parties to a dispute if they were to settle it on the day of filing suit, taking into account the necessity of filing suit, but without actually filing it").

(3) *Bernhardt v. Polygraphic Co. of America, 350 U.S. 198 (1956).* Defendant removed this state-court action to federal court and sought a stay of proceedings pending arbitration, in accordance with a contract between the parties. The state law provided that an agreement to arbitrate was revocable. The Supreme Court relied heavily on the outcome-determinative test in holding that the state law was controlling: "If the federal court allows arbitration where the state court would disallow it, the outcome of litigation might depend on the courthouse where the suit is brought. . . . The change from a court of law to an arbitration panel might make a radical difference in the ultimate result." Note that *Bernhardt* was decided after *Ragan* and before *Byrd*; the question is, does *Byrd* implicitly overrule *Bernhardt*? [Note: If the "definitiveness" of outcome determination is the issue, perhaps it does, because the change in fact-finder from jury to arbiter does not seem qualitatively different from changing from jury to judge. But if interest-balancing is the proper approach, perhaps the cases are consistent, because in *Byrd* the result is "influenced" by a strong federal policy expressed in the Seventh Amendment to the Constitution.] Notice that *Byrd* cites the *Bernhardt* holding with apparent approval.

[C] Controlling Federal Rules and the Policies of *Erie*

HOW TO READ *HANNA v. PLUMER*

Hanna v. Plumer involved a service-of-process provision incorporated in a statute of limitations (as did *Ragan*, but of a different kind). The defendant in *Hanna* relied heavily upon the outcome-determination test, which would have resulted in his immediate victory. But the Court rejects an "automatic, 'litmus paper' criterion," and into this area in which you have already seen so much inconsistency, it injects at least two additional approaches. First, there are some rules that "are rationally capable of classification as either" substance or procedure, and within this "gray area," deference should be given to a valid and controlling Federal Rule if there is one applicable. Second, the policies underlying *Erie* are important criteria for distinguishing substance and procedure. "The 'outcome-determination' test therefore cannot be read without reference to the twin aims of the *Erie* rule: discouragement of forum-shopping and avoidance of inequitable administration of the laws." You will have to determine for yourself whether *Hanna* rationalizes or further confuses the *Erie* doctrine.

HANNA v. PLUMER
380 U.S. 460 (1965)

[Hanna filed a diversity suit in a federal court in Massachusetts, alleging that Louise Plumer Osgood had negligently caused her injuries in an automobile accident. Because Osgood was deceased, Hanna named Plumer, the executor of her estate, as the defendant. Hanna had the complaint and summons served by leaving them at Plumer's residence with his wife. It was undisputed that this service complied with Fed. R. Civ. P. 4, which provides for "leaving [copies at the defendant's] dwelling or usual place of abode. . . ." Plumer later filed an answer, however, asserting a defense under a Massachusetts state statute providing that "an executor or administrator shall not be held to answer to an action by a creditor of the deceased which is not commenced within one year from the time of his giving bond . . . or to such an action which is commenced within said year unless before the expiration thereof the writ in such action has been served by delivery in hand upon such executor or administrator. . . ." The papers in Hanna's suit had been served within the one-year period, but they had not been served on the executor "in hand" within that period, as the Massachusetts statute required. The District Court, citing *York* and *Ragan*, granted summary judgment for defendant Plumer. The Court of Appeals affirmed, finding that "[r]elatively recent amendments to [the Massachusetts statute] evidence a clear legislative purpose to require personal notification within one year." The Supreme Court granted certiorari "[b]ecause of the threat to the goal of uniformity of federal procedure."]

MR. CHIEF JUSTICE WARREN delivered the opinion of the Court.

. . . .

We conclude that the adoption of Rule 4(d)(1) [now Rule 4(e)(2)], designed to control service of process in diversity actions, neither exceeded the congressional mandate embodied in the Rules Enabling Act nor transgressed constitutional bounds, and that the Rule is therefore the standard against which the District Court should have measured the adequacy of the service. Accordingly, we reverse the decision of the Court of Appeals.

The Rules Enabling Act, 28 U.S.C. § 2072 (1958 ed.), provides, in pertinent part:

> The Supreme Court shall have the power to prescribe, by general rules, the forms of process, writs, pleadings, and motions, and the practice and procedure of the district courts of the United States in civil actions.
>
> Such rules shall not abridge, enlarge or modify any substantive right and shall preserve the right of trial by jury. . . .

Under the cases construing the scope of the Enabling Act, Rule [4] clearly passes muster. . . . [I]t relates to the "practice and procedure of the district courts." . . .

> The test must be whether a rule really regulates procedure, — the judicial process for enforcing rights and duties recognized by substantive law and for justly administering remedy and redress for disregard or infraction of them.

Sibbach v. Wilson & Co. . . . In *Mississippi Pub. Corp. v. Murphree*, 326 U.S. 438, this Court upheld [another part of Rule 4, then codified as] Rule 4(f), which permits service of a summons anywhere within the State (and not merely the district) in which a district court sits:

> We think that Rule 4(f) is in harmony with the Enabling Act. . . . Undoubtedly most alterations of the rules of practice and procedure may and often do affect the rights of litigants. Congress' prohibition of any alteration of substantive rights of litigants was obviously not addressed to such incidental effects. . . . The fact that the application of Rule 4(f) will operate to subject petitioner's rights to adjudication by the district court for northern Mississippi will undoubtedly affect those rights. But it does not operate to abridge, enlarge or modify the rules of decision by which, that court will adjudicate its rights.

Id., at 445-446.

Thus were there no conflicting state procedure, [Rule 4] would clearly control. . . . However, respondent, focusing on the contrary Massachusetts rule, calls to the Court's attention another line of cases, a line which — like the Federal Rules — had its birth in 1938. *Erie R. Co. v. Tompkins*, 304 U.S. 64. . . . [A]s subsequent cases sharpened the distinction between substance and procedure, the line of cases following *Erie* diverged markedly from the line construing the Enabling Act. *Guaranty Trust Co. v. York*, 326 U.S. 99, made it clear that *Erie*-type problems were not to be solved by reference to any traditional or common-sense substance-procedure distinction:

> And so the question is not whether a statute of limitations is deemed a matter of "procedure" in some sense. The question is . . . does it significantly affect the result of a litigation for a federal court to disregard a law of a State that would be controlling in an action upon the same claim by the same parties in a State court?

Respondent, by placing primary reliance on *York* and *Ragan*, suggests that the *Erie* doctrine acts as a check on the Federal Rules of Civil Procedure, that despite the clear command of [Rule 4], *Erie* and its progeny demand the application of the Massachusetts rule. Reduced to essentials, the argument is: (1) *Erie*, as refined in *York*, demands that federal courts apply state law whenever application of federal law in its stead will alter the outcome of the case. (2) In this case, a determination that the Massachusetts service requirements obtain will result in immediate victory for respondent. If, on the other hand, it should be held that [Rule 4] is applicable, the litigation will continue, with possible victory for petitioner. (3) Therefore, *Erie* demands application of the Massachusetts rule. The syllogism possesses an appealing simplicity, but is for several reasons invalid.

In the first place, it is doubtful that, even if there were no Federal Rule making it clear that in-hand service is not required in diversity actions, the *Erie* rule would have obligated the District Court to follow the Massachusetts procedure. "Outcome-determination" analysis was never intended to serve as a talisman. *Byrd v. Blue Ridge Cooperative*, 356 U.S. 525, 537. Indeed, the message of *York* itself is that choices between state and federal law are to be made not by application of any automatic, "litmus paper" criterion, but rather by reference to the policies underlying the *Erie* rule. . . .

The *Erie* rule is rooted in part in a realization that it would be unfair for the character or result of a litigation materially to differ because the suit had been brought in a federal court. . . . The decision was also in part a reaction to the practice of "forum-shopping" which had grown up in response to the rule of *Swift v. Tyson*. 304 U.S., at 73-74. That the *York* test was an attempt to effectuate these policies is demonstrated by the fact that the opinion framed the inquiry in terms of "substantial" variations between state and federal litigation. 326 U.S., at 109. Not only are nonsubstantial, or trivial, variations not likely to raise the sort of equal protection problems which troubled the Court in *Erie*; they are also unlikely to influence the choice of a forum. The "outcome-determination" test therefore cannot be read without reference to the twin aims of the *Erie* rule: discouragement of forum-shopping and avoidance of inequitable administration of the laws.

The difference between the conclusion that the Massachusetts rule is applicable, and the conclusion that it is not, is of course at this point "outcome-determinative" in the sense that if we hold the state rule to apply, respondent prevails, whereas if we hold that [Rule 4] governs, the litigation will continue. But in this sense *every* procedural variation is "outcome-determinative." For example, having brought suit in a federal court, a plaintiff cannot then insist on the right to file subsequent pleadings in accord with the time limits applicable in the state courts, even though enforcement of the federal timetable will, if he continues to insist that he must meet only the state time limit, result in determination of the controversy against him. So it is here. Though choice of the federal or state rule will at this point have a marked effect upon the outcome of the litigation, the difference between the two rules would be of scant, if any, relevance to the choice of a forum. Petitioner, in choosing her forum, was not presented with a situation where application of the state rule would wholly bar recovery; rather, adherence to the state rule would have resulted only in altering the way in which process was served. Moreover, it is difficult to argue that permitting service of defendant's wife to take the place of in-hand service of defendant himself alters the mode of enforcement of state-created rights in a fashion sufficiently "substantial" to raise the sort of equal protection problems to which the *Erie* opinion alluded.

There is, however, a more fundamental flaw in respondent's syllogism: the incorrect assumption that the rule of *Erie R. Co. v. Tompkins* constitutes the appropriate test of the validity and therefore the applicability of a Federal Rule of Civil Procedure. The *Erie* rule has never been invoked to void a Federal Rule. . . . (Here, of course, the clash is unavoidable; [Rule 4] says — implicitly, but with unmistakable clarity — that in-hand service is not required in federal courts.) At the same time, in cases adjudicating the validity of Federal Rules, we have not applied the *York* rule or other refinements of *Erie*, but have to this day continued to decide questions concerning the scope of the Enabling Act and the constitutionality of specific Federal rules in light of the distinction set forth in *Sibbach*. . . .

Nor has the development of two separate lines of cases been inadvertent. The line between "substance" and "procedure" shifts as the legal context changes. . . . When a situation is covered by one of the Federal Rules, the question facing the court is a far cry from the typical, relatively unguided *Erie* choice: the court has been instructed to apply the Federal Rule, and can refuse to do so only if the Advisory Committee, this Court, and Congress erred in their *prima facie* judgment that the Rule in question transgresses neither the terms of the Enabling Act nor constitutional restrictions.

We are reminded by the *Erie* opinion that neither Congress nor the federal courts can, under the guise of formulating rules of decision for federal courts, fashion rules which are not supported by a grant of federal authority contained in Article I or some other section of the Constitution; in such areas state law must govern because there can be no other law. But the opinion in *Erie*, which involved no Federal Rule and dealt with a question which was "substantive" in every traditional sense . . . , surely neither said nor implied that measures like [Rule 4] are unconstitutional. For the constitutional provision for a federal court system (augmented by the Necessary and Proper Clause) carries with it congressional power to make rules governing the practice and pleading in those courts, which in turn includes a power to regulate matters which, though falling within the uncertain area between substance and procedure, are rationally capable of classification as either. . . . Although this Court has never before been confronted with a case where the applicable Federal Rule is in direct collision with the law of the relevant State, courts of appeals faced with such clashes have rightly discerned the implications of our decisions.

> One of the shaping purposes of the Federal Rules is to bring about uniformity in the federal courts by getting away from local rules. This is especially true of matters which relate to the administration of legal proceedings, an area in which federal courts have traditionally exerted strong inherent power, completely aside from the powers Congress expressly conferred in the Rules. The purpose of the *Erie* doctrine, even as extended

in *York* and *Ragan*, was never to bottle up federal courts with "outcome-determinative" and "integral-relations" stoppers — when there are "affirmative countervailing [federal] considerations" and when there is a Congressional mandate (the Rules) supported by constitutional authority.

Lumbermen's Mutual Casualty Co. v. Wright, 322 F.2d 759, 764 (C.A. 5th Cir. 1963).

Erie and its offspring cast no doubt on the long-recognized power of Congress to prescribe housekeeping rules for federal courts even though some of those rules will inevitably differ from comparable state rules. . . . To hold that a Federal Rule of Civil Procedure must cease to function whenever it alters the mode of enforcing state-created rights would be to disembowel either the Constitution's grant of power over federal procedure or Congress' attempt to exercise that power in the Enabling Act. [Rule 4] is valid and controls the instant case.

Reversed.

MR. JUSTICE BLACK concurs in the result.

MR. JUSTICE HARLAN, concurring. . . .

Erie was something more than an opinion which worried about "forum-shopping and avoidance of inequitable administration of the laws," although to be sure these were important elements of the decision. I have always regarded that decision as one of the modern corner-stones of our federalism, expressing policies that profoundly touch the allocation of judicial power between the state and federal systems. . . .

The shorthand formulations which have appeared in some past decisions are prone to carry untoward results that frequently arise from oversimplification. The Court is quite right in stating that the "outcome-determinative" test of *Guaranty Trust Co. v. York*, 326 U.S. 99, if taken literally, proves too much, for any rule, no matter how clearly "procedural," can affect the outcome of litigation if it is not obeyed. In turning from the "outcome" test of *York* back to the unadorned forum-shopping rationale of *Erie*, however, the Court falls prey to like over-simplification, for a simple forum-shopping rule also proves too much; litigants often choose a federal forum merely to obtain what they consider the advantages of the Federal Rules of Civil Procedure or to try their cases before a supposedly more favorable judge. To my mind the proper line of approach in determining whether to apply a state or a federal rule, whether "substantive" or "procedural," is to stay close to basic principles by inquiring if the choice of rule would substantially affect those primary decisions respecting human conduct which our constitutional system leaves to state regulation. If so, *Erie* and the Constitution require that the state rule prevail, even in the face of a conflicting federal rule.

The Court weakens, if indeed it does not submerge, this basic principle by finding, in effect, a grant of substantive legislative power in the constitutional provision for a federal court system (*compare Swift v. Tyson*, 16 Pet. 1), and through it, setting up the Federal Rules as a body of law inviolate. . . . So long as a reasonable man could characterize any duly adopted federal rule as "procedural," the Court, unless I misapprehend what is said, would have it apply no matter how seriously it frustrated a State's substantive regulation of the primary conduct and affairs of its citizens.Since the members of the Advisory Committee, the Judicial Conference, and this Court who formulated the Federal Rules are presumably reasonable men, it follows that the integrity of the Federal Rules is absolute. . . .

The courts below relied upon this Court's decisions in *Ragan v. Merchants Transfer Co.*, 337 U.S. 530, and *Cohen v. Beneficial Loan Corp.*, 337 U.S. 541. Those cases deserve more attention than this Court has given them, particularly *Ragan* which, if still good law, would in my opinion call for affirmance of the result reached by the Court of Appeals. . . .

In *Ragan* a Kansas statute of limitations provided that an action was deemed commenced when service was made on the defendant. Despite Federal Rule 3 which provides that an action commences with the filing of the complaint, the Court held that for purposes of the Kansas statute of limitations a diversity tort action commenced only when service was made upon the defendant .. . . I think that the decision was wrong. At most, application of the Federal Rule would have meant that potential Kansas tort defendants would have to defer for a few days the satisfaction of knowing that they had not been sued within the limitations period. The choice of the Federal Rule would have had no effect on the primary stages of private activity from which torts arise, and only the most minimal effect on behavior following the commission of the tort. In such circumstances the interest of the federal system in proceeding under its own rules should have prevailed.

Cohen v. Beneficial Loan Corp. held that a federal diversity court must apply a state statute requiring a small stockholder in a stockholder derivative suit to post a bond securing payment of defense costs as a condition to prosecuting an action. . . . The proper view of *Cohen* is, in my opinion, that the statute was meant to inhibit small stockholders from instituting "strike suits," and thus it was designed and could be expected to have a substantial impact on private primary activity. . . . I think it wholly legitimate to view Federal Rule 23 as not purporting to deal with the problem. But even had the Federal Rules purported to do so, and in so doing provided a substantially less effective deterrent to strike suits, I think the state rule should still have prevailed. That is where I believe the Court's view differs from mine; for the Court attributes such overriding force to the Federal Rules that it is hard to think of a case where a conflicting state rule would be allowed to operate, even though the state rule reflected policy considerations which, under *Erie*, would lie within the realm of state legislative authority.

It remains to apply what has been said to the present case. . . . If the Federal District Court in Massachusetts applies Rule 4(d)(1) of the Federal Rules of Civil Procedure instead of the Massachusetts service rule, what effect would that have on the speed and assurance with which estates are distributed? As I see it, the effect would not be substantial. It would mean simply that an executor would have to check at his own house or the federal courthouse as well as the registry of probate before he could distribute the estate with impunity. As this does not seem enough to give rise to any real impingement on the vitality of the state policy which the Massachusetts rule is intended to serve, I concur in the judgment of the Court.

NOTES AND QUESTIONS

(1) *Counting and Evaluating the Various "Tests." York* introduced (1) the "outcome determinative" test. Later, *Byrd* arguably redefined the test as (2) a requirement of "absolute" or "definitive" outcome determination. *Byrd* also illustrates (3) the "state-federal interest balancing" approach. *Hanna* relies on (4) a "controlling Federal Rules" analysis, as well as (5) a "policies of *Erie*" test. *See* McCoid, *Hanna v. Plumer: The Erie Doctrine Changes Shape*, 51 Va. L. Rev. 884 (1965). Is there any way to rationalize all of these tests or to say which one is "the best"? *See* Redish & Phillips, *Erie and*

the Rules of Decision Act: In Search of the Appropriate Dilemma, 91 Harv. L. Rev. 356 (1977) (arguing for a "refined balancing test").

(2) *Is There Still Hope for Consistency? Walker v. Armco Steel Corp., 446 U.S. 740 (1980).* In *Hanna*, above, Justice Harlan's concurring opinion implies that *Hanna* overrules *Ragan*. But then, in *Walker*, the Court was faced with another case presenting the *Ragan* problem. The plaintiff's suit was filed before, but service was made after, the running of a state statute of limitations defining commencement by the time of service. The Court unanimously upheld the *Ragan* result. Rule 3 provides only that a civil action "is commenced by filing a complaint . . . ." As the Court analyzed the matter, "There is no indication that the Rule was intended . . . to displace state tolling rules for purposes of . . . limitations. In our view, in diversity actions Rule 3 governs the date from which various timing requirements of the federal rules begin to run, but does not affect state statutes of limitations." Is this an outcome-determinative analysis, or interest balancing, or a policies-of-*Erie* approach? The court did distinguish the *Hanna* "controlling federal rule" approach by saying that the question was whether the Federal Rule was "sufficiently broad" to control; since it was not, the state and federal rule could "exist side by side, . . . each controlling in its own intended sphere . . . without conflict."

(3) *Dean Ely's Analysis: Focus on the Governing Act of Congress.* In Ely, *The Irrepressible Myth of Erie*, 87 Harv. L. Rev. 693 (1974), Dean Ely argues that much of the confusion disappears if one distinguishes between cases controlled by the Rules of Decision Act (*York, Byrd*) and those controlled by the Rules Enabling Act (*Hanna*). In the Rules-of-Decision-Act cases, Congress has directed the federal courts to apply state law (at least when the "policies of *Erie*" are involved) unless it is overridden by significant federal procedural policies, such as the constitutional preference for jury trial. In the Rules-Enabling-Act cases, Congress has directed application of the controlling Federal Rule of Civil Procedure unless it would abridge state substantive rights. The most difficult cases, such as *Walker v. Armco Steel Corp.*, may be read as reflecting efforts to avoid a clash between the two statutes, through narrow interpretation of the Federal Rules.

(4) *Applying the Hanna Analysis to Forum Clauses.* In *Stewart Organization, Inc. v. Ricoh Corporation*, 487 U.S. 22 (1988), the Supreme Court held the federal venue transfer statute (§ 1404(a)) controlled the question whether to consider the parties' forum selection clause despite Alabama state law that disfavored such clauses. The majority found no need to consider the "twin aims" of *Erie* when federal statutory law was involved. Justice Scalia in dissent argued that *Erie*'s twin aims require the federal court to follow state law to decide the validity of the forum selection clause. *See also* § 2.02[F][2] *supra*.

BURLINGTON NORTHERN RY. v. WOODS, 480 U.S. 1 (1987). The Woods sued Burlington Northern in Alabama state court to recover damages for injuries they sustained in a motorcycle accident. After removal to federal court, a jury awarded the Woods over $300,000 in damages. Their judgment was affirmed on appeal, and the federal appellate court imposed a 10% mandatory affirmance penalty against Burlington Northern as required by Alabama statute. Burlington challenged the application of this statute as "a procedural rule . . . inapplicable in federal court under the doctrine of *Erie Railroad Company v. Tompkins*, . . . and its progeny . . . ." The Court, per Justice Marshall, held that the Alabama statute was inapplicable:

> [Burlington] contends that the [Alabama] statute's underlying purposes and mandatory mode of operation conflict with the purposes and operation of Rule 38 of the

Federal Rules of Appellate Procedure, and therefore that the statute should not be applied by federal courts sitting in diversity. . . . Under this Rule, "damages are awarded by the court in its discretion in the case of a frivolous appeal as a matter of justice to the appellee and as a penalty against the appellant." Advisory Committee's Notes on Fed. Rule App. Proc. 38. . . .

In *Hanna v. Plumer*, 380 U.S. 460 . . . (1965), we set forth the appropriate test for resolving conflicts between state law and the Federal Rules. The initial step is to determine whether, when fairly construed, the scope of Federal Rule 38 is "sufficiently broad" to cause a "direct collision" with the state law or, implicitly, to "control the issue" before the court, thereby leaving no room for the operation of that law. [Citations omitted.] The Rule must then be applied if it represents a valid exercise of Congress' rule-making authority, which originates in the Constitution and has been bestowed on this Court by the Rules Enabling Act, 28 U.S.C. § 2072. . . .

The constitutional constraints on the exercise of this rulemaking authority define a test of reasonableness. Rules regulating matters indisputably procedural are *a priori* constitutional. Rules regulating matters "which, though falling within the uncertain area between substance and procedure, are rationally capable of classification as either," also satisfy this constitutional standard. . . . The Rules Enabling Act, however, contains an additional requirement. The Federal Rule must not "abridge, enlarge or modify any substantive right . . . ." 28 U.S.C. § 2072. . . .

Rule 38 affords a Court of Appeals plenary discretion to assess "just damages" in order to penalize an appellant who takes a frivolous appeal and to compensate the injured appellee for the delay and added expense of defending the District Court's judgment. Thus, the Rule's discretionary mode of operation unmistakably conflicts with the mandatory provision of Alabama's affirmance penalty statute. Moreover, the purposes underlying the Rule are sufficiently co-extensive with the asserted purposes of the Alabama statute to indicate that the Rule occupies the statute's field of operation so as to preclude its application in federal diversity actions. . . .

Federal Rule 38 regulates matters which can reasonably be classified as procedural, thereby satisfying the constitutional standard for validity. Its displacement of the Alabama statute also satisfies the statutory constraints of the Rules Enabling Act. The choice made by the drafters of the Federal Rules in favor of a discretionary procedure affects only the process of enforcing litigants' rights and not the rights themselves.

GASPERINI v. CENTER FOR HUMANITIES, INC.

518 U.S. 415 (1996)

JUSTICE GINSBURG delivered the opinion of the Court.

Under the law of New York, appellate courts are empowered to review the size of jury verdicts and to order new trials when the jury's award "deviates materially from what would be reasonable compensation." N.Y. Civ. Prac. Law and Rules (CPLR) § 5501(c) (McKinney 1995). Under the Seventh Amendment, which governs proceedings in federal court, but not in state court, "the right of trial by jury shall be preserved, and no fact tried by a jury, shall be otherwise re-examined in any Court of the United States, than according to the rules of the common law." U.S. Const., Amdt. 7. The compatibility of these provisions, in an action based on New York law but tried in federal court by reason of the parties' diverse citizenship, is the issue we confront in this case. We hold that New York's law controlling compensation awards for excessiveness or inadequacy can be given effect, without detriment to the Seventh Amendment, if the review standard set out in CPLR § 5501(c) is applied by the federal trial court judge, with appellate control of the trial court's ruling limited to review for "abuse of discretion."

[The Center for Humanities, Inc. lost hundreds of original color slide transparencies taken during Gasperini's seven-year stint in Central America as a journalist. The transparencies had been given to the Center to use in producing an educational videotape. Gasperini brought a diversity suit against the Center in the United States District Court for the Southern District of New York, alleging state-law claims for breach of contract, conversion, and negligence. The Center conceded liability, and the issue of damages was tried before a jury. Gasperini's expert witness testified that the "industry standard" within the photographic publishing community valued a lost transparency at $1,500. The jury awarded Gasperini $450,000 ($1,500 each for 300 slides lost) in compensatory damages. Alleging that the damage award was excessive, the Center moved for a new trial under Rule 59. The District Court denied the motion. The Second Circuit, applying the New York law standard to determine whether "an award is excessive or inadequate if it deviates materially from what would be reasonable compensation," concluded that testimony on industry standard alone was insufficient to justify a verdict and vacated the judgment. The Second Circuit then ordered a new trial unless Gasperini agreed to an award of $100,000.]

Before 1986, state and federal courts in New York generally invoked the same judge-made formulation in responding to excessiveness attacks on jury verdicts: courts would not disturb an award unless the amount was so exorbitant that it "shocked the conscience of the court."

In both state and federal courts, trial judges made the excessiveness assessment in the first instance, and appellate judges ordinarily deferred to the trial court's judgment. In 1986, as part of a series of tort reform measures, New York codified a standard for judicial review of the size of jury awards. Placed in CPLR § 5501(c), the prescription reads:

> "In reviewing a money judgment . . . in which it is contended that the award is excessive or inadequate and that a new trial should have been granted unless a stipulation is entered to a different award, the appellate division shall determine that an award is excessive or inadequate if it deviates materially from what would be reasonable compensation."

As stated in Legislative Findings and Declarations accompanying New York's adoption of the "deviates materially" formulation, the lawmakers found the "shock the conscience" test an insufficient check on damage awards; the legislature therefore installed a standard "inviting more careful appellate scrutiny."

III

In cases like Gasperini's, in which New York law governs the claims for relief, does New York law also supply the test for federal court review of the size of the verdict? The Center answers yes. The "deviates materially" standard, it argues, is a substantive standard that must be applied by federal appellate courts in diversity cases. Gasperini . . . characterizes the provision as procedural, an allocation of decisionmaking authority regarding damages, not a hard cap on the amount recoverable. Correctly comprehended, Gasperini urges, § 5501(c)'s direction to the Appellate Division cannot be given effect by federal appellate courts without violating the Seventh Amendment's re-examination clause.

As the parties' arguments suggest, CPLR § 5501(c), appraised under *Erie R. Co. v. Tompkins,* 304 U.S. 64 (1938) and decisions in *Erie*'s path, is both "substantive" and "procedural": "substantive" in that § 5501(c)'s "deviates materially" standard controls how much a plaintiff can be awarded; "procedural" in that § 5501(c) assigns decisionmaking authority to New York's Appellate Division. Parallel application of § 5501(c) at the federal appellate level would be out of sync with the federal system's division of trial and appellate court functions, an allocation weighted by the Seventh Amendment. The dispositive question, therefore, is whether federal courts can give effect to the substantive thrust of § 5501(c) without untoward alteration of the federal scheme for the trial and decision of civil cases. . . . Under the *Erie* doctrine, federal courts sitting in diversity apply state substantive law and federal procedural law.

Classification of a law as "substantive" or "procedural" for *Erie* purposes is sometimes a challenging endeavor.[7] *Guaranty Trust Co. v. York* . . ., an early interpretation of *Erie*, propounded an "outcome-determination" test . . . . A later path marking case, qualifying *Guaranty Trust,* explained that the "outcome-determination" test must not be applied mechanically to sweep in all manner of variations; instead its application must be guided by "the twin aims of the *Erie* rule: discouragement of forum-shopping and avoidance of inequitable administration of the laws." *Hanna v. Plumer* . . . .

Informed by these decisions, we address the question whether New York's "deviates materially" standard, codified in CPLR § 5501(c), is outcome-affective in this sense: Would "application of the [standard] . . . have so important an effect upon the fortunes of one or both of the litigants that failure to [apply] it would [unfairly discriminate against citizens of the forum State, or] be likely to cause a plaintiff to choose the federal court"?

We start from a point the parties do not debate. Gasperini acknowledges that a statutory cap on damages would supply substantive law for *Erie* purposes. . . . Although CPLR § 5501(c) is less readily classified, it was designed to provide an analogous control. . . . We think it a fair conclusion that CPLR § 5501(c) differs from a statutory cap principally "in that the maximum amount recoverable is not set by statute, but rather is determined by case law." In sum, § 5501(c) contains a procedural instruction, . . . but the State's objective is manifestly substantive.

It thus appears that if federal courts ignore the change in the New York standard and persist in applying the "shock the conscience" test to damage awards on claims governed by New York law, " 'substantial' variations between state and federal [money judgments]" may be expected. *See Hanna*, 380 U.S. at 467-468. We therefore agree with

---

[7] Concerning matters covered by the Federal Rules of Civil Procedure, the characterization question is usually unproblematic: It is settled that if the Rule in point is consonant with the Rules Enabling Act, 28 U.S.C. § 2072, and the Constitution, the Federal Rule applies regardless of contrary state law. *See Hanna v. Plumer*, 380 U.S. 460, 469-474, 85 S. Ct. 1136, 1142-1145, 14 L.Ed.2d 8 (1965); *Burlington Northern R. Co. v. Woods*, 480 U.S. 1, 4-5, 107 S.Ct. 967, 969-970, 94 L.Ed.2d 1 (1987). Federal courts have interpreted the Federal Rules, however, with sensitivity to important state interests and regulatory policies. *See, e.g., Walker v. Armco Steel Corp.*, 446 U.S. 740, 750-752, 100 S. Ct. 1978, 1985-1986, 64 L.Ed.2d 659 (1980) (reaffirming decision in *Ragan v. Merchants Transfer & Warehouse Co.*, 337 U.S. 530, 69 S. Ct. 1233, 93 L.Ed. 1520 (1949), that state law rather than Rule 3 determines when a diversity action commences for the purposes of tolling the state statute of limitations; Rule 3 makes no reference to the tolling of state limitations, the Court observed, and accordingly found no "direct conflict"); *S.A. Healy Co. v. Milwaukee Metropolitan Sewerage Dist.*, 60 F.3d 305, 310-312 (7th Cir. 1995) (state provision for offers of settlement by plaintiffs is compatible with Federal Rule 68, which is limited to offers by defendants).

the Second Circuit that New York's check on excessive damages implicates what we have called *Erie*'s "twin aims." Just as the *Erie* principle precludes a federal court from giving a state-created claim "longer life . . . than [the claim] would have had in the state court," *Ragan,* 337 U.S. at 533-534, so *Erie* precludes a recovery in federal court significantly larger than the recovery that would have been tolerated in state court.

. . . Acting essentially as a surrogate for a New York appellate forum, the Court of Appeals reviewed Gasperini's award to determine if it "deviated materially" from damage awards the Appellate Division permitted in similar circumstances. Concentrating on the authority § 5501(c) gives to the Appellate Division, Gasperini urges that the provision shifts fact-finding responsibility from the jury and the trial judge to the appellate court. Assigning such responsibility to an appellate court, he maintains, is incompatible with the Seventh Amendment's re-examination clause, and therefore, Gasperini concludes, § 5501(c) cannot be given effect in federal court. Although we reach a different conclusion than Gasperini, we agree that the Second Circuit did not attend to "an essential characteristic of [the federal-court] system," *Byrd v. Blue Ridge Rural Elec. Cooperative, Inc.,* 356 U.S. 525, 537 (1958), when it used § 5501(c) as "the standard for [federal] appellate review." . . .

The Seventh Amendment, which governs proceedings in federal court, but not in state court, bears not only on the allocation of trial functions between judge and jury, the issue in *Byrd*; it also controls the allocation of authority to review verdicts, the issue of concern here. *Byrd* involved the first clause of the Amendment, the "trial by jury" clause. This case involves the second, the "re-examination" clause. In keeping with the historic understanding, the re-examination clause does not inhibit the authority of trial judges to grant new trials "for any of the reasons for which new trials have heretofore been granted in actions at law in the courts of the United States." Rule 59(a). That authority is large. . . . This discretion includes overturning verdicts for excessiveness and ordering a new trial without qualification, or conditioned on the verdict winner's refusal to agree to a reduction (remittitur). . . .

In contrast, appellate review of a federal trial court's denial of a motion to set aside a jury's verdict as excessive is a relatively late, and less secure, development. Such review was once deemed inconsonant with the Seventh Amendment's re-examination clause. . . .

Before today, we have not "expressly [held] that the Seventh Amendment allows appellate review of a district court's denial of a motion to set aside an award as excessive." *Browning-Ferris Industries of Vt., Inc. v. Kelco Disposal, Inc.,* 492 U.S. 257, 279, n.25 (1989). But in successive [cases] . . . we noted, without disapproval, that courts of appeals engage in review of district court excessiveness determinations, applying "abuse of discretion" as their standard. . . . [In] *Browning-Ferris,* we again referred to appellate court abuse-of-discretion review:

> "The role of the district court is to determine whether the jury's verdict is within the confines set by state law, and to determine, by reference to federal standards developed under Rule 59, whether a new trial or remittitur should be ordered. The court of appeals should then review the district court's determination under an abuse-of-discretion standard."

As the Second Circuit explained, appellate review for abuse of discretion is reconcilable with the Seventh Amendment as a control necessary and proper to the fair administration of justice: "We must give the benefit of every doubt to the judgment of the trial judge;

but surely there must be an upper limit, and whether that has been surpassed is not a question of fact with respect to which reasonable men may differ, but a question of law." . . .

In *Byrd,* the Court faced a one-or-the-other choice: trial by judge as in state court, or trial by jury according to the federal practice. In the case before us, a choice of that order is not required, for the principal state and federal interests can be accommodated. The Second Circuit correctly recognized that when New York substantive law governs a claim for relief, New York law and decisions guide the allowable damages. But that court did not take into account the characteristic of the federal-court system that caused us to reaffirm: "The proper role of the trial and appellate courts in the federal system in reviewing the size of jury verdicts is . . . a matter of federal law." *Donovan v. Penn Shipping Co.*, 429 U.S. 648, 649 (1977) (per curiam); *see also Browning-Ferris*. . . .

Within the federal system, practical reasons combine with Seventh Amendment constraints to lodge in the district court, not the court of appeals, primary responsibility for application of § 5501(c)'s "deviates materially" check. Trial judges have the "unique opportunity to consider the evidence in the living courtroom context," *Taylor v. Washington Terminal Co.,* 133 U.S. App. D.C. 110, 409 F.2d 145, 148 (D.C. Cir. 1969), while appellate judges see only the "cold paper record," 66 F.3d at 431.

District court applications of the "deviates materially" standard would be subject to appellate review under the standard the Circuits now employ when inadequacy or excessiveness is asserted on appeal: abuse of discretion. . . . In light of *Erie's* doctrine, the federal appeals court must be guided by the damage-control standard state law supplies, but as the Second Circuit itself has said: "If we reverse, it must be because of an abuse of discretion. . . . The very nature of the problem counsels restraint. . . . We must give the benefit of every doubt to the judgment of the trial judge."

It does not appear that the District Court checked the jury's verdict against the relevant New York decisions demanding more than "industry standard" testimony to support an award of the size the jury returned in this case. As the Court of Appeals recognized, the uniqueness of the photographs and the plaintiff's earnings as photographer — past and reasonably projected — are factors relevant to appraisal of the award. Accordingly, we vacate the judgment of the Court of Appeals and instruct that court to remand the case to the District Court so that the trial judge, revisiting his ruling on the new trial motion, may test the jury's verdict against CLPR § 5501(c)'s "deviates materially" standard.

It is so ordered.

[Justice Stevens' and Justice Scalia's dissents are omitted.]

NOTES AND QUESTIONS

(1) *Is This Balancing the Same as Employed in Byrd?* Rather than choosing between federal and state interests, Justice Ginsburg sculpts an accommodation between the interests. Is this what *Byrd* meant as balancing interests? And how do you balance an essential characteristic of the federal system against an undeniable state substantive policy choice?

(2) *Is the Gasperini Approach Consistent With Hanna's Federal Rule Approach (or With an Outcome-Determinative Approach)?* The Court purports to ask whether the state rule is "outcome-affective in this sense" and it goes on to paraphrase *Hanna*'s policies-of-*Erie* approach, asking whether the state rule would have "so important an effect" that

non-application would discriminate or produce forum shopping. But this approach sidesteps *Hanna*'s federal rule approach: If a federal rule controls and its application is constitutionally acceptable, the federal court should simply apply the federal rule. In *Gasperini*, Federal Rule 59, which had been interpreted to embrace the excessiveness standard used in New York before 1986 ("shocked the conscience" test), coupled with the Seventh Amendment's Reexamination Clause, constituted the pertinent federal standards. Should the Court have simply applied them at the trial court level under the Supremacy Clause or under *Hanna*? What is the Court trying to tell us in footnote 7?

(3) *Commentary. See also* Stein, *Erie and Court Access*, 100 Yale L.J. 1935 (1991). Professor Stein suggests that "[t]he appropriate inquiry . . . is not how state law is categorized, but whether the policies driving the state law are undermined by federal nonconformity." This formula might avoid the procedure-substance quagmire. For another article evaluating the various approaches and opting for a modified interest-balancing test tilted toward the state law, see Crump, *The Twilight Zone of the Erie Doctrine: Is There Really a Different Choice of Equitable Remedies in the "Court a Block Away"?*, 1991 Wis. L. Rev. 1233 (1991). *See generally* Freer, *Erie's Mid-Life Crisis*, 63 Tul. L. Rev. 1087 (1989) (excellent assessment of *Erie*'s history and analysis of flurry of recent, divergent decisions). If *Erie* indeed is suffering a "mid-life crisis," is this perhaps caused by arrested development during *Erie*'s wayward youth? *See* Crump, *supra*.

§ 4.03 Determining What the State Law Is

[A] Which State's Law? Interstate Choice of Law

NOTE ON INTERSTATE CHOICE OF LAW

The Erie Case Itself: Choice of New York or Pennsylvania Law. We have omitted one important aspect of *Erie* from our discussion thus far. The *Erie* rule, of course, is that the federal court follows the substantive law of the state where the suit is brought. In *Erie*, that would have been New York. But Justice Brandeis's opinion says that the federal court was not "free to disregard the alleged rule of the Pennsylvania common law" making Tompkins a trespasser. Why Pennsylvania, if the court was in New York? The answer is logical: The federal court in New York would have to follow the law that a New York State court would follow, but Justice Brandeis assumed that a New York court would, in this instance, follow the law of Pennsylvania.

Different Approaches to Choice of Law. Every state has principles of law that tell its courts when to follow the law of some other state. This problem is called the "conflict of laws" or "choice of law." For example, if a tort occurs in state *Y*, and suit is brought for damages in state *X*, it may be that the court will follow the "law of the place of the injury" (in Latin, "*lex loci delicti*"). However, another approach is for state *X* to consider which state has the "most significant relationship" to the occurrence and the parties, as is advocated by the Second Restatement of Conflict of Laws. In the *Erie* case, either approach would have given the same result, because Pennsylvania was the place of the injury and also was the state with the most significant relationship to the claim. But consider the following case.

PENNINGTON v. DYE, 456 So. 2d 507 (Fla. App. 1984). A couple from Ohio was vacationing in Florida when they were involved in an automobile accident. Plaintiff, the wife, sued her husband and his liability insurer for injuries she received due to his alleged negligence. The Ohio doctrine of interspousal immunity would have barred the claim had it been brought in that state. Plaintiff filed the action in a Florida court, where she argued that there was no such immunity.

The court noted that, historically, Florida had followed the *lex loci delicti* principle (*i.e.*, the law of the place of the injury), which would mean that Florida law would apply to this Florida accident, and plaintiff might recover. However, in *Bishop v. Florida Specialty Paint Co.*, 389 So. 2d 999 (Fla. 1980), the Florida Supreme Court had adopted the "most significant relationship" test of the Second Restatement. *Bishop* had been a personal injury action arising from the crash of a small aircraft in South Carolina while en route from Florida to North Carolina; the court had applied Florida law because the connections of all parties to Florida were strong. Therefore, the Court in *Pennington v. Dye* concluded that the claim before it, between two Ohio citizens, must be tested by the most-significant-relationship test.

In deciding whether Florida or Ohio had the most significant relationship to the parties and occurrence, the court recognized that the incident had happened in Florida (which had an interest in regulating drivers within its borders). But the Restatement indicated that the state of domicile (in this case, Ohio) would have the "dominant interest" in the values of marital harmony and prevention of collusive claims against insurers of its citizens that were the basis of the interspousal immunity doctrine. Therefore, the Florida court held that the interspousal immunity question would be governed by the substantive law of Ohio, which barred the claim.

KLAXON CO. v. STENTOR ELECTRIC MFG. CO., 313 U.S. 487 (1941). This case was the first in which the Supreme Court directly addressed the question whether choice of law principles were "substantive" laws controlled by the *Erie* doctrine. Plaintiff brought suit in a federal court in Delaware for damages arising from the breach of a New York contract. The Court of Appeals, without examining Delaware law, held that a New York statute providing for interest in contract actions applied because it represented the "better" rule. The Supreme Court reversed, holding that the court must follow the choice of law principles of Delaware, where the action was brought:

> We are of the opinion that . . . *Erie* . . . extends to the field of conflict of laws. . . . Otherwise, the accident of diversity of citizenship would constantly disturb equal administration of justice in coordinate state and federal courts sitting side by side. Any other ruling would do violence to the principle of uniformity within a state, upon which the *Tompkins* decision is based. . . . [T]he proper function of the Delaware federal court is to determine what the state law is, not what it ought to be.

NOTES AND QUESTIONS

(1) *Law School Courses in Conflict of Laws.* Most law schools offer courses in conflict of laws. Typically, those courses are two, three, or four semester hours in length. As you can see, our discussion of the subject here is necessarily very general: We hope to give you enough of a sense of it so that you can understand its interrelationship with the *Erie* doctrine. *See* Randall, *The Erie Doctrine and State Conflict of Laws*, 17 S.C. L. Rev. 494 (1965).

(2) *Which Is Better: Lex Loci or Most Significant Relationship?* Most states that have confronted the question have chosen to replace the older *lex loci* rule with a modern variant of the significant relationship test (or modern "state's interest analysis"). *See* R.

Weintraub, *Commentary on the Conflict of Laws* 323-27 (3d ed. 1986). However, some states have chosen to retain the law of the place of the wrong for various reasons, including greater certainty or predictability (although that point is debatable). *Id.* For a hybrid approach, see *Hardly Able Coal Co. v. International Harvester Co.*, 494 F. Supp. 249 (N.D. Ill. 1980) (federal court, applying Illinois conflicts principles, found that significant relationships were equally divided between Illinois and Kentucky, and it therefore followed the law of the situs of the wrong, which was Kentucky).

(3) *Non-Tort Choice of Law.* The preceding discussion, for simplicity, is confined to tort cases. Different kinds of principles apply in cases concerning contracts, property, matrimonial actions, etc. *See generally* R. Weintraub, *supra.*

(4) *Constitutional Limitations on Choice of Law.* What should happen if a state with no legitimate policy interest applies its own law in derogation of a state that has significant interests? In *Phillips Petroleum Co. v. Shutts*, 472 U.S. 797 (1985), the Supreme Court of Kansas applied Kansas law to the claims of all members of a class of royalty owners, notwithstanding the fact that 99 percent of the gas leases in question and 97 percent of the plaintiffs had no connection to Kansas. The Supreme Court reversed. It cited an earlier decision, *Allstate Ins. Co. v. Hague*, 449 U.S. 302 (1981), which held that the Due Process Clause required "a significant contact or aggregation of contacts, creating state interests, such that [the] choice . . . is neither arbitrary nor fundamentally unfair." *See also* Williams, *The Impact of Allstate Insurance Co. v. Hague on Constitutional Limitations on Choice of Law*, 17 U. Rich. L. Rev. 489 (1983); Lowenfeld, *Choice of Law and the Supreme Court: A Dialogue Inspired By Allstate Insurance Co. v. Hague*, 14 U.C. Davis L. Rev. 841 (1981).

(5) *But After Shutts, the Kansas Courts Had the Last Laugh.* In *Sun Oil Co. v. Wortman*, 486 U.S. 717 (1988), the Kansas court contrived to reach the same result it had reached in *Shutts* — by the device of decreeing that three other affected states coincidentally would use the same interest rates as Kansas, even though all three had statutes specifying different rates.(!) The Kansas court reasoned that the other states' statutes were inapplicable to the case. The United States Supreme Court affirmed on the ground that only the clear contradiction of "clearly established" foreign law could be unconstitutional. [Question: Did the Court simply "fold" after being beaten into submission by the Kansas court's persistence?]

(6) *A More Complex Case: In re Air Crash Disaster Near Chicago, 644 F.2d 594 (7th Cir. 1981).* One hundred eighteen wrongful death claims, originally filed in six different jurisdictions, were transferred and consolidated in this single federal action against an airline and others arising out of a crash in Illinois. The court held (in accordance with the rule of *Van Dusen v. Barrack*, discussed in subsection 2.05[B][2], above) that the availability of punitive damages would be controlled by choice of law rules of the jurisdictions in which the various suits were originally filed. Thus, actions filed in New York or Illinois would be governed by the "most significant relationship" test, those filed in California by the comparative impairment approach, and those in Michigan or Puerto Rico by the law of the place of the injury. As for actions filed in Hawaii, said the court, since the applicable rules were not identified by the parties, the law of the forum would supply the choice of law rule. In the final analysis, however, the court determined that "under each of the applicable state choice-of-law rules, punitive damages cannot be allowed. . . ."(!)

(7) *Should Congress Pass a Federal Choice of Law Rule?* For complex or multiple-party cases, or those in which the dispute has such diffuse contacts with so many states

that highly refined choice of law may be counterproductive, it has been suggested that Congress should pass a choice of law rule for diversity cases. Would such a law be wise (or constitutional)? In a complex case, might it be that the current approach pressures the court toward "judicial fudging" to produce a uniform choice of law — which often is pragmatically necessary to simplify the dispute and make it manageable? *Cf.* note (6), *supra; see also In re "Agent Orange" Product Liability Litigation*, 100 F.R.D. 718, 723 (E.D.N.Y. 1983) (rather than apply 50 different sets of state laws, the court simply declared that there was a nationwide "consensus" and that all states thus would apply similar product liability laws (!)). We will reconsider this question in connection with §§ 4.04 and 4.05, below.

(8) *Uniform State Laws.* Perhaps this controversy should make us more interested in promulgating uniform laws for adoption by the states. The Uniform Commercial Code is the best-known example, but there are many. Through this mechanism, *Swift v. Tyson* may still have some modern vitality. The substantive rule of *Swift* — that an antecedent debt is "value" sufficient to establish holder-in-due-course status — is still good law, because U.C.C. § 3-308 has made this substantive principle a "uniform" law!

[B] Unsettled State Law: The "*Erie* Educated Guess"

NOTE ON "*ERIE* EDUCATED GUESSES"

You will see in this section that a federal court follows the decisions of the state supreme court to determine state law. But what if there is no controlling decision of the state supreme court? In that event, the court considers the decisions of the lower courts of the state as persuasive, but not binding, authority. What if there is no indication in *any* decision of any state court? In that event, the federal court makes what is sometimes called an "*Erie* educated guess" about what the state supreme court would do. And finally, what should be done if, after a federal Court of Appeals has already remanded the case to the District Court, a state court decides the same issue the opposite way? That is what the following series of cases is about. The issue here arises in the intriguing context of Elvis Presley's "right of publicity."

FACTORS ETC., INC. v. PRO ARTS, INC., 652 F.2d 278 (2d Cir. 1981). During his lifetime, Elvis Presley formed a Tennessee corporation and assigned to it exclusive ownership of all rights to the commercial use of his name and likeness. This bundle of rights is often referred to as the "right of publicity." After Presley's death, the defendant, Pro Arts, published and commercially sold a poster of Presley. Presley's assignee corporation promptly sued for an injunction in federal court in New York. In defense, Pro Arts argued that the right of publicity does not survive the death of the subject. The district court granted the injunction, and Pro Arts appealed to the Second Circuit Court of Appeals. The Second Circuit concluded that Tennessee law was controlling, but there was no authority on point in that state. As the court put it, "Tennessee statutory and decisional law affords no answer to the question." However, the Sixth Circuit, in a similar case, had concluded that Tennessee would not recognize any right of publicity after death. Since the Sixth Circuit includes Tennessee, the Second Circuit followed the Sixth Circuit's decision. It therefore held that the right of publicity died with Elvis, and it denied the injunction.

Judge Mansfield dissented. He argued that the Sixth Circuit's reasoning, in the Tennessee diversity case then before it, "was not in any way derived from the local law of Tennessee." He quoted the Sixth Circuit: "Since the issue is one of first impression, we are left to review the question in light of practical and policy considerations, the relative weight of the conflicting interests of the parties, and certain moral presuppositions concerning death, privacy, inheritability, and economic opportunity." The Sixth Circuit had cited such authorities as John Rawls' *A Theory of Justice* and the Restatement of Torts, rather than attempting to discern the views of the Tennessee Supreme Court. Therefore, its decision should not be regarded as controlling. On the merits, Judge Mansfield argued: "[T]he right of publicity involved here is in the nature of a valuable property right, representing the fruits of an individual's investment in the commercial development of his personality. It differs from a mere right of privacy, which is personal in nature and hence only protected from invasion as long as the individual lives." Because the majority's holding was "inconsistent with that of nearly every other case that has considered the issue" and "contrary to all current views of scholarly commentators," Judge Mansfield predicted that Tennessee would uphold the right of publicity after death. [Tennessee promptly did what Judge Mansfield predicted, in the next case in this book].

COMMERCE UNION BANK v. COORS, 7 Media L. Rptr. 2204 (Tenn. Chancery Ct. Davidson Co. 1981). Shortly after the Second Circuit's decision in *Factors Etc.*, above, this Tennessee trial court came to the opposite conclusion from the *Factors Etc.* majority. The estate of the late country music giant Lester Flatt sued to prevent Coors' use of his likeness in two beer advertisements. In a thorough opinion, the court discussed the relevant decisions in Tennessee and elsewhere, described the scholarly works on the right of publicity, chronicled the careers of Flatt and Scruggs at the Grand Ole Opry, and granted the injunction. It reasoned, "The Tennessee Supreme Court has recognized that the exclusive right to use a trade name can survive the termination of business by a business entity which used it [citation omitted]. The Tennessee Court of Appeals held that the exclusive right to use the name of a Memphis drugstore passed from the decedent-sole proprietor to his widow who continued to operate the business [citation omitted]." "Judge Mansfield," said the Tennessee court in closing, "makes a pointedly perceptive comment when he said 'it would be rational for Tennessee courts to adopt a policy enhancing the continued growth of Nashville and Memphis as centers for the lives and activities of music industry personalities.' . . . This Court agrees with Judge Mansfield. It would be unreasonable not to protect the efforts and energies of so many Tennessee artists."

FACTORS ETC., INC. v. PRO ARTS, INC.

541 F. Supp. 231 (S.D.N.Y. 1982) (on remand)

[The Elvis Presley right-of-publicity case had been remanded to the District Court when the Lester Flatt case (*Commerce Union Bank v. Coors*, above) was decided. In this opinion, the District Court traced the decisions and stayed further proceedings to allow the plaintiff to petition the Second Circuit to withdraw its mandate.]

TENNEY, DISTRICT JUDGE.

Plaintiffs Factors Etc., Inc. ("Factors") and Boxcar Enterprises, Inc. ("Boxcar") brought this action alleging that defendants Pro Arts, Inc. ("Pro Arts") and Stop and Shop Companies, Inc. ("Stop and Shop") infringed their exclusive right to exploit the name and likeness of Elvis Presley. . . . The Court subsequently entered summary judgment in favor of plaintiffs and issued a permanent injunction prohibiting defendants from marketing Presley memorabilia and directing that proceedings be held before a magistrate to determine damages, 496 F. Supp. 1090 (S.D.N.Y. 1980). That decision was reversed on appeal by the Second Circuit. . . .

Defendants now move for summary judgment and for damages for wrongful injunction; plaintiffs cross-move for summary judgment or, alternatively, request the Court to stay entry of judgment in this action. For the reasons discussed below, the Court will stay entry of judgment to permit plaintiffs to petition the Second Circuit for recall of its mandate and for rehearing. . . .

. . . Factors' right to an exclusive license to exploit commercially Presley's name and likeness was challenged in another suit. The Memphis Development Foundation sued Factors in federal court in Tennessee to prevent Factors from interfering with its plan to erect a large statue of Presley in downtown Memphis and to raise funds for its project by selling small pewter replicas of the proposed statue. Factors counterclaimed to restrain distribution of the statues. The district court entered a permanent injunction in Factors' favor, *see Memphis Development Foundation v. Factors Etc., Inc.*, 441 F. Supp. 1323 (W.D. Tenn. 1977), but its decision was reversed by the Sixth Circuit, 616 F.2d 956. . . . Maintaining that "Tennessee courts have not addressed this issue directly or indirectly, and we have no way to assess their predisposition," the Sixth Circuit nevertheless concluded, based on policy considerations, that the right of publicity is not descendible. . . .

When Factors subsequently moved for summary judgment in this action, the Court granted the motion and issued a permanent injunction.. . . [T]he Second Circuit reversed, concluding that . . . it should defer to the Sixth Circuit's holding in *Memphis Development*. . . .

On the basis of the Second Circuit's decision, defendants now move for summary judgment in their favor and for an assessment of damages for wrongful injunction against plaintiffs. Plaintiffs cross-move for summary judgment in their favor, citing *Commerce Union Bank v. Coors*, 7 Med. L. Rptr. 2204 (No. 81-1252-III. Tenn. Ch., Oct. 2, 1981), a recent decision of the Tennessee Chancery Court holding that under Tennessee law, the right of publicity is descendible. Alternatively, plaintiff's have requested the Court to stay entry of judgment in this action, so that they may petition the Second Circuit to recall its mandate and rehear this case on the basis of the *Commerce Union Bank* decision.

A federal court sitting in diversity has a duty to apply a new rule of state law that relates to an action *sub judice. Vandenbark v. Owens-Illinois Glass Co.*, 311 U.S. 538, 543, 61 S. Ct. 347, 350, 85 L. Ed. 327 (1941). Although in *Vandenbark*, the Court specifically referred to state law "in accordance with the then controlling decision of the highest state court," *id.*, it has long been recognized that the responsibility of federal courts in a diversity action to ascertain and apply state law is not limited to decisions of a state's highest court. . . .

Although *Commerce Union Bank*, as a trial court decision, does not bind the federal courts, it is nevertheless entitled to "proper regard."

Both *Factors II* and *Memphis Development* were decided before the Tennessee court's decisions in *Commerce Union Bank;* both circuit courts stated that their holdings were made in the absence of *any* Tennessee case to guide them. Thus, the *Commerce Union Bank* decision is particularly significant as the first Tennessee case to address the issue to hold that the right of publicity is descendible.

For these reasons, this Court will stay entry of judgment in this case to permit plaintiffs to petition the Second Circuit to recall its mandate and to rehear this case.

NOTES AND QUESTIONS

(1) *What Should the Second Circuit Now Do?* How much deference must the Second Circuit give to the Lester Flatt case (*Commerce Union Bank v. Coors*), and how should it go about deciding whether to reverse itself? *See* Gibbs, *How Does the Federal Judge Determine What Is the Law of the State?* 17 S.C. L. Rev. 487 (1965).

(2) *Abstention; State Provisions for Certification of Questions.* As we saw in Chapter 3, the federal courts sometimes abstain so that suits may be re-filed in state court (but abstention is confined to exceptional circumstances). Also, some states have provided mechanisms for federal courts to certify questions to state supreme courts. That procedure would have been helpful in the *Factors Etc.* case. However, it is important to recognize that certification is not a panacea. There simply are too many diversity cases for federal courts to certify every ambiguous issue, and the process effectively adds another layer to an already lengthy appellate process.

(3) *Don't Give Up Yet! There's More to the Elvis Presley Case: Factors, Etc., Inc. v. Pro Arts, Inc., 701 F.2d 11 (2d Cir. 1983).* If you think you know what the Second Circuit ought to do about the recall-of-mandate petition, you may be surprised by its actual decision — which might be called "*Factors Etc. No. IV*" (or "*V*" or "*VI*"). In accordance with the District Court's opinion, Factors Etc. did petition the Second Circuit to recall its mandate. But in the meantime, *another* Tennessee Chancery Court judge ruled on the question — and this judge came to the opposite conclusion! As the Second Circuit put it,

> Fortunately, a recent development . . . has made it unnecessary for us to determine whether *Commerce Union Bank* [the Lester Flatt decision] is of sufficient authoritativeness to warrant [recall of the mandate]. On November 24, 1982, the Chancery Court, acting through a different judge from the one who rendered the decision in *Commerce Union Bank*, ruled that Tennessee does not recognize a descendible right of publicity. *Lancaster v. Factors Etc., Inc.*, 8 Media L. Rptr. — (Chan. Ct. Shelby Co. Tenn. 1982). The *Lancaster* decision is surely entitled to no less weight than the decision in *Commerce Union Bank* and may even have a special pertinence since it involves a claim by the same parties who are plaintiffs in the instant litigation with respect to a descendible right of publicity concerning Elvis Presley.

Judge Mansfield again dissented, saying that the conflicting decisions "only serve to emphasize that . . . we are in as good a position as [the Sixth Circuit] to divine what would be the position of the Supreme Court of Tennessee . . . ." What does this case tell you about *Erie* educated guesses? *See also State ex rel. Elvis Presley Int'l Memorial Found. v. Crowell*, 733 S.W.2d 89 (Tenn. App. 1987) (holding that right of publicity did indeed survive Elvis' death under Tennessee law).

§ 4.04 Filling the Gaps in Federal Law

[A] Federal Common Law

NOTE ON THE JUSTIFICATION FOR FEDERAL COMMON LAW

Federal Common Law in Interstate Disputes. In *Erie*, Justice Brandeis flatly said: "There is no general federal common law." In certain selected areas, however, "federal common law" unquestionably does exist. In fact, in another case decided the same day as *Erie*, Justice Brandeis wrote that an interstate water rights dispute was "a question of 'federal common law' upon which neither the statutes nor the decisions of either state can be conclusive." *Hinderlider v. La Plata River & Cherry Creek Ditch Co.*, 304 U.S. 92 (1938). Obviously, there is good reason for not deciding a dispute between two states by the laws of either.

Uniquely Federal Interests: Clearfield Trust Co. v. United States, 318 U.S. 363 (1943). In this famous federal common law case, the United States sued a bank that had guaranteed and presented a forged check issued by the United States. The Court decided that it would be inappropriate to apply the law of the state where the transaction took place, which would have placed the loss on the United States because of a delay in notifying the bank. "The issuance of commercial paper by the United States is on a vast scale and transactions in that paper from issuance to payment will ordinarily occur in several states. The application of state law . . . would subject the rights and duties of the United States to exceptional uncertainty. . . . The desirability of a uniform rule is plain." The Court reached that result by federal common law. *See also Boyle v. United Technologies Corp.*, 487 U.S. 500 (1988) (adopting as federal common law, a "military contractor" defense, exempting military contractors from tort damages for accidents caused by products produced in conformity with military procurement orders; holding that such a defense implicates two kinds of "uniquely federal interests" — federal obligations, as in *Clearfield Trust*, and federal military procurement). But consider the following case.

ATHERTON v. FEDERAL DEPOSIT INSURANCE CORPORATION, 519 U.S. 213 (1997). City Federal Savings Bank was a federally chartered and insured savings institution that became insolvent. The Federal Deposit Insurance Company succeeded to its rights as receiver. The FDIC sued Atherton and other former officers and directors of City Federal on the theory that they had made bad loans and should personally repay the losses.

The FDIC's suit was affected by a federal statute codified as 12 U.S.C. § 1821(k), which provided: "A director or officer of a federally insured bank may be held personally liable for monetary damages [to the FDIC] for gross negligence [or] similar conduct . . . that demonstrates a greater disregard of a duty of care [than gross negligence]. Nothing in this paragraph shall impair or affect any right of the [FDIC] under other applicable law." The FDIC's position was that this statute allowed it to recover either on the gross negligence standard set by the statute or on a standard set by federal common law (which might allow recovery, for example, for breach of fiduciary duty). The defendants disagreed, arguing that federal common law was inapplicable and that nothing less than gross negligence would do.

The District Court agreed with the defendants and dismissed all but the gross negligence claims. The Court of Appeals, however, reversed. It held that federal common law was included in the "other applicable law" that would control aside from the gross negligence standard of § 1821(k). The Supreme Court, per Justice Breyer, reversed the reversal and held that the state common law, not federal common law, was the "other applicable law" that controlled:

> We begin by temporarily setting the federal "gross negligence" statute to the side, and by asking whether, were there no such statute, federal common law would provide the applicable legal standard. We recognize, as did the Third Circuit, that this Court did once articulate federal common-law corporate governance standards, applicable to federally chartered banks. *Briggs v. Spaulding,* 141 U.S. 132 (1891). *See also Martin v. Webb,* 110 U.S. 7 (1884) (directors must "use ordinary diligence . . . and . . . exercise reasonable control"). . . . But the Court found its rules of decision in federal common law long before it held, in *Erie R. Co. v. Tompkins* that "[t]here is no federal general common law." The Third Circuit, while considering itself bound by *Briggs*, asked whether relevant federal common-law standards could have survived *Erie*. We conclude that they did not and that [generally] state law, not federal common law, provides the applicable rules for decision.
>
> This Court has recently discussed what one might call "federal common law" in the strictest sense, i.e., a rule of decision that amounts, not simply to an interpretation of a federal statute or a properly promulgated administrative rule, but, rather, to the judicial "creation" of a special federal rule of decision. The Court has said that "cases in which judicial creation of a special federal rule would be justified . . . are . . . 'few and restricted.' " *O'Melveny & Myers v. FDIC*, 512 U.S. 79, 87 (1994). . . . "Whether latent federal power should be exercised to displace state law is primarily a decision for Congress," not the federal courts. . . . Thus, normally, when courts decide to fashion rules of federal common law, "the guiding principle is that a significant conflict between some federal policy or interest and the use of state law . . . must first be specifically shown." Indeed, such a "conflict" is normally a "precondition." . . .
>
> . . . Consequently, we must decide whether the application of state-law standards of care to [federally chartered] banks would conflict with, and thereby significantly threaten, a federal policy or interest. . . .
>
> First, the FDIC invokes the need for "uniformity." Federal common law, it says, will provide uniformity, but "[s]uperimposing state standards of fiduciary responsibility over standards developed by a federal chartering authority would . . . 'upset the balance' that the federal chartering authority 'may strike. . . .' " . . . To invoke the concept of "uniformity," however, is not to prove its need. . . .
>
> For one thing, the number of federally insured banks is about equally divided between federally chartered and state-chartered banks, . . . and a federal standard that increases uniformity among the former would increase disparity with the latter.
>
> For another, our Nation's banking system has thrived despite disparities in matters of corporate governance. Consider, for example, the divergent state law governance standards applicable to banks chartered in different States [here the Court cites various state statutes and decisions]. Indeed, the Comptroller of the Currency, acting through regulation, permits considerable disparity in the standard of care applicable to federally chartered banks other than savings banks (which are under the jurisdiction of the Office of Thrift Supervision, 12 U.S.C. §§ 1462a, 1463(a)). . . .
>
> Second, the FDIC at times suggests that courts must apply a federal common-law standard of care simply because the banks in question are federally chartered. This

argument, with little more, might have seemed a strong one during most of the first century of our Nation's history, for then state-chartered banks were the norm and federally chartered banks an exception—and federal banks often encountered hostility and deleterious state laws. . . .

After President Madison helped to create the second Bank of the United States, for example, many States enacted laws that taxed the federal bank in an effort to weaken it. This Court held those taxes unconstitutional. *McCulloch v. Maryland,* 4 Wheat. 316, 431, 4 L. Ed. 579 (1819) ("[T]he power to tax involves the power to destroy"). . . . Still, 10 years later President Andrew Jackson effectively killed the Bank. His Secretary of the Treasury Roger Taney (later Chief Justice), believing state banks fully able to serve the Nation, took steps to "ushe[r] in the era of expansive state banking." . . .

During and after the Civil War a federal banking system reemerged. . . .

This latter history is relevant because in 1870 and thereafter this Court held that federally chartered banks are subject to state law. *See National Bank v. Commonwealth,* 9 Wall. 353, 361, 19 L. Ed. 701 (1869). In *National Bank* the Court distinguished *McCulloch* by recalling that Maryland's taxes were "used . . . to destroy," and it added that federal banks "are subject to the laws of the State, and are governed in their daily course of business far more by the laws of the State than of the nation. All their contracts are governed and construed by State laws. Their acquisition and transfer of property, their right to collect their debts, and their liability to be sued for debts, are all based on State law. It is only when the State law incapacitates the banks from discharging their duties to the government that it becomes unconstitutional." 9 Wall., at 362. . . .

For present purposes, the consequence is the following: To point to a federal charter by itself shows no conflict, threat, or need for "federal common law." It does not answer the critical question. . . .

In sum, we can find no significant conflict with, or threat to, a federal interest. The federal need is far weaker than was present in what the Court has called the "few and restricted instances" in which this Court has created a federal common law. Consider, for example, *Hinderlider v. La Plata River & Cherry Creek Ditch Co.,* 304 U.S. 92 (1938) ([creating federal common law to govern] controversy between two States regarding apportionment of streamwater [within the two States]); *Boyle v. United Technologies Corp.,* 487 U.S. 500 (1988) ([creating federal common law defense to state tort claims for] Federal Government contractors and civil liability of federal officials). . . .

NOTES AND QUESTIONS

(1) *The (Rare) Conditions for Federal Common Law: Conflict Between Sovereign States, as in Hinderlider, or Between State Law and Federal Law, as in Boyle.* In a dispute between two states over water rights, it makes sense that neither sovereign's law should apply. Likewise, if a state's law would hold a federal contractor liable in tort for fulfilling his or her contract, it is apparent that state law should not apply. These are kinds of conflicts that create the rare phenomenon of federal common law. Be sure that you see why the *Atherton* case, above, does not fit either pattern.

(2) *Democratic Values, Federalism, Erie, and Federal Common Law.* A fundamental dilemma of American government lies behind the concept of federal common law. The

federal courts are not democratic institutions. Therefore, they should defer to Congress on major policy questions not controlled by the Constitution. But if Congress hasn't acted on a matter the courts obviously have to decide, doesn't that mean that it has left the issue for the courts to determine as best they can? There is also another dilemma, that of the relationship between the national government and the states in our federal system. *Hinderlider*, which was decided the same day as *Erie*, recognizes federal common law; but every time that federal common law is applied, it displaces state law in a way that conflicts with the deference required by *Erie*. Where should the line be drawn? Is the Supreme Court's formulation, confining federal common law to cases of "conflict" with "uniquely federal interests," practical and workable? *See* Field, *Sources of Law: The Scope of Federal Common Law*, 99 Harv. L. Rev. 881 (1986).

(3) *"Implied Rights of Action" Versus "Federal Common Law."* Reconsider *Bivens v. Six Unknown Agents*, in Chapter 3, above. The Court there held that the Fourth Amendment to the Constitution gave rise to an implied right of action for damages. Is *Bivens* a case of federal common law? The answer is no. There is a difference; federal common law is derived from non-textual sources, whereas in *Bivens*, the Court ostensibly based its reasoning on the relevant constitutional provisions. Its decision is a kind of "statutory interpretation." However, reasoning based on implication rather than textual interpretation, as in *Bivens*, is sometimes loosely referred to as "federal common law." *Cf. Pierson v. Ray*, 386 U.S. 547 (1967) (civil rights statute, although it mentions no defenses, held subject to absolute judicial immunity and to defense of good faith, because there was no indication Congress intended to abolish these longstanding common law defenses). *See also* Kreimer, *The Source of Law in Civil Rights Actions: Some Old Light on Section 1988*, 133 U. Pa. L. Rev. 601 (1985).

[B] "Borrowed" State Law Used as Federal Law

DELCOSTELLO v. INTERNATIONAL BROTHERHOOD OF TEAMSTERS, 462 U.S. 151 (1983). DelCostello brought a grievance against his employer for wrongful discharge. He was represented in grievance arbitration proceedings by his union, according to a collective bargaining agreement. When the proceedings terminated adversely to him, he sued the employer — and also sued his union on the claim that it had breached its duty fairly to represent him as required by federal labor legislation. The District Court granted summary judgment for the defendants, holding that DelCostello had not complied with the Maryland 30-day statute of limitations for actions to vacate arbitration awards. The court concluded that it was required to apply this state statute of limitations to these federal labor law claims by the Supreme Court's decision in *United Parcel Service, Inc. v. Mitchell*, 451 U.S. 56 (1981). In an opinion that distinguished *Mitchell* (but appears by implication to overrule it), the Supreme Court reversed. It held that DelCostello's claim must be governed by the six-month period provided under federal law for filing an unfair labor practice charge, set forth in § 10(b) of the National Labor Relations Act. Justice Brennan's opinion for the Court reasoned as follows:

> As is often the case in federal civil law, there is no federal statute of limitations expressly applicable to this suit. [O]ur task is to "borrow" the most suitable statute or other rule of timeliness from some other source. We have generally concluded that Congress intended that the courts apply the most closely analogous statute of limitations under state law. [The federal Rules of Decision Act provides that the laws of the several states are the rules of decision in the courts of the United States "except

where the Constitution, treaties or statutes of the United States shall otherwise require or provide."] . . .

In some circumstances, however, state statutes of limitations can be unsatisfactory vehicles for the enforcement of federal law. In those instances, it may be inappropriate to conclude that Congress would choose to adopt state rules at odds with the purpose or operation of federal substantive law. . . .

In *Mitchell*, we analogized the employee's claim against the employer to an action to vacate an arbitration award in a commercial setting . . . . [T]he parallel is imperfect in operation. The main difference is that a party to commercial arbitration will ordinarily be represented by counsel or, at least, will have some experience in matters of commercial dealings and contract negotiations. . . . In the labor setting, by contrast, the employee will often be unsophisticated in collective-bargaining matters, and he will almost always be represented by the union. . . . Yet state arbitration statutes typically provide very short times in which to sue for vacation of arbitration awards. . . .

These objections to the resort to state law might have to be tolerated if state law were the only source reasonably available for borrowing, as it often is. In this case, however, we have available a federal statute of limitations actually designed to accommodate a balance of interests very similar to that at stake here. . . . We refer to § 10(b) of the National Labor Relations Act, which establishes a six-month period for making charges of unfair labor practices before the [National Labor Relations Board].

[The Court reasoned that § 10(b) was intended to balance the national interest in stable bargaining relationships and encouragement of private labor settlements, which would call for a short period of repose, against the employee's interest in setting aside an unjust settlement reached under the collective bargaining system, which would call for a longer period. It concluded that the same balance was at issue in DelCostello's case.]

. . . We do not mean to suggest that federal courts should eschew use of state limitations periods anytime state law fails to provide a perfect analogy. . . . [R]esort to state law remains the norm for borrowing of limitations periods. Nevertheless, when a rule from elsewhere in federal law provides a closer analogy . . . , and when the federal policies at stake . . . make that rule a significantly more appropriate vehicle for interstitial lawmaking, we have not hesitated to turn away from state law. . . .

Justices Stevens and O'Connor dissented. Justice Stevens said: "For the past century, judges have 'borrowed' state statutes of limitation, not because they thought it was a sensible form of 'interstitial lawmaking,' but because they were directed to do so by the Congress of the United States." In particular, since he saw nothing in the laws of the United States that "required or provided" otherwise, Justice Stevens would have held that the Rules of Decision Act required application of the analogous state statute of limitations.

NOTES AND QUESTIONS

(1) *What Law Should Be Borrowed?* The *DelCostello* case shows the ambiguities inherent in borrowing "analogous" law. The trial judge had first borrowed Maryland's three-year statute for contract actions. Then the *Mitchell* case was decided, and he borrowed Maryland's 30-day vacation-of-arbitration statute. Justice Stevens' concurrence

argued that the state statute of limitations for malpractice by attorneys should be applied (because he saw it as most analogous to breach of the union's duty of fair representation). The majority, however, chose the six-month period of § 10(b). Can you see why it might be undesirable for the limitations period to be uncertain?

(2) *Congress Acts on the Statute-of-Limitations Problem (But Only Partially): A Federal Four-Year Statute for Future Federal Enactments.* Congress eventually reacted to this confusion by enacting a federal four-year limitations statute, applicable to future Acts of Congress that do not otherwise specify. 28 U.S.C. § 1658. But since this limitation period only applies to Acts of Congress passed *after* its enactment in 1990, all then-existing federal claims (which comprise *most* federal claims, even today) still raise the same problem of borrowing a state statute of limitations. Should Congress have made this statute applicable to existing federal claims, too? (That approach, of course, might not satisfactorily cover federal claims of a kind that should be subject to a short cutoff — but would the resulting increase in certainty be helpful?)

(3) *"Federalizing" the Borrowed Law: Holmberg v. Armbrecht, 327 U.S. 392 (1946).* In *Holmberg*, plaintiff's suit to enforce the liability of bank shareholders under the Federal Farm Loan Act would have been barred by the New York state statute of limitations. The Court applied the New York statute — but it "federalized" it by subjecting it to the condition, recognized by federal courts of equity, that delay caused by the fraud of defendants is not to be counted in the limitations period.

(4) *Other Instances of Borrowing.* The Federal Tort Claims Act makes the government liable for torts when a "private person" would be liable under local law. 28 U.S.C. §§ 1346(b), 2672. This enactment is only one of many in which Congress has adopted state law as federal law. For another example of state law used by courts to fill gaps in federal law, see *De Sylva v. Ballentine*, 351 U.S. 570 (1956) (in suit to construe federal copyright law to determine whether party was one of the "children" of the copyright owner, court looked to state law owing to the absence of a federal law of domestic relations).

§ 4.05 Improving the System of Federal-State Choice of Law: Notes and Questions

(1) *A Federal Choice-of-Law Provision for Complex Diversity Cases?* In 1985, the American Law Institute considered the question whether Congress could create federal choice-of-law rules in diversity cases. *See* 7:2 ALI Rep. 1 (Jan. 1985).

Among the proposals before the ALI was one applicable to certain kinds of complex diversity cases, providing that "the [federal] court may make its own determination as to which State rule of decision is applicable." The proposal continued: "In making this determination, the court may consider, among other factors, the following: the law that might have governed if the [federal] jurisdiction . . . did not exist; the forums in which the claims were or might have been brought; the desirability of application of uniform law . . . ; whether a change in applicable law in connection with removal or transfer of the action would cause unfairness; and the danger of creation of unnecessary incentives for forum shopping."

To see why this sort of proposal might be useful, consider *In re Agent Orange Product Liab. Litig.*, 100 F.R.D. 718, 723 (E.D.N.Y. 1983). In this uniquely complex action, brought by scores of thousands of veterans and their families for injuries allegedly caused by defoliants in Vietnam, the application of fifty different sets of laws would have made the case unmanageable. The District Court initially adopted federal common law. Then, when the Court of Appeals reversed this holding, the District Court judge adopted the dubious but pragmatic solution of declaring that there was a nationwide "consensus" — by which all states would apply identical product liability laws to the case. Wouldn't it be better if this kind of policymaking were explicit and authorized by Congress (as per the ALI proposal)?

Note that the quoted choice-of-law proposal would apply only to complex (multi-party, multi-state) cases. In that context, is it desirable? Is it constitutional?

(2) *Diversity Reform; Uniform Acts.* Abolition or reduction of diversity jurisdiction obviously would proportionally reduce the number of *Erie* questions to be decided by the federal courts. Does this factor provide another reason for diversity reform? *See* Westen, *Is There Life for Erie After the Death of Diversity?*, 78 Mich. L. Rev. 311 (1980). Similarly, *Erie* issues could be simplified by uniform state laws. The Uniform Commercial Code is an example. Should more uniform laws be adopted by more states? Finally, certification to the state courts sometimes can provide a solution.

(3) *More Careful Borrowing; Federal Statutes of Limitations.* Federal borrowing of state law is a good solution in some cases (*e.g.*, rules of conduct for federal enclaves, which usually should not be subject to radically different rules from the state that surrounds them). But in other areas, borrowing seems undesirable. Consider the following:

> It seems to me that the federal practitioner often has trouble enough finding out what the statute of limitations is in his case . . . .
>
> . . . [D]etermining the applicable statute of limitations in federal practice requires a preliminary determination of what the basis is for subject matter jurisdiction. [*Erie* requires use of the state statute in diversity cases.] But if the claim arises under federal law, . . . federal law may send the practitioner looking into state law anyway. . . . If Congress [enacted a limitations period for the case] — as it has done for many cases — the . . . plaintiff can be thankful at least for having to look no further. But for many other claims there is a "void," as the Supreme Court has itself called it. . . . Into this void steps confusion and uncertainty. The federal courts in such cases must "borrow." . . . And so begins the search: What is most analogous in state law?
>
> [The author gives several examples of the resulting confusion, including one in which courts in New York came up with three different statutes of limitations applicable to claims under 42 U.S.C. § 1983, the federal civil rights statute.]
>
> . . . Federal practitioners in other states can cite similar examples, often with unhappy results: a wrong guess and a barred action.
>
> This all too regular federal condition is to my mind intolerable. First, speaking generally, it seems to me that if a point is to be unclear or ambiguous, let it be on some other subject than the statute of limitations. Second, it must strike any observer as incongruous that something as fundamentally "federal" as a federal civil rights claim should be subject to varying periods from state to state. . . .

Siegel, *Practice Commentary on Amendment of Federal Rule 4 with Special Statute of Limitations Precautions*, 96 F.R.D. 88, 97-99 (1983).* Is this argument persuasive? Should Congress enact a series of generally applicable limitations periods, similar to those in effect in each of the states? Should Rule 3 be supplemented by a Congressional enactment making the filing date the date of commencement for limitations purposes?

(4) *Should the Future-Oriented General Federal Statute of Limitations Apply to Existing Claims?* The new general federal statute of limitations, 28 U.S.C. § 1658, provides a four-year time limit for *future* federal enactments that do not otherwise specify. Should Congress have expanded this limit to cover existing federal claims (which, after all, are most of the federal claims that exist)?

CHAPTER 5

PLEADINGS

§ 5.01 How Modern Pleading Developed

[A] Common Law Pleadings

"They Still Rule Us From Their Graves." The great Professor Maitland said that we may think we have buried common law pleadings, but "they still rule us from their graves." Maitland, *Equity* 296 (1909). It is true. Today's affirmative defense is an updated version of common law "confession and avoidance." California still permits the pleading of "common counts," which developed in connection with a common law form of action called general assumpsit. In Texas, litigation over land titles is done by a method resembling the common law action of "ejectment." And in the year these words in our first edition were written, the Supreme Court decided a case from Pennsylvania that depended upon vestiges of common law demurrers in that state's practice. *Smalis v. Pennsylvania*, 476 U.S. 140 (1986).

Why Study Common Law Pleading? Much of the discussion that follows is adapted from B. Shipman, *Handbook of Common Law Pleading* (Ballantyne 3d ed. 1923). The introduction to Shipman's book points out that, understandably, many students doubt the usefulness of learning about common law pleadings! *Id.* at 4. But there are reasons. Not only does this system rule us from its grave, but it has a structured logic that will help you understand today's more open, but in many ways analogous, procedures. And there is yet another, perhaps more important, purpose. Common law pleading will provide you with a perspective from which to judge a persistent policy question: Should pleading rules be tightened, or loosened?

[1] The Plaintiff's Suit: Writ and Declaration

Oral and Written Pleadings; The "Single Issue." Early common law pleadings actually were oral. It was not until the late Fourteenth Century that written pleadings began to replace this procedure. To simplify the dispute, oral pleadings were structured into alternating brief statements by the respective parties. This practice may have been one reason for the extraordinary determination with which the common law judges later insisted upon narrowing the pleadings to a "single issue."

The System of Writs. The plaintiff began his or her suit by obtaining a "writ" from the chancellor, who was the king's representative. The search for the single issue was under way even at this point, for the writ was not a general-purpose device for getting the defendant into court; instead, it was confined to the particular "form of action" that the plaintiff thought his claim might fit. The plaintiff was required to obtain a writ in trespass, for example, if that was the kind of suit she wanted to bring. In its earliest form, the "*capias ad respondendum*," the writ commanded the sheriff to seize the defendant's person. Later, the writ was simply served on the defendant. One of the oddities of the common law practice was that the jurisdiction of the King's Bench sometimes depended upon the custody of the defendant at Marshalsea prison — and therefore, the plaintiff's declaration alleged this confinement even if it was a complete fiction.

Plaintiff's Declaration. The analogue to today's complaint was the "declaration" filed by the plaintiff. But the declaration was full of formal elements, as the example of fictitious custody demonstrates. The function of the pleading was only partially to give notice to the defendant of the general nature of the claim, as would be the objective of a federal complaint today. For example, the following declaration might be used to charge a trespass to the plaintiff's horse:*

Declaration in Trespass for Injury to Personalty

In the King's Bench

On ________, the ________ Day of _____, in
________ Term, 1 Wm. IV

A.B. (to wit) the plaintiff in this suit, complains of C.D., the defendant in this suit, being in the custody of the marshal of Marshalsea of our said lord the now king, before the king himself, of a plea of trespass, for that the said defendant, on etc. (date of injury, or about it), with force and arms, etc., at etc. (venue; e.g., at ________, in the county of ________), drove a certain cart, with great force and violence, upon and against a certain horse of the said plaintiff, of great value, to wit, of the value of £______, there and then being, and there and then with one of the shafts, and other pieces of the said cart of the said defendant, so greatly pierced, cut, hurt, lacerated and wounded the said horse of the said plaintiff that by reason thereof the said horse, being of the value aforesaid, afterwards, to wit, on the day and year aforesaid, died, to wit, at etc. (venue), aforesaid.

And other wrongs to the said plaintiff then and there did, to the great damage of the said plaintiff, against the peace of our said lord the king. Wherefore the said plaintiff saith, that he is injured, and hath sustained damage to the amount of £______, and therefore brings his suit, etc.

The allegation of "force and arms," like that of imprisonment at Marshalsea, was not always to be taken seriously; it was an essential element of all trespasses, but sometimes was "constructive."

[2] The Defendant's Pleading: Demurrer, Traverse, or Confession and Avoidance

Demurrer. The defendant had several choices. First, if the declaration was insufficient on its face to show a right of action even if the truth of all the facts was admitted, or if it was technically defective in form, the defendant could prevail on a "demurrer." This pleading takes its name from the Latin "demorari" or French "demorrer," meaning to wait or stay; and as the etymology implies, the pleading asserts that defendant need do

* Reprinted from Shipman, *Common Law Pleading*, with permission of the West Publishing Company.

nothing because the declaration does not entitle the plaintiff to relief even if its allegations are undisputed. Thus if the plaintiff had omitted the allegation of "force and arms" from the declaration of trespass to his horse, a demurrer would be granted. The plaintiff could usually begin the suit again, but the delay and difficulty were advantageous to the defendant.

Dilatory Pleas: Pleas to the Jurisdiction or in Abatement. These pleadings asserted fundamental defects in the way suit was brought. A "plea to the jurisdiction" attacked subject-matter jurisdiction. A "plea in abatement" was used for a variety of purposes, including attacks on misjoinder or non-joinder of parties.

"Peremptory" Pleas (or Pleas "in Bar"); Traverse and Confession and Avoidance. These were pleas to the merits of the action. A "traverse" was the common law analogue of today's denials. For example, if the defendant wished to deny that he ran his cart into the plaintiff's horse, he would traverse that allegation. "Confession and avoidance" was the other kind of plea in bar. If the defendant wanted to say that he ran into the horse, but he was acting in self-defense because the plaintiff, while on his horse, was threatening him, he would plead by way of confession and avoidance. The modern analogue is the affirmative defense, sometimes called the "defense of new matter." In essence, the demurrer says: "It's true, but so what?"; the traverse says, "It isn't true"; and a defense in confession and avoidance says, "It's true, but here are some other facts that the plaintiff hasn't told you."

Back to the Plaintiff: Demur, Plead, or Join Issue? The ball was again in the plaintiff's court. He or she could respond with a demurrer; for example, a demurrer to the defendant's plea of self-defense would test its legal sufficiency. It would amount to an assertion that the plea could not avoid liability, even if true. Alternatively, the plaintiff could "join issue": he could signify that he accepted the issue formed by his opponent's traverse.

Replication, Rejoinder, Rebutter, Etc. Or, the plaintiff could continue the paper war by a "replication." This plea would be responsive to the defendant's peremptory plea. Thus the plaintiff might traverse the self-defense allegations and put their truth in issue, or he could plead in confession and avoidance — *e.g.*, he did threaten the defendant, but acted in defense of a third person. This plea would send the ball back to the defendant, who could demur, plead, or join issue. His plea would be a "rejoinder." The plaintiff could then respond with a "surrejoinder," to which the defendant would in turn file a "rebutter," followed by the plaintiff's "surrebutter." Theoretically, this process could go on indefinitely, but as a practical matter issue usually was joined after the first few exchanges.

[3] The Single Issue: Herein of "Color," "Duplicity," "Departure," and the "General Issue"

The "Single Issue" and the Prohibition on "Duplicity" or "Departure." What if the defendant had two different defenses to the merits? For example, it would be quite plausible for him to claim that he acted in self-defense and also that he did not cause the horse's death. But this "duplicity," as the common law labelled it, was strictly prohibited, and the plaintiff could attack it by demurrer. In fact, the system also prohibited a more intricate pleading error called a "departure." Each pleading had to be responsive to the opponent's before it and consistent with the party's own prior pleas. For example, if (1) the plaintiff's declaration was for trespass to his horse, (2) the defendant's peremptory plea was self-defense, (3) the plaintiff's replication was defense of a third person, and (4) the defendant's rejoinder was that the claim had been settled and released, the defendant would have committed the sin of departure. His plea of release would be nonresponsive to the replication and inconsistent with his own peremptory plea. The plaintiff would demur and have judgment.

Demurrer as an Admission; "Searching the Record." Initially, demurrers were subject to the single issue approach, too. A demurrer was an admission of the facts properly alleged in the declaration. Thus a "general" demurrer was an all-or-nothing proposition: If the declaration was technically defective, the defendant prevailed, but the defendant would lose, whatever the true facts, if the declaration was good on its face. Later, this process was changed by statute; a "special" demurrer, by which the defendant attacked a defect of form by specifically pointing it out, was not an admission, and even the general demurrer, which attacked the substance of the declaration, was permitted to be asserted without binding admission. Still another oddity of the demurrer practice was that the demurrer "opened" or "searched" the record. All errors in previous pleadings were to be sought out, and judgment would be granted against the pleader who made the first error. Thus if the defendant demurred to the replication, the court would also examine the defendant's peremptory plea for sufficiency; and if it was bad, the court would grant judgment for the plaintiff — unless the declaration was also bad, in which event judgment would be for the defendant.

The Plea of the "General Issue." In some cases, the common law relaxed completely its insistence on narrow pleadings and permitted the defendant to plead "the general issue." In trespassory actions, the plea was "not guilty"; in assumpsit, it was "non assumpsit' ("he did not promise"). These pleas allowed the defendant to contest most of the allegations that the plaintiff would be required to prove and, in addition, to raise certain affirmative defenses. With characteristic pragmatism, the law appears to have invented this procedure in reaction to the perversion of narrow pleading, which became an obstacle to justice. Ironically, the general issue itself was criticized because it obscured the issues in controversy, and its availability was restricted.

The Merits and Demerits of this System. You may well have doubts about this system. But its defenders did not. The vigor of their praise has to be read to be believed. Sir Matthew Hale said that common law pleading had reached a "comparatively perfect state" in the reign of Edward I, when it was "methodically formed and cultivated as a science." In 1855, Professor Samuel Tyler called it "the greatest of all judicial inventions." According to Sir William Jones, "The science of special pleading is an excellent logic. It is admirably calculated for the purpose of analyzing a cause — of extracting, like the roots in an equation, the true points in dispute . . . ." But there was trouble in this paradise. Lord Mansfield said that while the rules of pleading "are founded in strong sense, . . . they are often made use of as instruments of chicane." And Shipman puts it best: "Competent critics have asserted that common law pleading became a mere game of skill, and, instead of being the servant, became [a]n end in itself, instead of a means to the determination of substantial rights."

NOTES AND QUESTIONS

(1) *Some Examples.* Try your hand at identifying the next proper pleading or the proper result in each of the following cases.

(a) *Plaintiff Responds to a Legally Insufficient Defense.* The plaintiff properly pleads a trespass by assault and battery. The defendant's peremptory plea is by way of confession and avoidance, asserting in effect that the plaintiff was contributorily negligent. This plea cannot furnish a defense to assault and battery as a matter of law. How should the plaintiff plead?

(b) *Departure.* The plaintiff properly pleads an indebtedness on a promissory note. The defendant's peremptory plea is that the action is barred by the statute of limitations. The plaintiff's replication is that the statute is tolled, because the defendant was absent from the jurisdiction during most of the time before suit. The defendant's rejoinder is that the note has been paid. The plaintiff demurs. What result? [Notice that the plea of payment is unresponsive to the limitations and tolling pleas.]

(c) *Demurrer Searches the Record.* The plaintiff's declaration charges that the defendant drove his cart over the plaintiff's land and that this trespass destroyed vegetation. But the declaration omits to state that the defendant acted "with force and arms." The defendant's peremptory plea admits the trespass but alleges as an excuse that he was pursued by highway robbers. Since this plea cannot avoid liability for trespass, the plaintiff demurs. What result? [Remember that the party making the first pleading error loses.]

(2) *Advantages of This Pleading System.* Obviously, this system is hypertechnical. But it does have some arguable advantages. What are they?

[4] The Forms of Action

Substance, Remedy, and Procedure Intertwined. The purest essence of the common law was comprised in the "forms of action." Each form defined a substantive theory of recovery, but these forms did more than that. They also provided idiosyncratic remedies and an entire system of procedure unique to it. There was no general-usage civil action, and if the pleader misconceived her case at the outset, she could obtain no relief.

Development of the Forms of Action. Remember that the plaintiff began suit by obtaining a writ from the chancellor. The writ was necessary because no one could use the King's Court without his permission. But there were frequent struggles between the king and other powerful nobles, and in 1258, by the Provisions of Oxford, the king's power to generate new writs was severely limited. At times, new writs were added by Parliament, and new ones evolved slowly through fictions. In the reign of Henry VIII, the Registrum Brevium, or "Register of Writs," was published, organizing this complex field of knowledge. Shipman, at 62, lists five actions *ex delicto* (or "for wrongs done"): trespass, case, trover, detinue, and replevin. Contractual actions included assumpsit, covenant, debt, and account. As for real property, there were several ancient writs, but they were supplanted by others, principally ejectment.

Early Torts: The Action of Trespass. Breach of the king's peace was the source of one of the earlier writs, called trespass. It required three elements: first, a wrongful act done with "force"; second, an "immediate" injury (and not merely a "consequential" one); and third, if the injury was to property, actual or constructive possession of it. Mere nonfeasance could not support a trespass because it involved no force; hence the wrongful detention of goods could not be trespass, although a wrongful taking could. But the more intricate requirement was that of immediate injury. Thus "[i]f a person, in the act of throwing a log into the highway hits and injures a passer-by, the injury is immediate and trespass will lie; but if, after a log has been wrongfully thrown onto the highway, a passer-by falls over it, trespass will not lie." Shipman at 70. Trespass was further divided into trespass *quare clausum fregit* ("because [defendant] broke [plaintiff's] close," for trespass to realty); trespass *de bonis asportatis* ("of goods carried away"); trespass *per quod servitium amisit* ("by reason of his enticing away [plaintiff's] servant"); and trespass by assault and battery.

"Trespass on the Case" (or, Simply, "Case"). The example of the passer-by falling over the log shows the need for a later-developed form called trespass on the case, or simply "case." If a plaintiff suffered an injury that should be redressable, but it was not done with "force" or was "consequential" rather than immediate, trespass would not lie — and, slowly, it became recognized that trespass "on the case" was a proper form. The distinctions between trespass and case sometimes were almost metaphysical. If a person poured water on another's land, the injury was immediate and trespass would lie, but if he put a spout on his roof so that water ran from his building, collected, and overflowed onto the plaintiff's land, the injury was consequential and the only proper form was trespass on the case. Shipman at 89.

Personal Property: Detinue, Replevin, and Trover. "Detinue" was an early writ used to require the return of personalty. It had serious procedural deficiencies and allowed recovery only of the goods themselves, not of damages. "Replevin," at first, was a narrow remedy that allowed both recovery of the goods and damages for wrongful "distraint" or seizure; it later was extended to most kinds of unlawful takings, but not to cases in which the property was rightfully taken but wrongfully detained. Finally, the action of "trover" (or trover and conversion) evolved from trespass and case. It was a damage remedy for the defendant's conversion of personalty to his own use, whether by taking or detention. However, trover, too, had its restrictions. For example, if the defendant simply lost property that had been entrusted to his possession, there was no conversion, and trover would not lie.

The Early Contract Actions: Debt, Covenant, and Account. The recovery of a "liquidated" (*i.e.*, fixed or certain) sum of money could be accomplished by the action of "debt." This was one of the oldest forms, applicable, for example, in the instance of a loan; but it could not be used if the plaintiff sued for general or consequential damages, for installments, or in various other instances. "Covenant" was the action for damages for breach of a covenant under seal (that is, with the defendant's agreement signified by his seal affixed to it). But "the law is economical; the fact that a man has one action is no reason for giving him another," and so covenant in the early days would not lie if debt was available. "Account" was a form used in certain circumstances to recover funds from a fiduciary. There were many deficiencies in these actions, and a general-purpose damage remedy for breach of contract did not exist.

Recovery of Real Property: Ejectment. Ancient real property actions were cumbersome to the point of ineffectiveness. Therefore, the genius of the common law invented "ejectment." This form evolved, of all things, out of trespass, through a wonderfully far-fetched fiction. If the plaintiff entered the land and the defendant ejected him by force, trespass would lie. The defendant would plead "not guilty" (not guilty of what? Of the trespass, of course; because he claimed the land and therefore the right to eject the plaintiff). Thus the trespass action would put the question of title in issue. Later, inventive claimants who were themselves unable to use this form because of technical restrictions used "lessees" as stand-ins to be ejected; still later plaintiffs used two lessees, an ejector (known as the "casual ejector") and an ejectee. Fictional assertion of the ejectment became acceptable, so that actual force was not required, and even a plaintiff in undisturbed possession could use this form to quiet title to his property.

[5] Methods of "Trial," Variances, and the Rise of Assumpsit

The Variance Problem. Pleading was not the only stage where there were technicalities. Evidence at trial had to conform to the pleadings with a surprisingly strict kind of accuracy. If the declaration set out a promise made by the defendant, but the proof showed that the promise contained an additional qualification or condition, there was a fatal "variance" — and the plaintiff lost even if he proved that the additional requirement had been satisfied. In one case, an allegation of an absolute contract to deliver "40 bags of wheat" was not sustained by proof of a contract to deliver "40 or 50 bags of wheat." Shipman at 245-46.

Trial by Battle, Ordeal, and Wager of Law. Furthermore, trial by rational development of evidence before a judge or jury was not always available. There was a time when "trial" was by battle between the parties or their champions, or by an "ordeal," in which truth was to be revealed by divine intervention. One method of ordeal was to cast the defendant into water, which would "reject" the guilty; innocent defendants could be rescued by ropes around their waists. A later but only slightly more advanced procedure was "wager of law." If the defendant swore that he did not owe the debt and was supported by twelve "oath helpers" who swore that they believed him, the result was equivalent to a verdict in his favor. This "system of licensed perjury," as Shipman puts it, was available until comparatively recently in the actions of debt, detinue, and account. A plaintiff who had loaned money obviously regarded debt as an unattractive remedy since the defaulting debtor could defeat it merely by submitting the requisite thirteen oaths.

Assumpsit Replaces Debt; "Common Counts" and "General Assumpsit." To avoid wager of law in a debt action, plaintiffs developed a new action called assumpsit. At first, "special assumpsit" was a narrow remedy and could readily be defeated by variances in proof. Plaintiffs therefore asserted additional counts, or "common" counts, in their pleadings, covering variations in the theory of recovery. Eventually, in the Seventeenth Century, a new form called "general assumpsit" was recognized. It allowed recovery for such divergent theories as an unpaid promissory note or money paid over by mistake or even embezzled, in which the "assumpsit" allegation — literally, "he promised" — was fictitious or, as we would say today, implied only in law. Its breadth and simplicity made general assumpsit popular with plaintiffs (so much so that tort claimants sometimes tried to recharacterize their actions in contract terms). As in the case of the defense of the general issue, the common law had come full circle: general assumpsit was subject to criticism because, in removing technicalities, it had taken a form that completely failed to narrow the issues.

NOTES AND QUESTIONS

(1) *Which Form of Action?* Consider which form you would plead if you represented a common law plaintiff in each of these cases.

(a) *The Case of the Purloined Car.* The defendant moves the plaintiff's car outside the garage so he can get his own car to his parking place. He neglects to move the plaintiff's car back into the garage, and it is stolen. The plaintiff sues in trover; what result? [In *Bushel v. Miller*, 1 Strange 128, 93 Eng. Rep. 428 (K.B. 1718), an analogous case, the plaintiff lost on a declaration in trover because it was "clear" to the court that the defendant's conduct "could not amount to a conversion." The court added that "there might be a doubt" if trespass had been alleged. Actually, wouldn't case fit better than trespass?]

(b) *The Case of the Distrained Billiard Table.* A thief steals the plaintiff's billiard table and sells it to the defendant. The plaintiff asks for it back, but the defendant refuses; later, when he discovers the true facts, the defendant offers to let the plaintiff take it. But in the meantime, the defendant's landlord has distrained the billiard table for the defendant's past-due rent! The plaintiff sues in trover; the defendant pleads the general issue ("not guilty"). What result? [In *Burroughs v. Bayne*, 5 Hurlstone & Norman 296 (Exch. 1860), the court discussed (1) trespass, which would not fit because it would require a "taking" by the defendant "out of the possession of the owner"; (2) replevin, which probably would not fit because it was for goods distrained by the defendant but "restored to the owner by process of law"; (3) detinue, which was "a direct remedy . . . where a chattel was detained" but was undesirable because it allowed wager of law; (4) general assumpsit, for a "broken promise," express or implied; and, finally, (5) trover, which was "the action whereby a person entitled to the possession of goods wrongfully detained from him was entitled to recover damages for their detention." The requirement of a "conversion," said the court, was an "unfortunate expression," but it merely signified a detention by the defendant "so as to deprive the [plaintiff] of his dominion over" the property. Held, on trover for the loss of the billiard table, for the plaintiff. Are the *Bushel* and *Burroughs* decisions consistent?]

(2) *Advantages and Disadvantages.* Try to verbalize what is advantageous about the forms of action, if anything. Also, try to enumerate and explain the disadvantages of this system in light of the above cases.

(3) *The Case of the Wayward Bullet.* The defendant shoots at a target. He is inattentive and fails to notice that an unknown party has left a metal object behind the target. The bullet ricochets and strikes the plaintiff. Is the injury sufficiently "immediate" to allow the plaintiff to recover from the defendant in trespass, or is it "consequential" so that the plaintiff can recover from the defendant in case, or is the defendant not liable to the plaintiff? Consider *Scott v. Shepherd*, which follows (but which is distinguishable from the case of the wayward bullet).

SCOTT v. SHEPHERD

2 Blackstone 892 (Common Pleas 1773)

Trespass and assault for throwing, casting, and tossing a lighted squib at and against the plaintiff, and striking him therewith on the face, and so burning one of his eyes, that he lost the sight of it, whereby, &c.

On Not Guilty pleaded, . . . the jury found a verdict for the plaintiff. . . .

On the evening of the fair-day at Milborne Port, . . . the defendant threw a lighted squib, made of gunpowder, &c. from the street into the market-house, which is a covered building, supported by arches, and enclosed at one end, but open at the other and both the sides, where a large concourse of people were assembled; which lighted squib . . . fell upon the standing of one Yates, who sold gingerbread, &c. That one Willis instantly, and to prevent injury to himself and the said wares of the said Yates, took up the said lighted squib . . . and then threw it across the said market-house, where it fell upon another standing there of one Ryal, who sold the same sort of wares, who instantly, and to save his own goods from being injured, took up the lighted squib . . . and then threw it to another part of the said market-house, and, in so throwing it, struck the plaintiff then in the said market-house in the face therewith, and the combustible matter then bursting, put out one of the plaintiff's eyes.

Qu. If this action be maintainable? . . .

Nares, J., . . . The principle I go upon is what is laid down in Reynolds and Clark, Stra. 634, that if the act in the first instance be unlawful, trespass will lie. Wherever therefore an act is unlawful at first, trespass will lie for the consequences of it. So in 12 Hen. 4, trespass lay for stopping a sewer with earth, so as to overflow the plaintiff's land. . . . I do not think it necessary, to maintain trespass, that the defendant should personally touch the plaintiff. . . . He is the person, who, in the present case, gave the mischievous faculty to the squib. That mischievous faculty remained in it till the explosion. No new power of doing mischief was communicated to it by Willis or Ryal. It is like the case of a mad ox turned loose in a crowd. The person who turns him loose is answerable in trespass for whatever mischief he may do. . . .

Blackstone, J., was of the opinion, that an action of trespass did not lie for Scott against Shepherd upon this case. He took the settled distinction to be, that where the injury is immediate an action of trespass will lie; where it is only consequential, it must be an action on the case: Reynolds and Clarke, Ld. Raym. 1401, Stra. 634 . . . . [I]f I throw a log of timber into the highway (which is an unlawful act), and another man tumbles over it, and is hurt, an action on the case only lies, it being a consequential damage; but if in throwing it I hit another man, he may bring trespass; because it is an immediate wrong. . . . So that lawful or unlawful is quite out of the case; the solid distinction is between direct or immediate injuries on the one hand, and mediate or consequential on the other. And trespass never lay for the latter.

If this be so, the only question will be, whether the injury which the plaintiff suffered was immediate, or consequential only; and I hold it to be the latter. [S]hepherd, I think, is not answerable in an action of trespass and assault for the mischief done by the squib in the new motion impressed upon it, and the new direction given it, by either Willis or Ryal; who both were free agents, and acted upon their own judgment. [N]or is it like diverting the course of an enraged ox, or of a stone thrown, or an arrow glancing against a tree; because there the original motion, the *vis impressa*, is continued, though diverted. Here the instrument of mischief was at rest, till a new impetus and a new direction are given it, not once only, but by two successive rational agents. . . .

But it is said, if Scott has no action against Shepherd, against whom must he seek his remedy? I give no opinion whether case would lie against Shepherd for the consequential damage; though, as at present advised, I think, upon the circumstances, it would. But I think, in strictness of law, trespass would lie against Ryal, the immediate actor in this unhappy business. . . . So in the case . . . relied on in Raym. 467, — "If a man assaults me, so that I can avoid him, and I lift up my staff to defend myself, and, in lifting it up, undesignedly hit another who is behind me, an action lies by that person against me; and yet I did a lawful act in endeavoring to defend myself." But none . . . ever thought that trespass would lie, by the person struck, against him who first assaulted the striker.

. . . The same evidence that will maintain trespass, may also frequently maintain case, but not converso. . . . [I]f I bring trespass for an immediate injury, and prove at most only a consequential damage, judgment must be for the defendant. . . .

It is said by Lord Raymond, and very justly, in Reynolds and Clarke, "We must keep up the boundaries of actions, otherwise we shall introduce the utmost confusion." [I] am of opinion, that in this action judgment ought to be for the defendant.

Gould, J., was of the same opinion with Nares, J., that this action was well maintainable. . . . The line is very nice between case and trespass upon these occasions:

I am persuaded there are many instances wherein both or either will lie. . . . But, exclusive of this, I think the defendant may be considered in the same view as if he himself had personally thrown the squib in the plaintiff's face. The terror impressed upon Willis and Ryal excited self-defence, and deprived them of the power of recollection. What they did was therefore the inevitable consequence of the defendant's unlawful act. . . .

De Grey, C.J. . . . The question here is, whether the injury received by the plaintiff arises from the force of the original act of the defendant, or from a new force by a third person.

I agree with my Brother Blackstone as to the principles he has laid down, but not in his application of those principles to the present case. The real question certainly does not turn upon the lawfulness or unlawfulness of the original act; for actions of trespass will lie for legal acts when they become trespasses by accident; as in the cases cited cutting thorns, lopping of a tree, shooting at a mark, defending oneself by a stick which strikes another behind, &c. — they may also not lie for the consequences even of illegal acts, as that of casting a log in the highway,&c. — But the true question is, whether the injury is the direct and immediate act of the defendant; and I am of opinion, that in this case it is.

. . . I look upon all that was done subsequent to the original throwing as a continuation of the first force and first act, which will continue till the squib was spent by bursting. [T]he blame lights upon the first thrower. The new direction and new force flow out of the first force, and are not a new trespass. . . . On these reasons I concur with Brothers Gould and Nares, that the present action is maintainable.

[*Judgment for the*] . . . *Plaintiff.*

[B] Equity: An Alternative System Develops

During the development of these elaborate forms of action and rules of pleading of the common law, another system was also evolving. The other, radically different, system was called "equity."

The Origins of Equity. The chancellor functioned as a kind of secretary of state to the king. He was keeper of the great seal and supervised the massive amount of writing that had to be done in the king's name. Usually, he was a bishop and was thought of as the king's "conscience." As we have seen, he also had the duty of issuing writs to commence common law actions; and, in fact, if an aggrieved person could find no established writ for his case, the king remained as a reserve of justice, and in practice the dispensation of that justice by the invention of new writs fell largely to the chancellor. By the Fourteenth Century, the common law courts had become hostile to new forms and would quash writs that differed from those in recognized use. The chancellor developed a more direct route for these cases. He would summon the "defendant" and examine him concerning the "plaintiff's" cause, without referring the matter to a court. The process became formalized, with the petitioner filing a "bill" in Chancery, and the chancellor using a subpoena to compel the defendant to appear and answer it.

"No Adequate Remedy at Law." In the Fourteenth Century, the two systems overlapped, because the chancellors did not perceive any particular restrictions on their authority. But the common law judges were jealous of their jurisdiction, and they used political and judicial power to confine the chancellor to cases in which the law courts did not provide an adequate remedy. For example, the efficiency of the common law

led it to refuse enforcement to "uses" or trusts. If the trustee refused to use the property for the beneficiary, or even if he arrogated it to himself, the common law would not intervene, because the trustee had legal title and therefore all the title that the law courts recognized. The chancellor therefore took over the enforcement of trusts, which were very popular. Furthermore, the common law provided no adequate remedy in various cases of "fraud, accident, or breach of confidence," according to a famous saying. Equity provided redress for these claims. The subjects of equity jurisdiction bore no necessary relationship to each other, because the key determinant of that jurisdiction was that the plaintiff had to show that he had "no adequate remedy at law."

The Transition from Ecclesiastics to Trained Lawyers: Sir Thomas More. The Lord Chancellor best known today is probably Sir Thomas More, who served from 1529 to 1532. Educated as a lawyer at common law, he marks the shift in administration of equity from ecclesiastics and canons to trained lawyers. His conscience was such that, during the reign of Henry VIII (who needed independence from the papacy to void his marriage), he was executed for violation of the Act of Supremacy because he refused the oath of the king's supremacy as head of the church. He later was canonized by the Roman Catholic Church.

Intersystem Injunctions: The Coke-Ellesmere Dispute. Equity grew so powerful that there were cases in which the winning plaintiff in a case at law would be enjoined from enforcing his judgment because equity saw the underlying transaction as unfair or fraudulent. In the Seventeenth Century, during the reign of James I, this practice led to a famous dispute between the Chief Justice of the King's Bench, Sir Edward Coke, and Lord Chancellor Robert Ellesmere. Coke declared that parties seeking these injunctions were guilty of calling into question the judgments of the king's courts, which was a criminal offense under the Statute of Praemunire. King James took the opportunity to resolve the dispute as a means of evidencing his supremacy. In an opinion resembling a court decision, the king "gave his Judgment," in which he "approved, ratified and affirmed" the practices of the Court of Chancery. He ordered the chancellor to continue giving his subjects "such Relief in Equity (notwithstanding any Proceedings at the Common Law against Them) as shall stand with the Merit and Justice of their Case."

Equitable Remedies. The common law executed its judgments by seizing property. The chancellors had no such authority, but they did have behind them the power of the king to arrest and imprison the individual before them. Therefore, equity acted "in personam": it would order the respondent to do or refrain from doing an act and imprison him if he disobeyed. This remedy, in fact, was the greatest invention of equity: the injunction. It plugged a serious gap in the common law, which could never compel the doing of an act. But even today, a claimant seeking an injunction must show the absence of an adequate remedy at law, and if a suit for damages would give complete relief, an injunction cannot issue. A closely related idea also invented by equity was the remedy of specific performance. If the plaintiff had contracted for the purchase of a unique tract of land, so that damages could not remedy the defendant's refusal to convey it, the equity courts could order specific performance — again, because there was no adequate remedy at law.

The Chancellor's Discretion and the Absence of Jury Trial. The principles of equity were loose and highly discretionary. The chancellor could refuse relief to a person who had "unclean hands," or who was acting fraudulently himself. Furthermore, the chancellor would balance the equities in deciding on the precise contours of the relief he would tailor to the particular case. In fact, the evolution of new equitable remedies continues to the modern day; the school desegregation cases, in which courts invented zoning, pairing, faculty ratios, and the like, are a prime example. But while the flexibility to meet new needs was desirable, the unpredictability and ostensibly unlimited nature of the power of the chancellor was not. It was said that equity depended on "the length of the chancellor's foot." Given the character of equitable relief, it was clear (and still is clear today) that there was no right to trial by jury in equity. How could the jury draft an injunction? How could it function as the king's conscience in developing new remedies?

Equitable Procedure: Pleadings, Discovery, Depositions, and Trials. The equitable bill was a marvelous instrument. It came to contain three distinct parts that repeated the claim in different ways. First, the "narrative" part was the affirmative statement of the claim. Then, the "charging" part anticipated and rebutted defendant's defenses. Finally, the "interrogative" part was used to "probe the defendant's conscience." Since the bill had to be answered in detail, these intricate inquiries would cut off escape if skillfully employed. The investigative power of a bill in Chancery was such that litigants in the common law courts filed equitable bills, called "bills of discovery," to aid their suits. And equity invented the deposition. In fact, one of the oddities of equity procedure was that live witnesses were not used at trial; instead, all testimony was presented by deposition.

Equity in America. In some but not all of the thirteen American colonies, Courts of Chancery existed alongside the courts at law, and dispensed English equity. There are separate Courts of Chancery in a few states still today, and in many if not most states, the jurisdiction of the courts is partly defined by whether the relief sought is legal or equitable. (California and New York are examples; *see* § 3.02, above).

NOTES AND QUESTIONS

(1) *The Law-Equity Split and Its Disadvantages: Hahl v. Sugo, 169 N.Y. 109, 62 N.E. 135 (1901).* The defendant built a building so that it encroached on the plaintiff's land. The plaintiff sued in ejectment and obtained judgment, but the sheriff's office was not equipped to demolish a building and therefore it was impractical to enforce the judgment. The plaintiff brought a bill in equity, seeking an injunction that would require the defendant himself to remove the building. Because of the existing judgment, however, the equity side of the court denied relief. It appeared that the plaintiff would otherwise have been entitled to the injunction, since he could clearly show that he had no adequate remedy at law.

(2) *"Doing Equity"; The Evolution of Equitable Remedies.* Imagine that an equity court is asked to grant an injunction against a minor encroachment on the plaintiff's land. But the defendant will have to destroy a large building at a huge loss to remove the encroachment. The encroachment resulted because, before the building was built, the defendant and the plaintiff conferred about the boundary line between their properties and both were in error about its location. How should the equity court approach this case?

(3) *Delay in Chancery: Dickens' Bleak House.* Early equity proceedings were efficient, but several problems developed. First, the Chancery's insistence upon trial solely by depositions was slow and very expensive. Secondly, equity insisted upon joining all persons in the suit whose interests might be remotely affected. Bills were long but became longer, numerous parties with contingent interests clogged the proceedings, and settlements were impeded. "This is the Court of Chancery," wrote Charles Dickens in *Bleak House* (1852). "Suffer any wrong that can be done you, rather than come here!"

> Jarndyce and Jarndyce drones on. This scarecrow of a suit has . . . become so complicated that no man alive knows what it means. . . . [I]t has been observed that no two Chancery lawyers can talk about it for five minutes, without coming to a total disagreement as to all the premises. Innumerable children have been born into the cause: innumerable old people have died out of it. . . . [B]ut Jarndyce and Jarndyce still drags its dreary length before the Court. . . .
>
> How many people out of the suit, Jarndyce and Jarndyce has stretched forth its unwholesome hand to corrupt, would be a very wide question. From the master, upon whose impaling files [are] reams of dusty warrants . . . down to the copying-clerk in the Six Clerks' Office, who has copied his tens of thousands of Chancery-folio pages under that heading, no man's nature has been made better by it. [S]hirking and shirking . . . have been sown broadcast by the ill-fated cause. . . .

Jarndyce and Jarndyce "drags its weary length" through Dickens' book until the expenses of suit consume the entire fund at issue.

[C] "Code" Pleading

Reform: The Republic of Texas and the New York Commission. The middle of the Nineteenth Century saw serious efforts at reform. In 1840, the Fourth Congress of the Republic of Texas provided that Texas' adoption of the common law "shall not be construed to adopt the common law system of pleading." It also abolished the forms of action, merged law and equity, and provided for a simple "petition and answer" based on the Spanish system of pleading. *See* W. Dorsaneo, D. Crump, E. Carlson & E. Thornburg, *Texas Civil Procedure: Pretrial Litigation* § 5.01 (2007–08 ed.). A few years later, New York's Commission on Practice and Pleading became one of the most influential voices in the reform movement. It proposed a system in which "no action . . . need be designated . . . by any name, form, or distinction of action . . .; but that the only test of the right of the party complaining, [s]hall be, whether in his complaint he sets forth a sufficient legal right and a violation or withholding of such right by the party complained against." Preliminary Report of the Commissioners on Practice and Pleadings of New York 14-16 (1847).

The "Field Codes." The year after the Commission's preliminary report, New York adopted a new Code known as the Field Code, after the head of the New York Commission, David Dudley Field. The Code became the model for similar reform in other states, whose codes were also loosely called Field codes. The New York Code contained the following provisions:

> § 62. The distinction between actions at law and suits in equity, and the forms of all such actions and suits . . . are abolished; and there shall be in this state, hereafter, but one form of action, . . . which shall be denominated a civil action.
>
> § 120(2). The complaint shall contain . . . [a] statement of the facts constituting the cause of action, in ordinary and concise language, . . . in such a manner as to enable a person of common understanding to know what is intended. . . .
>
> § 132. No other pleading shall be allowed, than the complaint, demurrer, answer, and reply.
>
> § 151. The court shall, at every stage of an action, disregard any error, or defect in the pleadings or proceedings, which shall not affect the substantial rights of the adverse party. . . .

In summary, the Field Code abolished the forms of action, merged law and equity, limited pleadings to four functional categories, limited the effects of technical errors, and required pleading of "facts constituting the cause of action."

Pleading "the Facts" Constituting the "Cause of Action": Remaining Problems. The Field Code did not solve all of the problems. First, the forms of action were still the basis of the substantive law. Secondly, it was unrealistic to expect attitudes formed during more than 500 years of history to change overnight. Furthermore, there were hidden difficulties in the requirement that the plaintiff plead "the facts constituting the cause of action." A cause of action was the set of ultimate facts that the plaintiff must plead and prove to prevail on a given claim; for example, a negligence complaint must state the facts giving rise to the defendant's duty, the breach of that duty, proximate causation, the injury to the plaintiff, and the plaintiff's damages. The omission of any element would make the complaint defective.

"Facts," as Opposed to "Conclusions" or "Evidence." But the more difficult requirement was that the complaint must state "facts." A pleading asserting that the defendant "assaulted" the plaintiff, for example, would not suffice, because it stated only a conclusion. Likewise, a pleading containing details of the kind that a witness might relate would not be correct, because it would state evidence. The courts often found themselves mired in differentiating among "facts," "conclusions," and "evidence," particularly since these conceptions expressed differences only of degree and were inherently difficult to distinguish. *See generally* C. Clark, *Code Pleading* (2d ed. 1947).

[1] Pleading "Facts" Constituting a "Cause of Action"

GILLISPIE v. GOODYEAR SERVICE STORES

258 N.C. 487, 128 S.E.2d 762 (1963)

The hearing below was on demurrers to the complaint. . . .

The [relevant] [a]llegations of the complaint and the prayer for relief are as follows:

4. On or about May 5, 1959, and May 6, 1959, the defendants, without cause or just excuse and maliciously came upon and trespassed upon the premises occupied by the plaintiff as a residence, and by the use of harsh and threatening language and physical force directed against the plaintiff assaulted the plaintiff and placed her in great fear, and humiliated and embarrassed her by subjecting her to public scorn and ridicule, and caused her to be seized and exhibited to the public as a prisoner, and to be confined in a public jail, all to her great humiliation, embarrassment and harm.

5. By reason of the defendants' malicious and intentional assault against and humiliation of the plaintiff, the plaintiff was and has been damaged and injured in the amount of $25,000.00.

6. The acts of the defendants as aforesaid were deliberate, malicious, and with the deliberate intention of harming the plaintiff, and the plaintiff is entitled to recover her actual damages as well as punitive damages from the defendants and each of them.

. . .

Does the complaint state *facts* sufficient to constitute *any* cause of action?

A complaint must contain "[a] plain and concise statement of the facts constituting a cause of action . . . . " G.S. § 1-122. "The cardinal requirement of this statute . . . is that the facts constituting a cause of action, rather than the conclusions of the pleader, must be set out in the complaint, so as to disclose the issuable facts determinative of the plaintiff's right to relief." . . .

"The liability for tort grows out of the violation of some legal duty by the defendant, not arising out of contract, and the complaint should state facts sufficient to show such legal duty and its violation, resulting in injury to the plaintiff. What these facts are must depend upon the elements which go to make up the particular tort complained of, under the substantive law." McIntosh, *North Carolina Practice and Procedure*, § 388. . . .

"In an action or defense based upon negligence, it is not sufficient to allege the mere happening of an event of an injurious nature and call it negligence on the part of the party sought to be charged. This is necessarily so because negligence is not a fact in itself, but is the legal result of certain facts. Therefore, the facts which constitute the negligence charged and also the facts which establish such negligence as the proximate cause, or as one of the proximate causes, of the injury must be alleged." . . .

Plaintiff alleges, in a single sentence, that defendant, "without cause or just excuse and maliciously," trespassed upon premises occupied by her as a residence, assaulted her and caused her to be seized and confined as a prisoner. The complaint states no facts upon which these legal conclusions may be predicated. Plaintiff's allegations do not disclose *what* occurred, *when* it occurred, *where* it occurred, *who* did *what*, the relationships between defendants and plaintiff or of defendants *inter se*, or any other factual data that might identify the occasion or describe the circumstances of the alleged wrongful conduct of defendants. . . .

The judgments sustaining the demurrers are affirmed on the ground the complaint does not state facts sufficient to constitute any cause of action. It would seem appropriate that plaintiff, in accordance with leave granted in the judgments from which she appealed, now file an amended complaint and therein allege the facts upon which she bases her right to recover.

NOTES AND QUESTIONS

(1) *How Could Gillispie Properly Plead Her Cause of Action?* Try to describe the kinds of expressions that would suffice to state a "cause of action" within this pleading system. What words should the plaintiff use?

(2) *The Advantages of this Pleading System.* This pleading system does not require any particular form of words or designation of the claim (although it is squeamish about the particularity with which the facts are pleaded). It is thus more liberal than the common law system. Furthermore, it should lead to rapid development of the issues. The plaintiff will need to decide with some care which kinds of claims to assert. Marginal or innocent defendants are likely to be exonerated more easily.

(3) *The Disadvantages of this Pleading System: Pleading "Negative"; Undue Emphasis on Pleadings; Variances; Etc.* Imagine that Gillispie wanted to assert a cause of action against Goodyear for malicious prosecution. One of the elements of this tort is that a defendant caused a prosecution to be initiated against the plaintiff without probable cause. How does one go about stating all the "facts" showing that there was no probable cause without at some point saying, in some fashion, "There was no probable cause"? But that would be a conclusion, wouldn't it? The emphasis on pleading facts thus led to an overemphasis on pleadings, in which energies were expended without resolving controversies — or sometimes with resolutions on purely procedural grounds, rather than on

the merits. Furthermore, this pleading system produced more variances between allegations and proof than a looser system would. Consider the following cases.

[2] The "Theory of the Pleadings" Doctrine; Variances

CITY OF UNION CITY v. MURPHY, 176 Ind. 597, 96 N.E. 584 (1911). The City converted a small sanitary sewer into a storm-and-surface-water sewer, with the result that the sewer became overloaded and water and sewage backed into Murphy's cellar. At trial, the jury was instructed both that it should find for Murphy if the City had caused his damages by negligence and, also, that it should find for him if the City had wilfully created a nuisance. The jury found in Murphy's favor.

The appellate court reversed. It pointed out that the complaint contained elements of both negligence and wilful or intentional injury. For example, it alleged that the defendant had "knowingly, wilfully, and negligently turned large volumes of surface water into said sewer." However, the court concluded that the "theory of the pleadings" was intentional injury: "We think that the theory of the complaint, judged from its general scope and tenor, is that (Murphy) was damaged wilfully or intentionally." Then came the key element in the court's reasoning: A pleading must have a single theory, which is to be judged by reading it as a whole, and only on that theory can the plaintiff recover:

> [T]he case must be tried upon a single theory, and plaintiff must recover on that theory or not at all. . . . There is a clear distinction between cases which count on negligence as a ground of action and those which are founded on acts of aggressive wrong or wilfulness, and a pleading should not be tolerated which proceeds upon the idea that it may be good [for either]. . . . If the complaint proceeded on the theory of wilful injury, [Murphy] could not recover for injury caused by the negligence of [the City], even though the court should find facts in his favor showing that he had an action for this cause. Therefore, it was error to give instructions under which [Murphy] could recover either for wilful injury or for injury resulting from negligence. . . .

The judgment is reversed.

NOTES AND QUESTIONS

(1) *Is the Problem About Rules of Joinder Rather Than Rules of Pleading?* The common law courts were very strict about the joining of different claims in a single declaration. The "theory of the pleadings" doctrine is a throwback to this common law approach. Perhaps, therefore, a large share of the blame for the problems of common law pleading — and of strict code pleading — is due to rules about joinder rather than rules of pleading.

(2) *Should the Pleading of Inconsistent Theories Be Permitted?* The common law, with its search of the single issue, would obviously regard as anathema the pleading of two inconsistent theories in the declaration. But aren't there good reasons for permitting inconsistent pleading? For example, similar evidence might lead one jury to conclude that the defendant's acts were unintentional but negligent, while another jury might conclude that they were intentionally wrongful. Should the plaintiff be penalized by a take-nothing judgment if he guesses wrong about that?

(3) *Variances.* You should recall that the common law courts were subject to criticism for injustices due to variance. In a system with strict requirements that "facts" rather

than conclusions be pleaded and with a narrow "theory of the pleadings" doctrine, the variance problem is enhanced. Consider the following case.

MESSICK v. TURNAGE, 240 N.C. 625, 83 S.E.2d 654 (1954). While the plaintiff was seated as a patron in the defendant's movie theatre, falling plaster and water from the ceiling above her frightened her, so that she involuntarily jumped from her seat, striking the metal seat in front of her and injuring her leg. Her complaint charged the defendant with negligence, in that "the defendant failed to maintain a safe theatre . . . in that the defendant knew or should have known by reasonable observation which was his duty, that [the defendant's] roof was leaking and in bad repair." However, the plaintiff's proof at trial did not show a leaking roof. Instead, it showed that a fixture in the balcony restroom failed to close, the restroom filled with water, the water did not drain because the drainpipe was clogged with cigarette butts and other debris, the water seeped into the balcony carpet, and it loosened the plaster below it, causing it to fall. The trial judge granted judgment for the defendant at the conclusion of the plaintiff's evidence. The appellate court affirmed:

> . . . It was incumbent upon the plaintiff not only to prove negligence proximately causing her injury, but it was her duty to prove negligence substantially as alleged in her complaint. This she failed to do. Proof without allegation is as unavailing as allegation without proof. . . .

[D] Modern State Practice Requiring the Pleading of a "Cause of Action"

One Modern Approach to Pleading: Abolish the Requirement that Plaintiff Plead a Cause of Action. One way to address the problems illustrated by the preceding cases is to remove the requirement that the plaintiff plead a "cause of action." This is the approach adopted by the Federal Rules and, following their example, by many of the states. In such a system, the pleadings are not designed to narrow the issues or to separate legal questions from factual ones. Those functions are to be addressed by other processes, such as discovery or pretrial conferences. The relationship between the evidence and the pleadings still has to exist, but conformity is easier because the joinder of claims is liberally allowed and pleadings can be very general in their allegations.

Another Modern Approach to Pleading, Followed By Some States: Retain The Requirement That A Cause of Action Be Pleaded, But With Liberalized Rules. Some states have declined to follow the federal model and still require the pleading of a "cause of action." Is this approach an acceptable middle ground? Arguably it is, if the state adopts rules that avoid the difficulties of strict code pleading — as many of these states have. First, modern state pleadings do not place as much emphasis on the pleading of "facts" versus conclusions or evidence as did the courts in the early days of code pleading. The elements of the cause of action must be present in the pleading, but if the pleading gives notice of the plaintiff's factual theory of the elements, it is sufficient. Furthermore, these modern state rules liberalize the joinder of claims, just as the federal system does, so that alternate or inconsistent theories are permissible. More liberal allowance of amendment (including amendment at and after trial) helps to avoid variances. The result, again arguably, is a system that serves the function of narrowing issues, without the disadvantageous baggage of common law or strict code pleading. We will examine examples of state pleadings and pleading requirements at the end of this chapter — after we take up the federal system.

§ 5.02 The Functions Served by the Pleadings

Shipman, COMMON LAW PLEADING

*9-10 Ballantyne 3d ed. 1923**

. . . The various possible objects and purposes of pleading may be enumerated somewhat as follows: (1) To separate questions of law from questions of fact and decide them so far as possible prior to the trial of the facts. (2) To reduce questions of fact to clear-cut issues, by eliminating admitted, immaterial, and incidental matters, and narrowing the case to the one or more definite propositions on which the controversy really turns. (3) To notify parties of the claims, defenses, and cross-demands of their adversaries. (4) To serve as the formal basis of the judgment. (5) To place on record the questions raised and give litigants the advantage of a plea of *res judicata*, if the same questions should be raised again in other causes. (6) Lastly, there may be added the function of serving as an index of the points to be proved at the trial and apportioning the burden of proof and rebuttal as between the plaintiff and the defendant. Some of these functions of pleading are vastly more important than others, numbers (4) and (5) being sometimes unduly magnified.

[I]n both common-law and code pleading, [t]he issue-raising function far overshadows the notice-giving one, and is the source of the principal rules of pleading. . . .

NOTES AND QUESTIONS

(1) *Should Pleadings Serve the Function of Encouraging Truth?* The Massachusetts commissioners of 1851 stated the purposes of civil pleading as including "(1) that each party may be under the most effectual influences, which the nature of the case admits of, so far as he admits or denies anything, to tell the truth; . . . ." Why does Shipman's list not include this purpose? Perhaps the pleadings are not themselves the best device for ascertaining the truth of contested allegations, but isn't encouraging truth a factor in how to design rules governing them?

(2) *Ranking the Purposes.* How important are Shipman's first three purposes — those of giving notice, separating law from fact, and defining the issues? Should a pleading system be set up so that it emphasizes "notice" pleading to the virtual exclusion of the other purposes? *Cf.* Whittier, *Notice Pleading*, 31 Harv. L. Rev. 501 (1918).

PROBLEM A
CHAPTER 5 SUMMARY PROBLEM

ALICE DELAGROI'S MEDICAL MALPRACTICE CLAIM. Mrs. Alice Delagroi consults you about alleged malpractice during the removal of her appendix at Singleton Hospital. She emerged from the operation with a severely impaired left arm, in which various injections had been administered by various individuals. Because the impairment of an arm due to an appendix operation is unusual, and you surmise it would not normally occur in the absence of malpractice, you believe you may have a claim against one or more of the following: Mrs. Delagroi's physician; the anesthesiologist; the scrub nurse; various interns; the duty nurse; the hospital; and various other unknown persons or entities. Your suit will be filed in a federal court.

---

* Reprinted with permission of the West Publishing Company.

Upon checking, you find that the statute of limitations is two years, and it runs in precisely twenty days. You have a copy of the medical records for this operation, but you have little time to investigate further, and you are uncertain about which substantive law theories — negligence, warranty, strict liability, agency theories, or consumer legislation — might apply to which defendants. You face a dilemma: If you file suit against all the defendants and sort the matter out later, you may violate Rule 11, and these defendants are among those most likely to move for sanctions; but if you leave out any potential defendant, you may find your claim time-barred, especially because the defendants you do sue may point to the absent person as the guilty one. What should you do?

You may read this problem now, but you will need to read the rest of the Chapter to answer it (or, as always, you should treat it as your instructor directs). In analyzing the problem, you might consider the following issues:

1. How solid does your pleading of the claims need to be, in order to avoid the granting of a motion to dismiss?
2. What degree of specificity is required, to avoid the granting of a motion for more definite statement?
3. If you fail to include a given person as a defendant, and if a jury later determines that that person was solely responsible for your client's injuries, what might be the consequences for your client — and for you?
4. If you omit a party now because of uncertain liability, will you be able to amend to include that party after discovery, and have your pleading relate back to a time before the statute of limitations ran? (What can you do to enhance this possibility?)
5. What sanctions are possible under Fed. R. Civ. P. 11 if you carelessly file suit against an innocent party, and what can you do to minimize the likelihood of such sanctions?

[Note: Some jurisdictions follow the rule of *Ybarra v. Spangard*, 25 Cal. 2d 486, 154 P.2d 687, 162 A.L.R. 1258 (1944), which places the burden of "giving an explanation" on the defendants, when the plaintiff shows that she had "unusual" injuries and that the defendants had "control" over her body. This rule affects the plaintiff's dilemma, here — but it does not solve it. Why not?]

§ 5.03 The Complaint in Federal Court

[A] "Notice Pleading": The Standard for Specificity

Read Fed. R. Civ. P. 7; 8(a), (e), (f); 10; and 84. Also, read Federal Forms 11, 12, and 21.

CONLEY v. GIBSON, 355 U.S. 41 (1957). The text of this opinion appears above at § 1.04 of Chapter 1, and it should be read (or re-read) at this point. In essence, the Supreme Court rejected the defendant's arguments that the complaint had to set out specific facts in support of its allegations of racial discrimination. The Court instead construed Rule 8(a)'s requirement of "a short and plain statement of the claim" to require only "notice pleading," *i.e.*, sufficient specificity to "[give] the respondents fair notice of its basis."

DIOGUARDI v. DURNING
139 F.2d 774 (2d Cir. 1944)

CLARK, CIRCUIT JUDGE.

In his complaint, obviously home drawn, plaintiff attempts to assert a series of grievances against the Collector of Customs at the Port of New York growing out of his endeavors to import merchandise from Italy "of great value," consisting of bottles of "tonics." We may pass certain of his claims as either inadequate or inadequately stated and consider only these two: (1) that on the auction day, October 9, 1940, when defendant sold the merchandise at "public custom," "he sold my merchandise to another bidder with my price of $110, and not of his price of $120," and (2) "that three weeks before the sale, two cases, of 19 bottles each case, disappeared." Plaintiff does not make wholly clear how these goods came into the collector's hands, since he alleges compliance with the revenue laws; but he does say he made a claim for "refund of merchandise which was two-thirds paid in Milano, Italy," and that the collector denied the claim. These and other circumstances alleged indicate (what, indeed, plaintiff's brief asserts) that his original dispute was with his consignor as to whether anything more was due upon the merchandise, and that the collector, having held it for a year (presumably as unclaimed merchandise under 19 U.S.C.A. § 1491), then sold it, or such part of it as was left, at public auction. For his asserted injuries plaintiff claimed $5,000 damages, together with interest and costs, against the defendant individually and as collector. This complaint was dismissed by the District Court, with leave, however, to plaintiff to amend, on motion of the United States Attorney, appearing for the defendant, on the ground that it "fails to state facts sufficient to constitute a cause of action."

Thereupon plaintiff filed an amended complaint, wherein, with an obviously heightened conviction that he was being unjustly treated, he vigorously reiterates his claims, including those quoted above and now stated as that his "medicinal extracts" were given to the Springdale Distilling Company "with my betting [bidding?] price of $110: and not their price of $120," and "It isn't so easy to do away with two cases with 37 bottles of one quart. Being protected, they can take this chance." An earlier paragraph suggests that defendant had explained the loss of the two cases by "saying that they had leaked, which could never be true in the manner they were bottled." On defendant's motion for dismissal on the same ground as before, the court made a final judgment dismissing the complaint, and plaintiff now comes to us with increased volubility, if not clarity.

It would seem, however, that he has stated enough to withstand a mere formal motion, directed only to the face of the complaint, and that here is another instance of judicial haste which in the long run makes waste. Under the new rules of civil procedure, there is no pleading requirement of stating "facts sufficient to constitute a cause of action," but only that there be "a short and plain statement of the claim showing that the pleader is entitled to relief," [a]nd the motion for dismissal under Rule 12(b) is for failure to state "a claim upon which relief can be granted." The District Court does not state why it concluded that the complaints showed no claim upon which relief could be granted; and the United States Attorney's brief before us does not help us, for it is limited to the prognostication — unfortunately ill founded so far as we are concerned — that "the most cursory examination" of them will show the correctness of the District Court's action.

We think that, however inartistically they may be stated, the plaintiff has disclosed his claims that the collector has converted or otherwise done away with two of his cases of medicinal tonics and has sold the rest in a manner incompatible with the public auction he had announced — and, indeed, required by 19 U.S.C.A. § 1491, above cited, and the Treasury Regulations promulgated under it. . . . As to this latter claim, it may be that the collector's only error is a failure to collect an additional ten dollars from the Springdale Distilling Company; but giving the plaintiff the benefit of reasonable intendments in his allegations (as we must on this motion), the claim appears to be in effect that he was actually the first bidder at the price for which they were sold, and hence was entitled to the merchandise. Of course, defendant did not need to move on the complaint alone; he could have disclosed the facts from his point of view, in advance of a trial if he chose, by asking for a pre-trial hearing or by moving for a summary judgment with supporting affidavits. But, as it stands, we do not see how the plaintiff may properly be deprived of his day in court to show what he obviously so firmly believes and what for present purposes defendant must be taken as admitting. It appears to be well settled that the collector may be held personally for a default or for negligence in the performance of his duties.

On remand, the District Court may find substance in other claims asserted by plaintiff, which include a failure properly to catalogue the items (as the cited Regulations provide), or to allow plaintiff to buy at a discount from the catalogue price just before the auction sale (a claim whose basis is not apparent), and a violation of an agreement to deliver the merchandise to the plaintiff as soon as he paid for it, by stopping the payments. In view of plaintiff's limited ability to write and speak English, it will be difficult for the District Court to arrive at justice unless he consents to receive legal assistance in the presentation of his case. . . .

Judgment is reversed and the action is remanded for further proceedings not inconsistent with this opinion.

CRITICISM OF *DIOGUARDI v. DURNING:* McCaskill, THE MODERN PHILOSOPHY OF PLEADING: A DIALOGUE OUTSIDE THE SHADES, 38 A.B.A.J. 123, 124-26 (1952).* There has been a great deal of commentary on *Dioguardi*. Much is favorable, but a significant portion is unfavorable. Consider the following excerpts from Professor McCaskill's imaginary "dialogue" between a lawyer who extols the new pleading and his skeptical law-student son:

> SON: . . . Dad, in my pleading course, we are trying to find out what a fact is for pleading purposes. We are told that it is not a legal conclusion and not something commonly expressed in a witness' language. . . .
>
> FATHER: I see, son, that your pleading instructor is somewhat behind the times. In the days of common law pleading, the Bar had to struggle with the problem which is bothering you, but under the modern philosophy concerning pleadings they have the function only of providing fair notice. They make no attempt to form issues. . . .
>
> SON: We have been over that in our course. . . . Our professor thinks Clark and Moore are overstressing conciseness and ordinary language . . . in their zeal to escape from all form. . . . He says their interpretation of the New Federal Rules, and of the codes, lowers the standards of pleading to fit the incompetent or lazy lawyer, instead of keeping the standards where pleading will be of some use to the courts, and making those who wish to practice in the courts meet those standards. . . .

[Some weeks later. (The Father) enters the library whistling.]

SON: Won a case, Dad?

FATHER: Not exactly, but I taught some federal pleading to one of the old timers who moved to dismiss my complaint. . . .

SON: You convinced the judge it stated a cause of action?

FATHER: I did not even try to do that. It wasn't necessary. . . . I read him Judge Clark's opinion in the *Dioguardi* case. . . . Unless the pleader has been foolish enough to put some allegations in the complaint which show that under no circumstances can he have relief in the law, . . . the mover . . . cannot show the pleader is not entitled to relief. Mere omissions to state anything in a complaint do not show that a plaintiff is not entitled to relief. It is a neat trick of construction which works a reverse English on anyone foolish enough to move to dismiss a complaint on the pleadings alone. . . .

SON: There was merit in your case, was there not? You investigated it before bringing the action, I assume?

FATHER: As a matter of fact, I did not, and have not yet done so. I suppose it has merit. The client was in a hurry and wanted suit brought right away. I was busy. . . .

[Professor McCaskill has the "father" explain that after remand, Dioguardi went to trial and lost. He appealed again, but this time the Second Circuit affirmed the judgment against him. *Dioguardi v. Durning*, 151 F.2d 501 (2d Cir. 1945). The "son" sees this result as wasteful and oppressive of the defendant; his "father" answers by saying, "You are forgetting the satisfaction given Dioguardi and the public by the full hearing of the evidence."]

Are McCaskill's criticisms appropriate? Of what relevance is Dioguardi's subsequent loss on the merits? How effective do you think the federal system is likely to be in screening out vaguely pleaded claims against factually innocent defendants? Is there a better way?

NOTES AND QUESTIONS

(1) *What, If Anything, Does "Notice Pleading" Mean?* The drafters of the Rules did not use the term "notice pleading." Judge Clark, who was a principal drafter of them and who was the author of *Dioguardi v. Durning*, has criticized the term. He preferred the language of Rule 8, requiring a short and plain statement, and he pointed to the Forms appended to the Rules as illustrations. Clark, *Pleading Under the Federal Rules*, 12 Wyo. L.J. 177 (1958). Note that Rule 84 incorporates the Forms as examples and expressly makes them sufficient under the Rules. As for the nomenclature, although the authors of this book recognize the imperfections of the term "notice pleading," we have nevertheless used it. First, the Supreme Court called it that in *Conley v. Gibson*. Second, even if it has no precise definition, the standard at least needs a name. Third, this name has "stuck" and is in widespread use.

(2) *Does "Notice Pleading" Require the Plaintiff to Plead All of the Elements of the Alleged Offense?* In *Doe v. Smith*, 429 F.3d 706 (7th Cir. 2005), the district court had dismissed the complaint filed under the federal wiretapping statute for failing to allege "interception" within the meaning of the statute. The court of appeals reversed, stating that "pleadings in federal court need not allege facts corresponding to each 'element'

of a statute. . . . Usually they need do no more than narrate a grievance simply and directly, so that the defendant knows what he has been accused of."

(3) *"Filling in the Details" by Discovery.* The premise underlying the Federal Rules is that pleadings can be general because discovery supplies the details. What are the justifications for this approach? On the other hand, how successful do you think Durning would be in sending interrogatories to Dioguardi asking him to particularize his contentions (and, even if he could succeed, is it fair to place the cost of that process on Durning)?

(4) *Which Philosophy Is the "Modern" Theory of Pleading?* The approach of *Dioguardi* is often referred to as exemplifying the "modern" theory of pleading. However, several of the states have deliberately retained updated versions of Code pleading after considering the federal alternative. Which is the "modern" theory? Is there a middle ground between slavish insistence on factual detail and what McCaskill calls "escape from all form"? *See* Note, *Fact Pleading vs. Notice Pleading: The Eternal Debate*, 22 Loyola L. Rev. 47 (1975).

(5) *"Claim" and "Cause of Action."* Code pleading required the statement of a "cause of action." The Federal Rules deliberately avoid that term and require only the statement of a "claim." What is the difference between a "cause of action" and a "claim"? *See* James, *The Objective and Function of the Complaint: Common Law Codes — Federal Rules*, 14 Vand. L. Rev. 899 (1961); *Claim or Cause of Action?*, 13 F.R.D. 253 (1952).

(6) *Has the Supreme Court modified the Conley v. Gibson standard?* In 2007, the Supreme Court issued its opinion in *Bell Atlantic Corp. v. Twombly*, 550 U.S. —, 127 S. Ct. 1955 (2007). In the excerpt of the case that follows, ask yourself how this opinion affects the *Conley v. Gibson* standard.

BELL ATLANTIC CORP. v. TWOMBLY

127 S. Ct. 1955 (2007)

JUSTICE SOUTER delivered the opinion of the Court.

Liability under § 1 of the Sherman Act, 15 U.S.C. § 1, requires a "contract, combination . . ., or conspiracy, in restraint of trade or commerce." The question in this putative class action is whether a § 1 complaint can survive a motion to dismiss when it alleges that major telecommunications providers engaged in certain parallel conduct unfavorable to competition, absent some factual context suggesting agreement, as distinct from identical, independent action. We hold that such a complaint should be dismissed.

I

The upshot of the 1984 divestiture of the American Telephone & Telegraph Company's (AT&T) local telephone business was a system of regional service monopolies (variously called "Regional Bell Operating Companies," "Baby Bells," or "Incumbent Local Exchange Carriers" (ILECs)), and a separate, competitive market for long-distance service from which the ILECs were excluded. More than a decade later, Congress withdrew approval of the ILECs' monopolies by enacting the Telecommunications Act of 1996 (1996 Act), . . . which "fundamentally restructure[d] local telephone markets" and "subject[ed] [ILECs] to a host of duties intended to facilitate market entry." . . . In recompense, the 1996 Act set conditions for authorizing ILECs to enter the long-distance market. . . .

"Central to the [new] scheme [was each ILEC's] obligation . . . to share its network with competitors," . . . which came to be known as "competitive local exchange carriers" (CLECs) . . . . A CLEC could make use of an ILEC's network in any of three ways: by (1) "purchas[ing] local telephone services at wholesale rates for resale to end users," (2) "leas[ing] elements of the [ILEC's] network 'on an unbundled basis,'" or (3) "interconnect[ing] its own facilities with the [ILEC's] network." . . .

Respondents William Twombly and Lawrence Marcus (hereinafter plaintiffs) represent a putative class consisting of all "subscribers of local telephone and/or high speed internet services . . . from February 8, 1996 to present." . . . In this action against petitioners, a group of ILECs, plaintiffs seek treble damages and declaratory and injunctive relief for claimed violations of § 1 of the Sherman Act, . . . which prohibits "[e]very contract, combination in the form of trust or otherwise, or conspiracy, in restraint of trade or commerce among the several States, or with foreign nations."

The complaint alleges that the ILECs conspired to restrain trade in two ways, each supposedly inflating charges for local telephone and high-speed Internet services. Plaintiffs say, first, that the ILECs "engaged in parallel conduct" in their respective service areas to inhibit the growth of upstart CLECs. . . .

Second, the complaint charges agreements by the ILECs to refrain from competing against one another. . . .

The complaint couches its ultimate allegations this way:

> "In the absence of any meaningful competition between the [ILECs] in one another's markets, and in light of the parallel course of conduct that each engaged in to prevent competition from CLECs within their respective local telephone and/or high speed internet services markets and the other facts and market circumstances alleged above, Plaintiffs allege upon information and belief that [the ILECs] have entered into a contract, combination or conspiracy to prevent competitive entry in their respective local telephone and/or high speed internet services markets and have agreed not to compete with one another and otherwise allocated customers and markets to one another." . . .

The United States District Court for the Southern District of New York dismissed the complaint for failure to state a claim upon which relief can be granted. The District Court acknowledged that "plaintiffs may allege a conspiracy by citing instances of parallel business behavior that suggest an agreement," but emphasized that . . . "conscious parallelism" has not yet read conspiracy out of the Sherman Act entirely. . . . Thus, the District Court understood that allegations of parallel business conduct, taken alone, do not state a claim under § 1; plaintiffs must allege additional facts that "ten[d] to exclude independent self-interested conduct as an explanation for defendants' parallel behavior." . . . The District Court found plaintiffs' allegations of parallel ILEC actions to discourage competition inadequate because "the behavior of each ILEC in resisting the incursion of CLECs is fully explained by the ILEC's own interests in defending its individual territory." . . . As to the ILECs' supposed agreement against competing with each other, the District Court found that the complaint does not "alleg[e] facts . . . suggesting that refraining from competing in other territories as CLECs was contrary to [the ILECs'] apparent economic interests, and consequently [does] not rais[e] an inference that [the ILECs'] actions were the result of a conspiracy." . . .

The Court of Appeals for the Second Circuit reversed, holding that the District Court tested the complaint by the wrong standard. It held that "plus factors are not required to be pleaded to permit an antitrust claim based on parallel conduct to survive dismissal."

. . .

We granted certiorari to address the proper standard for pleading an antitrust conspiracy through allegations of parallel conduct, . . . and now reverse.

II

A

Because § 1 of the Sherman Act "does not prohibit [all] unreasonable restraints of trade . . . but only restraints effected by a contract, combination, or conspiracy," . . . "[t]he crucial question" is whether the challenged anticompetitive conduct "stem[s] from independent decision or from an agreement, tacit or express" . . . . While a showing of parallel "business behavior is admissible circumstantial evidence from which the fact finder may infer agreement," it falls short of "conclusively establish[ing] agreement or . . . itself constitut[ing] a Sherman Act offense." . . . Even "conscious parallelism," a common reaction of "firms in a concentrated market [that] recogniz[e] their shared economic interests and their interdependence with respect to price and output decisions" is "not in itself unlawful." . . .

The inadequacy of showing parallel conduct or interdependence, without more, mirrors the ambiguity of the behavior: consistent with conspiracy, but just as much in line with a wide swath of rational and competitive business strategy unilaterally prompted by common perceptions of the market. . . .

B

This case presents the antecedent question of what a plaintiff must plead in order to state a claim under § 1 of the Sherman Act. Federal Rule of Civil Procedure 8(a)(2) requires only "a short and plain statement of the claim showing that the pleader is entitled to relief," in order to "give the defendant fair notice of what the . . . claim is and the grounds upon which it rests," *Conley v. Gibson*, 355 U.S. 41, 47 (1957). While a complaint attacked by a Rule 12(b)(6) motion to dismiss does not need detailed factual allegations, . . . a plaintiff's obligation to provide the "grounds" of his "entitle[ment] to relief" requires more than labels and conclusions, and a formulaic recitation of the elements of a cause of action will not do. . . . Factual allegations must be enough to raise a right to relief above the speculative level, *see* 5 C. Wright & A. Miller, *Federal Practice and Procedure* § 1216, pp. 235-236 (3d ed. 2004) (hereinafter Wright & Miller) ("[T]he pleading must contain something more . . . than . . . a statement of facts that merely creates a suspicion [of] a legally cognizable right of action").[1] . . .

In applying these general standards to a § 1 claim, we hold that stating such a claim requires a complaint with enough factual matter (taken as true) to suggest that an agreement was made. Asking for plausible grounds to infer an agreement does not impose a probability requirement at the pleading stage; it simply calls for enough fact to raise a reasonable expectation that discovery will reveal evidence of illegal agreement. . . .

---

[1] . . . While, for most types of cases, the Federal Rules eliminated the cumbersome requirement that a claimant "set out *in detail* the facts upon which he bases his claim," *Conley v. Gibson*, 355 U.S. 41, 47 (1957) (emphasis added); Rule 8(a)(2) still requires a "showing," rather than a blanket assertion, of entitlement to relief. Without some factual allegation in the complaint, it is hard to see how a claimant could satisfy the requirement of providing not only "fair notice" of the nature of the claim, but also "grounds" on which the claim rests. . . .

And, of course, a well-pleaded complaint may proceed even if it strikes a savvy judge that actual proof of those facts is improbable, and "that a recovery is very remote and unlikely." . . . [L]awful parallel conduct fails to bespeak unlawful agreement. It makes sense to say, therefore, that an allegation of parallel conduct and a bare assertion of conspiracy will not suffice. Without more, parallel conduct does not suggest conspiracy, and a conclusory allegation of agreement at some unidentified point does not supply facts adequate to show illegality. Hence, when allegations of parallel conduct are set out in order to make a § 1 claim, they must be placed in a context that raises a suggestion of a preceding agreement, not merely parallel conduct that could just as well be independent action.

The need at the pleading stage for allegations plausibly suggesting (not merely consistent with) agreement reflects the threshold requirement of Rule 8(a)(2) that the "plain statement" possess enough heft to "sho[w] that the pleader is entitled to relief." A statement of parallel conduct, even conduct consciously undertaken, needs some setting suggesting the agreement necessary to make out a § 1 claim; without that further circumstance pointing toward a meeting of the minds, an account of a defendant's commercial efforts stays in neutral territory. . . .

. . . As we indicated over 20 years ago in *Associated Gen. Contractors of Cal., Inc. v. Carpenters*, 459 U.S. 519, 528, n.17 (1983), "a district court must retain the power to insist upon some specificity in pleading before allowing a potentially massive factual controversy to proceed." *See also Car Carriers, Inc. v. Ford Motor Co.*, 745 F.2d 1101, 1106 (7th Cir. 1984) ("[T]he costs of modern federal antitrust litigation and the increasing caseload of the federal courts counsel against sending the parties into discovery when there is no reasonable likelihood that the plaintiffs can construct a claim from the events related in the complaint") . . . . That potential expense is obvious enough in the present case: plaintiffs represent a putative class of at least 90 percent of all subscribers to local telephone or high-speed Internet service in the continental United States, in an action against America's largest telecommunications firms (with many thousands of employees generating reams and gigabytes of business records) for unspecified (if any) instances of antitrust violations that allegedly occurred over a period of seven years.

It is no answer to say that a claim just shy of a plausible entitlement to relief can, if groundless, be weeded out early in the discovery process through "careful case management," . . . given the common lament that the success of judicial supervision in checking discovery abuse has been on the modest side. . . . Probably, then, it is only by taking care to require allegations that reach the level suggesting conspiracy that we can hope to avoid the potentially enormous expense of discovery in cases with no "reasonably founded hope that the [discovery] process will reveal relevant evidence" to support a § 1 claim. . . .

Plaintiffs do not, of course, dispute the requirement of plausibility and the need for something more than merely parallel behavior . . ., and their main argument against the plausibility standard at the pleading stage is its ostensible conflict with an early statement of ours construing Rule 8. Justice Black's opinion for the Court in *Conley v. Gibson* spoke not only of the need for fair notice of the grounds for entitlement to relief but of "the accepted rule that a complaint should not be dismissed for failure to state a claim unless it appears beyond doubt that the plaintiff can prove no set of facts in support of his claim which would entitle him to relief." . . . This "no set of facts" language can be read in isolation as saying that any statement revealing the theory of the claim will suffice unless its factual impossibility may be shown from the face of the pleadings . . . .

On such a focused and literal reading of *Conley*'s "no set of facts," a wholly conclusory statement of claim would survive a motion to dismiss whenever the pleadings left open the possibility that a plaintiff might later establish some "set of [undisclosed] facts" to support recovery. So here, the Court of Appeals specifically found the prospect of unearthing direct evidence of conspiracy sufficient to preclude dismissal, even though the complaint does not set forth a single fact in a context that suggests an agreement. . . .

. . . *Conley*'s "no set of facts" language has been questioned, criticized, and explained away long enough. To be fair to the *Conley* Court, the passage should be understood in light of the opinion's preceding summary of the complaint's concrete allegations, which the Court quite reasonably understood as amply stating a claim for relief. But the passage so often quoted fails to mention this understanding on the part of the Court, and after puzzling the profession for 50 years, this famous observation has earned its retirement. The phrase is best forgotten as an incomplete, negative gloss on an accepted pleading standard: once a claim has been stated adequately, it may be supported by showing any set of facts consistent with the allegations in the complaint. . . . *Conley*, then, described the breadth of opportunity to prove what an adequate complaint claims, not the minimum standard of adequate pleading to govern a complaint's survival. . . .

. . . .

The judgment of the Court of Appeals for the Second Circuit is reversed, and the cause is remanded for further proceedings consistent with this opinion.

. . . .

JUSTICE STEVENS with whom JUSTICE GINSBURG joins except as to Part IV, dissenting.

. . . .

II

. . . .

. . . Once it is clear that a plaintiff has stated a claim that, if true, would entitle him to relief, matters of proof are appropriately relegated to other stages of the trial process. Today, however, in its explanation of a decision to dismiss a complaint that it regards as a fishing expedition, the Court scraps *Conley*'s "no set of facts" language. Concluding that the phrase has been "questioned, criticized, and explained away long enough," . . . the Court dismisses it as careless composition.

If *Conley*'s "no set of facts" language is to be interred, let it not be without a eulogy. That exact language, which the majority says has "puzzl[ed] the profession for 50 years," . . . has been cited as authority in a dozen opinions of this Court and four separate writings. In not one of those 16 opinions was the language "questioned," "criticized," or "explained away." Indeed, today's opinion is the first by any Member of this Court to express *any* doubt as to the adequacy of the *Conley* formulation. Taking their cues from the federal courts, 26 States and the District of Columbia utilize as their standard for dismissal of a complaint the very language the majority repudiates: whether it appears "beyond doubt" that "no set of facts" in support of the claim would entitle the plaintiff to relief.

. . . .

. . . *Conley*'s statement that a complaint is not to be dismissed unless "no set of facts" in support thereof would entitle the plaintiff to relief is hardly "puzzling" . . . . It reflects a philosophy that, unlike in the days of code pleading, separating the wheat from the chaff is a task assigned to the pretrial and trial process. *Conley*'s language, in short, captures the policy choice embodied in the Federal Rules and binding on the federal courts.

We have consistently reaffirmed that basic understanding of the Federal Rules in the half century since *Conley*. . . .

. . . .

Everything today's majority says would . . . make perfect sense if it were ruling on a Rule 56 motion for summary judgment and the evidence included nothing more than the Court has described. . . . The majority rejects the complaint in this case because — in light of the fact that the parallel conduct alleged is consistent with ordinary market behavior — the claimed conspiracy is "conceivable" but not "plausible" . . . . I have my doubts about the majority's assessment of the plausibility of this alleged conspiracy. . . . But even if the majority's speculation is correct, its "plausibility" standard is irreconcilable with Rule 8 and with our governing precedents. As we made clear in [previous cases], fear of the burdens of litigation does not justify factual conclusions supported only by lawyers' arguments rather than sworn denials or admissible evidence.

This case is a poor vehicle for the Court's new pleading rule, for we have observed that "in antitrust cases, where 'the proof is largely in the hands of the alleged conspirators,' . . . dismissals prior to giving the plaintiff ample opportunity for discovery should be granted very sparingly." . . . Moreover, the fact that the Sherman Act authorizes the recovery of treble damages and attorney's fees for successful plaintiffs indicates that Congress intended to encourage, rather than discourage, private enforcement of the law. . . .

. . . .

III

. . . .

. . . Many years ago a truly great economist perceptively observed that "[p]eople of the same trade seldom meet together, even for merriment and diversion, but the conversation ends in a conspiracy against the public, or in some contrivance to raise prices." A. Smith, *An Inquiry Into the Nature and Causes of the Wealth of Nations*, *in* 39 Great Books of the Western World 55 (R. Hutchins & M. Adler eds. 1952). . . .

. . . .

IV

. . . [T]he intentions of the drafters of three important sources of law — the Sherman Act, the Telecommunications Act of 1996, and the Federal Rules of Civil Procedure — all point unmistakably in the same direction, yet the Court marches resolutely the other way. Whether the Court's actions will benefit only defendants in antitrust treble-damages cases, or whether its test for the sufficiency of a complaint will inure to the benefit of all civil defendants, is a question that the future will answer. But that the Court has announced a significant new rule that does not even purport to respond to any congressional command is glaringly obvious.

The transparent policy concern that drives the decision is the interest in protecting antitrust defendants — who in this case are some of the wealthiest corporations in our economy — from the burdens of pretrial discovery. . . . Even if it were not apparent that the legal fees petitioners have incurred in arguing the merits of their Rule 12(b) motion have far exceeded the cost of limited discovery, or that those discovery costs would burden respondents as well as petitioners, that concern would not provide an adequate justification for this law-changing decision. . . .

If the allegation of conspiracy happens to be true, today's decision obstructs the congressional policy favoring competition that undergirds both the Telecommunications Act of 1996 and the Sherman Act itself. More importantly, even if there is abundant evidence that the allegation is untrue, directing that the case be dismissed without even looking at any of that evidence marks a fundamental — and unjustified — change in the character of pretrial practice.

Accordingly, I respectfully dissent.

NOTES AND QUESTIONS

(1) Does *Bell Atlantic*'s approach to the *Conley v. Gibson* standard apply only to antitrust cases or does the case reach further? Is there language in the case to support both positions?

(2) What concerns does the Court identify regarding a more generous pleading standard in the context of antitrust cases?

(3) What additional information would the plaintiffs need to add to satisfy the Court's standard? Is there a risk that such information would not be available to the plaintiffs until the discovery phase?

(4) Despite the *Twombly* majority's criticism of *Conley v. Gibson*'s "no set of facts" language; despite the dissent's characterization of the majority opinion as creating "the Court's new pleading rule"; and despite eager arguments from some lawyers and commentators that *Twombly* eradicated the *Conley* pleading standard, it is far from clear that *Twombly* has, in fact, changed Rule 8's pleading standard. Indeed, in *Erickson v. Pardus*, 127 S. Ct. 2197 (2007), decided shortly after *Twombly*, the Supreme Court reaffirmed that Rule 8(a) "requires only a short and plain statement of the claim showing that the pleader is entitled to relief," that "[s]pecific facts are not necessary," and that the statement "need only give the defendant fair notice." *Id.* at 2200. One thoughtful court of appeals decision observed that "whatever the Court is requiring in *Bell Atlantic* might be limited to, or at least applied most rigorously in, the context of either all section 1 [antitrust] allegations or perhaps only those section 1 allegations relying on competitors' parallel conduct." *Iqbal v. Hasty*, 490 F.3d 143, 156 (2d Cir. 2007). Ultimately, after noting *Twombly*'s "conflicting signals" and the "uncertainty as to [its] intended scope," the most that the *Iqbal* court was willing to say was that *Twombly* might be "oblig[ing] a pleader to amplify a claim with some factual allegations in those contexts where such amplification is needed to render the claim plausible." *Id.* at 157-58.

PROBLEM B

SPECIFICITY: HOW MUCH IS ENOUGH TO STATE A "CLAIM"? HOW MUCH IS ENOUGH TO STATE A "CAUSE OF ACTION"? Read Federal Form 11, and then consider the following hypothetical pleadings. They are arranged in order of increasing specificity. Which ones state a "claim"? Which ones state a "cause of action"?

(a) The defendant should pay damages to the plaintiff because the defendant was negligent.

(b) The defendant should pay damages to the plaintiff because on or about May 7, 2006, he caused personal injuries to the plaintiff by his negligence.

(c) On May 7, 2006, the defendant maintained its premises in a negligent manner, and by reason of that negligence, the plaintiff suffered a broken wrist and other personal injuries, for which the defendant is liable to the plaintiff in the amount of $100,000.

(d) On May 7, 2006, the defendant negligently maintained the floor of its store by allowing it to be in a slippery condition. By reason of that negligence, the plaintiff suffered personal injuries, for which the defendant is liable to the plaintiff in the amount of $100,000.

(e) On May 7, 2006, the defendant negligently maintained its floor by allowing it to be in a slippery condition. That negligence proximately caused the plaintiff, who was a customer of the defendant's, to slip and fall on the floor and to suffer personal injuries, including a broken wrist. The defendant is liable to the plaintiff for those injuries in the amount of $100,000.

(f) On May 7, 2006, the defendant waxed its floor with Acme Polychloridine and left this substance inadequately buffed. Also on that date, the defendant posted a sign warning customers of the floor's condition, but the sign said only "Warning/Wax on Floor" and, since it was only in 11-point type on a three-by-six inch background, it was too inconspicuous for a reasonable person to see. These actions of the defendant were negligent, in that they produced a dangerous slippery floor, of which the defendant knew or should have known. This negligence proximately caused the plaintiff to slip and fall on the floor and to suffer personal injuries including a broken wrist. For these reasons, the defendant is liable to the plaintiff in the amount of $100,000.

[B] Stating a "Claim": Substantive Sufficiency as Tested by Rule 12 Motions

PARTRIDGE v. TWO UNKNOWN POLICE OFFICERS, 791 F.2d 1182 (5th Cir. 1986). This is the case for which edited pleadings appear in § 1.04, above, under the name *Wytinger v. Two Unknown Police Officers*. Plaintiffs Ralph and Betty Partridge claimed damages arising from the suicide of their son, Michael, while he was a pretrial detainee in a municipal jail. The District Court dismissed the complaint for failure to state a claim, citing *Estelle v. Gamble*, 429 U.S. 97 (1976), to the effect that only an allegation of "deliberate indifference" to "serious medical need" would suffice in such a case. The Court of Appeals first reversed, with one judge dissenting; it then withdrew its opinion; and finally, it substituted another opinion, with the same judge dissenting. The court upheld the dismissal with respect to one police officer, whom the complaint unambiguously charged only with negligence. But otherwise, it reversed the dismissal:

> . . . We read the complaint as amended as alleging that the defendants had deliberately adopted a policy that constituted indifference to the medical needs of detained persons and, pursuant to policy, failed to render reasonable medical aid to Michael Partridge and to persons similarly subject to suicidal tendencies, that this failure was not the result of an individual act of negligence but was the result of systematic indifference to serious medical needs of pretrial detainees and of a "deliberate pattern of conduct"; that is, of a custom or policy. Those allegations go beyond negligence . . . .

The district court styled its action as a dismissal under Fed R. Civ. P. 12(b)(6). In reviewing such a dismissal, we may not go outside the pleadings. We accept all well-pleaded facts as true and view them in the light most favorable to the plaintiff. We cannot uphold the dismissal "unless it appears beyond doubt that the plaintiff can prove no set of facts in support of his claim which would entitle him to relief" [citing *Conley v. Gibson, supra*]. . . .

The complaint, in part, satisfied the requirements of *Monell.* The plaintiffs alleged that the Houston Police Department had a custom of inadequate monitoring of suicidal detainees which amounted to a policy of denying them medical care. . . . Furthermore, the facts alleged in the [amended] complaint are sufficient to support an allegation that the custom of inadequate care was persistent and widespread.

McLAREN v. UNITED STATES INC., 2 F. Supp. 2d 48 (D.D.C. 1998). This odd case provides a clear example of a suit subject to dismissal because even if the plaintiff's factual allegations were taken as true, he was entitled to no relief, as a matter of law. McLaren proclaimed himself the "Chief Ambassador and Consul General" of the "Republic of Texas." He and his followers maintained that Texas never was legitimately annexed by the United States, never became a State, and therefore remained a Republic. So vehement were these separatists' beliefs that they took hostages and engaged in an armed standoff with state law enforcement officers in Jeff Davis County in western Texas. As part of a "cease fire agreement," McLaren agreed to "commence legal actions in the District Court of The District of Columbia for the rights of the inhabitants on the soil of Texas to by popular vote decide [the] issue of Texas Independence."

McLaren filed the suit. The United States filed a motion to dismiss or for summary judgment. The district judge decided that whether Texas was a State was a pure question of law — and that McLaren's basic legal premise was flawed. The court therefore granted the motion to dismiss.

Read Fed. R. Civ. P. 12(b)-(f). Also, reconsider Rule 8(a).

NOTE ON RULE 12 MOTIONS

Substantive Sufficiency. What should happen if a complaint is crystal clear, but (unlike the one in *Partridge,* above) it shows without question that the law does not allow the plaintiff to recover? For example, the plaintiff may be seeking redress for grievances that the law simply does not recognize. Or the complaint may show on its face that it is unambiguously subject to a complete defense (*e.g.,* statute of limitations or statute of frauds). In these situations, the complaint may be subject to dismissal.

The Rule 12(b)(6) Motion to Dismiss for Failure to State a Claim Upon Which Relief May Be Granted. At this point, of course, there has been no trial, and the court cannot consider any evidence in support of the claims. There may not have been any discovery. The court can consider only the complaint. Therefore, a 12(b)(6) motion to dismiss for failure to state a claim has to be judged by a stringent standard. The complaint must be liberally read in the pleader's favor. It must be assumed that the pleader would be able to prove everything asserted in the complaint (because, after all, the court is considering dismissal without hearing any of her proof). Under *Conley v. Gibson,* only if it can be said with reasonable certainty that the plaintiff can prove no set of facts that would entitle her to any of the requested relief can the dismissal be granted. [A warning: If you have difficulty with this standard, remember that the court at this stage does not consider any evidence.] Does *Bell Atlantic v. Twombly* change the result?

The Rule 12(c) Motion for Judgment on the Pleadings. What if the motion to dismiss is filed after the defendant has filed an answer to the complaint? Although the same standard applies to both motions, technically after an answer to the complaint has been filed, the proper motion is a motion for judgment on the pleadings.

Whether under Rule 12(b)(6) or (c), when the court considers matters outside the pleadings, it must treat the motion as one for summary judgment under Rule 56. In this situation, all parties must be given a reasonable opportunity to present summary judgment evidence to the trial court.

The Rule 12(e) Motion for More Definite Statement. What if the pleading is vague? The court may grant a motion for a more definite statement. Note that while the standard for specificity ("notice" pleading) is distinct from the standard for substantive sufficiency, ultimately they are related, and a complaint that does not suffice to give notice is sometimes characterized as failing to state a claim.

The Rule 12(f) Motion to Strike. What if the complaint states a claim when read in its entirety, but it contains inappropriate material? For example, what if a suit on a promissory note contains an allegation that "The defendant's spouse has been arrested three times for assault"? Or what if there are several claims, one of which is unambiguously unsupportable? In these situations, the opponent may be able to obtain a ruling in response to a motion to strike.

How to Read the Case of Fox v. Lummus Co. The *Fox* case, which follows, is a good illustration of all three of these attacks on a complaint. There is a motion to dismiss directed at some of the claims, and you should bear in mind the relatively stringent standard for this motion and consider whether the court's ruling here is correct. The one remaining claim is attacked by a motion for more definite statement, and the court's ruling on this motion is not carefully explained. You should consider what standard should apply to the granting of the motion and whether the court's ruling, here, could be supported by a principled explanation. Finally, there is a motion to strike one allegation in the remaining count. Thus, this case will give you a "grand tour" of the possible attacks on substance and form of a complaint.

FOX v. LUMMUS COMPANY
524 F. Supp. 27 (S.D.N.Y. 1981)

MOTLEY, DISTRICT JUDGE.

This action arises out of an employment agreement between plaintiff, Ian Fox, . . . and defendant, The Lummus Company. . . . The agreement, entitled "Iraqi Jobsite Agreement" (the Employment Agreement), related to plaintiff's employment as a sub-contract administrator at defendant's construction project in Basrah, Iraq. Plaintiff claims that defendant breached the contract by unjustly withholding salary earned by plaintiff and by denying plaintiff holiday leave and in other ways "harassing" him. Defendant has moved for an order 1) dismissing the first three [claims] of the complaint for failure to state a claim upon which relief can be granted, pursuant to Rule 12(b)(6) of the Federal Rules of Civil Procedure; 2) directing plaintiff to give a more definite statement of the fourth [claim], pursuant to Rule 12(e); and 3) striking allegations of pain and suffering and related requests for relief from the fourth [claim], pursuant to Rule 12(f). For the reasons discussed below, defendant's motions are granted.

[The Employment Agreement contained a provision, Paragraph 5, which was intended to equalize the after-tax salaries of employees of different nationalities, no matter what tax regimes they might be subjected to, so as to avoid discord among them. Plaintiff Fox quoted this Paragraph 5 in his complaint: "The Employee's salary will be reduced by monthly amounts based upon the attached compensation worksheet for theoretical taxes calculated on base pay plus overtime. The Company will hold the Employee harmless for Iraqi and/or home taxes on Company earned income. . . ." Attachment B to the contract, which also was set forth in the plaintiff's complaint, contained exact monthly figures for the "theoretical tax" by which plaintiff's compensation was to be reduced, and it also set forth the precise "net monthly salary" that plaintiff was to receive.

[The complaint also alleged that "the foregoing constituted the entire understanding between the parties," and that the parties had never entered into any subsequent oral or written agreement on the subject. Then, in his first three claims, plaintiff alleged that since no tax ever was levied upon his salary by any governmental authority, defendant's deduction of "theoretical taxes" was improper. Plaintiff's first three claims included implied contract, equitable unjust enrichment, and quasi-contract theories based on this allegation.

[The court first considered the motion to dismiss, by which defendant had attacked these first three claims. You should recall that this motion calls for the complaint to be read liberally in Fox's favor; the court must assume that he would be able to prove all of his assertions and can dismiss only if it is reasonably certain that he would be entitled to none of the requested relief even after making such proof.]

It is clear that the complaint does not allege that defendant breached the express terms of the Employment Agreement. Indeed, plaintiff's claim is that defendant did exactly what the contract stated it would do — reduce plaintiff's salary by a theoretical tax in the amount set forth on the earnings calculation addendum of the agreement. The contract nowhere provided for subsequent payment to plaintiff of the amount deducted, as plaintiff now requests. Plaintiff, however, argues that the court should imply such a payment term. This the court may not do, in light of the express provision of paragraph 5 of the Employment Agreement.

While the fact that particular provision has not been expressly stated in a contract does not necessarily mean that no such promise exists, "a party who asserts the existence of an implied-in-fact covenant bears a heavy burden, for it is not the function of the courts to remake the contract agreed to by the parties, but rather to enforce it as it exists." *Rowe v. Great Atlantic and Pacific Tea Co., Inc.*, 46 N.Y.2d 62, 69, 412 N.Y.S.2d 827, 831, 385 N.E.2d 566 (1978). This burden is met only by proving that the particular unexpressed promise is in fact implicit in the agreement viewed as a whole. *Id.* The additional payment term plaintiff would have this court imply is inconsistent with the provision in paragraph 5 of the Employment Agreement that plaintiff's salary would be reduced each month by a specified amount. It is well established under New York law that, "where the expressed intention of contracting parties is clear, a contrary intent will not be created by implication." *Neuman v. Pike*, 591 F.2d 191, 194 (2d Cir. 1979).

Plaintiff alternatively contends that he is entitled to payment by the defendant under a theory of unjust enrichment or recovery in quasi-contract, which allows the courts to impose a duty to refund money to the person to whom it rightfully belongs. This argument also must fail. A quasi or constructive contract rests upon the equitable principle that a person shall not be allowed to enrich himself at the expense of another. It is an obligation created by law only in the absence of an agreement between the parties. *Bradkin v. Leverton*, 26 N.Y.2d 192, 309 N.Y.S.2d 192, 257 N.E.2d 643 (1970). As already noted above, where, as here, a written contract does exist, the duty of the courts is to enforce it. Accordingly, defendant's motion to dismiss plaintiff's first three [claims] pertaining to the reduction of plaintiff's salary is granted.

Plaintiff's fourth [claim] alleges that defendant also breached the employment contract by failing to provide plaintiff with back salary and with various leaves and expenses and by "a course of constant harrassment (sic) and pressure the object of which was to make the plaintiff leave his position prematurely . . . ." Defendant claims that the allegation of "harrassment and pressure" is so vague and ambiguous that defendant cannot reasonably be required to frame a responsive pleading and that it warrants a more definite statement in accordance with Rule 12(e) of the Federal Rules of Civil Procedure. The court agrees. Plaintiff, therefore, is directed to amend his complaint to state which acts of defendant constituted the alleged "harrassment and pressure," when such acts occurred, and which persons committed such acts.

Finally, defendant moves for an order striking from paragraph 22 of the complaint plaintiff's allegation that defendant's breach of the employment contract caused him "great mental and physical anguish and suffering" and paragraph 23 which alleges that plaintiff has sustained injuries in the amount of $100,000 as a result of the alleged breach. Defendant argues that such alleged non-economic injury is not cognizable as a matter of law.

> The New York rule is that damages for breach of an employment contract are limited to the unpaid salary to which the employee would be entitled under the contract less the amount by which he should have mitigated his damages.

Quinn v. Straus Broadcasting Group, Inc., 309 F. Supp. 1208, 1209 (S.D.N.Y. 1970). New York courts have accordingly stricken from the complaint allegations of and demands for damages resulting from mental anguish in breach of employment contract cases. *See Amaducci v. Metropolitan Opera Association*, 33 App. Div. 2d 542, 304 N.Y.S. 2d 322 (1st Dept. 1969). Since, under New York law, plaintiff's damages are limited to his economic injuries, the allegation of mental distress is immaterial and will be stricken pursuant to Rule 12(f). For the same reason, paragraph 23 of the complaint and subparagraph 4 of the *ad damnum* clause demanding $100,000 . . . will also be stricken.

In his Memorandum in opposition to defendant's motions plaintiff suggests that the complaint states a cause of action in tort, for which damages for intentionally inflicted emotional distress may be awarded. The complaint, however, does not state any allegations that would amount to a claim that defendant committed a tort, specifically intentional infliction of emotional harm, in a manner that would fairly notify defendant of such a claim or reasonably allow defendant to respond.

In summary, defendant's motions for an order dismissing the first three [claims], directing plaintiff to state more definitely the fourth [claim], and striking allegations of mental anguish and suffering in paragraph 22, as well as paragraph 23 and subparagraph 24 of the *ad damnum* clause, are all granted. Plaintiff may file an amended complaint in accordance with this opinion within 20 days of the filing of the order which accompanies this opinion.

NOTES AND QUESTIONS

(1) *Changing the Facts in Fox v. Lummus Company.* Would the result have been the same if Fox had claimed an oral modification of the employment agreement, in that his supervisor induced him to stay in Iraq by promising him that he would be docked only

the amount of taxes actually paid? What if Fox had alleged that the company consistently paid over the unpaid taxes to every employee, except Fox?

(2) *The Motion to Dismiss.* Is the dismissal consistent with the reasoning in *Conley v. Gibson* and *Dioguardi v. Durning*? Perhaps contract disputes in which the contract language is unambiguous make the most appealing cases for dismissal for failure to state a claim, even under the relatively strict standard of those cases.

(3) *The Motion for More Definite Statement.* The court does not give much explanation of the reasons for granting the more definite statement, and the cases construing Rule 12(e) are inconsistent. Some courts have reasoned that a more definite statement can be ordered only if the complaint fails to give notice or to conform to Rule 8(a). A variation of this approach is to grant the motion if the complaint is so vague that the defendant cannot be expected to make a responsive pleading. But if this standard is used here, shouldn't the motion be denied, since the complaint gives enough notice so that the judge can decipher what the claim is about? On the other hand, some courts have concluded that the motion should be granted if further details will be useful in resolving the case (if addition of the date of the alleged violation might establish a defense of limitations, for example). Yet a third approach is to defer to the discretion of the trial judge, who may order a statement above and beyond the requirements of notice pleading simply to narrow the issues. Would the judge's holding in *Fox v. Lummus Co.* be justified under any of these approaches? Which approach seems best to you? *Cf.* Marcus, *The Revival of Fact Pleading Under the Federal Rules of Civil Procedure*, 86 Colum. L. Rev. 433 (1986) (arguing that a role remains for pleadings in resolving the merits, and that this consideration explains why the courts have often required more factual detail, although they have not wisely distinguished cases in which more particularized pleading actually helps speed disposition). Is it arguable that Rule 12(e) itself provides a standard ("so vague or ambiguous that the party cannot reasonably prepare a response")?

(4) *The Motion to Strike.* This motion is like a miniature "motion to dismiss," aimed at a single allegation or set of allegations instead of at the entire complaint. (In fact, a purist might insist that the "motion to dismiss" the first three claims in this case actually was a motion to strike, since it did not seek dismissal of the complaint as a whole.)

(5) *Amendment of the Complaint by the Plaintiff.* The court is required to be liberal in allowing amendment after granting a Rule 12 motion. If you represented the plaintiff, how would you go about this task? Do you think you could revise the first three claims so that you could salvage them? How would you revise the fourth claim (for example, would you plead the tort of intentionally inflicted mental distress)? [Note: There is always the option of counseling the plaintiff that the claim is unmeritorious.]

PROBLEM C

PLEADINGS IN BROWN v. DILLER BREWING CO. The following pleadings were filed in a real case, although the names have been changed and the allegations are edited. Should the motion to dismiss be granted?

IN THE UNITED STATES DISTRICT COURT
FOR THE MIDDLE DISTRICT OF WEST YORK
LONDON DIVISION

ALBERT H. BROWN v. DILLER BREWING CO, ET AL.	CIVIL ACTION NO. CA-86-3481-D

PLAINTIFF'S COMPLAINT

[The plaintiff's complaint contains sufficient allegations of jurisdiction. It alleges that the defendant Martha Lyman, a minor, purchased Diller Lite Beer from defendant Go-N-Tote Stores, Inc., which was negligent in selling it to her when she was in an intoxicated condition. It alleges that these acts of negligence, concurrently with the negligent driving of Martha Lyman, proximately caused severe injuries to the plaintiff in a highway accident. It then contains the following allegations in paragraphs 11 and 12. In considering them, you should be aware that the law of West York makes a manufacturer strictly liable for injuries produced, whether to a user or third person, by a defective product, which is a product that is "unreasonably dangerous" in its design, manufacture, or marketing. A marketing defect can include an unreasonable failure to warn of dangers.]

. . . .

11. The Diller Lite Beer that was purchased by the defendant Martha Lyman was defective and unsafe at the time it left the control of the defendant Diller. . . . Specifically, the Diller beer fails to warn of the dangerous characteristics of the product. The product has no warning that consumption may cause intoxication and the possible inability of a person to control a motor vehicle safely. This marketing defect was a producing cause of plaintiff's damages. Therefore, defendant Diller is strictly liable to plaintiff for those damages under the law of the state of West York.

12. Diller knew or should have known that its product was extremely dangerous when used by a person under age operating a motor vehicle. It took no action to prevent the occurrence in question. Further, it has at all times encouraged consumption of Diller beer in greater quantities, including spending millions of dollars for advertising that is especially attractive to an under-aged person. . . .

IN THE UNITED STATES DISTRICT COURT
FOR THE MIDDLE DISTRICT OF WEST YORK
LONDON DIVISION

ALBERT H. BROWN v. DILLER BREWING COMPANY	CIVIL ACTION NO. CA-86-3481-D

DEFENDANT DILLER BREWING CO.'S RULE 12 MOTIONS

Defendant Diller Brewing Company ("Diller") moves the court as follows:

1. To dismiss the complaint against it under Rule 12(b)(6) on the ground that it fails to state a claim upon which relief may be granted.

2. In the alternative, to strike all allegations against Diller under Rule 12(f).

3. In the alternative, for a more definite statement pursuant to Rule 12(e). In accordance with that Rule, defendant hereby points out the defects complained of and the details desired:

a. Paragraph 11 fails to give notice of any duty violated by defendant, and defendant desires details giving notice of any duty claimed to have been violated.

b. Paragraph 12 fails to set out any marketing defect, and defendant desires details giving notice of any wrongful conduct of defendant and any duty it allegedly violated.

. . .

---

(1) *Should the Motion to Dismiss be Granted?* What if the plaintiff might be able to show at trial that the defendant's advertisements, which say that Diller Beer is "less filling," caused confusion in the public mind and led Martha Lyman, in the absence of any label warning, to believe that she could drink substantially greater quantities without impairment? If so, does this additional fact need to be expressly alleged in the complaint?

(2) *Can Dismissal Be Based Upon Extrinsic Information?* In the real litigation of *Brown v. Diller Brewing Co.*, the true fact was that the defendant Go-N-Tote had leased its premises to an independent operator. It was not responsible for the sale of beer to an intoxicated minor because it simply did not commit that act. However, it did not file a Rule 12(b) motion to dismiss because that procedure would not have been successful. Why not?

[C] Particularized Pleading Requirements

[1] Pleading Fraud, Damages, and Other Special Matters

Read Fed. R. Civ. P. 9(b), (c), (f), and (g). Also, read Federal Form 13.

SWEENY CO. v. ENGINEERS-CONSTRUCTORS, INC.
109 F.R.D. 358 (E.D. Va. 1986)

WARRINER, DISTRICT JUDGE.

Presently under consideration by the Court is defendant's motion to dismiss plaintiff's amended Count III of its amended complaint on the ground that the pleading fails to allege fraud with particularity as required by Rule 9(b) of the Federal Rules of Civil Procedure. . . .

[T]he complaint consisted of three counts, the third of which alleged that defendant fraudulently induced plaintiff, a subcontractor, to continue to provide labor and material when defendant actually intended to terminate the subcontract without cause and without making payment for amounts already due, at a time when plaintiff's work was essentially complete.

Defendant then filed its initial motion [t]o dismiss the third count for failure to allege fraud with particularity, and plaintiff responded by filing an amended pleading on 3 January 1986.

Plaintiff's amended complaint set forth essentially the same allegations. Again, the complaint alleged that during the "spring or summer of 1985," defendants through their "agents and employees" represented that plaintiff would be paid for all of its work under the subcontract. The amended pleading described for the first time defendants as having previously "secretly determined" to wrongfully terminate the subcontract, whereas the original complaint referred to a prior "scheme or device" to effect such wrongful termination.

After extensively researching the question of how much particularity is required in a complaint alleging fraud, I have concluded that plaintiff's amended count fails to meet the standard required by statute. For the following reasons I grant defendant's motion for dismissal of amended Count III.

Rule 9(b) provides that in averments of fraud, "the circumstances constituting fraud or mistake shall be stated with particularity." The purposes advanced by this requirement are to insure that allegations are specific enough to inform defendant and enable him to prepare an effective response and defense, to eliminate complaints filed in order to find unknown wrongs through discovery, and to protect defendants from unfounded charges that involve moral turpitude. . . . The purposes of the rule are accomplished when a plaintiff alleges the "time, place, and content of the false misrepresentation, the fact misrepresented and what was gained or given up as a consequence of the fraud." . . .

Clearly, however, the requirements of Rule 9(b) must be read in conjunction with Rule 8 of the Federal Rules of Civil Procedure, which establishes the general rules of pleading. [W]hen the sufficiency of a complaint under Rule 9(b) is challenged, "it is the duty of the Court to balance" the requirements of each of the rules. . . . If, for instance, plaintiffs do not have access to information, "some relaxation of Rule 9(b) is necessary when plaintiffs are not likely to have more specific information until after discovery." . . . It seems fair that in a case such as this in which the facts apparently are not hidden in a maze of convoluted transactions, the plaintiff should plead in the complaint who allegedly has done what, when, where, and why. . . .

[I] [f]ind no support for allowing this plaintiff to plead such general allegations as are found in amended Count III. The complaint instead should be specific enough to allege who made the secret plan and approximately when it was conceived. It should also identify some or all of the employees or agents of defendants who allegedly carried out such a plan and, likewise in regard to plaintiff, should state who allegedly received and relied on this information. The complaint should state as well when and why the defendants knew they were unable to pay plaintiff. . . .

Finally, I must consider whether plaintiff should be allowed a third opportunity to amend its complaint to try to overcome the lack of particularity required. Rule 15(a) of the Federal Rules of Civil Procedure places this determination within the discretion of the Court. I find that, based on the similarity of the first complaint and the amended pleading and the fact that plaintiff chose not to respond to defendant's second motion to dismiss, plaintiff would not alter its pleading sufficiently to cure the defects. If it could have done so and chose not to, it will have to abide with the result of its decision. To allow an amendment would cause undue delay and would not be in the interest of furthering the purposes of Rule 9(b). Therefore the motion to dismiss is GRANTED without leave to amend the complaint further.

NOTES AND QUESTIONS

(1) *Is the Result in Sweeny Good Policy?* On the one hand, the *Sweeny* result might be seen as a dysfunctional procedural cutoff of a possibly meritorious claim. But on the other hand, aren't the allegations in *Sweeny* the kind that will usually signal a dubious claim? To succeed, the plaintiff has to show that, at the time of contracting, the defendant had the fraudulent intent to obtain the plaintiff's performance and pay nothing. Note that the plaintiff still has viable contract claims, and this dispute is primarily about the contract. What evidence will the plaintiff find of "fraud," other than non-performance by the defendant (which is obviously insufficient as a matter of law)? Of course, another way to look at the matter is that, if the purpose of Rule 9 is to give notice, avoid harm to reputation from lightly made claims, minimize strike suits, and discourage filing of inadequately investigated claims, why shouldn't these objectives apply to every claim, not just to fraud? *See* Sovern, *Reconsidering Federal Civil Rule 9(b): Do We Need Particularized Pleading Requirements in Fraud Cases?* 104 F.R.D. 143 (1985).

(2) *"Tight" Versus "Loose" Interpretations of Rule 9.* The Rule 9 cases are not consistent. Some are more stringent than *Sweeny*; for example, in *Ross v. A.H. Robins Co.*, 607 F.2d 545, 557-58 (2d Cir. 1979), the court reasoned that the Rule 9 standard was distinct from that of Rule 8. Perhaps Rule 9 should not be read in harmony with Rule 8, since (after all) it reflects a deliberate intention of the drafters to set a different standard. Is this reasoning persuasive (or is the *Sweeny* court's effort to harmonize Rule 9 with Rule 8 better reasoned)? On the other hand, there is a line of cases that holds that the "particularity" requirement just extends to the method of committing the alleged fraud, so that the plaintiff need not detail the time, place, person, etc. *E.g., Denny v. Carey*, 72 F.R.D. 574 (E.D. Pa. 1976) (burden of pleading fraud is not a "rigorous" one; pleading that briefly stated that method of fraud was to underrepresent losses and overrepresent gains on financial statements complied with Rule 9, when harmonized with

Rule 8). If the *Sweeny* court had adopted this latter standard, what would have been the result?

SMITH v. DEBARTOLI, 769 F.2d 451 (7th Cir. 1985). In this strange case, the court construed the Rule 9 requirement that "special damages" must be "specifically stated." Inmate Smith alleged that he had been found guilty by the prison disciplinary committee of refusing to leave administrative segregation. His punishment: confinement to administrative segregation. His hearing was unlawful, however, because corrections officer DeBartoli was a member of the panel, and DeBartoli had previously participated in the decision to require Smith to leave segregation. The evidence was clear, so that Smith was unambiguously guilty of the violation; furthermore, his act of refusing to leave segregation blunted his claim for damages from that very segregation. Nevertheless, the trial court held that Smith's civil right to due process had been violated in a manner redressable under 42 U.S.C. § 1983. It awarded only $1 as "nominal" damages. Smith appealed in an effort to obtain greater damages.

The Court of Appeals affirmed. For the confinement itself, nominal damages were appropriate in these circumstances. Furthermore, Smith's pleading would not support recovery of other elements of damage such as claimed "emotional distress, stemming from the due process violation itself," because these were "special damages." The court defined special damages as "the kinds of injuries that do not *necessarily* flow from" the violation of rights that the plaintiff has proved.

NOTES AND QUESTIONS

(1) *How and What to Plead as Special Damages.* Your client's husband was killed in an automobile accident, and you have filed suit against the negligent driver in federal court. Your client has suffered the loss of his earnings, counsel, companionship, and consortium; psychiatric expenses for herself; medical expenses for him before his death; mental and emotional distress; diminished value in the estate she might have expected to recover from him; and possibly other damage elements. State law may permit recovery of attorney's fees and prejudgment interest, and you think the other driver was grossly negligent. How would you plead the damages?

(2) *With What Degree of Specificity Must Special Damages Be Pleaded?* The damages need not be pleaded in evidentiary detail. Several cases hold that Rule 9(g) is to be read together with Rule 8, so that "notice" of the nature of the special damage items is all that is required. *E.g., Great American Indem. Co. v. Brown*, 307 F.2d 306 (5th Cir. 1962) (complaint sufficient where it lumped items, thus: "For all of his personal injuries, permanent injuries, physical pain and suffering and mental anguish, loss of earnings past and future, and expenses and damages, plaintiff claims the sum of $114,000.00," and where other items, such as property damage to plaintiff's automobile, were specifically pleaded in other paragraphs).

[2] "Heightened Pleading Requirements" Imposed for Public Policy Reasons: A Shift Away from Notice Pleading?

SIEGERT v. GILLEY, 500 U.S. 226 (1991). Siegert brought a civil rights suit under § 1983 against Gilley, his former supervisor at a government hospital, for issuing a blisteringly negative employment reference that Siegert claimed was false and prevented him from getting a job at another government hospital. Gilley's defense included the defense of qualified immunity, which prevented liability if Gilley had written the reference in good faith. Gilley moved to dismiss on the ground, among others, that Siegert's complaint was subject to this immunity as a matter of law on its face.

The Court of Appeals held that the complaint was subject to a "heightened pleading" standard. This was so, according to the Court of Appeals, because good faith immunity was a special kind of defense: it was supposed to protect the good-faith public official not only from liability, but also from suffering the process of the lawsuit itself. This protection could be provided only by immediate dismissal at the complaint stage. Therefore, if the defendant raised the defense of good faith immunity, the complaint would be dismissed if it did not set forth specific facts sufficient to overcome this immunity (the "heightened pleading standard").

The majority of the Supreme Court affirmed, but it did not base its decision on the heightened pleading standard. Instead, it held that injury to reputation by defamation did not give rise to a § 1983 action because it did not deprive a person of any federally secured right. In the course of reaching this holding, the majority discussed the heightened pleading standard without directly analyzing it, causing many observers to infer that the majority might approve it (but cf. the *Leatherman* case, below). Three Justices dissented, but even they would have adopted a kind of heightened pleading standard to protect the immunity. The only Justice who would have based affirmance on the heightened pleading standard was Justice Kennedy, who reasoned as follows:

> JUSTICE KENNEDY, concurring in the judgment. . . .
>
> I would affirm for the reasons given by the Court of Appeals. Here malice is a requisite showing to avoid the bar of qualified immunity. The heightened pleading standard is a necessary and appropriate accommodation between the state of mind component of malice and the objective test that prevails in qualified immunity analysis as a general matter. *See Harlow v. Fitzgerald*, 457 U.S. 800 (1982). There is tension between the rationale of *Harlow* and the requirement of malice, and it seems to me that the heightened pleading requirement is the most workable means to resolve it. The heightened pleading standard is a departure from the usual pleading requirements of Federal Rules of Civil Procedure 8 and 9(b), and departs also from the normal standard for summary judgment under Rule 56. But avoidance of disruptive discovery is one of the very purposes for the official immunity doctrine, and it is no answer to say that the plaintiff has not yet had the opportunity to engage in discovery. The substantive defense of immunity controls.
>
> Upon the assertion of a qualified immunity defense the plaintiff must put forward specific, nonconclusory factual allegations which establish malice, or face dismissal. I would reject, however, the Court of Appeals' statement that a plaintiff must present direct, as opposed to circumstantial, evidence. Circumstantial evidence may be as probative as testimonial evidence. *See Holland v. United States*, 348 U.S. 121, 140 (1954). . . .

NOTES AND QUESTIONS

(1) *How Does Siegert v. Gilley's Treatment of the Heightened Pleading Requirement Square with Rules 8 and 9?* Note that even the dissenters appear to accept a heightened pleading requirement. (Perhaps all of the justices have become persuaded that there is

a need to deal effectively with unmeritorious civil rights claims and to shield public officials from them.) But is this pragmatic solution really an unprincipled shift away from Rule 8 without going through the rules amendment process? Justice Kennedy explains that, although a heightened pleading requirement is a "departure from the usual" rules, it nevertheless is a necessary implication of the "substantive defense of immunity," which "controls."

(2) *Does a Heightened Pleading Standard Reflect a Return to Common Law or Field Code Pleading of "the Facts" That Underlie a "Cause of Action"? Does It Overrule Dioguardi?* Note that the Court of Appeals would have required Siegert to plead "direct evidence." (How can one supply "direct" evidence of subjective intent, unless perhaps the defendant gives a confession?) Justice Kennedy would also recognize circumstantial evidence, but he seems to approve the concept of "evidence" pleading developed by the lower court. Is this reasoning a return to common law or Code pleading (or indeed, beyond it, because even common law and Code pleading did not require pleading of one's "evidence")? Or is this imprecise language merely an inelegantly phrased expression that there are, after all, some advantages to modern cause-of-action pleading?

(3) *The Precedent for Judge-Created Particularity Requirements in Civil Rights Cases. Siegert* actually was preceded by a long line of cases. "It is well established that in an action for damages against public officials under the Civil Rights Act, the plaintiff must allege highly specific facts to defeat a motion to dismiss." *Friedman v. Younger*, 282 F. Supp. 710, 713 (C.D. Cal. 1968); *accord, Martin v. Merola*, 532 F.2d 191 (2d Cir. 1976) ("general" charges not enough); *Ruppert v. Lehigh County*, 496 F. Supp. 954 (E.D. Pa. 1980) (standard of "greater" particularity).

(4) *The Volume of Pro Se Pleadings: But Is There Actually a Lesser Particularity Requirement?* It is no accident that *Dioguardi v. Durning*, above, was a *pro se* case. Should the judge be more lenient in evaluating the particularity of pleadings in a *pro se* case? Reconsider the newspaper excerpt following *Conley v. Gibson* in § 1.04, above ("Inmate Lawsuits Mushroom"). However, the past approach to laypersons' *pro se* complaints has been to subject them to "less stringent standards" than lawyers' complaints. *Haines v. Kerner*, 404 U.S. 519 (1972). With this principle in mind, what should be done with the complaint of the inmate, described in the newspaper article, for damages because his dinner plate contained fewer meatballs than other inmates'? Can it be dismissed? It may not be possible to know with certainty that such a plaintiff does not have claims with merit. On the other hand, shouldn't the resources consumed by such complaints be devoted to claims with more probable merit?

(5) *Judge-Created Particularity Requirements in "Big" Cases.* Judges have sometimes attempted to control "big case" litigation by more strict pleading requirements. *Compare* Dawson, *The Place of the Pleading in a Proper Definition of the Issues in the "Big Case,"* 23 F.R.D. 430 (1958), *with* Clark, *Comment on Judge Dawson's Paper on the Place of the Pleading in a Proper Definition of the Issues in the "Big Case,"* 23 F.R.D. 435 (1958). Perhaps antitrust litigation, shareholder's derivative suits, and allegations under the Racketeer-Influenced, Corrupt Organizations ("RICO") statute do raise problems similar to those of fraud claims. However, the appellate courts sometimes have reversed trial judges who have imposed strict pleading requirements, holding that Rule 8 is applicable even to "big cases" unless Rule 9 is involved. *E.g., Control Data Corp. v. International Business Machines Corp.*, 421 F.2d 323 (8th Cir. 1970). *But see* Marcus, *The Revival of Fact Pleading Under the Federal Rules of Civil Procedure*, 86 Colum L. Rev. 433 (1986). Should a judge be considered to be on firmer ground in using Rule

12(e)'s provision for a more definite statement, rather than Rule 12(b), as the vehicle for requiring specificity in these cases?

(6) *Use of the Motion for More Definite Statement as the Basis for Greater Particularity Requirements.* Some courts have declined to grant dismissals for failure to state a claim, but, at the same time, have required greater particularity by the device of ordering a more definite statement. *Ruppert v. Lehigh County, supra,* is an example. If a court uses this methodology to impose a more particularized standard of pleading, is the order more likely to be valid than if the court orders dismissal? (If not, it would appear that the motion for a more definite statement serves no function that is not already served by the motion to dismiss.)

(7) *The Supreme Court Surprises Heightened-Pleading Supporters in Leatherman, below.* Notwithstanding the implications in *Siegert v. Gilley,* the Supreme Court held, in the case that follows, that a civil rights case was governed by Rule 8, not by a heightened pleading standard.

LEATHERMAN v. TARRANT COUNTY NARCOTICS INTELLIGENCE AND COORDINATION UNIT

507 U.S. 163 (1993)

CHIEF JUSTICE REHNQUIST delivered the opinion of the [unanimous] Court.

We granted certiorari to decide whether a federal court may apply a "heightened pleading standard" — more stringent than the usual pleading requirements of Rule 8(a) of the Federal Rules of Civil Procedure — in civil rights cases alleging municipal liability under 42 U.S.C. § 1983. We hold it may not.

This action arose out of two separate incidents involving the execution of search warrants by local law enforcement officers. . . . Plaintiffs sued several local officials in their official capacity and the county and two municipal corporations that employed the police officers involved in the incidents, asserting that the police conduct had violated the Fourth Amendment to the United States Constitution. The stated basis for municipal liability under *Monell v. New York Department of Social Services,* 436 U.S. 658 (1978), was the failure of these bodies adequately to train the police officers involved. . . .

The United States District Court for the Northern District of Texas ordered the complaints dismissed, because they failed to meet the "heightened pleading standard" required by the decisional law of the Court of Appeals for the Fifth Circuit. . . . The Fifth Circuit, in turn, affirmed the judgment of dismissal . . . and we granted certiorari. . . . We now reverse.

Respondents seek to defend the Fifth Circuit's application of a more rigorous pleading standard on two grounds. First, respondents claim that municipalities' freedom from respondeat superior liability, *see Monell, supra,* necessarily includes immunity from suit. In this sense, respondents assert, municipalities are no different from state or local officials sued in their individual capacity. . . .

This argument wrongly equates freedom from liability with immunity from suit. To be sure, we reaffirmed in *Monell* that "a municipality cannot be held liable under § 1983 on a respondeat superior theory." . . . [But in] *Monell,* we overruled *Monroe v. Pape,* 365 U.S. 167 (1961), insofar as it held that local governments were wholly immune from suit under § 1983. [And in] *Owen v. City of Independence,* 445 U.S. 622, 650 (1980), we rejected a claim that municipalities should be afforded qualified immunity, . . . based on the good faith of their agents. These decisions make it quite clear that . . . a municipality can be sued under § 1983, but it cannot be held liable unless a municipal policy or custom caused the constitutional injury. We thus have no occasion to consider whether our qualified immunity jurisprudence would require a heightened pleading in cases involving individual government officials.

Second, respondents contend that the Fifth Circuit's heightened pleading standard is not really that at all. . . . According to respondents, the degree of factual specificity required of a complaint by the Federal Rules of Civil Procedure varies according to the complexity of the underlying substantive law. To establish municipal liability under § 1983, respondents argue, a plaintiff must do more than plead a single instance of misconduct. This requirement, respondents insist, is consistent with a plaintiff's Rule 11 obligation to make a reasonable pre-filing inquiry into the facts.

But examination of the Fifth Circuit's decision in this case makes it quite evident that the "heightened pleading standard" is just what it purports to be: a more demanding rule for pleading a complaint under § 1983 than for pleading other kinds of claims for relief. This rule was adopted by the Fifth Circuit in *Elliot v. Perez,* 751 F.2d 1472 (1985), and described in this language:

> "In cases against government officials involving the likely defense of immunity we require of trial judges that they demand that the plaintiff's complaints state with factual detail and particularity the basis for the claim which necessarily includes why the defendant-official cannot successfully maintain the defense of immunity." *Id.*, at 1473.

. . .

We think that it is impossible to square the "heightened pleading standard" applied by the Fifth Circuit in this case with the liberal system of "notice pleading" set up by the Federal Rules. Rule 8(a)(2) requires that a complaint include only "a short and plain statement of the claim showing that the pleader is entitled to relief." In *Conley v. Gibson,* 355 U.S. 41 (1957), we said in effect that the Rule meant what it said:

> "The Federal Rules of Civil Procedure do not require a claimant to set out in detail the facts upon which he bases his claim. To the contrary, all the Rules require is a "short and plain statement of the claim that will give the defendant fair notice of what the plaintiff's claim is and the grounds upon which it rests." *Id.* at 47 (footnote omitted).

Rule 9(b) does impose a particularity requirement in two specific instances. It provides that "in all averments of fraud or mistake, the circumstances constituting fraud or mistake shall be stated with particularity." Thus, the Federal Rules do address in Rule 9(b) the question of the need for greater particularity in pleading certain actions, but do not include among the enumerated actions any reference to complaints alleging municipal liability under § 1983. . . .

. . . Perhaps if Rules 8 and 9 were re-written today, claims against municipalities under § 1983 might be subjected to the added specificity requirement of Rule 9(b). But that is a result which must be obtained by the process of amending the Federal Rules, and not by judicial interpretation. In the absence of such an amendment, federal courts and litigants must rely on summary judgment and control of discovery to weed out unmeritorious claims sooner rather than later.

The judgment of the Court of Appeals is reversed, and the case remanded for further proceedings consistent with this opinion.

It is so ordered.

NOTES AND QUESTIONS

(1) *Does Leatherman v. Tarrant County Overrule Siegert v. Gilley?* The *Leatherman* opinion never mentioned *Siegert v. Gilley* in unanimously rejecting a heightened pleading standard for § 1983 municipal liability actions. And the Court expressly noted it was not deciding whether "our qualified immunity jurisprudence would require a heightened pleading in cases involving individual government officials." But aren't some of the arguments based on the absence of immunity from suit and inconsistency with notice pleading applicable to actions against individuals as well as municipalities?

(2) *The Fifth Circuit Uses the Requirement of a Rule 7(a) Reply to Preserve the Heightened Pleading Standard for Cases Against Individuals.* The Fifth Circuit has continued to impose heightened pleading requirements in § 1983 actions against public officials by using Rule 7(a) to require a detailed response tailored to a defendant's qualified immunity defense. *Schultea v. Wood,* 47 F.3d 1427 (5th Cir. 1995) (en banc). Rule 7(a) authorizes a federal court to order a plaintiff to file a reply to a defendant's defense, and unlike the complaint, it is not expressly subject to Rule 8 notice pleading.

(3) *In Case No One Was Listening, the Supreme Court Rules Against Heightened Pleading Twice More.* In *Swierkiewicz v. Sorema, N.A.*, 534 U.S. 506 (2002), the plaintiff, a native of Hungary, alleged he had been fired by the defendant on account of his national origin and age. The district court and the Second Circuit, applying a heightened pleading standard to all cases of employment discrimination, dismissed Swierkiewicz's complaint because it did not specifically allege each of the elements of the "prima facie" discrimination case based on the framework set out in *McDonnell Douglas Corp. v. Green*, 411 U.S. 792 (1973). A unanimous Supreme Court reversed. Writing for the Court, Justice Thomas noted that the *McDonnell Douglas* standard is an evidentiary standard, not a pleading standard, and does not apply in every employment discrimination case. "Given that the prima facie case operates as a flexible evidentiary standard, it should not be transposed into a rigid pleading standard for discrimination cases." 534 U.S. at 512-13. Moreover, the Court held, "imposing the Court of Appeals' heightened pleading standard in employment discrimination cases conflicts with Federal Rule of Civil Procedure 8(a)(2)," which requires only that plaintiff's statement of the claim "'give the defendant fair notice of what the plaintiff's claim is and the grounds upon which it rests.'" *Id.* (citing *Conley v. Gibson*, 355 U.S. 41, 47 (1957)). The Court reiterated that "Rule 8(a)'s simplified pleading standard applies to all civil actions, with limited exceptions." *Id.* Referring to Rule 9(b), the Court noted it "has declined to extend such exceptions in other contexts," citing *Leatherman v. Tarrant County Narcotics Intelligence and Coordination Unit*, 507 U.S. 163 (1993).

The Court subsequently again refused to create a heightened pleading standard in *Jones v. Bock*, 549 U.S. —, 127 S. Ct. 910 (2007). The *Jones* case concerned the Prison Litigation Reform Act of 1995 (PLRA), which requires prisoners to exhaust prison grievance procedures before filing suit. The Sixth Circuit, in its procedural rules, required prisoners to allege and demonstrate such exhaustion in their complaints. The Supreme Court held that although exhaustion is mandatory under the PLRA, Federal Rule of Civil Procedure 8(a) requires only a "short and plain statement of the claim" and the PLRA does not itself require prisoners to plead exhaustion. Accordingly, the Court held that failure to exhaust is an affirmative defense; prisoners are not required to plead or demonstrate exhaustion in their complaints.

In a portion of the Supreme Court's recent decision in *Bell Atlantic Corp. v. Twombly* not reproduced above, the Court specifically addressed the *Swierkiewicz* case, stating:

> Plaintiffs say that our analysis runs counter to *Swierkiewicz v. Sorema N.A.*, 534 U.S. 506, 508 (2002), which held that "a complaint in an employment discrimination lawsuit [need] not contain specific facts establishing a prima facie case of discrimination . . . ." They argue that just as the prima facie case is a "flexible evidentiary standard" that "should not be transposed into a rigid pleading standard for discrimination cases, . . . transpos[ing] 'plus factor' summary judgment analysis woodenly into a rigid Rule 12(b)(6) pleading standard . . . would be unwise." . . . As the District Court correctly understood, however, "*Swierkiewicz* did not change the law of pleading, but simply re-emphasized . . . that the Second Circuit's use of a heightened pleading standard for Title VII cases was contrary to the Federal Rules' structure of liberal pleading requirements." . . . Even though Swierkiewicz's pleadings "detailed the events leading to his termination, provided relevant dates, and included the ages and nationalities of at least some of the relevant persons involved with his termination," the Court of Appeals dismissed his complaint for failing to allege certain additional facts that Swierkiewicz would need at the trial stage to support his claim in the absence of direct evidence of discrimination. . . . We reversed on the ground that the Court of Appeals had impermissibly applied what amounted to a heightened pleading requirement by insisting that Swierkiewicz allege "specific facts" beyond those necessary to state his claim and the grounds showing entitlement to relief. . . .
>
> Here, in contrast, we do not require heightened fact pleading of specifics, but only enough facts to state a claim to relief that is plausible on its face. Because the plaintiffs here have not nudged their claims across the line from conceivable to plausible, their complaint must be dismissed. . . .

In another portion of the *Bell Atlantic* case, the Supreme Court insisted that in reaching its conclusion "we do not apply any 'heightened' pleading standard, nor do we seek to broaden the scope of Federal Rule of Civil Procedure 9 . . . . Here, our concern is not that the allegations in the complaint were insufficiently 'particular[ized],' . . . rather, the complaint warranted dismissal because it failed in toto to render plaintiffs' entitlement to relief plausible." 550 U.S. —, n.14.

NOTE ON THE PRIVATE SECURITIES LITIGATION REFORM ACT: A CONGRESSIONALLY-MANDATED HEIGHTENED PLEADING REQUIREMENT

Passed over President Clinton's veto, the Private Securities Litigation Reform Act of 1995 made numerous changes in the litigation procedures for actions brought under both the Securities Act of 1933 and the Securities Exchange Act of 1934. [P.L. 104-67, 109 Stat. 737 (1995) (*see* 15 U.S.C. §§ 77z-1, 78u-4); *see also Barrie v. Intervoice-Brite, Inc.*, 397 F.3d 249, *modified and reh'g denied*, 409 F.3d 653 (5th Cir. 2005).] Section 21D of the Act requires that the complaint in a securities fraud action brought under the 1934 Act in which the plaintiff alleges that the defendant made an untrue statement of a material fact or material omission, "shall specify each statement alleged to have been misleading, the reason or reasons why the statement is misleading, and if an allegation regarding the statement or omission is made on information and belief, the complaint shall state *with particularity* all facts on which that belief is formed." (Emphasis added) [109 Stat. 747.] State of mind allegations similarly require "with particularity facts giving rise to a strong inference that the defendant acted with the required state of mind."

[*Id.*] Other changes include mandatory Rule 11 sanctions, restoring that part of Rule 11 to its 1983-1993 formulation, special certifications by plaintiffs seeking to serve as representative parties, early notice to class members, and special requirements for discovery on the question of whether an alleged class plaintiff is the most adequate plaintiff. Whatever the merits of these changes, they represent yet another step away from universal (or "transubstantive") federal rules, that is, a single set of rules that will apply to all cases regardless of the substantive law basis for the claim or defense.

[3] Requirements of Pleading Evidentiary Matters in Compliance With Screening Mechanisms

DeLUNA v. ST. ELIZABETH'S HOSPITAL, 147 Ill. 2d 57, 588 N.E.2d 1139 (1992). Would it be a good idea to impose pleading requirements that force the plaintiff to show specifically that the plaintiff has inquired into the factual basis for the suit? Illinois Code of Civil Procedure § 2-622 requires that the plaintiff in a medical malpractice action attach to the complaint an affidavit stating that he or she has consulted with a health professional, in whose opinion there is a "reasonable and meritorious cause" for the filing of the action. In addition, the plaintiff is required to attach a copy of a written report from the health professional, detailing the grounds for his or her opinion.

In the *DeLuna* case, a medical malpractice plaintiff challenged the constitutionality of § 2-622 under various provisions of the Federal and Illinois Constitutions, including arguments asserting violation of equal protection, due process, separation of powers, certainty of remedy, and "special legislation" provisions. The court rejected all of these arguments and upheld the statute. It reasoned, for example, that § 2-622 did not violate equal protection or due process because it was "rationally related to a legitimate governmental interest": It was intended to reduce the number of frivolous actions that might otherwise be filed. By requiring litigants to obtain, at an early point, the opinion of an expert who agreed that a meritorious cause of action exists, the court reasoned, this statute should help ensure that only claims with some merit are presented. (One justice dissented on the ground that the Illinois statute granted to health care professionals the authority to abort the judiciary's role in applying principles of law to the facts of the case without a possibility for judicial review, and it thus violated the doctrine of separation of powers.)

NOTES AND QUESTIONS

(1) *Should the Plaintiff Be Required to Plead Compliance With Screening Requirements Designed to Ensure Pre-Filing Review of Merits?* The requirement that a plaintiff specifically plead compliance with a particularized inquiry requirement is unusual in American practice. And a requirement that the plaintiff produce a factual report indicating lawsuit merit, before filing, is even more unusual. Are these requirements sensible, or will they simply increase the cost and difficulty of filing for plaintiffs?

(2) *Court-Imposed Requirements of "Case Statements" in RICO Cases.* Several federal district judges have initiated the requirement of a "case statement" to be filed by plaintiffs in certain kinds of complex litigation under readily-abused statutes, such as the RICO statute. *See, e.g.,* Order entered by Chief Judge Lucius D. Bunton, *Sogelease Corp. v. Farnel,* No. MO-88-CA-87 (W.D. Tex. Jan. 23, 1989). Judge Bunton's order required that the plaintiff's "case statement" consist of reports on 20 separate items, numbered to correspond to the numbers in the Order. Some of the 20 items had as many as seven subparts, each calling for specific legal or factual information. Is such a "case statement,"

which obviously will impose an expensive burden on the plaintiff's lawyer, a legitimate screening device? (The requirement is subject to the strong suspicion that it is designed to deter the filing of RICO claims unless the pleader is extraordinarily serious about them; if so, is the requirement sensible and lawful?) In any event, similar requirements have been imposed by other judges.

[D] Alternate and Inconsistent Allegations

LAMBERT v. SOUTHERN COUNTIES GAS CO., 52 Cal. 2d 347, 340 P.2d 608 (1959). The plaintiffs sought damages for the loss of a bulldozer, which they had rented to certain ranch owners. It was totally destroyed by fire when it struck and punctured a high-pressure gas pipeline less than 15 inches below the surface of the ground. Count one of the complaint alleged negligence on the part of the ranch owners in operating the bulldozer over the pipeline. Count two alleged that, in the alternative, the gas company was negligent in permitting its pipeline to remain so near the surface.

The gas company, however, filed a general demurrer, arguing that the two counts were inconsistent. Section 402 of the California Vehicle Code provided that negligence in the use of a motor vehicle (including a bulldozer) "shall be imputed to the owner for all purposes of civil damages." Under this provision, any negligence on the part of the ranch owners was attributable to the plaintiffs. Thus the plaintiffs, in count one, had affirmatively pleaded their own contributory negligence, and California at that time followed the rule that contributory negligence barred any recovery. The trial court accepted this reasoning and sustained the gas company's demurrer (this holding was analogous to the granting of a motion to dismiss). The California Supreme Court, while agreeing that the negligence of the ranch owners was attributable to the plaintiffs and that the claims were inconsistent, nevertheless reversed the grant of the demurrer:

> But a plaintiff may plead inconsistent causes of action in separate counts of a single complaint. . . . [A] count sufficient within itself may not ordinarily be defeated by importing, from another count, an allegation to which the sufficient count makes no reference. . . .
>
> Here the gas company alone is named defendant in count two, and only its alleged negligence is involved in count two. Count two does not concern the alleged negligence of the ranch owners, which rests on a different premise for the recovery of damages as stated in count one. In short, the two counts in their respective separate statements of alleged negligence — that of the ranch owners, on the one hand, and that of the gas company, on the other — indicate that plaintiffs are in doubt as to which defendants should be held liable. . . . Plaintiffs may do this under the right of joinder of defendants afforded by our system. . . .

[E] The Form of the Pleadings: No "Magic Words"

FAULKNER v. FORT BEND INDEPENDENT SCHOOL DIST., No. H-85-2281 (S.D. Tex. April 24, 1986). In this case, Judge Lynn N. Hughes entered an order reading, in its entirety, as follows:

> First, the motion to dismiss by the defendants is denied.
>
> Secondly, the plaintiffs are ordered to replead by May 1, 1986, eliminating from the amended complaint all excessive capitalization, empty formalisms, obscure abstractions, and other conceptual and grammatical imbecilities.

Thirdly, at the pretrial conference on May 5, the issues will be narrowly focused.

NOTES AND QUESTIONS

(1) *Should a Pleader Write, "Now Comes" the Plaintiff, or "Comes Now" the Plaintiff?* Beginning attorneys have been known to puzzle over this question. It should be apparent from Rule 8, as well as from the order quoted above, that it makes no difference which of these two forms the plaintiff uses. In fact, it makes no difference if the pleader leaves out this "empty formalism."

(2) *Are There Any "Magic Words"?* The short answer to this question is "No." The real issue is whether the pleading conveys the substance that is intended. However, there are occasions when small differences in wording can make a difference, and it should be emphasized that the absence of a "magic words" requirement does not mean that any words will do or that the pleader does not need to exercise care. For example, what happens if the plaintiff pleads that the parties are of diverse "residence," when what is intended is to establish diversity of citizenship? The pleading is insufficient, not because of a magic words approach, but because the meaning of the words is inadequate to confer jurisdiction. *Robertson v. Cease*, 97 U.S. 646, 648 (1878); *Prescription Plan Serv. Corp. v. Franco*, 552 F.2d 493, 498 n.6 (2d Cir. 1977). The pleading of jurisdiction comes as close to a "magic words" approach as is to be found, probably because of the strong policy of limited federal jurisdiction. Even in this area, however, the cases tend to disregard poor word choice if the meaning of the words adequately conveys the jurisdictional requirements. *E.g., National Farmers Union Property & Casualty Co. v. Fisher*, 284 F.2d 421 (8th Cir. 1960) (error in pleading diversity of "residence" is not fatal if it is clear that citizenship was what the pleader intended).

(3) *Rule 10: Style, Caption, Paragraphs, Etc.* Rule 10 requires a "caption" containing the names of the parties, etc., or what lawyers often call the "style" of the pleading. Each pleading must be given a "designation" (*e.g.*, "Complaint"). The Rule requires numbered paragraphs, "each limited as far as practicable to a single set of circumstances." It also requires that separate claims or defenses be set out in different "counts" (*e.g.*, "First Claim," etc.). There is nothing in the Rule that requires a specific method of laying out the caption, and indeed defective compliance with Rule 10 is often overlooked. There is some advantage, however, in ensuring that one's pleadings "look right" to the judge and to opposing parties. Before some judges, that concern might even justify "empty formalisms" such as "Now Comes the Plaintiff."

§ 5.03 Appendix Drafting the Complaint

PLEADINGS IN *WYTINGER v. TWO UNKNOWN POLICE OFFICERS*

[Reproduced above in Appendix to § 1.04.]

For a concrete example of a federal complaint, motion to dismiss, and order of dismissal, read (or re-read) the appendix to § 1.04, above, which contains the pleadings in *Wytinger v. Two Unknown Police Officers*. Notice the particularity with which the facts are set forth in the complaint. Why? Notice the Court's disposition of the matter by dismissal. Is this result consistent with the substantive law and with the Federal Rules? Do you agree with the Court's decision?

§ 5.04 The Answer in Federal Court

[A] Dilatory Pleas and Attacks on the Complaint

"Dilatory Pleas and Demurrers." In common law practice, fundamental defects in the suit were raised by a demurrer, a plea to the jurisdiction, or by a "plea in abatement" (which was a device for raising various kinds of defects but was most frequently used to raise improper venue or nonjoinder of parties). Pleas to the jurisdiction or in abatement were known as "dilatory pleas" — in part, because they were often used precisely as the name implies. Dilatory pleas were required to be raised early in the proceedings, in "due order."

The Modern Federal Approach: Rule 12. Today, in the Federal Rules, there is no special category for dilatory pleas or demurrers. The Rules replace these pleadings with the Rule 12(b) motion to dismiss. Personal jurisdiction, subject-matter jurisdiction, venue, process, service, failure to state a claim, and failure to join a party, are all raised in federal practice by the motion to dismiss. Notice that several of these matters will be waived if not timely raised. *See* Rule 12(h). Many states follow the same approach (but there are some states in which demurrers and pleas in abatement are still used). Notice that Rule 12(g) allows the pleader to consolidate multiple defenses or requests in one motion, and in fact it provides that defenses omitted from such a motion are prohibited, in some instances, from inclusion in any later motion.

Inclusion of Dilatory Pleas in the Answer. The defendant can simply include these matters in the answer, rather than filing a motion. Thus the first paragraph may assert that the complaint fails to state a claim, while later paragraphs may contain admissions and denials and affirmative defenses. However, a defendant who seriously wants to assert a jurisdictional issue, or an attack on the complaint, usually prefers to file a motion to dismiss.

[B] Admissions and Denials

Read Fed. R. Civ. P. 8(b), (c), and (d) and Rule 12(a), (g), and (h). Also, read Federal Forms 30, 31, and 40.

NOTE CONTRASTING THE GENERAL DENIAL WITH FEDERAL PRACTICE

What Is a "General Denial"? Some states permit the defendant to plead a general denial: "The defendant denies each and every, all and singular, the material allegations of the plaintiff's complaint, and demands strict proof thereof before a jury." No particular form of expression is required, so long as the answer makes the point that the defendant is generally denying the plaintiff's allegations. This pleading is derived from the common law plea of the "general issue," which allowed the defendant to offer evidence rebutting the plaintiff's allegations without particularizing any positions in the answer.

The Effect of the General Denial. The effect of a general denial is to put in issue all of the ultimate facts required to sustain the plaintiff's claim. Some students perceive this plea as "dishonest," but this perception reflects a misunderstanding. In those states in which it is permitted, the general denial is not literally an assertion that all of the plaintiff's allegations are false; it merely amounts to a demand that the plaintiff "prove it."

Strategy and Desirability of the General Denial. A defendant would prefer to assert a general denial, if it is available. In those jurisdictions in which it is permitted, a defendant often files an answer that consists of a single sentence. Why? The defendant's greatest benefit is that he avoids narrowing the issues available to him at trial and therefore minimizes the probability of variances between proof and pleading of his defensive theories.

The Federal Approach: Admissions and Denials. The Federal Rules take a different approach. The defendant is required to sift through the complaint and state a position on the truth or falsehood of each allegation in it. Rule 8(b) says that denials "must fairly respond to the substance of the allegation." Furthermore, "[a] party that intends in good faith to deny only part of an allegation must admit the part that is true and deny the rest." (Don't be confused by the reference in Rule 8(b) to a "general denial"; the rule also says that defendant "must admit" the allegations that are true. This language means that, contrary to many state court practices, a defendant who files a general denial must indeed be denying *every* allegation in the pleading.)

WHITE v. SMITH
91 F.R.D. 607 (W.D.N.Y. 1981)

ELFVIN, DISTRICT JUDGE.

Plaintiff in this *pro se* civil rights action was granted permission to proceed *in forma pauperis* January 26, 1981. In my Memorandum and Order I outlined plaintiff's allegations and cited legal authority to the effect that, as presented, plaintiff's contentions pose tenable constitutional claims.

The Complaint was served on defendants January 29, 1981. By their attorney, New York State Assistant Attorney General Douglas S. Cream, defendants moved for additional time to answer in order to obtain information concerning a purportedly related action filed by plaintiff in the United States District Court for the Northern District of New York. At oral argument March 9, 1981 I granted defendants' request over plaintiff's written objections.

April 1, 1981, two months after they were served, all four defendants jointly filed their Answer, recounted in full below.[1]

---

[1] The body of defendants' Answer is as follows:

Defendants, HAROLD SMITH, DORIS BEITZ, CHARLES SCULLY, EDITH ALMETER, as and for their answer to the complaint, by their attorney, Robert Abrams, Attorney General of the State of New York, Douglas S. Cream, Assistant Attorney General, of counsel, set forth as follows:

1. DENY each and every allegation of the complaint which allege [sic] or tends to allege that they violated any of plaintiff's constitutionally protected rights.

AS AND FOR AN ADDITIONAL AND FURTHER DEFENSE:

2. The complaint fails to state a claim upon which relief can be granted.

AS AND FOR AN ADDITIONAL AND FURTHER DEFENSE:

3. The defendants are immune from liability.

AS AND FOR AN ADDITIONAL AND FURTHER DEFENSE:

4. At all times herein relevant, the defendants were employed by the New York State Department of Correctional Services.

5. All acts performed by the defendants were performed by them within the scope of their duties.

6. All acts performed by defendants were performed in the reasonable and good faith belief that those acts would not violate any of plaintiff's constitutionally protected rights.

As a general rule, federal court pleadings need not be extensive or detailed. On the contrary, Fed. R. Civ. P. Rule 8(b) requires only that defenses shall be stated "in short and plain terms." For the most part, denials are to be "specific denials of designated averments or paragraphs." [Today, the Rule states, "A party that does not intend to deny all the allegations must either specifically deny designated allegations or generally deny all except those specifically admitted." — Eds.] However, general denials which controvert all of a complaint's averments are acceptable under the rule if they are made "in good faith" subject to the obligations of Fed. R. Civ. P. rule 11.

. . . The federal rule does not contemplate an elaborate reply to every allegation of a complaint. . . . It does not even condemn averments of insufficient information or knowledge upon which to form a belief as to the truth of the complainant's allegations. . . . Nonetheless, the "form answer" submitted by defendants in this action does not come close to complying with the Federal Rules of Civil Procedure, not to mention basic notions of due process, adequate notice and fair play.

Although plaintiff is proceeding *pro se*, his claims are plainly and cogently presented. Admittedly, there is no numbering or other denomination of his separate allegations; but, essentially, he alleges that, despite the pendency of a state habeas corpus challenge to his extradition to North Carolina, defendants delivered him to the North Carolina authorities before the hearing.

Unlike many other *pro se* complaints filed in this court, this Complaint raises allegations which do not hinge solely on plaintiff's word against the defendants' words. Such a situation arises, for instance, where a prisoner alleges that a certain correctional officer physically assaulted him or denied him adequate medical care. In those types of cases, the use of a general denial, while not necessarily condonable, is more understandable due to the obvious difficulty of discussing an incident which defendants deny having occurred at all.

On the contrary, plaintiff's description of the events surrounding his extradition are meticulously detailed and quite specific. He includes all critical names and dates. Finally, attached to the Complaint are various documents pertaining to his detainer, state habeas corpus petition, and subsequent extradition which, in the court's view, tend to support his claim.

Surely it would not have been an onerous burden for defendants' attorney to compare plaintiff's averments and attached documents to defendants' own records to enable him to frame meaningful and responsible answers to plaintiff's charges. . . .

The absurdity of defendants' general denial appears all the more flagrant when the answer is compared to plaintiff's claims. Three examples will suffice, though many more are obvious. If defendants' general denial is to be believed, then notwithstanding the Complaint and its Exhibit B, the District Attorney of North Carolina did not request a detainer against plaintiff; notwithstanding the Complaint and its Exhibit F, Acting Superintendent Scully did not sign and send an "Offer to Deliver Temporary Custody" of plaintiff July 13, 1978; and notwithstanding the Complaint and its Exhibit I, Doris Beitz neither was informed that plaintiff's petition for habeas corpus was made returnable before the Honorable John S. Conable August 23, 1978 nor informed plaintiff of the hearing date in an inter-office communication dated August 7, 1978.

On the basis of defendants' wholly inadequate response to plaintiff's clearly framed allegations, I can only conclude that defendants' general denial is neither offered in "good faith," Fed. R. Civ. P. rule 8(b), nor complies with Fed. R. Civ. P. rule 11. For all the reasons discussed above, I would be stretching attorney Cream's credibility far beyond the realm of rationality were I to find that "to the best of his knowledge, information, and belief there is good ground to support [his general denial]." Fed. R. Civ. P. rule 11. . . .

Under the circumstances of this case, appropriate sanctions are more than justified. As noted *supra*, footnote 2, a pleading filed in violation of Fed. R. Civ. P. rule 11 may be stricken as sham and false and the action may proceed as though the pleading had not been served. I am satisfied that such a penalty is fully warranted in this matter . . . .

Nevertheless, because counsel for defendants has been permitted in the past to use this same type of unresponsive answer and because he and his office should have some advance warning prior to the imposition of the ultimate sanction of entry of a default and the proving up of a default judgment — and this Memorandum and Order is such a warning that such will occur in future similar situations — it is hereby

ORDERED that the defendants' Answer is stricken; and it is further hereby

ORDERED that defendants shall file an answer or answers to the Complaint not later than twenty (20) days after the entry of this Order.

NOTES AND QUESTIONS

(1) *Plaintiff's Strategy in Pleading a Federal Complaint.* Federal plaintiffs often plead in greater detail than the Rules require, since the defendants must respond to each allegation. By using separate paragraphs to set out each individual allegation of fact that the defendant in good faith must admit, the plaintiff may be able to prod the defendant into admissions that will establish these facts early. However, the plaintiffs usually stay with broad and general language in pleading allegations that are at the heart of the claim (*e.g.*, allegations of the defendant's actions in a negligence case). This latter strategy helps to avoid variances between allegations and proof.

(2) *Is There Justification for the General Denial?* The defendant, after all, has only twenty days to answer the complaint under the Rules, and therefore may not have had time to investigate the claims fully. The plaintiff has a strategic motivation to press the defendant with a complaint containing a large array of facts that should be admitted. If the plaintiff amends the complaint (as happens in a large percentage of cases), the defendant will be required to answer again. In any event, the particulars of the defendant's contentions can be specified through discovery or a pretrial order. Are these arguments persuasive justifications for the allowance of a more generous general denial (as often used in state courts) instead of the federal requirement of early specific admissions and denials (and the use of a general denial only when the pleader is denying every allegation)?

[C] Affirmative Defenses

NOTE: WHAT IS AN AFFIRMATIVE DEFENSE?

The affirmative defense is a modern version of the common law plea in confession and avoidance. It is also sometimes called the "defense of new matter." Rather than denying or rebutting an element of the plaintiff's claim, the affirmative defense adds a new fact or set of facts that defeats the claim even if the plaintiff proves all of the elements. Rule 8(c) lists certain affirmative defenses, of which contributory negligence, estoppel, fraud, limitations, and waiver are among the most common. By definition, a denial is insufficient to raise an affirmative defense; it must be set forth affirmatively. In general, the burden of proving the elements of the defense is also assigned to the defendant. Consider the following case.

GOMEZ v. TOLEDO
446 U.S. 635 (1980)

MR. JUSTICE MARSHALL delivered the opinion of the Court.

The question presented is whether, in an action brought under 42 U.S.C. § 1983 against a public official whose position might entitle him to qualified immunity, a plaintiff must allege that the official has acted in bad faith in order to state a claim for relief or, alternatively, whether the defendant must plead good faith as an affirmative defense.

I

Petitioner Carlos Rivera Gomez brought this action against respondent, the Superintendent of the Police of the Commonwealth of Puerto Rico, contending that respondent had violated his right to procedural due process by discharging him from employment with the Police Department's Bureau of Criminal Investigation. Basing jurisdiction on 28 U.S.C. § 1343(3), petitioner alleged the following facts in his complaint. Petitioner had been employed as an agent with the Puerto Rican police since 1968. In April 1975, he submitted a sworn statement to his supervisor in which he asserted that two other agents had offered false evidence for use in a criminal case under their investigation. As a result of this statement, petitioner was immediately transferred from the Criminal Investigation Corps for the Southern Area to Police Headquarters in San Juan, and a few weeks later to the Police Academy in Gurabo, where he was given no investigative authority. In the meantime respondent ordered an investigation of petitioner's claims, and the Legal Division of the Police Department concluded that all of petitioner's factual allegations were true.

[Gomez's complaint further alleged that Gomez was charged with wiretaping, then suspended and discharged by Superintendent Toledo. It alleged that the charge against Gomez ultimately was found not to have been based on probable cause and that he was ordered reinstated to his job.]

Based on the foregoing factual allegations, petitioner brought this suit for damages, contending that his discharge violated his right to procedural due process, and that it had caused him anxiety, embarrassment, and injury to his reputation in the community. In his answer, respondent denied a number of petitioner's allegations of fact and asserted several affirmative defenses. Respondent then moved to dismiss the complaint for failure to state a cause of action, *see* Fed. Rule Civ. Proc. 12(b)(6), and the District Court granted the motion. Observing that respondent was entitled to qualified immunity for acts done in good faith within the scope of his official duties, it concluded that petitioner was required to plead as part of his claim for relief that, in committing the actions alleged, respondent was motivated by bad faith. The absence of any such allegation, it held, required dismissal of the complaint. The United States Court of Appeals for the First Circuit affirmed. . . .

II

Section 1983 provides a cause of action for "the deprivation of any rights, privileges, or immunities secured by the Constitution and laws" by any person acting "under color of any statute, ordinance, regulation, custom, or usage, of any State or Territory. 42 U.S.C. § 1983." . . . As remedial legislation, § 1983 is to be construed generously to further its primary purpose. . . .

In certain limited circumstances, we have held that public officers are entitled to a qualified immunity from damages liability under § 1983. This conclusion has been based on an unwillingness to infer from legislative silence a congressional intention to abrogate immunities that were both "well established at common law" and "compatible with the purposes of the Civil Rights Act." . . .

Nothing in the language or legislative history of § 1983, however, suggests that in an action brought against a public official whose position might entitle him to immunity if he acted in good faith, a plaintiff must allege bad faith in order to state a claim for relief. By the plain terms of § 1983, two — and only two — allegations are required in order to state a cause of action under that statute. First, the plaintiff must allege that some person has deprived him of a federal right. Second, he must allege that the person who has deprived him of that right acted under color of state or territorial law. . . .

Moreover, this Court has never indicated that qualified immunity is relevant to the existence of the plaintiff's cause of action; instead we have described it as a defense available to the official in question. . . . Since qualified immunity is a defense, the burden of pleading it rests with the defendant. *See* Fed. Rule Civ. Proc. 8(c) (defendant must plead any "matter constituting an avoidance or affirmative defense"). . . . It is for the official to claim that his conduct was justified by an objectively reasonable belief that it was lawful. We see no basis for imposing on the plaintiff an obligation to anticipate such a defense by stating in his complaint that the defendant acted in bad faith.

Our conclusion as to the allocation of the burden of pleading is supported by the nature of the qualified immunity defense. As our decisions make clear, whether such immunity has been established depends on facts peculiarly within the knowledge and control of the defendant. Thus we have stated that "[i]t is the existence of reasonable grounds for the belief formed at the time and in light of all the circumstances, coupled with good-faith belief, that affords a basis for qualified immunity of executive officers for acts performed in the course of official conduct." . . .

. . . There may be no way for a plaintiff to know in advance whether the official has such a belief or, indeed, whether he will even claim that he does. The existence of a subjective belief will frequently turn on factors which a plaintiff cannot reasonably be expected to know. For example, the official's belief may be based on state or local law, advice of counsel, administrative practice, or some other factor of which the official alone is aware. To impose the pleading burden on the plaintiff would ignore this elementary fact and be contrary to the established practice in analogous areas of the law.

The decision of the Court of Appeals is reversed, and the case is remanded to that court for further proceedings consistent with this opinion.

Mr. Justice Rehnquist joins the opinion of the Court, reading it as he does to leave open the issue of the burden of persuasion, as opposed to the burden of pleading, with respect to a defense of qualified immunity.

PROBLEM D

DEFENSIVE THEORIES NOT LISTED IN RULE 8(c) — WHICH ONES ARE AFFIRMATIVE DEFENSES? Rule 8(c) does not purport to be an exhaustive list of affirmative defenses. In fact, whether a defensive theory is an affirmative defense is determined by reference to the substantive law governing the claim. Considerations of fairness and policy may enter into the determination. *Jicarilla Apache Tribe v. Andrus*, 687 F.2d 1324 (10th Cir. 1982). Consider the following examples:

(a) *Novation.* A "novation," in the law of contracts, is "a mutual agreement . . . for the discharge of a valid existing obligation by the substitution of a new valid obligation on the part of the debtor . . . ." Is novation an affirmative defense? *See Charles Kahn & Co. v. Sobery,* 355 F. Supp. 156 (E.D. Mo. 1972) ("The burden of establishing that a novation occurred is upon the party claiming" it, "and in this regard [it] is an affirmative defense under Rule 8(c)").

(b) *Unavoidable Accident.* The doctrine of unavoidable accident is to the effect that if a natural occurrence that could not be avoided was the actual and sole cause of the plaintiff's injuries, the defendant cannot have been guilty of negligence proximately causing those injuries. Is unavoidable accident an affirmative defense? *See Sanden v. Mayo Clinic*, 495 F.2d 221 (8th Cir. 1974) (held, no; "a defense that merely negates some element of plaintiff's *prima facie* case is not a true affirmative defense and need not be pleaded." The defendant may introduce evidence of unavoidable accident, and obtain jury instructions if provided by law on that subject, without pleading the doctrine).

NOTES AND QUESTIONS

(1) *State Law Conflicting with Rule 8(c).* In a diversity case, what happens if Rule 8(c) lists an "affirmative defense" that is not an affirmative defense under state law? The cases are inconsistent. In *Amelio v. Yazoo Mfg. Co.*, 98 F.R.D. 691 (N.D. Ill. 1983), the court struck the defendant's pleading of contributory negligence. Although this defense is listed in Rule 8(c) as an affirmative one, Illinois law made it only a partial defense, and therefore the court concluded that it could be raised in federal court without being pleaded. *See also Sundstrand Corp. v. Standard Kollsman Indus., Inc.*, 488 F.2d 807 (7th Cir. 1973) (defendant need plead affirmatively only those defenses upon which it bears burden of proof under governing state law). But the majority, and better reasoned, view appears to be that Rule 8(c) is a procedural requirement, governing which party must plead a given defensive theory, even though state law may allocate the burden of proof to the other party, and even though the court will follow the state burden of proof at trial. *Gilmore v. Witschorek*, 411 F. Supp. 491 (E.D. Ill. 1976) (where state law requires plaintiff to prove freedom from contributory negligence, that burden is governed by state law under the *Erie* doctrine, but 8(c) requires defendant to plead the defense).

(2) *Sufficiency of Pleading: "Notice" Pleading.* The adequacy of the defendant's pleadings to raise a given affirmative defense is tested by standards similar to those governing the complaint. *E.g., Barnwell & Hays, Inc. v. Sloan*, 564 F.2d 254 (8th Cir. 1977) (plea of waiver, even though it did not use the word "waiver" but instead alleged the existence of an oral agreement relied on by the defendant, was adequate because it "apprised" the plaintiff of the defense).

(3) *What Do You Do When You Are Unsure Whether Your Theory Is an Affirmative Defense?* If in doubt, plead the defensive theory affirmatively. As the above materials make clear, there is often room for doubt. The paper on which your secretary types the defense is cheap, but paying a malpractice judgment because your client was precluded from offering evidence of the defense at trial is expensive.

[D] The Plaintiff's Reply

What Is a Reply? A reply is the modern derivative of the plaintiff's replication in common law pleading. Under Federal Rule 7, a plaintiff is required to file a reply "to a counterclaim designated as a counterclaim"; this kind of reply resembles an answer to a complaint, and indeed Rule 7 refers to this pleading as "an answer to a counterclaim." The Rule otherwise does not require or allow the filing of a reply unless "the court orders one." In this situation, the reply probably will take the form of responses denying or avoiding the answer. If the court does not order a reply, Rule 8(b)(6) says that the allegations of the answer automatically will be "considered denied or avoided."

Avoidance of Matters in the Answer. The utility of having the court order a reply to the answer can best be illustrated by example. Say that the plaintiff has pleaded a contract claim; the defendant has responded with an answer stating the affirmative defense of limitations; and the plaintiff avoids the defense by arguing that the limitations period is tolled by the absence of the defendant from the jurisdiction. But this "tolling" argument is a kind of "affirmative defense to the affirmative defense," and so if the plaintiff is not required to plead it, how will the defendant find out about it? Possibly through discovery; but it seems inappropriate to require the defendant to conduct discovery on every basic legal theory that the plaintiff might invoke at trial. A requirement of a reply would place the same duty of pleading upon the plaintiff that is placed on the defendant. Another example: The plaintiff pleads a negligence claim; the defendant asserts the affirmative defense that the claim has been released; and the plaintiff plans to prove at trial that the release is avoidable because it was procured by fraud. By ordering a reply, the court could ensure that this matter in avoidance would be pleaded.

Should a Reply Be Required for Every Matter in Avoidance of an Affirmative Defense? Some jurisdictions, while following the federal principle that denials of allegations in the answer are deemed automatically to exist, require the plaintiff affirmatively to plead new matters that he plans to offer in avoidance of the defendant's affirmative defenses. Should the Federal Rules be amended to provide the same?

§ 5.04 Appendix Drafting the Answer

ANSWER IN *GEORGE MILLER CO. v. COMPUDATA, INC.*

[Reproduced above in Subsection E of the Appendix to Chapter 2]

For a concrete example of a federal answer, read (or re-read) the answer of Defendant Compudata in *George Miller Co. v. Compudata, Inc.*, reproduced above in the Appendix to Chapter 2, Subsection E. Notice how the answer is structured, in separate paragraphs, with the two defenses separated. Notice also that the admissions or denials are responsive to every allegation in the complaint; *i.e.*, no allegation is left unaddressed. Notice the separate pleading of the limitations defense: Why is this theory set out distinctly from the admissions and denials?

§ 5.05 Devices for Deterring Abuse of Liberal Pleading Rules

Read Fed. R. Civ. P. 23.1 and Rule 11.

[A] Older Approaches: Verification, etc.

SUROWITZ v. HILTON HOTELS CORP., 383 U.S. 363 (1966). Dora Surowitz was a Polish immigrant with little education. From her work as a seamstress, she earned money which she invested in stock of Hilton Hotels Corporation. One day, she received a communication from Hilton disclosing its plan to purchase a large amount of its own stock, and she promptly consulted her son-in-law. He happened to have an economics degree from Columbia and a law degree from Harvard and was named, appropriately enough, Irving Brilliant. Brilliant undertook an investigation of the transaction. He concluded that it reflected fraudulent activities by officers and directors of Hilton that had cost the corporation millions of dollars. Brilliant explained the scheme to Dora Surowitz. She agreed to file a shareholder's derivative suit, which is a type of action that seeks to recover from corporate employees for the benefit of the corporation.

Fed. R. Civ. P. 23.1 provides that a shareholder's derivative complaint "must be verified." The verification requirement was imposed in an effort to prevent "strike suits," or suits by obstreperous shareholders seeking to influence corporate policy by the sheer cost of unmeritorious litigation.

The defendants promptly took Ms. Surowitz's deposition. Her answers showed that she "did not understand the complaint at all . . . and in fact in signing the verification she had merely relied on what her son-in-law had explained to her about the facts in the case." The District Court accordingly dismissed the complaint as a "sham," and the Court of Appeals affirmed. The Supreme Court reversed: "We cannot construe . . . the Federal Rules as compelling courts to summarily dismiss [c]ases like this where grave charges of fraud are shown by the record to be based on reasonable beliefs growing out of careful investigation. . . . [The verification requirement], like the other civil rules, was written to further, not defeat the ends of justice."

NOTES AND QUESTIONS

(1) *The Meaning of "Verification" (What Is "Verified"?).* The Federal Rule requires only that the complaint in a shareholder's derivative suit be "verified," without explaining what that means. After *Surowitz v. Hilton Hotels*, what does it mean? Is it a requirement that the plaintiff personally know that the allegations are true, or that the plaintiff has a reasonable basis for believing them to be true, or that the plaintiff subjectively and in good faith thinks they are true, or that plaintiff thinks they might be true? The effectiveness of the Rule in achieving its purpose would obviously be different under each interpretation.

(2) *The Effectiveness of Verification.* Consider the following comments from D. Siegel, *New York Practice* 281 (1978):

> The requirement of verification is supposed to encourage honesty in pleading. A false verification is technically a perjury, but district attorneys seldom become involved, excusing themselves on grounds of more pressing problems. Earlier in our legal history the requirement of swearing may have been underwritten by a genuine fear of hell, but hell has little impact on New York practice. Quite the contrary. Verification, in a word, has nothing more to recommend it than the Legislature.

(3) *State Rules Requiring Verification.* In federal court, the general rule is that pleadings need not be verified, and requirements to that effect (such as Rule 23.1) are exceptions. Some states, however, have rules requiring numerous kinds of pleadings to be verified. *E.g.*, Tex. R. Civ. P. 93 (lengthy list, ranging from denials of existence of a partnership or corporation to pleadings asserting usury or lack or failure of consideration). New York and California also have verification rules.

[B] Rule 11: Certifications and Sanctions

NOTE ON THE MODERN APPROACH: RULE 11

The Certification Requirement. In *Surowitz v. Hilton Hotels Corp.*, above, an earlier version of Rule 11 was applicable. That rule provided that the attorney's signature on a pleading automatically constituted a "certification" that, among other things, the attorney believed there was "good ground to support it." That standard was vague and subjective; it was rare that violations could clearly be established. The burden on the plaintiff, in *Surowitz*, came from Rule 23.1, which applies only to shareholders' derivative suits. The court interpreted the rule as satisfied because the plaintiff had acted in reliance upon a reasonable investigation by her attorney. Question: Why not require this sort of investigation in every case? Answer: Rule 11 has been amended to require it.

The Rule 11 Certifications: An Objective Test? In 1983, Rule 11 was amended to make an attorney's signature an implied, automatic certification of several matters. The most important is that "to the best of the person's knowledge, information, and belief, formed after an inquiry reasonable under the circumstances," the allegations have "evidentiary support" (or are likely to, after discovery), and "are warranted by existing law" (or by a nonfrivolous argument for a change in existing law). The requirement of "reasonable" inquiry made Rule 11 a potent force. It set forth an objective standard. That is, an attorney acting in ignorance of facts and law that would be disclosed by a reasonable investigation could not take refuge in good faith or purity of heart alone.

"An Appropriate Sanction," Discretionary Impositions, and the Later "Safe Harbor." Rule 11 also provides that if a paper is signed in violation of the Rule, "the court may . . . impose an appropriate sanction . . . ." At one point in time, the terms of the Rule were mandatory; the Rule required the imposition of a sanction whenever a violation was found. *See* Schwartzer, *Sanctions under the New Federal Rule 11 — A Closer Look*, 104 F.R.D. 181 (1985). The 1993 amendments removed the mandatory requirement by substituting the word "may," thus giving the judge discretion. The amendments also introduced a requirement of notice and time to cure as a "safe harbor" or protection for the pleader. Whether Rule 11 sanctions are too loosely allowed, or too narrowly restricted, is a matter of continuing controversy.

The Three Historically Sequential Versions of Rule 11. To recapitulate, Rule 11 has had three different versions. To understand the controversy about sanctions, you have to know all three. (1) Before 1983, Rule 11 required proof of subjective bad faith. It had to be shown that the attorney actually did not believe the pleading was proper. This standard meant that the rule rarely could be enforced. (2) Therefore, in 1983, the rule was amended so that an attorney whose improper pleading was not based on a "reasonable investigation" was subject to a mandatory sanction. This was an objective, negligence-like standard. But later, the mandatory sanction was thought to be too draconian, and so (3) in 1993, a third version of the rule required notice and an opportunity to cure, and made sanctions discretionary. (Perhaps there is an argument that Rule 11 is now too weak.)

[1] An Objective Standard Requiring a "Reasonable Inquiry": The 1983 Amendment to Rule 11

EASTWAY CONSTRUCTION CORP. v. CITY OF NEW YORK, 762 F.2d 243 (2d Cir. 1985). This was one of the early influential decisions under the 1983 version of Rule 11, which defined violations objectively and prescribed mandatory sanctions. Eastway Construction Corporation was excluded from contracts on New York City construction projects after conduct of its officers involving bribes and defaults. This exclusion put Eastway out of business. Eastway then brought this action, "[s]omewhat desperately, perhaps," alleging that the City and other defendants were guilty of antitrust and civil rights violations. Judge Weinstein granted summary judgment for the defendants because (1) there was no basis for Eastway to claim the type of injury required for an antitrust claim (namely injury to the competitive market, as opposed to injury to an individual firm such as Eastway) and (2) a company merely hoping to obtain public contracts could not claim a property interest that could give rise to a due process or civil rights violation. The City, which had expended public funds defending against this groundless suit, moved for Rule 11 sanctions. But Judge Weinstein refused to impose sanctions on Eastway, explaining that "I can't say this was a frivolous case."

The Court of Appeals reversed and remanded the case to Judge Weinstein with orders to impose an "appropriate sanction." The court emphasized that after the 1983 amendments, the standard for determining a Rule 11 violation was objective reasonableness, not the more lax, subjective good faith standard that had applied prior to that time. Moreover, sanctions under the 1983 amendments were mandatory (a feature which since has been changed by the more recent 1993 amendments):

> The addition [to Rule 11] of the words "formed after reasonable inquiry" demand that we revise our inquiry. . . . No longer is it enough for an attorney to claim that he acted in good faith, or that he personally was unaware of the groundless nature of an argument or claim. For the language of the new Rule explicitly and unambiguously imposes an affirmative duty on each attorney to conduct a reasonable inquiry into the viability of a pleading before it is signed. Simply put, good faith no longer provides the safe harbor it once did. . . .
>
> [Moreover,] sanctions shall be imposed against an attorney and on his client [for any violation]. [Note: This mandatory-sanctions feature was a consequence of the wording of the 1983 version, and it has since been changed by the 1993 amendments].
>
> In framing this [objective] standard, we do not intend to stifle the enthusiasm or chill the creativity that is the very lifeblood of the law. . . . Courts must strive to avoid the wisdom of hindsight in determining whether a pleading was valid when signed, and all doubts must be resolved in favor of the signer. But where it is patently clear that the claim has absolutely no chance of success under the existing precedents, and where no reasonable argument can be advanced to extend, modify or reverse the law as it stands, Rule 11 has been violated. . . .
>
> Returning to the facts of this appeal, we cannot say that Eastway or its counsel acted in subjective bad faith. . . . [W]e can say, however, that its claim of an antitrust violation, . . . without any allegation of an antitrust injury, was destined to fail. [Separately, the court analyzed the civil rights claim, which similarly was unfounded.] Moreover, a competent attorney, after reasonable inquiry, would have had to reach the same conclusion.

On remand, the City showed that a reasonable attorney's fee for responding to Eastway's unfounded claims was $58,550, and it sought recovery of this sum as a sanction. Judge Weinstein, however, regarded Eastway's suit as only "marginally frivolous," and so he imposed a sanction of only $1,000, requiring the City to bear the rest of its $58,500 loss. The Court of Appeals again reversed. It held that this $1,000 sanction was an abuse of discretion, and it ordered Judge Weinstein to impose a sanction of $10,000 "to serve the . . . purpose of the rule." *Eastway Construction Corp. v. City of New York,* 821 F.2d 121 (2d Cir. 1987).

[Question: after the 1993 amendments, which replaced the mandatory requirement that the judge "shall" impose sanctions with a discretionary provision that the judge "may" do so, would the result have been different?]

NOTES AND QUESTIONS

(1) *Was Good Faith Relevant under the 1983 Rule? The Case of the Litigious Law Student: Heimbaugh v. City and County of San Francisco, 591 F. Supp. 1573 (N.D. Cal. 1984).* Heimbaugh had just finished law school and taken the bar examination. He filed a suit claiming that prohibitions upon his playing softball in a portion of a public park violated his constitutional rights. The court found this argument to be unwarranted by existing law or by a good faith argument for modification of existing law. It assessed a sanction against Heimbaugh pursuant to Rule 11 for the defendant's expenses in successfully opposing his frivolous suit, but because of Heimbaugh's "economic situation" and "inexperience" the court limited the sanction to $50.

What, then, was the relevance of good faith under the 1983 Rule? As Heimbaugh's case indicates, perhaps good faith or other subjective mental states ("inexperience") could affect the sanction that was "appropriate." On the other hand, is this approach justified? If a litigant acts with pure heart, but acts stupidly and recklessly, should the opposing party be deprived of reimbursement for its expenses when the pleadings are frivolous?

(2) *What Is a "Reasonable" Inquiry?* Just how much information must a litigant have had, to avoid sanctions under Rule 11? *See generally* Shaffer, *Rule 11 and the Prefiling Duty*, Nat. L.J. Aug. 18, 1986, at 28, col. 1. In *General Accident Ins. Co. of America v. Fidelity & Deposit Co. of Md.*, 598 F. Supp. 1223 (E.D. Pa. 1984), the defendant filed a third-party complaint that incorporated the allegations made in the plaintiff's original complaint. The court denied sanctions on the ground that the defendant had not merely pleaded the third-party allegations in sole reliance on the original complaint but had at least minimally discussed those allegations with officials of the plaintiff before filing the third-party complaint. On the other hand, in *Florida Monument Builders v. All Faiths Memorial Gardens*, 605 F. Supp. 1324 (S.D. Fla. 1984), the plaintiffs filed an antitrust complaint with no independent investigation, basing allegations of conspiracy solely upon the beliefs and experience of one of the plaintiff's attorneys derived from similar litigation in other parts of the country. The court upheld a sanction in the amount of $25,000 assessed against the plaintiff and its attorneys jointly. The cases produce mixed results when the facts are difficult to investigate or are known primarily to the opponents. *E.g.*, *Mohammed v. Union Carbide Corp.*, 606 F. Supp. 252 (E.D. Mich. 1985) (difficulty of investigating conspiracy and monopolization lessens the effort required for "reasonable" inquiry). What about a technically complex case in which reliance on an expert is necessary? *Compare Anderson v. Cryovac, Inc.*, 96 F.R.D. 431 (D. Mass. 1983) (no sanctions where plaintiff's attorney testified that he checked the complaint line by line with his retained expert and was advised that each line was justified), *with Duncan v. WJLA-TV, Inc.*, 106 F.R.D. 4 (D.D.C. 1984) (sanctions assessed where pleading was based on information from unqualified expert and where plaintiff and her counsel had failed to investigate the "expert's" qualifications).

(3) *Under the 1983 Rule, the Pleader Was Well Advised to Document the "Reasonable Inquiry."* Consider the following advice:

First of all, before signing any pleading that you have reason to believe, realistically or unrealistically, may subject you to a motion for sanctions, specifically take Rule 11 into account and review it. This is important not so much as an exercise but so that one can file an affidavit when resisting Rule 11 sanctions. . . .

In this regard you should determine the steps taken to make the reasonable inquiry required by the rule. . . .

Consider the source of the information you are relying upon in filing a certain pleading. In many instances the information must come from the client. What other sources of information besides the client are there, and, as a practical matter, is any additional inquiry necessary or fruitful? Be sure . . . to lay out in detail the nature of the inquiry or the reason that the inquiry was limited. . . .

Dombroff, *Attorneys in Affirming Pleadings Risk Sanctions*, Nat. L.J., Jan. 27, 1986, at 15, col. 3.

What other steps should the attorney take? First, before filing suit, a plaintiff's lawyer should write a demand letter to the opponent. The letter should invite response. Second, the attorney should thoroughly cross-examine the client and seek to verify the information thus received. Third, if appropriate, the attorney should employ an expert whose credentials have been examined. Fourth, the attorney should undertake at least minimal legal research. Fifth, the attorney should promptly undertake discovery and react to information revealing the inaccuracy of any allegations or denials.

(4) *Determining the Amount of Monetary Sanctions.* Sometimes the amount of a monetary sanction is very large. Consider, *e.g., Dayan v. McDonald's Corp.*, 126 Ill. App. 3d 11, 466 N.E.2d 945 (1984) (assessing over $1.8 million sanction under Illinois state rule, after 65-day trial with 1,072 photographs showed plaintiff's allegations to be baseless). The award of over $1.8 million is unusual in amount, but the appellate court emphasized that it was justified by proof of the amount and reasonableness of actual attorney's fees and expenses incurred by McDonald's. The Illinois provision at issue limited recovery to fees and expenses only, but Federal Rule 11 does not; it merely provides for an "appropriate" sanction.

(5) *Non-Monetary Sanctions.* Rule 11 provides for sanctions which "may include" expenses, but it is not confined by its terms to expenses, or for that matter to monetary penalties. Can the court dismiss or grant default judgment for a serious violation? Can (or should) it issue an opinion or order publicly reprimanding the attorney?

(6) *Did the 1983 Version of the Rule Discourage Novel or Difficult Claims?* There always was concern that, in discouraging frivolous claims, Rule 11 would also discourage attorneys from bringing claims that were difficult, novel, or ambiguous but that ought to be aired in the courts. *See* Note, *Reasonable Inquiry Under Rule 11 — Is the Stop, Look and Investigate Requirement a Litigant's Roadblock?*, 18 Ind. L. Rev. 751 (1982). However, judges generally were willing to take into account the novelty or difficulty of the claim. *E.g., John S. Griffith Constr. Co. v. Southern Calif. Cement Masons Negotiating Comm.*, 607 F. Supp. 809 (C.D. Cal. 1984) (where motion to dismiss for lack of jurisdiction was denied as a matter of law but had presented question of first impression, sanctions denied); *Ank Shipping Co. v. Seychelles Nat. Commodity Co.*, 596 F. Supp. 1455 (S.D.N.Y. 1984) (although claims were barred by *res judicata* from disposition of prior suit, sanctions denied because efforts to escape *res judicata* were at least arguable). These cases should be contrasted with such cases as *Booker v. City of Atlanta*, 586 F. Supp. 340 (N.D. Ga. 1984), in which the city's attorneys pleaded a theory that had been

rejected in a lengthy and unbroken line of previous cases, and they failed to come forward with any justification in response to a motion to show cause. The court assessed the plaintiff's expenses against the attorneys themselves.

(7) The Volume of Sanctions Motions under "Old" (1983) Rule 11. The 1983 version of Rule 11 generated an entire new field of satellite litigation over the criteria for deciding whether a pleading or motion was improper and what sanction was warranted when the Rule was violated. It is impossible to say how much needless litigation the Rule discouraged. However, the Rule certainly became a new weapon in the adversary system, leading to more than 700 court decisions in the five years after its amendment. Margolick, "At the Bar," *New York Times*, Mar. 11, 1988. There were many new commentaries on the Rule. *See* Miller, *The New Certification Standard under Rule 11*, 130 F.R.D. 479 (1990); Burbank, *The Transformation of American Civil Procedure: The Example of Rule 11*, 137 U. Pa. L. Rev. 1925 (1989); *e.g.*, Schwarzer, *Rule 11 Revisited*, 101 Harv. L. Rev. 1013 (1988); Maute, *Sporting Theory of Justice: Taming Adversary Zeal With a Logical Sanctions Doctrine*, 20 Conn. L. Rev. 7 (1987) (arguing that a logical, carefully implemented sanctions doctrine, including Rule 11, is needed and desirable to deter litigation misconduct); Nelken, *Sanctions Under Amended Federal Rule 11 — Some "Chilling" Problems in the Struggle Between Compensation and Punishment*, 74 Geo. L.J. 1313 (1986); Note, *Plausible Pleadings: Developing Standards for Rule 11 Sanctions*, 100 Harv. L. Rev. 630 (1987); Note, *An Attorney's Primer on Federal Rule of Civil Procedure 11*, 23 Tulsa L.J. 149 (1987).

[2] Dissatisfaction with Automatic Mandatory Sanctions

NOTES AND QUESTIONS

(1) *An Anxiety-Provoking Case under 1983's Rule 11: Business Guides, Inc. v. Chromatic Communications Enterprises, Inc., 498 U.S. 533 (1991).* In this case, the lower courts imposed sanctions against both a represented party and its attorneys. The Supreme Court affirmed the sanctions against the represented party, with the law firm having already gone bankrupt. The controversy began when Business Guides sought injunctive relief against Chromatic for allegedly copying its business directory. Business Guides claimed that its directory included bits of false information, called "seeds," and that ten entries in Chromatic's directory were copies of these seeds, leading to the conclusion that the directory had been copied. After various maneuvers, however, it turned out that 9 out of the 10 "seeds" were not seeds at all, because they contained no incorrect information. It took the District Court's law clerk only one hour to telephone the allegedly seeded businesses and to discover the correctness of the entries.

Meanwhile, Chromatic had spent $13,865.66 in opposing Business Guides's unfounded allegations. The magistrate recommended this amount as a sanction against Business Guides. Then, after deciding that the law firm had received enough information so that it should have ceased to rely on its client's statements about the seeds, the magistrate recommended that the sanctions be imposed on the lawyers too.

The Supreme Court affirmed as to the party sanctions. It did not review the recommended sanctions against the law firm (which never had been imposed because of the bankruptcy stay), but its opinion recounted the facts about those sanctions. The Court emphasized the mandatory nature of the 1983 Rule, and it relied on the text that required sanctions for signed papers, since Business Guides's personnel had signed some of the papers supporting the injunctive request.

Four justices dissented and concluded, "[P]atience . . . must be an attribute of the judicial system . . . . Our annoyance at spurious and frivolous claims . . . must not drive us to adopt interpretations of the rules that make honest litigants fear to petition the courts."

(2) *An Anxiety-Provoking Case Because It Focused on the Investigation that the Signer Could Have Performed, Rather than on the Investigation the Signer Actually Did Perform.* The District Court had characterized Business Guides's suit as a "mistake," a characterization the Supreme Court adopted. Presumably, however, a "mistake" alone is not enough to make a Rule 11 violation, even under the 1983 version. It appears that certain individuals in a large company possessed information that other individuals (and the company's attorneys) did not possess, and the signers never knew to inquire of the individuals who possessed the relevant knowledge. But isn't that situation, in which the "right hand doesn't know what the left hand is doing," common in what the Court called a "sophisticated" corporation? The Court also emphasizes that the lawyers later received information leading them to abandon three seeds. However, aren't a party and its attorney often justified in continuing to believe the thrust of the information they generated at the beginning of suit, in spite of some amount of contradiction (because contradictory evidence abounds in litigation)?

Neither the party nor its attorney conceived of the investigation that the District Court's law clerk conducted, *i.e.*, a process of telephoning the listed businesses. But consider the propriety and fairness of a district court, itself undertaking an investigation, in secret, and then comparing its investigation to that of the signer of the pleadings. To some of the authors of this casebook, these circumstances combine to make this decision an anxiety-provoking one for both clients and attorneys.

(3) *To What Extent Can an Attorney Rely on a Client's Representations of Fact (and to What Extent Does Rule 11 Make the Client an "Adversary")?* Notice that *Business Guides*, above, raises serious questions about the extent to which an attorney may believe the client. Does Rule 11 force the attorney to interview a client as an adversary? Furthermore, when the opponent's motion for sanctions expressly or implicitly raises the issue whether the attorney, the client, or both were responsible for a possible violation, attorney and client may be adversaries in fact, with a real conflict of interest that may require the attorney's withdrawal.

(4) *Should Amendment of the Rules Change Either the Holding or Result in Business Guides?* After this decision, the 1993 amendments limited the effect of the certification requirements to "an attorney or unrepresented party." This amendment would appear to change the holding: Business Guides would not trigger liability for itself merely because it signed papers negligently. Is it appropriate to exempt from sanctions a party who actually does sign court papers, merely because of representation by counsel? On the other hand, the amendment would still impose sanctions on "parties determined . . . to be responsible for a violation." But "responsible" is not defined, and perhaps it could be interpreted to depend upon the party's failure to conduct a reasonable inquiry. In that event, exempting the represented parties from the certification would make little difference, in that they would be held to substantially the same burden. Does the amendment, therefore, actually preserve the effect of *Business Guides*?

(5) *Should the Signer's Law Firm Also Be Subject to Sanctions (or Only the Signer Individually)?: Pavelic & LeFlore v. Marvel Entertainment Group, 493 U.S. 120 (1989).* In this case, the Supreme Court held that the text of then-existing Rule 11, in its 1983 version, did not permit sanctions against the law firm in which the violator was an

attorney; it permitted sanctions only against the signing attorney, individually. The firm benefits from the activities of the lawyer and arguably should have incentive to induce its members to comply with the Rules. The 1993 amendment reversed this result: even though the certification is done by an individual attorney, the amended rule provides for sanctions against responsible "law firms" as well as individuals. Indeed, the current version of Rule 11 states that, "Absent exceptional circumstances, a law firm must be held jointly responsible for a violation committed by its partner, associate, or employee." Is such a change appropriate? What "exceptional circumstances" would make a lawyer, but not the lawyer's law firm, "responsible"?

(6) *Should Withdrawal of the Pleading, or Voluntary Dismissal, Avoid Sanctions?: Cooter & Gell v. Hartmarx Corp., 496 U.S. 384 (1990).* In this case, the Supreme Court held that under the 1983 version, a voluntary dismissal did not deprive a District Court of jurisdiction over a Rule 11 violation by the dismissing plaintiff. "If a litigant could purge his violation of Rule 11 merely by taking a dismissal, he would lose all incentive to stop, think and investigate more carefully before serving and filing papers." Therefore, the Rule 11 violation had occurred the moment the offending pleading was filed, and it could not be eliminated by subsequent acts. Note that new Rule 11, with its safe harbor provisions, changes this process.

(7) *The Standard for Appellate Reversal — Abuse of Discretion, or De Novo Review?: Cooter & Gell, supra.* In *Cooter & Gell*, the Supreme Court also held that a District Court's finding of a violation or imposition of sanctions was to be reversed only if the District Judge had abused his discretion. Perhaps such a standard, deferring to the court's discretion, can be justified by the uniqueness of most Rule 11 compliance issues, which generally require resolution of factual or reasonableness questions. On the other hand, does an abuse-of-discretion standard hamper the appellate courts' ability to promote uniformity in the application of Rule 11, as compared to a standard by which the court of appeals would review the sanctions *de novo*?

(8) *The 21-Day "Safe Harbor' Notice Provision in the 1993 Amendments: Does It Protect Good-but-Mistaken Attorneys, or Does It Encourage Reckless Ones?* Perhaps, however, it would make sense to allow an attorney to avoid sanctions if he or she acts diligently to minimize the harm after being notified of a mistake. Therefore, the 1993 amendments have the effect of requiring the opposing attorney, before filing a motion for sanctions, to serve the motion first on the alleged offender, describing the specific conduct alleged as a violation; this change would nullify the sanctions motion if the violation is corrected within 21 days. Does it make sense for the Rule to include such a notice-and-grace-period provision, or does that approach simply encourage thoughtless or even intentional violations? [Note: Texas once had a rule requiring a court finding of violation, followed by a refusal to withdraw the offending pleading, before sanctions could be imposed; but the rule proved largely ineffective and was amended to delete this step. *See* Tex. R. Civ. P. 13.]

(9) *Minimizing Sanctions: Should There Be a "Least Sufficient Sanction" Limit?* The current version of Rule 11 states that sanctions "must be limited to what suffices to deter repetition of the conduct or comparable conduct by others similarly situated." What does this phraseology mean, and is it a useful limit?

(10) *But Maybe There's Another Side to All of This: Should Chromatic Not Recover the Damages It Suffered from the Negligent Conduct of Its Opponents, Who Imposed Costs on Chromatic by Filing Papers No Reasonable Person Would Have Filed?* An automobile driver, doctor, architect, or homeowner who negligently causes another person

to suffer damages generally is liable for the loss. By definition, a Rule 11 violator does the same, by failing to follow "reasonable" steps. Perhaps Chromatic, which suffered a loss caused by the unreasonable (negligent) conduct of Business Guides, in violation of the duties imposed by Rule 11, should recover its loss for the same reasons. Why are we resistant to the recovery of actual damages, caused by actual fault, in this situation? (Is it because the sanctions might be imposed on allegedly negligent attorneys, as opposed to members of other professions?)

[3] The 21-Day Safe Harbor and Limited, Discretionary Sanctions: The 1993 Amendments to Rule 11

NOTE ON THE 1993 AMENDMENTS TO RULE 11: IS IT BETTER — OR TOOTHLESS?

The controversy over Rule 11 led to its amendment in 1993. The most significant change was to make Rule 11 sanctions discretionary with the court [Rule 11(c)]. The amended rule also provided a "safe harbor." Under the safe harbor provision, once a motion for sanctions is served [but not yet filed], the alleged offender has 21 days to withdraw or correct the challenged paper or representation with no adverse consequences. Only if no corrective action is taken may the motion be filed with the court for further action [Rule 11(c)].

When the Supreme Court adopted the rule amendments, Justice Scalia filed a dissenting statement asserting that making sanctions discretionary and providing the safe harbor would "render the Rule toothless."

Other changes in the rule abandon the "snapshot" approach of judging a paper's merit only at the moment it is filed. Following the 1993 amendments, sanctions may be imposed for later advocating a position without sufficient basis although there was a sufficient basis for the position when the paper was filed [Rule 11(b)]. Sanctions are limited to "what suffices to deter repetition of the conduct or comparable conduct by others," and ordinarily monetary sanctions will be paid to the court, not the other party [Rule 11(c)(4)]. The amended rule does affect the result of several of the Supreme Court's Rule 11 cases. Law firms will ordinarily be held jointly responsible for violations of individual attorneys [Rule 11(c)(1)], overcoming *Pavelic & LeFlore v. Marvel Entertainment Group,* 493 U.S. 120 (1989), and there is a limitation on sanctioning represented parties for frivolous legal arguments [Rule 11(c)(5)(A)] that could have affected the outcome of *Business Guides, Inc. v. Chromatic Communications Enterprises, Inc.,* 498 U.S. 533 (1991). The result of the amendments has been a decrease in Rule 11 motions and sanction awards. Consider the following decision.

HADGES v. YONKERS RACING CORP.

48 F.3d 1320 (2d Cir. 1995)

[The District Court imposed sanctions against the plaintiff, George Hadges, and also against his well-known lawyer, the late William M. Kunstler. The underlying dispute centered on Hadges's efforts "to compel various racetracks and state agencies to permit him to pursue his career as a harness racehorse driver, trainer and owner." Hadges had submitted a sworn statement that 1993 was his "fifth year . . . out of work" due to a boycott and secret agreement among all the racetracks. Kunstler also submitted a signed memorandum of law, asserting that Hadges "has not worked for more than four years."

Defendant produced documents revealing that Hadges had in fact raced five times in 1991 and seven times in 1993, the last time within a month of submitting his affidavit. After defendant requested sanctions, Hadges admitted he had raced in 1991 and 1993 but said that he considered the races insignificant since he had earned less than $100 total over the two years. The trial judge imposed Rule 11 sanctions of $2,000 on Hadges and censured Kunstler for failing to make adequate inquiry as to the truth of Hadges' affidavits.

[The Second Circuit reversed both sanctions. With regard to Hadges, the court found that defendant Yonkers Racing Corp. ("YRC") had failed to comply with the revised procedural requirements of Rule 11, which created the 21-day safe harbor:]

In this case, YRC did not submit the sanction request separately from all other requests, and there is no evidence in the record indicating that YRC served Hadges with the request for sanctions 21 days before presenting it to the court. Thus, YRC denied Hadges the "safe-harbor" period that the current version of the Rule specifically mandates. . . . If Hadges had received the benefit of the safe-harbor period, the record indicates that he would have "withdrawn or appropriately corrected" his misstatements, thus avoiding sanctions altogether. . . . In addition to sanctioning Hadges for his factual representations, the district court ruled that sanctions were justified in part by the disqualification motion filed on Hadges's behalf. . . . In relying on the latter ground, the court imposed monetary sanctions on a represented party for making a legal contention that the court believed was not warranted by existing law or by a nonfrivolous argument for a change in existing law. Revised Rule 11 specifically prohibits imposition of monetary sanctions on the party on this basis. Fed.R.Civ.P. 11(b)(2) & [11(c)(5)(A)].

[The appellate court also rejected the possibility of imposing sanction on the trial court's own initiative. There was no proper order describing the specific conduct that appeared to violate the rule. Moreover, the court held:]

We doubt that sua sponte sanctions would have been justified here. The advisory committee note on the 1993 amendment specifically states that such sanctions "will ordinarily be [imposed] only in situations that are akin to a contempt of court." Hadges's conduct did not rise to that level.

[Kunstler's censure was inappropriate, the Second Circuit held, because he also did not receive the benefit of the safe-harbor rule. Furthermore, Kunstler's censure based on failing to adequately investigate the truth of Hadges's representations before submitting them to the court was inconsistent with established Second Circuit law and the amended Rule 11:]

The new version of Rule 11 makes it even clearer that an attorney is entitled to rely on the objectively reasonable representations of the client. No longer are attorneys required to certify that their representations are "well grounded in fact." The current version of the Rule requires only that an attorney conduct "an inquiry reasonable under the circumstances" into whether "factual contentions have evidentiary support." Fed.R.Civ.P. 11(b) & (b)(3). Thus, the new version of Rule 11 is in keeping with the emphasis . . . on looking to the record before imposing sanctions.

[According to the court of appeals, "It is clear that the record before the district court contained evidentiary support for Kunstler's incorrect statements."]

NOTES AND QUESTIONS

(1) *Do the Safe Harbor and Other 1993 Amendments Protect the Innovative-but-Mistaken Lawyer, or Do They Instead Shift to Innocent Litigants Costs Created by*

Bad-Faith and Reckless Rambos? Cases like this one (and attorneys who champion them) raise the most difficult kinds of Rule 11 issues. On the one hand, advocacy for persons such as Hadges, who claim they wrongfully have been shut out of the system, often involves innovative theories, controversial factual inferences, and arguments that force the lawyer out on a limb. The notice-and-cure provision, relaxed certification requirements, and limits on severity of sanctions probably reduce the deterrence of this kind of advocacy. On the other hand, somebody winds up paying the cost, and arguably it should not be the innocent litigant who faces an innovative but reckless pleading. Groundless litigation can be catastrophic, even ruinous, for some parties who are its victims (consider Chromatic, in the *Business Guides* case above). Such litigants may rightly consider that the safe harbor shifts to them the costs generated by the reckless Rambo who doesn't conduct a reasonable inquiry, and they may ask why they should pay for the investigation that the sloppy pleader should have done but didn't. Thus, the question is: Do the 1993 amendments strike the right balance?

(2) *When the Court, Rather than Counsel, Initiates Rule 11 Sanctions, Does the Standard Change?* Contrast *Jenkins v. Methodist Hospitals of Dallas, Inc.*, 478 F.3d 255 (5th Cir. 2007), with *In re Pennie & Edmonds, LLP*, 323 F.3d 86 (2d Cir. 2003). Under Rule 11(c)(3), a court may initiate a Rule 11 sanction proceeding on its own motion. However, as the Advisory Committee Notes to the 1993 Amendments explain, no "safe harbor" opportunity exists to withdraw or correct a submission challenged in such a court-initiated proceeding. In *Pennie & Edmonds*, the Second Circuit held that although the mental state generally applicable to liability for Rule 11 sanctions is objective unreasonableness, a different standard applies to court-initiated Rule 11 proceedings — at least for those proceedings initiated at a point in time when the challenged submission can no longer be corrected or withdrawn as part of the lawyer's response to the show cause order. Such circumstances, according to the Second Circuit, require the use of a subjective "bad faith" standard. The Fifth Circuit, in *Jenkins v. Methodist Hospitals of Dallas*, rejected this proposition, instead concluding that the same objective standard applies regardless of whether it is the court or counsel that initiates the sanction process. Which court reached the better result?

(3) *A Safe-Harbor Nightmare: The Clever, Persistent Bad-Faith Litigant.* Imagine that a litigant files an unfounded pleading with numerous complex factual allegations and issues of law. The opponent, at great expense, documents the errors in a 21-day notice. On the 20th day, the bad-faith litigant withdraws the offending pleading as is contemplated by Rule 11, thus avoiding sanctions. But the same litigant immediately files an amended pleading containing new, equally groundless allegations. Now the innocent opponent must begin the costly process of investigating the errors all over again (and perhaps this is exactly what the bad-faith litigant intended)! Does Rule 11 provide a practical solution? [See the next section for other sanction doctrines, although probably none can completely address this problem in the real world.]

(4) *The Other Side of the Issue: Reducing the Sometimes Excessive Costs of Complying With the Earlier, More Severe Version of Rule 11.* But the safe harbor has advantages. Experienced litigators immediately noticed the increased costs associated with Rule 11 after the 1983 amendments. To avoid being blindsided by the effects of their own innocent misapprehensions, they redundantly investigated even facts that were not likely to be disputed and law that seemed well established, driving up costs for their clients and pricing some clients out of the market. Do the 1993 amendments seem an appropriate means to reduce this effect?

(5) *The Expansions in the 1993 Amendments: Liability for "Responsible" Parties and Firms and for "Advocating" Pleadings — O'Brien v. Alexander, 101 F.3d 1479 (2d Cir. 1996).* But the 1993 Amendments are not purely pleader-friendly. There is new authority to sanction parties and law firms that are "responsible" for violations. "Responsible" is not defined in the Rule, but Rule 11(c)(1) states that a law firm should be held responsible under agency principles (*i.e.*, respondent superior) "[a]bsent exceptional circumstances." Additionally, the definition of violation is expanded to include "advocating" a pleading after its filing. The *O'Brien* case makes clear, however, that not just any oral statement made in the course of defending a challenged pleading can qualify as a violation, even if the pleading turns out to be groundless. To be sanctionable, the oral statement must (1) violate the certification requirement in Rule 11, (2) relate directly to a matter addressed in the challenged paper, and (3) be in furtherance of that matter. As a result, the appellate court in *O'Brien* held that only one of two challenged oral statements made by counsel in advocating a paper could justify sanctions.

(6) *Sanctions Still Are Mandatory in Securities Litigation.* The Private Securities Litigation Reform Act of 1995 was intended to reduce the volume of securities litigation perceived as unwarranted. In addition to other provisions tightening pleading standards, the Act makes certain sanctions mandatory, somewhat as did earlier Rule 11. See the Heightened Pleading Requirements coverage in § 5.03[C] above.

(7) *Severity of the Sanction: Is the Shift from Compensatory Standards to Minimal Deterrence Justified?: Bergeron v. Northwest Publications, Inc., 165 F.R.D. 518 (D. Minn. 1996).* Applying amended Rule 11's emphasis on deterrence rather than compensation, the district court in this case made the following sanction order:

> [The sanctioned lawyer] is required, at his own expense, to successfully complete a course in the Federal Rules of Civil Procedure, and the Local Rules of this Court. . . . The course shall be taught by a professor at an accredited law school, including any of the three Minnesota law schools. It shall consist of at least 40 hours of individualized instruction, and may require more if the professor finds additional instruction is necessary for successful completion of the course.

Now aren't you glad you paid attention in class? (But on the other hand, if you did pay attention in class, you may feel that the opponent who didn't should pay the resulting costs, rather than your client, who will pay an increased fee pursuant to this sort of order under a minimalist-sanctions rule.)

PROBLEM E

"BLACKWELL v. CARSON" — ADAPTED FROM EDITORIAL, *MR. BLACKWELL: FASHION CRITIC'S SUIT CLOGS COURTS AND COSTS PUBLIC*, Houston Chronicle, Mar. 21, 1992, at 10B. This editorial began by observing, "Over the years [the fashion critic who calls himself Mr. Blackwell] has gained international attention by putting celebrities on his 10 worst-dressed list and savaging them with vitriolic comments." But then, it relates, Johnny Carson (who was host of the Tonight Show on NBC and Jay Leno's predecessor) made fun of Mr. Blackwell by joking that Blackwell had criticized Nobel Prize winner Mother Teresa as a "nerdy nun" and a "fashion no-no." Blackwell promptly filed suit in a California state court for defamation, saying (correctly) that he had made no such statements and alleging that Carson's humorous monologue had subjected him to "hatred, contempt, and ridicule."

The editorial called Blackwell's suit "frivolous," saying that it would "add another little clog to the court system and cost taxpayers a few dollars more." And indeed, the suit does seem to be unmeritorious, because the Supreme Court has held that parody, even if outrageous and even if intended to cause emotional distress, is protected from suit under the First Amendment to the Constitution. *See Hustler Magazine v. Falwell*, 485 U.S. 46 (1988) (holding that parody was protected by the First Amendment even though it fictitiously depicted Moral Majority leader Jerry Falwell as confessing to a drunken incestuous rendezvous with his mother in an outhouse).

The editorial concluded that the California court "should [impose] whatever sanctions it can if it deems the lawsuit frivolous. The courts should not be part of show biz." *Questions:* If it had been filed in a federal court, could Mr. Blackwell's suit properly have invoked sanctions? If so, what kind, against whom, and under what procedures?

[C] Beyond Rule 11: "Inherent" Power and Other Sanction Powers

NOTE ON SANCTIONS FOR CONDUCT OTHER THAN FILING OR ADVOCATING PLEADINGS

Other Federal Sanction Powers. Rule 11 is not the only source of federal sanctions; there are other devices that can deter litigation misconduct. After all, Rule 11 is limited to papers filed. Section 1927 of Title 28 authorizes sanctions against any attorney who "multiplies the proceedings in any case unreasonably and vexatiously," whether by pleadings or otherwise. Sanctions for frivolous appeals are available through 28 U.S.C. § 1912 and Federal Rule of Appellate Procedure 38. Federal courts also claim an "inherent power" to sanction attorneys for misconduct in any proceedings. *Roadway Express Inc. v. Piper*, 447 U.S. 752 (1980). (Consider, also, the case below.) Further, we will see in Chapter 7 that there are separate rules (Rules 26(g) and 37), governing sanctions for discovery abuse, and in Chapter 9 we will revisit the concept of sanctions in connection with Rule 41 (governing dismissals). Finally, 28 U.S.C. § 1915(d) empowers the court even to "pierce the veil" of pleadings when they are *in forma pauperis*, by going beyond the face of the papers to determine whether they are "frivolous or malicious." *See* Joseph, *Rule 11 Is Only the Beginning*, ABA Journal, May 1, 1988, at 62.

State Analogues of Rule 11. Sanctions are also available in state courts under many state statutes. *See, e.g.*, Cal. Code Civ. Pro. § 128.5 (similar to current Rule 11); *see also* Tex. R. Civ. P. 13 (similar in effect to the 1993 version of Rule 11 though differently phrased).

CHAMBERS v. NASCO, INC., 501 U.S. 32 (1991). Do courts have inherent power to impose sanctions when Rule 11 is unavailable? In *Chambers*, the Supreme Court answered this question in the affirmative. The District Court relied on its inherent power to shift nearly $1 million in sanctions in the form of attorney's fees and expenses to Chambers. The alleged sanctionable conduct occurring both in and out of court and included even conduct occurring before suit was filed, by which the defendant fraudulently attempted to defeat jurisdiction. The Court deemed Rule 11 insufficient to support the sanction against Chambers, since the rule does not reach conduct other than the filing or advocacy of pleadings or motions.

Chambers entered into a written contract to sell a television license and station facilities to Nasco. He changed his mind and so informed Nasco. Nasco gave Chambers notice, required by federal rules, that it intended to file suit and seek a restraining order to prevent

Chambers from otherwise transferring the contracted-for property. Then, Chambers and his attorney quickly acted to transfer the property to relatives for the purpose of placing it beyond the reach of the court before the restraining order could be issued. They determined that a recorded sale to a third party would have this effect under applicable law because the contract with Nasco was not recorded.

The District Court rendered judgment for Nasco on the merits, and it imposed sanctions on Chambers of approximately $1 million — representing Nasco's entire attorney's fee. The court relied on its "inherent power" to sanction bad-faith litigation conduct, not on any federal or state rules or statutes. It based sanctions on Chambers' attempt to deprive the court of jurisdiction by acts of fraud, as well as other conduct that occurred both in and out of court (including the filing of false and frivolous pleadings and using tactics of delay and expense to "reduce [Nasco] to exhausted compliance"). The Court of Appeals affirmed the sanctions.

The Supreme Court also upheld the sanction, holding that federal courts have the discretionary, inherent power to punish bad-faith litigation conduct. The Court rejected the argument that 28 U.S.C. § 1927, Rule 11, and other express sanctioning authority displace courts' inherent power to impose attorney's fees as a sanction for bad faith conduct. Moreover, there is no need to resort to these express sanction provisions before invoking the inherent power. Finally, the Court rejected Chambers' argument that the sanction violated *Erie* principles.

Justice Kennedy, in dissent, characterized the decision as a "vast expansion of the power of federal courts, unauthorized by rule or statute." He would require federal district courts to exhaust their express sanctioning authority before resorting to inherent power. He also concluded that sanctions for pre-litigation conduct violated the *Erie* doctrine.

NOTES AND QUESTIONS

(1) *What Due Process Protections Should Accompany a Court's Use of Its Inherent Sanction Powers? F.J. Hanshaw Enterprises, Inc. v. Emerald River Development, Inc., 244 F.3d 1128 (9th Cir. 2001).* In its current version, Rule 11 requires notice and a reasonable opportunity to respond before the court can impose sanctions. Are similar protections available when the court relies on its inherent sanction power? In this extreme case in which the district court imposed a $500,000 monetary sanction payable to the United States on a party found to have offered a bribe to the court-appointed receiver, the Ninth Circuit held that the sanction should have been treated as equivalent to criminal contempt, requiring "the procedural protections appropriate to a criminal case." 244 F.3d at 1139. Because the sanctioned conduct occurred outside the court's presence, these protections require the use of an independent prosecutor, a jury trial, and a standard of proof beyond a reasonable doubt. According to the appellate court, "[t]he more punitive the nature of the sanction, the greater the protection to which an individual is entitled." *Id.* at 1137. Applying this rule, the Ninth Circuit found that because the sanctioned party had received sufficient notice and an opportunity to be heard, and because the court made an express finding of bad faith, an additional sanction of $200,000 to compensate the counter-claimant for expenses incurred as a result of the misconduct was within the court's inherent power. *Id.* at 1143.

(2) *Sanctions Awarded Under Court's Inherent Power Must Consider Ability to Pay: Martin v. Automobili Lamborghini Exclusive, Inc., 307 F.3d 1332 (11th Cir. 2002).* In *Martin*, the Eleventh Circuit vacated a $1.5 million sanction awarded jointly and severally against a plaintiff, his counsel, and a paralegal under the court's inherent power because

the district court judge failed to consider each individual's financial circumstances. "[W]hen exercising its discretion to sanction under its inherent power, a court must take into consideration the financial circumstances of the party being sanctioned." *Id.* at 1337. Considering the parties' combined financial ability to pay the award was insufficient to cure the error, according to the Eleventh Circuit, because each was individually responsible for the entire obligation. Accordingly, the Eleventh Circuit vacated the sanctions award and remanded the matter to the district court to assess an appropriate sanction based on the individual resources of each party.

NOTE:
HOW DOES THE LAWYER PAY THE SANCTIONS?

The Nightmare: Personal Liability for a Large Sanction Soon after the Lawyer Begins Practice. A student of one of the authors (before Rule 11 was amended) was required to pay more than $200,000 as a sanction under amended Rule 11 a short time after he started practice. He and his partners underwent several difficult years while they personally paid the sanction.

Will or Should Offending Lawyers' Malpractice Insurance Pay Their Sanctions (And What Effect Would That Rule Have Upon the Cost of Your Own Insurance)?: Bar Plan v. Campbell, No. 57946, 1991 Mo. App. LEXIS 1429, 60 U.S.L.W. 2225 (Mo. App. Sept. 17, 1991). The answer depends upon (1) the insurance policy, (2) the violation and (3) state law. In this Missouri case, the "pay all sums" clause of the policy required the insurer to "pay [a]ll sums [w]hich the Insured shall become legally obligated to pay as damages as a result of [claims made during the policy period] by reason of any fact or omission by the Insured [in his] professional capacity providing legal services." "Damages," in turn, was defined in the policy as "a monetary judgment award [not including] fines or statutory penalties." The policy excluded "fraudulent" or "maliciously or deliberately wrongful acts." The Missouri court concluded that Rule 11 imposed a standard "similar to [n]egligence," that the sanctions were not a "statutory penalty" or a "fine," and that they met the policy definition of "damages" even though they might be imposed as a deterrent. The court also reasoned that the malpractice policy was intended to protect the lawyer from the results of his negligent acts and that it "loses much of its value if it fails to provide coverage for negligent conduct [sanctioned] pursuant to Rule 11." But should the cost of your own malpractice insurance be increased to pay for penalties imposed on attorneys in cases such as *Eastway* or *Chambers v. Nasco*? Does the added protection to you outweigh that cost? Note that many beginning lawyers elect to "go bare," or practice without insurance, because they find the cost already prohibitive. Finally, is the Missouri court's reasoning persuasive?

§ 5.05 Appendix Sample Documents from a Sanctions Controversy

BACKGROUND: A CONTROVERSY ADAPTED FROM DOCUMENTS IN THE SUPREME COURT CASE OF *WILLY v. THE COASTAL CORPORATION*

The Controversy: Bayne v. The Proctor Corporation. Plaintiff George M. Bayne was an in-house lawyer for The Proctor Corporation until it terminated him. Bayne filed a state-court lawsuit, claiming that in violation of the law of the (hypothetical) State of West York, Proctor had wrongfully discharged him for his attempts to avoid illegal and criminal conduct under state and federal regulatory statutes. The Proctor Corporation removed the action to federal court. There, it defended, in part, on the theory that Bayne instead had sought to impose on Proctor his views of legal questions rather than counseling and representing it. Further, Proctor pointed out that applicable disciplinary rules permitted a client freely to disengage a lawyer, based on the lawyer's duty to withdraw, without fear of a claim for wrongful discharge.

Plaintiff Bayne's Motions to Remand, for Sanctions, and for Summary Judgment. Bayne, acting through his attorney, moved to remand. He pointed out that diversity was lacking, and he argued that the claim "arose under" state law of wrongful discharge (and not the federal statutes that he alleged he had sought to avoid violating). He also moved for sanctions, alleging technical violations of removal procedure (that the removal papers were not "signed" properly [is that a likely ground for sanctions?]). Then, with discovery still to be undertaken, he filed a motion for summary judgment, accompanied by a lengthy brief and a large stack of unnumbered pages.

Defendant's Response on Summary Judgment; Defendant's Motion for Sanctions. The defendant then filed the Response and Motion for Sanctions that follows.

The District Court Imposes Sanctions — but the Court of Appeals Holds the Removal Improper. The District Court entered an order for sanctions (see below). The Court of Appeals subsequently upheld the imposition of sanctions but it also held that the removal had been improper. (Question: Does this holding make sense?)

Simulation from a Real Supreme Court Case with Comparable Kinds of Events: Willy v. The Coastal Corporation, cert. granted, 501 U.S. 1216 (1991). This set of documents is simulated from the relevant papers in the *Willy* case, which the Supreme Court since has decided. The events narrated above and the documents below, however, are simplified and changed for teaching purposes. For that reason, most names and identifying features, as well as the state of origin, also have been changed. The authors thank James L. Reed, Jr., who served as counsel for The Coastal Corporation, for furnishing information from which these documents were simulated.

IN THE UNITED STATES DISTRICT COURT
FOR THE CENTRAL DISTRICT OF WEST YORK
LONDON DIVISION

GEORGE M. BAYNE v. THE PROCTOR CORPORATION	CIVIL ACTION NO. H-85-1234

DEFENDANT'S RESPONSE TO PLAINTIFF'S MOTION FOR PARTIAL SUMMARY JUDGMENT AND REQUEST FOR RULE 11 SANCTIONS

It is obvious that Plaintiff's Motion and Brief were filed without meeting the most rudimentary requirements of a motion for summary judgment. There is no evidence to support the summary judgment. Defendant requests that the Court impose sanctions under Rule 11, 28 U.S.C. § 1927, and the Court's inherent power, against Plaintiff and/or his attorney for filing such an unwarranted and wholly inadequate motion.

1. The Brief in support of the Partial Motion for Summary Judgment is 110 pages in length. The Brief is replete with references to exhibits which Plaintiff made no attempt to authenticate and prove as admissible evidence. There are no depositions in the cause

and there are no affidavits to support the Motion. In short, there is absolutely no competent summary judgment evidence. The Motion and Brief are so clearly inappropriate that they could not have been filed in good faith.

2. For example, at page 83 of the brief Plaintiff states as follows:

> For purposes of analysis of the claims of the Plaintiff and the evidence and other documents which this Court must consider in reaching a decision, Plaintiff has incorporated this analysis as Exhibit "A" attached and incorporated by reference in this brief.
>
> Attached to this brief is the evidence in the possession of the Plaintiff, and this evidence together with the admissions of the defendants supports summary judgment on all issue needed to make a cause of action for Plaintiff against each defendant.

The only exhibit attached to the brief was a draft of a Motion to Stay Discovery which was filed by Defendant. Defendant has no idea what "analysis" Plaintiff is referencing. Likewise, Defendant does not know the extent and content of the "evidence in the possession of the Plaintiff" which was allegedly attached to the Brief.

3. [The motion here briefly explains the application of Rule 11, § 1927, and inherent power sanctions.]

WHEREFORE, Defendant respectfully requests that Plaintiff's Partial Motion for Summary Judgment be denied and that the Court impose sanctions against Plaintiff and/or his attorney in an amount deemed appropriate by the Court, and for such other and further relief as the Court may deem appropriate.

Respectfully submitted,
BOURNE & TYLER
By <u>David E. Tyler</u>

IN THE UNITED STATES DISTRICT COURT
FOR THE CENTRAL DISTRICT OF WEST YORK
LONDON DIVISION

GEORGE M. BAYNE, Plaintiff v. THE PROCTOR CORPORATION, Defendant	CIVIL ACTION NO. H-85-1234

BRIEF IN SUPPORT OF DEFENDANT'S MOTION FOR SANCTIONS

Pursuant to Rule 11 of the Federal Rules of Civil Procedure, 28 U.S.C. § 1927, and the Court's inherent power, Defendant files this Brief in Support of its Motion for Sanctions against Plaintiff and his attorney.

BASIS FOR MOTION

As the basis for its initial Motion for Sanctions, Defendant cited several misleading and patently inappropriate pleadings filed by Plaintiff in the course of this action. During the August 18 hearing before this Court, Plaintiff and his attorney not only failed to offer a reasonable explanation for the inappropriate action cited by Defendant, but actually compounded their improprieties further in open court. Such conduct, as witnessed by this Court, fully justifies the imposition of sanctions upon Plaintiff and his attorney pursuant to Rule 11, 28 U.S.C. § 1927, and the Court's inherent power.

Several examples of the specific conduct upon which Defendant relies in support of its Motion for Sanctions are summarized briefly below. Defendant notes, however, that the following examples are by no means all-inclusive but only indicative.

1. Despite the virtual absence of an evidentially record, Plaintiff, on June 20, filed a Motion for Partial Summary Judgment purportedly addressing *every* material issue and defense raised in this action, with the exception of damages. (Brief, p. 83). Plaintiff's Brief in Support of this Motion is in many respects incomprehensible. Substantial portions of the Brief are devoid of legal citation and the Brief itself raises a myriad of disputed factual issues. For example, in discussing his blacklisting claim, Plaintiff actually concedes the existence of a material factual issue by stating that "[t]he question of fact is whether [Defendant] placed the name of the Plaintiff on a list with the intention of preventing him from obtaining employment." (Brief, p. 55). Plaintiff also states repeatedly in his Brief that discovery is needed on certain issues, while at the same time urging this Court to grant summary judgment on those very issues. (Brief, pp. 3, 4, 6-7, 55, 106, 107, 108, 109). The Brief also contains vague references to a multitude of documents which were in the possession of Plaintiff, but which did not accompany his Motion at the time of filing.

2. In a July 3 Reply Brief on Defendant's Motion to Dismiss, Plaintiff set forth a substantial discussion of the applicability to this matter of "Rule 503 of the Federal Rules of Evidence." (Reply Brief, pp. 4, 21, 24, 26). As this Court is well aware, there is no Rule 503 contained in the Federal Rules of Evidence, and Plaintiff's citation of this provision shows the absence of even a rudimentary inquiry into the law governing this case. Moreover, plaintiff later persisted in citing "Rule 503" in documents presented at the August 18 hearing, even though Defendant had pointed out in the intervening time that no such Rule existed.

3. In a July 18 Supplemental Brief, Plaintiff relied upon briefs from other cases which were not on file with this Court and which did not accompany his Supplemental Brief. (Supplemental Brief, pp. 5-6). In addition, Plaintiff sets forth in his Supplemental Brief an incomplete quotation of DR 2-110 of the West York Code of Professional Responsibility, which establishes the duty of an attorney to withdraw from representation when discharged by his client. (Supplemental Brief, p. 9). Defendant had relied upon this provision in a prior brief and had noted that it applies to all forms of representation. The incomplete quotation by Plaintiff omits the language of the rule that is specifically applicable to him, and the ensuing discussion would lead the Court to believe that the omitted language does not even exist. (Supplemental Brief, pp. 9-10).

4. At the August 18 hearing, Plaintiff's counsel informed the Court that he was finally prepared to provide Defendant with copies of the documents cited in Plaintiff's June 20 Brief in Support of his Motion for Partial Summary Judgment. Plaintiff's counsel then proceeded in open court to present Defendant's counsel with no less than 1200 pages of documentation. Defendant's counsel subsequently have been required to review that voluminous mass of documentation, which is now on file with this Court. Even a cursory review by the Court of the material produced will reflect that it consists of unnumbered, random documents, the majority of which have no conceivable relevance to this action.

Moreover, it is for the most part impossible to determine the proposition for which any particular document is purportedly submitted.

The mass of irrelevant documentation filed by Plaintiff is accompanied by a fourteen-page affidavit. In a single paragraph of that affidavit, Plaintiff himself purports to authenticate every single document submitted, relying upon Rule 803 (Hearsay Exceptions) and 902 (Self-Authentication) of the Federal Rules of Evidence. Plaintiff attests on page 2 of his Affidavit merely that the documents are true and correct copies of "what they appear to be." The affidavit contains two signature pages and two differing versions of its final pages.

ARGUMENT AND CITATION OF AUTHORITIES

[The Brief here sets out Rule 11, § 1927, and excerpts from authorities recognizing inherent power. It further explains the principles of interpretation applicable to these sources of law; *e.g.*, Rule 11 does not require any "showing of subjective bad faith . . . ." Similarly, "28 U.S.C. § 925 provides for the imposition of sanctions upon an attorney who unreasonably or vexatiously multiplies the proceedings in any case before a federal court."]

Plaintiff's blatant disregard for evidentiary and procedural requirements is most readily apparent from his June 20 Motion for Partial Summary Judgment. The ponderous Brief filed in support of that Motion consists primarily of Plaintiff's conclusory version of the facts and law involved in this case. *See Galindo v. Precision American Corp.*, 754 F.2d 1212, 1221 (5th Cir. 1985) ("We have long recognized that mere statements of conclusions of law or ultimate fact cannot shift the summary judgment burden to the nonmovant."). In its Response, Defendant specifically placed in issue virtually every material factual allegation set forth by Plaintiff. Nevertheless, Plaintiff persists in representing to this Court that these facts are not in dispute for purposes of his Motion for Partial Summary Judgment.

Ironically, the documentation submitted by Plaintiff in support of his Motion is itself replete with statements by other individuals that directly contradict Plaintiff's factual claims in this action. *See Hamilton v. Keystone Tankship Corp.*, 539 F.2d 684, 686 (9th Cir. 1976) (summary judgment denied "where the movant's papers are insufficient on their face or themselves demonstrate the existence of a material issue of fact."). For example, Plaintiff has submitted prior statements by two individuals that state clearly that the termination of his employment was in no way related to his advice on environmental matters. Plaintiff utterly ignores these statements by representing to this Court that there is no genuine issue of material fact concerning his claims of wrongful discharge.

There can be no question that the conduct of Plaintiff and his attorney in this matter rises to that level of irresponsible pleading that would justify the imposition of sanctions. The facts in this matter parallel those in *Limerick v. Greenwald*, 749 F.2d 97 (1st Cir. 1984), wherein the Court noted as follows:

> Counsel's course of conduct in the filing of hundreds of pages of irrelevant documents, in citing to dozens of cases unrelated to the real issues in these appeals, in bringing repetitive motions without a shred of rational basis, and in seeking to resurrect matters long since finally concluded has been at least irresponsible and has come perilously close to an abuse of process.

Id. at 101 (attorneys' fees assessed under 28 U.S.C. § 1927). Neither this court nor other courts within the Fifth Circuit have been hesitant to impose sanctions under Rule 11 in appropriate situations. *See, e.g., Hale v. Harney,* 786 F.2d 688 (5th Cir. 1986) (copy attached) (sanctions upheld in purported civil rights suit, against judge who divorced claimant, containing claimant's baseless allegations of conspiracy and improper conduct).

As a result of Plaintiff's actions in this case, Defendants have incurred substantial expense in responding to burdensome motions having no basis in fact or in law. [Elsewhere, defendant particularized these expenses by time records and disbursements, authenticated by affidavit. — Eds.] More significantly, Plaintiff and his counsel have unnecessarily burdened the judicial resources of this Court with their voluminous and unwarranted filings. As a result, Defendant requests that this Court impose monetary sanctions upon Plaintiff and his attorney, for the purpose of compensating Defendants for the excess attorneys' fees incurred in responding to Plaintiff's improper pleadings. In addition, Defendant requests that the Court strike from the record the inappropriate pleadings, affidavits and documents filed by Plaintiff in this action. . . .

IN THE UNITED STATES DISTRICT COURT
FOR THE CENTRAL DISTRICT OF WEST YORK
LONDON DIVISION

GEORGE M. BAYNE, Plaintiff v. THE PROCTOR CORPORATION, Defendant	CIVIL ACTION NO. H-85-1234

ORDER FOR SANCTIONS

Pending before this Court is Defendant's Motion for Sanctions. Having considered the pleadings with the reams of allegedly relevant supplemental material, the oral statements made on the record at hearings, the Defendant's affidavits for attorney's fees, the Plaintiff's (Pro Se) Response to Defendant's Affidavits in Support of Sanction, and the court rules and law applicable thereto, this Court is of the opinion that Defendant's Motion for Sanctions is well advised.

[The Court here sets out the relevant provisions of Rule 11.]

Plaintiff filed this suit in an apparent attempt to establish new law, at least as to one cause of action. Under such circumstances, the Court would expect Plaintiff, an attorney himself, and his counsel, to shed what light they could upon the issue in clear focus. [W]hen the Plaintiff's attorney signed his 110-page brief in support of a Motion for Partial Summary Judgment, he made the Rule 11 certifications to this Court. Furthermore, Plaintiff asked and received permission of this Court to file what Plaintiff's attorney certifies to be appropriate and competent summary judgment evidence. What Plaintiff's attorney filed, however, was a 1,200-page, unindexed, unnumbered, foot-high pile of material which this Court is unable, after examination, to fathom and which is determined to be a conscious and wanton affront to the judicial process, this Court, and opposing counsel. This Court finds the submission and the Plaintiff's accompanying affidavit to this Court to be irresponsible at a minimum and at worst intentionally harassing. The material is generally incompetent hearsay, supported only by the Plaintiff's own conclusions and averments. *See Galindo v. Precision Am. Corp.*, 754 F.2d 1212, 1216 (5th Cir. 1985).

Unfortunately, the transgressions do not stop here. Plaintiff's response(s) to Defendant's Motion to Dismiss are also careless and confusing. For example, at page 4 of Defendants' Response to Plaintiff's Briefs Regarding Defendants' Motion to Dismiss, the Plaintiff relies upon Rule 503 of the Federal Rules of Evidence. At the August [h]earing, this Court asked Plaintiff to find Federal Rule of Evidence 503. Plaintiff could not. At the September [h]earing, Plaintiff acknowledged that Rule 503 was never adopted by the United States Supreme Court. This is but an example of Plaintiff's and Plaintiff's counsel's careless pleading and a strong indication of intentional harassment.

[The order did not contain findings of specific violations relied on by the Court or findings concerning sanction amounts and was remanded for that reason (see below) — Eds.]

[T]he conduct of this suit has been inexcusable and can hardly be seen as a good faith attempt at making new law. It is therefore

ORDERED that Defendant's Motion for Sanctions be GRANTED. Plaintiff and Plaintiff's counsel, jointly and severally, are to pay $22,625 to the Defendants for the purpose of compensating the Defendant for the attorneys fees incurred in responding to Plaintiff's improper pleadings; in particular, Plaintiff's Motion for Partial Summary Judgment and Responses to Defendants' Motion to Dismiss. The $22,625 will be tendered to Defendant's attorney-in-charge on or before December 1. Proof of payment will be filed with the Court on or before December 1. . . .

JAMES BRATLER,
United States District Judge

NOTES AND QUESTIONS

1. *The Supreme Court's Grant of Certiorari to Determine Power to Sanction in an Improperly Removed Case: Willy v. The Coastal Corporation, cert. granted, 501 U.S. 1216 (1991).* Remember that the Court of Appeals later held that the case should have been remanded to state court. Does this mean that the District Court lacked the power to impose sanctions? The Supreme Court granted review in the case on which these documents were based. See below.

2. *Procedure, Evidence and Findings.* In *Willy*, the Court of Appeals initially remanded for a redetermination of sanctions. Then it affirmed the redetermined order of the District Court. Then, the Supreme Court accepted the case for review. Note that due process requires sanctions to be based on competent evidence (in this case, evidence of the violation and attorney's fee amounts). The absence of findings in this regard in the above order was one basis for the reversal and remand by the Court of Appeals. The revised order of the District Court, unlike its initial order, contained detailed findings of the incidents constituting violations as well as of attorney's fee amounts, leading to affirmance.

3. *Novel Issues; An Attorney's Duty When Making New Law.* Notice the trial judge's conclusion that since the plaintiff was "attempt[ing] to establish new law," the plaintiff and his counsel were expected "to shed what light they could upon the issue in clear focus." How should the novelty of the issues and the plaintiff's disclosure of the law bear on the case?

4. *Which Applies — Rule 11, § 1927, or Inherent Power?: The Safe Harbor Provision.* Note the court's reliance on Rule 11. The defendant's motion and brief also relied on § 1927 and inherent power. These doctrines require subjective mental states (*e.g.*, bad faith) that Rule 11 does not, but Rule 11 may not cover some of the allegedly offending conduct (*e.g.*, the voluminous unauthenticated evidence). Which doctrine is best to support the sanctions, if any?

Also, notice that this case arose at a time when "old" Rule 11 was in place, with no safe harbor and mandatory sanctions. The process would be different under "new" Rule 11. Would it be better under the new rule, or would the new rule simply allow violations to produce unredressable harm?

5. *"Represented Party" Sanctions or Attorney Sanctions?* "Bayne" pointed out that he did not sign any of the offending pleadings, and although he was a lawyer himself, he clearly relied at least to some extent on counsel. Is the imposition of sanctions, both on counsel and on the represented party, appropriate?

6. *The Causes of Controversies Like This One.* What are some of the reasons why a case such as this one can arise?

WILLY v. COASTAL CORP.
503 U.S. 131 (1992)

THE CHIEF JUSTICE delivered the opinion of the Court.

We granted certiorari to decide whether a federal district court may impose sanctions pursuant to Rule 11 of the Federal Rules of Civil Procedure in a case in which the district court is later determined to be without subject-matter jurisdiction. We conclude that in the circumstances presented here it may do so.

Petitioner Willy sued respondent Coastal Corporation (Coastal) in Texas state court, raising a variety of claims relating to Coastal's decision to terminate his employment as "in-house" counsel. Petitioner alleged that he had been fired due to his refusal to participate in respondent's violation of various federal and state environmental laws and that this violated, among other things, the "whistle-blower" provisions of those statutes. Respondent removed the case to Federal District Court, claiming original federal-question jurisdiction under 28 U.S.C. §§ 1331, 1441. Petitioner objected to the removal, claiming that his case did not "arise under" federal law, *see* § 1331, but the District Court disagreed and concluded that it had subject-matter jurisdiction. The District Court subsequently granted respondent's motion to dismiss for failure to state a claim, Fed. Rule Civ. Pro. 12(b)(6), and dismissed petitioner's pendent state claims.

At the same time, the District Court granted respondent's motion for Rule 11 sanctions, awarding attorney's fees of $22,625 against Willy and his attorney, Young, jointly and severally. The District Court found that the filings made by plaintiff's counsel "create[d] a blur of absolute confusion." These included a 1,200-page, unindexed, unnumbered pile of materials that the District Court determined "to be a conscious and wanton affront to the judicial process, this Court, and opposing counsel" that was "irresponsible at a minimum and at worst intentionally harassing." Petitioner's sanctionable behavior also included careless pleading, such as reliance on a nonexistent Federal Rule of Evidence. None of the sanctionable conduct was related to petitioner's initial effort to convince the District Court that it was without subject-matter jurisdiction.

On appeal, the Court of Appeals for the Fifth Circuit concluded that the District Court had lacked subject-matter jurisdiction because the complaint raised no claims arising under federal law. . . . The court also upheld the District Court's decision to award Rule 11 sanctions, although it remanded the case to the District Court to determine the amount. On remand the District Court recomputed the Rule 11 sanctions and imposed sanctions in the amount of $19,307, the amount of attorney's fees that respondent had incurred in responding to petitioner's sanctionable conduct. The Court of Appeals affirmed. . . .

Petitioner [points] out that Article III limits the subject-matter jurisdiction of the federal courts to certain "cases or controversies." He then contends that the District Court's exercise of judicial power to grant Rule 11 sanctions must have been an unconstitutional act because, in the absence of subject-matter jurisdiction, the District Court lacks "a substantive source of judicial power, beyond that conferred by Article III." . . .

We think petitioner's contentions flawed in several respects. Article I, Section 8, cl. 1, authorizes Congress to establish the lower federal courts. From almost the founding days of this country, it has been firmly established that Congress, acting pursuant to its authority to make all laws "necessary and proper" to their establishment, also may enact laws regulating the conduct of those courts and the means by which their judgments are enforced.

This leaves only petitioner's contention that Rule 11 sanctions must be aborted because at a time after the sanctionable conduct occurred, it was determined by the Court of Appeals that the district court lacked subject-matter jurisdiction. A final determination of lack of subject-matter jurisdiction of a case in a federal court, of course, precludes further adjudication of it. But such a determination does not automatically wipe out all proceedings had in the district court at a time when the district court operated under the misapprehension that it had jurisdiction. . . .

The District Court order which the petitioner seeks to upset is one that is collateral to the merits. We recently had occasion to examine Rule 11's scope and purpose in great detail in *Cooter & Gell v. Hartmarx Corp.*, 496 U.S. 384 (1990). The challenge in that case was to an order imposing Rule 11 sanctions for filing a frivolous complaint, entered after the plaintiff had voluntarily dismissed his action. In the course of our discussion we noted that "[i]t is well established that a federal court may consider collateral issues after an action is no longer pending . . . ." Such an order implicates no constitutional concern because it "does not signify a district court's assessment of the legal merits of the complaint." . . .

The interest in having rules of procedure obeyed [] does not disappear upon a subsequent determination that the court was without subject-matter jurisdiction. . . .

For the foregoing reasons, the judgment of the Court of Appeals is *Affirmed.*

§ 5.06 Amendment

Read Fed. R. Civ. P. 15.

[A] Amendment by Right or by Leave

BEECK v. AQUASLIDE 'N' DIVE CORP.

562 F.2d 537 (8th Cir. 1977)

BENSON, DISTRICT JUDGE.

This case is an appeal from the trial court's exercise of discretion on procedural matters in a diversity personal injury action.

Jerry A. Beeck was severely injured on July 15, 1972, while using a water slide. He and his wife, Judy A. Beeck, sued Aquaslide 'N' Dive Corporation (Aquaslide), a Texas corporation, alleging it manufactured the slide involved in the accident, and sought to recover substantial damages on theories of negligence, strict liability and breach of implied warranty.

Aquaslide initially admitted manufacture of the slide, but later moved to amend its answer to deny manufacture; the motion was resisted. The district court granted leave to amend. On motion of the defendant, a separate trial was held on the issue of "whether the defendant designed, manufactured or sold the slide in question." This motion was also resisted by the plaintiffs. The issue was tried to a jury, which returned a verdict for the defendant, after which the trial court entered summary judgment of dismissal of the case. Plaintiffs took this appeal, and stated the issues presented for review to be: [first, whether the trial court abused its discretion in permitting an amendment that denied manufacture after the statute of limitations had run, and second, whether the separate trial was an abuse of discretion].

I. Facts. . . .

In 1971 Kimberly Village Home Association of Davenport, Iowa, ordered an Aquaslide product from one George Boldt, who was a local distributor handling defendant's products. The order was forwarded by Boldt to Sentry Pool and Chemical Supply Co. in Rock Island, Illinois, and Sentry forwarded the order to Purity Swimming Pool Supply in Hammond, Indiana. A slide was delivered from a Purity warehouse to Kimberly Village, and was installed by Kimberly employees. On July 15, 1972, Jerry A. Beeck was injured while using the slide at a social gathering sponsored at Kimberly Village by his employer, Harker Wholesale Meats, Inc. Soon after the accident investigations were undertaken by representatives of the separate insurers of Harker and Kimberly Village. On October 31, 1972, Aquaslide first learned of the accident through a letter sent by a representative of Kimberly's insurer to Aquaslide, advising that "one of your Queen Model # Q-3D slides" was involved in the accident. Aquaslide forwarded this notification to its insurer. Aquaslide's insurance adjuster made an on-site investigation of the slide in May, 1973, and also interviewed persons connected with the ordering and assembly of the slide. An inter-office letter dated September 23, 1973, indicates that Aquaslide's insurer was of the opinion the "Aquaslide in question was definitely manufactured by our insured." The complaint was filed October 15, 1973. Investigators for three different insurance companies, representing Harker, Kimberly and the defendant, had concluded that the slide had been manufactured by Aquaslide, and the defendant, with no information to the contrary, answered the complaint on December 12, 1973, and admitted that it "designed, manufactured, assembled and sold" the slide in question.

The statute of limitations on plaintiff's personal injury claim expired on July 15, 1974. About six and one-half months later Carl Meyer, president and owner of Aquaslide, visited the site of the accident prior to the taking of his deposition by the plaintiff. From his on-site inspection of the slide, he determined it was not a product of the defendant. Thereafter, Aquaslide moved the court for leave to amend its answer to deny manufacture of the slide.

II. Leave to Amend

Amendment of pleadings in civil actions is governed by Rule 15(a), Fed. R. Civ. P., which provides in part that once issue is joined in a lawsuit, a party may amend his pleading ["only with the opposing party's written consent or the court's leave. The court should freely give leave when justice so requires"].

In *Foman v. Davis*, 371 U.S. 178, 83 S. Ct. 227, 9 L. Ed. 2d 222 (1962), the Supreme Court had occasion to construe that portion of Rule 15(a) set out above:

> Rule 15(a) declares that leave to amend "shall be freely given when justice so requires," this mandate is to be heeded. . . . In the absence of any apparent or declared reason — such as undue delay, bad faith or dilatory motive on the part of the movant, repeated failure to cure deficiencies by amendments previously allowed, undue prejudice to the opposing party by virtue of allowance of the amendment, futility of amendment, etc. — the leave sought should, as the rules require, be "freely given." Of course, the grant or denial of an opportunity to amend is within the discretion of the District Court. . . .

This Court in *Hanson v. Hunt Oil Co.*, 398 F.2d 578, 582 (8th Cir. 1968), held that "[p]rejudice *must be shown*." (Emphasis added). The burden is on the party opposing the amendment to show such prejudice. In ruling on a motion for leave to amend, the trial court must inquire into the issue of prejudice to the opposing party, in light of the particular facts of the case. . . .

It is evident from the order of the district court that in the exercise of its discretion in ruling on defendant's motion for leave to amend, it searched the record for evidence of bad faith, prejudice and undue delay which might be sufficient to overbalance the mandate of Rule 15(a), F.R. Civ. P., and *Foman v. Davis*, that leave to amend should be "freely given." Plaintiff had not at any time conceded that the slide in question had not been manufactured by the defendant, and at the time the motion for leave to amend was at issue, the court had to decide whether the defendant should be permitted to litigate a material factual issue on its merits.

[The Defendant's] reliance upon investigations of three insurance companies, and the fact that "no contention has been made by anyone that the defendant influenced this possibly erroneous conclusion," persuaded the court that "defendant has not acted in such bad faith as to be precluded from contesting the issue of manufacture at trial." The court further found "[t]o the extent that 'blame' is to be spread regarding the original identification, the record indicates that it should be shared equally."

In considering the issue of prejudice that might result to the plaintiffs from the granting of the motion for leave to amend, the trial court held that the facts presented to it did not support plaintiffs' assertion that, because of the running of the two year Iowa statute of limitations on personal injury claims, the allowance of the amendment would sound the "death knell" of the litigation. In order to accept plaintiffs' argument, the court would have had to assume that the defendant would prevail at trial on the factual issue of manufacture of the slide, and further that plaintiffs would be foreclosed, should the amendment be allowed, from proceeding against other parties if they were unsuccessful in pressing their claim against Aquaslide. On the state of the record before it, the trial court was unwilling to make such assumptions, and concluded "[u]nder these circumstances, the Court deems that the possible prejudice to the plaintiffs is an insufficient basis on which to deny the proposed amendment." The court reasoned that the amendment would merely allow the defendant to contest a disputed factual issue at trial, and further that it would be prejudicial to the defendant to deny the amendment.

The court also held that defendant and its insurance carrier, in investigating the circumstances surrounding the accident, had not been so lacking in diligence as to dictate a denial of the right to litigate the factual issue of manufacture of the slide.

On this record we hold that the trial court did not abuse its discretion in allowing the defendant to amend its answer.

III. Separate Trials

[Aquaslide had moved for separate trial of the issue of manufacture on the ground that it would "save considerable trial time" and would "protect Aquaslide from substantial prejudice." The court granted the motion under Fed. R. Civ. P. 42, which allows the trial judge discretion. The Court of Appeals held that the separate trial was not an abuse of discretion because the issue of manufacture was a substantial one, other issues would require lengthy trial, and evidence about the severe injuries of plaintiff Beeck could prejudice the defendant's claim of non-manufacture.]

The judgment of the district court is affirmed.

NOTES AND QUESTIONS

(1) *Amendment as of Right.* Rule 15(a) provides that a party may amend "once as a matter of course" before being served with a "responsive pleading," *i.e.*, an answer. Thus, if the defendant files only a motion to dismiss and the plaintiff wishes to amend for the first time, the Rule provides her a right to do so. Likewise, the defendant may amend an original answer or a third-party answer, if the answer does not include a counterclaim "designated as a counterclaim" [*see* Rule 7(a)], once "as a matter of course" "within 20 days after serving the pleading" because a reply to an answer is not allowed (unless ordered by the court) assuming that the action has not been placed on the trial calendar.

(2) *Leave "Freely Given"; Discretion to Deny.* The Rule is written so as to support liberal granting of leave to amend. For example, the mere passage of time between the complaint and its amendment is not ground by itself for denying leave. *Chitimacha Tribe v. Harry L. Laws Co., Inc.*, 690 F.2d 1157 (5th Cir. 1982). The amendment may assert a wholly new theory, and there are cases in which leave has been granted although the court recognized that the amendment might be insufficient to state a claim as a matter of law. *Harper v. Holiday Inns, Inc.*, 498 F. Supp. 910 (E.D. Tenn.), *aff'd,* 633 F.2d 215 (1978). However, this "liberal allowance" approach should not be taken too expansively. There still is good reason to take care in filing federal pleadings and not to rely upon the ability to amend. The trial judge has considerable discretion in taking into account the counterweights of delay, insubstantiality, number of previous amendments, prejudice to the opponent, and other factors. *E.g., Chitimacha Tribe v. Harry L.*

Laws Co., supra (trial court should consider whether amendment would cause undue delay, previous failure to cure deficiencies with prior amendments, whether amendment would lead to expeditious disposition, whether amendment adds substance, and whether it is germane to the original claim). In addition, a trial court may enter a scheduling or docket control order imposing a cutoff date for amendment.

[B] Amendment and the Statute of Limitations: Rule 15(c)

NOTE ON THE *SCHIAVONE* CASE AND INTERVENING RULE CHANGES

What happens if the plaintiff sues the wrong defendant and the limitations period runs before the plaintiff can amend? The case that follows sets a standard for amendments that avoid the bar of limitations. It applies the rule in a manner that some critics have found overly strict. Therefore, an amendment to Rule 15 was proposed to change the result. But interestingly, most of the reasoning of this case will still be good law in many cases. You will have to read both the case and the amended rule to see how they interact.

SCHIAVONE v. FORTUNE, a/k/a TIME, INCORPORATED
477 U.S. 21 (1986)

[Plaintiffs filed diversity suits alleging that they had been libeled by a story in *Fortune Magazine*. Their complaints designated the defendant solely as "Fortune" and described it as a "foreign corporation" with offices in New York. However, "Fortune" is only a trademark and internal division of Time, Inc. Time's registered agent refused service because Time itself was not named as a defendant. Plaintiffs then amended their complaints to designate the defendant as "Fortune, also known as Time, Incorporated." Time promptly moved to dismiss because both the original and amended pleadings were served after the statute of limitations had run. Plaintiffs argued that, under Rule 15(c), the pleadings "related back" to the original filing. The District Court rejected this argument, upheld Time's limitations defense, and dismissed. The Court of Appeals affirmed.

[The Supreme Court also affirmed the dismissal. The important question was whether the amendment "related back" to the earlier filing, which concededly had been made within the applicable limitations period. The Court reasoned as follows:]

Central to the resolution of this issue is the language of Rule 15(c). . . . Relation back is dependent upon four factors, all of which must be satisfied: (1) the basic claim must have arisen out of the conduct set forth in the original pleading; (2) the party to be brought in must have received such notice that it will not be prejudiced in maintaining its defense; (3) that party must or should have known that, but for a mistake concerning identity, the action would have been brought against it; and (4) the second and third requirements must have been fulfilled within the prescribed limitations period. We are not concerned here with the first factor, but we are concerned with the satisfaction of the remaining three.

The first intimation that Time had of the institution and maintenance of the . . . suits took place after May 19, 1983, the date the Court of Appeals said the statute ran "at the latest." . . . Only on May 20 did petitioners' counsel mail the [original] complaints to Time's registered agent in New Jersey. Only on May 23 were those complaints received by the registered agent, and then refused. Only on July 19 did each petitioner amend his complaint. And only on July 21 were the amended complaints served on Time.

It seems to us inevitably to follow that notice to Time and the necessary knowledge did not come into being "within the period provided by law for commencing the action against" Time, as is so clearly required by Rule 15(c). . . .

We do not have before us a choice between a "liberal" approach toward Rule 15(c), on the one hand, and a "technical" interpretation of the Rule, on the other hand. The choice, instead, is between recognizing or ignoring what the Rule provides in plain language. We accept the rule as meaning what it says. . . .

The linchpin is notice, and notice within the limitations period. Of course, there is an element of arbitrariness here, but that is a characteristic of any limitations period. And it is an arbitrariness imposed by the legislature and not by the judicial process. . . .

[Three Justices dissented in an opinion by Justice Stevens, which pointed out that Time, Inc.'s law department had been notified on the same day of the service of the initial complaints by the registered agent, who wrote: "Letter from Atty. indicates papers are for Time, Inc. . . ." There was no suggestion of prejudice to Time, Inc. Furthermore, the four requirements set out by the Court were applicable only to an amendment "changing the party" sued; as the dissenters saw it, this amendment could not be described fairly as "changing" or "bringing in" a new party within the meaning of Rule 15(c) because Fortune was a division of Time, Inc. The plain language of the Rule "disclosed an obvious purpose to protect parties . . . from prejudice," which was not even a remote risk in this case. The Court's misdesignation approach could conceivably apply with equal force to a mere misspelling, or perhaps even to a designation of "Time, Inc." instead of "Time, Incorporated." While statutes of limitations always involve arbitrary line-drawing to a degree, the dissent criticized the "Court's willingness to aggravate . . . that arbitrariness."

NOTES AND QUESTIONS

(1) *1991 Amendments Add the Cutoff Time for Service as a Grace Period to the Schiavone Holding — and Allow Relation Back Allowed under State Law.* The 1991 amendments, as adopted by the Court, provide for relation back if the new defendant has the requisite notice "within the period provided by [Rule 4] for serving the summons and complaint." The advisory committee expressly acted to "change the result in *Schiavone*." Although the result in *Schiavone* is changed because Time, Inc.'s registered agent received the original and the amended complaints within "120 days after the filing of the complaint[s]," this grace period may not be sufficient to change the result in other cases in which the mistake is not discovered in sufficient time to provide the right defendant with notice. As an alternative, the new rule allows relation back whenever "the law that provides the applicable statute of limitations allows relation back."

(2) *Suing the Wrong Defendant: A Common Problem!* The problem disclosed by this case is much more common than you might surmise. It arises frequently when interrelated businesses are involved. For example, you have claimed against Jones & Smith (a partnership), but the true entity against which your client has a valid claim is Jones & Smith, Inc. (a corporation controlled by the same individuals). In that situation, would Rule 15(c) make your later amendment to correct the party "relate back" to the original filing? Quite possibly, but of course it would be preferable not to have to find out. Alternatively, in a complex transaction in which the actors undertook various roles, one or more may have negligently injured your client, but sorting out the roles takes longer than the limitations period. Finally, consider the case in which your client may have a claim against the operators of an establishment called Temple's Fried Chicken; you sue Temple Corporation only to discover, after limitations has run, that the store was actually

owned and operated by the Acme Company, which is unrelated to Temple except that it is licensed to use the Temple name. Does 15(c) apply in this case? Unless there is more to it, relation back seems doubtful.

(3) *How Do You Avoid Suing the Wrong Defendant?* The uniform use of careful steps to minimize errors is a part of professionalism. There is good reason for using a demand letter in every case, whether the case seems likely to settle or not. Further, a skillful and diligent plaintiff's attorney would promptly take steps, after filing suit, to verify that the defendant sued is really the right defendant. For example, the use of discovery, including a request that the defendant admit that it operated the Temple Fried Chicken establishment at the time and place in question and that the personnel were within its employ, would be appropriate. (Many states require posting or filing of trade name information, but records are not always accurate or current and use of discovery in addition to this information is generally advisable.) Of course, there remain extraordinary cases — *Beeck v. Aquaslide 'N' Dive Corp.*, above, is an excellent example — in which even these steps will not suffice. It should go without saying that a plaintiff's attorney should immediately ascertain and calendar the limitations date for every claim in the office "tickler" system. *Cf.* Note, *Amendments That Add Plaintiffs Under Federal Rule of Civil Procedure 15(c)*, 50 Geo. Wash. L. Rev. 671 (1982).

[C] Trial and Post-Trial Amendments: Rule 15(b)

CUNNINGHAM v. QUAKER OATS COMPANY, FISHER-PRICE DIVISION, 107 F.R.D. 66 (W.D.N.Y. 1985). This action was brought by the father of a child who had suffered severe brain damage when he ingested a small toy manufactured by defendant, causing blockage of oxygen to his brain. A jury found the product defective owing to its size and ingestibility. By its verdict, the jury found damages for the child, for the father, and for the mother. The problem was, that the mother was not named as a plaintiff in the complaint. Plaintiff sought to make an amendment under Rule 15(b) to conform to the evidence. The court granted the motion, as follows: "[T]he issue of Mrs. Cunningham's damages was actually tried before the jury in this case [w]ith defendant's knowledge. Mr. and Mrs. Cunningham were cross-examined in the same way. The proof elicited from Mrs. Cunningham in the questions relating to value of services and loss of guidance and companionship was no less a matter of concern for the defendant than the proof elicited from Mr. Cunningham on these same points. [T]his case would not have been defended in a substantially different manner if Mrs. Cunningham's name appeared on the complaint . . . ." The court added that Rule 15(b) of the Federal Rules of Civil Procedure provides that ["[w]hen an issue not raised by the pleadings is tried by the parties' express or implied consent, it must be treated in all respects as if raised in the pleadings"]. Amending the pleadings to conform to the proof at trial may be done "at any time, even after judgment."

§ 5.07 State-Court Pleadings Today: Stating a "Cause of Action" Under Modern Rules

[A] New York: Liberal Cause-of-Action Pleading, but with Bill of Particulars

Pleading the Cause of Action in New York. The New York Commission on Practice and Procedure was a major force in reform of common law pleading, but the Field Code that it produced required pleading of "facts" rather than "evidence" or "conclusions." This provision meant that courts often became mired in controversies over whether a statement was a fact, a conclusion, or an item of evidence. *See* § 5.01[C], above. In 1957, New York's Rules Advisory Committee recommended the elimination of the word "facts" from the pleading requirements in the Civil Practice Act. The resulting provision is CPLR 3013, which provides:

> Statements in a pleading shall be sufficiently particular to give the court and the parties notice of the transactions . . . intended to be proved and the material elements of each cause of action or defense.

The New York standard is thus akin to federal "notice" pleading, with one exception: the allegations must give "notice" with respect to each material element of each cause of action or defense. The word "statement," which replaces the word "facts," indicates that this notice can be accomplished by conclusions, evidence, or facts, so long as the requisite notice is provided. Rule 3016, which is the analogue to Federal Rule 9, provides a slightly longer list of particularity requirements, applicable to actions for defamation, fraud, and divorce, among others.

The Answer in New York. Admissions and denials are governed by CPLR 3018(a), which is roughly analogous to federal practice (with the inclusion of a category of denials on information and belief). The defendant must address each allegation of the complaint in good faith and may not use a general denial, unless denying every single allegation of the complaint factually. Affirmative defenses must be pleaded.

Official Forms. As in the case of the Federal Rules, the CPLR is accompanied by official forms that illustrate "the simplicity and brevity of statement" that is contemplated. The forms are in many instances close to the federal forms. For example, New York's Form 12 is strikingly similar to Federal Form 9; it alleges, "On June 1, 1966, in a public highway called Broadway in New York City, defendant C.D. negligently drove a motor vehicle against plaintiff who was then crossing the highway." This first paragraph differs from the same paragraph of the Federal Form principally in that it alleges a location in New York.

Bill of Particulars. One major difference between New York and federal practice is that a party must serve a "bill of particulars" upon proper demand. For example, CPLR 3043(a) provides a list of particulars that a defendant may require of a personal injury plaintiff, including:

(1) the date and approximate time of the occurrence;

(2) the approximate location of the occurrence;

(3) a general statement of the acts or omissions constituting the negligence claimed to have caused the plaintiff's injuries;

(4) whether actual or constructive notice is claimed (when notice is an element of the cause of action);

(5) to whom and when actual notice was given, if any;

(6) a statement of the injuries and a description of those claimed to be permanent (as well as certain other particulars in certain actions governed by the No-fault Insurance Law);

(7) the length of time plaintiff was confined to bed or house;

(8) the length of time plaintiff was incapacitated from employment; and

(9) the total amounts claimed as special damages for physicians' services, medical supplies, lost earnings (with name and address of employer), hospital expenses, and nurses' services.

In other cases, there is no "laundry list" of proper particulars, and the cases tend to be confined to their individual facts as to which particulars can be demanded. Keep in mind, however, that a party may be required to provide particulars only with respect to contentions on which he or she bears the burden of proof.

Use of the Bill of Particulars. The purpose of the bill of particulars is akin to that of pleadings at common law: to narrow the issues. It creates, to some extent, the same dangers of inadvertent variance, as the case below indicates. However, the opponent cannot capitalize on the variance unless he has actually been misled by the bill of particulars and has been prejudiced as a result.

The "Motion to Preclude." If a party serves an inadequate bill of particulars, his opponent's remedy is a motion to preclude proof of the item not properly particularized. Typically, if it grants the motion, a court will do so conditionally, that is, if the proper particulars are not forthcoming within a specified period of time. In addition, the court can provide for payment of costs as a condition of denial of the preclusion order. *See generally* O. Chase, 1 *Weinstein, Korn & Miller, CPLR Manual* ch. 19 (1997); D. Siegel, *New York Practice* 291-98 (2d ed. 1991).

MAMMARELLA v. CONSOLIDATED EDISON CO., 44 A.D.2d 571, 353 N.Y.S.2d 38 (1974). The plaintiff's pleading in this wrongful death case evidently complied with the requirements of CPLR 3013 and was comparable in specificity to New York Form 12 (*see* above). The defendants sought a bill of particulars, itemizing the decedent's employment and loss of earnings claimed. The plaintiff responded to these items by a bill that said, "not applicable." At trial, however, the plaintiff proved that the decedent was employed and his earnings records were received into evidence. The jury returned a verdict for $55,000. The appellate division ordered a new trial unless the plaintiff accepted a reduction of the award to $20,000, representing what the verdict would have been if the lost earnings, which were omitted from the bill of particulars, were subtracted.

[B] Texas: Fair Notice of Factual Contentions

Plaintiff's Petition in Texas. A plaintiff's complaint in Texas must state a cause of action and give fair notice of the plaintiff's factual contentions as well as the plaintiff's legal theories. Dorsaneo, Crump, Carlson and Thornburg, *Texas Civil Procedure: Pretrial Litigation*, Ch. 5 (2007–08 ed.). The fair notice requirement requires a statement of the factual bases of the plaintiff's claim, but it is not necessary that the plaintiff plead the evidence on which the plaintiff places reliance. Thus, a general allegation of "negligence" is not sufficient to give fair notice of the plaintiff's factual claim. Older cases seem to require an identification of specific acts or omissions. *See, e.g., White v. Jackson*, 358 S.W.2d 174 (Tex. Civ. App.-Waco 1962, writ ref'd n.r.e.). Modern Texas cases interpret the fair notice standard to require roughly the same degree of factual specificity as Federal Form 9. *See, e.g., Willock v. Bui*, 734 S.W.2d 390 (Tex. App.-Houston [1st Dist.] 1987, no writ).

Defendant's Pleadings: Preliminary Matters ("Dilatory Pleas") and Special Exceptions. The defendant asserts that the court lacks subject matter jurisdiction by a plea to the jurisdiction; that it lacks personal jurisdiction by a special appearance; and that venue is improper or inconvenient by a motion to transfer venue. Most other matters not involving the merits (*e.g.*, failure to join a person needed for just adjudication) are raised by a plea in abatement (which, you should recall, is a common law legacy). Texas has abolished the general demurrer. A party's attack on the formal or substantive sufficiency of another party's pleadings in Texas is called a "special exception" and is related to the common law special demurrer. The special exception is used to attack vagueness, inappropriate matter, or legal insufficiency, and thus, this single type of pleading performs the functions fulfilled by the motion to dismiss for failure to state a claim, the motion to strike, and the motion for more definite statement in federal court.

General Denial and Other Defensive Pleadings on the Merits. Texas permits the defendant to assert a general denial in most instances. There are many kinds of denials that must be specific. Many of these denials must be "verified" (*i.e.*, supported by affidavit). Affirmative defenses must be "set forth affirmatively" under Tex. R. Civ. P. 94, which is modeled on Rule 8(c) of the Federal Rules.

WILLOCK v. BUI, 724 S.W.2d 390 (Tex. App.–Houston [1st Dist.] 1987, no writ). The plaintiff obtained a default judgment which the defendant challenged on appeal asserting, among other things, that the petition was inadequate to support a default judgment.

The pertinent part of Plaintiff Bui's petition reads as follows:

III.

On January 9, 1985 at approximately 8:00 a.m., Toan Viet Bui sustained serious personal injuries while driving a 1985 Toyota pickup truck which was involved in a rear-end collision, which forced his vehicle into the car in front of him. The automobile which Toan Viet Bui was operating was struck from behind during the collision which involved a Pontiac, Texas license number 3232-ADH, driven by George Michael Willock. The collision occured at 130 Hays Road, Houston Texas.

IV.

The collision described in paragraph III above and made the basis of this suit was directly and proximately caused by the negligence of George Michael Willock. On the occasion in question, George Michael Willock was guilty of acts of negligence each of which were a proximate cause of the collision made the basis of this suit.

A majority of the three-judge court of appeals' panel determined that the petition, though "inartfully drawn," gave the defendant fair notice of the claim involved. "A fair interpretation of the petition is that the appellee claims that he and the appellant were involved in an automobile collision, and that he was injured as a result of the appellant's negligence. The petition adequately informed appellant of the nature of the claim against him in compliance with Tex. R. Civ. P. 45 and 47." Another member of the panel dissented, reasoning that "the pleading fails to apprise the appellant of what his specific involvement was in the collision. Appellee's assertion that the appellant's vehicle was 'involved' in a collision with him, that also involved several other vehicles, does not assert a violation of any duty or responsibility owed by the appellant to the appellee."

[C] California: Pre-Printed Official Complaints, Common Counts, and Fictitious "Doe" Defendants

Official Pre-Printed Forms; Pleading a Cause of Action. Under the authority of CCP § 425.12, the California Judicial Council has promulgated officially approved forms for the "drafting" of the complaint. A plaintiff actually files two different kinds of documents — a "complaint," which contains fill-in-the-blank-and-check-the-box designations of parties, jurisdiction, damages, and type of claim, supplemented by an "attachment," stating the particularized cause of action, and also containing blanks and boxes. Plaintiff uses these forms to comply with the rules, which require that the cause of action be stated in terms of the "ultimate facts," not conclusions or evidence — although the cases interpret this requirement more liberally than the common law or Code pleading requirements. The pleading forms are optional, not mandatory.

Fictitious Defendants. One interesting aspect of California practice is the treatment of "Doe" defendants. *See* J. Hogan, *California's Unique Doe Defendant Practice: A Fiction Stranger than Truth*, 30 Stan. L. Rev. 51 (1977). If the complaint states that the name of a defendant is unknown to plaintiff, the defendant may be designated by this fictitious name, and, if the complaint is properly filed, plaintiff thus may avoid the bar of the statute of limitations. Doe defendants are used in situations in which plaintiff believes that certain individuals are liable but does not know their names, as well as in cases in which plaintiff is not sure whether the unknown defendants even exist (or whether they acted together with known defendants). Most of the cases indicate that the plaintiff's ignorance of the Doe defendants' identities must be real and not feigned, and the plaintiff must act promptly to identify them in the pleading when their true identities are learned. *Id.*

"Common Counts." As a holdover from the common law action of general assumpsit, California allows the pleading of common counts, in which it is sufficient to allege in a general way that the defendant "became indebted to the plaintiff" upon an open account (or a written account, or in some other manner, or for money had and received, etc.).

Defendant's Pleadings. The defendant may attack the form or legal sufficiency of the complaint by demurrer. (Certain kinds of motions are also available; *e.g.*, the motion for judgment on the pleadings, motion to strike, and motion to dismiss.) The answer is roughly analogous to that in federal practice, in that the defendant is required to sift the complaint and deny specific allegations; however, the defendant need not state expressly which allegations are admitted, in that those that are not denied are admitted. Also, denials must be more specific in form, in that the defendant must identify those allegations that are denied outright, those that are denied on "information and belief," and those that are denied "because of lack of sufficient information or belief." Again, the Judicial Council has promulgated Official Forms, which provide space for each variation in their truth and therefore denies them. Affirmative defenses must be separately pleaded.One interesting exception to these requirements: If the plaintiff's demand does not exceed $1,000, the defendant may use a general denial rather than admissions and denials. Cal. Code Civ. Pro. §§ 431.30 & 431.40.

SCHERER v. MARK, 64 Cal. App. 3d 834, 135 Cal. Rptr. 90 (1976). The plaintiff's original complaint alleged that defendant Memorial Hospital and "Does I through XXX, inclusive" were "each . . . responsible for the events and happenings hereinafter alleged." The complaint charged that all the defendants had "negligently and carelessly treated the plaintiff in that they failed to follow a standard of care in common practice," including watching over her while she was taking a bath and providing her with a safe place to bathe while handicapped and under medication, and that as a result she fell and was injured. After the running of the statute of limitations, she amended the complaint to insert the name of her physician, Howard Mark, in place of Doe I. Defendant Mark filed a demurrer, which was sustained evidently on the theory that the complaint stated no cause of action against him because, unlike the hospital, he had no duty with respect to the events in question. The plaintiff was given leave to amend.

The plaintiff's second amended complaint contained, first, the same cause of action in the original complaint. Second, it added a cause of action against Mark and Does 26, 27 and 28, to the effect that these "defendants . . . so negligently prescribed instructions and drugs and bathroom privileges and related treatment . . . that plaintiff was caused to" suffer injury. This time, Mark filed an answer containing denials as well as the affirmative defenses of contributory negligence and statute of limitations. The trial court granted summary judgment on the limitations defense, because the second cause of action was pleaded after limitations had run, and the appellate court affirmed. First, assuming the plaintiff was entitled to use John Doe practice as to her doctor, whose name she knew, "Ignorance of the facts giving rise to a cause of action, like ignorance of the true name, should be real and not feigned." Here, "plaintiff knew all of the basic facts" at the outset. Furthermore, the pleading against Mark could not relate back to the original filing because the cause of action alleged against him had been itself added after limitations had run. "[A]n amendment purporting to state a new cause of action against such Doe defendant in his true name will be barred if filed after the expiration of the statute of limitations."

§ 5.08 Improving the Rules of Pleading: Notes and Questions

(1) *Should We Require Pleading of a "Claim" or of a "Cause of Action"?* This question is an important issue raised by this chapter. One can validly object to the narrow kind of "fact" pleading required under the Field Codes, but no such objection can be leveled at modern state rules governing the pleading of a cause of action. Those rules probably result in somewhat earlier definition of issues and screening of inappropriate claims; the tradeoff may be that they require greater attention to pleading procedures and may result in a slightly higher number of variances (although this effect can be reduced by liberal allowance of trial and post-trial amendments) than federal "notice" pleading would. Which approach do you think is better?

(2) *Amendments; Limitations.* Under some state systems (*e.g.*, Texas), amendments are allowed without leave of court until a certain number of days before trial unless the opponent objects and shows prejudice. Might this approach be preferable to requiring judges to rule on each motion to amend, particularly since the leave is supposed to be "freely given"? [Note: The answer might depend upon the complexity of the case — and upon whether defendant is required to replead the answer each time.] As for limitations, should the federal system adopt an approach similar to California's "Doe Defendant" practice? [Note: That method would be disadvantageous to some defendants, who would experience delay in their investigations of claims against them, and might dilute the purposes of the statute of limitations in avoiding stale claims; on the other hand, it would protect a plaintiff who has a genuine claim if, and only if, the plaintiff was genuinely unable to name the defendant at the time of suit.]

(3) *Sanctions.* Rule 11 in its current form requires notice and an opportunity to cure (the 21-day safe harbor). Is this provision necessary to avoid discouraging innovation,

or does it result unfairly in putting the burden of investigation on innocent opponents? Should sanctions be mandatory on the initial violation?

(4) *The Form of Denials.* Should the general denial be permissible? [Note: Its use can better be appreciated when one considers that the plaintiff has the limitations period in which to plead, but the defendant has only a few days (unless the time is extended by agreement of the parties or order of the court); furthermore, the defendant can be compelled to admit or deny facts through a request for admissions.] In the alternative, should the federal courts consider California's compromise, which allows the general denial to be used in small cases? Should the federal courts adopt California practice, allowing defendant to plead against only those facts that he denies, taking the rest as admitted? [The difference is subtle, but the federal requirement of express admission may encourage the denial of facts that would otherwise remain uncontested.]

(5) *"Printed Form" Pleadings.* What advantages are there in California's promulgation of check-the-box and fill-in-the-blank pleadings? What disadvantages? Should the federal courts adopt a similar approach?

(6) *Coordination Among Pleadings, Discovery, and Pretrial Conferences and Orders.* In considering a system of pleading rules, one must keep in mind the relationship between pleadings, discovery, and pretrial conferences and orders. The federal system allows "notice" pleading, in part because it assumes that the opponent can obtain sufficient definition of facts and issues from discovery, and the court can narrow the issues at pretrial. At what stage in the lawsuit should the judge attempt to narrow the issues?

APPENDIX TO CHAPTER 5

SAMPLE PLEADINGS FROM THREE JURISDICTIONS

§ A New York: Palsgraf v. Long Island R.R. Co.

SUPREME COURT OF THE STATE OF NEW YORK
County of Kings

HELEN PALSGRAF, Plaintiff, against THE LONG ISLAND RR. CO., Defendant.	COMPLAINT Index No. ______

Plaintiff, complaining of the defendant through MATTHEW W. WOOD, her attorney, alleges:

FIRST: Upon information and belief, that at all of the times hereinafter mentioned the above named defendant was and still is a railway corporation duly organized and existing under and by virtue of the laws of the State of New York.

SECOND: [Alleges that defendant operated a railroad through Brooklyn.]

THIRD: [Alleges that defendant operated the East New York station.]

FOURTH: That it was the duty of the above named defendant at all of the times hereinafter mentioned to operate its trains so that the plaintiff and other persons . . . could use the said platform or station at the said East New York station without danger of being injured by the passing of defendant's trains through said station, and it was the further duty of the defendant to provide a suitable and sufficient number of employees or agents at said station . . . when . . . there was habitually accustomed to be a large number of passengers congregated on said station, . . . and it was further the duty of the defendant to make and enforce proper rules and regulations for the guidance and control of its employees . . . so that . . . the persons on the platform thereof might be reasonably free from injury. It was further the duty of the defendant to . . . exercise such care, caution and prudence in the premises that passengers or other persons would not be allowed to bring upon and into its said stations or cars or trains any fireworks or other combustible or explosive substances.

FIFTH: That the defendant was negligent and remiss in the performance of one or more of its several duties in that on Sunday, the 24th day of August, 1924, between the hours of ten and eleven o'clock in the forenoon of said day, it failed and neglected to provide a suitable and sufficient number of employees and agents at said station at a time when, to the knowledge of the defendant, the said station was accustomed to be and was used by a large number of passengers for the purpose of boarding its said cars at said station, . . . and further that it failed and neglected to make, promulgate and enforce proper rules and regulations for the guidance and control of its employees at said station so that the plaintiff and other persons on said station might be reasonably free from injury, and in that it failed to prevent the bringing in or upon the said passenger station or the carrying into its said passenger cars at said station or at some other station or place of fireworks or other explosive or combustible substances, and that by reason of the neglect of the defendant, its agents or servants, . . . the plaintiff herein, through the negligence and carelessness of the defendant, was negligently and carelessly invited, directed, permitted and allowed to enter upon the said platform then and there crowded with people, and in close proximity to a dangerous and unexploded blast of gunpowder or some other explosive at said time and place, and that while plaintiff was lawfully upon the platform, . . . an explosion of gunpowder or some other explosive substance suddenly and violently took place, by reason of which and as a direct result thereof the plaintiff was violently jostled, shoved, crowded or pushed by the force of said explosion or by the crowd of other passengers, which the defendant had negligently allowed to congregate and remain on said station at said time, or by both said explosion and jostling, so that plaintiff was knocked down or against certain of the platform stairs, inflicting upon plaintiff grievous, serious and painful injuries. . . . [The complaint describes plaintiff's injuries and damages, including past and future mental and physical pain; past and future medical and health-care expenses; and loss of earnings and earning capacity.]

SIXTH: That the said injuries to the plaintiff were caused solely through the carelessness and negligence of the defendant, its agents or servants, and through no fault on the part of the plaintiff in any way contributing thereto.

SEVENTH: That by reason of the premises plaintiff has been damaged in the sum of Fifty thousand dollars ($50,000.).

WHEREFORE plaintiff demands judgment against the defendant in the sum of Fifty thousand dollars ($50,000.) together with the costs and disbursements of this action.

MATTHEW W. WOOD,
Attorney for Plaintiff

SUPREME COURT OF THE STATE OF NEW YORK
County of Kings

HELEN PALSGRAF, Plaintiff, against THE LONG ISLAND RR. CO., Defendant.	ANSWER Index No. _______

The defendant answering the complaint herein alleges:

I. It admits that at all times mentioned in the complaint, it was and still is a domestic railroad corporation, duly organized and existing under and by virtue of the laws of the State of New York, and that at all of said times, it owned, operated and controlled a railroad together with its appurtenances in and through the Borough of Brooklyn, City and State of New York, and that in connection with its said railroad, it maintained a passenger station and platform known as the East New York Station in the said Borough of Brooklyn, City of New York.

II. On information and belief it denies each and every other allegation contained in the complaint.

WHEREFORE, the defendant asks that the complaint herein be dismissed with costs.

JOSEPH F. KEANY,
Attorney for Defendant

NOTES AND QUESTIONS

(1) *Stating "the Facts" Constituting the "Cause of Action."* A cause of action for negligence consists of the following elements: (1) defendant's duty, (2) defendant's breach of the duty by a negligent act or omission, (3) causation, (4) injury, and (5) damages. Are all of these elements present as properly pleaded "facts"? How might a pleading under modern rules differ from this one? [Note: Current New York rules require the statement of a "cause of action," CPLR 3211(a)(8), but do not require pleading of "facts." *See* § 5.07 [A], above.]

(2) *The Burden of Pleading Contributory Negligence.* Notice that the plaintiff pleads freedom from contributory negligence (Complaint, paragraph 6). For claims accruing after September 1, 1975, New York treats contributory negligence by a comparative system rather than as a bar, and it is an affirmative defense. CPLR 1412. How would this change affect pleadings such as these if the accident happened today?

(3) *Does the Answer Properly Address the Allegations?* Notice that the defendant's denial, in Paragraph II of the Answer, of "each and every other allegation" of the complaint, amounts to a denial of many allegations that must be true — such as that the defendant had a duty to provide sufficient employees to ensure safety and that the plaintiff was injured. How might a modern answer differ?

(4) *Palsgraf v. Long Island R.R.*, 248 N.Y.339, 162 N.E. 99 (1928), is one of the most famous cases in all of Anglo-American jurisprudence. The proof at trial showed that a conductor assisting a passenger to board a moving train dislodged a package containing fireworks, which exploded and knocked down a set of scales, which struck and injured the plaintiff. Chief Judge Cardozo's opinion reversed a judgment for the plaintiff on the ground that the element we know today as foreseeability was lacking. Question: Might the plaintiff have lost because of a variance, since her pleading alleged that her injuries resulted from the explosion itself or from the crowd jostling her, rather than from scales falling upon her?

§ B Texas: Pleadings in Pennzoil Co. v. Texaco Inc.

No. 84-05905

PENNZOIL COMPANY, a Delaware Corporation, Plaintiff, v. TEXACO INC., a Delaware Corporation, Defendant.	IN THE DISTRICT COURT OF HARRIS COUNTY, TEXAS 151ST JUDICIAL DISTRICT

PLAINTIFF'S THIRD AMENDED ORIGINAL PETITION

Pennzoil Company files this Third Amended Original Petition complaining of Texaco Inc., and would respectfully show the following:

I. THE PARTIES

1. Pennzoil Company ("Pennzoil") is a corporation organized and existing under the laws of the State of Delaware with its principal executive offices in Houston, Texas. . . .

2. . . . Texaco Inc. ("Texaco") is a corporation organized and existing under the laws of the State of Delaware with its principal executive (offices located at 2000 Westchester Avenue, White Plains, New York. Texaco has substantial offices located in Houston, Texas, and is qualified to do business in the State of Texas. Texaco has been served with [process] by serving its registered agent, Donald A. Buckner, 1111 Rusk Avenue, Houston, Texas 77002.

II. THE FACTS

3. On December 28, 1983, Pennzoil (through its wholly-owned subsidiary Holdings Incorporated) commenced a tender offer for up to 16,000,000 shares of the common stock of Getty Oil Company ("Getty"), at a per share price of $100 ("Tender Offer"). As of November 7, 1983, there were 79,132,352 shares of Getty common stock outstanding (the "Shares"). . . . The $100 per Share Tender Offer price represented a 25% premium above the closing price of the Shares on the day preceding the commencement of the Tender Offer. . . .

4. The J. Paul Getty Museum ("Museum") at the time of the Tender Offer was the beneficial owner of 9,320,340 Shares (approximately 11.8% of the total outstanding). . . . [T]he Museum . . . is a charitable trust organized under the laws of California. . . .

5. Gordon P. Getty, as Trustee ("Trustee") of the Sarah C. Getty Trust dated December 31, 1934 ("Trust"), was at the time of the Tender Offer the beneficial owner of 31,805,088 Shares (approximately 40.2% of the total outstanding). . . .

6. On Friday, December 30, 1983, representatives of the Trustee and Pennzoil met in New York City. At this meeting, the Trustee's representatives stated that the Trustee would be willing to enter into negotiations with Pennzoil to acquire Getty on the condition that the Trustee would own a controlling 4/7 ths of the stock of the Company (or 57%) and Pennzoil would limit itself to 3/7ths (or 43%).

[Paragraphs 7, 8 and 9 describe the negotiations by which Pennzoil, the Trustee, and the Museum entered into a Memorandum of Agreement which established a plan for Pennzoil's acquisition of Getty stock, to be presented to Getty's board of directors. These paragraphs also describe a "Letter Agreement" by which the Trustee agreed to support the Memorandum and Plan before the Getty board. A copy of the Letter Agreement is attached to the Petition as Exhibit A.

[Paragraph 10 describes restrictions imposed by the charitable trust instrument on the Museum's disposition of its assets. The paragraph also describes how the transaction was structured to comply with these requirements.]

11. On the evening of January 2, the Getty board of directors met in New York for the purpose of considering the Tender Offer and other related matters. At that meeting, the Trustee and the Museum together formally signed and presented to the board the Memorandum with certain insubstantial handwritten interlineations, a copy of which is attached hereto as Exhibit B. . . . The Memorandum recites that the Plan "has been developed and approved by" the Trustee, the Museum and Pennzoil. The board initially declined to approve the Plan as reflected in the Memorandum because of the $110 price, although the Trustee and the Museum's President, both members of the board, as well as four other non-management directors, voted in favor of the Plan.

[Paragraph 12 describes a series of counteroffers and negotiations. Exhibit D is a letter proposal that Pennzoil alleges became part of the final contract.]

13. On Tuesday, January 3, Pennzoil further offered to modify its proposal to pay $110 per Share in cash, plus a "stub" of $3 per Share at such time as [ERC Corporation, a Getty subsidiary] could be sold or otherwise liquidated (the "ERC stub"). Later that day, upon being advised that Pennzoil might be willing to increase the $3 ERC stub if the Getty board required it, the board voted 15 to 1 to accept the Pennzoil proposal so long as the stub was $5. The fifteen affirmative votes included the votes of Getty's Chairman, the Trustee and the President of the Museum. Pennzoil there-upon accepted this counterproposal. At that point, the Trustee, the Museum, Getty and Pennzoil had reached an agreement embodying all essential terms and conditions of a transaction in which Pennzoil and the Trustee would become the sole owners of Getty, and all of Getty's stockholders, other than the Trustee and Pennzoil, would receive cash and other considerations for their Shares. This agreement constituted a legally binding contract which had been approved not only by the Getty board of directors, but also by the holders of a majority of the Shares (*i.e.*, the Trustee and the Museum, who together owned 52% of the Shares).

14. On Wednesday morning, January 4, . . . Getty, the Museum and the Trustee jointly announced to the public their agreement with Pennzoil by issuing the following press release on Getty letterhead (a copy of which is attached hereto as Exhibit E):

> Los Angeles — Getty Oil Company, The J. Paul Getty Museum and Gordon P. Getty, as Trustee of the Sarah C. Getty Trust, announced today that they have agreed in principle with Pennzoil Company to a merger of Getty Oil and a newly formed entity owned by Pennzoil and the Trustee.
>
> In connection with the transaction, the shareholders of Getty Oil other than Pennzoil and the Trustee will receive $110 per share cash plus the right to receive deferred cash considerations in a formula amount. [Portions of the release are omitted here, though it was quoted in full in the petition.] . . .

> The transaction is subject to execution of a definitive merger agreement, approval by the stockholders of Getty Oil and completion of various governmental filing and waiting period requirements.
>
> Following consummation of the merger, the Trust will own 4/7ths of the outstanding common stock of Getty Oil and Pennzoil will own 3/7ths. The Trust and Pennzoil have also agreed in principle that following consummation of the merger they will endeavor in good faith to agree upon a plan for restructuring Getty Oil. . . .

Also on January 4, Pennzoil adopted the press release and reissued it to the public and Pennzoil's employees.

15. The January 3 agreement between Pennzoil and the three Getty entities imposed a good faith obligation on the parties to negotiate the details of the agreement and to execute definitive documentation to implement the essential terms already agreed upon. During the evening of January 3 and through the days of January 4 and 5, attorneys for Pennzoil and the Trustee worked on the formal documentation necessary to implement the agreement.

16. Texaco . . . induced the Museum and Getty management to violate their agreement with Pennzoil. To assure the success of its new proposal and to assure that the prior Pennzoil agreement would be thwarted, the Museum's chief counsel, Martin Lipton, in league with Texaco, instructed his primary assistant attorney not to meet with Pennzoil on January 5 to complete the formal closing papers.

[Paragraph 17 describes Texaco's transaction with the Trustee and the Museum. The Trustee agreed to recommend Texaco's proposal to the Getty board.]

18. Pennzoil did not learn of Texaco's interference with its agreement until at approximately 8:00 a.m., on Friday, January 6, the following announcement was carried by the Dow Jones New Service:

> White Plains, NY—DJ—John K. McKinley, Chairman of Texaco, Inc., announced that Texaco signed an agreement with the J. Paul Getty Museum, owner of 11.8% of the outstanding common stock of Getty Oil Company, to purchase all of that stock for $125 per share in cash. [The remainder of the announcement is omitted here but was quoted in full in the petition.]

[Paragraph 19 sets out the text of a letter in which Pennzoil advised the Getty board that Pennzoil expected its agreement to be honored and would commence suit if it was not.

[Paragraph 20 sets out Getty's announcement of an agreement in principle with Texaco.

[Paragraphs 21-22 allege that Texaco's inducements to Getty, the Museum and the Trustee to breach their agreement with Pennzoil included Texaco's indemnifying them against any claims of Pennzoil and accepting the Shares without warranty as to Pennzoil's rights.

[Paragraphs 23-27 describe the consummation of the Texaco-Getty acquisition at $128 per share and allege that this transaction caused Pennzoil "grievous damages."]

III. THE [CAUSES OF ACTION]

28. Texaco knew of the existence of the valid contract between and among Pennzoil, the Trustee, the Museum and Getty, and intentionally procured the breach of such contract, all to Pennzoil's detriment.

29. Texaco has consummated its agreements with the Trustee, the Museum and Getty in direct violation of Pennzoil's pre-existing rights, of which Texaco was well aware. Through this continuing interference with Pennzoil's pre-existing rights, Texaco has inflicted grievous damages on Pennzoil, for which Pennzoil should be compensated to the fullest extent possible by an award of money damages.

30. Pennzoil seeks actual damages representing its loss of bargain resulting from such wrongful conduct in an amount the jury deems appropriate. Pennzoil submits that its loss of bargain amounts to at least $7.53 billion.

31. Moreover, since Texaco's conduct was in willful, wanton and reckless disregard of the rights of Pennzoil, Pennzoil seeks recovery of punitive damages in an amount the jury deems appropriate. Pennzoil submits that Texaco's outrageous and intentional misconduct warrants an award of at least $7.53 billion.

32. Pennzoil further requests pre-judgment and post-judgment interest on the jury's award to the maximum extent permitted by law.

WHEREUPON, premises considered, Pennzoil respectfully prays that upon trial by jury this Court enter judgment against Texaco in such amount as is proper, which Pennzoil believes to be at least $7.53 billion actual damages and $7.53 billion punitive damages, plus pre-judgment and post-judgment interest thereon to the maximum extent permitted by law, that Pennzoil be awarded court costs, and that Pennzoil have such other and further relief as may be just.

Respectfully submitted,

OF COUNSEL:
BAKER & BOTTS
John L. Jeffers

JAMAIL & KOLIUS
By: Joseph D. Jamail

NO. 84-05905

PENNZOIL COMPANY, Plaintiff, v. TEXACO INC., Defendant	IN THE DISTRICT COURT OF HARRIS COUNTY, TEXAS 151ST JUDICIAL DISTRICT

TEXACO'S OBJECTION TO THE FILING OF PENNZOIL'S . . . AMENDED ORIGINAL PETITION, SPECIAL EXCEPTIONS, AND . . . AMENDED ANSWER AND COUNTERCLAIM

TO THE HONORABLE COURT:

NOW COMES Texaco Inc. ("Texaco"), defendant in the captioned case, and . . . would respectfully show the Court and jury as follows:

OBJECTION [TO AMENDMENT OF PETITION]

1. Texaco objects to the filing of Pennzoil's . . . Amended Original Petition and moves to strike the Petition. The filing is untimely in that it occurs after the pleadings have been closed by prior Court orders, after Pennzoil has represented that the pleadings are in order and the case ready for trial and after the Court [has] certified the case for trial. . . .

CHALLENGES TO THE SUFFICIENCY OF THE PETITION

[At this point, Texaco's pleading interposes 18 different challenges to Pennzoil's petition. The challenges are made by "special exception," which is the Texas procedure for raising matters either of form or of substance. The following is an example of a special exception directed to the form of the Petition.] . . .

5. Texaco specially excepts to that part of paragraph 13 of the Petition which reads as follows:

> At that point, the Trustee, the Museum, Getty and Pennzoil had reached an agreement embodying all essential terms and conditions of [the] transaction. . . . This agreement constituted a legally binding contract.
>
> . .

On the grounds that the allegations are opinions and conclusions without any or sufficient allegations of fact to support such conclusions. . . .

[The following is an example of Texaco's challenges to the substance of the petition.]

19. Texaco specially excepts to [paragraph 32] of the Petition on the grounds that prejudgment interest is not recoverable in this case.

. . . ANSWER [ON THE MERITS]

20. Texaco enters its general denial, as authorized by the rules of this Court, to the charges, claims, and allegations of Pennzoil, and respectfully requests that Pennzoil be required to prove all of those matters by a preponderance of the evidence as required by law.

21. The Pennzoil "Plan" or "Memorandum of Agreement" was at all times a unitary plan fixed by its terms which expired upon the withdrawal of any of the original parties to the plan. If any of the parties agreed to the plan then the agreement was by mutual mistake or mistakes and no party was bound by the terms once the mistake or mistakes were discovered.

22. Pennzoil repudiated and breached its alleged agreement with at least one of the members of the original "Plan" or "Memorandum of Agreement." The plan was a unitary plan and Pennzoil's breach left the parties free to negotiate with and contract with third parties.

23. Any private arrangements or agreements to purchase shares of stock in Getty Oil Company which Pennzoil made or is alleged to have made after January 1, 1984, were in violation of the securities laws of the United States including the Securities Exchange Act of 1934, 15 U.S.C. §§ 78a et seq., and Rule 10b-13, 17 C.F.R. § 240.10b-13, and the antitrust laws of the United States, including the Sherman Act, 15 U.S.C. § 1 and the Clayton Act, 15 U.S.C. § 19, and any owner of stock in Getty Oil Company with

whom Pennzoil dealt or attempted to deal with on this basis was free to sell such owner's stock regardless of any such agreement with Pennzoil.

[Paragraphs 24-27 allege other affirmative defenses, including duress (Getty was "under duress" by Pennzoil's tender offer) and illegality (because the alleged agreement would have violated the trust instrument that had set up the Museum). These paragraphs also set forth Texaco's position that the alleged transaction "was not a contract" or a "binding agreement."]

COUNTERCLAIM

[Paragraphs 28 through 46 contain Texaco's counterclaim for Pennzoil's alleged interference with Texaco's contract, for *prima facie* tort, for unfair competition, and for abuse of process.]

PREMISES CONSIDERED, Texaco Inc. prays that its Objection and Motion to Strike Pennzoil's . . . Amended Petition be sustained, and, subject to such Objection and Motion to Strike, that its special exceptions be granted with appropriate orders; that Pennzoil take nothing from Texaco Inc. on its claims; that Texaco Inc. have judgment against Pennzoil on its counterclaim; that all cost be charged to Pennzoil; and for such other and further orders and relief as may be appropriate, general or special, at law or in equity.

Respectfully submitted,
MILLER, KEETON,
BRISTOW & BROWN
[By] Richard B. Miller

NOTES AND QUESTIONS

(1) *The Petition.* Notice the structure of the petition. In particular, note that "The Facts" are set out in a section separate from the causes of action. In this manner, Pennzoil can state the facts once and apply them to each of its cause of action; furthermore, it avoids the need to particularize which facts relate to which cause of action. This method is economical and tactically sound in a jurisdiction requiring the pleading of a cause of action.

(2) *Specificity.* The allegations in this petition may have been set forth in greater detail than is required under Texas law, which requires "fair notice" of factual theories. But the plaintiff has minimized the likelihood of variances by pleading the causes of action separately from the facts. The defendant's special exceptions are attacks both on the content of the petition and, also, upon its specificity. Remember, this jurisdiction requires fair notice not only of the plaintiff's legal theory, but also of its factual theory.

(3) *The Answer.* Notice the use of the general denial by Texaco. How would a federal answer differ? Also, note the pleading of numerous affirmative defenses. Some of the matters that are affirmatively pleaded may not, in truth, be affirmative defenses (the defendant's assertion that there was no contract is an example); however, affirmative pleading is appropriate whenever there is doubt whether it is required. Texas has liberal amendment rules (more liberal than the federal approach), and the trial court overruled the defendant's objections to the amended petition.

§ C California: Pre-Printed Products Liability Complaint Form

[See Figure 5A below.]

NOTES AND QUESTIONS

(1) *Relationship of this "Attachment" to Other Form Pleadings.* This form is the place where the "guts" of a plaintiff's cause of action will be set out, but note that it is an "Attachment." It is designed, in fact, to be attached to a longer check-the-box-and-fill-in-the-blank "Complaint" form, upon which the plaintiff is to set forth information about the parties, jurisdiction, etc. Several different "Attachments" can be annexed to a single complaint to state different counts or causes of action against the same defendants. A check-the-box-and-fill-in-the-blank "Answer" form is also provided — it provides spaces for admissions, denials, and affirmative defenses. Note that the forms do not dispense with the necessity of drafting the claims or defenses; the attorney still has to do the thinking and writing that attorneys have traditionally done in this regard.

(2) *Advantages and Disadvantages.* What are the advantages and disadvantages of this approach?

SHORT TITLE:	CASE NUMBER

______ (number) **CAUSE OF ACTION—Products Liability** Page ______

ATTACHMENT TO □ Complaint □ Cross-Complaint

(Use a separate cause of action form for each cause of action.)

Plaintiff *(name)*:

Prod.L-1. On or about *(date)*: plaintiff was injured by the following product:

Prod.L-2. Each of the defendants knew the product would be purchased and used without inspection for defects. The product was defective when it left the control of each defendant. The product at the time of injury was being
□ used in the manner intended by the defendants.
□ used in a manner that was reasonably foreseeable by defendants as involving a substantial danger not readily apparent. Adequate warnings of the danger were not given.

Prod.L-3. Plaintiff was a
□ purchaser of the product. □ user of the product.
□ bystander to the use of the product. □ other *(specify)*:

PLAINTIFF'S INJURY WAS THE LEGAL (PROXIMATE) RESULT OF THE FOLLOWING:

Prod.L-4. □ **Count One—Strict liability** of the following defendants who
a. □ manufactured or assembled the product *(names)*:

□ Does ______ to ______
b. □ designed and manufactured component parts supplied to the manufacturer *(names)*:

□ Does ______ to ______
c. □ sold the product to the public *(names)*:

□ Does ______ to ______

Prod.L-5. □ **Count Two—Negligence** of the following defendants who owed a duty to plaintiff *(names)*:

□ Does ______ to ______

Prod.L-6. □ **Count Three—Breach of warranty** by the following defendants *(names)*:

□ Does ______ to ______
a. □ who breached an implied warranty
b. □ who breached an express warranty which was
□ written □ oral

Prod.L-7. □ The defendants who are liable to plaintiffs for other reasons and the reasons for the liability are
□ listed in Attachment—Prod.L-7 □ as follows:

Form Approved by the Judicial Council of California Effective January 1, 1982 Rule 982.1(8)

CAUSE OF ACTION—Products Liability

CCP 425.12

CHAPTER 6

MULTIPLE PARTIES AND CLAIMS

§ 6.01 An Overview of the Devices for Joining Multiple Parties or Claims

A Simplified Introduction. In this chapter, we take up procedural devices for combining (or separating) multiple parties or claims. These devices arise in litigation situations that are abstractly defined and hard to visualize. In addition, they create their own knotty procedural problems. Students sometimes find this material difficult, and accordingly, this overview is designed to give you a simplified introduction.

Perhaps the best way to visualize these concepts — which include third-party joinder ("impleader"), permissive joinder, counterclaims, cross-claims, compulsory joinder, interpleader, intervention, class actions, multi-district litigation, consolidation, separate trial, and severance — is to consider them simply as different ways of putting together or taking apart the parties and claims that make up a lawsuit. The various rules complement each other, and they are designed to allow the suit to have as large a number of parties or claims, or as few a number, as conveniently fits the factual situation in dispute. This overview will give you an idea of the purpose of each of these devices.

Third-Party Practice ("Impleader") (Rule 14). Assume that Paul Plaintiff is driving his car, begins to stop for a stop sign, and is rear-ended by Dan Defendant. Paul sues Dan for his injuries. But Dan, upon receiving the complaint, recalls that an instant before hitting Paul, he, Dan, was struck from the rear by an automobile driven by Tom Thirdparty. It was this impact which caused him to be propelled into Paul's vehicle. For a diagram of this accident, see Figure 6A, below.

If you represented Dan Defendant, you of course would want to defend him against Paul's claim. But is there anything else that you might want to do to represent Dan?

Of course there is! Tom Thirdparty is conspicuously left out. The device for bringing Tom into the suit is called a "third-party claim." More formally, it is known as "impleader": We say that Dan "impleads" Tom. For a diagram of impleader or third-party joinder, see Figure 6B.

FIGURES 6A—6E
THIRD-PARTY IMPLEADER, COUNTERCLAIM, AND CROSS-CLAIM

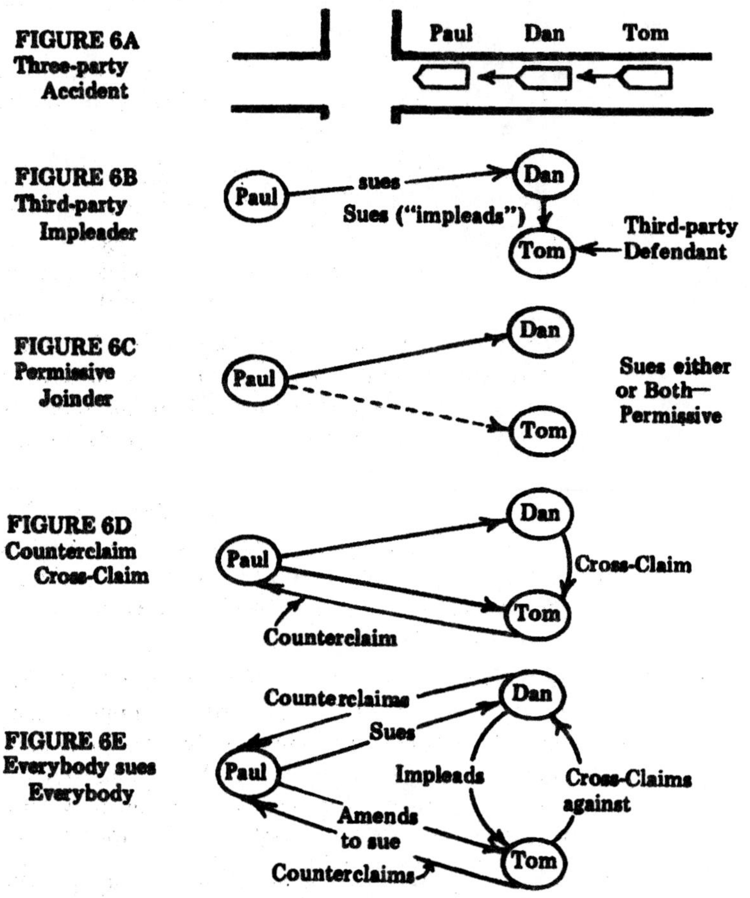

Why might Dan Defendant decide to implead Tom Thirdparty? Because if Dan is found liable to Paul, he may still be able to recover part or all of that liability from Tom if he can show that Tom was at fault. Of course, Dan is not required to implead Tom; that is a question of tactics.

Permissive Joinder of Parties (Rule 20). In the situation above, involving Paul, Dan, and Tom, what would you do if you represented Paul Plaintiff from the beginning, and you were trying to decide whom to sue?

If there were a basis for saying that either or both Dan and Tom were negligent, you could (and probably should) join both of them in one suit. You might do well to claim a right to relief against them severally (*i.e.*, they are both liable for the full judgment);

jointly (*i.e.*, they are each liable for portions of the judgment); and in the alternative (*i.e.*, if it wasn't Dan's fault, it was Tom's, and vice versa).

Figure 6C is a diagram of this type of joinder, called "permissive joinder."

What if you wanted to sue one or the other (that is, either Dan or Tom), but not both? The rules allow you to do that, too, if you prefer.

That is why this procedure is called "permissive" joinder. Paul can choose whether to sue one, sue the other, or sue both. If Paul thinks that Dan has sufficient assets to cover a judgment and was guilty of negligence, and if Tom was relatively free from negligence and his addition would only complicate matters, Paul may decide to sue Dan only. On the other hand, if Tom is guilty of negligence, while Dan has cooperated and settled his claim with Paul, Paul may decide to sue Tom only. Or, finally, if both appear to have been responsible, he may join both of them.

What if Dan Defendant is sued alone, and Dan doesn't like it? That's too bad; he can't complain about the non-joinder of Tom. His remedy is to file his own claim, in the form of a third-party action against Tom, if he wants to do so.

Counterclaims and Cross-Claims (Rule 13). The next two claim-joinder devices are diagrammed in Figure 6D. The simplest example of a "cross-claim" is an action by one defendant against another defendant. Thus if Paul has sued both Dan and Tom, Dan may assert a cross-claim against his co-party, Tom, to recover for damages to his person or property or for contribution to any liability to Paul, in case Dan is found liable to Paul. The simplest example of a counterclaim (also illustrated in Figure 6D) is a suit by the defendant against the plaintiff.

In the situation depicted here, Dan's or Tom's potential counterclaim against Paul would be a "compulsory" counterclaim. A compulsory counterclaim is one that arises out of the same transaction or occurrence as the plaintiff's suit. Because all of the claims in question here arose from the same automobile accident, the counterclaims are compulsory. A compulsory counterclaim must be asserted at the time of the plaintiff's suit, or it is barred.

Everybody Claims Against Everybody Else. These devices — impleader, permissive joinder, counterclaims, and cross-claims — were invented so that the litigation between and among Paul, Dan and Tom can be efficiently resolved. Legal terminology should not prevent all of their related claims from being heard in a single suit, if that is the most efficient procedure. These devices allow this flexibility, no matter who sues whom — and regardless of who is nominally called the plaintiff.

In our situation involving Tom, Dan, and Paul, the case could start with a simple claim by Paul against Dan and could escalate (through any one of a number of different patterns) into a case in which everyone was claiming against everyone else. Say, for example, that Paul sued Dan; Dan then counterclaimed against Paul and filed a third-party action against Tom; Paul then amended his complaint so that he was suing Tom, too (which Paul can do under the permissive joinder rules); and Tom then counterclaimed against Paul and cross-claimed against Dan. A diagram of all this appears in Figure E.

Or the case could start, and remain, very simple, with just one claim by Paul against Dan. But no matter how simple or complicated the lawsuit becomes, it is helpful to remember that the rules are set up to allow assertion of all related claims a party has, even if the result is that everyone claims against everyone else.

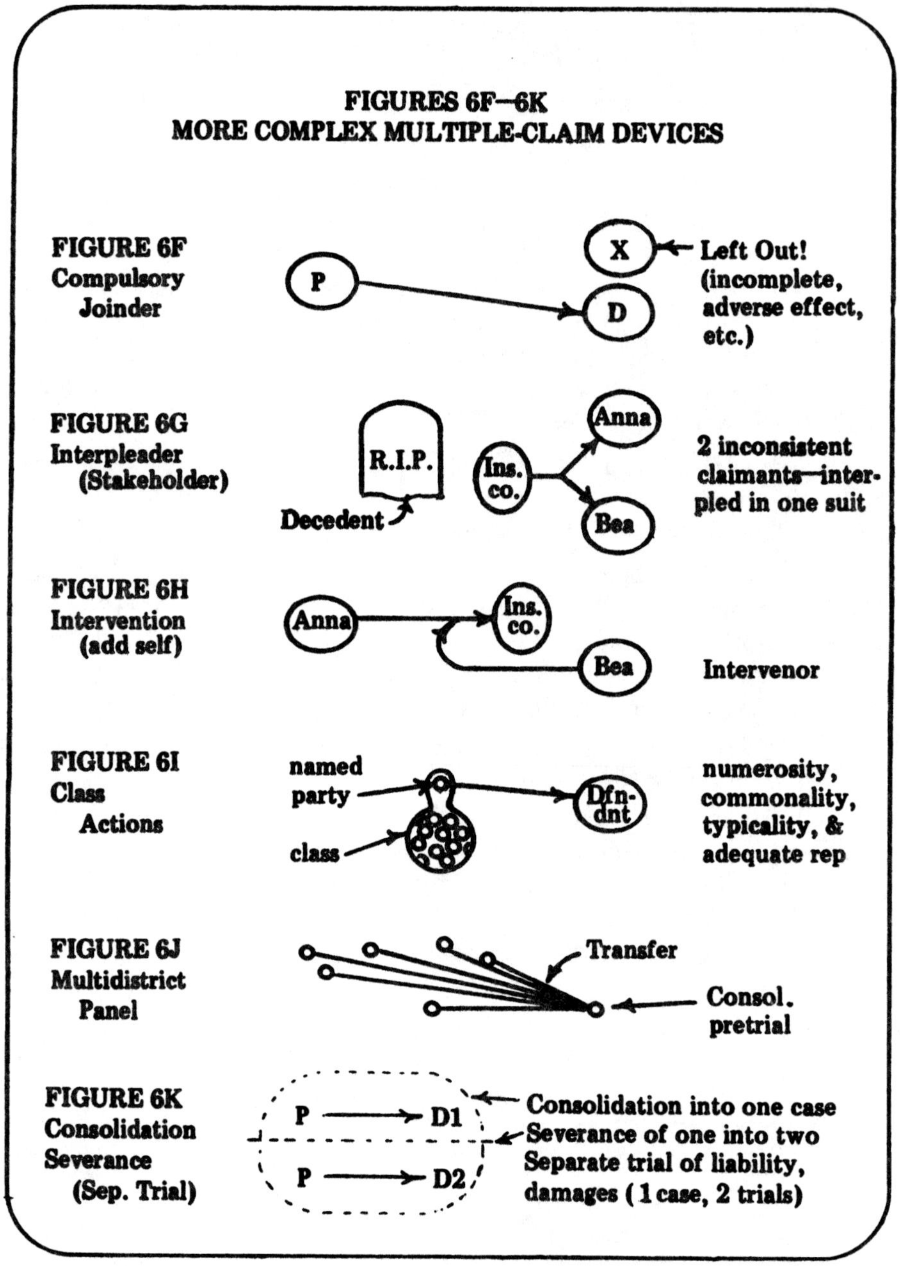

Compulsory Joinder: Persons Needed for Just Adjudication (Rule 19). Most situations involving multiple parties are permissive joinder situations, because there is no harm in allowing the plaintiff to have a choice of whom to sue. But there are some situations in which someone could be harmed because a potential party is left out. Also, there are some situations in which the lawsuit cannot effectively serve its purpose, or would result in an unfair judgment, because someone is left out.

What happens then?

The situation is diagrammed in Figure 6F, above. We say that the absent person is a "person[] required to be joined if feasible," in the terminology of Rule 19. And upon request, the courts will compel the plaintiff to join this absent party, if it is feasible to join him, before allowing the plaintiff to proceed with the action. That is why this situation is called "compulsory" joinder, as opposed to "permissive."

What sorts of situations give rise to compulsory joinder?

Here is one simple example. Assume that a decedent, *D*, has just died, leaving a will that gives his estate to certain persons. One of *D*'s relatives is left out of the will. He sues to contest the will, claiming that it is invalid. But the only person who this disgruntled relative sues is the executor named in the will. The persons who would receive property under the will, and the persons who would receive property if the will were thrown out, are not parties. Obviously, there is something wrong here; this lawsuit is more than a dispute between this named plaintiff and the defendant, because it will unavoidably affect the rights of other people. The action should not proceed until and unless the disgruntled relative names all the other potential recipients as plaintiffs or defendants in the suit, assuming it is feasible to do so.

Figure 6F illustrates this situation. Notice that *X* is left out of the suit, and that this omission means that complete relief cannot be granted to the existing parties, or the interests of the omitted party will be affected, or the defendant may be subjected to multiple liability; those are the situations that give rise to compulsory joinder.

Interpleader (Rule 22; 28 U.S.C. § 1335). Interpleader is designed to solve the problem of a "stakeholder" faced with conflicting demands. This device is illustrated by Figure 6G.

Assume that a life insurance company has issued a policy to an insured who is now deceased. The insured had designated as the beneficiary "my wife, Anna." But before he died, he and Anna were divorced, and after that he married his second wife, Bea. However, he never formally made any change in the designation of the beneficiary as "my wife Anna," and now he is unable to change it, because he is dead.

Anna says to the insurance company, "Pay me the $100,000 policy amount! I'm the named beneficiary." But Bea says, "No! Pay ME the $100,000. I'm his wife, and his intent was obviously that it should be paid to me!"

Now, the insurer has several options. First, it could simply pay out the money to the one it thinks is entitled to it. But that course of action may be unwise because, if it guesses wrong, it may be liable for another $100,000 to the claimant it didn't pay. Second, it could wait until it is sued by one of the claimants. It runs the risk, however, of being sued in two separate actions by the two different claimants, and it could be subjected to two judgments for $100,000.

The device of interpleader was invented to handle this kind of "stakeholder's dilemma."

The insurance company can file a complaint for interpleader and have both Bea and Anna served as defendants (or interpleader claimants). This procedure will, in effect, say to Anna and Bea, "The insurance company is faced with conflicting demands from you two. Come into this lawsuit and litigate your entitlement against each other."

The insurance company is the interpleader plaintiff, and Anna and Bea are the interpleader defendants (or claimants). But the interpleader plaintiff is not an ordinary plaintiff, nor are the interpleader defendants like ordinary defendants. One significant difference is that the interpleader plaintiff does not have the burden of proof; instead, the claimants — the interpleader defendants — each have the burden of proof against each other. Furthermore, Anna and Bea can be forced to make their claims in this suit, and only in this suit. It is usually possible for the insurance company to get an injunction against Anna and Bea, ordering them not to file suit in any other court for this fund.

Intervention (Rule 24). What if there is someone who might have an interest in a lawsuit, but who has not been made a party? Is there anything that this person can do to get into the lawsuit to protect her interests — *i.e.*, to intervene in the lawsuit?

Yes, there is. It is a procedure that is called, appropriately enough, "intervention."

Take the situation of Anna, Bea, and the life insurance company, which we have already discussed. Assume that the insurer refuses to pay out the $100,000, but does not file an interpleader action, and so Anna files suit against it. This turn of events might disturb Bea, because she is left out of the suit. If she wants, Bea can file a motion to intervene under Rule 24.

Will the judge grant Bea's motion?

If the intervention is "permissive," the judge has discretion. She would not be required to allow Bea to intervene. Even so, she probably would allow intervention in this situation, if the motion was filed early enough.

In fact, the judge might conclude that she is required to grant the motion to intervene here. Rule 24 says that intervention is a matter "of right" when the intervenor's interest "may as a practical matter" be "impair[ed] or impede[d]" by the disposition of the lawsuit. Here, if the insurer is forced to pay the money to Anna, it is likely that this disposition will impair Bea's ability to protect her interest.

Class Actions (Rule 23). This device is illustrated by Figure 6I. Although Rule 23 is sometimes difficult to apply, the justification for class actions is relatively simple. A class action is a way of disposing of a case expeditiously, when there are a very large number of plaintiffs or defendants, by combining all their claims in one case and having representative parties litigate. (Some scholars, however, see class actions as a means of adjudicating public litigation, rather than as a mere joinder device.)

For instance, assume that a corporation called the Superhuge Holding Company has issued a large number of shares of stock to the public. The number of people who have purchased the shares runs into the thousands. But something goes wrong, and Superhuge stock becomes worthless. It then develops that the brokerage firm that sold Superhuge stock made a number of fraudulent representations. As a result, each of the stock purchasers has a potential claim against the brokerage firm.

The plaintiffs (1) will be too numerous to join in a single suit. Their claims, however, (2) share common issues. Among these, there may be members of the class of defrauded persons who can (3) present typical claims and (4) adequately represent the class. These four requirements (which are abbreviated "numerosity," "commonality," "typicality," and "adequate representation") are the prerequisites to a class action under Rule 23. That does not mean that the courts necessarily will recognize (or "certify") the class action. There are several other hurdles that the representative parties have to overcome, and we shall see these later in the chapter.

The Judicial Panel on Multidistrict Litigation (28 U.S.C. § 1407). Let's continue to consider the situation of the brokerage firm that has allegedly defrauded tens of thousands of buyers of Superhuge Holding Company stock.

A class action is not the only possible result. It can, and probably will, happen that people all over the country will sue the brokerage firm in their respective districts. The brokerage firm may be sued in every district of every state. If that happens, the brokerage firm may go broke just from having to defend hundreds of different suits in different locations, even if it wins every suit.

The brokerage firm's lawyers may say to themselves, in effect, "We don't like class actions very much, but we sure wish there was some way to put all these lawsuits in one case! Because the plaintiffs didn't bring a class action, is there anything we, as the defendant's lawyers, can do to protect our client?"

Yes, there is, and it is illustrated in Figure 6J. There is a statute, 28 U.S.C. § 1407, that sets up a "Judicial Panel on Multidistrict Litigation." The brokerage firm may apply to the Panel to transfer all the cases to one place for consolidated and coordinated pretrial proceedings. There is one catch: The consolidation is for pretrial only, and each matter must be transferred back to its original district for trial. But still, this procedure is a great help to the defendant; most multidistrict cases are settled rather than tried anyway.

Consolidation, Severance, and Separate Trial (Rules 42, 21, 13(i), 14(a), and 20(b)). The court has broad discretion to consolidate multiple lawsuits into a single action if they share common questions. In addition, the court has broad discretion to order separate trials. In this respect, it may separate combined claims, or it may even order multiple trials for a single claim (*e.g.*, a first trial on liability, and if liability is established, a second trial on damages). Rules 14(a) and 21 mention, in addition, a "severance." Although the rules do not make the distinction, a severance is generally understood as the separation of different claims into different suits, as opposed to separate trials for a single claim.

§ 6.02 Adding or Subtracting Single Claims or Parties

[A] Counterclaims and Cross-Claims

Read Fed. R. Civ. P. 13 (counterclaim and cross-claim).

CAVANAUGH v. WESTERN MARYLAND RAILWAY CO.
729 F.2d 289 (4th Cir. 1984)

DONALD RUSSELL, CIRCUIT JUDGE.

. . . Western Maryland Railway Company (Western) and Baltimore & Ohio Railroad Company (B & O) appeal from an order of the district court dismissing their counterclaim for property damage in an action brought by Robert M. Cavanaugh (Cavanaugh) under the Federal Employers' Liability Act (FELA), 45 U.S.C. §§ 51 *et seq.* The district court held that the maintenance of the railroads' counterclaim would violate §§ 5 and 10 of the FELA, 45 U.S.C. §§ 55 and 60, and thus would be contrary to the public policy reflected in such Act. We disagree and reverse.

Cavanaugh was employed by Western or B & O as a railroad engineer. On February 12, 1980, the B & O train on which Cavanaugh was serving as engineer collided head-on with another B & O train proceeding in the opposite direction on tracks owned and controlled by B & O near Orleans Road in Morgan County, West Virginia. On November 19, 1981, Cavanaugh instituted this FELA action to recover one and a half million ($1,500,000) dollars for personal injuries sustained by him as a result of the collision. The railroads answered and counterclaimed under state law for property damage in the amount of one million, seven hundred thousand ($1,700,000) dollars, sustained by them as a result of the same accident. Cavanaugh moved to dismiss this counterclaim. The district court granted the motion. . . .

In determining whether the railroads have a right of action which they can assert as a counterclaim in an FELA action begun by a railroad employee, we begin by recognizing that there is a well accepted common law principle that a master or employer has a right of action against his employee for property damages suffered by him "arising out of ordinary acts of negligence committed within the scope of [his] employment" by the offending employee. . . .

Moreover, this right of action in favor of the employer or master may be asserted either in an independent action by the employer against the offending employee or by a counterclaim filed by the employer in the employee's action to recover for injuries sustained by him in the same occurrence. But, if the employee sues the employer in federal court for injuries sustained in the occurrence the employer has no option; federal practice compels the employer-master to assert by way of a counterclaim his claim against the employee for damages caused by the employee's negligence to his (employer's) property under penalty of loss of his right of action.[4] . . . It follows that if the railroads in this case are denied the right to assert their claim against the plaintiff by way of a counterclaim, they could be denied any right of action ever to recover for the damages to their property suffered as a result exclusively of plaintiff's negligence and the plaintiff in turn could be given absolute immunity from any liability for his negligence both in this action and in any other action begun after judgment in the present action.

It is difficult to believe that such an unfair result is compelled. However, the plaintiff argues that the railroads are foreclosed by the terms of the FELA from asserting their claim against him by way of a counterclaim in his FELA action. The plaintiff does not point to any explicit language in the Act which could be said to require, or even suggest, such a sacrifice of the railroads' rights.[5] . . . The plaintiff is accordingly reduced to contending that the proscription of such a counterclaim by the defending railroads is implicit in the language and the purpose of the Act. He would find the basis for such implication of a prohibition against a counterclaim by the railroads in the language of Sections 5 and 10 of the Act. . . .

Section 5 of the Act provides in pertinent part that "[a]ny contract, rule, regulation, or device whatsoever, the purpose or intent of which shall be to enable any common carrier to exempt itself from any liability created by this chapter, shall to that extent be void. . . . " The plaintiff would find that the maintenance of the present counterclaim under review constituted a device contrived in violation of Section 5 "to deprive plaintiffs [in FELA actions] of their right to an adequate recovery" and "to chill justifiable FELA claims." We do not find the argument persuasive.

. . . The term "device" is defined in the section. It is [any] "contract, rule, regulation, or device whatsoever, *the purpose or intent of which shall be to enable any common carrier to exempt itself from any liability created by this chapter* (Italics added)."

. . . The critical word in this definition of "device" is "exemption." It is only when the "contract . . . or device" qualifies as an "exempt[ion] itself from any liability" that

---

[4] This result is a consequence of Rule 13(a), Fed. R. Civ. P., which defines a compulsory counterclaim under federal practice. Claims which must be asserted by counterclaim are ["any claim that — at the time of its service — the pleader has against an opposing party if the claim: (A) arises out of the transaction or occurrence that is the subject matter of the opposing party's claim; and (B) does not require adding another party over whom the court cannot acquire jurisdiction]."

[5] We express no opinion as to whether barring in an FELA action of such a counterclaim, if coupled with Fed. R. Civ. P. 13(a)'s prohibition of assertion of the claim except by counterclaim, would amount to confiscation and bring into play constitutional considerations.

it is "void[ed]" under Section 5. But a counterclaim by the railroad for its own damages is plainly not an "exempt[ion] . . . from any liability" and is thus not a "device" within the contemplation of Congress.

The second section from which the plaintiff would deduce a basis for implying a statutory bar against the railroads' counterclaim is section 10 of the Act. Section 10 proscribes any "device" the "purpose, intent, or effect" of which would "prevent employees of any common carrier from furnishing voluntarily information to a person in interest as to the facts incident to the injury or death of any employee . . . ." As the language plainly indicates, this section was intended to prevent the railroad from making inaccessible to an injured employee other railroad employees whose testimony might be helpful to the injured employee if he chose to sue the railroad. . . .

The plaintiff, however, finds lurking obscurely in the language of Sections 5 and 10 a legislative purpose to interdict counterclaims by defending railroads in FELA suits because the filing of such counterclaims will unfairly coerce or intimidate the injured employee from filing and pursuing his FELA action. As we have already observed, there is nothing in the language of the Act or its legislative history that supports this reasoning. More than that, there is no authority for an assumption that the possibility of a counterclaim being filed creates an unfair advantage in favor of the defendant or improperly coerces or intimidates the injured party from seeking redress for his injuries. . . .

We would pose this hypothetical situation: The ruling of the district court would not prevent the railroads in this case from filing an independent action against the plaintiff-employee herein as a defendant to recover damages to its property as a result of his negligence. Assuming that the railroads can maintain such action, is the plaintiff-employee required under Rule 13(a), to assert his FELA claim as a counterclaim? If he is, we have substantially the same situation as we would have if the right of the railroads to counterclaim in the plaintiff's FELA action is recognized. If, however, the plaintiff-employee is not required to assert his FELA claim as a counterclaim in the railroads' independent action, will the plaintiff be barred by Rule 13(a) from asserting such claim in an action under FELA against the railroads after judgment in the railroads' independent action? We do not seek to answer these questions but pose them simply to emphasize the illogic of the ruling denying the railroads the right to counterclaim in the FELA action for their damages to their property resulting from the accident.

We recognize that the plaintiff finds support for his contrary conclusions in *Stack v. Chicago, M. St. P. & P.R. Co., supra*, 615 P.2d 457. In fact the reasoning of *Stack* is the basis for plaintiff's argument in this Court. We are not persuaded by such reasoning. So far as we have found, *Stack* has only been approved in one unreported district court case. . . . However, there are at least two unreported district court opinions in which the same view as expressed by us was adopted. . . .

Finding nothing in either section 5 or section 10 of the FELA from which it can be reasonably implied that Congress intended the illogical result of proscribing the filing of a counterclaim by the railroads in an FELA case to recover for property damages sustained by reason of the sole negligence of the plaintiff-employee in that action, we reverse the ruling of the district court dismissing the defendant-railroads' counterclaim and remand the cause for further proceedings not inconsistent with this decision. In remanding, however, we direct that, the district court shall, on remand, order the FELA case and the counterclaim be tried separately. This has been the manner in which similar cases seem to have been handled. . . .

K.K. Hall, Circuit Judge, dissenting. . . .

Contrary to the majority's assertion, the language of the FELA supports the conclusion that Congress intended to prohibit counterclaims, such as the one filed by the railroad here,[1] because the filing of such counterclaims will unfairly coerce or intimidate the injured employee from filing and pursuing his FELA action. . . .

The Supreme Court of Washington considered these statutes in *Stack v. Chicago, Milwaukee, St. Paul and Pacific Railroad Company*, 94 Wash. 2d 155, 615 P.2d 457 (1980) (*en banc*). In *Stack*, a brakeman injured in a head-on collision of two trains and the widow of an engineer killed in the same collision brought actions against the railroad under the FELA. The railroad counterclaimed against the engineer and filed a third-party claim against the remaining crew members seeking 1.5 million dollars in property damage resulting from the collision. The Supreme Court of Washington held unanimously that the railroad's counterclaim and third-party claim "constituted 'devices' contrived to deprive plaintiffs of their right to an adequate recovery and operated to chill justifiable FELA claims in violation of 45 U.S.C. 55 and 60." 94 Wash. 2d at 159, 615 P.2d at 459. I agree. . . .

In my view, the railroads' counterclaim is a "device" calculated to intimidate and exert economic pressure upon Cavanaugh, to curtail and chill his rights, and ultimately to exempt the railroads from liability under the FELA. Here, as in *Stack*, the railroads' counterclaim violates 45 U.S.C. § 55 "because the ultimate threat of 'retaliatory' legal action would have the effect of limiting [the railroads'] liability by discouraging employees from filing FELA actions. Further, it would have the effect of reducing an employee's FELA recovery by the amount of property damage negligently caused by the employee." . . .

NOTES AND QUESTIONS

(1) *The Strategic Use of Counterclaims.* Is this a case of "the best defense is a good offense"? Certainly, counterclaims are frequently used strategically for that reason. A plaintiff encountering a counterclaim must take it into account in settlement negotiations even if it is of marginal validity, because the discovery and other procedures necessary to defeat it will entail significant cost — and because there is always the chance that the trier of fact may give more credit to its validity than the plaintiff does.

On the other hand, doesn't the majority's reasoning in *Cavanaugh* have significant appeal? The FELA certainly doesn't say that a railroad is deprived of its right of action

---

[1] At oral argument before the district court, counsel for the railroads acknowledged that railroads generally do not bring actions against their employees for property damage because they have no reasonable expectation of recovery and because their employees may in fact be judgment proof. In this case, the railroads did not assert their claim for property damage until approximately one year and nine months after the accident when Cavanaugh instituted his FELA action. In fact, counsel for the railroads admitted to the district court that:

> In this case, [Cavanaugh] is not going to be judgment proof when he recovers a vast sum of money, which he is attempting to recover from the Railroads.
>
> As a matter of fact, he is going to be a rich man once he recovers, and can establish a right to recovery. And that is why this [counterclaim] has been asserted. . . .

Tr. 78. Thus, it is clear to me that the railroads filed their counterclaim either to coerce Cavanaugh into settling his claim or, if his FELA action proceeded to trial, to strip him of any damages by means of an offset. I cannot agree that Congress intended to sanction such a motive.

for property damage. Nor does it prohibit railroad counterclaims. In fact, it often occurs that the "real" plaintiff is the counterclaimant; a potential defendant, knowing that suit is imminent, beats the "plaintiff" to the punch by filing suit against the plaintiff, leaving that party to counterclaim. As the court points out, if the railroad sued first, wouldn't Cavanaugh be left to counterclaim?

(2) *"Compulsory" Counterclaims: Is the Rule Too Harsh?* The majority's reasoning in *Cavanaugh* is strengthened because the counterclaim is a "compulsory" counterclaim. As the court says, if the railroad does not assert the claim in this same suit, it will be forever barred. The courts have not been consistent in the theories they have used to justify the bar in a subsequent suit. Some reason that the failure to counterclaim operates as a waiver, while some say that it works as estoppel of the later claim; an apparently greater number of courts reason that the previous judgment is *res judicata* of any compulsory counterclaim. But the simplest rationale is just to say that Rule 13 bars the subsequent claim. This is the reasoning in *Cavanaugh. See* C. Wright, *Estoppel by Rule: The Compulsory Counterclaim Under Modern Pleading,* 39 Iowa. L. Rev. 255 (1954). On the other hand, some commentators have argued that the compulsory bar is an excessively harsh penalty for mere omission to make the counterclaim and that it would make more sense to require the relitigator to pay the opponent's added court costs and attorney's fees. *See* Kennedy, *Counterclaims under Rule 13,* 11 Hous. L. Rev. 255 (1974). In fact, some states' rules do not provide for compulsory counterclaims, including those of New York and Illinois. CPLR 3019; Ill. Rev. Stat. ch. 110, § 2-608. Should we abolish the rule?

(3) *Examples of the Compulsory Counterclaim Bar.* In *J. Aron & Co., Inc. v. Service Transp. Co.,* 515 F. Supp. 428 (D. Md. 1981), an insurer sued for a declaratory judgment of noncoverage. In a subsequent suit, the insured claimed that the insurer had failed to provide appropriate insurance coverage to it. The court held that the subsequent suit arose out of the same transaction or occurrence as that in the initial suit; it was therefore barred by the compulsory counterclaim rule. In *John Alden Life Ins. Co. v. Cavendes,* 591 F. Supp. 362 (S.D. Fla. 1984), the first suit was for breach of contract and depended upon the proper interpretation of the agreement between the parties. The defendant later filed a second suit against the plaintiff, asserting that the agreement itself was the product of extrinsic fraud. The court held this suit barred under the compulsory counterclaim rule. In one amusing case, *Smith v. McDaniel,* 503 F. Supp. 13 (N.D. Ga. 1980), *aff'd,* 633 F.2d 581 (11th Cir. 1981), the plaintiff initially sued a professional wrestler for injuring him in a scuffle at a public match at which the plaintiff was a spectator. The plaintiff-spectator obtained a judgment on this suit, which was in Virginia; he then brought an action on the judgment in Georgia, where the wrestler's assets were. In that suit, the wrestler asserted a counterclaim to the effect that the plaintiff-spectator had instead assaulted the wrestler as he sought to enter the ring. The court held that this claim was "inextricably" intertwined with the plaintiff's Virginia suit and was barred by the wrestler's failure to assert it there.

Are these cases correctly decided under the "same transaction or occurrence" test? In particular, is an act of fraud that leads to a contract the "same transaction" as the contract itself? Do the cases make more sense if they are viewed in terms of the purpose of the compulsory counterclaim rule — to prevent unnecessarily repetitive litigation?

(4) *The "Logical Relationship" Test: Moore v. New York Cotton Exchange, 270 U.S. 593, 610 (1926).* The Supreme Court defined "same transaction" in the following terms in this landmark case:

> "Transaction" is a word of flexible meaning. It may comprehend a series of many occurrences, depending not so much upon the immediateness of their connection as upon their logical relationship. The [defendant's conduct in *Moore* allegedly leading to the plaintiff's claim] is one of the links in the chain which constitutes the transaction upon which [defendant] bases its [counterclaim]. . . . Essential facts alleged by [the plaintiff] enter into and constitute in part the cause of action set forth in the counterclaim. That they are not precisely identical, or that the counterclaim embraces additional allegations, . . . does not matter. To hold otherwise would be to rob this branch of the rule of all serviceable meaning, since the facts relied upon by the plaintiff rarely, if ever, are in all particulars, the same as those constituting the defendant's counterclaim. . . .

Is this test useful? One criticism is that anything can have a "logical relationship" to anything else; at the very least, any counterclaim will have some relationship to the principal claim in that both have the same plaintiff and defendant as parties. The "logical relationship" must be read as "a relationship that would justify insistence that the claims be tried together." If it is read in this manner, perhaps the test does help. For example, it is clearer why a contract claim and a related fraud claim, even though depending on distinct events, may constitute the "same transaction" (*see* Note (3), above).

(5) *Permissive Counterclaims.* Any other kind of counterclaim, not a compulsory one, is termed "permissive." It "may" be asserted in the same action, *see* Rule 13(b), but it is not barred in a subsequent suit. For example, in *Meinrath v. Singer Co.*, 87 F.R.D. 422 (S.D.N.Y. 1980), a broker sued for "bonus" commissions allegedly due him under a compensation agreement. The defendant asserted a counterclaim alleging that, on prior occasions, it had paid "bonus" commissions exceeding what was due under the agreement, and demanding repayment of those amounts. The court held that this counterclaim was merely permissive, not compulsory, and that ancillary jurisdiction could not extend to it. [Is this decision correct? Can't it be said that the previous excess payments have a logical relationship to the currently claimed underpayment?]

(6) *Cross-Claims.* A counterclaim is exemplified by a suit by a defendant against a plaintiff, while a cross-claim is a suit by one co-party against another (*e.g.*, one defendant demands contribution or indemnity from another defendant). Rule 13(g) says that a cross-claim is permitted if it arises out of the same transaction or occurrence as the principal action. As *United Mine Workers v. Gibbs* indicates, these claims are within the court's supplemental jurisdiction. Consider the following case.

PETERSON v. WATT, 666 F.2d 361 (9th Cir. 1982). The Petersons purchased certain land on the east bank of the Colorado River in Arizona. The Colorado River then moved eastward. Believing that they were entitled to the land that eventually emerged on the west bank in Nevada, the Petersons filed a complaint seeking to quiet title to the land in their name. The United States, as riparian owner of the land on the west bank of the river, was named as defendant (through its Secretary of the Interior, James Watt). Because the United States had contracted to sell to the State of Nevada some 15,000 acres in the area, the Petersons later added Nevada as a second defendant.

On the first day of trial of the Petersons' suit, attorneys for Nevada orally announced in open court that they wished to preserve whatever rights Nevada might have as a result of a decision of the United States Supreme Court rendered that morning and giving states potential title claims under executory contracts. Nevada made no specific claim, however, and it never filed a cross-claim against the United States.

The trial court held against the Petersons, entering judgment that they did not own the land. The court then went on to decide the rights of the United States and Nevada against each other. Specifically, the court's "comprehensive and detailed opinion" held that the United States owned all the land up to the westerly high water mark before permanent channelization and that Nevada owned approximately 90 acres located between the land awarded to the United States and the present high water mark after channelization. The United States and Nevada then both joined in a motion to set aside this portion of the judgment on the ground that there had been no "case or controversy" between them. The District Court denied the motion. The United States appealed. During the appeal, Nevada changed its position to argue that the award of the acreage to it was proper, because although there was never any express claim asserted by Nevada, the record showed an "actual adversarial presentation of the question of title as between the United States and Nevada." The Court of Appeals reversed:

> . . . Nevada never asserted any cross-claim against the United States as it could have done under Federal Rule of Civil Procedure 13(g). Such cross-claims are permissive rather than mandatory. Fed. R. Civ. P. 13(g) states: "A pleading *may* state as a crossclaim any claim by one party against a coparty [if the claim arises out of the transaction or occurrence that is the subject matter of the original action . . .]." *Compare* Fed. R. Civ. P. 13(a) (compulsory counterclaims), 13(b) (permissive counterclaims). . . . Thus, if such a claim is neither asserted nor litigated, the parties cannot be barred from asserting it in a later action by principles of *res judicata*, waiver, or estoppel. . . . [A] party to an action having a claim in the nature of a cross-claim has the option to pursue it in an independent action. . . . The most that Nevada did in this case with respect to any claim independent of the [Petersons' suit] was to indicate that it would protect its position in light of the decision of the United States Supreme Court. . . . Although the case remained in the briefing stage for many months following trial, Nevada addressed the merits of any claim against the United States only in the most cursory fashion. The United States never saw any need to respond. . . .
>
> Thus, while the parties remain free to litigate the matter, when they were before the trial court they desired the same result and had no conflicting interests. The trial court was therefore deprived of the "clash of adverse parties" which "sharpens the presentation of issues . . . ."

NOTES AND QUESTIONS

(1) *Should Cross-Claims Be Made Compulsory?* By definition, a cross-claim arises out of the same transaction or occurrence as the plaintiff's claim. Its assertion in the same suit would normally serve judicial economy. Rule 13(g) could be rewritten to make cross-claims compulsory. Is this approach superior to that of the Federal Rules, which authorize a second suit covering issues and evidence overlapping the first?

(2) *Can Cross-Claims Be Compulsory Under Rule 13(g)?* Although a cross-claim is not normally compulsory, it can sometimes become a compulsory counterclaim. For example, in *Peterson v. Watt*, if Nevada had claimed against the United States on the basis of its contract of purchase, then any claim that the United States might have, arising out of the same transaction, would not only be a cross-claim, but also would fit the definition of a compulsory counterclaim under Rule 13(a).

[B] Third-Party Practice ("Impleader")

Read Fed. R. Civ. P. 14; also, read Federal Forms 4, 16, and 41 (third-party practice).

NOTE ON HOW TO READ THE CASE OF *BARAB v. MENFORD*

The case that follows, *Barab v. Menford,* is short but moderately complex. You should have the following thoughts in mind when you read it.

The Third Party May Implead a "Fourth" Party. Rule 14 provides that the third party may herself bring in a third (or "fourth") party. In fact, that party may implead a "fifth" party. In *Barab v. Menford,* the defendant brought in a third party, and that third party attempted — unsuccessfully, as it happens — to implead someone else as a third party.

A Third-Party Defendant Must Be Derivatively Liable (i.e., Liable to the Third-Party Plaintiff for Indemnity or Contribution) and Not Merely Liable to the Original Plaintiff. Rule 14 says that a defendant may bring in a third party who "is or may be liable to [the third-party plaintiff] for all or part of the claim against it." It is not enough for the defendant to show that the original plaintiff could assert a claim against the third party; the defendant must allege that she, the defendant, has a claim against the third party (usually for contribution in payment of the claim by the plaintiff, or for indemnity). This requirement operates to prevent the fourth-party claim in *Barab v. Menford.* The notes after the case will ask you whether the requirement should be abolished.

The Court's Discretion to Deny Impleader. Unless the third-party claim is asserted within ten days after answer, the claimant must obtain leave of court, which the court has discretion to grant or deny. In this case, the court first holds that the third-party claim is improper under the rules, and then, as a second reason for the result, explains why it would exercise its discretion to deny leave anyway.

BARAB v. MENFORD

98 F.R.D. 455 (E.D. Pa. 1983)

VAN ARTSDALEN, DISTRICT JUDGE.

[The plaintiff, Barab, was injured when she slipped on a doormat at an inn operated by Menford, and she sued Menford for her injuries. Menford brought a third-party action against Channel Home Centers, Inc., alleging that it had sold the doormat to Menford and was liable to indemnify Menford for the entire amount of any judgment taken by Barab. Channel answered with a denial that it had sold the doormat, and it also sought leave to implead Joy Plastics, Inc., as a third (or "fourth") party, on the allegation that Joy was the true supplier of the doormat to Menford. In the following opinion, the court denies leave for Channel to implead Joy.]

Third-party defendant Channel Home Centers, Inc. (Channel) has filed a motion to file and serve a third-party complaint upon Joy Plastics, Inc. . . . Notwithstanding that Channel's motion is unopposed, the motion will be denied for the reasons set forth herein.

Federal Rule of Civil Procedure 14(a) provides in part that "a defending party [may, as third-party plaintiff, serve a summons and complaint on a nonparty *who is or may be liable to it for all or part of the claim against it.*]" Fed. R. Civ. P. 14(a) (emphasis added). It is no longer possible under Rule 14, as it was prior to the 1948 amendment to the rule, to implead a third party claimed to be solely liable to the plaintiff. . . . A proposed third-party plaintiff must allege facts sufficient to establish the derivative or secondary liability of the proposed third-party defendant. . . . Thus, under Rule 14(a), a third-party complaint is appropriate only in cases where the proposed third-party defendant would be secondarily liable to the original defendant in the event the latter is held to be liable to the plaintiff.

In this action, Channel, the proposed third-party plaintiff, is alleged to have sold to the defendant the doormat which allegedly caused the injuries to plaintiff Mildred Barab. Channel denied selling the doormat to the defendant and, after discovery, continues to assert that denial. Channel contends that after having the doormat inspected by one of its buyers, it was able to identify the proposed third-party defendant, Joy Plastics, Inc., as the manufacturer and/or seller. Channel further contends that it could not reasonably have discovered the identity and involvement of the proposed third-party defendant at an earlier date because Channel had no records of the sale or purchase of the product and Joy Plastics, Inc., was *not* a supplier of the product to Channel.

It is clear from Channel's allegations that Channel has established no basis for the derivative or secondary liability of Joy Plastics, Inc. Channel's contentions, if accepted as true, would be a total defense to the defendant's third-party complaint against Channel. The fact that Joy Plastics, Inc., may be liable to the original defendant [Menford] does not form a basis for *Channel* to implead Joy Plastics, Inc., as a third-party defendant. Channel has alleged no facts which would suggest any possibility that Joy Plastics, Inc., could be liable to Channel. It is Channel's position that it never sold the doormat in question: that Joy Plastics, Inc., never supplied the product to Channel, and that Channel and Joy Plastics, Inc., had no relationship with each other in reference to the sale of the doormat to the Hacienda Inn.

The discovery deadline in this action was initially set for February 15, 1982. By agreement of the parties, and upon approval by the court, discovery was extended to April 15, 1982. On March 3, 1982, a third-party summons was issued to Channel as a third-party defendant. Discovery has continued in this action, notwithstanding the April 15, 1982 discovery deadline. To permit Channel to implead Joy Plastics, Inc., at this stage of the litigation would inevitably impede trial of this action. Of necessity, Joy Plastics, Inc., would need additional time for discovery to determine its relative position in the litigation. In the event that Channel does establish that it did not manufacture or supply the doormat at issue, the original defendant may have a claim against Joy Plastics, Inc. However, this is not a matter to be determined in these proceedings.

NOTES AND QUESTIONS

(1) *Dependency on Main Action: Third Party Must Be Potentially Liable to the "Defending Party," Not Merely to the Plaintiff.* The principal basis of the court's opinion is that Channel did not plead that Joy was derivatively liable to Channel, as Rule 14 requires. For another example of this requirement, see *Robbins v. Yamaha Motor Corp.*, 98 F.R.D. 36 (E.D. Pa. 1983). There, a motorcyclist sued the motorcycle manufacturer for injuries sustained in a collision with an automobile, alleging that the motorcycle was not "crashworthy." The manufacturer attempted to implead the automobile driver as a third-party defendant. Under Pennsylvania law, however, the manufacturer had no right of contribution or indemnity against the automobile driver because the two were not "joint and several tortfeasors" in a "crashworthiness" case. The motorcyclist had potential rights against the driver, but had not sued him. The manufacturer therefore had no basis for a third-party claim under Pennsylvania substantive law, and the court disallowed it.

Although the third party must be potentially liable to the plaintiff for the plaintiff's injuries, the third-party claim need not proceed on the same theory as the main action. Thus if the plaintiff's claim is based on negligence, impleader of a third party who is bound by contract to indemnify the defendant is proper. The key question is whether the liability is in some way dependent upon the outcome of the main claim. *Crude Crew v. McGinnis & Associates*, 572 F. Supp. 103 (E.D. Wis. 1983).

(2) *A Third Party Who "Is or May Be" Liable.* In *Barab v. Menford*, the court did allow the third-party action by Menford against Channel. But notice that there is as yet no existing claim for indemnity by Menford against Channel, because Menford has not yet been held liable. If Barab loses the main action, in fact, Menford will never have any right to recover against Channel. Isn't the third-party claim, therefore, premature and subject to dismissal? The answer turns on the wording of Rule 14, which authorizes impleader of a party who is "or may be" liable. Thus, Menford's third-party action is proper, because Channel "may" someday become liable. *Cf. Jeub v. B.G. Foods, Inc.*, 2 F.R.D. 238 (D. Minn. 1942) (in suit by consumer of allegedly unwholesome ham served by restauranteur, defendant could implead manufacturer of ham, even though manufacturer moved to dismiss on the ground that restauranteur had no claim yet because restauranteur itself was not yet liable). Should this Rule be changed, given that it subjects third-party defendants to expensive proceedings that might prove to be moot? [Note: This question requires a balancing of costs and benefits. Are the detriments to a third party, who may be forced to make a wasted defense, greater than the judicial economy and fairness to existing parties that result from allowance of impleader?]

(3) *The Discretionary Denial of Leave.* In *Barab v. Menford*, even if Channel's complaint against Joy was a proper third-party action, the court would deny leave to implead Joy because the motion is untimely. Third-party claims are not compulsory, and Menford or Channel can sue Joy in a later action. Nevertheless, is this denial of leave a proper exercise of the court's discretion? Note that Channel was itself brought into the case only shortly before the extended discovery cutoff date. Consider the following note.

(4) *What Factors Should Control the Court's Discretion?* Rule 14 provides that the defendant may implead a third party without leave of court if she does it within ten days after she serves her answer. But if she wants to implead after the ten-day period, she must obtain leave of court, and the court has discretion to deny it. How should the court go about exercising this discretion? In *Collins v. General Motors Corp.*, 101 F.R.D. 4 (W.D. Pa. 1983), the court identified three factors to consider: (1) the timeliness of the motion for leave; (2) whether the third-party action would introduce an unrelated controversy or unduly complicate the case so as to prejudice the plaintiff; and (3) whether it would serve the policy of Rule 14 by avoiding circuity of actions and settling related matters in one suit. In theory, there should also be another factor: the possibility of inconsistent judgments. That is, if the claims were separated, a jury might find Channel liable to Menford, but a later jury might deny Channel's claim for contribution against Joy, because it did not believe Channel was liable to Menford in the first place.

(5) *Third Party's Answer.* The third-party defendant may set up in its answer any defense it has against the third-party claim and, in addition, "may assert against the plaintiff any defense that the third-party plaintiff has to the plaintiff's claim." Rule 14(a). This provision enables the third party adequately to defend in the event that the defendant refuses or neglects to assert a given theory of defense. For example, if there is an argument that the plaintiff's claim is barred by limitations, but the defendant decides that this defense is too tenuous to plead, the third party, if it disagrees, may plead it.

(6) *Supplemental Jurisdiction.* Supplemental jurisdiction generally extends to third-party claims that otherwise might not be within the court's jurisdiction. We studied supplemental jurisdiction generally in Chapter 3, and we will return to this subject later in this Chapter, when we study class actions.

[C] Permissive Joinder of Parties and Claims by Plaintiff

Read Fed. R. Civ. P. 20 (permissive joinder), 18 (joinder of claims).

GROGAN v. BABSON BROTHERS CO.

101 F.R.D. 697 (N.D.N.Y. 1984)

MUNSON, CHIEF JUDGE . . . .

This action was commenced in the Supreme Court of the State of New York, Oneida County, by service of the summons and complaint on October 18, 1983. On November 14, 1983 the action was removed to this court pursuant to [the removal statutes]. Plaintiff subsequently moved to remand for "equitable reasons" but adjourned the motion, and in the interim filed a new motion seeking to amend his complaint to join two additional non-diverse defendants pursuant to Rules 15 and 20, Fed. R. Civ. P. For the reasons hereinafter stated the plaintiff's motion to amend his complaint joining the additional non-diverse defendants is granted. Because such joinder will divest this court of diversity jurisdiction, this case must be remanded to state court.

FACTS

Plaintiff initiated the present action against Babson Brothers Co. of Illinois alleging, *inter alia*, negligence and breach of warranty. Plaintiff's claims relate to certain livestock milking equipment manufactured by Babson Brothers Co. of Illinois, distributed by Surge Inc. of Babson Brothers Co., and retailed and distributed by Don Carrier Surge Inc. Don Carrier Surge Inc. [Don Carrier] installed the milking equipment on the plaintiff's premises. Plaintiff alleges that the equipment caused electric current to come into contact with the livestock during the milking operations. Don Carrier undertook to modify and correct the defect but allegedly abandoned its efforts without having corrected the problem.

Plaintiff seeks to amend his complaint joining Surge Inc. of Babson Brothers and Don Carrier Surge Inc. to the present action. Plaintiff had previously commenced a separate action in state court against these two proposed defendants. Plaintiff argues that by granting the instant motion the court will preserve precious judicial resources and avoid multiplicity of litigation. Defendant contends that the motion should be denied because plaintiff's sole motive in seeking joinder is to destroy diversity of citizenship thereby subverting the defendant's right to defend this litigation in a federal forum.

DISCUSSION

This case presents the interesting but seldom addressed question of whether a plaintiff is entitled to join additional non-diverse parties to a validly removed action when the effect is to destroy federal subject-matter jurisdiction, thereby necessitating a remand to state court. As a threshold matter, however, the court must determine whether joinder under Rule 20 is permissible in the first instance. . . .

Rule 20(a) imposes two specific requisites for the joinder of parties: (1) a right to relief must be asserted by, or against, each plaintiff or defendant [with respect] to or arising out of the same transaction or occurrence; and (2) some question of law or fact common to all the parties will arise in the action. . . . Joinder is to be construed liberally "in order to promote trial convenience and to expedite the final determination of disputes, thereby preventing multiple lawsuits." . . . Moreover, under the federal rules "the impulse is toward the broadest possible scope of action consistent with fairness to the parties; joinder of claims, parties and remedies is strongly encouraged." *United Mine Workers of America v. Gibbs* . . . .

In the case at bar these requisites are clearly satisfied. Plaintiff's action arises out of the defective nature of certain milking equipment, liability for which may rest with one or more of the proposed defendants. Questions of law and fact are common to all these parties. There is no question that the joinder of these parties will promote trial convenience and will prevent the possibility, if not likelihood, of multiple litigation.

In opposition to plaintiff's motions the defendant has pointed to the oft-stated general rule that the plaintiff cannot act so as to divest a court of jurisdiction over a case that has been properly removed. However, the majority of federal courts which have addressed this issue have concluded that when there is no showing that the plaintiff seeks to join the additional defendants *solely* to effectuate a remand, "in the exercise of . . . sound discretion the court may permit a new party to be added, although his citizenship destroys diversity and requires a remand." . . .

In the present case there is no evidence to suggest that plaintiff seeks to join additional defendants solely to effectuate a remand to state court. When plaintiff filed his original complaint he was apparently under the impression that Surge Inc. of Babson Brothers Co. was the exclusive manufacturer of the defective equipment. He subsequently discovered that Babson Brothers Co. of Illinois was the manufacturer of the defective product and thus the instant lawsuit was commenced. The plaintiff's motive in bringing this suit is simply to consolidate the pending suit with the state court action. While the court is at a complete loss to understand why the plaintiff did not merely join the instant defendant to his pending state court action, this tactical blunder should not effect the outcome of the present motion. If this motion were denied it would necessitate the continuance of parallel cases resulting in a great waste of judicial resources. Moreover, granting the motion will not prejudice the defendant because both lawsuits are in their infancy.

Having concluded that the reasons for bringing this motion are legitimate, the court grants the plaintiff's motion to amend its complaint adding the two non-diverse defendants. Because their joinder destroys this court's jurisdiction over the lawsuit, the case must be remanded to the New York State Supreme Court, Oneida County, pursuant to 28 U.S.C. § 1447(c).

NOTES AND QUESTIONS

(1) *"Same . . . Series of Transactions or Occurrences."* Notice that the three defendants technically engaged in different transactions: Babson Illinois manufactured the equipment; Surge Inc. of Babson distributed it; and Don Carrier installed it. Since these acts technically were different, isn't the court wrong in saying that each defendant's potential liability arose from the "same transaction or occurrence"? Technically, perhaps, but the court's holding on this point is justified anyway, because the court has not quoted the entire rule which includes not only the same transaction or occurrence, but the same

"series" of transactions or occurrences. The chain of manufacture, distribution and installation has the sort of sequential relationship that constitutes a series of transactions.

(2) *How Different May Events Be and Still Be Part of the Same "Series" of Transactions or Occurrences?* In *King v. Ralston Purina Co.,* 97 F.R.D. 477 (W.D.N.C. 1983), the three plaintiffs worked in different places and different divisions of the company they sued under the Age Discrimination in Employment Act. But because they alleged a companywide policy of discrimination, they were permitted to join as plaintiffs in a single suit. The court held that it was without discretion, in fact, to order severance. *See also United States v. Mississippi,* 380 U.S. 128 (1965) ("common practice" among voter registrars made different denials of votes to black citizens part of the same series). If the Ralston Purina employees each alleged that his own supervisor, acting individually, was solely responsible for the acts of discrimination against him, would joinder of the claims be permitted?

For a case on the other side of the line, consider *Movie Systems, Inc. v. Abel,* 99 F.R.D. 129 (D. Minn. 1983). A television program distributor sued 1,795 individual defendants in 18 actions with approximately 100 defendants allocated to each, all charged with similarly worded misconduct in the form of alleged piracy of microwave signals. The court held that the "same transaction . . . or series" requirement was not met where there was no allegation of concerted action and each defendant was alleged to have acted independently.

(3) *"Common Questions" of Law or Fact.* It has been said that "common questions must be of substantial importance as compared with all of the issues, and . . . the question of the comparative weight and importance of common and separate issues . . . is quite largely a matter of judgment" for the trial court. *Akely v. Kinnicutt,* 144 N.E. 682, 684, 238 N.Y. 466, 473 (1924). In *Akely,* 193 investors joined to sue the promoters of a sham corporation. Although each plaintiff's case included separate issues such as whether he received and relied on the fraudulent representations, the common question whether the scheme itself was fraudulent outweighed those separate questions and justified joinder.

(4) *Supplemental Jurisdiction.* Is there supplemental jurisdiction of claims by plaintiffs against nondiverse persons made parties who are originally or subsequently joined in the lawsuit under Rule 20? *See* 28 U.S.C. § 1367(a)-(b). If two plaintiffs jointly file suit in federal court on the basis of diversity jurisdiction, and one plaintiff satisfies the amount-in-controversy but the other does not, can the second plaintiff use supplemental jurisdiction? *See Exxon Mobil Corp. v. Allapattah Services,* 545 U.S. 546 (2005).

[D] Consolidation, Separate Trial, and Severance

> Read Fed. R. Civ. P. 42 (consolidation; separate trials). Also, read Rules 21 (misjoinder, nonjoinder, and severance) and 25 (substitution of parties).

HENZ v. SUPERIOR TRUCKING CO., 96 F.R.D. 219 (M.D. Pa. 1982). The plaintiffs, Sherry and Joseph Henz, husband and wife, sued the defendant, Superior Trucking Co. The defendant wished to assert a claim for contribution against the husband, Joseph, for any damages it might be required to pay to the wife. However, technical aspects of Rules 13 and 14 prevented the assertion of the contribution claim.

First, the claim could not be asserted as a counterclaim because Rule 13 requires counterclaims to be matured and in existence at the time of pleading. The Rule does not contain any provision for claims that "may" exist in the future. The defendant's claim for contribution was not yet in existence under applicable state law because yhe defendant had not yet been held liable to the wife. Secondly, the contribution claim could not be a third-party claim. Rule 14 does allow a defendant to implead a person who "is *or may be*" liable, and therefore it was no impediment that the contribution claim was not matured; however, Rule 14 does not permit a third-party claim to be asserted against a person who is already a party to the suit.

The court's elegant solution to this problem was to grant a severance. Then, there were two separate suits, one by the husband against the defendant, the other by the wife against the defendant. In the wife's suit, the husband was not a party, and therefore the defendant could seek contribution from him by a third-party claim. The court indicated that, once this result was accomplished, it probably could put the two suits back together by consolidation, under Rule 42(!)

NOTES AND QUESTIONS

(1) *Typical Uses of Separate Trial or Severance: Convenience, Judicial Economy, or Avoidance of Prejudice.* The *Henz* case involves a legitimate, but unusual, use of Rule 42. A more typical use is shown in *Beeck v. Aquaslide'N' Dive Corp.* (Chapter 5, above). There, the court granted a separate trial to determine whether the defendant had manufactured the allegedly defective product. A negative verdict avoided the need to determine other issues and therefore conserved judicial resources. Furthermore, this issue could be determined without presenting evidence about the plaintiff's injuries, which might be prejudicial to the defendant's claim of non-manufacture.

(2) *Consolidation.* Notice that consolidation under Rule 42, unlike permissive joinder, does not contain a "same transaction" requirement. It therefore can be used to put together multiple cases that arise from unrelated incidents, but have important common issues. For example, suppose that a lender wishes to file suits against many unrelated borrowers, each of which relies on the same legal defense. The court, in the exercise of its discretion, can consolidate the suits, resolve the common issues, and order separate trials of the other issues.

[E] Compulsory Joinder

Read Fed. R. Civ. P. 19 (compulsory joinder).

HOW TO UNDERSTAND RULE 19

"Persons Needed for Just Adjudication." Rule 19(a) defines "persons required to be joined if feasible." The terminology of the Rule is complex, but in simple terms, these cases include those in which the existing suit cannot properly accomplish its purpose (give "complete relief") or in which there may be unfair repercussions to the absent person or to the parties.

What If Joinder Isn't Feasible? Sometimes the joinder of a particular new party isn't feasible. (For example, no one may have thought about the absent person until after the court has granted judgment, and ordinarily it isn't feasible to join a new party at that point.) Rule 19(b) then tells the judge to decide whether, "in equity and good conscience," the judgment should stand. The Rule identifies four factors the court should consider.

Read Rules 19(a) and (b) with Care. Before you read the next case, you should understand the basic concept of "persons required to be joined if feasible," as well as the four-factor test that determines whether the court can proceed if it is "not feasible" to join such a person.

HOW TO READ THE CASE OF
PROVIDENT TRADESMENS BANK & TRUST CO. v. PATTERSON

The next case is one of the most difficult cases in this book. You need to keep Rules 19(a)-(b) firmly in mind as you read it. Furthermore, the case is factually very complicated.

A Synopsis. In its simplest outline, the *Provident Tradesmens* case results in a holding that an absent individual, named Dutcher, is a "person required to be joined if feasible." It is not "feasible" to join him at this point. The court determines, however, that the judgment can be upheld under the four-factor "equity and good conscience" test. The reasons for each of these holdings are complicated, however.

Step 1: Dutcher's Insurance. Dutcher had a policy of insurance issued by Lumbermen's Mutual Casualty Co. The policy contained standard language extending coverage, also, to any person using Dutcher's car with his consent. The policy limit was $100,000. If Dutcher (or a person using Dutcher's car with his consent) became liable for any amount greater than $100,000 in any accident, he would be without insurance coverage for that amount.

Step 2: The Accident and the Initial Suits. Dutcher loaned his car to a person named Cionci. Cionci, with passengers in the car, had a serious accident. Cionci was killed, and so were two other people named Lynch and Smith. Another individual named Harris was injured. Each of these individuals (or his estate) sued Cionci's estate. Some of them also sued Dutcher, claiming that he was liable for entrusting the car to Cionci.

Step 3: The Present Suit for a Declaratory Judgment of Insurance Coverage. In the present suit, Lynch's executor (Provident Tradesmens) sued to obtain a declaratory judgment that Dutcher's insurance covers Cionci's liability. It would cover him if he was using the car within the scope of Dutcher's permission.

Step 4: Dutcher as a "Person Required to Be Joined if Feasible." Dutcher was not made a party to the declaratory judgment suit, although he arguably was a "person required to be joined if feasible" under Rule 19(a). Why? Because he obviously had an interest in the insurance policy. If the $100,000 were all paid out to cover Cionci's estate's liability, Dutcher would be left with no insurance covering his own potential liability for having entrusted the car to Cionci. However, as sometimes happens, nobody made an issue of Dutcher's absence until after the trial court's judgment. Now, the question is: Can the judgment stand? The answer depends on the four-factor "equity and good conscience" test of Rule 19(b).

PROVIDENT TRADESMENS BANK & TRUST CO. v. PATTERSON
390 U.S. 102 (1968)

Mr. Justice Harlan delivered the opinion of the Court.

This controversy, involving in its present posture the dismissal of a declaratory judgment action for nonjoinder of an "indispensable" party, began nearly 10 years ago with a traffic accident. An automobile owned by Edward Dutcher, who was not present when the accident occurred, was being driven by Donald Cionci, to whom Dutcher had given the keys. John Lynch and John Harris were passengers. The automobile crossed the median strip of the highway and collided with a truck being driven by Thomas Smith. Cionci, Lynch, and Smith were killed and Harris was severely injured.

Three tort actions were brought. Provident Tradesmens Bank, the administrator of the estate of passenger Lynch and petitioner here, sued the estate of the driver, Cionci, in a diversity action. Smith's administratrix, and Harris in person, each brought a state-court action against the estate of Cionci, Dutcher the owner, and the estate of Lynch. These Smith and Harris actions, for unknown reasons, have never gone to trial and are still pending. The Lynch action against Cionci's estate was settled for $50,000, which the estate of Cionci, being penniless, has never paid.

Dutcher, the owner of the automobile and a defendant in the as yet untried tort actions, had an automobile liability insurance policy with Lumbermens Mutual Casualty Company, a respondent here. That policy had an upper limit of $100,000 for all claims arising out of a single accident. This fund was potentially subject to two different sorts of claims by the tort plaintiffs. First, Dutcher himself might be held vicariously liable as Cionci's "principal"; the likelihood of such a judgment against Dutcher is a matter of considerable doubt and dispute. Second, the policy by its terms covered the direct liability of any person driving Dutcher's car with Dutcher's "permission."

The insurance company [asserted] that Cionci had not had permission and hence was not covered by the policy. The facts allegedly were that Dutcher had entrusted his car to Cionci, but that Cionci had made a detour from the errand for which Dutcher allowed his car to be taken. The estate of Lynch, armed with its $50,000 liquidated claim against the estate of Cionci, brought the present diversity action for a declaration that Cionci's use of the car had been "with permission" of Dutcher. The only named defendants were the company and the estate of Cionci. The other two tort plaintiffs were joined as plaintiffs. Dutcher, a resident of the State of Pennsylvania as were all the plaintiffs, was not joined either as plaintiff or defendant. The failure to join him was not adverted to at the trial level.

[At trial, the issues centered upon state-law questions in relating to the scope of permission and admissibility of evidence. The court directed verdicts in favor of Smith's administratrix and Provident Tradesmens Bank as the representative of Lynch's estate. The jury found that Cionci had been given permission by Dutcher and awarded a verdict to Harris. The district court rendered a declaratory judgment that the plaintiffs' claims were covered by Lumbermens' policy. The defendant insurance company appealed, raising questions of state law only.

[Without reaching the state law questions, the Court of Appeals for the Third Circuit reversed on grounds not raised at all in the trial court. It noted that Dutcher had interests adverse to the claimants. Specifically, he had a potential need to call on the insurance fund to pay any judgments that might be taken against him, and therefore he had an interest in not having the $100,000 fund depleted by payment of Cionci's liability.

[Thus, the Court of Appeals concluded] that Dutcher was an indispensable party. The court held that [Dutcher's] "adverse interests" . . . required him to be made a party. The court did not consider whether the fact that a verdict had already been rendered, without objection to the nonjoinder of Dutcher, affected the matter. Nor did it follow the provision of Rule 19 of the Federal Rules of Civil Procedure that findings of "indispensability" must be based on stated pragmatic considerations. [Note: Rule 19(b) formerly referred to "indispensable" parties, but no longer does so — Eds.] It held, to the contrary, that the right of a person who "may be affected" by the judgment to be joined is a "substantive" right, unaffected by the Federal Rules; that a trial court "may not proceed" in the absence of such a person; and that since Dutcher could not be joined as a defendant without destroying diversity jurisdiction the action had to be dismissed.

Since this ruling presented a serious challenge to the scope of the newly amended Rule 19, we granted certiorari . . . . Concluding that the inflexible approach adopted by the Court of Appeals in this case exemplifies the kind of reasoning that the Rule was designed to avoid, we reverse.

I

The applicable part of Rule 19 read as follows: [The Court here sets out the entire text of Rules 19(a)-(b).]

We may assume, at the outset, that Dutcher falls within the category of persons who, under § (a), should be "joined if feasible." The action was for an adjudication of the validity of certain claims against a fund. Dutcher, faced with the possibility of judgments against him, had an interest in having the fund preserved to cover that potential liability. Hence there existed, when this case went to trial, at least the possibility that a judgment might impede Dutcher's ability to protect his interest, or lead to later relitigation by him.

The optimum solution, an adjudication of the permission question that would be binding on all interested persons, was not "feasible," however, for Dutcher could not be made a defendant without destroying diversity. Hence the problem was the one to which Rule 19(b) appears to address itself: in the absence of a person who "should be joined if feasible," should the court dismiss the action or proceed without him? Since this problem emerged for the first time in the Court of Appeals, there were also two subsidiary questions. First, what was the effect, if any, of the failure of the defendants to raise the matter in the District Court? Second, what was the importance, if any, of the fact that a judgment, binding on the parties although not binding on Dutcher, had already been reached after extensive litigation? The three questions prove, on examination, to be interwoven.

We conclude, upon consideration of the record and applying the "equity and good conscience" test of Rule 19(b), that the Court of Appeals erred in not allowing the judgment to stand.

Rule 19(b) suggests four "interests" that must be examined in each case to determine whether, in equity and good conscience, the court should proceed without a [person whom it is not feasible to join]. . . . First, the plaintiff has an interest in having a forum. . . . Second, the defendant may properly wish to avoid multiple litigation, or inconsistent relief, or sole responsibility for a liability he shares with another. . . .

Third, there is the interest of the outsider whom it would have been desirable to join. Of course, since the outsider is not before the court, he cannot be bound by the judgment rendered. This means, however, only that a judgment is not *res judicata* as to, or legally enforceable against, a nonparty. . . . [But] as Rule 19(a) expresses it, the court must consider the extent to which the judgment may "as a practical matter impair or impede [the person's] ability to protect" his interest in the subject matter. . . .

Fourth, there remains the interest of the courts and the public in complete, consistent, and efficient settlement of controversies. We read the Rule's third criterion, whether the judgment issued in the absence of the nonjoined person will be "adequate," to refer to this public stake in settling disputes. . . .

Rule 19(b) also directs a district court to consider the possibility of shaping relief to accommodate these four interests. . . . [T]he Rule now makes it explicit that a court should consider modification of a judgment as an alternative to dismissal. Needless to say, a court of appeals may also properly require suitable modification as a condition of affirmance.

Had the Court of Appeals applied Rule 19's criteria to the facts of the present case, it could hardly have reached the conclusion it did. We begin with the plaintiffs' viewpoint. It is difficult to decide at this stage whether they would have had an "adequate" remedy had the action been dismissed before trial for nonjoinder: we cannot here determine whether the plaintiffs could have brought the same action, against the same parties plus Dutcher, in a state court. After trial, however, the "adequacy" of this hypothetical alternative, from the plaintiffs' point of view, was obviously greatly diminished. Their interest in preserving a fully litigated judgment should be overborne only by rather greater opposing considerations than would be required at an earlier stage. . . .

Opposing considerations in this case are hard to find. The defendants had no stake, either asserted or real, in the joinder of Dutcher. They showed no interest in joinder until the Court of Appeals took the matter into its own hands. This properly forecloses any interest of theirs, but for purposes of clarity we note that the insurance company, whose liability was limited to $100,000, had or will have full opportunity to litigate each claim on that fund against the claimant involved. Its only concern with the absence of Dutcher was and is to obtain a windfall escape from its defeat at trial.

The interest of the outsider, Dutcher, is more difficult to reckon. The Court of Appeals, concluding that it should not follow Rule 19's command to determine whether, as a practical matter, the judgment impaired the nonparty's ability to protect his rights, [concluded] that Dutcher had a "right" to be joined: . . .

. . . There remains . . . the practical question whether Dutcher is [harmed]. The only possible threat to him is that if the fund is used to pay judgments against Cionci the money may in fact have disappeared before Dutcher has an opportunity to assert his interest. Upon examination, we find this supposed threat neither large nor unavoidable.

The state-court actions against Dutcher had lain dormant for years at the pleading stage by the time the Court of Appeals acted. Petitioner asserts here that under the applicable Pennsylvania vicarious liability law there is virtually no chance of recovery against Dutcher. We do not accept this assertion as fact, but the matter could have been explored below. Furthermore, even in the event of tort judgments against Dutcher, it is unlikely that he will be prejudiced by the outcome here. The potential claimants against Dutcher himself are identical with the potential claimants against Cionci's estate. Should the claimants seek to collect from Dutcher personally, he may be able to raise the permission issue defensively, making it irrelevant that the actual monies paid from the fund may have disappeared: Dutcher can assert that Cionci did not have his permission and that therefore the payments made on Cionci's behalf out of Dutcher's insurance policy should properly be credited against Dutcher's own liability. Of course, when Dutcher raises this defense he may lose, either on the merits of the permission issue or on the ground that the issue is foreclosed by Dutcher's failure to intervene in the present case, but Dutcher will not have been prejudiced by the failure of the District Court here to order him joined.

If the Court of Appeals was unconvinced that the threat to Dutcher was trivial, it could nevertheless have avoided all difficulties by proper phrasing of the decree. . . . Payment could have been withheld pending the suits against Dutcher and relitigation (if that became necessary) by him. In this Court, furthermore, counsel for petitioner represented orally that the tort plaintiffs would accept a limitation of all claims to the amount of the insurance policy. Obviously such a compromise could have been reached below had the Court of Appeals been willing to abandon its rigid approach and seek ways to preserve what was, as to the parties, subject to the appellant's other contentions, a perfectly valid judgment.

The suggestion of potential relitigation of the question of "permission" raises the fourth "interest" at stake in joinder cases — efficiency. It might have been preferable, at the trial level, if there were a forum available in which both the company and Dutcher could have been made defendants, to dismiss the action and force the plaintiffs to go elsewhere. Even this preference would have been highly problematical. . . . By the time the case reached the Court of Appeals, however, the problematical preference on efficiency grounds had entirely disappeared: there was no reason then to throw away a valid judgment just because it did not theoretically settle the whole controversy.

II

[The Court of Appeals also reasoned that Dutcher's right to be joined was a "substantive right." Since the Rules Enabling Act does not allow the Federal Rules to override "substantive" rights, the Court of Appeals held that it was required to reverse, no matter what interpretation might be made of Rule 19(b). The Supreme Court, here, rejects this reasoning.

[The Court of Appeals' reasoning was based on the argument that (1) there was a category of persons called "indispensable parties"; (2) that this category was defined by substantive law and could not be changed by rule; and (3) that an indispensable party, such as Dutcher, thus had an absolute right to be joined, irrespective of the rule.

[The Supreme Court points out that an "indispensable party" can be identified "only . . . in the context of particular litigation." Rule 19 requires exactly that consideration: It "commands the courts to examine each controversy to make certain" that the absent person really is needed. "To say that a court'must' dismiss in the absence of an indispensable party and that it'cannot proceed' without him puts the matter the wrong way around: a court does not know whether a particular person is'indispensable' until it has examined the situation to see whether it can proceed without him."

[The Supreme Court also points out that the lower court relied upon certain "19th century" joinder cases in finding a substantive right of certain classes of people to be joined in a suit. These cases, of course, were decided long before the adoption of Rule 19. The Supreme Court rejects the argument that those earlier cases created substantive rights contravening Rule 19. Under the older terminology, mere "necessary" persons were those who had an interest in the controversy that could be left unaffected by the judgment. While they "ought" to be made parties, "necessary" persons were not indispensable. The court would be deprived of power to adjudicate, however, by the absence of an "indispensable" person — one whose interest was such that "a final decree cannot be made . . . without affecting that interest . . . ."]

The majority of the Court of Appeals read *Shields v. Barrow* [58 U.S. (17 How.) 130 (1854)] to say that a person whose interests "may be affected" by the decree of the court is an indispensable party, and that all indispensable parties have a "substantive right" to have suits dismissed in their absence. We are unable to read *Shields* as saying either. It dealt only with persons whose interests must, unavoidably, be affected by a decree and it said nothing about substantive rights. Rule 19(b), which the Court of Appeals dismissed as an ineffective attempt to change the substantive rights stated in *Shields*, is, on the contrary, a valid statement of the criteria for determining whether to proceed or dismiss in the forced absence of an interested person. It takes, for aught that now appears, adequate account of the very real, very substantive claims to fairness on the part of outsiders that may arise in some cases. This, however, simply is not such a case.

The judgment is vacated and the case is remanded to the Court of Appeals for consideration of those issues raised on appeal that have not been considered, and, should the Court of Appeals affirm the District Court as to those issues, for appropriate disposition preserving the judgment of the District Court and protecting the interests of nonjoined persons.

NOTES AND QUESTIONS

(1) *The Old Approach — Rigid Categories of "Indispensable" Parties, Defined by Reference to Substantive Rights: Shields v. Barrow, 58 U.S. (17 How.) 130 (1854).* The older, now discredited, approach to compulsory joinder was to classify parties rigidly, depending upon the kinds of substantive rights they asserted. The leading case was *Shields v. Barrow, supra*, which required joinder when the rights were "joint" (rather than joint and several). Thus, persons who owned joint interests in the subject of the action (or who claimed joint interests) had to be joined, and if they were not, the court did not have jurisdiction. This rule was particularly disadvantageous when non-joinder became an issue after judgment (as in *Provident Tradesmens*).

(2) *"Bleak House": The Historical Problem of Compulsory Joinder in Equity.* From our discussion of equity (Chapter 5, § 5.01[B], above), you should recall that the over developed law of compulsory joinder was a principal factor underlying the advice of Charles Dickens in *Bleak House*: Suffer any wrong, rather than come to the Court of Chancery!

[F] Intervention and the Real-Party-in-Interest Requirement

Read Fed. R. Civ. P. 24 (intervention). Also, read Rule 17(a) (real party in interest).

HOW TO READ THE CASE OF *NOPSI v. UNITED GAS*

Intervention "of Right" Versus "Permissive" Intervention. Rule 24 sets out two different kinds of intervention. In the absence of a federal statute covering the precise situation, Rule 24(a) provides for intervention "of right" when the intervenor claims a legally protectable "interest" in the case that may be impaired and is not adequately represented by any existing party. "Permissive" intervention, on the other hand, is discretionary with the court and may be granted pursuant to Rule 24(b) whenever the claim or defense presented by the applicant for intervention has a question of law or fact in common with the existing action. *See* Kennedy, *Let's All Join In: Intervention under Federal Rule 24*, 57 Ky. L.J. 329 (1969).

New Orleans Public Service, Inc. v. United Gas: Is the Denial of Intervention Correct? The case that follows is moderately complex. Essentially, it is a contract dispute between an electric utility and its principal fuel supplier. In this dispute, certain city officials and ratepayers want to intervene. At first blush, it seems they should be allowed to, because after all, they are the ones who will pay higher rates if the fuel supplier prevails. But the trial court denied intervention. Is this holding correct? The issue is so controversial that the entire Fifth Circuit, en banc, hears the case. It must consider both kinds of intervention. First, as to intervention of right: The city officials and ratepayers obviously have some kind of "interest" in the case, but do they have a legally protected interest of the sort that is required for intervention of right, since the dispute is essentially a contract dispute between the two parties already in the case? Second, as to permissive intervention: Because the trial court had discretion to grant or deny it, can the intervenors overcome the deference that must be given to the decision below?

NEW ORLEANS PUBLIC SERVICE, INC. v. UNITED GAS PIPE LINE CO.
732 F.2d 452 (5th Cir. 1984) (en banc)

GARWOOD, CIRCUIT JUDGE:

This diversity case brings to our en banc consideration questions pertaining to the entitlement of third parties to intervene as plaintiffs in a contract action brought by a local electric utility against its major fuel supplier. The district court denied all requested intervention. The decision of the panel, as modified on rehearing, though declining to disturb both the denial of intervention to the electricity consumers and the determination that officials of the city which franchised the electric utility were not entitled to intervene as of right, held that the district court abused its discretion in denying the city officials permissive intervention. . . . This court en banc, disagreeing with the latter determination, now holds that the city officials were properly denied intervention.

[New Orleans Public Service, Inc. (or "NOPSI," pronounced to rhyme with "Flopsy"), provided electric service to the City of New Orleans. United Gas Pipe Line Co. ("United") was its principal fuel supplier. NOPSI and United had entered into a long-term natural gas contract in 1952, to expire in 1975. In anticipation of its expiration, NOPSI entered into an "interim agreement" to buy gas from United until the Federal Power Commission permitted United to abandon the service. The price initially was set at United's weighted average cost of gas ("WACOG") plus 61.84 cents per thousand cubic feet. But this interim agreement also purported to give United the authority to redetermine the price unilaterally at one-year intervals; NOPSI could reject the price and cease to take any gas. The pricing formula continued in effect, with some modifications, until, in 1981, United sent NOPSI a notice that it was exercising its right to redetermine the rate. The redetermined rate would vary according to the quantity purchased, but for large volumes, it was tied to the price of fuel oil and would be considerably higher than it had been the year before.

[NOPSI signed a letter agreement providing for the redetermined rate, but contemporaneously informed United that it was doing so "with reservation of rights." It then filed suit against United, claiming that it had been forced to sign the agreement under "duress" and that the redetermination provision was invalid under certain provisions of the Louisiana Civil Code because it provided for "an uncertain price." United answered by denying "duress," denying invalidity of the agreement, and pleading the affirmative defenses of laches, waiver and estoppel.]

. . . .

On August 26, 1981 [New Orleans Mayor] Ernest Morial moved to intervene in the litigation "as a party plaintiff," individually and as representative of the class of NOPSI electric customers. [O]n October 6, 1981 an amended motion was filed seeking intervention "as party plaintiffs herein" under Rule 24(a), Fed. R. Civ. P., on behalf of Morial, several other persons and businesses, and the City of New Orleans, in each case individually and as representatives of the class composed of all NOPSI electric rate payers. The then tendered amended petition in intervention recites that the intervenors are NOPSI electricity customers, . . . and that "the increased cost of power plant gas, which NOPSI uses to generate electricity, is charged to Intervenors in the form of increased fuel adjustment charges. Intervenors are thus paying the most significant portion of the increased cost of power plant gas." The amended petition in intervention expressly adopts the allegations of NOPSI's complaint, but does not otherwise allege any substantive claim or ground for relief.

[T]he district court in February 1982 denied all intervention. It ruled, *inter alia*, that . . . "none of the applicants for intervention . . . have a direct, legally protected interest in this contract action between the two parties to the contract," and that the applicants had not overcome the presumption of adequate representation by NOPSI. This appeal by the applicants for intervention followed. . . . [A panel of the Fifth Circuit reversed this decision as to the City and its officials; the entire court then accepted the case for en banc review.]

Intervention of Right

Respecting intervention under Rule 24(a)(2), Fed. R. Civ. P., we adhere to the statement in *International Tank Terminals, Ltd. v. M/V Acadia Forest*, 579 F.2d 964, 967 (5th Cir. 1978):

> It is well-settled that to intervene as of right each of the four requirements of the rule must be met: (1) the application for intervention must be timely; (2) the applicant must have an interest relating to the property or transaction which is the subject of the action; (3) the applicant must be so situated that the disposition of the action may, as a practical matter, impair or impede his ability to protect that interest; (4) the applicant's interest must be inadequately represented by the existing parties to the suit.

Interest of Applicant

Here our focus is on the second requirement, that the applicant for intervention have an interest relating to the transaction which forms the subject matter of the action. What *kind* of interest is required? . . .

[T]he Supreme Court in *Donaldson v. United States*, 400 U.S. 517 (1971), stated that the applicant's interest had to be "a significantly protectable interest." It is apparent that the Supreme Court in *Donaldson* used "protectable" in the sense of legally protectable, and it is difficult to conceive of any other sense in which the Court might have been employing "protectable" in that context.

By requiring that the applicant's interest be not only "direct" and "substantial," but also "legally protectable," it is plain that something more than an economic interest is necessary. What is required is that the interest be one which the *substantive* law recognizes as belonging to or being owned by the applicant. This is reflected by the requirement that the claim the applicant seeks intervention in order to assert be a claim as to which the applicant is the real party in interest. The real party in interest requirement of Rule 17(a), Fed. R. Civ. P., "applies to intervenors as well as plaintiffs," as does also the rule that "a party has no standing to assert a right if it is not his own." . . . As we stated in *United States v. 936.71 Acres of Land:* . . .

> The "real party in interest" is the party who, by substantive law, possesses the right sought to be enforced, and not necessarily the person who will ultimately benefit from the recovery.

[H]ere the suit is on the contract between NOPSI and United and the dispute concerns the contract price for the Power Plant Gas. Relief is not sought by the City officials (or NOPSI) against United on the basis of the Natural Gas Act or any asserted power to regulate or approve NOPSI's purchase of or contracts for Power Plant Gas (or United's sale or contracts for sale of such gas). [O]ther than the City's now lapsed regulatory role and the claim of third-party beneficiary rights under the NOPSI-United contract, the *only* "interest" asserted as a basis for intervention is a purely economic interest. We hold that an economic interest alone is insufficient, as a legally protectable interest is required for intervention under Rule 24(a)(2). . . .

Third-Party Beneficiary Contract

Louisiana law [g]overns the question of who possesses substantive legal rights under the NOPSI-United contract. [H]ere, the only basis on which it is claimed that anyone other than NOPSI and United has substantive rights under the contract is the assertion that it is a third-party beneficiary contract, a *stipulation pour autrui* under Louisiana law. . . .

Where the promisor's performance is to be made to, and is subject to the control of, the promisee, the Louisiana courts have refused to find a *stipulation pour autrui* despite the fact that the promisor and promisee may have contemplated that the promisor's performance would as a practical matter enable or facilitate the promisee's performance of its obligations to a third party. . . .

The Louisiana approach appears to be consistent with the general common law rule in this regard, which would plainly consider the NOPSI-United agreement not to be a third-party beneficiary contract. . . .

Conclusion, Intervention of Right

[W]e accordingly hold that the City officials were properly denied intervention as of right because they lacked the character of interest required by Rule 24(a)(2).

Permissive Intervention

The district court also denied the City officials permissive intervention under Rule 24(b)(2). Permissive intervention "is wholly discretionary with the [district] court . . . even though there is a common question of law or fact, or the requirements of Rule 24(b) are otherwise satisfied." . . . Accordingly, [t]he question on appeal is "[w]hether the trial court committed a clear abuse of discretion in denying the motion." . . .

In acting on a request for permissive intervention, it is proper to consider, among other things, "whether the intervenors' interests are adequately represented by other parties" and whether they "will significantly contribute to full development of the underlying factual issues in the suit." . . .

In the present case, both the City officials and NOPSI seek exactly the same relief, on exactly the same grounds, from and as against United. There is neither indication nor assertion that NOPSI has been or will be in any way remiss or inadequate in pursuing these claims against United, or that there is any character of collusion between NOPSI and United. Under these circumstances, NOPSI's representation is presumed to be adequate. . . .

The effect on the existing parties is also to be considered. When the intervention is for all purposes with full party rights [t]he control of the original parties over their own lawsuit is significantly diminished. . . . NOPSI and United clearly had the power to settle their differences without the permission of the City officials, if suit had not been filed. Yet, if the City officials are granted the intervention they seek they could prevent any settlement between NOPSI and United, or prevent those parties from simply accepting a judgment of the district court by allowing it to become final without appeal. . . . The position of amicus may be considered more appropriate than an intervention with full-party status, if, as here, such intervention may materially diminish the original parties' rights. . . .

We are unable to find that the district court clearly abused its discretion in denying the City officials permissive intervention. . . .

CONCLUSION

We hold that the City officials are not entitled to intervene as of right under Rule 24(a), and that the district court did not clearly abuse its discretion in denying them permissive intervention under Rule 24(b). . . .

JERRE S. WILLIAMS, CIRCUIT JUDGE, with whom GOLDBERG, ALVIN B. RUBIN, TATE and JOHNSON, CIRCUIT JUDGES, join, dissenting:

This is not just a little breach of contract case between two corporations. This litigation will inescapably decide how much the citizens of the City of New Orleans will pay their enfranchised monopoly, New Orleans Public Service, Inc., for their electric power. . . . The majority holding strikes a serious blow against the heralded modern development in law protecting the rights of consumers by allowing them to participate in administrative and judicial decisions for which they ultimately pay the full price out of their own pockets.

. . . I am in full agreement of that carefully reasoned portion of the opinion which holds that the Mayor and City Council of New Orleans, are not entitled to intervention as a matter of right. . . .

I accept the proposition set out in the opinion for the Court that it is unusual to upset a denial of permissive intervention by the district court. . . . Further, I concede that the standard to be applied is one of "clear abuse." . . .

We cannot close our eyes to the realities of the "pass-through". . . . [N]OPSI knows it can fall back with confidence in any ratemaking proceeding before the Commission on a guarantee of "fair return." . . . The *issue* which NOPSI and New Orleans presents is the same, but the *interests* which NOPSI represents do not fully encompass the *interests* which should be represented by the Mayor and City Council on behalf of the electorate — the citizens who put them in office and who pay the electric bills. . . .

NOTES AND QUESTIONS

(1) *Sufficiency of the Claimed Interest: South v. Rowe, 759 F.2d 610 (7th Cir. 1985).* While the principal case above, *NOPSI v. United*, shows the kind of interest that will not do, *South v. Rowe* shows the kind that will. The intervenor was a prison inmate who sought to claim that the prison law library failed to conform to a consent decree negotiated by a former inmate (who had since left prison) and the State of Illinois. The Court of Appeals held that his right to intervene should have been recognized. He asserted his own interest in the use of the law library, and the consent decree contemplated him as a third-party beneficiary in that its terms clearly were intended to benefit all inmates. Is this decision consistent with *NOPSI v. United*?

(2) *Adequate Representation by Existing Parties: Morgan v. McDonough, 726 F.2d 11 (1st Cir. 1984).* In a school desegregation case, can parents of non-plaintiff schoolchildren intervene to oppose remedies that are proposed by the plaintiffs? In *Morgan v. McDonough*, the court held that adequate representation of all citizens' interests by the school district was to be presumed — but that the presumption could be overcome, and intervention of right recognized, if there was collusion between the school district and the plaintiffs, or if the intervenors' interests were adverse to those of the school board, or if the school district failed to fulfill its duty of adequate representation. Does this holding make sense? Given that school desegregation decrees often result in the uneven distribution of benefits and burdens of compliance, and given that the school district will be forced to advocate the placement of these burdens in some manner if the case reaches the remedy stage, doesn't every parent of schoolchildren have interests that diverge from those of the school district as a whole — at least to some degree? But it hardly would make sense to hold that every parent has a right to intervene!

(3) *Permissive Intervention.* Courts considering permissive intervention have considered such factors as whether the intervention will prejudice existing parties by undue delay or by complicating the action; whether the intervenor will benefit from intervention; the nature and extent of the intervenor's interests in the subject of the action; whether the intervenor's interests are adequately represented by existing parties; and whether the intervenor will contribute to the development of the issues. *See, e.g., United States Postal Service v. Brennan*, 579 F.2d 188 (2d Cir. 1978). Given these factors, was the Court of Appeals correct in upholding the denial of permissive intervention in *NOPSI v. United*, the principal case above? [Note: Some factors favor intervention, and some do not. Does this split mean that the District Court's discretion should be upheld — or are some factors ranked higher than others? The *NOPSI v. United* dissent seems to suggest that the absence of prejudice is more important than others.] Shreve, *Questioning Intervention of Right — Toward a New Methodology of Decisionmaking*, 74 Nw. U. L. Rev. 894 (1980).

§ 6.03 Devices for Handling Numerous Parties

[A] Interpleader: The Modern "Stakeholder's Remedy"

Read Fed. R. Civ. P. 22 and 28 U.S.C. § 1335 (interpleader); also, read Federal Form 20.

HOW TO READ THE CASE OF *STATE FARM FIRE & CAS. CO. v. TASHIRE*

Rule 22 Versus Statutory Interpleader. The interpleader statute, 28 U.S.C. § 1335, has several bells and whistles that are not present in Rule 22 alone. For example, federal courts have interpleader jurisdiction on "minimal" diversity — that is, if any one claimant is diverse from any other. Furthermore, interpleader is available even if the claims are merely potential and not yet matured, because the statute covers persons who "may" claim (the Rule probably does too, but is less clear). Both of these threshold issues arose in *State Farm v. Tashire.*

The Accident and the Interpleader Action. A Greyhound bus and a truck collided in California, killing two people and injuring many more. State Farm insured the truck driver. It therefore had two obligations: (1) to pay its insured's liability up to policy limits (in this case, $20,000) and (2) to furnish its insured with a defense in suits or claims irrespective of cost. In this case, in which suits in multiple forums were likely, the defense obligation probably would cost much more than $20,000. State Farm filed an interpleader action in Oregon concerning the $20,000 policy limits. It sought to use the interpleader action to bring not only all claims against this fund, but all claims against its insured, into this one forum. It hoped to reduce litigation costs.

The Equitable Origins of Interpleader; The Injunction. It should not surprise you to learn that interpleader is a creature of equity. Furthermore, the equity courts would help the interpleader plaintiff by issuing an injunction to prevent the interpleader defendants from suing in multiple forums. In *State Farm v. Tashire*, State Farm naturally sought an injunction. The trial court granted a very broad injunction: In effect, it required all claims from the accident — not just those against the $20,000 fund — to be prosecuted in the same suit. That result was efficient. The question, in *State Farm v. Tashire*, was: Is it lawful?

Inconsistency of Claims, or in Other Words, Adverse Claims Between Rival Claimants, as the Key to Interpleader. A person cannot interplead anyone and everyone merely to obtain a convenient forum. The key requirement is that the claims must be inconsistent. The claims against State Farm's $20,000 were potentially inconsistent, because they would probably total many millions and far exceed this limited fund. But is there any inconsistency if Greyhound is held liable to every claimant? Or, for that matter, if State Farm's insured is held liable many times in different forums? The answer is, there is no inconsistency in these claims at all. In *State Farm v. Tashire*, the Supreme Court confined the scope of the interpleader, and therefore the scope of the injunction, for these reasons.

STATE FARM FIRE & CAS. CO. v. TASHIRE

386 U.S. 523 (1967)

MR. JUSTICE FORTAS delivered the opinion of the Court.

Early one September morning in 1964, a Greyhound bus proceeding northward through Shasta County, California, collided with a southbound pickup truck. Two of the passengers aboard the bus were killed. Thirty-three others were injured, as were the bus driver, the driver of the truck and its lone passenger. One of the dead and 10 of the injured passengers were Canadians; the rest of the individuals involved were citizens of five American States. The ensuing litigation led to the present case, which raises important questions concerning administration of the interpleader remedy in the federal courts.

The litigation began when four of the injured passengers filed suit in California state courts, seeking damages in excess of $1,000,000. Named as defendants were Greyhound Lines, Inc., a California corporation; Theron Nauta, the bus driver; Ellis Clark, who drove the truck; and Kenneth Glasgow, the passenger in the truck who was apparently its owner as well. Each of the individual defendants was a citizen and resident of Oregon. Before these cases could come to trial and before other suits were filed in California or elsewhere, petitioner State Farm Fire & Casualty Company, an Illinois corporation, brought this action in the nature of interpleader in the United States District Court for the District of Oregon.

In its complaint State Farm asserted that at the time of the Shasta County collision it had in force an insurance policy with respect to Ellis Clark, driver of the truck, providing for bodily injury liability up to $10,000 per person and $20,000 per occurrence and for legal representation of Clark in actions covered by the policy. It asserted that actions already filed in California and others which it anticipated would be filed far exceeded in aggregate damages sought the amount of its maximum liability under the policy. Accordingly, it paid into court the sum of $20,000 and asked the court (1) to require all claimants to establish their claims against Clark and his insurer in this single proceeding and in no other, and (2) to discharge State Farm from all further obligations under its policy — including its duty to defend Clark in lawsuits arising from the accident. Alternatively, State Farm expressed its conviction that the policy issued to Clark excluded from coverage accidents resulting from his operation of a truck which belonged to another and was being used in the business of another. The complaint, therefore, requested that the court decree that the insurer owed no duty to Clark and was not liable on the policy, and it asked the court to refund the $20,000 deposit.

Joined as defendants were Clark, Glasgow, Nauta, Greyhound Lines, and each of the prospective claimants. Jurisdiction was predicated upon 28 U.S.C. § 1335, the federal interpleader statute, and upon general diversity of citizenship, there being diversity between two or more of the claimants to the fund and between State Farm and all of the named defendants.

An order issued, requiring the defendants to show cause why they should not be restrained from filing or prosecuting "any proceeding in any state or United States Court affecting the property or obligation involved in this interpleader action, and specifically against the plaintiff and the defendant Ellis D. Clark." . . . Defendants Nauta, Greyhound, and several of the injured passengers responded, contending that the policy did cover this accident and advancing various arguments for the position that interpleader was either impermissible or inappropriate in the present circumstances. Greyhound, however, soon switched sides and moved that the court broaden any injunction to include Nauta and Greyhound among those who could not be sued except within the confines of the interpleader proceeding.

[A] temporary injunction along the lines sought by State Farm was issued by the United States District Court for the District of Oregon. . . . The injunction was later broadened to include the protection sought by Greyhound, but modified to permit the filing — although not the prosecution — of suits. The injunction, therefore, provided that all suits against Clark, State Farm, Greyhound, and Nauta be prosecuted in the interpleader proceeding.

On interlocutory appeal, the Court of Appeals for the Ninth Circuit reversed . . . The court . . . concluded that interpleader was not available in the circumstances of this case. It held that in States like Oregon which do not permit "direct action" suits against insurance companies until judgments are obtained against the insured, the insurance companies may not invoke federal interpleader until the claims against the insured, the alleged tortfeasor, have been reduced to judgment. Until that is done, said the court, claimants with unliquidated tort claims are not "claimants" within the meaning of § 1335, nor are they "persons [with] claims [that may expose a plaintiff to double or multiple liability]" within the meaning of Rule 22 of the Federal Rules of Civil Procedure. . . . Although we reverse the decision of the Court of Appeals upon the jurisdictional question, we direct a substantial modification of the District Court's injunction for reasons which will appear.

Before considering the issues presented by the petition for certiorari, we find it necessary to dispose of a question neither raised by the parties nor passed upon by the courts below. Since the matter concerns our jurisdiction, we raise it on our own motion. . . . The interpleader statute, 28 U.S.C. § 1335, applies where there are "[t]wo or more adverse claimants, of diverse citizenship . . . ." This provision has been uniformly construed to require only "minimal diversity," that is, diversity of citizenship between two or more claimants, without regard to the circumstance that other rival claimants may be co-citizens. The language of the statute, the legislative purpose broadly to remedy the problems posed by multiple claimants to a single fund, and the consistent judicial interpretation tacitly accepted by Congress, persuade us that the statute requires no more. There remains, however, the question whether such a statutory construction is consistent with Article III of our Constitution, which extends the federal judicial power to "Controversies . . . between Citizens of different States . . . and between a State, or the Citizens thereof, and foreign States, Citizens or Subjects." In *Strawbridge v. Curtiss*, 3 Cranch 267 (1806), this Court held that the diversity of citizenship statute required "complete diversity": where co-citizens appeared on both sides of a dispute, jurisdiction was lost. But Chief Justice Marshall there purported to construe only "[t]he words of the act of Congress," not the Constitution itself. And in a variety of contexts this Court and the lower courts have concluded that Article III poses no obstacle to the legislative extension of federal jurisdiction, founded on diversity, so long as any two adverse parties are not co-citizens. Accordingly, we conclude that the present case is properly in the federal courts.

II.

We do not agree with the Court of Appeals that, in the absence of a state law or contractual provision for "direct action" suits against the insurance company, the company must wait until persons asserting claims against its insured have reduced those claims to judgment before seeking to invoke the benefits of federal interpleader. That may have been a tenable position under the 1926 and 1936 interpleader statutes. These statutes did not carry forward the language in the 1917 Act authorizing interpleader where adverse claimants "may claim" benefits as well as where they "are claiming" them. In 1948, however, in the revision of the Judicial Code, the "may claim" language was restored. Until the decision below, every court confronted by the question has concluded that the 1948 revision removed whatever requirement there might previously have been that the insurance company wait until at least two claimants reduced their claims to judgments. . . .

. . . Were an insurance company required to await reduction of claims to judgment, the first claimant to obtain such a judgment or to negotiate a settlement might appropriate all or a disproportionate slice of the fund before his fellow claimants were able to establish their claims. The difficulties such a race to judgment pose for the insurer, and the unfairness which may result to some claimants, were among the principal evils the interpleader device was intended to remedy.

III.

The fact that State Farm had properly invoked the interpleader jurisdiction under § 1335 did not, however, entitle it to an order both enjoining prosecution of suits against it outside the confines of the interpleader proceeding and also extending such protection to its insured, the alleged tortfeasor. Still less was Greyhound Lines entitled to have that order expanded so as to protect itself and its driver, also alleged to be tortfeasors, from suits brought by its passengers in various state or federal courts. Here, the scope of the litigation, in terms of parties and claims, was vastly more extensive than the confines of the "fund," the deposited proceeds of the insurance policy. In these circumstances, the mere existence of such a fund cannot, by use of interpleader, be employed to accomplish purposes that exceed the needs of orderly contest with respect to the fund.

There are situations, of a type not present here, where the effect of interpleader is to confine the total litigation to a single forum and proceeding. One such case is where a stakes holder, faced with rival claims to the fund itself, acknowledges — or denies — his liability to one or the other of the claimants. In this situation, the fund itself is the target of the claimants. It marks the outer limits of the controversy. It is, therefore, reasonable and sensible that interpleader, in discharge of its office to protect the fund, should also protect the stakeholder from vexatious and multiple litigation. In this context, the suits sought to be enjoined are squarely within the language of 28 U.S.C. § 2361, which provides in part:

> In any civil action of interpleader or in the nature of interpleader under section 1335 of this title, a district court may issue its process for all claimants and enter its order restraining them from instituting or prosecuting *any proceeding* in any State or United States court *affecting the property, instrument or obligation involved in the interpleader action*. . . . (Emphasis added.)

But the present case is another matter. Here, an accident has happened. Thirty-five passengers or their representatives have claims which they wish to press against a variety of defendants: the bus company, its driver, the owner of the truck, and the truck driver. The circumstance that one of the prospective defendants happens to have an insurance policy is a fortuitous event which should not of itself shape the nature of the ensuing litigation. For example, a resident of California, injured in California aboard a bus owned by a California corporation should not be forced to sue that corporation anywhere but in California simply because another prospective defendant carried an insurance policy. And an insurance company whose maximum interest in the case cannot exceed $20,000 and who in fact asserts that it has no interest at all, should not be allowed to determine that dozens of tort plaintiffs must be compelled to press their claims — even those claims which are not against the insured and which in no event could be satisfied out of the meager insurance fund — in a single forum of the insurance company's choosing. There is nothing in the statutory scheme, and very little in the judicial and academic commentary upon that scheme, which requires that the tail be allowed to wag the dog in this fashion.

State Farm's interest in this case, which is the fulcrum of the interpleader procedure, is confined to its $20,000 fund. That interest receives full vindication when the court restrains claimants from seeking to enforce against the insurance company any judgment obtained against its insured, except in the interpleader proceeding itself. To the extent that the District Court sought to control claimants' lawsuits against the insured and other alleged tortfeasors, it exceeded the powers granted to it by the statutory scheme.

We recognize, of course, that our view of interpleader means that it cannot be used to solve all the vexing problems of multiparty litigation arising out of a mass tort. But interpleader was never intended to perform such a function, to be an all-purpose "bill of peace." None of the legislative and academic sponsors of a modern federal interpleader device viewed their accomplishment as a "bill of peace," capable of sweeping dozens of lawsuits out of the various state and federal courts in which they were brought and into a single interpleader proceeding. . . .

[W]e hold that the interpleader statute did not authorize the injunction entered in the present case. Upon remand, the injunction is to be modified consistently with this opinion.

[Reversed.]

[The dissent of JUSTICE DOUGLAS is omitted.]

NOTES AND QUESTIONS

(1) *The Requirement of Inconsistency: A Plaintiff Who "May Be Exposed to Double or Multiple Liability" on a Single Obligation.* Since interpleader is not an all-purpose "bill of peace," a potential debtor cannot interplead claimants if they all have rights to recovery that are not inconsistent. *See* Ilsen & Sardell, *Interpleader in the Federal Courts,* 35 St. John's L. Rev. 1 (1960). If, for example, a careless driver injures two people in one accident, the driver cannot use interpleader to prevent them from suing her in separate suits. There is no reason why both of them cannot recover from her, so interpleader is not available. In fact, that is why Greyhound cannot interplead the claimants in *State Farm v. Tashire* and cannot be protected by an injunction.

Consider the case of *Charles H. Tompkins Co. v. Lloyd E. Mitchell, Inc.*, 259 F.2d 177 (D.C. Cir. 1958). A general contractor, despite two adverse awards in arbitration proceedings that had become final, claimed that either its electrical subcontractor or its mechanical subcontractor had failed to perform certain disputed work that it, the general contractor, had therefore been required to do. From the subcontract payments, it withheld a "fund" covering the value of the disputed work and sought to interplead the two subcontractors. The Court of Appeals held that interpleader was not available because the claim of inconsistent "double or multiple" liability was fictitious. Is this holding correct? *See also Metropolitan Life Ins. Co. v. Prater,* 508 F. Supp. 667 (E.D. Ky. 1981) (where only potential claimant disclaimed fund, and where state statute absolved insurer for paying fund to sole claimant, there was no "substantial" prospect of multiple liability, and insurer could not interplead fund).

(2) *"Rule 22 Interpleader" Versus "Statutory Interpleader."* In reality, there are two different interpleader provisions in federal practice: Rule 22 interpleader and statutory interpleader. In addition to the jurisdictional differences pointed out above, there are other distinctions. Statutory interpleader requires only $500 in controversy, while Rule 22 requires ordinary diversity jurisdiction (in excess of $75,000). The statutory version has a special venue provision allowing suit at the residence of one or more claimants; Rule 22 does not cover the matter, and the ordinary venue provisions control in a Rule 22 case. You may be tempted to conclude that statutory interpleader has all the advantages and that Rule 22 has no place, but that conclusion would be erroneous. Diversity under Rule 22 is determined by traditional plaintiff-defendant distinctions, so Rule 22 interpleader comes within diversity jurisdiction if the claimants are all of the same citizenship, so long as the stakeholder is diverse from them. *Aetna Life & Cas. Co. v. Spain,* 556 F.2d 747 (5th Cir. 1977). Statutory interpleader requires diversity between adverse claimants, or between the claimants and an interested stakeholder.

Statutory interpleader also provides for nationwide service of process, which is discussed below.

(3) *What Could State Farm Have Done to Protect Its Interests Better in the Tashire Case?* State Farm is now protected by the interpleader action against inconsistent claims to the $20,000 fund, and the injunction permitted by the Supreme Court can prevent claims against this fund in other forums. But State Farm still is faced with the prospect of having to defend claims against its insured in multiple, scattered forums, possibly at great (and from its point of view, unnecessary) expense. Is there anything that State Farm

can do about this latter problem? [Note: State Farm would benefit from transfer of all the actions to a single forum for consolidated pretrial proceedings. How might it accomplish this result? If you are uncertain, review the Overview at the beginning of this chapter. A mechanism does exist for accomplishing this purpose, at least with respect to actions filed in federal courts. For actions in different state courts, or in state and federal courts, no means exists, unless the state actions can be removed to federal court.]

In this regard, the Court in *State Farm v. Tashire* says that interpleader is not an "all-purpose bill of peace." The "bill of peace" was an equitable proceeding, related to interpleader, that allowed a person subject to vexatious multiple litigation to require consolidation of the claims in certain circumstances. Should there be such a device today? Is the Court, in *State Farm v. Tashire*, correct in refusing to invent it? *See* Comment, *Promoting Judicial Economy Through the Extension of Interpleader to the Tortfeasor in the Mass Tort Area*, 17 Wayne L. Rev. 1241 (1971).

(4) *Attorney's Fees: How Much Doubt Must the Stakeholder Have?* Ordinarily, an interpleader plaintiff is entitled to recover attorney's fees, at least if she is a disinterested stakeholder who seeks only to be discharged from liability. It is not necessary that the prospect of multiple liability be certain, but only that there be a substantial or reasonable possibility, so that the interpleader plaintiff should not be required to run the risk. *United States v. Browne Elec. Co.*, 168 F. Supp. 806 (E.D. Va. 1959). This relief is within the equitable discretion of the court. *Cf. Murphy v. Travelers Ins. Co.*, 534 F.2d 1155 (5th Cir. 1976) (abuse of discretion found when court required disinterested stakeholder, which was neither dilatory nor in bad faith, to shoulder its own costs and attorney's fees). The usual procedure is to award costs and fees against the losing party — *i.e.*, the one whose claim made the interpleader necessary — although this principle, too, is within the court's discretion.

(5) *Nationwide Service, "Minimal" Diversity, and the Abolition of Traditional Jurisdictional Restrictions on Interpleader.* Congress passed the Federal Interpleader Act, 28 U.S.C. §§ 1335, 1397, 2361, partly as a response to *New York Life Ins. Co. v. Dunlevy*, 241 U.S. 518 (1916). There, the stakeholder was unable to use interpleader because it could not obtain personal jurisdiction of one claimant in the forum where it had been sued by the other claimant. That case had produced a clearly unfair result and made interpleader unavailable whenever two inconsistent claimants were not subject to process in the same jurisdiction. *See* Chafee, *Modernizing Interpleader*, 30 Yale L.J. 814 (1921). The Federal Interpleader Act provides for nationwide service, so that personal jurisdiction no longer is an impediment to impleader in the *Dunlevy* situation. Furthermore, to ensure that restrictions on subject — matter jurisdiction do not leave the interpleader plaintiff unable to use the federal remedy in a multi-state situation, the Act provides for jurisdiction in cases of "minimal" diversity (as *State Farm v. Tashire* illustrates).

[B] Class Actions

[1] Development of the Class Action Concept

Origins of Class Actions. Class actions originated in the English equity courts as an exception to procedural rules of compulsory joinder, when justice otherwise would fail (you should recall that equity had cumbersome joinder requirements). One plaintiff (or one defendant) "stood for" others similarly situated. This general device was known as the "representative suit," and it was closely related to other equity concepts and remedies (such as the "bill of peace," which had the objective of consolidating multiple and vexatious litigation). In American courts, the classic case was *Smith v. Swormstedt*, 57 U.S. (16 How.) 288 (1853), which was a representative suit on behalf of all ministers of the newly formed southern branch of the Methodist Church, seeking division of assets of the whole Church existing before its north-south split. The Court, through Justice Story, held that "the decree binds all of them the same as if all were before the court."

The Due Process Issues. But one of the most serious problems was: How could the court be assured that the "representative suit" would protect the great, passive mass known as the class, whose members (unlike the representative parties) had no contact with the court? At one time, the Federal Rules avoided this problem by granting the judge discretion to dispense with the joinder of impracticably numerous parties if it had "sufficient parties before it to represent all the adverse interest[s]," with the proviso: "But, in such cases, the decree shall be without prejudice to the rights and claims of the absent parties." Federal Rule of Equity 48. The "without prejudice" proviso was removed in 1912, and the issue has persisted, because the absent parties now can be bound. The case of *Richardson v. Kelly*, 191 S.W.2d 857, 144 Tex. 497 (1945), is an illustration: An entire class of defendants was held bound by a judgment against certain members of the class allegedly hand-picked by the plaintiff, although these representatives offered little defense and had only a small financial stake. In modern times, due process problems of notice and adequate representation have had great influence in shaping the class action. Consider the following landmark case.

HANSBERRY v. LEE, 311 U.S. 32 (1940). Lee and others sued to enjoin the Hansberrys, who were black, from residing in a predominantly white area of Chicago in alleged violation of a racially restrictive covenant. The case arose several years before the Supreme Court's decision in *Shelley v. Kraemer*, 334 U.S. 1 (1948), and racial covenants were then ostensibly enforceable. The Hansberrys defended by asserting that the covenant was ineffective by its own terms. It would be effective only if it had been signed by owners of 95% of the frontage, but it had been signed by owners of only about 54%. The plaintiffs responded that the issue was settled by *res judicata*, since an earlier suit, *Burke v. Kleiman*, 277 Ill. App. 519 (1934), had resulted in a final judgment including a determination, based on a stipulation of all parties, that owners of 95% had signed. The Hansberrys were not themselves parties to the earlier suit, and they took the position that the stipulation was false and fraudulent and that they were not bound by it. The Illinois Supreme Court concluded, however, that *Burke v. Kleiman* had been "a 'class' or 'representative' suit," and that "where the remedy is pursued by a plaintiff who has the right to represent the class to which he belongs, other members of the class are bound by the results in the case unless it is reversed or set aside on direct proceedings." The Illinois court also determined, ironically, that the Hansberrys had been members of the class seeking to enforce the racial covenant, since they were residents of the area and therefore within the definition of the class; hence, even though the court also thought that the 95% stipulation was contrary to fact, the Hansberrys were bound by it. The Supreme Court granted certiorari to determine whether this application of the class decree violated due process. It reversed.

> It is a principle of general application in Anglo-American jurisprudence that one is not bound by a judgment *in personam* in a litigation in which he has not been . . . made a party[.] . . .
>
> To these general rules there is a recognized exception that, to an extent not precisely defined by judicial opinion, the judgment in a "class" or "representative" suit . . .

may bind members of the class or those represented who were not made parties to it. . . .

The class suit was an invention of equity to enable it to proceed to a decree in suits where the number of those interested in the subject of the litigation is so great that their joinder as parties in conformity to the usual rules of procedure is impractical. Courts are not infrequently called upon to proceed with causes in which the number of those interested in the litigation is so great as to make difficult or impossible the joinder of all because some are not within the jurisdiction or because their whereabouts is unknown. . . . In such cases where the interests of those not joined are of the same class as the interests of those who are, and where it is considered that the latter fairly represent the former in the prosecution of the litigation of the issues in which all have a common interest, the court will proceed to a decree. . . .

. . . [T]here is scope within the framework of the Constitution for holding in appropriate cases that a judgment rendered in a class suit is *res judicata* as to members of the class who are not formal parties to the suit. . . . [T]his Court is justified in saying that there has been a failure of due process only in those cases where it cannot be said that the procedure adopted fairly insures the protection of the interest of absent parties who are to be bound by it. . . .

. . . It is plain that . . . all those alleged to be bound by the [racially restrictive] agreement would not constitute a single class in any litigation brought to enforce it. Those who sought to secure its benefits by enforcing it could not be said to be in the same class with or represent those whose interest was in resisting performance. . . .

Because of the dual and potentially conflicting interests of those who are putative parties to the agreement in compelling or resisting its performance, it is impossible to say, . . . that any two of them are of the same class.

It is one thing to say that some members of a class may represent other members in a litigation where the sole and common interest . . . is either to assert a common right or to challenge an asserted obligation. . . . It is quite another to hold that all those who are free alternatively either to assert rights or to challenge them are a single class. . . . Apart from the opportunities it would provide for the fraudulent sacrifice of the rights of absent parties, we think that the representation in this case no more satisfies the requirements of due process than a trial by a judicial officer who [has] an interest in the outcome of the litigation in conflict with that of the litigants. . . .

Reversed

NOTES AND QUESTIONS

History: Equitable Origins and "True," "Hybrid," and "Spurious" Actions. Consistently with its origins in equity practice (as exemplified by *Smith v. Swormstedt*), the federal class action rule in force at the time of *Hansberry v. Lee* provided for "joint" actions (in which class members held joint interests together), "hybrid" (in which they sought to enforce rights held in common, as through an association) or "spurious" (in which each member's right was independent but all presented common questions). These designations had more to do with the binding effect of the judgment than with the functional characteristics of class actions, and they have given way today to modern Rule 23 (*see* below). For an interesting history of the *Hansberry* case itself, see Kamp, *The History Behind Hansberry v. Lee,* 20 U.C. Davis L. Rev. 481 (1987).

[2] Class Actions Under Modern Rule 23

Read Fed. R. Civ. P. 23 (class actions).

NOTE ON UNDERSTANDING RULE 23

Rule 23 is carefully structured. In the next case, you will encounter issues that bring into play nearly every major section of the Rule. Its first two sections define the conditions under which class actions are permitted, and the remaining sections govern procedural matters.

(a) Prerequisites: "Numerosity," "Commonality," "Typicality," and "Adequate Representation." Rule 23(a) sets out the basic requirements that every class action must satisfy. The most obvious is (1) that the members must be "so numerous" that their joinder is "impracticable." If all of the members could be normal parties to a suit, a class action is unnecessary. This first element is often called "numerosity" by class action lawyers. (2) There must be "questions of law or fact common to the class." It would make no sense to put together a large number of claims that were all unrelated, because they would need to be decided individually anyway. Class action lawyers call this element "commonality." (3) The entire class will be represented by the named party or parties — that is, by one or a few members of the class. These representatives will do a better job, perhaps, if they have the same interests as the rest of the class. To ensure this incentive, the third requirement is that the representatives' claims or defenses must be "typical" of the class. This element, as you probably can predict, is called "typicality." (4) Finally, the court must satisfy itself that the named parties "will fairly and adequately protect the interests" of the class — the "adequate representation" requirement. Historically, courts interpreted Rule 23(a)(4)'s adequacy of representation requirement to encompass both the class representatives and class counsel. Revisions to Rule 23 have eliminated the need for this case law extension. Instead, Rule 23(a)(4) continues to apply to the class representatives, and Rule 23(g) now imposes an express adequacy of representation requirement upon class counsel.

(b) The Three Types of Class Actions. But these four universal prerequisites are not all of the requirements. Once they are satisfied, the class action also must be shown to fall within one of the three types of class actions that section (b) says are "maintainable." These are:

> *(b)(1): Inconsistent Results.* If there is a risk that individual suits would create inconsistent results, a class action is maintainable. The "inconsistency" can be either in the form of inconsistent standards for the party opposing the class, or results in earlier cases that would affect later class members. The prototype case under this subsection is one involving a limited fund with numerous claimants. If all members of the class are not brought into the litigation, the party opposing them might face court orders in separate suits that would require it to pay out more than the fund limits. Or early individual victors would obtain amounts greater than their proportional shares of the fund. (It should be clear to you that a "subsection (b)(1) class action" is analogous to a big interpleader action.)
>
> *(b)(2): Uniform Injunctive or Declaratory Relief.* The prototype "(b)(2) class action" is the civil rights class action, in which class representatives sue to have a statute declared unconstitutional. The relief is granted with respect to the class as a whole.

(b)(3): Common Questions "Predominate" and a Class Action Is the "Superior" Means of Managing the Case. The "(b)(3) class action" is the type that we visualize when we think of a class action, and it is the type most frequently brought in actual practice. The claims, under this subsection, can be independent, so long as they arise in a context of sufficiently common questions. Consumer class actions, antitrust class actions, and securities fraud class actions are examples. In each of these cases, there are many claimed victims of a single course of conduct by the party opposing the class. There are two requirements: The common questions must "predominate" over questions that are individual to each member, and the class format must be the "superior" means of managing their resolution. If these two requisites were not met, a class action would probably not be useful, and the Rule therefore makes them required elements.

The Four-Factor Test for (b)(3) Class Actions. Subsection (b)(3) is slightly more complex than this review would indicate, however, because it goes on to specify four factors that are "pertinent" to the determination. Briefly put, the factors are: (A) class members' possible interest in "individually controlling" their own actions; (B) other pending litigation, if any; (C) the appropriateness of the forum; and (D) the "likely difficulties in managing" a class action.

Remember, a class action must clear each of the hurdles set out in subsection (a) — the prerequisites — and, in addition, must conform to at least one of the three types of actions described in subsection (b).

(c) Certification and Notice. Section (c) of the Rule requires the court to conduct a hearing "[a]t an early practicable time" to determine whether the class action may be maintained. This determination is called "certification" of the class action. At the hearing, the court determines whether the four prerequisites of Rule 23(a) are met and, in addition, whether the action fits one of the three types set out in Rule 23(b). In addition, subsection (c) requires the court to direct notice to class members in a (b)(3) action. The notice must be "the best . . . practicable under the circumstances," must be written in "plain, easily understood language," and must include individual notice, usually by mail, to all class members "who can be identified through reasonable effort." This section also provides for members to request "exclusion" (to "opt out") if they desire.

(d) Flexible Orders in Conduct of Actions. Section (d) of the Rule is intended to give the court flexible authority to tailor the notice, pleadings, and pretrial orders to the shape of the particular class action, as well as ability to deal with "similar procedural matters." Class actions are different from ordinary litigation, and they sometimes require creativity on the part of the judge. In the case that you will read next, the court attempts to structure both the notice and the possible relief in novel ways.

(e) Settlement, Voluntary Dismissal or Compromise. Since the representative parties have obligations to the class, section (e) requires that the court approve any settlement, voluntary dismissal, or compromise of a certified class, that notice be given to class members of these events, and that the court may refuse to approve a class settlement unless class members are provided with a second opportunity to opt out of the class once they know the terms of the settlement.

(f) Class Action Fairness Act of 2005 (CAFA). The Class Action Fairness Act (CAFA) expanded federal court jurisdiction over large, multi-state class actions. The Act amended 28 U.S.C. § 1332, the diversity jurisdiction statute, to permit federal subject-matter jurisdiction of class actions in which the aggregated amount-in-controversy exceeds $5

million and at least one plaintiff is a citizen of a State different from a defendant, subject to limited exceptions. *See* 28 U.S.C. § 1332(d). The Act also liberalized removal procedures in such class actions, authorizing the removal of a CAFA class action (1) by any defendant, even if one or more other defendants do not consent, (2) even if one of the defendants is a citizen of the State in which the lawsuit was filed, and (3) without regard to the one-year limit imposed by section 1446. *See* 28 U.S.C. § 1453(b). CAFA also requires that each defendant must notify appropriate State and federal officials of any proposed CAFA class action settlement. *See* 28 U.S.C. § 1715.

PROBLEM A

STAR DEALERSHIP, INC. v. CONTINENTAL MOTORS COMPANY. This problem is designed to take you through each of the steps required for certification of a class action. Your client owns Star Dealership, which is one of the authorized dealers of automobiles manufactured by Continental Motors — one of the largest corporations in the world, which has a large share of the national automobile market.

Your client has a complaint about the way that Continental Motors distributes advertising allowances to dealers. He says that the distribution violates the antitrust laws, and, after looking into the matter, you determine that he may have a point (then again, he may not — that's the way antitrust cases are). It appears that Star may be able to prove something on the order of $50,000 in damages. That amount may sound large, but you determine that for an expensive, uncertain kind of claim such as one under the antitrust laws, you would not be willing to bring suit with damages of such size.

Your client tells you, however, that there are about fifty to a hundred other Continental dealers who are adversely affected by the advertising distribution scheme. They are located throughout the country, but there are many in your state. Each one has a separate contract with Continental, and therefore, the proof of the claim will entail slight differences from dealer to dealer. Of course, each one has different damage amounts. Upon checking, you learn that two individual dealers have brought suits in distant states already. Your client would like to see the present method of distribution stopped by an injunction or by declaratory relief, if possible, and a uniform, lawful method adopted; he would also like to see Star Dealership obtain damages if that is possible.

Answer the following questions:

(a) Are the four prerequisites — numerosity, commonality, typicality, and adequate representation — present?

(b)(1) Can the action be maintained as a (b)(1) action? This subsection requires a "risk" of inconsistent results.

(b)(2) Can it be maintained as a (b)(2) action? This subsection requires that the thrust of the action be for "injunctive or declaratory relief" applicable to the class as a whole. No other relief can be sought unless it is "incidental."

(b)(3) Can it be maintained as a (b)(3) action? This subsection requires that common questions predominate and that a class action be the superior means of management. You must evaluate the four factors of (A) the members' interest in individually controlling their own actions, (B) the relevance of pending litigation, (C) the desirability of concentrating all the litigation in your district, and (D) the "manageability" of this particular action.

(c) Will notice be a problem? What about the cohesiveness of the class? Might it be necessary to define subclasses for the different categories of claims that the dealers might have because of their different treatment by Continental?

(d) Will you take the case for your client and the class? The court must set your fee, as to the class, if (and only if) you prevail.

EISEN v. CARLISLE & JACQUELIN
417 U.S. 156 (1974)

MR. JUSTICE POWELL delivered the opinion of the Court.

On May 2, 1966, petitioner filed a class action on behalf of himself and all other odd-lot[1] traders on the New York Stock Exchange (the Exchange). The complaint charged respondents with violations of the antitrust and securities laws and demanded damages for petitioner and his class. Eight years have elapsed, but there has been no trial on the merits of these claims. Both the parties and the courts are still wrestling with the complex questions surrounding petitioner's attempt to maintain his suit as a class action under Fed. Rule Civ. Proc. 23. We granted certiorari to resolve some of these difficulties. . . .

I

Petitioner brought this class action in the United States District Court for the Southern District of New York. Originally, he sued on behalf of all buyers and sellers of odd lots on the Exchange, but subsequently the class was limited to those who traded in odd lots during the period from May 1, 1962, through June 30,1966. . . . Respondent brokerage firms Carlisle & Jacquelin and DeCoppet & Doremus together handled 99% of the Exchange's odd-lot business. . . . They were compensated by the odd-lot differential, a surcharge imposed on the odd-lot investor in addition to the standard brokerage commission applicable to round-lot transactions. . . .

Petitioner charged that respondent brokerage firms had monopolized odd-lot trading and set the differential at an excessive level in violation of §§ 1 and 2 of the Sherman Act, 15 U.S.C. §§ 1 and 2, and he demanded treble damages for the amount of the overcharge [and other relief].

A critical fact in this litigation is that petitioner's individual stake in the damages award he seeks is only $70. No competent attorney would undertake this complex antitrust action to recover so inconsequential an amount. Economic reality dictates that petitioner's suit proceed as a class action or not at all. Opposing counsel have therefore engaged in prolonged combat over the various requirements of Rule 23. . . .

Eisen I

As we have seen, petitioner began this action in May 1966. In September of that year the District Court dismissed the suit as a class action. [*Eisen I* dealt with issues of appellate procedure. The Court of Appeals ultimately determined that it properly could consider an appeal of this order.]

---

[1] Odd lots are shares traded in lots of fewer than a hundred. Shares traded in units of a hundred or multiple thereof are round-lots.

Eisen II

Nearly 18 months later the Court of Appeals reversed the dismissal of the class action in a decision known as *Eisen II* . . . . In reaching this result the court undertook an exhaustive but ultimately inconclusive analysis of Rule 23. Subdivision (a) of the Rule sets forth four prerequisites to the maintenance of any suit as a class action: [the Court here sets out the (1) numerosity, (2) commonality, (3) typicality, and (4) adequate, representation requirements]. The District Court had experienced little difficulty in finding that petitioner satisfied the first three prerequisites but had concluded that petitioner might not "fairly and adequately protect the interests of the class" as required by Rule 23(a)(4). The Court of Appeals indicated its disagreement with the reasoning behind the latter conclusion and directed the District Court to reconsider the point.

In addition to meeting the four conjunctive requirements of 23(a), a class action must also qualify under one of the three subdivisions of 23(b). Petitioner argued that the suit was maintainable as a class action under all three subdivisions. The Court of Appeals held the first two subdivisions inapplicable to this suit and therefore turned its attention to the third subdivision, (b)(3). That subdivision requires a court to determine whether "questions of law or fact common to the [class members] predominate over any questions affecting only individual members" and whether "a class action is superior to other available methods for [fairly and efficiently adjudicating] the controversy." More specifically, it identifies four factors relevant to these inquiries. After a detailed review of these provisions, the Court of Appeals concluded that the only potential barrier to maintenance of this suit as a class action was the Rule 23(b)(3)(D) directive that a court evaluate "the [likely difficulties in managing] a class action." Commonly referred to as "manageability," this consideration encompasses the whole range of practical problems that may render the class action format inappropriate for a particular suit. With reference to this litigation, the Court of Appeals noted that the difficulties of distributing any ultimate recovery to the class members would be formidable, though not necessarily insuperable, and commented that it was "reluctant to permit actions to proceed where they are not likely to benefit anyone but the lawyers who bring them." . . . The Court therefore directed the District Court to conduct "a further inquiry . . . in order to consider the mechanics involved in the administration of the present action." . . .

Finally, the Court of Appeals turned to the most imposing obstacle to this class action — the notice requirement of Rule 23(c)(2). The District Court had held that both the Rule and the Due Process Clause of the Fifth Amendment required individual notice to all class members who could be identified. . . . Petitioner objected that mailed notice to the entire class would be prohibitively expensive and argued that some form of publication notice would suffice. The Court of Appeals declined to settle this issue. . . .

Eisen III

After it held the evidentiary hearing on remand, which together with affidavits and stipulations provided the basis for extensive findings of fact, the District Court issued an opinion and order holding the suit maintainable as a class action. . . . The court first noted that petitioner satisfied the criteria identified by the Court of Appeals for determining adequacy of representation under Rule 23(a)(4). Then it turned to the more difficult question of manageability. Under this general rubric the court dealt with problems of the computation of damages, the mechanics of administering this suit as a class action, and the distribution of any eventual recovery. . . . The District Court attempted to resolve this difficulty by embracing the idea of a "fluid class" recovery whereby damages would be distributed to future odd-lot traders rather than to the specific class members who were actually injured. The court suggested that "a fund equivalent to the amount of unclaimed damages might be established and the odd-lot differential reduced in an amount determined reasonable by the court until such time as the fund is depleted." . . . The need to resort to this expedient of recovery by the "next best class" arose from the prohibitively high cost of computing and awarding multitudinous small damages claims on an individual basis.

Finally, the District Court took up the problem of notice. The court found that the prospective class included some six million individuals, institutions, and intermediaries of various sorts; that with reasonable effort some two million of these odd-lot investors could be identified by name and address; and that the names and addresses of an additional 250,000 persons who had participated in special investment programs involving odd-lot trading could also be identified with reasonable effort. . . . Thus individual notice to all identifiable class members would cost $225,000, and additional expense would be incurred for suitable publication notice designed to reach the other four million class members.

The District Court concluded, however, that neither Rule 23(c)(2) nor the Due Process Clause required so substantial an expenditure at the outset of this litigation. Instead, it proposed a notification scheme consisting of four elements: (1) individual notice to all member firms of the Exchange and to commercial banks with large trust departments; (2) individual notice to the approximately 2,000 identifiable class members with 10 or more odd-lot transactions during the relevant period; (3) individual notice to an additional 5,000 class members selected at random; and (4) prominent publication notice in the Wall Street Journal and in other newspapers in New York and California. The court calculated that this package would cost approximately $21,720.

The only issue not resolved by the District Court in its first opinion on remand from *Eisen II* was who should bear the cost of notice. Because petitioner understandably declined to pay $21,720 in order to litigate an action involving an individual stake of only $70, this question presented something of a dilemma. . . . Analogizing to the laws of preliminary injunctions, the court decided to impose the notice cost on respondents if petitioner could show a strong likelihood of success on the merits, and it scheduled a preliminary hearing on the merits to facilitate this determination. After this hearing the District Court issued an opinion and order ruling that petitioner was "more than likely" to prevail at trial and that respondents should bear 90% of the cost of notice, or $19,548 . . . .

On May 1, 1973, the Court of Appeals issued *Eisen III* . . . . The majority disapproved the District Court's partial reliance on publication notice, holding that Rule 23(c)(2) required individual notice to all identifiable class members. The majority further ruled that the District Court had no authority to conduct a preliminary hearing on the merits for the purpose of allocating costs and that the entire expense of notice necessarily fell on petitioner as representative plaintiff. Finally, the Court of Appeals rejected the expedient of a fluid-class recovery and concluded that the proposed class action was unmanageable under Rule 23(b)(3)(D). For all of these reasons the Court of Appeals ordered the suit dismissed as a class action. . . .

Thus, after six and one-half years and three published decisions, the Court of Appeals endorsed the conclusion reached by the District Court in its original order in 1966 — that petitioner's suit could not proceed as a class action. In its procedural history, at least, this litigation has lived up to Judge Lumbard's characterization of it as a "Frankenstein monster posing as a class action." . . .

II

[The Court first considered whether the Court of Appeals had jurisdiction to consider the appeal and concluded that it did.]

III

Turning to the merits of the case, we find that the District Court's resolution of the notice problems was erroneous in two respects. First, it failed to comply with the notice requirements of Rule 23(c)(2), and second, it imposed part of the cost of notice on respondents.

A

Rule 23(c)(2) provides that, in any class action maintained under subdivision (b)(3), each class member shall be advised that he has the right to exclude himself from the action on request or to enter an appearance through counsel, and further that the judgment, whether favorable or not, will bind all class members not requesting exclusion. To this end, the court is required to direct to class members "the best notice [that is] practicable under the circumstances, *including individual notice to all members who can be identified through reasonable effort*." We think the import of this language is unmistakable. Individual notice must be sent to all class members whose names and addresses may be ascertained through reasonable effort.

The Advisory Committee's Note to Rule 23 reinforces this conclusion. . . . The Advisory Committee described subdivision (c)(2) as "not merely discretionary" and added that the "mandatory notice pursuant to subdivision (c)(2) . . . is designed to fulfill requirements of due process to which the class action procedure is of course subject." . . . The Committee explicated its incorporation of due process standards by citation to *Mullane v. Central Hanover Bank & Trust Co.*, 339 U.S. 306 (1950), and like cases.

In *Mullane* the Court addressed the constitutional sufficiency of publication notice rather than mailed individual notice to known beneficiaries of a common trust fund as part of a judicial settlement of accounts. . . . It further stated that notice must be "reasonably calculated, under all the circumstances, to apprise interested parties of the pendency of the action and afford them an opportunity to present their objections." . . . The Court then held that publication notice could not satisfy due process where the names and addresses of the beneficiaries were known. In such cases, "the reasons disappear for resort to means less likely than the mails to apprise them of [an action's] pendency." . . .

. . . In the present case, the names and addresses of 2,250,000 class members are easily ascertainable, and there is nothing to show that individual notice cannot be mailed to each. For these class members, individual notice is clearly the "best notice practicable" within the meaning of Rule 23(c)(2) and our prior decisions.

Petitioner contends, however, that we should dispense with the requirement of individual notice in this case, and he advances two reasons for our doing so. First, the prohibitively high cost of providing individual notice to 2,250,000 class members would end this suit as a class action and effectively frustrate petitioner's attempt to vindicate the policies underlying the antitrust and securities laws. Second, petitioner contends that individual notice is unnecessary in this case, because no prospective class member has a large enough stake in the matter to justify separate litigation of his individual claim. Hence, class members lack any incentive to opt out of the class action even if notified.

The short answer to these arguments is that individual notice to identifiable class members is not a discretionary consideration to be waived in a particular case. It is, rather, an unambiguous requirement of Rule 23. As the Advisory Committee's Note explained, the Rule was intended to insure that the judgment, whether favorable or not, would bind all class members who did not request exclusion from the suit. . . . There is nothing in Rule 23 to suggest that the notice requirements can be tailored to fit the pocketbooks of particular plaintiffs.

Petitioner further contends that adequate representation, rather than notice, is the touchstone of due process in a class action and therefore satisfies Rule 23. We think this view has little to commend it. To begin with, Rule 23 speaks to notice as well as to adequacy of representation and requires that both be provided. Moreover, petitioner's argument proves too much, for it quickly leads to the conclusion that no notice at all, published or otherwise, would be required in the present case. This cannot be so, for quite apart from what due process may require, the command of Rule 23 is clearly to the contrary.

B

We also agree with the Court of Appeals that petitioner must bear the cost of notice to the members of his class. The District Court reached the contrary conclusion and imposed 90% of the notice cost on respondents. . . .

We find nothing in either the language or history of Rule 23 that gives a court any authority to conduct a preliminary inquiry into the merits of a suit in order to determine whether it may be maintained as a class action. . . . This procedure is directly contrary to the command of subdivision (c)(1) that the court determine whether a suit denominated a class action may be maintained as such "[a]s soon as practicable after the commencement of [the] action . . . ." [This language subsequently was changed to "[a]t an early practicable time" — Eds.] Additionally, we might note that a preliminary determination of the merits may result in substantial prejudice to a defendant, since of necessity it is not accompanied by the traditional rules and procedures applicable to civil trials. The court's tentative findings, made in the absence of established safeguards, may color the subsequent proceedings and place an unfair burden on the defendant. . . .

Petitioner has consistently maintained, however, that he will not bear the cost of notice under subdivision (c)(2) to members of the class as defined in his original complaint. . . . We therefore remand the cause with instructions to dismiss the class action as so defined.[16]

The judgment of the Court of Appeals is vacated and the cause remanded for proceedings consistent with this opinion. . . .

[Justice Douglas wrote a separate opinion, concurred in by three members of the Court, emphasizing that on remand, the District Court could modify its certification order to define a different and more manageable class.]

---

[16] The record does not reveal whether a smaller class of odd-lot traders could be defined, and if so, whether petitioner would be willing to pay the cost of notice to members of such a class. We intimate no view on whether any such subclass would satisfy the requirements of Rule 23. We do note, however, that our dismissal of the class action as originally defined is without prejudice to any efforts petitioner may make to redefine his class either under Rule 23(c)(4) or Fed. Rule Civ. Proc. 15.

NOTES AND QUESTIONS

(1) *Certification.* Was the District Court's certification order correct, assuming plaintiffs would be willing to pay the cost of notice? Or was Judge Lumbard correct in his now-famous statement, quoted by the Supreme Court, that the *Eisen* case involved a "Frankenstein monster posing as a class action"? *See also* D. Crump, *What Really Happens During Class Certification? A Primer for the First-Time Defense Attorney*, 10 Rev. of Litigation 1 (1990); D. Crump, *Defending a Class Action at the Certification Stage*, 38 Fed. B.J. 146 (1991).

Notice that the plaintiffs argued for certification under subsections (b)(1) and (b)(2), as well as (b)(3), but the lower courts rejected this argument. Because the (c)(2) requirement of notice applies by its express terms only to (b)(3) actions, the plaintiffs might have succeeded in avoiding the notice requirement if they had persuaded the courts to certify a (b)(1) or (b)(2) action.

Notice, also, how important the certification issue is. If the action is certified as a class action, it becomes viable; if not certified, it is not viable. As in this case, both parties may expend considerable energy arguing about the certification stage of the case.

(2) *A Frankenstein Monster — Or a Means to Vindicate the "Little Guy"?* Class actions invite emotional reactions from many people. *See generally* A. Miller, *Of Frankenstein Monsters and Shining Knights: Myth, Reality, and the "Class Action Problem,"* 92 Harv. L. Rev. 664 (1979). At different times in the modern history of Rule 23, the courts have viewed it with great favor; at other times, they have been more gloomy about it. This latter attitude seems to surface in *Eisen*. The Court almost appears to be using the requirement of notice as a restraint on overly exuberant uses of class actions — as a means to "chain down" the "Frankenstein monster." For a different perspective, see *Phillips Petroleum Co. v. Shutts*, 472 U.S. 797 (1985) ("Class actions . . . permit the plaintiffs to pool claims which would be uneconomical to litigate individually. [T]his lawsuit involves claims averaging about $100 per plaintiff; most of the plaintiffs would have no realistic day in court if a class action were not available"). *See also* A. Miller & D. Crump, *Jurisdiction and Choice of Law in Multistate Class Actions After Phillips Petroleum Co. v. Shutts*, 96 Yale L.J. 1 (1986); J. Alexander, *Do the Merits Matter? A Study of Settlements in Securities Class Actions*, 43 Stan. L. Rev. 497 (1991); D. Bassett, *Constructing Class Action Reality*, 2006 BYU L. Rev. 1415.

To the surprise of many, a 2004 study by Professors Theodore Eisenberg and Geoffrey P. Miller — a study financed neither by corporations nor by trial lawyers — concluded that if the effects of inflation are taken into account, then from 1993 through 2002, "contrary to popular belief, we find no robust evidence that either recoveries for plaintiffs or fees for their attorneys as a percentage of the class recovery increased." The study also found that "neither the mean nor the median level of fee awards has increased over time." As noted in the January 14, 2004 issue of *The New York Times*, the study undermines companies' claims that class action lawsuits "are driving up the cost of doing business, hurting the economy and lining lawyers' pockets." A 2005 study by the Federal Judicial Center similarly concluded that attorney fees, as a percentage of class action recoveries, have not increased substantially since 1996.

[C] The Judicial Panel on Multidistrict Litigation: Notes and Questions

Read 28 U.S.C. § 1407 (multidistrict litigation).

(1) *Purpose of the Multidistrict Litigation Statute.* 28 U.S.C. § 1407 addresses the problem of scattered, duplicative litigation that would waste judicial and private resources unless consolidated. *See* Herndon & Higginbotham, *Complex Multidistrict Litigation — An Overview of 28 U.S.C.A. § 1407*, 31 Baylor L. Rev. 33 (1979).

(2) *Procedure.* Section 1407 sets up a "Judicial Panel on Multidistrict Litigation," consisting of seven Circuit and District judges designated by the Chief Justice of the United States. Either on its own initiative or upon the motion of a party in any action, the Panel may order actions "involving one or more common questions of fact," pending in different Districts, transferred for "coordinated or consolidated pretrial proceedings." The Panel takes action on the vote of four members, pursuant to "a record of [a] hearing at which material evidence may be offered by any party . . . ." The standard for transfer is very general: The panel need only determine that transfer "will be for the convenience of parties and witnesses and will promote the just and efficient conduct of [the] actions." Multidistrict consolidation is used in antitrust, mass tort, securities, patent, and civil rights cases, and indeed it can be used in any type of dispute that generates dispersed but overlapping litigation.

The Class Action Fairness Act of 2005 may have an unexpected impact on multidistrict litigation procedure. Under the Act, mass actions sent to a federal court "may not thereafter be transferred to any court" — which would include the Multidistrict Litigation Panel and coordination under the multidistrict litigation statute — unless a majority of the plaintiffs in the cases request the transfer. Thus, the federal courts could face related actions spread among many districts, without the streamlining options available under section 1407.

(3) *Perspective of the Attorney for the Individual Litigant; Of the Defendant.* To an attorney pursuing an individual claim, multidistrict consolidation is often undesirable. She perceives the Panel as having "yanked" "her" case away from her, sending it to a distant place where it will not be heard from again for a long time. The individual attorney frequently perceives the Panel's procedures as cumbersome; for example, motion papers may be required to be sent to a mailing list of hundreds of other lawyers. To the defendant, however, the procedure may be a godsend. The defendant can avoid the duplication of expense it would otherwise incur (and, not incidentally, is spared the leverage in settlement negotiations that this expense otherwise gives the individual litigant). Some plaintiffs' counsel may share this favorable view, particularly class action counsel or attorneys likely to play prominent roles in the platoon system that will be devised to handle the litigation.

(4) *Restrictions on Multidistrict Consolidation.* Section 1407 allows consolidation only of federal litigation. Scattered litigation in courts of different states cannot be consolidated by this procedure (unless, of course, the individual cases can be removed to federal courts). Furthermore, multidistrict consolidation is for pretrial proceedings only; the panel is required to remand each case for trial to the district from which it was transferred (unless it is settled or otherwise terminated in pretrial proceedings, as happens in the great majority of cases). Are these limits desirable? Would it be appropriate for Congress to create a mechanism for consolidating scattered state and federal litigation?

(5) *The Presiding Judge Cannot Keep the Case for Trial, but Must Transfer It Back.* For many years, there was a practice by which the presiding judge sometimes would receive (or solicit) a motion for transfer under § 1404(a) of the entire case in all the consolidated suits. Since this was a pretrial matter, the judge might grant the motion, transferring all trials to the consolidated court as well. Was this an impermissible "end run" around the limits of § 1407? Yes, said the Supreme Court in *Lexecon v. Milberg Weiss Bershad Hynes & Lerach*, 523 U.S. 26 (1998). The language of § 1407 says that "[e]ach action so transferred *shall* be remanded" to the initial district for trial (emphasis added). This "plain command," said the Court, means that the district court cannot transfer all the actions to itself, but must transfer back all that are not settled — in spite of the "longstanding practice" to the contrary.

IN RE ASBESTOS PROD. LIAB. LITIG. (No. VI), 771 F. Supp. 415 (Jud. Pan. Mult. Lit. July 29, 1991). In this case, the Judicial Panel took the extraordinary step of transferring all pending federal asbestos cases involving allegations of personal injury or death to Judge Charles R. Weiner of the Eastern District of Pennsylvania. The Panel chose Judge Weiner because of his experience in complex litigation in general and in asbestos cases in particular (and his willingness to accept the assignment). The plaintiffs who supported consolidation predicted that it would lead to a single national class action with improved efficiency. Some defendants opposed transfer by arguing that factual controversies unique to individual cases predominated and that these controversies were well advanced in many pending cases. The Panel observed that Judge Weiner would have to address the class action question; he also would have to address the suggestion by many defendants for "reverse bifurcation," in which issues of causation and actual damages (usually the dispositive issues) would be tried before liability. The Panel concluded that the increased numbers of asbestos cases justified transfer and consolidation under § 1407. [Later, the attorneys entered into a global settlement agreement.]

[D] The Multiparty, Multiforum Trial Jurisdiction Act of 2002

The Multiparty, Multiforum Trial Jurisdiction Act of 2002 added section 1369 to title 28 of the United States Code. Section 1369 authorizes original jurisdiction in mass tort cases involving 75 or more deaths at a single location when minimal diversity exists between adverse parties. Special provisions govern venue, removal, service of process, and subpoenas in section 1369 actions. The Act also indicates a preference for remand to state courts for individual damage determinations after common liability determinations. The legislative history behind the Act is sparse, and the Act has been criticized as reflecting haste. What advantages does the Act serve procedurally? Should the Act be broadened to encompass mass torts involving fewer victims — or restricted to actions involving more victims?

Section 1369(b) requires the district court to abstain from hearing a case satisfying the prerequisites of section 1369(a) when the substantial majority of the plaintiffs and the primary defendants are all citizens of the same state, and the claims asserted will be governed primarily by the laws of that state. Although section 1369(b) is a mandatory abstention provision, it applies only to those cases in which original jurisdiction exists pursuant to section 1369(a). Accordingly, the abstention requirement of section 1369(b) does not apply to actions removed to federal court under section 1441(e)(1)(B), which expressly authorizes removal when original jurisdiction is lacking under section 1369(a). *See Wallace v. Louisiana Citizens Property Ins. Corp.*, 444 F.3d 697 (5th Cir. 2006).

[E] Global Settlement Class Actions: May a Court Manage an Intractable Dispute by Cutting the Gordian Knot?

AMCHEM PRODUCTS, INC. v. WINDSOR
521 U.S. 591 (1997)

JUSTICE GINSBURG delivered the opinion of the Court.

This case concerns the legitimacy under Rule 23 of the Federal Rules of Civil Procedure of a class-action certification sought to achieve global settlement of current and future asbestos-related claims. The class proposed for certification potentially encompasses hundreds of thousands, perhaps millions, of individuals tied together by this commonality: each was, or some day may be, adversely affected by past exposure to asbestos products manufactured by one or more of 20 companies. . . .

The United States District Court for the Eastern District of Pennsylvania certified the class for settlement only, finding that the proposed settlement was fair and that representation and notice had been adequate. That court enjoined class members [who did not timely opt out] from separately pursuing asbestos-related personal-injury suits in any court, federal or state, pending the issuance of a final order. The Court of Appeals for the Third Circuit vacated the District Court's orders, holding that the class certification failed to satisfy Rule 23's requirements in several critical respects. We affirm the Court of Appeals' judgment.

I

A

The settlement-class certification we confront evolved in response to an asbestos-litigation crisis. A United States Judicial Conference Ad Hoc Committee on Asbestos Litigation . . . described facets of the problem in a 1991 report: " . . . On the basis of past and current filing data, and because of a latency period that may last as long as 40 years for some asbestos related diseases, a continuing stream of claims can be expected. . . . Predictions have been made of 200,000 asbestos disease deaths before the year 2000 and as many as 265,000 by the year 2015.

> "The most objectionable aspects of asbestos litigation can be briefly summarized: dockets in both federal and state courts continue to grow; long delays are routine; trials are too long; the same issues are litigated over and over; transaction costs exceed the victims' recovery by nearly two to one; exhaustion of assets threatens and distorts the process; and future claimants may lose altogether."

Real reform, the report concluded, required federal legislation creating a national asbestos dispute-resolution scheme.. . . To this date, however, no congressional response has emerged.

In the face of legislative inaction, the federal courts . . . endeavored to work with the procedural tools available to improve management of federal asbestos litigation. Eight federal judges, experienced in the superintendence of asbestos cases, urged the Judicial Panel on Multidistrict Litigation (MDL Panel) to consolidate in a single district all asbestos complaints then pending in federal courts. Accepting the recommendation, the MDL Panel transferred all asbestos cases then filed, but not yet on trial in federal courts to a single district, the United States District Court for the Eastern District of Pennsylvania; pursuant to the transfer order, the collected cases were consolidated for pretrial proceedings before Judge Weiner. *See In re Asbestos Products Liability Litigation (No. VI)* [above]. The order aggregated pending cases only; no authority resides in the MDL Panel to license for consolidated proceedings claims not yet filed.

B

After the consolidation, attorneys for plaintiffs and defendants formed separate steering committees and began settlement negotiations. Ronald L. Motley and Gene Locks — later appointed, along with Motley's law partner Joseph F. Rice, to represent the plaintiff class in this action — co-chaired the Plaintiffs' Steering Committee. Counsel for the Center for Claims Resolution (CCR), the consortium of 20 former asbestos manufacturers now before us as petitioners, participated in the Defendants' Steering Committee. Although the MDL order collected, transferred, and consolidated only cases already commenced in federal courts, settlement negotiations included efforts to find a "means of resolving . . . future cases." . . .

To that end, CCR counsel approached the lawyers who had headed the Plaintiffs' Steering Committee in the [initial] unsuccessful negotiations, and a new round of negotiations began; that round yielded the mass settlement agreement now in controversy. At the time, the former heads of the Plaintiffs' Steering Committee represented thousands of plaintiffs with then-pending asbestos-related claims — claimants the parties to this suit call "inventory" plaintiffs. CCR indicated in these discussions that it would resist settlement of inventory cases absent "some kind of protection for the future." . . .

Settlement talks thus concentrated on devising an administrative scheme for disposition of asbestos claims not yet in litigation. In these negotiations, counsel for masses of inventory plaintiffs endeavored to represent the interests of the anticipated future claimants, although those lawyers then had no attorney-client relationship with such claimants.

Once negotiations seemed likely to produce an agreement purporting to bind potential plaintiffs, CCR agreed to settle, through separate agreements, the claims of plaintiffs who had already filed asbestos-related lawsuits. In one such agreement, CCR defendants promised to pay more than $200 million to gain release of the claims of numerous inventory plaintiffs. . . .

C

[To implement the settlement, the settling parties presented the District Court with a package consisting of a class action complaint, an answer, a proposed settlement agreement, and a joint motion for conditional class certification, all on the same day. They had no intent to litigate the class complaint, which was a vehicle for settlement only. The complaint identified nine plaintiffs and their families, all as representatives of the entire class. The class was defined as all persons (and certain of their family members) who had ever been exposed to asbestos products manufactured by one of the defendants, but who had never filed suit.

[The settlement agreement proposed to determine all claims of the class members and preclude all other litigation by them. It set up an administrative mechanism for distributing designated payments to class members who had met defined medical and exposure qualifications. It also fixed the range of damages for four types of cancers and other conditions. It denied compensation, however, for numerous conditions even if state law otherwise allowed it, including loss of consortium, emotional distress based on exposure alone, enhanced risk, medical monitoring, and pleural claims related to lung plaques without physical impairment. The compensation categories were not adjusted for inflation.]

D

[The trial judge conditionally certified the class and appointed Locks, Motley, and Rice as class counsel. No subclasses were created. The judge then assigned another judge to conduct "fairness proceedings" regarding the settlement. This judge approved elaborate plans for notice to class members by media and otherwise. The notice informed class members of a three-month period in which they could opt out.]

Objectors raised numerous challenges to the settlement. They urged that the settlement unfairly disadvantaged those without currently compensable conditions in that it failed to adjust for inflation or to account for changes, over time, in medical understanding. They maintained that compensation levels were intolerably low in comparison to awards available in tort litigation or payments received by the inventory plaintiffs. And they objected to the absence of any compensation for certain claims, for example, medical monitoring, compensable under the tort law of several States. Rejecting these and all other objections, Judge Reed concluded that the settlement terms were fair and had been negotiated without collusion. He also found that adequate notice had been given to class members and that final class certification under Rule 23(b)(3) was appropriate. . . .

Strenuous objections had been asserted regarding the adequacy of representation, a Rule 23(a)(4) requirement. Objectors maintained that class counsel and class representatives had disqualifying conflicts of interests. In particular, objectors urged, claimants whose injuries had become manifest and claimants without manifest injuries should not have common counsel and should not be aggregated in a single class. Furthermore, objectors argued, lawyers representing inventory plaintiffs should not represent the newly-formed class.

Satisfied that class counsel had ably negotiated the settlement in the best interests of all concerned, and that the named parties served as adequate representatives, the District Court rejected these objections. Subclasses were unnecessary, the District Court held, bearing in mind the added cost and confusion they would entail and the ability of class members to exclude themselves from the class during the three-month opt-out period. Reasoning that the representative plaintiffs "have a strong interest that recovery for all of the medical categories be maximized because they may have claims in any, or several categories," the District Court found "no antagonism of interest between class members with various medical conditions, or between persons with and without currently manifest asbestos impairment." Declaring class certification appropriate and the settlement fair, the District Court preliminarily enjoined all class members from commencing any asbestos-related suit against the CCR defendants in any state or federal court. The objectors appealed. The United States Court of Appeals for the Third Circuit vacated the certification, holding that the requirements of Rule 23 had not been satisfied. . . .

We granted certiorari and now affirm [the Court of Appeals decision decertifying the class].

II

Objectors assert in this Court, as they did in the District Court and Court of Appeals, an array of jurisdictional barriers. Most fundamentally, they maintain that the settlement proceeding instituted by class counsel and CCR is not a justiciable case or controversy within the confines of Article III of the Federal Constitution. In the main, they say, the proceeding is a nonadversarial endeavor to impose on countless individuals without currently ripe claims an administrative compensation regime binding on those individuals if and when they manifest injuries. [The Court declines to consider these jurisdictional issues because they "would not exist but for the [class action] certification," and decertification thus avoids them.]

III

To place this controversy in context, we briefly describe the characteristics of class actions for which the Federal Rules provide. [The opinion here examines the history and provisions of Rule 23.]

A proposed amendment to Rule 23 would expressly authorize settlement class certification, in conjunction with a motion by the settling parties for Rule 23(b)(3) certification, "even though the requirements of subdivision (b)(3) might not be met for purposes of trial." [This amendment would have changed the analysis, but it was not adopted. — Eds.] We consider the certification at issue under the rule as it is currently framed.

IV

We granted review to decide the role settlement may play, under existing Rule 23, in determining the propriety of class certification. The Third Circuit's opinion stated that each of the requirements of Rule 23(a) and (b)(3) "must be satisfied without taking into account the settlement." That statement, petitioners urge, is incorrect.

We agree with petitioners to this limited extent: settlement is relevant to a class certification. The Third Circuit's opinion bears modification in that respect. But . . . the Court of Appeals in fact did not ignore the settlement; instead, that court homed in on settlement terms in explaining why it found the absentees' interests inadequately represented. The Third Circuit's close inspection of the settlement in that regard was altogether proper.

Confronted with a request for settlement-only class certification, a district court need not inquire whether the case, if tried, would present intractable management problems, *see* Fed. R. Civ. Proc. 23(b)(3)(D), for the proposal is that there be no trial. But other specifications of the rule — those designed to protect absentees by blocking unwarranted or overbroad class definitions — demand undiluted, even heightened, attention in the settlement context. Such attention is of vital importance, for a court asked to certify a settlement class will lack the opportunity, present when a case is litigated, to adjust the class, informed by the proceedings as they unfold. *See* Fed. Rule Civ. Proc. 23(c), (d).

Rule 23(e), on settlement of class actions, reads in its entirety: "A class action shall not be dismissed or compromised without the approval of the court, and notice of the proposed dismissal or compromise shall be given to all members of the class in such manner as the court directs." [This language was modified in 2007 — Eds.] This prescription was designed to function as an additional requirement, not a superseding direction, for the "class action" to which Rule 23(e) refers is one qualified for certification under Rule 23(a) and (b). *Cf. Eisen,* 417 U.S. at 176-177 (adequate representation does not eliminate additional requirement to provide notice). Subdivisions (a) and (b) focus court attention on whether a proposed class has sufficient unity so that absent members can fairly be bound by decisions of class representatives. That dominant concern persists when settlement, rather than trial, is proposed. . . .

Federal courts, in any case, lack authority to substitute for Rule 23's certification criteria a standard never adopted — that if a settlement is "fair," then certification is proper. . . . The Court of Appeals' opinion amply demonstrates why — with or without a settlement on the table — the sprawling class the District Court certified does not satisfy Rule 23's requirements.

A

We address first the requirement of Rule 23(b)(3) that "[common] questions of law or fact . . . predominate over any questions affecting only individual members." The District Court concluded that predominance was satisfied based on two factors: class members' shared experience of asbestos exposure and their common "interest in receiving prompt and fair compensation for their claims, while minimizing the risks and transaction costs inherent in the asbestos litigation process as it occurs presently in the tort system." The settling parties also contend that the settlement's fairness is a common question, predominating over disparate legal issues that might be pivotal in litigation but become irrelevant under the settlement.

The predominance requirement stated in Rule 23(b)(3), we hold, is not met by the factors on which the District Court relied. The benefits asbestos-exposed persons might gain from the establishment of a grand-scale compensation scheme is a matter fit for legislative consideration, but it is not pertinent to the predominance inquiry. That inquiry trains on the legal or factual questions that qualify each class member's case as a genuine controversy, questions that preexist any settlement.

The Rule 23(b)(3) predominance inquiry tests whether proposed classes are sufficiently cohesive to warrant adjudication by representation. The inquiry appropriate under Rule 23(e), on the other hand, protects unnamed class members "from unjust or unfair settlements affecting their rights when the representatives become fainthearted before the action is adjudicated or are able to secure satisfaction of their individual claims by a compromise." But it is not the mission of Rule 23(e) to assure the class cohesion that legitimizes representative action in the first place. If a common interest in a fair compromise could satisfy the predominance requirement of Rule 23(b)(3), that vital prescription would be stripped of any meaning in the settlement context. . . .

The Third Circuit highlighted the disparate questions undermining class cohesion in this case: "Class members were exposed to different asbestos-containing products, for different amounts of time, in different ways, and over different periods. Some class members suffer no physical injury or have only asymptomatic pleural changes, while others suffer from lung cancer, disabling asbestosis, or from mesothelioma. . . . Each has a different history of cigarette smoking, a factor that complicates the causation inquiry.

> "The [exposure-only] plaintiffs especially share little in common, either with each other or with the presently injured class members. It is unclear whether they will contract asbestos-related disease and, if so, what disease each will suffer. They will also incur different medical expenses because their monitoring and treatment will depend on singular circumstances and individual medical histories."

Differences in state law, the Court of Appeals observed, compound these disparities. No settlement class called to our attention is as sprawling as this one. Predominance is a test readily met in certain cases alleging consumer or securities fraud or violations of the antitrust laws. Even mass tort cases arising from a common cause or disaster may, depending upon the circumstances, satisfy the predominance requirement. . . . [This] certification cannot be upheld, [however,] for it rests on a conception of Rule 23(b)(3)'s predominance requirement irreconcilable with the rule's design.

B

Nor can the class approved by the District Court satisfy Rule 23(a)(4)'s requirement that the named parties "will fairly and adequately protect the interests of the class." The adequacy inquiry under Rule 23(a)(4) serves to uncover conflicts of interest between named parties and the class they seek to represent. "[A] class representative must be part of the class and possess the same interest and suffer the same injury' as the class members." . . .

As the Third Circuit pointed out, named parties with diverse medical conditions sought to act on behalf of a single giant class rather than on behalf of discrete subclasses. In significant respects, the interests of those within the single class are not aligned. Most saliently, for the currently injured, the critical goal is generous immediate payments. That goal tugs against the interest of exposure-only plaintiffs in ensuring an ample, inflation-protected fund for the future. . . .

The Third Circuit found no assurance here — either in the terms of the settlement or in the structure of the negotiations — that the named plaintiffs operated under a proper understanding of their representational responsibilities. That assessment, we conclude, is on the mark.

C

Impediments to the provision of adequate notice, the Third Circuit emphasized, rendered highly problematic any endeavor to tie to a settlement class persons with no perceptible asbestos-related disease at the time of the settlement. Many persons in the exposure-only category, the Court of Appeals stressed, may not even know of their exposure, or realize the extent of the harm they may incur. Even if they fully appreciate the significance of class notice, those without current afflictions may not have the information or foresight needed to decide, intelligently, whether to stay in or opt out. . . .

Because we have concluded that the class in this case cannot satisfy the requirements of common issue predominance and adequacy of representation, we need not rule, definitively, on the notice given here. In accord with the Third Circuit, however, we recognize the gravity of the question whether class action notice sufficient under the Constitution and Rule 23 could ever be given to legions so unselfconscious and amorphous.

V

The argument is sensibly made that a nationwide administrative claims processing regime would provide the most secure, fair, and efficient means of compensating victims of asbestos exposure. Congress, however, has not adopted such a solution. And Rule 23 . . . cannot carry the large load CCR, class counsel, and the District Court heaped upon it. [Affirmed.]

JUSTICE BREYER, with whom JUSTICE STEVENS joins, concurring in part and dissenting in part.

Although I agree with the Court's basic holding that "settlement is relevant to a class certification," I find several problems in its approach that lead me to a different conclusion. First, I believe that the need for settlement in this mass tort case, with hundreds of thousands of lawsuits, is greater than the Court's opinion suggests. Second, I would give more weight than would the majority to settlement-related issues for purposes of determining whether common issues predominate. Third, I am uncertain about the Court's determination of adequacy of representation, and do not believe it appropriate for this Court to second-guess the District Court on the matter without first having the Court of Appeals consider it. Fourth, I am uncertain about the tenor of an opinion that seems to suggest the settlement is unfair. And fifth, in the absence of further review by the Court of Appeals, I cannot accept the majority's suggestions that "notice" is inadequate.

These difficulties flow from the majority's review of what are highly fact-based, complex, and difficult matters, matters that are inappropriate for initial review before this Court. The law gives broad leeway to district courts in making class certification decisions, and their judgments are to be reviewed by the Court of Appeals only for abuse of discretion. . . .

I do not believe that we can rely upon the Court of Appeals' review of the District Court record, for that review, and its ultimate conclusions, are infected by a legal error. *E.g.*, 83 F.3d 610, 626 (3d Cir. 1996) (holding that "considered as a *litigation* class," the class cannot meet Rule 23's requirements) (emphasis added). . . . I find, moreover, the fact-related issues presented here sufficiently close to warrant further detailed appellate court review under the correct legal standard.

I

First, I believe the majority understates the importance of settlement in this case. Between 13 and 21 million workers have been exposed to asbestos in the workplace — over the past 40 or 50 years — but the most severe instances of such exposure probably occurred three or four decades ago. Some of those who suffer from the most serious injuries, however, have received little or no compensation. . . . ("[U]p to one-half of asbestos claims are now being filed by people who have little or no physical impairment. Many of these claims produce substantial payments (and substantial costs) even though the individual litigants will never become impaired"). These lawsuits have taken up more than 6% of all federal civil filings in one recent year, and are subject to a delay that is twice that of other civil suits.

Delays, high costs, and a random pattern of noncompensation led the Judicial Conference Ad Hoc Committee on Asbestos Litigation to transfer all federal asbestos personal-injury cases to the Eastern District of Pennsylvania in an effort to bring about a fair and comprehensive settlement. . . .

. . . In the end, the negotiations produced a settlement that, the District Court determined based on its detailed review of the process, was "the result of arms-length adversarial negotiations by extraordinarily competent and experienced attorneys."

The District Court, when approving the settlement, concluded that it improved the plaintiffs' chances of compensation and reduced total legal fees and other transaction costs by a significant amount. Under the previous system, according to the court, "[t]he sickest of victims often go uncompensated for years while valuable funds go to others who remain unimpaired by their mild asbestos disease." The court believed the settlement would create a compensation system that would make more money available for plaintiffs who later develop serious illnesses.

I mention this matter because it suggests that the settlement before us is unusual in terms of its importance, both to many potential plaintiffs and to defendants, and with respect to the time, effort, and expenditure that it reflects. All of which leads me to be reluctant to set aside the District Court's findings without more assurance than I have that they are wrong. . . .

Second, the majority . . . says that the predominance "inquiry trains on the legal or factual questions that qualify each class member's case as a genuine controversy, questions that preexist any settlement." I find it difficult to interpret this sentence in a way that could lead me to the majority's conclusion. If the majority means that these pre-settlement questions are what matters, then how does it reconcile its statement with its basic conclusion that "settlement is relevant" to class certification, or with the numerous lower court authority that says that settlement is not only relevant, but important? . . .

Of course, as the majority points out, there are also important differences among class members. Different plaintiffs were exposed to different products for different times; each has a distinct medical history and a different history of smoking; and many cases arise under the laws of different States. The relevant question, however, is how much these differences matter in respect to the legal proceedings that lie ahead. Many, if not all, toxic tort class actions involve plaintiffs with such differences. And the differences in state law are of diminished importance in respect to a proposed settlement in which the defendants have waived all defenses and agreed to compensate all those who were injured. . . .

I agree that there is a serious problem, but it is a problem that often exists in toxic tort cases. . . . [C]onflict "between present and future claimants" "is almost always present in some form in mass tort cases because long latency periods are needed to discover injuries." . . .

Further, certain details of the settlement that are not discussed in the majority opinion suggest that the settlement may be of greater benefit to future plaintiffs than the majority suggests. The District Court concluded that future plaintiffs receive a "significant value" from the settlement due to variety of its items that benefit future plaintiffs, such as: (1) tolling the statute of limitations so that class members "will no longer be forced to file premature lawsuits or risk their claims being time-barred"; (2) waiver of defenses to liability; (3) payment of claims, if and when members become sick, pursuant to the settlement's compensation standards, which avoids "the uncertainties, long delays and high transaction costs [including attorney's fees] of the tort system"; (4) "some assurance that there will be funds available if and when they get sick," based on the finding that each defendant "has shown an ability to fund the payment of all qualifying claims" under the settlement; and (5) the right to additional compensation if cancer develops (many settlements for plaintiffs with noncancerous conditions bar such additional claims). For these reasons, and others, the District Court found that the distinction between present and future plaintiffs was "illusory."

I do not know whether or not the benefits are more or less valuable than an inflation adjustment. But I can certainly recognize an argument that they are. . . .

Fourth, I am more agnostic than is the majority about the basic fairness of the settlement. The District Court's conclusions rested upon complicated factual findings that are not easily cast aside. . . . I do not intend to pass judgment upon the settlement's fairness, but I do believe that these matters would have to be explored in far greater depth before I could reach a conclusion about fairness. And that task, as I have said, is one for the Court of Appeals.

Finally, I believe it is up to the District Court, rather than this Court, to review the legal sufficiency of notice to members of the class. . . . And in the end, the District Court was "confident" that Rule 23 and due process requirements were satisfied because, as a result of this "extensive and expensive notice procedure," "over six million" individuals "received actual notice materials," and "millions more" were reached by the media campaign. . . .

II

The issues in this case are complicated and difficult. The District Court might have been correct. Or not. Subclasses might be appropriate. Or not. . . . I would provide the courts below with an opportunity to analyze the factual questions involved in certification by vacating the judgment, and remanding the case for further proceedings.

NOTES AND QUESTIONS

(1) *Should the Supreme Court Have Been More Accommodating of Settlement Classes? Comparing the Amchem Majority and Dissent.* Every Justice in *Amchem* seems to agree that the asbestos claims at issue are intractable without either Congressional action, which has not been forthcoming, or novel interpretation of Rule 23. In fact, they all seem to agree that asbestos claims are a "crisis." Given this consensus, perhaps the dissent should have been more persuasive. Should the majority have "followed the law," as it purports to do, or should it have tried harder instead to "make sense of" the law in Rule 23 by "cutting the Gordian knot"?

(2) *The Supreme Court Revisits the Amchem Issue, But With a Twist: Ortiz v. Fibreboard Corp., 527 U.S. 815 (1999).* In 1993, before the *Amchem* decision, Fibreboard, another former asbestos products manufacturer, reached a $1.5 billion "global" settlement of asbestos claims (including past, present, and future claims) against it in a nationwide, mandatory, non-opt-out, Rule 23(b)(1)(B) class action. In 1995, the settlement was approved in Texas federal district court and affirmed by the Fifth Circuit Court of Appeals. Following the *Amchem* decision, the Supreme Court remanded the case to the Fifth Circuit for reconsideration in light of *Amchem*, but the Fifth Circuit again upheld the settlement.

The Supreme Court reversed. The seven-Justice majority rejected the Fifth Circuit's use of a "limited fund" theory under Rule 23(b)(1)(B) to craft the mandatory settlement. According to Justice Souter's opinion, the limited fund concept should stay close to the historical model of a "fund" with a definitely ascertained limit that is inadequate to pay all claims against it. The parties did not demonstrate that the fund was limited except by agreement of the parties, figures uncritically adopted by the lower courts. The majority was also critical of the acceptance by the Fifth Circuit of a fund that was less than all the assets available (it allowed Fibreboard to retain virtually its entire net worth) for payment of the mandatory class members' claims.

The settlement also allowed exclusions from the class and allocations of assets inconsistent with limited fund treatment and without critical structural protections suggested by Amchem. In particular, it lacked subclasses to separate conflicting claimants. "It is obvious after *Amchem* that a class divided between holders of present and future claims (some of the latter involving no physical injury and to claimants not yet born) requires division into homogenous subclasses under Rule 23(c)(4)(B), with separate representation to eliminate conflicting interests of counsel."

(3) *Class Actions Struggle in the Appellate Courts.* In a series of appellate decisions beginning with *In re Rhone-Poulenc Rorer Inc.,* 51 F.3d 1293 (7th Cir. 1995), lower courts' efforts to use the class action device to resolve mass tort claims frequently were rebuffed. *In Rhone-Poulenc,* Chief Judge Posner granted a writ of mandamus to overturn the district court's approval of a partial class action in a nationwide class of hemophiliacs who became infected with HIV from using defendants' blood products on grounds the selective class treatment would deny defendants their Seventh Amendment right to a jury trial. This controversial decision subsequently was rejected by a district court judge in *In re Copley Pharmaceutical Inc.,* 161 F.R.D. 456, 459-61 (D. Wyo. 1995).

The Fifth Circuit rejected class action treatment for a mammoth multistate tobacco addiction in *Castano v. American Tobacco Co.,* 84 F.3d 734 (5th Cir. 1996), citing "predominance" and "superiority" issues due to conflicting state laws. The overall effect of these decisions has been that class actions, at least in federal court, are harder to bring in the context of mass torts. There have continued to be mixed results.

(4) *Class Actions Under the Private Securities Litigation Reform Act of 1995 (PSLRA).* The same complaints about class actions generally that we hear today were raised previously in the specific context of securities fraud class actions. Concerned with a perceived problem of abusive securities litigation, Congress enacted the Private Securities Litigation Reform Act (PSLRA), discussed *supra* at § 5.03[C][2], in 1995. The PSLRA imposes significant procedural requirements on federal securities litigation, including securities fraud class actions. These requirements include, among others, the imposition of heightened pleading requirements requiring plaintiffs to plead specific facts in support of securities fraud allegations (*see* § 5.03[C][2], *supra*). 15 U.S.C. § 78u-4(b)(2). In addition to the requirements for class actions imposed by Rule 23, the PSLRA provides that any plaintiff may seek lead plaintiff/class representative status, but the court must appoint as lead plaintiff the individual(s) most capable of adequately representing the interests of the class members. There is a rebuttable presumption that the court should select the individual (or group of individuals) with the "largest financial interest in the relief sought." The court-appointed lead plaintiff(s) then select and retain class counsel, subject to the court's approval. 15 U.S.C. § 78u-4(a)(3). The PSLRA also requires additional specific disclosures concerning any proposed settlement, 15 U.S.C. § 78u-4(a)(7), and prohibits any attorney fees award that exceeds a "reasonable percentage of the amount of any damages and prejudgment interest actually paid to the class." 15 U.S.C. § 78u-4(a)(6).

(5) *The Securities Litigation Uniform Standards Act of 1998.* In reaction to the PSLRA, litigants shifted securities class action lawsuits from federal to state courts. As a result, Congress enacted the Securities Litigation Uniform Standards Act (SLUSA), which preempts most securities fraud class actions involving nationally traded securities that are brought in state court under state law alleging "a misrepresentation or omission of a material fact in connection with the purchase or sale of a covered security" or "that the defendant used or employed any manipulative or deceptive device or contrivance in connection with the purchase or sale of a covered security." 15 U.S.C. §§ 77p(f)(1)-(2), 78bb(f)(1)(5)(b). An important provision of the SLUSA provides that a covered class action is removable to the federal district court for the district in which the action is pending, and is subject to federal law, including the provisions of the PSLRA. 15 U.S.C. §§ 77p(c), 78bb(f)(3).

In 2006, the Supreme Court held that the statutory phrase "in connection with the purchase or sale" of securities is not limited to cases in which the plaintiff was defrauded into purchasing or selling particular securities. The phrase must be read more broadly to include fraud that coincides with a securities transaction, whether the transaction involves the plaintiff or someone else. *Merrill Lynch, Pierce, Fenner & Smith, Inc. v. Dabit*, 547 U.S. — , 126 S. Ct. 1503, 1513 (2006). The Court held that a purported class action by holders of securities was preempted by SLUSA; the status of the plaintiffs as holders, rather than as purchasers or sellers, was not determinative of whether the complaint alleged fraud "in connection with the purchase or sale" of securities. 126 S. Ct. at 1515.

Taken together, the PSLRA and the SLUSA make it virtually impossible to bring most securities fraud class actions in state court.

[F] Class Action Alternatives: The "Bellwether Case" Method

In re CHEVRON U.S.A., INC.
109 F.3d 1016 (5th Cir. 1997)

Robert M. Parker, Circuit Judge:

Chevron U.S.A., Inc. ("Chevron") petitions this Court for a Writ of Mandamus seeking relief from an order of the district court . . . containing a trial plan for this litigation. We DENY the petition as it relates to the scheduled trial of the thirty selected plaintiffs referenced in the district court's order, but GRANT the petition as it relates to utilization of the results of such trial for the purpose of issue or claim preclusion.

UNDERLYING FACTS AND PROCEDURAL HISTORY

This controversy arose out of the alleged injuries suffered by over 3,000 plaintiffs and intervenors ("Plaintiffs"), who claim damages for personal injuries, wrongful death, and property contamination allegedly caused by Chevron's acts and omissions. The Plaintiffs and their allegedly contaminated property are located in the Kennedy Heights section of Houston, Texas. The Plaintiffs contend that their subdivision was constructed on land used in the 1920's by Chevron for a crude oil storage waste pit. According to the Plaintiffs, when Chevron ceased using the property as a tank farm, it failed to take appropriate measures to secure the site, thereby allowing other waste to be deposited on the land [which ultimately allegedly caused differing kinds of damages to each of the plaintiffs]. . . .

. . . [T]he district court approved a trial plan. The trial plan provided for a unitary trial on the issues of "general liability or causation" on behalf of the remaining plaintiffs, as well as the individual causation and damage issues of the selected plaintiffs, and ordered the selection of a bellwether group of thirty (30) claimants, fifteen (15) to be chosen by the plaintiffs and fifteen (15) to be chosen by Chevron. Chevron contends that the goal of the "unitary trial" was to determine its liability, or lack thereof, in a single trial and to establish bellwether verdicts to which the remaining claims could be matched for settlement purposes. It is this selection process which Chevron argues will not result in a representative group of bellwether plaintiffs. . . .

DISCUSSION

1. Standard of Review

[The trial court's order can be overturned only to the extent it is an abuse of discretion.]

2. The Plan . . .

The district court, after designating the case as complex, then articulated the goals of its trial plan as seeking to achieve the greatest efficiency and expedition in the resolution of all issues involved in the case. Pursuant to those goals, it structured the trial as follows:

> 1. Composed of thirty (30) plaintiffs, fifteen (15) chosen by the plaintiffs and fifteen (15) chosen by the defendants. The thirty (30) plaintiffs chosen shall come from the lists submitted by the parties to the state court in April of 1996. However, each side is permitted to substitute or replace not more than five (5) plaintiffs, within its discretion, on or before January 1, 1997.
>
> 2. All chosen plaintiffs shall be adults, to the exclusion of minor children, unless the children are part of a household represented by at least one adult.
>
> 3. Each individual shall be counted as a single plaintiff, as opposed to a household as a single plaintiff.
>
> 4. The trial shall focus on the individual claims of each of the selected plaintiffs and on the issue of the existence or nonexistence of liability on the part of Chevron for the pollutants that, allegedly, give rise to all of the plaintiffs' claims.
>
> Thus, a unitary trial on the issues of general liability or causation as well as the individual causation and damage issues of the selected plaintiffs shall occur.
>
> 5. The Court reserves the right to: (a) place a time limit on the length of the trial, limit the testimony of certain witnesses, limit the number of witnesses to be called on a particular issue, amend this Order, and issue additional orders.

Initially, we note the obvious. The trial plan, while clearly designed to resolve the issue of liability on the part of Chevron to all the plaintiffs by referring to a unitary trial on the issues of general liability or causation, does not identify any common issues or explain how the verdicts in the thirty (30) selected cases are supposed to resolve liability for the remaining 2,970 plaintiffs. . . .

3. A Bellwether Trial

The term bellwether is derived from the ancient practice of belling a wether (a male sheep) selected to lead his flock. The ultimate success of the wether selected to wear the bell was determined by whether the flock had confidence that the wether would not lead them astray, and so it is in the mass tort context.

The notion that the trial of some members of a large group of claimants may provide a basis for enhancing prospects of settlement or for resolving common issues or claims is a sound one that has achieved general acceptance by both bench and bar. References to bellwether trials have long been included in the Manual for Complex Litigation.*See* Manual for Complex Litigation § 33.27-.28 (3d ed. 1995). . . . If a representative group of claimants are tried to verdict, the results of such trials can be beneficial for litigants who desire to settle such claims by providing information on the value of the cases as reflected by the jury verdicts. Common issues or even general liability may also be resolved in a bellwether context in appropriate cases.

Whatever may be said about the trial contemplated by the district court's . . . order, one thing is clear. It is not a bellwether trial. It is simply a trial of fifteen (15) of the "best" and fifteen (15) of the "worst" cases contained in the universe of claims involved in this litigation. There is no pretense that the thirty (30) cases selected are representative of the 3,000 member group of plaintiffs.

A bellwether trial designed to achieve its value ascertainment function for settlement purposes or to answer troubling causation or liability issues common to the universe of claimants has as a core element representativeness — that is, the sample must be a randomly selected one of sufficient size so as to achieve statistical significance to the desired level of confidence in the result obtained. Such samples are selected by the application of the science of inferential statistics. The essence of the science of inferential statistics is that one may confidently draw inferences about the whole from a representative sample of the whole. The applicability of inferential statistics have long been recognized by the courts. . . .

[T]he results that would be obtained from a trial of these thirty (30) cases lack the requisite level of representativeness so that the results could permit a court to draw sufficiently reliable inferences about the whole that could, in turn, form the basis for a judgment affecting cases other than the selected thirty. While this particular sample of thirty cases is lacking in representativeness, statistical sampling with an appropriate level of representativeness has been utilized and approved. As recognized by the Ninth Circuit, "[i]nferential statistics with random sampling produces an acceptable due process solution to the troublesome area of mass tort litigation." *In re Estate of Marcos Human Rights Litigation,* 910 F. Supp. 1460, 1467 (D. Haw. 1995), *aff'd. sub. nom. Hilao v. Estate of Marcos,* 103 F.3d 767 (9th Cir. 1996) (holding that the random sampling procedures used by the district court do not violate due process).

We, therefore, hold that before a trial court may utilize results from a bellwether trial for a purpose that extends beyond the individual cases tried, it must, prior to any extrapolation, find that the cases tried are representative of the larger group of cases or claims from which they are selected. Typically, such a finding must be based on competent, scientific, statistical evidence that identifies the variables involved and that provides a sample of sufficient size so as to permit a finding that there is a sufficient level of confidence that the results obtained reflect results that would be obtained from trials of the whole. . . .

The elements of basic fairness contained in our historical understanding of both procedural and substantive due process therefore dictate that when a unitary trial is conducted where common issues, issues of general liability, or issues of causation are coupled with a sample of individual claims or cases, the sample must be one that is a randomly selected, statistically significant sample. *See Hilao,* 103 F.3d at 782-84, 786.

. . .

EDITH H. JONES, CIRCUIT JUDGE, specially concurring:

I agree with Judge Parker's conclusions that mandamus must be granted in this case, that the district judge's method of selecting "bellwether" cases is fatally flawed, and that the most expeditious remedy is, without interfering with the setting of these cases, to deprive them of preclusive consequences. . . . I . . . have serious doubts[, however,] about the major premise of Judge Parker's opinion, i.e., his confidence that a bellwether trial of representative cases is permissible to extrapolate findings relevant to and somehow preclusive upon a larger group of cases. . . .

. . . Although Judge Parker need not have reached this larger question, he appears to have done so, asserting that the notion of a bellwether trial "is a sound one that has achieved general acceptance by both bench and bar." He further asserts that common issues or even general liability may be resolved in a bellwether context in appropriate cases. I have serious doubts about the procedure even where, as here, Chevron agreed to use of a statistically sound bellwether trial process.

The only case cited in the Manual for Complex Litigation concerning a bellwether strategy was tried by Judge Parker when he sat on the district court. *Cimino v. Raymark,* 751 F. Supp. 649, 653, 664-65 (E.D. Tex. 1990), cited in Manual for Complex Litigation § 33.27–.28 (3d ed. 1995) [but reversed on appeal; see below — Eds.]. One other recent case, affirmed in a split verdict of the Ninth Circuit, also used a bellwether technique. *Hilao v. Estate of Marcos,* 103 F.3d 767 (9th Cir. 1996). These are not necessarily the only examples of bellwether trials, but they appear to be most unusual.

The use of statistical sampling as a means to identify and resolve common issues in tort litigation has, however, been severely criticized. . . . Additionally, as Judge Higginbotham cautioned in *In re Fibreboard Corp.,* there is a fine line between deriving results from trials based on statistical sampling and pure legislation. Judges must be sensitive to stay within our proper bounds of adjudicating individual disputes. We are not authorized by the Constitution or statutes to legislate solutions to cases in pursuit of efficiency and expeditiousness. . . .

NOTES AND QUESTIONS

(1) *Bellwether Cases as a Settlement-Inducing Device.* One concept of a bellwether case is also referred to as a "test case" approach. The parties (or the luck of the draw) may select one case or several for initial trial in the hope that results will facilitate evaluation of numerous others for settlement. Alternatively, the court may designate several test cases or may decree a process for their designation (as the court did in the case, above). Should it make a difference if the court, rather than the parties, chooses the test cases (does the selection constitute a judicial act subject to review for abuse of discretion, or is it purely administrative)?

(2) *Bellwether Cases as Preclusive (i.e., as Having Res Judicata or Collateral Estoppel Effect.* The bellwether concept is taken into another dimension if the court intends to apply the resulting verdicts to decide an issue in all the other cases through the mechanism of collateral estoppel. Usually, the issue that is proposed for preclusive effect is either the question of so called "general" liability (*e.g.*, whether a given product is unreasonably dangerous) or so-called "general" causation (*i.e.*, whether the defendant's act or product is at all capable of legally causing the claimed injuries). The trial court in the principal case, above, proposed to give preclusive effect to the verdict on general liability (*i.e.*, whether Chevron was negligent) and on general causation (*i.e.*, whether Chevron's acts were capable of causing the damage claimed by not only the bellwether plaintiffs but all others of the Kennedy Heights claimants). That is, if the bellwether trial resulted in a plaintiff's verdict the judge would apply it against Chevron, and if it resulted in a defendant's verdict the judge would apply it not only to the bellwether plaintiffs but to all other plaintiffs. Consider whether this concept of a bellwether trial is consistent with due process and whether it is wise. If so, is Judge Parker correct in concluding that it needs to be done with statistically representative cases rather than by trying a group of "best" and "worst" ones selected by the parties?

(3) *Bellwether Cases as Furnishing a Vehicle for Resolution of All Cases by Extrapolation from a Representative Sample: The Cimino and Hilao Decisions.* These two decisions, cited in the principal case, involve bellwether cases selected by statistical sampling techniques with an eye toward resolving not only general liability and causation, but all other issues, in a large number of other cases. This is the most controversial use of the bellwether case doctrine. The concept is that, after a jury has decided liability and damages for various categories of representative cases, that jury (or another) can use these results, plus limited individual data about each of the other cases within each category, to resolve all others. Judge Parker appears to accept this bellwether application, conditioned on proper statistical science; Judge Jones does not. Which is correct? In any event, it will be challenging to create a viable trial plan. The *Cimino* case was reversed on appeal, and a revised trial plan also was reversed years later, 151 F.3d 297 (5th Cir. 1998).

APPENDIX TO CHAPTER 6

COMPLEX CLASS LITIGATION

§ A JURISDICTION AND CHOICE OF LAW IN MULTISTATE CLASS ACTIONS

Subject Matter Jurisdiction: Diversity. If a nationwide class action is based upon state law, at least some of the class members are likely to be of non-diverse citizenship from the defendant. For example, if the defendant is a Delaware corporation with its principal place of business in Indiana, all class members who are citizens of those states will be non-diverse from it. *Strawbridge v. Curtiss* provides that there must be complete diversity; does that mean that all citizens of Delaware and Indiana must be left out of the class? Fortunately for them, in *Supreme Tribe of Ben-Hur v. Cauble*, 255 U.S. 356 (1921), the Court held that only the citizenship of the representative parties was to be considered for diversity purposes. (The Court based its reasoning upon older cases, in which non-diverse claimants were allowed to intervene in an existing suit, and analogized that procedure to class actions.)

Jurisdictional Amount. As you have previously studied, the diversity statute requires both complete diversity of citizenship and an amount in controversy exceeding $75,000. Originally, in *Snyder v. Harris*, 394 U.S. 332 (1969), the Supreme Court held that the claims of multiple plaintiffs could not be aggregated to achieve the jurisdictional amount. Moreover, in *Zahn v. International Paper Co.*, 414 U.S. 291 (1973), the Court held that each claimant in a diversity-based Rule 23(b)(3) class action must satisfy the jurisdictional amount. The result of these cases was that many class actions could only be filed in state court. A combination of changes has lifted this restrictive view.

- *Supplemental Jurisdiction.* Congress enacted section 1367, the supplemental jurisdiction statute, after the *Snyder* and *Zahn* decisions. Section 1367 resulted in a split in the circuit courts as to whether supplemental jurisdiction authorized a court to assert jurisdiction over all claims in a class action, including smaller claims, if the court had jurisdiction over one or more claims that did exceed the minimum amount. In 2005, the Supreme Court overruled its prior *Zahn* decision in *Exxon Mobil Corp. v. Allapattah Services, Inc.*, 545 U.S. 546 (2005). According to the Court, under section 1367 so long as one of the named plaintiffs satisfies the requisite amount in controversy, the court may exercise supplemental jurisdiction over the remaining claims.

- *Aggregation and the Class Action Fairness Act.* Moreover, the Class Action Fairness Act (CAFA) expressly authorizes the filing of a class action in federal court (or the removal of a class action to federal court) if "the matter in controversy exceeds the sum or value of $5,000,000." Early court decisions have held that the $5 million jurisdictional amount may be satisfied if either the aggregate value to the class members, or the aggregate cost to the defendant, exceeds $5 million. In addition to satisfying the $5 million jurisdictional amount, the class action must also satisfy minimal diversity requirements — most commonly that any member of the plaintiff class is a citizen of a State different from any defendant. CAFA applies only prospectively — to lawsuits "commenced on or after" the date of its enactment.

Personal Jurisdiction and Choice of Law in Multistate Class Actions. The *International Shoe* case requires that, in order for a court to have power to adjudicate the rights of an individual, that individual must have affiliating circumstances tying him to the forum, or must have consented to the adjudication. Class members, of course, are in the position of having their rights permanently adjudicated, often by distant forums, and almost always without their express consent. Is this practice constitutional? Additionally, there is the question: What state's law should a court apply to a class action? Some courts, confronted with the modern nationwide class action, concluded that they were required to apply the laws of all fifty states plus foreign countries—a difficult undertaking. Other courts applied forum law to all claims, including those to which the forum had no connection.

Kennedy, THE SUPREME COURT MEETS THE BRIDE OF FRANKENSTEIN: *PHILLIPS PETROLEUM CO. v. SHUTTS* AND THE STATE MULTISTATE CLASS ACTION

*34 U. Kan. L. Rev. 255 (1985) (footnotes omitted)**

In *Eisen v. Carlisle & Jacquelin*, the Supreme Court first met a "Frankenstein monster posing as a class action." The Supreme Court restrained the monster by requiring the named plaintiff to pay for individual opt-out notice to members of the class before the plaintiff could obtain any determination of liability. Now, eleven years later in *Phillips Petroleum v. Shutts* the Supreme Court has met the Bride of Frankenstein. She appeared in the form of the state court, multistate class action. This time the Supreme Court unshackled Frankenstein's mate by refusing to require that nonresident members of the plaintiff class have minimum contacts with the forum state. The Court did, however, require that the Bride be governed by the laws of the several states.

PHILLIPS PETROLEUM CO. v. SHUTTS
472 U.S. 797 (1985)

[Phillips collected increased payments for natural gas that were allowed by Federal Power Commission opinions. Since it received the increases subject to refund, Phillips paid correspondingly increased royalties to landowners only after judicial review was finally concluded. At that time, however, it paid no interest on the funds it had withheld. Shutts and others brought a class action in a state trial court in Seward County, Kansas, on behalf of royalty owners residing in all fifty states, the District of Columbia, and numerous foreign countries, alleging that Phillips's refusal to pay interest on the increases was wrongful.

[Phillips objected to the Kansas court's exercise of jurisdiction over the claims of nonresidents who had no connection with Kansas. The Kansas Supreme Court rejected Phillips's argument and affirmed a judgment in favor of the entire royalty owner class. Furthermore, Phillips objected to the substantive law applied by the trial court, which had recognized an equitable claim under Kansas law based on unjust enrichment at the highest arguable interest rate in favor of all class members, including those having no connection with Kansas. Again, the Kansas Supreme Court rejected Phillips' arguments, and it upheld the application of a uniform substantive rule of law to all members of the class.

[The Supreme Court granted certiorari. Before reaching the real issues, however, the Court considered whether Phillips had standing to raise the question of personal jurisdiction over absent class members. The Court held that Phillips did have standing, because it had a concrete interest in ensuring that absent class members would be bound by the judgment, just as Phillips would be. The Court then proceeded to consider the determinative issues of jurisdiction and choice of law.]

II

Reduced to its essentials, petitioner's argument is that unless out-of-state plaintiffs affirmatively consent, the Kansas courts may not exert jurisdiction over their claims. Petitioner claims that failure to execute and return the "request for exclusion" provided with the class notice cannot constitute consent of the out-of-state plaintiffs; thus Kansas courts may exercise jurisdiction over these plaintiffs only if the plaintiffs possess the sufficient "minimum contacts" with Kansas as that term is used in cases involving personal jurisdiction over out-of-state defendants. *E.g., International Shoe Co. v. Washington*, 326 U.S. 310 (1945); *Shaffer v. Heitner*, 433 U.S. 186 (1977); *World-Wide Volkswagen Corp. v. Woodson*, 444 U.S. 286 (1980). Since Kansas had no prelitigation contact with many of the plaintiffs and leases involved, petitioner claims that Kansas has exceeded its jurisdictional reach and thereby violated the due process rights of the absent plaintiffs. . . .

Although the cases like *Shaffer* and *Woodson* which petitioner relies on for a minimum contacts requirement all dealt with out-of-state defendants or parties in the procedural posture of a defendant, . . . petitioner claims that the same analysis must apply to absent class-action plaintiffs. In this regard petitioner correctly points out that a chose in action is a constitutionally recognized property interest possessed by each of the plaintiffs. *Mullane v. Central Hanover Bank & Trust Co.*, 339 U.S. 306 (1950). An adverse judgment by Kansas courts in this case may extinguish the chose in action forever through *res judicata.* [T]hus, the same due process protections should apply to absent plaintiffs: Kansas should not be able to exert jurisdiction over the plaintiff's claims unless the plaintiffs have sufficient minimum contacts with Kansas.

We think petitioner's premise is in error. The burdens placed by a State upon an absent class-action plaintiff are not of the same order or magnitude as those it places upon an absent defendant. An out-of-state defendant summoned by a plaintiff is faced with the full powers of the forum State to render judgment *against* it. [T]he defendant may also face liability for court costs and attorney's fees. These burdens are substantial, and the minimum contacts requirement of the Due Process Clause prevents the forum State from unfairly imposing them upon the defendant.

A class-action plaintiff, however, is in quite a different posture. The Court noted this difference in *Hansberry v. Lee*, 311 U.S. 32, 40-41 (1940), which explained that a "class" or "representative" suit was an exception to the rule that one could not be bound by judgment *in personam* unless one was made fully a party in the traditional sense. . . .

Modern plaintiff class actions follow the same goals, permitting litigation of a suit involving common questions when there are too many plaintiffs for proper joinder. . . . For example, this lawsuit involves claims averaging about $100 per plaintiff; most of the plaintiffs would have no realistic day in court if a class action were not available.

In sharp contrast to the predicament of a defendant haled into an out-of-state forum, the plaintiffs in this suit were not haled anywhere to defend themselves upon pain of a default judgment. As commentators have noted, from the plaintiffs' point of view a class action resembles a "quasi-administrative proceeding, conducted by the judge." . . .

. . . Unlike a defendant in a civil suit, a class-action plaintiff is not required to fend for himself. The court and named plaintiffs protect his interests. . . .

Besides this continuing solicitude for their rights, absent plaintiff class members are not subject to other burdens imposed upon defendants. They need not hire counsel or appear. They are almost never subject to counterclaims or cross-claims, or liability for fees or costs.[2] Absent plaintiff class members are not subject to coercive or punitive remedies. Nor will an adverse judgment typically bind an absent plaintiff for any damages, although a valid adverse judgment may extinguish any of the plaintiff's claim which was litigated.

. . . In most class actions an absent plaintiff is provided at least with an opportunity to "opt out" of the class, and if he takes advantage of that opportunity he is removed from the litigation entirely. This was true of the Kansas proceedings in this case. The Kansas procedure provided for the mailing of a notice to each class member by first-class mail. . . . The notice further stated that class members would be included in the class and bound by the judgment unless they "opted out" by executing and returning a "request for exclusion" that was included in the notice. . . .

Because States place fewer burdens upon absent class plaintiffs than they do upon absent defendants in nonclass suits, the Due Process Clause need not and does not afford the former as much protection from state-court jurisdiction as it does the latter. The Fourteenth Amendment does protect "persons," not "defendants," however, so absent plaintiffs as well as absent defendants are entitled to some protection from the jurisdiction of a forum State which seeks to adjudicate their claims. In this case we hold that a forum State may exercise jurisdiction over the claim of an absent class-action plaintiff, even though that plaintiff may not possess the minimum contacts with the forum which would support personal jurisdiction over a defendant. If the forum State wishes to bind an absent plaintiff concerning a claim for money damages or similar relief at law, it must provide minimal procedural due process protection. The plaintiff must receive notice plus an opportunity to be heard and participate in the litigation, whether in person or through counsel. The notice must be the best practicable, "reasonably calculated, under all the circumstances, to apprise interested parties of the pendency of the action and afford them an opportunity to present their objections." *Mullane*, 399 U.S., at 314-315; *cf. Eisen v. Carlisle & Jacquelin*, 417 U.S. 156, 174-175 (1974). The notice should describe the action and the plaintiffs' rights in it. Additionally, we hold that due process requires at a minimum that an absent plaintiff be provided with an opportunity to remove himself from the class by executing and returning an "opt out" or "request for exclusion" form to the court. Finally, the Due Process Clause of course requires that the named plaintiff at all times adequately represent the interests of the absent class members. *Hansberry*, 311 U.S., at 42-43.

We reject petitioner's contention that the Due Process Clause of the Fourteenth Amendment requires that absent plaintiffs affirmatively "opt in" to the class, rather than

---

[2] Petitioner places emphasis on the fact that absent class members might be subject to discovery, counterclaims, cross-claims or court costs. Petitioner cites no cases involving any such imposition upon plaintiffs, however. We are convinced that such burdens are rarely imposed upon plaintiff class members, and that the disposition of these issues is best left to a case which presents them in a more concrete way.

be deemed members of the class if they do not "opt out." We think that such a contention is supported by little, if any precedent, and that it ignores the differences between class action plaintiffs, on the one hand, and defendants in non-class civil suits on the other. Any plaintiff may consent to jurisdiction. *Keeton v. Hustler Magazine, Inc.*, 465 U.S. 770 (1984). The essential question, then, is how stringent the requirement for a showing of consent will be.

We think that the procedure followed by Kansas, where a fully descriptive notice is sent first-class mail to each class member, with an explanation of the right to "opt out," satisfies due process.

III

The Kansas courts applied Kansas contract and Kansas equity law to every claim in this case, notwithstanding that over 99% of the gas leases and some 97% of the plaintiffs in the case had no apparent connection to the State of Kansas except for this lawsuit. . . .

Petitioner contends that total application of Kansas substantive law violated the constitutional limitations on choice of law mandated by the Due Process Clause of the Fourteenth Amendment and the Full Faith and Credit Clause of Article IV, § 1. We must first determine whether Kansas law conflicts in any material way with any other law which could apply. There can be no injury in applying Kansas law if it is not in conflict with that of any other jurisdiction connected to this suit.

Petitioner claims that Kansas law conflicts with that of a number of States connected to this litigation, especially Texas and Oklahoma. These putative conflicts range from the direct to the tangential, and may be addressed by the Supreme Court of Kansas on remand under the correct constitutional standard. For example, there is no recorded Oklahoma decision dealing with interest liability for suspended royalties: whether Oklahoma is likely to impose liability would require a survey of Oklahoma oil and gas law. Even if Oklahoma found such liability, petitioner shows that Oklahoma would most likely apply its constitutional and statutory 6% interest rate rather than the much higher Kansas rates applied in this litigation [citing Oklahoma authorities]. . . .

Additionally, petitioner points to an Oklahoma statute which excuses liability for interest if a creditor accepts payment of the full principal without a claim for interest, Okla. Stat., Tit. 23, § 8 (1951). [P]etitioner contends that by ignoring this statute the Kansas courts created liability that does not exist in Oklahoma.

Petitioner also points out several conflicts between Kansas and Texas law. Although Texas recognizes interest liability for suspended royalties, Texas has never awarded any such interest at a rate greater than 6%, which corresponds with the Texas constitutional and statutory rate [citing and discussing Texas authorities]. . . .

The conflicts on the applicable interest rates, alone—which we do not think can be labeled "false conflicts" without a more thorough-going treatment than was accorded them by the Supreme Court of Kansas—certainly amounted to millions of dollars in liability. We think that the Supreme Court of Kansas erred in deciding on the basis that it did that the application of its laws to all claims would be constitutional. . . .

The Supreme Court of Kansas in its opinion in this case expressed the view that by reason of the fact that it was adjudicating a nationwide class action, it had much greater latitude in applying its own law to the transactions in question than might otherwise be the case. . . .

We think that this is something of a "bootstrap" argument. The Kansas class action statute, like those of most other jurisdictions, requires that there be "common issues of law or fact." But while a state may, for the reasons we have previously stated, assume jurisdiction over the claims of plaintiffs whose principal contacts are with other States, it may not use this assumption of jurisdiction as an added weight in the scale when considering the permissible constitutional limits on choice of substantive law. . . .

Kansas must have a "significant contact or aggregation of contacts" to the claims asserted by each member of the plaintiff class, contacts "creating state interests" in order to ensure that the choice of Kansas law is not arbitrary or unfair. [*Allstate Ins. Co. v. Hague,* 449 U.S. 302 (1981).] Given Kansas' lack of "interest" in claims unrelated to that State, and the substantive conflict with jurisdictions such as Texas, we conclude that application of Kansas law to every claim in this case is sufficiently arbitrary and unfair as to exceed constitutional limits.

When considering fairness in this context, an important element is the expectation of the parties. *See Allstate, supra*, 449 U.S., at 333 (opinion of POWELL, J.). There is no indication that when the leases involving land and royalty owners outside of Kansas were executed, the parties had any idea that Kansas law would control. . . .

[W]e make no effort to determine for ourselves which law must apply to the various transactions involved in this lawsuit, and we reaffirm our observation in *Allstate* that in many situations a state court may be free to apply one of several choices of law. But the constitutional limitations laid down in cases such as *Allstate* . . . be respected even in a nationwide class action.

We therefore affirm the judgment of the Supreme Court of Kansas insofar as it upheld the jurisdiction of the Kansas courts over the plaintiff class members in this case, and reverse its judgment insofar as it held that Kansas law was applicable to all of the transactions which it sought to adjudicate. We remand the case to that Court for further proceedings not inconsistent with this opinion.

JUSTICE POWELL took no part in the decision of this case.

JUSTICE STEVENS, concurring in part and dissenting in part. . . .

As the Court recognizes, there "can be no [constitutional] injury in applying Kansas law if it is not in conflict with that of any other jurisdiction connected to this suit." A fair reading of the Kansas Supreme Court's opinion [r]eveals that the Kansas court has examined the laws of connected jurisdictions and has correctly concluded that there is no "direct" or "substantive" conflict between the law applied by Kansas and the laws of those other States. Kansas has merely developed general common law principles to accommodate the novel facts of this litigation—other State courts either agree with Kansas or have not yet addressed precisely similar claims. Consequently, I conclude that the Full Faith and Credit Clause of the Constitution did not require Kansas to apply the law of any other State, and the Fourteenth Amendment's Due Process Clause did not prevent Kansas from applying its own law in this case. . . .

[R]ather than potential, "putative," or even "likely" conflicts, I would require demonstration of an *unambiguous* conflict with the *established* law of another State as an essential element of a constitutional choice-of-law claim. Arguments that a State court has merely applied general common law principles in a novel manner, or reconciled arguably conflicting laws erroneously in the face of unprecedented factual circumstances, should not suffice to make out a constitutional issue. . . .

Kennedy, THE SUPREME COURT MEETS THE BRIDE OF FRANKENSTEIN: *PHILLIPS PETROLEUM CO. v. SHUTTS* AND THE STATE MULTISTATE CLASS ACTION*

34 U. Kan. L. Rev. 255, 279-89 (1985) (footnotes omitted)

The [*Shutts*] opinion rests upon a simplistic syllogism and abstract premises so unqualified as to be inaccurate. However, the most disquieting aspect of the opinion is that the Court, even in its abstract formalism, abandons any pretense of neutrality. Instead, the Court makes the startling announcement that a rule of procedure is intended to provide a remedy for plaintiffs against defendants but not the reverse.

From the opening characterization of the issue, Justice Rehnquist misleadingly and repeatedly labels the potential passive class members with the party concept "plaintiffs." Throughout the opinion he fails to maintain any careful and important distinctions between the named party plaintiff who authorizes the filing of the action, the lawyer who seeks authority to represent the class, the passive potential members who fail to opt out, and the class entity as a judicially created legal fiction. Unlike Justice Rehnquist's reliance on the label "plaintiff" to describe the class members, the better approach taken in the lower courts is that because of their right to remain passive, members defined into a class are neither "plaintiffs" nor "defendants." Members of the public who fail to opt out of a judicially created class are sui generis. . . .

Justice Rehnquist uses the abstraction "plaintiff" to assert half-truths, to make distorted comparisons, and to alchemize a new fiction of consent. . . . From under this "plaintiff" shell, he finally produces a fictional class entity that is a super oxymoron plaintiff—one that has all the benefits, but none of the burdens of its name. . . .

[T]here is another troubling, fundamental point. . . . Justice Rehnquist also disguises the reality that the opt-out device changes and expands the nature of judicial power itself.

The historical fundamental premise of the common law adversarial system is that judicial power is dependent upon active party initiative affirmatively requesting relief from the court. . . . The *Shutts* opinion, authored by Justice Rehnquist, reveals that the classical view of passive judicial power has become outmoded. Instead, the view is now pervasive that the modern judicial function is like that of an active administrative agency—exercising efficient power to accomplish law enforcement and justice for large groups of individuals upon the initiative of free-market, enterprising, private attorney generals. . . .

The result reached by the Court in this case is a good one. However, the opinion is irritating for either its self-delusion, or lack of candor or craft, and its ideological compulsion to feign judicial humility. But this criticism reflects academic irritation. *Shutts* is a grand opinion with grand objectives in the formal style of classic Supreme Court opinions. . . .

NOTES AND QUESTIONS

(1) *Jurisdiction and Certification: Should a Forum With No Interest in the Dispute Hear a Class Action?* The *Shutts* decision indicates that, as a matter of raw jurisdictional power, a court located in Maine or Hawaii could have decided the *Shutts* case, even if literally none of its citizens were affected and even if the forum had no connection with

the dispute at all. Should such a court hear the case? [Note: *See* Fed. R. Civ. P. 23(b)(3)(C), which makes the "desirability" of concentrating the claims in the particular forum a factor in deciding whether to certify a class action. Remember that only about 3% of the *Shutts* plaintiffs resided in Kansas and fewer than 1% of the leases were located there.]

(2) *"Magnet" Forums.* If an attorney representing a class has a wide-open choice among forums nationwide, wouldn't she naturally choose the "best" plaintiff's forum? For this reason, one might hypothesize that "magnet forums" will develop, attracting class actions concerning consumer laws, environmental issues, or royalty-owner interest payments. This possibility is not merely speculative. The reporter system discloses that Kansas appellate courts have decided at least eight royalty-interest class actions similar to *Shutts*, and its trial courts have considered more. No other state has a reported *Shutts*-type case. *See* A. Miller & D. Crump, *Jurisdiction and Choice of Law in Multistate Class Actions After Phillips Petroleum Co. v. Shutts*, 96 Yale L.J. 1 (1986). Is it fair to defendants to allow such "magnet forums" to exist? After *Shutts*, does the defendant have any remedy against the filing of a class action in a "magnet" forum?

(3) *Consent—and Related Notice Issues.* The *Shutts* opinion recognizes, and appears to preserve, litigants' interest in not having their rights cut off by distant forums to which they have no relationship. It avoids this issue, however, by attributing consent to class members who fail to opt out. This rationale, in turn, places greater emphasis on notice to the class member. Would a class member with a substantial claim, who loses it because the notice is never received, be bound by the court's decree on this implied consent theory? The *Shutts* claims were small, but the same issue could arise with a large claimant; consider the *Skywalk* case, below, in which potential class claims were worth millions of dollars. [The *Shutts* opinion generates confusion, since it says the class member has the right "to receive" notice, but it affirms the lower court without proof of actual receipt, and it cites cases that require only the sending of notice.]

(4) *Choice of Law in the Fifty-State-Plus-Foreign-Countries Class Action: An Impossible Dream?: Sun Oil Co. v. Wortman*, 486 U.S. 717 (1988). Can a state judge, such as the one in *Shutts*, really apply fifty-plus sets of laws to a class action? Won't there be irresistible pressure toward recognizing "uniformity" that does not exist? *See* Miller & Crump, below. For instance, in *Wortman* (which was a sequel to *Shutts*), the Kansas Supreme Court decided that Texas, Oklahoma and Louisiana all would apply the FPC rate (which happened to be the highest arguable rate), just as Kansas would. The Kansas court avoided the interest-rate statutes of all three states by saying they did not apply. The United States Supreme Court affirmed.

(5) *Other Issues of Jurisdictional Power After Shutts: "Competing" Nationwide Class Actions. Shutts* is like most landmark decisions: It raises new questions while solving old ones. Does it apply to federal as well as state courts? Does it apply to classes where all members have connections with the forum? Does it prohibit "defendant classes," or discovery from class members? *See* Miller & Crump, *supra*; *see generally Class Action Symposium: The Twentieth Anniversary of Phillips Petroleum Co. v. Shutts*, 74 UMKC L. Rev. 487–97 (2006). And does it apply to "competing" nationwide class actions that proceed simultaneously, each including the same passive class? Consider the following.

A. Miller & D. Crump, JURISDICTION AND CHOICE OF LAW IN MULTISTATE CLASS ACTIONS AFTER *PHILLIPS PETROLEUM CO. v. SHUTTS*

*96 Yale L.J. 1 (1986) (footnotes omitted)**

The possibility that courts in two or more states might certify different actions covering the same nationwide class raises a separate issue of adjudicatory power. Both actions would proceed with a passive class virtually intact in each. Professor Kennedy describes the problem best:

> Among the hypothetical parade of horribles which can be projected is the scenario in which 50 competing, national, multistate opt-out class actions are brought on the same claims and all members remain silent in response to the fifty notices. . . . [T]his dilemma of interstate federalism perhaps can only be solved by the United States Supreme Court constitutionally requiring pre-trial opt-in as to nonresident class members who have no minimum contacts with the forum. [Citing Kennedy, *Class Actions: The Right to Opt Out*, 25 Ariz. L. Rev. 3, 81 (1983).]

In *Shutts* however, the Supreme Court declined to adopt this solution, and the issue of adjudicatory power in competing class actions remains open.

Presumably, competing class actions could be resolved only by a race to judgment if no national means for selecting among different courts is developed. Race to judgment would induce several undesirable kinds of behavior. For example, defendants could forum-shop by delaying or accelerating particular actions. Plaintiffs could collude with similarly aligned parties in "stalking horse litigation," diverting their opponents' attention or seeking collateral advantages such as the cumulative benefits of inconsistent discovery rulings. Whatever form it takes, a race is an irrational method of adjudicating controversies of overlapping jurisdiction.

Injunctions against litigants or courts are unlikely to provide a satisfactory solution. Parallel state sovereignties probably lack the authority to enforce their orders. A federal court's authority to enjoin a pending state action is circumscribed by the Anti-Injunction Act [28 U.S.C. § 2283], which protects federalism by preventing these orders, with narrow exceptions. . . . A better solution would be for the less appropriate forum to stay (or, in some cases, dismiss) its own proceedings.

Thus far, competing multistate class actions have not been frequent enough to create a highly visible problem. The situation has occurred, however, and it is possible that the *Shutts* holding will give rise to more. If so, the recognition of comity principles may enable the courts to avoid wasteful proceedings in which they spend years determining where litigation will take place or whether there can be parallel state and federal proceedings.

§ B CERTIFICATION HEARING

The Importance of the Certification Issue

The Impact of Certification on the Economics of the Action. If the attorneys for representative plaintiffs can persuade the court to certify a class action, they can convert even small claims into a vehicle for economically viable recovery. Even if individual claims might be viable, class attorneys can obtain many more "clients" by certification. Additionally, the stakes increase enormously for both parties, so that settlement becomes more likely after certification. [Rule 23 does not use the term "certification," but cases often use it to refer to the hearing and order.] The defendant, on the other hand, may be able to defeat the action as a practical matter by persuading the court to deny certification. As a result, the certification hearing is a major pressure point in a class action, calling forth vigorous efforts from both sides.

Games Lawyers Play at Certification: "Prerequisites" Under Rule 23(a). The class attorneys, of course, must satisfy all four of the formal prerequisites of Rule 23(a). The defendant (or party opposing the class) is likely to attack all four of the prerequisites (as well as two other factors, *i.e.*, class existence and membership determinability). Any potential conflicts among class members will be used to oppose findings of typicality or commonality. *Cf. Hansberry v. Lee*, above. And perhaps most ironically, defendants sometimes oppose findings of "adequate representation" on the ground that the proposed class attorneys are not skillful or experienced enough to sue the defendant effectively! (The defendant has an interest in ensuring the binding effect of the judgment—but it is understandable if that proposition does not remove your belief that the argument is a little disingenuous.)

More Games Lawyers Play: "Maintainable" Actions or Issues Under Subdivisions (b)(1), (b)(2), and (b)(3). The class action must fit at least one of the three subdivisions of Rule 23(b). Just as opponents often argue the absence of all four prerequisites under 23(a), proponents often argue that all three subdivisions of 23(b) are satisfied, so that it is not uncommon for every single provision of the Rule affecting certification to be at issue simultaneously! Proponents particularly want certification under subdivisions (b)(1) and (b)(2), because then, Rule 23 may not require notice to the class. Thus, if they succeed under these subdivisions, class attorneys may be able to avoid entirely the expense imposed by *Eisen v. Carlisle & Jacquelin, supra.* And in some cases they may even succeed in preventing class members from opting out and thus ensure a larger group of captive clients.

CHAPTER 7

DISCOVERY AND DISCLOSURE

§ 7.01 The Objectives, Policies and Planning of Discovery

[A] Objectives of Discovery

The Importance of Discovery to a Trial Lawyer. The discovery phase of a modern lawsuit consumes more time, effort, expense and energy than any other phase. The tendency of lawyers to leave no stonc unturned, a lawyer's adversarial resistance to sharing harmful information, fear of failure in court, and the nature of the discovery rules themselves, all contribute to this phenomenon. Critics of the current system identify excessive and abusive discovery and unjustified resistance to proper discovery as major problems. In an adversary system, the purposes for which attorneys use discovery may include some or all of the following:

Purpose No. 1: Finding Out about the Lawsuit. The first and most obvious purpose of discovery is to find out everything possible about the transaction or occurrence that is at the heart of the lawsuit. If, during a deposition, an attorney finds out that the opposing party admits to having driven 5 miles per hour in excess of the speed limit, the attorney probably has advanced toward winning the suit. But note that the strategy is not limited to the discovery of helpful information. If the opposing party's contention is that the client ran a red light, the attorney will try to discover this claimed fact also. Having discovered it, he or she can consider how to explain, qualify, limit, or destroy the contention. Thus the attorney seeks to discover unfavorable as well as favorable information.

Purpose No. 2: "Freezing" the Harmful Evidence. A second function of discovery is to "freeze" the testimony of harmful witnesses. Does the opposing party claim that the plaintiff was traveling at 5 miles per hour in excess of the speed limit? In that event, the opponent will have difficulty if she testifies at trial that the plaintiff was going "at least seventy." The deposition does not prevent such a change in testimony, but it can be used to impeach the credibility of the witness if she testifies contrary to it. For this reason, skillful litigators are adept at getting deposition witnesses to give detailed answers.

Purpose No. 3: Preserving Evidence or Putting It in Usable Form. A third purpose of discovery is to put useful evidence in a form admissible at trial or in pretrial hearings. Let us say, for example, that the plaintiff's principal expert witness has written the plaintiff's attorney a letter summarizing the findings made after examining the product that is the subject of the action. The expert's schedule is such that she will not be available for trial, and it is permissible under applicable law to use a deposition as a substitute for the expert's live testimony. Under these circumstances, the letter itself is not admissible in evidence (it would be excluded as hearsay). The plaintiff may wish to take the expert's deposition — not to discover information this time, and not to freeze the expert's testimony, but simply because the deposition, unlike the letter, will be admissible at trial.

Purpose No. 4: Deliberately Abusive Discovery. Discovery may also be used in an abusive manner. In the right kind of case, most skillful litigators would be able to write interrogatories within an hour that could cost tens of thousands of dollars to answer. Even if the information sought is relevant and not privileged, the discovering party's objective may be to expose sensitive information or to impose unnecessary costs. By the same token, various methods can be used to shield discoverable information from discovery or to increase the cost of obtaining it. This conduct generally is improper, but if you are to understand the process, you must recognize that discovery sometimes is used or resisted for abusive reasons.

PROBLEM A: CHAPTER 7 SUMMARY PROBLEM

PAYNE v. WEST YORK HERALD-TRIBUNE: A PROBLEM RELATING TO DISCOVERY SCOPE, METHODOLOGY, SANCTIONS AND USAGE. Plaintiff John Payne has filed a diversity suit against the *West York Herald-Tribune*, alleging that the newspaper libeled him. His complaint alleges that the newspaper carried a story falsely reporting that Payne "acted as a bribe collector for certain West York politicians." The story was written by a reporter named Rob Woodwind, who relied upon statements by two individuals to whom he promised anonymity. The newspaper company's answer asserts that the report was true, denies its falsity, and denies that the newspaper acted negligently, with knowledge of the statement's falsity or reckless disregard for its falsity.

After the Rule 26(f) conference was conducted, Payne sought to discover "the identities of any persons who furnished information upon which the story about Payne allegedly was based." Payne also has requested production of "any written statement of or concerning any person who allegedly supplied any fact tending to show that Payne acted as a bribe collector, whether obtained before or after the filing of suit." The newspaper company desires to avoid producing any of these items, and reporter Woodwind states that he "never" will disclose his confidential sources, "no matter what happens to me or to the newspaper." Consider the following questions:

1. Is the requested information within the scope of discovery?
2. Is any of the information covered by provisions codifying the "work product" doctrine, and if so, can the plaintiff satisfy the conditions for obtaining it?
3. What other methods or doctrines can the newspaper company invoke in an effort to obtain protection, and what are its chances of success?
4. What sanctions might be imposed if the *Herald-Tribune* refuses to disclose any of the information requested: (1) before being ordered to do so by the court, or (2) after the court has ordered full responses?
5. Formulate a full plan for all discovery by the plaintiff in such a case. (Assume, for this purpose, that the interrogatory and the request quoted here have not yet been propounded.)
6. Describe the initial and expert disclosures that would be required by each party and compute the latest possible date for filing the initial ones (not easy to do

— you will need to cross-reference Rules 26(a), 26(f), and 16(b)). Assume that the suit was filed less that a month ago and was answered on the first day of the month in which you solve this problem.

[B] The Policies Behind Broad Discovery — and the Limits

Modern Discovery Is Broad in Scope. Federal Rule 26 generally extends to any matter that is "relevant to any party's claim or defense." Further, the court may order discovery of any matter relevant to the subject matter involved in the action "[f]or good cause." Rule 26 also provides that "[r]elevant information need not be admissible at the trial if the discovery appears reasonably calculated to lead to the discovery of admissible evidence." Fed. R. Civ. P. 26(b)(1). It may be perfectly permissible, for example, for a party to discover hearsay information or witness speculation, even if it will be excluded at trial.

The Purposes of Broad Discovery. Broad discovery, it is often said, makes the adversary process a better instrument for arriving at the truth. It decreases "Perry Mason" tactics and it discourages trial by ambush. It provides each party with greater knowledge about the case, and thus it arguably leads to fairer trials and, probably, to a higher proportion of disputes settled without trial. The latter result is sometimes said to be reflected in a more efficient system of justice, although this point is the subject of considerable debate.

Limits on the Scope of Discovery. Nevertheless, there are limits. First, the information may be so remote that its likelihood of turning up admissible evidence is marginal. In such a case, some courts might conclude that the information is not "reasonably calculated" to lead to the discovery of admissible evidence (or not "relevant"). Second, the information may be privileged, in which event it is exempted from discovery not because it is irrelevant to the issues, but on policy grounds. For example, the attorney-client privilege shields most confidential communications between attorney and client from discovery, even though they are highly relevant to the action. Third, the trial judge has discretion to impose limits on discovery to shield a person from embarrassment or undue expense. *See* Fed. R. Civ. P. 26(c) (protective orders).

The expense, burden, and intrusiveness of discovery have led to other kinds of limits, too. The Federal Rules now limit the number of written interrogatories, the number of depositions, and the length of depositions. *See* Fed. R. Civ. P. 30(d)(1) ("a deposition is limited to 1 day of 7 hours") and 33 (written interrogatories may not exceed 25, including "all discrete subparts," per party "[u]nless otherwise stipulated or ordered by the court"). Some courts require conferences or plans early in the case. And some assign each case to particular discovery "levels" or limits, based on complexity or amount in controversy.

The "Broad-versus-Narrow-Discovery" Controversy has a long history and is still ongoing. Ironically, in criminal cases, there is far less formal discovery than in civil cases — yet this fact does not seem to decrease the incidence of settlement without trial in criminal cases, and it is difficult to assert that criminal trials are less fair or accurate than civil ones as a result. The aims of discovery, then, are simply ultimate goals that the rules may, or may not, actually achieve. *See* G. Hazard, *Discovery Vices and Trans-Substantive Virtues in the Federal Rules of Civil Procedure*, in *Symposium*, 137 U. Pa. L. Rev. 1873 (1989).

[C] The Discovery Tools and the Concept of Required Disclosures

The following discovery mechanisms are provided for in the Federal Rules of Civil Procedure. Similar mechanisms have been adopted in the vast majority of states.

Oral Depositions (and Other Kinds of Depositions). Depositions are questions asked of a witness before trial, answered under oath in the presence of a court reporter, with opposing parties having the right to be present and ask questions also. (The term is also used to describe the session at which questions are asked and answered.) This type of discovery may be used both as to party and non-party witnesses. It is set up by a written notice to all other parties and, for a non-party witness, issuance of a subpoena. Depositions are usually the most effective means for obtaining useful information from adverse witnesses because the examiner may ask follow-up questions in the event of evasion.

As an alternative to the oral deposition, a party may send written questions to a person authorized to administer a written deposition to the deponent. The other side may, in response, file cross-questions. The "deposition on written questions" is a weak form of discovery for several reasons, including the fact that the deposition officer cannot revise the questions or ask follow-up questions. Its most frequent use is for authentication of documents.

Another alternative is the "deposition to perpetuate testimony." If a person expects to be a party to a lawsuit that has not yet been filed, and wishes to depose a witness now, she may petition a court for allowance of a deposition to perpetuate that witness' testimony. The court may do so if it finds that a failure of justice will otherwise occur.

Subpoena Duces Tecum; Production from Nonparties. The witness may be ordered to produce documents at the deposition by a subpoena duces tecum (literally meaning, "bring with you"). Amended Rule 45 now allows the subpoena to be used for third-party document production alone, without any deposition.

Written Interrogatories to Parties. Interrogatories are written questions directed by one party to another, to be answered under oath. Because this discovery device allows the opponent leisure to consider her response, and because opposing counsel generally determines the form of the answers, responses are frequently evasive, and thus interrogatories are not an effective method for obtaining controversial information from an adverse party. However, interrogatories may be an inexpensive way to acquire basic, background information, to establish the positions of opposing parties on some kinds of factual issues, and to identify dates, documents, witnesses and similar information. (Note that interrogatories may be directed to parties only. Written discovery from non-party witnesses must be obtained by the similar but separate mechanism of the deposition on written questions.)

Requests for Admission. A party opponent may be requested to admit or deny factual propositions submitted to her. This kind of discovery is useful for eliminating issues about which there is no real dispute.

Requests to Produce or Inspect (for Discovering Documents, Tangible Things or Realty). The request to produce constitutes the basic method for obtaining discovery of documents and other tangible things from other parties to the action. Under the request procedure, a party sends to another party a written request listing the documents, tangible things or realty she wishes to photograph, copy or inspect. (For nonparties, the appropriate device is a subpoena (see above).) Carlisle, *Nonparty Document Discovery From Corporations and Governmental Entities Under the Federal Rules of Civil Procedure*, 32 N.Y.L. Sch. L. Rev. 9 (1987).

Motions for Physical or Mental Examinations. Upon a motion showing good cause, the court may order the physical or mental examination of a person whose condition is in controversy.

Opposing Discovery: Objections and Motions for Protective Orders. A person who is the target of a discovery effort who thinks the requests are not allowed by the Rules can object and obtain a court ruling on the issue. And even if the Rules do not prohibit the discovery request, the discoveree may invoke the court's discretion by a motion for a protective order. Upon motion by a party or by the person from whom discovery is sought, and for good cause, the court may protect the movant from harassment, embarrassment, oppression or undue burden or expense, by making a protective order limiting discovery.

The Concept of Required, Self-Initiated Disclosures. Rule 26 requires all parties to make (1) "Initial Disclosures" "at or within 14 days after the parties' Rule 26(f) conference," which itself must be held "as soon as practicable — and in any event at least 21 days before a scheduling conference is held or a scheduling order is due under Rule 16(b)"; (2) "Disclosure of Expert Testimony" "at least 90 days before the date set for trial or for the case to be ready for trial," or if the expert testimony "is intended solely to contradict or rebut evidence on the same subject matter identified by another party under Rule 26(a)(2)(B), within 30 days after the other party's disclosure"; and (3) "Pretrial Disclosures" of fact witnesses and exhibits "at least 30 days before trial." In each instance, the rule describes the required information. The key feature of these disclosure requirements, however, is that they are automatically imposed on the party, without the need for any request. *See generally* W. Brazil, *The Adversary Character of Civil Discovery: A Critique and Proposals for Change*, 31 Vand. L. Rev. 1348 (1978); W. Schwarzer, *The Federal Rules, the Adversary Process, and Discovery Reform*, 50 U. Pitt. L. Rev. 703, 721-23 (1989).

[D] Basics of Discovery Planning

"Waves" of Discovery. The discovery phase of the litigation begins after the parties conduct a Rule 26(f) conference in order to develop a proposed discovery plan and to make or arrange for the disclosures required by Rule 26(a)(1). These disclosures include the name, address, and telephone number of each individual likely to have discoverable information that supports the claims or defenses of the disclosing party; a copy or description by category and location of all documents, electronically stored information, and tangible things in the possession, custody, or control of the disclosing party and that may be used to support the disclosing party's claims and defenses; the computation of any category of damages claimed by the disclosing party, and a copy of any liability insurance policy that may be available to satisfy part or all of the judgment that may be entered in the action. These disclosures must be made within 14 days after the Rule 26(f) conference, unless a different time is set by stipulation or court order, or unless a party objects during the discovery conference and states the party's objection in the Rule 26(f) discovery plan.

Typically, the discovery plan developed by the parties at the Rule 26(f) conference will not go into great detail concerning the use of the discovery tools or the sequence in which they will be used by the parties. Regardless of the approach taken by particular judges or local rules about the scope of the discovery plan and the court's Rule 16(b) scheduling order, the "second wave" of discovery will usually consist of interrogatories to obtain basic information not covered by the Rule 26(a)(1) disclosures. For example, interrogatories may be used to ask the other party to identify persons having knowledge of relevant facts other than those individuals who will be used to support the other party's claims and defenses; the identity and location of documents, other than those used to support the other party's claims and defenses, that are relevant or will lead to relevant evidence; the identity and location of other potential parties to the suit; whether the defendant has been sued in the correct name, and to ask the other party to explain contentions alleged generally in the party's pleadings, among other things.

Once the basics are established by disclosures and answers to interrogatories, the next or "third wave" of discovery, frequently consisting of requests for document production, will be conducted. While human testimony may vary, documents contain what they contain, and they are useful to have available when one takes depositions. The "fourth wave" may be depositions of witnesses or parties who know about the transaction at issue. These depositions may lead to a fifth or sixth wave of discovery, consisting of additional interrogatories, document requests, or other depositions. Finally, a request for admissions may be used as a last step in the discovery process to eliminate issues that the discovery process has shown to be undisputed and to authenticate documents to be introduced at trial.

Fitting the Discovery to the Case. Cost considerations affect and limit discovery strategy in every law suit. An automobile accident with minor injuries may justify only a brief deposition or two, if even that. An antitrust case, on the other hand, may easily call for the expenditure of hundreds of thousands of dollars in attorneys' fees for discovery.

PROBLEM B

USING THE DISCOVERY DEVICES. What device or devices might enable you to obtain each of the following items or information? Which of the following items or information would be disclosed in self-initiated disclosures? Explain.

(a) Information related to the plaintiff's medical expenses in a personal injury suit for personal injuries, including such matters as the doctors she consulted, the amount of money she paid and the treatment she underwent. You represent the defendant.

(b) The bank statements or cancelled checks of the plaintiff for these expenditures.

(c) In an action on a contract, the genuineness of the copy of the contract in your client's possession, which you wish to establish for trial.

(d) In a suit over an automobile accident, the opposing party's version of facts surrounding the accident.

(e) Records maintained by an automobile repair shop, which is not a party to the suit, concerning the condition of the brakes of the automobile driven by the opposing party.

PROBLEM C

RESPONDING TO DISCOVERY REQUESTS. What would you consider doing in each of the following situations?

(a) In an antitrust case, your opponent subjects your client to interrogatories which, although relevant to the issue of damages, would require disclosure of the names and addresses of all your client's customers, your client's method of doing business, and the process by which your client's product is made.

(b) In a contract action for loss of profits, your opponent seeks production of all your client's income tax records, claiming that they are relevant to the issue of damages.

(c) Your opponent seeks production from your client of "all documents produced as a result of any investigation by you or your attorneys of the accident upon which this suit is founded."

Morris, STRATEGY OF DISCOVERY

*18 For the Defense 83 (1977)**

[The following outline gives the author's suggestions for the planning of discovery in the defense of a medical malpractice case. You should consider the extent to which it is applicable to other kinds of cases. How, for example, would these approaches have to be adapted if you represented the plaintiff in a medical malpractice case? What about an automobile negligence case in which the damages were small? What about an antitrust case? — Eds.]

I. INTRODUCTION

Discovery for the defense begins with the defense — not with thc plaintiff

For it is the law that determines

(1) What facts are needed

(2) What form these facts must take to be admissible

Ideally — defense counsel should know as much about the law of his case before starting discovery as after conclusion of the appeal

II. THE LAW OF THE CASE

A. *Ways to achieve*

(1) Review the petition and the file and resolve — in your own mind — the legal issues

(2) Review your experiences re trials of similar cases — what were the issues. . . .

(3) Review the experience of others in similar cases

(a) *Reported cases* [Morris suggests reading not only the opinions, but also such sources as briefs and records.]

(b) *Unreported cases* [Morris suggests talking to lawyers and judges in such cases.]

B. *Purpose*

(1) *Define the issues*

(a) *re negligence*. . . .

(b) *re responsibility*

Who else involved

By what legal route:

---

* Copyright © 1969. Reprinted with the permission of the Practicing Law Institute and the author. The format has been changed in some respects to fit this book better.

[Morris suggests consideration of such diverse theories as the "captain of the ship" doctrine, administrative negligence, joint venture, etc.]

(2) *Delineate proof needed*

(a) *re substance*

Contractual relationships between the parties

Actual relationship between the parties

Representations to the patient

(b) *re form.* . . .

III. DISCOVERY OF DEFENSE

"Know thyself"

— as completely as possible

Rules of Thumb

Rule 1: Assume nothing — Take nothing for granted; cross-check everything and everyone including time-honored assumptions

Rule 2: Be resourceful. . . .

Rule 3: Be thorough. . . .

Rule 4: Preserve evidence — As you go, record: identifying information, serial numbers, etc.

A. *Primary sources* (of the fact)

(1) *Records involved*

1. *The hospital record (patient's medical chart)* covering the event in question

(a) Is your copy *complete* — *Caveat*: You must know the format for any hospital records: admission sheet, admitting history and physical, doctor order sheets, lab sheets, nurse's notes, etc.

(b) Is your copy *legible* — *Caveat*: What you can't read may be vital

(c) *Understanding your copy*

1. Lay out chronologically — not easy to do

2. Get doctor to explain significance — of all recorded events; of all missing events

2. *Accessory Records* [These include Emergency Room, Out-Patient, Physiotherapy, Clinic, Pathology, and Autopsy Records.]

3. *Records behind the records*

Original entries in original books from which hospital records are made up:

(a) *Laboratory*: [including work notebooks, logs, and routing slips]

(b) *Pathology*: [including work notebooks, slides, paraffin blocks, and amputated parts]

(c) *Operating Room*: [including log schedules, material schedules, and financial charges]

(d) *Equipment & Supplies*: [including purchase orders, maintenance and service, and financial charges]

(e) *Financial records*: [oxygen given, R.N. service, etc.]

(f) *X-ray*: [films, therapy dosage, and charts]

(g) *Doctors' notes*: [Summaries, etc. (if any)]

4. *Legal records*

Caveat: Probably privileged from discovery by plaintiffs. *Sierra Vista Hospital v. Superior Court of California* (Ct. App. 1967), 56 Cal. Rptr. 387 [Hospital's incident report privileged from plaintiff's discovery]; *Brown v. Superior Court* (Dist. Ct. App. 1963) 32 Cal. Rptr. 527 [Malpractice Committee Review of case privileged from plaintiff's discovery.]

(a) Incident report

(b) Correspondence and file, etc.

5. *Medical investigating records reviewing case — Caveat*: Probably privileged from discovery by plaintiffs. *Judd v. Park Avenue Hospital* (Sup. Ct. N.Y.), 235 N.Y.S.2d 843, *aff'd*, 235 N.Y.S.2d 1023 ["any and all medical staff discussions and meetings of committees" privileged from plaintiff's discovery.]

(a) *Hospital review committees* [Tissue, Disciplinary, and Mortality committees, etc.]

(b) *Outside committees. . . .*

Comment: Probably privileged from discovery by anyone but may have been published anonymously and can be recognized from factual situation [citations omitted].

(c) *Medical literature*

Comment: Occasionally a doctor will have published (before suit filed) an article on the case at bar itself because of its scientific interest. Check medical literature under authors for doctors' names involved and under subject matter involved from year of incident to date. [*E.g.*,] *Rizzo, Admrx, etc. v. American Cyanamid Co. et al.*, (Common Pleas Ct., Cuyahoga County, Ohio, Docket No. 748722) [Death from allergic reaction to Kynex; prior to suit being filed one of defendant doctors published article about the very case: JAMA, 172: 155-57 (1-9-60) *Fatal Thrombocytopenic Purpura after Administration of Sulfamethoxpyridazine*].

6. *Regulations applicable*

(a) *Joint Commission on Accreditation* — Was hospital accredited; If so, when last inspected; report on inspection and recommendations; Compliance by hospital with recommendations

(b) *Hospital's own regulations* [including Constitution, Bylaws, Minutes of Trustees meetings or Medical Counsel, departmental rules, nursing rules]

(c) *Handbooks* [Nursing and operating procedures]

(d) *Standing orders of doctors* — especially defendant doctor

(2) *Personnel involved*

Each must be identified; each must be interviewed

1. *Identify*

(a) *Operating room*

— Everyone present at any time

Prima facie: Surgeon, 1st Asst. Surgeon (resident), 2nd Asst. Surgeon (intern), Anesthesiologist (including all replacement doctors), Asst. Anesthesiologist . . . , Instrument or scrub nurse, Circulating nurse. *Perhaps also present*: Family doctor, Teams of specialists [heart-lung specialists, etc.], Observers [including doctors, students, and patient's family]

(b) *Laboratories*: Head of department, all technicians doing the lab work, all who had personal contact with the patient.

(c) *Nursing and Room Care*

(1) *Hospital Personnel*

Registered Nurses: Supervisor of floor, all R.N.'s on duty, all R.N.'s seeing patient

Licensed Practical Nurses: All seeing patient

Nurse's aides: All seeing patient

Orderlies: Any involved

(2) *Non-hospital Personnel*: Registered nurse, licensed practical nurses, friends and relatives rendering aid

(3) *Roommates*: Get addresses from financial records. . . .

(4) *Visitors*: Family, friends, relations, priest, social workers, etc.

Comment: Check hospital nurse's notes, financial records, and registry of nurses, etc. to locate above

(d) *Medical Care*: Attending physician [including replacement attending physician]; consultants; family doctor; specialists; residents; interns; Any doctor anywhere in hospital records, including nurse's notes, doctor's order sheets, etc.

(e) *Special Departments*: Check all personnel on duty or seeing patient Examples: Physiotherapy Department, X-ray Department, Emergency Room, Out-Patient Clinics, etc.

2. *Interview*

(a) Refresh their recollections — from hospital records, etc.

(b) Commit to writing — even if negative statement

(c) Inquire re collateral sources — which may lead to other evidence

(d) Get permanent address — for later location, including future plans

(e) Ask if they ever gave statement to plaintiffs

(f) Advise need not talk to plaintiff's side if don't want to and contact you if approached

(g) Qualifications: All education, all positions held, professional associations, honors, Board-certified in specialty

(h) All scientific writings by each

(i) Who they recommend to you as expert in their field

(j) Medical theories of case — theirs; others they know about

(k) Make them "level" with you re unpleasant facts about case or about themselves you should know

— "cross-examine" them on this

— any colleagues who hate them

3. *Investigate*

(a) *Personnel file*

— Review re each employee of hospital in question

— Review re each doctor on staff. . . .

(b) *Talk to colleagues*

— re general reputation of personnel in question

— re specific incident

4. *Equipment involved*

(a) *Identify*: locate, examine, get copy of instructional manual

Record: Serial number, model number, type number, manufacturer's name

(b) *Preserve* (for trial): perhaps photograph; allow no changes

(c) *Investigate*: Purchase records, maintenance records, outside service records, adaptations and changes records, performance records, installation records

(d) *Collateral Investigation*

— State of art of manufacturer at time installed

— Safety features on other makes not on this one

— Later safety features for this one since manufacture but before incident which might have been installed before incident

(e) *Testing*: Have expert examine and test re alleged incident and re its maintenance status

(f) *Scene of Accident*: Operating room, etc. (1) Inspect it yourself; (2) Prepare scale diagram, etc.; (3) Photograph

(g) *Third-party suits*: Discovery may reveal others owing hospital indemnity (1) Manufacturers of defective equipment; (2) Suppliers of drugs; (3) Independent contractor actors [anesthesiologists, etc.]

B. *Secondary Sources* (before the fact; after the fact)

(1) *Before the fact*

1. Hospital's experience re this type of incident: re legal "notice" to hospital; re causes

2. Hospital's experience re this type of equipment: re notice; re modifications

3. Hospital experience re this personnel

— *quality* — prior training, prior experience, record in general, colleagues' opinions

— *quantity* — how much experience with this operation, etc. (a) Has hospital had; (b) Has this surgeon had. . . .

(2) *After the fact*

What changes have occurred since this incident which bear on this incident — In practice, in procedure, in rules and regulations, in personnel, in equipment, etc.

C. *Collateral Sources*

Comment: All versions must be checked against independent expert sources to ascertain probable medical truth of matter.

(1) *Experts*

(a) *Quality* — the best obtainable

(b) *Quantity* — at least two in each specialty to check on each other

(c) *Review* — Careful review of all important known data and full hospital records by each expert

(2) *Medical and Scientific literature*: Check it yourself

(a) *Re medicine* — medical library articles and texts

(b) *Re drugs* — Manufacturer's brochure; Physicians Desk Reference; Pharmacology texts; pharmacologist; medical literature

(c) *Re equipment* — manufacturer's brochure, scientific texts and journals, scientific experts

IV. DISCOVERY OF THE PLAINTIFF

Comment: Now that you "know thyself" you are ready for discovery into plaintiff's case

A. *Discovery is discovery* — no magic; same as any other lawsuit

(1) *Interrogatories*

Cover all hospital admissions birth to date

Include hospital of birth and all doctors, medications, illnesses, etc.

(2) *Depositions*

(a) Plaintiff-patient especially re alleged verbal admissions by defendants and others

(b) All relatives and friends seeing patient in the hospital

(3) *All Hospital Records* — a gold mine

Birth to death whether relevant or not

All admissions — all Emergency and Out-patient Departments

B. *Check on plaintiff's version*

(1) With all doctors and hospital personnel

(2) Investigators: Neighborhood checks, etc.

C. *Ascertain plaintiff's experts and their theory of case*

(1) *Discovery*

(a) interrogatories

(b) motions to produce [citation omitted]

(c) snooping — gossip

(d) ask your doctors who likely

(e) pre-trial hearings

(2) *Check on plaintiff's expert*

(a) ask other doctors

(b) research literature for his articles

(c) ask local academy re his qualifications

(d) text of medical specialists

D. *Physical examinations of plaintiff*

(a) Re recovery and present status

(b) Re causation and etiology

(c) Thorough: all experts necessary; all tests necessary — chromosome studies, allergy studies, X-ray studies, physical exam, laboratory studies, etc.

Comment: Generally, plaintiff's deposition should wait until after defense's discovery of defense is complete. *Reason*: Operative facts are highly medical and beyond knowledge of plaintiff and within knowledge of defendants — unlike auto accident case, etc.

However: Occasionally, defendant's discovery must begin with plaintiff and plaintiff's witnesses. *Examples*: (1) Plaintiff's claim Emergency Room treatment — yet defendant hospital has no record of same [citation omitted]. (2) Plaintiff claims an R.N. injured his sciatic nerve with I-M injection of medicine and hospital records shows many shots — which does he blame [citation omitted]?

V. CONCLUSION

Suits against hospitals fall into two main categories

(1) Complicated medical situations — operating room accidents, etc.

(2) Very simple factual situations — fall out of bed; hot water bottle burns, etc.

Above format especially important re category (1); category (2) may proceed with discovery of plaintiff first

But in both (1) and (2) No substitute for full discovery of defendant and of plaintiff

Thorough and painstaking discovery and preparation is [the] keynote of success. . . .

NOTES AND QUESTIONS

(1) *Beginning the Discovery Plan.* Why should discovery by the defense "begin with the defense"? What is the strategic reason for doing so? What is the reason for beginning "not with the facts, but the law"? Is this really "discovery"?

(2) *The Volume of Paper Discovery.* In a suit involving a "complicated medical situation," as the author puts it, how many documents would you guess might be generated by discovery? Note that the number might be increased by the existence of multiple defendants, cross-claims, addition of claims based on products liability, etc. What problems would be created by the sheer number of documents, and how would the lawyers solve these problems?

(3) *Interviewing (Versus Deposing) Cooperative Witnesses.* The author says, "persons involved . . . each must be interviewed." Why "interviewed," rather than deposed?

(4) *The Breadth of the "Relevance" Concept in Discovery.* Why should interrogatories to the plaintiff "cover all hospital admissions, birth to date"? Will a plaintiff willingly comply with a request for such information in all cases? What does the author mean by suggesting that the plaintiff's hospital records, which he calls a "gold mine," be sought "birth to death whether relevant or not"?

(5) *Verifying the Client's Version.* Why must "all versions" — including, presumably, your client's version and versions of those friendly to your client — be "checked against independent expert sources to ascertain probable medical truth"? Can't a lawyer assume that her client is telling her the truth?

(6) *The Cost of Discovery.* What would be the cost of investigation and discovery in a case involving a "complicated medical situation"? What sort of financial resources would the plaintiff's lawyers have to possess in such a case, and why? Could discovery this thorough be done if the injuries are minor (a case in which potential damages are perhaps $10,000)? Is it possible the defense might engage in discovery that would cause the plaintiff to expend many times the $10,000 potentially at stake in such a case? What does this possibility suggest about the way that discovery rules should be written or interpreted?

(7) *Privileges and Discovery Limits.* Note the reference to defense material that may be "privileged," such as internal incident reports, review committee documents and the like. Why would the plaintiff want to obtain such documents? [Note: the plaintiff will want them irrespective of whether they contain admissible evidence.] What sort of financial difference might it make to the plaintiff's attorney if such documents are privileged? Why should they be privileged?

(8) *Theoretical Treatment of this Process: Tillers & Schum, A Theory of Preliminary Fact Investigation, 24 U.C. Davis L. Rev. 931 (1991).* Tillers and Schum describe the process of "marshalling" information to construct, refine and "coarsen" hypotheses according to various organizing strategies. They also describe how scenarios can be used to generate further hypotheses (or to eliminate them). The complexity of the article is such that it is not for the faint of heart, but it shows how a good lawyer conducting discovery would simultaneously follow multiple tracks and develop further tracks.

§ 7.02 The Scope of Discovery

Read Fed. R. Civ. P. 26(b)(1)-(2) (basic scope of discovery).

[A] The Discovery "Relevance" Standard: Information "Reasonably Calculated" to Lead to the Discovery of Admissible Evidence

KERR v. DISTRICT COURT, 511 F.2d 192 (9th Cir.), *aff'd*, 426 U.S. 394 (1976). You should read (or re-read) this case, which appears in § 1.06 of Chapter 1, above. The plaintiffs were California prison inmates who sued to have certain claimed procedural rights recognized in parole proceedings. Through interrogatories and requests for production, they sought extensive personnel files, internal memoranda and other information from the parole authority. The defendants argued that the information was not relevant, was privileged, and should be subjected to a protective order. The District Court granted the discovery. The appellate court denied mandamus, holding the materials were "relevant" in that, by showing the qualifications of parole personnel, the plaintiffs might be able to enhance their arguments for procedural reform.

BANK OF THE ORIENT v. SUPERIOR COURT, 67 Cal. App. 3d 588, 136 Cal. Rptr. 741 (1977). San Francisco Federal Savings Association sued Bank of the Orient, claiming that the Bank had permitted one of the Association's branch managers to deposit unauthorized checks in his personal account at the Bank and, further, had negligently permitted him to withdraw, and thereby embezzle, the funds. During the course of discovery, the Bank sought to obtain production of a report by an accounting firm (the "Coopers & Lybrand report") commissioned by the Association's board of directors two days after the discovery of the embezzlement, as well as a special audit committee report entitled "Suggestions for Improvement to Our System of Internal Control." Both reports contained details of the manner in which the embezzlement occurred and discussed weaknesses in the Association's internal auditing procedures.

The Association claimed that the reports were not discoverable. Among other grounds, it relied on § 1151 of the California Evidence Code, which provides that subsequent remedial measures are not admissible in evidence to prove fault: "When, after the occurrence of an event, remedial or precautionary measures are taken, which, if taken previously, would have tended to make the event less likely to occur, evidence of such subsequent remedial measures is inadmissible to prove negligence or culpable conduct in connection with the event." The provision is designed to prevent a person from being disadvantaged by having taken corrective measures, as well as to prevent confusion of the issues and undue prejudice before the jury (which might attach excessive importance to such evidence).

The District Court of Appeal, however, held that the reports were discoverable, even though they might not be admissible in evidence. They were "relevant" in the discovery sense because they obviously were reasonably calculated to lead to admissible evidence, even if not admissible themselves:

Evidence Code section 1151 [does not] provide support for [the Association's] refusal to produce documents or to answer questions related thereto. . . . [T]he section is a prohibition on the admissibility of evidence at trial. It does not purport to limit the scope of discovery. . . .

We conclude that the refusal of the [trial] court to compel production of the Coopers & Lybrand report and the document entitled "Suggestions for Improvement to Our System of Internal Control" was an abuse of discretion. . . .

NOTES AND QUESTIONS

(1) *Breadth of Discovery Relevance* As a result of amendments made in 2000 (and restyled in 2007), the general scope of discovery relevance was changed from "any matter, not privileged, that is relevant to the subject matter involved in the pending action," to "any nonprivileged matter that is relevant to any party's claim or defense." For good cause, the court may order discovery of any matter relevant to the subject matter involved in the action. Fed. R. Civ. P. 26(b)(1). The change was made to blunt attempts by some parties to justify overbroad discovery requests "that sweep far beyond the claims and defenses of the parties." Fed. R. Civ. P. 26(b)(1), cmt. In *Oppenheimer Fund, Inc. v. Sanders*, 437 U.S. 340, 353-54 (1978), the Supreme Court explained that the earlier "subject matter" phrase "has been construed broadly to encompass any matter that bears on, or that reasonably could lead to other matter that could bear on, any issue that is or may be in the case . . . ." In effect, under the "subject matter" relevance standard, the outer boundaries of discovery relevance is less than clear. The amendments generally conform the discovery relevance standard to the standard contained in the Federal Rules of Evidence. *See* Fed. R. Evid. 401-403. As summarized by one federal court, "[Although Rule 26] does not specifically explain the difference in scope between discovery relevant to 'claims and defenses' in the litigation, and discovery relevant to the 'subject matter,' it is clear that the former is intended to be narrower than the latter, and that the broader discovery is only to be allowed for 'good cause.'" *Thompson v. Department of Housing & Urban Development*, 199 F.R.D. 168, 171 (D. Md. 2001).

(2) *Depth of Discovery Relevance: Jampole v. Touchy, 673 S.W.2d 569 (Tex. 1984).* The *Kerr* case indicates that compliance can be an expensive and extremely disadvantageous proposition. The *Jampole* case is another illustration, in another context. The suit was for actual and punitive damages arising when a 1976 Vega automobile caught fire in a collision. The plaintiff sought a variety of documents relating to GM automobiles over a twelve-year span. The trial court limited the discovery to similar models over a shorter year span. The state supreme court reversed this "unduly restrictive" approach: the "feasibility of alternative designs" is germane to such a claim, and "[w]hether a safer fuel system design suitable for one vehicle is adaptable to another . . . is a question to be decided by the trier of fact." How much did it cost GMC to produce alternative design information for GMC passenger cars for 1967-79? This case illustrates the problems of discovery "depth" (*i.e.*, the number of documents requested of a given kind) as well as breadth (*i.e.*, the number of different kinds of documents). Many lawyers consider the "depth" problem a more serious issue than the "breadth" problem.

(3) *Relevance of Burden on the Party from Whom Discovery is Sought: Bauer v. Huber, 127 Misc. 2d 672, 487 N.Y.S.2d 303 (Sup. Ct. 1985).* Does it make a difference that the information sought is sensitive or confidential even though it is not privileged? In *Bauer v. Huber, supra*, Bauer claimed lost earnings as damages. Huber sought to discover Bauer's income tax returns as relevant to his past earnings, and therefore to his future

earnings. The court said that discovery of tax returns is not favored, but it may be allowed when other sources are "unreliable, lacking, or overly burdensome." *Bauer v. Huber* thus implies that a balancing process is involved in making the initial discoverability determination. Under the federal rules, the burden on the person from whom discovery is sought is a consideration when a protective order is sought. *See* Fed. R. Civ. P. 26(c). Burdensomeness is also a part of the initial discovery calculus, which requires a consideration of whether "the burden or expense of the proposed discovery outweighs its likely benefit, considering the needs of the case, the amount in controversy, the parties' resources, the importance of the issues at stake in the action, and the importance of the discovery in resolving the issues." Fed. R. Civ. P. 26(b)(2)(C)(iii).

[B] The Relevance Standard for Self-Initiated Disclosures

NOTE ON THE STANDARD FOR DISCLOSURES

Rule 26(a)(1) says that "a party must, without awaiting a discovery request," disclose persons or documents likely to have information "that the disclosing party may use to support its claims or defenses, unless the use would be solely for impeachment . . . ." This provision differs from other forms of discovery in that no request is necessary, and is discussed in more detail later in this Chapter.

[C] Information That Is "Not Privileged"

On policy grounds, certain confidential communications are privileged in the sense that their disclosure cannot be compelled either at trial or during the discovery process. Rule 501 of the Federal Rules of Evidence provides that in civil actions where federal law governs, privilege in the federal courts is to "be governed by the principles of the common law as they may be interpreted by the courts of the United States in the light of reason and experience." Judge-made privileges at common law include the attorney-client privilege, the physician-patient privilege, the psychotherapist-patient privilege, and a privilege for spousal communications. In civil actions where state law governs, as in diversity cases, privilege is a matter of state law. Fed. R. Evid. 501. Many states have enacted statutory schemes that both codify and extend the cloak of privilege to communications in other contexts, including the physician-patient relationship, the relationship between clergy and parishioners, and the psychotherapist-patient relationship.

KERR v. DISTRICT COURT, 511 F.2d 192 (9th Cir.), *aff'd*, 426 U.S. 394 (1976). You should read (or re-read) this case which appears in § 1.06 of Chapter 1, above. Note that, although determined to be relevant, the information in question was not discoverable if it was privileged. The defendants claimed three different kinds of privilege — one of which, the common law privilege for confidential information kept by a governmental entity, remained potentially viable on remand.

UPJOHN CO. v. UNITED STATES
449 U.S. 383 (1981)

JUSTICE REHNQUIST delivered the opinion of the Court.

[This case involved the scope of the attorney-client privilege in the corporate context.

[Upjohn Co. was a pharmaceutical company which discovered in 1976 that one of its foreign subsidiaries had made "questionable payments" for the benefit of foreign governmental officials to gain business abroad. Upjohn decided to conduct an internal investigation, and its attorneys prepared a letter and questionnaire to "All Foreign General and Area Managers." The letter informed the addressees about the possibly illegal payments and named Gerald Thomas, "the company's General Counsel," as the head of the "highly confidential" investigation. The questionnaire sought detailed information about payments to foreign governmental officials. General Counsel Thomas received responses whereupon he and outside counsel interviewed the recipients of the questionnaire and 33 other Upjohn officers and employees.

[In 1976, Upjohn reported certain questionable payments to the Securities and Exchange Commission and to the Internal Revenue Service. The latter agency instituted an investigation and issued a summons demanding production of "written questionnaires sent to managers of the Upjohn Company's foreign affiliates, and memorandums or notes of the interviews conducted in the United States and abroad with officers and employees of the Upjohn Company and its subsidiaries."

[Upjohn declined to comply, and the government began an enforcement proceeding. The District Court determined that Upjohn had waived the attorney-client privilege by communicating the information so broadly to employees. On appeal, the Sixth Circuit rejected this conclusion but held that the privilege did not apply to "communications . . . made by officers and agents not responsible for directing Upjohn's actions in response to legal advice . . . for the simple reason that the communications were not the 'client's.' " The Sixth Circuit remanded the case for a determination of the persons responsible for determining the company's actions "in response to legal advice."

[The Supreme Court granted certiorari to address the scope of the attorney-client privilege.]

Federal Rule of Evidence 501 provides that "the privilege of a witness . . . shall be governed by the principles of the common law as they may be interpreted by the courts of the United States in light of reason and experience." The attorney-client privilege is the oldest of the privileges for confidential communications known to the common law. 8 J. Wigmore, *Evidence* § 2290 (McNaughton rev. 1961). Its purpose is to encourage full and frank communication between attorneys and their clients and thereby promote broader public interests in the observance of law and administration of justice. . . . Admittedly complications in the application of the privilege arise when the client is a corporation, which in theory is an artificial creature of the law, and not an individual; but this Court has assumed that the privilege applies when the client is a corporation . . . and the Government does not contest the general proposition.

The Court of Appeals, however, considered the application of the privilege in the corporate context to present a "different problem," since the client was an inanimate entity and "only the senior management, guiding and integrating the several operations . . . can be said to possess an identity analogous to the corporation as a whole." 600 F.2d, at 1226. The first case to articulate the so-called "control group test" adopted by the court below, *Philadelphia v. Westinghouse Electric Corp.*, 210 F. Supp. 483, 485 (E.D. Pa. [1961]) . . . reflected a similar conceptual approach:

> Keeping in mind that the question is, Is it the corporation which is seeking the lawyer's advice when the asserted privileged communication is made?, the most satisfactory solution, I think, is that if the employee making the communication . . . is in a position to control or even to take a substantial part in a decision about any action which the corporation may take upon the advice of the attorney, . . . then, in effect,

> *he is (or personifies) the corporation* when he makes his disclosure to the lawyer and the privilege would apply. (Emphasis supplied.)

Such a view, we think, overlooks the fact that the privilege exists to protect not only the giving of professional advice to those who can act on it but also the giving of information to the lawyer to enable him to give sound and informed advice. . . .

In the case of the individual client the provider of information and the person who acts on the lawyer's advice are one and the same. In the corporate context, however, it will frequently be employees beyond the control group . . . who will possess the information needed by the corporation's lawyers. Middle-level — and indeed lower-level — employees can, by actions within the scope of their employment, embroil the corporation in serious legal difficulties, and it is only natural that these employees would have the relevant information needed by corporate counsel if he is adequately to advise the client with respect to such actual or potential difficulties. . . .

The control group test adopted by the court below thus frustrates the very purpose of the privilege by discouraging the communication of relevant information by employees of the client to attorneys seeking to render legal advice to the client corporation. The attorney's advice will also frequently be more significant to noncontrol group members than to those who officially sanction the advice, and the control group test makes it more difficult to convey full and frank legal advice to the employees who will put into effect the client corporation's policy. . . .

. . . The test adopted by the court below is difficult to apply in practice, though no abstractly formulated and unvarying "test" will necessarily enable courts to decide questions such as this with mathematical precision. But if the purpose of the attorney-client privilege is to be served, the attorney and client must be able to predict with some degree of certainty whether particular discussions will be protected. An uncertain privilege, or one which purports to be certain but results in widely varying applications by the courts, is little better than no privilege at all. . . .

The communications in issue were made by Upjohn employees[8] for Upjohn acting as such to secure legal counsel. As the Magistrate found, "Mr. Thomas consulted with the Chairman of the Board and outside counsel and thereafter conducted a factual investigation to determine the nature and extent of the questionable payments *and to be in a position to give legal advice to the company with respect to the payments*." (Emphasis supplied.) . . . Information, not available from upper-echelon management, was needed to supply a basis for legal advice concerning compliance with securities and tax laws, foreign laws, currency regulations, duties to shareholders, and potential litigation in each of these areas. The communications concerned matters within the scope of the employees' corporate duties, and the employees themselves were sufficiently aware that they were being questioned in order that the corporation could obtain legal advice. The questionnaire identified Thomas as "the company's General Counsel" and referred in its opening sentence to the possible illegality of payments such as the ones on which information was sought. App. 40a. A statement of policy accompanying the questionnaire clearly indicated the legal implications of the investigation. The policy statement was issued "in

---

8 Seven of the eighty-six employees interviewed by counsel had terminated their employment with Upjohn at the time of the interview. App. 33a-38a. Petitioner argues that the privilege should nonetheless apply to communications by these former employees concerning activities during their period of employment. Neither the District Court nor the Court of Appeals had occasion to address this issue, and we decline to decide it without the benefit of treatment below.

order that there be no uncertainty in the future as to the policy with respect to the practices which are the subject of this investigation." It began "Upjohn will comply with all laws and regulations," and stated that commissions or payments "will not be used as a subterfuge for bribes or illegal payments" and that all payments must be "proper and legal." Any future agreements with foreign distributors or agents were to be approved "by a company attorney" and any questions concerning the policy were to be referred "to the company's General Counsel." *Id.*, at 1655a-1666a. This statement was issued to Upjohn employees worldwide, so that even those interviewees not receiving a questionnaire were aware of the legal implications of the interviews. Pursuant to explicit instructions from the Chairman of the Board, the communications were considered "highly confidential" when made, *id.*, at 39a, 43a, and have been kept confidential by the company. Consistent with the underlying purposes of the attorney-client privilege, these communications must be protected against compelled disclosure.

The privilege only protects disclosure of communications; it does not protect disclosure of the underlying facts by those who communicated with the attorney. . . . Here the Government was free to question the employees who communicated with Thomas and outside counsel. Upjohn has provided the IRS with a list of such employees, and the IRS has already interviewed some 25 of them. While it would probably be more convenient for the Government to secure the results of petitioner's internal investigation by simply subpoenaing the questionnaires and notes taken by petitioner's attorneys, such considerations of convenience do not overcome the policies served by the attorney-client privilege. . . .

Accordingly, the judgment of the Court of Appeals is reversed, and the case remanded for further proceedings.

NOTES AND QUESTIONS

(1) *Waiver.* The protections afforded by a particular statutory or common law privilege can be waived by a client in appropriate circumstances. As a general rule, the law will imply a waiver whenever the holder of the privilege voluntarily discloses or allows to be disclosed any significant part of the privileged matter. But what if the disclosure is inadvertent? One common topic discussed at legal seminars concerning discovery is whether waiver occurs in a case involving a multitude of documents when counsel or counsel's legal assistant includes some privileged documentary evidence in a response to a discovery request. *Compare Hercules, Inc. v. Exxon Corp.*, 434 F. Supp. 136 (D. Del. 1977) (no waiver when disclosure is inadvertent), *with Underwater Storage, Inc. v. United States Rubber Co.*, 314 F. Supp. 546, 549 (D.D.C. 1970) (inadvertent disclosure constitutes waiver). *See also* R. Marcus, *The Perils of the Privilege: Waiver and the Litigator*, 84 Mich. L. Rev. 1605 (1986). Rule 26(b)(5)(B) now addresses this issue, permitting a party who has produced information in discovery that is subject to a claim of privilege or work product to notify the recipient of this claim. Upon notice of such a claim, the recipient "must promptly return, sequester, or destroy the specified information and any copies it has . . . [and] must not use or disclose the information until the claim is resolved . . . ."

(2) *Assistants and Investigators.* It is also recognized generally that the attorney-client privilege extends to representatives of both the client (as in *Upjohn*) and the attorney. For example, in *Ballew v. State*, 640 S.W.2d 237 (Tex. Crim. App. 1982), the court recognized that confidential communications to a psychiatrist retained by an attorney were within the protection of the privilege.

(3) *Other Statutory Privileges.* As is indicated above, many states have statutory provisions for husband-wife, clergy-penitent, physician-patient, and psychotherapist-patient privileges. The privilege against self-incrimination is protected by the Constitution and has been asserted successfully in some civil cases. Other possible privileges include an accountant-client privilege, a news reporter's privilege, a social worker-client privilege, a privilege for trade secrets, and a privilege for professional peer review committees (such as those operating in hospitals). The existence and scope of these privileges vary from state to state.

PROBLEM D

DISCOVERY RELEVANCE AND PRIVILEGE QUESTIONS RAISED IN SHAW v. SHOPPING CENTER ASSOCIATES, INC. Shaw brought suit to recover a brokerage commission allegedly due him in a case concerning a complex transaction to purchase an existing shopping center. During the deposition of Dr. Phillip Moskwitz, one of the limited partners in the venture, the plaintiff's attorney asked a number of questions concerning the witness' interpretation, as a layperson, of the legal meanings of several documents related to the transaction. He also asked about conversations with the deponent's attorney, undertaken in the presence of all the joint venturers, all of whom the attorney represented, as well as about the deponent's personal attorneys in matters unrelated to the subject of the suit. The following materials are adapted from a real case and fairly reflect the nature and substance of the actual questions, although the names have been changed and the questions have been altered for simplicity and continuity.

Excerpts from Certified Questions in the
Deposition of Dr. Phillip Moskwitz:

Q (by Mr. Jensen [plaintiff Shaw's attorney]): Now, doctor, you can read this little management and consulting agreement, which is just a little one-page form, right?

A: Yes, sir.

Q: It doesn't contain any legal terminology, does it?

Mr. Stone [defendant's attorney]: Just a minute. Whether or not a management agreement contains legal terminology and the meaning of it would be a legal question, and it obviously does contain legal terminology, because it's a contract.

Q [ignoring defendant's counsel]: Why don't you just read that contract, doctor, and tell me what you think it means?

A: I don't understand what it means.

Q: Why don't you read it, first? And then tell me what you think it means, or what you understand it to mean, as a layman.

A: I frankly don't have any idea what it is. I've never seen it before, and I don't know how it relates to this lawsuit, if it does.

Mr. Stone: I don't think that asking a witness to interpret a legal document for counsel is a proper question.

Mr. Jensen: I am asking him what it means to him. It is a one-page, double spaced document that he can read in about 20 seconds.

Mr. Stone: I am going to instruct the witness not to do that.

Q [ignoring defendant's attorney]: Now that the objection is on the record, you can go ahead and answer, if you would, sir.

Mr. Stone: Just a minute. [to the witness]: I am instructing you not to answer that question.

A: I'm going to follow my attorney's advice.

Mr. Stone: He is not going to answer that question. Ask him another one.

Mr. Jensen [to the court reporter]: Certify the question [*i.e.*, "Transcribe that series of questions separately for use in connection with a motion to the court to compel answers"].

Q [by Mr. Jensen]: Now, doctor, do you presently have a lawyer or lawyers with whom you consult on business other than what's related to this suit?

The Witness: I personally feel it's a private matter, because I consult attorneys about all kinds of matters, in all kinds of firms. I don't think that has to be brought out in this lawsuit.

Mr. Stone: Well, I will instruct the witness not to answer about what matters he may have consulted whatever other attorneys on, in matters unrelated to this lawsuit or to the shopping center deal that is at issue here.

Q: [by Mr. Jensen]: Are you going to answer my question, sir?

A: Absolutely not.

Mr. Jensen: Certify the question.

Q: Now, have you had any lawyers whom you have consulted on your personal matters since the date of this shopping center matter?

A: That's the same question as before!

Mr. Stone: I will instruct the witness not to answer.

Q: Are you going to answer my question, sir?

A: No, sir.

Mr. Jensen: Certify the question.

Q: Now, I want to talk to you about a meeting that took place after my client, Mr. Shaw, contacted Shopping Center Associates about his brokerage fee, with you and Mr. Williamson and possibly other people. Please tell me what the conversation was at that meeting.

Mr. Stone: Just a minute. Mr. Williamson was your lawyer then?

The Witness: Yes. And he served as the business manager and accountant for the venture.

Mr. Stone: And the other people present, did he represent them? Were they the other people in the venture with you?

The Witness: Yes, to my knowledge.

Mr. Stone: And did he give you legal advice, or did you discuss legal matters confidentially?

The Witness: Yes, sir.

Mr. Stone: I object to the question on grounds it is privileged, and I'm going to instruct the witness not to answer.

Q: But now that the objection is on the record, you can go ahead and answer the question, doctor.

Mr. Stone: Just a minute. [To the witness:] Don't answer the question. Just say, I'm not going to answer.

A [The Witness]: I'm not going to answer.

Q: Now, what was the subject of the discussions?

Mr. Stone: Just a minute. He's not going to answer that.

Mr. Jensen: Certify the question.

(1) *Relevance.* Consider the relevance, in discovery terms, of (a) asking a lay witness to interpret the meaning of a contract that forms a part of the transaction, but that she has never seen; (b) asking the witness to name her personal lawyers in unrelated matters; (c) asking the witness to detail discussions with her attorney-business manager-accountant.

(2) *Privilege.* Is the claim of privilege well taken? [What if the discussion at the "meeting" concerned accounting or business matters that, although confidential, were relevant to the suit?]

(3) *Persistent Questions, Objections, and Instructions to the Witness.* Why does Mr. Jensen ignore the objections and continue to urge the witness to answer? [Suggestion: What would be the result if Mr. Stone was asleep at the switch, and the witness happened to answer a general question about the discussions at the meeting?] Why does Mr. Stone not merely object, but also specifically instruct the witness not to answer? Notice that some of the questions — including those dealing with the witness' lay interpretation of legal questions and the identities of his other lawyers — probably wouldn't be harmful to the substance of the lawsuit if the witness answered. And answering would remove the controversy over those items. Why shouldn't Mr. Stone just tell his client to answer them? And — perhaps the most puzzling question — why did the real "Mr. Jensen" ask these questions? [Suggestion: There is a fair amount of gamesmanship in some lawsuits.]

[D] Work Product and Related Exceptions

[1] Trial Preparation Materials

The Problem. Imagine that, in the course of discovery, one party serves upon the other a request for production of "the entire file maintained by your attorney relating to this case, and all documents that are included in it, except those that are covered by the attorney-client privilege." This request would cover the attorney's investigation and research, including notes of witness interviews, diagrams, written statements by anyone other than the client, legal memoranda, etc. The contents of the lawyer's file clearly would be "relevant" in the discovery sense, and they would not be "privileged" except insofar as they embodied confidential communications between attorney and client (as opposed to information obtained from other sources).

The Invention of the "Work Product" Doctrine: Hickman v. Taylor. At the time the following case (*Hickman v. Taylor*) arose, the Rules did not address this kind of discovery request, and their literal terms suggested that the information was discoverable because it was "relevant" and "not privileged." It presumably would be possible to set up a fair system of procedure in which discovery this broad would be allowed; but our system, by deliberate design, is maintained as an "adversary" system. *Cf.* Waits, *Work Product Protection for Witness Statements: Time for Abolition*, 1985 Wis. L. Rev. 305. In *Hickman*, the courts invented the phrase "work product of the lawyer" to describe this kind of information. Today, Rule 26(b)(3) codifies a conditional protection for attorneys' work product (or "trial preparation" materials, to use the language of the Rule) in a manner adapted from *Hickman.*

Read Fed. R. Civ. P. 26(b)(3) (trial preparation materials or "work product").

HICKMAN v. TAYLOR
329 U.S. 495 (1947)

MR. JUSTICE MURPHY delivered the opinion of the Court.

[This case arose out of the sinking of the tugboat "J.M. Taylor" in 1943. Five of the nine crew members drowned, but four survived. Three days after the tug sank, the tug owners and their insurers hired a law firm to investigate and to defend against potential claims. Fortenbaugh, one of the members of the defendants' law firm, interviewed the survivors and took signed witness statements from them "with an eye toward the anticipated litigation." Fortenbaugh also interviewed other persons believed to have some information relating to the accident, and in some cases he made memoranda of what they told him. Later, a public hearing was held, at which most of these witnesses testified, and their testimony was publicly available.

[Ultimately, suit was brought in federal court by one of the survivors' representatives. The claimant's attorney made a discovery request for "copies of all statements of the [witnesses] if in writing, and if oral . . . the exact provisions of any such oral statements or reports."

[The tug owners resisted discovery of the written statements and refused to summarize or set forth the contents of the oral communications made to Fortenbaugh on the ground that "such requests called for 'privileged matter obtained in preparation for litigation' and constituted 'an attempt to obtain indirectly counsel's private files.' "]

[The District Court ordered discovery. The Third Circuit reversed. The Supreme Court granted certiorari.] . . .

In urging that he has a right to inquire into the materials secured and prepared by Fortenbaugh, petitioner emphasizes that the deposition-discovery portions of the Federal Rules of Civil Procedure are designed to enable the parties to discover the true facts and to compel their disclosure wherever they may be found. It is said that inquiry may be made under these rules, epitomized by Rule 26, as to any relevant matter which is not privileged; and since the discovery provisions are to be applied as broadly and liberally as possible, the privilege limitation must be restricted to its narrowest bounds. On the premise that the attorney-client privilege is the one involved in this case, petitioner argues that it must be strictly confined to confidential communications made by a client to his attorney. And since the materials here in issue were secured by Fortenbaugh from third persons rather than from his clients, the tug owners, the conclusion is reached that these materials are proper subjects for discovery under Rule 26. . . .

We agree, of course, that the deposition-discovery rules are to be accorded a broad and liberal treatment. No longer can the time-honored cry of "fishing expedition" serve to preclude a party from inquiring into the facts underlying his opponent's case. Mutual knowledge of all the relevant facts gathered by both parties is essential to proper litigation. To that end, either party may compel the other to disgorge whatever facts he has in his possession. The deposition-discovery procedure simply advances the stage at which the disclosure can be compelled from the time of trial to the period preceding it, thus reducing the possibility of surprise. But discovery, like all matters of procedure, has ultimate and necessary boundaries. . . .

We also agree that the memoranda, statements and mental impressions in issue in this case fall outside the scope of the attorney-client privilege and hence are not protected from discovery on that basis. . . . [T]his privilege does not extend to information which an attorney secures from a witness while acting for his client in anticipation of litigation. Nor does this privilege concern the memoranda, briefs, communications and other writings prepared by counsel for his own use in prosecuting his client's case; and it is equally unrelated to writings which reflect an attorney's mental impressions, conclusions, opinions or legal theories.

But the impropriety of invoking that privilege does not provide an answer to the problem before us. Petitioner has made more than an ordinary request for relevant, non-privileged facts in the possession of his adversaries or their counsel. He has sought discovery as of right of oral and written statements of witnesses whose identity is well known and whose availability to petitioner appears unimpaired. He has sought production of these matters after making the most searching inquiries of his opponents as to the circumstances surrounding the fatal accident, which inquiries were sworn to have been answered to the best of their information and belief. Interrogatories were directed toward all the events prior to, during and subsequent to the sinking of the tug. Full and honest answers to such broad inquiries would necessarily have included all pertinent information gleaned by Fortenbaugh through his interviews with the witnesses. Petitioner makes no suggestion, and we cannot assume, that the tug owners or Fortenbaugh were incomplete or dishonest in the framing of their answers. In addition, petitioner was free to examine the public testimony of the witnesses taken before the United States Steamboat Inspectors. We are thus dealing with an attempt to secure the production of written statements and mental impressions contained in the files and the mind of the attorney Fortenbaugh without any showing of necessity or any indication or claim that denial of such production would unduly prejudice the preparation of petitioner's case or cause him any hardship or injustice. For aught that appears, the essence of what petitioner seeks either has been revealed to him already through the interrogatories or is readily available to him direct from the witnesses for the asking.

The District Court, after hearing objections to petitioner's request, commanded Fortenbaugh to produce all written statements of witnesses and to state in substance any facts learned through oral statements of witnesses to him. Fortenbaugh was to submit any memoranda he had made of the oral statements so that the court might determine what portions should be revealed to petitioner. All of this was ordered without any showing by petitioner, or any requirement that he make a proper showing, of the necessity for the production of any of this material or any demonstration that denial of production would cause hardship or injustice. The court simply ordered production on the theory that the facts sought were material and were not privileged as constituting attorney-client communications.

In our opinion, neither Rule 26 nor any other rule dealing with discovery contemplates production under such circumstances. That is not because the subject matter is privileged or irrelevant, as those concepts are used in these rules. . . . It falls outside the arena of discovery and contravenes the public policy underlying the orderly prosecution and defense of legal claims. . . .

Historically, a lawyer is an officer of the court and is bound to work for the advancement of justice while faithfully protecting the rightful interests of his clients. In performing his various duties, however, it is essential that a lawyer work with a certain degree of privacy, free from unnecessary intrusion by opposing parties and their counsel. . . . This work is reflected, of course, in interviews, statements, memoranda, correspondence, briefs, mental impressions, personal beliefs, and countless other tangible and intangible ways — aptly though roughly termed by the Circuit Court of Appeals in this case as the "work product of the lawyer." Were such materials open to opposing counsel on mere demand, much of what is now put down in writing would remain unwritten. An attorney's thoughts, heretofore inviolate, would not be his own. Inefficiency, unfairness and sharp practices would inevitably develop in the giving of legal advice and in the preparation of cases for trial. The effect on the legal profession would be demoralizing. And the interests of the clients and the cause of justice would be poorly served.

We do not mean to say that all written materials obtained or prepared by an adversary's counsel with an eye toward litigation are necessarily free from discovery in all cases. Where relevant and non-privileged facts remain hidden in an attorney's file and where production of those facts is essential to the preparation of one's case, discovery may properly be had. Such written statements and documents might, under certain circumstances, be admissible in evidence or give clues as to the existence or location of relevant facts. Or they might be useful for purposes of impeachment or corroboration. And production might be justified where the witnesses are no longer available or can be reached only with difficulty. . . . But the general policy against invading the privacy of an attorney's course of preparation is so well recognized and so essential to an orderly working of our system of legal procedure that a burden rests on the one who would invade that privacy to establish adequate reasons to justify production through a subpoena or court order. . . .

No attempt was made [in this case] to establish any reason why Fortenbaugh should be forced to produce the written statements. There was only a naked, general demand for these materials as of right and a finding by the District Court that no recognizable privilege was involved. That was insufficient to justify discovery under these circumstances and the court should have sustained the refusal of the tug owners and Fortenbaugh to produce.

But as to oral statements made by witnesses to Fortenbaugh, whether presently in the form of his mental impressions or memoranda, we do not believe that any showing of necessity can be made under the circumstances of this case so as to justify production. . . . The practice forces the attorney to testify as to what he remembers or what he saw fit to write down regarding witnesses' remarks. Such testimony could not qualify as evidence; and to use it for impeachment or corroborative purposes would make the attorney much less an officer of the court and much more an ordinary witness. The standards of the profession would thereby suffer.

Denial of production of this nature does not mean that any material, non-privileged facts can be hidden from the petitioner in this case. . . . Searching interrogatories directed to Fortenbaugh and the tug owners, production of written documents and statements upon a proper showing and direct interviews with the witnesses themselves all serve to reveal the facts in Fortenbaugh's possession to the fullest possible extent consistent with public policy. Petitioner's counsel frankly admits that he wants the oral statements only to help prepare himself to examine witnesses and to make sure that he has overlooked nothing.

That is insufficient under the circumstances to permit him an exception to the policy underlying the privacy of Fortenbaugh's professional activities. . . .

We therefore affirm the judgment of the Circuit Court of Appeals.

MR. JUSTICE JACKSON, concurring.

[Justice Jackson pointed out that the demand for counsel's recollection of oral statements was particularly troublesome. "I can conceive of no practice more demoralizing to the Bar than to require a lawyer to write out and deliver to his adversary an account of what witnesses have told him. . . . [T]he statement would be his language permeated with his inferences. Everyone who has tried it knows it is almost impossible so fairly to record the expressions and emphasis of a witness that when he testifies in the environment of the court and under the influence of the leading question there will not be departures in some respects." And whenever the witness varied from the lawyer's account, the lawyer would be called by the adversary as an impeaching witness. "Counsel producing his adversary's 'inexact' statement could lose nothing by saying, 'Here is a contradiction, ladies and gentlemen of the jury. I do not know whether it is my adversary or his witness who is not telling the truth, but one is not.' "

[But above all, Justice Jackson emphasized that even if the discovery sought here could be fitted into the "literal language" of the Rules, it was inconsistent with "the background of custom and practice which was assumed by those who wrote and should be by those who apply them." Plaintiff's counsel did not have urgent need of the statements: "He bases his claim to it . . . on the view that the Rules were to do away with the old situation where a law suit developed into 'a battle of wits between counsel.' But a common law trial is and always should be an adversary proceeding. Discovery was hardly intended to enable a learned profession to perform its functions either without wits or on wits borrowed from the adversary."]

BANK OF THE ORIENT v. SUPERIOR COURT, 67 Cal. App. 3d 588, 136 Cal. Rptr. 741 (1977). A fuller version of this case appears in § 7.02[A], *supra.* The Bank sought discovery from its opponent of two confidential reports, one by an accounting firm (the "Coopers & Lybrand Report"), which had been ordered by the opponent's board of directors two days after discovery of the embezzlement that was the subject of the suit, and one a report by a committee of the opponent's board of directors entitled "Suggestions for Improvement to Our System of Internal Control," which contained details of the embezzlement and discussed weaknesses in the opponent's internal controls. The Court of Appeals rejected arguments that these documents were not "relevant" for discovery purposes (*see* § 7.02). It also concluded that they were not work product because they had not been commissioned by an attorney with an eye toward litigation:

> [T]he Coopers & Lybrand report was requested by the board of directors of plaintiff . . . two days after discovery of the embezzlement. . . . Thus, as [the Bank] points out, the report was commissioned not by an attorney but by the board of directors, some four months prior to the time the complaint was filed. A report which is not the product of the attorney or his agents or employees is not work product, and an attorney "cannot, by retroactive adoption, convert the independent work of another, already performed, into his own." . . .

SPORCK v. PEIL, 759 F.2d 312 (3d Cir. 1985). During pretrial discovery in a securities fraud action, plaintiff Peil served numerous sets of combined interrogatory and document requests on the defendants. Defendants produced hundreds of thousands of documents. Thereafter, counsel for defendant Sporck prepared him for an expected week-long deposition by showing him "an unknown quantity of the numerous documents produced by defendants in response to plaintiff's discovery requests." These documents had been "selected" and "compiled" by defense counsel and "the selected documents represented, as a group, counsel's legal opinion as to the evidence relevant both to the allegations in the case and the possible legal defenses." None of the individual documents contained work product.

At Sporck's deposition and later by written motion pursuant to Federal Rule 34, Peil's counsel requested production of "[a]ll documents examined, reviewed or referred to by Charles E. Sporck in preparation for the session of his deposition." Defense counsel objected because the documents had already been produced and because the selection and grouping of the documents constituted work product, even if the documents, taken individually, did not. Peil filed a motion to compel identification and production of the selected documents. The district judge granted the motion. Sporck sought a writ of mandamus directing the district judge to vacate his rulings. The Third Circuit concluded that the district judge had committed an error of law in ordering production because "the selection and compilation of documents by counsel in this case in preparation for pretrial discovery falls within the highly protected category of opinion work product."

After noting that Federal Rule 26(b)(3) recognizes the distinction between "ordinary" work product which can be invaded on the moving party's "showing of substantial need and undue hardship" and "opinion" work product which remains entitled to protection despite "need" and "hardship," the Circuit Court explained that:

> [o]pinion work product includes such items as an attorney's legal strategy, his intended lines of proof, his evaluation of the strengths and weaknesses of his case, and the inferences he draws from interviews of witnesses. . . . Such material is accorded almost absolute protection from discovery because any slight factual content that such items may have is generally outweighed by the adversary system's interest in maintaining the privacy of an attorney's thought processes and in ensuring that each side relies on its own wit in preparing their respective cases.

NOTES AND QUESTIONS

(1) *Impact of the Scope of Discovery on Pleading.* Under *Hickman v. Taylor*, above, information is "relevant to the subject matter" if it might reasonably assist a party in evaluating the case, preparing for trial, or facilitating settlement. Remember, however, that due to the amendments to Rule 26, this broad scope of discovery is no longer available as a matter of right. Matters that are merely "relevant to the subject matter" are discoverable only with leave of court for "good cause" shown. One prominent treatise has observed that this modification to the scope of discovery may have an impact on pleading: "[Under the amendments to Rule 26, a] party's pleadings become strategically important for discovery purposes. To assure the right to obtain discovery and mandatory disclosures from the opposing party, counsel may decide to make pleadings more specific than otherwise required under the rules governing pleading. Indeed, they may be forced to amend their pleadings in order to obtain discovery. In practice, this may alter the practice of 'notice pleading.'" W. Schwarzer, A. Tashima & J. Wagstaffe, Rutter Group Practice Guide: Federal Civil Procedure Before Trial, ¶ 11:21.3 (2002).

(2) *Materials Prepared by Agents of an Attorney: United States v. Nobles, 422 U.S. 225, 238-39 (1975).* One of the aspects of the work product doctrine left unanswered by *Hickman v. Taylor* was whether materials prepared by an attorney's agent in anticipation of litigation were likewise entitled to a qualified immunity from discovery. In *United States v. Nobles*, the Supreme Court answered the question affirmatively:

> [T]he doctrine is an intensely practical one, grounded in the realities of litigation in our adversary system. One of the realities is that attorneys often must rely on the assistance of investigators and other agents in the compilation of materials in preparation for trial. It is therefore necessary that the doctrine protect material prepared by agents for the attorney as well as those prepared by the attorney himself.

See generally Special Project, *The Work Product Doctrine*, 68 Cornell L. Rev. 760 (1983). *See also* E. Thornburg, *Rethinking Work Product*, 77 Va. L. Rev. 1515 (1991).

(3) *Materials Prepared by a Party or its Agents in Anticipation of Litigation.* The *Bank of the Orient* case holds that "A report which is not the product of the attorney or of his agents or employees is not an attorney work product, and an attorney 'cannot, by retroactive adoption, convert the independent work of another, already performed, into his own.' " Is this view too narrow? What if the party, in that case, had undertaken to investigate the matter using its own employees, and it did so precisely because it expected a lawsuit but had not had time to hire an attorney? Can the *Bank of the Orient* case better be rationalized by observing that the reports there were not prepared in anticipation of litigation, but instead were intended to improve the plaintiff's systems of internal controls?

(4) *Anticipation of Litigation.* When is a report prepared in anticipation of litigation or in preparation for trial? Would an accident report prepared by a bus driver, and required by the company every time there is an accident, qualify? Would a hospital "incident report" qualify if hospital employees are directed to prepare one every time an accident occurs? *See* Note, *The Work Product Doctrine: Why Have an Ordinary Course of Business Exception?*, 1988 Colum. Bus. L. Rev. 587.

[2] Testifying Experts and Consultants

Read Fed. R. Civ. P. 26(b)(4) (trial preparation — experts).

AGER v. JANE C. STORMONT HOSPITAL & TRAINING, ETC.
622 F.2d 496 (10th Cir. 1980)

[Emily Ager filed a medical malpractice case in which she alleged that the negligence of Dr. Dan L. Tappen, together with that of the Hospital, "joined and concurred in causing plaintiff's mother's death and plaintiff's bodily injuries and damages and resultant disability."

[Dr. Tappen propounded the following interrogatories to the plaintiff:

1. Have you contacted any person or persons, whether they are going to testify or not, in regard to the care and treatment rendered by Dr. Dan Tappen involved herein?

2. If the answer to the question immediately above is in the affirmative, please set forth the name of said person or persons and their present residential and/or business addresses.

3. If the answer to question #1 is in the affirmative, do you have any statements or written reports from said person or persons?

[The plaintiff objected to the interrogatories. Dr. Tappen sought relief in the form of an order compelling discovery. The United States Magistrate ordered the plaintiff to answer the interrogatories but ruled that the plaintiff need not identify "an expert who was informally consulted in preparation for trial, but who was never retained or specially employed and will not be called as a witness."

[The plaintiff's counsel answered the interrogatories in part, but failed to provide any information concerning experts not expected to testify. Ultimately, after the Magistrate ordered plaintiff to provide further answers concerning the identity of nontestifying consultants and after the order was affirmed by the District Court, the District Court held the plaintiff's lawyer in contempt because of his refusal to comply. Execution of the order was stayed pending appeal.

[After determining that the viability of the order of contempt depended upon the validity of the underlying discovery order, the Court of Appeals considered the subject of expert discovery in detail. It set forth the provisions of Rule 26(b)(4), which the court said separates experts into four categories: (1) experts expected to testify at trial; (2) consultants "retained or specially employed" for the litigation, but not expected to testify; (3) experts consulted informally, and not "retained or specially employed"; and (4) experts contacted for purposes unrelated to the litigation. "We are here concerned," said the court, "only with the second and third category of experts" — experts retained or informally consulted by a party, but not expected to testify at trial.]

A. Discovery of Experts Informally Consulted, But Not Retained or Specially Employed

No provision in . . . Rule 26(b)(4) . . . expressly deals with non-witness experts who are informally consulted by a party in preparation for trial, but not retained or specially employed in anticipation of litigation. The advisory committee notes to the rule indicate, however, that subdivision (b)(4)(B) "precludes discovery against experts who [are] informally consulted in preparation for trial, but not retained or specially employed." We agree with the District Court that this preclusion not only encompasses information and opinions developed in anticipation of litigation, but also insulates discovery of the identity and other collateral information concerning experts consulted informally. . . .

Ager urges that "an 'expert' would be considered informally consulted if, for any reason, the consulting party did not consider the expert of any assistance,' and that '[a] consulting party may consider the expert of no assistance because of his insufficient credentials, his unattractive demeanor, or his excessive fees.' " . . . This view is, of course, at odds with the Trial Court's ruling that:

> The commonly accepted meaning of the term "informally consulted" necessarily implied a consultation without formality. If one makes an appointment with a medical expert to discuss a case or examine records and give advice or opinion for which a charge is made and the charge is paid or promised — what is informal about such consultation? On the other hand, an attorney meets a doctor friend at a social occasion or on the golf course and a discussion occurs concerning the case — no charge is made or contemplated — no written report rendered — such could clearly . . . be an "informal consultation." . . .

We decline to embrace either approach in its entirety. In our view, the status for each expert must be determined on an *ad hoc* basis. Several factors should be considered: (1) the manner in which the consultation was initiated; (2) the nature, type and extent of information or material provided to, or determined by, the expert in connection with his review; (3) the duration and intensity of the consultative relationship; and (4) the terms of the consultation, if any (*e.g.*, payment, confidentiality of test data or opinions, etc.). Of course, additional factors bearing on this determination may be examined if relevant. . . .

The determination of the status of the expert rests, in the first instance, with the party resisting discovery. . . . The propounding party should then be provided the opportunity of requesting a determination of the expert's status based on an *in camera* review by the court. Inasmuch as the District Court failed to express its views on this question, we deem it appropriate to remand rather than attempt to deal with the merits of this issue on appeal. . . . If the expert is considered to have been only informally consulted in anticipation of litigation, discovery is barred.

B. Discovery of the Identities of Experts
Retained or Specially Employed

Subdivision (b)(4)(B) of Rule 26 specifically deals with non-witness experts who have been retained or specially employed by a party in anticipation of litigation. The text of that subdivision provides that "facts [known] or opinions [held]" by non-witness experts retained or specially employed may only be discovered upon a showing of "exceptional circumstances under which it is impracticable for the party to obtain facts or opinions on the same subject by other means." Inasmuch as discovery of the identities of these experts, absent a showing of exceptional circumstances, was not expressly precluded by the text of subdivision (b)(4)(B), the District Court found the general provisions of Rule 26(b)(1) controlling. . . .

The advisory committee notes indicate that the structure of Rule 26 was largely developed around the doctrine of unfairness — designed to prevent a party from building his own case by means of his opponent's financial resources, superior diligence and more aggressive preparation. Dr. Tappen contends that "[d]iscoverability of the identity of an expert [h]ardly gives the discovering party a material advantage or benefit at the expense of the opposing party's preparation. Once those identities are disclosed, the discovering party is left to his own diligence and resourcefulness in contacting such experts and seeking to enlist whatever assistance they may be both able and willing to offer." The drafters of Rule 26 did not contemplate such a result:

> [A]s an ancillary procedure, a party may *on a proper showing* require the other party to *name* experts retained or specially employed, but not those informally consulted. [Emphasis supplied.] . . .

There are several policy considerations supporting our view. Contrary to Dr. Tappen's view, once the identities of retained or specially employed experts are disclosed, the protective provisions of the rule concerning facts known or opinions held by such experts are subverted. The expert may be contacted or his records obtained and information normally non-discoverable, under Rule 26(b)(4)(B), revealed. Similarly, although perhaps rarer, the opponent may attempt to compel an expert retained or specially employed by an adverse party in anticipation of trial, but whom the adverse party does not intend to call, to testify at trial. *Kaufman v. Edelstein*, 539 F.2d 811 (2d Cir. 1976).[6] The possibility

[6] We do not here decide the propriety of this action.

also exists, although we do not suggest it would occur in this case, or that it would be proper, that a party may call his opponent to the stand and ask if certain experts were retained in anticipation of trial, but not called as a witness, thereby leaving with the jury an inference that the retaining party is attempting to suppress adverse facts or opinions. Finally, we agree with Ager's view that "[d]isclosure of the identities of [medical] consultative experts would inevitably lessen the number of candid opinions available as well as the number of consultants willing to even discuss a potential medical malpractice claim with counsel. . . . If one assumes that access to informed opinions is desirable in both prosecuting valid claims and eliminating groundless ones, a discovery practice that would do harm to these objectives should not be condoned." Brief of Appellant at pp. 27-28, 29-30.

In sum, we hold that the identity, and other collateral information concerning an expert who is retained or specially employed in anticipation of litigation, but not expected to be called as a witness at trial, is not discoverable except as "provided in Rule 35(b)[7] or [on showing] exceptional circumstances under which it is impracticable for the party . . . to obtain facts or opinions on the same subject by other means."[8] Fed. Rules Civ. Proc., Rule 26(b)(4)(B), 28 U.S.C.A. The party "seeking disclosure under Rule 26(b)(4)(B) carries a heavy burden" in demonstrating the existence of exceptional circumstances. . . .

Disposition

. . . On remand, the status of the non-witness experts against whom discovery is sought should be undertaken as a two-step process. First, was the expert informally consulted in anticipation of litigation but not retained or specially employed? If so, no discovery may be had as to the identity or opinions of the expert. Second, if the expert *was not* informally consulted, but rather retained or specially employed in anticipation of litigation, but not expected to testify at trial, do exceptional circumstances exist justifying disclosure of the expert's identity, opinions or other collateral information?

PROBLEM E

DISCOVERY FROM EXPERTS. How would the following experts be treated under the current Federal Rule? (a) Expert A, consulted over the telephone by Ms. Ager's counsel about Dr. Tappen's general reputation, who will not testify at trial and who has not helped in the preparation of the case; (b) Expert B, consulted in connection with

---

[7] Rule 35(b), Fed. Rules Civ. Proc., 28 U.S.C.A., deals with the exchange of information concerning physical or mental examinations of persons. These provisions are not at issue here.

[8] Professor Albert Sacks, reporter to the advisory committee, listed two examples of exceptional circumstances at a Practicing Law Institute Seminar on Discovery held in Atlanta, Georgia, September 25-26, 1970:

> (a) Circumstances in which an expert employed by the party seeking discovery could not conduct important experiments and test[s] because an item of equipment, etc., needed for the test[s] has been destroyed or is otherwise no longer available. If the party from whom discovery is sought had been able to have its experts test the item before its destruction or nonavailability, then information obtained from those tests might be discoverable.
>
> (b) Circumstances in which it might be impossible for a party to obtain its own expert. Such circumstances would occur when the number of experts in a field is small and their time is already fully retained by others.

See: ALI-ABA, *Civil Trial Manual* p. 189.

the case and who will testify at a hearing or trial; (c) Expert C, consulted in connection with the case for compensation and to prepare Expert B for cross-examination; (d) Expert D, who was not consulted in connection with any litigation, but who has assisted the defendant in complying with health and safety regulations before the event giving rise to the litigation occurred. *See generally* Day, *Expert Discovery in the Eighth Circuit: An Empirical Study*, 122 F.R.D. 35 (1988); Note, *Blind Man's Bluff: An Analysis of the Discovery of Expert Witnesses Under Federal Rule of Civil Procedure 26(b)(4) and a Proposed Amendment*, 64 Ind. L.J. 925 (1989); Note, *Gimme Shelter? Not If You Are a Non-Witness Expert Under Rule 26(b)(4)(B)*, 56 U. Cin. L. Rev. 1027 (1988).

NOTES AND QUESTIONS

(1) *State Rules with Broader or Narrower Coverage.* The subject of discovery from experts is extremely important, owing to the frequency of use of experts and the sensitive relationship they have to the parties. *See* Note, *Discovery of Retained Nontestifying Experts' Identities under the Federal Rules of Civil Procedure*, 80 Mich. L. Rev. 513 (1982). The subject therefore is given elaborate treatment in the Federal Rules and in many state provisions regarding discovery. Rule 193.3 of the Texas Rules of Civil Procedure appears to allow broader discovery than the Federal Rules because it authorizes discovery from a nontestifying consultant "whose mental impressions or opinions have been reviewed by a testifying expert." New York State's CPLR 3101(d) appears somewhat more restrictive of discovery than both the Texas and Federal Rules.

(2) *Expert Used in the Party's Ordinary Business: Marine Petroleum Co. v. Champlin Petroleum Co., 641 F.2d 984 (D.C. Cir. 1979).* An expert who was not contacted in connection with existing or expected litigation — such as a staff engineer or intern at a hospital that is a party — is not ordinarily shielded from discovery. But suppose the expert is hired initially in a consultative capacity, not in anticipation of litigation, and that the expert subsequently secures an expanded role to include assistance in defending against a particular claim? In *Marine Petroleum Co.*, the court held that the discovering party could obtain discovery of facts known or opinions held by the expert before his role changed, but not with respect to information developed thereafter, absent exceptional circumstances. *See also* Note, *The In-House Expert Witness: Discovery Under the Federal Rules of Civil Procedure*, 33 S.D. L. Rev. 283 (1988).

(3) *Determination of Expert's Status: "Gamesmanship."* Attorneys often are motivated to engage in "gamesmanship" about identities of experts. By delaying disclosure, they may hope to react to their opponents' designations, keep their adversaries in the dark, or hold their own options open. Thus it often happens that an interrogatory, asking a party to identify experts whom that party anticipates calling at trial, is answered by the sentence: "This has not been determined." When does the matter have to be determined? *See* Fed. R. Civ. P. 26(e) (party has duty to supplement answers regarding experts "by the time the party's pretrial disclosures under Rule 26(a)(3) are due"); *see also* Fed. R. Civ. P. 26(a)(2) (party must disclose identity of expert witnesses "at least 90 days before the date set for trial or for the case to be ready for trial"). *Compare Washington Hospital Center v. Cheeks*, 394 F.2d 964 (D.C. Cir. 1968) (trial recess granted to take deposition of undisclosed expert), *with Tabatchnick v. G.D. Searle & Co.*, 67 F.R.D. 49 (1975) (excluding testimony of expert). How should the Rules deal with this problem of "gamesmanship"? *See also* Preiser, *Cross-Examining the Expert Witness: Proceeding Without a Discovery Deposition*, 25 Trial 83 (1989); Day, *Discovery Standards for the Testimonial Expert Under Federal Rule of Civil Procedure 26(b)(4): A Twentieth Anniversary Assessment*, 133 F.R.D. 209 (1991).

[E] Protective Orders

Read Fed. R. Civ. P. 26(b)(2), (c)-(d) (limitations on discovery scope; protective orders; sequence and timing of discovery); Fed. R. Civ. P. 30(d)(4) (limits on taking oral depositions).

CENTURION INDUSTRIES, INC. v. WARREN STEURER AND ASSOCIATES

665 F.2d 323 (10th Cir. 1981)

SEYMOUR, CIRCUIT JUDGE.

Cybernetic Systems, Inc. (Cybernetic), a nonparty witness in a patent infringement action, appeals from an order of the United States District Court of New Mexico, requiring it to disclose certain computer software trade secrets to Centurion Industries, Inc. and Eric F. Burtis (hereinafter together referred to as "Centurion"). Cybernetic argues that Centurion has not met its burden of proof showing that Cybernetic's trade secrets are relevant and necessary to the patent suit. We disagree and affirm the order of the district court.

Cybernetic is a manufacturer of electronic "teaching machines" used in arithmetic instruction. . . .

Almost all functions of the Cybernetic teaching machines are controlled by a miniature programmed computer, a standard electronic product purchased by Cybernetic. This miniature computer, referred to in the computer industry as "hardware," must be programmed by its user to perform the desired tasks. In computer industry parlance, such programs are known as "software." Cybernetic itself created the software or program used in its purchased miniature computers, and claims that the software constitutes a trade secret.

Centurion owns a patent for a "teaching device having [the] means [for] producing a self-generated program," which it claims is infringed by the Cybernetic teaching machines. Centurion brought a patent infringement action in the United States District Court for the Central District of California.

Cybernetic is not a party to that action,[3] but its deposition was noticed in New Mexico by Centurion pursuant to Fed. R. Civ. P. 30(b)(6). The notice required production of certain documents from Cybernetic's files. Following the service of an appropriate subpoena and the designation of a witness by Cybernetic, Cybernetic filed a Notice of Objection to Subpoena under Fed. R. Civ. P. 45(d)(1), protesting discovery of materials listed in the notice and subpoena concerning software or programming information.

In response to Cybernetic's Rule 45(d) objection, Centurion filed a motion to compel production of the software information in the District Court for the District of New Mexico. The United States Magistrate ruled in favor of Centurion, issuing an order: (1) requiring Cybernetic to disclose its software information; and (2) requiring Centurion to abide by the conditions of a protective order restricting use of the trade secrets. On review, the district court affirmed the magistrate's order. . . .

---

[3] Cybernetic was originally joined as a defendant in the action in the Central District of California, but was dismissed for lack of personal jurisdiction. The defendants are either both customers of Cybernetic, or one is a Cybernetic manufacturer's representative and the other is a customer. . . .

"[T]here is no absolute privilege for trade secrets and similar confidential information." *Federal Open Market Committee v. Merrill*, 443 U.S. 340, 362 (1979). . . . To resist discovery under Rule 26(c) . . ., a person must first establish that the information sought is a trade secret and then demonstrate that its disclosure might be harmful. . . . If these requirements are met, the burden shifts to the party seeking discovery to establish that the disclosure of trade secrets is relevant and necessary to the action. . . . The district court must balance the need for the trade secrets against the claim of injury resulting from disclosure. . . .

It is within the sound discretion of the trial court to decide whether trade secrets are relevant and whether the need outweighs the harm of disclosure. Likewise, if the trade secrets are deemed relevant and necessary, the appropriate safeguards that should attend their disclosure by means of a protective order are also a matter within the trial court's discretion. We may only reverse the district court if it has abused its discretion. . . .

Cybernetic contends that Centurion, the party seeking discovery, has failed to discharge its burden of demonstrating that Cybernetic's software trade secrets are relevant and necessary to the patent infringement action before us. We disagree.

Fed. R. Civ. P. 26(b)(1) states that "[relevant information need not be admissible at the trial] if the [discovery] appears reasonably calculated to lead to the discovery of admissible evidence." Thus, relevancy is construed more broadly during discovery than at trial. . . .

Centurion's basic position is that information about Cybernetic's software is both relevant and necessary to determine if the teaching machines infringe its patent. From the defendants' response to interrogatories in the original action, it appears that the defendants' experts will have access to Cybernetic's software and will use their knowledge of the software and other operating details of the teaching devices to testify that Centurion's patent has not been infringed. We conclude from a reading of the record that the district court did not abuse its discretion in deciding that the technical operating details of the teaching devices, including the software, are relevant and necessary to the resolution of this patent suit. The information appears needed to provide a basis for Centurion's experts to adequately form an opinion of infringement and to rebut any assertions of noninfringement in the action. . . .

In trade secret discovery battles, "[t]he claim of irreparable competitive injury must be balanced against the need for the information in the preparation of the defense." . . . In the case at bar, we believe that enforcement of the subpoenas is reasonable: the need for the information outweighs the possible injury to Cybernetic, and the lower court issued a carefully fashioned protective order to guard against improper disclosure of the secrets.[7] In our opinion the trial court displayed a sound exercise of discretion.

---

[7] The district court upheld the magistrate's order, which provides that:

Cybernetic Systems, Inc. shall with [sic] twenty (20) days of the entry of this Order produce at its place of business in Albuquerque, New Mexico, to Charles H. Thomas, attorney for plaintiffs, all writings and materials relating to software or programming information of all its Mathiputer Learning Systems and shall immediately thereafter give deposition testimony concerning the technical operating details of such Systems.

The information obtained shall be treated as confidential by counsel for plaintiffs and used only for purposes of litigation in the United States District Court for the Central District of California, 76-2628-HP.

The attendance at the production and deposition shall be limited to the deponent, court reporter, counsel for plaintiffs, and counsel for Cybernetic Systems, Inc.

The decision of the district court is affirmed.

PROBLEM F

CHANGING THE PROTECTIVE ORDER RULING IN CENTURION INDUSTRIES INC. v. WARREN STEURER & ASSOCIATES. Reconsider *Centurion* (the principal case, above). Would the trial court have abused its discretion: (1) If it had entered a protective order absolutely prohibiting discovery of Cybernetic's software trade secrets? (2) If it appointed a "neutral" expert to receive the information from Cybernetic, and to convey it to Centurion, in such quantity and form as to maximize Centurion's knowledge of the facts relevant to the lawsuit while minimizing the competitive disadvantage to Cybernetic? *Cf. Triangle Mfg. Co. v. Paramount Bag Mfg. Co.*, 35 F.R.D. 540 (E.D.N.Y. 1964) (trial judge ordered "impartial third party" to give discoverer "the maximum amount of information while at the same time maintaining the secrecy of the actual" underlying trade secrets). (3) If it had limited discovery to written questions, rather than document production or depositions, in the hope that unnecessary invasion of trade secrets thus could be minimized? And, (4), a final question: Assuming that various alternatives might be within the court's discretion, how should the court go about deciding which alternative to choose (*i.e.*, which approach is "best")?

NOTES AND QUESTIONS

(1) *"Good Cause": When Does a Trial Judge Abuse His or Her Discretion by Denying a Protective Order? Silkwood v. Kerr-McGee Corp., 563 F.2d 433 (10th Cir. 1977).* The trial judge in this case denied a protective order sought by a news reporter who sought to avoid disclosing confidential sources. The Court of Appeals reversed and remanded on the ground that the trial judge had not considered the nature of the evidence sought, the discoveror's efforts to obtain it from other sources, or the necessity or relevance of the evidence. *See also Automatic Drilling Machines, Inc. v. Miller*, 515 S.W.2d 256 (Tex. 1974) (trial judge's summary denial of motion for protective order, sought by non-party inventor, reversed, where proof supporting motion showed that discoverer was in direct competition with inventor, information was highly confidential, and it probably would be the subject of an application for letters patent). *See also* Smith, *A Practical Approach to Rule 26(c) Protective Orders in Aviation Litigation*, 56 J. Air L. & Com. 765 (1991); Campbell, *The Protective Order in Products Liability Litigation: Safeguard or Misnomer?*, 31 B.C.L. Rev. 771 (1990).

A related question is, when does a trial judge abuse his or her discretion by *granting* a protective order removing information from discovery? *Cf. Williams v. City of Dothan*, 745 F.2d 1406 (11th Cir. 1984) (District Court erred in granting protective order shielding

---

Disclosure of the information obtained shall be limited to United States Federal Courts, plaintiffs' counsel and, [sic] plaintiffs' experts employed to testify in the action, provided Cybernetic Systems, Inc. be notified in writing by plaintiffs' counsel at least twenty (20) days prior to such disclosure of the names and addresses of such experts, and the date and place of such disclosure.

The transcript of the deposition shall remain sealed.

Cybernetic Systems, Inc. shall be notified by plaintiffs in writing at least twenty (20) days prior to plaintiffs [sic] tender of any of the materials obtained pursuant to this Order, into evidence, other than in closed session of a United States Federal Court.

Plaintiffs and Cybernetic Systems, Inc. shall pay their respective costs incurred in connection with the depositions and this Motion. . . .

from discovery the City's earlier payments for municipal projects, where the plaintiffs alleged racial discrimination in such payments, where the pattern in earlier years was clearly relevant to the issue of discriminatory intent, and where the potential harm from disclosure was slight).

(2) *Undue Burden or Expense: Jones v. Holy Cross Hospital Silver Spring, Inc.*, 64 F.R.D. 586 (D. Md. 1974). The *Centurion* case deals with information whose confidentiality is a key issue. Protective orders also are frequently sought because the information, although not particularly sensitive, is so voluminous that its compilation would impose an undue burden or expense on the party from whom discovery is sought. Interrogatories, for example, frequently ask questions calling for answers that are "relevant" in the discovery sense, but that require the other party to assemble and process very large amounts of information. In the *Jones* case, the plaintiff, in an action for alleged racially discriminatory employment practices filed before the discovery limits now set forth in Rule 33, served a set of 70 interrogatories on the defendant. Many contained from two to 23 subparts. They sought both racial and gender-related statistical information over a period of many years — indeed, beginning before the incorporation of the defendant and the opening of the hospital where the alleged discrimination took place. The trial court granted a protective order, curtailing some of the requested discovery. Note, however, that the granting of such an order and the form of protection are subject to the broad discretion of the trial judge, and denial of protection in such a situation normally is a proper option, too. *Cf. Burns v. Thiokol Chem. Corp.*, in § 7.03[A][2], *infra*. The court must decide what weight to give to the estimated cost of compliance, the need for the information, the nature of the claims, and the financial resources of the parties (some cases indicate that greater burdens can be placed on parties with greater resources).

(3) *The Type of Protection Granted; The Broad Range of Alternatives.* Rule 26(c) lists a wide range of options available to the court, including curtailing discovery, specifying conditions or methods, protecting confidentiality, etc. *See* Note, *Protective Orders Restricting Disclosure of Discovery in Federal Civil Proceedings*, 56 Chi.-Kent L. Rev. 943 (1980). Consider the following cases and questions:

(a) *Curtailing Discovery of Relevant Information: Farnsworth v. Procter & Gamble Co.*, 758 F.2d 1545 (11th Cir. 1985). In a product liability claim for a death allegedly due to toxic shock syndrome resulting from use of the defendant's tampons, the plaintiff sought extensive discovery from the Center for Disease Control, a non-party and agency of the United States government. The District Court granted a protective order disallowing the plaintiff from discovering the names of individual tampon users who participated in a study conducted by the Center, principally on the ground that such disclosure would damage the Center's ability to obtain survey participants in the future. The Court of Appeals affirmed.

(b) *Staying All Discovery: Crown Central Petroleum Co. v. Department of Energy*, 102 F.R.D. 95 (D. Md. 1984). The defendant Department sought and obtained a protective order staying all discovery in an action for declaratory relief by a petroleum products marketer, upon the Department's showing that there was a pending administrative proceeding presenting overlapping issues in which the plaintiff was seeking many of the same items in discovery.

(c) *Specifying a Different Method of Discovery Than That Used by the Party Seeking Discovery: Fishman v. A.H. Riise Gift Shop, Inc.*, 68 F.R.D. 704 (D.V.I. 1975). The party that was the target of discovery sought a protective order requiring the use of depositions rather than interrogatories. The court granted the motion, observing that the discoverer had attempted to misuse interrogatories in a manner not directed at obtaining information that might lead to admissible evidence.

(d) *Conditions for Discovery — Prepayment of Expenses: In re Coordinated Proceedings in Petroleum Products Antitrust Litig.*, 669 F.2d 620 (10th Cir. 1982). The plaintiff, the State of Florida, sought discovery from a nonparty. The discovery was time-consuming and could not inure to the benefit of the nonparty, and therefore, the trial court required the plaintiff to advance the costs of the requested document production. The Court of Appeals affirmed.

(e) *Designation of Time and Place: Detweiler Bros., Inc. v. John Graham & Co.*, 412 F. Supp. 416 (E.D. Wash. 1976). The plaintiff sought to prohibit the taking of its employee's deposition on the ground that he lacked knowledge of the subject of inquiry and was out of state. The court refused to prohibit the taking of the deposition, but held that the plaintiff could properly seek to control the time and place of the deposition by protective order. Also, consider the following materials.

[F] "Umbrella" Confidentiality Agreements and Orders

ZENITH RADIO CORP. v. MATSUSHITA ELEC. INDUS. CO., 529 F. Supp. 866 (E.D. Pa. 1981). The plaintiffs in an international antitrust suit moved to vacate an agreed-upon "umbrella" confidentiality order ("PTO 35") which provided that "confidential information" (defined as "any information that is designated 'confidential' at the time of its disclosure by the disclosing party") not be disclosed to persons other than "qualified persons" (defined to include counsel and designated representatives of the parties). PTO 35 provided further "that confidential information shall be used only in the preparation for trial and/or trial of these actions, and not for any other purpose whatsoever." The agreement also set forth procedures for challenging a party's claim of confidentiality and placed the ultimate burden of establishing a right to the court's protection on the party "seeking confidential treatment of information."

The plaintiffs sought to vacate the confidentiality order in its entirety and, alternatively, sought declassification of: (1) all pleadings and other papers filed of record that had been stamped "confidential" under PTO 35; (2) all documents offered by the parties at the pretrial evidentiary hearings; and (3) all documents produced in discovery which had been stamped confidential. The defendant (which, like the plaintiff, had trade secrets at issue) had produced many thousands of documents photocopied on paper already labeled "confidential" with a conspicuous, pre-printed legend.

After determining that the plaintiffs had ratified PTO 35 such that it was appropriate to treat it as a "consent order," the court concluded that PTO 35 was a valid protective order under Fed. R. Civ. P. 26(c) because: "(1) the material that it protects is confidential commercial information; (2) the harm ['competitive disadvantage'] is cognizable under Rule 26(c); and both at the time it was entered and at the present time, defendants (as well as plaintiffs) have shown good cause for the protective order to issue." The court also concluded that neither the common law right of access to judicial records nor the First Amendment required wholesale declassification of documents entitled to protection under Fed. R. Civ. P. 26. Finally, the court added: "We are unaware of any case in the past half-dozen years of even a modicum of complexity where an umbrella protective order has not been agreed to by the parties and approved by the court."

NOTES AND QUESTIONS

(1) *Do "Umbrella" Protective Orders Violate the First Amendment? Seattle Times Co. v. Rhinehart, 467 U.S. 20 (1984).* Rhinehart brought a defamation action against the *Seattle Times*, which sought to discover information about members and donors of Rhinehart's religious organization, the Aquarian Foundation. The trial court granted the discovery but imposed a confidentiality order. The *Seattle Times* argued, among other contentions, that this order violated the First Amendment. The U.S. Supreme Court upheld the order because disclosure of the information might result in annoyance, embarrassment and oppression of these individuals, and the trial court was in the best position "to weigh fairly the competing needs and interests." But does this reasoning apply to "blanket" or "umbrella" protective orders such as the one in *Zenith v. Matsushita*, in which the need for confidentiality of individual items is not "weighed"? *See* R. Marcus, *The Discovery Confidentiality Controversy*, 1991 U. Ill. L. Rev. 457.

(2) *The Practical Issues.* If there is a breach of an agreement such as that in *Zenith v. Matsushita* (perhaps years after disposition of the litigation), how is the agreement or the order resulting from it to be enforced? For that matter, how does the aggrieved party even detect a violation? Isn't it entirely possible that the parties may engage in inadvertent or unintended violations in the nature of "leaks" of sensitive information, or that designated contact employees may use the information in later assignments? On the other hand, is there any better alternative? *See* Joslin, *Confidentiality Orders in Complex Litigation*, 4 Rev. Litigation 109 (1985).

(3) *Rule Amendment Governing Protective Agreements.* A relatively recent amendment legitimizes umbrella agreements by eliminating the requirement of "good cause" when confidentiality is agreed to. But it also contemplates that any "person" may be "allowed to intervene to seek modification or dissolution" — *e.g.*, a news reporter in a high profile case.

§ 7.03 The Mechanics of Discovery

[A] Mandatory Self-Initiated Disclosures

(1) *An Overview: Disclosure, Limits, Conference Plans, Etc.* Fed. R. Civ. P. 26 requires mandatory disclosure of core information, including initial disclosure without any formal request of (1) the names, addresses and telephone numbers (if known) of any persons "likely to have discoverable information — along with the subjects of that information — that the disclosing party may use to support its claims or defenses . . ."; (2) copies or descriptions of documents that may be used; (3) a computation of any category of damages claimed; and (4) copies of insurance agreements that may be liable to satisfy any judgment [Rule 26(a)(1)(A)]. The rule also requires disclosure of expert testimony [Rule 26(a)(2)] and pretrial disclosure of witnesses who may be called to testify [Rule 26(a)(3)]. The rule requires the parties to meet to discuss and arrange disclosures before the Rule 16(b) judicial scheduling conference [Rule 26(f)]. The rule also contains a separate certification and signing requirement [Rule 26(g)].

(2) *The Controversy Over Disclosure Requirements: A Patchwork System at First; Now Uniform Nationwide.* Previously, the disclosure rules gave the local courts, by order or rule, the right to "opt out" of the disclosure, presumptive limits, and other provisions of the new rules. Many district courts did just that. As of March 22, 1996, exactly half of the 94 federal districts had implemented the initial disclosures rule (26(a)(1)) and half had not. Twenty-one of the 47 districts opting out allowed or required some disclosures.

Still, 26 districts exempted all cases from initial disclosures. Two-thirds of the districts had implemented Rule 26(f)'s requirement that the parties meet and prepare a discovery plan, but again, that meant one-third of the districts did not have this rule in effect. *Summary of Federal District Courts' Response to Rule 26 Amendments*, Implementation of Disclosure in United States District Courts, March 22, 1996.

This situation was widely criticized on the ground that the federal courts ought to follow a uniform nationwide set of procedural rules — and the opt-outs had created a patchwork system. Accordingly, the option of "opting out" was eliminated in 2000. On a case-by-case basis, a court can exempt the parties to a given controversy from disclosures, and the rule itself exempts certain categories of cases, but generally, the rules are mandatory nationwide.

BIGGARS v. ROMANS

2006 U.S. Dist. LEXIS 30015 (D. Kan. 2006)

MEMORANDUM AND ORDER

DONALD W. BOSTWICK, Magistrate Judge.

Before the Court are Defendant's Motion to Compel and supporting Memorandum (Docs. 22, 23), which request an order compelling Plaintiff to fully answer Defendant's Interrogatory No. 12 regarding Plaintiff's category of damages. Defendant further seeks an order for Plaintiff to be compelled to fully answer his Interrogatories No. 5, 6, 8, 9, 10, 16, and 21, including the address and telephone number of each person identified. Plaintiff did not file a response to Defendant's motion and the time to do so expired on March 28, 2006. . . .

BACKGROUND

Plaintiff filed her complaint on August 17, 2005, claiming that her employment was wrongfully and retaliatorily terminated by Defendant because she "asserted her rights under the Worker's Compensation law, and complained of unlawful working conditions" after allegedly suffering from mercury poisoning. (Doc. 1 at ¶ 19.) Plaintiff alleges that, as a result of Defendant's actions, she has suffered injury and damage, including "loss of time and income in the past, which is reasonably likely to continue in the future; medical expenses in the past, which are reasonably likely to continue in the future; and non-economic damages in the past, which are reasonably likely to continue in the future; and other damages." (Doc. 1 at ¶ 21.)

On November 9, 2005, Plaintiff served her Initial Disclosures on Defendant pursuant to Fed. R. Civ. P. 26(a)(1). Plaintiff's disclosure of individuals likely to have discoverable information pursuant to Rule 26(a)(1)(A) listed 25 specific individuals and two categories of individuals. The listing did not include an address or telephone number for any of these individuals, (Doc. 23, Exh. 1), although the rule requires disclosure of this information, if known. The disclosure regarding Plaintiff's claimed damages stated only "Economic Loss: $750,000.00" and "Non-Economic Loss: $750,000.00." (Doc. 23, Exh. 1.) The disclosure did not contain a computation of damages as required by Rule 26(a)(1)(C).

Defendant served his first discovery requests to Plaintiff on December 20, 2005. (Doc. 23, Exh. 2.) Plaintiff served her responses on February 14, 2006. (Doc. 23, Exh. 3.) Defendant's Interrogatory No. 12 requested that Plaintiff state the total amount of damages she claimed, including an itemization of each element thereof. (Doc. 23, Exh.

2.) In response, Plaintiff listed $343,640.00 for past and future economic loss, calculated at $15,620.00 per year for 22 years (while providing no basis for the $15,620.00 figure). She also listed past non-economic losses of $578,180.00 and future non-economic losses of $578,180.00, absent any supporting information or calculation thereof. (Doc. 23, Exh. 3.)

Various other interrogatories requested that Plaintiff "identify" certain categories of individuals. (Doc. 23, Exh.2, Interrogatories 5, 6, 8, 9, 10, 16, and 21.) Defendant's definition of "identify" indicated that Plaintiff should state the last known address and telephone number for such individuals. (*Id.*) In response to these interrogatories, Plaintiff either directed Defendant to her medical records without listing responsive individuals or listed various individuals by name with no reference to their last known addresses or telephone numbers. (Doc. 23, Exh. 3.)

Defense counsel appropriately conferred with Plaintiff's counsel by letter in an attempt to resolve this discovery dispute. (Doc. 23, Exh. 4.) Despite assurances from Plaintiff's counsel's staff that additional information would be forthcoming (Doc. 23, Exh. 5), Defense counsel filed the present motion . . . . Based on subsequent communication between the Court and counsel for both parties, it is the understanding of the Court that the parties have been unable to resolve these discovery issues. As such, the Court is prepared to rule on Defendant's motion.

DISCUSSION

. . . .

Suffice it to say, Plaintiff's responses to Defendant's Interrogatories 5, 6, 8, 9, 10, 12, 16, and 21 are inadequate. This is particularly true when the discovery responses are reviewed in the context of Plaintiff's initial disclosures.

Fed. R. Civ. P. 26(a)(1)(A) specifically requires disclosure of the address and telephone numbers of each individual likely to have discoverable information relevant to disputed facts, if known. *See Dixon v. Certainteed Corporation*, 164 F.R.D. 685, 689 (D. Kan. 1996). Therefore, Plaintiff should have provided much of the requested information to Defendant prior to the service of Defendant's interrogatories. The Court is aware that addresses and telephone numbers of many of these individuals are available to defense counsel from other sources, such as local telephone directories or Plaintiff's medical records. This does not, however, relieve Plaintiff from the obligation to disclose such information in discovery.

Fed. R. Civ. P. 26(a)(1) . . . requires Plaintiff to provide "a computation of [each] category of damages claimed" in her initial disclosures. Although Plaintiff's initial disclosures contained a general statement of her monetary damages, they did not contain any "computation" of such damages. Subsequently, Defendant's Interrogatory No. 12 directed Plaintiff to "state with specificity the total amount of damages you are claiming, and itemize each element thereof (e.g., loss of past wages, medical expenses, pain, suffering, mental anguish, disability, loss of future wages, etc.)." (Doc. 23, Exh. 2.) Plaintiff's response contained a very rough calculation of her alleged past and future economic loss. (Doc. 23, Exh. 3.) She did not, however, indicate whether this loss is the result of medical expenses, potential lost wages, potential lost benefits, or some other element of damages. She also listed the categories of past non-economic loss and future non-economic loss, giving each a value of $578,180.00. There is, however, no computation of these claimed damages nor has Plaintiff made any effort to itemize the elements of these damage categories. Thus, Plaintiff's response to Defendant's Interrogatory No. 12 is insufficient.

Because Plaintiff did not respond to Defendant's motion, the Court does not know what, if any, objection Plaintiff may have had to providing the requested information. The Court is not willing to surmise or assume what objections Plaintiff may have had. Regardless, the requested information is both discoverable and relevant. . . . As such, the Court finds Defendant's motion to be both unopposed and facially valid. Defendant's Motion to Compel should therefore be granted.

NOTES AND QUESTIONS

(1) *Reduction of Cost and Delay — or Encouragement of Waste and Gamesmanship?* One of the most hotly debated issues about initial disclosures is whether they will reduce cost and delay — or increase it. Notice that the defendant's interrogatories sought information that should have been revealed in the plaintiff's initial disclosures — a repetition of time and expense.

(2) *Limiting Disclosure to the Party's Own Claims or Defenses (as Opposed to Requiring Each Party to Figure Out the Opponent's Theories).* The disclosure requirements generally are restricted to information "that the disclosing party may use to support its claims or defenses, unless the use would be solely for impeachment." The earlier rule covered "every individual likely to have discoverable information relevant to disputed facts," whether the facts concerned the discloser's theories or the opponent's. The discloser, arguably, was required to adopt the opponent's frame of mind, to figure out what would help the opponent's case. The current language lets the discloser limit its search to "its claims or defenses." Perhaps this change lightens the burden. But then again, the improvement may not be as great as it seems, because one's own claims and defenses are closely related to the opponent's; they are the flip side of the opponent's, in a way.

(3) *Sanctions for Inadequate Disclosures: Paradigm Sales Inc. v. Weber Marking Systems, Inc., 151 F.R.D. 98 (N.D. Ind. 1993).* Although the *Biggars* case above did not impose sanctions, note that sanctions for nondisclosure can include exclusion of the undisclosed documents from evidence or of the undisclosed witness from testifying. In the *Paradigm* case, the plaintiff made a motion to exclude any evidence supporting any defense that the defendant had not yet pleaded as of the time of the initial disclosures. The court held that a "common-sense interpretation" of the Rule's requirement of disclosure did not extend to unpleaded claims or defenses. But the court added:

> [I]f full disclosure has been made and no additional defenses are raised, Weber has complied with the disclosure order. If full disclosure has not been made, Weber will find it difficult to introduce undisclosed evidence (including evidence on Paradigm's claim for damages) at trial or on summary judgment. . . . [If] Paradigm suspects Weber is holding back other defenses for tactical purposes, Paradigm may object on that ground to any motion to amend the pleadings. . . .

Note the severe impact of the potential sanction of exclusion. Also, note that the disclosure requirement seems to have prompted this court to imply a duty to plead claims or defenses earlier than the Rule governing amendments otherwise might require. Imagine a case in which the defendant is aware of a defense which the facts might or might not support, and which requires discovery before it can be pleaded in good faith. Might this defendant (or claimant) legitimately fear that a failure of early pleading and disclosure might cause the defense (or claim) to be precluded if the judge decides that there was enough information?

(4) *Sanctions for Failing to Disclose Obvious Witnesses: An Example.* The language of Rule 26(a)(1) would indicate that disclosures are still required even if the information is presumed to be known to the adversary. One of the problems that this principle raises is that of the undisclosed witness who is overlooked because she is obvious. Imagine that you have filed a claim on a promissory note for principal, interest, and attorney's fees, and your opponent answers with defenses of fraud, usury, and the defendant's status as an alleged "accommodation maker" who simply signed to satisfy the lender's requirements on a promise that he would not be liable. These defenses are pleaded with sufficient particularity to trigger disclosure requirements but remain factually general. Can you begin to make a list of the categories of witnesses and documents that you would disclose? [Note: If you didn't think of disclosing yourself as a witness, you may be precluded from supplying testimony necessary to recover attorney's fees! The complexity of the other issues, combined with the obviousness of the required testimony for attorney's fees, might lull a lawyer into nondisclosure — but how useful will it be to point out that the opponent "must have known" this testimony would be offered?]

(5) *Is "Good Faith" Enough?* Consider the situation of a party who finds, at trial, that an important piece of information has not been disclosed, but who has acted in good faith, in that the party simply did not realize that the information was relevant. Is such a party protected from the sanction of exclusion by an argument that the disclosures were made in good faith?

(6) *Disclosure of Damage Computations.* As observed in the *Biggars* case above, Rule 26 requires that a party disclose the "computation" of any category of claimed damages. Does the term "computation" connote the specification of a figure, mathematical formula, or calculation? Consider an attorney who has filed suit on behalf of a plaintiff with paraplegic injuries and who seeks to comply fully with this Rule with respect to such damages as future medical expenses, future pain and suffering, loss of consortium, and like categories. How would the initial disclosures be written to cover the "computation" of these damages?

NGUYEN v. IBP, INC.
162 F.R.D. 675 (D. Kan. 1995)

NEWMAN, UNITED STATES MAGISTRATE JUDGE.

Defendant moves to exclude any testimony at the trial of the action from plaintiff's retained expert witness, Nathan Shechter, M.D., on the grounds that plaintiff has failed to serve a proper disclosure under Fed.R.Civ.P. 26(a)(2) [the expert-witness disclosure provision]. . . .

A medical report signed by the expert witness and setting forth a summary of his physical examination and medical opinions was provided by Dr. Shechter. . . . Plaintiff also supplied an unsigned curriculum vitae and a list of patients about whom Dr. Shechter had given deposition testimony. The list identified the patient, either the patient's attorney or the attorney scheduling the deposition, and the date of the deposition. . . . Plaintiff also served a supplemental answer to [an] interrogatory [stating] that Dr. Shechter was to be paid the sum of $750.00 for his study and testimony in the case.

Defendant argues that the plaintiff has failed to make the appropriate disclosures. . . . Plaintiff boldly proclaims that "[p]laintiff has in fact fully complied with all disclosures pertaining to his expert witness. . . ."

[Rule 26(a)(2)(B)] clearly identifies the manner of disclosure as well as the specific disclosures to be made concerning a retained expert witness. A written report must be prepared and signed by the witness. The information to be disclosed in the report shall include: a) a complete statement of all opinions to be expressed and the reasons and basis underlying the opinions; b) the data or other information considered by the witness in forming the opinions; c) any exhibits to be used as a summary of or support for the opinions; d) the qualifications of the witness including a list of publications authored within the past 10 years; e) the compensation to be paid for the study and testimony; and f) a list of any other cases in which the witness has testified within the preceding four years, whether by deposition or at trial.

The disclosures served by plaintiff clearly and indisputably do not comply with Fed. R. Civ. P. 26(a)(2)(B). The only document signed by the expert witness was a letter addressing the expert's opinions and the basis therefor, the data considered by the expert, and exhibits to be used as a summary of or support for the opinions. While a curriculum vitae was provided, it was not signed by the witness and did not include publications authored by the witness within the past 10 years. Although plaintiff, by interrogatory answer, provided the compensation agreement, this agreement was not a part of the report signed by the witness. Plaintiff's counsel supplied a list of 137 patients about whom the witness had apparently testified during the 34 month period prior to October 28, 1994, and the dates of the deposition testimony. No identification of the "cases" in which these depositions were given is provided. The court or administrative agency in which the depositions were taken is not provided. Although an attorney's name is provided as to most of the patients, in many instances the first or last name of the attorney is missing. The telephone numbers are not supplied for the attorneys for 55 patients. The list is not signed by the witness. It includes entries for less than three years rather than for four years as required by the rule.

Fed. R. Civ. P. 37(c)(1) supplies the sanctions to be imposed in the event that a party fails to make the required disclosures. . . .

Under Rule 37(c)(1), the court must first consider whether the party has established "substantial[] justifi[cation]" for the failure to disclose and then consider whether the failure to disclose was "harmless." Substantial justification requires justification to a degree that could satisfy a reasonable person that parties could differ as to whether the party was required to comply with the disclosure request. . . . Failure to comply with the mandate of the Rule is harmless when there is no prejudice to the party entitled to the disclosure. The burden of establishing substantial justification and harmlessness is upon the party who is claimed to have failed to make the required disclosure.

. . . Plaintiff states that, while the witness has testified in hundreds of cases over the years, the only information retained by him related to his previous testimony is "the patient's name, the attorney's name who scheduled the deposition, the attorney's phone number and the date the deposition was given." Plaintiff's counsel states that he, personally, spent approximately eight hours compiling the information provided from the records retained by the witness for the preceding three years. He alleges that no record of deposition testimony beyond three years has been retained by the witness. Plaintiff argues that since all "reasonably available information listing the cases in which Dr. Shechter has testified" has been provided, the testimony of the witness should not be excluded. . . .

The court finds that the plaintiff has not established that the failure to disclose is substantially justified. . . .

Plaintiff has provided the facts required by five of the six subject matters required to be disclosed, notwithstanding plaintiff's failure to disclose all facts in the manner required by the Rule. The court will, therefore, primarily focus on the sixth subject matter or the failure to disclose "a listing of any other cases in which the witness has testified as an expert at trial or by deposition within the preceding four years."

Plaintiff argues that although the identity of the cases themselves may not have been provided, the information which "would enable the defendant to obtain the appropriate court or administrative records of Dr. Shechter's previous testimony" is disclosed. While counsel represents in plaintiff's memorandum that "all reasonably available information" has been disclosed, the witness has not adopted the representation or any of the disclosed information.

The court has great difficulty accepting at face value plaintiff's representation that all available information regarding cases in which the witness has testified as an expert during the past four years has been disclosed. The witness does not provide an affidavit to this effect. . . . Apparently, the plaintiff would have the court believe that Dr. Shechter has not maintained copies of any correspondence with attorneys which would have identified cases in which the expert's patients have been involved or in which depositions have been taken. Although Dr. Shechter may not have maintained a list of cases in which he has testified, one would expect a physician to have maintained records in the ordinary course of business from which the required disclosures could be assimilated. While perhaps the facts are as represented, notwithstanding the court's reservations, there is no evidence before the court which would require the court to find the existence of these facts and, without such, the court declines to make such findings. . . .

. . . An expert's failure to maintain records in the ordinary course of his business sufficient to allow the disclosures to be made, does not constitute "substantial justification" for the failure to provide required disclosures as to any retained expert expected to testify at the trial of the case. The requirements of the Rule 26(a) are mandatory as to any expert retained to testify. If the expert is unable or unwilling to make the disclosures he should be excluded as a possibility for retention as an expert witness in the case.

Plaintiff offers no explanation for the employment of an expert witness who was unable or unwilling to provide a report which complied with the rule. A party may not simply retain an expert and then make whatever disclosures the expert is willing or able to make notwithstanding the known requirements of Rule 26. . . . To the extent that there is a disadvantage created by the expert's failure to disclose it must be borne by the party retaining the expert witness. . . .

Plaintiff argues that any "minor disclosure omission" is harmless. The characterization of the failure to comply with Rule 26(a)(2)(B) as a minor omission, demonstrates plaintiff's lack of appreciation for the clear requirements of the Rule. The depositions of experts are precluded until the required disclosures have been made. . . . It was also contemplated that in many cases depositions would not be necessary due to the extent of the required disclosure. Obviously, a further reason for requirement of the disclosure in issue was to allow the adverse party to locate other testimony given by the expert witness which might be relevant to his proposed testimony in the pending case.

The information required to be disclosed are "cases" in which the witness has testified. The identification of "cases" at a minimum should include the courts or administrative agencies, the names of the parties, the case number, and whether the testimony was by deposition or at trial. Such information should be sufficient to allow a party to review the proceedings to determine whether relevant testimony was given. With the information supplied herein, the defendant would be required to contact each of the attorneys listed and obtain the identification of the "cases." Such is not contemplated by Fed. R. Civ. P. 26(a)(2)(B). . . . Cooperation of more than 100 attorneys who are not involved in this case in any way would also be required.

On the facts presented, the court finds that the failure to disclose the facts which could reasonably allow the defendant to review prior testimony by the witness is not "harmless."

Plaintiff's failure to provide a report including a statement of the expert's compensation agreement, the expert's qualifications, or an identity of the publications authored by the expert during the past 10 years, in light of the lack of any such publications, is harmless since the facts were otherwise supplied and the failure may be cured by simply having the witness sign a disclosure to these facts. As noted above, the failure to provide the listing of cases is not harmless. The court will allow the plaintiff to provide a supplemental disclosure which corrects the deficiencies identified herein within 40 days from the date of the filing of this order, otherwise, Dr. Shechter will not be permitted to testify at the trial of the action.

NOTES AND QUESTIONS

(1) *Cost and Delay Reduction — Or Cost and Delay Increase?* Assembly of the information required by the court here will require large expenditures of time and money by the party offering the witness. Note that the attorney already has spend eight hours together with the expert preparing (inadequate) responses; the market value of this fruitless effort almost certainly exceeds the entire $750 fee charged by the expert witness. The information may be exceedingly expensive to compile from raw records, particularly if it requires the physician to inspect all patient data during the last four years. The value of the information and the likelihood that this is the most efficient form for discovering it are doubtful. Does this judge's application of the disclosure rule reduce cost and delay or increase them?

(2) *What If the Information Simply Is Unavailable?: Considering the Court's Holding That the Rule Is "Mandatory."* The expert apparently has not kept records for all of the past four years and has kept only partial records in any event. People who are not attorneys often do not retain their documentation according to categories responsive to possible future litigation. Consider what should happen if the records simply do not permit a full listing of all prior cases with the precision that this opinion demands. (The judge hints that the problem is lack of an affidavit to this effect, but then holds that the disclosures are "mandatory." Is this holding appropriate, given that the rule expressly empowers the court to order that disclosures are not required in a particular case?) The judge also concludes that if the information is unavailable, the party for that reason alone should discard the expert. (Is this conclusion appropriate?)

(3) *What Kinds of "Experts" Are Subject to the Disclosure Requirements? — The Example of Treating Physicians: Salas v. United States, 165 F.R.D. 31 (W.D.N.Y. 1995).* In contrast to the strictness of the case above, several cases have held that treating physicians are not subject to the disclosure requirement, even though they are experts whose testimony fits the terms of the disclosure rule. The reasoning is that treating physicians are not "specially retained" within the meaning of the rule but instead are "viewers" or "actors" who testify to what they observed or did — even though they also testify to diagnosis, causation, indicated treatment, prognosis, etc. In *Salas*, the judge exempted five different physicians from disclosure requirements:

> As a general rule, a treating physician considers not just the plaintiff's diagnosis and prognosis, but also the cause of the plaintiff's injuries. In this case, there is no

> indication that these treating physicians reviewed any medical records other than those involved in their care and treatment of the patient. Plaintiff is not asking these doctors to comment upon or review the opinions of other doctors. Each of these physicians in fact treated the plaintiff in the area of their specialty. Accordingly, questioning these physicians as to whether the injuries for which they treated the plaintiff can be causally related to the accident would appear to be within the scope of the patient's care and treatment. . . .
>
> In sum, plaintiff's plan to elicit testimony from the treating physicians identified above as to causation does not bring those witnesses within the strict disclosure requirements of Rule 26(a)(2)(B).

Obviously, there can be important differences between experts hired to testify and those who testify after having been hired to treat the patient. The important subjects of the testimony, however, usually are similar: diagnosis, causation, etc. and usually even treating physicians are paid for time spent testifying. Is the difference in disclosures appropriate?

Appendix to § 7.03[A]: Self-Initiated Disclosures in Practice

NOTE ON THE LITIGATION IN THE DYNATECH CASE

Source of these Disclosures. The disclosures that follow are adapted from those in a real case involving contracts and subcontracts for NASA's space shuttle program. The names, terms, and all significant details of the disclosures are altered, and the dispute is reformulated to involve the space station program rather than the space shuttle. In the actual case, Professor Crump was counsel of record for Plaintiff Dynatech.

The Litigation. You may assume that Dynatech's Complaint alleges that the defendants violated a participation contract by which Dynatech was to be a subcontractor under a prime contract agreed to between NASA and the defendants for the space station program. Also, the complaint alleges that the defendants misappropriated several hundred of Dynatech's employees, together with trade secrets possessed by those employees. The complaint contains a number of different contract and business tort claims. Assume that the allegations show damages exceeding 50 million dollars. The defendants, you may assume, have answered with admissions and denials and with various statutory and common law defenses. (These descriptions of the claims and defenses are similar in format to those in the real case but differ in important respects.)

The broader 1993 version of the Rule, requiring disclosure of information "relevant to [any] disputed facts" advocated by either party, was in effect at the time. The current version might affect the extent of disclosures somewhat, by requiring only information "that the disclosing party may use to support its [own] claims or defenses." But the amendment probably would not decrease the volume of disclosures significantly.

Federal Jurisdiction(?) Assume that the plaintiff's suit was filed in state court, but the defendants have removed the action. Assume that there is no diversity, and the defendants' basis for removal is that the plaintiff's claims, although they purport to be based on state law, are necessarily federal because (the defendants contend) the claims concern subcontracts for the space program, in which there are uniquely federal interests. (In the real case, the trial judge ruled against a similar kind of argument and remanded the action to state court. But the remand occurred after the parties had undertaken the delay and expense necessary to file their disclosures, which were not required in the state court. Does this kind of result support an argument against requiring disclosures?)

UNITED STATES DISTRICT COURT
SOUTHERN DISTRICT OF TEXAS
HOUSTON DIVISION

DYNATECH CORPORATION, Plaintiff, vs. AMERICAN AEROSPACE PARTNERSHIP, L.L.C., NORWOOD INTERNATIONAL, INC., NORWOOD SPACE OPERATIONS, INC., and ARNOLD MASTERS CORP., Defendants.	CIVIL ACTION NO. X-96-2560 (JURY)

PLAINTIFF'S INITIAL DISCLOSURES
Under Rule 26(a)(1) of the Federal Rules of Civil Procedure

Pursuant to Fed. R. Civ. P. 26(a)(1), Plaintiff Dynatech Corporation ("Dynatech") here makes its initial disclosures as follows:

I. INDIVIDUALS WITH INFORMATION RELEVANT TO DISPUTED FACTS

Pursuant to Fed. R. Civ. P. 26(a)(1)(A), Dynatech believes the following persons are likely to have discoverable information [that fits the requirements for disclosure]:

Names **Address/Phone**	**Subjects of Which Witness May Have Knowledge**
Adley, John H. American Aerospace Partnership 1200 Mercury Avenue Houston, Texas 77058 (281) 542-7200	Program participation; quality of Dynatech's performance; termination of the original space station plan; the misappropriation of Dynatech's employees, data and/or business; formation of American Aerospace Partnership; pursuit of the new space station plans; and Defendants' conduct at Space Center.
Baker, Kevin American Aerospace Partnership 1200 Mercury Avenue Houston, Texas 77058 (281) 542-7200	Program participation; quality of Dynatech's performance; termination of the space station plan; the misappropriation of Dynatech's employees, data and/or business; formation of American Aerospace Partnership; and pursuit of the new plan.

Blank, Jimmy American Aerospace Partnership 1200 Mercury Avenue Houston, Texas 77058 (281) 542-7200	Dynatech's role in the program; contract negotiations; and program participation.
Brown, Adam 1018 Greenpark Altoona, PA 92390	Dynatech's role in the program; initial contract negotiations; and program participation.
Brykska, Daniel P. Western Switch 1210 Mercury Avenue Houston, Texas 77058 (281) 551-9722	Original space station plan team effort; termination of the space station plan; Dynatech's role in the program; pursuit of the new plan; and Defendants' conduct at Space Center. . . .

[At this point, approximately sixty (60) additional persons' names are listed, together with the subjects of which each may have knowledge. The names end as follows:]

Names **Address/Phone**	**Subjects of Which Witness May Have Knowledge**
Wurlitz, David American Aerospace Partnership 1200 Mercury Avenue Houston, Texas 77058 (281) 542-7200	Dynatech's role in the program; contract negotiations; termination of the plan; formation of American Aerospace Partnership; pursuit of the new plan; quality of Dynatech's performance; program participation; and the misappropriation of Dynatech's employees, data and/or business.
Zlotnik, Charles Houston, TX (281) 945-3612	Contract negotiations; Dynatech's role in the program; program participation; and quality of Dynatech's performance.

II. DOCUMENTS RELEVANT TO DISPUTED FACTS

Pursuant to Fed. R. Civ. P. 26(a)(1)(B), Dynatech hereby provides a description by category of the documents, data compilations and tangible things in its possession, custody or control that are not privileged and that are [within the disclosure requirements]. The items described below currently are located at one of the following locations: Dynatech Corporation, 1005 Alpha Drive, Greenwood, Virginia 23101; Dynatech Corporation, 1010 Mercury Avenue, Houston, Texas 77058 or [Dynatech's law firm], 300 Elm Street, Suite 1100, Dallas, Texas 75201.

1. Certain correspondence and memoranda from 1986 to the present relating to Dynatech's participation in the space operations program, including but not necessarily limited to certain documents in the following subcategories:
   a. Dynatech internal communications;
   c. Communications with third parties:
   d. Limited numbers of assorted other documents.
2. Requests for proposals and proposals (and related documents) from 1986 to the present relating to the space operations program, including but not necessarily limited to the following subcategories:

a. Requests for Proposals to or from the Defendants;

b. Responses to such Requests for Proposals;

c. Cost Proposals made by the parties;

d. Manpower Proposals made by the parties;

e. Offers made by the parties.

3. Certain contract materials (including change notices, statements of work, amendments, attachments, addenda and memoranda) from 1986 to the present relating to Dynatech's participation in the space operations program:

a. Drafts of and documents related to Subcontract No. Q7J5KRR-7575203 (SXRC OR "X" Contract);

b. Drafts of and documents related to Letter Agreement Q5A5KRR-88803K;. . . . [Here the document lists numerous additional contract materials, and it goes on to list several other categories of documents over several pages. The last item is:] 18. Certain assorted kinds of other documents from 1986 to the present relating to Dynatech's participation in the space station program.

III. DAMAGES CLAIMED

Because this case is in the early stages of discovery, Plaintiff is unable to provide an exact computation of its damages pursuant to Fed. R. Civ. P. 26(a)(1)(C) at this time. At this early stage of the litigation, Dynatech believes that its actual damages include (a) lost profits on the new space station plan contract, (b) unabsorbed overhead, and general administrative costs, and other direct costs that would have been absorbed by the new plan contract, (c) lost enterprise value and lost business opportunities resulting from the misappropriation and misuse of Dynatech's employees and proprietary information, and (d) restitution for lost profits derived by Defendants on the new plan and other contracts made possible by such misappropriation.

IV. INSURANCE AGREEMENTS

None.

Respectfully submitted,
[signed by James C. Adams]
JAMES C. ADAMS
[Firm name]
[Firm address, etc.]
ATTORNEY FOR PLAINTIFF
DYNATECH CORPORATION

NOTES AND QUESTIONS

(1) *Cost*. In Chapter 14, you will encounter the case of *Riverside v. Rivera*, which deals with the recovery of attorney's fees. The plaintiffs there recovered roughly $20,000 for preparation of a pretrial order draft in a case that produced verdicts for roughly $30,000, using fee rates that are half (or less) of current rates for comparable work. A pretrial order requires more kinds of information than disclosures, but it usually occurs after discovery, and thus perhaps the effort is comparable to that for a set of disclosures, which require raw data collection instead. This reasoning might lead to a cost estimate

of $50,000 at today's rates for disclosures in a small case. What would be the cost in a multi-million dollar case?

(2) *Alternatives; Opt-Out.* It immediately should be added that traditional discovery almost certainly would involve interrogatories requesting the same information as would be disclosed in such a case, and so perhaps the disclosures are not what "produces" these kinds of costs. But then again, imagine that the parties settle the case before substantial discovery (as happens in an appreciable minority of cases). In this event, disclosures might cause significant waste.

(3) *The Court's Evaluation of Disclosure Adequacy.* A "strict" court can multiply wasted costs by insisting on a high degree of precision in disclosures. Notice the document description for assorted documents and the description of damages, which are set out in terms appropriate for the early stage of a case. What would be the result if a given court were to insist upon a high degree of precision in these early disclosures?

[B] The Discovery Devices

[1] Oral Depositions

Read Fed. R. Civ. P. 28(a), 29, 30, 31, 32 (depositions), and 45 (subpoenas).

SALTER v. UPJOHN CO.
593 F.2d 649 (5th Cir. 1979)

[Susie Salter, as the executrix of the estate of Rufus Salter, brought a survival action against Upjohn and sought to take the deposition of Upjohn by deposing its President, Dr. William Hubbard.

[After her first deposition notice was vacated on Upjohn's motion for a protective order, Ms. Salter's counsel again sought to take Dr. Hubbard's deposition on two other occasions. Each time the judge denied her request.]

Of course, if after taking the other depositions, plaintiff was not satisfied and again properly gave notice of or requested taking Dr. Hubbard's deposition, the judge probably should have allowed the deposition. After the first protective order, however, plaintiff never again properly raised the issue in the trial court. In May 1976, plaintiff moved for the court to compel Dr. Hubbard to appear in Montgomery, Alabama for a deposition. Upjohn's principal place of business and Dr. Hubbard's residence was Kalamazoo, Michigan. It is well settled that "[t]he deposition of a corporation by its agents and officers should ordinarily be taken at its principal place of business," especially when, as in this case, the corporation is the defendant. . . . Before neither the trial court nor this court has plaintiff argued any peculiar circumstances that would justify her request to depose Dr. Hubbard in Montgomery. Therefore, the trial judge correctly denied plaintiff's motion to depose Dr. Hubbard in Alabama.

At oral argument plaintiff's attorneys asserted that when they made this second motion they were willing to go to Kalamazoo to take the deposition if necessary. Even if we accept this assertion as true, it is irrelevant. Plaintiff did not express her willingness to defendant or the trial judge. . . .

In October 1976 plaintiff moved for a third time to take Dr. Hubbard's deposition. This motion stated: "plaintiff requests that this Court either order the defendant to produce Dr. Hubbard in Montgomery, Alabama, for his testimony or to pay to plaintiff's attorney a reasonable charge for the time involved and also to pay his expenses to and from Kalamazoo, Michigan, to take this deposition of Dr. Hubbard." This motion was properly denied for several reasons. First, as noted above, the court did not abuse its discretion in refusing to compel Dr. Hubbard to appear in Montgomery. Second, the same policies validate the court's refusal to require defendant to pay plaintiff's expenses of taking the deposition in Kalamazoo. Plaintiff has never asserted any extraordinary circumstances that would have justified the unusual order she requested and we do not believe the trial judge's refusal to issue the order was an abuse of discretion. Third, on September 20, 1976, the court had entered a pretrial order, with the agreement of the parties, that "all discovery in this case be completed on or before October 1, 1976." On October 21, 1976, plaintiff made her third request to take Dr. Hubbard's deposition. Plaintiff has failed to even acknowledge that she made this request after the date by which the district court had ordered the parties to complete discovery. Therefore, she has of course not argued how the trial judge abused his discretion in imposing this limitation. . . . The judgment of the district court is therefore affirmed.

NOTES AND QUESTIONS

(1) *Setting up the Deposition: Notice.* The process of taking a deposition is begun by giving a deposition notice to every other party to the action. Fed. R. Civ. P. 30(b)(1). The notice must be "reasonable," although no fixed rule can be laid down as to what constitutes a reasonable time. *Compare Stover v. Universal Moulded Prod. Corp.*, 11 F.R.D. 90 (E.D. Pa. 1950) (two days' notice unreasonable in absence of showing of special need), *with Radio Corp. of America v. Rauland Corp.*, 21 F.R.D. 113 (N.D. Ill. 1957) (one day's notice not unreasonable when counsel were all in a foreign city for the taking of depositions at that time.) The notice is required to include the name and address, if known, of the witness, the time and place of the deposition, and a description of the documents or tangible things to be produced by the witness. As the principal case suggests, under the Federal Rules, a non-party witness who resides in a place that is far distant from the place in which the action is pending normally cannot be deposed in the forum; however, the court has broad discretion in this regard. *See* Fed. R. Civ. P. 45(c); *see also Baker v. Standard Indus., Inc.*, 55 F.R.D. 178 (D. P.R. 1972) (defendant could not avoid depositions in Puerto Rico by protective order, when its officers often travelled there and it had operations there).

(2) *Compelling Appearance.* A subpoena is necessary to compel the appearance of a non-party witness. Under the Federal Rules, subpoenas may be issued only from the court for the district in which the deposition is to be taken. Fed. R. Civ. P. 45(a)(2). When the witness is a party to the action, service of notice on the party's counsel has the same effect as a subpoena for the purpose of compelling attendance; thus a subpoena is not needed for a party-witness. *See* Fed. R. Civ. P. 37(d). Rule 45 requires the trial court to quash or modify a deposition subpoena that requires a person who is not a party or an officer of a party to travel more than 100 miles from the place where that person resides, is employed, or regularly transacts business. Fed. R. Civ. P. 45(c)(3)(A). Rule 45 also requires that a deposition subpoena state the manner in which the deposition will be taken.

(3) *Compelling Production.* When production of documents is desired from a non-party, the subpoena must set forth the documents to be produced. When information is withheld because it is privileged, the response must "expressly make [this] claim, and . . . describe the nature of the withheld" items sufficient to "enable the parties to assess the claim."

Fed. R. Civ. P. 45(d). Written objection to inspection or copying of any or all of the materials designated in the subpoena must be served within 14 days after service of the subpoena or before the time specified for compliance if such time is less than 14 days after service. Fed. R. Civ. P. 45(c)(2)(B). A person who is served with a subpoena duces tecum must produce the subpoenaed documents "as they are kept in the ordinary course of business or . . . organize and label them to correspond to the categories in the demand." Fed. R. Civ. P. 45(d). Likewise, the notice of deposition to a party may be accompanied by a request for production of documents made in compliance with Rule 34, which governs production. Fed. R. Civ. P. 30(b)(2).

(4) *Manner of Taking the Deposition.* In federal practice, persons authorized by the laws of the United States to preside at depositions, as well as persons authorized by state law to so preside, may record the testimony. Thus a state-certified court reporter may perform the task. Fed. R. Civ. P. 28. The witness is required to be placed under oath by the deposition officer. Fed. R. Civ. P. 30(c). A party may also take a deposition by nonstenographic means (*i.e.* by recording or videotape) by so stating in the notice, unless the court orders otherwise. Fed. R. Civ. P. 30(b)(3). The Federal Rules also provide that the parties may stipulate in writing, or the court on motion may order, that a deposition be taken by telephone or other remote means. Fed. R. Civ. P. 30(b)(4).

(5) *Objections to Procedural Defects.* Rule 32(d) requires prompt objection to certain types of procedural defects, such as irregularities in the notice, disqualification of the reporter, and deficiencies in the form of questions or answers. If not made promptly, these objections are waived. Most evidentiary objections, on the other hand, can be made at the time the deposition is offered in evidence (except objections to the form of questions or answers or other matters that could be cured on timely objection during the deposition). Thus, for example, the opponent does not need to object to preserve her right to exclude inadmissible prejudicial testimony in a deposition. She probably does need to object during the deposition, however, to a leading question directed to a non-adversary witness, if she wants to exclude the answer on that basis at trial — because it concerns the "form" of the question and because it could have been cured on timely objection.

(6) *Signature, Certification, Return and Filing.* A party or deponent may request, before the completion of the deposition, review of the transcript or recording. If this request is made, the deponent has 30 days after the transcript or recording is available to review it. If there are changes in form or substance, the deponent must make a statement regarding the changes and sign the statement. Fed. R. Civ. P. 30(e). Any errors or irregularities in the deposition are waived unless a motion to suppress the deposition or some part of it is made "promptly" after the defect is discovered or "with reasonable diligence" could have been discovered. Fed. R. Civ. P. 32(d)(4).

(7) *Stipulations Regarding Discovery Procedure Under Rule 29: The "Usual Agreements."* Rule 29 allows the parties to make stipulations about the taking of depositions and to modify most other discovery procedures. For example, attorneys frequently agree to waive the requirement that the witness sign the deposition (or agree that it may be signed before any notary, rather than before the court reporter). Agreements concerning the taking of the deposition by a non-certified court reporter, or concerning the allocation of deposition expenses, also sometimes occur. Indeed, the parties sometimes unnecessarily stipulate to matters already provided for by Rule, such as agreeing to waive notice defects (provided for by Rule 32(d)(1)). But perhaps the most frequent stipulation is that all objections to admissibility may be made at the time of trial, even if they otherwise would be required to be made contemporaneously under Rule 32. (If you propose to offer the

deposition at trial, you must consider carefully whether to enter into this stipulation. If you agree to the stipulation, objections to the form of questions and answers can be postponed until trial, rather than made during the deposition when you can cure them. But the stipulation still may be useful, since it avoids the need for the opponent to interrupt the deposition frequently. Without such a stipulation, many opposing attorneys will interpose lengthy objections to all questions, just to protect the record.) So widespread is the use of Rule 29 stipulations that attorneys often begin the deposition by directing the court reporter to insert "the usual agreements." This shorthand may be acceptable if all parties have the same "usual agreements" in mind, but local custom does vary. If there is any doubt, you should ask: "And what do you understand the 'usual agreements' to be?" For a discussion of deposition strategy, see Blumenkopk, *Deposition Strategy and Tactics*, 5 Am. J. Trial Advocacy 231 (1981).

(8) *Presumptive Limits of Ten Depositions; Time Limits on Depositions*. Rule 30(a) places a presumptive limit of ten depositions upon the parties (subject to stipulation otherwise by the parties, and to the court's authority to modify the limit for a particular case). Is such a rule a good idea? In addition, Rule 30(d) limits each deposition to no more than "1 day of 7 hours."

§ 7.03[B][1] Appendix Deposition Practice

Groce, CHECKLIST FOR TAKING PLAINTIFF'S DEPOSITION*

From State Bar of Texas, Practice Skills Course

This is not intended to be all-inclusive. Each case, of course, requires an interrogation indicated largely by the investigation file, but this is intended to give pointers that are sometimes overlooked.

1. Ask the (1) name; (2) social security number; (3) exact date of birth of the witness; (4) and whether he has ever gone under any other name; (5) or different spelling of the same name.
2. General history of the witness, including: (1) where he was born; (2) all places where he has lived; (3) names and location of (a) father; (b) mother; (c) brothers and (d) sisters; (4) education.
3. Marital history — (1) whether he is married or divorced; (2) where marriage or marriages took place; (3) and if divorced how many times; (4) how many children; (5) where former spouse or spouses can be located; (6) their maiden and present name; (7) and where divorce was granted.
4. (1) Description of the accident, letting witness first describe it in narrative form; (2) and then questioning him specifically; (3) condition of the street or other scene of accident; (4) weather condition.
5. Names and addresses of all witnesses known to plaintiff. Pin him down as to who saw the accident.
6. Whether or not any statements were made at the time of the accident or any admissions were made by any of the parties to the accident.
7. What occurred immediately after the accident; whether claimant went to the hospital and, if so, how.

---

* Reprinted by permission of the State Bar of Texas, Professional Development Program, the Estate of Josh H. Groce, Esq., and Groce, Locke and Hebdon, San Antonio, Texas.

8. Names and addresses of all doctors who have treated him prior and subsequent to the accident and who selected such doctors. He should identify his "family doctor," if he has one, and just what treatments for anything that he has received.

9. Have witness sign authorization in the following form: "All doctors who have treated me and all hospitals in which I have ever been a patient are hereby authorized to give to the bearer of this authorization or of any facsimile copy hereof, all information relative to my physical condition, past, present or future." This should be dated and signed by the witness and witnessed by his attorney.

10. Ask if claimant is willing to submit to a medical examination by doctors of defendant's selection and if not then will he agree to an examination by doctors selected by the court.

11. Ask witness whether he or any member of his family, as far as he knows, has ever had a claim for personal injury against any person, firm, corporation or governmental agency, and follow this up, depending upon the answer of the witness.

12. (1) Ask the witness whether he has ever had any previous accidents or injuries of any character; (2) any subsequent accidents or injuries to this one; (3) does he have any health and accident insurance paying money for prior injuries or the injury made the basis of this suit; (4) is he receiving any government benefits for disability, unemployment, etc. (5) has he applied for any jobs or insurance that required a physical examination either shortly before or at any time after the accident.

13. (1) Determine the nature of previous jobs; (2) how much he was making; (3) for whom he was working; (4) why employment was terminated; (5) what qualifications and experience the witness had for the type of work he was doing when injured; (6) and ask what income tax he paid, demand a copy of return; (7) inquire as to what work witness has done since accident, and describe just what his duties are or were; (8) determine his employers and earnings with particular care for the year preceding his injury.

14. (1) Definitely determine what part or parts of the witness' body were injured and eliminate all other portions; (2) if there is any particular member of the body injured, have him state what he can or cannot do with that particular member; (3) go into details as to what witness can and cannot do. This becomes important when movies are used.

15. (1) Ask for his status during the last war; (2) where his draft board was, and (3) if he was turned down, why; (4) obtain a signed authorization permitting bearer to review his army records and examine his records at any Veterans' Administration hospital; (5) obtain his service serial number and Veterans Administration Claim Number for identification purposes.

16. Inquire whether witness has ever been arrested, indicted or convicted of felony or crime, offense or misdemeanor and whether or not he has ever been in jail or prison. Geographically locate where the offenses occurred.

17. In automobile cases (1) obtain his driver's license number; (2) ask if his license has ever been revoked, suspended or put on probation together with details; (3) ask for history of all prior automobile accidents and moving traffic violations.

18. Explain to plaintiff that the purpose of the deposition is to bring out all the relevant facts from the plaintiff's standpoint and then ask: "Is there any other

fact relevant to this matter about which I have not asked but which might have a bearing on this case?"

NOTES AND QUESTIONS

(1) *Relevance and Work Product Problems in the Checklist.* Consider the last item in the above checklist (the inquiry as to whether there is "any other fact relevant to this matter"). Imagine that you represent the plaintiff who is being deposed and this question is asked of her in your presence. What would you do? (If you have interviewed the plaintiff yourself and discussed the case with her, what is the probable source of answers she would likely give as to what is "relevant"?) If you decide that this question is outside the bounds of discovery, on what ground? How would you enforce your client's rights in this situation?

(2) *Limits of Discovery.* Aside from the last item in the checklist (the general inquiry into "any other relevant fact"), are there other items in the checklist that you would consider outside the bounds of discovery if you represented the deponent?

(3) *Treatment of Non-Discoverable Inquiries.* What happens if a question is asked that is outside the bounds of discovery but the deponent's attorney does nothing? What happens if there is a genuine difference of opinion between the two attorneys as to what are the proper bounds (as there may be with several items here)?

(4) *Witness Background.* What is the relevance of questions about the deponent's family? Education? Military history? Whether she has ever been in jail? Are all of these items discoverable?

(5) *Encouraging the Witness to Narrate First: The "Funnel" Sequence.* In connection with the inquiry into the accident or event itself, the writer advises the examiner to let the "witness first describe it in narrative form." Only after that is done does the writer advise "questioning him specifically." Why? What would be lost if the examiner began with pointed questions of a leading nature? How will this examination differ from the cross-examination of this witness at trial? Would a skillful cross-examiner simply ask the witness to describe the accident in his own words? What does this tell you about the aims and goals of taking a deposition?

(6) *Prompting Further Narrative.* Suppose you are trying to get the witness to describe the accident "in narrative form," as the writer here advises, and the witness responds with a brief and incomplete statement. What would you do? Would you then go to pointed and specific questions, or would you try to get a complete narrative (and if so, by what techniques)?

(7) *Discovery of Other Information Sources.* Notice that there is an effort to find out about all witnesses, statements or other sources of information. Why?

NOTE ON PREPARING A WITNESS TO BE DEPOSED

A skillful deposer can obtain information from a witness, even if the witness is truthful, tending to embarrass the witness at trial — for the simple reason that no one has a perfect memory. Ambiguities in language also tend to create credibility difficulties with truthful witnesses. Therefore, the preparation of a client for deposition is as much an art as taking a deposition. The following ideas may help:

a. Explain to the witness the purpose of the taking of the deposition. It is to help the other side, not the client.

b. Anticipate the areas of questions, tell the client what you anticipate and discuss the answers he gives.

c. Explain how questions are asked — general questions, leading questions and the like.

d. Give the client specific advice on the deposition procedure, on how to act and on the format that questions and answers should take. Simulation is helpful and appropriate.

e. Be explicit and emphatic in advising the client to tell the truth.

Many litigators give their clients written advice. The following, used by the law office of Montgomery & Lee, is a sample.

MONTGOMERY & LEE, YOUR DEPOSITION

(unpublished law office document)

What is a Deposition?

In its simplest form, a deposition is the oral testimony of a witness, taken under oath, before trial. The basic rule is that the questions asked need only address themselves to information which is relevant to the case or to discovering relevant facts. The rules by which [c]ourts operate allow either side in a lawsuit to take a deposition of the other side and/or of any witness. Your deposition may be taken in our office, the office of the opposing attorney, a courtroom, or some other place. We will tell you where to be and when. There will be no judge present. However, what you say *will* be recorded, either by shorthand, court reporter, or perhaps videotape. We represent you in this important matter, but it is *your* deposition. We cannot answer the questions for you, and depending upon how you answer the questions and your attitude, your truthfulness, and your appearance, *your* case will be helped or hurt! . . .

Purpose

Why is your deposition being taken? That's simple — the opposing side wants to "pick your mind"! They want to find out what facts you know regarding this lawsuit and they want to pin you down to a specific story. If you answer a question one way during the deposition and another way during the trial, you will make it very difficult for us to help you. So we can avoid such difficulties, here are a few "DOs" and "DON'Ts" to remember:

1. DON'T hurry — DO take your time answering all questions; speak slowly and clearly.

2. DON'T volunteer — DO answer the question you are asked and *stop* talking. Never try to explain your answer. If you can answer "yes" or "no," do so and *stop*.

3. DON'T get excited or angry — DO relax and listen calmly. The opposing attorney may try to make you angry in hopes you will say something you will regret later (like at trial!).

4. DON'T guess — which means don't speculate; don't give your "opinion"; and don't estimate things like time, speed, or distance unless you have a good reason for knowing such matters. DO stick to the *basic* facts and testify only to that which you *personally* know.

5. DON'T fib — which is a nice way of saying *don't lie!* (DO believe us when we say the truth, in a lawsuit, never is as damaging as a lie!)

6. DON'T joke — while you may think a particular question or a possible answer to a question is cute or funny, we doubt you think your lawsuit is funny. DO treat the whole deposition seriously.

7. DON'T memorize — DO just answer the questions to the best of your ability.

8. DON'T worry — especially if you honestly don't know the answer to a question. If you don't, then admit it with the simple response, "I don't know."

9. DON'T be chummy — either with the opponents or their attorneys, before, during, and after the deposition. DO be on guard. Remember, the *other* attorney is your "legal enemy." Do not let his friendly manner cause you to drop your guard or become chatty. A deposition is *not* a social event!

10. DON'T magnify your injuries or losses. DO be conservative in describing them, but don't leave any out.

Your Attitude & Appearance

The first opportunity the opposing attorney has to see you usually comes at the deposition. He or she will use the occasion to try and size up you and your case. Therefore, it is important that you make a good impression. [Y]ou should prepare as if you were going to trial, and that means *you should:*

1. Be clean and neat and wear clean and neat clothing.

2. Treat all persons in the deposition room with respect.

3. Come prepared to exhibit any and all injuries which you have suffered.

4. Bring facts and figures with respect to the time you lost from work, amount of wages lost, doctor bills, hospital bills, and any other information pertaining to your lawsuit.

A SAMPLE DEPOSITION:
DEPOSITION OF PLAINTIFF JANET PRINGLE IN *PRINGLE v. JIM DANDY FAST FOODS, INC.*

The Dispute Background: The plaintiff's pleading alleges that she purchased a chicken dinner from the defendant's fast food restaurant and was injured because the chicken breast had an "improperly cut bone" that lodged in her throat. The claims are for negligence, product liability, and breach of warranty. The deposition was set up by a notice sent to the plaintiff's counsel by defense counsel. It is taken from the real case of *Jim Dandy Fast Foods, Inc. v. Carpenter*, 535 S.W.2d 786 (Tex. Civ. App.-Houston [1st Dist.] 1976), although it is edited and has been transformed to the hypothetical City of London, Manero County, West York, with some dates and names also changed. The defendant did business under the name "Church's Fried Chicken," which was the name that appeared on the restaurant sign; accordingly, the deposition contains references to the defendant as "Church's."

Not a "Model" Deposition, but Typical. Our efforts to find a deposition appropriate for this book have convinced the authors that "model" depositions must be rare. This investigative device simply does not lend itself easily to evaluation by academic or aesthetic standards. This deposition, however, is typical for a relatively simple personal injury case.

IN THE 199th DISTRICT COURT
NEW DUBLIN COUNTY, WEST YORK

JANET PRINGLE v. JIM DANDY FAST FOODS, INC., d/b/a CHURCH'S FRIED CHICKEN	NO. 23,150

DEPOSITION OF JANET PRINGLE

Deposition of Janet Pringle, taken on the 17th day of November, 1982, at 9:30 a.m., in the offices of Simpson, Morgan & Burwell, 619 Eighth Avenue North, Iberia City, West York, before Charles W. Conroy, Jr., a notary public in and for the County of Manero, State of West York; notice, signature of the witness and return being waived, with all objections to be reserved until the time of trial.

IT WAS FURTHER STIPULATED AND AGREED by and between counsel that the reporter could swear the witness with the same force and effect as though he were a notary public in and for New Dublin County, West York.

JANET PRINGLE,

the plaintiff, was called as a witness by the defendants, and, having been first duly sworn, testified as follows:

EXAMINATION by Mr. Bryan

Q: Your name is what, please, ma'am?

A: Janet Pringle.

Q: Where do you live?

A: Arcadia, West York.

Q: All right. What is your address in Arcadia?

A: . . . It is 3338 Cemetery Road. . . .

Q: How old a person are you, please?

A: I am 40 years old.

Q: Are you married?

A: Yes, sir.

Q: What is your husband's name?

A: Brandon Lee Pringle.

Q: Do you have any children?

A: Yes, sir.

Q: How many?

A: Three children.

Q: What are their ages, names and sexes?

A: Barbara Hinzer, she is 21. Jennara Lee Mandell. She is married now. Bertram Allen Sams, he is 17.

Q: All right. Now when did you marry your present husband?

A: In January, '80.

Q: All right. Now is he your second or third or what?

A: No. This is my fourth marriage. . . .

Q: All right. With whom is your present husband connected in business or professionally?

A: He works with West York A & M oceanographic department.

Q: Is that down in New Dublin?

A: Yes, sir.

Q: What are his duties generally, his title, so forth, as you know them?

A: He is a boatswain on one of their ships.

Q: I see. All right. Who was number three?

A: Christopher McCandless, a boy I went to school with. McCandless.

Q: Then none of these children are by your present husband?

A: No, sir. By my first marriage. . . .

[At this point, Mr. Bryan asks Mrs. Pringle about each of her previous marriages — the dates of each, the names of her husbands, and when she was divorced from each.]

Q: In any of those divorces, did you ask for a divorce on the basis of any physical mistreatment of any kind?

A: It wasn't physical, just mental. I guess mental and physical.

Q: Mental and physical mistreatment, is that correct? . . .

A: On my first marriage only.

Q: I see. That wasn't true of your application in the petition for divorce in numbers two and three?

A: Just mental. . . .

Q: I see. Mental cruelty. All right. Now, where were you born and raised?

A: I was born in Millbrook, Alabama. I was raised in different towns of Alabama.

Q: Did you go through the schools there?

A: Up until junior high school, when I came to West York. . . .

Q: Have you taken any courses of any kind since leaving high school?

A: Yes, sir. I am in college now.

Q: I see. All right. Which college?

A: New Dublin Community College.

Q: All right. What courses are you taking, please?

A: Courses to be a Registered Nurse, an R.N. nurse. . . .

[Mr. Bryan has Mrs. Pringle describe her other schooling, which included one previous year of junior college plus the learning of secretarial skills.]

Q: All right. Now who have you worked for starting at this time and going backwards; who have you worked for?

A: Since what time?

Q: Starting now and going back.

A: I worked for the University of West York Medical Branch.

Q: In New Dublin?

A: Two different positions. Yes.

Q: When was that, please?

A: '76 to '78 I was medical insurance clerk. From there I took a better position. I was executive secretary with Cablevision from '78 to '80. And at the present time I am in school.

Q: I see. What generally was your pay in those positions?

A: In Cablevision I made $550 plus expenses.

[Mrs. Pringle testified that she worked for the University of West York, the Manero County Welfare Department, the Dow Hospital, and Black's Hardware Store. Mr. Bryan asked her salary in each job. He asked, "do you remember anybody else that you worked for?" and Mrs. Pringle replied that she worked as a bookkeeper for a bank.]

[Mr. Bryan then asked about Mrs. Pringle's family, her father and mother. He asks about her medical history. Then he turns to the lawsuit itself.]

Q: All right. In reading your complaint and so forth, I gather you have some complaint about chicken and so forth at Church's Chicken place?

A: Yes, sir.

Q: All right. When did this occur?

A: About the middle of September. You mean when I swallowed the bone?

Q: Yes, ma'am. Whatever you are contending in your suit here.

A: Yes, sir.

[Mrs. Pringle fixed the date at September 16, and she said that the Church's store was on Palmer Highway, in the city of Iberia City, West York, with a sign saying "59¢."]

Q: All right. I take it you had been there before, had you?

A: No. I wasn't familiar with Iberia City at all.

Q: I see. How did you happen to go into the Church's place here in Iberia City?

A: I had taken that part — I had remarried and took that part-time job with Sears. Sears is down the road, so it was on the way.

Q: Well, we haven't heard about Sears. That is why I don't know. I don't believe you told me about Sears, did you?

A: I thought [I already told you] about it.

Q: No, ma'am.

A: I am sorry.

Q: . . . When did you go to work for Sears?

A: I went to work, that was my first day of work at Sears. I took a part-time job there.

Q: Doing what, please?

A: Telephone promotion, sales promotion.

[Mr. Bryan had the witness describe how she entered the store and purchased a chicken dinner, including a breast.]

Q: I see. All right. What else did you get with it, anything besides the piece of breast?

A: I ordered a Coke.

Q: All right. Is that what you customarily ordered, the piece of breast, so forth?

A: I usually have or most of the time I might have a small cole slaw.

Q: No. No. The piece of chicken that you mostly order, it is a breast of chicken, is that correct, when you go?

A: Yes, sir.

Q: What other places have you eaten in where they have fried chicken that way?

A: Shep's Fried Chicken. . . .

Q: I see. All right. Now, how long have you been going to these fried chicken places, so forth, and buying this breast section, either one side or the other, or with the wing on it? . . .

A: I guess in the last five years.

Q: I see. All right. Have you been in there a number of times during the last five years? . . .

A: Yes, sir.

[Mr. Bryan asked several questions concerning Mrs. Pringle's understanding of how chicken is cut. "You have to cut through the bones that make up the rib cage, don't you?" he asked at one point. She answered, "I don't know. I guess so." Mr. Bryan then returned to the sequence of events.]

Q: I see. All right. Now, did you get the real crisp type or just the regular fried chicken?

A: I believe all they had was the crisp. . . .

Q: All right. Now as I understand it, you went in to Church's place there and bought chicken and sat down and ate it there or attempted to eat it there at Church's, is that correct?

A: Yes. I sat down and had one bite of it.

Q: I see. All right. You saw the chicken. Was it delivered to you on a platter of some kind or a plate? . . .

A: A little open thing they serve in, they put it in like that. I picked it up and took my Coke and sat down.

Q: You had a Coke. Now, did you have anything else there with it at that time?

A: They give you a biscuit. . . .

Q: All right. So all you ordered, that you recall, was chicken, Coke and a biscuit?

A: Yes, sir. . . .

Q: All right. When you bought the chicken, were you given any receipt of any kind by the cashier there who took your money?

A: No, sir. I wasn't given a receipt. They may have. Sometimes they will stick it in a little tray there, but I don't remember about the receipt.

Q: I see. You don't have it now though, do you?

A: No.

Q: I see. Can you describe for me who was the cashier there at that time?

A: There was just a young man and woman in the place. . . .

Q: All right. What did the man look like, height, color of his hair, how he was dressed or whatever you can tell me about him?

A: I don't know if I can really explain what he looked like. He had [a] little paper hat on, I remember that.

[Mr. Bryan asked several more questions about the two employees in the store, then returned to the sequence of events.]

Q: I see. Now, you got your chicken at the counter. Do they have a dining room there; is the dining room part of the place there?

A: It's all one room. . . .

Q: That is where you sat down and ate it?

A: That is where I took one bite.

Q: One bite. All right. We have gotten you from the counter over to the benches now. Tell me what happened.

A: All right, sir. Well, I have a bridge. I can't bite down too hard to eat chicken, so I pulled a piece off like this. I put it in my mouth.

Q: Let me get that in the record there: In other words, you took your hand — I am not trying to misquote you. You follow me because I do want to get it in the record. You took your hand instead of — since you have a bridge which keeps you from biting down too hard, you took your hand and pulled the meat off?

A: Just one hand. . . .

Q: You pulled a piece of breast off of the piece that you bought and put it in your mouth, is that correct?

A: Yes, sir.

Q: All right. Then what happened?

A: I chewed and swallowed. As I swallowed, I felt a scratchiness which I thought was the crust because it was very crusty. I swallowed the second time and there was still something there. I thought, well, it must be that crust, you know, so I took a bite of the bread and then swallowed again and it didn't relieve it. So I got up immediately and went to the restroom, thinking that if I put my finger there that it would come up. Nothing but pure blood came up when I did that. . . .

Q: Okay. What did you do after that?

A: I went up to the counter and asked or told them that I thought possibly I had swallowed a bone. I was gasping and said, "I am not familiar with Iberia City. Could you direct me to a doctor, please?" They stood and just looked at me a moment. Then they said, "Well, the only thing we know is there is a dentist across the street." So I went and got in my car and drove across the street.

Q: Which dentist?

A: I don't even know the man's name. I just went on in. I was already just gasping like that.

Q: I see. All right. What did you do with the piece of chicken?

A: I just left it there.

Q: You didn't preserve it in any way?

A: No, sir. [Later I did preserve the bone, but not then, because it was still in my throat.]

Q: I see. All right. Now, did you make any complaints about the piece of chicken that you had there to those people at Church's place at that time?

A: No. I just left and hunted the doctor, went across to the doctor.

Q: Did you ever go back and make any complaint to them?

A: I never went back in there at all. . . .

[Mrs. Pringle described her contacts with Church's in an effort to get her medical bills paid. She testified that she received a communication, ultimately, from an insurance company in another state, denying her claim.]

Q: All right. Any other contact that you had with Church's Fried Chicken people or their companies?

A: Well, this man taped, you know, my story. He did tape it. He told me he was taping it as I talked on the telephone.

Q: Which man is that that taped it?

A: I think one insurance agent. There were some.

Q: Church's people?

A: Representing them in some sort of way. I don't know whether an insurance agent or what, just by phone, just a short conversation. He just told me he was going to tape it. I said, "Fine, I will tell you."

Q: About how long after September 16, 1980 was that? . . .

A: Oh, let's see. I would say within a month.

Q: All right. Now were there any other contacts that you have had with Church's Fried Chicken or Jim Dandy Fast Foods, and so forth? . . .

A: No, sir. Not after they declined [to pay the medical bills].

Q: Did you go to a doctor after this incident?

A: Yes, sir.

Q: Which one?

A: They sent me 20-some blocks to this one who looked — I don't know who he is. He sent me to another one. I was driving all around and finally wound up at this other one who was Dr. Niemann who did remove the bone.

Q: I see. You still have the bone?

A: Yes, sir.

Q: I see. What size bone is it?

A: I don't know. Would you like to see it?

Q: Yes, if you would, please.

A: It is in the same container the doctor handed me.

Q: Okay. What would you say that was, about an inch, an inch long, this piece of breastbone?

A: I don't know.

A: MR. BRYAN: You have seen it?

A: MR. BURWELL: Yes.

Q: (By Mr. Bryan) That is what it looks like to me, an inch long piece of breastbone.

MR. BURWELL: I don't know. About an inch long. I can get a measuring thing. I don't know.

MR. BRYAN: I think that is close enough.

THE WITNESS: Okay.

Q: (By Mr. Bryan) Then you went to — can you tell me the name of the doctor — Dr. Niemann?

A: Yes, sir. . . .

Q: How long after the occurrence where you say you put this piece of breast in your mouth there was it?

A: That he removed it, you mean?

Q: Yes, ma'am.

A: It was that night around — I don't know what time. I was admitted to the hospital. I heard them say something about he would be here at 6:00.

Q: Well, four, five, six hours, something like that, after you say that you were at Church's?

A: I would say between — yes, at least that long.

Q: I see. All right. Now, which hospital did you go in?

A: On the highway out here, New Dublin Memorial Hospital. . . .

Q: I see. Did you go back to Dr. Niemann in connection with your throat there any time after you were discharged from the hospital?

A: Yes, sir.

Q: How many times?

A: I went back, I believe, twice.

Q: All right. What did he do for you on those occasions?

A: Well, the first time was just like a checkup, you know. He said it looked like it was going well, just, you know —

Q: Had you opened your mouth and he had one of those little paddles and you said "Ahh, ahh, ahh"; is that what he had you to do?

A: Sort of.

Q: I see. On the second time, what did he do, the same thing as the first?

A: No, sir. I told him I was still having some trouble with my breathing and all. He said he would like to run an esophagram on it to make sure.

Q: Did he run an esophagram on it?

A: Yes, sir.

Q: What did he tell you that he found?

A: He told me that he thought I was all right, you know, to that date. I was doing all right.

Q: I see. That was about how long after the 16th of September, 1980?

A: About four or five months. . . .

Q: All right. Now did you go on with your job at Sears & Roebuck?

A: Yes. . . . [A]s I said, I did sales promotion, which is a lot of talking. I was very weak. I would have to stop talking. I couldn't even — I just got real weak. I did this several weeks, I'd even have to go straight to bed from being weak from that.

Q: Yes, ma'am. What was your pay at Sears & Roebuck?

A: I was just part time. It was $1.60 an hour.

Q: What were you averaging a week, please, ma'am?

A: Well, I worked about 40 hours a week. . . .

[Here there is further testimony concerning Mrs. Pringle's employment and her wage rates.]

Q: All right. Tell me this: How big was that piece?

A: That I put in my mouth?

Q: Yes, ma'am.

A: Just a normal size.

Q: Well, an inch by an inch?

A: I don't know how to say that, you know.

Q: All right. Well, when you say "normal," that doesn't mean anything. Normal to one person may mean a bunch of little pieces; and normal to another may mean the breast in layers, so you may take the whole layer of breast off. That is why I am trying to get some idea what size of piece it was.

A: I don't know the size. I just know it was [a] chewable size. . . . I am very bad on sizes, as you can see. I don't know how to say what is an inch or two inches. I have to measure. . . .

Q: Give me your best estimate.

A: Okay. About like that, about like that (indicating).

Q: In other words, about four inches, roughly four inches long, roughly about an inch thick?

A: If that is an inch thick. I don't really know.

Q: All right. I know you are estimating. All right. Now, how much chewing did you do of your food? Napoleon used to chew his, I think, 26 times or something like that.

A: Twenty-seven times.

Q: Before you swallow every mouthful, how much do you usually chew?

A: I don't know, but I didn't chew 27 times.

Q: All right. Well, you generally chew five times, ten times, fifteen, so forth?

A: I mean, who knows how many times you chew. . . .

Q: Wouldn't you imagine it would take at least ten chews to kind of tear a piece of chicken up to get it to pulverize it, so forth, so you could swallow it?

A: I don't know how many times I chew. . . .

Q: Are you generally familiar with the fact that when you eat a chicken, that you expect to find bones in the chicken?

A: Yes, there are bones in a chicken.

[At this point, there are many questions concerning Mrs. Pringle's understanding of chicken anatomy.]

Q: . . . All right. Have you ever been involved in any other litigation of any kind, any suits besides your divorce suits?

A: No, sir. . . .

Q: Ever made a claim for workmen's compensation benefits at any time?

A: No, sir.

Q: Ever reported an injury of any kind that required you to go to a nurse or to a doctor or so forth on any job?

A: No, sir. Never.

Q: Ever been injured in any way in an automobile accident where you were riding or driving?

A: No, sir.

Q: Ever had any injuries from slipping or falling in any way?

A: No, sir.

Q: Ever found it necessary to go to a psychiatrist for any reason?

A: No, sir.

[At this point, Mr. Bryan went into Mrs. Pringle's previous medical history, including the doctors she has seen and hospitals she has been to for medical treatment. He then returned to the injury at issue.]

Q: I see. Now Dr. Niemann has not told you that you have any permanent injury of any kind to your throat, has he?

A: He said it looked all right to him. . . .

Q: No doctor, since Dr. Niemann saw you and told you that he didn't think it was a permanent condition, has told you that it was a permanent condition, has he?

A: No.

Q: All right. Do you do the housekeeping at your place? . . .

A: Yes sir.

Q: All right. Ever prepared a chicken?

A: Yes, sir. But usually I buy them cut up.

[At this point, Mr. Bryan asked a number of questions designed to show that Mrs. Pringle knows that chicken, when cut, may have some cut bones.]

Q: Now what did Dr. Niemann charge you, please ma'am?

A: The best I can remember, about $157. That was just his fee.

Q: What was the hospital?

A: Approximately $140. I paid for the X-rays before they would even X-ray me, $14. That is not counting an esophagram and everything afterwards.

Q: What has been the total of your hospital and test costs, so forth?

A: I don't have the bills. I can get them for you.

MR. BRYAN: Do you have the bills?

MR. BURWELL: I don't have all of them either, Mr. Bryan.

MR. BRYAN: Would you get those, please, and let me have them? Do you have by any chance an oral narrative report from the doctor?

MR. BURWELL: Yes, sir.

MR. BRYAN: Would you mind letting me have a copy of it?

MR. BURWELL: Not at all. . . .

MR. BRYAN: Do you by any chance have a resume of the hospital discharge report?

MR. BURWELL: I do not. I will get a copy and furnish it to you.

Q: (By Mr. Bryan) As to where actually this piece of bone that you have got there and have shown me came from, to your own knowledge, you don't know, do you?

A: I don't know what you mean by that, "where it came from." What part of the chicken it came from?

Q: Yes, ma'am. . . .

MR. BURWELL: Do you know what part that bone is?

THE WITNESS: I don't know about that.

Q: (By Mr. Bryan) I see. All right. As to whether or not this came from that piece of chicken, to your own knowledge, you don't know, do you?

MR. BURWELL: You don't know whether that was a bone off that chicken or a bone off some other chicken?

THE WITNESS: No, I don't know. It was just in the piece I ate. That is all I know.

Q: (By Mr. Bryan) I see. All right. Now you are not contending, are you, that the piece of chicken, that that meat was spoiled in any way or was not wholesome for you to eat, are you? . . .

A: It wasn't a spoiled piece of chicken. No. . . .

Q: All right. It was not unfit for human consumption, was it?

A: Well, if the bone was there, it was. . . .

Q: All right. Mrs. Pringle, is it customary with you that when you are chewing anything that has meat that has bones in it or about it, that when you are masticating it in your mouth, to use your tongue to feel the thing and to see whether there is anything rough or hard, so forth, in it before you swallow it, isn't that customary to you?

A: Generally, sir.

Q: But you didn't do that on this occasion, is that correct?

A: Well, that is what puzzles me, too. I did not feel the bone at all. In fact, I thought it was the crust that I had swallowed.

Q: I see. All right. But you really didn't take your tongue — as you told me you normally would do — and work it around through the food and so forth to see that there were no hard rough places that could in anywise bother your throat?

A: Well, to my knowledge, I chewed in the normal way.

Q: I see. All right. Now, . . . you are not in a position to say that this chicken piece that you had there was improperly cut up by Church's or anybody else, are you?

A: I am not that much of an expert to know how you cut it, or whether it was proper or improper.

Q: I see. All right. . . . You are not in a position, to your own knowledge, to say that the piece of breast of that chicken, that there was anything dangerous about it when you bought it, are you?

A: Not when I purchased the piece of chicken.

MR. BRYAN: I see. I think that is all.

NOTES AND QUESTIONS

(1) *Setting up the Deposition.* This deposition was taken pursuant to notice. However, the notice was preceded by telephone agreements between the parties. In many jurisdictions, it is discourteous and counterproductive to set up a deposition by unilateral notice in the absence of efforts to find a mutually convenient time.

(2) *Preliminaries: Stipulations, Introduction, and "Impeachment Enhancement."* Rule 29 allows the parties to make stipulations about the manner in which the deposition is to be taken. Notice the agreement to reserve objections until time of trial. When a deposition of an adverse witness is taken, this agreement is frequently made, so that the deponent's attorney does not feel the need to make objections during the course of the deposition. When might it be unwise to make this kind of agreement? *See* Rule 32(d)(3) (objections to the form of questions and answers, or to other matters that can be cured at the time of taking the deposition, are not reserved until trial in the absence of a

stipulation). Also, note that deposers often begin by establishing that the witness understands what a deposition is and knows that it can be used to impeach variant testimony at trial. The reason: One of the purposes of the deposition is to "freeze" the testimony so the witness cannot freely vary it, and this sort of exchange is useful in enhancing the impeachment value of the deposition. There are, however, reasons why attorneys might not include this step. The defendant's attorney omitted it here.

(3) *The Structure of the Deposition.* A "standard" personal injury deposition might be thought of as including (1) preliminaries, (2) witness background, (3) the claimed incident causing injury, and (4) cataloguing of all damages. How well does this deposition fit the "standard" structure?

(4) *Questioning Patterns: Getting the Witness to Talk.* Usually, the deposer wants the deponent to talk as much as possible. What techniques does the defendant's attorney use here to accomplish that result, and how successful is he? Consider the "funnel" or "T-funnel" sequence that is described in the preceding set of notes, above. How closely did this attorney conform to this pattern? [Note: The "funnel" sequence is not appropriate for questioning an adverse witness at trial. Can you see why there is such a large difference between deposition questioning techniques and trial techniques?]

(5) *Relevancy; Nondiscoverable Information.* Why is it relevant for the deponent to describe all employment she has held? Or the grounds of her divorces? It is conceivable that objections could be directed to some of these matters, but the plaintiff's attorney does not object. Why not? Even with respect to a statement taken from the plaintiff's physician, which probably is work product, the plaintiff's attorney readily agrees to production. Why?

(6) *Thoroughness.* Does the defendant's attorney find out everything that he should? How well does his deposition stand up against Groce's "checklist"?

(7) *The Outcome.* The jury rendered a verdict on special interrogatories to the effect that the chicken was defective, that the defect caused the plaintiff's injuries, that the plaintiff was not contributory negligent and did not assume the risk, and that the sum of $1,500 would compensate for the plaintiff's damages. The judge granted judgment accordingly. The appellate court affirmed. For the plaintiff's attorneys, the "victory" obviously was a financial loss; for the defendant, the cost of the defense undoubtedly exceeded the judgment several times over.

A NOTE ON DEPOSITIONS ON WRITTEN QUESTIONS

Most procedural systems provide for taking depositions on written questions. This discovery device bears a stronger resemblance to written interrogatories than to oral depositions. The questions are prepared in advance and served with the deposition notice. Cross and redirect questions may also be prepared. The deposition officer propounds the questions and takes the answers. *See* Fed. R. Civ. P. 31.

The deposition on written questions is a weak form of discovery in comparison to an oral deposition because there is no opportunity to follow a witness' response with more probing questions. The written deposition can be useful to authenticate documents, such as non-party business records.

[2] Interrogatories

Read Fed. R. Civ. P. 26(b)(2) and (c) (limitations on discovery scope; protective orders), and 33 (interrogatories).

BURNS v. THIOKOL CHEMICAL CORPORATION
483 F.2d 300 (5th Cir. 1973)

JOHN R. BROWN, CHIEF JUDGE: . . .

Suit was filed by the appellant Burns under Title VII of the Civil Rights Act of 1964, 42 U.S.C.A. § 2000e et seq. and 42 U.S.C.A. § 1981, against his former employer, the Thiokol Chemical Corporation, both in an individual capacity and as a "private attorney-general" representing a class of aggrieved Blacks. . . .

A Gadfly In The Porridge

Neither party challenges the factual accuracy of the statement that over the course of his fourteen years in the employ of Thiokol, Claxton Burns developed "bad chemistry" with management. Indeed, both parties seek to use this fact to their advantage. Thiokol expends a considerable amount of space in its brief urging that not only did Burns develop such caustic personality and attitudinal traits that he became incapable of adequately performing his job, but also that he was a bellicose maverick without sufficient rapport with his fellow Black workers to represent them as a class.

The District Court found that Burns' attitude and his actions were anathema to the management of Thiokol. The Court also held that Burns was discharged, not because of his race, but because he spread false rumors around the business community about Thiokol's alleged failure to render medical aid to him after he collapsed. . . .

Discovery

In an effort to amass statistical evidence and define the contours of his case, Burns propounded interrogatories to Thiokol under F.R. Civ. P. 33 on May 14, 1970. Among other things, the interrogatories sought information regarding the name, age, sex, educational background, and employment history of all white employees at Thiokol's Huntsville plant dating from January 1, 1960;[4] a list of both permanent[5] and temporary[6]

---

[4] 9. List the name, age, address, sex, and school years completed by/of each white person hired by the Company at its Huntsville plant since January 1, 1960 and presently employed by the Company and with respect to each such employee state

(a) date of initial employment:

(b) all job classifications held since date of initial employment, including present job classification;

(c) date of each job classification change;

(d) plant age;

(e) department age;

(f) line of promotion age.

[5] 10. List each permanent vacancy which has occurred in each job classification at the Huntsville plant since January 1, 1960 and with respect to each such vacancy state

(a) date of each such vacancy;

(b) name, race, date of initial hire, department, job classification, all seniority dates of each person who bid for the vacancy;

job vacancies within the Huntsville plant and background information on both those applicants who competed for the jobs and those who were selected; and a job description of each non-bargaining unit job at the Huntsville plant.[7] The Company filed timely objection to these interrogatories contending, *inter alia*, that they sought irrelevant information and that they would be unduly burdensome to answer. Because the District Court sustained these objections in an oral, unrecorded order, we are unable to determine which — if either — of these grounds for objection was the basis for its decision. But it matters not, for neither will suffice on this record. . . .

Relevancy

"In the problem of racial discrimination, statistics often tell much, and Courts listen." *Alabama v. United States*, 5 Cir., 1962, 304 F.2d 583, 586, *aff'd*, 1962, 371 U.S. 37, 83 S. Ct. 145, 9 L. Ed. 2d 112. Our wide experience with cases involving racial discrimination in education, employment, and other segments of society have led us to rely heavily in Title VII cases on the empirical data which show an employer's overall pattern of conduct in determining whether he has discriminated against particular individuals or a class as a whole. . . .

Without making any pretense of exhaustively cataloguing possible uses of this information to Burns we note that one of Thiokol's chief witnesses was the personnel manager of its Huntsville Plant, Charles G. Babcock. Mr. Babcock testified at length about the employment practices of Thiokol during his fourteen year association with the Company. He undertook to give certain data relating to the size of the Thiokol work force during various periods of time, and the general manner in which vacancies were filled. On cross-examination of Babcock, Burns' counsel was obviously unable to ask intelligent, informed questions relating to any specifics. Perhaps the information sought by their interrogatories would have served to bolster Babcock's exclamatory testimony in behalf of the Company. Then again, it might have allowed plaintiff's counsel to pin the witness down to some unexplainable particulars. We do not know. The point is that open disclosure of all potentially relevant information is the keynote of the Federal Discovery Rules.In this case, that focal point has been ignored. . . .

(c) name of successful bidder;

(d) whether the successful bidder had previously worked in the job posted for bid, and, if so, dates worked in job posted for bid.

[6] 11. List each temporary vacancy of eight (8) hours or more which has occurred in each job classification in the Huntsville plant since July 1, 1964 and with respect to each such vacancy state

(a) reason for the vacancy, and length thereof;

(b) name and race of each employee who filled the vacancy;

(c) all seniority dates of persons filling the vacancy;

(d) prior job status of employee filling the vacancy;

(e) length of time employee remained in the vacancy;

(f) subsequent and current status of the employee who filled the vacancy.

[7] 18. State the job description of each non-bargaining unit job at the Company's Huntsville plant; the wage rates for each such job; and the name, address, age, race, sex, present position, and prior job classification of each employee currently employed in a non-bargaining unit position. Also indicate the date on which each such person holding a nonbargaining unit position was entered his present position.

The Burden

Thiokol argues that even if the information sought by Burns' interrogatories is somewhat relevant to his claim, [t]he onerous burden of compiling, assimilating, and synthesizing voluminous employment records into cogent, responsive answers to the interrogatories outweighs the utility of the information. We disagree. . . .

Of course the particular details of the discovery process are committed to the sound discretion of the trial court. Knowing, by virtue of our mandate, that the information is relevant, and therefore, discoverable, the judge may wish to require full answers to the interrogatories. But that is not his only option.

[Rule 33(d) may, under certain conditions, give] Thiokol the option to "[specify[] the records that must be reviewed, in sufficient detail to enable the interrogating party to locate and identify them as readily as the responding party could; and . . . giving the interrogating party a reasonable opportunity to examine and audit the records and to make copies, compilations, abstracts, or summaries.]"

The judge may also exercise the full extent of his discovery powers under Fed. R. Civ. P. 26(c) with appropriate protective orders as to time, place, manner, etc., in which the interrogatories will be answered.

Finally, our determination of the relevancy of this information does not irrevocably commit the judge and the parties to the process of discovery by interrogatories under Rule 33. If the judge determines that this particular manner of disseminating the information is in fact unduly burdensome on Thiokol, he may direct that alternative means be employed. Our paramount concern is that the information be available to the plaintiff. [Reversed and remanded for a new trial.]

SARGENT-WELCH SCIENTIFIC CO. v. VENTRON CORP., 59 F.R.D. 500 (N.D. Ill. 1973). In language complying with the "notice pleading" requirements of the Federal Rules governing pleadings, the plaintiff charged the defendants with "monopolization" and certain other violations of the antitrust laws. The defendants served four interrogatories on the plaintiff, of the kind sometimes called "contention interrogatories" because they seek to discover the opponent's contentions. Specifically, with reference to the "monopolization" claim, the defendants asked the plaintiff to state the factual basis of the plaintiff's allegations, in its pleadings, that the defendants possessed "market power and dominance," which, according to the complaint, had been "maintained, strengthened and enhanced" and had "created substantial competitive advantages for" the defendants. Similar "contention interrogatories" asked the plaintiff to specify the factual basis for the plaintiff's allegations of competitive injury and of generally stated violations by the defendants. The plaintiff objected to these interrogatories on the ground that they sought to elicit the plaintiff's legal theories and extended to issues of "pure law" not properly the subject of interrogatories. The court ordered the plaintiff to answer, pointing out that Rule 33(b) [now Rule 33(a)(2) — Eds.] specifically permitted interrogatories of this kind:

> It is well settled that an interrogatory is not objectionable merely because it calls for an opinion or contention that relates to fact or the application of law to fact. . . . [Citing Advisory Committee Note to Rule 33(b).] [now Rule 33(a)(2) — Eds.]
>
> The clear trend of recent cases has been to require "factual opinions" or opinions calling for the application of law to fact since this type of discovery can be most useful in narrowing and sharpening the issues, which is a major purpose of discovery. . . .

An interrogatory which inquires into the facts upon which certain vague and general allegations of a complaint are founded and the claimed relationship between such facts is not objectionable on the ground that it calls for a legal conclusion. . . .

[Motion to compel answers granted.]

NOTES AND QUESTIONS

(1) *Updating Burns v. Thiokol: Hollander v. American Cyanamid Co.*, 895 F.2d 80 (2d Cir. 1990). In this case, the Second Circuit reached a similar result to that of the Fifth Circuit, above. The plaintiff in an age discrimination case sought detailed statistical information covering a five-year period. The District Court refused to order discovery and granted summary judgment. The Court of Appeals reversed: "Because employers rarely leave a paper trail — or 'smoking gun' — attesting to a discriminatory intent, disparate treatment plaintiffs often must build their cases from pieces of circumstantial evidence which cumulatively undercut the credibility of the various explanations offered by the employer."

(2) *Time and Expense; Corporation's "Composite" Knowledge Required.* How much time and expense would it take Thiokol to answer Burns' interrogatories? What persons will actually prepare the answers? *See* Haydock & Herr, *Interrogatories: Questions and Answers*, 1 Rev. Litigation 263 (1981). The answers of corporate parties to interrogatories call for the "composite" knowledge of the corporation. *General Dynamics Corp. v. Selb Manufacturing Co.*, 481 F.2d 1204 (8th Cir. 1973), *cert. den.*, 414 U.S. 1162 (1974) (interpreting Fed. R. Civ. P. 33). This characteristic of interrogatories is significant because an attempt to force a corporation to give its corporate knowledge by a deposition is not easy to accomplish when that knowledge is possessed by numerous different persons.

(3) *Rules Limiting the Number of Interrogatories.* Certain District Courts have adopted local rules limiting the number of interrogatories, including subparts. Rule 33 creates a presumptive limit of 25 interrogatories (subject to stipulation and to the court's power to modify the limit). The number 25 reflects the Rule requiring self-initiated disclosures, which would cover similar subjects. Similar limitations are imposed under Texas procedural law, which limits discovery by interrogatories to "25 written interrogatories, excluding interrogatories asking a party to identify or authenticate specific documents" absent agreement of counsel or a court order. *See* Tex. R. Civ. P. 190.2(c)(3), 190.3(b)(3) and 190.4(b).

(4) *Self-Initiated "Disclosures" as a Substitute for Interrogatories.* The Rules adopt a system of automatic disclosures, which are required to be made without request. *See* § 7.01[C], above. This mechanism substitutes for some of the function of interrogatories. Is the "disclosure" idea a good one? Notice that in *Burns v. Thiokol,* the defendant would face the daunting task of identifying every possible document, as well as every person, with information relevant to the plaintiff's claims at the very onset of suit, irrespective of the alternative options referred to by the Court of Appeals.

(5) *Opinions, Contentions and Legal Theories.* As indicated in the *Sargent-Welch Scientific Co.* case, an interrogatory is not objectionable under the Federal Rules merely because the interrogatory "asks for an opinion or contention that relates to fact or the application of law to fact," but "pure" questions of law remain objectionable. What advantages does this approach have (as versus limiting discovery to "facts")?

(6) *Business Records; Protective Orders; Judicial Management.* Notice that, under Federal Rule 33, it is permissible to produce business records as an answer to

interrogatories under certain circumstances. (Note that you should not advise your client to exercise this option before looking through the records to see whether they include any privileged information.) Does this rule, by its terms, help Thiokol? Can Thiokol obtain any relief from application of Rule 26(b)(2)'s discovery limits or through Rule 26(c)'s provision for protective orders, which may curtail or set conditions for discovery? Finally, would more thorough judicial management (*see* Chapter 8, below) help Thiokol?

§ 7.03[B][2]Appendix Interrogatories in Practice

INTERROGATORIES IN *GEORGE MILLER CO. v. COMPUDATA, INC.*

[Reproduced above in § [C] of Appendix to Chapter 2, *supra.*]

For a concrete example of interrogatories, answers, and objections, read (or re-read) the documents in *George Miller Co. v. Compudata, Inc.*, in § [C] of the Appendix to Chapter 2. You should particularly note: (1) the specificity of the questions that get useful answers; (2) the kinds of objections (note that objections based on applications of legal conclusions, as in interrogatory 5, are inappropriate); and (3) use of the option to produce business records (interrogatory 11).

Seitz, GET MORE INFORMATION AND LESS INDIGESTION FROM YOUR INTERROGATORIES*

71 A.B.A.J. 74 (1985)

Do you feel you're doing more for your interrogatories than they're doing for you? . . .

Do you dream of force-feeding the last lecturer who convinced you that "the interrogatory is THE effective, cheap discovery device" with the last set you slaved over, which not only got zip for answers but also had the judge jumping all over you for sending [them]? . . .

Here's the secret

Despair not — there is hope. [T]he secret is to throw out the hyperbole and harassment mind-set that made interrogatories synonymous with the Black Death. The days of intimidation through tons of paper are over, thanks to Rules 11 and 26(e) [a]nd the outbreak of rules controlling the maximum number of questions. . . .

Before plunging headlong into blanket discovery, develop an overall plan and decide how your interrogatories fit into that plan. This is crucial because successful interrogatories do not exist in a vacuum. They must have a purpose; they must lead to a specific objective. If they don't, you are wasting your time and your client's money, which makes for a very unhappy client and in turn an unhappy lawyer. . . .

The most important thing to remember when you prepare interrogatories is that your opposing counsel, not the party, writes the final answers, with 30 days notice and exceptional care to present your adversary's response in the most favorable light. Remember this so you won't have dashed expectations of spontaneous true confessions.

There are four more things that those of us with short attention spans need to tattoo on a ready reference spot. One, there is no way for a quick follow-up to an answer. If you need a follow-up, save the question for a deposition. Two, expect the answer to be "more of less." Attorneys like to play hide and seek with information, giving the least amount possible. Three, do not ask questions to which you already know the answer. Instead, serve a request for admissions to tie the fact down. Four, keep interrogatories simple. Deliver yourself from drafting drudgery.

Why do we bother?

Why do we bother with interrogatories? Because they are frequently our best first line of discovery [especially in courts that do not enforce disclosure requirements]. They are the most efficient way to learn: (1) who knows the facts supporting the claims [or] defenses, (2) what documents exist pertaining to the claims or defenses, (3) the when and whereas relevant to each claim or defense, (4) the areas meriting deposition discovery and (5) general background details.

Note there isn't a "why" in the list. If you want subjective or interpretive information — information that depends on the credibility or demeanor of the answering party, or complex or confusing types of information — use depositions.

Here is a checklist of the information that interrogatories can deliver:

● The identity of all lay witnesses who have knowledge of the facts of the case (claims or defenses). If the responding party doesn't know these names, however, it does not have to conduct an investigation beyond the scope of Rule 26 to uncover them. [Also, disclosures may supply this.]

● The identity of the persons from whom the other side obtained statements or interviewed in the course of trial preparation. [T]he caveat is you can obtain attorney work product information [o]nly if you can show good cause, but sometimes the other side will give them to you.

● Greater factual particularity of the claims or defenses. . . .

● The identity of expert witnesses the opposition will call at trial, the subject matter and substance of facts and opinions about which each will testify and a summary of the grounds of each opinion. [Again, disclosures may supply this.]

● The identity of others allegedly liable to the opposition and the basis of that liability.

● Information regarding relevant insurance coverage (either liability or collateral source). [Disclosures may supply this.]

● A detailed description of injuries or damages, including the elements of damages and the measure by which the opposition claims they should be computed. [Disclosures may partially supply this.]

● The identity of those with a subrogation interest in the claim and the basis and extent of that interest.

● The existence, description, custody, condition and location of documents and tangible things relating to the subject matter, including items that a party or witness has written, signed, read or composed; contracts or transactions between or relating to the parties before and after the events of the case; similar incidents, complaints or problems the party or third persons has encountered relating to the subject matter of the case; financial information relevant to the case; and governmental licenses that affect a party's conduct. [Disclosures may supply some of this.]

● Business entity background, the nature of the business, principal place of business, state of incorporation and so forth.

● Personal background, including family history, work and school experience, other litigation or claims and criminal records.

● Facts pertaining to the court's jurisdiction.

● The identity of persons who were consulted or assisted in the preparation of the answers.

When to send them

You can serve successive sets of interrogatories. This often is the simplest way to obtain information if the answers to your first set are incomplete or objected to, rather than pursuing the time-consuming and expensive Rule 37 motion to compel and sanction route. The successive set of interrogatories gives you the added dividend [o]f a record to show the court you have bent over backwards to be reasonable. . . .

Ask clear, precise, direct questions. Brief questions requiring brief answers are winners because they are downright difficult to dodge. Stay away from vague, broad or overconclusive questions. They not only produce zero answers but also give your opponent a chance to strike them, which often is accompanied by a judge's verbal thrashing and an awkward explanation to the client. If you send out cumbersome, complex interrogatories, don't be surprised if the other side just photocopies them, adds a new cover sheet and sends them back to you.

When you draft questions, ask yourself:

● Could each question be simpler?

● Could some be eliminated or consolidated?

● What helpful information will I get from each answer?

● What loophole will my opponent find to avoid a complete answer? . . .

[3] Requests For Admissions

Read Fed. R. Civ. P. 36; Federal Form 51 (requests for admission).

TREVINO v. CENTRAL FREIGHT LINES, INC.
613 S.W.2d 356 (Tex. Civ. App.-Waco 1981, no writ)

[Central Freight sued J. Trevino "d/b/a Academy Surplus No. 5" claiming that it sold merchandise to Trevino that was accepted by Trevino's agent, Billy Brooks, at Trevino's Academy Surplus store. Central Freight also alleged that Trevino had provided Brooks "written authorization" to make purchases but that the check that Brooks gave Central Freight was drawn against insufficient funds to Central Freight's damage in the amount of $989.50. Central Freight also sought recovery of attorney's fees.

[Trevino filed an answer that denied Central Freight's allegations. Central Freight then served a request for admissions.]

The requested admissions were these:

1. The attached exhibit "A" is a genuine copy of a letter presented to Central Freight Lines, Inc., on September 28, 1976, by or on behalf of J. TREVINO, Defendant herein.

2. The original of the attached exhibit "A" is written on stationery of Academy Surplus.

3. The original of the attached exhibit "A" is written on paper on which the Academy Surplus logo is printed along with the address and phone number of Academy Surplus No. 5 Store.

4. J. TREVINO personally wrote the following on the original of the attached exhibit "A":

Dear Jerry

Please Let Bill Brooks Purchase Any Merchandise He Wishes For Us Here At Academy Surplus. My Tax Exempt # is 1-74-1707803-1

Thanks

5. J. TREVINO personally signed the original of the attached exhibit "A."

6. J. TREVINO has never, personally, or through any agent, servant or employee withdrawn, amended or contradicted the statement quoted in request for admission number four.

7. J. TREVINO is the sole owner of Academy Surplus No. 5.

8. J. TREVINO is the manager and operator of Academy Surplus No. 5.

9. On September 28, 1976, Bill Brooks purchased each item listed in the attached exhibit "B" from Central Freight Lines, Inc.

10. On September 28, 1976, Bill Brooks agreed to pay the prices listed in the attached exhibit "B" for each item listed in the attached exhibit "B."

11. The items listed in the attached exhibit "B" were delivered into the custody of Bill Brooks by Central Freight Lines, Inc.

12. Prior to the delivery referred to in request for admission number eleven, the items listed in the attached exhibit "B" were owned by Central Freight Lines, Inc.

13. The total purchase price of the items listed in the attached exhibit "B" was $989.50.

14. Bill Brooks delivered a check to Central Freight Lines, Inc. to pay the purchase price referred to in request for admission number thirteen.

15. The attached exhibit "C" is a genuine copy of the check referred to in request for admission number fourteen.

16. The check referred to in request for admission number fourteen was not paid due to insufficient funds.

17. Bill Brooks paid Central Freight Lines, Inc. $50.00 towards the check referred to in request for admission number fourteen.

18. Other than the $50.00 payment referred to in request for admission number seventeen, no payment has been made on the purchase price of $989.50.

It is undisputed that defendant did not respond to plaintiff's request for admissions.

. . .

On June 3, 1980, defendant filed, under oath, his first amended original answer. In addition to a general denial, defendant pleaded that at the time of the "alleged execution" by defendant of the written authorization relied upon by plaintiff, defendant was vice-president of Killeen Surplus, Inc., "and any acts alleged by Plaintiff to have been committed by Defendant in the execution of said instrument would have been done on behalf of Killeen Surplus, Inc., and not on behalf of Defendant individually"; that defendant did not, either orally or in writing, authorize the purchase of merchandise upon which this suit is based; and that he did not authorize anyone to make the purchase for him or for Killeen Surplus, Inc.

The case was called for trial on June 23, 1980. On that day, immediately prior to the trial, defendant filed a motion for extension of time for filing answers to plaintiff's request for admissions. Defendant alleged that in July, 1979, he furnished his attorney handwritten answers to the requested admissions; that he relied upon the attorney to answer the request; that he "did not know until now" the request was not answered; that his failure to answer was not the result of conscious indifference or disregard; that his amended original answer sets forth his position, and, therefore, the granting of the extension of time would not operate as a surprise to plaintiff; that the request for admissions was "overly broad" . . . in that it inquired into all elements of plaintiff's case, and also included matters outside defendant's personal knowledge; and that if all of the requested admissions should be deemed admitted because of defendant's failure to answer, then "Defendant would be required to stand mute at his own trial." . . .

After [a] hearing, the court denied the motion and adjudged that all eighteen matters of which admissions were requested by plaintiff were "deemed admitted." The case was then tried on its merits without a jury.

On the merits, plaintiff rested upon the introduction of its request for admissions and evidence supporting its plea for attorney's fees. Defendant then attempted to testify that he was not the sole owner of Academy Surplus No. 5, and was not doing business as Academy Surplus No. 5, in September, 1976, the time in question in this case. Plaintiff objected to this testimony on the ground that it contradicted the request for admissions, specifically requested admissions seven and eight. The objection was sustained. Defendant then sought and received permission of the court "to make a Bill of Exception as to what we would like to prove regarding the sole ownership of the store." Defendant testified on the Bill that on September 28, 1976, Academy Surplus No. 5 was owned by Killeen Surplus, Inc.; that at that time he was a stockholder in Killeen Surplus, Inc., and was manager of Academy Surplus No. 5; that as manager of Academy Surplus No. 5, he was "authorized to act, to purchase, to sell, to run the store on behalf of the corporation"; that he was one of the original incorporators of Killeen Surplus, in 1972; and that in August, 1979, he sold all of his interest in Killeen Surplus.

After defendant perfected his bill of exception, judgment was rendered that plaintiff recover from defendant $939.50 plus $450.00 attorney's fees, and costs.

Defendant brought this appeal on two points of error, asserting the court erred (1) in overruling his motion for extension of time for answering the request for admissions, and (2) in granting plaintiff's motion to deem the requested admissions admitted. We overrule these contentions. . . .

Defendant's uncontradicted testimony established that his failure to timely answer the request for admissions was due solely to the neglect of his attorney. Under the agency relationship of attorney and client, the neglect of the attorney is attributable to the client. . . . In the light of this rule, and the facts, the trial court did not abuse its discretion in overruling defendant's motion for extension of time to answer the request for admissions.

Under his second point, defendant contends the court erred in deeming admitted requested admissions nine through eighteen. He asserts that these requests dealt with facts not known to him, and which plaintiff would have the burden of proving at the trial. He cites several decisions in which it is stated that the purpose of [admissions] "is to simplify the trial by eliminating matters that really are not in controversy" and that the Rule "was not intended to be used as a demand upon a plaintiff or defendant to admit that he had no cause of action or ground of defense." Defendant then argues that requested admissions nine through eighteen violated [the Rules] because they "cast upon defendant the burden of admitting or denying matters which (a) were in controversy and (b) were not known to defendant nor readily ascertainable to him." We overrule these contentions. . . .

The "obvious purpose" of [admissions] "is to expedite trials and to relieve parties of the cost of proving facts which will not be disputed on trial, the truth of which can be ascertained by reasonable inquiry." . . . In our case, if defendant did not have personal knowledge of the matters in question, he should have ascertained their accuracy if that could have been done without cost or considerable burden. If that could not have been done, then defendant should have filed a sworn statement setting forth in detail why he could not truthfully admit or deny without assuming a costly and unreasonable burden. Defendant did not do this. Therefore, the trial court did not abuse its discretion in deeming the requests admitted. . . .

NOTES AND QUESTIONS

(1) *Scope of Admissions: They Can Include Matters of Opinion.* At the time that the principal case was decided, the state request for admission rule provided that requests could be made concerning the truth of "relevant facts." This limiting language was taken from the 1937 version of Federal Rule 33 and has since been removed from both Rules, which now provide that requests requiring the application of law to fact, or requiring opinions or conclusions, are not objectionable. The basis for these amendments was to eliminate discovery gamesmanship. *See* Advisory Committee Notes on Amendments to Federal Rule 36:

> Not only is it difficult as a practical matter to separate "fact" from "opinion," . . . but an admission on a matter of opinion may facilitate proof or narrow the issues or both. An admission of a matter involving the application of law to fact may, in a given case, even more clearly narrow the issues. For example, an admission that an employee acted in the scope of his employment may remove a major issue from the trial.

(2) *Effect of Failure to Answer.* On its face, Fed. R. Civ. P. 36 is self-enforcing. When answers are not made, the requests are deemed admitted merely by the operation of the rule. Nonetheless, courts have broad discretion to allow late responses. *See French v. United States*, 416 F.2d 1149 (9th Cir. 1969). Hence in districts where judges are lenient, as a practical matter, the requesting party cannot safely consider the matters deemed admitted unless a motion to deem has been granted. *See* Garner & Wolfe, *Late Responses to Requests to Admit: When Should Courts Allow Them?*, 78 Ill. B.J. 502 (1990).

(3) *Proof After Inappropriate Denial Authorizes Recovery of Expenses of Making Proof.* There is another way in which admissions are ostensibly self-enforcing. If a party denies a request and the requesting party later proves the requested matter, the answering party may be taxed the costs of such proof, including reasonable attorneys' fees, unless the court finds that one of several good faith reasons exists for the failure to admit. Fed. R. Civ. P. 37(c).

(4) *Effect of Admissions.* Unlike answers to interrogatories and to deposition questions, admissions have conclusive effect and cannot be contradicted by the admitting party. *See* Fed. R. Civ. P. 36(b) (procedure for withdrawing an admission).

§ 7.03[B][3] Appendix Requests for Admissions in Practice

REQUESTS AND ADMISSIONS IN *GEORGE MILLER CO. v. COMPUDATA, INC.*

[Reproduced in § [C] of the Appendix to Chapter 2, *supra.*]

For a concrete example of requests for admission and responses to them, see the admissions and responses in *George Miller Co. v. Compudata, Inc.*, in § [C] of the Appendix to Chapter 2. Note the wording of the requests; are the objections valid?

[4] Production of Documents and Tangible Things

Read Fed. R. Civ. P. 34; Federal Form 50 (production); Rule 45 (subpoenas).

ZUBULAKE v. UBS WARBURG LLC
217 F.R.D. 309 (S.D.N.Y. 2003)

. . . As individuals and corporations increasingly do business electronically — using computers to create and store documents, make deals, and exchange e-mails — the universe of discoverable material has expanded exponentially. . . . This case provides a textbook example of the difficulty of balancing the competing needs of broad discovery and manageable costs. Laura Zubulake is suing UBS Warburg LLC, UBS Warburg, and UBS AG (collectively, "UBS" or the "Firm") under Federal, State, and City law for gender discrimination and illegal retaliation. Zubulake's case is certainly not frivolous and if she prevails, her damages may be substantial. She contends that key evidence is located in various e-mails exchanged among UBS employees that now exist only on backup tapes and perhaps other archived media. According to UBS, restoring those e-mails would cost approximately $175,000.00, exclusive of attorney time in reviewing the e-mails. Zubulake now moves for an order compelling UBS to produce those e-mails at its expense. . . .

Discovery in this action commenced on or about June 3, 2002, when Zubulake served UBS with her first document request. At issue here is request number twenty-eight, for "[a]ll documents concerning any communication by or between UBS employees concerning Plaintiff." The term "document" in Zubulake's request "includ[es], without limitation, electronic or computerized data compilations." On July 8, 2002, UBS responded by producing approximately 350 pages of documents, including approximately 100 pages of e-mails. . . . [By subsequent agreement,] UBS agreed unconditionally to produce responsive e-mails from the accounts of five [specific] individuals . . . . UBS, however, produced no additional e-mails and insisted that its initial production (the 100 pages of e-mails) was complete. . . . Zubulake knew that there were additional responsive e-mails that UBS had failed to produce because she herself had produced approximately 450 pages of e-mail correspondence. Clearly, numerous responsive e-mails had been created and deleted at UBS,[19] and Zubulake wanted them. . . .

---

[19] The term "deleted" is sticky in the context of electronic data. "'Deleting' a file does not actually erase that data from the computer's storage devices. Rather, it simply finds the data's entry

Because it apparently recognizes that Zubulake is entitled to the requested discovery, UBS expends most of its efforts urging the court to shift the cost of production to "protect [it] . . . from undue burden or expense." . . . Courts must remember that cost-shifting may effectively end discovery, especially when private parties are engaged in litigation with large corporations. . . . Thus, cost-shifting should be considered only when electronic discovery imposes an "undue burden or expense" on the responding party. The burden or expense of discovery is, in turn, "undue" when it "outweighs its likely benefit, taking into account the needs of the case, the amount in controversy, the parties' resources, the importance of the issues at stake in the litigation, and the importance of the proposed discovery in resolving the issues." . . .

Many courts have automatically assumed that an undue burden or expense may arise simply because electronic evidence is involved. This makes no sense. Electronic evidence is frequently cheaper and easier to produce than paper evidence because it can be searched automatically, key words can be run for privilege checks, and the production can be made in electronic form obviating the need for mass photocopying. . . .

In fact, whether production of documents is unduly burdensome or expensive turns primarily on whether it is kept in an accessible or inaccessible format (a distinction that corresponds closely to the expense of production). . . . Whether electronic data is accessible or inaccessible turns largely on the media on which it is stored. . . .

The case at bar is a perfect illustration of the range of accessibility of electronic data. . . . UBS maintains e-mail files in three forms: (1) active user e-mail files; (2) archived e-mails on optical disks; and (3) backup data stored on tapes. The active (HP OpenMail) data is obviously the most accessible: it is online data that resides on an active server, and can be accessed immediately. The optical disk (Tumbleweed) data is only slightly less accessible . . . . The e-mails are on optical disks that need to be located and read with the correct hardware, but the system is configured to make searching the optical disks simple and automated once they are located. For these sources of e-mails — active mail files and e-mails stored on optical disks — it would be wholly inappropriate to even consider cost-shifting. UBS maintains the data in an accessible and usable format, and can respond to Zubulake's request cheaply and quickly. Like most typical discovery requests, therefore, the producing party should bear the cost of production.

E-mails stored on backup tapes (via NetBackup), however, are an entirely different matter. Although UBS has already identified the ninety-four potentially responsive backup tapes, those tapes are not currently accessible. In order to search the tapes for responsive e-mails, UBS would have to engage in [a] costly and time-consuming process . . . . It is therefore appropriate to consider cost-shifting. . . .

[The district court then reviewed the eight-factor test set forth in *Rowe Entertainment, Inc. v. William Morris Agency, Inc.*, 205 F.R.D. 421 (S.D.N.Y. 2002), and found the test inadequate. In particular, the court observed that the *Rowe* factors strongly favor

---

in the disk directory and changes it to a 'not used' status — thus permitting the computer to write over the 'deleted' data. Until the computer writes over the 'deleted' data, however, it may be recovered by searching the disk itself rather than the disk's directory. Accordingly, many files are recoverable long after they have been deleted — even if neither the computer user nor the computer itself is aware of their existence. Such data is referred to as 'residual data.'" Shira A. Scheindlin & Jeffrey Rabkin, *Electronic Discovery in Federal Civil Litigation: Is Rule 34 Up to the Task?*, 41 B.C. L. Rev. 327, 337 (2000) (footnotes omitted). Deleted data may also exist because it was backed up before it was deleted. Thus, it may reside on backup tapes or similar media. . . .

cost-shifting and that the *Rowe* factors needed adjustments, including that certain factors should predominate.]

In summary, deciding disputes regarding the scope and cost of discovery of electronic data requires a three-step analysis:

First, it is necessary to thoroughly understand the responding party's computer system, both with respect to active and stored data. For data that is kept in an accessible format, the usual rules of discovery apply: the responding party should pay the costs of producing responsive data. A court should consider cost-shifting only when electronic data is relatively inaccessible, such as in backup tapes.

Second, because the cost-shifting analysis is so fact-intensive, it is necessary to determine what data may be found on the inaccessible media. Requiring the responding party to restore and produce responsive documents from a small sample of the requested backup tapes is a sensible approach in most cases.

Third, and finally, in conducting the cost-shifting analysis, the following factors should be considered, weighted more-or-less in the following order:

1. The extent to which the request is specifically tailored to discover relevant information;
2. The availability of such information from other sources;
3. The total cost of production, compared to the amount in controversy;
4. The total cost of production, compared to the resources available to each party;
5. The relative ability of each party to control costs and its incentive to do so;
6. The importance of the issues at stake in the litigation; and
7. The relative benefits to the parties of obtaining the information.

Accordingly, UBS is ordered to produce all responsive e-mails that exist on its optical disks or on its active servers (i.e., in HP OpenMail files) at its own expense. UBS is also ordered to produce, at its expense, responsive e-mails from any five backup tapes selected by Zubulake. UBS should then prepare an affidavit detailing the results of its search, as well as the time and money spent. After reviewing the contents of the backup tapes and UBS's certification, the Court will conduct the appropriate cost-shifting analysis.

NOTES AND QUESTIONS

(1) In a subsequent ruling, the *Zubulake* court sanctioned the employer for destroying e-mail messages that were relevant to the lawsuit's claims. *See Zubulake v. UBS Warburg LLC*, 382 F. Supp. 2d 536 (S.D.N.Y. 2005).

(2) *Electronic Data and the Federal Rules.* The Federal Rules were amended in 2006 to address electronic data, which necessitated amendments to a number of the discovery rules. In particular, Rule 26 now includes a reference to "electronically stored information" within its initial disclosures provision, imposes a duty to preserve electronic data (but creates a "safe harbor" for data destroyed as part of a regular purging process), and includes electronically stored information within the definition of what is discoverable. Rule 26 creates two tiers of discovery for electronically stored information. Electronically stored information that is "reasonably accessible" must be searched and produced; if not reasonably accessible, the court may order discovery for good cause and with conditions,

including cost-shifting. Rule 34 now specifically includes "electronically stored information" within the purview of requests for production of documents and requires that if the request does not specify a form for producing electronically stored information, the party responding to such a request "must produce [the information] in a form or forms in which it is ordinarily maintained or in a reasonably usable form or forms." Absent exceptional circumstances, Rule 37 precludes the imposition of sanctions for "failing to provide electronically stored information lost as a result of the routine, good-faith operation of an electronic information system." Rule 45, dealing with subpoenas, also now contains provisions referring to "electronically stored information."

(3) *Scope of Request: Documents.* Fed. R. Civ. P. 34(b) provides that "The request . . . must describe with reasonable particularity each item or category of items to be inspected." *See Robbins v. Camden City Bd. of Educ.*, 105 F.R.D. 49 (D.N.J. 1985) (holding that request for production of documents that "relate or refer to" plaintiff, in employment discrimination suit, was not "reasonably particular" since every document in the defendant's possession could be said to relate to the plaintiff's employment).

(4) *Necessity of Providing Requested Documents in Usable Form.* Courts have held that an inadequate or unwieldy filing system does not excuse a party from producing requested documents in a usable form. *See, e.g., Rowlin v. Alabama Dep't of Public Safety*, 200 F.R.D. 459, 461 (M.D. Ala. 2001) ("To allow a [party] whose business generates massive records to frustrate discovery by creating an inadequate filing system, and then claim undue burden, would defeat the purposes of the discovery rules"); *Northern Natural Gas Co. v. Teksystems Global Applications, Outsourcing, LLC*, 2006 U.S. Dist. Lexis 64149 (D. Neb. 2006) (concluding that the responding party "must produce the responsive data in a form usable by [the requesting party]," including providing the requesting party with access to the software necessary to access the responding party's data systems).

(5) *Choice in Organizing the Response.* Rule 34(b) states that "A party must produce documents as they are kept in the usual course of business or must organize and label them to correspond to the categories in the request." Is this choice — between organizing the documents "as they are kept in the usual course of business" or organizing the documents "to correspond to the categories in the request" — a decision made by the requesting party or by the responding party? *See Board of Educ. v. Admiral Heating and Ventilating, Inc.*, 104 F.R.D. 23 (N.D. Ill. 1984) (permitting the requesting party to make the choice); *but see American Int'l Specialty Lines Ins. Co. v. NWI-I, Inc.*, 2007 U.S. Dist. LEXIS 3025 (N.D. Ill. 2007) (suggesting that the responding party has the choice). The majority view seems to give the choice to the responding party. *See, e.g., CP Solutions PTE, Ltd. v. General Elec. Co.*, 2006 U.S. Dist. LEXIS 27053 (D. Conn. 2006) ("Rule 34(b) clearly provides two alternative options for complying with a document production request. Defendants, having chosen to produce the documents as kept in the ordinary course of business, do not need to categorize them or label and organize them to correspond to specific requests for production.").

(6) *Possession, Custody or Control.* Under federal practice, inspection can be required if the party to whom the request is made has the right to obtain physical possession of the document, even though in fact the party has no copy. *Schwartz v. Travelers Ins. Co.*, 17 F.R.D. 330 (S.D.N.Y. 1954); *In re Ruppert*, 309 F.2d 97 (6th Cir. 1962) (document previously given to attorney).

[5] Physical and Mental Examinations

Read Fed. R. Civ. P. 35 (physical and mental examinations).

SCHLAGENHAUF v. HOLDER

379 U.S. 104 (1964)

MR. JUSTICE GOLDBERG delivered the opinion of the Court.

This case involves the validity and construction of Rule 35(a) of the Federal Rules of Civil Procedure as applied to the examination of a defendant in a negligence action. . . .

An action based on diversity of citizenship was brought in the District Court seeking damages arising from personal injuries suffered by passengers of a bus which collided with the rear of a tractor-trailer. The named defendants were The Greyhound Corporation, owner of the bus; petitioner, Robert L. Schlagenhauf, the bus driver; Contract Carriers, Inc., owner of the tractor; Joseph L. McCorkhill, driver of the tractor; and National Lead Company, owner of the trailer. Answers were filed by each of the defendants denying negligence.

Greyhound then cross-claimed against Contract Carriers and National Lead for damage to Greyhound's bus, alleging that the collision was due solely to their negligence in that the tractor-trailer was driven at an unreasonably low speed, had not remained in its lane, and was not equipped with proper rear lights. Contract Carriers filed an answer to this cross-claim denying its negligence and asserting "[t]hat the negligence of the driver of the . . . bus [petitioner Schlagenhauf] proximately caused and contributed to . . . Greyhound's damages."

Pursuant to a pretrial order, Contract Carriers filed a letter — which the trial court treated as, and we consider to be, part of the answer — alleging that Schlagenhauf was "not mentally or physically capable" of driving a bus at the time of the accident.

Contract Carriers and National Lead then petitioned the District Court for an order directing petitioner Schlagenhauf [the bus driver] to submit to both mental and physical examinations by one specialist in each of the following fields: (1) Internal medicine; (2) Ophthalmology; (3) Neurology; and (4) Psychiatry. For the purpose of offering a choice to the District Court of one specialist in each field, the petition recommended two specialists in internal medicine, ophthalmology, and psychiatry, respectively, and three specialists in neurology — a total of nine physicians. The petition alleged that the mental and physical condition of Schlagenhauf was "in controversy" as it had been raised by Contract Carriers' answer to Greyhound's cross-claim. This was supported by a brief of legal authorities and an affidavit of Contract Carriers' attorney stating that Schlagenhauf had seen red lights 10 to 15 seconds before the accident, that another witness had seen the rear lights of the trailer from a distance of three-quarters to one-half mile, and that Schlagenhauf had been involved in a prior accident. . . .

While disposition of this petition was pending, National Lead filed its answer to Greyhound's cross-claim and itself "cross-claimed" against Greyhound and Schlagenhauf for damage to its trailer. The answer asserted generally that Schlagenhauf's negligence proximately caused the accident. The cross-claim additionally alleged that Greyhound and Schlagenhauf were negligent

> [b]y permitting said bus to be operated over and upon said public highway . . . when both the said Greyhound Corporation and said Robert L. Schlagenhauf knew that the eyes and vision of the said Robert L. Schlagenhauf was [sic] impaired and deficient.

The District Court, on the basis of the petition filed by Contract Carriers, and without any hearing, ordered Schlagenhauf to submit to nine examinations — one by each of the recommended specialists — despite the fact that the petition clearly requested a total of only four examinations. [The trial judge later issued a "corrected" order that required only four examinations.] . . .

Rule 35 on its face applies to all "parties," which under any normal reading would include a defendant. Petitioner contends, however, that the application of the Rule to a defendant would be an unconstitutional invasion of his privacy, or, at the least, be a modification of substantive rights existing prior to the adoption of the Federal Rules of Civil Procedure and thus beyond the congressional mandate of the Rules Enabling Act.

These same contentions were raised in *Sibbach v. Wilson & Co.*, 312 U.S. 1, by a plaintiff in a negligence action who asserted a physical injury as a basis for recovery. The Court, by a closely divided vote, sustained the Rule as there applied. . . .

We hold that Rule 35, as applied to either plaintiffs or defendants to an action, is free of constitutional difficulty and is within the scope of the Enabling Act. . . .

Petitioner next contends that his mental or physical condition was not "in controversy" and "good cause" was not shown for the examinations, both as required by the express terms of Rule 35. . . .

It is notable, however, that in none of the other discovery provisions is there a restriction that the matter be "in controversy," and only in Rule 34 is there Rule 35's requirement that the movant affirmatively demonstrate "good cause." . . .

The "good cause" and "in controversy" requirements are not met by mere conclusory allegations of the pleadings — nor by mere relevance to the case — but require an affirmative showing by the movant that each condition as to which the examination is sought is really and genuinely in controversy and that good cause exists for ordering each particular examination. Obviously, what may be good cause for one type of examination may not be so for another. The ability of the movant to obtain the desired information by other means is also relevant.

Rule 35, therefore, requires discriminating application by the trial judge. . . . This does not, of course, mean that the movant must prove his case on the merits in order to meet the requirements for a mental or physical examination. Nor does it mean that an evidentiary hearing is required in all cases. This may be necessary in some cases, but in other cases the showing could be made by affidavits or other usual methods short of a hearing. It does mean, though, that the movant must produce sufficient information, by whatever means, so that the district judge can fulfill his function mandated by the Rule.

Of course, there are situations where the pleadings alone are sufficient to meet these requirements. A plaintiff in a negligence action who asserts mental or physical injury, *cf. Sibbach v. Wilson & Co., supra*, places that mental or physical injury clearly in controversy and provides the defendant with good cause for an examination to determine the existence and extent of such asserted injury. This is not only true as to a plaintiff, but applies equally to a defendant who asserts his mental or physical condition as a defense to a claim, such as, for example, where insanity is asserted as a defense to a divorce action. . . .

Here, however, Schlagenhauf did not assert his mental or physical condition either in support of or in defense of a claim. His condition was sought to be placed in issue by other parties. Thus, under the principles discussed above, Rule 35 required that these parties make an affirmative showing that petitioner's mental or physical condition was in controversy and that there was good cause for the examinations requested. This, the record plainly shows, they failed to do.

The only allegations in the pleadings relating to this subject were the general conclusory statement in Contract Carriers' answer to the cross-claim that "Schlagenhauf was not mentally or physically capable of operating" the bus at the time of the accident and the limited allegation in National Lead's cross-claim that, at the time of the accident, "the eyes and vision of . . . Schlagenhauf was [sic] impaired and deficient."

The attorney's affidavit attached to the petition for the examinations provided:

> That . . . Schlagenhauf, in his deposition . . . admitted that he saw red lights for 10 to 15 seconds prior to a collision with a semi-tractor trailer unit and yet drove his vehicle on without reducing speed and without altering the course thereof. . . .
>
> . . . Schlagenhauf has admitted in his deposition . . . that he was involved in a [prior] similar type rear end collision. . . .

This record cannot support even the corrected order which required one examination in each of the four specialties of internal medicine, ophthalmology, neurology, and psychiatry. Nothing in the pleadings or affidavit would afford a basis for a belief that Schlagenhauf was suffering from a mental or neurological illness warranting wide-ranging psychiatric or neurological examinations. Nor is there anything stated justifying the broad internal medicine examination.[16]

The only specific allegation made in support of the four examinations ordered was that the "eyes and vision" of Schlagenhauf were impaired. Considering this in conjunction with the affidavit, we would be hesitant to set aside a visual examination if it had been the only one ordered. However, as the case must be remanded to the District Court because of the other examinations ordered, it would be appropriate for the District Judge to reconsider also this order in light of the guidelines set forth in this opinion. . . .

MR. JUSTICE BLACK, with whom MR. JUSTICE CLARK joins, concurring in part and dissenting in part.

[Justice Black regarded evidence that might bear on Schlagenhauf's ability to drive as "of the highest relevance." He would have allowed broader examination, including Schlagenhauf's "mental or physical health." As he put it, when a driver twice rear-ends a visible moving truck on an open road, "one is . . . likely to ask, 'What is the matter with that driver? Is he blind or crazy?' "]

MR. JUSTICE DOUGLAS, dissenting in part.

[Justice Douglas feared that the plaintiff's doctors would "go on a fishing expedition in search of anything which will tend to prove that the defendant was unfit." And "a doctor for a fee can easily discover something wrong with any patient." Thus "the real

[16] Moreover, it seems clear that there was no compliance with Rule 35's requirement that the trial judge delineate the "conditions, and scope" of the examinations. Here the examinations were ordered in very broad, general areas. The internal medicine examination might for example, at the instance of the movant or its recommended physician extend to such things as blood tests, electrocardiograms, gastro-intestinal and other X-ray examinations. It is hard to conceive how some of these could be relevant under any possible theory of the case.

trial will be held there and not before the jury. . . . The doctor has a holiday in the privacy of his office." As Justice Douglas saw the matter, Congress and the Court had authorized medical examinations when the party had claimed a medical condition, as a personal injury plaintiff, but not otherwise, and the "right to keep one's person inviolate" should therefore prevail.]

[The dissenting opinion of Justice Harlan is omitted.]

NOTES AND QUESTIONS

(1) *Persons under Party's "Control."* Rule 35 states that "The court has the same authority to order a party to produce for examination a person who is in its custody or under its legal control." Some courts have held that this does not include a party's agents or employees. *See Kropp v. General Dynamics Corp.*, 202 F. Supp. 207 (E.D. Mich. 1962).

(2) *Who Chooses the Examining Physician?* As a general rule, the examining party has been the one to choose the examining physician, but it is within the trial court's discretion to select a neutral physician. *See Postell v. Amana Refrigeration, Inc.*, 87 F.R.D. 706 (N.D. Ga. 1980). *See also Employers Mut. Cas. Co. v. Street*, 702 S.W.2d 779 (Tex. App.-Ft. Worth 1986) (interpreting Tex. R. Civ. P. 167a, which is substantially identical to Fed. R. Civ. P. 35).

[6] "Discovery That Is Not Discovery": Freedom of Information Laws

Federal and state freedom of information laws were not enacted for the primary purpose of giving litigators another method for discovering facts. Nonetheless, it is permissible to take advantage of them for that purpose, and many lawyers do so. *See* Tomlinson, *Use of the Freedom of Information Act for Discovery Purposes*, 43 Md. L. Rev. 119 (1984).

The federal Freedom of Information Act, 5 U.S.C. § 552 (1982), requires federal agencies and departments to make their records available for inspection and copying upon request. No showing of need or status is required to make a request. The government's obligation to provide the records is subject to several exceptions, including one for trade secrets and commercial information which is privileged or confidential and another for "inter-agency or intra-agency memorandums or letters which would not be available by law to a party . . . in litigation with the agency." 5 U.S.C. § 552(b)(1)(A)(5). Do you see why the FOIA could be useful in litigation notwithstanding the last mentioned exception?

[7] Discovery in International Litigation: The Hague Evidence Convention

NOTE ON THE HAGUE EVIDENCE CONVENTION

Importance of International Litigation; The Hague Evidence Convention. The Hague Evidence Convention is an international agreement among certain "Contracting States" to provide for litigation that is not confined to one nation's borders. In Chapter 2, we described the Hague Convention as a method of obtaining international service of process; this related Evidence Convention provides mechanisms for discovery. Today, when transactional business may produce a dispute among a Japanese corporation assembling parts in the United States for sale in Germany, Italy or Brazil, this kind of litigation is more prevalent than ever, and discovery often presents unusual issues.

How Discovery Under the Hague Evidence Convention Can Be Used to Obtain Information Abroad, from Persons Not Present in the United States. Discovery under the Hague Evidence Convention most commonly begins with a "Letter of Request." (The best way to prepare such a letter probably is to work backwards; that is, begin with a form that is familiar to the Central Authority in the foreign jurisdiction, adapt it to case details in the foreign language, and then translate it into English.) The discoverer then moves the trial court in the United States to enter an Order approving the Letter of Request. The discoveror then sends the Order and Letter of Request, together with a certified official-language translation (that's why it is best to work backwards), to a "Central Authority," which the foreign jurisdiction is required under the Convention to designate. That authority forwards the Request to the "Competent Authority" that will execute it and then return the responsive documents through the same channels. But because extensive pretrial discovery is not favored outside the United States, it is difficult to obtain full responses. In fact, some nations have adopted "blocking" statutes designed to block American-style discovery. *E.g.*, French Penal Code Law No. 80-538, Art. 1A. *See generally* Alonso, *International Business Litigation*, in University of Houston, Advanced Business Litigation D1, D13-D16 (D. Crump ed. 1991). Consider the following case, which allows the discoveror to avoid these strictures.

SOCIETE NATIONALE INDUSTRIELLE AEROSPATIALE v. UNITED STATES DISTRICT COURT, 482 U.S. 522 (1987). When the suit is against a foreign national (or even a foreign government) that is present or doing business in the United States, must the claimant use the Hague Evidence Convention — or can the broader mechanisms of the Federal Rules be used? In the *Aerospatiale* case, the defendants were French corporations, owned by and operated as instrumentalities of the French government. Plaintiffs were persons injured by a crash of one of defendants' airplanes in Iowa. When the plaintiffs sued in a federal District Court and sought broad Federal-Rules-style discovery from the French defendants of documents and information located on French soil, the French defendants sought a protective order. The Supreme Court affirmed the denial of the protective order, holding that the Convention was "optional":

> [T]he text of the Evidence Convention, as well as the history of its proposal and ratification by the United States, unambiguously supports the conclusion that it was intended to establish optional procedures that would facilitate the taking of evidence abroad. [It] did not deprive the District Court of jurisdiction [t]o order a foreign national party before it to produce evidence physically located within a signatory nation. . . .

Four Justices joined in a separate opinion that would have called for a "general presumption" of first resort to the Convention.

NOTES AND QUESTIONS

1. *Is the Aerospatiale Decision Appropriate — Or Is It Merely Ethnocentric?* On the one hand, it can be argued that the court in this case is appropriately solicitous of the litigant's need for information. But on the other hand, why is it better to have procedures that make the extraction of sensitive information more certain? Might other nations have good reasons for not adopting the intrusiveness and expense that is unique to American discovery?

2. *Be Careful Doing Discovery Abroad.* In some countries, the taking of evidence is a governmental function, and privately conducted depositions on such a nation's soil can be a criminal act even if done in conjunction with litigation centered in the United States.

3. *Letters Rogatory.* What do you do if you need to obtain information from a person located in a foreign nation that is not a signatory of the Hague Evidence Convention? In that event, you may need to rely on "letters rogatory." Under this procedure, a United States court, by order, requests a court of the other nation to require a witness to be examined on interrogatories sent with the request or to otherwise take the testimony of the witness. The procedure is analogous to the Hague Evidence Convention, but the request is based only on international comity.

[C] The Duty to Supplement Responses

Read Fed. R. Civ. P. 26(e) (duty to supplement responses).

VOEGELI v. LEWIS, 568 F.2d 89 (8th Cir. 1977). The plaintiffs in this medical malpractice case made repeated efforts to obtain information about the defendant's expert witnesses, their professional backgrounds, their opinions, and the factual basis of those opinions. The defendant ultimately responded to interrogatories by stating that Drs. Gross and Van Demark "may be called as witnesses on behalf of Dr. Lewis, to explain that popliteal complications are very rare and difficult to diagnose and repair." The plaintiffs made further efforts to obtain specific answers, but the court denied enforcement of a second set of interrogatories and instead granted the plaintiffs permission to take the two experts' depositions. The plaintiffs took the deposition of Dr. Gross, but not that of Dr. Van Demark, because of written assurances that he had not been engaged and was not expected to be called.

At trial, Dr. Gross testified differently in crucial respects from what he had said in his deposition. There, he had conceded that it was unlikely for defendant Lewis to have obtained a pulse, as he testified he had, because the major artery in the area had been severed. At trial, however, Dr. Gross testified that it was possible for Dr. Lewis to have found a pulse from a "collateral source." When cross-examined about his change in position, Dr. Gross testified that he had read two articles after his deposition that had caused him to change his mind; however, neither he nor defendant advised the plaintiffs of this change. In addition, despite the assurance that Dr. Van Demark would not be called, the defendant did call him as a witness to testify to the rarity of the condition and the difficulty of diagnosis. The plaintiffs had not been apprised of this change and, indeed, had deliberately refrained even from examining potential jurors about whether they knew Dr. Van Demark, because they understood he would not be called. The jury found in defendant Lewis' favor.

The Court of Appeals reversed the judgment for the defendant and remanded for a new trial, citing Rule 26(e). Specifically, the court referred to the duty to supplement responses with respect to expert witnesses. In addition, it quoted the requirement that a party amend a response if the party learns that the response was "incorrect."

[D] The Use of Discovery in Hearings or Trials

Read Fed. R. Civ. P. 32(a) (use of discovery in court proceedings).

FRECHETTE v. WELCH
621 F.2d 11 (1st Cir. 1980)

LEVIN H. CAMPBELL, CIRCUIT JUDGE.

In this diversity tort action, plaintiffs' major contention on appeal is that the district court committed reversible error by admitting into evidence two depositions where the conditions for their use, as set forth in Fed. R. Civ. P. 32(a), were not satisfied.

Plaintiffs were seriously injured when defendant's automobile crossed the center line of a highway and struck, head on, the car in which they were riding. Defendant's defense was that the loss of control over his vehicle was the result of a sudden, unexpected, and unforeseeable blackout and therefore he was not negligent. *Savard v. Randall*, 103 N.H. 234, 169 A.2d 276 (1961). At trial, the defendant sought to substantiate his blackout defense with the testimony of three physicians, Drs. Blacklow, Zuckerman, and Turner. The jury, accepting this defense, returned a verdict for defendant. The depositions admitted into evidence that form the basis for this appeal were those of Drs. Blacklow and Zuckerman.

[W]ith respect to the videotape deposition of Dr. Zuckerman there was no exploration whether any of the conditions in Rule 32(a)(3) [pertaining to the witness' unavailability] were met. [Today this provision is found in Rule 32(a)(4) — Eds.] Rather, in accordance with the apparently standard practice of the federal district court of New Hampshire, the court stated in a pre-trial order that the videotape deposition was admissible "as a matter of course." With respect to two other non-videotape depositions of Drs. Turner and Blacklow the court ruled, in the same pre-trial order, that defendant was "to make every attempt to have [the doctors'] testimony live," but in the event the doctors were not available their depositions could be used. At trial only Dr. Turner was present, and a different judge admitted, over plaintiffs' objection, the deposition of Dr. Blacklow, without requiring defendant to establish the existence of any of the Rule 32(a)(3) [now Rule 32(a)(4)] conditions.[1]

The defendant now argues (1) that plaintiff agreed to the use of the depositions, and (2) that defendant's use of the depositions is sanctioned by New Hampshire state law which, under *Erie R.R. Co. v. Tompkins*, 304 U.S. 64, 58 S. Ct. 817, 82 L. Ed. 1188 (1938), should prevail in a federal diversity action.

We are unable to find that plaintiffs agreed to the use of the depositions in lieu of live witnesses. At the commencement of Dr. Zuckerman's videotape deposition, plaintiffs

[1] A colloquy directed to Rule 32(a)(3) [now Rule 32(a)(4)] preceded the admittance of Dr. Blacklow's deposition. The court took judicial notice that Dr. Blacklow's residence was within 100 miles of the court. Defense counsel then stated that he had been told, but had no firsthand knowledge, that Dr. Blacklow had just been through open heart surgery. Subsequent to the admission of Dr. Blacklow's deposition, defendant filed a statement from Dr. Blacklow mentioning two operations undergone six to seven months before trial. This was insufficient to establish that Dr. Blacklow was, at the time of trial, unable "[to] attend or testify because of . . . illness . . . ." Fed. R. Civ. P. 32(a)(3)(C) [now Fed. R. Civ. P. 32(a)(4)(C)]. No exceptional circumstances within the meaning of Rule 32(a)(3)(E) [now Rule 32(a)(4)(E)] were otherwise brought forward, and the court did not purport to rest its ruling on that basis.

recorded their opposition to the use of the videotape as a substitute for Dr. Zuckerman's actual presence unless the strictures of Fed. R. Civ. P. 32(a)(3) [now Rule 32(a)(4)] were met. This objection was renewed in a pre-trial memorandum and was repeated at the trial. Plaintiffs similarly objected, on the basis of Rule 32, when defendant offered Dr. Blacklow's deposition. Defendant would now rely upon a stipulation which prefaces Dr. Blacklow's deposition providing,

> It is stipulated and agreed that the deposition . . . when transcribed, may be used for all purposes for which depositions are competent under the laws of the State of New Hampshire.

The Blacklow deposition, as evidenced by the caption on its title page, was taken in conjunction not only with the present action but also with the case of Ernest Record (the driver of another car involved in the accident) versus defendant which was filed in the New Hampshire Superior Court. The stipulation, then made, relating to the purposes for which the deposition could be used, is insufficiently explicit to constitute a waiver of plaintiffs' federal rights under Rule 32.

A New Hampshire State statute, 5 N.H.R.S.A. 517:1, allows a deposition to be used in lieu of live testimony unless the party objecting to the use of the deposition procures the attendance at trial of the deponent. The statute provides:

> The deposition of any witness in a civil cause may be taken and used at the trial, unless the adverse party procures him to attend so that he may be called to testify when the deposition is offered.

Unlike federal practice under Fed. R. Civ. P. 32(a)(3) [now Rule 32(a)(4)], New Hampshire practice does not restrict the substantive use of deposition testimony to only those instances where a witness is unavailable for a particular reason such as death, illness, or the like. *Taylor v. Thomas*, 77 N.H. 410, 413, 92 A. 740 (1940). In New Hampshire, a sufficient reason for the use of a deposition is the adverse party's failure to produce the deponent in court. *Id.*, 413, 92 A. 740.

Rule 32(a)(3) [now Rule 32(a)(4)], however, prevails over the conflicting New Hampshire practice. . . . "When a situation is covered by one of the Federal Rules, the question facing the court is a far cry from the typical, relatively unguided *Erie* choice: the court . . . can refuse [to apply the federal rule] only . . . [if] the Rule in question transgresses . . . the terms of the Enabling Act [or] constitutional restrictions." *Hanna v. Plumer*. . . .

We therefore conclude that the district court erred in allowing defendant, over objection, to use the depositions of Drs. Zuckerman and Blacklow without an adequate showing that any of the conditions of Fed. R. Civ. P. 32(a)(3) [now Rule 32(a)(4)] were met. We further conclude, however, that the error was harmless, Fed. R. Civ. P. 61, and does not warrant reversal or a new trial.

[The court pointed out that Dr. Turner, who testified in person, had cared for defendant very soon after the accident, unlike the two doctors whose depositions were used. Therefore, the factors on which plaintiff cross-examined Dr. Turner, although they could also have furnished possible grounds for cross-examination of the other two physicians, were unlikely to make a difference if the others had testified in person too; as the court said, "we think it a remote possibility at best that such cross-examination could have affected the weight of their testimony."] Affirmed.

NOTES AND QUESTIONS

(1) *Unavailability: Should it Really Be Required?* Which approach to the admission of deposition evidence is preferable? The so-called unavailability requirements of Fed. R. Civ. P. 32(a)(4) are explainable in terms of a preference for live testimony. Note that the 100-mile distance in Rule 32(a)(4) corresponds with the scope of subpoenas under Rule 45. Fed. R. Civ. P. 45(c)(3)(A). This preference is shared by jurors, who generally are suspicious of or unimpressed by evidence read by counsel from a deposition that looks like a little book. (This jury suspicion does not seem to extend to videotaped depositions.) On the other hand, states that admit depositions irrespective of witness availability may reason that the proponent of the evidence takes the risk of this suspicion, and the opponent can bring the live witness if she considers it important. In other words, New Hampshire's rule is unlikely to harm the opponent. Furthermore, frequent resets of cases often make efforts to produce live witnesses chaotic. Aren't these considerations valid?

(2) *Should Experts Be Exempted From an Unavailability Requirement?* Federal amendments proposed for 1992 but not adopted would have exempted expert witnesses from the unavailability requirement. Given that experts are costly and often difficult to make available, does this proposal make sense?

(3) *Objections to the Reading of Inadmissible Parts of Depositions.* Because discovery relevance is broader than trial admissibility, it often happens that parts of a deposition, though properly taken, are inadmissible. Rule 32 enables the opponent to interpose most kinds of evidentiary objections at trial. Notice, however, that the Rule provides that objections to matters of form, or matters that could have been cured, are waived if not asserted during the deposition.

§ 7.04 Discovery Abuse and Sanctions

NOTE ON RULES 26 AND 37

Certifications and Conferences. In 1983, Rule 26 was amended to provide that upon sending or answering discovery requests, an attorney automatically makes certain "certifications." The certifications are roughly analogous to those in Rule 11 for pleadings. In addition, the rule provides for a discovery "conference" and for sanctions upon violation. Sherman, *The Judge's Role in Discovery,* 3 Rev. Litig. 89 (1982).

Sanctions. Rule 37 provides a range of sanctions for discovery abuse, ranging from simply ordering the discovery to very severe sanctions such as dismissal or default. Within limits, the choice of sanctions is within the discretion of the court. To understand the nature of discovery abuse, consider the following. (*See also* Note, *Discovery Abuse under the Federal Rules: Causes and Cures*, 92 Yale L.J. 352 (1982).)

Read Fed. R. Civ. P. 26(f)-(g) (discovery conference, automatic certifications, sanctions); also, read Rule 37 (sanctions).

[A] "Pushing" and "Tripping"

ROESBERG v. JOHNS-MANVILLE CORP., 85 F.R.D. 292 (E.D. Pa. 1980). In this asbestos personal injury case, the plaintiffs served fifty-seven interrogatories on each of several defendants. One defendant, GAF Corporation, answered six interrogatories but objected to the others as overly broad, burdensome, oppressive, not reasonably calculated to lead to admissible evidence, and privileged. The District Court granted a motion to compel answers to all fifty-seven. It noted, at the outset, that GAF had labelled virtually every interrogatory as "overly broad, burdensome, oppressive and irrelevant," but the court said: ". . . GAF cannot simply intone this familiar litany. Rather, GAF must show specifically how, despite the broad and liberal construction afforded by the federal discovery rules, each interrogatory is not relevant or how each question is overly broad, burdensome or oppressive . . . by submitting affidavits or offering evidence revealing the nature of the burden." The court then went on to give examples of cases in which interrogatories had been held unduly burdensome, as follows:

> . . . *Cf. In re United States Financial Securities Litigations*, [74 F.R.D. 497 (S.D. Cal. 1975)] (interrogatories three hundred eighty-one pages long and two inches high containing almost three thousand questions and costing over twenty-four thousand dollars to answer held unduly oppressive); *Alexander v. Rizzo*, 50 F.R.D. 374 (E.D. Pa. 1970) (objections to interrogatories denied even though answering would require hundreds of employees many years and hours, to "unearth" answers); *Krantz v. United States*, 56 F.R.D. 555 (W.D. Va. 1972) (fifteen hundred interrogatories held oppressive); *Frost v. Williams*, 46 F.R.D. 484 (D. Md. 1969) (two hundred interrogatories held oppressive); *Breeland v. Yale and Towne Manufacturing Co.*, 26 F.R.D. 119 (E.D.N.Y. 1960) (two hundred interrogatories held oppressive). . . .

NOTES AND QUESTIONS

(1) *Objecting to Unreasonable Requests (i.e., to "Pushing") Slatnick v. Leadership Housing Systems, 368 So. 2d 78 (Fla. App. 1979).* Is it reasonable for the court to take the position that a party always must object specifically to each individual interrogatory or other discovery request, and must show that each individually is oppressive? Or can the court consider the cumulative weight of the discovery requests? The use of unreasonable discovery requests is sometimes referred to as "pushing." Perhaps the world's champion reported case of "pushing" in discovery is *Slatnick v. Leadership Housing Systems*. The court described the interrogatories, there, as "composed of 2,300 legal size pages in small type (without excessive space between questions)." The court quoted one "choice sample" question, which called for detailed information about the load carried by each steel pipe column in each of eighteen condominium buildings. The court estimated that this single question (which occupied part of one of the 2,300 pages) "might take a week to answer" by itself. The discovering party argued that objections to the interrogatories must be overruled, because they were not particularized, question by question; the appellate court disagreed on the ground that the judge could not possibly review and hear argument on each individual interrogatory "unless he were to accept it as an exclusive line of work for weeks."

(2) *"Tripping": Unreasonable Noncompliance.* Another form of discovery abuse is to hinder unnecessarily the discovery of relevant non-privileged information by any one of a variety of means ranging from delay to concealment to destruction of evidence. This practice is euphemistically called "tripping" (and until the 1983 amendments to the federal discovery rules, this problem appeared to be the one with which the rulemakers had the most concern). Consider the conduct of GAF in *Roesberg v. Johns-Manville Corp.* GAF answered only six of the interrogatories. In other parts of its opinion, the court pointed out that GAF had objected to one interrogatory on the ground that it contained the

allegedly "vague and ambiguous" word "associated" (the court held that this term had a "clear" meaning in the context of the question); GAF claimed that a question calling for safety claims in advertising was "irrelevant" (the court held the relevancy of this interrogatory to be "obvious" in an asbestos products liability case); and there were similarly dubious objections throughout. Is this conduct properly characterized as "tripping"? Might it be difficult in some cases to tell the difference between tripping and *bona fide* objections with which a court simply disagrees?

(3) *"Canned" Interrogatories: SCM Societa Commercial SPA v. Industrial and Commercial Research Corp., 72 F.R.D. 110 (N.D. Tex. 1976).* Some kinds of cases, with recurring issues or fact patterns, may lend themselves to standardized interrogatories. In the *SCM* case, however, the court described the indiscriminate use of canned interrogatories as "an unprofessional and insulting practice." Would this statement be true, say, of a personal injury defense lawyer who sent interrogatories inquiring about the incident and the damages in similar form, with minor tailoring, in each intersectional collision case she handled?

(4) *Remedial Measures.* What is the best solution to the type of problem presented by the *Slatnick* case? Obviously this type of problem led to the general limits on the number of depositions and interrogatories. Should similar limits be placed on requests for production of documents? Should the party or the attorney who has committed the discovery abuse be fined or otherwise penalized? Should the trial judge play a more active managerial role in regulating the timing and extent of discovery? *See also* Sherman, *Federal Court Discovery in the 80's: Making the Rules Work,* 2 Rev. Litig. 10 (1981).

[B] Discovery Certifications and the Discovery Conference

ASSOCIATED RADIO SERVICE COMPANY v. PAGE AIRWAYS, INC., 73 F.R.D. 633 (D.C. Tex. 1977). In an antitrust case characterized by the district judge as one in which "Plaintiffs' allegations of antitrust have spilled over to the discovery process where nobody trusts anybody," the trial judge called a discovery conference and ordered counsel to attempt informal resolution of their discovery disputes and to submit a Discovery Conference Report. After both sides could not agree on what had been resolved at the discovery conference, two different reports were filed and the trial judge was required to conduct a hearing "in light of the disparity between the two conference report drafts." Then, because of the "failure to comply with my order concerning the discovery conference and the filing of the discovery conference report," the trial judge, pursuant to Fed. R. Civ. P. 37(b)(2), "decided to award expenses caused by the failure to comply with my order only against the attorneys."

The trial judge determined the amount of the monetary sanctions by considering the extent to which unnecessary legal expenses were incurred in preparation for and attendance at the hearing that itself was made necessary by the two conference reports. He ordered the respective law firms to pay the opposing clients this sum and further ordered that the law firms "shall not be indemnified or compensated in any other way by [their] clients or any party to this suit for the amount of this assessment."

[C] Sanctions

LEW v. KONA HOSPITAL

754 F.2d 1420 (9th Cir. 1985)

PREGERSON, CIRCUIT JUDGE.

Appellant Barry G. Lew, M.D., appeals a decision of the district court granting summary judgment to defendants on his claim of civil rights violations, unfair trade practices, and defamation. In addition, Dr. Lew challenges the district court's order that he pay costs and attorneys' fees incurred by defendants in connection with his deposition at which he failed to appear. We affirm the district court's grant of summary judgment and its award of costs and attorney's fees.

FACTS AND PROCEDURE

[Dr. Lew sued the Kona State hospital and various individuals because his probationary staff privileges were terminated. His complaint alleged violations of federal due process rights and also asserted state law claims for unfair trade practices and for defamation. After a series of interim orders, the defendants moved for summary judgment. The trial court, after a hearing and on the basis of the summary judgment record, granted summary judgment for all defendants on November 7, 1983.]

Defendants also filed a Motion to Dismiss for Dr. Lew's failure to appear for his deposition on October 7, 1983. Dr. Lew filed an opposition, claiming that he was unable to attend his deposition because of economic difficulties and because of the withdrawal of local counsel. At a hearing on October 31, 1983, the district judge denied the motion to dismiss, but ordered that Dr. Lew pay the attorneys' fees and costs that defendants incurred in connection with the scheduled deposition. Dr. Lew filed timely appeals from both actions of the district court. . . .

I. *Summary Judgment*

[The court affirms the summary judgment as to the federal due process claim because the defendants' affidavits show that Dr. Lew received a fair hearing in all challenged respects, and because Dr. Lew filed no affidavits or other competent factual material controverting this showing. The court affirms the judgment as to the state law claims because the alleged acts do not violate the state unfair trade practices statute as a matter of law and because a state statute furnishes a complete defense to defamation suits for statements uttered during a hospital peer review process.

[The court then turns to the issue of the sanctions assessed against Dr. Lew.]

II. *Imposition of Sanctions*

A. *Standard of Review*

The district court has great latitude in imposing sanctions under Fed. R. Civ. P. 37. We review the imposition of sanctions for failure to comply with discovery orders under an abuse of discretion standard. . . .

B. *Merits*

Rule 37(d) allows the district court to impose sanctions, including payment of expenses, on a party who fails to appear for his own deposition after receiving proper notice.

Pursuant to his authority under the rule, the district judge ordered Dr. Lew to pay $1,203.55 in costs and attorneys' fees for failure to appear at his deposition on Friday, October 7, 1983. Dr. Lew admits that the deposition was properly noticed, but argues that his failure to appear was "substantially justified" under the rule because he was not represented by local counsel at the time and his appearance at the deposition would therefore have been "futile."

The district judge was plainly acting within his discretion in ordering the payment of attorneys' fees and costs. The Advisory Committee Notes to Rule 37(d) themselves indicate that the failure to appear need not be willful. Rather, the Notes emphasize the discretion of the trial judge in deciding which sanctions to impose:

> In addition, in view of the possibility of light sanctions, even a negligent failure should come within Rule 37(d). If default is caused by counsel's ignorance of Federal practice, or by his preoccupation with another aspect of the case, dismissal of the action and default judgment are not justified, but the imposition of expenses and fees may well be.

(Citations omitted.) *See also Marquis v. Chrysler Corp.*, 577 F.2d 624, 642 (9th Cir. 1978) (even negligent failure to allow reasonable discovery may be punished). This circuit has upheld a sanction as severe as dismissal for failure to comply with discovery orders. *See, e.g., Sigliano v. Mendoza*, 642 F.2d 309, 310 (9th Cir. 1981) (dismissal for failure to answer interrogatories); *Pioche Mines Consolidated, Inc. v. Dolman*, 333 F.2d 257, 269 (9th Cir. 1964) (dismissal for willful failure to attend deposition) . . .; *Fong v. United States*, 300 F.2d 400, 409 (9th Cir.) (entry of default judgment for failure to resume depositions), . . . *See also Al Barnett & Son, Inc. v. Outboard Marine Corp.*, 611 F.2d 32, 35 (3d Cir. 1979) (dismissal for failure to attend deposition).

Other courts have specifically approved the award of attorneys' fees and costs to a party when the other party fails to appear for its own deposition. *See Weigel v. Shapiro*, 608 F.2d 268, 272 (7th Cir. 1979) (failure to answer any questions at deposition treated as failure to appear and expenses awarded accordingly); *Bosworth v. Record Data of Maryland, Inc.*, 102 F.R.D. 518 (D. Md. 1984) (plaintiff's financial indigency did not excuse her from liability for costs and fees for failure to attend properly noticed deposition). . . .

Dr. Lew's failure to attend his deposition could be characterized as "willful." Although he and his attorney received proper notice of the deposition, they concluded that appearance would be futile because Dr. Lew was not then represented by local counsel. After reaching this conclusion, however, neither Dr. Lew nor his attorney notified opposing counsel of their decision not to attend. In light of this "willful failure," the sanction the district court imposed was a light one.

Even if Dr. Lew's failure to attend was not willful, however, the sanctions the district court imposed were within the permissible range. Even a negligent failure to allow reasonable discovery may be punished. *Marquis*, 577 F.2d at 642 (9th Cir. 1978). The court considered defendant's claim for expenses, disallowed some of the fees, and allowed others. We uphold the reasonable expenses the district judge imposed because they were within his discretion under Rule 37(d). [Affirmed.]

NOTES AND QUESTIONS

(1) *Is "Gross Negligence" Enough for Severe Sanctions or Is "Willfulness" Required?: Cine Forty-Second Street Theatre Corp. v. Allied Artists Picture Corp., 602 F.2d 1062*

(2d Cir. 1979). Although the Ninth Circuit, in *Lew v. Kona Hospital*, above, implied that "willful" misconduct might be required for severe sanctions such as dismissal or default judgment, the Second Circuit in *Cine Forty-Second Street* concluded that "gross negligence" could suffice. In an antitrust case, the plaintiff, Cine, failed to answer interrogatories through a series of intermediate orders, which included several warnings by the magistrate. The magistrate ultimately entered a "preclusion order," precluding the plaintiff from making any proof of damages, since that was the subject of the interrogatories. This order had the same effect as a dismissal, since the plaintiff could recover nothing if it could not offer evidence of damages. The District Court, however, concluded that Cine's counsel could have been confused by the magistrate's oral orders, and it "regretfully" declined to uphold the magistrate's severe sanction. The Court of Appeals reversed and reinstated the sanction:

> . . . Cine's action was, at the very least, grossly negligent. . . .
>
> [S]anctions serve a threefold purpose. Preclusionary orders ensure that a party will not be able to profit from its own failure to comply. . . . Rule 37 strictures are also specific deterrents and, like civil contempt, they seek to secure compliance with the particular order at hand. . . . Finally, although the most drastic sanctions may not be imposed as "mere penalties," . . . courts are free to consider the general deterrent effect their orders may have . . . on other litigation, provided that the party on whom they are imposed is, in some sense, at fault. *National Hockey League v. Metropolitan Hockey Club, Inc.*, 427 U.S. 639 (1976) (per curiam); *Societe Internationale pour Participations Industrielles et Commercials v. Rogers*, 357 U.S. 197 (1958).
>
> [The court discussed the *Societe Internationale* case, which indicated that dismissal could be authorized against a party who engaged in "willfulness, bad faith, or . . . fault."]
>
> Unless we are to assume that the Court chose its words carelessly, we must accord the term "fault" a meaning of its own within the *Societe Internationale* triad. And plainly, if "fault" has any meaning not subsumed by "willfulness" and "bad faith," it must at least cover gross negligence of the type present in this case.

The courts have continued to struggle with the precise level of "fault" that should be required to justify severe sanctions. *Compare Cine Forty-Second Street*, above, *with Fjelstad v. American Honda Motor Co.*, 762 F.2d 1334 (9th Cir. 1985) (party that refused to answer interrogatories throughout several interim orders but could have misapprehended effects of orders, held, subject to sanctions, but not to severest sanctions; partial default judgment reversed). *See also* Heiderscheit, *Rule 37 Discovery Sanctions in the Ninth Circuit: The Collapse of the Deterrence Goal*, 68 Or. L. Rev. 57 (1989).

(2) *The Relevance of the Rule 26(g) Certifications: An Objective Standard of "Reasonable Inquiry" Analogous to Rule 11.* You should remember that Rule 26(g) attributes to every attorney signing a discovery request, response, or objection an automatic certification based upon a standard of "reasonable inquiry." This standard probably provides further support for the "negligence" standard adopted in *Lew v. Kona Hospital*, since both are objective standards of similar meaning (although 26(g) is not directly applicable to *Lew v. Kona* since it did not concern the signing of discovery requests). Does Rule 26(g) also support the result in such cases as *Cine Forty-Second Street*, which imposes a severe sanction for unintentional conduct? Notice that the Rule says that the court "must" impose an appropriate sanction, in language different from that of current Rule 11. Rule 26(g) apparently provides separate authority for sanctions,

in addition to Rule 37, although the purposes of the two Rules clearly overlap. *See* George, DeSalvo & Grose, *Rule 26(g) — The "Undiscovered Rule,"* 24 Trial 33 (1988).

(3) *The Permissible Purposes of Sanctions. Cine Forty-Second Street,* in Note 1, above, lists three purposes of sanctions: (1) adjusting the rights of the parties so that the disobedience does not create an advantage; (2) specific deterrence of future violations by other parties; and (3) general deterrence, *i.e.*, deterrence of violations by other parties in other, unrelated cases. To what extent is, or should, this third purpose of general deterrence be controlling? In earlier cases, the courts reasoned that mere "punishment" was inappropriate, and sometimes they confined sanctions to the minimum that would accomplish the purpose of solving the immediate discovery matter at issue. The difficulty with this standard was that some attorneys were adept at gauging precisely the point beyond which their noncompliance would invoke a sanction, and they obtained tactical advantages by pushing or tripping right up to that point. This behavior may be a problem still, but the knowledge that sanctions can be a general deterrent reduces it.

(4) *Procedural Considerations: Fjelstad v. American Honda Motor Co., 762 F.2d 1334 (9th Cir. 1985).* When the court contemplates imposing sanctions, what procedures must it follow? In *Fjelstad,* the sanctioned party made the following attacks: first, the order compelling discovery was so vague that sanctions based on its violation would not comply with due process; secondly, there was not sufficient notice given by the opponent's motion for sanctions; and third, the hearing held by the court on sanctions was inadequate. The court rejected these arguments because the underlying order made clear the party's duty to answer the questioned interrogatories completely, the motion clearly drew attention to the failure to do so, and the hearing transcript showed that the party had an adequate opportunity to address the issue. The due process clause presumably sets minimum levels for these matters. What procedures should be required if a party, rather than failing to answer completely, fails to answer at all? What procedures should be required for the most severe sanctions?

(5) *The Range of Sanctions. Cine Forty-Second Street,* in Note 1 above, gives a short summary of the range of sanctions, from ordering expenses at the milder end of the range, through taking facts as established, precluding evidence, or striking pleadings as intermediate sanctions; to dismissal, default, or contempt at the more severe end. For violation of a court order regarding discovery, however, these sanctions are merely examples, and the court actually has broad authority to "issue further just orders." Rule 37(b)(2). *See also* Note, *The Misuse of Inherent Powers When Imposing Sanctions for Discovery Abuse: The Exclusivity of Rule 37,* 9 Cardozo L. Rev. 1779 (1988).

(6) *Are a Pro Se Litigant's Costs of Representing Herself in a Discovery Dispute "Expenses Incurred" Under Rule 37?* In a case of first impression, the Court of Appeals for the Federal Circuit held that federal district courts may not award attorneys' fees to pro se litigants as a discovery sanction under Rule 37(a), because a pro se litigant's costs of representing herself do not constitute "reasonable expenses incurred" within the meaning of that provision. *Pickholtz v. Rainbow Technologies, Inc.*, 284 F.3d 1365 (Fed. Cir. 2002). However, such fees may be awarded under the court's inherent power to punish a party's willful disobedience of a court order or conduct that is in bad faith, vexatious, wanton, or oppressive.

§ 7.04 Appendix Sanctions in Practice

RULE 37 MOTION IN *GEORGE MILLER CO. v. COMPUDATA, INC.*

[Reproduced above in § [C] of Appendix to Chapter 2, *supra.*]

For a concrete example of the use of sanctions, read (or re-read) the Rule 37 Motion in *George Miller Co. v. Compudata, Inc.*, in § [C] of the Appendix to Chapter 2. Note that the respondent had refused to answer some questions and requests for admissions on "legal conclusion" grounds, in circumstances wherein the Rules clearly preclude this objection. What sanctions, if any, would be appropriate? In the real cases the court assessed no sanctions — but that was before the 1983 and 1993 amendments to Rule 11, the certification requirements in Rule 26, and the current "get tough" attitude on sanctions.

§ 7.05 Discovery Under State Rules

Variations on the Federal Theme. Many of the states follow the federal discovery model closely. To a greater or lesser degree, so do the states whose laws are discussed here. These notes are not complete descriptions of any of the systems discussed; they bring out a few interesting differences from the federal system.

California's Discovery Provisions. California's system is often closely analogous to the federal system, such as discovery scope defined by "any matter, not privileged, that is relevant to the subject matter involved in the pending action." CCP § 2017.010. Protective orders, however, are not confined to a single, central provision as in Federal Rule 26(c); instead, there are protective order and sanction provisions tailored to each of the discovery devices. For example, sixteen different oral deposition protective orders are specified in § 2025.420, plus a catchall provision. Some of the other California provisions that differ significantly from federal practice are § 2033.280, which requires the requesting party to seek a court order providing that unanswered requests for admission are deemed admitted (but requires the court to make the order unless the opposing party substantially complies before the hearing); §§ 2019.010(f), 2034.210 and 2034.430, which provide for simultaneous exchanges of expert witness information and also allow any party to depose a listed expert after tendering the expert's fee; §§ 2025.340 and 2025.620, which contain detailed provisions for videotaped depositions and allow videotaped experts' depositions to be used at trial irrespective of availability; and § 2032.220(a), which allows one routine physical examination of a personal injury plaintiff without leave of court. In addition, California has carefully created presumptive limits upon discovery. Under § 2025.610, only one deposition of a natural person is allowed, unless the court orders otherwise after a showing of good cause. And §§ 2030.030 and 2033.030 limit each party to 35 interrogatories and 35 requests for admission, although a party may exceed these limits by filing appropriate declarations.

California's Economic Litigation Act for Limited Civil Cases, CCP §§ 90–100. When the amount in controversy is $25,000 or less, this California Act prescribes a standard-form "case questionnaire" — and, beyond that, confines the parties to one (1) deposition plus any combination of thirty-five (35) interrogatories ("with no subparts"), demands to produce, and requests for admission. There are other provisions more generally applicable. [Is this a good idea?]

Texas: A Few Significant Differences from the Federal Rules. The Texas rules are more closely analogous to the Federal Rules than are California's. There are, however, important differences. The Texas discovery rules set up a three-tiered discovery scheme in an effort to tailor the amount of discovery to the complexity of the case. Level 1 applies to small cases (monetary recovery of $50,000 or less). Level 2 applies to most cases and Level 3, which requires a tailored discovery control plan, comparable to a Rule 16 scheduling order, is applicable to complex cases. Tex. R. Civ. P. 190.

In Level 1 cases, each party may have no more than six hours to examine all witnesses in oral depositions. The parties may agree to expand this limit to ten hours, but cannot agree to more than ten hours without a court order. In Level 2, each side is entitled to no more than 50 hours in oral depositions to examine opposing parties, experts and persons subject to the control of opposing parties. Other witnesses are not subject to the 50 hour limit. In Level 3, the court determines the amount of deposition discovery. *See* Tex. R. Civ. P. 190. In any event, unless otherwise agreed, no side may examine an individual witness for more than six hours. *See* Tex. R. Civ. P. 199.5.

Texas discovery also provides for disclosure of both favorable and unfavorable information in response to a "request for disclosure" of basic information. Tex. R. Civ. P. 194. This procedural device replaces the use of interrogatories for certain commonly relevant factual matters and for information regarding testifying experts. Tex R. Civ. P. 195.1. Interrogatories are reduced to no more than 25 under level 1 and level 2. Tex. R. Civ. P. 190. Depositions may be used at trial without any showing of unavailability. Tex. R. Civ. P. 203. Expert witnesses are covered differently than they are by the Federal Rules. Texas expressly provides for discovery of consultants' opinions if their work is reviewed by a testifying expert, but not otherwise. Tex. R. Civ. P. 192.3(e). Also the Texas version of work product, which otherwise resembles Federal Rule 26(b), does not protect witness statements from discovery. Tex. R. Civ. P. 192.5. A statement taken from a client may, however, be protected by the attorney-client privilege. Tex. R. Civ. P. 192, cmt. 9.

New York's "Disclosure" Provisions. "Disclosure" under the CPLR roughly parallels "discovery" under the Federal Rules, although the terminology is different and the scope is in some respects narrower. Chase, 1 *Weinstein, Korn & Miller CPLR Manual* §§ 20.01, 20.02 (1997). For example, CPLR 3101(a) extends disclosure to "all matter material and necessary in the prosecution or defense of an action . . . ." But this provision has been interpreted liberally, and despite its language, it is not limited to indispensable material; it applies to any facts "bearing on the controversy which will assist preparation for trial . . . ." Chase, *supra*, § 20.02(a). Interrogatories may not be used by a party who has demanded a bill of particulars (which is not, itself, a disclosure device, although it bears a relationship to disclosure), except in matrimonial actions. CPLR 3130. In some kinds of cases (most notably, personal injury negligence actions), a party may not take depositions and also serve interrogatories. CPLR 3130. "Discovery and inspection," which is the name of the device for production of documents or tangible things, can be used as to either parties or nonparties — but if the latter, it requires serving a subpoena. CPLR 3120, 3122-a. In some respects, such as the use of depositions, New York practice under CPLR 3117 closely parallels federal practice (but even here, there is a difference, in that the deposition of a person licensed to practice medicine may be used without a showing of unavailability).

§ 7.06 Improving the Discovery Rules: Notes and Questions

(1) *Small Cases.* One of the issues in cases without a large amount in controversy is conducting discovery without the cost exceeding the probable worth of plaintiff's claim. Consider the following proposals. Which ones, if any, would be worth adoption?

(a) *Standardized Bill of Particulars Practice as a Substitute for Individually Drafted Interrogatories.* New York has a bill of particulars practice, which actually is part of the pleading system in that state (*see* Chapter 5, *supra*), and which is standardized in terms of items that can be demanded, at least in personal injury cases. Texas has an analogous request for disclosure. A defendant need not draft interrogatories from scratch, and a plaintiff can know, at the time of the initial client interview, that there is a certain laundry list of information that will likely be required to be particularized. Would widespread adoption of this practice be wise? Could it be extended to, *e.g.*, consumer cases, suits on notes, etc.?

(b) *Informal "Meetings," Perhaps Conducted by Telephone, as Partial Substitutes for Depositions.* In some kinds of proceedings, unrecorded meetings are a substitute for discovery. In very small cases, might it not make sense for the attorneys to have the right to request a four-person meeting of the parties and attorneys, and to have it conducted by telephone, and not reported by a reporter, as a substitute for the more expensive deposition? A proviso would be necessary to the effect that either party could require a normal deposition.

(c) *California's Economic Litigation Act; How to Tell the Difference Between a Big Case and a Small One — And Whether to Treat Them Differently.* One problem with big-case-small-case distinctions is that the *ad damnum* may not show the real value of the case. Consider whether California's use of amount in controversy of $25,000 or less, to limit each party to one deposition and 35 written discovery requests, makes sense. If you object to different treatment of "large" and "small" cases, would it make sense to have the limited procedure be the norm in a small case, but allow either party to invoke more expansive procedures by motion to the court?

(2) *General Cost-Reduction Devices.* Evaluate the following proposals:

(a) *Required Disclosures; Limiting the Number of Interrogatories (or Required Answers).* Consider the required disclosures contained in the rules. Is this a useful device? Also, the rules create a "presumptive" limit of 25 interrogatories. What advantages or disadvantages would such a rule have? [Hint: Can't a single question be written so as to call for large amounts of information? *Cf. Slatnick v. Leadership Housing, supra.*] The parties could use more interrogatories either by agreement or by motion to the court, which the court should grant liberally, particularly in large cases.

(b) *Limiting the Number of Required Answers.* An alternative means of limiting interrogatory costs is to limit the number of answers. One problem is that, just as it is difficult to tell when one has twenty or thirty "questions," there can be varying judgments as to what is an "answer" (*e.g.*, plaintiff's attorney, with questionable ethics, answers a question about treating physicians with multiple names, treating each physician's first, middle and last name as a separate "answer").

(c) *Do Admissions Need to Be Limited?* Some, but many fewer, courts limit admission requests. This discovery device calls only for an "admitted" or "denied" and is less onerous to answer.

(d) *Limiting Production.* Document production is one of the more expensive aspects of discovery. It is difficult to limit, because two different cases with similar damages might require radically different numbers of documents. Might it make sense to provide that a production request may not call for more than 500 separate documents without a motion to the court? Indeed, might it make sense to require the discoverer to show "good cause" to obtain documents beyond a certain point? (Note that this proposal resurrects a form of Rule 34 that was discarded in 1970.)

(e) *Limiting the Number of Depositions.* Should a provision limit the number of depositions that either side could take in a case? Note California's Economic Litigation Act; Federal Rules (10 depositions). Would it make sense to impose a limit of, say, five depositions when the amount in controversy does not exceed $50,000, subject to court authority to allow further depositions upon motion showing need? Also, the presumptive seven-hour limit on each deposition protects witnesses and allows any deposition to be completed in one day. A good idea?

(3) *Privileges and Work Product.* One of the problems with respect to items such as trade secrets and work product is that the contours of the protection are vague and it is readily subject to being breached. As a result, there is a disproportionate amount of litigation over these items. Would the following proposals make sense?

(a) *A "Trade Secret" Privilege.* Some jurisdictions (*e.g.*, California) provide a privilege for trade secrets. The difficulty with this idea is that anything known to a firm and not shared with competitors arguably is a "trade secret," including most information relevant to a lawsuit, and so definition is difficult. Furthermore, even "hard core" trade secrets such as confidential information on advances in the state of the art can be highly relevant to litigation. A trade secret privilege cannot be absolute. Nevertheless, would it be useful?

(b) *Express, and Absolute, Immunity from Discovery as a Partial Substitute for the Work Product Doctrine.* Some jurisdictions (*e.g.*, Texas) historically have had absolute exemptions from discovery for some items that the Federal Rules would treat as work product. Would it make sense, in order to enhance predictability and reduce litigation, to supplement the general work product doctrine with specific provisions of this kind?

(4) *Experts.* Should it be easier to discover "consulting" experts, on the theory that witnesses whom one side decides not to call are likely to be good witnesses for the other side?

(5) *Use of Discovery at Trial.* Given the unpredictable nature of trial scheduling in most courts (*see* Chapter 8, *infra*), and given that the proponent usually takes the risk of jury skepticism, shouldn't Rule 32 be revised to allow the free use of depositions as evidence at trial?

(6) *Discovery Plans, Conference, and Sanctions.* Would the following proposals be wise to adopt?

(a) *Model Discovery Plans.* Just as there are forms of pleadings appended to the Rules, might it make sense for the Rules Advisory Committee to promulgate model forms of discovery plans for different kinds of cases and to incorporate them into the Rules? What disadvantages would such a proposal entail?

(b) *Automatic (or "Semi-Automatic") Sanctions.* One alleged deficiency in discovery sanctions is the lack of uniformity and predictability in their imposition. Would it make sense for District Courts, by local rule, to experiment with "automatic" sanction amounts in given situations? For example, a failure timely to answer interrogatories, in the absence of a showing of good cause, might invoke the imposition of a $500 sanction (unless the actual costs or losses of the opponent were greater). This idea has a great deal in common with the enactments in some states of determinate sentencing laws in criminal cases. What disadvantages would such a proposal have?

CHAPTER 8

PRETRIAL CONFERENCES AND CASE MANAGEMENT

§ 8.01 Pretrial Conferences and Pretrial Orders

Read Fed. R. Civ. P. 16 (pretrial conference; scheduling; management).

[A] The Purposes of Pretrial Conferences

CHEVRETTE v. MARKS, 558 F. Supp. 1133 (M.D. Pa. 1983). This *pro se* prisoner's suit should have been "rather uncomplicated," said the court, but it had swelled to eighty-nine documents and was pending before the District Court on ten recommendations by the magistrate relating to pending motions. The plaintiff's pleadings were confused; many of the plaintiff's motions were "inane" and had nothing to do with the proceedings, and the court suspected that the claim was groundless but could not be certain from the documents in the case. The District Court suggested that, in these circumstances, the magistrate could have used a pretrial conference under Rule 16 to simplify the case in a face-to-face meeting:

> Finally, the court observes that this might have been an appropriate case for the convening of a pretrial conference. When, as here, a case becomes "muddled" through the continuous filing of documents raising vacuous contentions, our Magistrates should feel free to convene a conference. Such a meeting can result in the elimination of insipid legal arguments and empty factual allegations, and can further promote judicial economy by sharpening the genuine questions involved in the dispute. [I]n the present case, the Magistrate had warned the plaintiff that he should confine his arguments to matters raised at the outset. The plaintiff ignored this caveat. [A] conference might very well have resolved the entire action. Indeed, this court previously has noted:
>
>> While a court may be reluctant to grant a motion for summary judgment in a *pro se* prisoner action where the prisoner's affidavit, liberally construed, may indicate a factual issue, such is not the case where the court has the opportunity at a pretrial conference to delve more deeply into the allegations and "separate the wheat from the chaff." . . .
>
> *Pifcho v. Brewer*, 77 F.R.D. 356, 357-58 (M.D. Pa. 1977). Thus, if the Magistrate had held a pretrial conference and concluded that the plaintiff had no proof to support his nonfrivolous claims, dismissal might have been appropriate. . . .

> Even if dismissal would not have resulted, the Magistrate would have been able to focus attention on the real issues and, at a minimum, would have avoided the task of wading through a flood of irrelevant documents — a "pointless" exercise. . . .

NOTES AND QUESTIONS

(1) *The Rule 16 List of Purposes; Breadth.* Notice the broad list of purposes contained in Rule 16. While *Chevrette* correctly states the general purpose of "sharpening the genuine questions involved in the dispute," the Rule 16 list gives a correct impression of considerable breadth.The *Chevrette* opinion indicates that the court may have an alternate purpose: to create a record that would justify dismissal if the complaint indeed is not supportable. Is this purpose proper? [Note: Can you think of any purpose related to the disposition of the action that, in fact, would not be covered by the broad purposes of Rule 16?] *See generally* Pollack, *Pretrial Procedures More Effectively Handled*, 65 F.R.D. 475 (1974).

(2) *The Advantage of Face-to-Face Exchange at a Pretrial Conference among the Judge, the Attorneys, and the Parties.* The conference allows the judge to direct follow-up statements or questions to the attorneys. It allows the judge to gauge responses, to induce desired behavior by the attorneys such as settlement negotiations, and even to persuade. In addition, there may be good reason to believe that attorneys will be less likely to advance unmeritorious positions if they are subject to an exchange with the court. In this regard, consider the following local rule that was once adopted by the Southern District of Texas:

> Henceforth, before any written motions are prepared and filed . . . , the attorneys will present them orally to the Court.
>
> Attorneys desiring to file any motion [w]ill [r]equest an appointment with the Court for a conference at which time the motion will be presented orally. . . .

Why do you think the court adopted this rule? Is it a wise and sensible requirement? [Regardless of its putative advantages, of course, a local rule must not be inconsistent with the Federal Rules of Civil Procedure (as this one arguably is). The rule later was repealed.]

(3) *Flexibility: No Conferences in Some Cases; Series of Conferences in Others.* Rule 16 does not require the court to hold a pretrial conference, and many cases may be resolved more expeditiously with none at all. Would that have been the case in *Chevrette v. Marks* if the case had not grown so complex?

On the other hand, "big" cases may require a whole series of pretrial conferences, perhaps held for different purposes. The *Manual for Complex Litigation* suggests multiple conferences: (1) an initial conference to begin the structuring of a case-management plan and scheduling order; (2) recurring conferences, the necessity of which is determined by the judge, to monitor the litigation and resolve problems as they arise; and (3) a final pretrial conference once discovery is complete and a firm trial date has been set. *See Manual for Complex Litigation* (Fourth), §§ 11.21-11.22 (2004).

[B] The Effects of Pretrial Orders

UNITED STATES v. FIRST NATIONAL BANK OF CIRCLE

652 F.2d 882 (9th Cir. 1981)

SCHWARZER, DISTRICT JUDGE:

The United States brought this action under Section 3505(b) of the Internal Revenue Code, 26 U.S.C. § 3505(b), to collect from the First National Bank of Circle (Bank) the unpaid withholding and Federal Insurance Contribution Act (F.I.C.A.) taxes owed by Fort Belknap Builders, Inc. (Builders). The District Court granted the Bank's motion for summary judgment, and the United States appeals. We reverse, having determined that the court's actions were not in conformity with Rule 16, Fed. R. Civ. P. . . .

Factual and Procedural Background

. . . In order to finance the purchase of a contract with the Department of Housing and Urban Development (H.U.D.) for the erection of 50 houses, Builders borrowed funds from the Bank and one of its affiliates in 1970. . . .

During the latter part of 1971, Builders' account with Bank was substantially overdrawn. Beginning in the fourth quarter of 1970 and through 1971, Builders paid its employees but failed to pay withholding and F.I.C.A. taxes.

This action was filed on July 18, 1974, to recover from the Bank under Section 3505(b) unpaid withholding and F.I.C.A. taxes owed by Builders for the fourth quarter of 1970 and all four quarters of 1971. That section imposes liability for federal withholding taxes on a person who supplies funds to an employer for the payment of wages, knowing that the employer does not intend or will not be able to pay those taxes.[1] The complaint alleged that during the relevant period the Bank supplied funds to Builders or for its account with knowledge that Builders did not intend or was not able to pay federal withholding taxes.

The Bank's answer consisted of a general denial.[a] Neither in its answer nor at any time thereafter until trial did the Bank specifically deny that it had been a supplier of funds to Builders. . . .

On March 28, 1978, appellant and the Bank entered into a pretrial order which included a statement of agreed facts and a summary of each party's contentions. Paragraph 20 of the agreed facts stated:

> Numerous loans and advances were made by the [Bank] together with various participating Banks or other affiliated entities between March 16, 1970, and December 31, 1971.

---

[1] Section 3505(b) provides:

> (b) Personal liability where funds are supplied. — If a lender, surety, or other person supplies funds to or for the account of an employer for the specific purpose of paying wages of the employees of such employer, with actual notice or knowledge (within the meaning of section 6323(i)(1)) that such employer does not intend to or will not be able to make timely payment or deposit of the amounts of tax required by this subtitle to be deducted and withheld by such employer from such wages, such lender, surety, or other person shall be liable in his own person and estate to the United States in a sum equal to the taxes (together with interest) which are not paid over to the United States by such employer with respect to such wages. . . .

[a] The United States apparently never moved to strike this answer (possibly because the pretrial order supplied details).

The Bank's contentions set forth in the pretrial order were in substance that (1) it did not have the requisite knowledge, (2) Builders was always able to pay the taxes, (3) the loans it made were ordinary working capital loans not for the specific purpose of paying wages, (4) the taxes owing by Builders had been paid, and (5) the action was barred by the statute of limitations and laches.

On the first day of trial the Bank moved for summary judgment on the ground that it had not been a supplier of funds. After appellant submitted an offer of proof as directed by the trial court, the court granted the motion. It held that the Bank, having only acted as agent for the participating banks in arranging for loans to Builders, had not supplied funds. It further held that the Bank had not supplied funds by honoring Builders' temporary overdrafts. The government now appeals from the judgment entered for the Bank.

Effect of the Pretrial Order

Appellant argues that it was error for the trial court to award judgment to the Bank on a theory which was not included among the Bank's contentions in the pretrial order and was at variance with the agreed facts stated in that order.

Rule 16, Fed. R. Civ. P., states in relevant part:

> The court shall make an order which recites the action taken at the [pretrial] conference . . . and the agreements made by the parties as to any of the matters considered, and which limits the issues for trial to those not disposed of by admissions or agreements of counsel; and such order when entered controls the subsequent course of the action, unless modified at the trial to prevent manifest injustice. [The language of Rule 16 subsequently was amended as explained in Note (1) following this case — Eds.]

Pretrial orders play a crucial role in implementing the purposes of the Federal Rules of Civil Procedure "to secure the just, speedy, and inexpensive determination of every action." Fed. R. Civ. P. 1. Unless pretrial orders are honored and enforced, the objectives of the pretrial conference to simplify issues and avoid unnecessary proof by obtaining admissions of fact will be jeopardized if not entirely nullified. Accordingly, a party need offer no proof at trial as to matters agreed to in the order, nor may a party offer evidence or advance theories at the trial which are not included in the order or which contradict its terms. Disregard of these principles would bring back the days of trial by ambush and discourage timely preparation by the parties for trial.

That is not to say that a pretrial order should not be liberally construed to permit evidence and theories at trial that can fairly be said to be embraced within its language. But particular evidence or theories which are not at least implicitly included in the order are barred unless the order is first "modified to prevent manifest injustice." Fed. R. Civ. P. 16.

Neither evidence that the loans to Builders during the relevant period were made by others than the Bank nor the contention that the Bank did not supply funds to Builders could be said to be included in the pretrial order even under the most liberal construction; in fact, that evidence and that contention are plainly contrary to the terms of the order.

Under Rule 16, the trial court had authority to modify the pretrial order if in the court's discretion modification was determined to be necessary "to prevent manifest injustice." The court, however, did not purport to make a modification of the order before granting the Bank's motion for summary judgment. For the court to have properly exercised its discretion to modify the order, it would have had to consider such factors as

(1) the degree of prejudice to the Bank resulting from a failure to modify;

(2) the degree of prejudice to plaintiff from a modification;

(3) the impact of a modification at that stage of the litigation on the orderly and efficient conduct of the case; and

(4) the degree of willfulness, bad faith or inexcusable neglect on the part of the Bank.

Where, upon consideration of factors such as those, the court determines that refusal to allow a modification might result in injustice while allowance would cause no substantial injury to the opponent and no more than slight inconvenience to the court, a modification should ordinarily be allowed. If necessary to prevent harm to the opponent, appropriate protective terms and conditions may be attached to the order allowing modification. But where as here the court departs substantially from the order to the prejudice of a party without exercise of its discretion informed by consideration of the relevant factors, the judgment must be reversed. . . .

NOTES AND QUESTIONS

(1) *"Restyling" of Rule 16's Language.* In 2007, Rule 16's language was "restyled." Two subsections now cover the language indicated in the case text above. Rule 16(d) provides: "After any conference under this rule, the court should issue an order reciting the action taken. This order controls the course of the action unless the court modifies it." Rule 16(e) provides: "The court may hold a final pretrial conference to formulate a trial plan, including a plan to facilitate the admission of evidence. The conference must be held as close to the start of trial as is reasonable, and must be attended by at least one attorney who will conduct the trial for each party and by any unrepresented party. The court may modify an order issued after a final pretrial conference only to prevent manifest injustice." Note that the ultimate standard — "to prevent manifest injustice" — remains the same. Does the "restyled" language make any substantive changes?

(2) *Preparation of the Pretrial Order: Drafts, Cooperation, and Burdens on Counsel and Parties.* It is typical for a pretrial order to specify all contested issues of fact, all contested issues of law, all agreed propositions of fact and law, all witnesses and the substance of their testimony, all exhibits (with designation of those objected to), all pending motions, and all requested charges to the jury. While there can be little question that an order containing these items, in detail, would simplify trial, it should be obvious that the drafting of the order can result in significant burdens on counsel and the parties. First, the sheer number of issues or exhibits can be a problem. In an antitrust case, for example, the parties may have produced documents numbering in the millions and may offer thousands before the jury. Given the possibilities of settlement, resolution on other issues, and other trial developments, might the judicial and private resources expended in attempting to catalogue all documents before trial be counterproductive? Second, the specification of the issues requires cooperation between the parties outside court; since they disagree about the dispute, they may well disagree about the specification of the issues that control it. In many courts, the plaintiff is given primary responsibility for ensuring that the draft pretrial order is prepared; is this allocation of the burden reasonable? [Note: What happens if the plaintiff's attorney has difficulty reaching the opponent by telephone, e-mail or otherwise, as often happens with busy attorneys?] Finally, since the trial will unfold unpredictably no matter how carefully it is planned, both parties

will attempt to avoid the situation disclosed in the *First National Bank of Circle* case, in which they are precluded from advancing claims or defenses that are omitted from the order.

(3) *Padovani v. Bruchhausen*, 293 F.2d 546 (2d Cir. 1961), is a classic example of the pressure that pretrial order drafts sometimes places on the parties. The plaintiff sued the Liggett & Myers Tobacco Company for negligence and breach of warranty that allegedly caused him to develop cancer of the larynx after smoking the defendant's products. The defendant demanded, and the judge issued an order requiring, a statement from the plaintiff of (1) "the facts," including those admitted and contested; (2) "plaintiff's legal theories of recovery"; (3) what facts the plaintiff intended to prove in support of each theory; (4) the "details" of the plaintiff's damage; (5) all proposed exhibits; (6) names, areas of specialization, and substance of the testimony of all expert witnesses; (7) names, addresses and substance of the testimony of all lay witnesses; and (8) any further discovery required. The plaintiff prepared these items, but the judge considered the plaintiff's statement too general. The plaintiff filed a second draft, then a third; finally, the judge entered a "preclusion order," which effectively prevented the plaintiff from offering evidence to prove his case. The Second Circuit reversed and said:

> [Rule 16] calls for a conference of counsel to prepare for, not to avert, trial, leading to an order which shall recite the "agreements made by the parties to any of the matters considered." It is subordinate and conciliatory, rather than compulsive, in character. Nothing in the Rule affords any basis for clubbing the parties into admissions they do not willingly make. . . .

This decision must be read with two caveats, however. First, the court did not disapprove of the matters that the trial court had inquired into, or to the proposition that attorneys could be required to prepare drafts for the pretrial order. Second, the *Padovani* case was decided before Rule 16 took its present form. Today, as we shall see, there is a greater emphasis on "management" of the case by trial judges. Do you think this emphasis might change the result in *Padovani* today?

(4) *Required Specificity in Pretrial Statements by Counsel: Gardner v. Safeway Stores, Inc., 99 F.R.D. 258 (D. Kan. 1983).* In this employment discrimination action, the trial court required that each party submit lists of witnesses and exhibits, adding that those that were not submitted "would not be permitted to testify or to be received in evidence, respectively." The plaintiff's list was non-specific and included "all witnesses identified in" other pending cases against Safeway. The plaintiff argued that the defendant knew in actuality who the witnesses would be. The court said:

> . . . The court believes that these procedures require candid and complete disclosure of both potential witnesses and exhibits. The rationale for such a requirement is obvious — to avoid surprise at trial. Thus the court agrees with the defendants that the plaintiff's original and supplemental list of exhibits and witnesses is deficient for lack of specificity. . . .

The court declined to invoke sanctions or to preclude proof, although it "acknowledged" that sanctions could be invoked. Is *Gardner* consistent with *Padovani v. Bruchhausen, supra*?

(5) *Construction of the Pretrial Order; Modification to Prevent "Manifest Injustice"; Court's Discretion.* Notice the way in which deviations from the letter of the pretrial order are to be evaluated. First, the court is to construe the order liberally. It is a general plan, not a straitjacket. *See Jones v. Nabisco, Inc.*, 95 F.R.D. 24 (E.D. Tenn. 1982) (parties

not bound by "precise" language of order). Question: in *First National Bank of Circle*, the principal case above, could the Bank have attempted to uphold its judgment successfully on this ground? The appellate court said no; was it correct?

Secondly, if a party deviates so that it is outside even a liberal construction of the pretrial order, the trial court is called upon to exercise its discretion in considering whether to modify the order. Note that in the *First Bank of Circle* case, the appellate court did not hold that a modification would be improper. Question: If the trial judge had expressly modified the order to allow First Bank of Circle to deny that it had supplied funds, would this action have been upheld on appeal? [Remember that this standard is to be evaluated on abuse-of-discretion grounds, by considering four factors: prejudice to the plaintiff; prejudice to the defendant; impact on orderly presentation; and degree of willfulness, bad faith, or inexcusable neglect.]

(6) *Relationship between Pleadings and Pretrial Order.* The pretrial order might be viewed as a kind of extension of the pleadings. The federal system does not insist upon specificity in pleadings, but it engages in heavy use of pretrial conferences and orders to narrow the issues. *See* Rule 16(d). Some state pleading systems instead use slightly more rigorous pleadings, coupled with discovery, to achieve similar purposes. At some point, the process must result in a narrowing of issues; perhaps the principal difference in these approaches depends on which stage, pleading or pretrial, does the narrowing.

Is there a functional difference between the two approaches? Which approach is better?

§ 8.01 Appendix Final Pretrial Order in *Bordelon v. Triangle J Co.*

[This simple pretrial order is adapted from a real case, although names and other particulars are changed, the forum has been shifted to the mythical "State of West York," and the order has been edited. Various attachments are omitted, including both parties' proposed jury selection questions, jury charge requests, etc., although these matters were a major part of the order and required considerable attorney effort. The format of the order is generally in conformity with a local rule of the court.]

IN THE UNITED STATES DISTRICT COURT
FOR THE MIDDLE DISTRICT OF WEST YORK
LONDON DIVISION

BRYAN BORDELON v. TRIANGLE J COMPANY, ET AL.	C.A. NO. H-83-4846

PRE-TRIAL ORDER
APPEARANCE OF COUNSEL

Plaintiff, Bryan Bordelon, through his attorney George Dewey, of Taylor, Gittleson, Dasher & Dewey, 2600 Center Bldg., London, West York, 77002, tel. 555-4433.

Defendants, Triangle J Company and Triangle J Drilling Company, through their attorney, John Small, of Brill, Steiner, Broinson & Stone, 700 Bank Building, Dublin, West York. . . .

STATEMENT OF THE CASE

This is a personal injury case brought by Bryan Bordelon against Triangle J Company and Triangle J Drilling Company.

Bryan Bordelon alleges he was injured on Triangle J rig number 95, which was situated at that time on Exxon platform number 54G on August 8, 2002. Exxon platform 54G is a fixed platform, permanently attached to the floor of the Gulf of Mexico. Mr. Bordelon alleges that his injury occurred when he, along with an employee of Triangle J, was attempting to reposition a scaffolding board. The drilling rig and platform in question were situated approximately fifty miles off the coast of the State of Calorida.

JURISDICTION

This Court has jurisdiction pursuant to the Outer Continental Shelf Lands Act, 43 U.S.C.A. Section 1333(b). The amount in controversy exceeds $10,000.00. [This federal statute grants jurisdiction to federal courts over certain matters pertaining to these ocean-bound lands and borrows, as the applicable federal law, the law of the upland state.]

MOTIONS

At the time that this Pre-Trial Order is being prepared, the Defendants have a Motion for Summary Judgment pending before this Court, to which the Plaintiff has filed his Response. Plaintiff's Motion in Limine is attached.

CONTENTIONS OF THE PLAINTIFF

1. Plaintiff contends that on the date of this accident, he was faced with the situation of having to move a rather large and heavy scaffolding board from one position to another on the rig in question. As was the custom, he approached one of the foremen for Triangle J and asked for the assistance of a Triangle J employee to assist him in the movement of the scaffolding board. At that time, the Triangle J foreman selected one of the Triangle J employees to assist Mr. Bordelon.

2. After explaining to the Triangle J foreman and the Triangle J employee what they were going to do in moving the board, Mr. Bordelon positioned himself at one point along the board and the Triangle J employee positioned himself at another point along the board. As they proceeded to move the scaffolding board from one position to another, the Triangle J employee made a reckless and negligent movement of the board, the effect of which was to cause almost the full weight of the board to shift onto Mr. Bordelon, thus precipitating the serious and permanent injuries that Mr. Bordelon has suffered and in reasonable medical probability will continue to suffer for the remainder of his life. Specifically, the Plaintiff contends that the Triangle J employee, acting within the course and scope of his employment for Triangle J and/or Triangle Drilling Company, was reckless and negligent in the following respects: [The Order goes on at this point to particularize the specific acts of alleged negligence, to particularize the claimed injuries and damages, and to state plaintiff's rebuttals of contributory negligence and other defensive theories.]

CONTENTIONS OF THE DEFENDANT

[Defendants here particularize their contentions that the Triangle J employee was neither reckless nor negligent, that Plaintiff's injuries are neither as serious as Plaintiff contends nor permanent, and that no action on Defendant's part did or could have proximately caused the event. Defendants point out that Bordelon and the Triangle J employee both were upon a scaffold owned by Bordelon's employer, Tomasino Construction Co.; the scaffold was being modified, and Bordelon and the Triangle J employee were engaged, actually, in work for Tomasino. Hence the Triangle J employee was not within the scope of his employment with Triangle J. Defendants conclude as follows:]

Triangle J contends that it was exercising no control whatsoever over the employee loaned to assist Mr. Bordelon, and that Mr. Bordelon was exercising exclusive control over this borrowed Triangle J employee at the time of his accident. Triangle J contends that it was the negligence of the Plaintiff himself which caused his accident and not any negligence on the part of Triangle J or its employee.

ADMISSIONS OF FACT

1. At the time of the accident in question, Mr. Bordelon was employed by Tomasino Construction Co.

2. Mr. Bordelon's employer, Tomasino Construction, was under contract with Exxon.

3. The platform on which the plaintiff alleges he was injured was located approximately 50 miles off the coast of Calorida and was a fixed platform.

CONTESTED ISSUES OF LAW

1. To the extent that it is an issue for the Court, and not the Jury, the Defendant has contended that, as a matter of law, at the time of the accident in question, the employee of Triangle J Company and/or Triangle J Drilling Company was a "borrowed servant" of Mr. Bordelon and Tomasino Construction. Plaintiff denies that the Triangle J employee was a "borrowed servant."

AGREED APPLICABLE PROPOSITIONS OF LAW

1. The substantive law of the State of Calorida applies in this case. Specifically, Article 2323, Calorida Civil Code applies and provides in pertinent part: "When contributory negligence is applicable to a claim for damages, . . . the claim for damages shall not thereby be defeated, but the amount of damages recoverable shall be reduced in proportion to the degree of percentage of negligence attributable to the person suffering the injury, death, or loss."

WITNESSES

A. Plaintiff's Witnesses

1. Bryan Bordelon, Box 208, Wellesley, West York. Mr. Bordelon will testify concerning the facts and circumstances surrounding this accident [and to] the elements of damage. . . .

2. Janet Bordelon, Box 208, Wellesley, West York. Mrs. Bordelon, the wife of Bryan Bordelon, will testify to her observation of the injuries and damages suffered by her husband. . . .

3. Dr. Philip J. Borgmann, videotaped deposition, 709 Medical Tower, London, West York. Dr. Borgmann will testify concerning the injuries which Mr. Bordelon suffered in this accident; his treatment of those injuries; and the effect of those injuries not only on his daily activities but also on his ability to work and retain employment in various occupations.

4. William D. Bradley, Ph.D. (economics), 306 Broadway, Jackson Hole, West York. Dr. Bradley will testify about the economic consequences of this injury up to the present time as well as the effect that this injury will have on Mr. Bordelon's earning capacity in the future. . . .

B. Defendant's Witnesses

1. An orthopedic surgeon who will examine the Plaintiff on behalf of Triangle J Company will testify regarding his current condition.

2. Billy Felder will testify regarding his knowledge of the facts of the accident.

In the event there are any other witnesses to be called at the trial, their names, addresses and the subject matter of their testimony shall be reported to opposing counsel as soon as they are known. This restriction shall not apply to rebuttal or impeaching witnesses, the necessity of whose testimony cannot reasonably be anticipated before the time of trial.

EXHIBITS

1. Medical records from Dr. Gregor A. Noll;
2. Medical records from Dr. Barry R. Winer;
3. Medical records from Dr. Philip J. Borgmann;
4. Medical records from Physical Therapy Department at Cuomo Memorial Hospital;

. . . .

7. Records from William D. Bradley, Ph.D.;
8. Wage and tax information on Bryan Bordelon;
9. Bill from Seton Medical Center; . . . .

SETTLEMENT

Although settlement discussions have been ongoing, it appears [that] the case cannot be settled and will have to be tried.

TRIAL

Counsel estimate that the probable length of trial will be two to three days, depending upon the amount of expert testimony offered into evidence.

REQUIRED PRETRIAL MATERIALS

[Plaintiff's and Defendants' proposed Questions for Voir Dire Examinations of Prospective Jurors are attached to this Order as exhibits A and B, respectively. Plaintiff's exhibit list is attached as exhibit C. Plaintiff's Motion in Limine is attached as exhibit D. Summaries of Qualifications of Plaintiff's Proposed Experts are attached as exhibits

E and F, respectively. Finally, Plaintiff's and Defendants' requested charges to the Jury have been attached hereto or will be submitted separately prior to trial.]

APPROVAL RECOMMENDED:

[signature]	[signature]
Counsel for Plaintiff	United States District Judge
[signature]	[dated]
Counsel for Defendant	Date

§ 8.02 The Trend Toward Judges as "Managers"

[A] How the Rules Encourage Judges to Manage Cases

J. Resnik, MANAGERIAL JUDGES

*96 Harv. L. Rev. 374 (1982)**

Until recently, the American legal establishment embraced a classical view of the judicial role. Under this view, judges are not supposed to have an involvement or interest in the controversies they adjudicate. Disengagement and dispassion supposedly enable judges to decide cases fairly. . . .

Today, federal district judges are assigned a case at the time of its filing and assume responsibility for shepherding the case to completion. Judges have described their new tasks as "case management" — hence my term "managerial judges." [T]hey negotiate with parties about the course, timing, and scope of both pretrial and posttrial litigation. These managerial responsibilities give judges greater power. Yet the restraints that formerly circumscribed judicial authority are conspicuously absent. . . .

. . . Professors Kaplan and von Mehren and Judge Schaefer marveled at the vigorous efforts of German judges to convince parties to settle. Ironically, their description of the German judge — "constantly descending to the level of the litigants, as an examiner, patient or hectoring, as counselor and adviser, [and] as insistent promoter of settlements" — now seems apt for the American judge as well. . . .

[Resnik constructs hypothetical cases to illustrate the managerial role. One of the cases is "Paulson v. Danforth Ltd.," in which Ms. Paulson claims that product defects in her new "Zip" automobile caused her injuries. She directed several interrogatories and document requests to defendant, which had moved to dismiss for lack of jurisdiction and responded to the discovery requests by a motion asking the trial judge, Judge Edward Kinser, for a moderately complex protective order. Plaintiff disagreed with all requested protective relief. Judge Kinser called the parties in for a conference in his chambers.]

. . . After listening for several minutes to the lawyers' posturing, Judge Kinser asked whether all these legal battles were really necessary: was not settlement the least expensive, quickest, and fairest resolution of most disputes? When the attorneys insisted upon pursuing their arguments, the judge asked whether the lawyers were acting in their clients' best interests. . . .

Judge Kinser then asked Mr. Adams to leave the room so that the judge could confer privately with defendant's lawyer.[58] Judge Kinser explained to Ms. Alford that he had learned a bit about plaintiff's case and that it looked "sound" to him. Did Danforth understand that a jury would surely be sympathetic to an injured plaintiff? What harm would there be in giving this injured victim some money? Had the parties talked numbers? Perhaps she should tell her client that $250,000 seemed "about right" to the judge. And perhaps she could mention that his court looked with disfavor upon uncompromising litigants.

Judge Kinser then called in plaintiff's counsel for a private meeting. Did Mr. Adams know how hard it was to prove a products liability claim? Had he thought about how long it might take to get to trial? What numbers would his client "go for"? The judge thought that $250,000 "sounded right" and that the case looked like one that "should settle."

Summoning both attorneys before him once more, Judge Kinser concluded the conference by announcing that he would defer ruling on the discovery motion until the parties had had time to negotiate further. He set a date to hold another conference in six weeks. . . .

"Replaying" *Paulson v. Danforth, Ltd.* as if proposed rule 16 were in effect[b] illustrates that the grant of pretrial power to federal judges would be expansive. In the hypothetical, Ms. Paulson's attorney, Mr. Adams, filed the complaint on January 4, 1982. But suppose that, instead of promptly replying, defendant asked for an additional twenty days to respond. Plaintiff's counsel readily agreed, and the parties filed a stipulation to that effect. However, Judge Kinser refused to permit any extension beyond the time permitted by the Federal Rules — twenty days after receipt of service.

On May 14, Judge Kinser held a rule 16 pretrial conference. Although he had not yet decided Danforth's pending motion to dismiss for lack of personal jurisdiction, rule 16 required him to issue a pretrial order "in no event more than 120 days after filing of the complaint." Ms. Alford argued that it would be a substantial waste of time and money for her to present discovery plans, because (she believed) the case should be dismissed on the jurisdictional ground. Mr. Adams was reluctant to discuss the case at all; he explained to the judge that, because no answer had been filed, he did not know what defenses would be raised, and he certainly did not want to suggest any.

Judge Kinser agreed that the conference was premature. He decided to postpone issuing a pretrial order (although he was not sure that rule 16 permitted the postponement). ["L]ooking down the road," the judge would neither tolerate further requests for delay nor let discovery "get out of hand." [H]e instructed the parties to return to his chambers on June 30 prepared to "talk settlement" with "real numbers." . . .

Subsequently, the parties requested and obtained changes in the original scheduling order. Experts for both sides were unavailable for most of the summer of 1982, and a shipment of documents disappeared in the mail and required several months to replace. At each of the three pretrial conferences that Judge Kinser has conducted to date, he has raised the issue of settlement, but with little success. As a result of his efforts, however, the parties have begun to discuss the same "ball park" settlement figures.

---

[58] Judge Kinser insisted on speaking to each side separately because real judges advised him to do so. [Resnik cites judicial authority recommending separate negotiations with the parties. *See also Kothe v. Smith*, in § 8.02[B], *infra*. — Eds.]

[b] [It since was adopted and is now in effect. — Eds.]

. . . [M]any federal judges manage their cases much as Judge Kinser did in the revised hypothetical. As they gain more experience with such new procedures, judges are acting more forcefully. Indeed, not all judges are as circumspect as Judge Kinser. Some warn the parties that the judge would take a dim, and possible hostile, view of either side's insistence on going to trial. . . .

I want to take away trial judges' roving commission and to bring back the blindfold. I want judges to balance the scales, not abandon them altogether in the press to dispose of cases quickly. No one has convincingly discredited the virtues of disinterest and disengagement, virtues that form the bases of the judiciary's authority. Our society has not yet openly and deliberately decided to discard the traditional adversarial model in favor of some version of the continental or inquisitorial model. Until we do, federal judges should remain true to their ancestry and emulate the goddess Justice. I fear that, as it moves closer to administration, adjudication may be in danger of ceasing to be.

S. Flanders, CASE MANAGEMENT AND COURT MANAGEMENT IN THE UNITED STATES DISTRICT COURTS (1977).

[Flanders sought to determine what procedures were associated with speed and productivity in court dispositions, consistently with the highest standards of justice. The study was based on data from ten courts.]

The following factors primarily distinguish the fast and/or highly productive courts from the others:

An automatic procedure ensures, for every civil case, that pleadings are strictly monitored, discovery begins quickly and is completed within a reasonable time, and a prompt trial follows if needed. . . .

Procedures minimize or eliminate judges' investment of time through the early stages of a case, until discovery is complete. Docket control, attorney contacts, and most conferences are delegated, generally to the courtroom deputy clerk or a magistrate. . . .

The role of the court in settlement is minimized; judges are highly selective in initiating settlement negotiations, and normally do so only when a case is ready, or nearly ready, for trial. Some judges also arrange to raise the issue early in each case, or have a magistrate do so.

Relatively few written opinions are prepared for publication.

All proceedings that do not specifically require a confidential atmosphere are held in open court. . . .

The . . . research revealed problems with some widely accepted notions about speed and productivity . . . . [Here, Flanders states that "strong case management" is not determinative since both fast and slow courts exhibited it; nor is a comprehensive pretrial order requirement determinative; and getting the lawyers in "early and often" seems "a poor use of time."] . . .

The key variable seems to be the time interval between the answer to the original complaint and the date on which the first pretrial was scheduled. [Flanders presents data from six courts in a chart form, showing convincingly that early initial pretrials correlated closely with short average disposition times.] The range of differences here is extraordinarily large, from 18 and 21 days, respectively, in Southern Florida and Central California [the faster courts], up to 595 days (in a very small number of cases) in Massachusetts [the slowest]. This appears to be a crucial variable. Eastern Pennsylvania, for example, could possibly save four or five months of "dead time" in many cases by earlier scheduling of the final pretrial conference. [The data also showed that realistic and effective discovery cutoff dates were useful.] . . .

Judicial participation in settlement produces mixed results. A limited role may be valuable, but data suggest that a large expenditure of judicial time is fruitless . . . .

NOTES AND QUESTIONS

(1) *Resnik's Doubts about Conclusions from Flanders' Study.* Resnik cites Flanders but questions reliance on his study for conclusions about cost savings (because Flanders did not directly measure parties' costs or court costs) or about management without diminution of decisional quality (because Flanders provides no measurement of quality; instead he assumes a "close positive relationship between speed and quality"). In fact, Resnik concludes, "Little empirical evidence supports the claim that judicial management 'works' either to settle cases or to provide cheaper, quicker, or fairer dispositions." Resnik, *supra*, at 380, 417-24. Are these suggestions valid? Isn't it highly probable that shortened disposition times, which Flanders' data do correlate with certain management techniques such as early initial pretrial, are correlated with lower costs — and isn't prompt resolution an ingredient of the quality of justice?

(2) *Flanders' Response to Resnik.* For Flanders' answer, see Flanders, *Blind Umpires — A Response to Professor Resnik*, 35 Hastings L.J. 505 (1984). *See also, e.g.*, Rubin, *The Managed Calendar: Some Pragmatic Suggestions about Achieving the Just, Speedy, and Inexpensive Determination of Civil Cases in Federal Courts*, 4 Justice System J. 135 (1978). Flanders concludes that Resnik does "a modest service by reminding [readers] of certain well-known problems" such as the dangers of "energetic judicial involvement in settlement negotiations," but that she "does her readers a remarkable disservice by overstating one problem and lumping together all forms of judicial case management." For this reason, says Flanders, Resnik's models are "fatally flawed," and "her attacks based on these models [are] marginally useful at best." Further, he says, Resnik "is far more radical than she imagines in suggesting so thorough a reassertion of an 'umpireal' role, or what I call a system of blind umpires." Are these conclusions valid (*i.e.*, is Resnik's work indeed only marginally useful)? Consider the *Kothe* case, below.

(3) *Resnik's Call for More Study before Amendment of Rule 16.* Is Resnik correct in arguing that Rule 16 should not be amended to encourage further management until more public debate is undertaken? *Cf.* Chase, *The Paradox of Procedural Reform*, 52 St. John's L. Rev. 163 (1988).

(4) *Amendment of Rule 16: Judicial Management as Part of the Job Description.* In 1983, several of the Federal Rules, including Rule 16, were amended to authorize more judicial management. *See also* Doerfer, *Why Judicial Case Management Pays Off at Trial*, 29 Judges' J. 12 (1990); Shapiro, *Federal Rule 16: A Look at the Theory and Practice of Rulemaking*, 137 U. Pa. L. Rev. 1969 (1989); Chase, *Civil Litigation Delay in Italy and the United States*, 36 Am. J. Compar. L. 41 (1987).

EXCERPTS FROM SECOND CIRCUIT JUDICIAL CONFERENCE OF 1983, DISCUSSING RULE 16 (PANEL DISCUSSION)

*101 F.R.D. 180 (1983)**

PROFESSOR ARTHUR R. MILLER: . . .

[I] have often wondered, if the man from Mars [o]r, in this day and age, E.T. appeared among us again, and you said to E.T., "Look at our system, what's wrong with it?" I think he would say, "You are a victim of your own propaganda."

E.T. would say, ". . . After all, 90 percent of your cases don't reach trial. You've really got a settlement system.

"Your Congress and your courts create new substantive rights almost on an annual basis . . . .

"[Y]our pleading rule, 8(a)(2), it says, 'Just give us a short and plain statement' — not the facts; God help us, not the facts — a short and plain statement. Just tell us where it hurts. . . .

"Oh, yes, then you've got these motions to dismiss, the 12(b)(6) motion for failure to state a claim, probably last granted in a meaningful way during the McKinley administration . . . .

"So, what do you expect? . . . That's the price you pay for your system."

Faced with that panorama, the Advisory Committee decided that the way to attack the litigation crunch problem, once it is realized that more than 90 percent of the cases do not reach trial, is attack the pretrial process . . . .

Now, the truth of the matter is, we intended to recognize judicial management as part of the judicial job description. [A]gain, the statistics seem to show that more management means shorter processing time for cases, and I think there are understandable reasons for that. I think it displays judicial seriousness and control . . . .

[I] think lawyers, who do not have death wishes by and large, are less likely to engage in fringe behavior if they know the judge is in command and involved in the case . . . .

It's like the commercial you see on television for the Fram oil filter, when the guy is standing there with the six-dollar oil filter next to a car that's smoking, with the engine blown, and he's saying, "You can pay me now or you can pay me later." I think a dollar of judicial energy up front saves five dollars of judicial energy at the back.

[Question: Is this view persuasive?]

[B] Sanctions for Failure to Participate "in Good Faith" in Conferences and Settlement Negotiations

KOTHE v. SMITH

771 F.2d 667 (2d Cir. 1985)

VAN GRAAFEILAND, CIRCUIT JUDGE:

Dr. James Smith appeals from a judgment of the United States District Court for the Southern District of New York (Sweet, J.), which directed him to pay $1,000 to plaintiff-appellee's attorney, $1,000 to plaintiff-appellee's medical witness, and $480 to the Clerk of the Court. For the reasons hereinafter discussed, we direct that the judgment be vacated.

Patricia Kothe brought this suit for medical malpractice against four defendants, Dr. Smith, Dr. Andrew Kerr, Dr. Kerr's professional corporation, and Doctors Hospital, seeking $2 million in damages. She discontinued her action against the hospital four months prior to trial. She discontinued against Dr. Kerr and his corporation on the opening day of trial.

Three weeks prior thereto, Judge Sweet held a pretrial conference, during which he directed counsel for the parties to conduct settlement negotiations. Although it is not clear from the record, it appears that Judge Sweet recommended that the case be settled for between $20,000 and $30,000. He also warned the parties that, if they settled for a comparable figure after trial had begun, he would impose sanctions against the dilatory party. Smith, whose defense has been conducted throughout this litigation by his malpractice insurer, offered $5,000 on the day before trial, but it was rejected.

Although Kothe's attorney had indicated to Judge Sweet that his client would settle for $20,000, he had requested that the figure not be disclosed to Smith. Kothe's counsel conceded at oral argument that the lowest pretrial settlement demand communicated to Smith was $50,000. Nevertheless, when the case was settled for $20,000 after one day of trial, the district court proceeded to penalize Smith alone. In imposing the penalty, the court stated that it was "determined to get the attention of the carrier" and that "the carriers are going to have to wake up when a judge tells them that they want [sic] to settle a case and they don't want to settle it." Under the circumstances of this case, we believe that the district court's imposition of a penalty against Smith was an abuse of the sanction power given it by Fed. R. Civ. P. 16(f). Although the law favors the voluntary settlement of civil suits, . . . it does not sanction efforts by trial judges to effect settlements through coercion . . . .

Rule 16 of the Fed. R. Civ. P. was not designed as a means for clubbing the parties — or one of them — into an involuntary compromise. *See Padovani v. Bruchhausen*, 293 F.2d 546, 548 (2d Cir. 1961) . . . .

We find the coercion in the instant case especially troublesome because the district court imposed sanctions on Smith alone. Offers to settle a claim are not made in a vacuum. They are part of a more complex process which includes "conferences, informal discussions, offers, counterdemands, more discussions, more haggling, and finally, in the great majority of cases, a compromise." J. & D. Sindell, *Let's Talk Settlement* 300 (1963). In other words, the process of settlement is a two-way street, and a defendant should not be expected to bid against himself. In the instant case, Smith never received a demand of less than $50,000. Having received no indication from Kothe that an offer somewhere in the vicinity of $20,000 would at least be given careful consideration, Smith should not have been required to make an offer in this amount simply because the court wanted him to.

Smith's attorney should not be condemned for changing his evaluation of the case after listening to Kothe's testimony during the first day of trial. [I]t is not at all unusual [f]or a defendant to change his perception of a case based on the plaintiff's performance on the witness stand . . . .

Although we commend Judge Sweet for his efforts to encourage settlement negotiations, his excessive zeal leaves us no recourse but to remand the matter with instructions to vacate the judgment.

NOTES AND QUESTIONS

(1) *Permissible Sanctions Regarding Settlement Efforts: G. Heileman Brewing Co., Inc. v. Joseph Oat Corp., 871 F.2d 648 (7th Cir. 1989) (en banc).* Are there circumstances in which a settlement arrived at after trial has begun could, properly, lead to sanctions? What if, for example, the defendant had contemptuously refused even to consider talking to the plaintiff in *Kothe v. Smith*, even after the judge's order to negotiate — and then, as in *Kothe v. Smith*, had agreed to settle for $20,000 after the beginning of trial? What if the defendant had merely pretended to negotiate but had insisted throughout on a figure that was unrealistic by any standard (nominal damages of $1 for a serious injury with disputed evidence of liability)? [How is the judge to gauge improper "pretensions" from the role-playing that is an integral part of most negotiations?] In the *Heileman* case, the magistrate ordered all parties to attend a pretrial conference not only through counsel, but also through a party representative with "full authority to settle." Three parties complied — but one defendant, which earlier had indicated its unwillingness to settle, sent only its attorneys, who the defendant said had "authority to settle," provided that they were not to agree to pay any money! The magistrate ultimately recommended sanctions in the amount of the opposing party's costs — and the Seventh Circuit, en banc, upheld these sanctions. The decision has been the subject of much commentary; *compare, e.g.*, Tozer, *The Heileman Power: Well-Honed Tool or Blunt Instrument?*, 66 Ind. L.J. 977 (1991) (decision "threatens the traditional role of American courts"), *with* Note, *Expanding the Federal Court's Power to Encourage Settlement Under Rule 16*, 1990 Wis. L. Rev. 1397 (1990) (recommending guidelines to prevent coercion), *and* Note, *Rule 16 and Pretrial Conferences: Have We Forgotten the Most Important Ingredient?*, 63 So. Cal. L. Rev. 1449 (1990) (recommending amendment of Rule 16 so that it "strongly encourages" the judge to require actual disputants' presence; "the parties [h]ave been absent for too long"). As amended in 1993, Rule 16 authorizes the imposition of sanctions under these circumstances.

(2) *Proper "Persuasion" Versus "Coercion."* Rule 16 obviously intends for the trial judge to have powers of persuasion that will make the parties behave more accommodatingly than they would otherwise. *See* Wall & Schiller, *Judicial Involvement in Pretrial Settlement: A Judge Is Not a Bump on a Log*, 6 Am. J. Trial Advoc. 27 (1982). How is this "persuasion" to be distinguished from prohibited "coercion"? Imagine a party whose attorney refuses to make any concession whatsoever at pretrial, even in narrowing issues or conceding unmeritorious ones. Can the judge make a show of exasperation, with the implication that discretionary rulings may take this background of uncooperative behavior into account? Can the judge impose monetary sanctions? If not, is there anything the judge can do? *Cf. Hess v. New Jersey Transit Rail Operations*, 846 F.2d 114 (2d Cir. 1988) (reversing sanctions imposed where defendant failed to make any offer after District Court's order to "make a *bona fide* offer").

(3) *Sanctions for Failure to Participate "in Good Faith"; Inducing Settlement.* Rule 16(f) authorizes the use of sanctions in connection with pretrial matters. Also, there should remain no question that inducing settlement negotiations is now "part of the job description" for federal judges. Note that the court in *Kothe v. Smith* makes a point of commending the trial judge's efforts even as it reverses his methods. But can the trial judge exercise this authority without adversely affecting the adjudication of cases that "need to be tried"?

[C] Reference to Magistrate Judges or Masters

Read Fed. R. Civ. P. 53 (masters); 72-73 (magistrate judges); 28 U.S.C. § 636(a), (b), (c)(1) (magistrate judges).

MATHEWS v. WEBER, 423 U.S. 261 (1976). The United States District Court for the Central District of California promulgated a local rule called General Order 104-D, which directed the clerk of the court to refer all Social Security review cases to magistrates. The magistrates were required to conduct "such factual hearings and legal argument as may be appropriate," to prepare a "proposed written order or decision" together with "proposed findings of fact and conclusions of law," and to send the file to the responsible district judge, together with any objections of the parties. The Secretary of Health, Education and Welfare argued that reference under General Order 104-D was illegal because it authorized magistrates to exercise decision-making authority in excess of that given by the Federal Magistrates Act. The Supreme Court, however, upheld the order of reference:

> After several years of study, Congress in 1968 enacted the Federal Magistrates Act . . . . The Act abolished the office of United States commissioner, and sought to "reform the first echelon of the federal judiciary into an effective component of a modern scheme of justice by establishing a system of U.S. magistrates." [The Act replaced the fee system with substantial salaries, required appointment of members of the bar whereover possible, and established definite terms of office.]
>
> [The Act] outlines a procedure by which the district courts may call upon magistrates to perform other functions, in both civil and criminal cases. It provides:
>
>> Any district court . . . may establish rules pursuant to which any . . . magistrate . . . may be assigned . . . such additional duties as are not inconsistent with the Constitution and laws of the United States. The additional duties authorized by rule may include, but are not restricted to —
>>
>>> (1) service as a special master in an appropriate civil action, pursuant to the applicable provisions of this title and the Federal Rules of Civil Procedure . . . ; [and]
>>>
>>> (2) assistance to a district judge in the conduct of pretrial or discovery proceedings in civil or criminal matters; . . .
>
> The [e]xamples [this section] sets out are, as the statute itself states, not exclusive. [The legislative history indicates that Congress hoped federal judges would be "innovative" in using magistrates in "new areas to increase the efficiency of their courts." Congress intended to "permit . . . district courts to assign magistrates . . . a variety of functions . . . presently performable only by the judges themselves."] . . .
>
> . . . Under the part of [General Order 104-D] at issue, the magistrates perform a limited function which falls well within the range of duties Congress empowered the district courts to assign to them. The magistrate is directed to conduct a preliminary review of a closed administrative record — closed because under . . . the Social Security Act, . . . neither party may put any additional evidence before the district court. The magistrate gives only a recommendation to the judge, and only on the single, narrow issue: is there in the record substantial evidence to support the Secretary's decision? . . . The district judge is free to follow it or wholly ignore it . . . .

NOTES AND QUESTIONS

(1) *Magistrate Judges' Authority and Typical Duties; Amendment of the Magistrates Act to Allow Evidence — Taking and to Change the Name to "Magistrate Judges."* Notice that the Court in *Mathews v. Weber* emphasizes the "closed record" in Social Security cases reviewed by magistrate judges. The Court implies that a closed record is a more appropriate matter to refer to a magistrate judge. Would a District Court violate the Magistrates Act if it referred to the magistrate judge a fact-finding matter in which the magistrate was required to hear evidence from live witnesses? Note that the Act has been amended to expressly allow the magistrate judge to "hear and determine any pretrial matter" (with exceptions for dispositive motions and certain other matters, and even as to the exceptions, the judge may "conduct hearings, including evidentiary hearings," from which he submits proposed findings and recommendations to the district judge). Does this procedure conform to the Constitution's requirement of an Article III judge appointed for life term? *See* Burnett, *Practical, Innovative, and Progressive Utilization of United States Magistrates to Improve the Administration of Justice in United States District Courts*, 28 Howard L.J. 293 (1985); Weinstein & Wiener, *Of Sailing Ships and Seeking Facts: Brief Reflections On Magistrates and the Federal Rules of Civil Procedure*, in *Symposium*, 62 St. John's L. Rev. 429 (1988). Even the name has been changed to "magistrate judge" to indicate greater authority.

(2) *Submission by Agreement to the Magistrate Judge (Including Jury Trials).* Section 636 of the Magistrates Act also provides that the parties may agree to have the magistrate perform functions that would otherwise be carried out by the judge, including presiding at jury or non-jury trials. In some districts substantial percentages of actual trials are conducted in this manner by magistrates. Consent to proceedings before a magistrate judge can be inferred from a party's conduct during litigation. *See Roell v. Withrow*, 538 U.S. 580 (2003). In *Roell*, the district court referred the case to a magistrate judge with the caveat that the defendants would be given an opportunity to consent to the magistrate judge's jurisdiction. The court clerk sent the magistrate referral order to counsel, together with a summons directing them to include, in either their answer or in a separate pleading, a statement regarding their consent, or refusal to consent, to the jurisdiction of the magistrate judge. One of the three defendants filed such a statement, but the other two defendants filed no such statement and their answers made no reference to consenting to the magistrate judge's jurisdiction. Only after the conclusion of the proceedings did the magistrate judge realize that express consent had not been obtained from all three defendants. The Supreme Court held that "the better rule is to accept implied consent where, as here, the litigant or counsel was made aware of the need for consent and the right to refuse it, and still voluntarily appeared to try the case before the Magistrate Judge. Inferring consent in these circumstances thus checks the risk of gamesmanship by depriving parties of the luxury of waiting for the outcome before denying the magistrate judge's authority."

(3) *When Is a Judge Better than a Magistrate Judge?* Consider the following excerpt from Second Circuit Judicial Conference, 101 F.R.D. 183, 186-187 (1983) (remarks of Peter M. Fishbein): "It is an entirely different order of magnitude for an attorney to sit at a pretrial conference and look the judge in the eye, who is an Article III judge, who is going to try the case, and explain why certain discovery is necessary than to do it with a magistrate who may never be involved again and will have nothing to do with the final disposition." Do you agree? (Incidentally, some District Courts intentionally use magistrates to supervise pretrial and encourage settlement for the very purpose of separating these functions from the conduct of the trial. Which approach is superior?)

§ 8.03 Docket Control and Case Flow Management

Read Fed. R. Civ. P. 6, 40, 78-79 (scheduling and time computation).

[A] Trial Settings and Continuances

OATES v. OATES, 533 S.W.2d 107 (Tex. Civ. App. 1976, no writ). Paul Oates's attorney was forced to trial in a federal case on the same day that Oates's divorce case was set. Oates's attorney sent a telegram to the divorce trial judge, as follows: "RE: NO. 74 CI-8328 OATES V. OATES PLEASE CONSIDER THIS AS RESPONDENT'S FIRST MOTION FOR CONTINUANCE REASON: RECORD ATTORNEY FOR PAUL OATES HAS PREVIOUS COMMITMENT FOR TRIAL IN U.S. DISTRICT COURT SHERMAN TEXAS ON APRIL 7 1975 STYLED EARL WATSON VS MKT RAILROAD. THIS MOTION IS NOT MADE FOR PURPOSES OF DELAY BUT THAT JUSTICE MAY BE DONE." The telegram concluded with a request for confirmation of the court's order by return wire. The trial judge, however, denied the continuance and proceeded to hear the divorce case in the absence of Oates and his attorney. The appellate court affirmed for two reasons. First, the motion for continuance was not in the proper form; among other defects, it was not supported by an affidavit. Secondly, continuance for absence of counsel is particularly within the discretion of the court, and the trial judge was not required to reschedule the trial merely because Oates's attorney was trying a case somewhere else.

NOTES AND QUESTIONS

(1) *The Federal Approach Is Similar.* Federal district judges have "broad discretion in supervision of the [time of] trial," and denial of continuance "will not be disturbed on appeal absent an abuse of discretion." *E.g., Sturgeon v. Airborne Freight Corp.*, 778 F.2d 1154 (5th Cir. 1985).

(2) *Why Perry Mason Should Read the Oates Case and Weep.* Full-time trial lawyers often have multiple, overlapping settings for trials, hearings, or other events. *See* Dorsaneo & Crump, *Texas Civil Procedure: Trial and Appellate Practice* 23 (Matthew Bender 2d ed. 1989) (reproducing actual calendar of typical metropolitan litigator, showing fifteen different events set during two-week period, including seven trial settings, one a "preferential" setting). The ability to manage one's time in a schedule in which these events fail to take place as scheduled or require simultaneous appearance in two different places is crucial to success as a litigator. Many trial judges, understanding the trial lawyer's plight, willingly reschedule trials upon learning, even informally, that counsel is in trial elsewhere; however, as *Oates* indicates, trial judges in most jurisdictions are not required to reschedule. Although statistics are unavailable, the authors' experience is that federal judges are less flexible in this regard than state judges.

(3) *Getting the Case to Trial: Delays and Repeated Settings.* The flip side of the continuance problem is the difficulty that counsel sometimes experiences in getting a prompt trial setting. A related, but perhaps more serious, problem is that sometimes cases are repeatedly rescheduled with long intervening periods, making preparation difficult. *See, e.g.*, Dorsaneo & Crump, *supra*, at 12–15 (documenting five different trial settings in prototypical personal injury case in metropolitan courts, with intervals ranging from less than a week to several months, resulting in trial four years after event). It may be

difficult to appreciate the effect that repeated settings of this kind can have. Witnesses and clients fail to understand the need for repeated subpoenas and often attribute this system characteristic to incompetence of counsel. They may become less cooperative. Trial preparation suffers when the trial may or may not take place. Students might consider the analogy of a final examination that is rescheduled without advance warning for a date six months in the future, only to be rescheduled on that date for a date when it is again rescheduled; for most attorneys, trials require a similar kind of preparation (and are at least as nerve-wracking) as their law school examinations. Modern docket management, which seeks to reduce the number of resettings and the intervals between them, may be a solution.

[B] Rules Forcing Action by Court or Counsel

Federal Requirement for Scheduling Order under Rule 16. Except in categories of actions exempted by district court rule as appropriate, the district judge, or a magistrate judge when authorized by district court rule, must issue and enter a scheduling order that limits the time to join parties, amend pleadings, file motions, and to complete discovery. The order may and usually does include other matters, such as the dates for conferences before trial, a final pretrial conference, and trial itself. The order must be issued "as soon as practicable, but in any event within the earlier of 120 days after any defendant has been served with the complaint or 90 days after any defendant has appeared." The following is an example of a blank form of scheduling order:

SCHEDULING ORDER

Issue having been joined herein, it is Ordered pursuant to Rule 16, Fed. R. Civ. P. and Local Rule 300-6, that:

1. Joining of other parties and the amending of the pleadings shall be on or before ___________ unless an extension is granted on good cause shown.

2. Filing of all motions shall be on or before ___________ unless an extension is granted on good cause shown.

3. Discovery shall be completed by the parties on or before ___________ unless an extension is granted on good cause shown.

4. A conference of attorneys shall be held on or before ___________ unless an extension is granted on good cause shown.

5. Counsel for the parties shall submit their proposed agreed pre-trial order to the Court on or before ___________ unless an extension is granted on good cause shown. The proposed order shall supply information required by Local Rule 300-6 and the pre-trial order check-list (Form PT-1), which is enclosed.

6. In the event counsel are unable to agree on the form of a proposed agreed pre-trial order, then counsel for each party is directed to submit his version of an approximate pre-trial order within ten (10) days after the expiration of the date set in paragraph 5 . . . . [The form contains five additional paragraphs of orders.]

Entered this _____ day of _____
20_____.

____

[United States District Judge]

State Administrative Rules. Consider the following set of "Administrative Rules," which were proposed but not adopted and which were designed to accomplish some of the same results as the Scheduling Order requirement under Federal Rule 16. This proposal was considered by the State of Texas, but the concept could be applied in any state. As is indicated below, attorneys' opposition defeated adoption of these particular rules.

Rule 1. The courts and bar of [this state] will manage their work to achieve the disposition of cases within the periods of time listed:

	50%	90%	98%
Domestic Actions and Actions for Liquidated Damages	90 days	180 days	360 days
All Other Civil Actions	180 days	360 days	540 days

Rule 2. [Requires each clerk of a trial court to report statistics to the administrative judge of the court district, including the ages of all disposed cases, a chart aging the cases, various information about tried cases, and "a report on the percentage of cases exceeding the designated limits . . . ."]

Rule 3. [Requires the judge to enter an order establishing a "plan" for completion of discovery and preparation for trial in every case, "as soon as practicable" after the lapse of certain deadlines for the parties to propose such "plans." Further, "Failure of a party to file the certification reports or other documents required by the Court or otherwise required by this rule shall be deemed a failure to comply with an order of the Court . . . ."]

NOTES AND QUESTIONS

(1) *Unified, Vociferous Opposition by Attorneys Defeated this Proposal.* As might be expected, attorneys vigorously opposed the adoption of these administrative rules. Their opposition was so united and so strong that it overwhelmed rule proponents, and the Texas proposals were resoundingly rejected by the state supreme court. The objections to such rules typically include the assertion that they unnecessarily channel energy into adversary proceedings over the collateral matter of scheduling when attorneys would otherwise arrive at the result by accommodation; that no harm is done if cases are allowed to remain pending on the docket for periods of time; that the result will be a more high-handed attitude necessarily adopted by the trial judge; that the rules will "federalize" state proceedings whereas many state practitioners consciously avoid federal courts in order to avoid precisely such an emphasis on formal procedures; and, most of all, that the cost required to handle a given case will increase owing to the need to comply with numerous artificial deadlines that are equivalent to multiple "statutes of limitations" for each case. Are these arguments meritorious? [Might the result actually be reductions in judicial time, earlier settlement, and less wasted motion for attorneys, since trials, which are currently often set on five to ten different occasions, would be more expeditiously held?] Note: In 1999, however, the Texas Supreme Court promulgated rules for pretrial discovery to streamline the discovery process. The rules provide for a "discovery control plan" for each case, depending on its size and complexity. These amendments establish a three-tiered system which regulates the amount and duration of permissible discovery according to the discovery level to which the case is assigned by rule or court order. *See* Tex. R. Civ. P. 190. The amended discovery rules bear a considerable resemblance to the rejected administrative rules.

(2) *Meaning of Deadlines.* Notice that the judges, under both the Federal Rules and the proposed state administrative rules indicated above, have authority to allow extensions for completion of discovery, etc. Does this power to extend mean that the deadlines are meaningless? If not, what "teeth" do the deadlines have?

(3) *Statistical Pressure on the Judge to Clear the Docket.* Notice that the state administrative rules above contain a feature that makes them different from the Federal Rules: a statistical target, in the form of percentages of cases disposed of within certain periods of time. The rules clearly contemplate that the trial judge will improve case dispositions, upon pain of having poor statistics (and possibly receiving reassignments or losing the vote of the electorate as a result). Will these rules have the undesirable effect of making judges excessively disposition-minded and high handed? [On the other hand, if they don't keep current dockets, can the judges perform their usual judging tasks adequately?]

[C] "Differential Case Management," "Fast Tracking," "Staging," and Other Docket-Management Techniques

NOTE: WHY THIS MATERIAL WILL AFFECT YOU AS A LAWYER

(1) *Differential Case Management.* "My opponent,who represents the lender, succeeded in persuading the court to assign this case to the expedited calendar because it is a suit on a note. That means a drastic reduction in the discovery I can get. I wanted it assigned to the complex track because I need plenty of discovery to support my novel defenses of usury, lender fraud and antitrust violations. What do I do?" [Is this problem overstated? How will the plaintiff see it differently?]

(2) *Staging and Fast Tracking.* "The other side just designated its experts. I agreed to let them do it late. Now the court-ordered cutoff has run for me to depose those experts. The clerk tells me the judge habitually refuses to extend these deadlines. What can I do?" [Is this problem also overstated? Can it be avoided?]

(3) *Adjudication by Missed Deadlines.* "The rules imposed a mandatory duty on the clerk to notify me that this deadline was set. He didn't, and that's why my case was dismissed. The statute of limitations has run, so I'm sure my client is going to look to me! How can I deal with this problem?" [The answer to this last question may be confined to reliance on one's malpractice insurance. In any event, the managerial revolution will create at least some of these kinds of questions, even though it arguably will improve case dispositions for the great majority of cases.]

Bakke & Solomon, CASE DIFFERENTIATION: AN APPROACH TO INDIVIDUALIZED CASE MANAGEMENT

*73 Judicature 17 (1989)**

[I]n traditional caseflow systems, [a]ll cases are treated alike, subject to the same procedures and time limits, under what colloquially has been termed the "FIFO" approach — first in, first-out. All cases have a status conference, all cases have a pretrial hearing, or all cases must be assigned to arbitration, etc. . . .

[M]any now see case differentiation as the next step in evolution of caseflow systems that provide early and continuous management. Differential treatment of cases is not entirely novel. In most courts, civil and criminal cases are managerially [d]istinguished. It also is common to segregate family and probate proceedings from general civil cases. Nevertheless, most systems are based on an assumption that within the conventional case categories, the same processing is appropriate for virtually all cases . . . .

The result has been either too much or too little case management . . . . For instance, disputes over relatively small sums, which would lend themselves to informal, inexpensive processing, are subjected to full-scale pleading, discovery and trial procedures. Conversely, a complicated environmental dispute that would benefit from early direct judicial oversight may not come to the court's attention until relatively late in the process, waiting its turn in the queue behind much less complicated cases filed earlier . . . .

Variations of civil differential case management ["DCM"] programs now are in place in a number of jurisdictions, including Alaska, California, Connecticut, Kentucky, Massachusetts, Michigan and Washington, DC . . . .

The DCM system developed in New Jersey consists of three tracks, and the track assignment is based on a number of factors including case type, amount of damages and the attorneys' assessment of the time needed to dispose of the case. New Jersey [r]epresents the fullest development of the case-differentiation concept to date . . . .

A civil case is initiated by the filing of a complaint accompanied by a case information statement containing supplementary case information . . . . When the answer is filed, the defendant(s) also submit an information statement. The case is assigned by the court to one of three processing tracks — expedited, standard, or complex — based on the information provided in the pleadings and the case information statement. [The New Jersey system also includes a case management plan with deadlines for each case, differentiation by track of methods and cutoff times for discovery, case monitoring throughout by the track coordinator, and trial scheduling that is based on case status and on the availability of the attorneys and judge.] . . .

[I]t is important to note that *no* type of case is presumptively complex. Attorneys must provide substantial justification when requesting assignment to the complex track . . . .

Track assignment includes designation of a track coordinator, responsible for monitoring the case through disposition. Initially, the coordinator reviews the track requested by counsel. [The authors state that in Bergen County, the court concurred in attorneys' track requests in 98 per cent of cases.] In the rare instance where counsel disagree on track selection, the track coordinator attempts to negotiate agreement. If necessary, a hearing will be held before the assigned judge . . . .

The brief duration of these projects forecloses presentation of substantial findings at this time. However, in Pierce County [c]ase samples show that "pre-DCM," the state's 90-day criminal case disposition time standard was exceeded in 27 per cent of the cases; since introduction of DCM, only 5 per cent of dispositions have occurred beyond the 90-day limit. Data collected in Bergen County showed that before introduction of DCM, about 7 per cent of civil cases were disposed of within six months of filing; during the first 18 months of DCM this figure increased to 39 per cent. During this same period, 87 per cent of the cases were terminated within one year of filing, comparing favorably with the American Bar Association Standard calling for disposition of 90 per cent of cases within one year of filing . . . .

Litan, SPEEDING UP CIVIL JUSTICE

*89 Judicature 162 (1989)**

Out of frustration with [litigation cost and delay], the chairman of the Senate Judiciary Committee, Joseph R. Biden (D-Del.), asked the Brookings Institution and the Foundation for Change to convene a task force [t]o consider how delay and costs in the courts can be reduced. The task force was formed in the summer of 1988 and ultimately consisted of 35 leading attorneys, law professors and former judges throughout the nation . . . .

District court plans. The core recommendation is that Congress direct each federal district court to develop its own "Civil Justice Reform Plan . . . ."

Case tracking. [T]he task force members believe that all plans should implement a system of case tracking or, as some have termed it, differentiated case management, whereby cases of different degrees of complexity are placed on different time tracks for discovery and trial. The State of New Jersey has experimented with a three-track system that could serve as a useful model for federal reform [see the preceding article] . . . .

[S]ignificantly, [the task force's survey results] show overwhelming support among plaintiffs' and defendants' attorneys for case tracking.

Time limits. Case tracking requires that time limits apply to each track . . . .

The task force believes that by far the most important deadline that should be set early in the case is the trial date. Nothing does more to convince the parties and their lawyers to move expeditiously toward a resolution of their dispute than knowing at the outset when they are scheduled for trial. In addition, an early firm trial date eliminates costly duplicative preparation . . . . Not surprisingly, therefore, strong majorities in the Survey supported the concept . . . .

Staging. Courts can accelerate the disposition of cases by "staging" discovery, which can take a variety of forms. One approach [l]imits the parties in the first stage to developing information needed for a realistic assessment of the case, perhaps by inspecting a few documents and taking a few depositions. If the case does not end, a second, more detailed, stage would begin.

Staging the disposition of key issues by judicial rulings can also be productive. For example, it is common in legal disputes for the parties to quarrel over the length and applicability of a relevant statute of limitations or the meaning of certain words in a contract. Often such disputes can be resolved quickly and inexpensively once a core issue is decided. Courts might also be encouraged, where appropriate, to bifurcate issues for trial — asking the jury to decide liability before damage issues, or vice-versa . . . .

[The article also refers to Task Force Recommendations for deadlines on judges' own dispositions, use of ADR, expanded judicial resources, and other devices.]

THE CIVIL JUSTICE REFORM ACT OF 1990, 28 U.S.C. §§ 471 et seq.: AN "EXPENSE AND DELAY REDUCTION PLAN" FOR EACH DISTRICT COURT — WAS IT A USEFUL EFFORT, OR A NOBLE EXPERIMENT THAT FAILED?

[This enactment, which followed the Task Force Report described above, required each District Court to adopt an "expense and delay reduction plan," which could include:]

(1) systematic, differential treatment of civil cases that tailors the level of individualized and case specific management to such criteria as case complexity, the amount of time reasonably needed to prepare the case for trial, and the judicial and other resources required and available . . . .

(2) early and ongoing control of the pretrial process through involvement of a judicial officer in — (A) assessing and planning the progress of a case; (B) setting early, firm trial dates, such that the trial is scheduled to occur within eighteen months after the filing of the complaint, unless [certain conditions exist]; (C) controlling [discovery]; and (D) setting, at the earliest practicable time, deadlines for filing motions and a time framework for their disposition;

[Next, the Act suggested systematic treatments of "complex" cases, encouragement of "cooperative" discovery, certain other devices] . . .; and

(6) authorization to refer appropriate cases to alternative dispute resolution programs, [i]ncluding mediation, minitrial, and summary jury trial.

Kakalik, et al., JUST, SPEEDY AND INEXPENSIVE? AN EVALUATION OF JUDICIAL CASE MANAGEMENT UNDER THE CIVIL JUSTICE REFORM ACT*
49 Ala. L. Rev. 17, 18–19 (1997)

The Judicial Conference and the Administrative Office of the U.S. Courts asked RAND's Institute for Civil Justice to evaluate the implementation and the effects of the CJRA in . . . [pilot] districts . . . .

To preview the main findings of the evaluation:

1. The CJRA pilot program, as the package was implemented, had little effect on time to disposition, litigation costs, and attorneys' satisfaction and views of the fairness of case management.
2. But our analysis of case management as practiced across districts and judges shows that what judges do to manage cases matters:
   - Early judicial case management, setting the trial schedule early, shortened time to discovery cutoff, and having litigants at or available for settlement conferences are associated with a significantly reduced time to disposition. Early judicial case management also is associated with significantly increased costs to litigants, as measured by attorney work hours.
   - Shortened time to discovery cutoff is associated with significantly decreased attorney work hours.
   - None of these policies significantly affect attorneys' satisfaction or views of fairness, either positively or negatively.
3. If early case management and early setting of the trial schedule are combined with shortened discovery cutoff, the increase in costs associated with the former can be offset by the decrease in costs associated with the latter. . . .
4. . . . Since adoption of the CJRA, the total number of all civil cases pending has increased, but the number of cases pending more than three years has dropped by about 25 percent from its pre-CJRA level.

NOTES AND QUESTIONS

(1) *Was the Civil Justice Reform Act Useful, or Was It Wasteful?* The Rand study excerpted above suggests that some of the effects of the CJRA were negative. The short of it is that management efforts to reduce costs and delay inevitably cause some amount of cost and delay, themselves. Was the CJRA useful or wasteful? Consider the issues in the following notes.

(2) *The Trouble with Tracking, Part 1: Attorneys' Expectations and Disputes about Assignment.* An attorney might say, "I think my civil rights suit against the city and its officers for beating my client should be on the 'complex case' track, but the tracking coordinator and the defendant persuaded the judge to put it on the 'expedited' track!" Early assignment to the expedited or standard track will reduce available discovery time and methods (in fact, that's the point of tracking). If the attorneys disagree, ultimately the judge must resolve the track assignment dispute (in yet another hearing that does not concern the merits). Bakke and Solomon report that courts adopted attorneys' track requests in 98 percent of the cases. (This figure is astounding. One might guess that the lawyers themselves would disagree in more than two (2) percent of the cases.)

(3) *The Trouble with Tracking, Part 2: Enforcing "Fast Track" Deadlines by Sanctions or Dismissals — Gorman v. City of Phoenix, 152 Ariz. 179, 731 P. 2d 74 (1987).* To solve a serious backlog, Maricopa County, Arizona adopted a "fast track" system with deadlines enforceable by dismissal under local Rule V(e). The Arizona Supreme Court observed in *Gorman* that "[l]awyers who fail to comply with [R]ule V(e) do so at their peril," even though the trial court should allow reinstatement in circumstances involving diligence and prejudice. *See also Flynn v. Cornoyer-Hedrick Architects & Planners, Inc.*, 160 Ariz. 187, 772 P.2d 10 (Ariz. App. 1988) (no reinstatement where initial delay in obtaining service caused plaintiff to get off-track). *See generally* Cates & Myers, *"Fast Track": Its Evolution and Future*, 21 Ariz. St. L.J. 219 (1989). Won't "tracking" inevitably produce more of these kinds of dispositions?

(4) *The Trouble With Tracking, Part 3: Increases in Attorney's Own Docket-Control Costs.* When Harris County [Houston, Texas] family court judges adopted case management strategies to reduce backlogs, divorce lawyers said that "inflexible judges with strict deadlines . . . increase the cost of an uncontested divorce by as much as 25 percent . . . ." Texas Lawyer, June 16, 1997, at 1. It takes effort, and therefore it costs money, to monitor and comply with tracking requirements. Tracking may also save money elsewhere, but the question is whether it costs more than it gains.

(5) *The Benefits of Tracking.* Perhaps, however, these "troubles" merely reflect the fact that the world is imperfect. Do the benefits outweigh the costs? Can the costs be minimized by employment of skillful coordinators, liberal reinstatement of dismissed cases, and experience with track assignments (what would Resnik and Flanders say)? *See also* Johnson, *What Can You Do With a 70,000 Case Backlog?*, 30 Judges' J. 16 (1991); Plotnikoff, *Case Control as Social Policy: Civil Case Management Legislation in the United States*, 10 Civ. Just. Q. 230 (1991); Luskin, *Making Sense of Calendaring Systems: A Reconsideration of Concept and Measurement*, 13 Just. Sys. J. 240 (1989).

(6) *"Staging" as Compared to "Tracking."* Note that "staging" is at least somewhat incompatible with an early plan setting deadlines (since it implies that deadlines will depend on intervening events). Can the two coexist (as the Task Force seems to think) — and if so, will staging contribute to prompt and fair dispositions?

(7) *The Alternative of Reducing the Federal Docket by Reshaping Jurisdiction, etc.: The Report of the Federal Courts Study Committee (1990).* Another approach would be to limit a court system to hard-core cases requiring its particular kind of judicial treatment. The Federal Courts Study Act, 28 U.S.C. § 331 (1988), resulted in a Committee Report, above, that recommended diversion of a large percentage of federal criminal cases to state courts, abolition of most diversity jurisdiction, unification of tax cases in one Tax Court, creation of an administrative forum for Social Security Act Disability Claims, and other alternatives. In one year (1988), during which 283, 137 actions were filed in the federal district courts, "the Committee's proposals would [have] eliminate[d] roughly 105,000 cases: roughly thirty-seven percent" of the filings. Slate, *Report of the Federal Courts Study Committee: An Update*, 21 Seton Hall L. Rev. 336 (1991). Is this approach preferable to "management" of a bigger caseload?

(8) *California's "Fast Track" Seeks a Two (2) Year Limit: The Trial Court Delay Reduction Act, Cal. Gov. Code §§ 68600 et seq. (1991).* California has adopted a proposal known colloquially as "Fast Track," requiring each Superior Court to adopt a "plan" that will result in trial or disposition of all civil cases within two years of filing, enforced by a reporting requirement. (Is this a good idea? If so, why did lawyers generally oppose it?)

(9) *The New York System for Calendaring Trials.* In New York, an action is put on the calendar by the filing of a "note of issue," pursuant to CPLR 3402. The note of issue, which contains a brief description of the action, must be accompanied by a "certificate of readiness," in which the party asserts that the pretrial proceedings are complete and that the action is ready to be tried. Standard forms for these papers have been promulgated by the Chief Administrator of the Courts. In the Supreme Court, each judge maintains an individual calendar of cases (which have, in general, been assigned to the various judges at random) and normally tries them in the order in which the note of issue was filed. Some types of cases, such as medical malpractice actions and cases in which the claimant has reached the age of seventy, are entitled to preferred treatment and are taken ahead of non-preferred cases. *See* CPLR 3403(a). New York does not have a set "outer limit," but it does allow actions to be dismissed for "laxness" in prosecution. Under CPLR 3216, if a year has expired since the joinder of issue in the case and a note of issue has not been served, the defendant may serve the plaintiff with a demand for a note of issue. The plaintiff then must serve the note within ninety days; if he does not, the action may be dismissed on motion. Even if a note of issue has been served, the action may be struck from the trial calendar if the plaintiff is not ready to proceed when the case is "called" for trial. The action thereafter will be dismissed as abandoned unless the plaintiff, within one year, obtains an order restoring the case to the calendar. *See* CPLR 3404. In addition, Uniform Rule 202.27 permits dismissal of the lawsuit without the 90-day notice protection when the plaintiff misses a calendar call or fails to appear at a pretrial conference.

(10) *The Texas System: Administrative Rules.* Although Texas did not initially adopt administrative rules mandating case "plans" for all cases (*see* § 8.03[B]), it did adopt time standards for the handling of civil litigation. Any case not disposed of within the time standards in the Texas Supreme Court's Administrative Rules "may be placed on a dismissal docket," which will mandate prompt action by the attorneys and will thereafter require strict deadlines. Tex. R. Civ. P. 165a. In addition, in 1999 Texas adopted discovery rules which require a "discovery control plan" for each case to streamline the discovery process by establishing a nine-month discovery period for each case and limiting the

amount of pretrial discovery that may be conducted during the discovery period. Tex. R. Civ. P. 190. Are these managerial techniques superior to New York's system, in which the initiative largely is with the parties and there is no outside limit or statistical target?

§ 8.04 Improving Pretrial Conferences and Case Management: Notes and Questions

(1) *Exemptions from Scheduling Orders.* Rule 16 contemplates that the District Courts, by local rules, will exempt given categories of cases from the requirements of scheduling orders. Which categories of cases should be exempted? One court with a long laundry list is the Western District of Texas, which exempts Social Security, habeas corpus, forfeiture, IRS summonses, bankruptcy, land condemnation, interpleader, pro se prisoner § 1983, student loan, VA overpayment, and certain other cases. Do these categories make sense? There is little consistency in these rules from district to district. Should the exempted categories be set forth in Rule 16 itself to ensure nationwide uniformity?

(2) *Should Scheduling Orders Be Required? Should Uniform Pretrial Orders Be Required?* Notice that Judge Sofaer opposes a requirement of case management in every case. Should the scheduling order requirement (which requires at least a little bit of management in every non-exempted case) be repealed? Should local rules that require uniform pretrial orders be repealed (or in the alternative, should they be dispensed with in "small" cases, such as those in which the probable damage amount is less than $50,000)?

(3) *Settlement Conferences.* There are several ways in which settlement could be treated in the pretrial process. One is to remove it from the list of factors to be considered in Rule 16 (but this approach has the arguable disadvantage that the trial judge's docket will increase rapidly and the parties may settle the case later with greater expense). A second idea is to separate the function of settlement mediation from that of ruling on the merits, such as by having a settlement conference presided over by a person otherwise not involved in the case (but this mediator will have less influence with the parties, the approach will require additional hearings and additional personnel usage, and it will be difficult to prevent the discussion of settlement at other hearings). A final approach is that of the current rules, which allow the judge to combine settlement mediation and adjudication. Which approach is most appropriate?

(4) *Trial-Setting Mechanisms.* Should setting for trial be initiated by action on the part of the attorneys, as it is in many cases in California and New York? Or should the court have a major scheduling function in initiating the process, as it does in most federal courts and as current California law permits?

(5) *"Individual" Dockets Versus "Unified" Dockets or "Master Calendar."* Individual dockets involve the assignment of cases at random to individual judges, who preside over all pretrial matters as well as the trial. "Unified" dockets, on the other hand, involve assignment of a trial judge immediately before trial. (In California, this method is referred to as a "master calendar system.") The theory is that a unified docket uses the court's resources fully because if a judge's docket for a given week "washes out" due to settlement or continuances, the individual docket would leave her with no cases to try. What disadvantages, however, can you perceive in the unified docket?

(6) *Encouraging Early Disposition.* The federal courts' scheduling order, California's "Fast-Track," and Texas' administrative rules all are different means of encouraging early disposition. Which is the best way of achieving this objective?

(7) *"Differential Case Management," "Staging," and the District Court's Plan Under the Civil Justice Reform Act of 1990.* What is the utility of these management techniques? How can we avoid the disadvantages of tracking (*i.e.*, disputes about track assignment and dismissals for missed deadlines)?

CHAPTER 9

ADJUDICATION WITHOUT TRIAL: SUMMARY JUDGMENT, DISMISSAL, DEFAULT, AND RELATED PROCEDURES

§ 9.01 Judgment on the Pleadings

NOTE ON JUDGMENT ON THE PLEADINGS

When Judgment on the Pleadings Can Be Granted. Suppose that the pleadings of both parties have been filed and the time for amendment, according to the court's scheduling order, has expired. Suppose, also, that the pleadings show that the parties agree on all of the factual issues. The case therefore depends solely on questions of law. Rule 12(c) provides a procedure, called a "judgment on the pleadings," that is proper in this relatively unusual set of circumstances.

Plaintiff's Motion for Judgment on the Pleadings. Imagine the following scenario. The plaintiff files a complaint that validly states a claim. A trial would be required if the defendant denied material allegations of the complaint, but instead, the defendant files an answer admitting all allegations of the complaint. The plaintiff now can obtain judgment by filing a Rule 12(c) motion for judgment on the pleadings.

Defendant's Motion for Judgment on the Pleadings. After the pleadings are closed, the defendant may move for judgment on the pleadings on the theory that the plaintiff's complaint fails to state a claim. As a practical matter, this procedure is similar to a motion to dismiss for failure to state a claim under Rule 12(b)(6); to be technical, the motion to dismiss is proper before the pleadings are closed and the motion for judgment on the pleadings is proper after.

Example. Consider the following case as an example of the successful use of the motion for judgment on the pleadings.

AUSTAD v. UNITED STATES, 386 F.2d 147 (9th Cir. 1967). The United States brought this action to foreclose a mortgage held by the Small Business Administration on property owned by the Austad Steel Company. It also sought a personal judgment against Johnny and Dorothy Austad, the owners of Austad Steel, who had signed an unconditional guarantee of Austad Steel's promissory note. The complaint alleged that Austad had defaulted on its note and that all conditions necessary to the foreclosure of the mortgage and to the Austads' personal liability on the guaranty had been satisfied. Copies of the note and guaranty agreement were attached to the complaint.

The defendants' answer admitted all relevant allegations of the complaint. But the individual defendants — the Austads — relied on three affirmative defenses: (1) that the United States failed to sue within sixty days after demand by the guarantors, thereby releasing them under state law; (2) that the delay estopped the United States; and (3) that the claim was barred by laches. The trial court rejected these defenses as a matter of law and granted judgment on the pleadings against all defendants.

The appellate court affirmed. The guaranty agreement was specifically worded to give the United States "uncontrolled discretion" in dealing with the debtor and the security (because the SBA should have discretion in dealing with defaulting debtors). As a matter of law, the three alleged defenses could not avoid liability. The judgment on the pleadings was proper as to Austad Steel Company because all elements of liability had been admitted. Furthermore, judgment on the pleadings was proper against the Austads personally, because once it was determined that their affirmative defenses were insufficient as a matter of law, their liability was established by their admission of all material allegations of the complaint.

§ 9.02 Summary Judgment

[A] The Standard for Granting Summary Judgment

Read Fed. R. Civ. P. 56 (summary judgment).

WARREN v. MEDLEY, 521 S.W.2d 137 (Tex. Civ. App. 1975, writ ref'd n.r.e.). The text of this opinion appears above at § 1.07 of Chapter 1 and should be read, or reread, at this point. After an evening at a nightclub with topless dancers as entertainment, Ms. Warren, Mr. Reynolds, and others went to Mr. Medley's home. There, Reynolds lifted Warren onto a glass-topped table against her wishes, urging her to demonstrate the dance. The table broke and Warren was injured. She sued Medley, the homeowner. After pointing out that summary judgment is not available "[i]f reasonable minds could differ as to the conclusions to be drawn from the summary judgment facts," the court affirmed the trial judge's grant of summary judgment in Medley's favor. Under the controlling law, the defendant could be liable only if he was grossly negligent. Warren's own deposition admitted that Medley "expressed surprise" at her plight, "couldn't have prevented it," and had nothing to do with it. Thus, the summary judgment materials negated gross negligence and causation on Medley's part, unequivocally and as a matter of law.

NOTES AND QUESTIONS

(1) *The Relationship Between Summary Judgment and Other Dispositive Procedures.* You may have noted a similarity among various procedures for disposition as a "matter of law," including (1) the Rule 12(b)(6) motion to dismiss for failure to state a claim; (2) the Rule 12(c) motion for judgment on the pleadings; (3) the motion for summary judgment; (4) the motion for judgment as a matter of law during trial ("directed verdict"); and (5) the motion for judgment as a matter of law after trial ("judgment notwithstanding the verdict"). What are the similarities, and what are the distinctions, among these procedures? See Figure 9A for a summary.

FIGURE 9A
SUMMARY JUDGMENT AND OTHER DEVICES FOR DECIDING A CASE "AS A MATTER OF LAW"

1. **DISMISSAL FOR FAILURE TO STATE A CLAIM**

   (when court can say, with reasonable certainty, that the plaintiff would not be able to obtain relief on any theory fairly encompassed within the complaint, even if supported by evidence; done before any evidence is received, so court must assume all allegations are true.)

2. **JUDGMENT ON THE PLEADINGS**

   (when pleadings leave no material fact to be decided, and the movant is entitled to judgment as a matter of law; done after the pleadings are closed, with no evidence yet received.)

3. **SUMMARY JUDGMENT**

   (when pleadings, affidavits, and discovery products demonstrate that there is no genuine issue of material fact, so that a reasonable juror properly applying the law could only find in favor of the movant; done on the basis of a paper record, so the judge must assume all inferences and credibility determinations would be made in favor of the non-movant.)

4. **JUDGMENT AS A MATTER OF LAW DURING TRIAL ("DIRECTED VERDICT")**

   (when the evidence that has been received, viewed in light most favorable to the non-movant, permits but one reasonable inference, in favor of the movant; done when the opponent rests or closes or at close of all evidence.)

5. **JUDGMENT AS A MATTER OF LAW AFTER TRIAL ("JUDGMENT NOTWITHSTANDING THE VERDICT")**

   (standard same as for judgment as a matter of law during trial, but done after the verdict has been received.)

6. **APPELLATE REVERSAL BECAUSE EVIDENCE DOESN'T SUPPORT VERDICT**

   (standard same as for judgment as a matter of law in trial court but done by the appellate court.)

(2) *The Basic Standard for Summary Judgment.* Rule 56 says that the summary judgment materials must show that there is no genuine dispute as to any material fact and that the moving party is entitled to prevail "as a matter of law." This language begs the question as to what conditions remove all genuine disputes about material fact or what entitles the movant to judgment "as a matter of law." *See* Schwarzer, *Summary Judgment under the Federal Rules: Defining Genuine Issues of Material Fact*, 99 F.R.D. 465 (1984). Can you restate the standard in language that is closer to a test that a judge could apply? [Note: it may help to focus upon conditions such that a reasonable juror correctly applying the governing law could come to only one conclusion. The trial judge cannot make fact inferences or judge credibility, but must assume that the jury would make all permissible inferences and all credibility determinations in favor of the non-moving party.] In this regard, compare the California standard: "no *triable* issue of material fact." CCP § 437c(c).

(3) *The Movant's Burden to Establish Entitlement to Summary Judgment.* As *Warren v. Medley* demonstrates, the movant has the burden to demonstrate the absence of genuine fact disputes about the elements of the non-movant's claims. The non-movant has no burden until and unless the state of the record is such that the movant would otherwise be entitled to summary judgment. Once the movant's burden is carried, then (and only then) the non-movant must show that there is a genuine issue for trial. *See* Louis, *Federal Summary Judgment Doctrine: A Critical Analysis,* 83 Yale L.J. 745 (1974).

At this point, we offer the following "Chapter Summary Problem." As usual, you should read it at this point but analyze it at the end of the Chapter (or, treat it as your instructor directs).

PROBLEM A: CHAPTER 9 SUMMARY PROBLEM

BROWNE v. SMITH: A PROBLEM INVOLVING SUMMARY JUDGMENT, DISMISSAL, AND DEFAULT. In this case, defendant Thomas Smith is a lawyer. Plaintiff David Browne is his former client. The complaint alleges that Browne at one time was employed by the City of London, in the hypothetical State of West York, as an airport police officer. On October 13, 2003, he was fired. Browne's complaint further alleges that he retained Smith to represent him in an appeal of his suspension to the City Civil Service Commission, but that Smith negligently failed to perfect the appeal in a timely manner and thereby proximately caused the loss of Browne's right to reinstatement.

The answer contains a defense of limitations. Browne sustained a legal injury on October 23, 2003, when Smith did not file the appeal within 10 days. But suit was not filed until October 30, 2005, apparently after the running of the applicable statute, which provides a two-year limit. West York follows the "discovery" rule in legal malpractice cases, which means that the claim does not accrue and the limitations period does not begin to run until the plaintiff "knew or should have known" in the exercise of reasonable diligence of the wrongful act and the resulting injury. Also, limitations can be "tolled" during any period of "fraudulent concealment" of the claim by the defendant.

The affidavits and discovery products on file show that Smith and Browne received a letter from the city on October 29, 2003, unequivocally advising them that the 10-day limit had passed and that no appeal would lie. But plaintiff Browne testified in his deposition that when he raised this issue with Smith, Smith said that "we would take them [the city] to court and sue them," and he believed Smith still could win him reinstatement. (For more detail, see the appendix to the section on summary judgment below, which reproduces the relevant documents).

1. Can the defendant successfully argue for summary judgment?
2. Can the plaintiff obtain voluntary dismissal of the claim if he senses that an adverse summary judgment is imminent?
3. If plaintiff Browne had obtained a default judgment because defendant Smith's lawyer had inadvertently misplaced the complaint and failed to answer it, would the defendant be able to set aside the default judgment?

ADICKES v. S.H. KRESS & CO.
398 U.S. 144 (1970)

MR. JUSTICE HARLAN delivered the opinion of the Court.

[On August 14, 1964, civil rights worker Sandra Adickes, a white woman, attempted to order food at a lunch counter in Kress' store in Hattiesburg, Mississippi, while in the company of six black students. Kress served the black students, but it refused to serve Ms. Adickes. When she left the store, Adickes promptly was arrested for vagrancy by Hattiesburg police officers. The Civil Rights Act of 1964 was not then interpreted as providing a damage remedy (even though Kress' conduct apparently violated the public accommodations sections of the Act). Therefore, Adickes sued under 42 U.S.C. § 1983, which provides a damage remedy against any person who deprives another person of federal civil rights while acting "under color of [state] law." Thus an essential ingredient of Adickes' recovery was that she allege and prove that Kress had acted under color of state law. In an effort to supply this required element, Adickes' complaint charges that Kress had "conspired" with Hattiesburg police to deny her food service and to cause her arrest on groundless charges.

[Defendant Kress moved for summary judgment. It argued that the affidavits and depositions on file did not permit the inference that it had acted under color of state law. The trial judge granted summary judgment for Kress, explaining that Adickes had failed to come forward with "any facts from which a conspiracy might be inferred." The Court of Appeals affirmed. The Supreme Court, in this opinion, reversed, holding that the lower courts had applied the wrong standard in considering whether Adickes, the non-movant, had come forward with any proof. Instead, the burden was on the movant, Kress, and the summary judgment should have been denied "because the Respondent [Kress] failed to show the absence of any disputed material fact."]

[I]n granting respondent's motion, the District Court simply stated that there was "no evidence in the complaint or in the affidavits and other papers from which a 'reasonably-minded person' might draw an inference of conspiracy" . . . . Our own scrutiny[,] however, convinces us that summary judgment was improper here, for we think respondent failed to carry its burden of showing the absence of any genuine issue of fact . . . .

In moving for summary judgment, Kress argued that "uncontested facts" established that no conspiracy existed between any Kress employee and the police. To support this assertion, Kress pointed first to the statements in the deposition of the store manager (Mr. Powell) that (a) he had not communicated with the police, and that (b) he had, by a prearranged tacit signal, ordered the food counter supervisor to see that Miss Adickes was refused service only because he was fearful of a riot in the store by customers angered at seeing a "mixed group" of whites and blacks eating together. Kress also relied on affidavits from the Hattiesburg chief of police, and the two arresting officers, to the effect that store manager Powell had not requested that petitioner be arrested. Finally, Kress pointed to the statements in petitioner's own deposition that she had no knowledge of any communication between any Kress employee and any member of the Hattiesburg police, and was relying on circumstantial evidence to support her contention that there was an arrangement between Kress and the police.

Petitioner [Adickes], in opposing summary judgment, pointed out that respondent had failed in its moving papers to dispute the allegation in petitioner's complaint, a statement at her deposition, and an unsworn statement by a Kress employee, all to the effect that there was a policeman in the store at the time of the refusal to serve her, and that this was the policeman who subsequently arrested her. Petitioner argued that [t]he sequence of events created a substantial enough possibility of a conspiracy to allow her to proceed to trial . . . .

[A]s the moving party, respondent [Kress] had the burden of showing the absence of a genuine issue as to any material fact, and for these purposes the material it lodged must be viewed in the light most favorable to the opposing party. Respondent here did not carry its burden because of its failure to foreclose the possibility that there was a policeman in the Kress store while petitioner was awaiting service, and that this policeman reached an understanding with some Kress employee that petitioner not be served.

[R]espondent [Kress] did not submit any affidavits from Miss Baggett, or from Miss Freeman, the waitress who actually refused petitioner service, either of whom might well have seen and communicated with a policeman in the store. Further, we find it particularly noteworthy that the two officers involved in the arrest each failed in his affidavit to foreclose the possibility (1) that he was in the store while petitioner was there; and (2) that, upon seeing petitioner with [blacks], he communicated his disapproval to a Kress employee, thereby influencing the decision not to serve petitioner . . . .

Pointing to Rule 56(e), as amended in 1963, respondent argues that it was incumbent on petitioner to come forward with an affidavit properly asserting the presence of the policeman in the store, if she were to rely on that fact to avoid summary judgment. Respondent notes in this regard that none of the materials upon which petitioner relied met the requirements of Rule 56(e).[19]

This argument does not withstand scrutiny, however, for [t]he 1963 amendment [w]as not intended to modify the burden of the moving party [t]o show initially the absence of a genuine issue concerning any material fact. The Advisory Committee [s]tated that "[w]here the evidentiary matter in support of the motion does not establish the absence of a genuine issue, summary judgment must be denied *even if no opposing evidentiary matter is presented.*" Because respondent did not meet its initial burden of establishing the absence of a policeman in the store, petitioner here was not required to come forward with suitable opposing affidavits.

If respondent had met its initial burden by, for example, submitting affidavits from the policemen denying their presence in the store at the time in question, Rule 56(e) would then have required petitioner to have done more than simply rely on the contrary allegation in her complaint. [P]etitioner would have had to come forward with either (1) the affidavit of someone who saw the policeman in the store or (2) an affidavit under Rule 56(f) explaining why at that time it was impractical to do so. Even though not essential here to defeat respondent's motion, the submission of such an affidavit would have been the preferable course for petitioner's counsel to have followed. . . .

NOTES AND QUESTIONS

(1) *Changing the Facts in Adickes v. S.H. Kress: Would It Make a Difference?* Suppose that, upon remand of the case to the trial court, the arresting officers both submit affidavits swearing that they were never inside the Kress store and that they arrested Adickes solely because of her earlier activities (the record showed that she had been involved in a demonstration at the public library, and police officers there had intervened and ordered

---

[19] [Adickes's deposition included her testimony to the effect that one of the students had told her that a police officer was inside the store. Also, defendant Kress had produced during discovery an unsworn written statement by one of its employees, Ms. Sullivan, who reported seeing a patrolman named Hillman enter the store and then leave close in time to Adickes, whom he arrested. However,] Petitioner's statement at her deposition . . . was, of course, hearsay; and the statement of Ms. Sullivan . . . was unsworn [and therefore could not qualify as an affidavit cognizable on summary judgment]. And, [Rule 56(e)] specifies that reliance on allegations in the complaint is insufficient . . . .

her to leave). Would Kress then be entitled to a summary judgment? What, if anything, could or should Adickes do to prevent an adverse summary judgment in that event?

(2) *The "Summary Judgment Evidence."* The Court points out that there are several items of information in the record that seem to support Adickes' conspiracy theory. There is Adickes' own deposition testimony, to the effect that a student told her an officer was in the store; there is the unsworn written statement of Ms. Sullivan that she saw the officer in the store; and there is the allegation, in the complaint, that Kress conspired with Hattiesburg police. But the Court refuses to consider any of these items in resolving the issue. Why? What's wrong with these items?

(3) *The Critical Difference Between a "Trial on a Stipulated Record" and a Summary Judgment Proceeding: John v. Louisiana Board of Trustees, 757 F.2d 698 (5th Cir. 1985).* Sometimes, the parties may agree on all the evidentiary facts, but not on the ultimate facts or conclusions that should be drawn from them. In that event, they may wish to agree to submit the case to the court on a stipulated record, allowing the court to make those inferences that the court, as fact finder, believes are correct. The crucial difference between this procedure and summary judgment is that in a trial on a stipulated record the trial judge is authorized to make inferences from disputed facts, but in a summary judgment proceeding, those inferences are absolutely prohibited. The *John* case is interesting in that there were contrary indications in the record as to whether the judgment was a summary judgment or a trial on a stipulated record. If the parties had in fact agreed to a trial on this kind of "paper record," it would have made no difference whether the record supported summary judgment, because the trial judge would have been authorized to find the facts. The Court of Appeals, however, reversed because the record as a whole did not show that the parties had agreed to present the case for trial on a stipulated record, and instead the trial judge had entered an invalid summary judgment.

[B] The Relevance of the Ultimate Burden of Proof: Summary Judgment Because the Opponent "Can't Prove Her Case"

DYER v. McDOUGALL, 201 F.2d 265 (2d Cir. 1952). Dyer sued McDougall for slander. The complaint alleged that McDougall had published the slanders by uttering them to two people, Mr. Almirall and Mrs. Hope. McDougall moved for summary judgment, supported by his own affidavit that he never uttered the alleged slander and by the affidavit of Mr. Almirall and the deposition of Mrs. Hope, both of whom stated that they had never heard the slander uttered. The court affirmed summary judgment for the defendants.

The court reasoned that, to obtain summary judgment, "The defendants had the burden of proving that there was no [genuine] issue" of material fact. "[O]n the other hand, at a trial the plaintiff would have the burden of proving the utterances; and therefore, if the defendants [s]ucceeded in proving that the plaintiff would not have enough evidence to go to the jury on the issue, the [summary] judgment was right." A jury would not be permitted to find slander from testimony that uniformly denied it. Thus, the defendant affirmatively had foreclosed all possible avenues of proof. The court also pointed out that the plaintiff had not sought to exercise his right under Rule 56(f) to obtain additional time for the taking of depositions or otherwise adding to the record by demonstrating that there were facts presently unavailable to him.

NOTE ON HOW TO READ THE CASE OF *CELOTEX CORP. v. CATRETT*

Showing that Plaintiff Has No Evidence — by Her Failure to Produce Any Evidence. Dyer v. McDougall shows one way a defendant can obtain summary judgment: by affidavits that affirmatively foreclose all possible sources of the plaintiff's proof. But there is another way. Rule 56 does not require the movant to produce affidavits; it just requires the movant to carry the burden of showing that there are no genuine disputes about the material facts. And so, if the defendant can show by inference that the plaintiff wouldn't be able to produce any evidence at a trial that would carry her burden to prove her case, the defendant may be entitled to summary judgment. That is what the following case is about.

Distinguishing the Celotex Case from Adickes. But remember: the threshold question isn't whether the plaintiff has come forward with evidence to raise a fact dispute; instead, it's whether the defendant has shown that there are no fact disputes. That's what we learned from *Adickes*, above. The case that follows has some arguable differences from *Adickes*; for example, the defendant in this case propounded interrogatories asking for all of the plaintiff's witnesses, and the plaintiff never gave the name of a single witness even after two years had passed. Does that fact justify an inference that the plaintiff "can't prove it"? (The majority and dissent disagree about the possible answers to that question.)

Ambiguities in Celotex. This case may appear difficult because some of its language is ambiguous. For instance, the Court never tells us exactly what the defendant has to do, to show that the plaintiff "can't prove it"; instead, it remands so that the Court of Appeals can consider that issue. Remember, the movant's burden still remains, that the movant must demonstrate — either directly or by inference — the absence of genuine disputes about the material facts.

CELOTEX CORP. v. CATRETT

477 U.S. 317 (1986)

JUSTICE REHNQUIST delivered the opinion of the Court.

The United States District Court for the District of Columbia granted the motion of petitioner Celotex Corporation for summary judgment against respondent Catrett because the latter was unable to produce evidence in support of her allegations in her wrongful death complaint that the decedent had been exposed to petitioner's asbestos products. A divided panel of the Court of Appeals for the District of Columbia Circuit reversed, however, holding that petitioner's failure to support its motion with evidence tending to *negate* such exposure precluded the entry of summary judgment in its favor . . . . This view conflicted with that of the Third Circuit in [another case]. We granted certiorari to resolve the conflict . . . .

[Catrett filed suit in 1980 seeking damages against 15 named asbestos manufacturers on negligence, warranty, and strict liability theories for the death of her husband. Defendant Celotex's motion argued that summary judgment was proper because Catrett had "failed to produce evidence that any [Celotex] product . . . was the proximate cause of the injuries alleged . . . ." In particular, Celotex noted that Catrett had been asked in interrogatories about witnesses who could testify to the decedent's exposure to Celotex's products, and in answering, had failed to identify any. In opposing summary judgment, Catrett relied on a hearsay transcript of the deposition of the decedent in a separate workers' compensation case, saying he had been exposed; an unsworn hearsay letter from another defendant's insurance company about the decedent's exposure; and an unsworn hearsay letter from the decedent's former supervisor describing the products to which he had been exposed. Celotex argued that none of these documents could be considered because all were inadmissible hearsay, not in affidavit form.

[In July 1982, almost two years after the filing of the suit, the District Court granted the motion on the stated ground that "there [was] no showing" of the decedent's exposure. A divided panel of the Court of Appeals reversed in reliance on *Adickes v. S.H. Kress & Co., supra,* which held that "the party opposing the motion for summary judgment bears the burden of responding *only after* the moving party has met its burden of coming forward with proof of the absence of any genuine issues of material fact." Judge Bork dissented, arguing that there was no requirement that a summary judgment movant "must always make an affirmative evidentiary showing . . ." and that the majority's holding "undermined the traditional authority of trial judges to grant summary judgment in meritless cases."]

We think that the position taken by the majority of the Court of Appeals is inconsistent with the standard for summary judgment set forth in Rule 56(c) of the Federal Rules of Civil Procedure. Under Rule 56(c), summary judgment is proper "if the pleadings, depositions, answers to interrogatories, and admissions on file, together with the affidavits, if any, show that there is no genuine issue as to any material fact and that the moving party is entitled to a judgment as a matter of law." [The 2007 "restyling" amendments to the Federal Rules of Civil Procedure made minor changes to the wording of Rule 56(c) — Eds.] In our view, the plain language of Rule 56(c) mandates the entry of summary judgment, after adequate time for discovery and upon motion, against a party who fails to make a showing sufficient to establish the existence of an element essential to that party's case, and on which that party will bear the burden of proof at trial. In such a situation, there can be "no genuine issue as to any material fact," since a complete failure of proof concerning an essential element of the nonmoving party's case necessarily renders all other facts immaterial. The moving party is "entitled to judgment as a matter of law" because the nonmoving party has failed to make a sufficient showing on an essential element of her case with respect to which she has the burden of proof. "[T]h[e] standard [for granting summary judgment] mirrors the standard for a directed verdict under Federal Rule of Civil Procedure 50(a). . . ." *Anderson v. Liberty Lobby, Inc.*, 477 U.S. 242, 250 (1986).

Of course, a party seeking summary judgment always bears the initial responsibility of informing the district court of the basis for its motion, and identifying those portions of "the pleadings, depositions, answers to interrogatories, and admissions on file, together with the affidavits, if any," which it believes demonstrate the absence of a genuine issue of material fact. But unlike the Court of Appeals, we find no express or implied requirement in Rule 56 that the moving party support its motion with affidavits or other similar materials *negating* the opponent's claim. On the contrary, Rule 56(c), which refers to "the affidavits, *if any*" (emphasis added), suggests the absence of such a requirement. And if there were any doubt about the meaning of Rule 56(c) in this regard, such doubt is clearly removed by Rules 56(a) and (b), which provide that claimants and defendants, respectively, may move for summary judgment "*with or without supporting affidavits*" (emphasis added). The import of these subsections is that, regardless of whether the moving party accompanies its summary judgment motion with affidavits, the motion may, and should, be granted so long as whatever is before the district court demonstrates that the standard for the entry of summary judgment, as set forth in Rule 56(c), is satisfied.

One of the principal purposes of the summary judgment rule is to isolate and dispose of factually unsupported claims or defenses, and we think it should be interpreted in a way that allows it to accomplish this purpose.

[I]n cases like the instant one, where the nonmoving party will bear the burden of proof at trial on a dispositive issue, a summary judgment motion may properly be made in reliance solely on the "pleadings, depositions, answers to interrogatories, and admissions on file." Such a motion, whether or not accompanied by affidavits, will be "made and supported as provided in this rule," and Rule 56(e) therefore requires the nonmoving party to go beyond the pleadings and by her own affidavits, or by the "depositions, answers to interrogatories, and admissions on file," designate "specific facts showing that there is a genuine issue for trial." [The 2007 "restyling" amendments to the Federal Rules of Civil Procedure also made minor changes to the wording of Rule 56(e) — Eds.]

We do not mean that the nonmoving party must produce evidence in a form that would be admissible at trial in order to avoid summary judgment. Obviously, Rule 56 does not require the nonmoving party to depose her own witnesses. Rule 56(e) permits a proper summary judgment motion to be opposed by any of the kinds of evidentiary materials listed in Rule 56(c), except the mere pleadings themselves, and it is from this list that one would normally expect the nonmoving party to make the showing to which we have referred.

The Court of Appeals in this case felt itself constrained, however, by language in our decision in *Adickes v. S.H. Kress & Co.*, 398 U.S. 144 (1970). [T]he *Adickes* Court said that "[t]he 1963 Amendment [w]as not intended to modify the burden of the moving party . . . to show initially the absence of a genuine issue concerning any material fact." [W]e think that this statement is accurate in a literal sense, since we fully agree with the *Adickes* Court that the 1963 Amendment to Rule 56(e) was not designed to modify the burden of making the showing generally required by Rule 56(c). It also appears to us that, on the basis of the showing before the Court in *Adickes*, the motion for summary judgment in that case should have been denied. But we do not think the *Adickes* language quoted above should be construed to mean that the burden is on the party moving for summary judgment to produce evidence showing the absence of a genuine issue of material fact, even with respect to an issue on which the nonmoving party bears the burden of proof. Instead, as we have explained, the burden on the moving party may be discharged by "showing" — that is, pointing out to the District Court — that there is an absence of evidence to support the nonmoving party's case . . . .

Respondent commenced this action in September 1980, and petitioner's motion was filed in September 1981. The parties had conducted discovery, and no serious claim can be made that respondent was in any sense "railroaded" by a premature motion for summary judgment. Any potential problem with such premature motions can be adequately dealt with under Rule 56(f), which allows a summary judgment motion to be denied, or the hearing on the motion to be continued, if the nonmoving party has not had an opportunity to make full discovery.

[T]he Court of Appeals declined to address either the adequacy of the showing made by respondent in opposition to petitioner's motion for summary judgment, or the question whether such a showing, if reduced to admissible evidence, would be sufficient to carry respondent's burden of proof at trial. We think the Court of Appeals with its superior knowledge of local law is better suited than we are to make these determinations in the first instance.

The Federal Rules of Civil Procedure have for more than 50 years authorized motions for summary judgment upon proper showings of the lack of a genuine, triable issue of material fact. Summary judgment procedure is properly regarded not as a disfavored procedural shortcut, but rather as an integral part of the Federal Rules as a whole, which are designed "to secure the just, speedy and inexpensive determination of every action." . . . Before the shift to "notice pleading" accomplished by the Federal Rules, motions to dismiss a complaint or to strike a defense were the principal tools by which factually insufficient claims or defenses could be isolated and prevented from going to trial with the attendant unwarranted consumption of public and private resources. But, with the advent of "notice pleading," the motion to dismiss seldom fulfills this function any more, and its place has been taken by the motion for summary judgment. Rule 56 must be construed with due regard not only for the rights of persons asserting claims and defenses that are adequately based in fact to have those claims and defenses tried to a jury, but also for the rights of persons opposing such claims and defenses to demonstrate in the manner provided by the Rule, prior to trial, that the claims and defenses have no factual basis.

The judgment of the Court of Appeals is accordingly reversed, and the case is remanded for further proceedings consistent with this opinion.

JUSTICE WHITE, concurring.

I agree that the Court of Appeals was wrong in holding that the moving defendant must always support his motion with evidence or affidavits showing the absence of a genuine dispute about a material fact. I also agree that the movant may rely on depositions, answers to interrogatories, and the like, to demonstrate that the plaintiff has no evidence to prove his case and hence that there can be no factual dispute. But the movant must discharge the burden the Rules place upon him: It is not enough to move for summary judgment without supporting the motion in any way or with a conclusory assertion that the plaintiff has no evidence to prove his case.

A plaintiff need not initiate any discovery or reveal his witnesses or evidence unless required to do so under the discovery Rules or by court order. Of course, he must respond if required to do so; but he need not also depose his witnesses or obtain their affidavits to defeat a summary judgment motion asserting only that he has failed to produce any support for his case. It is the defendant's task to negate, if he can, the claimed basis for the suit.

Petitioner Celotex does not dispute that if respondent has named a witness to support her claim summary judgment should not be granted without Celotex somehow showing that the named witness' possible testimony raises no genuine issue of material fact. . . . It asserts, however, that respondent has failed on request to produce any basis for her case. Respondent, on the other hand, does not contend that she was not obligated to reveal her witnesses and evidence but insists that she has revealed enough to defeat the motion for summary judgment. Because the Court of Appeals found it unnecessary to address this aspect of the case, I agree that the case should be remanded for further proceedings.

JUSTICE BRENNAN, with whom THE CHIEF JUSTICE and JUSTICE BLACKMUN join, dissenting.

[The dissenters "[did] not disagree with the Court's legal analysis" rejecting the requirement that the movant present affirmative evidence. But the dissenters believed that Celotex had not met its burden of production under Rule 56 and therefore they did not join in the remand to the Court of Appeals, concluding that the summary judgment should simply be reversed outright.]

[T]he burden of establishing the nonexistence of a "genuine issue" is on the party moving for summary judgment. This burden has two distinct components: an initial burden of production, which shifts to the nonmoving party if satisfied by the moving party; and an ultimate burden of persuasion, which always remains on the moving party . . . . *Adickes v. S.H. Kress & Co.*

[Justice Brennan delineates two types of defendants' summary judgments: the type in which the defendant makes an affirmative showing by uncontested evidence that destroys the claim, and the different type, at issue here, in which the defendant relies on the plaintiff's lack of evidence.]

Where the moving party [s]eeks summary judgment on the ground that the nonmoving party — who will bear the burden of persuasion at trial — has no evidence, the mechanics of discharging Rule 56's burden of production are somewhat trickier. Plainly, a conclusory assertion that the nonmoving party has no evidence is insufficient . . . . Rather, as the Court confirms, a party who moves for summary judgment on the ground that the nonmoving party has no evidence must affirmatively show the absence of evidence in the record . . . . This may require the moving party to depose the nonmoving party's witnesses or to establish the inadequacy of documentary evidence. If there is literally no evidence in the record, the moving party may demonstrate this by reviewing for the court the admissions, interrogatories and other exchanges between the parties that are in the record. Either way, however, the moving party must affirmatively demonstrate that there is no evidence in the record to support a judgment for the nonmoving party . . . .

The result in *Adickes v. S.H. Kress & Co., supra*, is fully consistent with these principles. [There, the Court] held that it was error to grant summary judgment "on the basis of this record" because respondent had "failed to fulfill its initial burden" of demonstrating that there was no evidence [by which plaintiff could prove her case] . . . .

The opinion [in] *Adickes* has sometimes been read to hold that summary judgment was inappropriate because the respondent had not submitted affirmative evidence to negate the possibility that [plaintiff might prove her case]. The Court of Appeals apparently read *Adickes* this way and therefore required Celotex to submit evidence establishing that plaintiff's decedent had not been exposed to Celotex asbestos. I agree with the Court that this reading of *Adickes* was erroneous and that Celotex could seek summary judgment on the ground that plaintiff could not prove exposure to Celotex asbestos at trial. However, Celotex was still required to satisfy its initial burden of production. . . .

I do not read the Court's opinion to say anything inconsistent with or different than the preceding discussion. My disagreement with the Court concerns the application of these principles to the facts of this case.

[The dissent points out that the three items produced by Catrett, although themselves inadmissible, included (1) a letter from an insurance representative of another defendant describing asbestos products to which the decedent had been exposed, (2) a letter from a former supervisor of decedent — whom Catrett indicated she intended to call as a witness at trial — describing asbestos products to which decedent had been exposed, and (3) a copy of decedent's deposition in an earlier workers' compensation hearing. Since the record thus did contain evidence — including at least one witness — that arguably supported plaintiff's claim, "there simply is no question that Celotex failed to discharge its initial burden of production." Justice Brennan concluded, "This case is indistinguishable from *Adickes*."

[The dissenting opinion of Justice Stevens is omitted.]

NOTES AND QUESTIONS

(1) *Celotex on Remand: The Court of Appeals Repeats Its Reversal.* On remand from the Supreme Court, the Court of Appeals decided that Celotex's motion for summary judgment must still be denied, because the record before the District Court regarding decedent's exposure to a Celotex product was not so one-sided that Celotex was entitled to judgment as a matter of law. That record included the letter from the decedent's former supervisor describing his exposure to a product attributable to Celotex (although the letter's admissibility remained in doubt), the former supervisor's possible trial testimony, and links between Celotex products and the decedent's former place of employment, supplied by Celotex. Judge Bork again dissented. *Catrett v. Johns-Manville Sales Corp.*, 826 F.2d 33 (D.C. Cir. 1987).

(2) *When Can Defendant Obtain Summary Judgment On the Ground that "Plaintiff Can't Prove It"? Comparing Dyer, Celotex, and Adickes.* What is the difference between the situation in *Dyer*, where the defendant affirmatively showed that the plaintiff could not prove the case, and *Celotex*? Notice that *Celotex* expresses a general agreement by the Justices that affirmative proof of the *Dyer* variety is not required. See whether you can state, briefly, just what is (or should be) required of a defendant in Celotex's position to prevail on its motion for summary judgment. Finally, what differences are there between the situation in *Celotex* and that in *Adickes*? [Note that Justice Brennan says the two cases are indistinguishable; is he correct?] *See* G. Miller, *The Pretrial Rush to Judgment: Are the "Litigation Explosion," "Liability Crisis," and Efficiency Cliches Eroding Our Day in Court and Jury Trial Commitments?*, 18 N.Y.U. L. Rev. 982 (2003); *see also* L. Mullenix, *Summary Judgment: Taming the Beast of Burdens*, 10 Am. J. Trial Ad. 433 (1987).

(3) *"When [Evidence Is] Unavailable": Rule 56(f).* The non-movant may be able to prevent summary judgment through the mechanism of Rule 56(f). This procedure is important to a non-movant who faces a motion supported by the movant's affidavits; it may be even more important if the absence of record evidence can suffice for summary judgment. Notice that the nonavailability of evidence must be shown by the non-movant through "affidavits," according to the Rule. What sort of showing by the non-movant should be required? For example, should the non-movant be able to obtain a continuance merely by showing that she has not obtained evidence yet, if she has had time to do so? What if the movant shows that evidence might conceivably exist, but the only witness with relevant knowledge cannot be deposed effectively because of a privilege (such as the Fifth Amendment)? *See* Note, *Summary Judgment Before the Completion of Discovery: A Proposed Revision of Federal Rule of Civil Procedure 56(f)*, 24 U. Mich. J.L. Ref. 253 (1990).

(4) *Should Summary Judgment in Complex Cases Be Governed by the Same Standards as in Simple Cases? Matsushita Electric Indus. Co. Ltd. v. Zenith Radio Corp., 475 U.S. 574 (1986).* In earlier cases, the Supreme Court said that "summary procedures should be used sparingly" in complex cases. *Poller v. Columbia Broadcasting System, Inc.*, 368 U.S. 464, 473 (1962). This dictum makes sense if it is understood as urging the trial judge to understand the complexities of the issues before granting summary judgment; but in general, if a trial would be a waste of time, wouldn't it be backward reasoning

to require it to be held anyway, merely because it would be lengthy and complex? *Cf. In re "Agent Orange" Prod. Liab. Litig.*, 611 F. Supp. 1223, 1256-57 (E.D.N.Y. 1985) (Weinstein, J.: "In complex and protracted litigation, waste of the trier's time is a particularly telling factor"). Finally, in the *Matsushita Electric* case, the Supreme Court upheld a summary judgment in a complex international antitrust case, saying that "metaphysical" doubts did not raise a genuine fact issue, without referring to the *Poller* dictum. This case, together with *Celotex* and *Anderson*, has widely been read as encouraging summary judgment where it is appropriate, even in complex cases. *See* Stewart, *Rulings Make Summary Judgment Possible in Complex Litigation*, Nat. L.J., Dec. 1, 1986, at 22, col. 1.

NOTE ON WIDER ACCEPTANCE OF SUMMARY JUDGMENT

There are signs that the Supreme Court's seeming encouragement of summary judgment in the *Celotex* and *Matsushita* cases has had an effect in the lower courts. Even before these decisions, the courts were headed in the same direction. In *Knight v. U.S. Fire Insurance Co.*, 804 F.2d 9, 12 (2d Cir. 1986), Chief Judge Feinberg stated:

> It appears that in this circuit some litigants are reluctant to make full use of the summary judgment process because of their perception that this court is unsympathetic to such motions and frequently reverses grants of summary judgment. Whatever may have been the accuracy of this view in years gone by, it is decidedly inaccurate at the present time, as borne out by a recent study by the Second Circuit Committee on the Pretrial Phase of Civil Litigation . . . . The Committee analyzed the published and unpublished decisions of the Second Circuit for the period from July 1, 1983 to June 30, 1985 and found that the affirmance rate on appeals from orders granting summary judgment was 79%. [Of course, there are few, if any, appeals from orders denying summary judgment, since such orders ordinarily are not appealable.] That figure is comparable to this circuit's 84% affirmance rate for appeals in civil cases generally.

For an excellent treatment of a broader thesis, see A. Kamp, *Federal Adjudication of Facts: The New Regime*, 12 Am. J. Trial Ad. 437 (1989). Professor Kamp persuasively argues that pretrial fact adjudication is expanding through a variety of procedural devices that include not only summary judgment but also rules governing pleading specificity and fact-oriented dismissals, among others.

§ 9.02[B] Appendix Proceedings in *Jones v. Clinton*

NOTE ON THE LITIGATION IN *JONES v. CLINTON*

During the presidency of William J. Clinton, a former Arkansas state employee named Paula Jones held a news conference to announce that, while he was Governor of Arkansas, the President had summoned her, through a state trooper named Danny Ferguson, to his hotel room. There, Ms. Jones alleged, the then-Governor had exposed himself to her and had made other advances. He also allegedly mentioned that her boss was his "good friend." She stated that she had declined his advances. As she left, she said, he told her, "You are smart. Let's keep this between ourselves."

Jones then filed a federal suit stating three different kinds of claims. First, she alleged sexual harassment under the federal civil rights statute, 42 U.S.C. § 1983. Actually, she alleged two types of sexual harassment: a "quid pro quo" claim, which requires proof that the defendant offered or threatened something (or took some rewarding or retaliatory action), and a "hostile environment" claim, which requires proof that the defendant so altered the job environment as to change the terms and conditions of employment. Second, she set out a conspiracy claim, alleging that the then-Governor and Trooper Ferguson conspired to sexually harass her. Finally, she included a state common law claim for harassment, or for what is more formally known as intentional infliction of emotional distress, under the law of Arkansas.

After various pretrial proceedings (which included review by the Supreme Court, which held that a lawsuit properly could proceed against a sitting president), and after extensive discovery, the President's attorneys filed the following motion for summary judgment, which was supported by a memorandum of authorities and by discovery materials.

IN THE UNITED STATES DISTRICT COURT
FOR THE EASTERN DISTRICT OF ARKANSAS
WESTERN DIVISION

PAULA CORBIN JONES, Plaintiff, v. WILLIAM JEFFERSON CLINTON and DANNY FERGUSON, Defendants.	CIVIL ACTION NO. LR-C-94-290

PRESIDENT CLINTON'S MOTION FOR SUMMARY JUDGMENT

President Clinton . . . hereby moves the Court pursuant to Federal Rule of Civil Procedure 56(b) to enter judgment for him on all claims in plaintiff's First Amended Complaint. [P]laintiff has failed to adduce evidence showing the existence of essential elements of each of her claims. Therefore, President Clinton is entitled to judgment as a matter of law.

PRELIMINARY STATEMENT

President Clinton adamantly denies that he sexually harassed Paula Corbin Jones at the Excelsior Hotel on May 8, 1991, or behaved improperly in any way towards her at any time. This factual dispute does not preclude summary judgment in this case however, because even as alleged by plaintiff, the purported encounter at the hotel is not actionable, and there has been a total failure of proof as to required elements of plaintiff's claims. . . .

Count I — Section 1983 Sexual Harassment Claim

In Count I, plaintiff alleges that President Clinton, while Governor of Arkansas, subjected her to sexual harassment and thereby deprived her of her constitutional right to equal protection in violation of 42 U.S.C. § 1983. President Clinton is entitled to judgment on this claim because plaintiff has failed to prove either *quid pro quo* or hostile environment sexual harassment.

To sustain a *quid pro quo* claim, a plaintiff must show that her purported refusal of a supervisor's alleged advances resulted in a tangible job detriment. Ms. Jones clearly failed to meet that burden here, because the record plainly demonstrates that President Clinton did not take any action to cause plaintiff to suffer any tangible job detriment. Plaintiff's counsel did not even bother to ask the President at his deposition whether he caused anyone to take any adverse job actions against plaintiff. But those witnesses who were asked about this — including plaintiff's three supervisors at the Arkansas Industrial Development Corporation — uniformly testified that he did not; they were wholly unaware of any incident between plaintiff and Mr. Clinton; they never discussed Ms. Jones with Governor Clinton; and neither the Governor nor anyone in his office ever asked them to take any action with respect to plaintiff, adverse or otherwise.

Plaintiff, moreover, did not in fact suffer any tangible job detriment. Notwithstanding that she has sued the President of the United States for employment discrimination, plaintiff admitted at her deposition that she filed suit without reviewing her employment records, and had not reviewed them since. Those records show — and Ms. Jones does not dispute — that she stayed in her AIDC job for nearly two years following the alleged indicent, and left the job of her own volition; that she received merit raises and cost-of-living increases throughout that period; that her job classification was up-graded two months after the alleged encounter; that she received several satisfactory job reviews during her tenure at AIDC; and that she suffered no material adverse job action. For all these reasons, plaintiff's *quid pro quo* claim fails.

To the extent plaintiff's Section 1983 claim rests on allegations of hostile environment sexual harassment, it also fails. Even if one were to resolve all factual disputes in favor of plaintiff for purposes of this Motion only, the alleged actions which plaintiff seeks to attribute to Mr. Clinton do not as a matter of law constitute severe or pervasive abusive conduct.

By plaintiff's own allegations, she encountered Governor Clinton only three times during her employment at AIDC — *a total of less than 20 minutes over a two-year period.* These alleged, sporadic encounters cannot possibly constitute the kind of sustained, severe and non-trivial harassment required to make out a hostile environment claim — let alone conduct that amounts to a deprivation of constitutional rights.

Even as described by plaintiff, the alleged encounter at the Excelsior Hotel does not constitute such abuse. By her own version of these alleged events, plaintiff was not threatened or coerced to go to the hotel room — she went voluntarily and was excited to meet the Governor, and was not induced by any promises related to her job. Most significantly, plaintiff herself alleges that the defendant did not use violence or make explicit threats; did not physically force sexual contact on her when she indicated she did not welcome his alleged advances; told her he did not want her to do anything she did not want to do; and she was allowed to leave the unlocked room as soon as she expressed a desire to do so. The conduct alleged here — an isolated advance rejected by plaintiff — is not actionable as hostile environment harassment. . . .

Count II — Civil Rights Conspiracy Claim

Count II asserts that Governor Clinton conspired with Arkansas State Trooper Danny Ferguson to deprive plaintiff of her equal protection rights, in violation of 42 U.S.C. § 1985(3). To prevail on a Section 1985 claim, it is not enough to allege simply that the defendants conspired; the conspiracy must have succeeded in depriving plaintiff of her civil rights. Accordingly, if the Court agrees that plaintiff has failed to make out a prima facie equal protection claim under Section 1983, Count II must fail as well.

Additionally, the record is barren of any evidence that Trooper Ferguson and Governor Clinton entered into any agreement to violate plaintiff's civil rights. Both defendants deny that they forged such an agreement, and there is no evidence to the contrary. For both these reasons, summary judgment should be entered for President Clinton on this claim as well.

Count III — State Tort/Outrage Claim

The last remaining Count asserts that Governor Clinton is liable under Arkansas state law for the tort of intentional infliction of emotional distress, or "outrage." President Clinton is entitled to summary judgment on this claim because plaintiff failed to adduce prima facie evidence of two independently essential elements — conduct that is outrageous as matter of Arkansas law, and distress so severe no reasonable person could be expected to endure it. It is undisputed that the purported conduct was brief and isolated; did not result in any physical harm or objective symptoms of the requisite severe distress; and President Clinton had no knowledge of any special condition of plaintiff that would render her particularly susceptible to distress — indeed she had none.

CONCLUSION

This Court has given plaintiff every opportunity to adduce evidence to survive summary judgment. Yet the record fails to support essential elements of her claims. We respectfully submit that if the Court were to permit such a veneer-thin case of sexual harassment and outrage as this to go forward against a sitting President, it would place future Presidents at risk for frivolous and vexatious litigation.

For these and all the reasons more fully set forth in the accompanying Memorandum and Exhibits, the Court should put an end to this case, and enter judgment for President Clinton.

Respectfully submitted,
Robert S. Bennett, Esq. . . .
Counsel to President William J. Clinton

NOTES AND QUESTIONS

(1) *The Relevance of the Celotex Decision to Jones v. Clinton.* Notice that the President's attorneys pursued the motion for summary judgment only after extensive discovery. Notice further that they make the point repeatedly that discovery has indicated the absence of evidence supporting the claim. Why? Explain how these tactics were dictated by the *Celotex* decision.

(2) *The District Court's Grant of Summary Judgment: Jones v. Clinton, 990 F. Supp. 657 (E.D. Ark. 1998).* The district judge labelled the alleged conduct "certainly boorish and offensive," but she granted summary judgment. Essentially, the court agreed with the President's arguments. For example, the court held that absent "tangible job detriments," a threat must be "clear and unambiguous" to warrant a *quid pro quo* claim. As for the hostile environment claim, the President's alleged conduct was not "one of the exceptional cases in which a single incident of sexual harassment, such as an assault, was deemed sufficient."

If you disagree with this holding, do you think your disagreement is with the application of the law to the facts, or is it with the state of the Arkansas and federal law? If the latter, then even if you were the judge, wouldn't you be bound to grant the same judgment?

(3) *Settlement of Jones v. Clinton.* After judgment, the parties settled for a monetary payment. Why, after obtaining summary judgment, was the defendant willing to settle?

[C] The "Summary Judgment Evidence"

CAMPBELL v. FORT WORTH BANK & TRUST CO., 705 S.W.2d 400, 401 (Tex. App.-Fort Worth 1986, writ ref'd n.r.e.). In a suit on a guaranty, the bank moved for summary judgment supported by affidavits, including affidavits showing the defendant's signature on the guaranty and circumstances indicating that the guaranty was in force at the time of default. The defendant countered with an affidavit saying, among other things, "To the best of my knowledge no liability was owed to Fort Worth Bank and Trust at the time of my resignation and sale of my stock [in the debtor corporation]. . . . To the best of my knowledge, subsequent guaranties were executed solely by [others] and Plaintiff no longer relied upon the prior Unconditional Guaranty upon which it now bases its suit against me." The defendant sought, by this affidavit, to dispute facts relating to his defenses of release, estoppel, and failure of consideration.

The appellate court held that these statements were not valid summary judgment evidence and affirmed the summary judgment:

> [A]ffidavits must be made upon personal knowledge. The statements in appellant's affidavit based upon "the best of his knowledge" constitute no evidence at all. A person could testify with impunity that to the best of his knowledge there are twenty-five hours in a day, eight days in a week, or thirteen months in a year. Such statements do not constitute factual proof in a summary judgment proceeding.

NOTES AND QUESTIONS

(1) *Affidavits and Discovery Materials as a Substitute for Evidence in the Summary Judgment Hearing.* In a summary judgment proceeding, the question is whether there are factual disputes that would require a trial. It makes sense, therefore, to test the affidavits and discovery materials by asking whether they show that the proponent could offer admissible evidence at the trial. In fact, the phrase "summary judgment evidence" is often used to describe the materials that the court considers at the summary judgment hearing.

(2) *After Celotex, Do the Summary Judgment Materials Need to Conform to the Rules of Evidence?* For affidavits and discovery products offered by the movant, the answer to this question is probably still "yes," even after *Celotex*. But for the non-movant, *Celotex* seems to set a more relaxed standard. "We do not mean that the non-moving party must produce evidence in a form that would be admissible at trial in order to avoid a summary judgment," says the Court. Should this issue be clarified by a Rule amendment?

(3) *Is Campbell v. Ft. Worth Bank & Trust, supra, Consistent with Celotex?* In the *Campbell* case, the court refused to consider an affidavit because it was not made on personal knowledge; the defendant said only that he swore to the facts "to the best of my knowledge." Is this result consistent with *Celotex*? [Note: If the movant had sustained its burden, showing entitlement to judgment as a matter of law, wasn't it incumbent on the non-movant to produce something to show that he could have controverting evidence at trial? Does an affidavit "to the best of his knowledge" fulfill this function?]

§ 9.02[C] Appendix Summary Judgment Documents in *Browne v. Smith*

[A] The Dispute Background

(*See also* the Chapter Summary Problem, above).

Source and Adaptation. The following materials are adapted from a real case, in which the court granted a summary judgment. The names and details have been changed, the documents have been edited, and the forum is shifted to the mythical "State of West York." You should analyze whether summary judgment properly can be granted. The authors express appreciation to Stephen Tipps of Baker & Botts, who supplied a modified set of documents from which these papers were adapted.

The Complaint. Thomas Smith, the defendant, is a lawyer. David L. Browne, the plaintiff, is his former client. The complaint alleges that Browne at one time was employed by the City of London, in the State of West York, as an airport police officer. On October 13, 2003, he was fired. Browne's complaint further alleges that he retained Smith to represent him in an "appeal" of his suspension to the city civil service commission, but that Smith failed to perfect the appeal in a timely manner. As a result, Browne lost all right to reinstatement. His complaint alleges that Smith's failure to perfect the appeal was negligence and proximately caused the loss of Browne's right to reinstatement.

The Answer. The answer contains a general denial (which you may assume is permitted in this state). It also contains the affirmative defense that the plaintiff's claim is barred by limitations. It is this last defense that is the subject of the motion for summary judgment that follows. According to the answer, the plaintiff's complaint shows on its face (by the file stamp) that it was not filed until October 30, 2005. The applicable statute of limitations, the answer says, is two years. Hence any claim accruing to Browne before October 30, 2003, is barred. But Browne's alleged claim, if he has any, accrued on October 23. This is so, according to the answer, because Browne was terminated on October 13, and the deadline for appeal was ten days. Hence any right to reinstatement was lost permanently on October 23, 2003, and any claim based upon that loss was barred because it was not filed before October 23, 2005, when two years expired.

The Reply: The "Discovery" Rule and the "Fraudulent Concealment" Rule. In avoidance of this limitations defense, the plaintiff's reply alleges (1) that the plaintiff did not discover the existence of the cause of action until a later date, and could not have discovered it by reasonable diligence earlier (but the defendant vigorously denies that this "discovery rule" helps the plaintiff); and (2) that the limitations period is tolled because the defendant "fraudulently concealed" the existence of the cause of action from the plaintiff.

[B] The Defendant's Motion for Summary Judgment and Supporting Affidavits

IN THE 199TH DISTRICT COURT
FOR THE STATE OF WEST YORK

DAVID L. BROWNE
vs. } CIVIL NO. 1,234,567
THOMAS SMITH

DEFENDANT'S MOTION FOR SUMMARY JUDGMENT

Thomas Smith, the defendant, moves that the Court grant summary judgment in his favor pursuant to Rule 56 of the West York Rules of Civil Procedure, and respectfully would show the Court the following:

1. Defendant Smith is entitled to summary judgment based upon the statute of limitations set forth in Article 5526 of the West York Revised Civil Statutes. The plaintiff's complaint alleges that the defendant committed negligence and malpractice by failing to file an appeal of the plaintiff's suspension form the Airport Security Force of the City of London on or before October 23, 2003. The basis of the plaintiff's lawsuit is set forth in his deposition testimony:

Q: And your complaint with Mr. Smith is that he didn't file the appeal timely?

A: That's correct.

Q: And you base that complaint on this letter that's marked Browne Exhibit 3?

A: My basis for that is the City, in this letter here, what they say was not filed timely. To answer your question, it would be yes. (Deposition of David L. Browne at 90).

Later in his deposition, plaintiff again summarized the essence of his complaint:

> My complaint against Mr. Smith is: He was hired to be my attorney to act in my best interest and he did not file this appeal within the deadline, the deadline as set up by the City Civil Service Department. That's my complaint against Mr. Smith. (Deposition of David L. Browne at 91).

A copy of the letter which plaintiff referred to as "Browne Exhibit No. 3" is attached to the Affidavit of Ollie Holmes filed among the papers of this cause.

2. Plaintiff did not file any action against defendant Smith until October 30, 2005 or more than two years after his cause of action, if any he has against defendant, accrued. The court can take judicial notice of the filing date from the court's own records — namely, the file mark on the complaint. Since the plaintiff's action against defendant was not filed on or before October 23, 2005, or within two years of the time his cause of action accrued, it is barred by limitations. The summary judgment proof shows that there exists no genuine issue concerning any fact material to this issue.

3. This defendant further would show that the only additional allegation made by the plaintiff against this defendant, that he concealed from the plaintiff his cause of action,

is wholly negated by the plaintiff's own testimony, making summary judgment proper. Plaintiff testified clearly concerning his understanding that his appeal had been denied in his deposition:

Q: When was the next time you talked with Mr. Smith after writing those words on that Browne Exhibit No. 2?

A: The next time I talked to Mr. Smith was when I got a certified letter from the Civil Service Commission Department turning down the appeal. (Deposition of Browne at 86).

The attached Affidavit of Ollie Holmes shows that the certified letter in question was received by Mr. Browne on October 29, 2003. Mr. Browne in his deposition then went on to explain his understanding of what had happened:

Q: What was the nature of your discussion?

A: Well, the letter obviously says that the appeal was denied and I asked him [Smith] why and he said the ten days, which is self-explanatory here. I asked him why he didn't file it on time and he said he had been real busy and just didn't get around to it. I said, well, okay, you didn't file; what legal recourse do we have now? And he said we would take them to court and sue them.

Q: Was that it?

A: That's all that I remember. (Deposition of Browne at 87.)

By the plaintiff's own testimony, nothing was concealed from him by this defendant or anyone else. As shown by the summary judgment proof, there exists no genuine issue concerning any fact material to this issue, and the defendant is on these facts entitled to judgment as a matter of law.

FOR THESE REASONS, Thomas Smith prays that summary judgment be granted in his favor.

Respectfully submitted,
LAUGHLIN & MORGAN
By William Morgan

AFFIDAVIT OF OLLIE HOLMES [OFFERED IN SUPPORT OF DEFENDANT'S MOTION FOR SUMMARY JUDGMENT]

My name is Ollie Holmes. I am over 18 years of age, am of sound mind, have never been convicted of any crime or offense, have personal knowledge of every statement herein made, and am fully competent to testify to the material stated.

I am the Assistant Director of the City of London Civil Service Department and custodian of the official records of that department. I have examined the personnel records maintained by the Civil Service Department and hereby certify that Exhibits A and B, attached to this affidavit, are true and accurate copies of a letter dated October 25, 2003 from H.S. Lanier, then Director of the Civil Service Department, to the Law Office of T.R. Smith, and the certified mail return receipt showing delivery of a copy of this letter to David L. Browne (received by Mrs. David Browne) on October 29, 2003. The originals of these instruments are maintained as part of David L. Browne's personnel file in the Civil Service Department.

I have care, custody and control of the City's records regarding hearings and suspensions, including this letter. Letters of this kind are prepared as part of the regularly conducted activity of the City in its ordinary course of business. It is the ordinary course of business for the City to prepare this kind of letter at or about the time of the events stated therein, whenever an inquiry concerning a suspension has been received after the ten-day period referred to. It is the business practice of the City to have this kind of letter prepared by someone with personal knowledge of the events described in the letter.

[signature: OLLIE HOLMES]

SUBSCRIBED AND SWORN TO BEFORE ME by the said Ollie Holmes on this the 8th day of May, A.D., 2005, to certify which witness my hand and seal of office.

[Notary signature and seal]

[Exhibit A to Ollie Holmes' Affidavit (on City letterhead):]

Dear Mr. Smith:

Someone apparently representing you delivered to this office a copy of the indefinite suspension letter directed to David L. Browne, Airport Police. On the second page of this letter was a hand-penned note signed by David L. Browne dated October 23, 2003. Mr. Browne's hand-penned note stated: "I authorize my attorney T.R. Smith as my attorney in fact to appeal my suspension from Airport Security, and I give him power of attorney to sign my name if necessary." These papers were received and stamped in the Civil Service office at 2:30 p.m. October 24, 2003.

However, Mr. Joseph A. Foster hand delivered Mr. Browne his letter of indefinite suspension during the early morning working hours in the offices of the Aviation Department on October 13, 2003.

Article V(a) on Civil Service, of the City Charter, Sec. 3, Removal of employees, states in part:

> . . . Within ten days after such suspension the employee so suspended may, if he desires, file an appeal with the civil service commission . . . .

Mr. Browne's request for a hearing before the Commission on the indefinite suspension is beyond the limits allowed by Charter specification and is therefore denied.

Yours very truly,
H.S. Lanier, Director
Civil Service Department

cc: Mr. David L. Browne

[Exhibit B, a certified mail receipt for a copy of this letter, signed by "Mrs. David Browne" and dated "Oct. 29, 2003," is omitted.]

AFFIDAVIT OF BEN CARDOZO [OFFERED IN SUPPORT OF DEFENDANT'S MOTION FOR SUMMARY JUDGMENT]

My name is Ben Cardozo. I am a lawyer, licensed to practice by the Supreme Court of West York. I have practiced law in London, West York, since receiving my law degree from West York A&M University in 1985. I specialize in the practice of municipal government law.

Prior to making this affidavit, I have reviewed a letter dated October 25, 2003, from H.S. Lanier to the Law Office of T.R. Smith. A true and accurate copy of the letter I reviewed is attached to this affidavit and is incorporated herein by reference. [The copy is identical to the one attached to Ollie Holmes's affidavit.] Assuming the facts set forth in the letter are true and correct, it is my professional opinion that Mr. Browne has no legal recourse from the decision of the Civil Service Department suspending him indefinitely from his job. Pursuant to Article V(a) of the Charter of the City of London, Section 3, all appeals from suspensions must be filed within ten (10) days of the date of suspension. If an appeal is not filed within that ten day period, there is no further recourse within the Civil Service Department. Moreover, the administrative decision will be considered final and will not be reviewed by any court.

All of the opinions expressed in this letter are based upon reasonable legal probability.

[signature: BEN CARDOZO]

[The jurat, oath and notarization are omitted from this reproduction.]

[C] Plaintiff's Response and Affidavits in Opposition to Summary Judgment

IN THE 199TH DISTRICT COURT
FOR THE STATE OF WEST YORK

DAVID L. BROWNE vs. THOMAS SMITH	CIVIL NO. 1,234,567

PLAINTIFF'S RESPONSE TO MOTION FOR
SUMMARY JUDGMENT

David L. Browne, the plaintiff, makes this response to the motion of defendant Thomas Smith for summary judgment in this case.

1. The summary judgment proof fails to establish as a matter of law when the limitations period began or when the claim accrued. In this regard, plaintiff objects to the use of deposition opinion testimony from plaintiff, a lay person, on this subject, specifically, all testimony in paragraph 1 of defendant's Motion for Summary Judgment. Further, plaintiff objects to the affidavit of Ollie Holmes and the letter and return receipt attached thereto, as containing opinion and hearsay for which no predicate is established.

2. Limitations on plaintiff's action runs not from the date of defendant's wrongful act or omission but rather from the date the nature of the injury was or should have been discovered by plaintiff. As set forth in the Affidavit of David L. Browne, which is on file among the papers in this cause, plaintiff did not discover, nor should he have discovered, the negligence of defendant until December 5, 2003, or thereafter. Under this discovery rule, plaintiff's action, therefore, is in all things timely brought.

3. In the alternative, plaintiff would show that defendant is estopped from relying on the defense of limitations by reason of his fraudulent concealment of the existence of plaintiff's cause of action against him as is set forth more fully in the aforementioned Affidavit of David L. Browne and in the Affidavit of Joseph Hawkins, attorney-at-law.

4. For these reasons, it is clear that a genuine issue exists concerning a fact material to the outcome of this action and that defendant is not, as he claims, entitled to judgment as a matter of law . . . .

Respectfully submitted,
Hobart A. Randell

AFFIDAVIT OF DAVID L. BROWNE [OFFERED IN OPPOSITION TO SUMMARY JUDGMENT]

My name is David L. Browne. I am the plaintiff in this action. I have personal knowledge of every fact stated in this affidavit and am competent to testify as to each such fact.

After I received the letter from the Civil Service Department on October 29, 2003 informing Mr. Smith that he had failed to make a timely filing of my appeal, I went down to Mr. Smith's office to find out what had happened. This was on the first day of November, 2003. I sat down with him and had a meeting that lasted at least 15 minutes. The first thing I asked him was why he had not filed the appeal on time. He said he had other things to do and simply did not get around to it. I then asked him what I was supposed to do. He told me that the Civil Service Department was obviously being overly technical in its interpretation of the City Charter because it had not been prejudiced by the late filing. He went on and said that since it was clear that my suspension was wrongful, we could go to court and have the decision reversed. Then I could get my job back. I told him to go ahead and file the necessary papers and to keep me advised.

When I did not hear anything from Mr. Smith for over a month, I tried to make an appointment to see him. Every time I called, his secretary told me either that he was in court or that he was out-of-town. Finally, I got fed up and went to see Mr. Joseph Hawkins who is another lawyer I know. When I explained the whole conversation to Mr. Hawkins, he told me that any lawyer who tries to fight City Hall should know that there is no appeal from a failure to meet the time deadlines. He said that I had no chance of getting the decision of the Civil Service Department changed and that Mr. Smith had simply been trying to cover up his mistake.

It was on December 5, 2003, that I talked to Mr. Hawkins. That was the first time that I knew that even though the suspension was a mistake in the first place, I would never be able to get my job back.

[signature: DAVID L. BROWNE]

[The jurat, oath and notarization are omitted from this reproduction. The affidavit of attorney Joseph Hawkins, which corroborates Browne's account of their conversation, is also omitted.]

[D] The Parties' Briefs

IN THE 199TH DISTRICT COURT
FOR THE STATE OF WEST YORK

DAVID L. BROWNE vs. THOMAS SMITH	CIVIL NO. 1,234,567

BRIEF OF DEFENDANT IN SUPPORT OF SUMMARY JUDGMENT

I. THE SUMMARY JUDGMENT EVIDENCE PRECLUDES RELIANCE BY PLAINTIFF ON THE DISCOVERY RULE

Even if the discovery rule is applied here, it causes plaintiff's claim to accrue when it should have been discovered. The summary judgment proof contains an affidavit and letter, shown by the summary judgment proof to have been received by plaintiff through his wife, on October 29, 2003, that clearly should have caused the claim, if any, to have been discovered. The letter unambiguously alerted plaintiff that his malpractice claim had accrued, in that it flatly told him that his reinstatement claim was barred.

A legal malpractice claim accrues when a reasonable person should have notice of the facts showing that the duty is breached, if any, and that "the legal wrong, if any occurred, is complete." *Anderson v. Sneed*, 615 S.W.2d 898, 900-01 (W.Y. App. 1981). That is when the statute begins to run, "not when it [actually] is discovered, or actual damage [is] fully ascertained." 615 S.W.2d at 900.

II. PLAINTIFF'S AFFIDAVIT AND DEPOSITION NEGATE THE EXISTENCE OF ANY FACT ISSUE WITH REGARD TO "FRAUDULENT CONCEALMENT"

[Defendant's brief argues that as a matter of law, Plaintiff's claim that Defendant said he had not gotten around to the appeal, and Defendant's prediction that Plaintiff could succeed by a suit in court, could not amount to "fraud."]

IN THE 199TH DISTRICT COURT
FOR THE STATE OF WEST YORK

DAVID L. BROWNE vs. THOMAS SMITH	CIVIL NO. 1,234,567

PLAINTIFF'S BRIEF IN OPPOSITION TO MOTION FOR SUMMARY JUDGMENT

The case of *Anderson v. Sneed*, 615 S.W.2d 898 (W.Y. App. 1981), is squarely on point, and is in opposition to defendant's motion. That case, too, was an attorney malpractice case. As here, the defendant relied on the statute of limitations. Plaintiff offered summary judgment proof closely resembling the evidence in this case. The lawyer allegedly had allowed a time period to run and allegedly had discussed the issue with his client in a manner that misled him. The district court of appeals held that summary judgment was improper.

The court in *Anderson v. Sneed* gave two grounds for this conclusion. First, the affidavit was sufficient to raise an issue of fraudulent concealment, if that was necessary. Secondly, the "discovery rule" was potentially applicable. The court found the applicability of this rule to be an "open question," and it found it unnecessary to decide on the discovery rule because the affidavits, similar to those here, did make out a fraudulent concealment case . . . .

Respectfully submitted,
Hobart A. Randell

NOTES AND QUESTIONS

(1) *Complexity.* The issues raised by this motion really are very simple, compared to those in other motions for summary judgment. The issues are (1) whether the summary judgment evidence establishes that the plaintiff should have discovered the relevant facts more than two years before filing and (2) if not, whether the summary judgment evidence precludes proof of tolling because of "fraudulent concealment" of the claim. Notice, however, that when the facts are compiled in a record, the case "looks" more complicated. The party opposing summary judgment naturally would want to create an appearance of greater complexity than really exists, in the hope that a court may deny summary judgment rather than expend the disproportionate effort required to understand the documents. [Did you find your eyes glazing over, and could that phenomenon have affected you if you were the judge?]

(2) *Movant's Tactics.* Given the eyes-glaze-over problem, what skills or techniques should a movant for summary judgment employ to maximize her chances of persuading the court? Should her briefing be lengthy and thorough — or short? *See* Stamper, *Rule 56: Using Summary Judgment Motions*, 7 Litigation 36 (Spring 1981).

(3) *Should the Motion Be Granted or Denied in This Case?* Notice that the defendant says the summary judgment evidence shows as a matter of law that the plaintiff "should have" discovered the existence of the claim at an early enough date to cause limitations to have run. And what about the "fraudulent concealment" allegation? There seems little question that Browne's evidence on this point is thin. Should summary judgment be granted or denied?

(4) *A Closely Similar Case: Braxton-Secret v. A.H. Robins Co., 769 F.2d 528 (9th Cir. 1985).* Braxton-Secret sued Robins on the theory that product defects in her Dalkon Shield IUD caused her to become pregnant and miscarry. She replied to Robins's limitations defense by claiming late discovery, in that she did not and could not reasonably have known of the existence of the claim at its accrual, and that Robins fraudulently concealed the existence of the claim from her and from the public by its statements. The District Court granted summary judgment which the Court of Appeals upheld, on the ground that her pregnancy should have put Braxton-Secret on inquiry of the "possible origin" of her damages as product defects in the Shield. Further, she could not claim fraudulent concealment when she had facts independent of Robins's statements that should have put her on inquiry. Would this court have held that summary judgment for

Smith against Browne would be proper, too? Wasn't Browne put on notice, very clearly, by the city's letter, which he received before October 30, 2003?

§ 9.03 Voluntary Dismissal

Read Fed. R. Civ. P. 41 (dismissal).

McCANTS v. FORD MOTOR CO., 781 F.2d 855 (11th Cir. 1986). The plaintiff's decedent was killed while riding in a military jeep on an army reserve training mission in Mississippi. The plaintiff filed a products liability action in Alabama against Ford, the manufacturer of the jeep. After discovery and certain pretrial motions, it became apparent that there was a substantial argument that the Alabama one-year statute of limitations was applicable, in which event the action would be time-barred. The plaintiff voluntarily moved to dismiss, intending to file a new action in Mississippi, where the applicable limitations period was six years. Rule 41(a)(2) provides that under these circumstances, an action "may be dismissed at the plaintiff's request only by court order, on terms that the court considers proper." The Rule also provides that such a dismissal is "without prejudice" to future litigation "[u]nless the order states otherwise." Ford opposed dismissal without prejudice, and it argued in the alternative that dismissal should be conditioned upon payment of the substantial expenses it had incurred and upon the continued applicability, in any other suit, of an order Ford had obtained precluding the plaintiff's use of expert witnesses as a discovery sanction. The District Court granted the plaintiff's motion and dismissed without prejudice and without attaching any conditions.

The Court of Appeals concluded that the dismissal without prejudice was not an abuse of discretion. It vacated the order, however, and remanded for the trial court to reconsider whether conditions should be attached to the dismissal. It reasoned as follows:

> . . . The purpose of [Rule 41(a)] "is primarily to prevent voluntary dismissals which unfairly affect the other side, and to permit the imposition of curative conditions." . . . Thus a district court considering a motion for dismissal without prejudice should bear in mind principally the interests of the defendant, for it is the defendant's position that the court should protect . . . .
>
> [H]owever, in most cases a dismissal should be granted unless the defendant will suffer clear legal prejudice, *other than the mere prospect of a subsequent lawsuit,* as a result. Thus it is no bar to a voluntary dismissal that a plaintiff may obtain some tactical advantage over the defendant in future litigation . . . . Rather, the district court must exercise its broad equitable discretion under Rule 41(a)(2)[,] [i]mposing such costs and attaching such conditions as are deemed appropriate . . . .
>
> [A]ppellant argues that it will suffer plain legal prejudice as a result of the district court's dismissal without prejudice, as it will lose the complete defense it claims it is afforded by the applicable statute of limitations in Alabama . . . .
>
> [W]hat little authority that exists on this particular question suggests that the likelihood that a dismissal without prejudice will deny the defendant a statute of limitations defense does not constitute plain legal prejudice and hence should not alone preclude such a dismissal . . . .
>
> . . . [In prior authority, the court has] considered it important that there was no evidence in the record of bad faith on the part of plaintiff's counsel in failing to [act]

in a timely manner. Here, too, we find no evidence in the record to suggest that appellee or her counsel acted in bad faith in filing this action in Alabama or in filing it more than one year after the accident occurred. Under the circumstances, we cannot find appellant to have suffered any plain legal prejudice other than the prospect of a second lawsuit on the same set of facts. The district court did not abuse its discretion in granting the dismissal without prejudice in this case . . . .

. . . Appellant claims the district court should have conditioned the dismissal on the payment by appellee of full compensation for the considerable time and effort it claims it wasted in defending this action. Further, appellant argues that the district court should have imposed non-monetary conditions that would have the effect of insuring that appellant retains the benefits it claims it is due under the terms of a discovery order . . . . [A]ppellee would not have been able to call any expert witnesses at trial if this case had not been dismissed . . . .

[T]he record now before this court is insufficient to allow us to evaluate the district court's exercise of its discretion in rejecting appellant's request for the attachment of conditions to its order dismissing the case . . . . Just how much of the work done by appellant in this case was wasted and how much will be useful in further litigation in Mississippi is not clear . . . . We thus remand the case, with instructions [to consider conditions and to state the findings that led to the trial court's decision] . . . .

NOTES AND QUESTIONS

(1) *Is There Prejudice to the Defendant?* Will the conditions (including compensation) actually remove any prejudice to the defendant? On the one hand, it loses a viable defense. On the other hand, it is placed in the same position as if the plaintiff had made the right strategic choice in the first place. For a different prejudice dilemma, see *Merit Ins. Co. v. Leatherby Ins. Co.*, 581 F.2d 137 (7th Cir. 1978). There, the Court of Appeals upheld a voluntary dismissal without prejudice that had the effect of negating an order to submit the suit to arbitration. Judge Swygert dissented and said, "Merit is able to dismiss its lawsuit, thereby negating . . . arbitration, and is given another opportunity to try its fortune in another forum. The majority condones the practice. I cannot." Is this reasoning persuasive, and if so, should it influence the outcome in the case above, *McCants v. Ford Motor Co.*?

(2) *The Court's Discretion in Attaching Conditions.* How should the trial court go about deciding how much of Ford's total Mississippi litigation costs to charge to the plaintiff, or whether to order that the plaintiff may not use experts in future litigation? On the one hand, the court's ability to enforce such an order may seem questionable. On the other hand, if the plaintiff can avoid the effect of the order, sanctions may be made less effective.

§ 9.04 Involuntary Dismissal for Want of Prosecution: The Court's Inherent Power

LINK v. WABASH RAILROAD, 370 U.S. 626 (1962). On the morning of a scheduled pretrial conference, the plaintiff's attorney had his secretary telephone the court to state that he would not be able to attend because he was working on some papers to file in the Indiana Supreme Court. The District Court found that the attorney had "failed to indicate . . . a reasonable" excuse for nonappearance and dismissed the case for want of prosecution, in the exercise of its "inherent power." The Supreme Court upheld the dismissal under the authority of Rule 41(b), which, in today's version, provides for dismissal "[i]f the plaintiff fails to prosecute or to comply with these rules or a court order":

> The authority of a federal trial court to dismiss a plaintiff's action with prejudice because of his failure to prosecute cannot be seriously doubted. The power to invoke this sanction is necessary in order to prevent undue delays in the disposition of pending cases and to avoid congestion in the calendars of the District Courts . . . .
>
> Petitioner contends that the language of this Rule . . . prohibits involuntary dismissals for failure of the plaintiff to prosecute except on motion of the defendant. In the present case there was no such motion.
>
> We do not read Rule 41(b) as implying any such restriction . . . .
>
> Nor does the absence of notice as to the possibility of dismissal or the failure to hold an adversary hearing necessarily render such a dismissal void . . . . The circumstances here were such as to dispense with the necessity for advance notice and hearing . . . .
>
> . . . Whether such an order can stand depends on whether it was within the permissible range of the court's discretion . . . .
>
> There is certainly no merit to the contention that dismissal of petitioner's claim because of his counsel's unexcused conduct imposes an unjust penalty on the client. Petitioner voluntarily chose this attorney . . . . Any other notion would be wholly inconsistent with our system of representative litigation, in which each party is deemed bound by the acts of his lawyer-agent . . . .
>
> We need not decide whether unexplained absence from a pretrial conference would alone justify a dismissal with prejudice . . . . For the District Court in this case relied on all the circumstances that were brought to its attention, including the earlier delays . . . .

NOTES AND QUESTIONS

(1) *"Dismissal Dockets."* In many courts, it is common practice to set up "dismissal dockets," consisting of cases that have been on file for lengthy periods without recent action. The court may then provide notice to the plaintiffs that their cases will be dismissed unless they undertake a given step (*e.g.*, filing a request for trial setting, or even filing a "Motion to Retain on the Docket"). Dismissal dockets are useful because there typically are many cases on a busy court's docket in which counsel have withdrawn, clients have disappeared, etc., and the parties are unlikely to resolve them. *See* Note, *Dismissal with Prejudice for Failure to Prosecute: Visiting the Sins of the Attorney Upon the Client*, 22 Ga. L. Rev. 195 (1987).

(2) *Dismissal Notice Periods: The Texas and New York Practice.* Tex. R. Civ. P. 165a provides for dismissal for want of prosecution when the plaintiff or her attorney fail to attend a hearing of which they had notice, absent a showing of good cause. Another basis for involuntary dismissal is noncompliance with time standards for disposal of civil cases promulgated by the Texas Supreme Court. The rule also provides a series of time limits during which the case can be reinstated, making the dismissal irrevocable after certain periods. This rule lends itself to the kind of dismissal dockets mentioned above. For a different approach with similar effects, consider New York's provisions for "laxness" dismissals, described in Note 9 of § 8.03[C], above.

(3) *Other Dismissals: For Failure to State a Claim, for Want of Jurisdiction, as a Discovery Sanction, Etc.* Notice that Rule 41(b) provides, "Unless the dismissal order states otherwise, a dismissal under this subdivision (b) and any dismissal not under this rule — except one for lack of jurisdiction, improper venue, or failure to join a party under Rule 19 — operates as an adjudication on the merits," *i.e.*, it is "with prejudice" to any future litigation. Thus a dismissal for want of jurisdiction would not bar the plaintiff from refiling in a proper court — but a dismissal for failure to state a claim would, unless it "otherwise specifies." If the judge has just indicated to you that she intends to dismiss your federal suit for failure to state a claim, but you think you might be able to present a closely similar claim successfully in the state courts, what would you ask the court to include in the order of dismissal? *See* Note, *Res Judicata Effects of Involuntary Dismissals: When Involuntary Dismissal Based Upon Prematurity or Failure to Satisfy a Precondition to Suit Should Bar a Second Action*, 70 Cornell L. Rev. 667 (1985). As to general sanctioning authority under the court's inherent power, see Chapter 5, above; *see also* Cogan, *The Inherent Power and Due Process Models in Conflict: Sanctions in the Fifth Circuit*, 42 Sw. L.J. 1011 (1989).

§ 9.05 Default Judgment

Read Fed. R. Civ. P. 55 (default).

BUTNER v. NEUSTADTER
324 F.2d 783 (9th Cir. 1963)

HAMLIN, CIRCUIT JUDGE.

This is an appeal from an order of the United States District Court for the Southern District of California denying appellant's motion to set aside a default judgment . . . .

[The defendant was served with process in a California state suit while he was in Los Angeles temporarily. At that time, California rules required an answer within ten days. The defendant sent the papers to his attorney in Little Rock, Arkansas, where defendant resided; he enclosed the name of Los Angeles attorney Samuel Reisman. By the time his Little Rock lawyer contacted Reisman's office to secure California counsel, answer time had nearly expired under the California state rules, and Reisman then was out of town. An associate of Reisman left messages with the plaintiff's attorney seeking an extension of time, but the plaintiff's attorney ultimately responded that he had already secured a default judgment on the day after answer day, which he refused to set aside. The defendant's attorneys then removed the case to federal court, where they (1) filed an answer, which they claimed superseded the default, since it was filed within the twenty-day period provided under the federal rules; and (2) moved in the alternative to have the federal court set aside the state default judgment, pursuant to Federal Rule 60(b). The district court refused to set aside the default. The Court of Appeals, in this opinion, reversed.]

The issues presented are: (1) Is defendant entitled to have the default judgment vacated as a matter of law upon removal to federal district court; and (2) if not, did the trial court abuse it discretion in not granting the motion to set aside?

Appellant contends that he is entitled to have the default judgment set aside as a matter of law upon removal to federal district court. His reasoning is as follows: section 1446(b) gives a defendant the right to remove within twenty days after service of process. Fed. R. Civ. P. 12 gives him twenty days within which to appear and plead. If a default judgment entered in a state court within ten days after service of process is allowed to take precedence over the removal statute which allows him twenty days to remove, then, he contends, the whole purpose of the removal statute is defeated. Appellee maintains, on the other hand, that although the removal after the default judgment is perfectly proper, it cannot be taken to supersede the default judgment which must be regarded as valid until set aside. We agree.

Although Fed. R. Civ. P. 81 (c) provides the time within which a defendant must answer in a removed action, it is obvious that it did not contemplate a situation in which the action had proceeded to a final judgment before removal. The federal rules apply after removal and "neither add to nor abrogate what has been done in the state court prior to removal." *Talley v. American Bakeries Co.*, 15 F.R.D. 391, 392 (E.D. Tenn. 1954). The federal court takes the case as it finds it on removal and treats everything that occurred in the state court as if it had taken place in federal court. Therefore, this default judgment should be treated as though it had been validly rendered in the federal proceeding. Appellant's argument that state law cannot prevent removal or defeat its effects is quite correct. That does not mean that the default judgment must be vacated as a matter of law. Instead, a motion to set aside a default may be made in the district court under Fed. R. Civ. P. 60(b) because of mistake, inadvertence, surprise, or excusable neglect.

Appellant argues that the trial court abused its discretion in denying the motion to vacate . . . . In *Karlein v. Karlein* [103 Cal. App. 2d 496, 229 P.2d 831 (1951)], the district court of appeal said:

> An appellate court listens more readily to an appeal from an order denying relief [from default]. The law is remedial and any doubt as to the propriety of setting aside a default should be resolved in favor of the application, even in a case where the showing . . . is not strong . . . . Neither party should be deprived of a hearing except when guilty of inexcusable neglect, and doubts should be resolved in favor of an application to set aside a default judgment.

These statements are a good guide to action in this case. Appellant contends he has a good defense on the merits, namely that the note in question was obtained by means of fraud and that appellee is not a holder in due course. Whether or not this is true, if he is not guilty of inexcusable neglect, he should have a hearing on the merits.

Appellee maintains that appellant was guilty of inexcusable neglect in that he sent the summons and complaint to his attorney in Arkansas with directions to contact Mr. Reisman in Los Angeles, that he was acquainted with lawyers in Los Angeles, and that he was an astute businessman and should have simply contacted Mr. Reisman himself. Then the fact that Mr. Reisman was out of town would not have made any difference, for appellant would have been aware of that circumstance and could have made appropriate arrangements to get another attorney. While there may be some doubt as to the wisdom of appellant's actions in this case, there are several possible explanations of his conduct. Having been a resident of Little Rock for more than a year, he might quite naturally wish to send all his legal business to his Little Rock attorney, and merely in this one instance have sent the name of Mr. Reisman along as a convenience to the Little Rock attorney. He might do this as a matter of routine, being, as appellee asserts, an "astute businessman." . . .

There is a possibility of a meritorious defense. An attempt was made to take action on the complaint within the allotted ten days but was frustrated by certain events. There is doubt as to whether the circumstances which frustrated the attempt could amount to inexcusable neglect. We have been cited to no case allowing a default judgment to stand under facts similar to those in this case. We hold that the order by the district court [refusing to set aside the default judgment] was an abuse of discretion.

The judgment is reversed.

NOTES AND QUESTIONS

(1) *Liberal Standards for Setting Aside Defaults upon "Excusable Neglect": Changing the Facts in Butner v. Neustadter.* Would (or should) it have made a difference in *Butner v. Neustadter* if default had resulted simply because the defendant had mislaid the summons and complaint and forgotten it? Or if it resulted because the defendant sent the papers to his attorney and the Post Office delayed for several weeks in delivery? Or if the defendant ignored the suit because he didn't understand the papers or was "too busy" to deal with them?

(2) *Proof Requirements for Default Judgments.* If the claim is "liquidated" (*i.e.*, if it is for "a sum certain or for a sum which by mathematical calculation can be made certain," as in the case of a promissory note), Rule 55(b)(1) says that the clerk shall enter judgment on proper application. But application must be made to the court if the sum is unliquidated. The court may order a hearing and evidence. Ordinarily, the damages must be proved by competent evidence, and the court may require liability facts to be proved under Rule 55(b)(2) when needed "to enter or effectuate judgment."

(3) *Technical Scrutiny of Default Judgments on Timely Direct Attack.* There can be little question that default judgments are more readily subject to setting aside than judgments after defense. Areas of attack may include: (1) inadequacy of the summons or return (*e.g.*, the return fails to describe the service properly); (2) absence of jurisdiction; (3) failure to make an adequate record at the default hearing; (4) in some jurisdictions, failure to have a reporter record the default hearing (on the theory that the defaulting defendant is entitled to appeal); (5) in some jurisdictions, lack of specificity in the complaint; and (6) lack of notice of default, or misleading instructions from the opposing party or court personnel. *See* Pohl & Hittner, *Judgments by Default in Texas*, 37 Sw. L.J. 421 (1983).

§ 9.06 Improving Summary Judgment and Other Non-Trial Disposition Methods: Notes and Questions

(1) *Clarifying the Standard for Summary Judgment Against the Party with the Burden of Proof.* After *Celotex*, it is clear that the party without the burden of proof can obtain summary judgment without putting her own evidence in the record. However, a comparison of the opinion of the Court with the separate opinion of Mr. Justice Brennan makes it clear that the standard remains ambiguous. Should the Rule be amended to make clear that summary judgment can be granted if the movant's interrogatories asking the non-movant to particularize her evidentiary basis for her contentions remain unanswered after the non-movant has had adequate time for discovery? Or should amendment limit considerations only to materials admissible in evidence?

(2) *Requiring a Response to the Motion for Summary Judgment; Encouraging Thorough Consideration by the Court.* Some jurisdictions require the non-movant to

respond to the motion, particularizing his or her contentions concerning why the motion should not be granted. If there is no response, summary judgment may be granted. How would this type of rule affect the result in *Celotex*, and is this type of rule a good idea? California requires the trial judge to give reasons and specify triable issues even when denying summary judgment (a requirement that presumably weighs against denial simply because of complexity). Cal. Code Civ. P. § 437c(f)-(g). Is this idea a good one?

(3) *Conditions on Voluntary Dismissal.* If the plaintiff has subjected the defendant to suit in a given forum and wishes to dismiss without prejudice, it seems only fair that the plaintiff should pay the expenses that this choice has occasioned for the defendant and that the issues actually determined in the defendant's favor should carry over to other litigation, absent reason to the contrary. Would it make sense to amend Rule 41 to provide that the plaintiff must pay the defendant's reasonable expenses and that the dismissal preserves rulings favorable to the defendant unless the court otherwise provides in its order?

(4) *Default.* Would it make sense to provide for the manner of making proof to support default judgment (*e.g.*, by expressly providing in the Rule that affidavits are satisfactory proof)? Should the time for setting aside default be enlarged so that it is longer than time limits for setting aside other kinds of judgments? Since setting aside defaults is *sui generis* — it really is a different kind of issue than setting aside other kinds of judgments based on fraud, newly discovered evidence, etc. — would it make sense to govern the process of setting aside default by a liberal provision contained in its own separate Rule?

CHAPTER 10

TRIAL

§ 10.01 The Order of Events in a Jury Trial

Although there are some jurisdictional variations, the events in a jury trial usually follow this sequence:

Trial Setting and Final Pretrial Conference. The trial may have been set for years, or it may have been set for a few weeks or months only. The federal system contemplates a final pretrial conference close in time to the trial, although practice varies. This process is covered in detail in Chapter 8, *supra*, but it is important to remember its relationship to the trial.

Motions on the Eve of Trial. These motions may include requests for particular orders relating to jury selection (*e.g.*, for individual examination of jurors), for evidence rulings, etc. A "motion in limine" is frequently asserted at this stage in some jurisdictions. "*In limine*" is Latin, meaning "at the threshold." The motion asks the court to exclude potentially prejudicial evidence in advance, unless the proponent of the evidence raises the issue outside the presence of the jury first. If there is serious question about the admissibility of important evidence, the motion may be very useful. In jurisdictions without extensive use of pretrial conferences, these motions may be presented and ruled upon the day trial begins.

Voir Dire Examination of Jurors. The trial itself begins with a panel of potential jurors in the courtroom. The judge, or the attorneys, or both — depending upon the jurisdiction and the court — question the panel members about their qualifications.

Challenges to Potential Jurors ("Jury Selection"). During the examination, attorneys may challenge disqualified jurors, and each side is allowed to remove a certain number of potential jurors without giving reasons. The first twelve (or, in some courts, the first six) panel members who remain are impaneled and sworn.

Opening Statements. The plaintiff's attorney gives an opening statement, followed by the defendant's attorney. In some jurisdictions, the defendant may choose to give an opening statement after the plaintiff rests, right before defendant's case begins.

Invoking "the Rule" (Sequestering Witnesses). At this stage (or sometimes earlier), many jurisdictions permit either attorney to demand that the court sequester the witnesses (*i.e.*, order them to refrain from listening to the evidence or discussing the case with persons other than the attorneys). This procedure is often called "invoking 'the rule' " ("Your honor, I invoke the rule.").

The Right to Open and Close. The party with the burden of proof on the whole case (usually the plaintiff) has the right to open and close the evidence and summations.

Plaintiff's Evidence. The plaintiff calls her first witness. The evidence for the plaintiff must be submitted in accordance with the Rules of Evidence, which govern what is admissible and the form in which it may be admitted. The plaintiff's evidence also may include stipulations, discovery products, or facts judicially noticed by the court. The plaintiff ends this phase of trial by saying, "plaintiff rests."

Motion for Judgment as a Matter of Law or "Directed Verdict." The defendant may move to have the case taken from the jury and decided by the judge on the ground that the plaintiff's evidence cannot support a verdict.

Defendant's Evidence. The defendant may choose to submit evidence. The same kinds of evidentiary rules control. At the conclusion, the defendant rests.

Rebuttal and Surrebuttal Evidence. The plaintiff now may move for judgment against the defendant. In addition, the plaintiff may offer evidence in rebuttal to the defendant's evidence. The defendant may offer surrebuttal, to which the plaintiff may again respond, etc.

Motion for Judgment as a Matter of Law or "Directed Verdict" at the Close of the Evidence. Either party may move for judgment as a matter of law (also called a "directed verdict") when all parties close.

The Charge Conference: Requests and Rulings. The attorneys must be given an opportunity to make requests for jury charges. In many federal courts, the requests must be made before trial; in some state courts, they may be made during trial. Typically, the court confers with the parties about the charge. The Federal Rules require that the judge inform the parties of its rulings on requested charges before the attorneys give their jury arguments.

The Court's Charge and Submission of the Case to the Jury (Verdict Forms). The court then instructs the jury on the applicable law and submits a question, or series of questions, to the jury, together with a form for its verdict. In some courts, the court charges the jury before the arguments of counsel.

Jury Argument (or "Summation"). The attorneys argue the law and the evidence to the jury, giving their explanations of the way in which the jurors should resolve the issues. The party with the burden of proof on the whole case (usually the plaintiff) opens the jury argument. The defendant gives the second jury argument. The plaintiff gives the final (rebuttal) argument.

Objections to the Charge. The attorneys must be given an opportunity to place their objections to the charge on the record. Many jurisdictions prohibit appellate consideration of errors in the charge unless they were objected to before the jury retired.

Jury Deliberations; Further Charges or Questions; Verdict. The jury retires to deliberate. In certain circumstances, the court may give further charges after the jury retires. The jury returns written answers, in the form of a verdict, to the questions asked. The judge receives the verdict if it is in order (or may send the jury back to deliberate further if it is not). After receipt of the verdict, either side may demand that the jury be "polled" (that is, that each juror be asked individually whether the verdict is his or her verdict). The jurors then may be discharged.

Post-Trial Motions and Judgment. These steps are not part of the trial proper, although they are related closely to it. The verdict loser may move for judgment as a matter of law (also known as a "judgment notwithstanding the verdict") and for a new trial. Under the federal rules, the verdict loser makes both motions after judgment. The judge may receive written briefs concerning these motions, and sometimes the attorneys present oral argument. The court has the responsibility of applying the law to the jury's verdict to produce a judgment, which is an order granting or denying the requested relief.

The Subjects in This Chapter. Here, we take up these events (with some omissions and some additions) in roughly the order in which they occur in a trial. We also will briefly consider trial before the court. First, however, we offer the following Chapter Summary Problem, which you should read now but analyze at the end of the chapter (or you should treat it as your instructor directs).

PROBLEM A: CHAPTER 10 SUMMARY PROBLEM

JUDGE OR JURY TRIAL IN STONE v. CRESTVIEW APARTMENT CO. You represent Myron and Charlotte Stone. While both were away at their jobs, their three-year-old daughter — who was in the care of her usual babysitter — wandered off, fell into the apartment swimming pool, and suffered severe brain damage. She will require extensive medical and custodial care for the rest of her life. Your complaint charges Crestview Apartment Company with negligence for failing to keep the gate in the fence surrounding the pool locked. Consider the following questions:

1. *Right to Trial by Jury?* To what extent could you have a right to trial by jury in a federal court if the negligence claim is joined with a claim for an injunction against a fraudulent transfer (because you fear that Crestview may shift its assets to a newly formed entity)?
2. *Should You Challenge the Array?* You are convinced that jury venires in the county of suit are underinclusive of young people, ages 18 to 25, because jury summonses are based on voter registration lists. Should you make a challenge to the array on these grounds (and if so, when and how)?
3. *Should You Demand a Jury — Or Waive It?* There are some cases in which you would be better off trying your case before a judge without a jury. Is this one of those cases — or would you demand a jury (and if so, when and how)?
4. *Examination by the Judge or by the Attorneys.* The state courts in your jurisdiction give the parties the right to question the potential jurors, through their attorneys. The federal judges in the region, however, usually exercise the option to conduct the examination themselves alone. The attorney opposing you is much more experienced in jury trials than you are. If diversity of citizenship gave you the choice, would you file suit in state court or federal court?
5. *Insurance Questions During Voir Dire.* Assuming you are in federal court, you have the opportunity to file written requests for questions to be asked by the judge. The probability exists that you will want to have the jurors questioned about their insurance affiliations, both because (1) you believe that insurance-affiliated persons will be unfavorable jurors and because (2) Crestview is a small family business, and you would not want the jurors to assume that your suit would make it insolvent. But there is a strict prohibition in this jurisdiction upon introducing before the jury the fact that the defendant is, or is not, covered by liability insurance. How would you word the requested questions so as to maximize the probability of obtaining information, obtaining a basis for challenges for cause

if they exist, and counteracting the possibility of prejudice in favor of the defendant as a "little guys" corporation?

6. *The "Ideal Juror."* Try to construct a profile of the kinds of jurors you would want. Would you want young people or old people? Rich or poor? College-educated jurors or high-school dropouts? Professional people or blue-collar workers? Law students?

7. *Peremptory Challenges Based upon Ethnicity or Gender.* Assume that a survey indicates that Asian-Americans are strongly disposed to favor the defendant in this case, and that women are much more favorable to the plaintiff than men. [In fact, a survey did show these predispositions; this problem is based on a real case — *see* Appendix to § 10.03, below.] Is a strike illegal or unethical if it is influenced by these considerations? What steps should you take if 100% of defendant's peremptory challenges are against women?

8. *Court's Charge and Verdict.* Assume that the jury returns a general verdict for $2 million, but it also returns special verdicts on each of the permissible elements of damage, adding up to only $1 million. What would you urge the judge to do?

[Ed. Note: On April 11, 1991, a jury in a state court in Houston delivered a verdict for $84 million in a case in which a baby drowned and her young sister suffered brain damage after entering an apartment pool area through an unlocked gate. *See Jury Delivers $84 Million Verdict in Drowning Case*, Houston Chronicle, April 12, 1991, at A-21, col.2. What performance by the plaintiff's and defendant's lawyers do you think made the difference between this verdict and one for $100,000 — or for that matter, between this verdict and a defendant's verdict? Consider The New Dublin Jury Study, reproduced below at § 10.03.]

§ 10.02 The Right to Trial by Jury

[A] In Federal "Suits at Common Law"

Read U.S. Const. amend. VII and Fed. R. Civ. P. 38 (right to jury trial).

NOTE ON THE KINDS OF CLAIMS THAT CARRY THE RIGHT TO TRIAL BY JURY

The Federal Rules and the Seventh Amendment. So accustomed are we to thinking of the right to trial by jury as fundamental, that it may surprise you to learn that the right does not exist in all federal suits. The Seventh Amendment provides, "in suits at common law, . . . the right of trial by jury shall be preserved . . . ." From Chapter 5, you should remember that "suits at common law" are distinct from suits in equity. The equity courts did not try cases by jury before the adoption of the Seventh Amendment in 1791; therefore, it follows that the Seventh Amendment does not preserve a right to trial by jury in these cases. There are certain other areas (*e.g.*, admiralty cases) in which no right to jury trial historically was recognized and to which the right does not extend today. Federal Rule 38 does not create any additional rights, but only states that the right exists "as declared by the Seventh Amendment to the Constitution — or as provided by a federal statute."

The Right to Trial by Jury After the Merger of Law and Equity; The "Clean-Up Doctrine." Until the merger of law and equity, there was little question in federal practice about when the jury trial right applied. The law courts used juries, the equity courts did not, and the issue was principally one of jurisdiction. In fact, the equity courts sometimes decided legal claims without jury trial under what was called the "clean-up" doctrine: to avoid two separate suits in these two independent court systems, equity would "clean up" legal issues intertwined with a predominantly equitable claim. After the merger of law and equity, "preservation" of the right to jury trial required recognition of the historical nature of the claim as "legal" or "equitable." The task would be easy if the law remained unchanged and if litigants never joined legal claims with equitable ones in the same suit. Few areas of the law remained static, however; most evolved or were changed by statute.

Claims That Evolved Since Adoption of the Constitution; Statutory Claims. Another question is that of "preservation" of the right to jury trial for claims that did not exist when the Seventh Amendment was adopted. For example, strict product liability claims as we know them today did not exist before the twentieth century. Also, modern statutes create new causes of action. Does the Seventh Amendment "preserve" a right to trial by jury in an employment discrimination claim based upon the Civil Rights Act of 1964? What about statutes giving rise to complex litigation, so that a jury would be required to sit for two to five years? The materials that follow address these questions as well. *See also* James, *Right to a Jury Trial in Civil Actions*, 72 Yale L.J. 655 (1963).

[1] Effects of the Nonexistence of the Right in Equity Cases

HOW TO READ THE CASE OF *BEACON THEATRES v. WESTOVER*

In the case that follows, the action is complicated because the plaintiff sued for two kinds of relief: an injunction and a declaratory judgment. The injunction is clearly equitable. The declaratory judgment is harder to characterize — but if it relates to a claim that is legal in origin, the Supreme Court apparently would treat it as legal. The problem, therefore, is that the case includes both legal issues, which carry the right to jury trial, and equitable issues, which do not. But similar facts control both kinds of issues. How, then, should the district court decide these facts — with a jury, or without? The district judge adopted a solution by which he, alone, effectively would decide them. That procedure would have been acceptable in the past (remember the clean-up doctrine). In this decision, however, the Court holds that modern procedures change the picture — and the right to a jury trial does apply. Is anything left of the clean-up doctrine? And is the decision faithful to the "preservation" language of the Seventh Amendment?

BEACON THEATRES, INC. v. WESTOVER
359 U.S. 500 (1959)

MR. JUSTICE BLACK delivered the opinion of the Court.

Petitioner, Beacon Theatres, Inc., sought by mandamus to require a district judge in the Southern District of California to vacate certain orders alleged to deprive it of a jury trial of issues arising in a suit brought against it by Fox West Coast Theatres, Inc. The Court of Appeals for the Ninth Circuit refused the writ, holding that the trial judge had acted within his proper discretion in denying petitioner's request for a jury. . . . We granted certiorari. . . .

[Fox had contracts giving it exclusive rights of distribution of motion pictures in a certain geographic area. Beacon notified Fox that it considered these contracts to be in violation of the antitrust laws. Fox then filed suit against Beacon, alleging that the contracts were valid under the antitrust laws (specifically, the Sherman and Clayton Acts). Fox prayed for declaratory relief, under the Declaratory Judgment Act, that the contracts were not in violation of the antitrust laws. However, Fox also sought "an injunction . . . to prevent Beacon from instituting any action against Fox and its distributors" on the ground that Beacon had made alleged threats of treble damage suits against Fox and its distributors which, Fox alleged, subjected Fox to "duress and coercion" and deprived it of a valuable property right (the right to negotiate for exclusive distribution contracts). This latter claim, for an injunction, was ostensibly equitable.

[Beacon answered and counterclaimed. The counterclaim raised many of the same legal and factual issues as the complaint, in reverse. Specifically, Beacon alleged that the exclusive distribution contracts violated the antitrust laws, and it prayed for the treble damages allowed by those laws. Beacon also demanded a jury trial of all factual issues.

[The district judge concluded that the claims presented by Fox's complaint were "essentially equitable." Acting under the authority of Rule 42 (which allows separate trial of any claim or issue) and Rule 57 (which empowers the judge to order a speedy trial of a declaratory judgment action and to advance it on the docket), the district judge held that these "equitable" claims would be tried first. Further, since he thus considered plaintiff Fox's claims to be "equitable," the judge planned to determine them himself, without a jury. This order of trial probably would effectively deprive Beacon of the right to have fact issues determined by a jury, since any fact findings made by the judge probably would be binding, under the principle of collateral estoppel, in a later trial of the issues raised by Beacon's counterclaim. Beacon sought mandamus as a means of having the appellate court order the trial judge not to determine the "equitable" issues first and, more importantly, to preserve the right to jury trial. The Supreme Court, in this opinion, accepts Beacon's arguments.]

The District Court's finding that the Complaint for Declaratory Relief presented basically equitable issues draws no support from the Declaratory Judgment Act, 28 U.S.C. §§ 2201, 2202. . . . That statute, while allowing prospective defendants to sue to establish their nonliability, specifically preserves the right to jury trial for both parties. It follows that [Beacon] cannot be deprived of that right merely because Fox took advantage of the availability of declaratory relief to sue Beacon first. Since the right to trial by jury applies to treble damage suits under the antitrust laws, . . . the Sherman and Clayton Act issues on which Fox sought a declaration were essentially jury questions.

Nevertheless the Court of Appeals refused to upset the order of the district judge. . . . A party who is entitled to maintain a suit in equity for an injunction, said the court, may have all the issues in his suit determined by the judge without a jury regardless of whether legal rights are involved. . . .

[T]he Court of Appeals [then] held it was not an abuse of discretion of the district judge, acting under Federal Rule of Civil Procedure 42(b), to try the equitable cause first even though this might, through collateral estoppel, prevent a full jury trial of the counterclaim and cross-claim which were as effectively stopped as by an equity injunction. . . .

Viewed in this manner, the use of discretion by the trial court under Rule 42(b) to deprive Beacon of a full jury trial on its counterclaim and cross-claim, as well as on Fox's plea for declaratory relief, cannot be justified. Under the Federal Rules the same court may try both legal and equitable causes in the same action. . . . [The court can preserve the status quo if necessary by issuing a temporary injunction, which does not have collateral estoppel effect.] Whatever permanent injunctive relief Fox might be entitled to on the basis of the decision in this case could, of course, be given by the court after the jury renders its verdict. In this way the issues between these parties could be settled in one suit giving Beacon a full jury trial of every antitrust issue. . . . By contrast, the holding of the court below while granting Fox no additional protection unless the avoidance of jury trial be considered as such, would compel Beacon to split its antitrust case, trying part to a judge and part to a jury. . . .

Our decision is consistent with the plan of the Federal Rules and the Declaratory Judgment Act to effect substantial procedural reform while retaining a distinction between jury and nonjury issues and leaving substantive rights unchanged. . . . Thus, the justification for equity's deciding legal issues once it obtains jurisdiction, and refusing to dismiss a case, merely because subsequently a legal remedy becomes available, must be re-evaluated in the light of the liberal joinder provisions of the Federal Rules which allow legal and equitable causes to be brought and resolved in one civil action. . . . This is not only in accord with the spirit of the Rules and the Act but is required by the provision in the Rules that "[t]he right to trial by jury as declared by the Seventh Amendment to the Constitution or as given by a statute of the United States shall be preserved . . . inviolate." [The 2007 "restyling" amendments to the Federal Rules of Civil Procedure changed this language slightly — Eds.]

If there should be cases where the availability of declaratory judgment or joinder in one suit of legal and equitable causes would not in all respects protect the plaintiff seeking equitable relief from irreparable harm while affording a jury trial in the legal cause, the trial court will necessarily have to use its discretion in deciding whether the legal or equitable cause should be tried first. Since the right to jury trial is a constitutional one, however, . . . that discretion is very narrowly limited and must, wherever possible, be exercised to preserve jury trial. . . . [O]nly under the most imperative circumstances, circumstances which in view of the flexible procedures of the Federal Rules we cannot now anticipate, can the right to a jury trial of legal issues be lost through prior determination of equitable claims. . . .

Reversed.

Mr. Justice Frankfurter took no part in the consideration or decision of this case.

Mr. Justice Stewart, with whom Mr. Justice Harlan and Mr. Justice Whittaker concur, dissenting.

. . . The district judge simply exercised his inherent discretion, now explicitly confirmed by the Federal Rules of Civil Procedure, to schedule the trial of an equitable claim in advance of an action at law. . . .

The Court's opinion does not, of course, hold or even suggest that a court of equity may never determine "legal rights." For indeed it is precisely such rights which the Chancellor, when his jurisdiction has been properly invoked, has often been called upon to decide. Issues of fact are rarely either "legal" or "equitable." All depends upon the context in which they arise.

. . . It has also been long settled that the District Court in its discretion may order the trial of a suit in equity in advance of an action at law between the same parties, even if there is a factual issue common to both. . . .

The Rules make possible the trial of legal and equitable claims in the same proceeding, but they expressly affirm the power of a trial judge to determine the order in which claims shall be heard. Rule 42(b). Certainly the Federal Rules were not intended to undermine the basic structure of equity jurisprudence, developed over the centuries and explicitly recognized in the United States Constitution.

For these reasons I think the petition for a writ of mandamus should have been dismissed.

NOTES AND QUESTIONS

(1) *Does the Clean-Up Doctrine Still Exist?* Is anything left of the clean-up doctrine after *Beacon Theatres v. Westover?* [Note: The Court says that "only under the most imperative circumstances, . . . which . . . we cannot now anticipate, can the right to jury trial of legal issues be lost through prior determination of equitable claims."] For a further nail in the coffin of the clean-up doctrine, see *Dairy Queen v. Wood*, below.

(2) *Is Beacon Theatres Consistent With the Historical Approach of the Seventh Amendment "Preservation" Requirement?* It repeatedly has been held that the Seventh Amendment adopts a historical approach. *Curtis v. Loether,* 415 U.S. 189 (1974); *cf. Parsons v. Bedford*, 28 U.S. (3 Pet.) 433 (1830). The language of the amendment "preserves" the right as it existed in England at the time of adoption of the Bill of Rights in 1791; it does not purport to create a broader right than then existed. There is little question, however, that *Beacon Theatres* extends a right to trial by jury to a case in which, at the time of adoption of the Bill of Rights, it would not have existed. Is *Beacon Theatres*, therefore, inconsistent with the historical approach of the Seventh Amendment, as Justice Stewart's dissent implies?

On the other hand, equity has never been static, and isn't the Court correct in arguing that an equitable doctrine may disappear if it is replaced with an adequate remedy at law? In that event, perhaps procedural changes (such as those of the Federal Rules) could indirectly limit equitable doctrines — and thereby affect the right to jury trial. Can this reasoning reconcile *Beacon Theatres* with an historical view of the Seventh Amendment?

(3) *"Suits at Common Law" as an Evolving Concept.* Perhaps the historical view of the Seventh Amendment has flexibility built into it, since the common law itself is evolutionary. Consider the following language from *Parsons v. Bedford, supra*, 28 U.S. (3 Pet.) at 447:

> [The drafters of the Constitution understood the "common law" to include] suits in which legal rights were to be ascertained and determined, in contradistinction to those where equitable rights [or other nonlegal rights] alone were recognized. . . . Probably, there were few, if any, states in the union, in which some new legal remedies, differing from the old common-law forms, were not in use; but in which, however, the trial by jury intervened. . . . [T]he amendment then may well be construed to embrace all suits, which are not of equity and admiralty jurisdiction, whatever may be the peculiar form which they may assume to settle legal rights.

Is *Beacon Theatres* consistent with an historical view of the Seventh Amendment when viewed in light of this "evolution" argument? *See* Rothstein, *Beacon Theatres and the Constitutional Right to Jury Trial*, 51 A.B.A.J. 1145 (1965).

(4) *The Disadvantages of a Jury Trial, and Advantages of Equity, in Beacon Theatres.* Fox, the plaintiff in *Beacon Theatres*, may well have been in a quandary and in need of a very rapid declaration of its rights. If it continued to use exclusive contracts, it might be in continued violation of the antitrust laws, and its conduct could make it liable for damages — treble damages, in fact, under the antitrust laws. But if it ceased to rely upon

exclusive contracts, it might later find that these arrangements were perfectly legal and gave an advantage in the meantime to its competitors. One of the serious disadvantages of jury trial is that it often entails lengthy delay. Under the arrangement ordered by the Supreme Court, the trial judge might hold for Fox in the preliminary injunction hearing, thus seemingly validating Fox's reliance on the legality of its conduct; but findings on preliminary injunction are not binding, and a jury could saddle Fox with treble damages, several years later. Yet in *Beacon Theatres*, the Court criticized the District Court's accelerated hearing plan on the ground that it "grant[ed] Fox no additional protection unless the avoidance of jury trial be considered as such." Is this statement really true? Has the Court, in fact, deprived Fox of the adaptability, flexibility, and accommodation to the needs of the lawsuit that are the principal characteristics of equitable remedies?

(5) *Avoiding Dependence of the Jury Trial Right Upon Who Sues First.* The holding in *Beacon Theatres* does have the advantage of avoiding dependence of the jury trial right on who sues, or has her claim determined, first. After *Beacon*, a potential defendant cannot deprive a plaintiff with a legal claim of her right to jury trial, merely by beating the plaintiff to the punch with an equitable suit and having it heard first. This concern gives rise to another question: Can a plaintiff avoid a jury trial by carefully structuring the claim as equitable when she might have sought legal relief? Consider *Dairy Queen v. Wood,* which follows.

DAIRY QUEEN, INC. v. WOOD, 369 U.S. 469 (1962). The respondent licensed petitioner to use the trademark "Dairy Queen" in certain parts of Pennsylvania, in exchange for contractual payments, which varied over time with the petitioner's receipts. The respondent claimed that the petitioner had failed to make the required payments and filed suit asking for three kinds of relief: (1) temporary and permanent injunctions against the petitioner's use of the trademark; (2) an accounting to determine the exact amount of money owed by the petitioner; and (3) an injunction against the petitioner's collecting any money from Dairy Queen stores during the accounting.

The requested injunctions were equitable claims. The request for an "accounting" also ostensibly invoked an equitable remedy. (An equitable "accounting" is available when the accounts between the parties are of such a "complicated nature" that they can satisfactorily be unraveled only by a court of equity.) The respondent had thus structured the complaint so that it appeared to seek purely equitable relief, apparently in an attempt to avoid jury trial; indeed when the petitioner demanded a trial by jury, the respondent moved to strike the demand. The District Court granted the motion, struck the jury demand, and explained that the action was "purely equitable" or, if it was not purely equitable, that whatever legal issues were raised were "incidental" to equitable issues and therefore triable before the Court without a jury.

The Supreme Court reversed, holding that the petitioner had the right to jury trial. It first rejected the argument that jury trial could be denied as to legal issues that were "incidental" to equitable issues. "[O]ur previous decisions make it plain that no such rule may be applied in the federal courts," said the Court. "The holding in *Beacon Theatres* was that where both legal and equitable issues are presented in a single case, 'only under the most imperative circumstances, circumstances which in view of the flexible procedures of the federal rules we cannot now anticipate, can the right to a jury trial legal issues be lost through prior determination of equitable claims.' " The Court then went on to hold that the claim for an "accounting" was really a legal claim rather than an equitable one because it was "an action on a debt allegedly due under a contract, seeking a 'money judgment' ":

> Petitioner's contention, as set forth in its petition for mandamus to the Court of Appeals and reiterated in its briefs before this Court, is that insofar as the complaint requests a money judgment it presents a claim which is unquestionably legal. We agree with that contention. The most natural construction of the respondents' claim for a money judgment would seem to be that it is a claim that they are entitled to recover whatever was owed them under the contract as of the date of its purported termination plus damages for infringement of their trade-mark since that date. . . . As an action on a debt allegedly due under a contract, it would be difficult to conceive of an action of a more traditionally legal character. And as an action for damages based upon a charge of trademark infringement, it would be no less subject to cognizance by a court of law.
>
> The respondent's contention that this money claim is "purely equitable" is based primarily upon the fact that their complaint is cast in terms of an "accounting," rather than in terms of an action for "debt" or "damages." But the constitutional right to trial by jury cannot be made to depend upon the choice of words used in the pleadings. The necessary prerequisite to the right to maintain a suit for an equitable accounting, like all other equitable remedies, is, as we pointed out in *Beacon Theatres*, the absence of an adequate remedy at law. Consequently, in order to maintain such a suit on a cause of action cognizable at law, as this one is, the plaintiff must be able to show that the "accounts between the parties" are of such a "complicated nature" that only a court of equity can satisfactorily unravel them. In view of the powers given to District Courts by Federal Rule of Civil Procedure 53(b) to appoint masters to assist the jury in those exceptional cases where the legal issues are too complicated for the jury adequately to handle alone, the burden of such a showing is considerably increased and it will indeed be a rare case in which it can be met. But be that as it may, this is certainly not such a case. A jury, under proper instructions from the court, could readily determine the recovery, if any, to be had here, whether the theory finally settled upon is that of breach of contract, that of trade-mark infringement, or any combination of the two. The legal remedy cannot be characterized as inadequate merely because the measure of damages may necessitate a look into petitioner's business records. . . .

NOTES AND QUESTIONS

(1) *Bankruptcy: Katchen v. Landy, 382 U.S. 323 (1966).* In *Katchen*, the petitioner filed a claim in a bankruptcy proceeding for debts allegedly due him by the bankrupt. The trustee in bankruptcy promptly sued the petitioner to recover payments made by the bankrupt to the petitioner as "voidable preferences" (a voidable preference is a transfer on the eve of bankruptcy that preferentially benefits an individual creditor at the expense of other creditors, and it is subject to being set aside). The petitioner demanded a jury trial of the voidable preference issue. He pointed out that he would have been entitled to a jury trial on that issue if sued in District Court, and therefore, to deny him a jury trial simply because he had filed a bankruptcy claim would be inconsistent with *Beacon Theatres* and *Dairy Queen.* The Supreme Court rejected the argument and denied the petitioner a jury trial. The Court admitted that petitioner might be entitled to a jury trial if he had presented no claim and had awaited a federal district court action by the trustee, but "when the same issue arises as part of the process of allowance and disallowance of [bankruptcy] claims, it is triable in equity. The Bankruptcy Act . . . converts the

creditor's legal claim into an equitable claim. . . ." The Court also pointed out that the "delay and expense" of jury trials would be inconsistent "with the equitable purposes of the Bankruptcy Act" because "petitioner's argument would require that in every case where a jury trial is demanded the proceeding on allowance of claims must be suspended." Is *Katchen v. Landy* consistent with *Beacon Theatres* and *Dairy Queen*? *See* Sabino, *Jury Trials in the Bankruptcy Court: A Continuing Controversy*, 90 Com. L.J. 342 (1985).

(2) *Ross v. Bernhard, 396 U.S. 531 (1970).* The petitioners brought a shareholders' derivative suit against corporate managers for allegedly paying excessive brokerage commissions to a firm with which they were affiliated. The trial court granted the petitioners' demand for jury trial; the Second Circuit reversed; and, finally, the Supreme Court reversed the reversal, upholding the right to jury trial. The Supreme Court admitted that a shareholders' derivative suit is a creature of equity, since the common law provided no remedy by which shareholders could make corporate officers and directors accountable. However, the Court noted that the shareholders' suit was simply an equitable device to allow shareholders to assert claims owned by the corporation against corporate managers. "The heart of the action is the corporate claim. If it presents a legal issue, one entitling the corporation to a jury trial under the Seventh Amendment, the right to a jury is not forfeited merely because the stockholders' right to sue must first be adjudicated as an equitable issue triable to the Court. *Beacon* and *Dairy Queen* require no less." Justice Stewart dissented, arguing that the shareholders' derivative suit historically could be brought only in equity and therefore carried no constitutional right to jury trial, as a matter of "the most elementary logic."

(3) *The "Ross Footnote": A Three-Part Test for the Right to Jury Trial.* In a famous footnote, the majority opinion in *Ross v. Bernhard* sets out three factors for distinguishing legal from equitable claims. 396 U.S. at 538 n. 10. "[T]he 'legal' nature of an issue is determined by considering, first, the . . . custom of reference to such questions [before the merger of law and equity]; second, the remedy sought; and third, the practical abilities and limitations of juries." The first factor in this "*Ross* Footnote Test" is the familiar historical approach supported by the language of the Seventh Amendment. The second factor, which looks to the remedy as well as the claim, may also be viewed historically. The third factor, "the practical abilities and limitations of juries," is new; it seems to imply an approach oriented more toward policy considerations. How should the third factor be taken into account in determining whether there is a right to jury trial of a claim created by statute? This issue is dealt with in subsection 10.02[A][2], below. How should the "*Ross* footnote" affect a huge, complex case — one that might take several years to try, include hundreds of thousands of documents as evidence, and require resolution of fact issues inseparable from legal questions? Should the "practical abilities and limitations of juries" then result in denial of jury trial where it would otherwise exist? *See* subsection 10.02[B], below.

(4) *Equitable Fact Findings That Collaterally Estop Later Legal Issues: Parklane Hosiery Co. v. Shore, 439 U.S. 322 (1979).* The Securities and Exchange Commission sued Parklane and twelve of its personnel for an injunction against the distribution of a proxy statement that the SEC alleged was materially false and misleading. After a four-day trial, the District Court found, as a fact, that the proxy statement was indeed materially false and misleading. Then, in a separate suit filed as a shareholders' derivative suit against the same defendants, the plaintiffs moved for partial summary judgment on the ground that the findings in the injunction action were binding against these defendants in the derivative suit also, under the doctrine of collateral estoppel. The lower courts

denied the motion on the ground that it would violate the Seventh Amendment for equity fact findings made by a judge to become binding determinations of legal issues that would otherwise be triable of right by a jury. The Supreme Court reversed, holding that collateral estoppel could apply. Justice Stewart (who had dissented in *Beacon Theatres* and *Ross*) wrote the opinion. He recognized that "there would have been no collateral estoppel in 1791," when the Seventh Amendment was adopted; the procedure of that day would not allow it "because of lack of mutuality" (*i.e.*, since Parklane and the other defendants would be bound but the shareholder plaintiffs would not). Today, however, many jurisdictions allow collateral estoppel despite lack of mutuality, and — said Justice Stewart — "nothing in the Seventh Amendment dictates a different result" merely because "[t]he law of collateral estoppel . . . has evolved since 1791."

Justice Rehnquist dissented, in part because of a "nagging sense of unfairness as to the way petitioners have been treated." More importantly, the majority reduced the jury trial right, "which Blackstone praised as 'the glory of English law,' to a mere 'neutral' factor . . . in the name of procedural reform." But procedural evolution, left unchecked, could "erode" this valued right. To Justice Rehnquist, proper protection lay in the historical approach to the Seventh Amendment: "If a jury would have been impaneled in a particular kind of case in 1791, then the Seventh Amendment requires a jury trial today, if either party so decides." Thus, Justice Rehnquist's solitary dissent would have extended the Bill of Rights where the other eight Justices would not. Are his arguments persuasive?

(5) *The Supreme Court "Rediscovers" the Right to Jury Trial: The Granfinanciera, Lytle, Tull, and Terry Cases.* In a quartet of cases, the Supreme Court returned to the jury trial issues it decided in *Katchen v. Landy* and *Parklane Hosiery Co. v. Shore* [Notes 1 & 4] and elaborated on the question of jury trial in modern statutory actions (*see* below). In each case, the right to jury trial was vindicated, and the Court seemed to return to the expansive approach found in *Beacon Theatres, Dairy Queen*, and *Ross*.

In *Granfinanciera, S.A. v. Nordberg*, 492 U.S. 33 (1989), the Supreme Court revisited *Katchen v. Landy*'s exception to jury trials in bankruptcy courts. The Court held that the Seventh Amendment entitles a person who has not submitted a claim against a bankruptcy estate to a jury trial in bankruptcy court when sued by the trustee in bankruptcy to recover an allegedly fraudulent monetary transfer. As in *Katchen*, the Court found the action one that would ordinarily carry with it a right to jury trial based upon its 18th Century English analogs and request for legal relief. In dissent, Justice White argued *Katchen* could not be distinguished on the basis of whether the funds in dispute were part of the bankruptcy estate and that the Court *sub silentio* had overruled *Katchen. See also Symposium, Jury Trials in Bankruptcy Courts*, 65 Am. Bankr. L.J. 1 (1991).

In *Lytle v. Household Manufacturing, Inc.*, 494 U.S. 545 (1990), the Supreme Court limited *Parklane Hosiery*, holding that the Seventh Amendment precludes giving collateral estoppel effect to a District Court's determination of issues common to equitable and legal claims when the court resolved the equitable claims first only because it erroneously dismissed the legal claims. Lytle, an African-American, had sued Household under both Title VII of the Civil Rights Act of 1964 and 42 U.S.C. § 1981 for allegedly discriminatory termination of his employment. The trial court dismissed the § 1981 claims that would have entitled Lytle to a jury trial and found against Lytle on the Title VII claims. The Court of Appeals affirmed the trial court's disposition (even though it noted the § 1981 dismissal was apparently erroneous), because the Title VII determinations would collaterally estop Lytle's § 1981 claims. The Supreme Court reversed, holding that *Beacon Theatres*, not *Parklane Hosiery*, governs when legal claims are erroneously dismissed from an action containing both legal and equitable claims. But for the erroneous dismissal, the court could not have resolved issues common to both claims without a jury.

The other two cases (*Tull v. United States* and *Chauffeurs, Teamsters and Helpers v. Terry*) are covered in the section that follows.

PROBLEM B

C & K ENGINEERING CONTRACTORS v. AMBER STEEL CO. (*see* § 10.02[D], below). The plaintiff sues under the terms of a contract. A contract action is a classic common law claim. However, in this case, the plaintiff attempts to base the action on the equitable doctrine of promissory estoppel (under which a party may be bound by a promise if it induces injurious reliance by the other). You may assume that state law would recognize such a claim and would hold the defendant bound to perform the promise; further, state law grants a right to monetary damages in such actions. You may also assume that the state courts, following a decision of the state supreme court interpreting the state constitution, would deny a jury trial (in fact, the California Supreme Court did, on the theory that the "gist of the action" was equitable; *see* § 10.02[D]).

If defendant removes the case to federal court and demands a jury trial, should the court grant it? [Note: perhaps it would be best to answer in terms of plaintiff's best arguments and defendant's best arguments.] Incidentally, you should not be influenced by what the state courts would do; federal law controls. [Why?]

[2] Statutory Actions

TULL v. UNITED STATES
481 U.S. 412 (1987)

JUSTICE BRENNAN delivered the opinion of the Court.

[Section 1913 of The Federal Clean Water Act subjects a violator to an injunction as well as to "a civil penalty not to exceed $10,000 per day" in some cases. The Government sued Tull, a real estate developer, for dumping fill on certain wetlands, and it sought both an injunction and a large civil penalty — in excess of $22 million. The District Court denied Tull's timely demand for a jury trial. Sitting without a jury, the trial judge found that Tull had committed violations of the Act, but he limited the civil penalty to a drastically reduced amount of no more than $325,000.

[The Clean Water Act, of course, did not exist at the time of adoption of the Seventh Amendment. The Supreme Court nevertheless holds that the jury trial right can apply to statutory claims, and that Tull is entitled to a jury trial on liability — but not on the amount of the penalty.]

II

. . . The Court has construed [the Seventh Amendment] to require a jury trial on the merits in those actions that are analogous to "Suits at common law." . . . This analysis applies not only to common law forms of action, but also to causes of action created by congressional enactment.

To determine whether a statutory action is more similar to cases that were tried in courts of law than to suits tried in courts of equity or admiralty, the Court must examine both the nature of the action and of the remedy sought. First, we compare the statutory action to 18th-century actions brought in the courts of England prior to the merger of the courts of law and equity. . . . Second, we examine the remedy sought and determine whether it is legal or equitable in nature. . . .

The petitioner analogizes this Government suit under § 1319(d) to an action in debt within the jurisdiction of English courts of law. Prior to the enactment of the Seventh Amendment, English courts had held that a civil penalty suit was a particular species of an action in debt that was within the jurisdiction of the courts of law. . . .

After the adoption of the Seventh Amendment, federal courts followed this English common law in treating the civil penalty suit as a particular type of an action in debt, requiring a jury trial. . . . Actions by the Government to recover civil penalties under statutory provisions therefore historically have been viewed as one type of action in debt requiring trial by jury. . . .

The Government argues, however, that [t]he closer historical analogue is an action to abate a public nuisance. . . .

Whether . . . a public nuisance action is a better analogy than an action in debt is debatable. But we need not decide the question. As *Pernell v. Southall Realty,* 416 U.S., at 375, 94 S. Ct., at 1729, cautioned, the fact that the subject matter of a modern statutory action and an 18th-century English action are close equivalents "is irrelevant for Seventh Amendment purposes," because "that Amendment requires trial by jury in actions unheard of at common law." It suffices that we conclude that both the public nuisance action and the action in debt are appropriate analogies to the instant statutory action. . . .

We reiterate our previously expressed view that characterizing the relief sought is "[m]ore important" than finding a precisely analogous common law cause of action in determining whether the Seventh Amendment guarantees a jury trial.

A civil penalty was a type of remedy at common law that could only be enforced in courts of law. The action authorized by subsection 1319(d) is of this character. Subsection (d) does not direct that the "civil penalty" imposed be calculated solely on the basis of equitable determinations, such as the profits gained from violations of the statute, but simply imposes a maximum penalty of $10,000 per day of violation. The legislative history of the Act reveals that Congress wanted the district court to consider the need for retribution and deterrence, in addition to restitution, when it imposed civil penalties. . . .

Thus, the petitioner has a constitutional right to a jury trial to determine his liability on the legal claims.

III

The remaining issue is whether the petitioner additionally has a Seventh Amendment right to a jury assessment of the civil penalties. The legislative history of the 1977 Amendments to the Clean Water Act shows [t]hat Congress intended that trial judges perform the highly discretionary calculations necessary to award civil penalties after liability is found. . . .

The answer must depend on whether the jury must shoulder this responsibility as necessary to preserve the "substance of the common-law right of trial by jury. . . ." Is a jury role necessary for that purpose? We do not think so. "Only those incidents which are regarded as fundamental, as inherent in and of the essence of the system of trial by jury, are placed beyond the reach of the legislature." The assessment of a civil penalty is not one of the "most fundamental elements." Congress' authority to fix the penalty by statute has not been questioned, and it was also the British practice. . . .

Since Congress itself may fix the civil penalties, it may delegate that determination to trial judges. In this case, highly discretionary calculations that take into account multiple factors are necessary in order to set civil penalties under the Clean Water Act. These are the kinds of calculations traditionally performed by judges. . . .

IV

We conclude that the Seventh Amendment required that the petitioner's demand for a jury trial be granted to determine his liability, but that the trial court and not the jury should determine the amount of penalties, if any. . . .

CHAUFFEURS, TEAMSTERS AND HELPERS, LOCAL NO. 391 v. TERRY
494 U.S. 558 (1990)

JUSTICE MARSHALL delivered the opinion of the Court except as to Part III-A.

This case presents the question whether an employee who seeks relief in the form of backpay for a union's alleged breach of its duty of fair representation has a right to trial by jury. We hold that the Seventh Amendment entitles such a plaintiff to a jury trial.

[Terry and other employees of McLean Trucking Company sued McLean and their union, alleging that McLean had breached its collective-bargaining agreement with the union in violation of § 301 of the Labor Management Relations Act and that the union had violated the duty of fair representation it owed to them by not pressing their grievances as a result of a series of transfers, layoffs and recalls by McLean. Terry requested a jury trial. The union moved to strike the jury demand on the ground that no right to a jury trial exists in a duty-of-fair-representation suit. The District Court denied the union's motion and the Court of Appeals affirmed.]

[The Supreme Court first holds that "[w]hether the employee sues both the labor union and the employer or only one of those entities, he must prove the same two facts to recover money damages: that the employer's action violated the terms of the collective bargaining agreement and that the union breached its duty of fair representation."]

III.

We turn now to the constitutional issue presented in this case — whether respondents are entitled to a jury trial. . . . The right to a jury trial included more than the common-law forms of action recognized in 1791; the phrase "Suits at common-law" refers to "suits in which *legal* rights [are] to be ascertained and determined, in contradistinction to those where equitable rights alone [are] recognized, and equitable remedies [are] administered." *Parsons v. Bedford*. . . . The right extends to causes of action created by Congress. *Tull v. United States*.

To determine whether a particular action will resolve legal rights, we examine both the nature of the issues involved and the remedy sought. "First, we compare the statutory action to 18th-century actions brought in the courts of England prior to the merger of the courts of law and equity. Second, we examine the remedy sought and determine whether it is legal or equitable in nature." *Tull*. The second inquiry is the more important in our analysis. *Grandfinanciera, S.A. v. Nordberg*.

A

An action for breach of a union's duty of fair representation was unknown in 18th-century England; in fact, collective-bargaining was unlawful. We must therefore look for an analogous cause of action that existed in the 18th century to determine whether the nature of this duty of fair representation suit is legal or equitable.

The Union contends that this duty of fair representation action resembles a suit brought to vacate an arbitration award because respondents seek to set aside the result of the grievance process. In the 18th Century, an action to set aside an arbitration award was considered equitable. . . .

The arbitration analogy is inapposite, however, to . . . this case. No grievance committee has considered respondents' claim that the Union violated its duty of fair representation; the grievance process was concerned only with the employer's alleged breach of the collective-bargaining agreement. . . .

The Union next argues that respondents' duty of fair representation action is comparable to an action by a trust beneficiary against a trustee for breach of fiduciary duty. Such actions were within the exclusive jurisdiction of courts of equity. This analogy is far more persuasive than the arbitration analogy. Just as a trustee must act in the best interests of the beneficiaries, a union, as the exclusive representative of the workers, must exercise its power to act on behalf of the employees in good faith. Moreover, just as a beneficiary does not directly control the action of a trustee, an individual employee lacks direct control over a union's actions taken on his behalf.

The trust analogy extends to a union's handling of grievances. In most cases, a trustee has the exclusive authority to sue third parties who injure the beneficiaries' interests in the trust. . . . Similarly, the union typically has broad discretion in its decision whether and how to pursue an employee's grievance against an employer. . . .

Respondents contend that their duty of fair representation suit is less like a trust action than an attorney malpractice action, which was historically an action at law. . . .

[But] [u]nlike employees represented by a union, a client controls the significant decisions concerning his representation. Moreover, a client can fire his attorney if he is dissatisfied with his attorney's performance. . . . Thus, we find the malpractice analogy less convincing than the trust analogy.

Nevertheless, the trust analogy does not persuade us to characterize respondents' claim as wholly equitable. . . . To recover from the Union here, respondents must prove both that McLean violated § 301 by breaching the collective bargaining agreement and that the Union breached its duty of fair representation. When viewed in isolation, the duty of fair representation is analogous to a claim against a trustee for breach of fiduciary duty. The § 301 issue, however, is comparable to a breach of contract claim — a legal issue.

Respondents' action against the Union thus encompasses both equitable and legal issues. The first part of our Seventh Amendment inquiry, then, leaves us in equipoise as to whether respondents are entitled to a jury trial.

[The Court here proceeds to the second part of the inquiry: whether the remedy is legal or equitable in nature.] [I]n this case, the only remedy sought is a request for compensatory damages representing backpay and benefits. Generally, an action for money damages was "the traditional form of relief offered in the courts of law.:" [B]ecause we conclude that the remedy respondents seek has none of the attributes that must be present before we will find an exception to the general rule and characterize damages as equitable, we find that the remedy sought by respondents is legal.

First, we have characterized damages as equitable where they are restitutionary, such as in "action[s] for disgorgement of improper profits," *Tull.* The backpay sought by respondents is not money wrongfully held by the Union, but wages and benefits they would have received from McLean had the Union processed the employees' grievances properly. Such relief is not restitutionary. . . .

The Union argues that the backpay relief sought here must nonetheless be considered equitable because this Court has labeled backpay awarded under Title VII [of the Civil Rights Act of 1964], 42 U.S.C. § 2000e *et seq.* (1982 ed.), as equitable. . . . We are not convinced.

The Court has never held that a plaintiff seeking backpay under Title VII has a right to a jury trial. Assuming, without deciding, that such a Title VII plaintiff has no right to a jury trial, the Union's argument does not persuade us that respondents are not entitled to a jury trial here. Congress specifically characterized backpay under Title VII as a form of "equitable relief." 42 U.S.C. § 2000e5(g). ("[T]he court may . . . order such affirmative action as may be appropriate, which may include, but is not limited to, reinstatement or hiring of employees, with or without back pay . . . , or any other equitable relief as the court deems appropriate"). *See also Curtis v. Loether* [415 U.S. 189 (1974)] (distinguishing backpay under Title VII from damages under Title VIII, the fair housing provision of the Civil Rights Act, 42 U.S.C. §§ 3609-3619, which the Court characterized as "legal" for Seventh Amendment purposes). Congress made no similar pronouncement regarding the duty of fair representation. Furthermore, the Court has noted that backpay sought from an employer under Title VII would generally be restitutionary in nature, *see Curtis v. Loether*, in contrast to the damages sought here from the union, Thus, the remedy sought in this duty of fair representation case is clearly different from backpay sought for violations of Title VII.

We hold, then, that the remedy of backpay sought in this duty of fair representation action is legal in nature. Considering both parts of the Seventh Amendment inquiry, we find that respondents are entitled to a jury trial on all issues presented in their suit.

IV

On balance, our analysis of the nature of respondents' duty of fair representation action and the remedy they seek convinces us that this action is a legal one. Although the search for an adequate 18th-century analog revealed that the claim includes both legal and equitable issues, the money damages respondents seek are the type of relief traditionally awarded by courts of law. Thus, the Seventh Amendment entitles respondents to a jury trial, and we therefore affirm the judgment of the Court of Appeals.

JUSTICE BRENNAN, concurring in part and concurring in the judgment.

I agree with the Court that respondents seek a remedy that is legal in nature and that the Seventh Amendment entitles respondents to a jury trial on their duty of fair representation claims. I do not join that part of the opinion which reprises the particular historical analysis this Court has employed to determine whether a claim is a "Suit at common law" under the Seventh Amendment, because I believe the historical test can and should be simplified.

I would decide Seventh Amendment questions on the basis of the relief sought. If the relief is legal in nature, I would hold that the parties have a constitutional right to trial by jury — unless Congress has permissibly delegated the particular dispute to a non-Article III decisionmaker and jury trials would frustrate Congress' purposes in enacting a particular statutory scheme.

. . . For the past decade and a half, this Court has explained that the two parts of the historical test are not equal in weight, that the nature of the remedy is more important than the nature of the right. [T]here remains little purpose to our rattling through dusty attics of ancient writs. The time has come to borrow William of Occam's razor and sever this portion of our analysis.

Requiring judges, with neither the training nor time necessary for reputable historical scholarship, to root through the tangle of primary and secondary sources to determine which of a hundred or so writs is analogous to the right at issue has embroiled courts in recondite controversies better left to legal historians. . . .

Indeed, . . . it is unlikely that the simplified Seventh Amendment analysis I propose will result in different decision than the analysis in current use. In the unusual circumstance that the nature of the remedy could be characterized equally as legal or equitable, [t]he comparison of a contemporary statutory action [t]o some ill-fitting ancient writ is too shaky a basis for the resolution of an issue as significant as the availability of a trial by jury. If, in the rare case, a tie-breaker is needed, let us break the tie in favor of a jury trial.

Justice Stevens, concurring in part and concurring the judgment.

. . . As I have suggested in the past, I believe that duty of fair representation action resembles a common law action against an attorney for malpractice more closely than it does any other form of action. . . .

Duty of fair representation suits are for the most part ordinary civil actions involving the stuff of contract and malpractice disputes. There is accordingly no ground for excluding these actions from the jury right. . . .

Justice Kennedy, with whom Justice O'Connor and Justice Scalia join, dissenting.

. . . .

I disagree with the analytic innovation of the Court that identification of the trust action as a model for modern duty of fair representation actions is insufficient to decide the case. The Seventh Amendment requires us to determine whether the duty of fair representation action "is more similar to cases that were tried in courts of law than to suits tried in courts of equity." *Tull v. United States*. Having made this decision in favor of an equitable action, our inquiry should end. Because the Court disagrees with this proposition, I dissent. . . .

The Court must adhere to the historical test in determining the right to a jury because the language of the Constitution requires it. The Seventh Amendment "preserves" the right to jury trial in civil cases . . . . Our obligation to the Constitution and its Bill of Rights, no less than the compact we have with the generation that wrote them for us, do not permit us to disregard provisions that some may think to be mere matters of historical form.

NOTES AND QUESTIONS

(1) *Tension Among Tests Emphasizing the Right, or the Remedy, or Functional (Practical) Concerns.* The views of the Justices illustrate the tension that exists between

the traditional historical approach and modern, more functional approaches. Should the focus be on remedies rather than analogies to 18th century forms of action? (Do we need a simpler test — is Justice Brennan correct that judges are poorly equipped as historical researchers?) But, given the text of the Seventh Amendment, isn't Justice Kennedy correct that the court simply must do the best it can using an historical approach?

(2) *Is the Court "Fudging" the Issue by Preferring Juries Even When the Constitution Doesn't?* Given *Granfinanciera, Lytle, Tull,* and *Terry,* hasn't the Court returned to an approach that prefers juries as factfinders "except under the most imperative circumstances," one that selectively uses the historical test only when it clearly supports the right to trial by jury?

(3) *Can the Terry Holding Persuasively Be Distinguished from the Confusing Issue of Monetary Relief in Civil Rights Cases?: Curtis v. Loether* [*cited in Terry*], *415 U.S. 189 (1974).* In the *Curtis* case, the Court held that a defendant sued for housing discrimination had a right to jury trial. The principal reason was that the applicable statute, Title VIII of the Civil Rights Act of 1968, created a straightforward damage remedy for a Fair Housing violation. But the *Curtis* Court sharply distinguished Title VII of the Civil Rights Act of 1964, which redresses employment discrimination. Title VII provides a remedy consisting of "such affirmative action as may be appropriate, which may include, but is not limited to, reinstatement or hiring of employees with or without back pay [or] any other equitable relief as the court deems appropriate." Thus, Congress expressly provided that the remedy for employment discrimination was to be called "equitable," and it gave it equitable characteristics. "In Title VII [employment discrimination] cases, [b]ackpay [is] an integral part of an equitable remedy, a form of restitution," said the *Curtis* Court. Furthermore, "the decision to award backpay is committed to the discretion of the judge," who flexibly considers and balances all forms of equitable relief contemplated by Title VII. Hence, denial of jury trial in Title VII actions was distinguishable. In 1991, Congress amended Title VII to provide a statutory right to trial by jury in connection with claims for compensatory damages (which do not include backpay or interest on backpay) and punitive damages in cases of intentional employment discrimination. *See* 42 U.S.C. § 1981a.

(4) *No Right to Jury Trial in Administrative Proceedings — A "Public Rights" Exception: Atlas Roofing Co. v. Occupational Safety & Health Review Commission, 430 U.S. 442 (1977).* Petitioners claimed the right to trial by jury in Occupational Safety & Health Act ("OSHA") proceedings, but the Commission's administrative law judges rejected this argument and imposed fines on petitioners in accordance with the administrative scheme of the Act. The Supreme Court upheld the denial of jury trial:

> At least in cases in which "public rights" are being litigated — *e.g.*, cases in which the government sues in its sovereign capacity to enforce public rights . . . — the Seventh Amendment does not prohibit Congress from assigning the fact finding function . . . to an administrative forum with which the jury would be incompatible.

The Court emphasized that "[w]holly private tort, contract and property cases . . . are not at all implicated," but it also said:

> More to the point, it is apparent from the history of jury trial and civil matters that fact finding . . . was never the exclusive province of the jury, . . . at the time of the adoption of the Seventh Amendment; and the question whether a fact would be found by a jury turned to a considerable degree on the nature of the forum in which a litigant found himself.

Is there, then, a right to trial by jury in a private tort matter that Congress might otherwise assign to an administrative tribunal? *See* Kirst, *Administrative Penalties and the Civil Jury: The Supreme Court's Assault on the Seventh Amendment*, 126 U. Pa. L. Rev. 1281 (1978).

(5) *The Court Zigzags Between the Functional Test and the Historical Approach.* In *Markman v. Westview Instruments, Inc.*, 517 U.S. 370 (1996), the Supreme Court appeared to opt for the functional test. In this patent infringement case, the Court considered whether the issue of interpretation of a patent claim is properly within the province of the judge or jury. Justice Souter first performed a detailed historical analysis and, finding no clear answers and no governing precedent, moved directly to the functional test. The functional test proved to be the deciding factor. The Court examined who was better suited to construe the patent, the judge or jury. Due to the judge's experience and background, the Court reasoned that the judge could more aptly give the patent terms the proper interpretation: "Where history and precedent provide no clear answers, functional considerations also play their part in the choice between judge and jury to define terms of art."

Then, however, in *Feltner v. Columbia Pictures Television, Inc.*, 523 U.S. 340 (1998), the Court considered the Copyright Act, which provides for "statutory damages" of "not less than $500 nor more than $20,000, as the Court considers just." This flexible range might seem to call for a functional approach, and one might expect, after *Tull*, that the judge would set the amount of damages, just as the judge sets the flexible penalty in a pollution case. But the Supreme Court followed a strict historical approach: Because the Act provided for damages, and because damages traditionally are a legal remedy, the jury must determine the amount.

And in *City of Monterey v. Del Monte Dunes at Monterey, Ltd.*, 526 U.S. 687 (1999), the Court again used a historical approach. The suit was for damages for a taking of property, brought under the civil rights statute, § 1983. The City argued that the better analogy was eminent domain, which does not carry the right to jury trial. The Court concluded that the better analogy was a suit for monetary relief or damages, and this historical link required a jury trial.

Perhaps one can sum these cases by saying that an historical approach dominates, but when the historical analysis is unclear, a functional test can tip the scales.

[B] Changing the Size or Function of the Jury

Read Fed. R. Civ. P. 48 (number of jurors).

COLGROVE v. BATTIN, 413 U.S. 149 (1973). Many district courts, by local rule, have provided for six-member juries in civil cases. In this case, petitioner demanded, instead, to have a twelve-member jury, which the common law courts would have provided. The Supreme Court upheld the use of the six-member jury. The Court said, "We . . . conclude . . . that by referring to the 'common law,' the framers of the Seventh Amendment were concerned with preserving the right of trial by jury . . . , rather than the various incidents of trial by jury. . . ." The Court also relied upon studies of the operations of juries to conclude that different size made "no discernible difference" in the results reached.

NOTES AND QUESTIONS

(1) *Changing the "Incidents": The Size and Function of the Jury.* How much of a change in the size or function of the jury can be made without violating the Seventh Amendment? Specifically, would a statute or rule violate the Constitution if it resulted in: (a) Authorizing the judge to void the jury's verdict, and grant a new trial, if she believed the verdict was against the "great weight" of the evidence? [Note: This authority may have existed at common law. *See Gasperini v. Center for Humanities, Inc.*, 518 U.S. 415 (1996).] (b) Making the jury responsible for deciding what the law is, as well as the facts? [Note: The common law provided a judge as decider of the law. *Patton v. United States,* below.] (c) Accepting non-unanimous verdicts, such as by the vote of a majority of jurors? [Note: The common law required unanimity. *Patton,* below.] (d) Changing the size of the jury to three members? [Note: *See Ballew v. Georgia,* below.] *See also* Bieger & Varrin, *Six-Member Juries in the Federal Courts,* 58 Judicature 425 (1975); *cf. Tull v. United States,* above (determination of penalty amount is not a "fundamental" incident of jury trial).

(2) *Criminal Jury Incidents: Patton v. United States, 281 U.S. 276 (1930).* In this criminal case, the Supreme Court held that the Sixth Amendment right to trial by jury included the "essential elements" recognized in England and the United States when the Constitution was adopted and that it specifically included (1) a twelve-person jury, (2) superintendence by a judge having power to instruct on the law and advise on the facts, and (3) a unanimous verdict. Later, however, in *Williams v. Florida,* 399 U.S. 78 (1970), the Court held that a six-person jury was constitutionally acceptable in state or federal criminal cases. In *Ballew v. Georgia,* 435 U.S. 223 (1978), the Court held that the use of five-person juries in state criminal cases was unconstitutional.

(3) *The Seventh Amendment has Not Been Applied to State (as Opposed to Federal) Trials.* The Supreme Court has never applied the Seventh Amendment directly to the states. The states, are, of course, bound by the Fourteenth Amendment's Due Process Clause. What difference would this (presumably) less stringent standard mean in the freedom of the states to change the nature of jury trial in civil cases?

[C] Demand and Waiver of the Right

Read Fed. R. Civ. P. 39, 81(c) (trial by jury or by the court).

NOTE ON WAIVER IN THE ABSENCE OF TIMELY DEMAND

A Person Who has the Right to Jury Trial Can Waive It. Rule 38 requires a demand within 10 days of the last pleading to preserve the right to jury trial. Failure to make this demand is generally a waiver of the right. However, in a removed case (such as *Lewis v. Time Inc.*, the case that follows), the rules governing demand are more complicated. Rule 81(c) provides that an "express demand" in state court obviates the need for further demand after removal, and if no express demand is required in state court, the Rule dispenses with the requirement in federal court also. In any event, unless Rule 81(c) is satisfied, a litigant must make demand within the ten-day period provided by Rule 38 to preserve the right. *See* Note, *Demanding a Jury Trial in the Federal Court System: Federal Rules of Civil Procedure 38 and 39*, 37 Fed'n Ins. & Corp. Couns. Q. 299 (1987).

Discretionary Relief from Waiver; Advisory Juries. If the jury right does not exist or has been waived, all may not be lost. Rule 39(c) allows the court to impanel an "advisory" jury (whose findings the court has authority to accept or reject) or the parties may consent to trial by jury. Under Rule 39(b), in the absence of timely demand, the court may also grant a motion for jury trial in the exercise of its discretion. The following case limits that discretion narrowly. Is the reasoning correct?

LEWIS v. TIME INC.
710 F.2d 549 (9th Cir. 1983)

DUNIWAY, CIRCUIT JUDGE:

Lawyer Jerome Lewis appeals from a judgment against him in his action against TIME Inc. for defamation. We affirm.

I. *Facts.*

The cover story of TIME magazine's April 10, 1978 issue was a 10-page article entitled "Those #*X§ !!! Lawyers." This case is about one subsection of that article, titled "Ethics Enforcement." In relevant part, it stated:

> If the legal profession has been reluctant to discipline its shadier practitioners, it has been swift to crack down on anyone threatening to cut fees or reduce business. . . .
>
> Under these circumstances, it is hardly surprising that some Americans have grown cynical about lawyers — and the law. What is more, every day's newspaper offers up fresh horror stories. . . . Thanks to painfully slow bar discipline, a northern California lawyer named Jerome Lewis is still practicing law despite a $100,000 malpractice judgment against him in 1970 and a $60,000 judgment including punitive damages in 1974 for defrauding clients of money. . . .

Lewis, the only lawyer criticized by name in this section of the article, sued in California state court on March 2, 1979. He alleged libel, slander, invasion of privacy, and intentional infliction of emotional distress. . . .

A month after TIME was served on April 30, it removed the case to the United States District Court for the Eastern District of California. . . .

. . . The court also granted a partial summary judgment in favor of TIME. First, it found that Lewis's libel, slander, invasion of privacy, and intentional infliction of emotional distress claims were all bound up into one claim for relief for defamation. Lewis does not contest the finding.

Second, the district court took judicial notice of two state court judgments entered against Lewis. In one of the cases, a jury had awarded damages of $100,000 to a client who had sued Lewis for malpractice. . . . In the other case, another client had won $60,000, including punitive damages, on a counterclaim against Lewis for fraud. The district court held that TIME's statements about the money judgments against Lewis were protected because they were truthful statements of matters of public record. With respect therefore to any of the article's clearly factual statements about Lewis, the court found that the only remaining question of fact was whether the assertion that Lewis defrauded "*clients*," when the fraud judgment against him was in favor of only a single *client*, was a material variance from the truth, and therefore a basis for liability for defamation as a derogatory falsehood. . . .

After the grant of partial summary judgment, the only remaining issue to be tried was the significance of the plural "clients." The district court granted Lewis's motion for relief from his untimely demand for a jury trial, but then on its own motion reconsidered and denied the motion. After trial to the court, the district judge found that the addition of the "s" in "clients" was not a material variance from the truth. Judgment for TIME was entered on December 15, 1981. . . .

[The court rejected attacks on the District Court's refusal to remand to state court as well as its partial summary judgment in Pts. II-III of the opinion. It then considered the final issue, the District Court's denial of Lewis' demand for jury trial, as follows.]

IV. *Demand for Jury Trial.*

Finally, Lewis argues that the district judge incorrectly denied his motion for a jury trial on the issue of whether the word "clients" was a material variance from the truth.

Under F.R. Civ. P. 81(c), the federal "rules apply to civil actions removed to the United States district courts from the state courts and govern procedure after removal." The rule further states in relevant part:

> A party who, prior to removal, has made an express demand for trial by jury in accordance with state law, need not make a demand after removal. If state law applicable in the court from which the case is removed does not require the parties to make express demands in order to claim trial by jury, they need not make demands after removal unless the court directs that they do so. . . . [The 2007 "restyling" amendments to the Federal Rules of Civil Procedure slightly changed this language — Eds.]

Lewis did not request a jury trial before his case was removed from California state court. Under California law, a litigant waives trial by jury by, *inter alia*, failing to "announce that one is required" when the trial is set. Cal. Civ. Proc. Code §§ 631, 631.01. (1982 Supp.). We understand that to mean that an "express demand" is required. Therefore, Fed. R. Civ. P. 38(d), made applicable by Rule 81(c), required Lewis to file a demand "not later than 10 days after the service of the last pleading directed to such issue [to be tried]." Failure to file within the time provided constituted a waiver of the right to trial by jury. Rule 38(d).

Lewis did not request a jury trial until March 17, 1980, nine months after TIME filed its answer, the last pleading on the issue to be tried. Lewis then filed a motion for relief from failure to make a timely demand for jury trial.

The district court, in its discretion, may order a jury trial on a motion by a party who has not filed a timely demand for one. Fed. R. Civ. P. 39(b). That discretion is narrow, however, and does not permit a court to grant relief when the failure to make a timely demand results from an oversight or inadvertence. *Chandler Supply Co. v. GAF Corp.*, 9 Cir., 1980, 650 F.2d 983, 987; *Mardesich v. Marciel*, 9 Cir., 1976, 538 F.2d 848, 849.

Lewis argues, however, that the discretion permitted the district court was defined by California state law, not by federal law under Rule 39(b). He relies on *Higgins v. Boeing Co.*, 2 Cir., 1975, 526 F.2d 1004, for the proposition that where state law would have permitted discretionary relief from waiver of jury trial, had the case not been removed from state court, the federal court has the same discretion as the state court to order relief.

There is some reason to believe that the discretion California law permits trial judges in granting relief from jury trial waivers is broader than the discretion we permit under Rule 39(b). *See, e.g., Byram v. Superior Court*, Cal. App., 1977, 74 Cal. App. 3d 648, 141 Cal. Rptr. 604; and Cal. Civ. Proc. Code §§ 631 and 631.01. We need not consider the issue, however, because we conclude that Rule 39(b) defined the discretion to be exercised by the district court here. . . .

Therefore, because Rule 39(b) does not permit relief where the waiver was caused by oversight or inadvertence, *see Chandler Supply* and *Mardesich, supra*, the district court correctly denied Lewis's motion for a jury trial. Lewis's further argument that it was error for the trial judge to reconsider his earlier ruling granting Lewis's untimely motion for jury trial is meritless.

Affirmed.

NOTES AND QUESTIONS

(1) *Sufficiency of the Demand: Pinemont Bank v. Belk, 722 F.2d 232 (5th Cir. 1984).* Rule 38 does not prescribe any formal language for the demand. The most frequent practice is to endorse the demand at the bottom of the pleading: "Plaintiff/Defendant demands trial by jury of all issues triable of right by jury." In *Pinemont Bank v. Belk*, local rules prescribed a cover sheet with a preprinted notation: "Jury Demand: Check 'Yes' only if demanded in complaint. Yes__________ No__________." The plaintiff checked the box marked "Yes," although in fact he had made no demand in the complaint. At the time of trial, the defendant claimed that he had relied in good faith upon the indication of jury demand on the cover sheet. The Fifth Circuit reversed the District Court's denial of jury trial. Although criticizing reliance upon the cover sheet as dangerous and "not the preferred method of compliance," it held that the right was preserved. Note that the defendant effectively may rely upon the plaintiff's demand because Rule 38(d) prohibits withdrawal without consent of the parties.

(2) *Liberal Allowance of Discretion.* Frequently, appellate courts say trial courts have "broad" discretion to allow a jury trial after waiver. The narrow scope of discretion allowed by the Ninth Circuit in *Lewis* differs sharply from the approach of some other courts. In fact, many of the decisions indicate narrow discretion to deny jury trial, rather than narrow discretion to grant it. *E.g., United States v. Unum, Inc.*, 658 F.2d 300 (5th Cir. 1981) (motion to relieve party from waiver of jury trial should be favorably received unless there are persuasive reasons to deny it). The Rule itself does not prevent a discretionary jury trial in the event of inadvertent or mistaken waiver; is the Ninth Circuit's implication of an exclusion in cases of inadvertence justified?

(3) *Discretionary Denial of Jury Trial.* Of course, jury trials are more time-consuming than trials to the court. Judge Posner has estimated that the average jury trial lasts 4.48 days compared to 2.21 days for the average non-jury trial. R. Posner, *The Federal Courts* 130 n.1 (1985). The court is likely to consider this fact. *See In re N-500L Cases*, 517 F. Supp. 821 (D.P.R. 1981) (district court considered issues to be tried, expenses to be incurred, time elapsed, possibility of prejudice resulting from trial without jury as opposed to trial by jury, as well as congestion of docket, and concluded that these factors did not weigh in favor of relieving movant of its waiver).

(4) *Should the Trial Judge Encourage Waiver After Demand of Jury Trial? Black, Sivalls & Bryson, Inc. v. Keystone Steel Fabrication, Inc., 584 F.2d 946 (10th Cir. 1978).* In this patent case, the plaintiff's counsel stated that an infringement question could properly be decided by the court since it was primarily technical, and the defendant's counsel responded to an inquiry by the court that he was "certainly more than happy" to have the court decide the issue in spite of an earlier jury demand. The Court of Appeals held that this oral stipulation, entered on the record, was sufficient to waive a jury in spite of an earlier demand. Should trial judges use pretrial conferences to attempt to persuade counsel to waive juries in complex cases?

[D] The Jury Trial Right in State Courts: Notes and Questions

(1) *California — The "Gist" of the Action: C & K Engineering Contractors v. Amber Steel Co., 23 Cal. 3d 1, 587 P.2d 1136, 151 Cal. Rptr. 323 (1978).* Cal. Const. Art. I sec. 16 preserves the right to jury trial as it existed at common law in 1850, when the state constitution was adopted. "[A]nd what that right is," said the California Supreme Court in *C & K Engineering*, "is a purely historical question, a fact which is to be ascertained like any other social, political or legal fact." In *C & K Engineering*, the plaintiff's damage suit for breach of contract was based entirely upon the equitable doctrine of promissory estoppel. Since promissory estoppel is an equitable doctrine, said the court, there was no right to jury trial. The court refused to look to whether legal questions might be involved in the case or to protect the jury trial right for those issues (as federal courts would do under the *Beacon Theatres* approach). Instead, Justice Richardson's opinion held that the right depended upon the "gist" of the action. Because, in this case, the "gist" was equitable, trial would be held before the court alone. Justice Newman's dissent, joined by Chief Justice Bird, focused "not on rights but on remedies," and concluded that a "plaintiff who seeks damages should be entitled to a jury." This case suggests a narrower range for the jury trial right in California state courts than is recognized in the federal system.

(2) *Texas — Extension of the Right to Equity Cases: State v. Texas Pet Foods, Inc., 591 S.W.2d 800, 803 (Tex. 1979).* The right to trial by jury in Texas is more extensive than in most jurisdictions, because Tex. Const. Art. 5, § 10 extends it to "all causes in the District Courts." The term "cause" has been given a broad construction and includes suits in equity as well as actions at law. Although a litigant has the right to trial by jury in an equitable action, only ultimate issues of fact are submitted for jury determination. The jury does not determine the propriety of equitable relief, and the determination whether to grant an injunction, as well as its scope, is for the trial court, exercising chancery powers. In *Texas Pet Foods*, the jury found numerous violations of pollution control statutes. Then, predicated on the past violations found by the jury, the trial court determined that future violations were likely to occur and granted injunctive relief. Texas also is liberal in allowing late demand for a jury, which can be made at any reasonable time, not less than 30 days before trial. *See* Tex. R. Civ. P. 216.

(3) *New York — An Historical Approach: Matter of Garfield, 14 N.Y.2d 251, 251 N.Y.S.2d 7, 200 N.E.2d 196 (1964).* The New York Constitution guarantees trial by jury "in all cases in which it has heretofore been guaranteed by constitutional provision." N.Y. Const. art. I, sec. 2; *see also* CPLR 4101-4102 (specific list of cases). In *Matter of Garfield*, the plaintiff was an attorney seeking to recover a fee allegedly owed by his deceased client. He made a claim for his fee by the statutory procedure, which was to petition for an accounting in the Surrogate's (*i.e.*, probate) Court. The executor contested the claim and demanded trial by jury, to which the Court of Appeals held that she was entitled. The fundamental claim was legal in nature, and its assertion in a "court of equity" (the Surrogate's Court) did not change the right. Thus the jury right in New York seems broader than in the federal system (which, under the holding in *Katchen v. Landy*, would deny it to legal issues in the analogous setting of bankruptcy). New York also extends jury trial to several matters by statute outside the CPLR (*e.g.*, divorce cases). A party waives the right to a jury trial by serving a note of issue that fails to include a jury demand (the note of issue is a preprinted form used to put the case on the trial calendar, and the jury demand is made by checking the appropriate box on the form). A party served with a note of issue that does not include a jury demand must serve a jury demand within

fifteen days to preserve the right to jury trial. Thus New York, as do many states, avoids forcing an early choice, or inducing inadvertent waiver, by not requiring a demand tied closely to the date of the pleadings, as do the Federal Rules.

(4) *Trial "by Referee" in New York.* In addition to trial by jury and trial by the court, New York has a third form: trial by referee. The referee is a person, usually a lawyer, appointed by the court under circumstances authorized by CPLR 4001 and 4317. One circumstance for trial by referee is when the parties so stipulate. CPLR 4317(b) also allows compulsory reference to a referee in certain cases, including certain kinds of complex accounting cases. Is this provision sensible?

§ 10.03 Jury Selection

[A] The "Fair Cross-Section" Requirement

THIEL v. SOUTHERN PACIFIC CO.
328 U.S. 217 (1946)

[Plaintiff Thiel's complaint alleged that the defendant railroad was liable to him for damages for its negligence, in that its agents knew that he was "out of his normal mind" and should not have been accepted as a passenger or should have been guarded. He jumped out of the window of a moving train and was injured.

[After demanding a jury trial, Thiel moved to strike the entire panel, alleging that it consisted of "mostly business executives or those having the employer's viewpoint" and that "poorer classes" were discriminated against. The judge denied this challenge to the jury array, and the trial resulted in a verdict for the railroad.

[The evidence in Thiel's challenge to the array included testimony of the clerk and the jury commissioner that they "deliberately and intentionally excluded from the jury list all persons who worked for a daily wage." They worked from the city directory. In the words of the clerk, "If I see in the directory the name of John Jones and it says he is a longshoreman, I do not put his name in, because I have found by experience that that man will not serve as a juror, and I will not get people who will qualify. The minute that a juror is called into court on a venire and says that he is working for $10 a day and cannot afford to work for four, the judge has never made one of those men serve. . . . Where I thought the designation indicated that they were day laborers, I mean they were people who were compensated solely when they were working by the day, I leave them out." The evidence indicated, however, that laborers who were paid weekly or monthly wages were placed on the jury list, as well as the wives of daily wage earners, and the judge in Thiel's trial specifically found that five of the twelve jurors "belong more closely and intimately with the working man and employee class than they do with any other class."

[In an opinion by Justice Murphy, the Supreme Court reversed and remanded for the following reasons:]

The American tradition of trial by jury, considered in connection with either criminal or civil proceedings, necessarily contemplates an impartial jury drawn from a cross-section of the community. . . . This does not mean, of course, that every jury must contain representatives of all the economic, social, religious, racial, political and geographical groups of the community; frequently such complete representation would be impossible. But it does mean that prospective jurors shall be selected by court officials without systematic and intentional exclusion of any of these groups. . . .

This exclusion of all those who earn a daily wage cannot be justified by federal or state law. Certainly nothing in the federal statutes warrants such an exclusion. . . .

It is clear that a federal judge would be justified in excusing a daily wage earner for whom jury service would entail an undue financial hardship. But that fact cannot support the complete exclusion of all daily wage earners regardless of whether there is actual hardship involved. Here there was no effort, no intention, to determine in advance which individual members of the daily wage earning class would suffer an undue hardship by serving on a jury at the rate of $4 a day. All were systematically and automatically excluded. . . .

It follows that we cannot sanction the method by which the jury panel was formed in this case. . . .

It is likewise immaterial that the jury which actually decided the factual issue in the case was found to contain at least five members of the laboring class. The evil lies in the admitted wholesale exclusion of a large class of wage earners in disregard of the high standards of jury selection. To reassert those standards, to guard against the subtle undermining of the jury system, requires a new trial by a jury drawn from a panel properly and fairly chosen.

Reversed.

MR. JUSTICE FRANKFURTER, with whom MR. JUSTICE REED concurs, dissenting. . . .

Trial by jury presupposes a jury drawn from a pool broadly representative of the community as well as impartial in a specific case. Since the color of a man's skin is unrelated to his fitness as a juror, [African Americans] cannot be excluded from jury service because they are [African Americans]. *E.g., Carter v. Texas*, 177 U.S. 442. A group may be excluded for reasons that are relevant not to their fitness but to competing considerations of public interest, as is true of the exclusion of doctors, ministers, lawyers, and the like. *Rawlins v. Georgia*, 201 U.S. 638. . . .

Obviously these accepted general considerations must have much leeway in application. In the abstract the Court acknowledges this. . . . But it is not without illumination that under California law all those belonging to this long string of occupations are exempted from jury service: judicial, civil, naval, and military officers of the United States or California; local government officials; attorneys, their clerks, secretaries, and stenographers; ministers; teachers; physicians, dentists, chiropodists, optometrists, and druggists; officers, keepers, and attendants at hospitals or other charitable institutions; officers in attendance at prisons and jails; employees on boats and ships in navigable waters; express agents, mail carriers, employees of telephone and telegraph companies; keepers of ferries or tollgates; national guardsmen and firemen; superintendents, engineers, firemen, brakemen, motormen, or conductors of railroads; practitioners treating the sick by prayer. California Code of Civil Procedure, § 200.

The precise issue must be freed from all atmospheric innuendoes. . . . If workmen were systematically not drawn for the jury, the practice would be indefensible. But concern over discrimination against wage earners must be put out of the reckoning. Concededly those who are paid weekly or monthly wages were placed by the jury lists. . . .

It is difficult to believe that this judgment would have been reversed if the trial judge had excused, one by one, all those wage earners whom the jury commissioner, acting on the practice of trial judges of San Francisco, excluded. . . .

FEIN v. PERMANENTE MEDICAL GROUP, 38 Cal. 3d 137, 695 P.2d 665, 211 Cal. Rptr. 368 (1985). The text of this case appears in § 1.08 of Chapter 1, above, and should be read (or re-read) at this point. In this medical malpractice case, in which the evidence "sharply conflict[ed]," the trial judge ordered a blanket exclusion of all prospective jurors who were members of the Kaiser medical plan. The defendant, Permanente, was an affiliate of the Kaiser Health Foundation, and the judge explained: "I am going to excuse you at this time because we've found that we can prolong the jury selection by just such a very long time by going through each and every juror under these circumstances." The court's ruling excused twenty-four of sixty jurors (or forty percent of the entire panel), and Kaiser objected to the exclusion. While conceding that "past decisions do not provide a clearcut answer," the California Supreme Court affirmed a judgment for the plaintiff. The court held, first, that the trial judge had broad discretion which he had not abused by his ruling, and second, that Kaiser members "were not a cognizable class" with the kind of "shared experiences, ideology or background" that prior cases had protected against "systematic exclusion."

NOTES AND QUESTIONS

(1) *Is the Requirement Really a "Fair Cross-Section" (Or Is There Only a Prohibition Upon "Systematic Exclusion" of "Cognizable Groups")?* In the *Thiel* case, the Supreme Court began its analysis by saying that trial by jury "necessarily contemplates an impartial jury drawn from a cross-section of the community." But is there really a requirement that the panel from which the jury is drawn be a "cross-section"? As the dissent points out, all government officials, attorneys, ministers, teachers, physicians, and members of certain other occupations were exempted from *Thiel*'s jury. And if a "cross-section" is required, how can *Thiel* be distinguished from *Fein v. Permanente*? The answer may be that the requirement is not one of a "cross-section" at all, but instead is a prohibition upon the "systematic exclusion" of "cognizable groups." It is on that basis that the California court distinguished *Thiel;* it reasoned that the Kaiser plan members were not a "cognizable group." Is the distinction persuasive? (Can it be that exclusion of day laborers, in *Thiel*, is unacceptable, but exclusion of upscale workers in the Kaiser plan, as in *Fein*, is acceptable?) *See* Druff, *The Cross-Section Requirement and Jury Impartiality*, 73 Calif. L. Rev. 1555 (1985).

(2) *The Jury Selection and Service Act of 1968.* The federal Jury Selection and Service Act, 28 U.S.C. § 1861 et seq., was passed since the *Thiel* decision. It requires selection at random from a "fair cross-section" and a "fair opportunity" to serve, as well and prohibits invidious discrimination. Each district court is to devise a "plan for random jury selection" with the following features: Management by a jury commission or by the court clerk; use of voter registration lists, lists of actual voters, or these lists plus supplementation from other sources; random selection of names for placement into a jury wheel; specification of exemptions by individual request and exemptions barring service; and other features. There are minimum qualifications (including citizenship, ability to read and write English, freedom from certain criminal charges or convictions, etc.). Furthermore, the Act provides a cutoff date for asserting a challenge to the array (*i.e.*, to the manner of summons). The challenge must be made before examination of the jury begins, or within seven days of the time when defects in the array should have been discovered, whichever is earlier.

(3) *Does "Widespread Juror Apathy" That Distorts Jury Composition Negate a "Fair Cross-Section"? United States v. Gometz, 730 F.2d 475 (7th Cir. 1984) (en banc).* In

this case, the appellant alleged that widespread juror apathy caused a large fraction of the persons to whom the district clerk sent juror qualification forms to fail to respond. The appellant's challenge to the array claimed that the resulting venire did not represent a "fair cross-section." It was alleged, further, that court officials took no special efforts to combat this widespread apathy. The Court of Appeals held that the challenge was properly denied. First, the Jury Selection and Service Act provides for selection from lists of registered voters. Thus the venire is limited to those persons who demonstrate a sense of civic obligation in the first place. Congress' approval of this "built-in screening element," said the court, shows that it never intended juries to be composed of every element within a community; in fact it suggests that Congress "wanted people who lacked a sense of civil obligation not to serve on federal juries. . . ." Nor could judges and clerks reasonably be expected to counteract juror apathy: an "angry juror," forced to serve against her will, "is a bad juror." In summary, "Congress was not concerned with anything so esoteric as nonresponse bias when it enacted the Jury Selection and Service Act." Is this reasoning persuasive?

(4) *Is the Use of Voter Registration Lists Unconstitutionally Underinclusive? People v. Harris, 36 Cal. 3d 36, 679 P.2d 433, 201 Cal. Rptr. 782 (1984).* In this criminal case, the California Supreme Court held unconstitutional a jury pool randomly selected from a voter registration list. The defendant offered total population figures showing a statistically significant underrepresentation of Blacks and Hispanics, compared to their proportions in the community. The court held that a "party is constitutionally entitled to a petit jury that is as near an approximation of the ideal cross section of the community as the process of random draw permits." Voter registration lists could have been supplemented by drivers' license records. Is this reasoning correct? Authority in other state and federal courts that have considered the question is to the contrary, with many decisions holding that the argument presents no constitutional issue. *E.g., United States v. Clifford*, 640 F.2d 150 (8th Cir. 1981); *United States v. Lewis*, 472 F.2d 252 (3d Cir. 1973); *Davis v. Zant*, 721 F.2d 1478 (11th Cir. 1984). For an interesting view of a different but related issue, see DiSalvo, *The Key-Man System for Composing Jury Lists in West Virginia — The Story of Abuse, the Case for Reform*, 87 W. Va. L. Rev. 219 (1985).

(5) *Disqualifications and Exemptions.* In addition to statutory disqualifications, such as noncitizenship and inability to read, write, or speak English (*see* 28 U.S.C. § 1865), a prospective juror may be excluded on the ground that the juror "may be unable to render impartial jury service or that his service as a juror would be likely to disrupt the proceedings, or . . . for good cause shown." 28 U.S.C. § 1866(c). The district court has wide discretion regarding challenges for cause and, on appeal, is reviewed on an abuse of discretion standard. *Vanskike v. ACF Indus., Inc.*, 665 F.2d 188, 207 (1981), *cert. denied,* 455 U.S. 1000. Regarding impartiality, the Supreme Court has said the following (in a criminal case although the same is no doubt true for civil cases): "In essence, the right to jury trial guarantees to the criminally accused a fair trial by a panel of impartial, 'indifferent' jurors. The failure to accord an accused a fair hearing violates even the minimal standards of due process. . . . It is not required, however, that the jurors be totally ignorant of the facts and issues involved. . . . It is sufficient if the juror can lay aside his impression or opinion and render a verdict based on the evidence presented in court." *Irvin v. Dowd,* 366 U.S. 722, 722-23 (1961).

[B] *Voir Dire* Examination and Challenges

NOTE ON HOW JURORS ARE "SELECTED": PREVIEWING *FLOWERS v. FLOWERS*

The Voir Dire Examination. The jury venire is seated in the courtroom, usually in the public seats. The venire generally consists of many more individuals than will ultimately serve on the jury, since some — perhaps most — of them will be removed by challenges. The process called "voir dire examination," or examination of the jurors to determine their qualifications or undesirability to either side, then begins. ("*Voir dire*" is taken from French words meaning "to see" and "to speak.") *See* Hittner, *Federal Voir Dire and Jury Selection*, 25 Trial 85 (March 1989).

"Peremptory" Challenges and Challenges "for Cause." The *voir dire* may show that some venire members do not meet the general requirements for service (*e.g.*, non-citizenship or illiteracy) or disqualification from serving in the particular case (most commonly, by an unavoidable bias against a party or against a principle of law at issue). Then, a party may remove this person by a challenge "for cause." Each party may exercise an unlimited number of challenges for cause. In addition, each party is entitled to a number of "peremptory" challenges set by rule or statute; in the federal courts, the Jury Selection and Service Act allows three peremptory challenges to each side. 28 U.S.C. § 1870. These three "strikes" can be exercised without the assignment of any reason. The idea is that both sides are more likely to appreciate that the jury is impartial if each party is allowed to remove a few potential jurors who seem most likely to be unfavorable. *See Symposium, The Selection and Function of the Modern Jury*, 40 Am. U. L. Rev. 541 (1991).

Procedure for Examination and Challenges. Rule 47 allows a federal judge discretion to conduct the *voir dire* examination herself, or to allow the attorneys to do it, or to conduct it herself with supplemental examination by the attorneys. (One question you should consider in this section is, what difference does the exercise of this discretion make?) When an individual subject to challenge for cause is identified, the attorney usually raises it at the time; the judge has responsibility for ruling on the challenge. The attorneys exercise peremptory challenges at the conclusion of the voir dire, customarily by drawing lines through the names of the challenged jurors on a list compiled by the clerk.

Tactics. The process seeks to impanel a fair and impartial jury, but the parties certainly don't. The adversary system very definitely is in effect at this stage. Each lawyer is alert even to small cues about possibly unfavorable thoughts among venire members, so as best to use peremptory challenges. If the attorneys conduct the voir dire, they inevitably use it to prepare jurors for the proof; sometimes they test the limits of propriety. And if it appears that a venire member is biased and subject to a party's challenge for cause — well, that may mean that the venire member is highly desirable to the opponent, who will attempt to "rehabilitate" this individual with questions designed to minimize the appearance of bias. *See* Fulero & Penrod, *The Myths and Realities of Attorney Jury Selection Folklore and Scientific Jury Selection: What Works?*, 17 Ohio N.U. L. Rev. 229 (1990).

The Judge's Function in Ruling on Challenges for Cause: A Preview of the Flowers Case. The judge applies the governing law of disqualification and, simultaneously, makes a fact finding (which often is implicit) about the individual venire member. The judge may have "wiggle room" in making this fact determination. Because every juror has opinions, a mere feeling about the issues is not sufficient basis for disqualification. (For example, in a negligence case, many potential jurors may have heard about the tort reform debate, but it would make no sense to remove all of those who have any thoughts about the subject.) The ultimate question is whether the putative bias or prejudice will unfairly affect the juror's decision or whether she is capable of deciding the case from the law and evidence. Often, judges are understandably reluctant to allow marginal challenges, for fear of distorting the balance of the jury pool or depleting it. Consider the following case — in which the trial judge's ruling may seem shocking at first blush, but which shows how the process works.

[1] Challenges "For Cause" Versus "Peremptory" Challenges

FLOWERS v. FLOWERS

397 S.W.2d 121 (Tex. Civ. App.-Amarillo 1965, no writ)

CHAPMAN, JUSTICE.

The subject matter of this suit involves a question of the disqualification of a juror in a child custody contest tried to a jury. . . .

This case was tried in a town and county of very small population where the record shows many members of the jury panel had heard what they referred to as gossip or rumors concerning the case. The parties to the suit are Billie Charlene Flowers, plaintiff below, the mother; and R.A. Flowers, Jr., the father. The victims of the unfortunate broken home are three little girls ranging in ages from two to ten at the time of the filing of divorce by their mother in January 1964. . . .

The jurors were told on voir dire examination that the evidence would show that plaintiff drank some socially and on one or two occasions had consumed alcoholic beverages to excess. They were questioned as to whether that fact standing alone would prejudice them against her as a fit and proper person to have custody of the children.

The record preserved upon examination of Mrs. Schmidt as a prospective juror shows that she first testified she was well acquainted with the Flowers family, belonged to the same Baptist church they did in the little town of Miami, and that she had no opinion formed in the case at all. Then when counsel said to her the evidence will show "that Billie does drink upon social occasions with the crowd at a dance, or something of that sort, she would have a highball or cocktail, and it will show on one occasion that she had too much, or two times had too much, what is your attitude —" she answered:

A: I am against drinking in any manner, any kind.

Q: Any way or any fashion at all?

A: Any type.

Q: Mrs. Schmidt, that would definitely affect your judgment in the case, wouldn't it?

A: If the evidence was true.

Q: Could you enter the — you would take a seat as a juror with a positive feeling that any drinking whatsoever is wrong, and it is bad so far as the mother of these little girls is concerned, —

A: Anybody else.

Q: If the evidence shows Billie has had one drink or two — drinks at a social occasion, you would hold that against her?

A: I don't approve.

The court then took over the examination and asked her a number of questions, one of which was:

Q: Well, are you saying by that, Mrs. Schmidt, that you wouldn't grant either party to this law suit custody of the children if they drank?

A: I am.

The court then turned to leading questions to the juror as to her attitude about passing upon whether the mother was a fit person to have the custody of the girls, saying:

Q: Dependent upon the testimony you hear in a trial; the mere fact that she got drunk a few times and threw a conniption fit or something, you wouldn't hold that against her and think she wasn't —

A: Not especially.

The court then overruled the challenge of the juror for cause. . . .

Article 1, Section 15 of the Texas Constitution, Vernon's Ann. St., guarantees the right to trial by jury, which our courts have held to be an impartial jury. . . .

Article 2134, Vernon's Ann. Tex. Civ. St., provides as one of the disqualifications: "Any person who has a bias or prejudice in favor of or against either of the parties."

This disqualification for bias or prejudice extends not only to the parties personally, but also to the subject matter of the litigation. . . . *Compton v. Henrie*, Tex., 364 S.W.2d. 179.

In defining the terms "bias" and "prejudice" as used in Article 2134 our Supreme Court in the *Henrie* case just cited has said:

> Bias, in its usual meaning, is an inclination toward one side of an issue rather than to the other, but to disqualify, it must appear that the state of mind of the juror leads to the natural inference that he will not or did not act with impartiality. Prejudice is more easily defined for it means pre-judgment, and consequently embraces bias; the converse is not true. . . .

Mrs. Schmidt's statements indicate to us both bias and prejudice factually and such a prejudgment of the case as to indicate she could not have acted with impartiality. If we are correct in this factual conclusion then under the authorities just cited her disqualification is not a matter of discretion with the trial court but a matter of law. We believe the record compels such holding on our part. . . .

Even if we are in error in our pronouncements in the preceding paragraphs, it cannot be gainsaid that the record shows bias and prejudice on the part of Mrs. Schmidt toward plaintiff and toward her alcoholic consumption her attorney admitted would be shown before the examination of the jury on voir dire. From the viewpoint of this writer, such feelings on the part of Mrs. Schmidt are to her credit even if it did disqualify her as a juror. But even if under the facts of this case bias or prejudice was a fact to be determined by the trial court, those feelings having been clearly established, her answer of "Yes, sir" to a leading question to the effect that she would be able to decide the case on the evidence submitted, should be disregarded. . . .

In cases involving juror disqualification the Complainant need not establish that probable injury resulted therefrom before a new trial may be granted. *Compton v. Henrie, supra.* However, under this record probable injury is established by the proof that there were other jurors who, under the known facts at the time the [peremptory] challenges were exercised, were less desirable than Mrs. Schmidt.

[*Reversed.*]

McDONOUGH POWER EQUIPMENT, INC. v. GREENWOOD, 464 U.S 548 (1984). Greenwood's son was seriously injured in an accident with a riding lawnmower manufactured by McDonough. After a three-week trial, the jury returned a verdict for the defendant McDonough. One of Greenwood's grounds for a new trial concerned questioning on voir dire about "injuries . . . that resulted in any disability or prolonged pain or suffering" to members of any potential juror's immediate family. One venire member named Payton, who actually served on the jury, failed to respond to this question, although his son had sustained a broken leg as a result of an exploding tire. The District Court denied a motion for new trial and entered judgment for McDonough. The Court of Appeals reversed, holding that juror Payton's failure to respond had prejudiced Greenwood's right of peremptory challenge. The court concluded that the "unrevealed information" indicated probable bias "because it revealed a particularly narrow concept of what constitutes a serious injury." The Court assumed that the juror had answered in good faith, but said, "Good faith . . . is irrelevant to our inquiry."

In an opinion by Justice Rehnquist, the Supreme Court reversed. It began with the principle of harmless error, pointing out that "[a] litigant is entitled to a fair trial but not a perfect one." The Court then reasoned as follows:

> Voir dire examination serves to protect [the right to an impartial jury] by exposing possible biases, both known and unknown, on the part of potential jurors. Demonstrated bias in the response to questions on voir dire may result in a juror being excused for cause; hints of bias not sufficient to warrant challenge for cause may assist parties in exercising their peremptory challenges. . . .
>
> . . . Juror Payton apparently believed that his son's broken leg sustained as a result of an exploding tire was not [a disabling or prolonged] injury. In response to a similar question from petitioner's counsel, however, another juror related such a minor incident as the fact that his six year old son once caught his finger in a bike chain. . . .
>
> The varied responses to respondent's questions on voir dire testified to the fact that jurors are not necessarily experts in English usage. . . . Thus, we cannot say, and we doubt that the Court of Appeals could say, which of these . . . jurors was closer to the "average juror" in his response to the question. . . .
>
> To invalidate the result of a three-week trial because of a juror's mistaken, though honest response to a question, is to insist on something closer to perfection than our judicial system can be expected to give. . . . We hold that to obtain a new trial in such a situation, a party must first demonstrate that a juror failed to answer honestly a material question on voir dire, and then further show that a correct response would have provided a valid basis for a challenge for cause. The motives for concealing information may vary, but only those reasons that affect a juror's impartiality can truly be said to affect the fairness of a trial. . . .

Justice Blackmun (joined by Justices Stevens and O'Connor) concurred on the ground that the Court's opinion did not "foreclose the normal avenue of relief available to a party who is asserting that he did not have the benefit of an impartial jury." Justice Brennan (joined by Justice Marshall) concurred only in the judgment: "I cannot join . . .

in the legal standard asserted by the Court's opinion. In my view, the proper focus when ruling on a motion for new trial in this situation should be on the bias of the juror and the resulting prejudice to the litigant." In other words, Justice Brennan would not have interposed a requirement that the juror failed to answer honestly. "Whether the juror answered a particular question on voir dire honestly or dishonestly, or whether an inaccurate answer was inadvertent or intentional, are simply factors to be considered in this latter determination of actual bias."

NOTES AND QUESTIONS

(1) *The Attorney's Burden in Setting Up Challenges for Cause.* In *Flowers v. Flowers*, what would have been the outcome: (a) If Mrs. Flowers' attorney, through inadvertence or deliberate choice, had refrained from asking about juror attitudes toward drinking during the voir dire examination? (b) If he had asked the whole panel whether any member automatically would refuse custody to a parent who drank, and Mrs. Schmidt remained silent? (c) If he had succeeded in identifying Mrs. Schmidt but failed to pin her down, beyond the expression of a general opposition to drinking? *See also* Note, *Juror Bias Undiscovered During Voir Dire: Reviewing Claims of a Denial of the Constitutional Right to an Impartial Jury*, 39 Drake L. Rev. 201 (1990).

(2) *The Difficulty of the "Bias" Inquiry.* Examining venire members like Mrs. Schmidt is a difficult art form. First, the attorney must succeed in causing these individuals to identify themselves. The general question, "Is anybody biased"? is unlikely to elicit appropriate responses, since few of us place ourselves in that category and even if we did, we might be reluctant to stand up in a courtroom and say so. Furthermore, a general attribution of bias may be insufficient; the question is whether the bias is severe enough to prevent the juror from deciding the case on the law and facts. Finally, some members of the venire ultimately will decide the lawyer's case, as jurors, and so heavy-handed efforts to pin a potential juror down may be counterproductive. In fact, the task calls for extreme diplomacy.

(3) *Peremptory Challenges: Are They Adequately Protected by the McDonough Holding?* Greenwood's principal argument, in *McDonough v. Greenwood*, appears to have been that he was denied a fair opportunity to make a peremptory challenge against juror Payton. But the Court's holding is that "to obtain a new trial . . ., [Greenwood] must . . . show that a correct response would have provided a valid basis for a challenge for cause." Notice that, if a correct answer would clearly indicate a peremptory challenge that any reasonable lawyer would have exercised, the standard in *McDonough* provides no protection of the right to make it. To take a concrete example, imagine that a venire member flatly and falsely denies being an insurance adjuster. As a result, the plaintiff's attorney withholds a peremptory challenge in circumstances in which any plaintiff's attorney in possession of accurate information would have exercised it. But since mere employment as an insurance adjuster is not alone sufficient to make "a valid basis for a challenge for cause," the literal language of *McDonough* would deny a new trial. Is this result appropriate? Why is the Court so restrictive of new trials based on jury challenges? *See* Crump, *Peremptory Challenges After McDonough Power Equipment, Inc. v. Greenwood: A Problem of Fairness, Finality, and Falsehood*, 69 Ore. L. Rev. 741 (1990).

(4) *The Judge's Discretion to Grant or Deny a Challenge for Cause.* In either retaining a panel member challenged as biased or excusing an individual on marginal evidence, the cases indicate broad discretion in the trial judge. *E.g., Kinty v. United Mine Workers,*

544 F.2d 706 (4th Cir. 1976) (judge did not abuse discretion in excusing wife of union pensioner, as well as an individual working in coal mines, in action seeking damages from union); *Neveaux v. Central Gulf S.S. Corp.*, 503 F.2d 961 (5th Cir. 1974) (judge did not abuse discretion in denying challenge of potential juror employed by a party).

(5) *Can the Reasons for Exercising Peremptory Challenges Be Illegal? Racially Motivated Strikes and Batson v. Kentucky, 476 U.S. 79 (1986).* In *Batson*, a criminal case, the Court held that it would be unconstitutional for a prosecutor to exercise racially motivated peremptory challenges. A *prima facie* showing by the defendant (such as removal of all blacks from the panel) would place upon the prosecutor the burden of justifying the challenges by reference to non-racial factors.

You should be aware that "label" characteristics — such as age, wealth, occupation, and social class — are frequent selection factors, and many attorneys probably would agree that at least some of these factors are legitimate. In an employment discrimination suit in which the plaintiff alleges a racially motivated discharge, won't both parties be considering these "label" characteristics in exercising peremptories — and will they be considering race as a factor, too? Should a principle prohibiting this consideration be adopted? *See* Salzburg & Powers, *Peremptory Challenges and the Clash between Impartiality and Group Representation*, 41 Md. L. Rev. 337 (1982); *see also* Note, *Race, Trial Strategy and Legal Ethics*, 24 U. Rich. L. Rev. 361 (1990). Consider the following decision, which extends the prohibition to civil cases.

EDMONSON v. LEESVILLE CONCRETE CO.
500 U.S. 614 (1991)

JUSTICE KENNEDY delivered the opinion of the Court.

[In *Batson v. Kentucky*, 476 U.S. 79 (1986), the Supreme Court prohibited the prosecutor in a criminal case from exercising peremptory challenges on the basis of race. Here, the Supreme Court extends that holding to private litigants in civil cases.

[Edmonson was injured in a job-site accident and alleged that a Leesville Concrete Company employee permitted one of the company's trucks to roll backward and pin him against some construction equipment. Leesville used two of its three peremptory challenges authorized by federal statute to remove black persons from the prospective jury. Edmonson, who was himself black, requested that the federal District Court require Leesville to articulate a race-neutral explanation for striking the two jurors. The District Court did not require Leesville to give any explanation or to exonerate itself from racial discrimination because it concluded that *Batson* did not apply. (The Equal Protection and Due Process Clauses apply only to conduct of the government; the Fourteenth Amendment, for example, provides that "[no] State" shall deny equal protection or due process.)

[The jury, which included eleven whites and one black, rendered a verdict for Edmonson, but it also attributed 80 percent of the fault to Edmonson's contributory negligence, so that he was awarded only $18,000. The Supreme Court here reverses.]

With a few exceptions, constitutional guarantees of individual liberty and equal protection do not apply to the actions of private entities. This fundamental limitation on the scope of constitutional guarantees "preserves an area of individual freedom by limiting the reach of federal law" and "avoids imposing on the State, its agencies or officials, responsibility for conduct for which they cannot fairly be blamed." *Lugar v. Edmondson Oil Co.*, 457 U.S. 922, 936-937 (1982). One great object of the Constitution is to permit citizens to structure their private relations as they choose subject only to the constraints of statutory or decisional law.

To implement these principles, courts must consider from time to time where the governmental sphere ends and the private sphere begins. . . . This is the jurisprudence of state action, which explores the "essential dichotomy" between the private sphere and the public sphere, with all its attendant constitutional obligations.

We begin our discussion within the framework for state action analysis set forth in *Lugar*. There we considered the state action question in the context of a due process challenge to a State's procedure allowing private parties to obtain prejudgment attachments. We asked first whether the claimed constitutional deprivation resulted from the exercise of a right or privilege having its source in state authority, and second, whether the private party charged with the deprivation could be described in all fairness as a state actor.

There can be no question that the first part of the *Lugar* inquiry is satisfied here. By their very nature, peremptory challenges have no significance outside a court of law. Their sole purpose is to permit litigants to assist the government in the selection of an impartial trier of fact. . . .

Legislative authorizations, as well as limitations, for the use of peremptory challenges date as far back as the founding of the Republic; and the common-law origins of peremptories predate that. [W]ithout this authorization, granted by an Act of Congress itself, Leesville would not have been able to engage in the alleged discriminatory acts.

Given that the statutory authorization for the challenges exercised in this case is clear, the remainder of our state action analysis centers around the second part of the *Lugar* test, whether a private litigant in all fairness must be deemed a government actor in the use of peremptory challenges. [O]ur precedents establish that, in determining whether a particular action or course of conduct is governmental in character, it is relevant to examine the following: the extent to which the actor relies on governmental assistance and benefits, *see* . . . *Burton v. Wilmington Parking Authority*, 365 U.S. 715 (1961); whether the actor is performing a traditional governmental function, *see Terry v. Adams*, 345 U.S. 461 (1953); *Marsh v. Alabama*, 326 U.S. 501 (1946); and whether the injury caused is aggravated in a unique way by the incidents of governmental authority, *see Shelley v. Kraemer*, 334 U.S. 1 (1948). . . .

[I]t cannot be disputed that, without the overt, significant participation of the government, the peremptory challenge system [s]imply could not exist. [C]ongress has established the qualifications for jury service, *see* 28 U.S.C. § 1865, and has outlined the procedures by which jurors are selected. To this end, each district court in the federal system must adopt a plan for locating and summoning to the court eligible prospective jurors. This plan, as with all other trial court procedures, must implement statutory policies of random juror selection from a fair cross section of the community, 28 U.S.C. § 1861, and nonexclusion on account of race, color, religion, sex, national origin, or economic status, 18 U.S.C. § 243; 28 U.S.C. § 1862. Statutes prescribe many of the details of the jury plan, 28 U.S.C. § 1863, defining the jury wheel, § 1863(b)(4), voter lists, §§ 1863(b)(2), 1869(c), and jury commissions, § 1863(b)(1). A statute also authorizes the establishment of procedures for assignment to grand and petit juries, § 1863(b)(8), and for lawful excuse from jury service, §§ 1863(b)(5), (6).

. . . The Clerk of the United States District Court, a federal official, summons potential jurors from their employment or other pursuits. They are required to travel to a United

States courthouse, where they must report to juror lounges, assembly rooms, and courtrooms at the direction of the court and its officers. . . . 28 U.S.C. § 1871.

The trial judge exercises substantial control over *voir dire* in the federal system. *See* Fed. Rule Civ. Proc. 47. The judge determines the range of information that may be discovered about a prospective juror, and so affects the exercise of both challenges for cause and peremptory challenges. In some cases, judges may even conduct the entire *voir dire* by themselves, a common practice in the District Court where the instant case was tried. *See* Louisiana Rules of Court, Local Rule W.D. La. 13.02 (1990). The judge oversees the exclusion of jurors for cause, in this way determining which jurors remain eligible for the exercise of peremptory strikes. In cases involving multiple parties, the trial judge decides how peremptory challenges shall be allocated among them. 28 U.S.C. § 1870. When a lawyer exercises a peremptory challenge, the judge advises the juror he or she has been excused.

. . . Without the direct and indispensable participation of the judge, who beyond all question is a state actor, the peremptory challenge system would serve no purpose. . . .

In determining Leesville's state-actor status, we next consider whether the action in question involves the performance of a traditional function of the government. A traditional function of government is evident here. The peremptory challenge is used in selecting an entity that is a quintessential governmental body, having no attributes of a private actor. [A]nd in all jurisdictions a true verdict will be incorporated in a judgment enforceable by the court. These are traditional functions of government, not of a select, private group beyond the reach of the Constitution. . . .

We find respondent's reliance on *Polk County v. Dodson*, 454 U.S. 312 (1981), unavailing. In that case, we held that a public defender is not a state actor in his general representation of a criminal defendant. . . . While recognizing the employment relation between the public defender and the government, we noted that the relation is otherwise adversarial in nature. "[H]eld to the same standards of competence and integrity as a private lawyer, . . . a public defender works under canons of professional responsibility that mandate his exercise of independent judgment on behalf of the client."

In the ordinary context of civil litigation in which the government is not a party, an adversarial relation does not exist between the government and a private litigant. In the jury-selection process, the government and private litigants work for the same end. [T]he selection of jurors represents a unique governmental function delegated to private litigants by the government and attributable to the government for purposes of invoking constitutional protections against discrimination by reason of race.

. . . If peremptory challenges based on race were permitted, persons could be required by summons to be put at risk of open and public discrimination as a condition of their participation in the justice system. The injury to excluded jurors would be the direct result of governmental delegation and participation.

Finally, we note that the injury caused by the discrimination is made more severe because the government permits it to occur within the courthouse itself. . . .

It may be true that the role of litigants in determining the jury's composition provides one reason for wide acceptance of the jury system and of its verdicts. But if race stereotypes are the price for acceptance of a jury panel as fair, the price is too high to meet the standard of the Constitution. Other means exist for litigants to satisfy themselves of a jury's impartiality without using skin color as a test. . . .

The judgment is reversed, and the case is remanded for further proceedings consistent with our opinion. . . .

. . . .

JUSTICE O'CONNOR, with whom the CHIEF JUSTICE and JUSTICE SCALIA join, dissenting.

. . . Because I believe that a peremptory strike by a private litigant is fundamentally a matter of private choice and not state action, I dissent.

I

In order to establish a constitutional violation, Edmonson must first demonstrate that Leesville's use of a peremptory challenge can fairly be attributed to the government. We have stated the rule in various ways, but at base, "constitutional standards are invoked only when it can be said that the [government] is *responsible* for the specific conduct of which the plaintiff complains." . . .

The Court concludes that this standard is met in the present case. It rests this conclusions primarily on two empirical assertions. First, that private parties use peremptory challenges with the "overt, significant participation of the government." Second, that the use of a peremptory challenge by a private party "involves the performance of a traditional function of the government." Neither of these assertions is correct.

A. . . .

. . . The peremptory challenge "allow[s] parties," in this case *private* parties, to exclude potential jurors. It is the nature of a peremptory that its exercise is left wholly within the discretion of the litigant. [B]y allowing the litigant to strike jurors for even the most subtle of discerned biases, the peremptory challenge fosters both the perception and reality of an impartial jury. . . . The peremptory is, by design, an enclave of private action in a government-managed proceeding.

The Court amasses much ostensible evidence of the Federal Government's "overt, significant participation" in the peremptory process. Most of this evidence is irrelevant to the issue at hand. The bulk of the practices the Court describes . . . are independent of the statutory entitlement to peremptory strikes, or of their use. . . . That these actions may be necessary to a peremptory challenge — in the sense that there could be no such challenge without a venire from which to select — no more makes the challenge state action than the building of roads and provision of public transportation makes state action of riding on a bus.

The entirety of the Government's actual participation in the peremptory process boils down to a single fact: "When a lawyer exercises a peremptory challenge, the judge advises the juror he or she has been excused." This is not significant participation. The government "normally can be held responsible for a private decision only when it has exercised coercive power or has provided such significant encouragement, either overt or covert, that the choice must in law be deemed to be that of the State." . . .

The alleged state action here is a far cry from that the Court found, for example, in *Shelley v. Kraemer*. In that case, state courts were called upon to enforce racially restrictive covenants against sellers of real property who did not wish to discriminate. The coercive power of the State was necessary in order to enforce the private choice of those who had created the covenants. . . ." In contrast, peremptory challenges are "exercised without a reason stated [and] without inquiry." A judge does not "significantly encourage" discrimination by the mere act of excusing a juror in response to an unexplained request. . . .

The Court relies also on *Burton v. Wilmington Parking Authority*. But the decision in that case depended on the perceived symbiotic relationship between a restaurant and the state parking authority from whom it leased space in a public building. As I have shown, the government's involvement in the use of peremptory challenges falls far short of "interdependence" or "joint participation." . . .

B

The Court errs also when it concludes that the exercise of a peremptory challenge is a traditional government function. . . . Whatever reason a private litigant may have for using a peremptory challenge, it is not the government's reason. . . . The Court is incorrect, and inconsistent with its own definition of the peremptory challenge, when it says that "[i]n the jury-selection process [in a civil trial], the government and private litigants work for the same end." . . .

C

None of this should be news, as this case is fairly well controlled by *Polk County v. Dodson*. We there held that a public defender, employed by the State, does not act under color of state law when representing a defendant in a criminal trial. . . . This is because a lawyer, when representing a private client, cannot at the same time represent the government. . . .

II

Racism is a terrible thing. It is irrational, destructive, and mean. . . . But not every opprobrious and inequitable act is a constitutional violation. . . . The Government is not responsible for a peremptory challenge by a private litigant. I respectfully dissent.

. . . .

JUSTICE SCALIA, dissenting.

I join Justice O'Connor's dissent, which demonstrates that today's opinion is wrong in principle. I write to observe that it is also unfortunate in its consequences.

. . . It will not necessarily be a net help rather than hindrance to minority litigants in obtaining racially diverse juries. In criminal cases, *Batson v. Kentucky* already prevents the *prosecution* from using race-based strikes. The effect of today's decision (which logically must apply to criminal prosecutions) will be to prevent the *defendant* from doing so — so that the minority defendant can no longer seek to prevent an all-white jury, or to seat as many jurors of his own race as possible. . . . So in criminal cases, today's decision represents a net loss to the minority litigant. In civil cases that is probably not true — but it does not represent an unqualified gain either. *Both* sides have peremptory challenges, and they are sometimes used to *assure* rather than to *prevent* a racially diverse jury.

The concrete costs of today's decision, on the other hand, are not at all doubtful; and they are enormous. [It] means that *both* sides, in *all* civil jury cases, no matter what their race (and indeed, even if they are artificial entities such as corporations), may lodge racial-challenge objections and, after those objections have been considered and denied, appeal the denials — with the consequence, if they are successful, of having the judgments against them overturned. Thus, yet another complexity is added to an increasingly Byzantine system of justice that devotes more and more of its energy to side-shows and less and less to the merits of the case. . . .

NOTES AND QUESTIONS

(1) *The Role and Objectives of a Private Lawyer in Exercising Peremptory Challenges.* Notice the disagreement between the majority and the dissent with respect to the role and objectives of a private lawyer. Is the majority correct in saying that he works for the "same end" as that of the government? Arguably, the lawyer is not trying to obtain a "fair" jury; rather, she seeks a "favorable" one. What exactly is the function that peremptory challenges serve? *See also* Morehead, *Prohibiting Race-Based Peremptory Challenges: Should the Principle of Equal Protection Be Extended to Private Litigants?*, 65 Tul. L. Rev. 833 (1991); Goldman, *Toward a Colorblind Jury Selection Process: Applying the "Batson Function" to Peremptory Challenges in Civil Trials*, 37 Santa Clara L. Rev. 147 (1990); Note, *Striking the Peremptory Challenge from Civil Litigation: "Hey Batson, Stay Where You Belong!"*, 11 Pace L. Rev. 357 (1991); Note, *Edmonson v. Leesville Concrete Company, Inc.: Can the "No State Action" Shibboleth Legitimize the Racist Use of Peremptory Challenges in Civil Actions?*, 23 J. Marshall L. Rev. 271 (1990).

(2) *Extending Edmonson — Will Extension Wipe Out the Peremptory Challenge?: Gender, Age, Social Status, Etc.* Does *Edmonson* implicitly outlaw peremptories exercised on the basis of gender? Age? Religion? Social status? Wealth? Any and every unexplainable basis? (*see below*) If so, doesn't it eliminate peremptories, since the nature of peremptories is that they are exercised on the basis of generalizations or "hunches," and without cause? For an argument that the Court's reasoning really requires abolition of peremptories, see Garcia, *Strike Three and It's Out: There Goes the Peremptory*, Hous. Lawyer, Nov.-Dec. 1991, at 22. *See also* Morehead, *Exploring the Frontiers of Batson v. Kentucky: Should the Safeguards of Equal Protection Extend to Gender?*, 14 Am. J. Trial Ad. 289 (1990); Sagawa, *Batson v. Kentucky: Will It Keep Women on the Jury?*, 3 Berkeley Women's L.J. 14 (1987).

(3) *The Batson/Edmonson Rule Extends to Prohibit Gender-Based Strikes: J.E.B. v. Alabama ex rel. T.B., 511 U.S. 127 (1994).* In this paternity/child support case, the state court empaneled an all-female jury after rejecting the father's Batson claim that the State's peremptory challenges to remove male jurors violated the Equal Protection Clause. The United States Supreme Court reversed the decision, holding that the Equal Protection Clause forbids using gender as a proxy for juror competence and impartiality. The majority also ruled that gender-based peremptory challenges did not substantially further the State's legitimate interest in achieving a fair and impartial trial. Justice Scalia, in a somewhat sarcastic dissent, argued that the gender-based challenges were permissible under the Equal Protection Clause. Scalia reasoned that the challenges were exercised properly to remove the men because they would be unfavorable to the State's case, rather than improper simply because of their gender. For this reason, Scalia found that the peremptory challenges did substantially further the State's legitimate interest in achieving a fair and impartial trial.

Interestingly, about one month after *J.E.B.* was decided, prohibiting gender-based peremptory challenges and opening the door to challenges based on other suspect categories, the Court denied certiorari in a Minnesota Supreme Court case allowing religion-based peremptory challenges, even though the opinion's reasoning was contrary to the J.E.B. extension of *Batson (Minnesota v. Davis*, 504 N.W.2d 767 (1993), *cert. denied,* 511 U.S. 1115 (1994)). The federal circuit courts currently are divided on the issue of whether the Constitution forbids the use of peremptory challenges against prospective jurors on the basis of their religious beliefs. In *United States v. DeJesus*, 347 F.3d 500 (3d Cir. 2003), the Third Circuit held that peremptory challenges on this basis are constitutional. The Seventh Circuit previously had reached the opposite conclusion in *United States v. Stafford*, 136 F.3d 1109 (7th Cir. 1998).

(4) *The "Complex" Matter of Making or Rebutting an Edmonson Challenge: How Do You Do It?* The progeny of *Batson* suggest that the objector must, in a timely fashion, make out a *prima facie* case, usually by statistics (*e.g.*, the opponent has exercised his peremptories disproportionately on persons of one race or ethnicity). The burden then shifts to the opponent to make a "neutral" explanation (*i.e.*, one not based on race). Many of the cases depend upon determining whether the race-neutral explanation is "pretextual," or in other words whether it is offered as a cover-up. But sometimes it may be difficult for the opponent to offer an articulate "explanation" even if she genuinely is *not* racially motivated, since peremptory challenges are supposed to include strikes exercised, quite properly, by mere "hunches." *See, e.g., Hernandez v. New York*, 498 U.S. 1065 (1991) (explanation held race-neutral, where trial court found that exercise of peremptories against Hispanic venirepersons was motivated by concern that, as Spanish-speakers, they would not be able to rely solely upon English translation by interpreter). There is no question that this inquiry adds "complexity" unrelated to the merits, as Justice Scalia suggests. Does he have a point (and if so, can the courts preserve the holding of *Edmonson* while successfully keeping the "complexity" in bounds?) *See also* Patton, *The Discriminatory Use of Peremptory Challenges in Civil Litigation: Practice, Procedure and Review*, 19 Texas Tech L. Rev. 921 (1988); Note, *Illinois Courts Struggle to Evaluate Race-Neutral Explanations for Peremptory Challenges under Batson v. Kentucky*, 22 J. Marshall L. Rev. 235 (1988); Note, *Rebutting the Inference of Purposeful Discrimination in Jury Selection under Batson v. Kentucky*, 57 UMKC L. Rev. 355 (1989).

(5) *Has the Supreme Court Eased the Burden for the Proponent of a Peremptory Challenge?* In *Purkett v. Elem,* 514 U.S. 765 (1995), in a per curiam opinion with Justices Stevens and Breyer dissenting, the Court reversed the Eighth Circuit Court of Appeals habeas corpus determination that a prosecutor had not sufficiently justified the peremptory strike of two black men from a jury panel. The prosecutor had explained that he struck one juror because he had long, unkempt hair, a mustache, and a beard. The Court emphasized that the proponent of a peremptory strike need not offer a reason that "makes sense," only one that "does not deny equal protection." It then becomes the trial judge's burden to determine as a matter of fact whether or not the strike was racially motivated.

[2] The Conduct of the *Voir Dire* Examination

Read Fed. R. Civ. P. 47 (jury examination and selection); also, read 28 U.S.C. § 1861 et seq. (the Jury Selection and Service Act).

WICHMANN v. UNITED DISPOSAL, INC., 553 F.2d 1104 (8th Cir. 1977). The defendant argued that the trial court had committed reversible error by voir dire questions to the jury that had improperly injected the inadmissible issue of insurance coverage into the case. First, the trial judge asked the entire panel: "Do you or does anyone in your family or do any of your close friends have any connection with the insurance business as an officer, employee, stockholder, claims adjuster or otherwise . . . ?" Secondly, the judge asked whether "The suspicion that one or more of the parties to this suit were or were not covered . . . by insurance" would affect the impartiality of any panel member. The appellate court affirmed:

> We find no error in the first insurance-related voir dire question. . . . Although the sensitive issue of insurance must be treated circumspectly in voir dire, it is permissible to determine whether any prospective juror harbors some bias due to direct or indirect involvement with an insurance company. . . .
>
> However, the second question overemphasizes the element of insurance. Upon establishing that prospective jurors maintain no direct or indirect ties with the business of insurance, the district court should not question them concerning their abstract feelings about insurance coverage. Such a question, by implication, injects the specter of insurance into the case to an unnecessary and undesirable degree. [The Court expressed no view on the propriety of this question if any prospective juror did disclose a direct or indirect relationship with the insurance industry; here, the Court's affirmance was based upon the doctrine of harmless error.]

NOTES AND QUESTIONS

(1) *The District Court's Discretion to Omit or Include Voir Dire Questions: Fietzer v. Ford Motor Co., 622 F.2d 281 (7th Cir. 1980).* In this products liability suit, arising out of a rear-end collision involving a Mercury Comet which burst into flames, the trial judge chose to conduct a limited voir dire examination, consisting of six very general questions, none of which focused on the nature of the claim. Ford requested the trial court to ask several additional questions, including whether any juror had been in a rear-end collision, whether any juror had been a witness to an accident involving fire, whether any juror or member of his or her family had ever suffered burn injuries, and like inquiries. The trial judge refused to inquire into these matters. The Court of Appeals reversed, stating that the issue was "whether the procedure used for testing impartiality created a reasonable assurance that prejudice would be discovered if present." It concluded, "[N]o such assurance could be found from the voir dire examination in this case." However, the cases generally disclose a wide discretion in the court to define the manner of examination and the subjects of inquiry. *E.g., Darbin v. Nourse*, 664 F.2d 1109 (9th Cir. 1981) (court need not follow questions submitted by parties if it covers substance of important areas); *Stephan v. Marlin Firearms Co.*, 353 F.2d 819 (2d Cir. 1965) (in suit for injuries sustained in hunting accident, trial judge's refusal to permit plaintiff to inquire into experience of prospective jurors with guns was not abuse of discretion); *Jamestown Farmers Elevator, Inc. v. General Mills, Inc.*, 413 F. Supp. 764 (D.N.D. 1976) (failure to ask whether jurors might own stock in or work for corporate defendant not abuse of discretion).

(2) *Prejudicial Remarks During Voir Dire Examination: Socony Mobil Oil v. Taylor, 388 F.2d 586 (5th Cir. 1968).* This case should be compared to *Wichmann v. United Disposal*, the principal case, above. The trial judge, through voir dire examination, injected into the case the possibility that the defendant corporation had insurance coverage. It was undisputed that the defendant in fact had no insurance coverage. The appellate court ordered a new trial.

NOTE ON BROADER STATE PROTECTION OF ATTORNEY *VOIR DIRE*

California, New York, and Texas, among other states, differ sharply from federal practice in voir dire examination. By rule or by custom, these states allow attorneys to conduct the bulk of the examination of jurors in civil cases (although California has sharply restricted it in criminal cases). The result is deeper inquiry into possible disqualification, but the disadvantages of attorney voir dire also are present.

The Discretionary Federal Practice prompts many, if not most, federal judges to conduct the voir dire examination themselves, alone. This approach undoubtedly conserves valuable time and avoids some of the abuses of voir dire. *See* Strand & Hart, *The Best Method of Selecting Jurors*, 29 Judges' J. 8 (1990). Why have state courts come to such a different resolution of the issue?

§ 10.03 Appendix The Realities of Jury Selection

D. Crump, ATTORNEYS' GOALS AND TACTICS IN *VOIR DIRE* EXAMINATION

*43 Tex. B.J. 244 (1980)**

The ostensible goal of voir dire examination is to obtain information upon which to base peremptory challenges and challenges for cause.

. . . However, most lawyers use it for other purposes as well. . . .

. . . Some of the uses of voir dire include:

1. *Emphasizing Favorable Law or Facts.* An attorney will usually simplify and explain law favorable to him in a way that makes it seem even more favorable. . . . A plaintiff's personal injury lawyer will explain that negligence means, simply, "carelessness."

2. *Limiting the Effect of Unfavorable Law.* . . . A personal injury defense lawyer will counter the plaintiff's gambit in equating negligence and carelessness by putting negligence in terms of having to find "my client guilty of an unreasonable act" before finding negligence. . . .

3. *Inoculation Against Unfavorable Facts.* If the client has a felony conviction that is going to become known to the jury when he testifies, a lawyer often decides that it would be unwise to wait until that time to introduce the jury to it. . . . This technique is called "inoculation." Just as in medicine a vaccine inoculates against disease by introducing an element of the disease-causing agent into the body, so this use of voir dire examination inoculates against the unfavorable fact. . . . "[T]he mere fact of conviction — that wouldn't prejudice you? You wouldn't be unfair to him?"

4. *Obtaining Commitments.* "If I introduce evidence showing that my client has suffered substantially, could you award him substantial damages — as the law requires? If you find that you're saying to yourself, 'It'd take more than a million dollars to compensate for that suffering,' would you have any hesitation in awarding such an amount?" . . . The theory is that after having given such a commitment, the jurors are . . . likely to follow [it].

5. *Personalizing the Client.* A lawyer may introduce his client, tell a little about him, or have him stand and face the jury. . . . The client is "John," not "Mr. Smith." . . . [A] corporation . . . becomes not "X Corporation," but . . . "John's company."

6. *Arguing the Case Itself.* Some lawyers use the voir dire examination as a kind of opening statement. . . . Some facts have to be given the jurors in order for them to answer

---

questions intelligently, . . . [and] it is inevitable that the facts become stated in an adversary light.

7. *Conditioning the Jurors to Accept One's Proof.* This is a subtle tactic. . . . If, for example, [a lawyer] has a lot of evidence but expects the other side to nibble at it and seek to exclude as much as possible, [he] might depict [himself] as just "trying to get all the facts out as expeditiously as possible" and might express the hope that [his] adversary, Mr. Jones, "will be trying to do the same thing." If, on the other hand, the lawyer has very little evidence . . . [,] he might point out that it is not the number of witnesses that counts, adding: "I always wonder about lawyers who drag a trial out with a string of witnesses. . . . But I believe in getting right to the heart of the matter, and I've boiled the testimony I'm going to present right down to the essentials." . . . This tactic works because the jurors do not know the lawyer who is using it tried another case last week in which he put on a complete dog-and-pony show. . . .

8. *Building Rapport.* Extreme diplomacy is called for . . . (but jurors will not respect a lawyer who doesn't protect his client adequately, so don't hold back from relevant questions unduly). The use of humor, homely analogies and folksy mannerisms . . . often pays off. "This case is sort of like what the old mountain man said about his pancakes: 'No matter how thin I slice'em, there is always two sides.' " . . . [N]ot very highbrow humor — but if used properly, it can bring broad smiles from jurors who are tired of being herded around and a little leery of lawyers anyway.

Another technique is to orient the jurors in a way that shows concern for their function [and] comfort. . . . "I know those benches are getting hard to sit on; I think they must order special, extra-hard benches for every courthouse."

9. *Stealing [the] Adversary's Thunder.* "At the end of this case, . . . Mr. Jones is going to argue that his client ought to get a huge sum of money. . . . It's his job. But if the evidence shows otherwise, can you ignore all that emotional argument and decide this case on the evidence?"

10. *Increasing or Decreasing the Impact of Concerns That Are Outside the Evidence.* This tactic is often ethically dubious. Even though insurance may be outside the allowable evidence, for instance, the plaintiff's lawyer may imply the existence of insurance — indirectly. "Anyone work for an insurance company? Can you be fair, even though you work for a company that furnishes defense lawyers to individuals . . . ?" This sort of comment would not only raise ethical questions; it might be grounds for mistrial. This kind of brinkmanship, however, is common in voir dire examination. . . .

There is even a legitimate place for comment along related lines, however. Jurors may feel sympathy and reluctance to award monetary damages if the defendant is an individual. . . . It may be proper to point out that the jurors should not be concerned about who is to pay any judgment rendered. . . . And of course, it is also proper to attempt to discover persons who work for insurance companies on the panel. This ethical line is difficult to draw. . . .

11. *Guiding the Conduct of the Jurors in Deliberations.* Attorneys have been known to "nominate" the foreperson during voir dire examination. "Mr. Smith, it may be necessary for you to serve as foreperson of the jury. Could you perform that function? . . ." It may even be possible for a lawyer to influence the methodology of jury procedure [by predicting how jurors will go about discussing the case]. . . .

12. *Disqualifying Unfavorable Jurors.* . . . [S]killful lawyers use [the grounds of disqualification] to identify, disqualify and remove persons whom they consider

unfavorable. . . . A highly skilled practitioner may first make the decision to remove an individual and pursue lines of questioning designed to disqualify that individual as a consequence.

The following tactics are often used:

— First, ask about the ground of disqualification in a way that makes a disqualifying position seem reasonable and attractive. . . .

— Second, elicit the response. "You say it'd be difficult. What you're really saying is, you don't think you'd do it, right?"

— Third, if the juror equivocates, force a decision. "Well, there comes a time when everybody has to stand up and be counted. . . ."

— Fourth, "clinch" the response. Your adversary will attempt to rehabilitate the juror; you can head [his efforts] off by saying, "Your answers won't change if I or Mr. Jones ask you a bunch of other questions, will they? . . ." . . .

Insofar as possible, lawyers try to question jurors they wish to disqualify outside the presence of the jurors — at the bench, for instance. . . .

13. *Using Members of the Panel as "Witnesses."* When one juror speaks, the rest of the panel hears what he/she says [unless the court has ordered individual voir dire examination, which is unusual]. Attorneys sometimes exploit this fact by using members of the panel as quasi-"witnesses" . . . . If an insurance company is trying to establish a defense of suicide, and one of the panel members happens to know something about suicide — an ambulance driver, etc. — the defense lawyer might ask: "So you have seen lots of suicide cases, right? Have you seen many where the deceased drove his car into a concrete pier, like in this case, or have you heard about cases like this?" A plaintiff's lawyer may elicit responses from jurors familiar with the type of instrument that injured his client in an effort to cause them to say things that will imply its dangerousness. . . . The response will be more credible "testimony" than any in the trial, because it comes from a disinterested juror chosen ostensibly at random.

It should be reemphasized that not all of these tactics are . . . ethical. The use of jurors as witnesses and efforts to use voir dire examination to place before the jurors considerations not admissible in evidence are examples of voir dire that will usually be improper.

. . . The voir dire examination gives greater play to attorneys' skill than most other parts of the trial. Unfortunately, it often starts the proceedings with a showboating, mud-slinging personality contest. In those jurisdictions that allow extensive voir dire by lawyers, however, one must learn how to deal with it.

VOIR DIRE EXAMINATION BY JOSEPH D. JAMAIL IN *PENNZOIL CO. v. TEXACO, INC.*, NO. 84-05905

151st Dist. Ct. Harris Cy., Tex. July 10, 1985

THE COURT: Are counsel ready?

MR. JAMAIL: Ready for Pennzoil, your honor.

MR. MILLER: We are ready [for Texaco].

THE COURT: Very well, proceed.

MR. JAMAIL: Judge Farris and ladies and gentlemen of the jury, yesterday Judge Farris told you that my name was Joe Jamail, and that I represent Pennzoil, and I do.

This lawsuit that we are here about arose out of evidence that you are going to hear of Texaco's executives and just a few people who wrongfully interfered with Pennzoil's contract for Getty Oil Company and the Getty interests.

There are going to be a lot of issues that you are going to hear, but after you sift through all the issues, only one thing is going to be clear to you. And that is, this is a case of promises, and what those promises meant to Pennzoil, and what they meant ultimately to Texaco.

Pennzoil had a promise with Getty Oil and the Getty interests to purchase three-sevenths of the assets of Getty Oil Company. That promise wasn't just your ordinary promise. It was made by people, not companies.

Hugh Liedtke who I represent and who is my friend, who is seated here today, was the chief executive officer and chairman of the board of Pennzoil. Wasn't a building that made these promises. It was people.

And the question ultimately that you are going to have to decide, those of you that get chosen to serve on this jury, is what a promise is worth, what your word is worth, what a handshake is worth, what a contract is worth. Because that's what a contract is, a promise. . . .

The ultimate question that you are going to get asked . . . and the twelve of you that get to sit and listen to this evidence [are] going to be very fortunate . . . [, is] whether or not people ought to keep their word. . . .

Whether or not you can rely on exchange of promises, evidenced by handshakes and there is something else, evidenced by writing. A memorandum of agreement. All of this happened. . . .

Now, I will come back to this argument in detail because we are going to be together for a while. I know these seats are hard, but you can appreciate my burden and it's a — I think [it's] the most important case ever brought in the history of America. . . .

Whether or not there is morality in the marketplace. . . . That's what it's about. . . .

[Mr. Jamail narrates his client's version of the events in controversy. His statements occupy roughly twenty transcript pages before he questions the venire members. "I'm going to try to keep it simple because it's the only way I can understand it. They made an offer. The [Getty] Museum and the Trustee accepted that offer, shook hands. . . ." The narrative includes simple illustrations: "Those of you who [have] bought a house know what I'm talking about. You make a deal, you agree to buy it, and the next day it's not done. You have to wait a few days and lawyers got to do their thing." For a version of the narrative of events, see Pennzoil's pleading, contained in the Appendix to Chapter 5, above. Mr. Jamail completes the narrative and questions the venire:]

. . . I remind you on the afternoon of the 4th of January, Pennzoil issued the very same press release that Getty had issued that morning showing that both parties were bound by it. You will have that press release. It will be in evidence.

Is there anyone who cannot accept that as evidence of whether Pennzoil and Getty thought they had a binding agreement on the 3rd of January?

If there is, I need to know by a show of hands.

[There is no response, indicating no disagreement.] . . .

Because they [Texaco] own Getty now, lock, stock and barrel and they've agreed to pay any damages that Getty or any of their representatives might incur as a result of inducing Getty to knowingly breach a contract that they had made with Pennzoil on January 3rd. [Mr. Jamail explains that Texaco's purchase contract with Getty included an agreement to indemnify Getty and its managers for breach of contract and related claims.]

I want to ask each one of you, and this is so vital, is there any member of this panel who could not and would not accept that indemnity that Texaco gave at the insistence of the Getty people, . . . as evidence that Texaco had knowledge of the Getty and Pennzoil agreement and binding contract? . . . If there is, I've got to know that now. . . . Raise your hands if there is anybody.

I see no hands. I didn't expect any. . . .

[Mr. Jamail explains that the sellers gave Texaco only a limited warranty of the stock, excluding any claims that Pennzoil might have.]

My question to you is, is there anyone here who would not accept that as evidence of, first, Getty's belief that they had a binding contract? . . .

Secondly, is there anyone here who has any reason to believe you could not accept as evidence, if proved by us, and we will, what I've just told you [as evidence] that Texaco . . . knew that Pennzoil and Getty had a binding agreement? . . .

I didn't think I would see any hands and I didn't. . . .

[Mr. Jamail continues with a different subject:]

[A] question was asked of Texaco's lawyer, what's a handshake worth these days out in the oil patch? And is it a binding agreement? . . . And this is Channel 11 [Television News, interviewing Texaco's lawyer, Mr. Miller] . . . .

Mr. Miller's reply [was,] "[I]f they want to say that there is some old tradition in the oil field, huh, Jesus Christ, they were in New York!" . . .

MR. MILLER: Your honor, excuse me. I'm sorry I was guilty of gross profanity when I said that. I was speaking privately —

THE COURT: Approach the bench. . . .

MR. MILLER: We are going to ask the Court for a mistrial. That's the grossest kind of error for the counsel for Pennzoil to read to the jury a part of the statement which I made to a reporter who was interviewing me, and I had no idea it would ever be abused in this courtroom. . . .

And I object particularly to the recitation of a curse word I used which I should not have used.

MR. KRONZER: [FOR PENNZOIL]: Your honor, it's clearly an extra-judicial admission by a person under the scope of his authority and [admissible in evidence before the jury] under Rule of Evidence 801(a). We mean to offer it in evidence at the appropriate time, too.

MR. MILLER: I don't object to what I said concerning this oil patch handshake. What I object to is in reading the curse word that I used. . . .

THE COURT: Consider it a phrase that I would not have used, but I do not consider it a curse word.

Motion for mistrial is denied.

MR. KEETON [FOR TEXACO]: Your honor, may I point out . . . that that statement . . . is directly in the teeth of their motion in limine about news media publication, portions thereof, purporting to relate to matters at issue [*i.e.*, Mr. Jamail's conduct violated an order of the court against mentioning matter from news reports before the jury without the court's permission, Mr. Keeton claims]. . . .

THE COURT: My ruling stands. No mistrial. . . .

MR. JAMAIL: [addressing the jury again, in open court]: . . .

My question to you: Is there anybody on this panel who has an opinion . . . that is in agreement with what . . . Mr. Miller says is Texaco's position in this, a handshake in New York is meaningless? . . . I take it that you do not.

[Mr. Jamail discusses some of Texaco's defenses. "One of them is that, well, we didn't start it. Getty's investment banker came to us first." Mr. Jamail explains that this argument would be no defense. "Is there anyone here who would accept that just carte blanche as an excuse for what Texaco did, after having knowledge?" He also discusses what he calls Texaco's "loophole defense:" the assertion that the agreement was not binding because it was subject to a definitive agreement. "We say that 'definitive agreement' means what it says, a formal lawyer document such as taking all the inventory and sticking it all in and those things."

[After this and other discussion of legal issues, Mr. Jamail turns to another subject:]

. . . Now, as [his] honor told you earlier . . . , [a]lso representing Pennzoil with me is . . . Baker [&] Botts law firm. I have my own small law firm. I was born here. I was raised here. I went to school and I live here. I'm pleased to be associated with Baker [&] Botts in this case but I need to ask you something because over the years, [it] has represented many companies and families and people. . . . [Here, Mr. Jamail goes through each of the attorneys and firms in the case and, row by row, ascertains which venire members know any member of any firm and ensures that there will be no adverse effects to his client. He then interrogates each venire member who owns any stock in any oil and gas company, or works for any; there are several who own stock in Pennzoil, Texaco or both. He then continues, with another subject:]

. . . What I tell you is what I intend to prove in this case. . . . It's not evidence but we're officers of the court. . . . That's what I tell you and you will see that we will prove it. We cannot under oath misstate things to you. . . . [T]he evidence that you decide the case from will be from that witness stand. . . .

. . . Every question that you get asked at the end of this case [*i.e.*, in the court's charge] will be prefaced with the words, "Find from a preponderance of the evidence" or "Do you find from a preponderance of the evidence."

. . . I need now to explain to you — in order to ask you [a certain] question — what a "preponderance of the evidence" . . . is. . . . By "preponderance of the evidence" is meant "the greater weight and degree of credible evidence."

It does not mean the number of witnesses. It means the believable testimony. I think I can give you an example of this best by asking you to visualize the scales of justice. . . . [P]reponderance of the evidence relative to those scales means [they] tilt[] just the slightest on one side. . . . Whatever way it falls. That will be your oath.

Now, my question to each of you is: Is there anyone here who feels that he or she would not be able to accept that instruction . . . that I believe will be given to you with the charge or issues at the end of this case . . . ? . . .

[A recess took place at this point, during which the following discussion was held outside the presence of the jury:]

THE COURT: . . . Mr. Jamail, I came that close to giving you one on the remark you made.

MR. JAMAIL: What? Quoting [Mr. Miller saying,] "Jesus Christ"?

THE COURT: That's your bite at the apple.

MR. KEETON: We want to renew . . . the motion that we get a new panel [of potential jurors] . . . after those remarks.

THE COURT: My ruling stands, but [to Mr. Jamail:] I've given you fair warning.

MR. JAMAIL: I really didn't realize that was objectionable, but I will not do it ever again. . . .

[After the recess, Mr. Jamail continued, as follows:]

MR. JAMAIL: [addressing the jury venire]: I had [begun] discussing with you, preponderance of the evidence. . . .

Conversely, is there anyone here who would require us to do more than the law does [*i.e.*, to prove the case by more than a preponderance of the evidence]? I take it you would not. . . . I see no hands. . . .

[Mr. Jamail qualifies the venire on the question whether its members would be able to accept testimony from witnesses whom the judge permits to testify as experts. He then explains what a deposition is and notifies the potential jurors that some of Pennzoil's testimony will be offered in deposition form.] . . .

My question to all of you is this, whatever portions of . . . deposition testimony that is let into evidence by Judge Farris, is there anyone here who has any reservation about being able to accept that . . . as evidence just because the witness isn't here? . . . Is there anyone who would not be able to accept deposition testimony in this case for any reason?

I take it that all of you could and would do so. . . .

Is there anyone on the panel who, for whatever reason . . . — I don't want to open a can of worms, but I mean serious business reasons — who feels that he or she could not concentrate . . . on listening to the evidence in this case because of some problem that you might have? If there is, raise your hand. . . .

[The venire already has been informed that the trial will be lengthy, lasting many weeks. Before the commencement of Mr. Jamail's voir dire, the court ruled on 27 venire members' requests to be excused on hardship grounds, overruling all but the most serious. Now, in response to Mr. Jamail's question, several of the same venire members whose claims were denied by the court, plus others, raise their hands. The court, again, considers these matters, questioning each venire member individually, outside the presence of the panel, again denying most requests. The first is Venireperson No. 6, whose request is typical:]

VENIREPERSON NO. 6: I'm the general manager of a country club. . . . I have about 75 people that work for me and I'm responsible for the complete day-to-day operations . . . and only on my ultimate decision totally. . . . [A]nd a long duration, especially, would be detrimental to the company I work for. . . .

MR. JAMAIL: Would it . . . hurt your concentration in this case?

VENIREPERSON NO. 6: Well, a prime example, sir, is like last night. I stayed here all day and I went in about 8:00 o'clock trying to clear up the problems that happened yesterday. I can't be there. There are contracts for asphalting, potholes. Goes on and on. . . . It's my responsibility.

. . . [A] week or something, fine. But possibly ten weeks, I think it would be tough.

MR. MILLER: . . . It's very important that we get responsible people on this jury. We can't try cases in front of unemployed people.

VENIREPERSON NO. 6: That's true.

MR. MILLER: We have to have people that have morality and judgment about them and some sense. It's a hardship on both Pennzoil and us if we can't get people like you. [Mr. Miller is trying to retain the venireperson, Mr. Jamail to have him excused. Why? — Eds.] . . .

MR. JAMAIL: Do you feel like you're going to be put against the wall?

VENIREPERSON NO. 6: I know for a fact I'm going to be put against the wall. Yesterday is a prime example. Every day when I leave here I have to take care of business back at the country club. . . .

MR. JAMAIL: [after the venireperson's examination, outside his presence]: What do you want to do with him, Judge? He can't concentrate.

THE COURT: I'm not going to excuse him. . . .

[The court next considers No. 7 (a Bank employee with only two people in her department, responsible for annual reports and advertising campaigns in the end-of-the-fiscal-year rush — excuse denied); No. 16 (sole proprietor of an antique store with a pending prepaid trip abroad to purchase a business — excuse denied); No. 19 (supervisor of 55 employees — excuse denied); No. 22 (manager of royalty owner relations for a small oil company without "much backup" — excuse denied); No. 24 ("I work the 3:00 to 11:00 shift and after I leave here I have to still report to work" — excused); and many others. The inquiries include the following:]

VENIREPERSON NO. 29: I am not sure this is appropriate, but my fiance works for Mayor, Day & Caldwell [another, unrelated law firm], and he has a case pending against Mr. Jamail, and he has worked with Mr. Miller's firm before. . . . I have heard a lot of stories. . . . [It is an aircraft crash case.]

MR. JAMAIL: Let me ask you this. . . . If he said something bad about me, are you going to let that slop over onto Pennzoil?

VENIREPERSON NO. 29: I am not really sure. I don't mean to be rude, but —

MR. JAMAIL: No, you need to give us the truth. I need to know. . . .

VENIREPERSON NO. 29: I know that he respects you. But I don't know if I could just negate all the other stuff that I have over the years heard. . . .

MR. JAMAIL: [I]n other words, we are not starting out even at this point, are we?

VENIREPERSON NO. 29: No. . . .

MR. JAMAIL: I am behind?

VENIREPERSON NO. 29: Yes.

MR. JAMAIL: [And] I would have to put on more proof or evidence to overcome whatever prejudice you have in your mind.

VENIREPERSON NO. 29: Yes.

MR. MILLER: . . . Now, this is not any kind of airplane case. . . . And your fiance is not in the case. . . . And you don't know Mr. Jamail. And, now, people talk about lawyers just like they talk about doctors and judges and carpenters and everybody else. And most of that gossip you hear is not true. You know that?

VENIREPERSON NO. 29: Yes. . . .

MR. MILLER: And you know, we hate to lose good people just because they happen to have heard something about one or the other of the lawyers.

Now if it was one of the parties, it would concern me. But we are not talking about any feeling you have got against any of the parties, right?

VENIREPERSON NO. 29: No. . . .

MR. MILLER: You think you could listen to the evidence and decide the case according to the evidence?

VENIREPERSON NO. 29: Yes. I think so.

MR. MILLER: That's what I thought. I don't think the lady is excused. . . .

MR. JAMAIL: . . . I move to strike her for cause.

MR. JEFFERS [ALSO FOR PENNZOIL]: Wouldn't be fair for us to use a [peremptory] strike on her. . . .

THE COURT: I will wait until I get the transcript [of the examination, which was prepared, during this trial, on a daily basis].

MR. JAMAIL: It's my position that that makes no difference. Once she said she was prejudiced, . . . [Mr. Miller could not] overcome it.

THE COURT [deferring a ruling on the challenge]: Let's wait till I read it. . . .

[The voir dire examination continued over several days. Mr. Jamail's examination continued for quite some time after this point and was followed by a shorter examination by another attorney for Pennzoil. In addition, Mr. Miller examined the panel for a comparable period of time on behalf of Texaco. Mr. Miller's questions were skillfully phrased, as were Mr. Jamail's, although in a different personal style. They covered many of the same areas of inquiry, but from the standpoint of Mr. Miller's client, Texaco.

[Immediately before concluding his voir dire examination, Mr. Jamail discussed Pennzoil's claimed damages, as follows:]

MR. JAMAIL: . . . Now, the evidence will show by at least one acceptable measure, by expert testimony that we'll present to you . . . that Pennzoil was damaged in the amount of seven billion five hundred [million] dollars, a great deal of money. . . .

Now, I know that that . . . is an astronomical amount of money, but . . . if we are right and we prove our case by a preponderance of the evidence, those of you who remain have already told me up to this point that you would have no problem saying so by your verdict. . . . [Here, using a chart, Mr. Jamail explains the methodology by which Pennzoil plans to prove its damages. He then asks:]

[I]s there anyone on this first row who has any . . . reason to believe that because this is such a large amount of money that regardless of the loss and the proof, . . . that you would not be able to assess these kinds of money damages if Pennzoil proves it in this case by a preponderance of the evidence? . . . [O]bviously, I cannot have asked you a more important question. . . .

[I]t's not wrong or an embarrassment to have a feeling. The only thing that would be wrong is if you had such an inhibition or a feeling, would be not to tell us about it because we would . . . be at a totally unfair disadvantage. . . . Is there anyone on this first row . . . ? Anyone on the second row . . . ? . . .

On the third row, is there anyone who has any reason to believe that you would not be able to assess [$7.5 billion as damages] if we by a preponderance of the evidence sustain our burden of proof? [Mr. Jamail repeats the question for the members of each separate row. A few venire members raise their hands and are questioned before the bench, separately. Mr. Jamail then concludes:]

I take it that all of you would.

Your honor, that concludes the questions from me now. . . .

NOTES AND QUESTIONS

(1) *The Goals and Tactics Illustrated in the Jamail Voir Dire.* The voir dire illustrates several of the goals and tactics described in the article preceding it. You should try to identify portions of the examination in which Mr. Jamail does the following: (a) personalizing the client; (b) obtaining commitments from potential jurors; (c) decreasing the impact of unfavorable law or facts; (d) "inoculation;" (e) increasing the jurors' understanding of (and increasing the impact of) favorable law or facts; (f) building rapport with the jurors; (g) conditioning the jurors to accept the proof; and (h) placing before the jurors inferences or evidence that may not be admitted in the record.

(2) *Ethical Limitations.* Are there any remarks or tactics in this examination that raise ethical problems?

(3) *Challenges for Cause.* Venireperson No. 29 has "heard a lot of stories" about Mr. Jamail, admits to a "prejudice," and would require "more proof of evidence" to overcome it. Mr. Miller elicits her statements that she has no feeling about the parties, "hopes" she could give a fair trial, and "thinks" she can decide the case on the law and evidence. First question: Should the judge grant Mr. Jamail's challenge for cause as to this venireperson? Second question: If the judge does not grant the challenge and makes a finding of fact that she can decide the case according to the evidence and that her feelings based upon stories she has heard will not make her unable to do so, is that ruling likely to be an abuse of the trial judge's broad discretion, so as to lead to reversible error?

(4) *The Defendant's (Texaco's) Voir Dire.* In a sense, this presentation gives a misleading impression that the voir dire was heavily slanted toward Pennzoil's side. But Texaco's lawyers had an equal chance to examine the potential jurors — and Mr. Miller is a skilled attorney with experience comparable to Mr. Jamail's. How should Mr. Miller use the opportunity he has with the jury? What subjects should he cover, and how should he go about the task? Try to construct suggestions for an effective voir dire examination on behalf of the defendant, Texaco.

(5) *Trying a Complex Case to a Jury.* What light does this material shed upon the question of trying highly complex cases to a jury, and upon whether there should be a "complex case exception" to the right to trial by jury? The materials probably do not support the theory that jurors "cannot understand" complex cases (in part because of necessary editing). But they do show the very serious difficulties of composing a jury in a complex case — not because it is complex, but because it is lengthy. This court is ruthless in denying hardship excuses (notice the antique shop sole proprietor who loses the prepaid trip abroad to investigate the purchase of a new business). Isn't the court

right to adopt this approach, since otherwise a representative jury would be impossible to obtain? But could the court reasonably adopt the same attitude if the trial were estimated to last two to five years?

(6) *Voir Dire Examination by Judge or by Attorney (or Both)?* The problem with attorney voir dire is that it starts the trial with a personality contest in which the attorneys try to do everything from obtaining commitments from the jurors to suggesting inadmissible considerations. The trouble with judge voir dire is that the judge is less familiar with the case and lacks the motive to probe for disqualification. (Would the judge have obtained disqualifying responses from venireperson No. 29, who is prejudiced against Mr. Jamail because she has "heard lots of stories?") Which is better? Might it be preferable to have the judge conduct the bulk of the examination, followed by more brief questioning from each attorney? *Compare* Stanley, *Who Should Conduct Voir Dire? The Judge*, 61 Judicature 70 (1977), *and* Begam, *Who Should Conduct Voir Dire? The Attorneys*, 61 Judicature 71 (1977).

(7) *What Kind of Jurors Does Each Side Want?* Mr. Miller, representing Texaco, obviously wants to keep the country club manager. As a crude generalization, the record taken as a whole seems to indicate that Mr. Miller wanted educated, experienced business and professional people. Why? And what sort of jurors would Mr. Jamail, representing plaintiff Pennzoil, want?

Consider the following theory (and it is only a theory). In almost every case, there is one side that would benefit more if the jurors undertook a thoughtful, unemotional analysis of the evidence and were willing to make tough decisions on the evidence, and one side that would benefit more if the jury reacted emotionally to the totality of the evidence. The first will prefer people who are experienced in making difficult decisions from evidence in their daily lives. The second will prefer people who are not — blue collar workers and beauticians. Is this theory valid, and does it fit this case?

(8) *Selection by "Label" Characteristics or by Voir Dire Responses?* The attorneys know various characteristics of the venire members quite clearly, such as their occupations, addresses, ages, marital status, gender, ethnicity, and education. Many of these characteristics, in fact, appear on information forms, filled out by the venire members and furnished to the attorneys for the purpose of simplifying the examination. An interesting question: Which would be a better predictor of the attorneys' peremptory challenges in the average case, the "label" characteristics or the individual responses to voir dire examination? [Note: Relying on labels may seem un-American. But isn't that data "hard," whereas the data from the examination frequently is "softer"?] Consider the following jury study, which emphasizes the "labels."

Murray & Tedin, THE NEW DUBLIN JURY STUDY

Unpublished Study for Use in Litigation *

[Attorney Hartley Hampton filed suit in *Smith v. Crestview Apartment Co.*, on behalf of the parents of a child, Stefanie Smith, who suffered brain damage from an accident in an apartment swimming pool in the (hypothetical) City of New Dublin, State of West York. The complaint accused the apartment owner of negligence in failing to keep the gate in the fence surrounding the pool locked. In preparation for jury selection, Mr. Hampton commissioned Professors Richard Murray and Kent Tedin to survey the

---

* Reprinted with permission.

attitudes of New Dublin County's people. The authors of this book wish to express appreciation to these attorneys and professors for furnishing the documents from which these brief excerpts, with names and details changed, were adapted.]

. . . This survey is based upon interviews of 505 registered voters in New Dublin County, West York. Voters are sampled from . . . a sample of precincts that closely resembles the ethnic, socio-economic, and urban-non-urban characteristics of the county's adult population. Interviews were conducted by telephone, from the central phone facility in [the] Department of Political Science, West York University. . . .

General Attitudes toward Safety Regulations. . . . [The researchers began their survey by asking various questions about safety regulations generally. The conclusion: "People are strongly disposed toward legal rules designed to promote safety." Further, given the existence of a swimming pool ordinance in New Dublin, the interviewees were asked their understanding of it. Most — 88 percent — knew little or nothing, but almost half inferred that it would cover a fence requirement. The overwhelming majority concluded that fences were required for safety reasons. "Virtually everyone (97 percent) said if a fence were built around a swimming pool, it should have a gate that could be closed and locked. Sixty eight percent thought . . . the gate should be closed and locked when the pool was not in use. Thirty-one percent said it would depend on the circumstances]. . . ."

Working Mothers. . . . [Since the accident had occurred while the mother was at work and the child in the care of a babysitter, the interviewees were asked about working mothers. ". . . 21 percent said they should not work; 55 percent said it depended on the circumstances, and one percent was unsure."] . . .

Reactions to the Case Scenario. The sample was read a short summary of the major issues [in] the lawsuit. They were then asked: "In a dispute of this nature, who do you think should win the lawsuit? . . ." . . . [A chart summarizing results is omitted.].

The [sample] tended to favor the mother, by a 57 percent to 21 percent margin, with 11 percent saying it was a tossup. . . .

After people had reacted to the scenario, we asked what factors . . . influenced people's opinions. . . . [T]he most mentioned item was the open gate.

On the other side, people were prone to place blame on the babysitter. Seventeen percent mentioned that she was at fault as their first comment, and 25 percent mentioned this at some point. A few people felt that the mother was at fault. . . .

No one mentioned the owner's rationale [asserted in the discovery and pleading phases of the lawsuit] that the fence was not a safety device in the first place except that several people mentioned that they found this reasoning to be offensive. . . .

[Several charts and accompanying analysis are omitted.]

When told that medical expenses in cases such as this one might amount to two million dollars, and that the average worker might earn a million dollars in their lifetime, people were more willing to [specify] amounts [of damages they thought appropriate]. Among the 55 percent willing to [specify] an amount, $2 million was the most common amount, followed by $1 million and $3 million or more. Relatively few people (less than 5 percent) would award less than $100,000, and a total of 12 percent would award less than a half million. . . .

. . . *Demographic Items and Scenario Preferences.* Much of our attention was directed to analyzing the demographic items' relationship to care preferences. Unlike the attitudinal items, we can be sure that many of the demographic characteristics of potential or actual jurors will be known to the attorneys. [An extensive chart, relating demographic characteristics of members of the sample with attitudes favoring the parents or the apartment owner, is omitted.]

. . . There is a strong [gender] bias in case preference, with men being less favorable [to the plaintiff] than women. And, upper socioeconomic status groups appear to be less good for the mother.

Men favor the mother by 57 percent to 27 percent, a 30 percent difference. However, women favor the plaintiff by 63 percent to 18 percent, a 45 percent difference. The most important predictor of male preferences we could find was whether or not the men had children. . . .

On the socioeconomic front, the plaintiff fared best with people that had finished high school or had less education. The owner did better with those who had attended college. Upper middle . . . and upper . . . income groups were much worse for the plaintiffs, although middle income families . . . were good for the mother. Comparing [gender] with socioeconomic status, we found little impact. Upper income men and women are both worse for the plaintiffs' side.

Racially, there were few differences between whites and blacks, although Mexican-Americans were much worse for the mother, and other [ethnic groups, such as Asian Americans] favored the owner by a substantial margin. The major religious groups in New Dublin did not differ much in preference, although Catholics and fundamentalist Protestants were somewhat [less favorable to the mother] than Baptists.

Responses by age did not follow a linear pattern. Those under 30 were favorable to the mother by a large margin, while those in their 60's or 70's were more likely to favor the owner. Interestingly, strongest support for the mother's side by age came from people in their 50's, who favored the mother by 17 percent compared to 7 percent for the owner.

Occupational data show some groups like medical personnel and college professors to be very good [for the mother], and [predominantly] "female" professions like clerks, secretaries and stenographers to be good. A number of groups like business managers and teachers/ministers appear to be about average in their preferences, while retired persons are worse. The worst occupational group of all was a catchall of "other white collar" types that included people in the construction business and assorted [specialized professions].

One should note that housewives were not especially good for the plaintiff. . . . The best of all women would appear to be those of middle socioeconomic status, currently working outside the home, with children. . . .

Only two farmers were interviewed in our sample, but it might be worth noting that both strongly favored the owner. One might surmise that the conditions of agricultural life would make most farm owners less than sympathetic to the plaintiff's case. However, . . . there is no evident advantage for the mother among urban residents as opposed to rural residents. In fact, those living in small towns and rural areas outside New Dublin City were most favorable of any area grouping. . . .

[A final selection of the Study, containing conclusions and advice for case strategy, is omitted. It included such observations as the concern that pro-owner members of the population, although the minority, were likely to be influential persons; that damages was a separate concern, and demographic characteristics of jurors likely to find liability might differ from those of jurors who would award significant damages; etc.]

§ 10.04 Opening Statements

NOTE ON THE OPENING STATEMENT

Purposes. The opening statement has been likened to the table of contents or introduction to a book. It is designed to let the jury know what to expect: What proof will be offered, how it correlates together, and how it fits with the legal issues. Depending on the case, for example, counsel might outline the testimony witness by witness. Some courts prohibit "argumentative" statements about legal propositions (but this approach tends to diminish the usefulness of the opening statement in relating the facts to the legal theories if it is too strict). In some jurisdictions, the opening statement may not be important, because of wide latitude in the *voir dire* examination.

Tactics. A good opening statement should be clear, direct, and positive. It should be expressed in laypersons' language. It should preview the evidence so that jurors can understand how it fits with the legal theory, and it should make the jurors interested in hearing the case. It should avoid overstating the case, however. Some of the opponent's best final arguments may take the form of: "They told you they would show you thus-and-so, and they did not keep that promise." *See* Shrager, *The Opening Statement*, 21 Trial 102 (Oct. 1985).

The Importance of Establishing Themes in Opening Statements: Major Impact on Juror Decisions. Recently, jury research has shown that jurors form tentative judgments very early in the case — at the voir dire or opening statement stage — and, in fact, they usually do not vary from those early judgments when they reach the verdict stage. This research suggests that close cases, at least, can be "won" in voir dire and opening statement. It also suggests that a chronological preview of the witnesses may be less effective than a thematic, or scenario, approach. "The defense will bring you three major themes: First, we will show you that the defendant was driving carefully; secondly, we will show that the child darted out so that he couldn't avoid hitting her; and third, we will show you that this tragic accident wouldn't have happened if her parents had showed her the proper way to cross the street." This approach works, not because jurors confuse the opening statement with the evidence, but because their reasoning is deductive rather than inductive: that is, they start with certain hypotheses and then seek support from the evidence, rather than building to a conclusion by weighing bits and pieces of evidence. The lawyer who most persuasively establishes these themes thus has established a "filtering system" for the jurors — or a lens through which they will look at all the evidence. *See* Vinson, *Jury Trials: The Psychology of Winning Strategy* (1986).

Legal Problems. In some jurisdictions, it is possible for the defendant to move for nonsuit at the conclusion of the opening statement, on the theory that the proof outlined in the statement would not support a verdict even if all received and believed. *Hurn v. Woods*, 183 Cal. Rptr. 495, 132 Cal. App. 3d 896 (1982). Another issue concerns opening statements telling the jury about evidence that turns out, later, to be inadmissible. What should be done then? In *Smith v. Covell*, 100 Cal. App. 3d 947, 161 Cal. Rptr. 377 (4th Dist. 1980), the court held that reversal should follow when an attorney makes harmful remarks in the opening statement, and when she knows that evidence to support them will not be admitted. [Question: This formulation hints that an appellate court would affirm if the attorney disclosed prejudicial inadmissible information believing in good faith that it possibly might be admissible. Why?]

§ 10.05 Presenting the Case: Evidence and "Proof"

[A] The Rules of Evidence

> Read Fed. R. Civ. P. 43, 45. Also, if your instructor assigns them, read Fed. R. Evid. 103, 401-403, 602, 701-702, 801(c), and 803(1), (2), (6), and (8).

What the Rules of Evidence Are About. The Anglo-American judicial system does not permit the parties to present to the jury any and every item of information they might choose. Instead, the form and content of the evidence is controlled by rules, which have a number of purposes. First, these rules are designed to focus inquiry on matters relevant to the issues, rather than matters that are collateral or prejudicial. Second, they are designed to screen out information that is particularly unreliable or incapable of verification. Third, they seek to allow each party a balanced opportunity to develop and test the evidence. Fourth, they insure the making of an organized and reproducible record. Like all rules, however, the principles of evidence are imperfect, and they can result in the exclusion of arguably useful information. Furthermore, they leave a great deal to the discretion of the judge, just as the rules of civil procedure do, and therefore they depend heavily upon correct interpretation on the spur of the moment, during trial. *See generally* Comment, *A Practitioner's Guide to the Federal Rules of Evidence*, 10 U. Rich. L. Rev. 169 (1975).

An Example to Work With: The Evidence in a Simple Automobile Accident. To illustrate the operation of the rules of evidence, let us take an example. Imagine a common, ordinary automobile-pedestrian accident. Paul Plaintiff alleges that he was injured by the negligence of Dan Defendant, who he alleges ran a red light after becoming intoxicated. Dan denies intoxication, claims that his brakes failed suddenly, and attributes the accident to Paul's negligence in walking outside the pedestrian crosswalk (which Paul denies). A passerby named Bill Bystander saw some of the relevant events. Let us use this example to see what kinds of evidence would likely be received if offered, and what items of information the court would probably exclude.

The Basic Rule of Admissibility: "Relevant" Evidence. Federal Rules of Evidence 401-402 express a general principle of admissibility. "Relevant" evidence is admissible at trial, unless it is excluded by a particular exclusionary rule. "Relevant" evidence, in turn, is defined as evidence having "any tendency" to make a fact that is of consequence to the determination of the action more probable or less probable than it would be without the evidence. This rule is, and should be, liberal; there is no requirement of certainty, and no requirement that the ultimate fact follow inevitably from the evidence, but only a requirement that it have some tendency — "any" tendency — to support the inference. For example, imagine that Paul offers testimony that he saw several empty beer cans in Dan's car immediately after the accident. There is no proof that beer from these cans contributed to Dan's alleged intoxication, or even that he drank them. Nevertheless, many courts would admit this evidence, because it does have a "tendency" to support an ultimate inference that is of consequence to the determination of the action. Therefore, the evidence is "relevant."

The Hearsay Rule of Exclusion. Given the broad rule of admissibility contained in Rules 401-402, it should not surprise you that many of the rules of evidence are rules of exclusion. One of the best known exclusionary rules is the hearsay rule, set forth in Federal Rules of Evidence 801-802. For example, if Dan attempted to show that Paul was outside the crosswalk by testifying that Bill Bystander told him so, the evidence would be relevant, but it would be excluded by the hearsay rule. However, the definition of hearsay is more complex than this simple example might imply. Rule 801 says that hearsay is "a statement, other than the one made by the declarant while testifying at the trial or hearing, offered in evidence to prove the truth of the matter asserted." Thus, it sometimes is proper to offer testimony including someone else's statement, if that statement is not offered to prove "the truth of the matter asserted." Furthermore, certain admissions of a party opponent are specifically excluded from the definition of hearsay. For example, imagine that Paul offers testimony that at the scene, Dan said: "I just ran into a train, didn't I?" Paul offers this testimony to show Dan's intoxication. This evidence would not be excluded by the hearsay rule for at least two reasons. First, it is an admission of a party opponent. Secondly, it is not offered to prove the truth of the matter asserted (because Paul is offering it to show intoxication, not to show that Dan "ran into a train").

Exceptions to the Hearsay Rule: From "Excited Utterances" to Business Records. The rule excluding hearsay is a good one, because hearsay evidence is hard to test for reliability and is usually unnecessary. There are, however, some kinds of hearsay that should be admitted. Some categories of hearsay have circumstantial guarantees of trustworthiness that substitute for the usual manner of testing by cross-examination, and also, certain forms of hearsay are likely to be the best available evidence of the facts they exhibit. Therefore, there is a long list of exceptions to the hearsay rule. For example, Rule 803 allows reception of hearsay statements relating "present sense impressions" as well as hearsay in the form of "excited utterances." For example, if Paul Plaintiff were to testify that Bill Bystander shouted, "That driver's not going to stop!" an instant before the accident, the repetition of this statement would be hearsay — but it probably would be admissible, under both of these exceptions. Another, very common, pair of exceptions admits business records and public records or reports. For example, imagine that Paul offers the repair records kept by Dan's automobile mechanic, which contain the mechanic's statement the day before the accident: "Checked brakes — working fine." This evidence, properly predicated, would be admissible. If courts excluded business records of this sort merely because they contained some hearsay assertions, the jury would be deprived of valuable evidence that might provide the only available means of proving crucial facts. Paul might also attempt to offer the police report compiled by officers who investigated the accident, although this evidence presents a more controversial question.

The Problem of Balancing Relevancy and Prejudice. As we have seen, the definition of relevant evidence is broad. However, a piece of evidence might have relevance so slight, in comparison to its prejudicial impact, that it should not be admitted. For example, suppose that Paul attempted to show that ten years ago, Dan got drunk and fell into the swimming pool at his high school prom. This information may have some tendency to show that Dan has an inclination toward intoxication in the present, but its probative value is slight. Rule 403 says that, if the relevance of a piece of evidence is "substantially outweighed" by unfair prejudice, confusion, misleading tendencies, delay, or inquiry into collateral issues, the judge has discretion to exclude it. Likewise, what if Paul wished to show that Dan had offered to settle the case, or if he presented character witnesses to testify to Dan's generally bad reputation, as a means of persuading the jury to infer that Dan probably was at fault? The rules would exclude this kind of proof.

The Requirement of Personal Knowledge and Limits on Opinion Testimony From Lay Witnesses. Rule 602 requires a showing that the witness has "personal knowledge" of the matter she is testifying about. In general, we want witnesses to testify about observations they actually have made, not about speculation or conjecture. But verbal expression is complicated, and it would not do to exclude testimony merely because it contains some element of "opinion." Therefore, Rule 701 says that opinion evidence is admissible if it is "rationally based on the perception of the witness" and is "helpful to a clear understanding" of her testimony. To take an example, if Paul Plaintiff calls Bill Bystander as a witness, Bill of course would be permitted to testify to what he observed. He could testify about Dan's "glassy-eyed stare" and about his inability to walk without stumbling. He even could give an opinion in the form of an estimate of the speed Dan was driving or a statement that Dan was intoxicated (these matters are clearly based on perception and are helpful to clear understanding). But the court is much less likely to receive Bill's generalized opinion testimony that "Dan handled the situation badly."

Expert Witnesses and Scientific Evidence: Greater Allowance of Opinion Testimony. A separate set of rules applies to expert witnesses. Rule 702 provides that an expert, qualified by "knowledge, skill, experience, training, or education," may testify in the form of an opinion that may encompass information not observed by the witness. The court probably would not allow Bill Bystander, if he is a lay person, to testify that "Paul has a Colles fracture with causalgia for which the prognosis is permanent twenty percent disability," but an expert witness (most likely a physician) could provide this testimony. Scientific expert testimony has been a particular concern of courts attempting to prevent "junk science" from becoming evidence. The Supreme Court's decisions require the trial judge to determine the "reliability" of scientific evidence or, in other words, that it arguably is the product of good science, and also that it "fits" the case, or is useful in correctly resolving the particular fact issues presented, before admitting the evidence.

Procedure: The Manner of Examination and Enforcement of the Rules. The Rules provide that leading questions ordinarily should not be used on direct examination. A leading question is one that suggests its own answer. The court has discretion to make exceptions, however, for such matters as background testimony, child witnesses, etc. Furthermore, testimonial evidence customarily is received in question-and-answer form, rather than as a free-flow narrative from the witness (to which objections would be difficult). Another procedural principle imbedded in the evidence rules is that the attorneys have important responsibilities in the enforcement of the rules. Rule 103 provides that error may not be predicated upon the admission of evidence unless the opponent has timely objected, stating a specific ground. And if the proponent of evidence claims error in its exclusion, she must make an "offer of proof": Either by explaining it, or by putting it in the record outside the presence of the jury, she must insure that "the substance of the evidence was made known to the court" and that it was made a part of the record. Thus, for example, if Paul's lawyer were to ask him, "You were crossing the street inside the crosswalk, weren't you?" Dan could object and should state his ground: The question is leading. On the other hand, if Paul believes that the judge has made an error in excluding evidence — for example, the judge did not permit Bill Bystander to say that Dan was "intoxicated" — Paul must get the substance of this evidence on the record, either by a verbal statement of what he would have proved or by questions and answers on the record, if he wants to be able subsequently to claim error in the judge's ruling.

Cross-Examination and Impeachment. There is no prohibition of leading questions in cross-examination. "You were outside the crosswalk in the street, weren't you?" is a proper question for Dan's lawyer to put to Paul. (In fact, some skilled lawyers maintain that every single question a cross-examiner asks should be a leading question.) And greater latitude is allowed in admitting evidence to impeach the opponent's witnesses. For example, Federal Rules of Evidence 608-611 allow the use of prior inconsistent statements, reputation for untruthfulness, and even convictions for certain crimes. Thus, Paul's lawyer (assuming he has a good-faith basis in information for each question) may ask Dan: "Even though your testimony here is that you were sober, isn't it a fact that last week you told your bartender that you were drunk at the time of the accident?" or "You have a reputation for untruthfulness, don't you?" or "Two years ago, you were convicted of aggravated perjury, weren't you?"

Documents, Objects, Photographs, etc. Unlike TV's Perry Mason, Paul's lawyer would not be successful if he offered an exhibit by standing up and simply saying: "This is a whiskey bottle, your honor, and we offer it into evidence." The exhibit first must be numbered (because it must be made a part of the record). It must be identified, shown to be relevant, and "authenticated" — that is, in the terms of Federal Rule of Evidence 901, it must be shown to be "what its proponent claims." The whiskey bottle would become admissible upon testimony from Bill Bystander, for example, as follows: "Exhibit 1 is a whiskey bottle. I saw it fall out of Dan's car immediately after the accident, and I recognize it because of markings on the label, the level of contents, and its general appearance." For similar reasons, photographs must be shown to "fairly and accurately depict" matters relevant to the suit. As for motion pictures, models, diagrams, or staged recreations, the judge has broad discretion to approve the showing of relevance and authenticity or to exclude the evidence. Finally, documents also must be supported by authentication and a showing of relevance; in addition, where the precise contents of the document are in issue, a party may force the opponent to offer the original or a close duplicate under some circumstances. Thus, if Dan claims to have received a written release from Paul, he must have it marked, identify it, show its relationship to the case, authenticate it ("that's Paul's signature"), offer it, and have it received in evidence.

An Example: Rainey v. Beech Aircraft Corp., below. For an example of the Rules of Evidence in actual operation, consider the *Rainey* case, which follows. The case turns on the difference in wording of two exceptions to the hearsay rule. Section 803(6) admits business records, including "opinions" and "diagnoses" contained in them. Section 803(8) admits public records containing certain "observations" and "fact findings." The question is: Can an unvarnished evaluative conclusion, which would qualify as an "opinion" be admitted into evidence if it is contained in a public document? As you read the case, notice the importance that the Rules of Evidence have for a trial lawyer. There is a separate, upper-level course in Evidence at every law school, in which you will have an opportunity to study the Federal Rules of Evidence in detail. In this course, our objective is more modest: to demonstrate how the Federal Rules of Evidence fit into the trial process and into the overall scheme of civil procedure.

RAINEY v. BEECH AIRCRAFT CORP., 784 F.2d 1523 (11th Cir. 1986) [see Note 1, below, as to the Supreme Court's reversal of this decision]. This case illustrates the impact of the rules of evidence, in that the appellate court reversed after the trial judge admitted what the appellate court concluded was inadmissible hearsay. The plaintiffs, who were the spouses of a Navy flight instructor and student killed in a training exercise, sued the aircraft manufacturer and other defendants on negligence and strict product liability grounds. The Judge Advocate General had conducted an investigation of the fatal aircraft accident, as authorized by law. The investigative report was a public document and contained a number of evaluative conclusions, in the form of the investigators' opinions, which tended to indicate that the accident was not due to negligence of the defendants or to product defects at all. The defendants offered the entire investigative report at trial. Although the report was hearsay, defendants argued that it was a "public record," admissible under Federal Rule of Evidence 803(8). The trial judge admitted the investigative report into evidence, including the investigators' opinions. The jury returned a verdict for the defendants.

The Court of Appeals reversed, holding that the investigators' opinions should not have been admitted into evidence because they were hearsay and did not fall within any exception to the hearsay rule. Federal Rule of Evidence 802 excludes hearsay unless it is subject to an exception. Rule 803(8), the "public records" exception, authorizes admission of the actual "observations" contained in the report. Rule 803(8) did not, however, contain any language referring to "opinions" of investigators contained in a public report. The Rule did admit "factual findings resulting from an investigation made pursuant to authority granted by law . . ."; the relevant question, therefore, was whether the opinions qualified as "factual findings." To determine the meaning of this term, the Court quoted prior authority:

> The language of Rule 803 suggests that "factual findings" define something different than "opinions" and "diagnoses," which are admissible under 803(6) when contained in [business records]. Rule 803(8), although similar to 803(6), substitutes the term "factual findings" for "opinions" and "diagnoses." Since these terms are used in similar contexts . . . it is logical to assume that Congress intended that the terms have different and distinct meanings.

If "factual findings" are distinguishable from "opinions" or "diagnoses," said the Court of Appeals, the difference must lie in the greater degree of formality, precision, and process implied by the phrase "factual findings." Here, the opinions did not qualify, and according to the Court of Appeals, they should have been excluded. [*But see* Note 1, below.]

NOTES AND QUESTIONS

(1) *The Supreme Court Reverses the Rainey Decision (above). Rainey* was affirmed by an evenly divided court on rehearing en banc by the Eleventh Circuit. 827 F.2d 1498 (11th Cir. 1987). However, the Supreme Court reversed the Court of Appeals decision on the scope of Evidence Rule 803(8). *Beech Aircraft Corp. v. Rainey*, 488 U.S. 153 (1988). The Court held that merely because a public record and report containing factual information also contains opinions and conclusions does not render those opinions and conclusions inadmissible. Thus, the trial judge properly allowed defendants to introduce the entire Judge Advocate General's investigative report, including the opinions that pilot error was the probable cause of the accident. This holding, indeed, was consistent with the majority view among the Circuits; the Eleventh Circuit's approach was aberrational. "The prevailing view . . . [is] that all evaluative conclusions are within the scope of Rule 803(8)(C)." *Walker v. Fairchild Industries*, 554 F. Supp. 650 (D. Nev. 1982). What if the investigative report contains hearsay statements taken from third-party witnesses?

(2) *Why Have the Rules of Evidence?* Why shouldn't we just take the approach that any information reasonably germane to a civil case can be admitted and then allow the jury to evaluate its credibility? Lawyers would be perfectly able to argue differences in reliability of different sources to the jury. For example, lay jurors come into court with an almost universal appreciation that hearsay is second-rate evidence. And if that is not enough, the court could instruct the jurors to be suspicious of hearsay. In fact, lawyers

and jurors deal with more difficult credibility issues when they evaluate conflicting witness testimony. Furthermore, exclusion of evidence has significant costs. Do the advantages of the Rules justify these costs? *See also* Berger, *The Federal Rules of Evidence: Defining and Refining the Goals of Codification*, 12 Hofstra L. Rev. 255 (1984).

(3) *Alternate Methods That Can Properly Get This Information Before the Jury.* If evaluative conclusions in a document are to be excluded because they are in the form of hearsay and do not qualify even under the Supreme Court's approach, that does not mean that the underlying information itself necessarily must be kept from the jury. All it means is that it cannot be introduced in this form. If you were the defendant's lawyer, and you felt that the jury should hear the substance of these evaluative opinions, how would you go about finding a way to do it?

[B] Making the Record

GUETERSLOH v. C.I.T. CORP., 451 S.W.2d 759 (Tex. Civ. App.-Amarillo 1970, writ ref'd n.r.e.). This was a suit on a promissory note by C.I.T. Corporation as plaintiff against M.F. Guetersloh, as maker of the note, and Herman Guetersloh, as co-maker and guarantor. The Court granted judgment for the plaintiff. On appeal, the defendant's first point of error was that plaintiff C.I.T. Corporation failed to introduce the note into evidence. It appears that, during the trial, plaintiff produced the original document; it was inspected by defendant's trial counsel; it was marked by the court reporter as "plaintiff's exhibit 1"; it was handed to the judge, and it was included by the court reporter among the exhibits that were part of the proceeding. However, plaintiff never offered it into evidence, and the judge never made a ruling ordering that it be received or admitted. Therefore, the defendant argued, neither it nor its contents could properly have been considered by the trial court. Without the note as an exhibit, the trial record would be inadequate to sustain a finding of the existence, possession, or terms of the note.

The appellate court affirmed. There is a requirement that a party offer the exhibit and that the court rule on its admittance. But the court reasoned that the precise word "offer" was not required, nor did the court's ruling have to take any particular form. Here, there was an *implied* offer and admittance:

> During the trial . . . the original document . . . was handed to and received by the Court, and it was placed in the [record of evidence received] by the court reporter. The defendant's trial counsel treated the note as though it were in evidence. In fact, during the testimony the defendant's counsel objected to a question on the ground that it would "vary the terms of the contract which is already in evidence." The circumstances here . . . indicate that the note was introduced in evidence.

NOTES AND QUESTIONS

(1) *Desirability of a Clear Record of Evidence to Support a Favorable Judgment.* Although the plaintiff prevailed and the decision leaves a sense that justice was done, it would have been better if this appellate issue had never arisen. The plaintiff could not be certain of victory, because there have been numerous cases in which courts have refused to consider evidence that was not a part of the record. *See, e.g., Adickes v. S.H. Kress & Co.*, in § 9.02 above (Supreme Court refused to consider summary judgment evidence that was not in proper form, although included in record). An attorney should

(1) prepare a proof outline before trial (it is surprising in some relatively simple cases how many discrete facts plaintiff must prove) and (2) consider it as a checklist before resting.

(2) *The Record as Including Both Admitted and Excluded Evidence.* The trial judge's ruling admitting an exhibit is necessary because the record includes both evidence that has been received for the jury's consideration and information that has been excluded (*e.g.*, offers of proof received outside the jury's presence).

(3) *Necessary Steps for Admitting an Exhibit.* In federal courts, exhibits may be marked and admitted in a pretrial conference. But in courts in which pretrial admission is not customary, the following is a list of steps that may be necessary: (1) Have the exhibit marked by the court reporter or courtroom deputy. "May I have this marked as plaintiff's exhibit 1, please?" (2) Have the sponsoring witness identify it. "It's a photograph of the accident scene." (3) Lay the predicate to authenticate and show relevancy. "And does plaintiff's exhibit 1 fairly and accurately depict the accident scene as you saw it?" "Yes." (4) Tender it to opposing counsel, who may object to its admission. (5) Formally offer it into evidence. "I offer plaintiff's exhibit 1 into evidence, Your Honor, after having tendered it to opposing counsel." (6) Be ready to argue its admissibility against an objection, if necessary. (7) Take affirmative steps to obtain a ruling from the court to the effect that the exhibit is "admitted" or "received" in evidence. "Is plaintiff's exhibit 1 admitted, Your Honor?" "Yes." (8) Take steps to have the exhibit communicated to the jury. "May the bailiff pass plaintiff's exhibit 1 to the jurors, Your Honor?" [Note: Custom varies; for example, in some jurisdictions an exhibit should be shown to opposing counsel before the witness speaks about it.]

[C] The "Burden of Proof"

NOTE ON THE BURDENS OF PRODUCTION AND OF PERSUASION

The "Burden of Production." The phrase "burden of proof" actually refers to two distinct concepts: the "burden of production" and the "burden of persuasion." The burden of production is the burden to introduce some evidence that is minimally sufficient to support a jury finding on a given issue. It sometimes is described as the burden to "make out a *prima facie* case" or the burden to introduce "sufficient evidence to get to the jury." In practical terms, the party who bears the burden of production is the one that would lose if neither side introduced any evidence.

The "Burden of Persuasion." The burden of persuasion, on the other hand, is the requirement that a party introduce evidence that persuades the trier of fact on a given issue. Usually, in a civil case, the preponderance-of-the-evidence standard defines the burden of persuasion. Thus the party with the burden of persuasion is the one that would lose if the jury viewed the evidence as precisely balanced.

Allocating the Burdens Between the Parties. On some issues, the plaintiff may have both the burden of production and the burden of persuasion; on others, the defendant may have both burdens. Sometimes, one party has the burden of production, the other the burden of persuasion; and there are some cases in which it can be said that one burden or the other "shifts" when one party makes out a *prima facie* case.

A Simple Example: Proof of Agency by a Presumption Based on the Defendant's Placement of Its Trade Name on Its Vehicle. In some jurisdictions, proof that a vehicle carries the defendant's trade name creates a "mandatory, rebuttable presumption" that the defendant's agent was operating the vehicle and that he was acting within the scope of his agency. In other words, proof of the trade name automatically establishes the responsibility of the defendant, unless the defendant offers evidence of non-agency. Thus, if the plaintiff meets her initial burden of production — by showing that the truck that struck her carried the defendant's trade name — she has presumptively established the defendant's responsibility, even if she can prove nothing else about the driver. That is so, unless the defendant responds by carrying his own burden of production (by offering some evidence, for example, from which a jury could conclude that the truck was stolen and missing at the time of the accident). In that event (*i.e.*, where both parties at least minimally have met their burdens of production), some jurisdictions would submit the case to the jury with the ultimate burden of persuasion placed on the plaintiff. *See* C. McCormick, Evidence §§ 343-344 (3d ed. 1984). The following case is a more complex application of the same principles.

TEXAS DEPARTMENT OF COMMUNITY AFFAIRS v. BURDINE
450 U.S. 248 (1981)

JUSTICE POWELL delivered the opinion of the Court.

This case requires us to address again the nature of the evidentiary burden placed upon the defendant in an employment discrimination suit brought under Title VII of the Civil Rights Act of 1964. . . . The narrow question presented is whether, after the plaintiff has proved a prima facie case of discriminatory treatment, the burden shifts to the defendant to persuade the court by a preponderance of the evidence that legitimate, non-discriminatory reasons for the challenged employment action existed. [Eds. Note: The precise placement of the burdens, in certain kinds of civil rights cases, has been adjusted since this case, although both the framework of this case and the precise holding probably remain authoritative today. See Notes 1–3, below.]

I

[Petitioner Texas Department of Community Affairs ("TDCA") hired respondent Burdine, a woman, for the position of accounting clerk. She was promoted to field services coordinator. She then applied for the supervisory position of project director, but TDCA employed a man from another division of the agency in this position. Subsequently, he reduced staff by firing respondent Burdine along with two other employees, retaining another man as the only professional employee in the division. Respondent Burdine soon was rehired by TDCA and assigned to another division, where she received the exact salary paid to the project director. Subsequent promotions kept her salary and responsibility commensurate with what she would have received as project director.

[Burdine sued TDCA, alleging gender discrimination. The District Court held for the defendant, TDCA. The defendant's evidence consisted of employees' testimony that the three terminated individuals did not work well together and that TDCA thought that eliminating this problem would improve efficiency. The District Court accepted this explanation. The Fifth Circuit reversed in part, disagreeing with the District Court's finding that the testimony sufficiently had rebutted Burdine's prima facie case of gender discrimination in the decision to terminate her employment. The court held that the defendant in a Title VII case bears the burden of proving by a preponderance of the evidence the existence of legitimate non-discriminatory reasons for the employment action and that the defendant also must prove by objective evidence that those hired or promoted were better qualified than the plaintiff. It remanded the case for computation of back pay. The Supreme Court granted certiorari and vacated the Fifth Circuit's decision.]

II

In *McDonnell Douglas Corp. v. Green*, 411 U.S. 792, 93 S. Ct. 1817, 36 L. Ed. 2d 668 (1973), we set forth the basic allocation of burdens and order of presentation of proof in a Title VII case alleging discriminatory treatment. First, the plaintiff has the burden of proving by the preponderance of the evidence a prima facie case of discrimination. Second, if the plaintiff succeeds in proving the prima facie case, the burden shifts to the defendant "to articulate some legitimate, nondiscriminatory reason for the employee's rejection." . . . Third, should the defendant carry this burden, the plaintiff must then have an opportunity to prove by a preponderance of the evidence that the legitimate reasons offered by the defendant were not its true reasons, but were a pretext for discrimination. . . .

The burden of establishing a prima facie case of disparate treatment is not onerous. The plaintiff must prove by a preponderance of the evidence that she applied for an available position for which she was qualified, but was rejected under circumstances which give rise to an inference of unlawful discrimination. [I]f the trier of fact believes the plaintiff's evidence, and if the employer is silent in the face of the presumption, the court must enter judgment for the plaintiff because no issue of fact remains in the case.[7]

The burden that shifts to the defendant, therefore, is to rebut the presumption of discrimination by producing evidence that the plaintiff was rejected, or someone else was preferred, for a legitimate, nondiscriminatory reason. . . . It is sufficient if the defendant's evidence raises a genuine issue of fact as to whether it discriminated against the plaintiff. . . . Placing this burden of production on the defendant thus serves simultaneously to meet the plaintiff's prima facie case by presenting a legitimate reason for the action and to frame the factual issue with sufficient clarity so that the plaintiff will have a full and fair opportunity to demonstrate pretext. The sufficiency of the defendant's evidence should be evaluated by the extent to which it fulfills these functions.

The plaintiff retains the burden of persuasion. She now must have the opportunity to demonstrate that the proffered reason was not the true reason for the employment decision. This burden now merges with the ultimate burden of persuading the court that she has been the victim of intentional discrimination. . . . *See McDonnell Douglas*. . . .

III

In reversing the judgment of the District Court that the discharge of respondent from PSC was unrelated to her sex, the Court of Appeals adhered to two rules it had developed to elaborate the defendant's burden of proof. First, the defendant must prove by a preponderance of the evidence that legitimate, nondiscriminatory reasons for the discharge existed. . . . Second, to satisfy this burden, the defendant "must prove that those he hired . . . were somehow *better* qualified than was plaintiff; in other words, comparative evidence is needed." . . .

---

[7] The phrase "prima facie case" not only may denote the establishment of a legally mandatory, rebuttable presumption, but also may be used by courts to describe the plaintiff's burden of producing enough evidence to permit the trier of fact to infer the fact at issue. 9 J. Wigmore, *Evidence* § 2494 (3d ed. 1940). *McDonnell Douglas* should have made it apparent that in the Title VII context we use "prima facie case" in the former sense.

The Court of Appeals has misconstrued the nature of the burden that *McDonnell Douglas* and its progeny place on the defendant. *See* Part II, *supra.* We stated . . . that "the employer's burden is satisfied if he simply 'explains what he has done' or 'produc[es] evidence of legitimate nondiscriminatory reasons.' " . . . It is plain that the Court of Appeals required much more: it placed on the defendant the burden of persuading the court that it had convincing, objective reasons for preferring the chosen applicant above the plaintiff. . . .

The Court of Appeals also erred in requiring the defendant to prove by objective evidence that the person hired or promoted was more qualified than the plaintiff. . . . The Court of Appeals' rule would require the employer to show that the plaintiff's objective qualifications were inferior to those of the person selected. If it cannot, a court would, in effect, conclude that it has discriminated.

The court's procedural rule harbors a substantive error. Title VII prohibits all discrimination in employment based upon race, sex, and national origin. . . . Title VII, however, does not demand that an employer give preferential treatment to minorities or women. . . .

The view of the Court of Appeals can be read, we think, as requiring the employer to hire the minority or female applicant whenever that person's objective qualifications were equal to those of a white male applicant. But Title VII does not obligate an employer to accord this preference. . . .

IV

In summary, the Court of Appeals erred by requiring the defendant to prove by a preponderance of the evidence the existence of nondiscriminatory reasons for terminating the respondent and that the person retained in her stead had superior objective qualifications for the position. When the plaintiff has proved a prima facie case of discrimination, the defendant bears only the burden of explaining clearly the nondiscriminatory reasons for its actions. The judgment of the Court of Appeals is vacated and the case is remanded for further proceedings consistent with this opinion.

NOTES AND QUESTIONS

(1) *Adjustment of the Burdens in Certain Civil Rights "Disparate Impact" Cases: The Civil Rights Act of 1991 and the Decisions after Burdine.* The Civil Rights Act of 1991 adjusts the burdens of production in some kinds of civil rights cases, particularly those of "disparate impact" (*i.e.*, cases in which the employer's general policies have a disparate statistical impact upon a protected class). For example, once a plaintiff has met her initial burden of production by showing a disparate impact on members of her race from a practice engaged in by her employer, it is no longer sufficient for the employer merely to offer a "race-neutral" explanation. Instead, under § 105(a) of the 1991 Act, the defendant's burden of production is to "demonstrate that the challenged practice is job related for the position in question and consistent with business necessity." This provision reverses the Supreme Court's decision in *Wards Cove Packing Co. v. Atonio*, 490 U.S. 642 (1989). The *Burdine* decision may be unaffected by the legislation, however, because it did not involve statistical proof or responses explaining the employer's general policies, but rather involved the treatment of a single employee (*i.e.*, it was a "disparate treatment" case involving an individual rather than a statistical "disparate impact" case). Note how the precision of definition in *Burdine* of the various burdens facilitates their adjustment,

whether by legislation or by decision. *See generally* Ware, *The Civil Rights Act of 1990: A Dream Deferred*, 10 St. Louis Pub. L. Rev. 1 (1991).

(2) *Is Proof of Pretext Alone Sufficient Under Burdine. St Mary's Honor Center v. Hicks, 509 U.S. 502 (1993).* In this Title VII civil rights action, plaintiff Hicks established a prima facie case of discriminatory treatment, and defendant St. Mary's offered non-discriminatory explanations for its actions that the trial court found to be pretextual. The Supreme Court held that finding a defendant's explanations pretextual does not entitle the plaintiff to judgment as a matter of law. According to the Court, plaintiff retains the ultimate burden of persuasion and is still required to prove that the defendant's actions were racially motivated. Subsequently, in *Reeves v. Sanderson Plumbing Products, Inc.*, 530 U.S. 133 (2000), the Supreme Court ruled that evidence of pretext alone, *i.e.*, that the employer's proffered reason is unworthy of credence, may be sufficient to prove unlawful discrimination by a preponderance of the evidence. On the other hand, the Supreme Court also explained that "[c]ertainly there will be instances where, although the plaintiff has established a prima facie case and set forth sufficient evidence to reject the defendant's explanation, no rational fact finder could conclude that the action was discriminatory." The *Reeves* opinion appears in the next subsection.

(3) *Burdens of Production and Persuasion in Burdine.* The Court's holding can be stated this way: The plaintiff has the initial burden of production. When that burden is satisfied, the defendant has the burden of production of a non-discriminatory explanation. If both burdens of production are met, the plaintiff has the burden of persuasion. Given this explanation, what should be the result if: (a) The plaintiff makes out a *prima facie* case sufficient to meet her burden of production, and the defendant offers no explanation whatever? (b) Both parties meet their burdens of production, and neither party offers any further evidence? (c) Both parties meet their burdens of production, and the plaintiff then offers further evidence, but the trier of fact is not persuaded by the plaintiff's evidence taken as a whole?

(4) *Presumptions, "Bursting Bubbles," and "Mandatory, Rebuttable Presumptions."* A "presumption" is a factual conclusion that the law permits or requires the factfinder to make if other specified facts (sometimes called the "base facts") are proved. In many jurisdictions, proof of the base facts compels a finding of the presumed fact, unless the opponent rebuts the proof. For example, evidence that a letter was mailed (with proper address and postage) creates a presumption that the letter was received by the addressee. Thus if the defendant offers no contrary evidence, the plaintiff would be entitled to have the court instruct the jury that it must find that the defendant received it. If the defendant actually testifies that she did not receive it, however, in some jurisdictions the presumption disappears like a "bursting bubble." (This "bursting bubble" theory is not applied in all jurisdictions or to all presumptions, but it is widespread.) In *Burdine*, the Supreme Court says (in footnote 7) that when a Title VII plaintiff makes out a *prima facie* case, she has established "a legally mandatory, rebuttable presumption." What does this jargon mean?

[D] Judgment as a Matter of Law (or "Directed Verdict")

Read U.S. Const. amend. VII (right to jury trial) and Fed. R. Civ. P. 50.

REEVES v. SANDERSON PLUMBING CO.
530 U.S. 133 (2000)

JUSTICE O'CONNOR delivered the opinion of the Court.

This case concerns the kind and amount of evidence necessary to sustain a jury's verdict that an employer has unlawfully discriminated on the basis of age. . . . We must also decide whether the employer was entitled to judgment as a matter of law under the particular circumstances presented here.

I

[This was an age discrimination suit under the federal Age Discrimination in Employment Act (ADEA). Roger Reeves, age 57, was a supervisor of Sanderson Plumbing's "Hinge Room," as it was called. Joe Oswalt, in his mid-thirties, also was a supervisor, and Russell Caldwell, age 45, was the manager of the Hinge Room. Powe Chesnut, who was company's director of manufacturing, ordered an audit of the Hinge Room's timesheets. The audit showed that unauthorized absenteeism was frequent in the Hinge Room, and it revealed numerous timekeeping errors and misrepresentations by Reeves, Caldwell, and Oswalt. Chesnut recommended that Reeves and Caldwell, age 57 and 45 respectively, be fired, but he did not recommend firing Oswalt, the one in his mid-thirties. Sandra Sanderson, the company's president, followed this recommendation and discharged Reeves and Caldwell.]

[In his suit, plaintiff Reeves claimed that his age was a motivating factor for his discharge, in violation of the ADEA. Defendant Sanderson Plumbing countered by contending that it had fired Reeves due to his failure to maintain adequate attendance records. But Reeves offered testimony tending to show that the company's explanation was a pretext. Reeve's evidence, if believed, would have shown that he accurately recorded attendance and that Chesnut, the man who had recommended Reeves's firing, had demonstrated age-based animus toward Reeves by making derogatory age-related remarks.]

During the trial, the District Court twice denied oral motions by respondent for judgment as a matter of law under Rule 50 of the Federal Rules of Civil Procedure, and the case went to the jury. The court instructed the jury that "[i]f the plaintiff fails to prove age was a determinative or motivating factor in the decision to terminate him, then your verdict shall be for the defendant." So charged, the jury returned a verdict in favor of [plaintiff Reeves]. . . . Respondent [later] renewed its motion for judgment as a matter of law and alternatively moved for a new trial. . . . The District Court denied respondent's motions and [entered judgment for nearly $100,000 in favor of Reeves].

The Court of Appeals for the Fifth Circuit reversed, holding that petitioner [Reeves] had not introduced sufficient evidence to sustain the jury's finding of unlawful discrimination. After noting respondent's proffered justification for petitioner's discharge, the court acknowledged that petitioner "very well may" have offered sufficient evidence for "a reasonable jury [to] have found that [respondent's] explanation for its employment decision was pretextual." The court explained, however, that this was "not dispositive" of the ultimate issue — namely, "whether Reeves presented sufficient evidence that his age motivated [respondent's] employment decision." Addressing this question, the court weighed petitioner's additional evidence of discrimination against other circumstances surrounding his discharge. Specifically, the court noted that Chesnut's age-based comments "were not made in the direct context of Reeves's termination"; there was no allegation that the two other individuals who had recommended that petitioner be fired (Jester and Whitaker) were motivated by age; two of the decisionmakers involved in petitioner's discharge (Jester and Sanderson) were over the age of 50; all three of the Hinge Room supervisors were accused of inaccurate recordkeeping; and several of respondent's management positions were filled by persons over age 50 when petitioner was fired. On this basis, the court concluded that petitioner had not introduced sufficient evidence for a rational jury to conclude that he had been discharged because of his age. [In performing this "weighing" of the evidence, the Fifth Circuit followed its previous decision in *Boeing Co. v. Shipman*, 411 F.2d 365 (5th Cir, 1969) (en banc), which held that a motion for judgment as a matter of law required review of the entire record, as opposed to consideration of only the evidence favoring the nonmovant.] . . .

[Part II of the Court's opinion, dealing with the text and proof structure of the ADEA, is omitted here. After its discussion of the ADEA, the Court turned to the general issue of motions for judgment as a matter of law, in Part III, as follows.]

III

A

. . . Under Rule 50, a court should render judgment as a matter of law when "a party has been fully heard on an issue and there is no legally sufficient evidentiary basis for a reasonable jury to find for that party on that issue." Fed. R. Civ. Proc. 50(a). [The 2007 "restyling" amendments to the Federal Rules of Civil Procedure have changed this language slightly — Eds.] The Courts of Appeals have articulated differing formulations as to what evidence a court is to consider in ruling on a Rule 50 motion. Some decisions have stated that review is limited to that evidence favorable to the non-moving party, *see, e.g., Aparicio v. Norfolk & Western R. Co.*, 84 F.3d 803, 807 (6th Cir. 1996); *Simpson v. Skelly Oil Co.*, 371 F.2d 563, 566 (8th Cir. 1967), while most have held that review extends to the entire record, drawing all reasonable inferences in favor of the nonmovant, *see, e.g., Tate v. Government Employees Ins. Co.*, 997 F.2d 1433, 1436 (11th Cir. 1993); *Boeing Co. v. Shipman*, 411 F.2d 365, 374 (5th Cir. 1969) (en banc).

On closer examination, this conflict seems more semantic than real. Those decisions holding that review under Rule 50 should be limited to evidence favorable to the nonmovant appear to have their genesis in *Wilkerson v. McCarthy*, 336 U.S. 53 (1949). *See* 9A C. Wright & A. Miller, Federal Practice and Procedure § 2529, pp. 297-301 (2d ed. 1995) (hereinafter Wright & Miller). In *Wilkerson*, we stated that "in passing upon whether there is sufficient evidence to submit an issue to the jury we need look only to the evidence and reasonable inferences which tend to support the case of" the nonmoving party. But subsequent decisions have clarified that this passage was referring to the evidence to which the trial court should give credence, not the evidence that the court should review. In the analogous context of summary judgment under Rule 56, we have stated that the court must review the record "taken as a whole." And the standard for granting summary judgment "mirrors" the standard for judgment as a matter of law, such that "the inquiry under each is the same." . . . *Celotex Corp. v. Catrett.* It therefore follows that, in entertaining a motion for judgment as a matter of law, the court should review all of the evidence in the record.

In doing so, however, the court must draw all reasonable inferences in favor of the nonmoving party, and it may not make credibility determinations or weigh the evidence. "Credibility determinations, the weighing of the evidence, and the drawing of legitimate inferences from the facts are jury functions, not those of a judge." Thus, although the court should review the record as a whole, it must disregard all evidence favorable to the moving party that the jury is not required to believe. *See* Wright & Miller 299. That is, the court should give credence to the evidence favoring the nonmovant as well as that "evidence supporting the moving party that is uncontradicted and unimpeached, at least to the extent that that evidence comes from disinterested witnesses."

B

Applying this standard here, it is apparent that respondent was not entitled to judgment as a matter of law. In this case, in addition to establishing a prima facie case of discrimination and creating a jury issue as to the falsity of the employer's explanation, petitioner introduced additional evidence that Chesnut was motivated by age-based animus and was principally responsible for petitioner's firing. Petitioner testified that Chesnut had told him that he "was so old [he] must have come over on the Mayflower" and, on one occasion when petitioner was having difficulty starting a machine, that he "was too damn old to do [his] job." According to petitioner, Chesnut would regularly "cuss at me and shake his finger in my face." Oswalt, roughly 24 years younger than petitioner, corroborated that there was an "obvious difference" in how Chesnut treated them. He stated that, although he and Chesnut "had [their] differences," "it was nothing compared to the way [Chesnut] treated Roger." Oswalt explained that Chesnut "tolerated quite a bit" from him even though he "defied" Chesnut "quite often," but that Chesnut treated petitioner "in a manner, as you would . . . treat . . . a child when . . . you're angry with [him]." Petitioner also demonstrated that, according to company records, he and Oswalt had nearly identical rates of productivity in 1993. Yet respondent conducted an efficiency study of only the regular line, supervised by petitioner, and placed only petitioner on probation. Chesnut conducted that efficiency study and, after having testified to the contrary on direct examination, acknowledged on cross-examination that he had recommended that petitioner be placed on probation following the study.

Further, petitioner introduced evidence that Chesnut was the actual decisionmaker behind his firing. Chesnut was married to Sanderson, who made the formal decision to discharge petitioner. Although Sanderson testified that she fired petitioner because he had "intentionally falsified company pay records," respondent only introduced evidence concerning the inaccuracy of the records, not their falsification. A 1994 letter authored by Chesnut indicated that he berated other company directors, who were supposedly his co-equals, about how to do their jobs. Moreover, Oswalt testified that all of respondent's employees feared Chesnut, and that Chesnut had exercised "absolute power" within the company for "as long as [he] can remember."

In holding that the record contained insufficient evidence to sustain the jury's verdict, the Court of Appeals misapplied the standard of review dictated by Rule 50. Again, the court disregarded critical evidence favorable to petitioner — namely, the evidence supporting petitioner's prima facie case and undermining respondent's nondiscriminatory explanation. The court also failed to draw all reasonable inferences in favor of petitioner. For instance, while acknowledging "the potentially damning nature" of Chesnut's age-related comments, the court discounted them on the ground that they "were not made in the direct context of Reeves's termination." And the court discredited petitioner's evidence that Chesnut was the actual decisionmaker by giving weight to the fact that there was "no evidence to suggest that any of the other decision makers were motivated by age." Moreover, the other evidence on which the court relied — that Caldwell and Oswalt were also cited for poor recordkeeping, and that respondent employed many managers over age 50 — although relevant, is certainly not dispositive. In concluding that these circumstances so overwhelmed the evidence favoring petitioner that no rational trier of fact could have found that petitioner was fired because of his age, the Court of Appeals impermissibly substituted its judgment concerning the weight of the evidence for the jury's.

[The judgment of the Court of Appeals is reversed.]

[The concurring opinion of Justice Ginsburg is omitted.]

W. Dorsaneo, REEXAMINING THE RIGHT TO JURY TRIAL*
54 SMU L. Rev. 1695 (2001)

[In this article, Professor Dorsaneo explains the impact of the *Reeves* case and the meaning of its holding.]

. . . .

[T]he *Reeves* Court addressed, and for the most part resolved, longstanding differences among the courts of appeals on the issue of the scope and standard of appellate review of fact findings. The Court explained that some decisions "have stated that review is limited to the evidence favorable to the nonmoving party while most hold that review extends to the entire record." But the Court regarded this distinction as "more semantic than real" and explained that while review of all of the evidence is required to determine a motion for judgment as a matter of law, the trial judge is required to give credence only to the evidence and reasonable inferences that tend to support the finding and to disregard all contrary evidence the jury was not required to believe. This means that the reasonableness of inferences involves a consideration of the evidence as a whole, but not that a reviewing court may make credibility determinations or weigh the evidence.

The high Court's most critical language concerning the method of legal sufficiency review states that:

> [T]he court must draw all reasonable inferences in favor of the nonmoving party, and it may not make credibility determinations or weigh the evidence. "Credibility determinations, the weighing of the evidence, and the drawing of legitimate inferences from the facts are jury functions, not those of a judge." Thus, although the court should review the record as a whole, it must disregard all evidence favorable to the moving party that the jury is not required to believe. That is, the court should give credence to the evidence favoring the nonmovant as well as that "evidence supporting the moving party that is uncontradicted and unimpeached, at least to the extent that [it] comes from disinterested witnesses."

Hence, the Court makes it very clear that it is the jury's role to draw reasonable inferences from the evidence and that any judge or court reviewing the record to determine whether legally sufficient evidence supports a verdict must disregard all direct and circumstantial evidence contrary to the verdict that the jury was not required to believe.

. . . .

A clear understanding of the Court's opinion in *Reeves* dictates how whole-record review is properly conducted. First, the whole record is reviewed to identify the direct and circumstantial evidence favoring the party with the burden of proving a particular issue as well as the limited range of evidence the fact finder is required to believe or credit. In the context of circumstantial evidence, this means that a reviewing court must determine from the evidence as a whole whether reasonable inferences can be drawn from the circumstantial evidence in support of the proponent's issue and what those inferences are.

Second, based on the evidence and inferences favorable to the proponent of an affirmative finding on an issue, a reviewing court must test the sufficiency of the evidence by "giving credence" only to the evidence that supports an affirmative finding on the proponent's issue and the undisputed evidence the jury was required to believe. By definition, this means that evidence contrary to the finding that the jury was not required to credit, and even reasonable inferences in derogation of the finding are not given credence and otherwise should not be part of the second step in the evaluative process.

The primary reason for this two-step method of whole-record review is for reviewing courts to avoid the temptation to weigh the evidence and make credibility determinations in cases involving conflicts in the direct evidence. On a more subtle level, the two-step approach recognizes and validates the companion principle that drawing legitimate inferences from the facts is a jury function, not a job for judges. Because the circumstantial evidence will frequently provide a reasonable basis for drawing legitimate but conflicting inferences about a particular issue, a consideration of both favorable and unfavorable inferences would require a reviewing court to identify and then overlook its own view about which reasonable inference is the most convincing. This approach simply expects too much from reviewers.

The better view on the basis of policy and precedent is that if the circumstantial evidence will support more than one reasonable inference, it is for the jury to decide which one is more convincing or more reasonable. The reviewing court's focus should be restricted to an evaluation of the reasonableness of the favorable inference, a matter that does not require the consideration of competing reasonable inferences.

Properly applied, whole-record review is conducted to identify the direct evidence and reasonable inferences that can be drawn from the circumstantial evidence that supports the challenged fact or finding, so this evidence can be evaluated under the substantive legal principles that are applicable to the case. Once this has been done, it is not necessary to reconsider contrary evidence or contrary inferences that the jury could have credited or reasonably drawn from the evidence, but was not required to credit or draw from the circumstantial evidence. In fact, reexamination of the evidence will inevitably lead a reviewing court to a consideration of whether an inference rejected by the jury is equally or, indeed, more probable than the jury's finding or verdict, thereby defeating the basic principle that a reviewing court must not weigh the evidence.

. . . .

[I]n *Pennsylvania R.R. v. Chamberlain*, a Federal Employers' Liability Act (FELA) case decided in 1933, the Supreme Court stated that "where proven facts give equal support to each of two inconsistent inferences; in which event, neither of them being established, judgment, as a matter of law, must go against the party upon whom rests the necessity of sustaining one of these inferences." This "equally probable inference" rule supported the trial judge's order directing the jury to find a verdict against claimants in a death action because the circumstantial evidence of a collision between two strings of railroad cars was counterbalanced and rendered insubstantial by other evidence that such a collision had not occurred. . . .

A decade later, the Supreme Court decided *Lavender v. Kurn*, another FELA case involving the death of a railroad employee. [*Lavender v. Kurn* appears infra in Chapter 11 — Eds.] As in *Chamberlain*, the cause of the employee's death was hotly contested. . . . [W]ithout expressly overruling or repudiating the "equally probable inference" rule set forth in *Chamberlain*, *Lavender* developed a "reasonable basis in the record" standard. Under this standard, the jury, not the trial judge, and certainly not any appellate court, performs the important function of drawing and rejecting (or weighing) inferences from the evidence. . . .

[T]he "equal inferences rule" is not merely unnecessary, it is actually quite harmful. In the hands of a reviewing judge who wants to violate the jury's province so as to impose his or her own idiosyncratic preferences on the case, the "equal inferences rule" provides an ideal tool. The abuse-of-power demons on the judge's shoulder need only whisper, "Just declare that the inferences are 'equal,' even if to do so requires an application of experience that our system entrusts to the jury." This is, in fact, what the Fifth Circuit panel did in *Reeves* when it analyzed the evidence by giving weight to the defense's case according to the panel's own preferences and declared that those inferences overcame the plaintiff's inferences. . . . Given its tendency to mislead, or rather to justify judicial imposition, the usefulness of the "equal inferences rule" is far outweighed by the mischief that it promotes. . . .

§ 10.06 Jury Argument or Summation

NOTE ON LEGITIMATE FUNCTIONS OF JURY ARGUMENT

When the evidence is concluded, the case must be submitted to the jury. Jury argument, or the attorney's summation to the jury, is a part of that process. Before considering jury argument, it will be useful to consider why it is included in a trial. What purposes does it serve?

Rational Analysis of Evidence in Light of the Law. The rational component of jury argument implies at least three separate functions. (1) Argument should help the jury better understand the court's charge, which may contain such confusing concepts as "proximate cause" or "promissory estoppel," by illustrating it with simple examples. (2) Counsel on both sides may legitimately use argument to select, arrange, and interpret those portions of the evidence that are relevant to their theories. (3) Counsel may guide the jury in judging the credibility of witnesses. *Cf.* Crump, *The Function and Limits of Prosecution Jury Argument*, 28 Sw. L.J. 505, 506-09 (1974).

Emotional or Social Policy Arguments. Emotionally based argument creates more difficult problems, but there are instances in which it is appropriate. (1) It can legitimately give the jury the determination to ignore prejudicial distractions, which may themselves be emotionally rooted and incapable of removal by logic. (2) It may properly remind the jury to take both sides of the case seriously. (3) It can assist the jury in setting community and social standards by which to resolve questions of degree that are at the heart of virtually every case. When a jury is asked whether the defendant's conduct was "negligent" or whether a contractual breach was "substantial," it is required to combine legal and factual elements with issues of policy that cannot be answered without exploration of societal values. *Id.*

The Pressures Toward Improper Argument. In an adversary context, these legitimate functions do not always prevail. "Brinkmanship" is encouraged because rules governing jury argument are vague and tractable. Attorneys may perceive advantage in misrepresenting the law, injecting prejudicial matter, arguing matters outside of the evidence, or making inflammatory personal attacks. Striking a balance between these abuses and the beneficial effects of sound adversary argument has long been a difficult problem for the courts. *See* Carlson, *Argument to the Jury: Passion, Persuasion, and Legal Controls*, 33 St. Louis U.L.J. 787 (1989).

BROKOPP v. FORD MOTOR CO.

71 Cal. App. 3d 841, 139 Cal. Rptr. 888 (4th Dist. 1977)

KAUFMAN, ASSOCIATE JUSTICE.

In this action to recover damages for personal injuries sustained in a single-vehicle accident, defendant Ford Motor Company ("Ford") appeals from a judgment entered upon a jury verdict in favor of plaintiffs Robert and Carol Brokopp ("plaintiffs") in the amount of $3,010,000. . . .

Misconduct of Counsel

Ford contends that, in arguing to the jury, counsel for plaintiffs was guilty of several acts of prejudicial misconduct, to wit: (1) he made a variant of the "golden rule" argument; (2) he made an appeal to the sympathy of the jury based on Ford's size and corporate status; (3) he expressed his personal opinion on the credibility of several of Ford's expert witnesses; (4) he made an appeal to the self-interest of the jurors as taxpayers; and (5) he argued a matter not in evidence and, indeed, contrary to all of the pertinent expert testimony. Although in all but one instance we agree that the substance of Ford's charges is correct, Ford is foreclosed from asserting these defects as grounds for reversal because it failed to make an adequate record below. Misconduct of counsel may not be urged as a ground for reversal absent both timely objection and request for admonition in the trial court. . . .

In his opening argument plaintiff's counsel made a number of statements from which the jury might have inferred it was proper in calculating damages to place themselves in Mr. Brokopp's shoes and award the amount they would "charge" to undergo equivalent disability, pain and suffering. This so-called "golden rule" argument . . . is impermissible.

But Ford's counsel neither objected to the statements nor requested any admonition. . . .

Counsel for plaintiffs also argued: "Save a buck, and that is the only reason I can think of why they would handle things the way they do. These large corporations, in effect, crippled Bob; they took his manhood away from him; they took his privacy from him; they took his body away from him; and they left him in pain. . . ."

Appeals to the sympathy of the jury based on the size or corporate status of a defendant are improper. However, Ford failed to object to this argument and requested no admonition.

In argument, counsel for plaintiffs also stated: "You know, in this trial, I never have had more evasive witnesses than Mr. Valant and Mr. Brink. I just never have seen witnesses as Mr. Valant and Mr. Brink who just would not answer a question."

Ford characterizes this as a statement of counsel's personal opinion on the credibility of these witnesses. We believe not. An attorney is permitted to argue all reasonable inferences from the evidence, and may with propriety comment on the demeanor of a witness indicating recalcitrance.

Moreover, again, Ford lodged no objection and requested no admonition with respect to this statement.

Counsel for plaintiffs also told the jury: "Bob doesn't have to stay at the V.A. hospital. I don't think that we, the taxpayers, ought to pay for Bob in preference to Ford, if they are liable." An appeal to the jurors' self-interest as taxpayers constitutes misconduct. . . . Although Ford objected to this statement, it failed to secure a definitive ruling and requested no admonition. Any impropriety could easily have been remedied by a prompt and proper admonition.

Ford's contention that plaintiff's counsel argued a matter not in evidence arises out of the following situation. It was important to plaintiffs' theory that the power steering belt came off its pulley while the pulley was in motion and not as a result of the crash. All the experts, including those called by plaintiffs, agreed that there were no marks on the belt from which it could be determined that the belt came off a moving pulley. Nevertheless, in his argument, counsel for plaintiffs insisted that he could see marks on the belt, implied that these marks indicated the belt had come off a moving pulley, and started to mark the belt with a yellow crayon. . . . Ford's counsel [objected]. The judge thereupon removed the crayon marks from the belt and ordered plaintiffs' counsel not to mark any exhibits. Proceedings were then resumed before the jury, and plaintiffs' counsel proceeded with his argument during which he told the jury that, if they would hold the belt down in the light, they would see two faint lines. No further objection, motion to strike, or request for admonition was interposed by the defense.

Ford urges that, although the belt was in evidence, there was no evidence whatever that any marks on the belt indicated the belt came off a moving pulley. Ford is correct. The belt was in evidence and counsel could argue that there were marks visible on it. It was improper, however, to suggest to the jury that these marks indicated the belt came off a moving pulley. While an attorney may argue all reasonable inferences from the evidence . . . it is misconduct to argue matters not in evidence or to assert as fact matters allegedly within counsel's personal knowledge. . . .

However, that was not the thrust of the defense objection. Although this particular portion of the argument covers several pages of transcript, it was not until plaintiffs' counsel started marking the belt with yellow crayon that the defense objected, and the trial court justifiably understood the objection as being against counsel's marking the exhibit. This impropriety the trial court corrected. Argument thereafter resumed without further objection or any request for admonition by defense counsel. The impropriety now asserted was waived. . . .

The judge is affirmed.

NOTES AND QUESTIONS

(1) *The Varieties of Improper Jury Argument.* Improper argument usually falls into one or more of the following categories:

(a) *Appeals to Prejudice: Texas Employers Ins. Ass'n v. Haywood, 266 S.W.2d 856 (Tex. 1954).* In this case, reversal resulted because the defendant's attorney argued that witnesses were not credible because they were black and said, "Why then didn't they

. . . bring some white fellow that you could see and know was telling the truth?" Even without objection, the Court reversed, holding the argument "incurable." Similar kinds of arguments, based upon race, religion, national origin, or other invidious distinctions, can be found in the digests of decisions in every state. *Cf. Cherry Creek National Bank v. Fidelity & Cas. Co.*, 207 A.D. 787, 202 N.Y.S. 611 (4th Dep't 1924). Generally, arguments against a party because of wealth, or because it is a corporation, are similarly improper; *but see Wayte v. Rollins International, Inc.*, 169 Cal. App. 3d 1, 215 Cal. Rptr. 59, (2d Dist. 1985) (defendant could argue about wealth of defendant corporations because it was relevant to punitive damages). But argument is not improper merely because it is hard-hitting or emotional, provided that it is related to the issues and is not based upon invidious categories. *See Leonard & Harral Packing Co. v. Hahn*, 571 S.W.2d 201 (Tex. Civ. App. — San Antonio 1978, writ ref'd n.r.e.) (in suit for wrongful death of young wife, plaintiff's attorney's argument on damages, including recitation of marriage vows and reference to popular song titles such as "Just Me and My Shadow" and "Little Things Mean a Lot," were not improper appeals to prejudice; attorney not required to be "apathetic").

(b) *Diverting the Jury From Following the Law: Wank v. Richman & Garrett, 165 Cal. App. 3d 1103, 211 Cal. Rptr. 919 (2d Dist. 1985).* In this case, the court had ordered separate trials on liability and damages. Defendant's attorney made several remarks suggesting to jurors that they should decide the liability trial against the plaintiff so they could avoid the separate damage trial, including the remark that jurors would have to come back and "sit for eight weeks" to decide the damage issues. The court concluded that these remarks were error, but declined to reverse. Such an argument (like the "golden rule" argument, disapproved in *Brokopp v. Ford Motor Co.*, above) is improper because it urges the jury to decide the case on a different standard than the legal standard contained in the court's instructions.

A similar, but more controversial, issue is presented by "per diem" arguments, in which the plaintiff's attorney breaks down units of time and multiplies them by dollar figures to obtain very large amounts as suggested pain-and-suffering verdicts. Some states (*e.g.*, California) rigidly confine these arguments, other states (*e.g.*, Texas) permit them, and in some states (such as New York) there has been no ruling by the state's highest court. *See Tate v. Colabello*, 58 N.Y.2d 84, 459 N.Y.S.2d 422, 445 N.E.2d 1101 (1983) (not improper, however, for the plaintiff's counsel to "suggest" a sum, based upon life expectancy of 64 years and upon series of rhetorical questions as to the value of pain over such a period of time). In any event, it is not improper for counsel to explain the law to the jury, by using simple examples or translations into everyday language. *E.g., State v. Haire*, 334 S.W.2d 488 (Tex. Civ. App.-Austin 1960, writ ref'd n.r.e.) (explanation of definition of market value, in jury argument in which attorney constructed hypothetical situation for jury, not improper).

(c) *Remarks Outside the Record and Not Inferable From It: Howard v. Faberge, Inc.*, 679 S.W.2d 644 (Tex. App.-Houston [1st Dist.] 1984 writ ref'd n.r.e.). In this product liability suit, the plaintiff claimed to have been burned by the defendant's product. In order to show that the plaintiff's theory was impossible, the defendant's attorney, during his jury argument, poured the product on his arm and attempted to light it, saying, "God, if I am wrong, burn me," adding that he had "tried a hundred times" without it burning. The court reversed without an objection, holding the argument incurable, since it injected facts not in evidence or subject to cross-examination.

But attorneys are given very broad latitude in making any reasonable inference from the evidence, even if it is not the only possible inference. The credibility arguments in

Brokopp, above, are examples. The attorney is even allowed some degree of poetic license — for hyperbole or literary allusion. Thus, in *Standard Fire Ins. Co. v. Reese*, 584 S.W.2d 835 (Tex. 1979), the Court held that the evidence authorized the defendant's lawyer's inference that the plaintiff's lawyer had sent him to a particular physician to inflate the damages and that the plaintiff had "driven past a thousand doctors." The Court quoted Shakespeare (*Romeo and Juliet*: "A thousand times good night!") and John Milton ("Thousands at his bidding speed, and post o'er land and ocean without rest") to hold that counsel's figure of speech was legitimate argument, even though "a thousand doctors" might have been an exaggeration. Levitt, *Rhetoric in Closing Argument*, 17 Litigation 25 (Winter 1991).

(d) *Invective and Arguments Ad Hominem: Wetherbee v. United Ins. Co. of America, 265 Cal. App. 2d 921, 71 Cal. Rptr. 764 (1968).* As is suggested in *Brokopp*, above, harsh rhetoric about credibility and conduct is not inappropriate if it is supported by the evidence. When it lacks support in the evidence, however, harsh invective is likely to be error. In *Wetherbee*, the insured's counsel argued that the case was one of "mass fraud." The court held this remark unwarranted by the fact that a letter received by the insured was a form letter, in the absence of a showing that similar letters went to other policyholders or were relied upon by them. *See also Fortenberry v. Fortenberry*, 582 S.W.2d 188 (Tex. Civ. App.-Beaumont 1979, writ ref'd n.r.e.) (reference to will proponents as "vultures circling in the air" above the testatrix, held improper).

(2) *"Preservation" of Error in Jury Argument Is Difficult, and Reversal Is Not Common.* To preserve error in jury argument for appeal requires extraordinary diligence, because an objection, followed by a request for admonition, must be made at the time. Furthermore, frequent objection may be tactically unwise in some jurisdictions, because objections may be required to be done in the jury's presence. The doctrines of "cured" or "harmless" error probably result in the affirmance of the majority of cases in which argument is held improper. *Cf. Hilliard v. A.H. Robins Co.*, 148 Cal. App. 3d 374, 196 Cal. Rptr. 117 (2d Dist. 1983) (reversal required only in the "extreme case" in which the impropriety cannot be removed by an instruction to disregard).

(3) *The Timing of Jury Argument: Before or After Court's Charge.* In some jurisdictions, jury argument by counsel is first and the court's charge follows afterward. Perhaps this order of proceeding puts the cart before the horse. How can counsel effectively argue to the jury how the court's instructions should be applied, if the court hasn't given the instructions yet? The Federal Rules address this problem by requiring the judge to rule on counsel's objections and requested charges to the jury before argument, even though the court's charge may be given after counsel's argument. This provision does not completely solve the problem, however, because counsel may be required to argue the case without quite knowing what the court is going to say to the jury. Thus, some courts, apparently for this reason, allow counsel to address argument to the jury after the court's charge. Is this approach better, or does it have its own disadvantages?

(4) *The Right to Open and Close the Final Jury Arguments: A Powerful Forensic Advantage.* It is customary in most jurisdictions for the party with the burden of proof on the whole case (usually the plaintiff) to open and close the argument. In other words, the plaintiff argues first; the defendant argues next; the plaintiff, finally, is allowed time for rebuttal. This sequence gives the plaintiff a powerful forensic advantage. The plaintiff can unleash her most emotional argument as the last word the jury hears before retiring. Also, the plaintiff has the opportunity to rebut the defendant's last argument, but the defendant does not have that right with respect to the plaintiff's final argument. Is there

a better way? (Many jurisdictions theoretically confine the plaintiff's rebuttal argument to matters raised in the preceding two arguments, but that is not much of a limitation in most cases.)

§ 10.07 Jury Instructions and Verdicts

[A] The General Charge Versus Special Interrogatories

Read Fed. R. Civ. P. 49 (special verdicts and interrogatories).

NOTE ON THE TWO BASIC FORMS OF VERDICTS

The General Charge. There are two fundamentally distinct methods of submitting a case to the jury. One is the "general charge," which involves instructing the jury on all applicable principles of law and asking it a single question: Who wins? If the verdict is for the plaintiff, a second finding may be necessary, for the amount of damages. It might be said that a general charge involves one single, long question. In a negligence case, for example, the jury might be instructed on such principles as the significance of negligence and proximate causation, the treatment of contributory negligence, the proper measure of damages, and the proof standard. But the jury would make no discrete fact findings.

The Charge with Special Verdicts. The other method of submission is by "special verdicts." The judge asks the jury factual questions: who was negligent, was the negligence a proximate cause of the occurrence, etc. The jury must be given definitions of terms (such as negligence or proximate cause), but it need not be told the significance of its answers, and it need not consider who is to win. For decades, the special verdict system was virtually the exclusive method of submission in Texas. It sometimes happened that the jury did not even know who had won after it rendered its verdict.

Discretionary, Mixed Systems (California; New York; Federal). In some jurisdictions, both methods are in use. California and New York, for example, afford the trial judge discretion. The federal system does also; Rule 49 effectively allows the judge to choose between special verdicts, the general charge, or both together.

The Advantages and Disadvantages of Each System. As is often the case with choices among procedural alternatives, both types of charge have advantages and disadvantages. Special verdicts are said to impose a logical structure on the jury's responses, requiring the jurors to "think with their heads rather than with their hearts." Prejudicial distractions, such as which party is more attractive personally, are reduced by the focus of the charge on factual issues, rather than upon who wins. Also, the special-verdict charge gives a record of the jury's fact findings. The trial judge renders judgment in accordance with the law, and if some of the findings are unsupported on the evidence, that outcome is not concealed as it would be with the general charge. If one of the claims or defenses is invalid as a matter of law, the appellate court may not need to reverse (as it would in the case of a general charge). On the other hand, the special-verdict charge can be criticized because, in some cases, it makes too much depend upon a single word or set of words in a single question. It has great potential for misleading the jury about what is being asked. As a result, attorneys haggle over every nuance — sometimes over every comma — in the questions. And there are some kinds of claims that are difficult to split into a series of questions about the "elements," because they are made up of different factors that have to be weighed against each other. Finally, the champions of the general charge point out that the jury is not, and never was intended to be, a mere factual computer. The general charge permits "play in the joints" so that the jury can round out the rough edges of the substantive law and temper its unfairness — which is a traditional function ascribed to the jury.

Broad Special Verdicts, Blending into a General Charge. The above discussion treats these two approaches as though they were completely different. But with special verdicts, it is possible to break the case down into very fine, discrete parts — or it is possible to ask very broad, very general questions, each combining several elements. For example, if the first interrogatory is "Whose negligence, if any, proximately caused the occurrence in question, and in what percentage did each party's causal negligence, if any, contribute to the occurrence?" and the second interrogatory inquires about damages, the charge technically may be a "special" charge — but it is very close to a general charge, in effect. Different jurisdictions have different approaches to the breadth or narrowness of the submissions that customarily are used.

HOW TO READ THE CASE OF *McLAUGHLIN v. FELLOWS GEAR SHAPER CO.*

In the case that follows, the trial judge used both a general verdict and a verdict on special interrogatories, in combination. But the answers the jury returns are inconsistent. What is to be done when that happens? If the special verdict answers are consistent with each other, Rule 49 says that the judge can ignore the general verdict and grant judgment on the special verdicts. Alternatively, she can send the jury back to deliberate further or grant a new trial. If the special verdicts are inconsistent with each other, the court is supposed to send the jury back to deliberate or grant a new trial. Here, the trial judge instead sent the jury back with more questions — and the result, including the trial judge's treatment of it, is confusing (and, even in the final analysis, a little unclear). In the process of comparing the analyses done by the majority and the dissent of this aberrational conduct by the trial judge, you will learn something about the advantages and disadvantages of both kinds of charges.

McLAUGHLIN v. FELLOWS GEAR SHAPER CO.

786 F.2d 592 (3d Cir. 1986)

Mansmann, Circuit Judge.

I.

This is a Pennsylvania diversity action in which plaintiffs were successful in recovering damages under the strict liability theory of Section 402A of the Restatement of Torts for personal injury caused by defectively designed machinery. On appeal, defendants have raised several trial errors, chiefly, that the district court erred in resubmitting the foreseeability issue to the jury and in *sua sponte* setting aside the jury's finding of assumption of the risk. Finding no merit in any of the allegations raised, we affirm.

II.

[Plaintiff Wilbur McLaughlin was manually doing "setup" on a hobbing machine (a machine that cuts indentations in metal to make gears) by standing on top of it and rotating it. When he engaged the machinery by lowering the "collar" of the device onto the workpiece, it amputated his left thumb.

[Plaintiffs' theory of liability was that the machine should have had an "interlock" or automatic shutoff. The defendant had two theories of defense. First, it claimed that the absence of an automatic shutoff did not make it responsible for McLaughlin's injuries, since the law required only that it make its product safe for foreseeable uses, whereas McLaughlin's injury had been caused by his standing on the machine, which was unforeseeable misuse. Secondly, defendant argued that McLaughlin had assumed the risk, which would provide an affirmative defense to liability.

[The court, in the exercise of its discretion under Rule 49, determined that it should submit both a general charge and special interrogatories to the jury. The court's instructions included all applicable principles of liability and damages. The verdict sheet consisted of four interrogatories on liability, plus an interrogatory on damages. The effect of the trial judge's instructions was that a positive answer to the damage interrogatory would be both a finding of the amount of damages and, also, a general verdict for plaintiff on liability.]

. . . The [five] interrogatories and the jury's answers [to them] were as follows:

1. When the hobbing machine was delivered [from Defendant] . . . , was it in a defective condition rendering it unsafe for its intended use?

   Yes X No ______

2. If so, was the defective condition of the hobbing machine a proximate cause of the accident and plaintiff's injury?

   Yes X No ______

3. Was it foreseeable to the manufacturer that operators would, on occasion, stand on the machine while carrying out the setting-up process?

   Yes ______ No X

4. Did plaintiff assume the risk?

   Yes X No ______

5. (To be completed only if your verdict is in favor of plaintiffs.)

We, the jury, award damages as follows:

Mr. McLaughlin $100,000

Mrs. McLaughlin $20,000

Upon learning the jury's answers, defendants moved for entry of judgment in their favor, and plaintiffs moved for a mistrial. The district court denied both requests. Instead, the court submitted two additional questions to the jury to clarify the foreseeability question, in particular, to determine the effect of McLaughlin's standing on the machine during the time it was being set up for operation. The supplemental interrogatories and answers were as follows:

3(a) Was the fact that plaintiff stood on the machine a substantial factor in causing the accident?

   Yes ______ No X

(b) Was it the sole cause of the accident? Yes ______ No X

After ascertaining that the jury was unanimous in its answers to these supplemental interrogatories, the district court asked the following questions of the jury in open court and received the following responses:

THE COURT: Finally, members of the jury, by the answers that you have given, is it your intention to find in favor of the plaintiffs or in favor of the defendant? Can somebody state what you have in mind?

[THE FOREPERSON]: Plaintiff.

THE COURT: You all agree you intend to find in favor of the plaintiffs in the sum of $120,000?

(The jury answered in the affirmative.)

Subsequently, the district court set aside the jury's finding of assumption of the risk and entered judgment in favor of the plaintiffs in the amount of $135,879.45, including delay damages. Defendants' subsequent motions for judgment notwithstanding the verdict and for a new trial were denied by the district court.

III.

Defendants' first argument faults the procedural course of the case. Specifically, defendants contend that the district court erred when it determined that the answers to the special interrogatories were inconsistent and when it set aside the jury's finding of assumption of the risk and entered judgment for plaintiffs, which defendants characterize as an entry of judgment n.o.v. in favor of plaintiffs on this issue. Given the record in this case, two things are clear: first, the district court followed the procedure for general verdicts and interrogatories outlined in Federal Rule of Civil Procedure 49(b) and second, this case does not involve a judgment n.o.v. and so does not turn upon the procedural dictates of Federal Rule of Civil Procedure 50 which governs motions for directed verdict and for judgment notwithstanding the verdict. For these reasons, we find defendants' first argument to be unpersuasive.

A. Rule 49(b)

When assessing [the] jury findings, the district court observed in its . . . opinion:

> Obviously, these answers were inconsistent with each other. Under the instructions of the court, the jury could not have found in favor of the plaintiffs and thus awarded them damages, while at the same time finding that plaintiff had assumed the risk. And it was equally apparent that the true import of the jury's answer to the third question could not be determined, because of the unfortunate incompleteness in the wording of the question. The finding that plaintiff's "misuse" of the machine was not foreseeable would absolve the defendants from liability if, but only if, there was a causal connection between the manner in which plaintiff was conducting the set-up operation, (*i.e.*, the misuse of the product) and the happening of the accident — and the jury had not been asked to make a finding on that subject.

Accordingly, at the time of trial, the district court submitted to the jury two supplemental interrogatories in order to clarify the effect of McLaughlin's standing on the hobbing machine while he was preparing it for operation. On this point the district court offered the following explanation:

> . . . If they find it was the sole cause of the accident, and it was not foreseeable, then I think certainly it is a defendants' verdict. And obviously if their finding of assumption of risk stands up that would be a defendants' verdict. . . .

Defendants complain that the district court was required by the Seventh Amendment to reconcile the inconsistencies in the original five jury interrogatories. Moreover, defendants contend that the answers to these five interrogatories were not inconsistent, that they could be reconciled and that a defense verdict was mandated.

In *Atlantic & Gulf Stevedores, Inc. v. Ellerman Lines, Ltd.*, 369 U.S. 355 (1962), the Supreme Court of the United States held:

> Where there is a view of the case that makes the jury's answers to special interrogatories consistent, they must be resolved that way. For a search for one possible view of the case which will make the jury's finding inconsistent results in a collision with the Seventh Amendment [which prohibits "reexamination" by the Court of a jury verdict except as allowed at common law.] . . .

In the case before us, however, the answers are inconsistent on their face and cannot be read to be consistent. Answers to the first and second questions are inconsistent with the answers to the third and fourth* questions. Moreover, the answers to the third and fourth questions are inconsistent with the general verdict in favor of plaintiffs. Recognizing this, the district court gave the jury further instructions and two supplemental questions and asked it to return for further deliberations. The district court did not redetermine the facts as found by the jury but rather asked the jury to reconsider its decision. In this there can be no Seventh Amendment violation.

Moreover, the decision to seek clarification from the jury in order to resolve the apparent conflict in the answers to the five original interrogatories is precisely what Rule 49(b) of the Federal Rules of Civil Procedure prescribes in such a situation, and the district court cannot be faulted for having followed it. In relevant part Rule 49(b) states [that the court] "*may return the jury for further consideration* of its answers and verdict or may order a new trial." (emphasis supplied). . . .

B. Judgment N.O.V.

[The defendant argues that the jury's initial finding of assumption of the risk should have been controlling, and that in refusing to follow it, the trial court granted an improper "judgment notwithstanding the verdict," or "judgment n.o.v.," for the plaintiff. The rules require that a party must move for directed verdict during trial before being entitled to move for judgment notwithstanding the verdict after. But the plaintiff did not move for directed verdict.

[The appellate court rejects this argument. It holds that the trial judge did not grant a "judgment notwithstanding the verdict" at all. At the time the judge received the final verdict of the jury, what he received was the general verdict. The plaintiff, under this verdict, had prevailed. The plaintiff had no need to file a motion for judgment notwithstanding the verdict to get the judge to set aside the assumption-of-the-risk finding. In fact, he would have had no right to have the trial judge consider such a motion if he filed it, because the assumption-of-the-risk finding no longer was any part of the case — the jury impliedly had invalidated it. The trial judge therefore was correct in "setting aside" the assumption of the risk finding without any motion for judgment notwithstanding the verdict, because what he did was to render judgment on the verdict.

[The appellate court bolsters this reasoning by analyzing the evidence of assumption of the risk. The evidence showed only that McLaughlin engaged the machine through

* [Eds. Note: Is the majority wrong about the fourth question? Couldn't a jury conclude that a defective product (question 1) was a cause of the accident (question 2), but that a given plaintiff assumed the risk (question 4)?]

inattention and inadvertence. There was no evidence from which the jury could have concluded that he "consciously or willingly accepted the risk of having his thumb amputated." As a matter of law, this evidence would not have supported a finding of assumption of risk. The court concludes:]

We have reviewed the district court's entire charge to the jury, especially that portion dealing with assumption of risk, and conclude that the court fully explained the legal principles which the jury was to apply in rendering its decision. We must only assume that the jury, hearing all of this, understood the charge and accordingly rendered a [general] verdict for plaintiffs. Having received a verdict in their favor, plaintiffs were not in a position to be seeking judgment n.o.v. . . .

The finding by the jury on the assumption of the risk issue was contrary to the evidence, and it was, therefore, appropriately set aside by the district court. Moreover, it was appropriate for the district court to enter judgment in favor of plaintiffs. . . .

Accordingly, we affirm the judgment of the district court.

Adams, Circuit Judge, dissenting.

I respectfully dissent because the majority in affirming the district court has sanctioned a violation of Rule 49(b) of the Federal Rules of Civil Procedure as well as a transgression of the time-honored rule of this Court, bottomed largely on the Seventh Amendment to the Constitution, that before judgment notwithstanding the verdict may be granted there must be a motion for a directed verdict. . . .

[The majority] reasons that the "resubmission" of additional special interrogatories was permissible under Federal Rule of Civil Procedure 49(b) [s]ince the jury's initial answers to special interrogatories were inconsistent with each other and with the general verdict. It further concludes that the trial judge did not err in setting aside the jury's finding of assumption of risk because that action did not amount to granting a judgment notwithstanding the verdict and thus was not governed by the procedural strictures of Federal Rule of Civil Procedure 50(b). . . .

I disagree that this case involves a matter of resubmission to the jury of inconsistent answers to special interrogatories. The special findings of the jury, both before and after the trial court submitted the supplemental questions, were reconcilable with one another. Although the findings by the jury were plainly inconsistent with the general verdict for plaintiffs, both the Seventh Amendment and Fed. R. Civ. P. 49(b) prohibit a federal court from choosing from among a jury's findings those that will be set aside and those that will be given effect. Under Fed. R. Civ. P. 49(b), when a jury's answers to special interrogatories are consistent with each other but inconsistent with the general verdict, the court may either request the jury to reconsider all of its answers, enter a judgment consistent with the jury's special findings, or grant a new trial. Even if the special findings of the jury in this case were inconsistent with one another, the appropriate course of action under Rule 49(b) was to order a new trial or to resubmit *all* of the answers to the jury to allow it to reconcile them itself.

Furthermore, the procedure employed in the district court violated the clear-cut requirement stated in Federal Rule of Civil Procedure 50(b) and emphasized in numerous opinions by this Court that a grant of judgment n.o.v. must be preceded by a motion for a directed verdict specifically identifying the ground upon which judgment n.o.v. is requested. This rule serves important practical purposes in ensuring that neither party is precluded from presenting the most persuasive case possible and in preventing unfair surprise after a matter has been submitted to the jury. More importantly, the rule has constitutional underpinnings in the Seventh Amendment's guarantee that "no fact tried by a jury, shall be otherwise re-examined in any court of the United States, than according to the rules of the common law."

. . . I would vacate the judgment for plaintiffs and order . . . a new trial. . . .

NOTES AND QUESTIONS

(1) *Does the Dissent Have It Right (And if So, Is There Any Way to Defend the Majority's Affirmance)?* In terms of hard analysis of the Rules, the dissent seems very persuasive. First, isn't the dissent right in concluding that the special verdicts were not inconsistent? Isn't it entirely possible that the machine was defective, and that the defect was a proximate cause of the occurrence, but, at the same time, the plaintiff's assumption of the risk was a cause too, and the plaintiff's act of standing on the machine was not a foreseeable use? Secondly, wasn't the trial judge precluded from "setting aside" the assumption of risk finding, since he could only do that by granting a motion for judgment n.o.v., which the plaintiff was not entitled to make since he had not made a motion for directed verdict? [But perhaps the majority's opinion can be defended thus: After they were sent back to deliberate, the jurors agreed once again on the general verdict in the plaintiff's favor, and that was the verdict they reported (orally) at the end of the proceedings, tacitly reversing their assumption-of-the-risk finding. The trouble is, first, the jury never changed its written finding that the plaintiff assumed the risk, and second, the majority repeatedly refers to the trial judge's action as "setting aside" the finding. Certainly, the trial judge couldn't set it aside just because he wanted to, could he?] *See* Comment, *Special Verdicts: Rule 49 of the Federal Rules of Civil Procedure*, 74 Yale L.J. 483 (1965).

(2) *Did the Jury Understand the Charge?* The jury returned a special verdict of assumption of risk that the majority says can not be reasonably inferred from the evidence. And it returned a general verdict that obviously was inconsistent with the finding of assumption of risk. Isn't it clear that the jury misunderstood the charge? For an excellent treatment of the problem of jury misunderstanding of the charge, see Tanford, *The Law and Psychology of Jury Instructions*, 69 Neb. L. Rev. 71 (1990).

(3) *General Verdict, Special Verdicts, or Both — Which Is Best?* What does this case tell you about the relative advantages of the various types of verdicts? It might be argued that the jury's inconsistent actions support the use of special verdicts, because they make the jury focus on the facts rather than jumping to conclusions that may be at variance with the facts. But it also might be argued that if the judge had submitted only a general verdict, he would have kept the jury from getting bogged down in minutiae that they are unlikely to understand. *See* Sunderland, *Verdicts, General and Special*, 29 Yale L.J. 253 (1920).

(4) *A New York Decision to Compare With McLaughlin: Pogo Holding Corp. v. New York Property Ins. Underwriting Ass'n, 62 N.Y.2d 969, 468 N.E.2d 291, 479 N.Y.S.2d 336 (1984).* Plaintiff Pogo sued on a fire loss policy for $55,000. The insurance company's defense was that the policy was voided by Pogo's fraudulent inflation of the value of its loss in both its proofs of loss and in subsequent sworn statements. (The evidence included an appraisal that showed the property worth only $10,500.) The trial judge submitted the case to the jury on five special interrogatories plus a general verdict form; the first question was "Did plaintiff falsely swear to or misrepresent a material fact?" The jury's written answer was "yes." The instructions told the jury, with this answer,

to leave all other questions blank and return a general verdict for the defendant. However, the jury never reported any general verdict.

The trial judge sent the jury back twice to deliberate further, with questions asking whether the falsehood was in the proofs of loss or in subsequent statements. The jury finally answered "no" to both. The trial judge then declared that the answers were in conflict and granted a new trial. The New York Court of Appeals reversed and ordered judgment for the defendant on the verdict; it tacitly assumed that the jury would have rendered a general verdict for defendant according to the instructions:

> Trial term erroneously refused to accept the jury's initial finding. . . . This was not a case where the jury's initial answers to interrogatories were . . . inconsistent with each other. . . . The inconsistent answers, reached only after trial term twice rejected its finding of misrepresentation, . . . cannot serve as a basis for rejecting the jury's initial interrogatory answer and the jury's [implied] general verdict [for defendant]. . . .

Is this reasoning correct? Is the case distinguishable from *McLaughlin v. Fellows Gear* (or does it show how that case should have been decided)? Consider the following problem, in which the court used a different approach.

PROBLEM C

SPECIAL INTERROGATORIES AND VERDICTS IN HOWARD v. BACHMAN. In this intersection collision case, the court's charge and the verdict included the following:

QUESTION NO. 1: On the occasion in question, did Bruce F. Bachman:

(a) Fail to keep such a lookout as a person using ordinary care would have done? Answer: No.

(b) Drive at a greater rate of speed than a person using ordinary care would have driven? Answer: Yes. . . .

If you have answered any subdivision of Question No. 1 "yes," and only in that event, then answer the corresponding subdivision of Question No. 2.

QUESTION NO. 2: Was such act or omission a proximate cause of the occurrence in question with respect to:

(a) Failure to keep . . . a lookout . . . ? Answer: [Unanswered.]

(b) Driving at a greater rate of speed than a person using ordinary care would have driven? Answer: No. . . .

QUESTION NO. 3: On the occasion in question, did Ollie B. Howard:

(a) Fail to keep such a lookout as a person using ordinary care would have kept? Answer: Yes.

(b) Fail to yield the right of way to the vehicle driven by Bruce Bachman? Answer: Yes.

[An instruction setting forth and explaining a state statute requiring observance of the right of way is omitted here.]

If you have answered any subdivision of Question 3 "yes," and only in that event, then answer the corresponding subdivision of Question No. 4.

QUESTION NO. 4: Was such act or omission a proximate cause of the occurrence with respect to:

(a) Failure to keep . . . a lookout . . . ? Answer: No.

(b) Failure to yield the right of way to Bruce Bachman as that term is above defined? Answer: Yes.

QUESTION NO. 5: What percentage of the negligence that caused the occurrence do you find from a preponderance of the evidence to be attributable to each of the parties found by you to have been negligent? . . . [Answer:] Bruce F. Bachman, 40%; Ollie B. Howard, 60%.

QUESTION NO. 6: Find from a preponderance of the evidence the reasonable cost in Manero County, West York, of repairs, if any, necessary to restore Bruce Bachman's vehicle to the condition in which it was immediately before the occurrence in question. . . . Answer: $1271.30.

(a) *Is the Verdict Complete?* Notice that at least one question, No. 2(a), remains unanswered. Yet the trial judge treated the verdict as complete, and this treatment was correct. Why?

(b) *The Wording of Question 3(b).* Question 3(b) asks whether Ollie Howard "failed to yield the right of way," but it doesn't ask whether this conduct was negligent or whether it violated a standard of ordinary care. Why not? Is there a factual issue omitted here that the jury should decide? [Note: From your Torts course, what is the consequence in a negligence action of proof of a statutory violation?]

(c) *Are the Answers Inconsistent, or Can They Be Reconciled?* Notice that the jury finds that Howard's negligence proximately caused the occurrence, but Bachman's didn't. Then, however, the jury attributes to Bachman 40 percent of the negligence "that caused" the occurrence. Are these findings reconcilable? [Note: The court in *Howard v. Bachman*, 524 S.W.2d 414 (Tex. Civ. App.-Eastland 1975, no writ) ruled that there was no conflict between them, as precedent had established the principle that the specific findings on liability control over the general findings apportioning percentages of liability to the parties. Therefore, the failure to find Bachman's action a proximate cause rendered the comparative apportionment finding immaterial. In addition, because the comparative causation question didn't result in a finding that Bachman "proximately" caused the occurrence, and because "proximate" causation not merely cause-in-fact is required before a causation finding has any significance, the percentage causation question had no significance to the outcome whatsoever. Do you agree? Would the Third Circuit or New York Court of Appeals, whose recent decisions appear above, agree?]

(d) *Who Wins, and How Much?* The court in *Howard v. Bachman, supra*, held that Bachman recovered 100% of his damages. Correct?

(e) *Is This a Good Way to Submit a Jury Charge?* It seems doubtful that the jury focused on the difference between "cause" and "proximate cause." One might speculate that the jury may not have understood the consequences; it may have thought it was awarding Bachman only 60% of his damages. Assuming it didn't understand, is that factor irrelevant on the theory that it shouldn't have been able to "fudge" its answers anyway? Is this charge a good method of submitting a case to a jury? [Note: Texas has repudiated the proliferation of narrow questions illustrated by *Howard v. Bachman*, and its rules now call for "broad form" questions. Today, questions 1 through 4 (with all of their subparts) would be compressed into a single interrogatory asking, in essence, "Whose negligence, if any, proximately caused the occurrence in question?" *See Lemos v. Montez*, 680 S.W.2d 798 (Tex. 1984). The verdict form would look as follows:

Question 1. Whose negligence, if any do you find from a preponderance of the evidence proximately caused the occurrence in question?

Answer "Yes" or "No" for each of the following:

	Yes	No
(a) John Doe	_____	_____
(b) Sally Smith	_____	_____

This question would be followed by one asking the jury to attribute to each party a percentage of the negligence (if any) (*i.e.,*a comparative apportionment question). Finally, the last question would inquire about damages, predicated on an affirmative finding of liability.

Is this approach preferable, or does it give up the advantages attributed to special verdicts? *See generally* William V. Dorsaneo, III, *Broad-Form Submission of Jury Questions and the Standard of Review,* 46 S.M.U. L. Rev. 601 (1992).]

[B] Instructions to the Jury

Read Fed. R. Civ. P. 51 (instructions to jury; objections).

[1] Explanation of the Law by the Judge

MEAGHER v. LONG ISLAND R.R. CO.

27 N.Y.2d 39, 313 N.Y.S.2d 378, 261 N.E.2d 384 (1970)

JASEN, JUDGE.

This is an action to recover for the death of plaintiff's testator alleged to have been caused through the negligence of the defendant. For a number of years, the decedent regularly used the Long Island Rail Road in commuting between his Williston Park home and his place of employment in New York City.

On July 20, 1966, the decedent called his wife to inform her that he had "missed his East Williston train" and was instead taking a train to the Mineola station. Although the train was not scheduled to stop at Mineola, it was customary for the train to travel slowly in the vicinity of the Mineola station, pending clearance to proceed through the crossover switch and onto the Oyster Bay Line. The decedent was fatally injured while disembarking from the train in the Mineola station. There is a conflict of evidence as to whether the train had stopped or was moving at the time of the accident, and also, whether the decedent was fatally injured as a result of his riding on the platform (vestibule) of the car in violation of section 83 of the Railroad Law.

A reversal and new trial is required here solely upon the ground that the trial court's instructions to the jury, with regard to the applicability of section 83 of the Railroad Law Consol. Laws, c. 49 and the issue of contributory negligence, were erroneous.

Section 83 of the Railroad Law provides in pertinent part:

> No railroad corporation shall be liable for any injury to any passenger while on the platform [vestibule] of a car . . . in violation of the printed regulations of the corporation, posted up at the time in a conspicuous place inside of the passenger cars, then in the train, if there shall be at the time sufficient room for the proper accommodation of the passenger inside such passenger cars.

Undisputed testimony indicated that on this train signs appeared in the front and rear vestibules of each car and inside each car, stating: "Please keep off the platform until the train stops." Also, it is undisputed that there were empty seats in the car from which the decedent exited. Thus, there was testimony that both prerequisites of section 83 were satisfied.

In a written request, defendant asked the court to instruct the jury that if the decedent went upon the car platform while the car was in motion, in violation of section 83 of the Railroad Law, and such act on the part of the decedent was the proximate cause of his injuries, the plaintiff could not recover. Instead, the court instructed the jury that section 83 does not apply "to a passenger preparing to leave the train at a station who enters upon the platform as the train enters the station."

There can be little dispute that the statute clearly relieves the railroad of liability if the passenger rides on the platform in violation of the posted regulations of the railroad. . . .

In addition to incorrectly instructing the jury with regard to the applicability of section 83 of the Railroad Law, the trial court improperly charged the jury as to the standard of contributory negligence.

In its written requests to charge, the defendant asked the court to charge that if the jury found decedent stepped or jumped off a moving train, then the jury must find for the defendant. Instead, the court instructed the jury:

> While a railroad is under a duty to allow its passengers a reasonable time in which to board or alight from a train, a passenger is guilty of contributory negligence, as a matter of law, if he attempts to get off a train that is moving at *other than* an exceedingly slow rate of speed, for example, not more than two or three miles per hour. (Emphasis added.)

The well-established rule of law in this State is that boarding or alighting from a moving train is negligence per se unless in so doing either the passenger was put to an election between alternative dangers, or some direction of a railroad employee to get on or off the train had diverted the passenger's attention from the danger and had created a confidence that the attempt could be made in safety. . . .

Although the instructions to the jury were erroneous, a question is raised as to whether each of these issues has been preserved for our review.

As mentioned, the defendant submitted proper written requests to charge with regard to the applicability of section 83 of the Railroad Law and the issue of contributory negligence. The trial court did not so charge. Immediately after the instruction to the jury, the following colloquy took place in open court:

> [The Court]: If there are any exceptions or requests to charge I will hear them in chambers. Are there any? Are there some?
>
> Mr. Donnelly [Defendant's attorney]: I have no exceptions, your Honor.
>
> The Court: Do you have any exceptions?
>
> Mr. Donnelly: I have no exceptions.
>
> Mr. Halpern: No, your Honor.
>
> The Court: Do you have requests to charge?
>
> Mr. Donnelly: Judge, it is not a request —

The Court: If you have, I will hear it in chambers.

Mr. Donnelly: It isn't a request, your Honor —

Mr. Halpern: May we step inside, sir?

Mr. Donnelly: It isn't a request.

The Court: All right.

Mr. Halpern: I have no requests, Judge.

Mr. Donnelly: Can we come up to the bench, Judge? It isn't a request, actually.

There followed a discussion off the record at the bench and then the jury was sent to begin their deliberations. Immediately thereafter, a conference was held in the Judge's chambers and defense counsel requested the Judge to charge the jury in a manner similar to the written requests earlier submitted. The court declined to so charge and noted: "Let the record show that defendant's attorney requested the following charges to the jury be made by the Court and that any of the requests to charge as hereinafter indicated that were not included in the Court's charge may be considered as having been declined by the Court to so charge."

CPLR 4017 provides:

> [A]t any time before the jury retires to consider its verdict, a party shall make known his objection to a charge to the jury or a failure or refusal to charge as requested. Failure to so make known objections may restrict review upon appeal in accordance with paragraphs three and four of subdivision (a) of section 5501. . . .

While the defendant herein did not object to the failure to charge as requested until after the jury had retired, we are of the opinion that the issue of the charge was adequately preserved for our review.

The trial court had indicated to counsel that it did not desire to have the exceptions and requests to charge heard before the jury, and instructed counsel that such be brought up in chambers. Counsel was entitled to rely upon this instruction of the court in withholding his exception until the conference in chambers. Moreover, the objection was raised in chambers immediately following submission of the case to the jury. Had the court accepted counsel's requests, the deleterious effect on the jury's deliberative process in recalling the jury and recharging them would have been *de minimis*. Furthermore, the response of the court in chambers to counsel's requests clearly indicates that the court had considered the earlier written requests and had made an irrevocable decision not to charge in accordance with those requests. In such a situation, it would exalt useless formalism over substance to hold that the issue of the charge had not adequately been preserved for review.

Accordingly, the order of the Appellate Division [which had affirmed the trial court] is reversed and the action remitted to the Supreme Court for a new trial. . . .

GIBSON, JUDGE (dissenting): . . .

[T]here was not, in my view, an adequate and timely exception to the trial court's omission to charge in accordance with either of the requests now argued; and, in fact, when the jury some time later returned for further instructions, the court, without objection or exception on the part of either party, reread its charge in respect of negligence and contributory negligence, including the interpretation of section 83 of which appellant now complains. To excuse noncompliance with CPLR 4017 is to deny effect to the salutary and well-recognized purpose underlying its enactment; and that purpose was not subserved by the blanket exception which defendant sought to make, after the jury had retired, to the court's disposition of a series of written requests.

SCILEPPI, BERGAN and BREITEL, JJ., concur with JASEN, J.

GIBSON, J., dissents and votes to affirm in a separate opinion in which FULD, C.J., and BURKE, J., concur.

NOTES AND QUESTIONS

(1) *The Requirement of Contemporaneous Objection to the Charge: Federal Rule 51; Pogo Holding Corp. v. New York Property Ins. Underwriters Ass'n, 62 N.Y.2d 969, 468 N.E.2d 291, 479 N.Y.S.2d 336 (1984).* Federal Rule 51 provides that if the trial court has informed a party of its proposed instructions before instructing the jury and before final jury arguments, the party is required to object "before the instructions and arguments are delivered." Fed. R. Civ. P. 51(b), (c). The New York law construed in *Meagher* is similar. In the *Pogo* case, the insurance company's defense was that the plaintiff had made fraudulently inflated claims, and the court erroneously instructed the jury that the defendant should prevail if the claim was "knowingly" false. This statement of the law was seriously misleading, because the defendant was required to prove an "intent to deceive" on plaintiff's part. The Court of Appeals, however, held that since the plaintiff had not objected before the jury retired, the erroneous instruction "is the law governing this case." Is this procedure unnecessarily harsh? In contrast, a failure to object to the submission of the wrong law in the charge does not make an erroneous instruction the "law of the case" in federal court. In *City of St. Louis v. Praprotnik*, 485 U.S. 112, 119-20 (1988), the Supreme Court held that regardless of whether a proper objection was made in the trial court, for the purposes of appellate review, the sufficiency of the evidence is evaluated under the law that should have been given in the court's charge rather than the law that was erroneously included in the court's jury charge. The Court reasoned that the importance of the issue required review and under these circumstances review will not "undermine the policy of judicial efficiency that underlies Rule 51." The concept of plain error is not mentioned in the Court's opinion.

(2) *The Charge Conference, Requests by Attorneys, and Objections.* It is typical for the court to hold a "charge conference" in the presence of the attorneys at the conclusion of the evidence, at which requested instructions and questions are received and discussed. The conference may be very short (if the case is "plain vanilla" and the attorneys are in substantial agreement about the proper charge) or it may last days, in unusual circumstances. In some federal courts, the attorneys are required to submit requested charges before trial, but the charge conference still may be necessary. The charge conference typically is informal and may be unreported; the court often is seeking to hear opposing views on how the charge should be given. The objections to the charge, on the other hand, must be made a part of the record, because their purpose is to preserve error. Note that, in the *Meagher* case, the trial judge told the attorneys that they could make objections in chambers; the jury already had begun to deliberate when the judge ruled on them. What would be the result under Federal Rule 51? What should the attorney have done? Could he reasonably have argued with the judge over the legality of that procedure? The attorney was "saved by the bell." The decision is by a four-to-three majority.

(3) *The Format and Drafting of the Instructions: Sprague v. Equifax Inc., 166 Cal. App. 3d 1012, 213 Cal. Rptr. 69 (2d Dist. 1985).* This California case illustrates the range of objections that can be addressed to the format, sources, and substance of the

instructions in that state. The jury rendered special verdict findings that resulted in a judgment holding the defendants liable for conspiring to defraud the plaintiff of insurance benefits to which he was entitled, with actual damages of $100,000 and punitive damages of $5 million assessed. The first objection was that the instructions on conspiracy were repetitious and excessive in number. Although the instructions occupied a major portion of the charge and were repetitious, the appellate court noted that when taken as a whole, the instructions on conspiracy did not "unfairly emphasize" the plaintiff's theory of the case. Furthermore, "repetition of a correct instruction rarely constitutes reversible error." [Does this principle make sense? If you were the plaintiff in a conspiracy case, wouldn't you request a lengthy charge on the subject?] Secondly, the defendants argued that the instructions were vague. The court concluded that again, the question was whether the charge as a whole was inadequate. Many otherwise vague phrases were understandable if viewed in the context of instructions at other points in the charge. [Does this holding make sense? Will the jury cross-reference all of the legal concepts in a charge that may be twenty-five or more pages long?] Third, the defendants objected that the conspiracy instructions were "argumentative." An argumentative instruction "is one which embodies detailed recitals of fact drawn from the evidence in such a manner as to constitute an argument to the jury in the guise of a statement of law." The charge did include the instruction that "direct evidence of a conspiracy is rare," imbedded in discussions of how the jury should treat the evidence; the court agreed that this remark "might better have been left for argument [by counsel]," but it was not reversible when the charge was read as a whole. [Is this analysis persuasive?] Fourth, the defendants argued that the charge "improperly used language from appellate opinions." Use of charges from approved charge sources, the court hinted, is safest. While it is inappropriate to use language verbatim from an appellate opinion without fitting it to the circumstances of the case on trial, the court held that no error was shown here. [Is this analysis sensible? If there is a principle of law contained in an appellate opinion, and it is important to the case, and expressed in no approved charge source, shouldn't the jury be told about it?] Finally, the instructions were attacked as inconsistent. Any inconsistencies, said the court, derived from the complexity of the case. [Note: The search for perfection in jury charges would result in a 100 percent reversal rate if unduly emphasized. Was this consideration behind the court's consideration of this case?]

(4) *The Impact of Substantively Erroneous or Misleading Instructions: Henderson v. United States Fidelity & Guaranty Co., 695 F.2d 109 (5th Cir. 1983).* The federal approach to instruction errors is deferential. The trial court has discretion in choosing the form of the charge and the method of conveying required information to the jury. Substantive error in the charge, however, may lead to reversal. The charge is to be read as a whole in the context of the evidence and pleadings, and only if the charge remains misleading is reversal required, even after objection. In *Henderson,* above, the trial judge instructed the jury that the sending of notice of cancellation of insurance would not result in cancellation if the insured did not receive it. This charge was contrary to the governing state law, but since the court elsewhere in the charge corrected it, and since the whole was not misleading, the appellate court held that the error was not reversible. *See also Polk v. Ford Motor Co.*, 529 F.2d 259 (8th Cir. 1976) (misleading instruction in crashworthiness case, which arguably could have led the jury to assess all damages from crash, and not merely those from alleged defect enhancing injuries from crash, was not reversible when viewed in context of entire charge). Apparently, only very serious distortions of the law, which persist after the entire charge is understood and absorbed, will result in reversal. *E.g., Brewer v. Jeep Corp.,* 724 F.2d 653 (8th Cir. 1983) (instruction

that allowed plaintiff benefit only of strict liability claim, and denied plaintiff opportunity to have breach of warranty claim carrying lesser proof requirements, held reversible error). *See generally* Steven A. Childress, *Federal Standard of Review,* (2d ed. Salem 1992).

Is the federal approach appropriate? It might lead to sloppiness by judges giving instructions and to "brinkmanship" by attorneys requesting them. Furthermore, guessing whether an erroneous instruction was misleading as read by lay jurors, is a chancy matter. (But might a stricter approach bring about inappropriate reversals?)

(5) *Omission of Properly Requested Instructions: Bueno v. City of Donna,* 714 F.2d 484 (5th Cir. 1983). What about omitted instructions? The parties are entitled to have the jury instructed adequately upon theories of the case that are supported by law and by the evidence. However, the trial court need not adopt the precise language requested. In the *Bueno* case, the defendants requested a charge on an affirmative defense, but the requested language would have placed the burden of proof, erroneously, on the plaintiff. The Court of Appeals nevertheless held that the "substance" of the requested charge was communicated to the court, and it reversed.

[2] Comments by the Judge on the Evidence

LEWIS v. BILL ROBERTSON & SONS, INC., 162 Cal. App. 3d 650, 208 Cal. Rptr. 699 (2d Dist. 1984). In this personal injury suit, in which the plaintiff claimed that he had slipped and fallen due to the defendant's negligent maintenance of his premises, the trial judge informed the jury after the attorney's arguments that he would exercise his authority, under Cal. Const. art. VI, § 10, to comment "on the evidence and the testimony and the credibility of any witness." He began his summary by telling the jurors that they had just heard an impassioned plea based upon prejudice from the plaintiff's attorney that was in no way based on the evidence.

The judge then told the jurors that (1) ninety percent of automobile lots had chains around them like the one plaintiff had tripped over and anyone over eight years of age knew they were meant to keep people out; (2) the plaintiff's argument that he could not have used a safer entrance was a smokescreen to cloud over the elements of negligence that the plaintiff was required to prove; (3) there was no horrendous pain and suffering in a broken arm that had healed perfectly; and (4) the plaintiff's doctor had not testified that he would have any permanent pain. The judge went on to say that the plaintiff's method of calculating damages was a false method, although the jurors were "perfectly free" to ignore the judge's opinion. He told the jurors that "no defect in these premises had anything to do with this fall." He repeated this statement but told the jurors they could ignore his comments and tell him to "go jump in the lake" if they thought the court was wrong. The plaintiff moved for an instruction to the jury that it disregard these comments, or for a mistrial; the judge refused. After beginning its deliberations, the jury asked to have the judge's comments read again; the judge refused this request on the ground that it was "[c]ompletely irrelevant to the jury's duties." The jury returned a 9-3 verdict for the defendant. The appellate court reversed:

> [The constitutional provision] allows the trial judge to use his experience and training in evaluating the evidence, so as to aid the jury in reaching a just verdict. . . . The court's function . . . goes well beyond a colorless recital of the evidence. A judge may analyze all or part of the testimony and express his views with respect to its credibility. . . .

Nevertheless, a judge's power to comment on the evidence is not unlimited. He cannot withdraw material evidence . . . or distort the testimony, and he must inform the jurors that they are the exclusive judges of fact and of the credibility of the witnesses. . . .

The record here discloses that the trial judge failed to comply with the limitations suggested in other cases. . . . [Those cases hold that the judge should avoid] commenting on the crucial issues of proximate causation, damages or credibility. . . .

Not only did the trial judge in this case comment on the crucial issue of proximate cause, but he distorted the testimony. . . . [Uncontroverted testimony showed that plaintiff sustained permanent damage from the fall.] . . .

The cumulative impact of the court's comments may well have swayed [the jury]. . . . [The judgment is reversed.]

NOTES AND QUESTIONS

(1) *The Scope of Proper Comments.* Notice that the judge's authority to comment, in this state, is broad, and the judge need not confine the comments to "colorless" summation. The federal law is generally similar. *E.g., Bass v. International Brotherhood of Boilermakers*, 630 F.2d 1058 (5th Cir. 1980) (judge has great discretion, but must be fair and impartial when commenting substantively on evidence).

(2) *Changing the Facts in the Lewis Case.* In *Lewis v. Bill Robertson*, above, would the judge have been upheld if his only comment had been, "The plaintiff says there was no safer way inside, but I don't think you should credit that testimony, because all the other evidence showed there was a normal gate at the front," coupled with an admonition that the jurors were the exclusive judges of the evidence?

(3) *The Texas View: Prohibiting Comment by the Trial Judge on the Weight of the Evidence.* Why should the judge be permitted to comment directly on the evidence to the jury at all? The Texas view is that the judge should not be. In fact, Tex. R. Civ. P. 277 expressly prohibits the judge from commenting directly on the weight of the evidence. One criticism of this approach is that it leads to large numbers of reversals, since it is difficult for the court to charge the jury meaningfully without commenting, at least indirectly, on the evidence. For this reason, the modern Texas rule relaxes the prohibition, outlawing only "direct" comments. *Cf. Brown v. Russell*, 703 S.W.2d 843 (Tex. App.-Fort Worth 1986, no writ) (reversal of child custody case where judge criticized former wife's failure to submit expert psychological evidence about second husband). Another possible objection to the Texas approach is that it deprives the jury of the judge's expertise. Does the Texas approach have advantages, however? *Cf.* Note, *Deadlocked Juries and the Allen Charge*, 37 Maine L. Rev. 167 (1985).

(4) *The Requirement that the Court's Charge Apply the Law to the Facts: Green v. Downs, 27 N.Y.2d 205, 316 N.Y.S.2d 221 (1970).* How is the law applied to the facts when special interrogatories are used? Reconsider the charge given in the *McLaughlin* case and in *Howard v. Bachman* above. New York frequently uses the general charge, and the decisions require specific application of the law to the evidence in the particular case. The defendant backed his car and struck the plaintiff, saying that he did not see her. The Court of Appeals reversed a verdict and judgment for the defendant on the ground that the charge failed to discuss the evidence and relate it to the principles of law charged; it should have "appl[ied] to each party's version [of the facts] the pertinent statutory and decisional law." "[M]ere abstract propositions of law . . . or mere statements of law

in general terms, even though correct, should not be given unless they are made applicable to the case at bar."

(5) *Should the Jury Be Told the Effects of Its Answers to a Special Verdict Charge?* Some jurisdictions prohibit the court from telling the jurors the legal effects of their answers to special verdict questions on the judgment. *Cf. Gulf Coast State Bank v. Emenhiser*, 562 S.W.2d 449 (Tex. 1978) (instruction that if jury found certain facts, it should "find for" defendants held error). The prohibition is based on the notion that telling the jurors might make them "fudge" their answers. On the other hand, many jurisdictions (including the federal courts) have no such prohibition, and there are some jurisdictions that actually require the judge to inform the jury. For example, in *Kaeo v. David*, 719 P.2d 387 (Hawaii 1986), the jury found that the City of Honolulu's negligence was causally responsible for only one percent of the plaintiff's damages — but under the law, this finding meant that the City was liable for nearly the entire damage award of $620,000. The Hawaii Supreme Court held that it was reversible error for the trial judge not to have told the jury the effect of its answers. *See* Comment, *Informing the Jury of the Legal Effect of Special Verdict Answers in Comparative Negligence Actions*, 1981 Duke L.J. 824.

§ 10.06-10.07 Appendix The Realities of the Court's Charge and of Jury Argument

COURT'S CHARGE AND JURY'S VERDICT IN *PENNZOIL CO. v. TEXACO INC.*, NO. 84-05905

151st Dist. Ct. Harris Cy., Tex. Nov. 15, 1985

MEMBERS OF THE JURY: This case is submitted to you on special [interrogatories] consisting of specific questions about the facts. . . . You are the sole judges of the credibility of the witnesses and the weight to be given their testimony, but in matters of law, you must be governed by the instructions in this charge. . . . [Y]ou will observe all the instructions which have previously been given to you. I shall now give you additional instructions . . . [to] follow during your deliberations.

1. Do not let bias, prejudice or sympathy play any part in your deliberations.

2. In arriving at your answers, consider only the evidence, . . . together with the law as given you by the court. . . .

4. You must not decide who you think should win, and then try to answer the questions accordingly. Simply answer the questions, and do not discuss nor concern yourselves with the effect of your answers. . . .

[Other general instructions tell the jurors not to conclude that any question is unimportant; not to "trade answers" or agree to be bound by an average; that a non-unanimous verdict of ten or more jurors is acceptable in this jurisdiction; that violation of the instructions may be misconduct and require a wasteful retrial; etc. The court then instructs the jury on the law applicable to the case:]

By the term "preponderance of the evidence" as used in this Charge, is meant the greater weight and degree of credible evidence before you. . . .

[INSTRUCTIONS RELATED TO SPECIAL INTERROGATORY NO. 1:]

1. An agreement may be oral, it may be written or it may be partly written and partly oral. Where an agreement is fully or partially in writing, the law provides that persons

may bind themselves to that agreement even though they do not sign it, where their assent is otherwise indicated.

2. In answering [Interrogatory] No. 1, you should look to the intent of Pennzoil and the Getty entities as outwardly or objectively demonstrated to each other by their words and deeds. The question is not determined by the parties' secret, inward, or subjective intentions.

3. Persons may intend to be bound to an agreement even though they plan to sign a more formal and detailed document at a later time. On the other hand, parties may intend not to be bound until such a document is signed.

4. There is no legal requirement that parties agree on all the matters incidental to their agreement before they can intend to be bound. Thus, even if certain matters were left for future negotiations, those matters may not have been regarded by Pennzoil and the Getty entities as essential to their agreement, if any, on January 3. On the other hand, you may find that the parties did not intend to be bound until each and every term of their transaction was resolved.

5. Every binding agreement carries with it a duty of good faith performance. If Pennzoil and the Getty entities intended to be bound at the end of the Getty Oil board meeting of January 3, they were obliged to negotiate in good faith the terms of the definitive merger agreement and to carry out the transaction. . . .

SPECIAL [INTERROGATORY] NO. 1: Do you find from a preponderance of the evidence that at the end of the Getty Oil board meeting of January 3, 1984, Pennzoil and each of the Getty entities, to wit, the Getty Oil Company, the Sarah C. Getty Trust and the J. Paul Getty Museum, intended to bind themselves to an agreement that included the following terms:

a. All Getty Oil shareholders except Pennzoil and the Sarah C. Getty Trust were to receive $110 per share, plus [other stated compensation];

b. Pennzoil was to own 3/7ths of the stock of Getty . . . ;

c. Pennzoil and the Sarah C. Getty Trust were to endeavor in good faith to agree upon a plan for restructuring Getty Oil on or before December 31, 1984, [and if unable to agree, they would divide the assets of Getty on a stated basis].

Answer: "We do" or "We do not." [ANSWER:] We do.

[Note to the student: The wording of this special interrogatory was the subject of several objections by Texaco, and it was the focus of a vigorous appellate attack. Can you see why?]

SPECIAL [INTERROGATORY] NO. 2: Do you find from a preponderance of the evidence that Texaco knowingly interfered with the agreement between Pennzoil and the Getty entities, if you have so found?

Answer: "We do" or "We do not." ANSWER: We do.

[Extensive instructions, which explained the concepts of knowledge and interference, followed this interrogatory but are omitted here.]

SPECIAL [INTERROGATORY] NO. 3: What sum of money, if any, do you find from a preponderance of the evidence would compensate Pennzoil for its actual damages, if any, suffered as a direct and natural result of Texaco's knowingly interfering with the agreement between Pennzoil and the Getty entities, if any?

Answer in dollar and cents. ANSWER: $7.53 Billion.

[Instructions relating to this issue are omitted.]

[Special interrogatories Nos. 4 (asking whether Texaco acted in intentional disregard of Pennzoil's rights), 5 (punitive damages), 6 (an alternate theory of the agreement), 7 (another alternate theory of the agreement), and 8 (whether the agreements reflected a fair price), are omitted here. The jury's answers to all of these questions were positive (and thus favorable to Pennzoil).]

After you retire to the jury room, you will select your own presiding juror. The first thing the presiding juror will do is to have this complete charge read aloud and then you will deliberate upon your answers to the questions asked. . . .

When you have answered all of the questions which you are required to answer . . . you will return into Court with your verdict.

Solomon Casseb, Judge Presiding

CERTIFICATE: We, the jury, have answered the above and foregoing special issues as herein indicated, and herewith return same into court as our verdict. [The instructions require the verdict to be signed by presiding juror if the jury is unanimous, or by all jurors rendering the verdict if not.]

Richard V. Lawler, Presiding Juror

EXCERPTS FROM CHARGE CONFERENCE AND OBJECTIONS IN *PENNZOIL CO. v. TEXACO, INC.*, NO. 84-05905

151st Dist. Ct. Harris Cy., Tex. Nov. 14, 1985

THE COURT: File these [written] objections for the Plaintiff, please, as of this time. And do you have the Defendant's [written objections]?

[THE CLERK]: Yes, your Honor.

[Numerous objections to the charge were made in writing. The following excerpts from the record of oral objections are only a small part of the transcript but show the nature of the objections and argument on the charge.] . . .

THE COURT: . . . All right. Mr. Keeton[a]

MR. KEETON [FOR TEXACO]: Your Honor, on Special [Interrogatory] No. 1, the next to last line before we get to the enumerated items [that contain the terms of the alleged agreement], . . . where it says, "intended to bind themselves to an agreement" . . . , [w]e request that the words "the same" be substituted for the word "an" . . . [s]o that somewhere in this charge, and in some fashion, the jury understands that [Pennzoil, the Trustee, the Museum, and Getty] must [have] agree[d] to the same agreement. Not four different agreements. . . .

---

[a] Dean Yudof explains that "the excerpted remarks were part of a continuing debate over New York contract law and general versus special submissions to the jury." Texaco, he says, viewed agreement on essential terms and intention to be bound as separate tests for contract formation. Pennzoil, on the other hand, viewed Texaco's arguments as reflecting long-discarded formalism. According to Pennzoil, the New York law followed the Restatement of Contracts: the controlling question was whether there was an agreement, and the question whether all essential terms were agreed to was subsumed within that ultimate inquiry. Letter from Dean Mark Yudof to David Crump, August 19, 1986. As Dean Yudof observes, the exchange is an interesting example of the interplay between substantive doctrine and civil procedure.

DEAN YUDOF [FOR PENNZOIL]: Your Honor, I think that the response to this [objection] is simply that the whole notion of a mutual intention to be [bound] suggests that the parties agreed to the same terms. . . .

. . . And if the jury concludes that that is not the case [*i.e.*, that the parties did not agree to the same terms], then presumably the jury will conclude that there was no intention to be bound, [in response to] Special [Interrogatory] No. 1.

MR. KEETON: Your Honor, that is simply an incorrect statement of the law.

. . . [T]his idea of intent to be bound is a wholly separate item from did they agree and have a meeting of the minds on the elements and terms of that contract. . . .

They can agree on all the elements and not intend to be bound.

You can intend to be bound and not agree on all the elements. [Either way,] you do not have a contract.

THE COURT: [Ultimately overrules the objection.] . . . Give me your next objection.

MR. KEETON: . . . [There is not] a definition of agreement in the instructions. . . .

THE COURT: Well, I believe in the original instruction, they had, "An agreement ordinarily takes the form of an offer or proposal made by one person to another followed by acceptance of the offer by the other." . . . That was left out [of the current draft]. . . .

MR. JAMAIL: . . . Judge, we had [that definition] in our first draft and we would like to have it in. . . .

MR. KEETON: [The defendant would] rather have none than that one. . . .

[The discussion focuses, again, on the objection that the first interrogatory does not require the jury to find that all parties contemplated "the same" agreement. At the conclusion of the argument, before ruling, the Court says:]

THE COURT: All right. Anything further from anybody on that?

MR. JAMAIL: Nothing else, your Honor. . . .

MR. KEETON: All talked out, your Honor.

THE COURT: All right. Those objections will be overruled except as to cosmetic changes that have been made.

And all of your [requested] special [interrogatories] and instructions [*i.e.*, those not incorporated into the charge] are refused as of this time.

And I am ready for the jury [which, after a recess, will hear the charge and the jury arguments]. . . .

NOTES AND QUESTIONS

(1) *Objections to the Charge.* If you represented Texaco, what additional objections would you have levelled at Interrogatory No. 1, with respect to its asking whether the parties "intended to be bound?" [Note: From your Contracts course, which controls — subjective "intent" or objective manifestations of agreement? Of course, the instructions tell the jury that "intent" is to be considered as it was "outwardly or objectively demonstrated" by the parties "to each other by their words and deeds." Does this instruction solve the problem, or is the use of the word "intended" in the question itself misleading enough to be error?] Additionally, if you represented Texaco, would you

consider the phrase "intended to be bound" to be a sufficient inquiry as to whether Pennzoil had a present, existing contract? [Can't parties presently "intend" to be bound in the sense that they are working toward that goal but have not yet reached it?]

(2) *Texaco's Appeal.* Texaco appealed, asserting numerous charge errors. The intermediate appellate court affirmed but granted a remittitur that (like the verdict) was the largest in history. *Texaco, Inc. v. Pennzoil Co.*, 729 S.W.2d 768 (Tex. App. — Houston [1st Dist.] 1987, writ ref'd n.r.e.). The Texas Supreme Court, in a one-sentence order, refused to review the decision. The verdict and judgment had originally exceeded $11 billion, but the parties settled for $3 billion while Texaco was preparing a petition for certiorari to the United States Supreme Court, which was later denied. 485 U.S. 994 (1988).

(3) *The General Verdict versus Special Verdicts.* How would the charge be structured differently if it were a general verdict charge — and what practical difference, if any, would that make to the parties?

(4) *Hypothesizing Different Answers by the Jury: What Difference in the Result?* What would be the result if the jury had answered the first interrogatory (existence of the contract) "yes," the second (whether there was interference) "no," and the third (damages) "$7.53 billion"? [Note that the third question does not purport to be a general verdict; it is only a measure of Pennzoil's loss and cannot supply the findings needed for liability, because the instructions do not make it a general verdict.] What would be the result if all questions were answered favorably to Pennzoil except the last one (to which, assume the jury answered that the price was not fair)? [Note: Such a finding arguably would have established an affirmative defense of illegality, since applicable law would require a contract at a fair price. Would the jurors have known the result? Would you have?]

(5) *The Effect of Special Verdicts on Jury Argument or Summation.* With a special verdict charge, the attorneys' summations must focus on the questions of fact that the jury must answer, rather than merely on who should win. Is this effect an advantage of special verdict charges? Consider the following.

D. Crump, EFFECTIVE JURY ARGUMENT: THE ORGANIZATION

*43 Tex. B.J. 468 (1980)**

Plaintiff's Opening Argument.

[Plaintiff's first argument] is not an occasion for histrionics [because the defendant's argument will follow, and plaintiff will have a final opportunity in rebuttal]. . . . Your opponent's best points may come from points you exaggerate.

[An outline of a well organized argument, if special interrogatories are used, might look something like this:]

1. *Introduction.* This [part] consists, often, of thanking the jurors and setting the stage. "It has been a long trial. . . . I want to thank you for your careful attention during it. I am a fan of the jury system, because I think it does more substantial justice than any other system devised on earth. . . . You are here today to say who is responsible for the accident. . . ."

2. *Explanation and Emphasis of Legal Considerations* [*In the Charge*]. "I want to go over the judge's charge with you. And . . . I want to remind you of the [voir dire]

examination, in which I told you that the court would define certain terms for you. Here's the court's definition of the term 'negligence,' for instance (read . . . the definition). . . . [I]t comes down to this: If a person . . . is careless — that is negligence. And what this defendant did certainly fits the definition. . . ." In the same manner, cover each of the other legal issues you want to emphasize. Simplify them in a manner favorable to the conclusion you are trying to guide the jury toward. . . .

3. *Take the Special Interrogatories, One by One, Marshal the Evidence Toward the Conclusion You Wish the Jury to Reach, and Tell the Jury the Finding You Believe It Should Make.* "The first special [interrogatory] asks this: 'Do you find from the preponderance of the evidence that the defendant [was negligent]?' All that means, ladies and gentlemen, is, was the defendant just a little careless . . . ? And I submit to you that the answer to that question must be 'yes.' . . . First of all, he plowed right into the plaintiff's car. . . . Second, the damage to the car is severe. That indicates undiminished speed. Third, the witnesses say he swerved only at the last minute. Fourth, the defendant's own testimony — with a little prodding from me — tells you that he saw the plaintiff when he was just about ten feet away. . . . Now, special [interrogatory] number two asks you. . . ."

Ordinarily, it is not good [strategy] to . . . summarize the evidence by going through what the first witness said, what the second said, and so forth. The evidence should be marshaled in a way that answers the questions the jury will have to answer.

4. *Make a Short, Unemotional Closing.* "I ask you . . . for a verdict that answers the questions the way I have just described. . . . I believe it is supported by the evidence. . . ." You have the right to close. Don't shoot off your biggest emotional guns now.

Defendant's Argument

Defendant has the disadvantage of having his entire argument sandwiched between the plaintiff's two arguments. Therefore, he must combine all of his points in one argument.

1. *Introduction.* This phase of the argument . . . might be very much like the plaintiff's introduction. . . .

2. *Answer . . . the Opposing Argument — In Short Fashion.* You have to answer the plaintiff's argument. However, you should not let the plaintiff's argument dominate yours. . . . Answer and get it over with. . . .

a. Tell the jury you are going to answer . . . [, but]

b. Tell the jury . . . you are not going to try to answer everything. "I'm not going to have time to answer every single point in the plaintiff's argument, because he has raised such a number of them."

c. Explain your adversary's role. "Mr. Jones, the plaintiff's lawyer, is of course representing the plaintiff. I have no quarrel with that. . . . But I think you have to realize that everything he said was calculated to get a recovery for the plaintiff. . . ."

d. Answer one, two or three points — briefly. "He tells you that the plaintiff is a young man, in the flower of his youth. That is an attempt to make you feel sympathy. . . . But what has the judge told you? 'Do not let bias, prejudice or sympathy play any part in your deliberations.' . . . He also tells you that the witnesses said John swerved at the last minute. Well, the answer to that, and Mr. Jones conveniently leaves it out, is that the plaintiff pulled out in front of him suddenly. . . ."

3. *Having Answered Briefly, Say: "Now, I Want to Get Down to What This Lawsuit is Really About."*

4. *Go Over the [Instructions] and the Special [Interrogatories] — But Not the Way the Plaintiff Did; the Way You Think They Should Be Answered.* "The judge tells you that negligence means 'unreasonable' conduct. Now, I just don't think [the evidence shows] John was guilty of any unreasonable conduct." . . . Then go over the special [interrogatories] individually, marshaling the evidence and giving the answers you believe appropriate [which will be the opposite ones from the plaintiff].

5. *Give the Jury the Emotional Basis for Holding for You.* "Ladies and gentlemen, anybody can sue anybody else. There's not even a screening panel that decides whether the lawsuit has any merit to it. . . . The only protection John here has is you, . . . even if he's completely right himself. It will be a terrible thing if, every time somebody pulls out in front of you suddenly and your car hits them because of it, you get sued for damages. . . ."

6. *Tell the Jury That Your Opponent Has the Last Word — You Can't Answer.* "In a moment I'll sit down, and I won't be able to answer Mr. Jones. . . . He may get emotional. . . . If he does just remember this: Emotionalism is the indication of a weak argument. He may distort things. . . . I must trust you, and I do . . . ; and if he says something wrong, you will recognize it."

Plaintiff's Closing Argument

Plaintiff may begin with an answer to the defense argument. It should take a form similar to the defendant's answer to the plaintiff. Then the plaintiff's lawyer should:

1. *Go Over the Issues Again, More Briefly This Time, Again Marshaling the Important Evidence.*

2. *Hit Hardest On the Fundamental Issue in the Case.*

3. *Give the Jury the Emotional Basis for Holding in the Plaintiff's Favor.* "When you're injured by someone else's carelessness, the law is very simple. If they refuse to assist you in bearing the cost of your injuries, you come before a jury of your peers and ask for justice. No man is an island. We are all responsible for assisting those whom we have injured . . . carelessly by our inattention, as the defendant did. His efforts to pin the blame on the plaintiff are disgraceful. . . . The plaintiff will go through the rest of his days with a part of his life taken from him. This is his only day in court for that [loss]. I pray you — I beg you: Do not turn a deaf ear on his plea for simple justice."

EXCERPTS FROM JURY ARGUMENTS OR SUMMATIONS IN *PENNZOIL CO. v. TEXACO, INC.*, NO. 84-05905

151st Dist Ct. Harris Cy., Tex. Nov. 14, 1985

THE COURT: . . . Mr. Jeffers, you may commence with your summation. . . .

MR. JEFFERS [FOR PENNZOIL]: Thank you, your Honor.

Good morning, ladies and gentlemen. . . .

. . . The charge of this court . . . under special [interrogatory] number 1, the instructions say that "an agreement may be oral and it may be written and it may be partly written and partly oral. . . . [T]he law provides that persons may bind themselves to [an] agreement even though they do not sign it where their assent is otherwise indicated."

"In answering [interrogatory] No. 1, you should look to the intent of Pennzoil and the Getty entities as outwardly or objectively demonstrated to each other by their words and deeds."

[Mr. Jeffers reads other instructions relating to interrogatory No. 1.] . . .

That is the law of this court under which this case is to be decided — that if the parties intended to be bound at the conclusion of the Getty board meeting on January 3 to an agreement that included the elements listed under Special [Interrogatory] No. 1, if they intended to be bound by their outward and objective manifestations, their conduct, then they were bound and they had an obligation to proceed in good faith. . . .

Special [Interrogatory] No. 1 says, "Do you find from a preponderance of the evidence that at the end of the Getty board meeting . . . Pennzoil and each of the Getty entities . . . intended to bind themselves to an agreement that . . . included the following terms [Mr. Jeffers reads them]?"

Now, of course, we believe that the answer to that question is, "We do."

You can start with the press release. Surely the press release shows that there was an intent to be bound, at the conclusion of that board meeting, to an agreement which included those terms. . . .

[Mr. Jeffers compiles the evidence showing the existence of the agreement. He uses the instructions, particularly the one calling attention to objective signs of behavior, to emphasize his evidence and to reject subjective interpretations of the events by hostile witnesses. The detailing of the evidence in support of, and refutation of Texaco's theories against, a "yes" answer to interrogatory 1, occupy roughly 100 transcript pages of Mr. Jeffers' argument.]

All right. So I have said about as much as I can say about Special [Interrogatory] No. 1. . . . [W]e again say the answer is, "[W]e do. . . ."

[In a similar manner, Mr. Jeffers covers other special interrogatories, with instructions, explanation of the law, and with compilation of the evidence. He concludes:]

In my humble opinion, the defenses to these issues have been an outrageous cover-up. If Texaco's witnesses can get away from the witness stand with the things they said here, if they can do to Pennzoil what they did in the marketplace, they can do it to someone else somewhere else. But they are here. . . . It's time for an accounting.

Thank you.

[Mr. Jeffers was followed by another attorney for Pennzoil, who concluded the plaintiff's opening argument. After a recess, Texaco's argument followed, given by Mr. Miller.]

THE COURT: Mr. Miller, you may proceed.

MR. MILLER [FOR TEXACO]: May it please your Honor.

Ladies and gentlemen of the jury, I had the feeling that if I waited long enough I would finally get to talk to you. . . .

[The following appears in the latter part of Mr. Miller's argument. The focus is upon special interrogatory 1:]

Now, you don't see in this charge the word "contract," but every time you see the word "agreement," that's what the Court's talking about. He's talking about a contract, a binding obligation, something that can be enforced in court.

So this is a contract case and a claim that Texaco tortiously interfered with a contract. And, of course, the first thing that has to be decided, your first obligation, is . . . "Did they have a contract?" I put it to you that simply and bluntly and plainly. . . .

This first [interrogatory] says, "Do you find from a preponderance of the evidence that at the end of the Getty Oil board meeting . . . Pennzoil and each of the Getty entities intended to bind themselves to an agreement that included the following terms?"

Now, . . . in order to answer that [interrogatory] yes, you must find that these four organizations . . . intended to be bound.

Point number two, the statement, "intended to bind themselves to an agreement," [means] "to commit themselves to a binding contract," not an agreement in principle, not a plan . . . , but a binding contract that you could take to court. . . .

And paragraph 3 says, "The parties may intend to be bound to an agreement even though they plan to sign a more formal and detailed document at a later time. On the other hand, parties may intend not to be bound until such a document is signed."

So there you have it. You may intend to be bound before you sign a document or you may not.

I spent quite a bit of time, when we were selecting you ladies and gentlemen on the jury, . . . asking you . . . if you would be willing to accord these Getty entities the right to withhold their assent to a contract until they saw it in writing and had their advisors examine it and test it. . . .

And I want to read some of the testimony to you. [Mr. Miller reads from the transcript of the testimony of Mr. Liman, a Pennzoil lawyer during the negotiations leading to the alleged contract:] . . .

Q: My question [was] . . . did Pennzoil want a full written agreement?

A: Pennzoil wanted a full written agreement, yes, sir. . . .

Q: What I'm trying to find out, is did you understand that it was some kind of a contract between Pennzoil and Gordon Getty when you left that meeting on the 1st? . . .

A: No, I think we had an exploratory meeting . . . but it was to be followed by something else.

Q: And [that] "something further," of course, was a written agreement, wasn't it?

A: We contemplated that there should be a written agreement . . . [signed by the parties].

Q: [You] contemplated [you] were going to have a written agreement that would set out the principal terms and that nobody would be bound until that happened?

A: I don't know that we really thought about it, but I assume that the idea was that, you know, I suppose the people could have backed out until they signed the agreement. . . . They were not bound and we understood that.

[Mr. Miller reads from the testimony of another Pennzoil witness, Mr. Hertz.]

Q: The thought was, the parties wanted a written agreement that was signed by all parties?

A: That is what was the expectation. . . .

Q: And . . . when they signed it, then there was to be an agreement; is that right?

A: I think that is right. . . .

Now, that's not my evidence. That's their [Pennzoil's] evidence. That's from their people. Every one of those people is a witness who is hostile to the interest of Texaco. And it's very clear that they wanted this document in writing and that they wanted everybody to sign it.

I've got more proof. The document itself is as good . . . proof as you could possibly have.

[Mr. Miller reads from the written "Plan":] "This is subject to the approval of the board of directors of [Getty]. . . . Upon such approval the company shall execute three or more counterparts of the joinder of the company . . . and deliver one such counterpart to each of the Trustee, the Museum, and Pennzoil." . . .

[Mr. Miller details the other evidence upon which he relies in his contention that the jury should not find the existence of an agreement. "I guess the most persuasive thing to me is [Pennzoil] left [its hostile tender offer for shares of Getty] in effect [during and after the negotiations]. . . . Do they need the tender offer if they've got that binding contract?"

[Mr. Miller argues other special interrogatories in a similar manner. His argument on the damage interrogatory begins with the reading of the issue and includes the following:]

. . . This [interrogatory] is dealing with damages that have been caused by tortious interference. And if there was not tortious interference, of course, there could be only one answer, and that would be zero. . . .

We don't owe these people anything, not a dime. . . . We owe them zero. . . .

I believe we're right. I believe you think we're right. I believe you're going to find "No" to that first issue. . . .

Remember what Harry Truman's mother said to him: "You do right and the case will come out like it ought to come out."

And, I thank you very much.

[After a recess, Mr. Jamail gave the plaintiff's closing argument.]

THE COURT: . . . You may proceed, Mr. Jamail.

MR. JAMAIL: Thank you, Judge Casseb. . . .

There were so many misstatements in what Mr. Miller told you that I'm not going to try to answer all of them. . . .

He starts out by giving you four hours of excuses for Texaco's conduct and ends it up by saying to you, "Don't take our company because if something went wrong, it was Getty that did it."

They bought and paid for this lawsuit when they gave the indemnities [to the Getty entities and personnel].

And for Mr. Miller to stand here and attempt to change the court's charge . . . by inserting things that he likes, is typical. . . .

If [the judge] had wanted to say to you "contract," he would have said it. . . .

The reason for that [*i.e.*, for Mr. Miller's argument] is this subtle way, . . . to try to get you, the jury, to . . . impose a harsher burden on Pennzoil than . . . the law does. . . .

[Mr. Jamail takes the jury, once again, through the charge and the evidence. His conclusion includes the following:]

You people here, you jur[ors], are the conscience, not only of this community . . . , but of this country.

What you decide is going to set the standard of morality in business for America for years and years to come.

Now, you can turn your back on Pennzoil and say, "Okay, that's fine. We like that kind of deal. That's slick stuff.

"Go on out and do this kind of thing. Take the company, fire the employees, lose the pension fund." . . . [O]r you can say: "No. Hold it, hold it, hold it now. That's not going to happen.

"I have got a chance. Me. Juror.

"I have got me a chance.

"I can stop this. And I am going to stop it.

"And you [Texaco] might pull this on somebody else, but you are not going to run it through me and tell me to wash it for you.

"I am not going to clean that dirty mess for you."

It's you. Nobody else but you. Not me. I am not big enough. Not Liedtke, not Kerr, not anybody. Not the judge. Only you, in our system, can do that.

Don't let this opportunity pass you. Do not. . . .

The evidence is clear. Punitive damages is meant for one reason, to stop this kind of conduct. . . .

And the reason is that you can send a message to corporate America, [to the] business world, because it's just people who make up those things.

And you can tell them that you are not going to get away with this. . . .

I know you are going to do the right thing.

You are people of morality and conscience and strength.

Don't let this opportunity pass you.

§ 10.08 Trial to the Court Without a Jury

Read Fed. R. Civ. P. 52 (findings by the court); also, read 28 U.S.C. §§ 144, 455 (bias of judge; disqualification).

NOTE ON TRIAL TO THE COURT

If you understand trial by jury, then, in general, you understand trial to the court. It is simpler in many respects — it is not necessary, obviously, to select or to charge the jury. There are, however, some important differences, and there are a few respects in which trial to the court involves complexities not present in jury trials.

Relaxation of Formalities in Evidence and Proof: Eagle-Picher Indus., Inc. v. Liberty Mut. Ins. Co., 682 F.2d 12 (1st Cir. 1982). In the absence of indications to the contrary, it will be assumed that the trial judge disregarded inadmissible evidence and based her fact findings on admissible evidence. In the *Eagle-Picher* case, which involved interpretation of contract language, the appellate court advised trial judges to admit "provisionally" all extrinsic evidence of the parties' intent, unless it is clearly inadmissible, privileged, or too time-consuming — to guard against reversal for failure to admit evidence. In a jury trial, receipt of harmful inadmissible evidence over objection brings about a quite different result (reversible error). Is the relaxation of this approach in trials to the court appropriate?

Recusal as a Means of Ensuring an Impartial Tribunal: Aetna Life Ins. Co. v. Lavoie, 475 U.S. 813 (1986). Unlike jury trials, trials to the court may furnish no opportunity for examining the trier of fact to expose potential bias. The remedy is a motion for recusal if a party knows or suspects prejudice. In the *Lavoie* case, the Alabama Supreme Court recognized a new cause of action against an insurer for bad faith refusal to pay legitimate claims. Aetna learned that one justice was the plaintiff in a pending bad faith suit against another insurer. Aetna filed a motion to recuse, which was denied, in an order that left recusal to each judge individually. The Supreme Court reversed. The issue was not whether this individual justice was biased, it said; instead, he should have recused himself if the circumstances "would offer a possible temptation . . . to the average [judge] . . . [to] lead him not to hold the balance nice, clear, and true." Should there be a procedure, as there is in jury trials, for another person to rule on the disqualification of the trier of fact (by having another judge decide it)? In some jurisdictions, a party may obtain at least one change of judge on demand (like a peremptory challenge); is this procedure sound?

Findings of Fact and Conclusions of Law. Probably the most complex difference between jury and judge trials involves the means of establishing the factual basis of the judgment. Knowing the "facts" that were found may be important in the appellate court, since a given legal theory may be viable or not, depending on how controverted facts were decided in the trial court. In a trial to the court, however, there are no instructions or verdicts. Federal Rule 52 fills this need by providing that the trial judge shall make findings of fact (or write an opinion or memorandum of decision) for purposes of review.

§ 10.09 Improving Trial Processes: Notes and Questions

(1) *Providing Jury Trial in the Right Cases (and Not in the Wrong Ones?)* Jury trials seem most important in cases in which citizens' perceptions of the balance of interests might diverge from the views of government, and when the issues are related to those in common experience. To the extent that there is constitutional room not to provide a jury, however, it may be appropriate to consider the fact that jury trials are more unpredictable, much more expensive for all concerned, and more likely to produce delay. Consider the following proposals:

(a) *Congress Should Expressly Consider Whether the Jury Trial Right Applies when Passing Legislation.* In cases in which the right might not otherwise attach under the Constitution and Rule 38, yet in which the arguments for jury trial are strong, Congress should provide for jury trial (*e.g.*, in enacting a civil rights law providing for a straightforward damage remedy). But in cases in which these policies are inapplicable, should Congress structure the legislation so that the right does not attach? *Compare Tull v. United States*, above (court followed Congress' intent that judge, not jury, should assess amount of penalty).

(b) *Should Legislatures Avoid Unnecessary Provision for Jury Trial in Complex Cases Requiring Special Experience?* For example, some states provide juries in child custody cases — but other states do not. The custody decision is one in which a judge's longer experience, including the experience of seeing how one's decisions in earlier cases have turned out, might be most valuable. Is this the kind of case in which a legislature should refrain from providing for jury trial? [On the other hand, family practitioners have observed that custody decisions of judges tend to be more influenced by gender bias than those of juries!]

(2) *Improving the Process of Voir Dire Examination and Jury Selection.* If the jury examination is done by the attorneys, the trial starts with a personality contest. If, on the other hand, voir dire is done exclusively by the judge, it is much less likely to ferret out unconscious prejudices. Neither method is perfect. Might we improve the system if we amended the rules to provide that the judge may conduct the bulk of the examination, but that she must provide a reasonable time for supplementary questioning of the venire by the attorneys? In the alternative, should the rules be amended to give the trial judge discretion to examine the jury herself about sensitive subjects such as insurance, and allow the attorneys to conduct the bulk of the examination?

(3) *Presentation of Evidence.* The rules of evidence are in large measure premised on the notion that juries will misuse many kinds of information and that this information must be kept from them. Both because these rules sometimes hide facts that are relevant and true, and because their enforcement is itself a factor that makes the trial more complex, there have sometimes been suggestions for streamlining the rules. Might it be better simply to place before the jury all facts of any kind that the attorneys wish to bring them (perhaps subject to a reasonable limit on the length of presentation) and to let the jurors sort out this information? On the other hand, those who support rules of exclusion sometimes point out that their enforcement by objection in the presence of the jury encourages the asking of improper questions. Would it be better to videotape trials and present a version to the jury that removed inadmissible material?

(4) *Jury Argument.* Improper jury argument is frequent. The contemporaneous objection requirement clearly is one reason; the application of harmless error principles is another. Would it be better to provide that an attorney may properly object at the end of the opponent's jury argument, rather than during it, and to provide for reversal in the event of clear violations whether or not they are harmful?

(5) *The Court's Authority to Comment to the Jury on the Evidence.* As you have seen, some jurisdictions (*e.g.*, California; the federal system) allow judges to comment liberally on the evidence, so long as the comments are not excessively one-sided. Other jurisdictions (*e.g.*, Texas) prohibit this practice. Which approach is better? [Might judicial comment cure some of the deficiencies in overzealous argument by counsel (or is it likely itself to invade the jury's function)?]

(6) *Submitting the Case to the Jury.* One of the more profound questions raised by this chapter is whether the general charge or special interrogatories should be the basic model for jury submission. What is your conclusion at this point? Also, consider the following possibilities:

(a) *"Broad" Special Interrogatories.* Perhaps a compromise between general and special interrogatories is possible. The court could be required or encouraged to submit the case on special interrogatories, but permitted to submit them broadly and generally. For example, a negligence case could consist of three questions: One asking the jury to decide whose negligence proximately caused the occurrence, one asking the jury to assign percentages of responsibility to the parties for comparative negligence purposes, and one inquiring about the amount of damages. Does this approach preserve the advantages of both verdict types?

(b) *Plain Language.* There may be room for skepticism about the "plain language" movement in some kinds of legal documents, but not in the area of jury instructions. Section 10.07, above, shows the difficulty jurors sometimes have in understanding the court's charge. *See generally* Tanford, *The Law and Psychology of Jury Instructions*, 69 Neb. L. Rev. 71 (1990). *See also* Sand & Reiss, *A Report on Seven Experiments Conducted by District Court Judges in the Second Circuit*, 60 N.Y.U. L. Rev. 423, 456 (1985) (efforts to ensure comprehension, including recording); Note, *Improving Jury Comprehension in Complex Civil Litigation*, 62 St. John's L. Rev. 549 (1988). But there is a major difficulty with "plain language" efforts: it is very difficult to draft complete and accurate instructions without using complex terminology. Thus, a readily comprehensible explanation in plain words may be subject to attack as inaccurate, and a fully accurate explanation may be difficult to comprehend.

(c) *Pattern Jury Instructions.* In some jurisdictions, official charge form books are available. California's "BAJI" (Book of Approved Jury Instructions) is a notable example. In other jurisdictions, there are unofficial but authoritative sources, such as the State Bar of Texas' Pattern Jury Charges. *See also* E. Devitt & C. Blackmar, *Federal Jury Practice and Instructions* vols. 1-3 (3d ed. 1977). Would it be preferable for each jurisdiction to adopt official charge forms and encourage their use?

(7) *The Vanishing Trial?* A study has documented the decreasing numbers of cases that proceed all the way to trial. The study, reported in the December 14, 2003 issue of The New York Times, noted that in 1962, 11.5 percent of all civil cases filed in federal court proceeded to trial. By 2002, that number had dropped to 1.8 percent. The decrease is reflected in the raw numbers as well: In 1985, 12,529 civil trials were conducted in federal court; in 2002, only 4,569 civil cases were tried in federal court. Is this reduction in civil trials entirely positive? *See* R. Perschbacher & D. Bassett, *The End of Law*, 84 B.U. L. Rev. 1 (2004) (noting the resultant privatized law, distorted norms, diminished case resolution and explanation, and other effects due to efforts to reduce trials).

(8) *Principles for Juries and Jury Trials.* The American Bar Association has issued "Principles for Juries and Jury Trials." These principles include a call for the return to the 12-person jury in civil trials, permitting jurors to take notes, and allowing the judge to meet with the jury if the jury has reached an impasse to see whether the judge can offer any clarifying instructions. These principles are available at http://www.abanet.org/juryprojectstandards/principles.pdf.

CHAPTER 11

POST-TRIAL MOTIONS

§ 11.01 Judicial Power to Take the Case Away from the Jury

Taking the Case away from the Jury. The right to trial by jury does not imply that the jury makes all decisions. At several points in the process — some of which we have already seen, including summary judgment and dismissal — the judge may be called upon to withdraw the case from the jury's decision.

The Procedures: Judgment on the Verdict, Judgment as a Matter of Law, New Trial, and Relief from Judgments. First, the judge may have a complex task in granting judgment on the verdict. In some cases, that step is clearcut; in others, it is not, and it may require the application of the law to the verdict in non-obvious ways. Secondly, the judge may be called upon, by a motion for judgment as a matter of law during trial (also called a "directed verdict") or after trial (also called a "judgment notwithstanding the verdict"), to countermand a verdict that is unsupportable by the record evidence. Third, the judge may be called upon to determine whether the trial has included procedural errors, misconduct, or lopsided results so serious as to constitute a miscarriage of justice. If so, the judge has discretionary authority to grant a new trial. Finally, there is the possibility that a final judgment, as to which all time limits for the usual kinds of attacks have expired, may be so egregiously unjust that the court should have narrow authority to set it aside. This authority is given the court by the Rule 60 Motion for Relief from Judgment. [Consider the following Chapter Summary Problem, which you should analyze at the end of the chapter (or otherwise treat as your instructor directs).]

PROBLEM A: CHAPTER 11 SUMMARY PROBLEM

THE AUTOMOBILE ACCIDENT BETWEEN PAULA GREEN AND THE WEST YORK BUS COMPANY: A POST-TRIAL MOTIONS PROBLEM. This case concerns a collision between an automobile driven by plaintiff Paula Green and a bus operated by the West York Bus Company. At trial, there was only one hotly contested issue related to Paula's negligence claim:

> The bus driver testified that plaintiff Paula drove across the median and collided with the bus on its side of the road, while Paula testified that she was in her proper lane a few seconds before the collision, when she suffered a heart attack that rendered her unconscious, and she woke up with her vehicle still in her lane. The trial judge excluded the testimony of an accident-reconstruction expert called by Paula. No other testimony on this issue was submitted. At the conclusion of all evidence, the defendant

moved for "judgment as a matter of law" on the ground that there was no legally sufficient evidence of negligence.

The judge instead submitted the case to the jury. But he erroneously instructed the jurors that the defendant had the burden of showing contributory negligence "by clear and convincing evidence." The defendant did not object to this instruction. After a verdict for the plaintiff, the defendant learned that plaintiff Paula had said in a live television interview broadcast at the scene of the accident, "I have no idea how the accident happened, but maybe I crossed the median." Paula's pretrial deposition contained her testimony that she was "unaware of any testimony or evidence that even remotely supports the bus driver's version."

1. If the defendant now (post-verdict) moves for "judgment as a matter of law," should the court grant the motion?
2. What are the defendant's chances of obtaining relief through a motion for new trial?
3. What should the plaintiff do if the Court of Appeals reverses the judgment for the plaintiff and, for the first time, grants judgment for the defendant on the ground that the plaintiff's evidence was legally insufficient?
4. What recourse would the defendant have had if it learned of the plaintiff's broadcast statement six months after the trial court had granted a judgment for the plaintiff? What if it learned two years after?

§ 11.02 Judgment on the Verdict

The Judge's Duty with Respect to the Verdict. If the jury has rendered a general verdict that is supported by the evidence and can be the basis for judgment in accordance with the law, the entry of judgment on the verdict is straightforward. But special verdicts may present a complex question of law. If there are many interrogatories, it may not be obvious to a neutral observer who has won. For a simple example, consider a case in which the jury finds that a defective product caused the occurrence and that the plaintiff concurred in causing it by her contributory negligence. But assume further that there is no statute or decision that makes clear whether contributory negligence is a defense to a strict product liability claim. It is entirely likely that both sides will claim to have "won" the right to judgment on the jury's verdict. The trial judge will face the decision of a case of first impression.

An Example: Fein v. Permanente Medical Group, 38 Cal. 3d 137, 695 P.2d 665, 211 Cal. Rptr. 368 (1985). In § 1.08 of Chapter 1, we considered the case of *Fein v. Permanente Medical Group.* The California Medical Injury Compensation Reform Act ("MICRA") placed a $250,000 "cap" on noneconomic damages (*i.e.*, pain and suffering) in medical malpractice cases. The jury's verdict fixed the plaintiff's noneconomic loss at $500,000. The verdict was not a determination that the plaintiff was entitled to recover that amount; it merely was a fact finding that the judge was required to use in rendering a final judgment. The judge determined that correct application of the law to the jury's findings resulted in a judgment for $250,000 (not $500,000) in noneconomic damages. In so deciding, the judge had to face several complex legal questions, including the question whether the cap was unconstitutional. Technically, however, the trial judge's decision did not set aside the jury's verdict. It was a judgment entered on the verdict, because the legal consequence of the jury's finding was the judgment actually rendered.

§ 11.03 Judgment as a Matter of Law

[A] During Trial

PROBLEM B

EVALUATING PLAINTIFF'S EVIDENCE IN WEBER v. JARNIGAN. The law of the (hypothetical) State of West York is that in medical malpractice cases, other than those involving negligence of a kind that laypersons are capable of evaluating clearly, the plaintiff must offer expert testimony to set the standard of care that the allegedly negligent physician should have observed. (This is the law in most states.) In his trial in a West York district court, plaintiff Weber testifies that he engaged Dr. Jarnigan to remove his appendix; that Dr. Jarnigan performed the operation; that after the operation, he, Weber, experienced pain in the area of his appendix; that Dr. Jarnigan informed him that infection had set in and that a second operation would be necessary; and that, as a result, he, Weber, experienced pain and discomfort. Weber also testifies that in his opinion as a layperson, Dr. Jarnigan was extremely sloppy and negligent in letting the infection set in. Weber then rests without submitting any other testimony. If you represented Dr. Jarnigan, what motion would you make to the court at this point? How should the court rule? [And, finally, here is a slightly more difficult question: Would your conclusions be the same if Weber also testified that Dr. Jarnigan admitted that his inadvertence in leaving a sponge inside the sutured wound probably was the source of the infection?]

NOTE ON "DIRECTED VERDICT," "JUDGMENT NOTWITHSTANDING THE VERDICT," AND "JUDGMENT AS A MATTER OF LAW"

Earlier Terminology: Directed Verdict (During Trial) and Judgment Notwithstanding the Verdict (After Trial). Long before the present rules, the judge had authority to grant a "directed verdict" in favor of a party that was entitled as a matter of law to prevail. A directed verdict aborted the trial after the nonmovant had rested, on the ground that reasonable minds could not differ with the position of the movant, i.e., that no legally sufficient evidence supported the finding or verdict sought by the nonmovant. The modern practice also allowed a motion for "judgment notwithstanding the verdict," which actually amounted to a renewal of a motion for directed verdict, but which was urged after the trial. In the federal courts, the motion literally was the same motion renewed after the trial, and it was considered by the same standard. (A judgment notwithstanding the verdict sometimes was called a "judgment non obstante verdicto" or "judgment N.O.V.," which means the same thing.)

The 1991 Amendments: Revision of Terminology by Adoption of the Single Phrase, "Judgment as a Matter of Law." In 1991, amendments to Rule 50 jettisoned both "directed verdict" and "judgment notwithstanding the verdict," and instead adopted the term, "judgment as a matter of law" to describe both processes. The purposes were to modernize the nomenclature and to emphasize the identity of the two motions. It is debatable whether this change was necessary or even beneficial.

The Legal Standard for Judgment as a Matter of Law. Rule 50 provides that a court should render judgment as a matter of law when "a party has been fully heard on an issue during a jury trial and the court finds that a reasonable jury would not have a legally sufficient evidentiary basis to find for the party on that issue." As you might expect, however, the concept cannot be fully conveyed by this one sentence. Consider the Rule and the following decision.

Read Fed. R. Civ. P. 50(a) (judgment as a matter of law during trial).

LAVENDER v. KURN

327 U.S. 645 (1946)

MR. JUSTICE MURPHY delivered the opinion of the Court.

The Federal Employers' Liability Act permits recovery for personal injuries to an employee of a railroad engaged in interstate commerce if such injuries result "in whole or in part from the negligence of [the railroad]." 45 U.S.C. § 51.

Petitioner, the administrator of the estate of L.E. Haney, brought this suit under the Act against the respondent trustees of the St. Louis-San Francisco Railway Company (Frisco) and the respondent Illinois Central Railroad Company. It was charged that Haney, while employed as a switch-tender by the respondents in the switchyard of the Grand Central Station in Memphis, Tennessee, was killed as a result of respondents' negligence. Following a trial in the Circuit Court of the City of St. Louis, Missouri, the jury returned a verdict in favor of petitioner and awarded damages in the amount of $30,000. Judgment was entered accordingly. On appeal, however, the Supreme Court of Missouri reversed the judgment, holding that there was no substantial evidence of negligence to support the submission of the case to the jury. . . . We granted certiorari to review the propriety of the [Missouri] Court's action under the circumstances of this case. . . .

The Illinois Central tracks run north and south directly past and into the Grand Central Station. About 2,700 feet south of the station the Frisco tracks cross at right angles to the Illinois Central tracks. A west-bound Frisco train wishing to use the station must stop some 250 feet or more west of this crossing and back into the station over a switch line curving east and north. . . .

It was very dark on the evening of December 21, 1939. At about 7:30 p.m. a west-bound interstate Frisco passenger train stopped on the Frisco main line, its rear some 20 or 30 feet west of the switch. Haney, in the performance of his duties, threw or opened the switch to permit the train to back into the station. The respondents claimed that Haney was then required to cross to the south side of the track before the train passed the switch; and the conductor of the train testified that he saw Haney so cross. But there was also evidence that Haney's duties required him to wait at the switch north of the track until the train had cleared, close the switch, return to his shanty near the crossing and change the signals from red to green to permit trains on the Illinois Central tracks to use the crossing. The Frisco train cleared the switch, backing at the rate of 8 or 10 miles per hour. But the switch remained open and the signals still were red. Upon investigation Haney was found north of the track near the switch lying face down on the ground, unconscious. An ambulance was called, but he was dead upon arrival at the hospital.

Haney had been struck in the back of the head, causing a fractured skull from which he died. There were no known eyewitnesses to the fatal blow. Although it is not clear, there is evidence that his body was extended north and south, the head to the south. Apparently he had fallen forward to the south; his face was bruised on the left side from hitting the ground and there were marks indicating that his toes had dragged a few inches southward as he fell. His head was about 5 feet north of the Frisco tracks. Estimates ranged from 2 feet to 14 feet as to how far west of the switch he lay.

The injury to Haney's head was evidenced by a gash about two inches long from which blood flowed. The back of Haney's white cap had a corresponding black mark about an inch and a half long and an inch wide, running at an angle downward to the right of the center of the back of the head. A spot of blood was later found at a point 3 or 4 feet north of the tracks. The conclusion following an autopsy was that Haney's skull was fractured by "some fast moving small round object." One of the examining doctors testified that such an object might have been attached to a train backing at the rate of 8 or 10 miles per hour. But he also admitted that the fracture might have resulted from a blow from a pipe or club or some similar round object in the hands of an individual.

Petitioner's theory is that Haney was struck by the curled end or tip of a mail hook hanging down loosely on the outside of the mail car of the backing train. This curled end was 73 inches above the top of the rail, which was 7 inches high. The overhang of the mail car in relation to the rails was about 2 to 2 1/2 feet. The evidence indicated that when the mail car swayed or moved around a curve the mail hook might pivot, its curled end swinging out as much as 12 to 14 inches. The curled end could thus be swung out to a point 3 to 3 1/2 feet from the rail and about 73 inches above the top of the rail. Both east and west of the switch, however, was an uneven mound of cinders and dirt rising at its highest points 18 to 24 inches above the top of the rails. Witnesses differed as to how close the mound approached the rails, the estimates varying from 3 to 15 feet. But taking the figures most favorable to the petitioner, the mound extended to a point 6 to 12 inches north of the overhanging side of the mail car. If the mail hook end swung out 12 to 14 inches it would be 49 to 55 inches above the highest parts of the mound. Haney was 67 inches tall. If he had been standing on the mound about a foot from the side of the mail car he could have been hit by the end of the mail hook, the exact point of contact depending upon the height of the mound at the particular point. His wound was about 4 inches below the top of his head, or 63 inches above the point where he stood on the mound — well within the possible range of the mail hook end.

Respondents' theory is that Haney was murdered. They point to the estimates that the mound was 10 to 15 feet north of the rail, making it impossible for the mail hook end to reach a point of contact with Haney's head. Photographs were placed in the record to support the claim that the ground was level north of the rail for at least 10 feet. Moreover, it appears that the area immediately surrounding the switch was quite dark. Witnesses stated that it was so dark that it was impossible to see a 3-inch pipe 25 feet away. It also appears that many hoboes and tramps frequented the area at night in order to get rides on freight trains. Haney carried a pistol to protect himself. This pistol was found loose under his body by those who came to his rescue. It was testified, however, that the pistol had apparently slipped out of his pocket or scabbard as he fell. Haney's clothes were not disarranged and there was no evidence of a struggle or fight. No rods, pipes or weapons of any kind, except Haney's own pistol, were found near the scene. Moreover, his gold watch and diamond ring were still on him after he was struck. Six days later his unsoiled billfold was found on a high board fence about a block from the place where Haney was struck and near the point where he had been placed in an ambulance. It contained his social security card and other effects, but no money. His wife testified that he "never carried very much money, not very much more than $10." Such were the facts in relation to respondents' theory of murder.

Finally, one of the Frisco foremen testified that he arrived at the scene shortly after Haney was found injured. He later examined the fireman's side of the train very carefully and found nothing sticking out or in disorder. In explaining why he examined this side of the train so carefully he stated that while he was at the scene of the accident "someone said they thought that train No. 106 backing into Grand Central Station is what struck this man" and that Haney "was supposed to have been struck by something protruding on the side of this train." The foreman testified that these statements were made by an unknown Illinois Central switchman standing near the fallen body of Haney. The foreman admitted that the switchman "didn't see the accident . . . ." This testimony was admitted by the trial court over the strenuous objections of respondents' counsel that it was mere hearsay falling outside the *res gestae* rule.*

The jury was instructed that Frisco's trustees were liable if it was found that they negligently permitted a rod or other object to extend out from the side of the train as it backed past Haney and that Haney was killed as the direct result of such negligence, if any. The jury was further told that Illinois Central was liable if it was found that the company negligently maintained an unsafe and dangerous place for Haney to work, in that the ground was high and uneven and the light insufficient and inadequate, and that Haney was injured and killed as a direct result of the said place being unsafe and dangerous. This latter instruction as to Illinois Central did not require the jury to find that Haney was killed by something protruding from the train.

The [Missouri] Court, in upsetting the jury's verdict against both the Frisco trustees and the Illinois Central, admitted that "It could be inferred from the facts that Haney could have been struck by the mail hook knob *if* he were standing on the south side of the mound and the mail hook extended out as far as 12 or 14 inches." But it held that "all reasonable minds would agree that it would be mere speculation and conjecture to say that Haney was struck by the mail hook" and that "plaintiff failed to make a submissible case on the question." It also ruled that there "was no substantial evidence that the uneven ground and insufficient light were causes or contributing causes of the death of Haney." Finally, the Supreme Court held that the testimony of the foreman as to the statement made to him by the unknown switchman was inadmissible under the *res gestae* rule since the switchman spoke from what he had heard rather than from his own knowledge.

We hold, however, that there was sufficient evidence of negligence on the part of both the Frisco trustees and the Illinois Central to justify the submission of the case to the jury and to require appellate courts to abide by the verdict rendered by the jury.

The evidence we have already detailed demonstrates that there was evidence from which it might be inferred that the end of the mail hook struck Haney in the back of the head, an inference that the Supreme Court admitted could be drawn. That inference is not rendered unreasonable by the fact that Haney apparently fell forward toward the main Frisco track so that his head was 5 feet north of the rail. He may well have been struck and then wandered in a daze to the point where he fell forward. . . .

It is true that there is evidence tending to show that it was physically and mathematically impossible for the hook to strike Haney. And there are facts from which it might reasonably be inferred that Haney was murdered. But such evidence has become irrelevant upon appeal, there being a reasonable basis in the record for inferring that the hook struck Haney. . . . Under these circumstances it would be an undue invasion of the jury's historic function for an appellate court to weigh the conflicting evidence, judge the

---

* [In the terminology of today's Rules of Evidence, we would say that the declaration was hearsay and did not fit either the exception for present sense impressions or the exception for excited utterances. *See* § 10.05, *supra*. — Eds.]

credibility of witnesses and arrive at a conclusion opposite from the one reached by the jury. . . .

It is no answer to say that the jury's verdict involved speculation and conjecture. Whenever facts are in dispute or the evidence is such that fair-minded men may draw different inferences, a measure of speculation and conjecture is required on the part of those whose duty it is to settle the dispute by choosing what seems to them to be the most reasonable inference. Only when there is a complete absence of probative facts to support the conclusion reached does a reversible error appear.

In view of the foregoing disposition of the case, it is unnecessary to decide whether the allegedly hearsay testimony was admissible under the *res gestae* rule. . . . [I]nasmuch as there is adequate support in the record for the jury's verdict apart from the hearsay testimony, we need not determine whether that discretion was abused in this instance.

The judgment of the Supreme Court of Missouri is reversed and the case is remanded for whatever further proceedings may be necessary not inconsistent with this opinion.

McLAUGHLIN v. FELLOWS GEAR SHAPER CO., 786 F.2d 592 (3d Cir. 1986). This case appears in Chapter 10 above and should be reconsidered at this point. The plaintiff sued on the theory that a defective machine had amputated his thumb. The jury rendered a special verdict of "Yes" to the question, "Did plaintiff assume the risk?" But the appellate court concluded, as a matter of law, that there was no evidence to support any finding of assumption of risk. Nevertheless, both the district judge and the appellate court were unable to grant the plaintiff a judgment as a matter of law *after* trial — because the plaintiff's lawyer had not specified the absence of evidence of assumption of risk as a ground for judgment as a matter of law *during* the trial. The court of appeals found other grounds for disregarding the assumption-of-risk finding, over the dissent of one judge who accused the court of violating Rule 50(b).

NOTES AND QUESTIONS

(1) *The Standard for Judgment as a Matter of Law.* Briefly put, a judgment as a matter of law is proper if there is no reasonable way that a jury, properly applying the law, could find the facts so as to return a verdict for the non-movant. This standard is sometimes expressed in terms of the non-movant's having introduced "no evidence" (which does not mean literally no evidence, but evidence insufficient to make a case) or no "substantial evidence." The judge is required to draw all reasonable inferences in favor of the non-movant and may not make credibility determinations or weigh the evidence. *See Reeves v. Sanderson Plumbing Co.*, 530 U.S. 133 (2000). *See also* Cooper, *Directions for Directed Verdicts: A Compass for Federal Courts*, 55 Minn. L. Rev. 903 (1971).

(2) *Is a Judgment as a Matter of Law a Violation of the Seventh Amendment Right to Jury Trial? Galloway v. United States, 319 U.S. 372 (1943).* Galloway sued for disability benefits owing to his insanity, claiming that it originated during his service in the Army in World War I. His evidence showed that on two occasions during his service he engaged in bizarre behavior, creating disturbances; that he was "a wreck" when he returned; and that he currently was disabled by insanity. But the evidence failed to account for lengthy periods of years between his service and the present. The Supreme Court therefore upheld a judgment as a matter of law for the government. The Court emphasized that the insanity needed to have been continuous to the present but that there was a lengthy gap of years that were open to "mere speculation [rather than] probative

facts," in the proof. "Insanity so long and continuously sustained does not hide itself from the eyes and ears of witnesses."

The more interesting issue in the case, however, was Galloway's argument that the judgment as a matter of law, in the form granted against him, was unknown to the common law at the time of the Seventh Amendment. The common law did provide a procedure called a "demurrer to the evidence," but it required that the defendant "conced[e] the full scope of the [plaintiff's] evidence," *i.e.*, if the ruling did not favor the defendant, the automatic result was judgment for the plaintiff. The Court rejected Galloway's argument. First, his argument actually denied a jury trial right to the defendant: "To force this choice and yet deny that afforded by the directed verdict would be to embed in the Constitution the hypertechnicality of common-law pleading and procedure. . . ." In addition, "[t]he Amendment did not bind the federal courts to the exact procedural incidents or details of jury trial . . . in 1791." . . .

Justice Black, joined by two other members of the Court, dissented. The federal courts, he argued, had improperly converted the directed verdict into a requirement of "substantial" evidence to carry the burden of proof, which "permitted directed verdict even though there was far more evidence in the case than a plaintiff would have needed to withstand a demurrer."

(3) *Evidence Amounting to a "Mere Scintilla."* Most courts state that a "mere scintilla" is not legally sufficient evidence from which a reasonable factfinder can draw a legitimate inference. For example, in *Boeing Co. v. Shipman*, 411 F.2d 365, 374 (5th Cir. 1969) (en banc), the court of appeals explained that a "mere scintilla" is insufficient to present a question for the jury. But "if there is substantial evidence . . ., that is evidence of such quality and weight that reasonable and fair-minded men in the exercise of impartial judgment might reach different conclusions . . . the case [must be] submitted to the jury." *See also Kaplan v. Burroughs Corp.*, 611 F.2d 286 (9th Cir. 1979); *see also Galloway v. United States, supra*. The "scintilla" rule does not apply to conflicts in the direct evidence, which normally present jury questions about what happened, *e.g.*, whether the traffic light was red or green. It only applies to the jury's ability to draw inferences from circumstantial evidence.

(4) *Circumstantial Evidence.* Many, if not most, cases require the factfinder, whether judge or jury, to draw inferences from the circumstantial evidence in reaching a verdict on broader issues, such as whether the defendant's conduct proximately caused the occurrence, whether the applicable standard of care was violated, or about other so-called mixed questions of law and fact that are within the jury's province. In this respect, *Lavender v. Kurn* is a typical case in which the Court held that "there was [circumstantial] evidence from which it might be inferred that the end of the mail hook struck the decedent," and therefore judgment as a matter of law was improper. The Court devised a "reasonable basis in the record standard" under which the jury, not the trial judge, and certainly not any appellate court, performs the important function of drawing reasonable inferences from the circumstantial evidence.

Although *Lavender v. Kurn* contains the potentially broader proposition that "[o]nly when there is a complete absence of probative facts to support the conclusion reached does reversible error occur," that aspect of the opinion is considered as a special verdict favorable rule restricted solely to FELA cases. Properly interpreted, the "reasonable basis in the record" standard spawned by *Lavender v. Kurn* has evolved into a "reasonable minds" standard under which judgment as a matter of law is inappropriate "[i]f reasonable minds could differ as to the import of the evidence." *Anderson v. Liberty Lobby, Inc.*,

477 U.S. 242, 250-51 (1986). An earlier FELA case, *Pennsylvania Railroad Corp. v. Chamberlain*, 288 U.S. 333 (1933), overruled sub silentio in *Lavender v. Kurn*, had used an "equally probable inference" standard under which the inference in support of the verdict is not permissible if the evidence tends to sustain two inconsistent propositions. For an analysis of how federal courts evaluate the reasonableness of inferences from circumstantial evidence, see Dorsaneo, *Reexamining the Right to Jury Trial*, 54 SMU L. Rev. 1695, 1706-10 (2001).

(5) *If a Fact Issue Can Be Resolved by the Exercise of Logic — If It Doesn't Require Some Degree of "Speculation" and "Conjecture" — Then Paradoxically, It Isn't a Jury Issue*! An interesting paradox lies hidden in *Lavender v. Kurn*. The Court says:

> It is no answer to say that the jury's verdict involved speculation and conjecture. Whenever facts are in dispute or the evidence is such that fair-minded men may draw different inferences, a measure of speculation and conjecture is required on the part of those whose duty it is to settle the dispute by choosing what seems to them to be the most reasonable inference.

And, conversely, if the case can be resolved by rigid, mathematical logic, there is no need for a jury decision of the facts, because there is no jury issue! A paradox thus arises: If there is no speculation and conjecture required, then judgment as a matter of law is proper; but if the reviewing court thinks that too much speculation and conjecture is required, then judgment as a matter of law also is proper. The resolution of the paradox lies in the recognition that reasonableness is the standard for permitted inferences: If different people, using a "reasonable" kind of "speculation and conjecture," could arrive at different inferences from the facts, then a jury issue is presented; otherwise, it is not.

(6) *Evidence that Contradicts Itself.* Internal inconsistencies in the plaintiff's evidence do not necessarily destroy its probative value. The jury may be able to reconcile the conflict in favor of the plaintiff in a reasonable way. *Cf. Wilson v. Bailey*, 257 F.2d 352 (10th Cir. 1958). On the other hand, when the internal contradiction is of such a kind that no reasonable juror could credit the plaintiff's theory, a judgment as a matter of law is proper.

PROCEDURAL ASPECTS OF JUDGMENT AS A MATTER OF LAW: NOTES AND QUESTIONS

Read Rule 50(a) (judgment during trial).

(1) *Statement of Grounds for the Motion.* Rule 50 says that the motion must "specify . . . the law and facts that entitle the movant to the judgment." How specific does it have to be? *Cf. United States Industries, Inc. v. Semco Mfg. Co.*, 562 F.2d 1061 (8th Cir. 1977), in which the plaintiff moved for judgment as a matter of law in a contract case simply by saying that there was a legally enforceable contract and overwhelming evidence of the defendant's breach; the court held the statement sufficient. The main reason for the requirement is to enable the opponent to correct the deficiency, if she can, while the jury still is present. Presumably, that purpose should be considered in judging the sufficiency of the statement.

(2) *Timing of the Motion.* The motion is proper when the opponent rests or closes, or when all parties close. *Compare Rocco v. Johns-Manville Corp.*, 754 F.2d 110 (3d Cir. 1985) (motion was clearly untimely and could not be considered when asserted for the first time after the jury had rendered its verdict), *with Panotex Pipe Line Co. v. Phillips*

Petroleum Co., 457 F.2d 1279 (5th Cir. 1972) (grant of motion in favor of defendants during defense testimony, even though not immediately after plaintiff's having rested, not improper).

(3) *Making the Motion Outside the Jury's Presence.* A defendant usually should take care to make the motion outside the presence of the jury. If the motion is overruled, the jury otherwise would hear the judge reject the defendant's arguments and may infer that the plaintiff's claim is meritorious. *But cf. Womble v. J.C. Penney & Co.*, 47 F.R.D. 350 (E.D. Tenn.), *aff'd*, 431 F.2d 985 (6th Cir. 1970) (failure to excuse jury during hearing before the bench on motion for judgment as a matter of law not improper).

[B] After Trial

Read Rule 50(b) (judgment after trial).

NOTE ON REQUIREMENTS FOR POST-TRIAL JUDGMENT AS A MATTER OF LAW

Reserving Decision of the Motion. If a Rule 50(a) motion is not granted, the trial judge is deemed to have submitted the action to the jury subject to a later determination of the legal questions raised by the motion. In other words, the trial judge can decide the motion after trial. For one thing, the jury might decide the case the "right" way and thus might avoid the need to decide the legal question. If not, the court can grant the motion under the same legal standard after the verdict is in — and, if the appellate court disagrees, it can reinstate the verdict without the necessity of a retrial. Note, *Rule 50(b), Judgment Notwithstanding the Verdict*, 58 Colum. L. Rev. 517 (1958). Arguably, this is the careful course of action in a close case, and it allows for briefing and deliberation rather than quick decision in the heat of trial.

The Motion During Trial as a Prerequisite. As a consequence of this reasoning, a motion during trial is a prerequisite for moving for judgment as a matter of law after trial. Indeed, under a prior version of Rule 50, a Rule 50(a) motion made *before* the close of all the evidence had to be renewed at the *close* of all the evidence in order to preserve the ability to bring a Rule 50(b) motion. Under the current version of Rule 50, however, any Rule 50(a) motion may be renewed in a Rule 50(b) motion after trial.

The Legal Standard After Trial Is the Same as that During Trial. It follows that a post-trial judgment as a matter of law "is nothing more than a directed verdict granted after, rather than before, the jury has had an opportunity to bring in its verdict." *Lester v. Dunn*, 475 F.2d 983 (D.C. Cir. 1973). The same legal standard is applicable to both. In fact, the same standard also applies to an appellate court's consideration of "matter of law" questions.

NOTES AND QUESTIONS

(1) *Motion During Trial as a Prerequisite to a Post-Trial Motion — A Trap for the Unwary: Guglielmo v. Scotti & Sons, Inc., 58 F.R.D. 413 (W.D. Pa. 1973).* Rule 50(b) confines the granting of a judgment as a matter of law to parties who have moved during trial. The theory is that, if the jury still is present, the opponent may be able to supply the missing element in her proof if apprised of the problem by the "specific statement of the grounds." In the *Gugliemo* case, *supra*, the defense attorney approached the bench

after the last witness in the case and informed the trial judge that he "did not have a motion" to make, but did have a written "point for binding instructions" to the jury. He then proceeded to make arguments about the contents of the jury instructions, including remarks about the standard of care, the gist of which was that the jury should be bound to hold for the defendant. Post-verdict, the defense attorney attempted to assert a motion for judgment as a matter of law on related grounds; the court held, however, that he had waived the motion, since his remarks to the court did not amount to a motion for a Rule 50(a) judgment as a matter of law.

Actually, Rule 50(b) issues can arise in several ways. For example, what if the movant requests a "dismissal" when she should request a judgment as a matter of law? *Cf. Peterson v. Hager*, 724 F.2d 851 (10th Cir. 1984) (held, although not proper in a jury trial, a "motion to dismiss" at the close of evidence will be treated as a motion for judgment as a matter of law). What if the grounds for the later motion for judgment after trial were not contained in the motion during trial? *Compare, e.g., Moran v. Raymond Corp.*, 484 F.2d 1008 (7th Cir. 1973) (written motion was insufficient by itself to preserve right to make later Rule 50(b) motion for judgment as a matter of law, because it contained no grounds; but since movant's oral argument made the grounds clear, no waiver), *with Western Oil Fields, Inc. v. Pennzoil United, Inc.*, 421 F.2d 387 (5th Cir. 1970) (where Rule 50(a) motion for judgment as a matter of law was filed but did not raise issue of damages, that issue could not later be urged as basis for a Rule 50(b) judgment as a matter of law or as basis for appellate reversal). For a particularly poignant case, consider *Wegner v. Rodeo Cowboys Ass'n*, 417 F.2d 881 (10th Cir. 1969), in which the defendant said, "We have a motion in addition, if your honor please; a renewal of it," and clearly alluded to a previous motion stating specific grounds. But the judge said he would hear and consider the motion later, outside the jury's presence, and the defendant never presented it further nor obtained a definitive ruling from the judge. Held, a waiver: The defendant should have insisted on a ruling.

(2) *Should the Prerequisite of a Motion During Trial Be Abolished? (If So, Is Its Abolition Constitutionally Permissible?): Slocum v. New York Life Ins. Co., 228 U.S. 364 (1913).* The frequency of procedural default, by which a party wins a judgment to which it is clearly not entitled on the merits, may be an argument for abolishing the prerequisite. In fact, many states allow a motion for judgment notwithstanding the verdict, without the necessity of an earlier motion for directed verdict. *See, e.g.*, California CCP § 629; N.Y. CPLR § 4404; Tex. R. Civ. P. 301. Perhaps the approach followed by California, New York, and Texas can be criticized for failing to notify the non-movant of the defect during trial; but the justification is that the non-movant has the obligation of making a case to go to the jury, and instances in which that party would be able to remedy defects in the evidence must be very rare.

If you conclude that the federal courts also should abolish the prerequisite, you must consider whether the change would be constitutionally permissible. The Seventh Amendment not only preserves jury trial but also contains the "reexamination" clause, which prohibits facts found by the jury to be reexamined other than in the ways provided by the common law. The common law did not allow bare post-trial motions for judgment as a matter of law; it only allowed the judge to take the directed verdict motion under advisement, to be decided after trial. Certain older cases, such as *Slocum*, above, suggest that the Seventh Amendment requires this procedure. *See also Baltimore & Carolina Line, Inc. v. Redman*, 295 U.S. 654 (1935); *see generally* Note, *Preservation of Judgment N.O.V. Motion under Rule 50(b): Renewal of Directed Verdict Motion*, 70 Iowa L. Rev.

269 (1985). The decisions have been criticized, and it is possible that they may not indicate what the Court would decide today.

(3) *Prerequisite to Appellate Consideration, Too.* Note that a motion during trial is also a prerequisite, as a practical matter, to an appellate attack on the sufficiency of the evidence to support the verdict. If no attack has been made in the trial court, there is no error to assign on appeal; and if there has been no attack by way of a motion during trial, there can be no attack by post-trial motion for judgment as a matter of law — and hence the trial court has not committed any error that can be the basis of a reversal. *E.g., Coughlin v. Capitol Cement Co.*, 571 F.2d 290 (5th Cir. 1978) (in absence of motion for directed verdict, sufficiency of evidence not reviewable on appeal).

[C] Judgment as a Matter of Law in Favor of the Party With the Burden of Persuasion

Relevance of the Burden of Persuasion. Assume that the plaintiff is the only living person who knows how the accident occurred. The plaintiff testifies in a manner that, if believed, shows the defendant to have been negligent in the extreme. The defendant's attorney cross-examines the plaintiff; however, the defendant never is able to offer evidence that squarely contradicts the plaintiff's evidence. Since it remains undisputed, does the plaintiff's evidence entitle her to a judgment as a matter of law? The answer is, not necessarily. The plaintiff has the burden of persuading the jury by the preponderance of the evidence, and, in these circumstances, many jurisdictions would not grant her judgment without having the jury pass on the question whether she has met that burden.

The Standard for Granting Judgment as a Matter of Law for the Party with the Burden of Proof. Some courts express the notion in terms of "conclusive" proof (which probably overstates the requirement). Fundamentally, the standard is the same as that applicable to the party without the burden: Can it be said that the plaintiff's proof is so definitive that no reasonable person could come to any other conclusion than in the plaintiff's favor? Consider the following case.

ARBEGAST v. BOARD OF EDUCATION OF SOUTH NEW BERLIN CENTRAL SCHOOL, 65 N.Y.2d 161, 480 N.E.2d 365, 490 N.Y.S.2d 751 (1985). The defendant, Buckeye Donkey Ball Co., assisted the South New Berlin Central School to put on two donkey basketball games as a fund-raising event for the senior class in exchange for a percentage of the receipts.* During the first game, between the faculty team and the local fire department, faculty member Christy Arbegast participated without mishap (and in fact, the faculty won). In the second game, however, Arbegast was furnished with what the New York Court of Appeals refers to as "a different, larger donkey." The unfortunate result: "She spent a good deal of the game walking the donkey around but, at the urging of another faculty member, mounted. Soon thereafter she was

* A "donkey basketball game" evidently has rules adapted from ordinary basketball, with the difference (among others) that participants must ride donkeys. The opinion of the New York Court of Appeals describes the event as "a donkey basketball game," with no more elaboration than if the accident had involved an automobile or bus. The reader is left to infer that this equestrian sport is so common in the vicinage as to justify the assumption of audience familiarity. Some authors of this book, however, gained their first acquaintance with donkey basketball from the New York High Court's opinion, and so may some students.

thrown over the donkey's head when it put its head down as it stopped, with resultant permanent injury to her left arm." Understandably, Arbegast sued the school board (with which she settled before trial) and the Buckeye Donkey Ball Co., against which she asserted the theory that it was liable as the owner of a domestic animal that had injured her "as a result of the animal's vicious propensity." Equally understandably, Buckeye asserted the affirmative defense of assumption of the risk. New York law provided that assumption of the risk generally was not a bar to recovery unless the assumption of the risk was express, in which event it was a complete defense. New York law also placed the burden of proof of this defense on the defendant.

At trial, Arbegast testified to these events and, in addition, testified that she was warned by a Buckeye employee, before the games, that she participated at her own risk. Specifically, it was undisputed that the instructions to participants included the statements that "the donkeys do buck and put their heads down causing people to fall off and . . . if injuries happened the participants were at their own risk." At the conclusion of the evidence, plaintiff Arbegast moved for a judgment as a matter of law in her favor, and defendant moved for a dismissal (the equivalent). The case eventually reached the Court of Appeals, which held that the defendant's motion should have been granted. Specifically, the Donkey Ball Company was entitled to a judgment as a matter of law on the theory that it had demonstrated express assumption of the risk as a matter of law.

Express assumption of the risk, said the court, "resulted from agreement in advance that defendant need not use reasonable care for the benefit of plaintiff and would not be liable for the consequence of conduct that would otherwise be negligent." Thus the defendant had a complete defense if, and only if, "by express consent of the injured party no duty exist[ed] and, therefore, no recovery may be had." The court concluded, finally, that the defendant Donkey Ball Company had carried its burden of showing these elements as a matter of law and was entitled to a judgment as a matter of law:

> The existence of such an express assumption of risk by the injured party is a matter of defense upon which the burden of proof will be on the party claiming to have thus been absolved of duty . . . and will be a factual issue for the jury, unless there is no real controversy as to the facts. . . .
>
> [Plaintiff would] have been entitled to a [jury determination of] implied assumption of the risk had she not conceded that she was told before the games began that "participants are at their own risk." In light of that concession, however, the Trial Judge should have directed a verdict for defendant. . . .

NOTES AND QUESTIONS

(1) *Was the Essential Agreement Shown Beyond Controversy*? The court concluded that there was "no real controversy as to the facts." If this statement is confined to evidentiary facts, such as what was said and done, the statement is true. But does that showing, alone, entitle the defendant to a directed verdict? The ultimate fact that the defendant must prove is that there was an "agreement . . . that defendant need not use reasonable care . . . and would not be liable for conduct that would otherwise be negligent." Did the evidence establish this inference beyond controversy? Can it be said that one who hears that she is participating "at her own risk" must be characterized as having agreed that the defendant need not use reasonable care, and that no other reasonable interpretation of these facts exists? [If not, the trial judge could not direct a verdict, and the Court of Appeals' decision is wrong.]

(2) *"Conclusive" Proof or Proof "as a Matter of Law."* In *Arbegast*, the facts at issue were deemed established as a matter of law because Arbegast, against whom the facts were used, admitted them to be true. The facts thus were not only undisputed, but agreed by both parties to be so. What should happen if the party with the burden of proof submits strong evidence, but the opponent does not agree that it is true?

§ 11.04 New Trial

Read Rule 50(c) (alternative motion for new trial) and Rule 59 (new trials and amendment of judgments).

Standard for the Motion for New Trial; Uses. Unlike the motion for judgment as a matter of law (which serves only a single purpose and is subject to a mechanical standard), the motion for new trial is a multi-purpose device and is highly discretionary. Although these two post-trial motions are often asserted simultaneously, they have very different functions.

Addressing a Broad Range of Miscarriages of Justice: Trial Error, Newly Discovered Evidence, Misconduct, Result Contrary to the Weight of the Evidence, Etc. While the purpose of a judgment as a matter of law is to give judgment to the party unambiguously entitled to it, the purpose of a new trial is to start the process over again because the current result reflects a possible miscarriage of justice. That purpose encompasses a wide variety of potential grounds. The most common, probably, is trial or pre-trial error. The trial judge can order a new trial because of error in the charge, admittance of inadmissible evidence, erroneous rulings during jury selection, etc. Furthermore, a trial judge can grant a new trial upon a showing of newly discovered evidence, under certain narrow circumstances. Also, misconduct of jurors, parties, or attorneys can be grounds for a new trial. And the motion for new trial even invokes the judge's authority to set aside the result because the judge believes the jury's verdict is against the "great weight" of the evidence — an idea that would be heresy in a judgment as a matter of law, where the judge is strictly prohibited from weighing the evidence (except in the sense of determining that there is "no weight" at all). The trial judge also has authority to grant a new trial because the amount of damages is excessive or inadequate when compared to the record — which also is a weight-of-the-evidence concept.

Reversible Error Is Not Required; Discretion. The trial judge can grant a new trial even if an appellate court could not. The reason need not amount to reversible error. For example, an error in the charge that was not objected to, still can be a ground for new trial if the judge decides to grant it. In theory, the judge should confine such a ruling to miscarriages that had a probable effect on the outcome, and Fed. R. Civ. P. 61 requires the disregard of any defects "that do not affect any party's substantial rights"; but usually, the trial judge's grant of a new trial in the federal system is final because it is reviewable on appeal only under the most deferential standard of abuse of discretion. *See* Case Comment, *Appellate Review of Trial Court's Ruling on a Motion for New Trial*, 9 Memphis St. U. L. Rev. 535 (1979).

[A] New Trial Based on Procedural Errors

CONWAY v. CHEMICAL LEAMAN TANK LINES, INC.
687 F.2d 108 (5th Cir. 1982)

JOHNSON, CIRCUIT JUDGE:

This is the fourth time this diversity action has been before this Court on appeal. This case has been tried before a jury on three different occasions: in June 1974, in January 1977, and in June 1977. The issue in the instant appeal is whether the district court abused its discretion in granting a new trial because the defendant, Chemical Leaman Tank Lines, Inc. (Chemical Leaman), introduced a surprise expert witness in the second trial. We hold that the district court did not abuse its discretion.

I. *Background*

This tort action arose when two heavy tank trucks sideswiped each other near the centerline of a highway in Liberty County, Texas at approximately 4:00 a.m. on September 14, 1972. The westbound truck, owned by Dixie Transport of Texas, Inc. (Dixie Transport), lost its left front tire at impact, veered off the road to the left, and overturned, killing its driver, Robert Eugene Conway. Conway's widow, sons, and Dixie Transport brought this action against Chemical Leaman, owner of the eastbound truck involved in the collision. The essence of plaintiffs' contention is that the Chemical Leaman truck negligently crossed over the centerline of the highway, striking the oncoming Dixie Transport truck driven by Conway.

The only living eyewitness to the collision was Chemical Leaman's driver, John Johnson, who testified that Conway suddenly turned onto Johnson's side of the road when the vehicles were about a truck-length apart, both traveling about fifty miles per hour. Crucial to Johnson's credibility before the jury was the expert witness testimony concerning the various marks made by the trucks at the site of the collision. The expert witness testimony involved the tire marks in Dixie Transport's (Conway's) westbound lane, in Chemical Leaman's (Johnson's) eastbound lane, the gouge marks, and the physical dimensions of the trucks and the road.

[*The First Trial: Judgment for Plaintiff Reversed on Appeal on Evidence Grounds.*] At the first jury trial in 1974, Dixie Transport's safety director and an accident reconstruction expert testified that the tire marks were skid marks which indicated that Conway was properly in his right hand lane just before the collision, while Johnson's left wheels were over the centerline in Conway's lane. Expert witnesses for the defendant, Charles Ruble and Dr. William Tonn, testified, however, that it was Conway's truck which was driven on the wrong side of the roadway at the time of the collision, while Johnson's truck was in its proper lane. After hearing this testimony, the jury returned its verdict which was favorable to the plaintiffs. On appeal, this Court reversed and remanded on the grounds that the district court failed to admit certain impeachment evidence. *Conway v. Chemical Leaman, Inc., (Conway I)*, 525 F.2d 927 (5th Cir.), *modified on petition for rehearing*, 540 F.2d 837 (5th Cir. 1976).

[*The Second Trial: A Surprise Witness and a Confusing Verdict.*] At the second jury trial in January of 1977, the plaintiffs' witnesses again testified that tire marks indicated Chemical Leaman's truck had crossed the centerline and caused the collision. After the plaintiffs had rested their case, the defendant's counsel failed to call to the stand the two expert witnesses it had called in the previous trial, Ruble and Tonn. Instead, Chemical Leaman's safety director, Arnold Hay, was called to testify.

Hay had been designated as the representative for Chemical Leaman at the beginning of the first trial and occupied that position throughout all of that proceeding. Hay's name was not placed on the list of witnesses in the court's pre-trial order and such order specifically required notification of any further witnesses to the other party five days prior to the trial. [H]ay sat at the defendant's counsel table as the representative of Chemical Leaman, assisting defendant's counsel throughout the entire trial.

When the second trial began, Hay again took his position as the representative of Chemical Leaman at the defendant's counsel table. Again, he was not listed as a witness. Again, he was not sworn to testify. [T]he time at which Hay was called is of particular note: It was [a]fter the plaintiffs' witnesses had been excused, and it was near the end of the second jury trial of the case. When Hay was called to take the stand plaintiffs' counsel immediately objected that he was a surprise witness, and the district court granted a running or continuing objection to all of his testimony.

Hay's testimony at this second trial included his opinion that the Chemical Leaman truck was not the source of the questioned eastbound tire marks. Rather, Hay testified that the eastbound marks were made when a vehicle of a different type later tracked asphalt from the asphalt spill left by Conway's overturned truck. Hay also testified that what he claimed to be Chemical Leaman tire marks were not skid or brake marks; he asserted they would have been lighter than the westbound tire marks. [H]ay's analysis allowed the jury to determine that both vehicles came so close to the centerline that they clipped mirrors as the cabs of the tractors passed on the highway, causing Conway to lose control of his vehicle.

Hay's testimony failed to point out that differences in weight between Conway's asphalt-loaded truck and the Chemical Leaman truck might explain the lighter tire marks in the eastbound lane. [I]n any event, the jury's response to the court's interrogatories in the second trial clearly imply that they were influenced by Hay's testimony.[2] The jury returned a verdict favorable to the defendant.

---

[2] The jury verdict in the second trial recites in pertinent part, as follows:

INTERROGATORY NO. 1

Do you find from a preponderance of the evidence that the Defendant, Chemical Leaman Tank Lines, Inc., its agents, servants or employees, committed some act or omission of negligence which was a proximate cause of the injuries and death of the deceased, Robert Eugene Conway?

Answer: "Yes" or "No".

ANSWER: Yes.

If you have answered interrogatory No. 1 "Yes" and only in that event, list below the acts or omissions of negligence you have so found.

We have decided the defendant was too close to center line, as was the plaintiff, causing the collision of mirrors, after which uncontrollable acts by both drivers caused the final collision.

INTERROGATORY NO. 2

Do you find from a preponderance of the evidence that the deceased, Robert Eugene Conway, committed some act or omission of negligence which was a proximate cause of the injuries and death of the deceased?

Answer: "Yes" or "No".

ANSWER: Yes.

If you have answered interrogatory No. 2 "Yes", and only in that event, list below the acts or omissions of negligence you have so found.

[*The Motion For New Trial: Erroneously Granted on the First Stated Ground of an Allegedly "Defective" Verdict.*] The plaintiffs thereafter filed a motion to set aside the verdict of the jury and to grant a new trial. The motions were based on two grounds: (1) the answers of the jury to the interrogatories did not support a judgment favorable to any party [this assertion was erroneous]; and (2) the district court erred in permitting the surprise witness, Hay, to testify for the defendant. The district court granted the motion for a new trial [erroneously] on the first ground only. The court did not address the plaintiffs' second ground concerning the surprise witness feature. No judgment was entered in this second jury trial.

[*The Third Trial: Judgment for Plaintiff Reversed on Appeal Because the "Defective Verdict" Ground for New Trial (After the Second Trial) Was Erroneous.*] The third jury trial was in June 1977. The jury returned a verdict favorable to the plaintiffs. Upon appeal this Court determined that the trial court erred in ordering a new trial (the third trial) because the jury's answers in the second trial supported a judgment for the defendant, Chemical Leaman. *Conway v. Chemical Leaman Tank Lines, Inc., Conway II*, 610 F.2d 360 (5th Cir. 1980). The case was reversed and remanded with instructions that the trial court enter judgment for Chemical Leaman based on the jury's answers in the second trial. The trial court complied and entered judgment for Chemical Leaman. 487 F. Supp. 647.

[*The Trial Court Re-Grants the New Trial — On the Other Ground, "Unfair Surprise."*] Plaintiffs once again filed a motion for new trial, reasserting the ground — previously urged but not ruled upon — set forth in plaintiffs' motion to set aside the verdict of the jury and to grant a new trial: that the trial court erred in allowing Hay to testify as an expert witness for defendant at the second trial. The trial court granted this motion for new trial, 87 F.R.D. 712, and entered judgment in favor of plaintiffs upon the jury verdict returned at the third trial. The trial court's power to consider the second ground of Conway's motion for new trial, and its order granting a new trial, were affirmed by this Court. In this Court's opinion, *Conway v. Chemical Leaman Tank Lines, Inc.* (*Conway III*), 644 F.2d 1059, 1062 (5th Cir. 1981), it was suggested that, instead of ordering a fourth trial, judgment might be rendered for Conway on the third trial, absent any errors in that trial. [The trial court did enter judgment on the third trial, and defendant brought this fourth and last appeal, attacking the Unfair Surprise ground.]

II. *The Unfair Surprise Claim*

Rule 59(a) of the Fed. R. Civ. P. states that a "new trial may be granted to . . . any of the parties . . . in an action in which there has been a trial by a jury, for any of the reasons for which new trials have heretofore been granted in actions at law in courts of the United States." Fed. R. Civ. P. 59(a). It is well settled that Rule 59 provides a means of relief in cases in which a party has been unfairly made the victim of surprise. 11 Wright & Miller, *Federal Practice and Procedure* § 2805 at 38 (1973). The surprise, however, must be "inconsistent with substantial justice" in order to justify a grant of a new trial. Fed. R. Civ. P. 61. The district court is therefore entitled to grant a new trial only if the admission of the surprise testimony actually prejudiced the plaintiffs' case. . . . This Court has limited reversible error from unfair surprise to situations where a completely new issue is suddenly raised or a previously unidentified expert witness is suddenly called to testify. . . .

We have decided the plaintiff was also too close to the center line, causing the collision of mirrors, after which uncontrollable acts by both drivers caused the final collision.

The determination of a trial judge to either grant or deny a motion for a new trial is reviewable under an abuse of discretion standard. . . .

In the instant case, Hay was a previously unidentified witness who was called without any forewarning to testify as an expert at the second trial. Hay's testimony was not cumulative; rather, it introduced the theory that the questioned eastbound tire marks were asphalt marks from another vehicle. No other party — plaintiff or defendant — had presented this theory. Under the circumstances, plaintiffs had no time or opportunity to prepare a response to this unexpected turn of events. The interrogatories answered by the jury in the second trial leave no doubt that the jury was influenced by Hay's testimony.[6]

Even assuming the testimony was unfair and prejudicial, Chemical Leaman nevertheless contends that the plaintiffs should have moved for a continuance rather than a new trial. Indeed, the granting of a continuance is a generally more appropriate remedy than exclusion of evidence when claims of unfair surprise are raised. *See* Advisory Committee's Note to Rule 403, Fed. R. Evid. The granting or denial of a continuance, however, is a procedural matter of the kind that this Court has repeatedly said is subject to the discretion of the trial judge. . . . At the time that Hay's testimony was admitted, the trial was almost completed. A continuance at this point may have been, from the vantage of the district court judge, impractical and inefficient. Although this Court has acknowledged that continuance is a preferable remedy for prejudicial error from unfair surprise, there is no ironclad rule requiring it. . . .

Accordingly, the district court did not abuse its discretion in granting a new trial on grounds of unfair surprise. . . .

NOTES AND QUESTIONS

(1) *Don't Let This Case Mislead You into Thinking That New Trials Are Easily Obtained.* The trial judge's behavior in granting repeated new trials after jury verdicts, in *Conway*, is quite unusual. A judge facing a motion for new trial generally is cognizant of the backlog in her docket, including many cases in which the parties have not yet had a single trial, let alone two or three. Furthermore, perfect trials are rare. And since losing a jury trial is a terrible experience for an attorney, it can be expected that whoever loses the new trial will vigorously point out the defects in that verdict, too. Thus, if anything, trial judges have a natural (and perhaps healthy) resistance to granting new trials even if there has been a defect in the proceedings unless the defect was a very serious one. *See* Sacramento Bee, April 8, 1984, at B-8, col. 1 (reporting on retirement of California Superior Court Judge Warren K. Taylor, who stated that his respect for juries was so strong that he set aside only two (2) jury verdicts in 21 years of service).

(2) *The Standard for Granting a New Trial Based on Evidence Rulings.* Was it error to admit Hay's testimony, and if it was not error, could the trial judge properly have granted a new trial? What is the relevance, if any, of the jury's answers to special interrogatories, and the fact that they adopted Hay's explanation of the accident as the verdict? If the trial judge had denied a new trial, would the appellate court be in a position to reverse the judgment? What does all of this tell you about the trial judge's authority to grant a new trial?

---

[6] At the third trial in June 1977, where the testimony of Arnold Hay was met with lengthy detailed questioning, the jury rejected his opinion.

(3) *Reversible Error in Granting a New Trial.* Notice, however, that (after the third trial) the court of appeals, in a previous appeal, held that ordering the third trial was a reversible abuse of discretion because the jury's answers in the second trial were not insufficient to support a judgment, as the trial judge had thought. A slightly different, *de facto* standard may apply in the instance of a new trial ordered because of insufficiency of the verdict. Whether the verdict will support a judgment is a pure question of law, with little if any room for discretion, and so "abuse" of discretion is easier to find. Note that this attack, which actually concerned the second trial, occurred after the third trial — because the grant of a new trial is not a final judgment, and therefore it ordinarily is not appealable. Thus, attacks on the third judgment included allegations of error in the third trial and, also, allegations that the third trial never should have been held because the second verdict should not have been set aside. After that appeal, as this opinion indicates, the trial judge set aside his order setting aside the second verdict, entered judgment on that verdict, but then immediately set aside the second verdict again on the alternate ground of Hay's testimony — leading to this appeal.

[B] New Trial Based Upon the "Great Weight" of the Evidence

UNITED STATES v. AN ARTICLE OF DRUG, 725 F.2d 976 (5th Cir. 1984). This case illustrates the trial judge's power to set aside a verdict that is contrary to the "great" weight of the evidence. The United States, through the Food and Drug Administration, sought to seize an animal drug called "Neo-Terra Powder" marketed by Pfizer, Inc., on the ground that it was not "generally recognized" by qualified experts as safe and effective, and, therefore, it was required to be FDA approved. It brought this judicial enforcement action for that purpose. Pfizer demanded a jury trial and obtained a favorable verdict. The jury credited Pfizer's experts and specifically found that the drug was "generally recognized" as safe and effective. The trial judge then granted a new trial on the ground that the great weight of the evidence was contrary to the jury's verdict. Later, the trial judge granted the government's motion for summary judgment on the separate ground, not raised in the jury trial, that Pfizer's studies of the drug were inadequate as a matter of law. The Court of Appeals affirmed both the summary judgment and the grant of new trial that led to it:

> Initially, we note that this case comes to us in a rather unusual posture — a grant of summary judgment following the grant of a new trial. It might seem, at first blush, that our disposition with regard to the summary judgment would be dispositive of the issue of the propriety of the district court's previous grant of a new trial. While this might be true in an appropriate case, we do not think that this is such a case. First, our affirmance of the district court's summary judgment is based . . . upon uncontroverted affidavits . . . which were not presented at the original trial. Moreover, the district court granted the motion for a new trial, not upon the ground of the legal deficiency of Pfizer's studies, as was our affirmance of the summary judgment, but upon the weight of the evidence. Therefore, we review the district court's grant of a new trial on the basis of the evidence presented at the original trial and upon its stated grounds for doing so.
>
> Pfizer first notes that, at the jury trial, it presented the testimony of seven experts who testified that Neo-Terra Powder is generally recognized as effective. Pfizer then argues, relying upon language from cases in which we have examined denials of . . . new trials, that the district court's grant of a new trial can be upheld only where there

is an "absolute absence" of evidence to support the verdict; therefore, since it presented evidence that would support the jury's verdict, Pfizer argues, we must reverse the district court's order and reinstate the jury verdict.

Pfizer miscomprehends our standard of review for a grant of a new trial. The trial judge can grant a new trial if he believes the verdict is contrary to the weight of the evidence. . . . In a motion for new trial, the judge is free to weigh the evidence. . . . As an appellate court, our review of the grant or denial of a new trial is severely limited; we may interfere only when the court abuses its discretion or fails to exercise it. . . . [W]e have held in cases reviewing the denial of a motion for new trial that the district judge does not abuse his discretion . . . unless there is an absolute absence of evidence to support the jury's verdict. . . .

This is no way intimates, however, that, in reviewing a grant of a new trial, we may sustain the district court only if there is an "absolute absence" of evidence to support the jury's verdict. There is no deference to the district court's discretion in such a standard. Rather, the district court's discretion, its freedom to weigh the evidence, and our limited scope of review, suggest the exact opposite: we may reverse the district court's grant of a new trial only if we find an abuse of discretion, *i.e.*, only where there is an "absolute absence" of evidence contrary to the jury's verdict.

. . . [I]n this case, [t]he United States presented the testimony of several experts who testified that Neo-Terra Powder is not generally recognized as effective. The district court, in weighing the evidence, could reasonably have determined that there was a severe conflict in the expert testimony that precluded a finding of general recognition. Accordingly, we do not find that the district court abused its discretion.

NOTES AND QUESTIONS

(1) *Shouldn't the Trial Judge Be Restricted to Considering the "Great" Weight of the Evidence, Not Merely the Preponderance?* If the judge sets aside the jury's verdict based merely on her opinion of the "weight" of the evidence, doesn't she thereby substitute her judgment of the preponderance of the evidence for the jury's? Shouldn't the judge be required to say that the verdict is based upon "grossly" insufficient evidence, or is against the "great" weight of the evidence, in order to grant a new trial on this ground? For a decision expressing the prevailing federal view that the judge may grant a new trial based upon the "great" weight — but not merely on the "greater" weight, or preponderance — see *Eyre v. McDonough Power Equip., Inc.*, 755 F.2d 416 (5th Cir. 1985). *See* Figure 11A.

Is the *Eyre v. McDonough* "great weight" standard consistent with *United States v. An Article of Drug* (the principal case, above)? [Note: *The Article of Drug* case deals with the standard for appellate reversal. Might it be possible to have a trial court standard requiring the judge to consider the "great" weight, but an appellate standard upholding the trial judge's discretion according to a looser test?] In any event, "[t]he holding [in *United States v. An Article of Drug*] means that it will be a rare case in which the trial judge will not have authority to grant a new trial because of factual disagreement with the jury." Crump & Crump, *The Year's Developments in Civil Procedure*, 16 Texas Tech. L. Rev. 115, 137 (1985).

(2) *Not Enough that Judge Disagrees with Jury: Foster v. Continental Can Corp., 101 F.R.D. 710 (E.D. Ind. 1984).* In this vehicular accident case, the judge concluded that the verdict, which was for the defendant, came "very close" to being contrary to

the weight of the evidence, and that the judge himself would have decided the case differently, but these conclusions were "not enough" to compel the granting of a new trial. *See also, e.g., Brown v. McGraw-Edison Co.*, 736 F.2d 609 (10th Cir. 1984) (new trial not warranted because verdict not "clearly, decidedly, or overwhelmingly" against evidence).

FIGURE 11A
STANDARDS FOR DIRECTED VERDICT, JUDGMENT NOTWITHSTANDING THE VERDICT, AND NEW TRIAL BASED ON "GREAT WEIGHT"

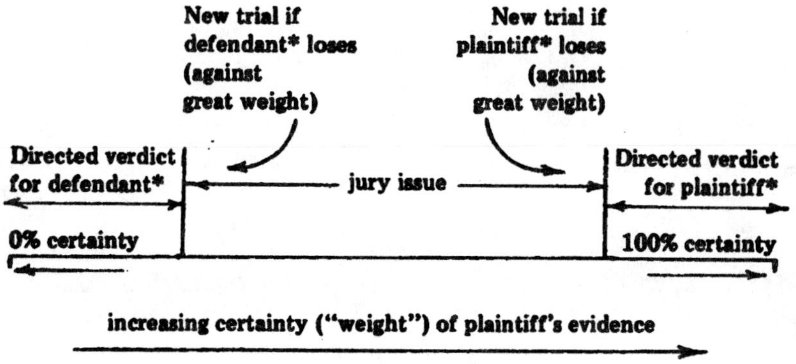

* Assuming plaintiff is the party with the burden of proof.

[C] New Trial Based on the Amount of Damages: "Remittitur" and "Additur"

Remittitur. The trial judge also can grant a new trial because the damage verdict is excessive or inadequate. Actually, this kind of new trial is really just a special case of a new trial based on the great weight of the evidence. When the trial judge concludes that the damage award is so high that it is against the great weight of the evidence, she may grant a "conditional" new trial; that is, she may order that the verdict will be set aside and a new trial held unless the plaintiff agrees to a judgment for a lesser amount specified by the judge. Such a conditional new trial is called a "remittitur." *See, e.g., United States v. 158.24 Acres of Land*, 696 F.2d 559 (8th Cir. 1982) (trial judge should have found that jury award of $43,200 for 6.9 particular acres was excessive, but somewhat less than $2,000 per acre was not, so that Court of Appeals would order trial judge to grant new trial unless remittitur of $30,200 was accepted by the plaintiff, in which event judge should grant judgment). The issue is sometimes put in terms of whether the jury's award shows that factors outside the evidence, such as passion or prejudice, must have influenced it. *T.D.S. Inc. v. Shelby Mut. Ins. Co.*, 760 F.2d 1520 (11th Cir. 1985); *see also Norfin, Inc. v. International Business Machines Corp.*, 81 F.R.D. 614 (D. Colo. 1979) (jury award of $7.5 million as lost profits in patent infringement action was not so high that it could "clearly be said to lie beyond the maximum limit of a reasonable range" and did not "shock the conscience of the court"). Review is confined to an abuse of discretion standard. *E.g., Steinberg v. Indemnity Ins. Co. of North America*, 364 F.2d 266 (5th Cir. 1966) (jury's award of $49,000 for injuries due to surgeon's negligence, where plaintiff suffered great pain, was permanently disabled, and had permanent disfiguring scars, could not be called excessive, and trial judge's remittitur of $20,400 was an abuse of discretion).

In 1987 the RAND Corporation's Institute for Civil Justice published a study of tort litigation in the United States, "Trends in Tort Litigation." Among its many interesting findings were that 20% of all jury awards are reduced by the court or through negotiations; that the higher the award, the more likely it will be cut; and that awards including punitive damages are cut an average 43%. *See also* Schnapper, *Judges Against Juries — Appellate Review of Federal Civil Jury Verdicts*, 1989 Wisc. L. Rev. 237.

Additur. The trial judge lacks authority, in the federal system, a grant a new trial conditioned upon "additur," or upon a defendant's agreement to an increase in damages. However, the trial judge can grant the plaintiff a new trial because the damages are inadequate. For a state court opinion upholding the use of additur, see *Jehl v. Southern Pacific Co.*, 66 Cal. 2d 821, 427 P.2d 988, 95 Cal. Rptr. 276 (1967) (where jury award of $100,000 was exceeded by clearly proved economic damages even without pain and suffering, trial judge could grant new trial, but also could consider additur).

[D] New Trial Based on Newly Discovered Evidence

OPE SHIPPING, LTD. v. UNDERWRITERS AT LLOYDS, 100 F.R.D. 428 (S.D.N.Y. 1983). The Managua was a vessel owned by a corporation that, in turn, was owned by the then-president of Nicaragua, General Anastasio Somoza. It was insured against war risks by Lloyds. The war risk policy, however, excluded losses due to seizure by the "Government . . . of the country in which the vessel is owned or registered." The evidence, at trial, showed that during the pendency of the Sandanista revolution in Nicaragua, the ship was in port in El Salvador and was there detained; she slipped out of the harbor, leaving behind crew members who refused to return to Nicaragua; and she was detained by Panamanian authorities and ultimately returned to Nicaragua, where she was registered, and where the ruling junta authorized the confiscation of all property of the Somoza family, but never acted specifically to carry it out with respect to this vessel. The trial court granted judgment for the defendants, holding that the loss was within the exclusion of the policy. The Second Circuit reversed, holding that the Sandanista junta was not the "Government" of Nicaragua at the time of the alleged "seizure." The court of appeals remanded for entry of judgment against the war risk insurers.

Upon remand, the defendant war risk insurers moved for a new trial based upon newly discovered evidence. They had a dramatic new theory: The Managua was seized not by the Sandanistas, but by the Somoza regime, which the Second Circuit had indicated was then the true "Government." The defendants supported the motion with affidavits showing that, at a new trial, they would offer the testimony of George Robakis, the former captain of the Managua, and abstracts of the ship's log prepared by him. This evidence would show that the Managua was lost, in fact, because she was commandeered by the existing government of Nicaragua under General Somoza, boarded by three Nicaraguan military officers and seventeen soldiers, equipped with three 40 mm. artillery pieces, and used in the bombardment of Sandanista shore positions for three hours. She left the area in haste after the Sandanistas returned fire; but then, after she made port in Nicaragua, she was taken over by Sandanista forces. The district court granted a new trial:

> A motion for a new trial may be based on the discovery of evidence; such a motion is addressed to the discretion of the court. . . . Federal case law, however, establishes a number of prerequisites to the court's exercise of that discretion.
>
> > Before a new trial may be granted on the basis of newly discovered evidence, there must be a showing that the allegedly newly discovered evidence was discovered since the trial; facts from which the court may infer reasonable diligence on the part of the moving party; that the evidence is not merely impeaching or cumulative; and the evidence is of such a character that on a new trial it will probably produce a different result. . . .
>
> "Newly discovered evidence" is "evidence of facts in existence at the time of trial of which the party seeking a new trial was justifiably ignorant." If such evidence was available or by the use of reasonable diligence could have been made available to the party seeking a new trial, that evidence cannot support an order for a new trial. . . . A narrow exception to this rule has been recognized: a new trial may be ordered to prevent a grave miscarriage of justice even though the "newly discovered" evidence . . . would have been available to the moving party had that party exercised reasonable diligence. . . . This exception, however, has been restricted to cases in which the evidence is practically conclusive. . . .
>
> Despite defendants' knowledge of the rumored use of the Managua to bombard Sandanista shore positions, this Court concludes that defendants could not have discovered prior to trial the evidence to be offered by Captain Robakis. Defendants claim, and plaintiffs do not deny, that plaintiff produced no Managua log books during discovery from which the existence or identity of Captain Robakis could have been learned. The evidence produced by plaintiffs at trial . . . was designed to demonstrate [only] what had . . . happened to the Managua after it reached [El Salvador]. . . . Defendants, moreover, claim that the sole source of their knowledge of the possibility that the vessel had been used as a Somocista gun boat was Albert Griffith [a plaintiffs' witness], . . . who denied at trial any such knowledge. Defendants claim . . . that they first learned of the activities of the Managua . . . from a person having first-hand knowledge thereof when Captain Robakis contacted them after trial.
>
> Even if the defendants in the exercise of due diligence could have discovered the evidence . . . , defendants' motion for a new trial would not be denied. Given the distinct possibility that plaintiffs herein knew of any prior use of the Managua and concealed such use from this court, a new trial must be ordered . . . to prevent the miscarriage of justice.
>
> At trial, plaintiffs called three witnesses who reasonably could be thought to have known of the use made of the Managua by the Nicaraguan military in May, 1979. . . .
>
> Given the great likelihood that plaintiffs knew of the prior use of the Managua . . . , a new trial would be warranted . . . even in the absence of a showing of "due diligence." Such a proceeding would be justified in order to prevent a miscarriage of justice, namely the commission of a fraud on this court. The evidence on which defendants base their motion, moreover, is practically conclusive in establishing the May, 1979 use of the Managua as a gunboat: this motion thus falls within the . . . "conclusive evidence" [exception] to the due diligence requirement.

The newly discovered evidence on which defendants predicate this motion is clearly material, and is neither cumulative nor impeaching. Thus, the only remaining issue this court must address in deciding this motion is whether introduction of that evidence at a new trial would likely result in a judgment for defendants. This court concludes that defendants' evidence would likely produce such a result. . . .

Had defendants discovered their proposed evidence at a later stage, *i.e.*, at a time too late to bring this motion for a new trial, they could have moved this court for relief from judgment . . . pursuant to Fed. R. Civ. P. 60(b)(2). . . .

A new trial of this action is ordered. . . .

NOTES AND QUESTIONS

(1) *The Restrictions on New Trials for Newly Discovered Evidence.* Notice that new trial for newly discovered evidence is narrowly circumscribed. A showing of non-discovery and diligence prior to trial is required, as this opinion shows. *See also Moore v. Rosecliff Realty Corp.*, 88 F. Supp. 956 (D.N.J. 1950) (where attorney attempted to find witness during three weeks preceding trial, diligence not sufficiently shown). But even these factors are not sufficient unless the evidence is itself very significant. *Cf. Pioneer Paper Stock Co. v. Miller Transport Co.*, 109 F. Supp. 502 (D.N.J. 1953) (photograph showing that vehicle lights were on, contrary to trial court finding, was merely cumulative and related to subordinate fact and probably would not have changed result). Why is the law so restrictive of new trials on newly discovered evidence?

(2) *"Conclusive" Evidence Preventing "Grave Miscarriage of Justice"; Fraud.* The court in *Ope Shipping*, above, recognizes a narrow exception by which a new trial may be granted even in the absence of diligence if it prevents a grave miscarriage of justice and if the evidence is "practically conclusive." Does this formulation improve the law without opening the floodgates to unmeritorious motions? The trial judge also infers the existence of a fraud on the court. If it exists in this case, should that ground be an independent reason for granting a new trial (or should the restricted grounds for newly discovered evidence apply)? Note the court's reference to procedures, under Rule 60, for reopening after time has expired for new trial, on grounds that can include fraud. We consider this issue further in § 11.06 below.

[E] New Trial on Grounds of Jury Misconduct

MULTIFLEX, INC. v. SAMUEL MOORE & CO., 709 F.2d 980 (5th Cir. 1983). The jury's damage verdict in this antitrust case exceeded the amount shown by the plaintiff's proof at trial. The district judge obtained the affidavits of two jurors, which suggested that the verdict might have included $200,000 to compensate the plaintiff for "injury to its reputation" or to "punish" the defendant. One juror also stated that the $200,000 figure was reached by taking an average of each juror's predilection regarding this added award — an improper "quotient verdict." Both the trial and appellate courts concluded that these theories of damages were not authorized by law. The trial judge addressed the issue by ordering a remittitur sufficient to conform to the maximum damage amount proved by the plaintiff at trial. Although ordering a partial new trial on damages for other reasons, the Court of Appeals held that these acts of jury misconduct could not be the basis of a new trial:

[W]e are also cognizant of the need to respect the finality of a jury's verdict. . . . Rule 606(b) of the Federal Rules of Evidence discusses the limited permissible inquiry into the validity of a verdict. An affidavit discussing the jury's decision-making process is cognizable only to discover whether "extraneous prejudicial information was improperly brought to bear upon any juror." Fed. R. Evid. 606(b). [Fed. R. Evid. 606(b) now also permits the use of juror testimony to prove that the verdict reported was the result of a clerical mistake, but otherwise leaves intact the narrow circumstances under which juror testimony or affidavits may be used to inquire into the validity of the verdict. — Eds.] The court, therefore, properly could not consider [defendant's charges] that the jury awarded impermissible punitive damages or arrived at a "quotient verdict." . . .

The district judge in this case examined the affidavits for the single purpose of determining whether the award was supported in the evidence. He . . . [ordered a] remittitur in the amount of the unsupportable excess. . . . The remittitur, acceptable to the plaintiff . . . , properly reduced the award only to the extent necessary to conform to the evidence. The district court properly handled the questions raised by the excessive amount of the verdict. Therefore, we refuse to consider [defendant's] arguments regarding the foundation of the verdict. . . .

NOTES AND QUESTIONS

(1) *The Exclusionary Rule for Jury Deliberations: Fed. R. Evid. 606(b).* Notice that the court of appeals does not hold that the jury's actions did not amount to misconduct. What the appellate court holds is that the jury's misconduct, although no one questions that it occurred, cannot be proved, because Rule 606(b) makes the jurors incompetent as witnesses to the misconduct, and they are the only possible source of proof. If the verdict was within the proof, there would be no basis for relieving the defendant of the verdict. Why do we restrict new trials based upon jury misconduct? [Note: How often does a jury deliberate at length on a difficult or controversial case without discussing insurance, or attorneys' fees, or personal experiences, or other improper considerations?] If we decide to restrict the availability of new trials for jury misconduct, however, is an exclusionary rule prohibiting the parties from proving that the events took place a rational way to accomplish that result? *See* S. Crump, *Jury Misconduct, Jury Interviews, and the Federal Rules of Evidence: Is the Broad Exclusionary Principle of Rule 606(b) Justified?*, 66 N.C. L. Rev. 509 (1988); Thompson, *Challenge to the Decisionmaking Process — Federal Rule of Evidence 606(b) and the Constitutional Right to a Fair Trial*, 38 Sw. L.J. 1187 (1985).

(2) *The Alleged "Quotient Verdict."* It is improper for jurors to agree, in advance, that they will be bound by the average of their damage award votes, as a substitute for the individual vote of each juror. But it is not a quotient verdict if jurors consider the predilections of each individual, or even if they consider the average, provided that each arrives at the acceptance of the final figure individually, rather than by an agreement to be bound by the result of mathematical calculations. Did the jury engage in misconduct of the quotient verdict variety?

(3) *What Kind of Misconduct Can Be the Basis of a New Trial? Budoff v. Holiday Inns, Inc., 732 F.2d 1523 (6th Cir. 1984).* The defendant's evidence on motion for new trial showed that an employee of the plaintiff's counsel communicated information to a relative of one juror, who communicated it to the juror. That juror became the presiding juror. This evidence was not excluded by Rule 606(b) (Why not?), and the Court of

Appeals reversed the trial judge's denial of a new trial, emphasizing its inference that the communication was made deliberately and probably influenced the verdict.

§ 11.05 The Interplay Between Motion for Judgment as a Matter of Law (or Notwithstanding the Verdict) and Motion for New Trial

Read Rule 50(c)-(e) (interplay between motion for judgment as a matter of law and motion for new trial).

The Verdict Loser Often Files Both a Motion for Judgment as a Matter of Law (or Notwithstanding the Verdict) and a Motion for New Trial. Remember, the two motions serve different, and complementary, purposes. The first motion serves the narrow purpose of giving judgment to a party unambiguously entitled to it on the basis of the evidence. The second motion (for new trial) ensures the fairness of the process and result. If you have lost the jury verdict, you may very well want to obtain the benefit of both kinds of motions at the post-trial stage.

Rule 50(c)-(e): A Confusing, but Logical, Procedure for Considering both Motions, with Only One Appeal. Subsections (c) through (e) of Rule 50 may confuse you at first. But they are ultimately logical. They are premised upon two policy considerations. First, any party aggrieved by the outcome of a trial should have the benefit of making both kinds of motions. Secondly, there should be only one appeal from both motions.

The Simplest Case: The Trial Judge Denies Both Motions. Overwhelmingly, the most frequent pattern is that the judge denies the motion for judgment as a matter of law (or notwithstanding the verdict), because the jury's verdict does have some support in the evidence, and also denies the motion for new trial, because the verdict is not against the great weight of the evidence and the process and result are not unfair. The losing party has had the opportunity to make both motions, and a single appeal can be taken from both rulings.

A More Difficult Case: The Trial Judge Grants the Motion for Judgment as a Matter of Law (or Notwithstanding the Verdict) and Then Must Rule Conditionally on the Same Party's Motion for New Trial (And Also on the Opponent's Motion for New Trial). Here, the process becomes confusing, but we ask the gentle reader to persevere, with the promise that there is a kind of logic to the Rule. If the trial judge grants the Motion for Judgment as a Matter of Law (or Notwithstanding the Verdict) ("MJN") the verdict loser is now the (satisfied) judgment winner. But the opponent (the verdict winner, now the judgment loser) isn't and may appeal. If the appellate court reverses and reinstates the verdict, the Rules contemplate a single appeal, and that result could not be accomplished if the appellate court had to remand for a ruling on the pending Motion for New Trial ("MNT"). Therefore, immediately after granting the MJN, the trial judge must rule conditionally on the MNT. In other words, she must say in advance what ruling she would make on the MNT, in case the MJN is reversed. *See* Rule 50(c)(1). And, finally, the verdict winner, who is now the judgment loser, also must have the opportunity to file a MNT, since this party, too, is entitled to the benefit of both motions. Although having lost the judgment, this party may take the position that rulings of the trial court unfairly forced that result (*e.g.*, the trial judge erroneously excluded evidence that would have proved the case, so that a new trial is appropriate). *See* Rule 50(d).

A Third Case: Appellate Reversal on Sufficiency-of-Evidence Grounds. Now, imagine that the verdict winner receives judgment, and has no dissatisfaction with the trial court's disposition of the case. But the court of appeals, for the first time, rules that the evidence did not support the verdict — and that the opponent's MJN should have been granted. The verdict winner is now the judgment loser, but has not had the benefit of a motion for new trial. As the following case, *Neely v. Martin K. Eby Constr. Co.*, indicates, the policy in favor of a single appeal has led to a requirement that the losing appellee must move for new trial in the court of appeals. (Notice that this is one of the few instances in which action in the appellate court is not predicated on action in the trial court.) *See* Rule 50(e). In *Neely*, the trouble was that this requirement, which today is reasonably clear, was not at all clear at that time.

NEELY v. MARTIN K. EBY CONSTRUCTION CO., INC.
386 U.S. 317 (1967)

Mr. Justice White delivered the opinion of the Court.

Petitioner brought this diversity action in the United States District Court for the District of Colorado alleging that respondent's negligent construction, maintenance, and supervision of a scaffold platform used in the construction of a missile silo near Elizabeth, Colorado, had proximately caused her father's fatal plunge from the platform during the course of his employment as Night Silo Captain for Sverdrup & Parcel, an engineering firm engaged in the construction of a missile launcher system in the silo. At the close of the petitioner's evidence and again at the close of all the evidence, respondent moved for a directed verdict. The trial judge denied both motions and submitted the case to a jury, which returned a verdict for petitioner for $25,000.

Respondent then moved for judgment notwithstanding the jury's verdict or, in the alternative, for a new trial, in accordance with Rule 50(b), Federal Rules of Civil Procedure. The trial court denied the motions and entered judgment for petitioner on the jury's verdict. Respondent appealed, claiming that its motion for judgment *n.o.v.* should have been granted. Petitioner, as appellee, urged only that the jury's verdict should be upheld.

The Court of Appeals held that the evidence at trial was insufficient to establish either negligence by respondent or proximate cause and reversed the judgment of the District Court "with instructions to dismiss the action." Without filing a petition for rehearing in the Court of Appeals, petitioner then sought a writ of certiorari, presenting the question whether the Court of Appeals could, consistent with the 1963 amendments to Rule 50 of the Federal Rules and with the Seventh Amendment's guarantee of a right to jury trial, direct the trial court to dismiss the action. Our order allowing certiorari directed the parties' attention to whether Rule 50(d) [now Rule 50(e) — Eds.] and our decisions in *Cone v. West Virginia Pulp & Paper Co.*, 330 U.S.212; *Globe Liquor Co. v. San Roman*, 332 U.S. 571; and *Weade v. Dichmann, Wright & Pugh, Inc.*, 337 U.S. 801, permit this disposition by a court of appeals despite Rule 50(c)(2) [now Rule 50(d) — Eds.], which gives a party whose jury verdict is set aside by a trial court 10 days in which to invoke the trial court's discretion to order a new trial. We affirm. . . .

The question here is whether the Court of Appeals, after reversing the denial of a defendant's Rule 50(b) motion for judgment notwithstanding the verdict, may itself order dismissal or direct entry of judgment for defendant. As far as the Seventh Amendment's right to jury trial is concerned, there is no greater restriction on the province of the jury when an appellate court enters judgment *n.o.v.* than when a trial court does; consequently, there is no constitutional bar to an appellate court granting judgment *n.o.v.*. . . .

This brings us to Federal Rules 50(c) and 50(d), which were added to Rule 50 in 1963 to clarify the proper practice under this Rule. Though Rule 50(d) is more pertinent to the facts of this case, it is useful to examine these interrelated provisions together. Rule 50(c) [now Rule 50(c)(2) — Eds.] governs the case where a trial court has granted a motion for judgment *n.o.v.* Rule 50(c)(1) explains that, if the verdict loser has joined a motion for new trial with his motion for judgment *n.o.v.*, the trial judge should rule conditionally on the new trial motion when he grants judgment *n.o.v.* If he conditionally grants a new trial, and if the court of appeals reverses his grant of judgment *n.o.v.*, Rule 50(c)(1) provides that "the new trial shall proceed unless the appellate court has otherwise ordered." On the other hand, if the trial judge conditionally denies the motion for new trial, and if his grant of judgment *n.o.v.* is reversed on appeal, "subsequent proceedings shall be in accordance with the order of the appellate court." [T]he appellate court [then] will review on appeal both the grant of judgment *n.o.v.*, and, if necessary, the trial court's conditional disposition of the motion for new trial. . . .

Rule 50(d) [now Rule 50(e)] is applicable to cases such as this one where the trial court has denied a motion for judgment *n.o.v.* Rule 50(d) [now Rule 50(e)] expressly preserves to the party who prevailed in the district court the right to urge that the court of appeals grant a new trial should the jury's verdict be set aside on appeal. Rule 50(d) also emphasizes that "nothing in this rule precludes" the court of appeals "from determining that the appellee is entitled to a new trial, or from directing the trial court to determine whether a new trial shall be granted." [Similar language today appears in Rule 50(e).] Quite properly, this Rule recognizes that the appellate court may prefer that the trial judge pass first upon the appellee's new trial suggestion. Nevertheless, consideration of the new trial question "in the first instance" is lodged with the court of appeals. . . .

As the Advisory Committee explained, these 1963 amendments were not intended to "alter the effects of a jury verdict or the scope of appellate review," as articulated in the prior decisions of this Court. [I]n *Weade v. Dichmann, Wright & Pugh, Inc., supra*, where a proper motion for judgment *n.o.v.* was made and denied in the trial court, we modified a Court of Appeals decision directing entry of judgment *n.o.v.* because there were "suggestions in the complaint and evidence" of an alternative theory of liability which had not been passed upon by the jury and therefore which might justify the grant of a new trial.

[T]he opinions in the above cases make it clear that an appellate court may not order judgment *n.o.v.* [w]here the record reveals a new trial issue which had not been resolved. Part of the Court's concern has been to protect the rights of the party whose jury verdict has been set aside on appeal and who may have valid grounds for a new trial, some or all of which should be passed upon by the district court, rather than the court of appeals, because of the trial judge's first-hand knowledge of witnesses, testimony, and issues — because of his "feel" for the overall case. These are very valid concerns to which the court of appeals should be constantly alert. . . .

But these considerations do not justify an ironclad rule that the court of appeals should never order dismissal or judgment for defendant when the plaintiff's verdict has been set aside on appeal. Such a rule would not serve the purpose of Rule 50 to speed litigation and to avoid unnecessary retrials. . . .

[W]here the court of appeals sets aside the jury's verdict because the evidence was insufficient to send the case to the jury, it is not so clear that the litigation should be terminated. [T]here remain important considerations which may entitle him to a new trial. The erroneous exclusion of evidence which would have strengthened his case is an important possibility. . . .

In our view, therefore, Rule 50(d) [now Rule 50(e)] makes express and adequate provision for the opportunity — which the plaintiff-appellee had without this rule — to present his grounds for a new trial in the event his verdict is set aside by the court of appeals. [He may do so] in his brief — or in a petition for rehearing. . . .

[In the case before us,] Petitioner, as appellee, suggested no grounds for a new trial in the event her judgment was reversed, nor did she petition for rehearing in the Court of Appeals, even though that court had directed a dismissal of her case. . . . Indeed, in her brief in the Court of Appeals, petitioner stated, "This law suit was fairly tried and the jury was properly instructed." . . .

Petitioner's case in this Court is pitched on the total lack of power in the Court of Appeals to direct entry of judgment for respondent. We have rejected that argument and therefore affirm.

It is so ordered.

MR. JUSTICE DOUGLAS and MR.. JUSTICE FORTAS, while agreeing with the Court's construction of Rule 50, would reverse the judgment because in their view the evidence of negligence and proximate cause was sufficient to go to the jury.

MR. JUSTICE BLACK, dissenting.

I dissent from the Court's decision in this case for three reasons: First, I think the evidence in this case was clearly sufficient to go to the jury on the issues of both negligence and proximate cause. Second, I think that under our prior decisions and Rule 50, a court of appeals, in reversing a trial court's refusal to enter judgment *n.o.v.* on the ground of insufficiency of the evidence, is entirely powerless to order the trial court to dismiss the case, thus depriving the verdict winner of any opportunity to present a motion for new trial to the trial judge who is thoroughly familiar with the case. Third, even if a court of appeals has that power, I find it manifestly unfair to affirm the Court of Appeals' judgment here without giving this petitioner a chance to present her grounds for a new trial to the Court of Appeals as the Court today for the first time holds she must. . . .

NOTES AND QUESTIONS

(1) *The Clairvoyance Required of the Trial Judge in Making a Conditional Ruling on the MNT.* After granting a MJN, the trial judge must rule conditionally on the same party's MNT (in case the MJN is reversed). Can you perceive any difficulty in this task? [Note: The trial judge must respond, in advance, to the reasoning of an opinion of the court of appeals that she can only imagine, reversing another ruling that she believes to be correct. The conditional ruling ordinarily will require her to determine whether the "great weight" of the evidence is contrary to a verdict that she had already decided is unsupportable as a matter of law, on the hypothesis that the appellate court will find that it presents a jury issue.] Is there a better way?

(2) *The Omniscience Required of the Court of Appeals in Ruling on the Losing Appellee's Motion for New Trial.* If it grants judgment on the theory a MJN should have been

granted against the appellee, Rule 50(d) (and the *Neely v. Martin K. Eby* case) tell us that the appellate court must consider the MNT in the first instance. Can you see any difficulty in this task? [Note: What if the characteristics of live witnesses' testimony are such that the trial judge would have granted a new trial, but those characteristics do not appear in the printed record? The Supreme Court points out, of course, that the Court of Appeals can remand to the trial court. But by definition, it would remand so that the trial court can take account of matters unknown to the Court of Appeals, and if the matters are unknown to the Court of Appeals, how can it know to remand?] We told you, at the beginning of this subsection, that the structure of Rule 50(c)-(d) is logical, and it is; we didn't say it was workable or sound policy. In fact, to the extent that we have had personal experience with the presentation of new trial grounds to appellate courts in the *Neely v. Martin K. Eby* situation, we have gained the impression that the process is both unfamiliar and unworkable from their viewpoint, particularly when it concerns — as it generally does — matters extraneous to the subject of the appeal itself.

(3) *"Preserving" Sufficiency of the Evidence Complaints on Appeal.* Still another consideration is the necessity of "preserving" the ability to make sufficiency of the evidence arguments on appeal. Consider the following.

UNITHERM FOOD SYSTEMS, INC. v. SWIFT-ECKRICH, INC.
126 S. Ct. 980 (2006)

Justice Thomas delivered the opinion of the Court.

Ordinarily, a party in a civil jury trial that believes the evidence is legally insufficient to support an adverse jury verdict will seek a judgment as a matter of law by filing a motion pursuant to Federal Rule of Civil Procedure 50(a) before submission of the case to the jury, and then (if the Rule 50(a) motion is not granted and the jury subsequently decides against that party) a motion pursuant to Rule 50(b). In this case, however, the respondent filed a Rule 50(a) motion before the verdict, but did not file a Rule 50(b) motion after the verdict. Nor did respondent request a new trial under Rule 59. The Court of Appeals nevertheless proceeded to review the sufficiency of the evidence and, upon a finding that the evidence was insufficient, remanded the case for a new trial. Because our cases addressing the requirements of Rule 50 compel a contrary result, we reverse.

I

The genesis of the underlying litigation in this case was ConAgra's attempt to enforce its patent for "A Method for Browning Precooked Whole Muscle Meat Products," U.S. Patent No. 5,952,027 (" '027 patent"). In early 2000, ConAgra issued a general warning to companies who sold equipment and processes for browning precooked meats, explaining that it intended to "aggressively protect all of [its] rights under [the '027] patent." 375 F.3d 1341, 1344 (Fed. Cir. 2004). Petitioner Unitherm sold such processes, but did not receive ConAgra's warning. ConAgra also contacted its direct competitors in the precooked meat business, announcing that it was "making the '027 Patent and corresponding patents that may issue available for license . . . ." *Id.* at 1345. Jennie-O, a direct competitor, received ConAgra's correspondence and undertook an investigation to determine its rights and responsibilities with regard to the '027 patent. Jennie-O determined that the browning process it had purchased from Unitherm was the same as the process described in the '027 patent. Jennie-O further determined that the '027 patent was invalid because Unitherm's president had invented the process described in that patent six years before ConAgra filed its patent application.

Consistent with these determinations, Jennie-O and Unitherm jointly sued ConAgra in the Western District of Oklahoma. As relevant here, Jennie-O and Unitherm sought a declaration that the '027 patent was invalid and unenforceable, and alleged that ConAgra had violated § 2 of the Sherman Act, 15 U.S.C. § 2, by attempting to enforce a patent that was obtained by committing fraud on the Patent and Trademark Office (PTO). . . . The District Court construed the '027 patent and determined that it was invalid based on Unitherm's prior public use and sale of the process described therein. . . . After dismissing Jennie-O [for lack of standing under the antitrust laws], the District Court allowed Unitherm's . . . claim to proceed to trial. Prior to the court's submission of the case to the jury, ConAgra moved for a directed verdict under Rule 50(a) based on legal insufficiency of the evidence. The District Court denied that motion. The jury returned a verdict for Unitherm, and ConAgra neither renewed its motion for judgment as a matter of law pursuant to Rule 50(b), nor moved for a new trial . . . pursuant to Rule 59. . . .

On appeal to the Federal Circuit, ConAgra maintained that there was insufficient evidence to sustain the jury's . . . verdict. Although the Federal Circuit has concluded that a party's "failure to present the district court with a post-verdict motion precludes appellate review of sufficiency of the evidence," *Biodex Corp. v. Loredan Biomedical, Inc.*, 946 F.2d 850, 862 (1991), in the instant case it was bound to apply the law of the Tenth Circuit. 375 F.3d, at 1365, n.7 ("On most issues related to Rule 50 motions . . . we generally apply regional circuit law unless the precise issue being appealed pertains uniquely to patent law"). Under Tenth Circuit law, a party that has failed to file a postverdict motion challenging the sufficiency of the evidence may nonetheless raise such a claim on appeal, so long as that party filed a Rule 50(a) motion prior to submission of the case to the jury. *Cummings v. General Motors Corp.*, 365 F.3d 944, 950-951 (2004). Notably, the only available relief in such a circumstance is a new trial. *Id.*, at 951.

Freed to examine the sufficiency of the evidence, the Federal Circuit concluded that, although Unitherm had presented sufficient evidence to support a determination that ConAgra had attempted to enforce a patent that it had obtained through fraud on the PTO, 375 F.3d, at 1362, Unitherm had failed to present evidence sufficient to support the remaining elements of its antitrust claim. . . . Accordingly, it vacated the jury's judgment in favor of Unitherm and remanded for a new trial. We granted certiorari, . . . and now reverse.

II

Federal Rule of Civil Procedure 50 sets forth the procedural requirements for challenging the sufficiency of the evidence in a civil jury trial and establishes two stages for such challenges — prior to submission of the case to the jury, and after the verdict and entry of judgment. Rule 50(a) allows a party to challenge the sufficiency of the evidence prior to submission of the case to the jury, and authorizes the District Court to grant such motions at the court's discretion . . . . Rule 50(b), by contrast, sets forth the procedural requirements for renewing a sufficiency of the evidence challenge after the jury verdict and entry of judgment. . . .

This Court has addressed the implications of a party's failure to file a postverdict motion under Rule 50(b) on several occasions and in a variety of procedural contexts. This Court has concluded that, "[i]n the absence of such a motion" an "appellate court [is] without power to direct the District Court to enter judgment contrary to the one it had permitted to stand." *Cone v. West Virginia Pulp & Paper Co.*, 330 U.S. 212, 218, 67 S.Ct. 752, 91 L.Ed. 849 (1947). This Court has similarly concluded that a party's failure to file a Rule 50(b) motion deprives the appellate court of the power to order the entry of judgment in favor of that party where the district court directed the jury's verdict, *Globe Liquor Co. v. San Roman*, 332 U.S. 571, 68 S.Ct. 246, 92 L.Ed. 177 (1948), and where the district court expressly reserved a party's preverdict motion for a directed verdict and then denied that motion after the verdict was returned. *Johnson v. New York, N.H. & H.R. Co.*, 344 U.S. 48, 73 S.Ct. 125, 97 L.Ed. 77 (1952). A postverdict motion is necessary because "[d]etermination of whether a new trial should be granted or a judgment entered under Rule 50(b) calls for the judgment in the first instance of the judge who saw and heard the witnesses and has the feel of the case which no appellate printed transcript can impart." *Cone, supra*, at 216, 67 S.Ct. 752. Moreover, the "requirement of a timely application for judgment after verdict is not an idle motion" because it "is . . . an essential part of the rule, firmly grounded in principles of fairness." *Johnson, supra*, at 53, 73 S.Ct. 125.

The foregoing authorities lead us to reverse the judgment below. Respondent correctly points out that these authorities address whether an appellate court may enter judgment in the absence of a postverdict motion, as opposed to whether an appellate court may order a new trial (as the Federal Circuit did here). But this distinction is immaterial. This Court's observations about the necessity of a postverdict motion under Rule 50(b), and the benefits of the district court's input at that stage, apply with equal force whether a party is seeking judgment as a matter of law or simply a new trial. In *Cone*, this Court concluded that, because Rule 50(b) permits the district court to exercise its discretion to choose between ordering a new trial and entering judgment, its "appraisal of the bona fides of the claims asserted by the litigants is of great value in reaching a conclusion as to whether a *new trial* should be granted." 330 U.S., at 216, 67 S.Ct. 752 (emphasis added). Similarly, this Court has determined that a party may only pursue on appeal a particular avenue of relief available under Rule 50(b), namely the entry of judgment *or a new trial*, when that party has complied with the Rule's filing requirements by requesting that particular relief below. *See Johnson, supra*, at 54, 73 S.Ct. 125 ("Respondent made a motion to set aside the verdict and for new trial within the time required by Rule 50(b). It failed to comply with permission given by 50(b) to move for judgment n.o.v. after the verdict. In this situation respondent is entitled only to a new trial, not to a judgment in its favor").

Despite the straightforward language employed in *Cone*, *Globe Liquor*, and *Johnson*, respondent maintains that those cases dictate affirmance here, because in each of those cases the litigants secured a new trial. But in each of those cases the appellants moved for a new trial postverdict in the District Court, and did not seek to establish their entitlement to a new trial solely on the basis of a denied Rule 50(a) motion. . . . Accordingly, these outcomes merely underscore our holding today — a party is not entitled to pursue a new trial on appeal unless that party makes an appropriate postverdict motion in the district court.

Our determination that respondent's failure to comply with Rule 50(b) forecloses its challenge to the sufficiency of the evidence is further validated by the purported basis of respondent's appeal, namely the District Court's denial of respondent's preverdict Rule 50(a) motion. As an initial matter, *Cone*, *Globe Liquor*, and *Johnson* unequivocally establish that the precise subject matter of a party's Rule 50(a) motion — namely, its entitlement to judgment as a matter of law — cannot be appealed unless that motion is renewed pursuant to Rule 50(b). Here, respondent does not seek to pursue on appeal the precise claim it raised in its Rule 50(a) motion before the District Court — namely, its entitlement to judgment as a matter of law. Rather, it seeks a *new trial* based on the legal insufficiency of the evidence. But if, as in *Cone*, *Globe Liquor*, and *Johnson*, a litigant that has failed to file a Rule 50(b) motion is foreclosed from seeking the relief it sought in its Rule 50(a) motion — *i.e.*, the entry of judgment — then surely respondent is foreclosed from seeking a new trial, relief it did not and could not seek in its preverdict motion. In short, respondent never sought a new trial before the District Court, and thus forfeited its right to do so on appeal. *Yakus v. United States*, 321 U.S. 414, 444, 64 S.Ct. 660, 88 L.Ed. 834 (1944) ("No procedural principle is more familiar to this Court than that a . . . right may be forfeited . . . by the failure to make timely assertion of the right before a tribunal having jurisdiction to determine it").

The text of Rule 50(b) confirms that respondent's preverdict Rule 50(a) motion did not present the District Court with the option of ordering a new trial. That text provides that a district court may only order a new trial on the basis of issues raised in a preverdict Rule 50(a) motion when "ruling on [the] renewed motion" under Rule 50(b). Accordingly, even if the District Court was inclined to grant a new trial on the basis of arguments raised in respondent's preverdict motion, it was without the power to do so under Rule 50(b) absent a postverdict motion pursuant to that Rule. Consequently, the Court of Appeals was similarly powerless.

Similarly, the text and application of Rule 50(a) support our determination that respondent may not challenge the sufficiency of the evidence on appeal on the basis of the District Court's denial of its Rule 50(a) motion. The Rule provides that "the court *may* determine" that "there is no legally sufficient evidentiary basis for a reasonable jury to find for [a] party on [a given] issue," and "*may* grant a motion for judgment as a matter of law against that party . . . ." (Emphasis added.) [The 2007 "restyling" amendments changed this language slightly — Eds.] Thus, while a district court is permitted to enter judgment as a matter of law when it concludes that the evidence is legally insufficient, it is not required to do so. To the contrary, the district courts are, if anything, encouraged to submit the case to the jury, rather than granting such motions. As Wright and Miller explain:

> "Even at the close of all the evidence it may be desirable to refrain from granting a motion for judgment as a matter of law despite the fact that it would be possible for the district court to do so. If judgment as a matter of law is granted and the appellate court holds that the evidence in fact was sufficient to go to the jury, an entire new trial must be had. If, on the other hand, the trial court submits the case to the jury, though it thinks the evidence insufficient, final determination of the case is expedited greatly. If the jury agrees with the court's appraisal of the evidence, and returns a verdict for the party who moved for judgment as a matter of law, the case is at an end. If the jury brings in a different verdict, the trial court can grant a renewed motion for judgment as a matter of law. Then if the appellate court holds that the trial court was in error in its appraisal of the evidence, it can reverse and order judgment on the verdict of the jury, without any need for a new trial. For this reason the appellate courts repeatedly have said that it usually is desirable to take a verdict, and then pass on the sufficiency of the evidence on a post-verdict motion." 9A Federal Practice § 2533, at 319 (footnote omitted).

Thus, the District Court's denial of respondent's preverdict motion cannot form the basis of respondent's appeal, because the denial of that motion was not error. It was merely an exercise of the District Court's discretion, in accordance with the text of the Rule and the accepted practice of permitting the jury to make an initial judgment about the sufficiency of the evidence. The only error here was counsel's failure to file a postverdict motion pursuant to Rule 50(b).

. . . .

For the foregoing reasons, we hold that since respondent failed to renew its preverdict motion as specified in Rule 50(b), there was no basis for review of respondent's sufficiency of the evidence challenge in the Court of Appeals. The judgment of the Court of Appeals is reversed.

[The dissenting opinion of Justice Stevens is omitted.]

§ 11.05 Appendix Post-Trial Motions in *Wilcox Development Co. v. First Interstate Bank*

Read (or re-read) the post-trial motions in *Wilcox Development Co. v. First Interstate Bank of Oregon*, which appear in § 1.09 of Chapter 1, above. Notice that the defendant has asserted in the same instrument both a Rule 50(b) motion for judgment as a matter of law and a motion for new trial. The motion for new trial is conditioned on denial of the motion for judgment as a matter of law. Notice, also, that the motion for new trial contains several different grounds, including attacks on the instructions (trial error) and attacks on the weight of the evidence. Finally, you should remember that the court granted the motion for judgment as a matter of law and then, as Rule 50 requires, conditionally ruled on the motion for new trial — by saying that, if reversed, a new trial would be granted on the ground that the verdict was against the great weight of the evidence.

§ 11.06 Relief From Final Judgments

[A] The Rule 60 Motion

Read Rule 60 (relief from judgments).

Reopening a Final Judgment. Imagine that a final judgment has been rendered against your client. You are not happy with it, but your client is resigned to it and is convinced that the process that led to it was fair. But suddenly one day, you discover that the written draft of the judgment entered with the clerk does not match the judgment rendered because the draft added two zeros — so that now, instead of liability for $10,000, your client faces liability for $1 million. (In the alternative, imagine that you learn, after all time limits for a new trial or appeal have run, that the opposing attorney obtained a default judgment by forging the return of service.) In these kinds of cases, there should be a narrow escape valve from the doctrine of finality.

Rule 60: Clerical Mistakes, Other Mistakes, Inadvertence, Excusable Neglect, Newly Discovered Evidence, Fraud, Etc. Rule 60(a) allows the court to correct clerical errors *sua sponte* at any time and, on motion made at a reasonable time not more than a year after entry, Rule 60(b) authorizes relief from judgments in cases of mistake, fraud, etc. Relief under Rule 60(b) is narrowly circumscribed, because of the strong policy favoring repose of final judgments. But it does exist, as the following case shows.

ROZIER v. FORD MOTOR CO., 573 F.2d 1332 (5th Cir. 1978). The plaintiff's decedent died from burns after his 1969 Ford Galaxie automobile was rear-ended. He directed interrogatories to Ford, including the question whether Ford had prepared any "written reports or analyses of the comparative advantages or disadvantages of alternate locations (*e.g.*, on top of the rear axle or in front of the rear axle) for fuel tanks in full-sized sedans and hard-tops, including the 1969 Galaxie. . . ." The trial judge overruled Ford's objections and required it to answer with respect to reports that included applicability to the 1969 Galaxie. Ford's response was that "Defendant cannot find [any] such written analysis covering the inquiry." A week-long jury trial resulted in a verdict for Ford.

Ten months later, the plaintiff's counsel learned of a Ford document, dated "2/9/71," entitled "Trend Cost Estimate — Fuel Tank Proposals (30 mph safety std.) — Prop[osal] I — Tank Over Rear Axle Surrounded by Body Sheet Metal Barrier & Prop[osal] II — Tank in Tank Filled With Polyurethane vs. 1971 Ford Design — 1975 Ford/Mercury." Within five days, the plaintiff's counsel had filed a motion for relief pursuant to Rule 60(b)(2), newly discovered evidence, and Rule 60(b)(3), fraud, misrepresentation and other misconduct. Attached to the motion were affidavits of two experts who said that the 1969 Ford Galaxie was "so similar in size, design, and fuel tank location to the 1971 Ford that the subject [Report] is as applicable and valid for the 1969 Ford as it is for the 1971 Ford." In response, Ford produced an affidavit by one of its in-house attorneys who had been involved in the case, stating that the report "would have no application to the 1969 Ford Galaxie" and that he was not aware of it at the time of the answers to interrogatories (although he was aware of it prior to trial). The trial judge denied the Rule 60 motion.

The Court of Appeals held this ruling an abuse of discretion and reversed. It first noted that the motion had been filed within one year and was not subject to the more stringent standard that would be applicable to an independent action, filed after one year. An independent action requires a showing of "fraud on the court," which requires the "most egregious misconduct, such as bribery of a judge or members of a jury, or the fabrication of evidence in which an attorney is implicated." In an independent action, "[l]ess egregious misconduct, such as nondisclosure to the court of facts allegedly pertinent . . . ," will not suffice. The standard under the true Rule 60(b)(3) motion, for fraud, misrepresentation, or other misconduct, is not so stringent, and, under that section, the plaintiff's motion should have been granted:

> One who asserts that an adverse party has obtained a verdict through fraud, misrepresentation or other misconduct has the burden of proving the assertion by clear and convincing evidence. . . . The conduct complained of must be such as prevented the losing party from fully and fairly presenting his case or defense. . . . Although Rule 60(b)(3) applies to misconduct in withholding information called for by discovery, . . . it does not require that the information be of such nature as to alter the result in the case. . . . This subsection of the Rule is aimed at judgments which were unfairly obtained, not at those which are factually incorrect. . . .
>
> We conclude that Mrs. Rozier has proved by clear and convincing evidence that Ford engaged in misrepresentation and other misconduct. Plaintiff's interrogatory 19, as limited by the district court's order, called for production of the Trend Cost Estimate. In its written response, Ford stated that it could find no such report. A month later, an in-house attorney for Ford involved in this case discovered the Trend Cost Estimate but failed to disclose it or to amend the inaccurate response to interrogatories. . . .
>
> The more vexing question is whether nondisclosure of the Trend Cost Estimate prevented Mrs. Rozier from fully and fairly presenting her case. . . . Inevitably, information developed in the discovery stages of the case influenced the decision as

to which theories would be emphasized at trial. We are left with the firm conviction that disclosure of the Trend Cost Estimate would "have made a difference in the way plaintiff's counsel approached the case or prepared for trial," . . . and that Mrs. Rozier was prejudiced by Ford's nondisclosure.

[Ford argued that the information was merely cumulative even if admissible and would not be admissible because it was a subsequent remedial measure excluded by Fed. R. Evid. 407. The court notes that inadmissibility is irrelevant in the discovery context if the information is reasonably calculated to lead to admissible evidence.] . . .

We do not reach the question of whether the district court abused its discretion in denying plaintiff's motion . . . based on newly discovered evidence, pursuant to Rule 60(b)(2). Under that Rule, the moving party must show, inter alia, that the newly discovered evidence is "such that a new trial would probably produce a different result." . . . To hold the plaintiff in this case to such a showing would be manifestly unfair:

> "[I]t cannot be stated with certainty that all of this would have changed the result of the case. But, as said by the Supreme Court, a litigant who has engaged in misconduct is not entitled to 'the benefit of calculation, which can be little better than speculation, as to the extent of the wrong inflicted on his opponent.' *Minneapolis, St. Paul & S.S.M. Ry. Co. v. Moquin*, 1931, 283 U.S. 520, 521-22. . . ."

We hold that the district court abused its discretion in denying plaintiff's Rule 60(b)(3) motion and that a new trial is required. . . .

NOTES AND QUESTIONS

(1) *Fraud, Misrepresentation and Other Misconduct: Metlyn Realty Corp. v. Esmark, Inc., 763 F.2d 826 (7th Cir. 1985).* Does the less rigorous standard for showing harmfulness in the event of fraud apply when a witness has made misstatements, but counsel are unaware of the misstatement? In *Metlyn Realty*, an expert witness made "misstatements," and the parties settled the case, entering a final judgment on the basis of the record including those misstatements. Afterward, one party moved for relief under the Rule 60 "fraud, misrepresentation and other misconduct" provision on this basis. The court held that where counsel were unaware of witness misconduct, the liberal standard for setting aside judgments based upon fraud was inapplicable, and the movant must show substantial danger that an unjust result actually was produced. Notice that Rule 60 may apply to settlements as well as judgments resulting from trial (which, after all, are a small minority of judgments).

(2) *Mistake, Inadvertence, Surprise, Excusable Neglect: Murray v. Ford Motor Co., 770 F.2d 461 (5th Cir. 1985).* Obviously, many kinds of "mistakes" must remain unredressable (*e.g.*, one party or the other did not prepare properly for the trial because of a mistake in interpreting the law). What kind of "mistake," etc., qualifies? In *Murray*, the plaintiff initially obtained a default judgment in a state court action. The defendant moved, in state court, to set aside the default, and then removed the case. The state court entered an order setting aside the default, which both parties mistakenly believed was effective. When the defendant realized, more than a year later, that the state court order was not effective because it had been entered after the removal was effectuated, it moved for relief under Rule 60. The court granted relief under the mistake, inadvertence, etc.

subdivision using the original state court motion to avoid the bar of the one-year limit for 60(b)(1) motions. The court concluded that the state-court motion, which had been filed within one year of the default judgment and still was pending in the removed action, was sufficient for this purpose. *See* Note, *Relief from Final Judgment Under Rule 60(b)(1) Due to Judicial Errors of Law*, 83 Mich. L. Rev. 1571 (1985).

(3) *Newly Discovered Evidence: Bradley Bank v. Hartford Acc. & Indem. Co., 562 F. Supp. 241 (W.D. Wis. 1983).* Since newly discovered evidence is a ground for new trial, and since the requirements there are stringent, it is reasonable to assume that the courts would be even more restrictive of newly discovered evidence as a ground for Rule 60 relief — and that is the case. In *Bradley Bank*, for example, the insurance company belatedly discovered evidence that showed that the policy in question had been redrafted in its present form for the very purpose of clarifying an ambiguous term. The bank had exploited this ambiguity in obtaining judgment. The insurance company also satisfied the court that it could not have learned of this evidence earlier by the exercise of due diligence. The court denied relief under Rule 60 on the ground that the evidence was not sufficiently significant to change the result.

(4) *Void Judgments, Satisfied Judgments, Etc.* Rule 60(b)(4)-(5) provides for relief from a variety of judgments that are not themselves substantively defective but that should not be enforced. If, for example, the court had no subject-matter jurisdiction — a small claims court entered a judgment for $1 million — the mechanism for setting it aside after time limits have run is the Rule 60(b)(4) attack on a void judgment. If the judgment is paid, it is customary to reflect that fact in the record (*e.g.*, by a release filed among the papers of the cause); if, however, that is not done, and the judgment remains as a cloud on title or even as a vehicle for enforcement efforts, the Rule 60(b)(5) attack on a satisfied or discharged judgment is appropriate. Rule 60(b)(6) contains a "catchall" provision for "other" reasons. Rule 60(b)(4)-(6) motions must be made "within a reasonable time," but, unlike motions under Rule 60(b)(1)-(3), are not subject to the outer limit of "no more than a year after the entry of the judgment or order or the date of the proceeding." *See McCorvey v. Hill*, 385 F.3d 846, 849-50 (5th Cir. [Tex.] 2004), *cert. denied*, 543 U.S. 1154 (2004) (Norma McCorvey a/k/a Jane Roe's attack on *Roe v. Wade* was not too late "as a matter of law" despite 30-year delay in making Rule 60(b)(6) motion, but mootness doctrine precluded review).

(5) *Mere Errors of Law or Fact in Rendering Judgment Ordinarily Are Not Redressable; Clerical Errors Distinguished.* Rule 60 ordinarily is not thought of as a means of correcting errors of fact or law that the court has made in rendering judgment. *Cf. McKnight v. U.S. Steel Corp.*, 726 F.2d 333 (7th Cir. 1984) (review should be sought, instead, by timely appeal). *But see Parks v. U.S. Life & Credit Corp.*, 677 F.2d 838 (11th Cir. 1982) (Rule 60 can encompass "mistakes in the application of the law"). On the other hand, "clerical" mistakes are subject to correction at any time, and the court may act on its own motion. *E.g., Chavez v. Balesh*, 704 F.2d 774 (5th Cir. 1983) (where judge inadvertently failed to include liquidated damages in signed judgment, although findings of fact entered same day unambiguously entitled plaintiff to them, later correction was clerical in nature). Sometimes it is difficult to distinguish "legal" errors, which are harder to correct, from "clerical" errors. The difference is based upon whether the matter requires judicial judgment. *Scola v. Boat Frances R., Inc.*, 618 F.2d 147 (1st Cir. 1980) (where "error" consisted in choosing wrong interest provision, it was not "clerical" in nature and was subject to correction only in timely fashion).

[1] Rule 60 as a Mechanism for Setting Aside Default

The Excusable Neglect Standard: Butner v. Neustadter, 324 F.2d 783 (9th Cir. 1963) (reproduced in § 9.05 of Chapter 9, above). If a default judgment is discovered within 10 days, the defendant can obtain relief by a motion for new trial, but after that time, the mechanism is the Rule 60 motion. The "excusable neglect" standard is often used for this purpose. In *Butner v. Neustadter*, the plaintiff took a default in state court under state rules that allowed only ten days to answer. The defendant promptly removed the action and sought to answer, still within the 20 days; however, the court held that the default prevented answer — although it could be set aside under Rule 60(b). Setting aside defaults, at least when the defendant has a potentially meritorious defense and there is no prejudice to the plaintiff, is more liberally granted than most other kinds of Rule 60 motions. *See* Project, *Relief from Default Judgments Under Rule 60(b) — A Study of Federal Case Law*, 49 Fordham L. Rev. 956 (1981).

[2] The Independent Action for Relief From Judgment

The One-Year Time Limit for Rule 60(b)(1)-(3) Motions. In *Rozier v. Ford Motor Co.*, a passage of the opinion not included above explains the one-year limit. It quotes the Supreme Court in *Hazel-Atlas Glass Co. v. Hartford-Empire Co.*, 322 U.S. 238, 244 (1944):

> Federal courts . . . long ago established the general rule that they would not alter or set aside their judgments after the expiration of the term at which the judgments were finally entered. This salutory general rule springs from the belief that in most instances society is best served by putting an end to litigation after a case has been tried and judgment entered. . . . From the beginning, there has existed alongside the term rule a rule of equity to the effect that under certain circumstances, one of which is after-discovered fraud, relief will be granted against the judgments regardless of the term of their entry.

"Rule 60 substitutes a general one year limitations period for the earlier 'term rule,' " but it "continues to reflect a strong policy favoring an end to litigation by severely restricting the relief available after the one year limit has run." *Rozier*, 573 F.2d at 1338. Subsections (4) and (5) are not limited, nor is section (a).

The More Stringent Standard for the Independent Action. Rozier points out that "only the most egregious misconduct, such as bribery of a judge or members of a jury, or the fabrication of evidence by a party in which an attorney is implicated, will constitute a fraud on the court." 573 F.2d at 1338. Question: If the plaintiff's counsel, in *Rozier*, had learned of the nondisclosure of the Trend Cost Estimate two months later, so that his motion was not filed within one year, would the requested relief have been granted? [Note that *Rozier* also points out that "[l]ess egregious misconduct, such as nondisclosure to the court of facts allegedly pertinent to the matter before it, will not ordinarily rise to the level of fraud on the court" for purposes of an independent action.]

CHAPTER 12

APPEALS

§ 12.01 The Scope of Appellate Review

[A] Errors of Law and Avoidance Doctrines

Read Fed. R. Civ. P. Rule 61 (harmless error) and 28 U.S.C. § 2111.

[1] Harmless Error Principles

McDONOUGH POWER EQUIPMENT, INC. v. GREENWOOD, 464 U.S. 548 (1984). This case appears in § 10.03[B][1] of Chapter 10, above, and should be read again at this point. The plaintiff appealed from the trial court's refusal to grant a new trial. The plaintiff's motion for new trial had been made on the basis that one of the jurors had concealed material information during the jury selection process. In reversing the Court of Appeals' reversal of the trial court's denial of a new trial, the Supreme Court held that under principles of "harmless error" a new trial is only appropriate in such a situation when a juror is shown to have been dishonest in failing to answer a material question on voir dire and it also is shown that a correct (honest) response would have provided a valid basis for a challenge for cause. The Court's explanation of "harmless error" is set forth in the following excerpt:

> We have also come a long way from the time when all trial error was presumed prejudicial and reviewing courts were considered "citadels of technicality." . . . The harmless error rules adopted by this Court and Congress embody the principle that courts should exercise judgment in preference to the automatic reversal for "error" and ignore errors that do not affect the essential fairness of the trial. . . . For example, the general rule governing motions for a new trial in the district courts is contained in Federal Rule of Civil Procedure 61, which provides:
>
>> No error . . . or defect in any ruling or order or in anything done or omitted by the court or by any of the parties is ground for granting a new trial or for setting aside a verdict . . . unless refusal to take such action appears to the court inconsistent with substantial justice. The court at every stage of the proceeding *must* disregard any error or defect in the proceeding which does not affect the substantial rights of the parties (emphasis added). [The 2007 "restyling" amendments changed this language slightly — Eds.]

While in a narrow sense Rule 61 applies only to the district courts, *see* Fed. Rule Civ. Proc. 1, it is well-settled that the appellate courts should act in accordance with the salutary policy embodied in Rule 61. . . . Congress has further reinforced the application of Rule 61 by enacting the harmless error statute, 28 U.S.C. § 2111, which applies directly to appellate courts and which incorporates the same principle as that found in Rule 61.

NOTES AND QUESTIONS

(1) *The Harmless Error Principle.* As the principal case indicates, a litigant is entitled to a "fair trial but not a perfect one." In other words, a showing that some misconduct occurred or that an erroneous ruling was made is not enough to obtain reversal of the trial court's judgment on appeal. What types of errors are reversible? At the federal level, Rule 61 provides that no error is ground for disturbing a judgment or order "[u]nless justice requires otherwise." *See also* 28 U.S.C. § 2111. *Compare* Tex. R. App. P. 44, which provides "[n]o judgment may be reversed on appeal on the ground that the trial court made an error of law unless the court of appeals concludes that the error complained of: (a) probably caused the rendition of an improper judgment; or (b) probably prevented the appellant from properly presenting the case to the court of appeals." *See also* Tex. R. App. P. 61, which provides the same "harmless error" standard for reversal of cases appealed to the Texas Supreme Court.

California, in a major development, held that even instructional errors do not warrant reversal of the judgment unless they cause actual prejudice. *Soule v. General Motors Corp.*, 8 Cal. 4th 548, 882 P.2d 298, 34 Cal. Rptr. 2d 607 (1994). The court found a jury in a design-defect case should not have been instructed on ordinary consumer expectations. However, the court was also persuaded that the error was harmless, because it was not reasonably probable that the defendant would have obtained a more favorable result in its absence. 34 Cal. Rptr. at 619.

(2) *Applying Harmless Error Principles.* How should the broad principle of "substantial justice" be applied to protect a party's "substantial rights"? Should harm ever be presumed because of the nature of the error? Imagine, for example, that the appellant claims that the trial judge erroneously denied him a trial by jury, but the appellee responds that even if the denial was error, it was harmless, because the evidence is so overwhelming that neither a judge nor a jury was likely to find in the appellant's favor.

PROBLEM A: CHAPTER 12 SUMMARY PROBLEM

DOBSON v. JONES: APPEALABILITY, GROUNDS, SUSPENSION AND APPELLATE STEPS. A federal district court has just entered what it labels a "Judgment Final Except for Periodic Reporting and Adjustment" against the City of New Dublin and in favor of a named plaintiff (Patrick Dobson) and a class consisting of all pretrial detainees arrested during the last four years. The judgment requires extensive changes in the management of the city police department in order to prevent a "pattern of violence . . . perpetrated by police officers on arrested or detained suspects," according to the Findings of Fact filed by the judge. The mayor, Sandra Jones, publicly has complained that the judge was biased, made "unbelievable" findings, and relied on experts who simply had no credentials or expertise. The order requires Jones to make monthly reports and provides for certain specified "adjustments" to the judgment, depending on future court findings that will be based on further evidence. The judgment also requires payment of more than $20 million by the city to the class members, but it leaves open the amount of attorneys' fees.

Mayor Jones wishes to appeal because the judgment is "destroying officers' morale, keeping us from responding to crime victims, and ruining the city's bond rating." She plaintively adds: "We actually have a better police department than most other cities our size, even though we all have problems." You have concluded that the findings involve extremely broad inferences from the evidence, and the intrusiveness of the order is unusual.

Assume that you represent the Mayor or, in the alternative, consider that you represent Patrick Dobson. Dobson believes that the trial judge erred in refusing to adopt certain findings tendered by him, awarded inadequate damages, and entered an order that "won't even begin to make a dent in the problem." Dobson bitterly denounces what he sees as an "out-of-control police department," and he points out that his own claim is enhanced by a citizen's videotape of two officers injuring him during his arrest.

1. Is this "final" judgment wholly or partly appealable?
2. What appellate steps are required next, and when?
3. Has the trial judge committed reversible error?
4. Can the city avoid complying with the judgment during the appeal?

[2] The Preservation Requirement; "Plain" Error

Read Fed. R. Civ. P. Rule 46, 50, 51, and 59.

NEU v. GRANT

548 F.2d 281 (10th Cir. 1977)

[Nina Neu brought a negligence action against Frank and Lorna Grant as a result of injuries she sustained in a car wreck as a passenger in a 1967 Plymouth Fury owned by the Grants and driven by Lorna. The accident was the result of a "speed contest" between a pickup truck operated by Frank and the Plymouth operated by Lorna on Poison Spider Road in Casper, Wyoming.]

Neu contends that the jury verdict resulted from an "unlawful" instruction, *i.e.*, that Neu was a guest in the Plymouth Fury and that, in light of the Wyoming Guest Statute, W.S. 31-233,[1] it was obligatory that Neu prove that Lorna Marie Grant was grossly negligent. Following a pre-trial conference, Neu filed a Motion to Strike Paragraph 6 of Grant's Answer to her Amended Complaint, which alleged that the Wyoming Guest Statute barred recovery, "upon the grounds that Wyoming's guest statute is unconstitutional, denies equal protection of law under the Constitution of the State of Wyoming and the Constitution of the United States of America and should be stricken." [The trial court overruled the Motion to Strike.]

---

[1] W.S. § 31-233. *Liability of owner to guest.* — No person transported by the owner or operator of a motor vehicle as his guest without payment for such transportation shall have a cause of action for damages against such owner or operator for injury, death or loss, in case of accident, unless such accident shall have been caused by the gross negligence or wilful and wanton misconduct of the owner or operator of such motor vehicle and unless such gross negligence or wilful and wanton misconduct contributed to the injury, death or loss for which the action is brought.

On appeal Neu attacks the judgment-verdict on the basis that the Wyoming Guest Statute is constitutionally infirm [under both the state and federal constitutions].

[The Court of Appeals first examines Neu's federal constitutional challenges to the Wyoming Guest Statute under the Fourteenth Amendment to the United States Constitution and concludes that they are "foreclosed" by a United States Supreme Court opinion that was handed down subsequent to the trial of the case. The court then proceeds to consider Neu's arguments under the Wyoming State Constitution, but rejects them on procedural grounds, as follows.]

Neu did not adequately preserve her objections to the Wyoming Guest Statute for appellate consideration.

Neu's pre-trial submission listed the legal issues as: (a) applicability of defense of guest statute, (b) applicability of assumption of risk or contributory negligence defenses and (c) constitutionality of the Wyoming Guest Statute. . . . The trial court instructed the jury in detail relative to the Wyoming Guest Statute. . . .

Critically, insofar as Neu's appeal is concerned, this record *does not* evidence (1) any objection following the Court's denial of Neu's Motion to Strike or Motion for Partial Summary Judgment, (2) any objection to the court's instructions on the applicability of the Wyoming Guest Statute and (3) any motions by Neu following the jury verdict or the court's judgment to set them aside or for a new trial. In fact, after the jury was discharged the trial court inquired if there were any motions. Counsel for Neu responded "No motions, your Honor." . . .

. . . While exceptions to trial court rulings adverse to a party have been abolished, Fed. Rules Civ. Proc., Rule 46 requires that in lieu thereof ". . . it is sufficient that a party, at the time of the ruling or order of the court is made or sought, makes known to the court the action which he desires the court to take or his objection to the action of the court and his grounds therefore; and, if a party has no opportunity to object to a ruling or order at the time it is made, the absence of an objection does not thereafter prejudice him." [The 2007 "restyling" amendments have streamlined this language — Eds.] The purpose for timely objection or motion as a precedent to review on appeal is two-fold. It provides the trial court with the opportunity to know the *specific* contentions and to take corrective action, if required. And — more importantly for appellate review — it *does not* permit a party to sit idly by, watching error being committed, and then take a "first" shot at the claimed error without having accorded the trial court the opportunity to correct its action. . . .

We affirm.

NOTES AND QUESTIONS

(1) *Preservation of Objections; Waiver.* As a general rule, a party must make known to the court the action which the party desires the court to take or the objection to the court's action and the grounds for objection at the time a ruling or order is made. Fed. R. Civ. P. 46; *see also* Fed. R. Civ. P. 51; Fed. R. Evid. 103. Otherwise, no complaint can be made about the court's action on appeal. The principal case points out that the purpose for a timely complaint is twofold: (1) to advise the trial court of the complainant's specific contentions so that the judge can take corrective action, and (2) to prevent litigants from "riding the verdict," protected by apparently reversible error. Given the fact that Nina Neu's counsel did challenge Wyoming's Guest Statute at the pretrial stage, in what respect did counsel violate Rule 46? A similar approach applies to the preservation of

appellate complaints about the sufficiency of the evidence. *See Unitherm Food Systems, Inc. v. Swift-Eckrich, Inc.*, 126 S. Ct. 980 (2006), in Chapter 11, *supra.*

(2) *Specificity of Objections.* The principal case points out that a party's objections to rulings on evidence, arguments of counsel, the jury charge and "all other matters throughout the trial" must be specific. Why is this the case? If a litigant makes a "Perry Mason"-style objection that certain evidence is "irrelevant, incompetent, and immaterial," should an appellate court later consider an argument that the evidence was inadmissible hearsay?

(3) *The Concept of "Plain" Error.* In many procedural systems, there is a concept called "plain" or "fundamental" error. *See* Fed. R. Civ. P. 51(d). When this type of error has been committed, failure to make an objection or obtain a ruling may be excused. Procedural systems differ in their attitude toward "plain" error. Some take a strict view that limits the scope of the doctrine to errors that go to the jurisdiction of the trial court. Others take a more relaxed approach that treats serious denial of a party's rights as plain error when it is apparent on the face of the appellate record. *See, e.g., Morreale v. Downing*, 630 F.2d 286 (5th Cir. 1980); *see also Miley v. Delta Marine Drilling Co.*, 473 F.2d 856, 857-58 (5th Cir. 1973) (excusing counsel's failure to object to trial judge's comments during trial on basis that "[w]here a trial judge's comments were so prejudicial as to deny a party an opportunity for a fair and impartial trial, the absence of objections will not preclude our review since counsel will be loathe to challenge the propriety of a trial judge's utterances for fear of antagonizing him and thereby prejudicing a client's case").

[B] Standards of Review: Deference to Trial Court Discretion

NEWMAN v. A.E. STALEY MANUFACTURING COMPANY, 648 F.2d 330 (5th Cir. 1981). Newman brought suit against Staley alleging that Staley manufactured and sold adulterated cattle feed to Newman that caused death to a great number of Newman's cattle, illness among his herd, interruption in his feeding and maintenance program and otherwise injured and damaged him. A jury verdict was rendered against Staley. Staley appealed on several grounds, including a complaint that the District Court abused its discretion in refusing to allow Staley to call a witness who was not identified on the defendant's pretrial witness list as required by the judge's pretrial order. In rejecting this appellate complaint, the Court of Appeals explained that "[t]he decision to modify or enforce a pretrial order is discretionary with the trial court and will not be disturbed on appeal absent an abuse of discretion. . . . Failure of a district court to allow defendant to present a witness who was not named in a required witness list to testify contrary to the plaintiff's evidence is not an abuse of discretion if the defendant was on notice that the plaintiff would present the evidence at issue. . . ."

NOTE ON TRIAL COURT'S DISCRETION

Any ruling that is within the discretion of the judge will be reviewed under an abuse of discretion standard. A discretionary decision will not be reversed unless the appellate court is convinced that the trial court was clearly wrong. This narrow scope of review extends to a wide range of matters that occur during the pretrial process or during trial, including the admission or exclusion of evidence, the conduct of the trial and the preparation of the jury charge.

Even when the abuse of discretion review standard applies, the degree of appellate deference depends on the specific context in which the trial court's ruling was made. For example, the trial judge has no discretion to misstate the applicable law in a jury charge. But the judge has considerable discretion in how the jury is charged. Finally, some rulings are subject to non-deferential *de novo* review. For example, a trial court's grant of summary judgment or another judgment as a matter of law are rulings that are subject to *de novo* review on appeal. The appellate court applies the same legal sufficiency standard as the trial judge in deciding whether the trial judge's ruling was correct. In contrast, the abuse of discretion standard of review applies to rulings on new trial motions.

[C] Review of Determinations of Fact

Read Fed. R. Civ. P. 52(a) (the "clearly erroneous" standard).

ANDERSON v. CITY OF BESSEMER CITY
470 U.S. 564 (1985)

[JUSTICE WHITE delivered the opinion of the Court . . . .

[Anderson, a 39-year-old female schoolteacher with college degrees in social studies and education, applied for the position of Recreational Director. A City committee instead hired Kincaid, a 24-year-old man who had recently obtained a physical education degree. After unsuccessful conciliation efforts in the Equal Employment Opportunity Commission, Anderson filed an action in federal District Court alleging that the City's decision was affected by gender discrimination in violation of Title VII of the Civil Rights Act of 1964. The District Court heard evidence at trial and issued a memorandum announcing its holding in favor of Anderson and requesting that she propose findings of fact and conclusions of law. The court also requested a response from the City. When the court issued its findings and conclusions, its finding that Anderson had been denied employment because of gender discrimination was based upon Anderson's proposed findings to some degree but also differed from those proposed findings. The court found that Anderson was the most qualified candidate for certain specified reasons, that she had been asked questions about her spouse's feelings that other candidates had not been asked, and that the male committee members were biased against hiring a woman.

[The Court of Appeals reversed. It held that the District Court's controlling findings of fact were "clearly erroneous" within the meaning of Rule 52(a). The Supreme Court granted certiorari and, in this opinion, reversed the Court of Appeals' decision.]

II

We must deal at the outset with the Fourth Circuit's suggestion that "close scrutiny of the record in this case [was] justified by the manner in which the opinion was prepared," . . . that is, by the District Court's adoption of petitioner's proposed findings of fact and conclusions of law. . . .

We, too, have criticized courts for their verbatim adoption of findings of fact prepared by prevailing parties, particularly when those findings have taken the form of conclusory statements unsupported by citation to the record. . . .

. . . Nonetheless, our previous discussions of the subject suggest that even when the trial judge adopts proposed findings verbatim, the findings are those of the court and may be reversed only if clearly erroneous.

In any event, the District Court in this case does not appear to have uncritically accepted findings prepared without judicial guidance by the prevailing party. The court itself provided the framework for the proposed findings when it issued its preliminary memorandum, which set forth its essential findings and directed petitioner's counsel to submit a more detailed set of findings consistent with them. Further, respondent was provided and availed itself of the opportunity to respond at length to the proposed findings. Nor did the District Court simply adopt petitioner's proposed findings: the findings it ultimately issued . . . vary considerably in organization and content from those submitted by petitioner's counsel. . . .

III

Because a finding of intentional discrimination is a finding of fact, the standard governing appellate review of a district court's finding of discrimination is that set forth in Federal Rule of Civil Procedure 52(a): "Findings of fact shall not be set aside unless clearly erroneous, and due regard shall be given to the opportunity of the trial court to judge of the credibility of the witnesses." . . .*

Although the meaning of the phrase "clearly erroneous" is not immediately apparent, certain general principles governing the exercise of the appellate court's power to overturn findings of a district court may be derived from our cases. The foremost of these principles, as the Fourth Circuit itself recognized, is that "a finding is 'clearly erroneous' when although there is evidence to support it, the reviewing court on the entire evidence is left with the definite and firm conviction that a mistake has been committed." *United States v. United States Gypsum Co.*, 333 U.S. 364 (1948). This standard plainly does not entitle a reviewing court to reverse the finding of the trier of fact simply because it is convinced that it would have decided the case differently. . . . If the district court's account of the evidence is plausible in light of the record viewed in its entirety, the court of appeals may not reverse it even though convinced that had it been sitting as the trier of fact, it would have weighed the evidence differently. Where there are two permissible views of the evidence, the fact-finder's choice between them cannot be clearly erroneous. . . .

This is so even when the district court's findings do not rest on credibility determinations, but are based instead on physical or documentary evidence or inferences from other facts. To be sure, various Courts of Appeals have on occasion asserted the theory that an appellate court may exercise *de novo* review over findings not based on credibility determinations. *See, e.g., Orvis v. Higgins*, 180 F.2d 537 (2d Cir. 1950). . . . This theory has an impressive genealogy . . . but it is impossible to trace the theory's lineage back to the text of Rule 52, which states straightforwardly that "findings of fact shall not be set aside unless clearly erroneous." . . .

The rationale for deference to the original finder of fact is not limited to the superiority of the trial judge's position to make determinations of credibility. The trial judge's major role is the determination of fact, and with experience in fulfilling that role comes expertise. Duplication of the trial judge's efforts in the court of appeals would very likely contribute only negligibly to the accuracy of fact determination at a huge cost in diversion of judicial resources. In addition, the parties to a case on appeal have already been forced

* As a result of the 2007 "restyling" amendments, the applicable subsection of Rule 52(a) provides: "Findings of fact, whether based on oral or other evidence, must not be set aside unless clearly erroneous, and the reviewing court must give due regard to the trial court's opportunity to judge the witnesses' credibility." Fed. R. Civ. P. 52(a)(6).

to concentrate their energies and resources on persuading the trial judge that their account of the facts is the correct one; requiring them to persuade three more judges at the appellate level is requiring too much. As the Court has stated in a different context, the trial on the merits should be "the 'main event' . . . rather than a 'tryout on the road.' " *Wainwright v. Sykes*, 433 U.S. 72, 90, 97 S. Ct. 2497, 2508, 53 L. Ed. 2d 594 (1977). For these reasons, review of factual findings under the clearly-erroneous standard — with its deference to the trier of fact — is the rule, not the exception.

When findings are based on determinations regarding the credibility of witnesses, Rule 52 demands even greater deference to the trial court's findings; for only the trial judge can be aware of the variations in demeanor and tone of voice that bear so heavily on the listener's understanding of and belief in what is said. . . . This is not to suggest that the trial judge may insulate his findings from review by denominating them credibility determinations, for factors other than demeanor and inflection go into the decision whether or not to believe a witness. Documents or objective evidence may contradict the witness' story; or the story itself may be so internally inconsistent or implausible on its face that a reasonable factfinder would not credit it. Where such factors are present, the court of appeals may well find clear error even in a finding purportedly based on a credibility determination. *See, e.g., United States v. United States Gypsum Co., supra*, 333 U.S., at 396. But when a trial judge's finding is based on his decision to credit the testimony of one of two or more witnesses, each of whom has told a coherent and facially plausible story that is not contradicted by extrinsic evidence, that finding, if not internally inconsistent, can virtually never be clear error.

IV

Application of the foregoing principles to the facts of the case lays bare the errors committed by the Fourth Circuit in its employment of the clearly-erroneous standard. In detecting clear error in the District Court's finding that petitioner was better qualified than Mr. Kincaid, the Fourth Circuit improperly conducted what amounted to a *de novo* weighing of the evidence in the record. The District Court's finding was based on essentially undisputed evidence regarding the respective backgrounds of petitioner and Mr. Kincaid and the duties that went with the position of Recreation Director. The District Court, after considering the evidence, concluded that the position of Recreation Director in Bessemer City carried with it broad responsibilities for creating and managing a recreation program involving not only athletics, but also other activities for citizens of all ages and interests. The court determined that petitioner's more varied educational and employment background and her extensive involvement in a variety of civic activities left her better qualified to implement such a rounded program than Mr. Kincaid, whose background was more narrowly focused on athletics.

The Fourth Circuit, reading the same record, concluded that the basic duty of the Recreation Director was to implement an athletic program, and that the essential qualification for a successful applicant would be either education or experience specifically related to athletics. Accordingly, it seemed evident to the Court of Appeals that Mr. Kincaid was in fact better qualified than petitioner.

Based on our own reading of the record, we cannot say that either interpretation of the facts is illogical or implausible. . . . The question we must answer, however, is not whether the Fourth Circuit's interpretation of the facts was clearly erroneous, but whether the District Court's finding was clearly erroneous. . . . When the record is examined in light of the appropriately deferential standard, it is apparent that it contains nothing that mandates a finding that the District Court's conclusion was clearly erroneous. . . .

[The Court also rejected the Court of Appeals' conclusion that the District Court's finding that Anderson was asked questions not asked of men was clearly erroneous. The evidence on this issue was ambiguous, and therefore it raised "somewhat different" concerns: The error of the Court of Appeals was its failure to "give due regard to the ability of the District Court to interpret and discern the credibility of oral testimony." Having disagreed with the Court of Appeals on these and other points, the Court concluded: "Accordingly, we hold that the Fourth Circuit erred in denying petitioner relief under Title VII."] . . . .

Reversed.

[The concurring opinions of Justices Powell and Blackmun are omitted.]

NOTES AND QUESTIONS

(1) *Applying the "Clearly Erroneous" Rule to a Mixed Question of Law and Fact: Commissioner v. Duberstein, 363 U.S. 278 (1960).* The "clearly erroneous" standard does not apply to questions of law, such as the interpretation of a statute or an unambiguous contract. "Law," as opposed to fact, questions are reversible by a Court of Appeals even if they are subject to differing interpretations; indeed, such decisions are the essence of the appellate court's responsibility. But what about a District Court finding that "mixes" law and fact? An example would be an ultimate factual conclusion that a person was "negligent" or that a particular transaction amounted to a "gift" for tax purposes. These findings do involve facts — but they may also contain implicit decisions about knotty legal questions, such as the definition of "negligence" or of a "gift." In *Commissioner v. Duberstein, supra*, the Supreme Court held that a trial judge's determination that a payment to a taxpayer was a "gift" was reviewable under the clearly erroneous standard, and it analyzed the evidence in accordance with Rule 52(a). But what if the Court had reason to suspect that the "finding of fact" was influenced by an erroneous view of the law defining "gifts" in the mind of the trial judge? [Note: The *Duberstein* Court indicated that the clearly erroneous standard applied whenever the decision was based upon a "fact-finding tribunal's experience with the mainsprings of human conduct."] *See* Nangle, *The Ever Widening Scope of Fact Review in Appellate Courts — Is the "Clearly Erroneous Rule" Being Avoided?*, 59 Wash U. L.Q. 409 (1981).

(2) *A Different Approach to Constitutional Cases: Fiske v. Kansas, 274 U.S. 380 (1927).* Many cases hold that fact findings governing an ultimate question of constitutionality are treated differently. Where the constitutional issues are intertwined with the facts found, *Fiske* and subsequent cases require a review by the appellate court of the entire record to decide those issues. Is this approach justifiable?

(3) *Contrasting the "Clearly Erroneous" Standard with the Standard for Review of Jury Verdicts: Reconsidering Reeves v. Sanderson Plumbing, supra, Chapter 10, and Lavender v. Kurn, supra, Chapter 11.* You should recall that a jury verdict is subject to being disregarded upon a motion for judgment as a matter of law only if reasonable persons properly applying the law could not differ as to the result. This standard is highly deferential, as is illustrated by *Lavender v. Kurn* in Chapter 11, *supra* (although that case, as a FELA case, may be unusually deferential). The weight of authority appears to favor the proposition that, under the "clearly erroneous" standard, appellate courts may review findings by judges more freely than findings by juries. There are, however, some decisions

that sensibly equate the standards for review of judge and jury findings. *E.g., Minnesota Amusement Co. v. Larkin*, 299 F.2d 142, 146 (8th Cir. 1962). Should the appellate court be freer to disagree with jury than with judge findings, or should the two standards be the same? How is the difference (if any) affected by the decision in the principal case above, *Anderson v. Bessemer City*? How does *Reeves v. Sanderson Plumbing*, the age discrimination case in Chapter 10, *supra*, fit into this picture?

§ 12.02 Appellate Procedure

Read Fed. R. App. P. 3, 4(a) (notice of appeal); 7 (cost bond); 10(a)-(b), 11, 12(a) (record); 28, 30(a), 31(a), 32(a)-(b) (briefs and appendix).

[A] Time Limits: Notice of Appeal, Record Preparation and Briefs

WILSON v. ATWOOD GROUP

725 F.2d 255 (5th Cir. 1984) (en banc)

. . . Alvin B. Rubin, Circuit Judge:

The appellants failed to file this appeal within thirty days after the district court entered judgment because, and only because, their counsel had relied on the clerk of court to give notice of the entry of judgment and the clerk failed to do so. Consequently, counsel did not learn of the judgment until the time for appeal had expired. Because the notice of appeal was filed too late, we dismiss the appeal.

This death action was filed in 1979 and later settled by the defendants, The Atwood Group and Occidental Petroleum Corporation. Before settling the primary lawsuit, the defendants filed a third-party complaint against Kirby L. Stark, Worldwide Drilling Consultants, Inc., and Hartford Accident and Indemnity Company. Because the third-party defendants declined to contribute to the settlement, the third-party claim was tried without a jury by Judge Jack M. Gordon in May 1981. Judge Gordon took the case under advisement, but died before rendering judgment. [I]n April 1982, the case was submitted to Judge Carr on the transcript of the first trial. Judge Carr rendered judgment against the third-party defendants, Stark, Worldwide and Hartford, and this was entered in June 1982. The third-party defendants made a timely motion for new trial. A hearing was scheduled, but, in the interim, Judge Henry Mentz was appointed to succeed Judge Gordon. In accordance with the usual procedure, all of the cases that had originally been assigned to Judge Gordon were assigned to Judge Mentz. Judge Mentz, therefore, heard the motion without objection by any party on August 11, 1982. He overruled it the next day.

The clerk mailed notice of the order to the third-party plaintiffs (the appellees) but, due to a clerical error, did not mail notice to the third-party defendants (the appellants). Counsel for the third-party defendants did not seek information from the clerk about the status of the motion or take any other step to determine when judgment might be entered. More than two months after judgment was entered, counsel for the third-party plaintiffs, Atwood Group and Occidental, demanded payment of the judgment. Counsel for the third-party defendants thus learned for the first time that the motion for a new trial had been denied. They moved promptly for an enlargement of time in which to file a notice of appeal.

Judge Mentz heard the motion on November 3, 1982. At the hearing it became apparent that, sometime in June, a deputy clerk had erroneously placed the word "out" beside the third-party defendants' (appellants') names on the docket sheet. The notation "out" indicated that these parties were no longer in the case. Consequently, the clerk had mailed no further notices to their counsel.

Judge Mentz granted the motion to enlarge the time to appeal, relying on Fed. R. Civ. P. 60(b). He vacated and then reentered his denial of the motion for new trial because he did "not find any fault on the part of counsel for third party defendants. In light of the eleven-month delay in the rendering of a decision in this case, it was not unreasonable for counsel to anticipate further delays with respect to a decision on the post-trial motions."

A panel of this court dismissed the appeal. 702 F.2d 77 (5th Cir. 1983). The full court granted rehearing en banc. We now reach the same result as the panel.

By its terms [at the time of this appeal,] Fed. R. Civ. P. 77(d) precludes this appeal. It states:

> Lack of notice of the entry by the clerk does not affect the time to appeal or relieve or authorize the court to relieve a party for failure to appeal within the time allowed. . . .

Advisory Committee Notes explain that this provision was inserted to prevent the procedure employed here. Under the rule previously established by *Hill v. Hawes*, 320 U.S. 520, 64 S. Ct. 334, 88 L. Ed. 283 (1944), if the district court clerk did not notify the parties of judgment, the district court could vacate and reenter its judgment. The Advisory Committee expressly rejected *Hill*, stating:

> the decision in *Hill v. Hawes* is to give the district court power, in its discretion and without time limit, and long after the term may have expired, to vacate a judgment and reenter it for the purpose of reviving the right of appeal. This seriously affects the finality of judgments. . . .
>
> Rule 77(d) as amended makes it clear that notification by the clerk of the entry of a judgment has nothing to do with the starting of the time for appeal; that time starts to run from the date of entry of judgment and not from the date of notice of the entry. . . .

The rule is strict, but its meaning and purpose are plain. We have consistently held that the simple failure of the clerk to mail notice of the entry of judgment, without more, does not permit relief to a party who has failed to appeal within the prescribed time. . . .

Because of what the panel opinion correctly called the "draconian effect" of Rule 77(d), courts have sought to palliate its results by invoking rule 60(b). This rule states that the court may relieve a party from a judgment or order for any "reason justifying relief from the operation of the judgment." In *Hensley v. Chesapeake & Ohio Railway Co.*, 651 F.2d 226 (4th Cir. 1981), the Fourth Circuit held that a court may rely on Rule 60(b) to supersede Rule 77(d) under "unique circumstances." The District of Columbia Circuit has been even more generous, holding that Rule 60(b) permits a district court to vacate and reenter a judgment if the appellant was not at fault in failing to appeal, timely notice was given to neither party, and the appellee will not be prejudiced. *Expeditions Unlimited Aquatic Enterprises, Inc. v. Smithsonian Institute*, 500 F.2d 808 (D.C. Cir. 1974).

[T]he effect of this interpretation is virtually a return to *Hill*, the decision that Rule 77(d) was designed to overturn. Accordingly, the Second Circuit has rejected this effort to circumvent Rule 77(d): "a Rule 60(b)(6) motion may not be granted absent some showing of diligent effort by counsel to ascertain the status of the case." *Mizell v. Attorney General of the State of New York*, 586 F.2d 942, 944-45 n. 2 (2d Cir. 1978), *cert. denied*, 440 U.S. 967, 99 S. Ct. 1519, 59 L. Ed. 2d 783 (1979).

We accept the district court's findings that this case presents "unique circumstances" and that it was not unreasonable for counsel to anticipate further delay in decision. Fed. R. Civ. P. 52(a). But counsel made no effort to determine whether the decision was likely to be or was being delayed and did not forego action because of his belief that decision was likely to be delayed. He simply relied on the clerk to give notice. Apparently, this was no departure from his usual practice: the record gives no reason to believe he would have acted otherwise under normal circumstances. Delay caused solely by unwarranted reliance on an expectation that notification routine would be followed does not permit intervention by the district court.

We have previously permitted relief from the 30-day limit when counsel who filed a belated notice of appeal had not relied on the clerk to give notice of the entry of judgment but had been diligent in attempting either to delay its entry or to inquire about the status of the case. *Smith v. Jackson Tool & Die, Inc.*, 426 F.2d 5 (5th Cir. 1970) . . . . Other circumstances might also be the basis for relief from a judgment in accordance with rule 60(b). Counsel is not guilty of inexcusable neglect if he fails to run a periodic docket check with the clerk on every pending case to determine whether a judgment has been entered without notice to him. But to be relieved from the effect of a judgment, a party must show more than mere reliance on the clerk to give notice of a judgment. . . .

Perhaps finality and judicial efficiency are not so important as to warrant the emphasis on timeliness required by [former] Rule 77(d). A rule that admits equitable considerations might be more desirable than this categorical command. But such values are for the redactors of rules, not their interpreters. [Former] Rule 77(d) evinces a decision by the Advisory Committee and by the Supreme Court, in adopting the Committee's recommendation, to choose a simple inexorable mandate over a flexible rule.

For these reasons, the appeal is dismissed.

CLARK, CHIEF JUDGE, with whom BROWN, TATE, JOHNSON, WILLIAMS and JOLLY, CIRCUIT JUDGES, join, dissenting:

In this simple-issue, fact-bound appeal, the majority has substituted its conclusion of fact for that reached by the trial court and has created a troubled, unnecessary reversal.

There is no disagreement between us about the language and intent of the pertinent Federal Rules of Civil Procedure. [T]he reason cannot be the clerk's failure to notify. There must be *something more*. The compulsion for this dissent comes not from the Rules, but from their application to the proper facts in this case, which show that something more was found. . . .

[The dissenters here quote the trial judge's memorandum opinion, which contained the following:]

> Because the case had been handled by three different judges, and presumably three different deputy clerks in the Clerk's office, this evidently caused some confusion with respect to what parties were "in" or "out" on the docket sheet. . . .
>
> [I]n light of the eleven-month delay in the rendering of a decision in this case, it was not unreasonable for counsel to anticipate further delays with respect to a decision on the post-trial motions. . . .

About as succinctly as can be put, the proper trier of fact tells us that the "unique circumstances" found to be present have nothing to do with the clerical error that resulted in a failure to notify counsel of the entry of the vacated judgment. . . . [T]he district court found there was *something more*. . . .

That *something more* was his own reasonably unexpected next-day entry of final judgment in a case that had passed through the hands of three judges and had experienced an eleven-month delay in decision. Based on these facts — not on the lack of notice — the district court expressly found "it was not unreasonable for counsel to anticipate further delays with respect to a decision on the post-trial motions." . . .

Because we ought to affirm, I respectfully dissent.

NOTE ON AMENDMENTS OF RULE 77(d) AND APPELLATE RULE 4

Rule 77(d) was amended to allow the trial court to grant extensions of time as allowed by amended Rule 4(a) of the Federal Rules of Appellate Procedure. Fed. R. Civ. P. 77(d)(2). Appellate Rule 4(a) now includes provisions for extending the time for filing a notice of appeal if the deadline is missed but the appellant shows "excusable neglect or good excuse" (*see* Fed. R. App. P. 4(a)(5)) and authorizing district judges to reopen the time to file an appeal (*see* Fed. R. App. P. 4(a)(6)) if the appellant did not receive notice under Rule 77(d). These amendments mitigate but do not altogether eliminate the harsh result in *Wilson v. Atwood Group*. The amendments also make the finality of judgments less clear.

NOTES AND QUESTIONS

(1) *Federal Rules of Appellate Procedure.* Under the Federal Rules of Appellate Procedure, the notice of appeal is the one "jurisdictional" prerequisite to an appeal. The contents of a notice of appeal are set forth in Fed. R. App. P. 3(c); *see also* Official Form 1 of the Appellate Rules. In addition to the notice of appeal, an appellant in a civil case may be required to file a cost bond (Fed. R. App. P. 7), will be required to file the record (Fed. R. App. P. 10, 11, 12(b)), and file a brief and an appendix (Fed. R. App. P. 28, 28.1, 30-32) in compliance with the appellate timing requirements contained in those rules. None of the latter steps is jurisdictional, but failure to accomplish them can result in dismissal of the appeal.

(2) *Extensions of Time.* As noted above, Appellate Rule 4(a)(5) provides that the District Court "upon a showing of excusable neglect or good cause, may extend the time for filing a notice of appeal upon motion filed not later than 30 days after the expiration of the time prescribed," but no "extension shall exceed 30 days past such prescribed time or 10 days from the date of entry of the order granting the motion, whichever occurs later." Fed. R. App. P. 4(a). Further, Appellate Rule 4(a)(4) extends the time for filing a notice of appeal in civil cases if any party files a motion for judgment as a matter of law (Fed. R. Civ. P. 50(b)); a motion to amend findings in a nonjury trial (Fed. R. Civ. P. 52(b)); a motion for new trial (Fed. R. Civ. P. 59); a motion to alter or amend the judgment (Fed. R. Civ. P. 59(e)); or a Rule 60(b) motion within 10 days after entry of judgment. The time "runs for all parties from the entry of the order disposing of the last such remaining motion." Fed. R. App. P. 4(a)(4).

(3) *Paralegal's Misreading of Rule May Constitute "Excusable Neglect."* In *Pincay v. Andrews*, 389 F.3d 853 (9th Cir. 2004), the en banc Ninth Circuit held that a lawyer's reliance on a paralegal, who miscalculated the deadline for filing an appeal, constituted

"excusable neglect" that would permit an extension of the filing deadline under Rule 4(a)(5) of the Federal Rules of Appellate Procedure. In reaching this conclusion, the Ninth Circuit rejected a rigid rule, instead imposing a four-part balancing test: (1) the danger of prejudice to the non-moving party; (2) the length of delay and its potential impact on judicial proceedings; (3) the reason for the delay, including whether it was within the movant's reasonable control; and (4) whether the movant's conduct was in good faith.

(4) *The Separate Document Requirement and Time for Appeal.* Rules 54 and 58 generally require the preparation and entry of a separate judgment document in the court's civil docket in order to trigger the commencement of the appellate timetable. *See* Fed. R. Civ. P. 54 (defining judgment as "any order from which an appeal lies"); Fed. R. Civ. P. 58 and Fed. R. App. P. 4(a)(7) (providing complex rules controlling time of entry).

(5) *Unnamed Class Members Can Appeal the Fairness of a Class Settlement Without Intervening.* In *Devlin v. Scardelletti*, 536 U.S. 1 (2002), the Supreme Court held that an unnamed class member, who had timely objected to the approval of a class action settlement at the fairness hearing but had not intervened, was a "party" empowered to appeal the order approving the settlement. Because the district court's approval of the settlement was binding on Devlin as a member of the class, this was a final decision of Devlin's claim "sufficient to trigger his right to appeal." The Eleventh Circuit subsequently distinguished *Devlin* in *AAL High Yield Bond Fund v. Deloitte & Touche LLP*, 361 F.3d 1305 (11th Cir. 2004), holding that objectors to a class settlement who have not moved to intervene lack standing to appeal the lower court's settlement.

[B] Suspending Enforcement Pending Appeal: Supersedeas Bonds

Read Fed. R. Civ. P. 62(a)-(d) (stay of enforcement of judgment; security requirements) and Fed. R. App. P. 8 (stay or injunction pending appeal).

TEXACO INC. v. PENNZOIL COMPANY, 784 F.2d 1133 (2d Cir. 1986). Pennzoil obtained a judgment for $11.12 billion from Texaco in a Texas state court. Under Texas law, it was necessary for a judgment debtor to post a relatively nominal cost bond in order to prosecute an appeal from a trial court's judgment. Under Texas law, the filing of a cost bond did not suspend execution or enforcement of a judgment. In order to stay enforcement of the judgment pending appeal, under Texas law, Texaco was required to post another bond, called a supersedeas bond, "in at least the amount of the judgment, interest and costs," which amounted to more than $12 billion.

Texaco filed a federal suit in the Southern District of New York, where it had its home office, seeking a preliminary injunction against Pennzoil's enforcement of the Texas judgment. Among other arguments, Texaco claimed that the Texas provisions for supersedeas bonds effectively denied it the right of appeal and therefore denied it due process and equal protection of the laws under the United States Constitution. Pennzoil, in response, disputed these arguments, and it pointed out that it had offered to stipulate to a supersedeas bond governed by provisions such as those in Fed. R. Civ. P. 62(d), which simply provide for a supersedeas bond "approved" by the court. Thus, federal law would allow the District Court wide discretion in setting the amount of the security, and this approach would have been applicable in the Pennzoil-Texaco dispute if Texaco had accepted the stipulation (or so Pennzoil argued). Pennzoil further argued that the preliminary injunction should not have issued because Texaco should have appealed within the Texas court system and because the injunction violated the restrictions on federal injunctions interfering with ongoing state proceedings.

The federal district judge granted the injunctive relief requested by Texaco, but he conditioned relief on the posting by Texaco of a $1 billion bond in order to protect Pennzoil against Texaco's transferring or encumbering assets that otherwise would be available to Pennzoil if the Texas judgment was affirmed by the Texas appellate courts. Texaco promptly posted the $1 billion bond. Pennzoil, however, appealed the preliminary injunction. In its opinion, the Second Circuit considered the allegedly irreparable harm that Texaco would suffer without the injunction, as well as other requisites of injunctive relief, and affirmed the trial judge's decision:

In this circuit the standard for issuance of preliminary injunctive relief is well-settled. The plaintiff has the burden of showing irreparable harm *and* (1) either probable success on the merits *or* (2) sufficiently serious questions going to the merits to make them a fair ground for litigation *plus* a balance of hardships tipping decidedly in the plaintiff's favor. . . . The effect of the grant or withholding of such relief upon the public interest must also be considered. . . .

It is beyond dispute that, absent injunctive relief, enforcement of Texas' lien and supersedeas bond provisions would rapidly produce a catastrophe of major proportions, causing substantial harm to Texaco itself and to thousands of others throughout the United States, including stockholders, customers, and suppliers. Pennzoil concedes that Texaco, although it has a liquidation value of $22 billion and a net worth of about $23 billion, could not possibly post a bond or security in the sum of the approximately $12 billion that is mandated by Tex. R. Civ. P. 362(b). The simultaneous attachment of a lien pursuant to Tex. Prop. Code Ann. §§ 52.001 *et seq.* on Texaco's real property in Texas, valued at $5 billion, would seal the company's fate. Unable to finance its operations or obtain credit lines needed for its continued existence, Texaco, the fifth largest business organization in the United States, would be forced into bankruptcy or liquidation. . . .

Against the hardship to Texaco from denial of a stay the district court was required to balance the threat to Pennzoil's interests caused by granting the stay. A judgment creditor's primary concern when a judgment in his favor is stayed pending appeal is that he be "secure . . . from loss resulting from the stay of execution." . . .

In the present case there is no serious dispute that, should Texaco be required to liquidate its substantial assets, it would be able to pay Pennzoil's judgment in full. Texaco's financial statement shows that, as of December 1984, it had an appraised net worth of $22.622 billion. . . . [The] Chairman of Pennzoil's Board stated that . . . "he did not doubt Texaco's ability to pay the damages." . . .

Pennzoil argues, however, that any necessity for preliminary relief is dispelled by its "stipulation" that the Texas trial court may apply the standards of Fed. R. Civ. P. 62 to determine the security required of Texaco pending appeal. Pennzoil's "stipulation" does not solve the problems Texaco faces in this action. . . . It is doubtful that a Texas trial court . . . would consider itself any more jurisdictionally obligated, much less willing, to obey Pennzoil's request, than it would be to apply Chinese or Russian procedural law simply because one party requested it. . . .

[The court also held that federal jurisdiction existed to grant the preliminary injunction, and that it was within the authority of the District Court, although the district judge did not have power to reconsider and decide other claims that had been presented to and resolved by the Texas courts.] . . .

NOTES AND QUESTIONS

(1) *The Supreme Court Reversed This Decision: Pennzoil Co. v. Texaco, Inc., 481 U.S. 1 (1987).* The Supreme Court overturned Texaco's injunction. The Court's unanimous decision rested on abstention grounds, stating, "Both the District Court and the Court of Appeals failed to recognize the significant interests harmed by their unprecedented intrusion into the Texas judicial system. Similarly, neither of those courts applied the appropriate standard in determining whether adequate relief was available in the Texas courts . . . ." Texaco immediately requested a stay from a Texas Court — which granted a temporary stay for one week until a full hearing could be held. On the sixth day, however, pressure from creditors and vendors was so strong that Texaco obtained a stay by filing a bankruptcy petition.

(2) *Pennzoil's Potential Interests in the Supersedeas Bond.* Does the Second Circuit's approach fully protect Pennzoil's legitimate interests? Imagine a litigant in Texaco's position that might be willing to take steps during the several years of pendency of appeals to frustrate recovery of the judgment. Hypothetically, such a litigant could arrange its affairs so as to favor other creditors (including suppliers who contracted with it after the plaintiff obtained judgment). In some cases, it might structure its transactions so as to provide maximum protection to holders of its securities as against the judgment holder. If faced with a definitive adverse ruling, it might have strong motive to undertake eleventh-hour transactions for these purposes while staving off enforcement by last-ditch applications for discretionary review. It also might seek the protection of the bankruptcy courts, years after the judgment.

(3) *The Merits of the Texas Supersedeas Approach Compared to Those of Federal Rule 62; Amendment of the Texas Rule.* The ostensible virtue of the federal approach under Rule 62 is that it is more flexible. On the other hand, doesn't the Texas approach have merit? It provides better assurance that the appellee — who, after all, has gone through all of the steps necessary to obtain a jury verdict and the judgment of a district court, often many years after the claimed injury — will find its judgment effectively collectible upon the exhaustion of appeals. [After this decision, Texas amended its rule to allow reduction of the bond if the amount required is likely to cause the judgment debtor substantial economic harm. *See* Tex. R. App. P. 24.2(b). Other amendments set the amount of the bond or other security at "the sum of compensatory damages awarded in the judgment," interest for the estimated duration of the appeal and costs, but cap the amount of the bond or other security at the lesser of 50 percent of the judgment debtor's net worth or 25 million dollars. Tex. R. App. P. 24.2(a).]

(4) *The Due Process Issue.* After *Pennzoil,* must a state procedural system provide a means for staying execution pending appeal? If so, must that mechanism resemble Fed. R. Civ. P. 62? *See also* Carlson, *Mandatory Supersedeas Bond Requirements: A Denial of Due Process Rights?*, 39 Baylor L. Rev. 29 (1987).

[C] The Record, Briefs, and Submission

The Record. After the notice and cost bond have been filed, the appellant has the responsibility for getting the trial court record prepared and filed. As a general proposition, any error that is raised on appeal must appear in the record. The record also must show that the error is reversible under the appropriate standard of review. In federal practice, Appellate Rules 10 and 11 indicate how the record is prepared and forwarded to the appellate court. *See* Fed. R. App. P. 10, 11.

Briefs, Submission, and (If Allowed) Oral Argument. After the record is filed the appellant is required to file a brief "within 40 days" unless this time is extended by court order "for good cause shown." *See* Fed. R. App. P. 31(a); Fed. R. App. P. 26 (Computation and Extension of Time). If no appellant's brief is filed within the time provided, an appellee may move for dismissal of the appeal. Fed. R. App. P. 31(c). The appellee is required to file a brief within 30 days after service of the appellant's brief or "the appellee will not be heard at oral argument except by permission of the court." Fed. R. App. P. 31(a), (c). The appellant may serve and file a reply brief within 14 days after service of the appellee's brief. Fed. R. App. P. 31(a). After briefs have been filed, the case is ready, or should be ready, for "submission." Submission may involve oral argument, but when the facts and legal arguments are adequately presented in the briefs, it is not uncommon for oral argument to be curtailed or eliminated altogether. *See* Fed. R. App. P. 34. In fact, although oral argument may seem more dramatic, experienced appellate advocates generally agree that in a well-prepared court, the brief is much, much more important.

Form of the Brief. The form and contents of briefs are set out in Fed. R. App. P. 28.

§ 12.03 Appealable Orders

Read 28 U.S.C. § 1291 (the final decision rule).

[A] The Final Judgment Rule

NOTE ON AUTHORIZATION OF SUPREME COURT RULES

The "Judicial Improvements Act of 1990" amended 28 U.S.C. § 2072 (The Rules Enabling Act) to give the Supreme Court rulemaking authority to specify the terms and conditions under which District Court decisions should be treated as "final" for purposes of 28 U.S.C. § 1291.

COOPERS & LYBRAND v. LIVESAY
437 U.S. 463 (1978)

MR. JUSTICE STEVENS delivered the opinion of the Court.

The question in this case is whether a district court's determination that an action may not be maintained as a class action pursuant to Fed. R. Civ. Proc. 23 is a "final decision" . . . within the meaning of 28 U.S.C. § 1291 and therefore appealable as a matter of right. Because there is a conflict in the Circuits over this issue, we granted certiorari and now hold that such an order is not appealable under § 1291.

Petitioner, Coopers & Lybrand, is an accounting firm that certified the financial statements in a prospectus issued in connection with a 1972 public offering of securities in Punta Gorda Isles for an aggregate price of over $18 million. Respondents purchased securities in reliance on that prospectus. In its next annual report to shareholders, Punta Gorda restated the earnings that had been reported in the prospectus for 1970 and 1971 by writing down its net income for each year by over $1 million. Thereafter, respondents sold their Punta Gorda securities and sustained a loss of $2,650 on their investment.

Respondents filed this action on behalf of themselves and a class of similarly situated purchasers. They alleged that petitioner and other defendants had violated various sections of the Securities Act of 1933 and the Securities Exchange Act of 1934. The District Court first certified, and then, after further proceedings, decertified the class.

Respondents did not request the District Court to certify its order for interlocutory review under 28 U.S.C. § 1292(b). Rather, they filed a notice of appeal pursuant to § 1291. The Court of Appeals regarded its appellate jurisdiction as depending on whether the decertification order had sounded the "death knell" of the action. After examining the amount of respondents' claims in relation to their financial resources and the probable cost of the litigation, the court concluded that they would not pursue their claims individually. The Court of Appeals therefore held that it had jurisdiction to hear the appeal and, on the merits, reversed the order decertifying the class.

. . . Federal appellate jurisdiction generally depends on the existence of a decision by the District Court that "ends the litigation on the merits and leaves nothing for the court to do but execute the judgment." An order refusing to certify, or decertifying, a class does not of its own force terminate the entire litigation because the plaintiff is free to proceed on his individual claim. Such an order is appealable, therefore, only if it comes within an appropriate exception to the final-judgment rule. . . .

I

[The Court first concluded that the denial of certification was not appealable under what is known as the "collateral order doctrine," which is discussed in a later section of this chapter, below.]

II

[T]he "death knell" doctrine assumes that without the incentive of a possible group recovery the individual plaintiff may find it economically imprudent to pursue his lawsuit to a final judgment and then seek appellate review of an adverse class determination. Without questioning this assumption, we hold that orders relating to class certification are not independently appealable under § 1291 prior to judgment. . . .

Though a refusal to certify a class is inherently interlocutory, it may induce a plaintiff to abandon his individual claim. On the other hand, the litigation will often survive an adverse class determination. What effect the economic disincentives created by an interlocutory order may have on the fate of any litigation will depend on a variety of factors.[15] . . .

In administering the "death knell" rule, the courts have used two quite different methods of identifying an appealable class ruling. Some courts have determined their jurisdiction by simply comparing the claims of the named plaintiffs with an arbitrarily selected jurisdictional amount; others have undertaken a thorough study of the possible impact of the class order on the fate of the litigation before determining their jurisdiction. Especially when consideration is given to the consequences of applying these tests to pretrial orders entered in non-class-action litigation, it becomes apparent that neither provides an acceptable basis for the exercise of appellate jurisdiction. . . .

The formulation of an appealability rule that turns on the amount of the plaintiff's claim is plainly a legislative, not a judicial, function. While Congress could grant an appeal of right to those whose claims fall below a specific amount in controversy, it has not done so. Rather, it has made "finality" the test of appealability. . . .

---

[15] *E.g.*, the plaintiff's resources; the size of his claim and his subjective willingness to finance prosecution of the claim; the probable cost of the litigation and the possibility of joining others who will share that cost; and the prospect of prevailing on the merits and reversing an order denying class certification.

While slightly less arbitrary, the alternative approach to the "death knell" rule would have a serious debilitating effect on the administration of justice. It requires class-action plaintiffs to build a record in the trial court that contains evidence of those factors deemed relevant to the "death knell" issue and district judges to make appropriate findings. . . .

The potential waste of judicial resources is plain. The district court must take evidence, entertain argument, and make findings; and the court of appeals must review that record and those findings simply to determine whether a discretionary class determination is subject to appellate review. And if the record provides an inadequate basis for this determination, a remand for further factual development may be required. Moreover, even if the court makes a "death knell" finding and reviews the class designation order on the merits, there is no assurance that the trial process will not again be disrupted by interlocutory review. For even if a ruling that the plaintiff does not adequately represent the class is reversed on appeal, the district court may still refuse to certify the class on the ground that, for example, common questions of law or fact do not predominate. Under the "death knell" theory, plaintiff would again be entitled to an appeal as a matter of right pursuant to § 1291. And since other kinds of interlocutory orders may also create the risk of a premature demise, the potential for multiple appeals in every complex case is apparent and serious.

Perhaps the principal vice of the "death knell" doctrine is that it authorizes *indiscriminate* interlocutory review of decisions made by the trial judge. The Interlocutory Appeals Act of 1958, 28 U.S.C. § 1292(b), was enacted to meet the recognized need for prompt review of certain nonfinal orders.

[Here, the Court discusses appeals by permission under § 1292(b), which are referred to as "discretionary" appeals and which are considered later in this chapter. The present appeal has not been taken in compliance with § 1292(b). Moreover, the Court points out that "Congress carefully confined the availability of such review" by requiring certain conditions and providing for "screening," in the form of discretion at both the trial and appellate court levels, governing whether the appeal may be taken. The death knell doctrine "circumvents these restrictions," the Court concludes.]

. . . Additional considerations reinforce our conclusion that the "death knell" doctrine does not support appellate jurisdiction of prejudgment orders denying class certification. First, the doctrine operates only in favor of plaintiffs even though the class issue — whether to certify, and if so, how large the class should be — will often be of critical importance to the defendant as well. [M]oreover, allowing appeals of right from nonfinal orders that turn on the facts of a particular case thrusts appellate courts indiscriminately into the trial process and thus defeats one vital purpose of the final-judgment rule — "that of maintaining the appropriate relationship between the respective courts. . . . This goal, in the absence of most compelling reasons to the contrary, is very much worth preserving." . . .

Accordingly, we hold that the fact that an interlocutory order may induce a party to abandon his claim before final judgment is not a sufficient reason for considering it a "final decision" within the meaning of § 1291. The judgment of the Court of Appeals is reversed with directions to dismiss the appeal.

NOTE ON AMENDMENT OF RULE 23

An amendment in 1998 added a new subdivision (f) to Rule 23. Rule 23(f) provides that a court of appeals "may permit an appeal from an order granting or denying class-action certification." This amendment changes the holding in *Coopers & Lybrand* in the narrow context of class actions. The certification decision, whichever way it is made, is so important to the viability of the action that a discretionary immediate appeal makes sense.

In other contexts, however, the *Coopers & Lybrand* holding remains viable. The general rule is that non-final orders, also called interlocutory orders, are not appealable.

NOTE ON THE FINAL JUDGMENT RULE

(1) *What the Rule Means: The Judgment Generally Must Be Final as to All Parties, All Claims, and All Requested Grounds of Relief.* The final judgment rule means that a judgment must dispose of the claim, not merely of some aspect of the claim. But it also means a great deal more than that; as the Supreme Court says in *Coopers & Lybrand v. Livesay*, a final judgment generally is one that "terminate[s] the entire litigation." Thus, as a general rule, the judgment must dispose of all claims and defenses in the case, must be final as to all parties, and must adjudicate all grounds for relief. Because students sometimes have difficulty with this concept, we will consider some examples here before going on. *See generally* Note, *Appealability in the Federal Courts,* 75 Harv. L. Rev. 351 (1961).

(2) *Some Examples.* Imagine that Plaintiff P sues two defendants, D1 and D2. Imagine further that Defendant D1 moves for summary judgment, and the trial court grants the motion. Is there a final judgment? The answer: No, because P's claim against D2 remains pending, and so the judgment is not final as to the "entire" litigation. For another example, imagine that P sues a single defendant D, asserting four different claims. The trial court dismisses the first two claims on the ground that they fail to state any basis upon which relief can be granted. Is the dismissal order a final judgment? Again, the answer is "No," because the plaintiff's other two claims are still pending.

(3) *The Policy Reasons for the Final Judgment Rule.* As the Supreme Court indicated in *Coopers & Lybrand,* the foremost policy underlying the final judgment rule is that of efficiency. Piecemeal appeals are wasteful. If P were to appeal the summary judgment granted to D1, and later appeal the outcome of his claim against D2, judicial and private resources would twice be devoted to the same factual context and perhaps to overlapping issues of law. Moreover, piecemeal appeals may cause delay, as final disposition awaits appellate decision of the correctness of some intermediate step. Finally, there is the more subtle matter of what *Coopers & Lybrand* calls "the appropriate relationship between the respective courts." If a case is partly in the trial court and partly in the appellate court, conflicts may arise, or there may be ambiguities as to which court has authority to decide an issue.

(4) *Difficult Questions of Finality; Brown Shoe Co. v. United States, 370 U.S. 294 (1962).* Occasionally there are cases in which it is difficult to decide whether a judgment should be called "final." Consider, also, a case in which a trial court dismisses on *forum non conveniens* grounds but retains limited jurisdiction to ensure that the foreign forum is adequate. Is the judgment final? An issue remains open, but it is remote and speculative, and the practical termination of the action may effectively be unreviewable if the judgment is not considered final. In the *Brown Shoe* case, the District Court ordered divestiture of a company acquired in a merger attacked under the antitrust laws, but ongoing issues required continuing negotiations and determinations in response to future changing conditions. The Court held the order final and appealable in spite of these concerns. (Otherwise, it might never have become appealable!) Fortunately, the vast majority of cases do not present such difficult problems.

(5) *Exceptions to the Finality Requirement.* A more significant concern arises in the case of orders that ought to be immediately appealable even though it is clear they are not final. (Non-final orders are called "interlocutory" orders.) For example, a preliminary injunction may irreparably alter the status quo, causing ongoing harm if not appealed until the end of the case. And sometimes, it may be more efficient to appeal a significant interlocutory order, such as when reversal would avoid the need for a complicated trial. As *Coopers & Lybrand* points out, there are special appeal mechanisms for just such cases. These mechanisms are considered in the later sections of this chapter.

(6) *Rule 54(b) and Sears v. Mackey.* In the case that follows, the trial court dismisses two of four claims, leaving the other two pending. The dismissal order, obviously, would normally not be final. But this case — *Sears Roebuck & Co. v. Mackey* — involves a special consideration. In effect, Rule 54(b) gives the trial judge the power artificially to make some non-final orders into final judgments by including certain recitations in them.

[B] Rule 54(b) Certification and Appealable Interlocutory Orders

Read 28 U.S.C. § 1292(a)-(b) (appealable interlocutory orders); also, read Fed. R. Civ. P. 54(b) (final judgment in cases involving multiple claims).

[1] Rule 54(b): Making the Judgment Final

SEARS, ROEBUCK & CO. v. MACKEY, 351 U.S. 427 (1956). The plaintiffs brought suit against Sears on four distinct claims. The district judge dismissed two of the claims without leave to amend. Pursuant to Rule 54(b) of the Federal Rules of Civil Procedure, the order of dismissal expressly directed that judgment be "entered" for Sears on the two dismissed claims and also expressly determined that there was "no just reason for delay" in entering judgment. These provisions ostensibly made the order into a "final judgment" under Rule 54(b). However, when plaintiff Mackey appealed, Sears moved to dismiss the appeal, contending that the trial court's order was not a "final decision" and could not be appealed under 28 U.S.C. § 1291, which provides that "The courts of appeals shall have jurisdiction of appeals from all final decisions of the district courts. . . ." The Seventh Circuit refused to dismiss the appeal. Sears then sought and obtained a writ of certiorari in the Supreme Court to determine the validity and proper interpretation of Fed. R. Civ. P. 54(b).

The Supreme Court first explained that the original formulation of Rule 54(b) had created confusion. The older Rule 54(b) allowed appeal of certain kinds of orders adjudicating "separable" claims, and the difficulty of interpreting this requirement meant that appealability often was unclear. Furthermore, since the application of the older Rule 54(b) did not depend upon findings by the trial court, litigants sometimes could not tell whether they might be required to appeal an interlocutory order upon pain of losing the right to appeal it. The volume of appeals swelled because prudent litigants took immediate appeals of any interlocutory orders whose appealability was in doubt. Nevertheless, the old Rule was upheld as valid. After thus discussing the old Rule and its deficiencies, the Court examined Rule 54(b) in its current, amended form:

> In this form, it does not relax the finality required of each decision, as an individual claim, to render it appealable, but it does provide a practical means of permitting an

appeal to be taken from one or more final decisions on individual claims, in multiple claims actions, without waiting for final decisions to be rendered on *all* the claims in the case. The amended rule does not apply to a single claim action nor to a multiple claims action in which all of the claims have been finally decided. It is limited expressly to multiple claims actions in which "one or more but less than all" of the multiple claims have been finally decided and are found otherwise to be ready for appeal.

To meet the demonstrated need for flexibility, the District Court is used as a "dispatcher." It is permitted to determine, in the first instance, the appropriate *time when each "final decision"* upon "one or more but less than all" of the claims in a multiple claims action is ready for appeal. This arrangement already has lent welcome certainty to the appellate procedure. Its "negative effect" has met with uniform approval. The effect so referred to is the rule's specific requirement that for "one or more but less than all" multiple claims to become appealable, the District Court must make both "an express determination that there is no just reason for delay" and "an express direction for the entry of judgment." A party adversely affected by a final decision thus knows that his time for appeal will *not* run against him until this certification has been made.

In the instant case, the District Court made this certification, but Sears, Roebuck & Co. nevertheless moved to dismiss the appeal for lack of appellate jurisdiction under § 1291. The grounds for such a motion ordinarily might be (1) that the judgment of the District Court was not a decision upon a "claim for relief," (2) that the decision was not a "final decision" in the sense of an ultimate disposition of an individual claim entered in the course of a multiple claims action, or (3) that the District Court abused its discretion in certifying the order.

In the case before us, there is no doubt that each of the claims dismissed is a "claim for relief" within the meaning of Rule 54(b), or that their dismissal constitutes a "final decision" on individual claims. Also, it cannot well be argued that the claims stated in Counts I and II are so inherently inseparable from, or closely related to, those stated in Counts III and IV that the District Court has abused its discretion in certifying that there exists no just reason for delay. They certainly *can* be decided independently of each other.[a]

Petitioner contends that amended Rule 54(b) attempts to make an unauthorized extension of § 1291. We disagree. . . .

. . . The District Court *cannot*, in the exercise of its discretion, treat as "final" that which is not "final" within the meaning of § 1291. But the District Court *may*, by the exercise of its discretion in the interest of sound judicial administration, release for appeal final decisions upon one or more, but less than all, claims in multiple claims action. . . .

Rule 54(b) . . . is [an] exercise of the rule-making authority of this Court. It does not supersede any statute controlling appellate jurisdiction. It scrupulously recognizes the statutory requirement of a "final decision" under § 1291 as a basic requirement for an appeal to the Court of Appeals. . . . By its negative effect, it operates to restrict in a valid manner the number of appeals in multiple claims actions.

We reach a like conclusion as to the validity of the amended rule where the District Court acts affirmatively and thus assists in properly timing the release of final decisions

---

[a] [The Court elsewhere pointed out that Count I was based on the Sherman Act, to which Counts III and IV did not even refer. Count II similarly was independent of III and IV. — Eds.]

in multiple claims actions. . . . Just as Rule 54(b), in its original form, resulted in the release of some decisions on claims in multiple claims actions before they otherwise would have been released, so amended Rule 54(b) now makes possible the release of more of such decisions subject to judicial supervision. The amended rule preserves the historic federal policy against piecemeal appeals in many cases more effectively than did the original rule.

Accordingly, the appellate jurisdiction of the Court of Appeals is sustained, and its judgment denying the motion to dismiss the appeal for lack of appellate jurisdiction is affirmed.

[The dissenting opinion of Justice Frankfurter, with whom Justice Harlan joined, is omitted].

NOTES AND QUESTIONS

(1) *One Final Judgment Rule.* Recall the social policies that support the general "one final judgment" rule. Is current Rule 54(b) consistent with those policies?

(2) *Defining a Claim.* For Rule 54(b) purposes, what is a claim? Can an order determining liability be appealed if the District Court "dispatches" it to the Court of Appeals, even though damages have not been determined?

[2] The "Collateral Order" Doctrine

COHEN v. BENEFICIAL INDUSTRIAL LOAN CORP., 337 U.S. 541 (1949). In a stockholder's derivative action brought in a federal District Court in New Jersey on diversity grounds, the trial judge denied the defendant's motion to require the plaintiff to give security for costs. The defendant's motion was based on a New Jersey statute that dealt with derivative actions against corporations. The trial judge held that the statute did not apply in federal court. The Court of Appeals reversed. The Supreme Court affirmed the reversal, but first it considered whether the order denying security, which obviously was an interlocutory order, properly could be appealed:

> At the threshold we are met with the question whether the District Court's order refusing to apply the statute was an appealable one. Title 28 U.S.C. 1948 ed § 1291 provides, as did its predecessors, for appeal only "from all final decisions of the district courts." . . .
>
> The effect of the statute is to disallow appeal from any decision which is tentative, informal or incomplete. Appeal gives the upper court a power of review, not one of intervention. So long as the matter remains open, unfinished or inconclusive, there may be no intrusion by appeal. But the District Court's action upon this application was concluded and closed and its decision final in that sense before the appeal was taken.
>
> Nor does the statute permit appeals, even from fully consummated decisions, where they are but steps towards final judgment in which they will merge. The purpose is to combine in one review all stages of the proceeding that effectively may be reviewed and corrected if and when final judgment results. But this order of the District Court did not make any step toward final disposition of the merits of the case and will not be merged in final judgment. When that time comes, it will be too late effectively to review the present order and the rights conferred by the statute, if it is applicable,

will have been lost, probably irreparably. We conclude that the matters embraced in the decision appealed from are not of such an interlocutory nature as to affect, or to be affected by, decision of the merits of this case.

This decision appears to fall in that small class which finally determine claims of right separable from, and collateral to, rights asserted in the action, too important to be denied review and too independent of the cause itself to require that appellate consideration be deferred until the whole case is adjudicated. The Court has long given this provision of the statute this practical rather than a technical construction. . . .

We hold this order appealable because it is a final disposition of a claimed right which is not an ingredient of the cause of action and does not require consideration with it. But we do not mean that every order fixing security is subject to appeal. Here it is the right to security that presents a serious and unsettled question. If the right were admitted or clear and the order involved only an exercise of discretion as to the amount of security, a matter the statute makes subject to reconsideration from time to time, appealability would present a different question. . . .

NOTES AND QUESTIONS

(1) *What Isn't a Collateral Order: Coopers & Lybrand, Above; Stringfellow v. Concerned Neighbors in Action, 480 U.S. 370 (1987).* "Concerned Neighbors" sought to intervene in litigation about a nearby toxic waste dump. The District Court allowed only very limited intervention, and Concerned Neighbors attempted to appeal. The Supreme Court held that the collateral order rule was not applicable because the denial of intervention was completely redressable in the main appeal (*i.e.*, if Concerned Neighbors could show error that affected the result, it could obtain reversal and a new trial). *See also Lauro Lines S.R.L. v. Chasser*, 490 U.S. 495 (1989) (district court's denial of dismissal pursuant to a forum selection clause was not an appealable collateral order because after a loss on the merits, defendant could appeal and secure reversal to enforce the forum clause; although "not perfect[]," this review "adequately" secured defendant's rights). Remember that, in *Coopers & Lybrand*, above, the Court held that the collateral order doctrine did not allow appeal of the denial of class certification. Why not? [Note: What factors govern class certification, and are they unrelated to the merits?] Today, by rule amendment, there is an appeal in class certification decisions (see the Note following the cases above).

(2) *Civil Rights Immunity Determinations (cf. Siegert v. Gilley, Ch. 5) as Collateral Orders: Williams v. Collins, 728 F.2d 721 (5th Cir. 1984).* Remember (from Chapter 5) that a defense of immunity to a civil rights claim not only prevents a public official's liability; it is designed to prevent an innocent official from even the requirement of defending an unmeritorious suit beyond the earliest stages. In the *Williams* case, the court held that denial of immunity was an appealable collateral order. Does this holding seem correct? The appealability of immunity denials seems inconsistent, however. *Compare Johnson v. Jones,* 515 U.S. 304 (1995) (denial of summary judgment was not appealable), *with Behrens v. Pelletier,* 516 U.S. 299 (1996) (denial of summary judgment, as well as denial of dismissal, was appealable).

(3) *What Else Isn't a Collateral Order: Cunningham v. Hamilton County, 527 U.S. 198 (1999).* A unanimous Supreme Court ruled that an order imposing discovery sanctions on an attorney is not immediately appealable even when the attorney no longer represents a party in the case. According to the Court, Rule 37(a) discovery sanctions are seldom completely separate from the merits, as the collateral order exception requires. Also,

immediate appeal would undermine the purpose of discovery sanctions and the judge's "discretion to structure a sanction in the most effective manner." Another example of something that is not a collateral order, according to the Seventh Circuit, is a federal district court's order refusing to certify a question of state law to the state's supreme court. In *Brown v. Argosy Gaming Co.*, 360 F.3d 703 (7th Cir. 2004), the court noted that certification is not among the statutory exceptions making interlocutory orders appealable under section 1292. The order also did not fall within the *Cohen* doctrine because an order denying certification does not conclusively determine the disputed issue, nor does it resolve an issue completely separate from the merits. Moreover, in this case, the order effectively would be reviewable if the district court were to issue a final order on the motion to dismiss.

(4) *The Scope of Collateral Orders Expands With the Adoption of Rule 23(f), Applicable Only to Class Actions.* As noted above, Rule 23(f) gives the court of appeals the discretion to permit an appeal from a district court order granting or denying class action certification. The scope of this discretion has been considered by courts from the First, Second, Third, Fourth, Seventh, Eleventh, and District of Columbia Circuits. The result is a melange of formulations. *In re Lorazepam & Clorazepate Antitrust Litigation*, 289 F.3d 98 (D.C. Cir. 2002), identified three circumstances under which immediate review of class certification decisions is ordinarily appropriate: "(1) when there is a death-knell situation for either the plaintiff or defendant that is independent of the merits of the underlying claims, coupled with a class certification decision by the district court that is questionable, taking into account the district court's discretion over class certification; (2) when the certification decision presents an unsettled and fundamental issue of law relating to class actions, important both to the specific litigation and generally, that is likely to evade end-of-the-case review; and (3) when the district court's class certification decision is manifestly erroneous." Since the petitioners' petition for review rested on a question of substantive antitrust law rather than an issue related to class certification, the D.C. Circuit denied interlocutory review.

[3] Injunctions and Receiverships: Section 1292(a)

LEVESQUE v. STATE OF MAINE, 587 F.2d 78 (1st Cir. 1978). Interlocutory appeals of decisions regarding injunctions are provided for in 28 U.S.C. § 1292(a)(1). The statute does not, by its terms, cover temporary restraining orders, although it does clearly extend to preliminary injunctions. Plaintiff Levesque was Commissioner of Manpower for the State of Maine for just under five years, leaving office in 1978. A factual dispute existed concerning whether the Governor had terminated him unlawfully and without cause, as Levesque contended, or whether he was removed for cause or simply resigned, as the state contended. He sought a temporary restraining order reinstating him and requiring a hearing prior to termination. The District Court denied the requested relief, and Levesque attempted to appeal. The court concluded that this particular temporary restraining order was to be treated as a preliminary injunction and that it therefore did have jurisdiction of the appeal:

> Temporary restraining orders are normally not appealable. . . . Exceptions to the general rule of nonappealability arise when the order in reality operates as a preliminary injunction . . . [or is in reality a final order].
>
> [To apply the first exception, the court] must find either that a full adversary hearing has been provided or that, in the absence of review, further interlocutory relief is unavailable. . . .

The trial court denied the requested order reinstating Levesque to his position and denied the request for a pre-termination hearing. The court . . . concluded that . . . [Levesque's] interests would be protected through a post-termination hearing. . . . [T]he court suggested that defendants begin the process of providing a post-termination hearing . . . one month following the lower court's decision. This means, of course, that, in fashioning this order, relief broader than that normally available under a temporary restraining order, whose duration is limited to ten days, Fed. R. Civ. P. 65(b), was envisioned by the court.

. . . [P]laintiff is effectively foreclosed from pursuing further interlocutory relief in the form of a preliminary injunction which would request the same remedy to which the court has already determined he is not entitled. Therefore, . . . we think this is the unusual case where denial of a temporary restraining order is tantamount to denial of a preliminary injunction and, hence, appealable under 28 U.S.C. § 1292(a)(1).

[The court went on, however, to affirm the trial court's denial of relief to Levesque on the merits.]

[4] "Discretionary" Appeals: Section 1292(b)

GARNER v. WOLFINBARGER

433 F.2d 117 (5th Cir. 1970)

GODBOLD, CIRCUIT JUDGE:

Plaintiffs sued the corporation in which they are shareholders, and various of the corporate directors, officers and controlling persons, claiming violations of federal and state securities laws, fraud and other wrongs. The District Court for the Northern District of Alabama transferred the cause to the Southern District of Alabama under 28 U.S.C. § 1404(a). The plaintiffs seek to review that order by interlocutory appeal under 28 U.S.C. § 1292(b). [The District Court certified to the factors required for appeal under § 1292(b).] . . .

This court granted permission for a § 1292(b) appeal from the transfer order but reserved ultimate determination of the appropriateness of the appeal for consideration along with the merits. We conclude that leave to appeal was improvidently granted. Also we deny the petition for mandamus.

To attempt to get within § 1292(b), the plaintiffs grasp for a controlling question of law as to which there is substantial ground for a difference of opinion by contending that a plaintiff's choice of forum should always be respected in actions brought under the Securities Act of 1933 and the Securities Act of 1934. . . .

This court has used the procedure of § 1292(b) to review both questions of law and the discretion of the trial judge in transfer cases. But we have not squarely adjudicated the propriety of review of discretion under § 1292(b). . . .

We are of the view that § 1292(b) review is inappropriate for challenges to a judge's discretion in granting or denying transfers under § 1404(a). The Congressional policy against piecemeal appeals, as expressed in the final judgment rule, 28 U.S.C. § 1291, to which § 1292(b) is a narrow exception, is eroded by permitting review of exercise of the judge's discretion under § 1404(a) as a "controlling question of law." Our conclusion is the same as that already reached by the Second, Third, and Sixth Circuits, and by the text writers. . . .

. . . There are several considerations against piecemeal appeals. It is contrary to the language of § 1292(b), which is in terms of the appealability where "*such order* involves a controlling question of law." The issue is not one of convenience to the litigants, or even to this court, but of appellate jurisdiction. The ad hoc approach invites the parties to inject a sham issue as the vehicle to bring the case to this court at the interlocutory stage for a declaration on an order not otherwise reviewable. And it confuses the courts and the parties, who assume that because a discretionary transfer order has been reviewed in one case it can be reviewed in any other. . . .

The transfer order is affirmed. . . .

JOHN R. BROWN, CHIEF JUDGE, concurring and dissenting in part:

I agree that the transfer from the Northern to the Southern District of Alabama should not be disturbed. . . . But I dissent as to the Court's holding that § 1292(b) is not available to test the grant or the denial of a transfer under § 1404(a) when the issue is the so-called "abuse of discretion" by the trial Judge. . . .

I think it is regrettable that we undertake to fix rigid classes of cases which are beyond the reach of § 1292(b). Our prior cases show the great utility of this device which is so flexible. I am positive that Judge Godbold sounds for all of the members of the full Court the concern that we have been too lax in allowing § 1292(b) appeals. We have of late, after argument, vacated such orders in a number of cases where we felt the allowance was improvidently granted. But the protection against such a practice is not to needlessly encumber a flexible apparatus. Rather it is for each of us to exercise great restraint so that only cases of any or every character which meet the controlling issue test as outlined here may be taken on interlocutory appeal. Indeed this is the answer to the criticism that our prior practice is too ad hoc. . . .

Section 1292(b) has worked well for us. We have taken a position much more adaptable, less rigid than other Circuits. . . . We do not need to fashion a rule that, while freeing us from the travail of our calling, unnecessarily ties our hands in a specific type of case to thus begin a construction of the statute which will become more and more technical.

NOTES AND QUESTIONS

(1) *Procedure.* Consider the exact procedure that must be followed under 28 U.S.C. § 1292(b). Given the facts that: (1) the trial judge must certify that the interlocutory order "involves a controlling question of law as to which there is substantial ground for difference of opinion and that an immediate appeal from the order may materially advance the ultimate termination of the litigation"; and (2) the Court of Appeals has "discretion" to "permit [or deny] an appeal," is there any real likelihood that § 1292(b) will be abused? Has Congress, in fact, authorized *ad hoc* review of interlocutory orders by enacting § 1292(b)? *See generally* Note, *Interlocutory Appeals in the Federal Courts Under 28 U.S.C.A. § 1292(b)*, 88 Harv. L. Rev. 607 (1975).

(2) *Controlling Question of Law.* How is the phrase "controlling question of law" interpreted in the principal case? Does the case hold that all interlocutory orders involving discretion are outside the purview of § 1292(b)?

(3) *Other Approaches to Interlocutory Review.* Section 1292 reflects two fundamentally different approaches to the problem of interim review of interlocutory orders. Subsection (a) identifies particular interlocutory orders and makes them appealable all of the time. Subsection (b) does not restrict itself to particular orders but its provisions are only

available when both the trial and appellate judges believe that an interlocutory appeal is appropriate.

[C] Mandamus and Other Writs

Read 28 U.S.C. § 1651 (the "All Writs Act," which authorizes issuance of mandamus and other writs by trial and appellate courts).

KERR v. UNITED STATES DISTRICT COURT, 511 F.2d 192 (9th Cir.), *aff'd*, 426 U.S. 394 (1976). This case appears in § 1.06 of Chapter 1, above, and should be read again at this point. The case was a class action brought by prisoners in the custody of the California Department of Corrections in which the plaintiffs sought to discover documents over the defendants' objection that the documents were confidential and privileged. The District Court ordered production of the documents. The defendants filed two petitions for a writ of mandamus under 28 U.S.C. § 1651(a), requesting the Court of Appeals to vacate the District Court's discovery order. The Court of Appeals denied both requests. On certiorari, the Supreme Court affirmed the Court of Appeals and explained why the remedy of mandamus was unavailable:

> The remedy of mandamus is a drastic one, to be invoked only in extraordinary situations. . . . As we have observed, the writ "has traditionally been used in the federal courts only 'to confine an inferior court to a lawful exercise of its prescribed jurisdiction or to compel it to exercise its authority when it is its duty to do so.' " . . . And, while we have not limited the use of mandamus by an unduly narrow and technical understanding of what constitutes a matter of "jurisdiction," . . . the fact still remains that "only exceptional circumstances amounting to a judicial 'usurpation of power' will justify the invocation of this extraordinary remedy." . . .
>
> Our treatment of mandamus within the federal court system as an extraordinary remedy is not without good reason. As we have recognized before, mandamus actions such as the one involved in the instant case "have the unfortunate consequence of making the [District Court] judge a litigant, obliged to obtain personal counsel or to leave his defense to one of the litigants [appearing] before him" in the underlying case. . . .
>
> . . . More importantly, particularly in an era of excessively crowded lower court dockets, it is in the interest of the fair and prompt administration of justice to discourage piecemeal litigation. It has been Congress' determination since the Judiciary Act of 1789 that as a general rule "appellate review should be postponed . . . until after final judgment has been rendered by the trial court." . . . A judicial readiness to issue the writ of mandamus in anything less than an extraordinary situation would run the real risk of defeating the very policies sought to be furthered by that judgment of Congress.
>
> As a means of implementing the rule that the writ will issue only in extraordinary circumstances, we have set forth various conditions for its issuance. Among these are that the party seeking issuance of the writ have no other adequate means to attain the relief he desires, . . . and that he satisfy "the burden of showing that [his] right to issuance of the writ is 'clear and indisputable.' " . . .
>
> Moreover, it is important to remember that issuance of the writ is in large part a matter of discretion with the court to which the petition is addressed. . . .
>
> When looked at in the framework of these factors, it would appear that the actions of the Court of Appeals in this case should be affirmed. What petitioners are seeking

here is not a declaration that the documents in question are absolutely privileged and that plaintiffs can never have access to any of them. On the contrary, petitioners request only that "production of the confidential documents not be compelled without a prior informed determination by the district court that plaintiffs' need for them in the action below outweighs their confidentiality." . . . Petitioners ask in essence only that the District Court review the challenged documents in camera before passing on whether each one individually should or should not be disclosed. But the Court of Appeals' opinion dealing with the Adult Authority files did not foreclose the possible necessity of such in camera review. Its denial of the writ was based largely on the grounds that the governmental privilege had not been asserted personally by anyone eligible to assert it, and that it had not been asserted with the requisite specificity. The court apparently left open the opportunity for petitioners to return to the District Court, assert the privilege more specifically and through responsible officials, and then have their request for an in camera review of the materials by the District Court reconsidered in a different light. . . .

We are thus confident that the Court of Appeals did in fact intend to afford the petitioners the opportunity to apply for and, upon proper application, receive in camera review. Accordingly the orders of the Court of Appeals are affirmed.

NOTES AND QUESTIONS

(1) *Availability of Mandamus: LaBuy v. Howes Leather Co., 352 U.S. 249 (1957).* As the principal case shows, the federal courts are reluctant to issue writs of mandamus in discovery matters, which generally involve highly discretionary interest balancing. The absence (or abuse) of discretion must be clear. For an example of the successful use of mandamus, consider *La Buy v. Howes Leather Co.*, in which the District Court referred a garden variety antitrust case to a master. The Supreme Court upheld the appellate court's writ of mandamus, because reference to a master is confined to "extraordinary" cases, and thus, the abuse of discretion was clear. *See also* Ward, *Can the Federal Courts Keep Order in Their Own House? Appellate Supervision Through Mandamus and Orders of Judicial Councils,* 1980 B.Y.U. L. Rev. 233.

(2) *Habeas Corpus.* One method of testing a pretrial order compelling conduct such as the production of documents is by temporarily refusing to obey the order and having oneself held in (civil) contempt. The lawfulness of the order of contempt depends, in these circumstances, on the lawfulness of the order that is being enforced. Thus, once the trial court has adjudicated the attorney in contempt, he may seek a writ of habeas corpus in the Court of Appeals (usually after being admitted to bail pending the outcome). If the underlying order is invalid, the contempt adjudication is reversed; if not, the attorney usually can purge himself of the contempt by complying with the order. This method was used in *Hickman v. Taylor* (the "work product" case), which appears in Chapter 7, above.

[D] An Alternative System: New York's "Wide Open" Definition of Appealable Orders

Consider the following description of New York's approach to appealability, taken from O. Chase, *2 Weinstein, Korn & Miller, CPLR Manual* § 26.03 (1997). New York has what might be called a "wide open" definition of appealable orders with respect to appeals to its Appellate Division:

CPLR 5701 is the basic provision governing appeal . . . to the Appellate Division. All judgments, whether interlocutory or final, are appealable as of right, subject only to an exception designed to prevent appeal as of right when all the issues in the case have already been decided by the Appellate Division on an earlier appeal.

Most non-final orders are also appealable as of right. Paragraph 2 of CPLR 5701(a) is the basic provision governing these so-called intermediate appeals; it authorizes appeal as of right from seven enumerated classes of orders, including among them the broad catchall provisions for any order that "involves some part of the merits" or "affects a substantial right."

It is generally recognized that this broad authority for appeal as of right from almost every kind of intermediate determination is a prime source of delay and expense in litigation and imposes an undue burden on the Appellate Division. Nevertheless, only in orders on motions to require a more definite statement or to strike scandalous or prejudicial matter in a pleading and orders in Article 78 proceedings does CPLR 5701(b) require permission to appeal. . . .

California has a different but analogous system allowing broad appealability. *See* Cal. Code of Civ. Proc. §§ 904.1, 904.2. In contrast, Texas law is considerably more restrictive in its allowance of appeals before entry of a final judgment. *See* Tex. Civ. Prac. & Rem. C. § 51.014. What advantages, and what disadvantages, would a "wide open" system such as New York's have? (Appeals to New York's Court of Appeals, the State's highest court, generally may be taken only from final judgments and only by permission of that court. CPLR 5601–5602.)

§ 12.04 The Supreme Court

NOTE ON THE JURISDICTION OF THE SUPREME COURT

Read 28 U.S.C. §§ 1251-1254, 1257 (jurisdiction of the Supreme Court).

Review by Writ of Certiorari. A writ of certiorari (literally, "to be made more certain") is a discretionary order allowing review of a lower court's decision. In the Supreme Court, 28 U.S.C. § 1254(1) provides broad authority for review by writ of certiorari, "before or after rendition of judgment or decree." Review extends to decisions of both federal and state courts, provided the issue is one of federal law. Today, almost all of the cases reviewed by the Supreme Court are reviewed by certiorari. However, the Court receives thousands of petitions for certiorari annually, and it must deny most of them. The percentage granted varies from year to year, but generally has been considerably less than 5 percent.

Late in 1988, Congress passed and the President signed legislation giving the Supreme Court almost total discretionary control over its docket. In all cases except direct appeals (see below), review must now proceed by writ of certiorari. Representative Robert Kastenmeier, D-Wis., a leader in getting the legislation adopted, called the new law the "most significant jurisdictional reform affecting the high Court in over 60 years." ABA Journal, Sept. 1, 1988, at 33. The Supreme Court also adopted a new set of Rules effective January 1, 1990, in part to reflect its expanded discretionary jurisdiction.

Direct Appeal from District Courts. There is a very narrow class of cases in which appeal to the Supreme Court lies directly from the District Courts, bypassing the Courts of Appeals.

Original Jurisdiction: The Supreme Court as the "Trial" Court. The Supreme Court has original jurisdiction in a narrow class of cases defined by the Constitution, particularly those "in which a State shall be a Party." U.S. Const. art. III, § 2. Typical examples would include suits by one state against another concerning boundaries, water rights, or the right to tax. *Cf. Ohio v. Wyandotte Chemicals Corp.*, 401 U.S. 493 (1971) (Court had, but declined to exercise, original jurisdiction of suit by state against alleged polluters of Lake Erie).

PROCEDURE FOR REVIEW BY CERTIORARI OR APPEAL

The Petition for Certiorari. Invocation of the Supreme Court's discretionary jurisdiction is an esoteric art. The applicant files a petition for certiorari. The purpose of this document is not to argue the merits; instead, it is to convince the Court that there are "special and important reasons" (in the language of Supreme Court Rule 17.1) why the Court should make the case one of the very few it hears. *See* Prettyman, *Petitioning the United States Supreme Court — A Primer for Hopeful Neophytes*, 51 Va. L. Rev. 582 (1965). Paradoxically, a demonstration that the case is unique, or that it is an aberration, or even that it is opposed by unanimous contrary authority, may actually be counterproductive(!). Instead, citations showing that the issue has been considered by many courts, and that some have decided for the petitioner and some the other way, are likely to be more persuasive.

Grant or Denial of Certiorari; The "Rule of Four." Affirmative votes by four members of the Court suffice to grant certiorari. This convention is known as the "rule of four." Denial of certiorari is of no precedential value, and the principle is well established that it means only that there were not four members of the Court who chose to hear this particular case at this time. *See Hughes Tool Co. v. Trans World Airlines*, 409 U.S. 363 (1973); Linzer, *The Meaning of Certiorari Denials*, 79 Colum. L. Rev. 1227 (1979).

Principles Guiding the Certiorari Decision. Justice to the individual parties is the concern underlying the provision for intermediate appellate review; contrary to popular conception, however, it is not the purpose of certiorari. Supreme Court Rule 17.1 sets out certain circumstances in which certiorari is indicated. Among the most important are those in which there are intolerable conflicts between Courts of Appeals, or between a Court of Appeals and a state court of last resort, or those in which substantial issues of federal law have not been, but should be, decided by the Supreme Court. Thus review by certiorari addresses systemic problems, rather than problems of individual justice.

Adequate State Grounds. Review of state court decisions is limited to federal questions, and the Court will decline to review even important issues of federal law if the lower court's decision rests upon an "adequate state ground" (*i.e.*, if it could be upheld without reference to the federal issue). However, the Court has indicated a greater willingness to consider cases in which state and federal grounds are interwoven and the basis for decision is ambiguous. *Michigan v. Long*, 463 U.S. 1032 (1983).

CHAPTER 13

RES JUDICATA, COLLATERAL ESTOPPEL, AND RELATED PRECLUSION DOCTRINES

§ 13.01 Res Judicata: Claim Preclusion

[A] The Elements: "Same" Claim, "Same" Parties, Final Judgment

The Effect of Judgments. The doctrine of *res judicata* deals generally with the conclusive effect of judgments. The term itself (*res judicata*, meaning "the subject has been adjudicated") is sometimes used broadly, to encompass the separate doctrines of (1) "claim" preclusion, or merger and bar (precluding relitigation when a subsequent suit is brought on the same claim), and (2) "issue" preclusion, or collateral estoppel (precluding relitigation of an issue settled in a prior suit, even if on a different claim). Here, we deal with the broader doctrine of *res judicata* as "claim" preclusion; a later section of this book deals with "issue" preclusion, or collateral estoppel.

The Restatement View of Res Judicata. Sections 18 and 19 of the Restatement (Second) of Judgments set out the principles of claim preclusion in the following manner:*

> § 18. Judgment for Plaintiff — The General Rule of Merger
>
> When a valid and final personal judgment is rendered in favor of the plaintiff: (1) The plaintiff cannot thereafter maintain an action on the original claim or any part thereof, but he may be able to maintain an action upon the judgment; and (2) In an action upon the judgment, the defendant cannot avail himself of defenses he might have interposed, or did interpose, in the first action.
>
> § 19. Judgment for Defendant — The General Rule of Bar
>
> A valid and final personal judgment rendered in favor of the defendant bars another action by the plaintiff on the same claim.

Policies Served by Res Judicata. These rules are said to rest upon the policy of protecting a party from being twice vexed for the same cause, together with that of achieving judicial economy by precluding a party who has had a fair trial from relitigating the same matter. Other policy considerations include the prevention of double recovery and the promotion of the stability or finality of decisions. *See generally* Cleary, *Res Judicata Reexamined*, 57 Yale L.J. 339, 344-49 (1948).

The Elements of Res Judicata or Claim Preclusion. It is impossible accurately to summarize the doctrine of *res judicata* in a few words, because each word will be susceptible to varying interpretations. Nevertheless, it may be useful to outline the doctrine by referring to three "elements," if the reader is careful to remember that each "element" is really a shorthand phrase for a whole complex of subsidiary questions. With these thoughts in mind, one might say that *res judicata* requires:

1. An existing, valid, final judgment on the merits;
2. Between the "same" parties (or, in some cases, parties sufficiently closely related to the present parties);
3. Concerning the "same claim" (or same cause of action, or a cause of action sufficiently closely related to the present one).

Cf. Ray v. Tennessee Valley Authority, 677 F.2d 818, 821 (11th Cir. 1982).

Different Approaches. As this statement of the "elements" implies, different jurisdictions vary in the breadth of the preclusive effects that they afford to judgments. Some preclude only claims that are very closely similar to the prior claim. Here, we call this approach the "individualized" or "same evidence" approach. Other jurisdictions have adopted broader preclusive doctrines, which we call the "transactional analysis" or "broad procedural duty" approaches. In the cases that follow, you will see that New York originally used one approach, but it has changed to another approach in more recent cases.

PROBLEM A: CHAPTER 13 SUMMARY PROBLEM

FIRST BANK v. DONALDSON CORPORATION: A PROBLEM OF RES JUDICATA AND COLLATERAL ESTOPPEL. The Donaldson Corporation executed a guaranty agreement that guaranteed two different promissory notes of The Alpha Company. Both of the notes were in default, and Alpha was completely insolvent. Therefore, the holder of the notes, The First Bank and Trust Co., filed suit against Donaldson in a state court in the (hypothetical) State of West York, to enforce the guaranty and make the Donaldson Corporation pay Alpha's debt.

However, for some unknown business or tactical reason, the Bank included the amount of only *one* of the notes in this suit — the older one, which was longer in default. Donaldson Corporation alleged a defensive theory of "economic duress" in an attempt to avoid the guaranty, but the court granted summary judgment rejecting this defense without giving a reason (although the record showed that Donaldson Corporation had not properly responded to the summary judgment motion under state procedural law). Plaintiff Bank obtained a final state court judgment on the guaranty, awarding it the amount of the older note.

Later, the bank filed a second suit on the same guaranty, seeking to enforce it for the amount of the second note — the one omitted from the first suit. This time the Bank also joined James Donaldson personally as an additional defendant. James Donaldson had also signed the guaranty personally, and at all times he was president and sole shareholder of the Donaldson Corporation. The defendants again alleged the "economic duress" defense. All parties then alleged various theories of preclusion in the second suit.

1. Can the defendants successfully assert that the second claim is barred by *res judicata*?
2. Can the plaintiff collaterally estop either the Donaldson Corporation, or James Donaldson personally, from asserting economic duress again as a defense in the second suit?

3. If the second suit were to be brought in a federal court in a different state, could the result be different?

[B] The "Same Claim" Requirement: How Broad is a "Claim"?

[1] The "Individualized/Same Evidence" Approach

SMITH v. KIRKPATRICK
305 N.Y. 66, 111 N.E.2d 209 (1953)

[The plaintiff originally instituted suit on the basis of the defendant's alleged breach of an employment contract. The defendant denied the existence of the agreement and filed a motion for summary judgment on the ground that the agreement pleaded by the plaintiff did not comply with the statute of frauds. The defendant's motion was granted, and the plaintiff was granted leave to serve an amended complaint "so that he might sue for the value of his services."

[The plaintiff served a second complaint "to establish a partnership and to obtain an accounting" or "to establish that plaintiff and defendant were joint venturers" who each were entitled to share the profits of the venture equally. At trial without a jury, the trial judge dismissed the amended complaint because "plaintiff has failed to establish his causes of action by a fair preponderance of the credible evidence."

[The plaintiff did not appeal the final judgment denying him recovery.

[Subsequently, the plaintiff did institute a second action in *quantum meruit* seeking to recover the reasonable value of services rendered. The defendant answered and interposed the defense of *res judicata*. The trial judge denied the defendant's motion to dismiss but the Appellate Division reversed and dismissed the complaint.

[On appeal to the Court of Appeals of New York, that court considered the availability of the defense of *res judicata*.]

It is familiar law that where a cause of action has been prosecuted to a final adjudication on the merits, the *same cause of action* may not be again litigated. It is said that the prior adjudication is conclusive as to all things which might have been litigated as well as those actually litigated but that where a subsequent proceeding is had upon a different cause of action between the same parties or their privies only such things as were actually and necessarily determined in the prior proceeding are held to be concluded, *Cromwell v. County of Sac*, 94 U.S. 351, 24 L. Ed. 195. . . .

The determination of what constitutes the "same" or "different" cause of action is not a matter free from difficulty. The definition of the term "cause of action" is a variable one and depends upon the context in which it appears. . . . The test for determining whether or not "causes of action" are the "same" for purposes of *res judicata* has been variously expressed. . . . "A cause of action does not consist of facts, but of the unlawful violation of a right which the facts show. The number and variety of the facts alleged do not establish more than one cause of action so long as their result, whether they be considered severally or in combination, is the violation of but one right by a single legal wrong."

. . . And in the leading case of *Schuylkill Fuel Corp. v. B. & C. Nieberg Realty Corp.*, 250 N.Y. 304, 306-307, 165 N.E. 456, 457, Cardozo, Ch. J., we said that a "judgment in one action is conclusive in a later one, not only as to any matters actually litigated therein, but also as to any that might have been so litigated, when the two causes of action have such a measure of identity that a different judgment in the second would destroy or impair rights or interests established by the first. *Cromwell v. County of Sac*, 94 U.S. 351, 24 L. Ed. 195. . . . It is not conclusive, however, to the same extent when the two causes of action are different, not in form only (case cited), but in the rights and interests affected. . . ."

By his [first suit] the plaintiff sought to enforce a right which arose out of an express agreement and from defendant's asserted ownership of accounts procured by him. Defendant's alleged wrong was the misappropriation of those accounts and the proceeds thereof. Plaintiff's right to all profits save the 50% intended to compensate defendant for the use of his facilities, sprang from an alleged relationship, established by the express agreement, which, though vaguely expressed in the complaint, appears to have been in the nature of that existing between joint venturers, partners or landlord and tenant. The redress sought was, as we have seen, an accounting, judgment for moneys found due in accordance with the terms fixed by the agreement and the transfer of accounts belonging to plaintiff. In that action it was determined that defendant had no liability by reason of his being a party to the relationships alleged and that plaintiff's title to the accounts was not superior to that of defendant.

In the present action plaintiff's alleged right rests upon an implied contract. The relationship allegedly existing between the parties is somewhat analogous to that found between master and servant. The wrong alleged is defendant's acceptance and retention of benefits, conferred upon him by plaintiff, without payment in return of fair compensation. The relief now sought is merely the reasonable value of the services rendered to defendant at his request or with his consent.

The two actions involve different "rights" and "wrongs." The requisite elements of proof and hence the evidence necessary to sustain recovery vary materially. The cause of action are different and distinct and the rights and interests established by the previous adjudication will not be impaired by a recovery, if that be the outcome in *quantum meruit*.

. . .

Defendant does not urge that the determination of [the trial court] — that the contract alleged in the first complaint failed to comply with the Statute of Frauds — bars the present action. Indeed he could not. Upon the dismissal of the first complaint, plaintiff was given leave to amend. There was no final adjudication on the merits. The conclusiveness of the determination dismissing the first complaint is confined to the precise issue then determined. That being so, the order of dismissal is conclusive only as to the point that the contract alleged in the first complaint did not comply with the Statute of Frauds. That narrow determination is insufficient to preclude the present action, the plaintiff here being entitled to a construction of his complaint most favorable to him.

NOTES AND QUESTIONS

(1) *Scope of Preclusion*. As the principal case indicates, under the "individualized/same evidence" approach to the definition of particular causes of action, even a minimal alteration of material facts may give rise to a new cause of action if the alteration makes available a new rule of substantive law. When a new rule of substantive law becomes involved, the cases are said to involve different "rights" and "wrongs." Under this approach, the operation of the doctrine of merger and bar is restricted and causes of action are "small sized." The approach has been criticized as being too narrow and oblivious to important policy considerations. *See* Steakley & Howell, *Ruminations on Res Judicata*, 28 Sw. L.J. 355, 361-62 (1974).

(2) *"Same Rights," "Same Evidence," and "Destruction of the Prior Adjudication": Are These Really Three Different Tests?* Actually, the *Smith* case may lump together several distinct approaches: one that asks whether the two suits depend on different rights and wrongs, one that asks whether they depend upon the same evidence, and one that asks whether the second adjudication effects a destruction of the prior one. Are these really three tests, even though they seem similar and may often lead to similar results?

(3) *Diligence and Tactics.* Why wasn't the *quantum meruit* claim included in the second complaint? Assuming that it is well known that the statute of frauds does not bar a *quantum meruit* claim under New York contract law, what do you think of counsel's diligence? Can you think of a tactical reason why the claim was not included? If you can, what is your attitude about the "individualized/same evidence" approach?

[2] The "Transactional Analysis" Approach

O'BRIEN v. CITY OF SYRACUSE
54 N.Y.2d 353, 429 N.E.2d 1158 (1981)

[The plaintiffs initially brought suit in 1973 alleging that their real property situated in an area of Syracuse subject to urban rehabilitation had been wrongfully appropriated by a governmental entity without just compensation. This action was dismissed after a nonjury trial on the merits because the plaintiffs failed to establish a *de facto* taking. The Appellate Division affirmed the dismissal.

[The plaintiffs filed a second suit in 1978, essentially alleging the same facts "but with the added averment that the city had taken the property by tax deed on June 1, 1977." Subsequently, the plaintiffs filed an amended complaint alleging that the defendants had trespassed upon and damaged the subject property "during the period 1967 to 1978." The trespass claim attempted to recover for the same actions on which the first claim for *de facto* taking had been based.

[The defendants moved to dismiss the complaint on various grounds including *res judicata.* The trial judge concluded that "no bar existed because there were involved materially different elements of proof for the two theories of recovery," citing *Smith v. Kirkpatrick.* The Appellate Division reversed on the reasoning that the entire action was barred. This order was affirmed by the New York Court of Appeals "but on a different basis," as follows.]

In analyzing the complaint, plaintiffs' allegations fall into two categories: (1) those concerning activities underlying the 1973 litigation; and (2) those asserting trespass generally. Only the claims encompassed by the first category are definitely barred by *res judicata.*

This State has adopted the transactional analysis approach in deciding *res judicata* issues (*Matter of Reilly v. Reid*, 45 N.Y.2d 24, 407 N.Y.S.2d 645, 379 N.E.2d 172). Under this approach, once a claim is brought to a final conclusion, all other claims arising out of the same transaction or series of transactions are barred, even if based upon different theories or if seeking a different remedy (*id.*, at pp. 29-30, 407 N.Y.S.2d 645). Here, all of defendants' conduct falling in the first category was also raised during the 1973 suit as the basis for that litigation. That proceeding having been brought to a final conclusion, no other claim may be predicated upon the same incidents.

Plaintiffs, relying on *Smith v. Kirkpatrick*, 305 N.Y. 66, 111 N.E.2d 209, *supra*, urge that *de facto* appropriation and trespass are actions having different theoretical bases and requiring different evidentiary proof. . . .

[E]ven if it were assumed that the two actions involved materially different elements of proof, the second suit would be barred as to the claim predicated upon the first category allegations. When alternative theories are available to recover what is essentially the same relief for harm arising out of the same or related facts such as would constitute a single "factual grouping" (*Restatement, Judgments 2d,* § 61 [Tent. Draft No. 5]), the circumstance that the theories involve materially different elements of proof will not justify presenting the claim by two different actions.[1] Consequently, plaintiffs' action is barred by the doctrine of *res judicata* insofar as the allegations in the first category are concerned.

Finally, the second category of allegations — the general trespass allegations — are not barred by *res judicata* to the extent that they describe acts occurring after the 1973 lawsuit. They are, however, barred by reason of plaintiffs' failure to serve timely a notice of claim. . . .

For the reasons stated, the order of the Appellate Division granting the defendants' motion and dismissing the complaint should be affirmed, with costs.

NOTES AND QUESTIONS

(1) *Scope of Preclusion: Transactional Approach.* The transactional approach defines the breadth of the term "claim" or "cause of action" for *res judicata* purposes to embrace all the remedial rights of a plaintiff against a defendant growing out of the relevant transaction or series of connected transactions. The unit or entity that may not be split is "coterminous with the transaction regardless of the number of substantive theories, or variant forms of relief flowing from those theories, that may be available to the plaintiff. . . ." *Restatement (Second) of Judgments,* § 24, comment a.

The expression "transaction or series of transactions" is one that "connotes a natural grouping or common nucleus of operative facts." Among the factors relevant to a determination whether the facts are so woven together as to constitute a single claim are their "relatedness in time, space, origin, or motivation, and whether, taken together, they form a convenient unit for trial purposes." *Restatement (Second) of Judgments,* § 24, comment b. The idea is very similar to, if not broader than, the compulsory counterclaim concept. Fed. R. Civ. P. 13(a).

(2) *Procedural Duty Analysis.* Some court opinions and commentators have asserted that the entire problem of claim preclusion could be dealt with more effectively by imposing a procedural duty on the plaintiff to join related claims and a procedural penalty such as payment of costs if he does not, rather than by attempting to decide whether the causes of action or claims are the same or different. *See* Schopflocher, *What is a Single Cause of Action for the Purpose of the Doctrine of Res Judicata?,* 21 Ore. L. Rev. 319, 320-23 (1942); *see also Griffin v. Holiday Inns of America,* 496 S.W.2d 535, 538 n.1 (Tex. 1973), expressly overruled in *Barr v. Resolution Trust Corp.,* 837 S.W.2d 627, 630-31 (Tex. 1992), which adopted the Restatement's "transactional approach to claim preclusion." Of course, if the procedural duty is defined in terms of an obligation to join all claims arising out of the same transaction, the procedural duty analysis becomes identical to the transactional analysis approach at least in terms of defining the duty. It should be noted, however, that the so-called procedural duty approach probably is more complex than the transactional analysis approach. *See, e.g., Ogletree v. Crates,* 363 S.W.2d 431 (Tex. 1963) (focusing on external policy considerations involved in child custody cases).

---

[1] To the extent *Smith v. Kirkpatrick,* 305 N.Y. 66, 111 N.E.2d 209, *supra* may be to the contrary, it is overruled.

(3) *Role of Policy Considerations.* Professor Cleary, a leading academic expert on the law of *res judicata*, has described the matter in these pragmatic terms in Cleary, *Res Judicata Reexamined,* 57 Yale L.J. 339, 346 (1948):

> Policy would seem to indicate that when a plaintiff has once attempted to obtain his entire relief based upon his entire damages, then the matter should be laid to rest. He should be denied a second attempt at substantially the same objective under a different guise. In deciding such cases, the concept of a cause of action possesses real validity if applied with realization of what actually is at issue.

[3] Public Policy Exceptions to Preclusion

BOGARD v. COOK, 586 F.2d 399 (5th Cir. 1978). Bogard, a former prisoner at the Mississippi State Penitentiary at Parchman, Mississippi, brought suit for personal injuries against various supervisory officials, employees and inmates at Parchman based on 42 U.S.C. § 1983 and pendent state tort claims. While he was an inmate, Bogard was subjected to corporal punishment and suffered two incidents of prison violence. The first incident was in February, 1971, when Bogard was struck in the foot by a rifle bullet fired by a prisoner who had been made a "trusty shooter" by prison officials. At Parchman, "trusty shooters" were inmate-guards armed with rifles and charged with the day-to-day guarding of other inmates. The second was in July, 1972, when another inmate knifed Bogard when Bogard was sent to get a sewing machine from the other inmate by a prison official. The knife wound rendered Bogard a permanent paraplegic because the knife blade severed his spine. Bogard alleged that both incidents were caused by the negligence of prison officials.

Prior to Bogard's damage suit, Bogard participated (as a class member) in *Gates v. Collier*, 349 F. Supp. 881 (N.D. Miss. 1972), *aff'd*, 501 F.2d 1291 (5th Cir. 1974). The *Gates* case was brought in 1971 seeking declaratory and equitable relief for inmates, including Bogard, from violations of civil rights. The District Court granted sweeping declaratory and injunctive relief. Consequently, because Bogard could have brought his damage claims in the *Gates* litigation, the defendants asserted that the claims were barred.

The Court of Appeals concluded that "[p]rinciples of res judicata are not ironclad . . . res judicata will not be applied when it contravenes an important public policy." Holding that the inmates were not given any indication that they could assert damage claims in *Gates* by the class action notice, the Court stated that "[i]t would be a harsh and improper application of res judicata to hold, on the basis of the notice sent out in *Gates*, that prisoners forfeited their rights to personal redress [of constitutional rights] for lack of knowledge that federal law . . . required that injunctive and monetary relief be sought in one action."

[C] The Other Elements — Identity of Parties and a Judgment That Should Be Given Preclusive Effect: Notes and Questions

(1) *What Kind of Judgment Is Sufficient? Restatement § 20.* The *Restatement (Second) of Judgments* provides a list of situations in which a valid judgment, even if final, should not be given preclusive effect. Examples include a dismissal on grounds such as jurisdiction, venue, misjoinder or nonjoinder; a nonsuit without prejudice; or a judgment to which preclusive effect is denied by statute. Many jurisdictions have statutes denying preclusive effect to small claims (and certain other) judgments. *See, e.g.,* Tex. Civ. Prac.

& Rem. C. §§ 31.004–31.005; *Gilberg v. Barbieri,* in § 13.02[C], below. Likewise, most take-nothing judgments based on prematurity or failure to satisfy a precondition to recovery are not preclusion of a later suit brought after the condition is satisfied. *See generally Restatement (Second) of Judgments* § 20 (1982). *Res judicata* may be based upon a judgment that still is subject to appeal, in some jurisdictions — although a judgment based upon preclusion is subject to being set aside if the earlier judgment ultimately is reversed. *See id.* §§ 13-16.

(2) *What Kinds of Persons Are Bound Though Not Themselves Parties to the Action? Restatement §§ 34-42.* The basic rule is that parties to the action and subject to the court's jurisdiction are bound. The more interesting question, however, concerns persons who are subject to the preclusive effect of the judgment although they are not parties to the action. For example, a person who "controls or substantially participates in the control of the presentation on behalf of a party" may be bound as though he were a party. *Id.* § 39. Persons "represented by" parties — such as trust beneficiaries represented by a trustee, estate beneficiaries represented by an executor, principals who authorize their agents to sue in their behalf, class members represented by named parties in a class action, and certain other kinds of nonparties — may be bound by a judgment to which they were not parties, with certain exceptions (based upon, *e.g.*, noncompliance with notice requirements). *Id.* §§ 41-42. For a discussion of some issues at the frontiers, *see Martin v. Wilks*, in § 13.02[C] of this chapter, below.

§ 13.02 Collateral Estoppel: Issue Preclusion

[A] The Basic Elements

The branch of the doctrine of *res judicata* that is termed "collateral estoppel" or "estoppel by judgment" by traditionalists, and "issue preclusion" by modernists, is applied when one of the parties to a civil action argues that preclusive effect should be given to one or more issues determined in an earlier civil action. *Restatement (Second) of Judgments*, introduction at 2, 263-265 (1982).

The elements of the doctrine are explained by Professor Rex Perschbacher as follows:

> . . . Throughout the last forty years, collateral estoppel has changed from a precisely defined and narrowly applied doctrine to a vaguely defined idea widely used by harried courts. Originally, collateral estoppel prevented relitigation only of factual issues that were *actually litigated* and *essential* to an earlier judgment on a *different cause of action* binding the *same parties*. In comparison, *res judicata* prevented relitigation of issues that might have been raised, but were not, following judgment on the same cause of action.
>
> Recently a refashioned and broadened doctrine of collateral estoppel has emerged with simplified formal requirements, best expressed in the *Restatement (Second) of Judgments.* Issues of either law or fact can be the basis of collateral estoppel. Mutuality is no longer necessary; only the estopped party need be bound by the prior determination. Nonjudicial bodies, particularly administrative agencies, can make this prior determination provided they operate "in a judicial capacity." Only a party who lacked a "full and fair opportunity" to litigate the issue in the first action is excepted from the doctrine's operation. Courts and commentators have generally welcomed this expansion of collateral estoppel as one way to deal with increasing caseloads.

R. Perschbacher, *Rethinking Collateral Estoppel: Limiting the Preclusive Effect of Administrative Determinations in Judicial Proceedings*, 35 U. Fla. L. Rev. 422, 423-24 (1983).*

Section 27 of the *Restatement (Second) of Judgments* contains the following general rule:**

> § 27. Issue Preclusion — General Rule
>
> When an issue of fact or law is actually litigated and determined by a valid and final judgment, and the determination is essential to the judgment, the determination is conclusive in a subsequent action between the parties, whether on the same or a different claim.

[B] The Requirement of "Actual Litigation" of the "Same" Issue, Which Was "Essential to" the Prior Judgment

CROMWELL v. COUNTY OF SAC, 94 U.S. 351 (1876). As in all collateral estoppel situations, this case involved two different actions. The first action was brought on Cromwell's behalf against Sac County, Iowa, for recovery of interest on twenty-five bond coupons. This action ended in a judgment for Sac County. The court found that the County had issued a number of bonds to raise money for the construction of a courthouse; but the contractor had given one of the bonds as a "gratuity" to the county executive, and the courthouse was never constructed. The court found the transaction to have been so tainted with fraud and illegality that only a *bona fide* purchaser for value could recover on any of the bonds or coupons. Since it was not shown in the first suit that Cromwell had paid value for the twenty-five coupons, the court rendered judgment against Cromwell.

Later, in the second action, Cromwell sued upon certain *other* bonds and coupons. The defendant, Sac County, pleaded the doctrine of collateral estoppel. The lower courts agreed with the defendant and held that Cromwell's right to recover in the second action was estopped by the prior judgment. The Supreme Court noted that the issue of fraud and illegality had been actually litigated in the prior suit. The issue was identical for all bonds, since if the transaction was fraudulent and illegal it affected all of them. Thus collateral estoppel did apply to this issue, and consequently, Cromwell would be required to prove in the second action that he had purchased the bonds and coupons for value. But the second suit involved *different* bonds and coupons than the first, and so the question whether Cromwell had been a *bona fide* purchaser for value in the second suit had not been decided in the first. Therefore, the payment-of-value issue was not subject to collateral estoppel, and the Supreme Court reversed the lower court's judgment for defendant. The Court reasoned as follows:

> [I]t should be borne in mind . . . that there is a difference between the effect of a judgment as a bar . . . against the prosecution of a second action upon the same claim or demand, and its effect as an estoppel in another action between the same parties upon a different claim or cause of action. In the former case, the judgment, if rendered upon the merits, constitutes an absolute bar to a subsequent action. It is

---

a finality as to the claim or demand in controversy, . . . not only as to every matter which was offered and received to sustain or defeat the claim or demand, but as to any other admissible matter which might have been offered for that purpose. Thus, for example, a judgment rendered upon a promissory note is conclusive as to the validity of the instrument and the amount due upon it, although it be subsequently alleged that perfect defenses actually existed, of which no proof was offered, such as forgery, want of consideration or payment. . . .

But where the second action between the same parties is upon a different claim or demand, the judgment in the prior action operates as an estoppel only as to those matters in issue or points controverted, upon the determination of which the finding or verdict was rendered. . . . [T]he inquiry must always be as to the point or question actually litigated and determined in the original action; not what might have been thus litigated and determined. Only upon such matters is the judgment conclusive in another action. . . .

If, now, we consider the main question presented for our determination by the light of the views thus expressed and the authorities cited, its solution will not be difficult. . . . [T]he matters adjudged in [the first] case were these: that the bonds were void as against the County in the hands of parties who did not acquire them before maturity and give value for them, and that plaintiff, not having proved that he gave such value, was not entitled to recover upon the coupons. Whatever illegality or fraud there was in the issue and delivery to the contractor of the bonds affected equally the coupons for interest attached to them. The finding and judgment upon the invalidity of the bonds, as against the County, must be held to estop the plaintiff here from averring to the contrary. But as the bonds were negotiable instruments, and their issue was authorized by a vote of the County, and they recite on their face a compliance with the law providing for their issue, they would be held as valid obligations against the County in the hands of a *bona fide* holder taking them for value before maturity, according to repeated decisions of this court upon the character of such obligations. If, therefore, the plaintiff received the bond and coupons in [the second] suit before maturity for value, as he offered to prove, he should have been permitted to show that fact. . . . The fact that a party may not have shown that he gave value for one bond or coupon is not even presumptive, much less conclusive, evidence that he may not have given value for another and different bond or coupon. . . .

Judgment reversed and cause remanded, for a new trial.

NOTES AND QUESTIONS

(1) *Different Cause of Action.* A principal distinction between the doctrine of claim preclusion (merger and bar) and the doctrine of issue preclusion (collateral estoppel) is that under the latter doctrine, the prior lawsuit can involve a different cause of action than the second action. In other words, even though claim preclusion principles are inapplicable, the prior adjudication can preclude relitigation of an issue in a subsequent suit if it can be shown from the record in the prior suit that the issue was already litigated. To test your understanding of this basic difference between claim preclusion and issue preclusion, why wasn't the second action against Sac County barred altogether? What was the precise effect that the prior adjudication had on the subsequent lawsuit?

(2) *The Requirement That the Finding Be "Essential" to the Prior Judgment: Rios v. Davis, 373 S.W.2d 386 (Tex. Civ. App.—Eastland 1963, writ ref'd).* Even though an issue is "actually litigated" and made the subject of jury findings, it will not affect the

judgment if the judgment rests on other findings. Thus collateral estoppel is limited to issues that were "essential to" the prior judgment. For example, in *Rios v. Davis*, a truck owned by Popular Dry Goods and driven by Rios collided with a vehicle driven by Davis. In the first suit, which was filed in a county-level court with an amount-in-controversy jurisdiction not exceeding $1,000, Popular sued Davis for damage to its truck, and Davis filed a "third-party" claim against Rios for damages to Davis's car. The jury found all three parties guilty of negligence proximately causing the collision, and since contributory negligence was then a complete bar under the governing law, neither Popular nor Davis recovered anything. Later, in the second suit brought in a district court, Rios sought to recover approximately $20,000 from Davis for his personal injuries. Davis pleaded that the jury's finding of Rios's causal negligence in the first suit collaterally estopped his recovery in the second suit. The lower courts applied the collateral estoppel doctrine as Davis requested, but the appellate court — correctly — held that collateral estoppel was inapplicable. Can you see why? [In the first suit, the finding that Rios was causally negligent was not "essential"; in fact, it was immaterial to the judgment. Davis did not recover from Rios on Davis's third-party claim because he, Davis, never became liable to Popular, and he could not recover his own damages in that action from Rios because of his own contributory negligence. Thus it made no difference whether Rios was found negligent or not negligent. Furthermore, Rios was not adversely affected by the first judgment, since it was in his favor. He would not have been allowed to complain about the finding of his negligence on appeal, and in fact he could not appeal the judgment at all on that ground.]

The reason why nonessential determinations are not binding is expressed in comment h to the *Restatement (Second) of Judgments* § 27 (1982), as follows:

> *h. Determinations not essential to the judgment* . . . have the characteristics of *dicta*, and may not ordinarily be the subject of an appeal by the party against whom they are made. In these circumstances, the interest in providing an opportunity for a considered determination, which if adverse may be the subject of an appeal, outweighs the interest in avoiding the burden of relitigation.

Under this analysis, should Davis be collaterally estopped to deny his negligence in Rios's suit against Davis?

RYAN v. NEW YORK TELEPHONE CO.

62 N.Y.2d 494, 478 N.Y.S.2d 823, 467 N.E.2d 487 (1984)

JASEN, J. . . .

[Ed. Note: In New York, this decision has been reversed legislatively. (See the Note that follows the case). It nevertheless illustrates common law reasoning of more general application, and your reading of it is essential to your understanding of the legislation.]

Plaintiff, Edward Ryan, was discharged from his employ with defendant New York Telephone Company for theft of company property. Defendants Lauriano and Perrino, company security investigators, had observed Ryan removing what appeared to be company property from the workplace. They stopped him and called the police who arrested Ryan and charged him with petit larceny and criminal possession of stolen property.

Following his discharge from work, Ryan applied for unemployment insurance benefits, but his application was rejected by a claims examiner of the Department of Labor on the ground that the discharge was the result of his own misconduct. Ryan filed an appeal from that initial determination and a hearing . . . was held before an Unemployment Insurance Administrative Law Judge. . . . After considering the testimony of witnesses, including Ryan, who were examined and cross-examined extensively, the Administrative Law Judge sustained the ruling of the claims examiner and disallowed benefits, finding, *inter alia*, that "claimant was seen . . . removing company property from the company premises" and holding that "[t]he evidence . . . establishes that claimant lost his employment for [possessing] company property without authorization [and therefore] he lost his employment due to misconduct in connection therewith." This determination was subsequently affirmed by the Unemployment Insurance Appeal Board whose decision was, in turn, upheld by the Appellate Division.

During the pendency of the foregoing administrative proceedings and judicial review, the criminal action in which Ryan was represented by counsel resulted in an adjournment in contemplation of dismissal. Ultimately, it was restored to the Trial Calendar on the motion of the defendant and, on the People's motion, the charges were dismissed "in the interest of justice." . . .

Between the conclusion of the criminal proceedings and the Appellate Division's affirmance of the administrative determination thereafter, plaintiffs commenced this action asserting claims for false arrest, malicious prosecution, slander and wrongful discharge, and an additional claim for the resultant injuries to Ryan's wife. Defendants pleaded an affirmative defense of *res judicata* and collateral estoppel on the basis of the prior administrative determination denying Ryan's claim for unemployment benefits. When plaintiffs moved to dismiss the affirmative defense, defendants cross-moved to dismiss the first, second, third, sixth and seventh causes of action comprising claims for false arrest, malicious prosecution, slander and two claims for wrongful discharge, respectively. [The lower courts granted plaintiff's motion and dismissed the affirmative defense, but the Appellate Division certified to the Court of Appeals the question whether this ruling was correct.] We now reverse, grant defendants' cross motion to dismiss, and answer the certified question in the negative. . . .

The doctrine of collateral estoppel, a narrower species of *res judicata*, precludes a party from relitigating in a subsequent action or proceeding an issue clearly raised in a prior action or proceeding and decided against that party or those in privity, whether or not the tribunals or causes of action are the same.

. . . What is controlling is the identity of the issue which has necessarily been decided in the prior action or proceeding.

Of course, the issue must have been material to the first action or proceeding and essential to the decision rendered therein . . . and it must be the point actually to be determined in the second action or proceeding such that "a different judgment in the second would destroy or impair rights or interests established by the first" . . . .

In addition, where the party against whom collateral estoppel is asserted claims that he was not afforded a full and fair opportunity in the prior administrative proceeding to contest the decision now said to be controlling, he must be allowed to do so. [The "full and fair opportunity" doctrine is discussed in § 13.02[C] of this chapter, below. The Court of Appeals determined that Ryan had had a "full and fair opportunity" to litigate the issue in the prior proceeding.] . . .

Applying the foregoing rules of law to this case demonstrates clearly that collateral estoppel bars plaintiffs from litigating the subject claims. A comparison of the material issues raised in this action with those resolved by the prior administrative determination, and an examination of the prior proceeding itself show that both requisite criteria, the identicality and decisiveness of the issues and the opportunity for a full and fair hearing have been satisfied.

The critical issue in the prior administrative proceeding was whether Ryan was discharged by reason of misconduct and, therefore, not entitled to unemployment benefits. The Administrative Law Judge's specific findings, essential to the disallowance of benefits to Ryan, was that the latter was guilty of unauthorized removal and possession of company property, and that he was discharged for that reason. That determination, affirmed by the Unemployment Insurance Appeal Board and ultimately by the Appellate Division, is conclusive between the parties in this action, and it is dispositive of the subject claims asserted by plaintiffs.

The first cause of action alleges false arrest resulting from the defendants' complaints against Ryan to the police. The lack of legal justification is an essential element of the tort of false arrest, but the administrative determination of criminally chargeable misconduct is dispositive of the presence of such justification and, consequently, grounds for dismissal of the cause of action. Likewise, the second cause of action alleging malicious prosecution requires a lack of probable cause for instituting the criminal proceeding, but the prior determination is decisive that defendants' investigators actually witnessed Ryan removing the property and, therefore, had probable cause to bring charges against him. The third cause of action asserts a slanderous remark against Ryan to the effect that he "stole something" from his workplace. The Administrative Law Judge's findings that Ryan was seen "removing company property from the company premises" and that his taking was "without authorization" were the essential predicate to the determination rendered that he was discharged for misconduct. Those findings, therefore, are entitled to the same conclusive effect as the determination itself and, inasmuch as they establish the truth of the remarks alleged to be slanderous, they constitute a complete defense. The sixth and seventh causes of action are grounded on allegations of wrongful discharge, but, again, the prior determination is dispositive of the fact that Ryan's termination from employment resulted from and was justified by his misconduct. Consequently, justification being a defense to the tort of wrongful discharge (*see Brandt v. Winchell*, 3 N.Y.2d 628, 633), the determination constitutes a basis for dismissal of those causes of action as well. It is clear, then, that the criterion of issue identicality and decisiveness is satisfied for each of the subject causes of action. . . .

Finally, the eventual dismissal of the criminal charges on the motion of the prosecutor "in the interest of justice" does not constitute an adjudication of the veracity of the receipts or of Ryan's innocence of the charges. Consequently, it in no way undermines the force and effect of the administrative determination. A dismissal "in the interest of justice" is neither an acquittal of the charges nor any determination of the merits. Rather, it leaves the question of guilt or innocence unanswered.

Thus, in view of plaintiffs' failure to demonstrate Ryan's lack of a full and fair opportunity to litigate his claim at the prior administrative hearing and inasmuch as the issues in that proceeding and the causes of action here in question are identical and dispositive, the doctrine of collateral estoppel applies and precludes relitigation of the prior determination. . . .

NOTE ON LEGISLATIVE REVERSAL OF *RYAN v. NEW YORK TELEPHONE CO.*

Ryan v. New York Telephone Co. has been legislatively overruled. New York Labor Law § 623, as amended, provides [in essence] that no finding of fact or law in a decision rendered on a claim for unemployment insurance may be given preclusive effect in subsequent litigation, unless the subsequent litigation also involves unemployment insurance.

[C] Parties Who Had "Full and Fair Opportunity" to Litigate the Issue

[1] When the First Action Is Minor or Informal

GILBERG v. BARBIERI, 53 N.Y.2d 285, 441 N.Y.S.2d 49, 423 N.E.2d 807 (1981). Gilberg and Barbieri were involved in an altercation. Gilberg filed a criminal complaint, charging Barbieri with "harassment," a petty offense designated as a "violation" by the New York Penal Law. After a brief non-jury trial, which was to be followed by a felony trial, the judge of the City Court of Mount Vernon, New York, immediately found Barbieri guilty and sentenced him to a one-year "conditional discharge," saying, "You're not found guilty of a crime, it's a violation. . . ." The day following the conviction, a summons was issued in Gilberg's civil suit against Barbieri for assault, in which Gilberg sought a quarter of a million dollars in damages. Gilberg moved for summary judgment, arguing that the City Court finding on the harassment charge collaterally estopped Barbieri's denial of liability. The trial court granted summary judgment, noting that the conviction was based on a finding that Barbieri had used "physical force against" Gilberg. The Appellate Division affirmed. The Court of Appeals, however, reversed because it found that Barbieri had not had a "full and fair opportunity" to litigate the issue in the prior proceeding:

> The doctrine of collateral estoppel is based on the notion that it is not fair to permit a party to relitigate an issue which has previously been decided against him in a proceeding in which he had a fair opportunity to fully litigate the point. . . .
>
> The City Court action was a relatively minor one. . . . As the drafters of the Penal Law noted, petty infractions below the grade of misdemeanor are, like traffic violations, more accurately described as "noncriminal offenses" . . . By statute collateral estoppel effect is denied to traffic convictions . . . and determinations in small claims actions. . . . Even in the absence of statute, however, these minor suits are illustrative of the type of determination which, under accepted common-law principles, should not be held conclusive in later cases [citing the *Restatement (Second) of Judgments*].
>
> Of course the defendant did not choose to litigate the matter first in the City Court. It was the plaintiff who had the initiative. . . .
>
> Because of the relative insignificance of the charge, the defendant had no constitutional or statutory right to a jury trial, as he would have . . . in the subsequently initiated civil action for damages. . . . Nor could he expect or be expected to defend with the same vigor. The brisk, often informal, way in which these matters must be tried, as well as the relative insignificance of the outcome, afford the party neither opportunity nor incentive to litigate . . . as thoroughly as he might if more were at stake. . . .

[*Reversed.*]

NOTES AND QUESTIONS

(1) *"Criminal-Civil" Estoppel; "Non-Mutual" Estoppel.* New York allows collateral estoppel to be based on a criminal judgment in a proper case. Furthermore, it applies

the collateral estoppel doctrine even if the non-estopped party was not a party to the prior suit, so that he could not have suffered estoppel (as was true of Gilberg, since he technically was not a party to the harassment action). The court recognized these principles in *Gilberg v. Barbieri*. However, the nature of the prior action obviously may affect the application of the "full and fair opportunity" doctrine. (For coverage of the "mutuality" issue, see § 13.02[D] below.)

(2) *Gilberg v. Barbieri as a Case of "Offensive" (Rather than "Defensive") Collateral Estoppel.* The distinction between offensive and defensive use of collateral estoppel is based on the relative positions of the parties as defendants or plaintiffs in the second action. When a litigant seeks to impose liability on a defending party in the second suit, the use of collateral estoppel is "offensive." When a litigant seeks to avoid liability to a claimant in the second action, the use of collateral estoppel is "defensive." *Gilberg v. Barbieri* involved an attempted use of offensive collateral estoppel; should this feature of the action have affected the outcome? *See Restatement (Second) of Judgments* § 29, comment d (pointing out that it may be relevant that the party "had no choice, or restricted choice, as to the forum" in the prior action, particularly in offensive collateral estoppel cases). Furthermore, offensive use of a fact finding in a prior case creates special problems when the second action involves a different claimant. For a more sophisticated discussion of these issues, and the related question whether so-called "mutuality" of estoppel is required, *see Parklane Hosiery Co., Inc. v. Shore*, which appears below in § 13.02[D].

[2] When the Parties Are Not Identical

MARTIN v. WILKS
490 U.S. 755 (1989)

CHIEF JUSTICE REHNQUIST delivered the opinion of the Court.

[A group of white firefighters sued the City of Birmingham, Alabama and the Jefferson County Personnel Board, alleging that the defendants illegally had denied promotions to the white plaintiffs in favor of less qualified black firefighters. The defendants relied in part on certain consent decrees resulting from a previous suit by black firefighters. In those decrees, the court had ordered an extensive remedial system requiring the hiring and promotion of black firefighters by the City and the Board. The white plaintiffs in the present action had not been parties to the earlier action, and they had not intervened in it.

[The District Court dismissed the white plaintiffs' claims. It held that the defendants had "establish[ed] that the promotions of the black individuals [w]ere in fact required by the [c]onsent decree[s]" and that the defendants therefore "[were] not guilty of [illegal] racial discrimination." The Court of Appeals, however, reversed. It held that "[b]ecause [the white plaintiffs] were neither parties nor privies to the consent decrees, [t]heir independent claims of unlawful discrimination are not precluded." The Court of Appeals also held that, on remand, the consent decrees should be given only the deference due to voluntary affirmative-action plans. The Supreme Court, per Chief Justice Rehnquist, affirmed:]

We [a]ffirm the Eleventh Circuit's judgment. All agree that "[i]t is a principle of general application in Anglo-American jurisprudence that one is not bound by a judgment [i]n a litigation in which he is not designated as a party or to which he has not been made a party by service of process." *Hansberry v. Lee*, 311 U.S. 32, 40 (1940). [A] judgment or decree among parties to a lawsuit resolves issues as among them, but it does not conclude the rights of strangers to those proceedings.[2]

Petitioners argue that, because respondents failed to timely intervene in the initial proceedings, their current challenge to actions taken under the consent decree constitutes an impermissible "collateral attack." [T]he position has sufficient appeal to have commanded the approval of the great majority of the federal courts of appeals, but we agree with the contrary view expressed by the Court of Appeals for the Eleventh Circuit in this case.

We begin with the words of Justice Brandeis in *Chase National Bank v. Norwalk*, 291 U.S. 431 (1934):

> The law does not impose upon any person [t]he burden of voluntary intervention in a suit to which he is a stranger. . . . Unless duly summoned to appear in a legal proceeding, a person not a privy may rest assured that a judgment recovered therein will not affect his legal rights.

[A]gainst the background of permissive intervention set forth in *Chase National Bank*, the drafters cast Rule 24, governing intervention, in permissive terms. *See* Fed. Rule Civ. Proc. 24(a) (intervention as of right) ("[on] timely [motion, the court must permit certain persons] to intervene"); Fed. Rule Civ. Proc. 24(b) (permissive intervention) ("[on] timely [motion, the court may permit] anyone . . . to intervene"). They determined that the concern for finality and completeness of judgments would be "better [served] by mandatory joinder procedures." Accordingly, Rule 19(a) provides for mandatory joinder in circumstances where a judgment rendered in the absence of a person may "leave [an existing party] subject to a substantial risk of incurring . . . inconsistent obligations. . . ." Rule 19(b) sets forth the factors to be considered by a court in deciding whether to allow an action to proceed in the absence of an interested party.

Joinder as a party, rather than knowledge of a lawsuit and an opportunity to intervene, is the method by which potential parties are subjected to the jurisdiction of the court and bound by a judgment or decree.[6] The parties to a lawsuit presumably know better than anyone else the nature and scope of relief sought in the action, and at whose expense such relief might be granted. It makes sense, therefore, to place on them a burden of bringing in additional parties where such a step is indicated. . . . The linchpin of the "impermissible collateral attack" doctrine [i]s therefore quite inconsistent with Rule 19 and Rule 24. . . .

---

[2] We have recognized an exception to the general rule when, in certain limited circumstances, a person, although not a party, has his interests adequately represented by someone with the same interests who is a party. *See Hansberry v. Lee. . . .*; *Montana v. United States*, 440 U.S. 147, 154-155 (1979) (control of litigation on behalf of one of the parties in the litigation). Additionally, where a special remedial scheme exists expressly foreclosing successive litigation by nonlitigants, as for example in bankruptcy or probate, legal proceedings may terminate preexisting rights if the scheme is otherwise consistent with due process. [N]either of these exceptions, however, applies in this case.

[6] The dissent argues on the one hand that respondents have not been "bound" by the decree but rather, that they are only suffering practical adverse affects from the consent decree. On the other hand, the dissent characterizes respondents' suit not as an assertion of their own independent rights, but as a collateral attack on the consent decree which, it is said, can only proceed on very limited grounds. [E]ither the fact that the disputed employment decisions are being made pursuant to a consent decree is a defense to respondents' Title VII claims or it is not. If it is a defense to challenges to employment practices which would otherwise violate Title VII, it is very difficult to see why respondents are not being "bound" by the decree.

Nor do we think that the system of joinder called for by the Rules is likely to produce more relitigation of issues than the converse rule. The breadth of a lawsuit and concomitant relief may be at least partially shaped in advance through Rule 19 to avoid needless clashes with future litigation. And even under a regime of mandatory intervention, parties who did not have adequate knowledge of the suit would relitigate issues. . . .

Petitioners also urge that the congressional policy favoring voluntary settlement of employment discrimination claims [a]lso supports the "impermissible collateral attack" doctrine. [But] [a] voluntary settlement in the form of a consent decree between one group of employees and their employer cannot possibly "settle," voluntarily or otherwise, the conflicting claims of another group of employees who do not join in the agreement.

[P]etitioners point to language in the District Court's findings of fact and conclusions of law which suggests that respondents will not prevail on the merits. We agree with the view of the Court of Appeals, however, that the proceedings in the District Court may have been affected by the mistaken view that respondents' claims on the merits were barred to the extent they were inconsistent with the consent decree.

Affirmed.

JUSTICE STEVENS, with whom JUSTICE BRENNAN, JUSTICE MARSHALL, and JUSTICE BLACKMUN join, dissenting . . . .

The District Court's rulings in this case have been described incorrectly by both the Court of Appeals and this Court. The Court of Appeals repeatedly stated that the District Court had "in effect" held that the white firefighters were "bound" by a decree to which they were not parties. . . .

[I]t is absolutely clear that the court did not hold that respondents were bound by the decree. Nowhere in the District Court's lengthy findings of fact and conclusions of law is there a single word suggesting that respondents were bound by the consent decree or that the court intended to treat them as though they had been actual parties to that litigation and not merely as persons whose interests, as a practical matter, had been affected. . . .

Regardless of whether the white firefighters were parties to the decrees granting relief to their black co-workers, it would be quite wrong to assume that they could never collaterally attack such a decree. If a litigant has standing, he or she can always collaterally attack a judgment for certain narrowly defined defects. [But] a broad allowance of collateral review would destroy the integrity of litigated judgments, would lead to an abundance of vexatious litigation, and would subvert the interest in comity between courts. Here, respondents have offered no circumstance that might justify reopening the District Court's settled judgment. . . .

[T]here is no basis for collaterally attacking the judgment as collusive, fraudulent, or transparently invalid. Moreover, respondents do not claim — nor has there been any showing of — mistake, duress, or lack of jurisdiction. Instead, respondents are left to argue that somewhat different relief would have been more appropriate than the relief that was actually granted. Although this sort of issue may provide the basis for a direct appeal, it cannot, and should not, serve to open the door to relitigation of a settled judgment.

The facts that respondents are not bound by the decree and that they have no basis for a collateral attack, moreover, do not compel the conclusion that the District Court should have treated the decree as nonexistent for purposes of respondents' discrimination suit. That the decree may not directly interfere with any of respondents' legal rights does not mean that it may not affect the factual setting in a way that negates respondents' claim. The fact that a criminal suspect is not a party to the issuance of a search warrant does not imply that the presence of a facially valid warrant may not be taken as evidence that the police acted in good faith. Similarly, the fact that an employer is acting under court compulsion may be evidence that the employer is acting in good faith and without discriminatory intent.

[A]ll of the reasons that support the Court's view that a police officer should not generally be held liable when he carries out the commands in a facially valid warrant apply with added force to city officials, or indeed to private employers, who obey the commands contained in a decree entered by a federal court. In fact, Equal Employment Opportunity Commission regulations concur in this assessment. They assert, "[t]he Commission interprets Title VII to mean that actions taken pursuant to the direction of a Court Order cannot give rise to liability under Title VII." [A]ny other conclusion would subject large employers who seek to comply with law by remedying past discrimination to a never-ending stream of litigation and potential liability. It is unfathomable that either Title VII or the Equal Protection Clause demands such a counter-productive result. . . .

MONTANA v. UNITED STATES, 440 U.S. 147 (1979). This case concerns the proper use of collateral estoppel against a person who "controlled" the earlier litigation. Montana imposed a tax on contractors who worked on public (but not private) construction projects. The United States, whose contractors were subject to this tax, considered that the tax was unconstitutionally discriminatory. Therefore, the federal government recruited one of its contractors (Peter Kiewit Sons' Co., which had worked on a federal dam project in Montana and had paid the tax) to sue Montana in a Montana state court. The United States was not a party to the state litigation, but "[t]he litigation was directed and financed by the United States." The state litigation terminated in a unanimous decision of the Montana Supreme Court upholding the Montana tax. The contractor at first sought review in the United States Supreme Court, but it then abandoned this effort — at the request of the United States.

Despite this loss, the United States pursued a separate suit against Montana, this time in the name of the United States, and in a United States District Court. The District Court rejected Montana's defense of collateral estoppel and struck down the tax. The Supreme Court reversed:

> [The purposes underlying collateral estoppel] are similarly implicated when nonparties assume control over litigation in which they have a direct financial [i]interest and then seek to redetermine issues previously resolved. [These litigants] cannot be said to be "strangers to the [earlier] cause." . . .
>
> That the United States exercised control over the [Kiewit] litigation is not in dispute. [T]hus, although not a party, the United States plainly had a sufficient "laboring oar" in the conduct of the state-court litigation to actuate principles of estoppel.

NOTES AND QUESTIONS

(1) *Did the District Court in Martin v. Wilks Erroneously "Collaterally Estop" the Plaintiffs — Or Did It Merely Prevent an "Impermissible Collateral Attack" by Them on a Decree That Indirectly Affected Them? (Is There a Difference?)* The majority sees

the District Court's action as erroneous collateral estoppel. The dissent sees it as the proper rejection of an impermissible collateral attack. When a court prevents you from collaterally attacking a judgment that affects your legal rights, is the result really the same as collateral estoppel (as the majority suggests)? Or is there a difference between collateral estoppel and the enforcement of a decree that has indirect effects on nonparties' legal rights (as the dissent suggests)? Cast in these terms, the debate seems as though it were about metaphysics!

(2) *The Impact of the Civil Rights Act of 1991 on Martin v. Wilks.* Section 108 of the Civil Rights Act of 1991 affects these problems. Employer conduct that implements a court order may not be challenged on federal employment discrimination grounds even by a nonparty, if the nonparty had sufficient actual notice and a reasonable opportunity to object or if the nonparty's interests were adequately represented. How much of the holding of *Martin v. Wilks* is left after this Act? (Note that the Act affects only federal employment discrimination legislation and only under the specified circumstances, leaving an area of continued vitality to the decision).

(3) *The Restatement Approach.* Both §§ 28 and 29 of the *Restatement (Second) of Judgments* recognize that a party is not precluded from relitigating an issue when the party "lacked full and fair opportunity to litigate the issue in the first action or other circumstances justify affording him an opportunity to relitigate the issue." *Restatement (Second) of Judgments* § 29 (1982). Neither section contemplates that a person who was not a party can be bound *unless* she is represented by a party or has interests that are derived from a party. The "Reporter's Note" to § 29 identifies this principle as "a rule of Constitutional law." Notice that the "identity of parties" concept overlaps the concept of a party who had a "full and fair opportunity to litigate" in the first action. Which concept is most useful in analyzing the cases in this section — the identity-of-parties requirement, or the full-and-fair opportunity doctrine?

[D] Mutuality: Is It (or Should It Be) Required?

PARKLANE HOSIERY COMPANY, INC. v. SHORE
439 U.S. 322 (1979)

MR. JUSTICE STEWART delivered the opinion of the Court.

[In the first lawsuit, the Securities and Exchange Commission ("SEC") obtained injunctive and declaratory relief against Parklane Hosiery Co. and others after a four-day nonjury trial. The basis for the judgment was that a proxy statement was materially false and misleading to shareholders.

[In the second lawsuit, individual shareholders, including Leo Shore, brought a stockholders' derivative suit for damages against the same defendants for damages on the ground that the proxy statement was materially false and misleading in essentially the same respects.

[Leo Shore moved for partial summary judgment on the basis that the defendants were collaterally estopped from relitigating the issues that had been resolved against them in the action brought by the SEC. The motion was denied by the district judge on the theory that such an estoppel would deny the defendants' Seventh Amendment right to a jury trial. The Second Circuit reversed. The Supreme Court granted certiorari.]

I

The threshold question to be considered is whether, quite apart from the right to a jury trial under the Seventh Amendment, the petitioners can be precluded from religating facts resolved adversely to them in a prior equitable proceeding with another party under the general law of collateral estoppel. Specifically, we must determine whether a litigant who was not a party to a prior judgment may nevertheless use that judgment "offensively" to prevent a defendant from relitigating issues resolved in the earlier proceeding.[4]

A

Collateral estoppel, like the related doctrine of res judicata, has the dual purpose of protecting litigants from the burden of relitigating an identical issue with the same party or his privy and of promoting judicial economy by preventing needless litigation. *Blonder-Tongue Laboratories, Inc. v. University of Illinois Foundation*, 402 U.S. 313, 328-329 . . . . Until relatively recently, however, the scope of collateral estoppel was limited by the doctrine of mutuality of parties. Under this mutuality doctrine, neither party could use a prior judgment as an estoppel against the other unless both parties were bound by the judgment. Based on the premise that it is somehow unfair to allow a party to use a prior judgment when he himself would not be so bound,[7] the mutuality requirement provided a party who had litigated and lost in a previous action an opportunity to relitigate identical issues with new parties.

By failing to recognize the obvious difference in position between a party who has never litigated an issue and one who has fully litigated and lost, the mutuality requirement was criticized almost from its inception. Recognizing the validity of this criticism, the Court in *Blonder-Tongue Laboratories, Inc. v. University of Illinois Foundation, supra*, abandoned the mutuality requirement, at least in cases where a patentee seeks to relitigate the validity of a patent after a federal court in a previous lawsuit has already declared it invalid. The "broader question" before the Court, however, was "whether it is any longer tenable to afford a litigant more than one full and fair opportunity for judicial resolution of the same issue." . . . The Court strongly suggested a negative answer to that question:

> In any lawsuit where a defendant, because of the mutuality principle, is forced to present a complete defense on the merits to a claim which the plaintiff has fully litigated and lost in a prior action, there is an arguable misallocation of resources. To the extent the defendant in the second suit may not win by asserting, without contradiction, that the plaintiff had fully and fairly, but unsuccessfully, litigated the same claim in the prior suit, the defendant's time and money are diverted from alternative uses — productive or otherwise — to relitigation of a decided issue. And, still assuming that the issue was resolved correctly in the first suit, there is reason to be concerned about the plaintiff's allocation of resources. Permitting repeated litigation of the same issue as long as the supply of unrelated defendants holds out reflects either the aura of the gaming table or "a lack of discipline and of disinterestedness

[4] In this context, offensive use of collateral estoppel occurs when the plaintiff seeks to foreclose the defendant from litigating an issue the defendant has previously litigated unsuccessfully in an action with another party. Defensive use occurs when a defendant seeks to prevent a plaintiff from asserting a claim the plaintiff has previously litigated and lost against another defendant.

[7] It is a violation of due process for a judgment to be binding on a litigant who was not a party or a privy and therefore has never had an opportunity to be heard. *Blonder-Tongue Laboratories, Inc. v. University of Illinois Foundation*. . . .

on the part of the lower courts, hardly a worthy or wise basis for fashioning rules of procedure." . . . Although neither judges, the parties, nor the adversary system performs perfectly in all cases, the requirement of determining whether the party against whom an estoppel is asserted had a full and fair opportunity to litigate is a most significant safeguard.

B

The *Blonder-Tongue* case involved defensive use of collateral estoppel — a plaintiff was estopped from asserting a claim that the plaintiff had previously litigated and lost against another defendant. The present case, by contrast, involves offensive use of collateral estoppel — a plaintiff is seeking to estop a defendant from relitigating the issues which the defendant previously litigated and lost against another plaintiff. In both the offensive and defensive use situations, the party against whom estoppel is asserted has litigated and lost in an earlier action. Nevertheless, several reasons have been advanced why the two situations should be treated differently.

First, offensive use of collateral estoppel does not promote judicial economy in the same manner as defensive use does. Defensive use of collateral estoppel precludes a plaintiff from relitigating identical issues by merely "switching adversaries." . . . Thus defensive collateral estoppel gives a plaintiff a strong incentive to join all potential defendants in the first action if possible. Offensive use of collateral estoppel, on the other hand, creates precisely the opposite incentive. Since a plaintiff will be able to rely on a previous judgment against a defendant but will not be bound by that judgment if the defendant wins, the plaintiff has every incentive to adopt a "wait and see" attitude, in the hope that the first action by another plaintiff will result in a favorable judgment. Thus offensive use of collateral estoppel will likely increase rather than decrease the total amount of litigation, since potential plaintiffs will have everything to gain and nothing to lose by not intervening in the first action.[13]

A second argument against offensive use of collateral estoppel is that it may be unfair to a defendant. If a defendant in the first action is sued for small or nominal damages, he may have little incentive to defend vigorously, particularly if future suits are not foreseeable. *The Evergreens v. Nunan*, 141 F.2d 927, 929 (2d Cir.); *cf. Berner v. British Commonwealth Pac. Airlines*, 346 F.2d 532 (2d Cir.) (application of offensive collateral estoppel denied where defendant did not appeal an adverse judgment awarding damages of $35,000 and defendant was later sued for over $7 million). Allowing offensive collateral estoppel may also be unfair to a defendant if the judgment relied upon as a basis for the estoppel is itself inconsistent with one or more previous judgments in favor of the defendant.[14] Still another situation where it might be unfair to apply offensive

---

[13] The *Restatement (Second) of Judgments* § 88(3) (Tent. Draft No. 2, Apr. 15, 1975), provides that application of collateral estoppel may be denied if the party asserting it "could have effected joinder in the first action between himself and his present adversary."

[14] In Professor Currie's familiar example, a railroad collision injures 50 passengers all of whom bring separate actions against the railroad. After the railroad wins the first 25 suits, a plaintiff wins in suit 26. Professor Currie argues that offensive use of collateral estoppel should not be applied so as to allow plaintiffs 27 through 50 automatically to recover. Currie, *supra*, 9 Stan. L. Rev., at 304. *See Restatement (Second) of Judgments* § 88(4), *supra*.

estoppel is where the second action affords the defendant procedural opportunities unavailable in the first action that could readily cause a different result.[15]

C

We have concluded that the preferable approach for dealing with these problems in the federal courts is not to preclude the use of offensive collateral estoppel, but to grant trial courts broad discretion to determine when it should be applied.[16] The general rule should be that in cases where a plaintiff could easily have joined in the earlier action or where, either for the reasons discussed above or for other reasons, the application of offensive estoppel would be unfair to a defendant, a trial judge should not allow the use of offensive collateral estoppel.

In the present case, however, none of the circumstances that might justify reluctance to allow the offensive use of collateral estoppel is present. The application of offensive collateral estoppel will not here reward a private plaintiff who could have joined in the previous action, since the respondent probably could not have joined in the injunctive action brought by the SEC even had he so desired. Similarly, there is no unfairness to the petitioners in applying offensive collateral estoppel in this case. First, in light of the serious allegations made in the SEC's complaint against the petitioners, as well as the foreseeability of subsequent private suits that typically follow a successful Government judgment, the petitioners had every incentive to litigate the SEC lawsuit fully and vigorously. Second, the judgment in the SEC action was not inconsistent with any previous decision. Finally, there will in the respondent's action be no procedural opportunities available to the petitioners that were unavailable in the first action of a kind that might be likely to cause a different result.[19]

We conclude, therefore, that none of the considerations that would justify a refusal to allow the use of offensive collateral estoppel is present in this case. Since the petitioners received a "full and fair" opportunity to litigate their claims in the SEC action, the contemporary law of collateral estoppel leads inescapably to the conclusion that the petitioners are collaterally estopped from relitigating the question of whether the proxy statement was materially false and misleading.

---

[15] If, for example, the defendant in the first action was forced to defend in an inconvenient forum and therefore was unable to engage in full scale discovery or call witnesses, application of offensive collateral estoppel may be unwarranted. Indeed, differences in available procedures may sometimes justify not allowing a prior judgment to have estoppel effect in a subsequent action even between the same parties, or where defensive estoppel is asserted against a plaintiff who has litigated and lost. The problem of unfairness is particularly acute in cases of offensive estoppel, however, because the defendant against whom estoppel is asserted typically will not have chosen the forum in the first action. *See, id.*, at § 88(2) and Comment *d.*

[16] This is essentially the approach of *id.*, at § 88, which recognizes that "the distinct trend if not the clear weight of recent authority is to the effect that there is no intrinsic difference between 'offensive' as distinct from 'defensive' issue preclusion, although a stronger showing that the prior opportunity to litigate was adequate may be required in the former situation than the latter." *Id.*, Reporter's Note, at 99.

[19] It is true, of course, that the petitioners in the present action would be entitled to a jury trial of the issues bearing on whether the proxy statement was materially false and misleading had the SEC action never been brought — a matter to be discussed in Part II of this opinion. But the presence or absence of a jury as fact finder is basically neutral, quite unlike, for example, the necessity of defending the first lawsuit in an inconvenient forum.

II

The question that remains is whether, notwithstanding the law of collateral estoppel, the use of offensive collateral estoppel in this case would violate the petitioners' Seventh Amendment right to a jury trial. . . .

[The Court held that application of collateral estoppel under the circumstances did not violate the Seventh Amendment, even though the prior judgment had been rendered in a proceeding to which the right to a jury trial did not attach. This aspect of the opinion, including Justice Rehnquist's dissent to the holding, is discussed in Section 10.02[A] of Chapter 10, above.

[The dissenting opinion of Mr. Justice Rehnquist is here omitted.]

NOTES AND QUESTIONS

(1) *New York's "Aggressive" Application of Offensive Collateral Estoppel: Kaufman v. Eli Lilly & Co., 65 N.Y.2d 449, 492 N.Y.S.2d 584, 482 N.E.2d 63 (1985).* Lilly was held liable in one of fifteen pending cases alleging damages sustained by the plaintiff's daughters from their mothers' ingestion of diethylsilbestrol (DES). Kaufman, the plaintiff in another of the fifteen cases, promptly moved for partial summary judgment based on offensive collateral estoppel. The New York Court of Appeals applied offensive collateral estoppel to a number of issues, including Lilly's negligence in testing DES. The court said: "[The case] fits the example described by James and Hazard of an instance in which there are several similar cases and the first tried is 'roughly typical' of the rest. In that situation, the professors noted, it is not unfair to preclude the defendant from retrying the issues previously litigated and decided adversely to it (James & Hazard, *Civil Procedure* § 11.24, at 581 [2d ed.])." Is this approach sensible? *See also Koch v. Consolidated Edison Co. of N.Y., Inc.*, 62 N.Y.2d 548, 479 N.Y.S.2d 163, 468 N.E.2d 1 (1984) (finding of utility's gross negligence in causing electrical blackout held binding in suits by other plaintiffs).

(2) *Non-Mutual Use of Defensive Collateral Estoppel: Hardy v. Fleming, 553 S.W.2d 790 (Tex. Civ. App.-El Paso 1977, writ ref'd n.r.e.).* Hardy suffered what he claimed was a heart attack on the job and filed a worker's compensation claim. The jury found that Hardy had suffered no injury, and the court rendered judgment that he take nothing. In a second suit, Hardy alleged that his physician, Dr. Fleming, had negligently caused him to suffer the same "heart attack." The Court of Appeals affirmed a summary judgment for defendant Fleming, based upon collateral estoppel. Defensive collateral estoppel, as in *Hardy v. Fleming*, poses fewer problems than the offensive variety when mutuality is lacking. *See also Ryan v. New York Telephone Co.*, § 13.02[B], above.

(3) *The Supreme Court Draws the Line on Parklane: Preserving the Right to Jury Trial in Lytle v. Household Mfg., Inc., 494 U.S. 545 (1990) (see also Ch. 10, above).* In this later case, the plaintiff argued that the District Court had erroneously dismissed the plaintiff's legal claims before adversely determining the plaintiff's equitable claims without a jury. The Court of Appeals applied collateral estoppel to preclude the plaintiff's legal claims, even though this disposition denied the plaintiff the right to jury trial and even though it arose from the District Court's arguable error. The Supreme Court reversed; it preserved the plaintiff's right to jury trial by rejecting the preclusion defense. [Can this decision be distinguished from *Parklane* on the theory that a deprivation of the right to jury trial based on a court's error is worse than the same deprivation based on a race to judgment won by an equitable claimant?]

§ 13.03 Interjurisdictional Preclusion: State-State and State-Federal Effects

Read 28 U.S.C. §§ 1738, 1738A (full faith and credit).

MARRESE v. AMERICAN ACADEMY OF ORTHOPAEDIC SURGEONS
470 U.S. 373 (1985)

JUSTICE O'CONNOR delivered the opinion of the Court.

This case concerns the preclusive effect of a state court judgment in a subsequent lawsuit involving federal antitrust claims within the exclusive jurisdiction of the federal courts. The Court of Appeals for the Seventh Circuit, sitting en banc, held as a matter of federal law that the earlier state court judgments barred the federal antitrust suit. Under 28 U.S.C. § 1738, a federal court generally is required to consider first the law of the State in which the judgment was rendered to determine its preclusive effect. Because the lower courts did not consider state preclusion law in this case, we reverse and remand.

[The defendant, American Academy of Orthopaedic Surgeons, denied the plaintiffs membership privileges. The plaintiffs filed suit in an Illinois state court, claiming that the membership denial had violated their associational rights under the common law of the state. The Illinois courts dismissed the plaintiffs' claims with prejudice, determining that they failed to state a cause of action under state law.

[Plaintiffs then filed an action in federal court, alleging that the membership denial was an illegal boycott in violation of the federal antitrust laws. The defendant moved to dismiss on the ground that the state court judgments precluded the federal action. The Court of Appeals agreed, holding that the federal antitrust action was barred by claim preclusion as a matter of federal law. This was so, said the Court, even though the antitrust claim was subject by statute to exclusive federal jurisdiction and could not have been asserted in the state court case. The Supreme Court here reverses and remands, so that the District Court may consider the preclusive effect of the state court judgments under Illinois law.]

The issue presented by this case is whether a state court judgment may have preclusive effect on a federal antitrust claim that could not have been raised in the state proceeding. [T]he Court of Appeals erred by suggesting that in these circumstances a federal court should determine the preclusive effect of a state court judgment without regard to the law of the State in which judgment was rendered.

The preclusive effect of a state court judgment in a subsequent federal lawsuit generally is determined by the full faith and credit statute, which provides that state judicial proceedings "shall have the same full faith and credit in every court within the United States . . . as they have by law or usage in the courts of such State . . . from which they are taken." 28 U.S.C. § 1738. "[I]t has long been established that § 1738 does not allow federal courts to employ their own rules of res judicata in determining the effect of state judgments. Rather, it goes beyond the common law and commands a federal court to accept the rules chosen by the State from which the judgment is taken." *Kremer v. Chemical Construction Corp.*, 456 U.S. 461, 481-482 (1982). . . . Section 1738 embodies concerns of comity and federalism that allow the States to determine, subject to the requirements of the statute and the Due Process Clause, the preclusive effect of judgment in their own courts. *Cf. Riley v. New York Trust Co.*, 315 U.S. 343, 349 (1942) (discussing preclusive effect of state judgment in proceedings in another State).

The fact that petitioners' antitrust claim is within the exclusive jurisdiction of the federal courts does not necessarily make § 1738 inapplicable to this case. Our decisions indicate that a state court judgment may in some circumstances have preclusive effect in a subsequent action within the exclusive jurisdiction of the federal courts. Without discussing § 1738, this Court has held that the issue preclusive effect of a state court judgment barred a subsequent patent suit that could not have been brought in state court. *Becher v. Contoure Laboratories, Inc.*, 279 U.S. 388 (1929). Moreover, *Kremer* held that § 1738 applies to a claim of employment discrimination under Title VII of the Civil Rights Act of 1964, although the Court expressly declined to decide whether Title VII claims can be brought only in federal courts. . . .

[K]remer observed that "an exception to § 1738 will not be recognized unless a later statute contains an express or implied repeal." [W]e conclude that the basic approach adopted in *Kremer* applies in a lawsuit involving a claim within the exclusive jurisdiction of the federal courts.

To be sure, a state court will not have occasion to address the specific question whether a state judgment has issue or claim preclusive effect in a later action that can be brought only in federal court. Nevertheless, a federal court may rely in the first instance on state preclusion principles to determine the extent to which an earlier state judgment bars subsequent litigation. *Kremer* illustrates that a federal court can apply state rules of issue preclusion to determine if a matter actually litigated in state court may be relitigated in a subsequent federal proceeding.

With respect to matters that were not decided in the state proceedings, we note that claim preclusion generally does not apply where "[t]he plaintiff was unable to rely on a certain theory of the case or to seek a certain remedy because of the limitations on the subject matter jurisdiction of the courts. . . ." *Restatement (Second) of Judgments* § 26(1)(c) (1982). If state preclusion law includes this requirement of prior jurisdictional competency, which is generally true, a state judgment will *not* have claim preclusive effect on a cause of action within the exclusive jurisdiction of the federal courts. . . .

[U]nless application of Illinois preclusion law suggests, contrary to the usual view, that petitioners' federal antitrust claim is somehow barred, there will be no need to decide in this case if there is an exception to § 1738.[3] . . .

In this case the Court of Appeals should have first referred to Illinois law to determine the preclusive effect of the state judgment. Only if state law indicates that a particular claim or issue would be barred, is it necessary to determine if an exception to § 1738 should apply. Although for purposes of this case, we need not decide if such an exception exists for federal antitrust claims, we observe that the more general question is whether the concerns underlying a particular grant of exclusive jurisdiction justify a finding of an implied partial repeal of § 1738. Resolution of this question will depend on the particular federal statute as well as the nature of the claim or issue involved in the subsequent federal action. Our previous decisions indicate that the primary consideration must be the intent of Congress. . . .

---

[3] The Chief Justice notes that preclusion rules bar the splitting of a cause of action between a court of limited jurisdiction and one of general jurisdiction. . . . [But] the rule that the judgment of a court of limited jurisdiction concludes the entire claim assumes that the plaintiff might have commenced his action in a court *in the same system of courts* that was competent to give full relief. *See Restatement (Second) of Judgments* § 24, Comment *g* (1982). [W]here state preclusion rules do not indicate that a claim is barred, we do not believe that federal courts should fashion a federal rule to preclude a claim that could not have been raised in the state proceedings.

The judgment of the Court of Appeals is reversed, and the case is remanded for further proceedings consistent with this opinion. . . .

CHIEF JUSTICE BURGER, concurring in the judgment.

[I] cannot agree with the Court's interpretation of the jurisdictional competency requirement. If state law provides a cause of action that is virtually identical with a federal statutory cause of action, a plaintiff suing in state court is able to rely on the same theory of the case and obtain the same remedy as would be available in federal court, even when the plaintiff cannot expressly invoke the federal statute because it is within the exclusive federal jurisdiction.

The states that recognize the jurisdictional competency requirement do not all define it in the same terms. Illinois courts have expressed the doctrine in the following manner: "The principle [of *res judicata*] extends not only to questions which were actually litigated but also to all *questions* which *could have been raised* or determined." *Spiller v. Continental Tube Co.*, 95 Ill. 2d 423, 432, 447 N.E.2d 834, 838 (1983) (emphasis added). . . . In the present case, each petitioner could have alleged a cause of action under the Illinois Antitrust Act in his prior state court lawsuit against respondent. The principles of the Illinois res judicata doctrine appear to be indeterminate as to whether petitioners' ability to raise state antitrust claims in their prior state court suits should preclude their assertion of essentially the same claims in the present federal action. [T]he Illinois courts have not addressed whether the notion of "questions which could have been raised" should be applied narrowly [1] or broadly. [2] No Illinois court has considered how the jurisdictional competency requirement should apply [w]here the same theory of recovery may be asserted under different statutes. Nor has any Illinois court considered whether res judicata precludes splitting a cause of action between a court of limited jurisdiction and one of general jurisdiction.

Hence it is likely that the principles of Illinois claim preclusion law do not speak to the preclusive effect that petitioners' state court judgments should have on the present action. In this situation, it may be consistent with § 1738 for a federal court to formulate a federal rule to resolve the matter. If state law is simply indeterminate, the concerns of comity and federalism underlying § 1738 do not come into play. At the same time, the federal courts have direct interests in ensuring that their resources are used efficiently and not as a means of harassing defendants with repetitive lawsuits, as well as in ensuring that parties asserting federal rights have an adequate opportunity to litigate those rights. Given the insubstantiality of the state interests and the weight of the federal interests, a strong argument could be made that a federal rule would be more appropriate than a creative interpretation of ambiguous state law. . . . [4]

A federal rule might be fashioned from the test, which this Court has applied in other contexts, that a party is precluded from asserting a claim that he had a "full and fair opportunity" to litigate in a prior action. Thus, if a state statute is identical in all material respects with a federal statute within exclusive federal jurisdiction, a party's ability to

---

[1] *E.g.*, by inquiring whether the plaintiff could have raised the question whether the defendant violated a particular statute.

[2] *E.g.*, by inquiring whether the plaintiff could have raised the question whether the defendant engaged in a group boycott.

[4] By contrast, when a federal court construes [substantive] state law in [a] diversity action, the federal interest is insignificant and the state's interest is much more direct[,] even if the relevant state law is ambiguous.

assert a claim under the state statute in a prior state court action might be said to have provided, in effect, a "full and fair opportunity" to litigate his rights under the federal statute.

The Court will eventually have to face these questions; I would resolve them now. . . .

NOTES AND QUESTIONS

(1) *State-to-State Preclusion: Riley v. New York Trust Co., 315 U.S. 343, 349 (1942).* Consider what preclusive effect a state court should give to another state's judgment. (For example, what should happen if Marrese next files an action in the courts of another state, asserting that state's antitrust laws?) Notice how § 1738 is written: It requires "every court within the United States" to give the same effect to a judgment as it would have under the law of the state that rendered it. The *Riley* case, cited in *Marrese,* discusses the general issue.

(2) *State Administrative Agency Decisions — Can They Preclude Federal Claims?: University of Tennessee v. Eliot, 478 U.S. 788 (1986).* In this case, an unreviewed state administrative hearing resulted in a finding of no discrimination. The plaintiff later brought a federal employment discrimination claim under Title VII of the Civil Rights Act of 1968. The Supreme Court held that the federal court must apply state preclusion law, under which an administrative finding did have preclusive effect that barred the Title VII action. Does this holding go too far? Does Section 1738 compel such a result? *See also* Shreve, *Preclusion and Federal Choice of Law*, 64 Tex. L. Rev. 1209 (1986).

(3) *Preclusive Effect of Federal Judgment.* Federal common law governs the preclusive effect of federal judgments in both federal question and diversity cases. If the federal judgment is rendered in a case based on diversity of citizenship jurisdiction, the claim preclusive effect of the federal judgment is determined by the law of the state in which the federal court was sitting, unless the state law is incompatible with federal interests. *Semtek Int'l v. Lockheed Martin*, 531 U.S. 497, 506-09 (2001). In contrast, federal judgments in federal question cases have the preclusive effect prescribed by federal law, without reference to state law. The same approach is probably applicable to the preclusive effect of federal judgments in connection with issue preclusion.

(4) *State Court Judgment Preclusion of Exclusive Federal Claims: Matsushita Electric Industrial Co. v. Epstein, 516 U.S. 367 (1996).* In *Matsushita,* the Supreme Court held that state court settlement judgments that release exclusive federal claims are entitled to full faith and credit in federal court. Citing *Marrese,* Justice Thomas' majority opinion stated that the full faith and credit statute, 28 U.S.C. § 1738, applied to a state court class action settlement even though it released claims within the exclusive jurisdiction of the federal courts.

(5) *Res Judicata Cannot Reduce Amount in Controversy.* In *Scherer v. Equitable Life Assurance Society*, 347 F.3d 394 (2d Cir. 2003), the Second Circuit held that, as an affirmative defense, res judicata cannot be used to exclude certain damages from the calculation of the amount in controversy needed for federal diversity jurisdiction. "The district court's use of preclusion doctrines to winnow down the amount in controversy so that it failed to reach the jurisdictional threshold does not comport with the rule that the amount in controversy is to be ascertained as of the time of filing, without regard to 'affirmative defenses.' . . . [B]ecause affirmative defenses can be waived, the court cannot at the time of filing be certain that any given affirmative defense will be applied to the case."

§ 13.04 The "Law of the Case" Doctrine

WILLIAMS v. CITY OF NEW ORLEANS, 763 F.2d 667 (5th Cir. 1985). During the course of a class action lawsuit that was brought against the New Orleans Police Department by black applicants and members on the basis of allegedly racially discriminatory policies, white, Hispanic and female members sought to intervene in the case. The District Court refused to allow the intervention but subsequently granted partial intervenor status to other members of the department. The district judge's order denying full intervenor status was appealed to the Court of Appeals which affirmed the District Court. Subsequently, the same persons again sought full intervenor status from the District Court. When this relief was denied again, they appealed again. The Court of Appeals dismissed the second appeal on the basis of the "law of the case" doctrine:

> We stated in *White v. Murtha*, 377 F.2d 428, 431-32 (5th Cir. 1967) (footnotes omitted):
>
> > While the "law of the case" doctrine is not an inexorable command, a decision of a legal issue or issues by an appellate court establishes the "law of the case" and must be followed in all subsequent proceedings in the same case in the trial court or on a later appeal in the appellate court, unless the evidence on a subsequent trial was substantially different, controlling authority has since made a contrary decision of the law applicable to such issues, or the decision was clearly erroneous and would work a manifest injustice. . . .
>
> Appellants have failed to meet the *White v. Murtha* test. They have presented no evidence which differs from that presented in their prior appeal to this court. The controlling law has not changed. Finally, appellants have not demonstrated that manifest injustice would result by rejecting this second appeal. The mere fact that the en banc court affirmed the District Court's vacation of the consent decree and has remanded for further proceedings fails to establish any reason to relitigate the grant of limited intervenor status. Plaintiffs retain this status and may thus object to any proposed settlement agreement. We fail to see how their interests are now less protected than before.

CHAPTER 14

REMEDIES, JUDGMENTS, AND THEIR ENFORCEMENT

§ 14.01 Emergency and Temporary Relief: "Provisional" Remedies

[A] Seizure of Assets Before Hearing on the Merits: Attachment, Garnishment, Sequestration, Replevin, etc.

Read Fed. R. Civ. P. 64 (provisional remedies).

Kheel, NEW YORK'S AMENDED ATTACHMENT STATUTE: A PREJUDGMENT REMEDY IN NEED OF FURTHER REVISION

*44 Brooklyn L. Rev. 199, 202 (1978)**

Consider . . . the situation of a businessman in financial trouble who fails to pay for goods purchased or consigned. If his creditor brings suit for payment, the debtor can rely on the fact that it will be months and — given the usual reluctance of the courts to grant summary judgment — perhaps years before he will be required to pay. . . . But if the creditor can obtain an attachment of the debtor's bank account, the debtor will no longer be able to use or control the creditor's money prior to judgment. . . . In this way attachment often motivates a defendant to settle a claim which he might not otherwise be willing to settle — at least at that time. For the same reason, an order of attachment could provide a swift and effective remedy against fraud or conversion and may even serve to deter a defendant from such acts. . . .

Attachment . . . also can cause a devastating impact on a defendant. Since orders of attachment often are granted *ex parte*, a defendant does not have notice and cannot protect himself against the unexpected disruptions they bring. Attachment of a bank account may cause checks to bounce, enrage employees who cannot be paid, or otherwise disrupt ongoing business relations. Under most lending agreements the entry of an order of attachment against the borrower's property constitutes an act of default; consequently, a defendant's obligations to his lenders may be accelerated. The disruption of business and acceleration of debts exert powerful pressure on the defendant to settle prior to any adjudication of the dispute.

On the other hand, to many a plaintiff who seeks the prompt return of property owed by a defendant, an early settlement may be the only solution. A court "victory" ordering the return of plaintiff's property after years or even months may be as bad as losing the battle. The pressure that a plaintiff can exert with an order of attachment is thus the countervailing force which can get him a prompt and meaningful remedy, through the courts.

PROBLEM A: CHAPTER 14 SUMMARY PROBLEM

THE EMBEZZLEMENT FROM ACME COMPANY AND EFFORTS TO RECOVER FROM ROBERT BAILEY: PROBLEMS OF PREJUDGMENT SEIZURE, TEMPORARY RELIEF, DAMAGES, EQUITABLE REMEDIES AND ENFORCEMENT. The Vice President for Finance of Acme Company is worried. He tells you that he has just detected a very large embezzlement, exceeding $2 million. He believes that a single individual, whom he identifies as Robert Bailey, committed the embezzlement over a period of some four years, and although he has no direct proof, the circumstantial evidence is such that "it couldn't have been anyone else." Bailey left the company's employment a few months ago.

Bailey is known to have extensive holdings of valuable business equipment, precious metals, and stocks; these items (or the certificates) are held partly by Bailey and partly by others. The Vice President believes that the value of Bailey's holdings has increased tremendously over the last few years. In effect, Bailey has invested the apparently stolen funds in a way that has enriched him handsomely. But the Vice President confides that Bailey has "underworld connections, and he once bragged to me that he could disappear in a day by going to a foreign country where there's no extradition treaty." [These facts are a dramatization of several more mundane (and frustrating) cases in which some of the authors of this casebook have from time to time been involved.]

Consider what possibilities exist of using the following collection tools or remedies, what conditions you would need to show for each, and what advantages or disadvantages each might entail:

1. Devices to secure property before suit, or to prevent Bailey's disappearance or transfer of property either before, during or after suit;
2. Damage and damage-related remedies;
3. Equitable remedies (might there be some such remedies that would afford greater recovery than damages?); and
4. Means of collecting or enforcing a judgment against Bailey at the post-judgment stage, if suit is successful.

FUENTES v. SHEVIN
407 U.S. 67 (1972)

MR. JUSTICE STEWART delivered the opinion of the Court.

We here review the decisions of two . . . federal District Courts that upheld the constitutionality of Florida and Pennsylvania laws authorizing the summary seizure of goods or chattels in a person's possession under a writ of replevin. Both statutes provide for the issuance of writs ordering state agents to seize a person's possessions, simply upon the *ex parte* application of any other person who claims a right to them and posts a security bond. Neither statute provides for notice to be given to the possessor of the property, and neither statute gives the possessor an opportunity to challenge the seizure at any kind of prior hearing. The question is whether these statutory procedures violate the Fourteenth Amendment's guarantee that no State shall deprive any person of property without due process of law.

I

[The appellants each had been subjected to seizures in dubious circumstances. For example, appellant Margarita Fuentes had bought certain appliances on a conditional sales contract for about $600, but she refused to pay approximately the last $200 because of a dispute about a related service agreement. Under the governing Florida law, the vendor had only to file an unsworn fill-in-the-blank form with the clerk of the small claims court to cause issuance of a writ of replevin that resulted in the seizure of the appliances the same day. Mrs. Fuentes filed this federal action shortly thereafter, attacking the Florida replevin procedure under the Due Process Clause. The Pennsylvania appellants, likewise, included three who had purchased goods on installment only to have them seized by replevin, plus one appellant whose experience was more bizarre: Her ex-husband, a deputy sheriff who was litigating the custody of their son with her and who was familiar with the procedures, obtained the seizure of the boy's toys, furniture and clothes.]

II

Under the Florida statute challenged here, "[a]ny person whose goods or chattels are wrongfully detained by any other person . . . may have a writ of replevin to recover them. . . ." Fla. Stat. Ann. § 78.01 (Supp. 1972-1973). There is no requirement that the applicant make a convincing showing before the seizure that the goods are, in fact, "wrongfully detained." Rather, Florida law automatically relies on the bare assertion of the party seeking the writ that he is entitled to one and allows a court clerk to issue the writ summarily. It requires only that the applicant file a complaint, [r]eciting in conclusory fashion that he is "lawfully entitled to the possession" of the property, and that he file a security bond. . . .

Thus, at the same moment that the defendant receives the complaint seeking repossession of property through court action, the property is seized from him. He is provided no prior notice and allowed no opportunity whatever to challenge the issues of the writ. *After* the property has been seized, he will eventually have an opportunity for a hearing, as the defendant in the trial of the court action for repossession, which the plaintiff is required to pursue. And he is also not wholly without recourse in the meantime. For under the Florida statute, the officer who seizes the property must keep it for three days, and during that period the defendant may reclaim possession of the property by posting his own security bond in double its value. . . .

The Pennsylvania law differs, though not in its essential nature, from that of Florida. . . . [A] private party may obtain a prejudgment writ of replevin through a summary process of *ex parte* application to a prothonotary. . . . Unlike the Florida statute, however, the Pennsylvania law does not require that there *ever* be opportunity for a hearing on the merits of the conflicting claims to possession of the replevied property. . . . If the party who loses property through replevin seizure is to get even a post-seizure hearing, he must initiate a lawsuit himself. He may also, as under Florida law, post his own counterbond [t]o regain possession. . . .

III

[The Court acknowledged that these replevin statutes were "descended from the common-law replevin action of six centuries ago," but it said, "they bear little resemblance to it." Common law replevin was used by tenants to recover property wrongfully distrained from them by their landlords; these statutes "are most commonly used by creditors to seize goods allegedly wrongfully detained . . . by debtors."]

IV

For more than a century the central meaning of procedural due process has been clear: "Parties whose rights are to be affected are entitled to be heard; and in order that they may enjoy that right they must first be notified." *Baldwin v. Hale*, 1 Wall. 223, 233. . . . It is equally fundamental that the right to notice and an opportunity to be heard "must be granted at a meaningful time and in a meaningful manner." *Armstrong v. Manzo*, 380 U.S. 545, 552. . . .

[I]ts purpose, more particularly, is to protect his use and possession of property from arbitrary encroachment — to minimize substantively unfair or mistaken deprivations of property, a danger that is especially great when the State seizes goods simply upon the application of and for the benefit of a private party. . . .

. . . For when a person has an opportunity to speak up in his own defense, and when the State must listen to what he has to say, substantively unfair and simply mistaken deprivations of property interests can be prevented. It has long been recognized that "fairness can rarely be obtained by secret, one-sided determination of facts decisive of rights. . . ."

If the right to notice and a hearing is to serve its full purpose, then, it is clear that it must be granted at a time when the deprivation can still be prevented. . . .

The Florida and Pennsylvania prejudgment replevin statutes fly in the face of this principle. To be sure, the requirements that a party seeking a writ must first post a bond, allege conclusorily that he is entitled to specific goods, and open himself to possible liability in damages if he is wrong, serve to deter wholly unfounded applications for a writ. But those requirements are hardly a substitute for a prior hearing, for they test no more than the strength of the applicant's own belief in his rights. [L]awyers and judges are familiar with the phenomenon of a party mistakenly but firmly convinced that his view of the facts and law will prevail, and therefore quite willing to risk the costs of litigation. . . .

V

The right to a prior hearing, of course, attaches only to the deprivation of an interest encompassed within the Fourteenth Amendment's protection. . . .

A

A deprivation of a person's possessions under a prejudgment writ of replevin, at least in theory, may be only temporary. [B]ut it is now well settled that a temporary nonfinal deprivation of property is nonetheless a "deprivation" in the terms of the Fourteenth Amendment. *Sniadach v. Family Finance Corp.*, 395 U.S. 337; *Bell v. Burson*, 402 U.S. 535. Both *Sniadach* and *Bell* involved takings of property pending a final judgment in an underlying dispute. In both cases the challenged statutes included recovery provisions, allowing the defendants to post security to quickly regain the property taken from them. Yet the Court firmly held that these were deprivations of property that had to be preceded by a fair hearing.

The present cases are no different. . . . The Fourteenth Amendment draws no bright lines around three-day, 10-day or 50-day deprivations of property. Any significant taking of property by the State is within the purview of the Due Process Clause. . . .

B

The appellants who signed conditional sales contracts lacked full legal title to the replevied goods. The Fourteenth Amendment's protection of "property," however, has never been interpreted to safeguard only the rights of undisputed ownership. Rather, it has been read broadly to extend protection to "any significant property interest". . . .

Their ultimate right to continued possession was, of course, in dispute. If it were shown at a hearing that the appellants had defaulted on their contractual obligations, it might well be that the sellers of the goods would be entitled to repossession. But even assuming that the appellants had fallen behind in their installment payments, and that they had no other valid defenses, that is immaterial here. The right to be heard does not depend upon an advance showing that one will surely prevail at the hearing. . . .

VI

There are "extraordinary situations" that justify postponing notice and opportunity for a hearing. *Boddie v. Connecticut*, 401 U.S., at 379. These situations, however, must be truly unusual. Only in a few limited situations has this Court allowed outright seizure without opportunity for a prior hearing. [T]hus, the Court has allowed summary seizure of property to collect the internal revenue of the United States, to meet the needs of a national war effort, to protect against the economic disaster of a bank failure, and to protect the public from misbranded drugs and contaminated food.

The Florida and Pennsylvania prejudgment replevin statutes serve no such important governmental or general public interest. . . .

VII

[The Court considered, and rejected, the creditors' arguments that the debtors had waived their rights to hearings by signing conditional sales contracts providing that the sellers had the power to "retake" or "repossess" the merchandise. These printed-form provisions appeared in small type. "[A] waiver of constitutional rights . . . must, at the very least, be clear." The contracts did not indicate "how or through what process — a final judgment, self-help, prejudgment replevin with a prior hearing, or prejudgment replevin without a prior hearing — the seller could take back the goods."]

VIII

We hold that the Florida and Pennsylvania prejudgment replevin provisions work a deprivation of property without due process of law insofar as they deny the right to a prior opportunity to be heard before chattels are taken from their possessor. Our holding, however, is a narrow one. We do not question the power of a State to seize goods before a final judgment in order to protect the security interests of creditors so long as those creditors have tested their claim to the goods through the process of a fair prior hearing. . . .

For the foregoing reasons, the judgments of the District Courts are vacated and these cases are remanded for further proceedings consistent with this opinion.

MR. JUSTICE POWELL and MR. JUSTICE REHNQUIST did not participate in the consideration or decision of these cases.

MR. JUSTICE WHITE, with whom THE CHIEF JUSTICE and MR. JUSTICE BLACKMUN join, dissenting. . . .

. . . It goes without saying that in the typical installment sale of personal property both seller and buyer have interests in the property until the purchase price is fully paid, the seller early in the transaction often having more at stake than the buyer. . . .

. . . The interests of the buyer and seller are obviously antagonistic during this interim period: the buyer wants the use of the property pending final judgment; the seller's interest is to prevent further use and deterioration of his security. By the Florida and Pennsylvania laws the property is to all intents and purposes placed in custody and immobilized during this time. The buyer loses use of the property temporarily but is protected against loss; the seller is protected against deterioration of the property but must undertake by bond to make the buyer whole in the event the latter prevails.

In considering whether this resolution of conflicting interests is unconstitutional, much depends on one's perceptions of the practical considerations involved. . . . If there is a default, it would seem not only "fair," but essential, that the creditor be allowed to repossess; and I cannot say that the likelihood of a mistaken claim of default is sufficiently real or recurring to justify a broad constitutional requirement that a creditor do more than the typical state law requires and permits him to do. Sellers are normally in the business of selling and collecting the price for their merchandise. I could be quite wrong, but it would not seem in the creditor's interest for a default occasioning repossession to occur; as a practical matter it would much better serve his interests if the transaction goes forward and is completed as planned. . . .

. . . Surely under the Court's own definition, the creditor has a "property" interest as deserving of protection as that of the debtor. At least the debtor, who is very likely uninterested in a speedy resolution that could terminate his use of the property, should be required to make those payments, into court or otherwise, upon which his right to possession is conditioned. . . .

. . . The Court's rhetoric is seductive, but in end analysis, the result it reaches will have little impact and represents no more than ideological tinkering with state law. It would appear that creditors could withstand attack under today's opinion simply by making clear in the controlling credit instruments that they may retake possession without a hearing, or, for that matter, without resort to judicial process at all. Alternatively, they need only give a few days' notice of a hearing, take possession if hearing is waived or if there is default; and if hearing is necessary merely establish probable cause for asserting that default has occurred. It is very doubtful in my mind that such a hearing would in fact result in protections for the debtor substantially different from those the present laws provide. On the contrary, the availability of credit may well be diminished or, in any event, the expense of securing it increased. . . .

NOTES AND QUESTIONS

(1) *Ironic Results of Fuentes v. Shevin, Part I: What Protection Is Left for Property Interests of Persons Not in Possession?* The creditor who seeks a provisional remedy may have a property interest in the chattel at issue, just as the purported debtor may. In some instances, the creditor may have title; in others, he may have a security interest; in many other instances, he may be entitled to immediate possession. In fact, consider

the case of a person whose property has been taken by force or fraud and is now in the possession of a thief. *Fuentes v. Shevin* provides protection of the interest of the alleged debtor in the first instance, and of the thief in the second; what, if any, protection does it provide for the creditor or true owner not in possession?

(2) *Ironic Results of Fuentes v. Shevin, Part II: Effects on Credit Costs.* As Note #1, above, implies, there may be a valid interest of creditors in a process for *ex parte* seizure. Ironically, might the *Fuentes* decision also harm the interests of some future buyers on credit? Prices of goods sold on credit in a market economy, of course, must reflect the losses attributable to bad debts and to costs of collection. If you were a purchaser on credit who intended to and were able to pay for the purchase as agreed, wouldn't you prefer to be in a jurisdiction where your creditor had expeditious remedies against defaulting parties, so that your own payments would not include costs attributable to them?

(3) *Ironic Results of Fuentes v. Shevin, Part III: Private Repossession Probably Is Not State Action and Is Not Subject to the Due Process Clause.* What happens if, instead of using the sheriff and the mechanisms of the law, the creditor employs an army of private "repo men," and they simply take chattels away from debtors whom the creditor considers to be in default? Note that the dissenters argue that the creditor can accomplish this result by putting provisions in an installment sales contract. Actually, it's easier than that, because § 9-503 of the Uniform Commercial Code provides, "Unless otherwise agreed a secured party has on default the right to take possession of the collateral. . . ." In general, self-help remedies do not invoke the protection of the Fourteenth Amendment, because it provides that "no State" shall deny due process, and self-help does not involve state action. *See Flagg Bros., Inc. v. Brooks*, 436 U.S. 149 (1978). Is it desirable to prohibit use of legal remedies and to substitute purely private conduct in this situation?

(4) *Is There a Middle Ground?* In *Fuentes*, the Court used its power of discretionary review to select cases in which a holding in favor of the possessory parties was attractive. Furthermore, the provisional remedies at issue lacked appropriate protections. Criticism of *Fuentes* might better be directed at its rhetoric and reasoning than at its holding. Is there a middle ground that can use the law to protect interests both of possessors and non-possessors? [Note that *Fuentes* is a four-to-three decision, in which neither Justice Rehnquist nor Justice Powell participated.] Consider the following decision, rendered a year and a half after *Fuentes*.

MITCHELL v. W.T. GRANT CO., 416 U.S. 600 (1974). Mitchell bought a refrigerator, range, stereo, and washing machine on an installment credit contract with W.T. Grant Co. On Grant's application showing that Mitchell was in default, and without a prior adversary hearing, a state court in New Orleans issued a writ of sequestration in conformity with a Louisiana statute, authorizing the seizure of the merchandise. Stressing the differences between the Louisiana procedure for seizure and the processes at issue in *Fuentes v. Shevin*, the Supreme Court upheld the sequestration order:

> Petitioner [Mitchell] no doubt "owned" the goods he had purchased under an installment sales contract, but his title was heavily encumbered. The seller, W.T. Grant Co., also had an interest in the property, for state law provided it with a vendor's lien to secure the unpaid balance of the purchase price. Because of the lien, Mitchell's right to possession and his title were subject to defeasance in the event of default in paying the installments due from him. . . .

> . . . The reality is that both seller and buyer had current, real interests in the property. . . . Resolution of the due process question must take account not only of the interests of the buyer of the property but those of the seller as well. . . .
>
> Louisiana statutes provide for sequestration where "one claims the ownership or right to possession of property, or a mortgage, lien, or privilege thereon . . . if it is within the power of the defendant to conceal, dispose of, or waste the property or the revenues therefrom, or remove the property from the parish, during the pendency of the action." . . .
>
> The Louisiana sequestration statute followed in this case mandates a considerably different procedure. A writ of sequestration is available . . . to forestall waste or alienation of the property, but, different from the Florida and Pennsylvania systems, bare, conclusory claims of ownership or lien will not suffice under the Louisiana statute. Article 3501 authorizes the writ "only when the nature of the claim and the amount thereof, if any, and the grounds relied upon for the issuance of the writ clearly appear from specific facts" shown by verified affidavit. Moreover, in the parish where this case arose, the requisite showing must be made to a judge, and judicial authorization obtained. Mitchell was not at the unsupervised mercy of the creditor and court functionaries. . . . [S]hould the writ be dissolved there are "damages for the wrongful issuance of a writ" and for attorneys' fees "whether the writ is dissolved on motion or after trial on the merits." . . .
>
> [I]n *Fuentes*, [a wrongful detention] standard for replevin was thought ill-suited for ex parte determination. In Louisiana, on the other hand, the facts relevant to obtaining a writ of sequestration are narrowly confined. . . .
>
> . . . Under Louisiana procedure, . . . the debtor, Mitchell, was not left in limbo to await a hearing that might or might not "eventually" occur, as the debtors were under the statutory schemes before the Court in *Fuentes*. Louisiana law expressly provides for an immediate hearing and dissolution of the writ "unless the plaintiff proves the grounds upon which the writ was issued." . . . [As in *Fuentes*, Louisiana also required the creditor to post security and allowed the debtor to obtain return of the property by posting security.]
>
> To summarize, the Louisiana system seeks to minimize the risk of error of a wrongful interim possession by the creditor. The system protects the debtor's interest in every conceivable way, except allowing him to have the property to start with, and this is done [t]o put the property in the possession of the party who furnishes protection against loss or damage to the other pending trial on the merits. . . .

Justice Powell concurred separately. Justices Brennan, Stewart, Douglas and Marshall dissented. Justice Stewart's opinion argued that an *ex parte* hearing did not adequately protect the debtor's interest and that the case was "identical to" *Fuentes*.

NOTES AND QUESTIONS

(1) *Is Mitchell Sufficiently Different from Fuentes to Make a Difference (or Is It the Result of Personnel Changes on the Court)?* The factors "protecting" the debtor in *Mitchell* include requirements of (a) sworn testimony by the creditor (b) showing specific facts (c) conforming to narrow grounds authorizing the writ (d) before a judicial officer (e) supported by a bond posted by the creditor, (f) subject to an "immediate" post-seizure hearing on the debtor's demand (g) at which the creditor must prove entitlement to the writ, with (h) the debtor having a right to possession on posting security and (i) to damages

if the writ is dissolved. Justice Stewart claimed that the Court had ignored the principle of *stare decisis*; is he right? [This question, in turn, depends both upon whether the case is sufficiently distinguishable and upon whether the broad language of *Fuentes*, requiring a prior adversary hearing for even a "temporary" deprivation, is controlling.]

(2) *The Debtor's Interest After Mitchell: Is It Adequately Protected?* Isn't it possible, after *Mitchell*, that a plaintiff could obtain a writ of sequestration in bad faith and avoid paying very large damages caused to the possessor because the plaintiff is judgment-proof? Does *Mitchell* adequately protect the possessor's legitimate interests? Is there a better way?

(3) *Reaffirming the Fuentes Holding after Mitchell: North Georgia Finishing, Inc. v. Di-Chem, Inc., 419 U.S. 601 (1975).* In this case, the creditor used a Georgia statute that allowed *ex parte* garnishment upon a sworn application before a judge or clerk, showing that the creditor "has reason to apprehend the loss" of the amount claimed, and supported by a bond. "The Georgia garnishment statute has none of the saving characteristics of the Louisiana statute" upheld in *Mitchell*, said the Court. It did not require that the sworn application be on personal knowledge, it could be conclusory, it did not require a judicial decision, and there was no provision for an early hearing. "This approach failed to take account of *Fuentes v. Shevin*," said the Court.

(4) *Extending Due Process Protection to Pre-Judgment Property Liens: Connecticut v. Doehr, 501 U.S. 1 (1991).* In *Doehr*, Connecticut law authorized the prejudgment attachment of real estate without affording the affected owner any prior notice or opportunity for a hearing. Nor was any bond required. Under this statute, DiGiovanni submitted an application to a Superior Court judge seeking an attachment of $75,000 against Doehr's home in connection with DiGiovanni's civil action for assault and battery against Doehr in the same court. The suit did not involve Doehr's real estate, nor did DiGiovanni have any pre-existing interest in any of Doehr's property. On the strength of DiGiovanni's five-sentence affidavit, the judge ordered the attachment. Doehr challenged the Connecticut statute in federal court, claiming that it violated the Due Process Clause of the Fourteenth Amendment. The lower court upheld the statute, but the Court of Appeals reversed, concluding that the statute violated due process because it permitted *ex parte* attachment absent a showing of extraordinary circumstances.

A unanimous Supreme Court affirmed the decision of the appellate court, concluding that the Connecticut law failed to protect the rights of those being sued. Not only would such liens permit the seizure of property based upon "one-sided, self-serving" affidavits, it could prevent Doehr from selling his home or obtaining future loans and damage his credit rating. The Court laid out a three-part inquiry to determine a statute's constitutionality: First, a consideration of the private interest that will be affected by the prejudgment measure; second, an examination of the risk of erroneous deprivation through the procedures under attack and the probable value of additional safeguards; and third, principal attention to the interest of the party seeking the prejudgment remedy with due regard for any governmental interest.

Applying this test, the Court found that the highly factual nature of the issues in an assault and battery claim significantly increased the risk of a wrongful attachment. Therefore, dispensing with notice and opportunity for a hearing until after the attachment without a showing of extraordinary circumstances, coupled with the statute's failure to require the petitioner to post a bond, rendered the statute unconstitutional. As a result, plaintiffs could not seize the property of defendants based solely on the plaintiff's sworn affidavit. There must be a showing of exigent circumstances to justify such seizure. Four members of the Court further concluded that due process also requires the plaintiff to post a bond or other security as a protection to the defendant.

NOTE ON THE MODERN USE OF PROVISIONAL REMEDIES

Replevin, Sequestration, or Other Seizure of Specific Chattels. Most jurisdictions provide a pre-judgment remedy involving seizure of a chattel on application of a person entitled to its possession, when it may be subjected to waste, removal, destruction, etc. The remedy may be named, variously, "replevin" (as in Florida and Pennsylvania), or "claim and delivery" (as in California) or "sequestration" (as in Louisiana and Texas), or merely "seizure" (New York). Of course, the statute and the procedure actually used must conform to the *Fuentes-Mitchell* requirements. This remedy is most often used by sellers of goods, although it is open to use by others in proper circumstances.

Self-Help Repossession Under the UCC. As is pointed out in the preceding text, the UCC provides for the repossession of collateral by a secured party upon default. One important condition is that the repossession must be undertaken without a "breach of the peace." Force, threats, or unauthorized entry into a building are examples of the kinds of private actions that may be breaches of the peace and may subject the repossessor to potentially large liability for damages. In the event of resistance, the creditor should withdraw and use a judicial remedy provided in the jurisdiction. *See also* Del Duca, *Pre-Notice, Pre-Hearing, Pre-Judgment Seizure of Assets — Self-Help Repossession Under UCC § 9-503, Its Antecedents and Future*, 79 Dick. L. Rev. 211 (1975).

Attachment. In many states, a separate remedy is provided to unsecured creditors allowing seizure of a debtor's non-exempt property in which the creditor does not have a specific security or other ownership interest, provided that the creditor makes a satisfactory showing of emergency need under the appropriate statute. Property that is exempt from execution under state or federal law also is not subject to attachment, which is regarded as execution before judgment. For example, imagine that Bank B loans funds to Debtor D in exchange for her promissory note. Debtor D is in default and the Bank is concerned because she is frittering away the assets she has purchased with the loan (or is transferring them to related persons so as to place them beyond the Bank's reach). Note that one problem the Bank will have is in demonstrating, by particularized facts satisfying the *Fuentes-Mitchell* criteria, the probable loss of its debt, since often the creditor does not have access to evidence that would support such a demonstration (and the mere fact of default is unlikely, after *Fuentes* and *Mitchell*, to be enough).

Pre-Judgment Garnishment. As the case of *North Georgia Finishing, Inc. v. Di-Chem, Inc.*, above, shows, many jurisdictions provide a pre-judgment remedy allowing seizure of property in the hands of a third person. (In some jurisdictions, including, for example, New York and California, pre-judgment garnishment is included in provisions for attachment.) The most common situation, as in *Di-Chem*, is that in which Debtor D is in default and has funds on deposit in a bank. The plaintiff files suit nominally against the bank as garnishee, with notice to Debtor D. Pre-judgment garnishment, today, requires conformity to the *Fuentes-Mitchell* due process protections, usually including proof that there is a need for pre-judgment seizure because the debt will otherwise be lost. Of course, post-judgment garnishment does not. Can you see why?

Real Property: Notice of Lis Pendens. A dispute over real estate title may give rise to the need for this procedure. A claimant, to prevent the possessory party's transfer of property to a *bona fide* purchaser without notice, may file a notice of pending dispute over title — or notice of lis pendens — in the real property records maintained by the local county clerk or other authorized officer. Strictly speaking, this notice may not be a "provisional remedy," but arguably is a form of self-help. It effectively discourages the transfer of title unless the purchaser is able to satisfy herself that it is safe to ignore the dispute. (Does *Connecticut v. Doehr*, above, impose due process limits despite the ostensibly "private" nature of this remedy?)

Real Property: Forcible Entry and Detainer; Eviction; Writ of Possession. Most jurisdictions provide expeditious remedies for possession of real property. The common law writ of possession obtained at the conclusion of a suit for forcible entry or forcible detainer is an example. Because of the nature of real property, as well as for historical reasons, it is not common for these remedies to be undertaken without notice or opportunity for hearing; instead, the usual pattern is for the service of process to notify the possessor of a prompt hearing. There are some states that provide for *ex parte* sequestration or other judicial seizure in narrow circumstances (*e.g.*, restoration of real property taken by actual force).

Receivership. Some states provide for provisional orders appointing receivers. The remedy at the post-judgment stage is dealt with in greater depth in a later section of this chapter.

NOTE ON DAMAGES FOR WRONGFUL USE OF PROVISIONAL REMEDIES

One aspect of provisional remedies that should be stressed is that they should not be lightly used. Most jurisdictions provide serious remedies for wrongful process. In some jurisdictions, fault is not required; all that is necessary is that the issuance of the order be wrongful. Consider the following cases.

BARFIELD v. BROGDON, 560 S.W.2d 787 (Tex. Civ. App.-Amarillo 1978, no writ). Barfield, an attorney, took his lawnmower for repairs to Brogdon. He disputed the price, refused to pay, and was met with Brogdon's retention of the lawnmower. Barfield then sued for, and obtained, a writ of sequestration, despite his lack of entitlement because (1) he had not supported his application by sworn testimony and (2) he had no right to possession (Brogdon had a possessory lien for the price of repairs under state law). Brogdon answered and claimed damages for wrongful sequestration. The court awarded Brogdon actual damages. It also awarded exemplary damages, which it held were generally recoverable when the writ was obtained without probable cause and maliciously. The original repair bill had been $24.32; Barfield became liable on a judgment for $74.32 actual damages and $3,000 exemplary damages, or $3,074.32 total.

RICHMAN v. RICHMAN, 52 A.D.2d 393, 384 N.Y.S.2d 220 (1976). After determining that the defendant was liable for wrongful attachment of certain savings accounts and stock of the plaintiff, the trial court granted (and the appellate court affirmed) judgment for $5,799.80 in damages and $4,500 in attorney's fees. The court fixed the amount of damages simply by applying the legal rate of interest to the value of the property over the 188 days that the attachment was in effect. *See also Beagle v. Vasold*, 65 Cal. 2d 166, 417 P.2d 673, 53 Cal. Rptr. 129 (1966) (per diem-based damages).

[B] Temporary Restraining Orders

Read Fed. R. Civ. P. 65 (injunctions).

Weber, SO YOU NEED A TEMPORARY RESTRAINING ORDER? 41 Tex. B.J. 728 (1978). Imagine this situation:*

> You are sitting at your desk at 2:00 p.m. on Friday. The telephone rings. One of your better clients, Sam Successful, is frantic! Sam has recently purchased a beautiful 50-acre tract of woodlands on which he and his wife plan to build a summer home. Today Sam received word from an adjoining landowner that Landeater Lumber Company has cut his fence and begun cutting the timber on his homesite. Landeater has a timber deed by which it claims the right to cut the timber. Landeater refuses to cease operations and hopes to have the land cleared before the weekend is over. Sam wants you to stop Landeater immediately, before the entire tract is ruined. You need a temporary restraining order!

The facts always differ, but two things are always the same: there is a crisis, and both you and your client are in a hurry. . . .

I. What Papers Do We Need?

These are the items the lawyer must have ready when he or she applies for a temporary restraining order:

A. The petition or complaint.

B. The temporary restraining order itself.

C. The restraining order bond.

D. The filing fee.

These items will be discussed in detail, but remember — by now it is 2:30 on Friday afternoon. You must make the practical arrangements to see that the necessary people are available to issue and serve the writ. This is "greasing the skids."

II. Greasing the Skids

You cannot issue and serve the temporary restraining order yourself. You will need the cooperation of the district judge (state or federal), the district clerk (state or federal), and the county sheriff or federal marshal. Each of these persons has a role to play and each must be available.[a]

A. *Call the District Clerk:* A personal call to the clerk's office and a conversation with the deputy who will be handling the application for the TRO is a must. Give the clerk an estimate of when the papers will be prepared and the application filed. In counties with multiple judges, one judge may be designated the injunction judge. The clerk can give you this information. . . .

B. *Contact the Judge:* You should immediately contact the injunction judge to determine his availability. Has he or she left for the weekend? Where can he or she be reached? Can another judge hear the matter? . . . The judge may want you to advise

---

[a] [Amendments to Fed. R. Civ. P. 4 now provide for the use of private process servers in lieu of the marshal. — Eds.]

Landeater or his lawyer to be present. [Note that Rule 65(b) requires the applicant to certify in writing the reasons for dispensing with notice, if that is the case, and also requires that the reasons appear in the order. — Eds.] . . . Furthermore, an advance call to the judge emphasizes the urgency of the proceedings. During this conference you may apprise the court of the circumstances of the case, thus minimizing the actual time required to present the matter to the court. Also, the judge might be asked the amount of the bond he or she is inclined to set so you can have it prepared in advance.

C. *Contact the Marshal or Sheriff:* The TRO is worthless to the lawyer unless he can get it served on Landeater and its employees. . . .

III. Preparing the Papers

A. *The Bond.* The bond is the last instrument you will need, but the first you need to prepare. [Federal Rule 65(c) requires] posting of a bond in almost all cases before issuance of a restraining order.

If you intend to post a corporate surety bond, you should contact the bonding or insurance agent immediately. By now it is 3:30 p.m. and the bond must be prepared quickly, before the bonding company closes. . . .

B. *Prepare the Facts.* Who and where are the parties? Sam must supply you with basic information concerning Landeater Lumber Company, including some address where the sheriff or marshall can find its management, in order to serve the TRO.

Get a good factual summary of the events giving rise to your case. Hard, specific facts are needed for the application for temporary restraining order, to show that Sam owns the property in question, that Landeater has actually begun cutting the timber without permission, and that, unless Landeater is restrained, Sam will suffer irreparable harm for which there is no adequate remedy at law. Remember you or your client must swear to the factual allegations (. . . Rule 65(b), F.R.C.P.) . . .

C. *The Petition or Complaint.* The petition or complaint will contain [several] parts, many of which are common to any original petition or original complaint:

(1) *The names of the parties* and places where the defendant can be served with [process];

(2) *The factual allegations* giving rise to your right to relief, *i.e.*, that Sam owns the land and that Landeater is cutting the timber without right or authority. Sam must further allege and show that irreparable harm will result if the temporary restraining order is not granted, to wit: that the land upon which he is hoping to build his summer home is being ruined by the cutting of the timber, that his remedy at law of money damages is not adequate to protect him, and that Landeater is unable to respond in money damages anyway. These allegations must be of specific facts — pleading legal conclusions is not sufficient.

(3) *The prayer* should ask for not only a temporary restraining order but also that Landeater be cited to appear and show cause why the restraining order should not be converted into a [preliminary] injunction. The prayer should further request a permanent injunction upon final hearing on the merits.

(4) *The affidavit:* [The Rules] require verified pleading, or alternatively, in the federal court, supporting affidavits. . . .

D. *Temporary Restraining Order.* The requirements of the order itself are set out in . . . Rules 65(b) and (d), F.R.C.P. The order should track the complaint. . . .

(1) defining the injury in specific factual terms;

(2) stating specifically why the injury is irreparable; mere conclusory statements will not suffice;

(3) stating why the order was granted without notice;

(4) providing for the posting of a bond as a prerequisite to the clerk's issuing writs of injunction (Note: the amount of the bond can be left blank to be filled in by the judge when the order is signed);

(5) *specifically* setting out the act or acts being enjoined;

(6) specifically stating the order is binding on the parties, their officers, agents, servants, employees, attorneys, and those persons in active concert with them who receive actual notice of the order by personal service or otherwise;

(7) setting a date, within ten days, for a hearing on application for temporary injunction.

IV. Hearing, Filing and Follow-up

A. *The Hearing.* Now that the skids are greased and the pleadings prepared, you are ready for the hearing. . . . [Y]ou should appear wherever you have arranged to meet the judge with your client, Sam Successful. Sam should be prepared to testify to the matters set out in your pleadings. If the judge grants your TRO, he will (a) fill in the amount of the bond; (b) set a date, within ten days, for hearing the application for [preliminary] injunction; and (c) sign the order.

B. *Don't Forget the Filing Fee.* Check state or federal costs schedules to determine the amount of the filing fee. . . .

[Here, the article describes how the attorney should obtain copies of the pleadings and certified copies of the TRO (to convince doubters), use special marshall's forms and form of summons in federal court, and obtain service of the TRO. The lawyer, it suggests, should go to the site of the activity both to help the sheriff or marshal serve defendant and to assist in obtaining compliance. In the rare instance of defiance, the lawyer may draw up an affidavit to support contempt.]

V. Congratulations!

By noon Saturday all is peaceful. Landeater has withdrawn from Sam's land. Sam lost a few trees, but serious damage has been averted. If you have obtained the TRO, had it served, and stopped the cutting smoothly and without a hitch, you have done an outstanding job of legal planning and organization. Sam should be pleased and impressed with a job well done.

PROBLEM B

THE CASE OF THE IMPOUNDED BULLDOG. The City of New London has a provision called Ordinance No. 81-235, which allows impoundment of a dog or other animal that has bitten a human being and, after a hearing with prior notice to the owners if they can be identified through reasonable effort, the eventual destruction of the animal. Wade and Sandra Collins have come to you because their bulldog, Spike, is impounded under the authority of 81-235. The hearing will take place tomorrow, but they have not been able to learn when Spike would be destroyed if the hearing goes against him. With their help, you determine that 81-235 does not have any explicit provision governing who must prove what at the hearing and does not provide for judicial review of the decision at the hearing (although it is doubtful that the Constitution requires judicial review in all cases). The Collinses want you to stop the hearing or, in the alternative, prevent the city from destroying Spike. What papers will you need, what specifics will they contain, and what are your chances?

§ 14.02 Damages: The Traditional Legal Remedy

[A] Compensatory Damages: Recoverable Elements

MEMPHIS COMMUNITY SCHOOL DISTRICT v. STACHURA, 477 U.S. 299 (1986). Parents' complaints, apparently based largely on inaccurate rumors, resulted in the suspension of tenured teacher Edward Stachura from the Memphis, Michigan, School District after he instructed students on human reproduction in a seventh-grade life sciences class. Stachura was reinstated, but he sued under 28 U.S.C. § 1983 on the allegation that his suspension deprived him of due process and violated the First Amendment to the Constitution. He had received his salary throughout the suspension period but claimed other elements of damage. The Supreme Court did not decide whether Stachura's constitutional claims were valid, because the liability issue was not presented to it; it considered only the correctness of certain instructions given by the trial judge on damages.

During its instructions to the jury, the District Court had made the following remarks regarding (1) compensatory damages: "You should consider in this regard any lost earnings; loss of earning capacity; out-of-pocket expenses; and any mental anguish or emotional distress that you find the plaintiff to have suffered as a result of conduct by the defendants depriving him of his civil rights." In addition, the court instructed the jury that (2) punitive damages could be awarded. Finally, at Stachura's request and over the defendants' objection, the court charged that (3) damages also could be awarded based upon the value or importance of the abstract constitutional rights that were allegedly violated, as follows:

> The precise value you place upon any constitutional right which you find was denied the plaintiff is within your discretion. You may wish to consider the importance of the right in our system of government, the role which this right has played in the history of our republic, [and] the significance of the right in the context of the activities which the plaintiff was engaged in at the time of the violation of the right.

The jury found the defendants liable and awarded a total of $275,000 in compensatory damages and $46,000 in punitive damages. The district court entered judgment against all but one defendant for a slightly reduced amount. The Court of Appeals affirmed. The Supreme Court reversed, holding that it was error to allow the jury to find damages for the alleged constitutional deprivation in the abstract, as opposed to damages suffered by the plaintiff:

> We have repeatedly noted that 42 U.S.C. § 1983 creates a "species of tort liability" in favor of persons who are deprived of "rights, privileges, or immunities secured" to them by the Constitution. *Carey v. Piphus*, 435 U.S. 247, 253 (1978). . . . Accordingly, when § 1983 plaintiffs seek damages for violations of constitutional rights, the level of damages is ordinarily according to principles derived from the common law of torts. . . .
>
> Punitive damages aside, damages in tort cases are designed to provide "*compensation* for the injury caused to plaintiff by defendant's breach of duty." . . . To that

end, compensatory damages may include not only out-of-pocket loss and other monetary harms, but also such injuries as "impairment of reputation . . . , personal humiliation, and mental anguish and suffering" . . . Deterrence is also an important purpose of this system, but it operates through the mechanism of damages that are *compensatory* — damages grounded in determinations of plaintiffs' actual losses.

[Plaintiff Stachura] further argues that the challenged instructions authorized a form of "presumed" damages — a remedy that is both compensatory in nature and traditionally part of the range of tort law remedies. . . .

Presumed damages are a *substitute* for ordinary compensatory damages, not a *supplement* for an award that fully compensates the alleged injury. When a plaintiff seeks compensation for an injury that is likely to have occurred but difficult to establish, some form of presumed damages may possibly be appropriate. [However,] no rough substitute for compensatory damages was required in this case, since the jury was fully authorized to compensate respondent for both monetary and non-monetary harms caused by [the defendants'] conduct. . . .

The judgment of the Court of Appeals is reversed and the case is remanded for further proceedings consistent with this opinion.

NOTES AND QUESTIONS

(1) *"Compensatory" Damages, "Presumed" Damages, or Damages for Loss of the "Abstract Right" to Vote? Nixon v. Herndon, 273 U.S. 536 (1927).* The efforts of the Court in *Memphis County School Dist. v. Stachura* to distinguish in a footnote the case of *Nixon v. Herndon,* illustrate the difficulty of measuring § 1983 damages. In *Nixon,* the Court had held that a plaintiff who was illegally prevented from voting had suffered a compensable injury. In *Stachura,* the Court says: "This holding did not rest on the 'value' of the right to vote as an abstract matter; rather, the Court recognized that the plaintiff had suffered a particular injury — his inability to vote in a particular election — that might be compensated through substantial money damages." But if so, how should the court instruct the jury? If it tells the jury to award damages for "the inability to vote," has it committed error similar to the error that caused reversal in *Stachura*? [What should the jury do if different jurors place values that range from $1 to $1 million and logically defend these different measures of damages?]

(2) *Pain and Suffering as a Compensable Element of Damages.* Obviously, the same kind of "measurement of damages" problem arises when the jury is required to determine monetary compensation for plaintiff's pain and suffering. Should the jury go about this task by putting a value on an hour's or day's suffering, and multiplying it by the number of hours or days that plaintiff has endured? Some jurisdictions restrict the plaintiff's attorney from arguing this measure, although many allow it. *Cf. Tate v. Colabello,* 58 N.Y.2d 84, 459 N.Y.S.2d 422, 445 N.E.2d 1101 (1983) (court did not need to determine whether "*per diem*" argument would be approved in New York; it was not improper, however, for plaintiff's counsel to "suggest" a sum based on life expectancy of 64 years and on series of rhetorical questions as to the value of pain over a period of time). If not by a *per diem* method, how should pain and suffering damages be fixed? By a "market value" approach (*i.e.,* the amount of money that a person would accept in exchange for undergoing the same pain)?

(3) *Damage "Caps": Fein v. Permanente Medical Group, 38 Cal. 3d 137, 211 Cal. Rptr. 368, 695 P.2d 665 (1985).* The *Fein* case has been dealt with in several earlier

parts of this book, most notably in § 1.08 of Chapter 1. The jury found the defendant liable for medical malpractice in failing to diagnose a heart condition of the plaintiff, and earlier excerpts have dealt with jury selection and instructions. There also were important damages issues.

In *Fein*, the court upheld and applied a "cap" on non-economic damages in medical malpractice cases. The California Act in question allowed full recovery for "hard" elements of damages, such as lost earnings or medical expenses, but limited "non-economic damages" by a $250,000 damage "cap." The California court, by a four-to-three majority, held that the cap was constitutional. Other jurisdictions have decided the constitutional question differently; for example, some states have interpreted state constitutions as invalidating similar damage caps.

Aside from the constitutional question, what about the wisdom of damages caps? One can debate whether it is good policy to limit damages for the most severely injured persons rather than for the least injured ones; after all, large awards may involve lower transaction costs and may be undervalued anyway since the compensatory dollars are worth less to a severely injured person. *See also* Schwartz & Cooper, *Should There Be a Cap on Personal Injury Awards?*, 64 Mich. B.J. 137 (1985).

(4) *"Tort Reform" — Changes in the Collateral Source Rule, Periodic Payments, and Other Features of Damage Awards: Fein v. Permanente Medical Group, supra.* The "collateral source rule" avoids reducing tort recoveries by insurance or other reparations receivable by the plaintiff. The rule is premised on the notion that the defendant should pay for damage she has caused as well as the desire to preserve incentives for farsighted plaintiffs who see to their own insurance. There has been considerable argument for the abrogation of the rule, and the California Act applied in *Fein* did, indeed, modify the rule to deny some "double recovery." Should the collateral source rule be abrogated? In addition, the California Act in *Fein* required awards to be paid periodically in some instances, rather than in a lump sum. Tort law generally has attempted to make lump sum awards for both past and future damages, rather than making payments depend upon either the passage of time or future contingencies. Would periodic payments be a superior method? Would it make more sense to make speculative kinds of damages — *e.g.*, future medical expenses — dependent upon future events? *See generally* ABA, *Report of the Action Commission to Improve the Tort Liability System* (R. McKay, ed. 1987).

(5) *Federal Tort Reform in 1995: The "Contract With America" and its Fallout.* As part of the Republicans' successful Fall 1994 campaign that ended with Republican control of both houses of Congress, the Republicans proposed a "Contract With America" — a promise to bring up a series of measures for votes. The Contract included, as item 9, "The Common Sense Legal Reform Act: 'Loser pays' laws, reasonable limits on punitive damages and reform of product liability laws to stem the tide of endless litigation." The House of Representatives passed a sweeping reform measure that would (1) cap punitive damages in all state and federal civil cases at $250,000 or treble economic damages, (2) adopt a version of "loser pays" in federal diversity tort cases in which a more favorable settlement offer has been rejected, (3) change joint-and-several liability to make liability for non-economic losses proportionate to fault, (4) create a complete defense against plaintiffs whose injuries are caused primarily by alcohol or drugs, and (5) rewrite Rule 11 to again make sanctions mandatory. President Clinton vetoed the bill.

[B] Proof of Economic Damages With Reasonable Certainty

HAWTHORNE INDUSTRIES, INC. v. BALFOUR MACLAINE INTERNATIONAL LTD., 676 F.2d 1385 (11th Cir. 1982). Balfour contracted to supply Hawthorne with jute carpet backing, which was required to conform to the standards and tolerances of the Jute Carpet Backing Council. The jute failed to conform, and in order to avoid "wrinkles, sagging and other undesirable effects" in its carpets, Hawthorne had to slow its machinery, make hand adjustments, and add extra latex adhesive. Its suit for breach of warranty was made more difficult, however, by the fact that "jute carpet backing is an imperfect commodity in which some deviation in quality and dimension is normally expected." As evidence of its consequential damages, therefore, Hawthorne offered testimony of three plant supervisors to the effect that the machinery was slowed from 20 feet per minute to only 3 feet per minute to process Balfour's jute; that the plant experienced approximately 30% down time; and that from two to four extra ounces of adhesive were applied per yard. Using these estimates, together with normal weekly production reports, Hawthorne's chief financial officer testified to a cost estimate for the lost efficiency and extra materials, supporting the prayer for $50,000 in Hawthorne's complaint. Balfour, pointing out that Hawthorne had kept no written records of the slowed production rate or additional materials, attacked this evidence as "guess work and speculation." The district judge found that Hawthorne suffered "a loss of machine efficiency in processing the Balfour jute," that down time caused "additional cost," and that extra adhesives also required "increased cost." However, since Hawthorne's "method of proving consequential damages failed to account adequately for the wide deviation in the rate of production with various types of jute," the District Court concluded that Hawthorne had "failed to prove its damages with a sufficient degree of certainty." The District Court therefore awarded Hawthorne no damages, but awarded Balfour the contract price. The Court of Appeals remanded, reasoning as follows:

> The District Court's findings plainly indicate that some consequential damages were caused by Balfour's breach. . . . [Under] the Uniform Commercial Code . . . , the rule preventing recovery of "speculative" damages referred "more especially to the uncertainty as to the cause, rather than uncertainty as to the measure or extent of damages." . . . There is no speculation in this case as to the causation of damages. With respect to certainty as to measure or extent of damages, Comment 4 to UCC § 2-715 . . . states the applicable rule as follows:
>
> > The burden of proving the extent of loss incurred by way of consequential damage is on the buyer, but the [UCC] section on liberal administration of remedies rejects any doctrine of certainty which requires almost mathematical precision in the proof of loss. Loss may be determined in any manner which is reasonable under the circumstances.
>
> . . . [The applicable] law requires "reasonable certainty" . . .
>
> Balfour is entirely correct that the "question of damages cannot be left to speculation and guesswork." . . . [H]owever, . . . compensation for undisputed injury should not be denied merely because the amount of damages cannot be precisely and exactly determined.
>
> The district court may very well have believed that the proof of damages was insufficient because the estimates of company witnesses were mere conjecture. . . . Unfortunately, we cannot tell from the record as it stands whether this was, in fact, the basis of the district court's opinion. On remand, if the district court feels that proof

of extent of damages is lacking, it should enter a finding to that effect. However, if the court determines upon reexamination of the record and its findings that an award of consequential damages can be ascertained with reasonable certainty, the court shall enter such an award. . . .

NOTES AND QUESTIONS

(1) *Unacceptably "Speculative" Methods of Proof of Damages: Freund v. Washington Square Press, Inc., 34 N.Y.2d 379, 314 N.E.2d 419, 357 N.Y.S.2d 857 (1974).* In *Freund,* the defendant publisher breached its contract by refusing to publish the plaintiff's book on modern drama. Freund claimed damages in the form of loss of anticipated royalties and alternative publication expenses. However, Freund had never published a work in the field, and there was no basis in the record for a finding of public acceptance of this work; accordingly, the court held that proof of damages was too speculative.

(2) *Proof of "Reasonableness" of Tort Damages: Jackson v. Lewis, 554 S.W.2d 21 (Tex. Civ. App.—Amarillo 1977, no writ).* This case demonstrates, in a tragic way, the technical requirements of proof of damages. In a wrongful death case for personal injuries, the plaintiff sought to recover for medical expenses. The proof for the medical expenses was offered by stipulation, as follows:

> [Counsel for Lewis]: Your Honor, we have agreed that these charges . . . are reasonable, customary, usual, and necessary charges in the vicinities in which they were rendered. [To opposing counsel:] Is that correct?
>
> [Counsel for Jackson]: Yes, sir, that is correct. We want this all to go to the jury, I doubt if any medical charge these days is reasonable, but we are not going to argue about that. But we would like all this to go to the jury, we just don't raise any objection on that.
>
> [Counsel for Lewis]: Okey, Your Honor, in other words, so we wouldn't have to call the doctors to testify.
>
> [The Court]: Let the record so show.
>
> [Counsel for Lewis]: We will offer then those bills into evidence.
>
> [The Court]: They will be accepted.

The jury, however, rendered a verdict finding "zero" damages for medical expenses. The trial judge noted that Lewis was required to prove (1) that the medical expenses actually were incurred, (2) that they were reasonable in amount in the place and at the time they were rendered, and (3) that they were reasonably medically necessary for the treatment of injuries resulting from the accident. The trial judge rendered judgment for Lewis in the amount shown by the medical bills. The appellate court reversed and rendered judgment that Lewis take nothing, according to the jury's verdict. Although the stipulation clearly established the reasonableness of the amount of the charges and the bills showed that Lewis had incurred them, there was no proof in the record that they were reasonably necessary to treat injuries resulting from the accident!

PROBLEM C

PROOF OF DAMAGES IN HOWARD v. BACHMAN. The jury instructions contained in Problem C, in Chapter 10, above, are fairly typical for the measurement of damages to a chattel resulting from the defendant's negligence. The instruction reads as follows:

> Find from the preponderance of the evidence the reasonable cost in Manero County, West York, of repairs, if any, necessary to restore Bruce Bachman's vehicle to the condition in which it was, immediately before the occurrence in question.

If you represented the claimant, Bachman, what witness(es) would you call, and what question(s) would you ask of them, to lay a predicate for the recovery of damages to Bachman's vehicle under this instruction?

[C] Punitive or "Exemplary" Damages

SMITH v. WADE, 461 U.S. 30 (1983). Smith, a prison guard, placed two other inmates in Wade's cell with him, who beat and sexually assaulted him. Wade had voluntarily sought administrative segregation because of prior assaults, and a vacant cell was available. Wade sued Smith under 42 U.S.C. § 1983, alleging that Smith violated the Eighth Amendment prohibition on cruel and unusual punishment because he knew or should have known that assault was likely. The trial court instructed the jury that Smith could be liable only if he acted with "gross negligence," defined as "a callous indifference or thoughtless disregard for the consequences of one's act or failure to act." Smith could not be liable even for compensatory damages on mere simple negligence. The trial judge also instructed the jury on punitive damages:

> If you find the issues in favor of the plaintiff, and if the conduct of one or more of the defendants is shown to be a reckless or callous disregard of, or indifference to, the rights or safety of others, then you may assess punitive or exemplary damages in addition to any award of actual damages.
>
> . . . The amount of punitive or exemplary damages assessed against any defendant may be such sum as you believe will serve to punish that defendant and to deter him and others from like conduct.

The jury found Smith liable and awarded $25,000 in compensatory and $5,000 in punitive damages. The Supreme Court affirmed a judgment on this verdict.

Smith argued that the punitive damage award should be reversed because the instruction should have limited punitive damages to situations involving "ill will, spite, or intent to injure" in a § 1983 case. The Supreme Court rejected this argument:

> Smith's argument, which he offers in several forms, is that an actual-intent standard is preferable to a recklessness standard because it is less vague. [H]e concedes, of course, that deterrence of future egregious conduct is a primary purpose of both § 1983 . . . and of punitive damages. . . . But deterrence, he contends, cannot be achieved unless the standard of conduct is stated with sufficient clarity to enable potential defendants to conform to the law and to avoid the proposed sanction. . . .
>
> . . . While, *arguendo*, an intent standard may be easier to understand and apply . . . , we are not persuaded that a recklessness standard is too vague to be fair or useful. . . .
>
> . . . The need for exceptional clarity in the standard for punitive damages arises only if one assumes that there are substantial numbers of officers who will not be deterred by compensatory damages; only such officers will seek to guide their conduct by the punitive damages standard. The presence of such officers is a powerful argument against raising the threshold for punitive damages. . . .

Justice Rehnquist, joined by the Chief Justice and Justice Powell, dissented. He argued that mature legal systems, respecting freedom of the human will, would require intent or wrongful animus before imposing punishment: "A relation between some mental element and punishment for a harmful act is almost as instinctive as the child's familiar exculpatory 'But I didn't mean to.' " Furthermore, the award of punitive damages on less than proof of intent would provide a powerful incentive to additional § 1983 litigation, which already flooded the courts; and "the uncertainty resulting from largely random awards of punitive damages will have serious effects upon the performance by state and local officers of their official duties."

NOTE ON THE ECONOMIC PURPOSE OF COMPENSATORY AND PUNITIVE DAMAGES

How the Price System Works to Allocate Resources. To an economist, the costs of various resources that a firm uses to provide a product or service are an inducement to efficiency. The price system forces the firm to produce in the most efficient manner possible, and it also induces the firm to provide those products or services that the consumers of a society most want.

The Function of Compensatory Damages in Addressing Market Imperfections. But this theory breaks down if the firm can avoid costs by "externalizing" them. Thus, if cheaper means of production result in environmental pollution or an unacceptably large proportion of accidents and injuries, the price system functions counterproductively to induce the firm to choose this undesirable method of production. The economist would see the law's imposition of damage liability as a counterpart to these externalities. To the economist, the desirable level of damage liability would be reached when it precisely balanced the consumer's desire for cheaply produced products against the desire to avoid the harmful consequences such as pollution or injuries that result from cheap production. Too little damage liability results in undesirably high levels of these "external" effects. Too much damage liability, on the other hand, results in undesirable reduction of the production of goods or services.

When Are Punitive Damages Appropriate? The economist would see compensatory damages as perfectly fulfilling this function, at least in theory. The price system induces the firm to produce goods and services efficiently, while the tort reparations system confronts the firm with the precise cost of losses to victims in the form of compensatory damages. This theory also breaks down because desirable levels of damage liability might not result. Transaction costs (such as attorney's or experts' fees) and proof difficulties are such that not all injured persons will recover all their losses. This is where the theory of punitive damages comes in, according to an economist. The function of these damages, in the eyes of an economist, is not so much that of "punishing" an individual based upon "wrongful intent" as that of adjusting the level and locus of damage liability to take account of undervaluation of external costs by the tort system of compensatory damages.

The Need to Limit Punitive Damages. But this theory suggests that punitive damages can be harmful as well as helpful, if they are excessively imposed. Therefore, there is a need to limit their availability and their amount. The economist would see a "gross negligence" threshold as a means of limiting the availability of punitive damages. If this standard did not perfectly calibrate the desired reduction in injuries or pollution with the desired level of production of goods and services, the economist would advise shifting to a different standard — *e.g.*, a requirement of intentional injury, if punitive damages were too high. In addition, the law has evolved various means of limiting the amount of punitive damages (such as requiring a relationship between the amount of actual damages awarded and the amount of punitive damages in some states).

Comparing Wade v. Smith to the Economic Theory. How do the opinions in *Wade v. Smith* measure up, in terms of these economic theories? Note that the majority speaks in terms of the lack of desirable levels of deterrence of some callous officers if an intent standard is imposed, while the dissent speaks in terms of the discouragement of official government duties if a lower standard is used. *See also* Cooter, *Economic Analysis of Punitive Damages*, 56 So. Cal. L. Rev. 79 (1982).

NOTES AND QUESTIONS

(1) *Limiting Punitive Damages by Relationships between Amounts of Punitive Damages and Amounts of Actual Damages: Doubleday & Co. v. Rogers, 674 S.W.2d 751 (Tex. 1984).* The jury found that Doubleday had libeled Rogers; awarded "zero" in actual damages, finding that he had suffered no harm; and awarded more than $1 million in punitive damages. An intermediate appellate court rendered judgment for Rogers for the amount of punitive damages. The state supreme court reversed on the basis of a rule requiring a relationship between the amount of punitive damages and the amount of actual damages; since there was no actual damage, there could be no recovery of punitive damages. This rule has been rejected in many jurisdictions; is it sound?

(2) *Limiting Punitive Damages as a Part of the "Tort Reform Movement": The Montana Statute.* Montana has enacted a statute that limits the recovery of certain kinds of punitive damages to $25,000 or two percent of the defendant's net worth, whichever is larger. Mont. Code Ann. § 27-1-22(6)(b) (1985). Is this approach sound?

As alternative approaches to the call for tort reform, would it make sense to enact specific ratio limitations (say, two-to-one) for punitive as compared to actual damages? To provide that all (or a substantial portion) of any punitive damages recovered would be paid to the state treasury? Consider the following case.

PACIFIC MUTUAL LIFE INS. CO. v. HASLIP
499 U.S. 1 (1991)

JUSTICE BLACKMUN delivered the opinion of the Court.

[Haslip's health insurance premiums were paid to an agent of Pacific Mutual. The agent was supposed to forward these premiums to Union Fidelity Life Insurance Co., but he did not do so; instead, he misappropriated most of them. Haslip was hospitalized, and eventually suffered a judgment against her for the costs because she was unable to obtain insurance coverage. She and others sued Pacific Mutual and the agent.

[In accordance with Alabama state law, the trial judge instructed the jury that if it found fraud, it could award punitive damages to "punish" the defendant[s] and to "protect[] the public." Further, he said, such an award "is entirely discretionary . . . that means you don't have to award it unless this jury feels that you should do so." The only other stated criteria were that the jury "must take into consideration the character and the degree of the wrong [a]nd the necessity of preventing similar wrong." Pacific Mutual did not object to the lack of specificity in the instructions, nor did it propose any more specific charge. After affirmance by the Alabama Supreme Court, Pacific Mutual obtained review in the United States Supreme Court of the question whether this allegedly "unbridled" jury discretion violated its due process rights. The Supreme Court here affirms.]

"Punitive damages have long been a part of traditional state tort law." *Silkwood v. Kerr-McGee Corp.*, 464 U.S. 238, 255 (1984). Blackstone appears to have noted their use. . . .

Under the traditional common-law approach, the amount of the punitive award is initially determined by a jury instructed to consider the gravity of the wrong and the need to deter similar wrongful conduct. The jury's determination is then reviewed by the trial and appellate courts to ensure that it is reasonable. . . .

So far as we have been able to determine, every state and federal court that has considered the question has ruled that the common-law method for assessing punitive damages does not in itself violate due process. "[If] a thing has been practiced for two hundred years by common consent, it will need a strong case for the Fourteenth Amendment to affect it." *Sun Oil Co. v. Wortman*, 486 U.S. 717, 730 (1988). . . .

This, however, is not the end of the matter. ("[N]either the antiquity of a practice nor the fact of steadfast legislative and judicial adherence to it through the centuries insulates it from constitutional attack. . . ."). We note once again our concern about punitive damages that "run wild." Having said that, we conclude that our task today is to determine whether the Due Process Clause renders the punitive damages award in this case constitutionally unacceptable. . . .

One must concede that unlimited jury discretion — or unlimited judicial discretion for that matter — in the fixing of punitive damages may invite extreme results that jar one's constitutional sensibilities. We need not, and indeed we cannot, draw a mathematical bright line between the constitutionally acceptable and the constitutionally unacceptable that would fit every case. We can say, however, that general concerns of reasonableness and adequate guidance from the court when the case is tried to a jury properly enter into the constitutional calculus. . . .

1\. . . . To be sure, the [Alabama trial court's] instructions gave the jury significant discretion in its determination of punitive damages. But that discretion was not unlimited. It was confined to deterrence and retribution, the state policy concerns sought to be advanced. And if punitive damages were to be awarded, the jury "must take into consideration the character and the degree of the wrong as shown by the evidence and necessity of preventing similar wrong." The instructions thus enlightened the jury as to the punitive damages' nature and purpose, identified the damages as punishment for civil wrongdoing of the kind involved, and explained that their imposition was not compulsory.

These instructions, we believe, reasonably accommodated Pacific Mutual's interest in rational decisionmaking and Alabama's interest in meaningful individualized assessment of appropriate deterrence and retribution. . . .[9]

2\. Before the trial in this case took place, the Supreme Court of Alabama had established post-trial procedures for scrutinizing punitive awards. . . .

3\. By its review of punitive awards, the Alabama Supreme Court provides an additional check on the jury's or trial court's discretion. It first undertakes a comparative analysis. It then applies the detailed substantive standards it has developed for evaluating punitive awards. In particular, it makes its review to ensure that the award does "not exceed an amount that will accomplish society's goals of punishment and deterrence." *Green Oil Co. v. Hornsby*, 539 So. 2d 218, 222 (1989). . . .

[9] The Alabama Legislature recently enacted a statute that places a $250,000 limit on punitive damages in most cases. *See* 1987 Ala. Acts, No. 87-185 §§ 1, 2, and 4. The legislation, however, became effective only on June 11, 1987, *see* § 12, after the cause of action in the present case arose and the complaint was filed.

The application of these standards, we conclude, imposes a sufficiently definite and meaningful constraint on the discretion of Alabama fact finders in awarding punitive damages. . . .

[Justice Scalia concurred only in the judgment. Since the Alabama instructions followed the "traditional practice of American courts," he said, "I would approve the procedure challenged here without further inquiry into its 'fairness' or 'reasonableness.' " Moreover, the majority's "jury-like" treatment of Alabama's procedure, according to Justice Scalia, "perpetuates the uncertainty" as to other punitive award procedures. "A harsh or unwise procedure is not necessarily unconstitutional," Justice Scalia concluded; and the states have power to "restrict or abolish the common-law practice [a]nd in recent years have increasingly done so."

[The concurring opinion of Justice Kennedy is omitted. Justice Souter did not participate.]

JUSTICE O'CONNOR, dissenting. . . .

Due process requires that a State provide meaningful standards to guide the application of its laws. *See Kolender v. Lawson*, 461 U.S. 352, 358 (1983). A state law that lacks such standards is void for vagueness. The void-for-vagueness doctrine applies not only to laws that proscribe conduct, but also to laws that vest standardless discretion in the jury to fix a penalty. *See United States v. Batchelder*, 442 U.S. 114, 123 (1979). I have no trouble concluding that Alabama's common-law scheme for imposing punitive damages is void for vagueness. . . .

Giaccio v. Pennsylvania, 382 U.S. 399 (1966), offers a compelling analogy. At issue in *Giaccio* was a statute that left to the discretion of the jury whether or not to assess costs against an acquitted criminal defendant. The statute did not set out any standards to guide the jury's determination. The Court did not hesitate in striking down the statute on vagueness grounds. . . .

[A]labama's punitive damages scheme places no substantive limits on the amount of a jury's award. Pacific Mutual was found liable for punitive damages of $840,000. [*S*]*ee* [*also*] App. to Brief for Alabama Defense Lawyer Association as *Amicus Curiae* 1a-19a (listing Alabama jury verdicts including punitive damages awards as high as $10 million, $25 million, and $50 million). . . .

[P]araphrased slightly, the court's terse instruction told the jury: "Think about how much you hate what the defendants did and teach them a lesson." [L]ike most common-law punitive damages instructions, this one has "an open-ended, anything-goes quality that can too easily stoke . . . the vindictive or sympathetic passions of juries." P. Huber, *Liability: The Legal Revolution and Its Consequences* 118 (1988) (hereinafter Huber). . . .

This is not a case where more precise standards are either impossible or impractical. Just the opposite. The Alabama Supreme Court has already formulated a list of seven factors that it considers relevant to the size of a punitive damages award:

> (1) Punitive damages should bear a reasonable relationship to the harm that is likely to occur from the defendant's conduct as well as to the harm that actually has occurred. If the actual or likely harm is slight, the damages should be relatively small. If grievous, the damages should be much greater.
>
> (2) The degree of reprehensibility of the defendant's conduct should be considered. The duration of this conduct, the degree of the defendant's awareness of any hazard

which his conduct has caused or is likely to cause, and any concealment or "cover-up" of that hazard, and the existence and frequency of similar past conduct should all be relevant in determining this degree of reprehensibility.

(3) If the wrongful conduct was profitable to the defendant, the punitive damages should remove the profit and should be in excess of the profit, so that the defendant recognizes a loss.

(4) The financial position of the defendant would be relevant.

(5) All the costs of litigation should be included, so as to encourage plaintiffs to bring wrongdoers to trial.

(6) If criminal sanctions have been imposed on the defendant for his conduct, this should be taken into account in mitigation of the punitive damages award.

(7) If there have been other civil actions against the same defendant, based on the same conduct, this should be taken into account in mitigation of the punitive damages award.

Green Oil Co. v. Hornsby, supra.

[U]nfortunately, Alabama courts do not give the *Green Oil* factors to the jury. . . .

Obviously, [appellate] *post hoc* application of the *Green Oil* factors does not cure the vagueness of the jury instructions. [A]fter-the-fact review of the amount in no way diminishes the fact that the State entrusts its juries with standardless discretion. . . .

I would require Alabama to adopt some method [t]o constrain the discretion of juries in deciding whether or not to impose punitive damages and in fixing the amount of such awards. As a number of effective procedural safeguards are available, we need not dictate to the States the precise manner in which they must address the problem. . . .

NOTES AND QUESTIONS

(1) *The Aftermath: Georgia Gives Haslip Only "Slight Regard" — Hospital Authority of Gwinnett County v. Jones, 261 Ga. 613, 409 S.E.2d 501 (1991).* In this Georgia case, a patient was only slightly injured in a helicopter accident during a transfer from his initial hospital to a hospital with a burn unit. The jury, after receiving instructions "quite similar" to those in Alabama, awarded approximately $5,000 in "nominal" damages — and then added a whopping $1.3 million in punitives. The Georgia Supreme Court affirmed without recognizing any need for a rule requiring that punitive damages "bear some relationship" to actual damages or to the defendant's net worth. *Haslip* did not mandate any such considerations, said the court. Is the Georgia Supreme Court's decision consistent with *Haslip*? [Law Week characterizes this reasoning as giving "slight regard" to the latter decision.]

(2) *Survey Confirmation of the Conditions for "Punitive Damages 'Run Wild' ": Wall St. Journal, Nov. 13, 1991, § B, at 3, col. 1.* The California research firm Metricus polled people eligible for jury duty nationwide. Among the findings: (1) 70% were more likely to favor an individual over a corporation even before knowing anything else about the dispute; (2) the respondents were "much more likely" to believe an accusation that a defense lawyer was not telling the truth than the same accusation about a plaintiff's lawyer; and (3) most significantly, "60% of [potential] jurors deemed a $1 million judgment just a 'slap on the wrist' for a corporation."

(3) *Should the Jury Be Told the Defendant's Total Net Worth Whenever Punitive Damages Are Sought?: Lunsford v. Morris, 746 S.W.2d 471 (Tex. 1988).* In this case,

a state supreme court held that evidence of the defendant's total net worth was relevant evidence in a case in which punitive damages were at issue. [In *Haslip*, net worth evidence was not admitted, although Justice O'Connor's opinion shows that the Alabama Supreme Court treats the defendant's "financial position" as "relevant."] Note that the usual procedure in a jury trial would mean that the evidence is to be admitted whenever the plaintiff has included a prayer for punitive damages in her complaint (and, perhaps, has offered minimally sufficient evidence that, if credited, might support them — although this latter requirement is not mandated by most states for most kinds of evidence). In a case involving a relatively small loss and doubtful liability, what effect would this rule of evidence, admitting total net worth, have in a suit against Microsoft, Exxon or AIG?

(4) *Settlement Impact: The Effect of Discretionary Punitive Damages.* Most cases are not tried; they are settled. Imagine that you are defending the hypothetical suit, above, for a relatively small loss based on dubious liability, but in which the net worth of your client (Microsoft, Exxon or AIG) will be presented to the jury in support of the plaintiff's prayer for many millions of dollars in punitive damages (and unavoidably will influence the jury in determining all other issues as well, including liability). How will the combination of these legal rules affect settlement negotiations?

NOTES ON THE CONTINUING PUNITIVE DAMAGES CONTROVERSY

(1) *What If, Unlike Haslip, the State Law Allows No Judicial Review of Excessiveness?: Honda Motor Co. v. Oberg, 512 U.S. 415 (1994).* Uniquely among the 50 States, Oregon provided no procedure for judicial review of punitive awards for excessiveness. The Supreme Court, in this case, distinguished Haslip and held that an award of $5 million in punitive damages was a violation of due process because of the Oregon procedure.

(2) *Constitutional Limits on the Amount of Punitive Damages: BMW of North America, Inc. v. Gore, 517 U.S. 559 (1996).* Aside from the process by which the jury is guided, the Supreme Court has struggled in several cases with substantive limits imposed by the Constitution on punitive damages amounts. In *TXO Production Corp. v. Allied Resources Corp.*, 509 U.S. 443 (1993), a divided Court upheld a $10 million punitive award against both substantive and procedural attacks, without articulating clear limits. Finally, in *BMW v. Gore,* the Court struck down a $2 million punitive award to an individual whose actual damages the jury fixed at $4,000. The opinion analyzed the award according to three factors: (1) the degree of reprehensibility of the defendant's conduct, (2) the ratio of the punitive award to actual damages, and (3) the amount of civil or criminal penalties provided by law for comparable conduct. Four Justices dissented. *See also* Crump, *Evidence, Economics, and Ethics: What Information Should Jurors Be Given to Determine the Amount of a Punitive-Damage Award?* 57 Md. L. Rev. 174 (1998).

(3) *The Supreme Court Opens the Door to Broad Appellate Review of the Constitutionality of Punitive Damage Awards, Part One.* In *Cooper Industries, Inc. v. Leatherman Tool Group, Inc.*, 532 U.S. 424 (2001), the Court, with only Justice Ginsburg dissenting, gave greatly enhanced power to appellate courts to review punitive damage awards by holding that Courts of Appeals should apply a *de novo* standard when reviewing district court determinations of the constitutionality of punitive damages awards. In this case, the Ninth Circuit had concluded that the district court did not abuse its discretion in declining to reduce Leatherman's jury award of $4.5 million in punitive damages based on a $50,000 compensatory award for Cooper Industries, Inc.'s use of photographs of a modified version of Leatherman's enhanced Swiss Army knife tool in advertising materials that introduced a competing tool. The Court held that a jury's imposition of

punitive damages is an expression of its moral condemnation and not an essentially factual determination requiring a more limited review standard. The Court believed a thorough, independent review of the district court's rejection of Cooper's due process objections to the punitive damage award, using the three Gore factors, might well have led to a different result had the Court of Appeals applied the more rigorous *de novo* review standard, and accordingly the case was remanded to the Ninth Circuit. Justice Ginsburg's dissent asserted that the majority was ignoring the Seventh Amendment's Reexamination Clause and other practical reasons that would support using an abuse-of-discretion standard. *See* Bassett, *"I Lost at Trial — In the Court of Appeals!": The Expanding Power of the Federal Appellate Courts to Reexamine Facts*, 38 Hous. L. Rev. 1129 (2001); Dorsaneo, *Reexamining the Right to Jury Trial*, 54 SMU L. Rev. 1695 (2001).

(4) *The Supreme Court and Appellate Review of the Constitutionality of Punitive Damage Awards, Part Two.* In *State Farm Mutual Automobile Insurance Co. v. Campbell*, 538 U.S. 408 (2003), a majority of the Supreme Court concluded that a $145 million punitive damage award based on a $1 million compensatory judgment for an insurer's bad faith failure to settle for the insured's policy limits was excessive and violated the Due Process Clause of the Fourteenth Amendment. Seemingly retreating from previous Supreme Court jurisprudence upholding punitive damages more than four times the amount of compensatory damages, the majority observed that "[s]ingle-digit multipliers are more likely to comport with due process, while still achieving the State's goals of deterrence and retribution . . . ." Justices Scalia and Thomas dissented, reiterating their previous views that the Due Process Clause provides no protections against large punitive damage awards. Justice Ginsburg also dissented, stating that "the numerical controls today's decision installs seem to me boldly out of order." The courts have not interpreted the *State Farm* decision consistently. For example, the Oregon Court of Appeals, in *Bocci v. Key Pharmaceuticals Inc.*, 79 P.3d 908 (Or. App. 2003), rejected a $22.5 million punitive damages award as unconstitutionally excessive due to its 45-to-1 ratio to the $500,000 compensatory damages award, and granted a defense motion for new trial unless the plaintiff agreed to a remittitur of punitive damages to $3.5 million. However, in *Mathias v. Accor Economy Lodging, Inc.*, 347 F.3d 672 (7th Cir. 2003), the Seventh Circuit stated that *State Farm* did not set an inflexible limit, and upheld a 37-to-1 ratio of punitive to compensatory damages to motel guests who were bitten by bedbugs, noting that the motel was aware of the infestation but refused to follow the exterminator's recommendation and instead merely moved guests from room to room.

§ 14.03 Equitable Remedies

[A] Injunctions

Origins and Nature of Equity. Reconsider § 5.01[B] of Chapter 5, above, which introduced the concept of equity jurisprudence. Equity developed remedies for wrongs that were not adequately addressed by the courts of law, under the stewardship of the Chancellor.

"Irreparable Injury" for Which There Is "No Adequate Remedy at Law." You should remember that jurisdictional disputes between law and equity resulted in the requirement that an equity suitor demonstrate that, in the absence of equitable relief, she would suffer "irreparable injury" for which there was "no adequate remedy at law." For example, if the harm anticipated by the plaintiff could be completely redressed by common law damages, an injunction would not issue. This requirement is a feature of the case that follows, *MidCon Corp. v. Freeport-McMoran, Inc.*

The Relationship Among Temporary Restraining Orders (TROs), Preliminary Injunctions, and Permanent Injunctions. To preserve the status quo, Rule 65(b) empowers the court to grant a temporary restraining order without notice to the opposing party, which can have a duration of no more than ten (10) days. A preliminary injunction under Rule 65(a) is issued with notice and after a hearing for the purpose of preventing irreparable injury during the pendency of suit, before final judgment. A permanent injunction is the final adjudication of the issue, pursuant to Rule 65(d).

Flexibility and Conditions; "Balancing the Equities." In granting or denying equitable relief, the court "balances" the equities. For example, in the case that follows, which involves a preliminary injunction, the court invokes a traditional four-part test for the relief, which involves balancing of various possibilities of harm. It also invokes a more novel test. [For another example of flexibility in the use of this remedy, and related remedies, see Brill, *The Citizen's Relief Against Inactive Federal Officials: Case Studies in Mandamus, Actions "in the Nature of Mandamus," and Mandatory Injunctions*, 16 Akron L. Rev. 339 (1983).]

[1] Preliminary Injunctions: The Requirements

MIDCON CORP. v. FREEPORT-McMORAN, INC.
625 F. Supp. 1475 (N.D. Ill. 1986)

DUFF, DISTRICT JUDGE.

This matter comes before the court on the plaintiff's motion for a preliminary injunction. Plaintiff MidCon Corporation ("MidCon") is the owner of a pipeline system which supplies natural gas to the St. Louis and Chicago areas, among others. Defendants Freeport-McMoran, Inc. [and other defendants] own or are affiliated with persons owning substantial natural gas properties in the United States.

On December 16, 1985, defendants announced a tender offer to acquire all outstanding shares of common stock of MidCon. MidCon asks this court to enjoin the acquisition alleging that it would violate §§ 1 and 2 of the Sherman Act, 15 U.S.C. §§ 1-2 and § 7 of the Clayton Act, 15 U.S.C. § 18. Section 7 of the Clayton Act provides in relevant part:

> No person engaged in commerce or in any activity affecting commerce shall acquire [t]he whole or any part of the stock or other share capital [o]f another person engaged also in commerce or in any activity affecting commerce, *where, in any line of commerce or in any activity affecting commerce in any section of the country, the effect of such acquisition may be substantially to lessen competition, or to tend to create a monopoly.* (Emphasis added.)

. . . After hearing two days of live testimony and considering the affidavits and depositions submitted, the court denied plaintiff's motion for a preliminary injunction. The court ruled orally on December 30, 1985. As stated then, to the extent that anything in this opinion is contrary to the oral ruling, the written opinion is controlling.

FACTS

Plaintiff bases its antitrust claim on the possibility that the defendants, once they gain control of the pipelines owned by MidCon's subsidiaries, will force those subsidiaries to purchase gas from the defendants at inflated prices, resulting in higher gas prices for MidCon's utility customers and, ultimately, for consumers. Nearly all of plaintiff's evidence was presented in an attempt to support this argument.

One MidCon subsidiary, Natural Gas Pipeline Company of America ("Natural"), supplies natural gas to the Chicago area. . . .

Plaintiff's theory that defendants would force high priced gas into MidCon's pipelines rests on what it called MidCon's "captive market." According to James J. McElligott, Natural's Assistant Vice President for rates, Natural has a captive market in the Chicago area because its competitors have the capacity to supply only 200 to 300 billion cubic feet ("bcf") of the 700 to 900 bcf of gas consumed in the Chicago area. This leaves a demand for 500 to 600 bcf that can be filled only by Natural. . . .

[Plaintiff offered testimony about Natural's policy of purchasing at the lowest available price. But it did not show that defendants would abandon this practice when purchasing, nor did it show that defendants, as sellers, had ever entered into contracts at prices exceeding prevailing market prices. Furthermore, Natural's "low price" purchases had involved "take-or-pay contracts," which required it to buy minimum quantities or pay for them even if not taken. In considering Natural's "low" purchase prices, said the court, McElligott "ignored the fact that as of January 1, 1986, Natural will have incurred approximately $1 billion in take-or-pay liability."]

In addition to the evidence about the particular policies of these parties, plaintiff's witnesses testified that generally, it is important for a pipeline to be independent from producers. Dan H. Grubb, President of Natural, testified that a pipeline company makes money by investing in pipelines and therefore has an incentive to keep prices low. A producer, on the other hand, makes money on the spread between the cost of finding the gas and the ultimate sales price and, thus, Grubb concluded, defendants would be motivated to keep prices high. Other than this vague speculation, plaintiff failed to provide any real evidence that defendants would, in fact, pursue such a high pricing policy which would be contrary to their own economic interests.

While urging the importance of independence between pipeline and producer, Natural acknowledged that it owns two gas-producing subsidiaries. Grubb testified that in 1985, Natural produced 51 bcf of natural gas. Defendants' combined production for 1984 was approximately 60 bcf. Grubb testified that despite the fact that both MidCon and the defendants are substantial gas producers, the relationship between MidCon and its gas-producing affiliates differs from the relationship MidCon would have with the defendants. Grubb did not adequately explain how or why MidCon's relationship with Natural would be different and seemed to rely on the "great personalities" of the defendants in predicting that they would force Natural to take its gas.

In addition to this analysis of the relevant markets and pricing policies of the parties, evidence was presented concerning the policies and procedures of the FERC, a federal agency with the power to regulate gas prices. Grubb and McElligott testified that although pipeline companies must submit their pricing policies for review by the FERC every six months, neither of them knew of any instance when the FERC had rejected a pipeline's request for a price increase. Both, however, acknowledged the FERC's power to reject unreasonable price increases. . . .

DISCUSSION

In determining whether to issue a preliminary injunction, the court must consider four factors: (1) whether plaintiff has an adequate remedy at law or will suffer irreparable harm if the injunction is denied; (2) whether this harm will be greater than the harm defendant will suffer if the injunction is granted; (3) whether plaintiff has shown a reasonable likelihood of success on the merits; and (4) whether the public interest will be affected by the issuance of an injunction. . . .

In *American Hospital Supply Corporation v. Hospital Products Limited*, 780 F.2d 589, 593 (7th Cir. 1986), Judge Posner reduced these factors to an algebraic formula and directed a district judge to

> . . . grant the preliminary injunction if but only if $P \times H_p > (1-P) \times H_d$, or, in other words, only if the harm to the plaintiff if the injunction is denied, multiplied by the probability that the denial would be an error (that the plaintiff, in other words, will win at trial), exceeds the harm to the defendant if the injunction is granted, multiplied by the probability that granting the injunction would be an error.

There is the potential here for irreparable injury on both sides of Judge Posner's equation. If this proposed merger violates § 7 of the Clayton Act, and it is not enjoined, plaintiff would suffer an irreparable injury. After the takeover, it would be virtually impossible to "unscramble the eggs" and return the two companies to the status quo.

On the other hand, if the proposed merger does not violate the Clayton Act and the defendants are enjoined, it might be difficult to make the defendants whole with a money judgment. It is difficult for the court to say that these defendants would be injured, however, since the court cannot predict what the loss would be if the takeover were erroneously enjoined. There are incalculable contingencies — actions by regulatory agencies, MidCon's rescue by a "white knight," actions by shareholders, changes in the natural gas market — which could obstruct this merger or make it unprofitable for the defendants. Nonetheless, courts have held that blocking an otherwise lawful tender offer is an irreparable injury.

In *Edgar v. MITE Corp.*, 457 U.S. 624 (1982), the Supreme Court discussed the injuries which flow from an injunction against a takeover as follows:

> The effects of allowing the [injunction of] a nationwide tender offer are substantial. Shareholders are deprived of the opportunity to sell their shares at a premium. The reallocation of economic resources to their highest valued use, a process which can improve efficiency and competition, is hindered. The incentive the tender offer mechanism provides incumbent management to perform well so that stock prices remain high is reduced.

457 U.S. at 643. . . .

As in *American Hospital Supply Corporation*, the magnitude of injury to the plaintiff if the injunction were erroneously denied is nearly equal to the injury to the defendants if the injunction were erroneously granted. Thus, under Judge Posner's formula, plaintiff must show "a better than 50 percent chance of winning the case." The court is hesitant to handicap a judicial contest and apply percentages to the likelihood of success on the merits; however, in this case plaintiff's chances of success can only be characterized as a long shot.

While the traditional threshold for establishing likelihood of success on the merits is low, plaintiff has failed to present any evidence or even any argument to suggest that it could ultimately prevail against these defendants. Under § 7 of the Clayton Act as quoted above plaintiff must show that this proposed merger may substantially lessen competition or tend to create a monopoly in any line of commerce and in any section of the country. In *Brown Shoe Co. v. United States*, 370 U.S. 294 (1962), the Supreme Court set forth the method for identifying violations of § 7. The court must determine the line of commerce or the relevant product market, the relevant section of the country or the geographic market, and whether the merger may substantially lessen competition.

There is no dispute that the line of commerce is the sale of natural gas. There is, however, a dispute over the relevant geographic market. At issue is whether the court should look at competition among natural gas producers at the top end of the pipeline (a nationwide market) or among utility companies who purchase gas at the bottom end of the pipeline for distribution to the ultimate users (a local market).

. . . [P]laintiff has failed to show that this merger will affect or lessen competition in either the producer or the utility market.

. . . Plaintiff's basic argument is that after the merger, defendants would force high-priced gas into MidCon's pipelines. The court cannot determine how this argument meets the *Brown Shoe* requirements or establishes that the merger will lessen competition, perhaps because plaintiff's evidence does not support [its] argument. . . .

While the defendants would acquire a substantial percentage of the market at the utility end of the pipeline, it is no different from that percentage of the market now controlled by the plaintiff. The merger will, therefore, not affect the market at the utility end of the pipeline. The vertical merger would appear to have the potential to affect the market at the producer end of the pipeline. Yet, plaintiff provided no evidence on the market of natural gas producers, on defendants' percentage of that market, or on the likelihood that defendants would foreclose any other producers from the natural gas market. . . .

It is clear from the foregoing that plaintiff has a negligible chance of succeeding on the merits. When this is multiplied against the equality of potential injury to each party, Judge Posner's formula looks like this: $P \times H_p < (1-P) \times H_d$ and plaintiff's request for a preliminary injunction should be denied.

At first blush, Judge Posner's formula seems to ignore the public interest. The public interest, however, may be factored with the injury on either side of the equation, depending on where the public interest lies. *See American Hospital* at 601-602.

[T]he public may be affected by the fact that such a large percentage of the market is supplied by a single pipeline. The court cannot say, however, that the public would be affected by a change in the ownership of that pipeline. [T]hus, an examination of the public interest in the issuance or denial of an injunction in this case does not add anything to either side of the equation.

For these reasons, plaintiff's motion for a preliminary injunction has been denied.

NOTES AND QUESTIONS

(1) *The Traditional "Four Factor Test" and Judge Posner's "Algebraic Formula" — Are They Equivalent?: Lawson Products, Inc. v. Avnet, 782 F.2d 1429 (7th Cir. 1986).* The traditional "four factor" test of equity contains a public interest element (at least in some cases), and this factor, according to the District Court in *MidCon*, must be added to both sides of Judge Posner's equation where applicable. With this addition, is the algebraic test the same as the traditional test? In *Lawson Products*, a different panel of the Seventh Circuit said that Judge Posner's mathematics "provide important insights which may be helpful in the exercise of a district judge's discretion" — but his test should not be read to undermine the rule that preliminary injunctive relief continues to be governed by the four traditional equitable factors of irreparable injury, the balance of the equities, the likelihood of success, and the public interest. In particular, said the

Lawson Products court, Judge Posner's *American Hospital* formula "[does] not limit in any way the ability of the district courts to flexibly weigh the competing considerations and mold appropriate relief in preliminary injunction cases." Is this advice helpful — or is it merely reflective of this panel's suspicion of algebra?

(2) *"Irreparable Injury": Los Angeles Memorial Coliseum Comm'n v. National Football League, 634 F.2d 1197 (9th Cir. 1980).* The Oakland Raiders football team proposed to move to Los Angeles, and the Los Angeles Memorial Coliseum Commission sought a preliminary injunction against the National Football League to prevent its potential invocation of a rule requiring a three-fourths vote of all franchises for such a transfer. The Commission claimed that the rule violated the antitrust laws, but the Court of Appeals vacated a preliminary injunction granted by the District Court without reaching the merits of the antitrust claim — because it concluded that the Commission had not shown the requisite "irreparable injury" for which there would be "no adequate remedy at law." It quoted the following from *Sampson v. Murray*, 415 U.S. 61, 90 (1974):

> [T]he temporary loss of income, ultimately to be recovered, does not usually constitute irreparable injury. . . . "The key word in this consideration is irreparable." Mere injuries, however substantial, . . . are not enough. The possibility that adequate compensation or other corrective relief will be available at a later date, in the ordinary course of litigation, weighs heavily against a claim of irreparable injury.

On this basis, the court held that the loss of the Commission's "only opportunity to obtain a professional football tenant" did not constitute "irreparable injury" for which there was no adequate remedy at law. Does this reasoning make sense? For reasoning that may be more realistic (and certainly is more emotionally satisfying), see *City of New York v. New York Yankees*, 117 Misc. 2d 332, 458 N.Y.S.2d 486 (1983), in which the court held that the City would suffer irreparable injury if the Yankees' home opening series were played in Denver, in violation of the baseball team's stadium lease. As the court put it, "The Yankee pin stripes belong to New York like Central Park, like the Statue of Liberty. . . . Dare one whisper the dreaded words: 'The Denver Yankees'?"

(3) *Should the Irreparable Injury Rule Be Abolished? Laycock, The Death of the Irreparable Injury Rule, 103 Harv. L. Rev. 687 (1990).* The cases in Note #2 may justify the suspicion that the irreparable injury rule obfuscates the real questions: Which kind of relief is better? Which gives the more appropriate remedy at the lesser cost? Professor Laycock argues for a more functional approach: Minimally adequate legal remedies should not be deemed automatically superior to equitable ones, but rather should be preferred only when they actually are better. Furthermore, perhaps the "death" of irreparable injury reflects not only what the courts should do, but what they really *are* doing (albeit sometimes by reasoning that reflects a degree of "fudging"). Would the replacement of irreparable injury with a functional approach be appropriate?

[2] Permanent Injunctions: Shaping the Relief to Balance the Equities

GALELLA v. ONASSIS, 487 F.2d 986 (2d Cir. 1973). Jacqueline Onassis, the widow of President John F. Kennedy, obtained a temporary injunction against Galella, a "paparazzo" photographer, who had "insinuated himself into the very fabric of" the lives of her and her children, often startling or endangering them or interfering with their privacy. Galella contemptuously violated the order. The trial judge consolidated the hearing on preliminary and permanent injunction. At this hearing, Galella "demonstrated a galling lack of respect for the truth. . . . Not only did he admit blatantly lying in his testimony, but he admitted attempting to have other witnesses lie for him." After a six-week trial, the District Court granted a permanent injunction ordering Galella not to (1) keep Mrs. Onassis or her children under surveillance; (2) approach within 100 yards of the home of Mrs. Onassis or her children, within 100 yards of either child's school, within 75 yards of either child, or within 50 yards of Mrs. Onassis; (3) use photographs of these persons for advertising; or (4) attempt to communicate with them except through her attorney. The Court of Appeals concluded,

> Injunctive relief is appropriate. . . .
>
> The injunction, however, is broader than is required to protect [Mrs. Onassis]. Relief must be tailored to protect Mrs. Onassis from the "paparazzo" attack which distinguishes Galella's behavior from that of other photographers; it should not unnecessarily infringe on reasonable efforts to "cover" [Mrs. Onassis]. Therefore, we modify the court's order to prohibit only (1) any approach within twenty-five (25) feet of defendant or any touching of the person of . . . Jacqueline Onassis; (2) any blocking of her movement in public places and thoroughfares; (3) any act foreseeably or reasonably calculated to place the life and safety of [Mrs. Onassis] in jeopardy; and (4) any conduct which would reasonably be foreseen to harass, alarm or frighten the defendant.
>
> Any further restriction on Galella's taking and selling pictures of [Mrs. Onassis] for news coverage is, however, improper and unwarranted by the evidence. . . . [The Court of Appeals similarly limited the injunction with reference to the children.]

Judge Timbers dissented from the restriction of the injunction. He pointed out that Galella had a "heavy" burden of showing abuse of discretion by the district judge, who had heard the evidence. The repeated violations of earlier orders showed that abstract prohibitions on "harassment" and the like were unworkable; the restraint needed to be clear, simple and effective; Galella's attitude was a proper consideration in tailoring the relief; and the injunction needed to leave no room for quibbling or evasion, as the district court had expressly found. The majority's unexplained restrictions reduced by 84% the distance ordered as to Mrs. Onassis and left such anomalous exceptions as the absence of any restriction on the distance Galella had to keep from Mrs. Onassis's home.

NOTES AND QUESTIONS

(1) *"Balancing the Equities."* Which of the judges "balanced the equities" properly? Should the Court of Appeals have deferred to the findings and holding of the trial judge, or was this question one of law that an appellate court could decide as well as the trial judge? What countervailing value caused the Court of Appeals majority to restrict the injunction, given that even those judges considered Galella's disrespect for the law "galling"? *See also* Urquhart, *The Most Extraordinary Remedy: The Injunction*, 45 Tex. B.J. 358 (1982).

(2) *Enforceability of the Decree by Contempt.* One of the main issues in drafting an injunction is whether it will be enforceable by criminal contempt. If Galella violates this injunction, contempt will be Mrs. Onassis's main remedy. For criminal contempt to lie, the injunction must be specific in its prohibitions. *See* § 14.06[E] below. Given these principles, what do the prohibitions on "blocking movements," "placing in jeopardy," and "harassment, alarm or fright" add to Mrs. Onassis's relief, in reality?

PROBLEM D

THE CASE OF THE IMPOUNDED BULLDOG (CONTINUED). Reconsider Problem B (in which the Collinses' bulldog has been impounded and is subject to being destroyed after a hearing). Would the Collinses be entitled to a preliminary injunction, given the test for such an injunction? What should the injunction order say?

[B] Specific Performance, Equitable Restitution, Constructive Trusts, and Other Equitable Relief: Notes and Questions

(1) *Specific Performance: Centex Homes Corp. v. Boag, 128 N.J. Super. 385, 320 A.2d 194 (1974).* Specific performance is an equitable remedy available when the performance required by a contract is so unique that damages will not provide an adequate remedy, so that equity is justified in intervening to order the performance. In the *Centex Homes* case, Boag signed a contract to purchase a condominium unit in a luxury high-rise building from Centex. The contract provided for Centex's retention of the deposit as liquidated damages upon breach. Boag refused to close the purchase or to make any further payments, thereby breaching the contract. Centex sued — but in order to avoid being limited to liquidated damages, it did not sue for contract damages; instead, it sued for specific performance. The court noted that a purchaser, as distinguished from a seller, of real property, ordinarily could invoke the remedy of specific performance, since parcels of land usually fulfill the "uniqueness" requirement. Although this principle had rarely if ever been applied in the instance of a condominium unit, the court indicated that it would so apply it, in an otherwise proper case. This rationale, however, did not extend to a seller such as Centex, which would receive money on performance of the contract — the money being "non-unique." The court recognized that remedies available to the parties would not be symmetrical, but held that "mutuality" of remedy was not required. It also recognized that the amount of liquidated damages might be smaller than Centex's actual damages, but this result was a consequence of the contract and not of the inadequacy of legal relief. *See generally* Schwartz, *The Case of Specific Performance*, 89 Yale L.J. 271 (1979).

(2) *Restitution: Prevention of "Unjust Enrichment."* Restitution is a complex subject; but put simply, it means "restoration" of something to the plaintiff. Restitutionary remedies exist both at law and in equity. For example, replevin (for recovering a chattel) and general assumpsit (*e.g.*, for the restoration of money paid by mistake) were common law writs that sometimes involved restitutionary remedies. The goal of restitution, however, may not in some cases be limited to that of restoring the plaintiff; often, it is to cause the defendant to disgorge "unjust enrichment." *See also* Kovacic, *A Proposal to Simplify Quantum Meruit Litigation*, 35 Am. U. L. Rev. 547 (1986).

(3) *Equitable Restitution Versus Compensatory Damages: Burger King Corp. v. Mason, 710 F.2d 1480 (11th Cir. 1983).* This case shows, in a striking way, the difference between equitable restitution, which is founded on disgorgement of unjust enrichment, and damages. The District Court found that Mason had breached his contract with Burger King in the operation of a restaurant franchise but rejected Burger King's arguments based upon trademark infringement and unfair competition. Then, in an erroneous effort to compensate for the breach of contract, the District Court awarded to Burger King the profits earned by Mason in the operation of the restaurant as "compensatory damages," finding that these profits coincidentally happened to equal Burger King's actual damages. The Court of Appeals reversed:

> As the parties recognize, a trademark infringer can be required to turn over the profits he earns during the period of the infringement subject to the discretion of the district judge and in light of the equities of the case. . . . However, the district judge did not find that Mason infringed upon a trademark. . . .

> . . . Disgorgement of profits earned is not the remedy for breach of contract. . . . [A] contract plaintiff may recover damages in an amount which will place him in the position that he would have obtained but for the breach. . . . In some cases, if the offending conduct causes the non-breaching party to lose profits, the defendant can be required to compensate the plaintiff for the [plaintiff's] *lost profits*. . . .
>
> There is no support on the record that the profits owned by Mason equaled [Burger King's] damages from the breach. That would be correct only if [Burger King] proved that it would have taken over the operation of the franchises after termination and [Burger King] reasonably could have earned the profits that were generated by Mason. . . .

In a footnote, the court rejected the trial judge's characterization of the profits award as preventing "unjust enrichment": "An accounting of profits may be appropriate to prevent the unjust enrichment of a trademark infringer, . . . but does not comport with the compensatory nature of breach of contract damages."

(4) *Constructive Trust: An Equitable Restitutionary Remedy.* Judge Cardozo said: "A constructive trust is the formula through which the conscience of equity finds expression. When property has been acquired in such circumstances that the holder of the legal title may not in good conscience retain the beneficial interest, equity converts him into a trustee." *Beatty v. Guggenheim Exploration Co.*, 225 N.Y. 380, 386, 122 N.E. 378, 380 (1919). While there are other equitable restitutionary devices, the flexible constructive trust is one of the most frequently used. It allows the plaintiff to obtain the increase in value of property; it may also enable him to "follow the property into its product" (*i.e.*, to obtain property, or its increased value, into which his lost property has been transmitted). The remedy is simple: the holder of unjust enrichment is deemed to be a trustee for the proper claimant. A constructive trust may be used, for example, to prevent unjust enrichment of a fiduciary who otherwise would be immune from a damage remedy because of such rules as the statute of frauds. In the case of *Snepp v. United States*, below, the constructive trust was used in a novel context, but in a way consistent with its history, because proof of damages would be difficult and would itself be unduly costly. *See also* Devin & David, *The Constructive Trust — A Valuable Salvage Tool*, 15 Forum 790 (1980).

(5) *Constructive Trust: Snepp v. United States, 444 U.S. 507 (1979).* Snepp's employment with the CIA involved a fiduciary relationship, as the Court put it, to an "extremely high degree." This fiduciary relationship was emphasized in a written contract signed by Snepp. The agreement specifically imposed the obligation not to publish any information relating to the agency without submitting the information for clearance. In breach of this agreement, Snepp published a book about certain CIA activities in South Vietnam. For purposes of the litigation, the government conceded that Snepp's book divulged no classified intelligence. However, it pointed out that a former intelligence agent's publication of unreviewed material is detrimental to vital national interests even if not classified, because it may expose classified information and confidential sources indirectly, may discourage agents from serving in dangerous posts dependent upon confidentiality, and may destroy the confidence of cooperative nations' intelligence sources. The District Court, based upon these findings, imposed a constructive trust on Snepp's profits from the sale of his book. The Court of Appeals agreed that Snepp was liable for the breach, but held that the remedy should be confined to compensatory and punitive damages. The Supreme Court reversed the Court of Appeals and reinstated the constructive trust:

The government could not pursue the only remedy that the Court of Appeals left it without losing the benefit of the bargain it seeks to enforce. Proof of the tortious conduct necessary to sustain an award of punitive damages might force the government to disclose some of the very confidences that Snepp promised to protect. . . .

A constructive trust, on the other hand, protects both the Government and the former agent from unwarranted risks. This remedy is the natural and customary consequence of a breach of trust. It deals fairly with both by conforming relief to the dimensions of the wrong. . . . If the agent publishes unreviewed material in violation of his fiduciary and contractual obligation, the trust remedy simply requires him to disgorge the benefits of his faithlessness. . . .

(6) *Resulting Trusts (As Compared to Constructive Trusts): Harris v. Sentry Title Co., 727 F.2d 1368 (5th Cir. 1984).* A "resulting" trust often is prayed for as an alternative to a constructive trust, although the two are quite different in concept. The resulting trust is a "true" trust, but it is implied rather than created by express contract. For example, in *Harris v. Sentry Title*, the plaintiff gave the defendant money with which to purchase real estate, on the understanding that the defendant would hold the property as a "nominee" for the plaintiff (the wealthy plaintiff was concerned that, otherwise, his involvement would increase the purchase price). The defendant, however, simply kept the real estate as his own, asserting the statute of frauds as a defense to any legal obligation to convey to the plaintiff! The trial court imposed a constructive trust, but the Court of Appeals, over a vigorous dissent, reversed — because the duration of the parties' relationship and its fiduciary nature were not sufficiently strong to comply with state law of constructive trust in the majority's view. Question: On remand to the District Court, may the plaintiff prevail on the theory of resulting trust? [Do the parties have an implied trust relationship?] You should also consider whether the decision rejecting the constructive trust remedy seems correct.

(7) *Other Restitutionary Equitable Remedies: Equitable Liens, Accountings, Back-pay, Subrogation, Rescission, and Reformation.* An "equitable lien" can be imposed by a court when wrongfully taken property is used to purchase a more substantial asset; the plaintiff has a lien against the asset to secure payment. (This remedy actually is a special case of the constructive trust.) An equitable "accounting" is available in situations of complex accounts (*cf. Dairy Queen v. Wood*, § 10.02[A][1], above); and an "accounting for profits" is a slightly different remedy, available for example when the defendant wrongfully has infringed the plaintiff's trademark (*see Burger King Corp. v. Mason*, above). A restitutionary "back-pay" award is within the court's discretionary authority in some kinds of civil rights actions, subject to balancing of the equities by the court. *See Curtis v. Loether*, discussed in § 10.02, above. "Subrogation" is analogous to constructive trust, but operates by allowing one person to "step into the shoes of another." The most common example is the casualty insurer who pays an injured person's loss; the remedy of subrogation allows the insurer, in some circumstances, to step into the shoes of its insured and sue a negligent third person for the amount of the loss. "Rescission" is a remedy by which a party to an illegal or otherwise improper transaction may have the court set it aside, and "reformation" is a restructuring of the agreement when the parties have inaccurately expressed it owing to mistake or fraud of a kind that equity will redress. All of these remedies partake of the character of, and might be loosely described as types of, "restitution."

(8) *The Continuing Evolution of Equitable Remedies: Marvin v. Marvin ["Marvin II"], 5 Fam. L. Rep. 3077 (Cal. Super. Ct. April 18, 1979).* This famous case dramatically

illustrates the continuing evolution of equitable remedies. In *Marvin I* [*Marvin v. Marvin*, 18 Cal. 3d 660, 134 Cal. Rptr. 815, 557 P.2d 106 (1976)], the California Supreme Court held that Michelle Triola, also known as Michelle Marvin, could recover from movie star Lee Marvin, with whom she had resided while unmarried, on an implied contract or on various legal or equitable theories. On remand, the trial court held that there was no express or implied contract, and it further found no basis for constructive trust, resulting trust, or any other traditional legal or equitable remedy. The trial court noted, however, that Michelle had resorted to unemployment benefits while Lee had substantial resources. The California Supreme Court's opinion had "[urged] the trial court to employ whatever equitable remedy may be proper." Therefore, the trial court ordered what might be called "equitable rehabilitative alimony." It said: "In view of these circumstances, the court in equity awards plaintiff $104,000 [*i.e.*, $1,000 per week, the highest scale plaintiff ever earned as a singer, paid over a two-year period] for rehabilitation purposes . . . so that she may return from her status as companion of a motion picture star to a separate, independent, but perhaps more prosaic existence."

The District Court of Appeals reversed this "equitable rehabilitative alimony" award in *Marvin v. Marvin* [*"Marvin III"*], 122 Cal. App. 3d 871, 176, Cal. Rptr. 555 (1981). The majority held that the trial court's findings of no contract, no unjust enrichment, and no wrongful act on Lee's part, gave no substantive basis for any award whatsoever. However, the *Marvin* case remains as an example of the continuing growth of equity.

(9) *"Institutional Reform" Remedies in Civil Rights Cases: Williams v. New Orleans, 729 F.2d 1554 (5th Cir. 1984) (en banc).* Black officers sued the city in a class action, claiming longstanding racial discrimination in employment in violation of Title VII of the Civil Rights Act of 1964. The parties agreed on a proposed settlement agreement that governed "virtually every phase of an officer's employment by the New Orleans Police Department." Among other subjects, the decree required recruitment by black officers in black neighborhoods; assignments of "buddies" to guide black applicants through the (shortened) application process; new examination procedures designed to ensure that blacks passed in the same proportion in which they entered the police academy; special training sessions; elimination of general intelligence tests; an "academy review panel" composed half of black officers to review any dismissals; creation of forty-four new supervisory positions, all to be filled by black officers; filling of all supervisory vacancies by fifty percent black officers; extensive reporting obligations; and a $300,000 back-pay fund to be distributed to black officers. The District Court adopted all of the decree except the fifty percent black promotion provision, concluding that it would impact adversely upon members of other minority groups. The en banc Court of Appeals, in a fragmented opinion, affirmed on the ground that the trial judge had the discretion of a court of equity, and he could either enter or reject the decree.

School desegregation cases provide another example of the broad, equitable discretion of the trial judge in "institutional reform" litigation. *Brown v. Board of Education*, 347 U.S. 483 (1954), required equitable remedies of desegregation to be carried out with "all deliberate speed." Later, in response to intractable segregation, the courts created such remedies as faculty ratios, minority-to-majority transfer policies, redrawing of zone lines, pairing of different schools, and "satellite" zoning. This last remedy required busing of children to schools in cross-town zones not contiguous to ones in which they resided, and it was approved in *Swann v. Charlotte-Mecklenburg Board of Education*, 402 U.S. 1 (1971).

(10) *Can an Equitable "Institutional Reform" Decree Go Beyond Prevention of Future Violations? Can It Replace the State's Decisionmaking Processes with Other Processes,*

Responsible to the Court? Can It Require Particular Votes by Government Officials? United States v. City of Parma, 661 F.2d 562 (6th Cir. 1981), cert. denied, 456 U.S. 926 (1982). In this unusual case, after finding that the city's housing policies were racially motivated, the District Court ordered the members of the city council to pass an ordinance welcoming "all persons of good will" to move to the city. It also set up a committee responsible to the court to review all zoning ordinances, and it required the city to conduct an advertising campaign for new residents. The Court of Appeals affirmed these portions of the order as within the broad equitable discretion of the trial judge. First, that a remedial decree may address matters beyond correction of future violations, because the intervention necessary to make the remedy often brings about other conditions that must be addressed. It is likewise clear that intrusions into the sovereignty of a state are within the authority of a court of equity redressing a civil rights violation (although the extent and nature of the intrusion is an equitable factor to be considered in limiting the decree). Given these equitable considerations, was the *Parma* decree appropriate? [Note: The *Parma* decree also included more direct remedies, such as requiring the city to build certain numbers of housing units on schedule, at the city's expense.]

§ 14.04 Declaratory Judgments

Read 28 U.S.C. §§ 2201-2202 and Fed. R. Civ. P. 57 (declaratory judgments).

Why are Declaratory Judgments Needed?: Beacon Theatres, Inc. v. Westover, 359 U.S. 500 (1958) (reproduced in § 10.02[A] of Chapter 10). It sometimes happens that a party needs a declaration of her rights, even though the controversy has not proceeded to a point where traditional coercive relief would be available. For example, Fox West Coast Theatres had exclusive distribution contracts for certain motion pictures. Beacon claimed that the contracts were invalid. It was important to Fox to know whether they were valid and enforceable. The mechanism for finding out was the declaratory judgment.

A Common Use of the Declaratory Judgment: Insurance Duty-to-Defend Cases. Typically, liability insurance contracts impose on the insurer a duty to furnish a defense to the insured in suits covered by the policy. But what if the insured is subjected to a suit that the insurer believes is not covered? The insurer can simply decline to defend — but then might be subjected to large liability if it is wrong. The typical solution to these difficulties is for the insurer to furnish a defense to the insured (which customarily is accompanied by a "reservation of rights" agreement, in which the insured and insurer agree that the furnishing of the defense is not a waiver of the insurer's rights), but simultaneously to commence a suit for declaratory judgment of nonliability. For an interesting discussion of a different but related issue, see Morris, *Conflicts of Interest in Defending Under Liability Insurance Policies: A Proposed Solution*, 1981 Utah L. Rev. 457 (1981).

§ 14.05 Attorney's Fees, Interest, and Costs

CITY OF RIVERSIDE v. RIVERA
477 U.S. 561 (1986)

JUSTICE BRENNAN announced the judgment of the Court and delivered an opinion in which JUSTICE MARSHALL, JUSTICE BLACKMUN, and JUSTICE STEVENS join.

The issue presented in this case is whether an award of attorney's fees under 42 U.S.C. § 1988 is *per se* "unreasonable" within the meaning of the statute if it exceeds the amount of damages recovered by the plaintiff in the underlying civil rights action.

I

Respondents, eight Chicano individuals, attended a party on the evening of August 1, 1975, at the Riverside, California, home of respondents Santos and Jennie Rivera. A large number of unidentified police officers, acting without a warrant, broke up the party using tear gas and, as found by the District Court, "unnecessary physical force." Many of the guests, including four of the respondents, were arrested. The District Court later found that "[t]he party was not creating a disturbance in the community at the time of the break-in" . . . . Criminal charges against the arrestees were ultimately dismissed for lack of probable cause.

[R]espondents sued the City of Riverside, its chief of police, and 30 individual police officers under 42 U.S.C. §§ 1981, 1983, 1985(3), and 1986 for allegedly violating their First, Fourth, and Fourteenth Amendment rights. The complaint, which also alleged numerous state-law claims, sought damages and declaratory and injunctive relief. . . . The jury returned a total of 37 individual verdicts in favor of the respondents and against the City and five individual officers. . . . Respondents were awarded $33,350 in compensatory and punitive damages: $13,300 for their federal claims, and $20,050 for their state-law claims.

Respondents also sought attorney's fees and costs under § 1988. They requested compensation for 1,942.75 hours expended by their two attorneys at a rate of $125 per hour, and for 84.5 hours expended by law clerks at a rate of $25.00 per hour, a total of $245,456.25. The District Court found both the hours and rates reasonable, and awarded respondents $245,456.25 in attorney's fees. The court rejected respondents' request for certain additional expenses, and for a multiplier sought by respondents to reflect the contingent nature of their success and the high quality of their attorneys' efforts.

[T]he Court of Appeals for the Ninth Circuit affirmed. . . .

[The Supreme Court vacated and remanded for reconsideration in light of *Hensley v. Eckerhart*, 461 U.S. 424 (1983), an intervening decision. The District Court again awarded precisely the same fee, with extensive additional findings, and again the Court of Appeals affirmed.]

Petitioners again sought a writ of certiorari from this Court, alleging that the District Court's fee award was not "reasonable" within the meaning of § 1988, because it was disproportionate to the amount of damages recovered by respondents. We granted the writ . . . and now affirm the Court of Appeals.

II

A

In *Alyeska Pipeline Service Co. v. Wilderness Society*, 421 U.S. 240 (1975), the Court reaffirmed the "American Rule" . . . each party to a lawsuit ordinarily shall bear its own attorney's fees. In response to *Alyeska*, Congress enacted the Civil Rights Attorney's Fees Awards Act of 1976, 42 U.S.C. § 1988, which authorized the district courts to award reasonable attorney's fees to prevailing parties in specified civil rights litigation. While the statute itself does not explain what constitutes a reasonable fee, both the House and Senate Reports accompanying § 1988 expressly endorse the analysis set forth in *Johnson v. Georgia Highway Express, Inc.*, 488 F.2d 714 (5th Cir. 1974). *Johnson* identifies 12 factors to be considered in calculating a reasonable attorney's fee.[3]

---

[3] These factors are: (1) the time and labor required; (2) the novelty and difficulty of the questions; (3) the skill requisite to perform the legal service properly; (4) the preclusion of employment by

Hensley v. Eckerhart, 461 U.S. 424 (1983), announced certain guidelines for calculating a reasonable attorney's fee under § 1988. *Hensley* stated that "[t]he most useful starting point for determining the amount of a reasonable fee is the number of hours reasonably expended on the litigation multiplied by a reasonable hourly rate." This figure, commonly referred to as the "lodestar," is presumed to be the reasonable fee contemplated by § 1988. The opinion cautioned that "[t]he district court . . . should exclude from this initial fee calculation hours that were not 'reasonably expended' " on the litigation.

Hensley then discussed other considerations that might lead the district court to adjust the lodestar figure upward or downward, including the "important factor of the 'results obtained.' " The opinion noted that where a prevailing plaintiff has succeeded on only some of his claims, an award of fees for time expended on unsuccessful claims may not be appropriate. In these situations, the Court held that the judge should consider whether or not the plaintiff's unsuccessful claims were related to the claims on which he succeeded, and whether the plaintiff achieved a level of success that makes it appropriate to award [these] attorney's fees for [u]nsuccessful claims. . . .

B

Petitioners argue that the District Court failed properly to follow *Hensley* in calculating respondents' fee award. We disagree. . . . First, the court found that "[t]he amount of time expended by counsel in conducting this litigation was reasonable and reflected sound legal judgment under the circumstances." App. 190.[4] The court also determined that counsels' excellent performances in this case entitled them to be compensated at prevailing market rates, even though they were relatively young when this litigation began. . . .

The District Court then concluded that it was inappropriate to adjust respondents' fee award downward to account for the fact that respondents had prevailed only on some of their claims, and against only some of the defendants. The court first determined that "it was never actually clear what officer did what until we had gotten through with the whole trial," so that "[u]nder the circumstances of this case, it was reasonable for plaintiffs initially to name thirty-one individual defendants. . . . as well as the City of Riverside as defendants in this action." . . .

The District Court also considered the amount of damages recovered, and determined that the size of the damages award did not imply that respondents' success was limited:

---

the attorney due to acceptance of the case; (5) the customary fee; (6) whether the fee is fixed or contingent; (7) time limitations imposed by the client or the circumstances; (8) the amount involved and the results obtained; (9) the experience, reputation, and ability of the attorneys; (10) the "undesirability" of the case; (11) the nature and length of the professional relationship with the client; and (12) awards in similar cases. 488 F.2d, at 717-719.

[4] *Hensley* stated that a fee applicant should "exercise 'billing judgment' with respect to hours worked." 461 U.S., at 437. Petitioners maintain that respondents failed to exercise "billing judgment" in this case, since they sought compensation for all time spent litigating this case. We think this argument misreads the mandate of *Hensley*. *Hensley* requires a fee applicant to exercise "billing judgment" not because he should necessarily be compensated for less than the actual number of hours spent litigating a case, but because the hours he does seek compensation for must be *reasonable*. . . .

Hensley also stated that a fee applicant should "maintain billing time records in a manner that will enable a reviewing court to identify distinct claims." *Id.*, at 437. Petitioners submit that the time records submitted by respondents' attorneys made it difficult for the District Court to identify and separate distinct claims. The District Court, however, does not appear to have shared this view. . . .

> [T]he size of the jury award resulted from (a) the general reluctance of jurors to make large awards against police officers, and (b) the dignified restraint which the plaintiffs exercised in describing their injuries to the jury. . . .

The court paid particular attention to the fact that the case "presented complex and interrelated issues of fact and law," and that "[a] fee award in this civil rights action will . . . advance the public interest." . . . Finally, the District Court "focus[ed] on the significance of the overall relief obtained by [respondents] in relation to the hours reasonably expended on the litigation." The court concluded that respondents had "achieved a level of success in this case that makes the total number of hours expended by counsel a proper basis for making the fee award." . . .

Based on our review of the record, we agree with the Court of Appeals that the District Court's findings were not clearly erroneous. We conclude that the District Court correctly applied the factors announced in *Hensley* in calculating respondents' fee award, and that the court did not abuse its discretion in awarding attorney's fees for all time reasonably spent litigating the case.

Petitioners, joined by the Solicitor General as *amicus curiae*, maintain that *Hensley*'s lodestar approach is inappropriate in civil rights cases where a plaintiff recovers only monetary damages. . . . Specifically, they suggest that fee awards in damages cases should be modeled upon the contingent fee arrangements commonly used in personal injury litigation. In this case, assuming a 33% contingency rate, this would entitle respondents to recover approximately $11,000 in attorney's fees.

The amount of damages a plaintiff recovers is certainly relevant to the amount of attorney's fees to be awarded under § 1988. It is, however, only one of many factors that a court should consider in calculating an award of attorney's fees. We reject the proposition that fee awards under § 1988 should necessarily be proportionate to the amount of damages a civil rights plaintiff actually recovers.

III

A

As an initial matter, we reject the notion that a civil rights action for damages constitutes nothing more than a private tort suit benefiting only the individual plaintiffs whose rights were violated. . . .

Congress expressly recognized that a plaintiff who obtains relief in a civil rights lawsuit "does so not for himself alone but also as a 'private attorney general,' vindicating a policy that Congress considered of the highest importance." House Report, at 2. . . .

Because damages awards do not reflect fully the public benefit advanced by civil rights litigation, Congress did not intend for fees in civil rights cases [t]o depend on obtaining substantial monetary relief. Rather, Congress made clear that it "intended that the amount of fees awarded under [§ 1988] be governed by the same standards which prevail in other types of equally complex Federal litigation, such as antitrust cases, and *not be reduced because the rights involved may be nonpecuniary in nature.*" Senate Report, at 6 (emphasis added). . . .

B

A rule of proportionality would make it difficult, if not impossible, for individuals with meritorious civil rights claims but relatively small potential damages to obtain redress from the courts. This is totally inconsistent with the Congress' purpose in enacting § 1988. . . .

This case illustrates why the enforcement of civil rights laws cannot be entrusted to private-sector fee arrangements. The District Court observed that "[g]iven the nature of this lawsuit and the type of defense presented, many attorneys in the community would have been reluctant to institute and to continue to prosecute this action." . . . [I]t is highly unlikely that the prospect of a fee equal to a fraction of the damages respondents might recover would have been sufficient to attract competent counsel. . . .

IV

. . . In the absence of any indication that Congress intended to adopt a strict rule that attorney's fees under § 1988 be proportionate to damages recovered, we decline to adopt such a rule ourselves. The judgment of the Court of Appeals is hereby affirmed.

JUSTICE POWELL, concurring in the judgment.

I join only the Court's judgment. The plurality opinion reads our decision in *Hensley v. Eckerhart*, 461 U.S. 424 (1983), [m]ore expansively than is necessary to decide this case. For me affirmance — quite simply — is required by the District Court's detailed findings of fact, which were approved by the Court of Appeals. On its face, the fee award seems unreasonable. But I find no basis for this Court to reject the findings made and approved [b]elow. . . .

CHIEF JUSTICE BURGER, dissenting.

I join Justice Rehnquist's dissenting opinion. I write only to add that it would be difficult to find a better example of legal nonsense than the fixing of attorney's fees by a judge at $245,456.25 for the recovery of $33,350 damages. . . .

JUSTICE REHNQUIST, with whom THE CHIEF JUSTICE, JUSTICE WHITE, and JUSTICE O'CONNOR join, dissenting.

In *Hensley v. Eckerhart*, 461 U.S. 424, 433 (1983), our leading case dealing with attorney's fees awarded pursuant to 42 U.S.C. § 1988, we said that "[t]he most useful starting point for determining the amount of a reasonable fee is the number of hours reasonably expended on the litigation multiplied by a reasonable hourly rate." As if we had foreseen the case now before us, we went on to emphasize that "[t]he district court . . . should exclude from this initial fee calculation hours that were not 'reasonably expended' on the litigation. . . ." I see no escape from the conclusion that the District Court's finding that respondents' attorneys "reasonably" spent 1,946.75 hours to recover a money judgment of $33,350 is clearly erroneous, and that therefore the District Court's award of $245,456.25 in attorney's fees to respondents should be reversed. The Court's affirmance of the fee award emasculates the principles laid down in *Hensley*, and turns § 1988 into a relief act for lawyers.

A brief look at the history of this case reveals just how "unreasonable" it was for respondents' lawyers to spend so much time on it. . . . Prior to trial, 17 of the police officers were dismissed from the case on motions for summary judgment, and respondents dropped their requests for injunctive and declaratory relief. More significantly, respondents also dropped their original allegation that the police had acted with discriminatory intent. The action proceeded to trial, and the jury completely exonerated nine additional police officers. Respondents ultimately prevailed against only the City and five police officers on various § 1983, false arrest and imprisonment, and common negligence claims.

No restraining orders or injunctions were ever issued against petitioners, nor was the City ever compelled to change a single practice or policy as a result of respondents' suit. The jury awarded respondents a total of $33,350 in compensatory and punitive damages. Only about one-third of this total, or $13,300, was awarded to respondents based on violations of their federal constitutional rights. . . .

It is obvious to me that the District Court viewed *Hensley* not as a constraint on its discretion, but instead as a blueprint for justifying, in an after-the-fact fashion, a fee award it had already decided to enter solely on the basis of the "lodestar." . . . A few examples should suffice: (1) The court approved almost 209 hours of "prelitigation time," for a total of $26,118.75. (2) The court approved some 197 hours of time spent in conversations between respondents' two attorneys, for a total of $24,625. (3) The court approved 143 hours of preparation of a pre-trial order, for a total of $17,875.00. (4) Perhaps most egregiously, the court approved 45.50 hours of "stand-by time," or time spent by one of respondents' attorneys, who was then based in San Diego, to wait in a Los Angeles hotel room for a jury verdict to be rendered in Los Angeles, where his co-counsel was then employed by the UCLA School of Law, less than 40 minutes' driving time from the courthouse. The award for "stand-by time" totaled $5,687.50. . . .

Indeed, on the basis of some of the statements made by the District Court in this case, I reluctantly conclude that the court may have attempted to make up to respondents in attorney's fees what it felt the jury had wrongfully withheld from them in damages. As the court noted in its opinion . . . :

> [T]he size of the jury award resulted from (a) the general reluctance of jurors to make large awards against police officers, and (b) the dignified restraint which the plaintiffs exercised in describing their injuries to the jury. . . .

But a District Court, in awarding attorney's fees under § 1988, does not sit to retry questions submitted to and decided by the jury. . . .

Suppose that A offers to sell Blackacre to B for $10,000. It is commonly known and accepted that Blackacre has a fair market value of $10,000. B consults an attorney and requests a determination whether A can convey good title to Blackacre. The attorney writes an elaborate memorandum concluding that A's title to Blackacre is defective and submits a bill to B for $25,000. . . . Does anyone seriously think that a court should award the attorney the full $25,000 which he claims? . . .

The amount of damages which a jury is likely to award in a tort case is of course more difficult to predict than the amount it is likely to award in a contract case. But even in a tort case some measure of the kind of "billing judgment" previously described must be brought to bear in computing a "reasonable" attorney's fee. Again, a hypothetical example will illustrate the point. If, at the time respondents filed their lawsuit in 1976, there had been in the Central District of California a widely publicized survey of jury verdicts in this type of civil rights action which showed that successful plaintiffs recovered between $10,000 and $75,000 in damages, could it possibly be said that it would have been "reasonable" for respondents' attorneys to put in on the case hours which, when multiplied by the attorneys' prevailing hourly rate, would result in an attorney's fee of over $245,000? In the absence of such a survey, it might be more difficult for a plaintiff's attorney to accurately estimate the amount of damages likely to be recovered, but this does not absolve the attorney of the responsibility for making such an estimate and using it as a guide in the exercise of "billing judgment." . . .

. . . I agree with the plurality that the importation of the contingent-fee model to govern fee awards under § 1988 is not warranted by the terms and legislative history of the statute. But I do not agree with the plurality if it means to reject the kind of "proportionality" that I have previously described. . . . One may agree with all of the glowing rhetoric contained in the plurality's opinion about Congress' noble purpose in authorizing attorney's fees under § 1988 without concluding that Congress intended to turn attorneys loose to spend as many hours as possible to prepare and try a case that could reasonably be expected to result only in a relatively minor award of monetary damages. . . .

NOTES AND QUESTIONS

(1) *Should Defendants Recover Attorney's Fees if They Prevail in Civil Rights Actions? Eastway Constr. Corp. v. City of New York, 762 F.2d 243 (2d Cir. 1985).* This case appears above in § 5.05[B] of Chapter 5, as a case dealing with sanctions under Rule 11. The court of appeals also recognized that the Civil Rights Attorney's Fees Act provides for awards to prevailing defendants. The court limited such awards to actions that were "frivolous, unreasonable, or without foundation," but it did not require "subjective bad faith." Under this standard, the court held that the trial judge must award fees to the defendant city in a suit in which there was no basis for the claim.

(2) *Should a "Multiplier" Be Applied to the Lodestar to Reflect Contingency? Pennsylvania v. Delaware Valley Citizens' Council for Clean Air, 483 U.S. 711 (1987).* In this Clean Air Act case, the District Court first computed the "lodestar" — hours worked, multiplied by a reasonable fee — and then doubled the fee by applying a "multiplier" of two to the lodestar, to reflect the contingent nature of the potential recovery. Given that a non-prevailing litigant recovers no fees, is the multiplier an appropriate means of addressing the contingent nature of the award? No, said the Supreme Court, at least in the case before it. Four Justices concluded that the attorney's fees statute at issue should not be construed as permitting enhancement of a reasonable lodestar fee to compensate an attorney for the risk of loss and of nonpayment, and that even if it were construed to permit enhancement in appropriate cases, it was error to do so in this case. Justice O'Connor concluded that Congress did not intend to foreclose consideration of contingency in setting a reasonable fee. But she agreed that the District Court erred in employing a risk multiplier in the circumstances of this case. Four more Justices concluded that Congress intended to allow an upward adjustment, in appropriate circumstances, for a case taken on a contingent basis, and that the award in this case should be vacated and remanded for further findings: "The court then should arrive at an enhancement for risk that parallels, as closely as possible, the premium for contingency that exists in prevailing market rates."

(3) *Does a Contingent Fee Agreement Limit the Amount of Attorney's Fees? Blanchard v. Bergeron, 489 U.S. 87 (1989).* The Supreme Court here held that a contingent fee agreement entered into between the plaintiff and his attorney, in which the attorney would get 40% of any award, did not place a ceiling on fees recoverable under the Civil Rights Attorney's Fees Award Act. The plaintiff, Blanchard, was awarded $10,000 on his claim that the defendant deputy sheriff violated his civil rights by beating him. The District Court awarded the plaintiff's attorney $7,500 as a reasonable attorney fee, but the Court of Appeals reduced the fee to $4,000 to reflect the plaintiff's and attorney's contingent fee agreement. The Supreme Court reversed, holding that § 1988's legislative history showed that Congress did not intend contingent fee agreements to cap the attorney's fee award. Such an agreement is simply a factor to be considered by the trial court in determining the award.

(4) *Do Nominal Damages of One Dollar Support Attorney's Fees in a § 1983 Civil Rights Action? Farrar v. Hobby, 506 U.S. 103 (1992).* After being indicted for the murder

of a patient, Dr. Farrar's residential treatment facility was temporarily shut down. The indictment was eventually dismissed, and the Farrars filed a civil rights suit against, among others, Lieutenant Governor Hobby, claiming there had been a conspiracy to deprive them of their livelihood. The Farrars sought compensatory damages of $17 million, but after 17 years and the death of Dr. Farrar, the plaintiffs were awarded $1 in nominal damages by the Federal District Court. In addition, the District Court awarded $280,000 in attorney's fees pursuant to 42 U.S.C. § 1988. The Court of Appeals reversed the award of attorney's fees on the ground that the plaintiffs were not "prevailing parties." The Supreme Court held that the plaintiffs had technically won on the merits, and were therefore prevailing parties. However, the Court went on to say that the determination of whether to award attorney's fees hinged on the degree of success achieved by the prevailing party. Here, because the plaintiffs were unable in 17 years to establish actual, compensable injury, the Court held that "the only reasonable fee is usually no fee at all."

NOTE ON AVAILABILITY AND IMPACT OF PRE-JUDGMENT INTEREST

General Rule Against Pre-Judgment Interest. The common law did not authorize recovery of prejudgment interest in most tort cases. Exceptions existed in contract cases and in tort cases in which the damages were liquidated and the harm occurred on a particular date before trial. This principle applied to simple contracts requiring payments on specific dates before trial and to conversion cases.

Judicial Imposition of Pre-Judgment Interest: Cavnar v. Quality Control Parking, Inc., 696 S.W.2d 549 (Tex. 1985). In *Cavnar*, a parking lot attendant struck the deceased while backing a van, then backed a second time and ran over her again. The deceased's three adult children sued. In addition to awarding damages, the Texas Supreme Court held for the first time that "as a matter of law, a prevailing plaintiff may recover prejudgment interest compounded daily (based on a 365-day year) on damages that have accrued by the time of the judgment." The court borrowed from a general statute setting rates of interest not otherwise provided, to set the rate of interest. The court further held that in wrongful death and non-death personal injury actions, interest begins to accrue six months after the occurrence. In survival actions, interest begins to accrue as of the date of death (or, if the deceased does not die within six months of the injury, interest begins as of the date of the occurrence). Pre-judgment interest was not to be permitted on future damages or on punitive damages. (Notice that this holding meant that there must be special verdicts separating survival damages from wrongful death damages and past damages from future damages; a single, lump-sum award would make calculation of pre-judgment interest impossible).

Pre-Judgment Interest as "Judicial Legislation." The holding in *Cavnar* looks like a statute, with its "daily" compounding, 365-day year, six-month periods, and precise separation of different categories of damages. In fact, it has widely been criticized as "judicial legislation." While courts have generally exercised power to adjust or extend common law claims and remedies, should a matter of this complexity, with so little basis in statute or precedent, have been left to the legislature? Subsequent legislation in Texas has modified and superseded *Cavnar.*

Motion to Add Pre-Judgment Interest Governed by Fed. R. Civ. P. 59(e). According to the Ninth Circuit, a post-judgment motion to add mandatory pre-judgment interest to a judgment is an amendment to the judgment, and therefore governed by Rule 59(e) —

not merely a correction of a clerical error under Rule 60(a). *McCalla v. Royal Maccabees Life Ins. Co.*, 369 F.3d 1128 (9th Cir. 2004).

NOTES AND QUESTIONS

(1) *Discounting Future Damages to Present Value; Other Adjustments.* If a plaintiff cannot work and has lost income of $50,000 per year, and has a life expectancy of 40 years, is the value of her lost earnings equal to (40 × $50,000), or $2 million? Not in present dollars, because the total must be discounted by a present-value factor (*e.g.*, current market interest rates), since the $50,000 payments in the 39th and 40th years are worth much less today than $50,000 paid today. Litigants frequently offer testimony of labor economists on issues such as these. The plaintiff will counter the discount by offering evidence that a worker earning $50,00 has a reasonable anticipation of increases in real dollars owing to raises or promotions. These adjustments can be significant in amount (the $2 million, for example, may be reduced to a small fraction of that amount by discounting to present value at a high rate of interest).

(2) *"Costs" to the Prevailing Party.* Most jurisdictions allow a prevailing party to recover "costs" unless the court provides otherwise. But costs of court do not compensate for all expenses, because they do not include the most significant items, such as attorney's fees or amounts paid expert witnesses; instead, they usually include filing fees, deposition reporting costs, witness fees and expenses, payments for record preparation, and the like. Consider the following:

> Bell Helicopter Textron is seeking almost $50,000 in out-of-pocket trial costs . . . from two women who sued the company over their husbands' deaths. . . .
>
> A federal jury ruled in favor of the widows in January 1985 and awarded them $3.65 million after finding that the Bell rotor system was "unreasonably dangerous."
>
> But the Fourth U.S. Circuit Court of Appeals in Richmond recently overturned the case after ruling defense contractors are not liable for defects in aircraft built for the military. . . .
>
> Federal law allows the winners of civil suits to seek certain trial expenses . . . , such as the costs of depositions, witness fees and some travel expenses. The district clerk of each court has wide discretion about which fees to allow. . . .
>
> Many of [Bell's] witnesses flew first-class from Fort Worth to Baltimore and stayed in expensive hotels, racking up airline and hotel bills of $17,145, according to court documents. . . .
>
> Joe Haas, the Maryland district court clerk who will hear Bell's request on Oct. 22, said most expense vouchers filed with him rarely exceed $1,000.
>
> "Maybe a dozen times a year I'll see one above $10,000," Haas said. "Now, I haven't looked at this case yet, but in general, I don't grant those kinds of things" listed in Bell's reimbursement request. . . .
>
> "I have talked to numerous judges and lawyers and they're all appalled," [plaintiff's attorney John] Green said. "They're appalled that Bell, who probably has already written off these expenses, and who had over $800 million in sales last year, would come back against two widows of servicemen." . . .

Houston Chronicle, Aug. 29, 1986, § 1, at 33, col. 1 (Scripps-Howard News Service).* Should observers be "appalled," or is this an instance of "hard cases make bad law"?

Shouldn't prevailing defendants recover actual, real costs of court? Isn't there a case to be made that either a plaintiff or a defendant should recover attorney's fees, too (which in Bell's situation undoubtedly exceed these costs by a factor of ten or more), not as a matter of imposing hardship on the losing party, but as a matter of appropriate relief to the prevailing party? In fact, some statutes treat attorney's fees as a part of "costs." *See Marek v. Chesny*, in Chapter 15, below, for the consequences.

§ 14.06 Enforcement of Judgments

[A] Execution and Judicial Sale

GRIGGS v. MILLER, 374 S.W.2d 119 (Mo. 1963). Plaintiff Griggs had purchased a 322-acre farm previously owned by W.A. Brookshire at a sheriff's sale following execution. But Brookshire declined to relinquish the premises, so Griggs brought this ejectment action against him. Later, Brookshire was incarcerated in the Missouri penitentiary, and Miller, who was appointed trustee of his estate, was substituted as defendant in the ejectment action.

Brookshire had had several judgments against him which he did not pay. In fact, this same parcel of land had been sold at sheriff's sale on a previous occasion; that sale had been set aside on grounds similar to those at issue in this case. On this occasion, Ray Crouch had an outstanding final judgment against Brookshire amounting to just over $2,000 including interest and costs; Dorothy Contestible had an outstanding judgment for $17,000 against Brookshire for wrongful death; there also were judgments for $600 and $13.00. Counsel in these cases sought and obtained general writs of execution, commanding the sheriff to investigate, advertise, seize, and sell property of the judgment debtor sufficient to pay the respective judgments. The sheriff advertised the sale of the 322-acre farm to pay the Crouch judgment (approximately $2,000), but did not advertise it in connection with the Contestible judgment (the one for $17,000). Brookshire appeared at the execution sale and protested to bidders that the farm was clear of liens and was worth $50,000; that he had advised the sheriff in writing to sell only the northeast 40 acres; and that "whoever bought the farm would buy a law suit." The sheriff sold the entire 322 acres to the highest bidder, Griggs, for $20,600.

The Missouri Supreme Court, while recognizing that "[f]orced sales of property usually do not bring full value," set forth several restrictions on execution sales. First, the sheriff is the agent of both the judgment creditor and the property owner, and it is his duty to protect their interests and to see that the property is not sacrificed. Secondly, a sufficiently large "disparity" between market value and sales price would require setting aside. Third, the sheriff may not levy execution upon all the debtor's property, but only so much as is sufficient to satisfy the judgment debt. Fourth, if real property is capable of division, it must be subdivided, and only that portion sold that is necessary to pay the debt. Finally, if the judgment debtor elects in writing three days before sale, the sheriff must follow the order of sale designated by the debtor.

Here, only the $2,000 judgment could be considered since it was the only one that had been advertised, even though the sheriff had levied on the fund for all four judgments. The sheriff's violations of these applicable principles restricting execution sales required the setting aside of the sale, said the court. However, it required Brookshire to "do equity" in order to obtain relief, holding that he would be entitled to a reversal of the lower court's judgment against him if, but only if, he deposited $20,600 plus six percent interest in the registry of the court within thirty days.

NOTES AND QUESTIONS

(1) *Changing the Facts: What if All Judgments Had Been Advertised?* If the sheriff had advertised the sale to pay all of the judgments against Brookshire (particularly the Contestible judgment, for $17,000), should the result have been different? If so, is the holding in *Griggs v. Miller* based on a "technicality"?

(2) *Other Typical Restrictions on Execution Sales.* The restrictions on execution sales set forth in *Griggs v. Miller* are representative of the laws of many states, and there are other restrictions to be found in some. *Cf. Matter of Silverman*, 6 B.R. 991 (D.N.J. 1980) (under New Jersey law, execution on real property is void unless preceded by good-faith effort to locate and levy upon debtor's personalty first).

(3) *Liability for Wrongful Execution; Sheriff's Insistence on Bond.* A common-law claim exists for wrongful execution. Given this prospect, not to mention federal civil rights liability under such statutes as § 1983, would you be prompt and energetic in enforcing judgments if you were a Missouri sheriff? [Note: In many jurisdictions, it is customary for the sheriff to withhold execution and sale until the judgment creditor furnishes a satisfactory indemnity bond.]

(4) *Are the Restrictions on Execution Sales Set Forth in Griggs v. Miller Appropriate?* There was nothing whatsoever preventing Brookshire from selling property in whatever order he chose, for the purpose of satisfying each judgment (which, after all, was a court order providing that the plaintiff recover from him). The purchaser, Griggs, sustains a significant net loss, including his attorney's fees (and other purchasers sometimes lose even larger amounts if the setting aside of a sale is not accompanied by an equitable requirement, as here, for repayment of the bid price). The law's protection of Brookshire comes at the expense, also, of judgment creditors (including those holding wrongful death judgments, such as Ms. Contestible, here). Who else loses? [Note: The Missouri court recognizes that "[f]orced sales of property usually do not bring full value"; isn't that so, because the purchaser knows she is buying a lawsuit? Consequently, the price is discounted even more than for other distress sales, and the judgment debtor whose property is sold has a greater deficiency than she otherwise might — or receives less than she otherwise would, since excess amounts are payable to the judgment debtor.] Would these considerations justify a more absolute sale mechanism, in the interest of both judgment creditors and judgment debtors? The New York legislature has so concluded. Consider the following.

GUARDIAN LOAN CO. v. EARLY
47 N.Y.2d 515, 392 N.E.2d 1240, 419 N.Y.S.2d 56 (1979)

COOKE, CHIEF JUDGE.

We determine here whether the provisions of CPLR 5240 may be utilized to set aside a lawfully consummated Sheriff's sale once the real property has been struck off and a deed delivered to a stranger to the underlying judgment. We hold that while the statute vests the court with broad discretion to prevent abuse in the use of the enforcement procedures of CPLR article 52, it furnishes no grounds for relief once those procedures have been carried out in accordance with law.

Plaintiff, not a party to this appeal, obtained a judgment against respondents Early for $1,268.93 which was docketed in the office of the Suffolk County Clerk on July 14, 1976. After respondents had failed to satisfy the judgment, plaintiff delivered a real property execution, with notice to respondents, to the Suffolk County Sheriff for the sale of respondents' residence. The sale was duly advertised for May 23, 1977 in accordance with CPLR 5236 (subd. [c]) but was adjourned twice at the request of respondents (*see* CPLR 5236, subd. [d]). Finally, on August 1, 1977, the property was struck off to appellant Berlin, a stranger to the underlying judgment, for the sum of $3,020. Two days later, the Sheriff, after deduction of his proper fees, distributed the proceeds of the sale to judgment creditors who had failed executions and delivered a deed to the property to appellant.

This proceeding to set aside the sale was brought on by order to show cause. In support of their request for relief, respondents averred that on August 1, 1977 they had approximately $1,100 in cash — a sum which would have been inadequate to redeem the property prior to the sale — but were unable to reach the place of sale on time because of a flat tire. It was asserted upon information and belief that the property had a market value of between $55,000 and $60,000 (later revised to $48,000) and was subject to a mortgage balance of approximately $9,000. In opposition, appellant disputed the value of the property and set forth an abstract of title showing an unsatisfied 1975 Federal tax lien in the amount of $5,688 plus interest as well as several prior unsatisfied liens totaling over $6,000. Supreme Court set aside the sale, relying on CPLR 5240. A divided Appellate Division affirmed (64 A.D.2d 689, 407 N.Y.S.2d 571). We must now reverse.

The enactment of CPLR article 52 effected sweeping changes of both substance and procedure in the law relating to the satisfaction of money judgments. Nowhere were these changes more apparent than those with respect to the procedures involving the sale of real property (*see* Sale of Real Property Pursuant to an Execution under the CPLR, Tenth Ann. Report of N.Y. Judicial Conference, 1965, p. 120). Perhaps the most striking change accomplished by the CPLR was the abolition of the debtor's right of redemption upon sales to enforce money judgments (CPLR 5236). The Civil Practice Act had previously contained a number of rather complex provisions under which the judgment debtor or his creditors could redeem property after it had been sold upon execution (Civ. Prac. Act. §§ 758-763). It was thought that substantially higher prices could be realized upon execution sales were the right to redeem eliminated (*see* 6 Weinstein-Korn-Miller, *N.Y. Civ. Prac.*, par. 5236.02). While this rationale may not have been borne out in actual experience (*see Community Capital Corp. v. Lee*, 58 Misc. 2d 34, 35-36, 294 N.Y.S.2d 336, 337-338), the purchaser at a Sheriff's sale now takes immediate title to the property and is placed in the same position as he would have been if the deed had been executed by the judgment debtor himself (*see Hetzel v. Barber*, 69 N.Y. 1, 10).

Any judicial sale, especially one involving the judgment debtor's residence, is a tragic event. Debtors are often divested of their only real asset to satisfy a previous obligation, however small. In many instances, the family home is sold for substantially less than the debtor's equity in it (*see Concord Landscapers v. Pincus*, 41 A.D.2d 759, 760, 341 N.Y.S.2d 538, 540; *Wandschneider v. Bekeny*, 75 Misc. 2d 32, 346 N.Y.S.2d 925). Even the very threat of a sale of a residence places enormous pressure on the debtor. This is particularly unfortunate where there are less drastic means by which a creditor may enforce his judgment (*see, generally*, CPLR 5231 [income execution]; CPLR 5232-5233 [levy and sale of personal property]). It is evident, however, that the Legislature was not unaware of this problem. For example, it has recently raised the homestead exemption, which provides that upon a judicial sale of the debtor's principal place of residence, the first $10,000 of the proceeds representing the debtor's equity may not be used in satisfaction of the judgment (CPLR 5205, subd. [a]).

CPLR 5240 is perhaps the most practical method to protect judgment debtors from the often harsh results of lawful enforcement procedures. The statute provides: "The court may at any time, on its own initiative or the motion of any interested person, and upon such notice as it may require, make an order denying, limiting, conditioning, regulating, extending or modifying the use of any enforcement procedure. Section 3104 is applicable to procedures under this article." Designed to replace myriad provisions of the Civil Practice Act which often led to conflicting results (*see* 10 Carmody-Wait 2d, *N.Y. Prac.*, § 64:434), CPLR 5240 grants the courts broad discretionary power to control and regulate the enforcement of a money judgment under article 52 to prevent "unreasonable annoyance, expense, embarrassment, disadvantage, or other prejudice to any person or the courts" (Third Preliminary Report of the Advisory Comm. on Practice and Procedure, 1959, p. 314; *see* Siegel, *Practice Commentaries, McKinney's Cons. Laws of N.Y.*, Book 7B, CPLR 5240:1, pp. 451-452; Siegel, *New York Practice*, § 522).

Although on the whole judgment debtors have failed to take advantage of the protective provisions of CPLR 5240, in many instances the statute has been applied in an extremely beneficial manner in accordance with its stated purpose. By way of illustration, courts have restrained impending sales of residences on the ground that creditors could easily resort to less intrusive means to satisfy judgments (*see Hammond v. Econo-Car of North Shore*, 71 Misc. 2d 546, 336 N.Y.S.2d 493; *Holmes v. W.T. Grant, Inc.*, 71 Misc. 2d 486, 336 N.Y.S.2d 601; *Gilchrist v. Commercial Credit Corp.*, 66 Misc. 2d 791, 322 N.Y.S.2d 200). In other cases, where there has been a showing that a judicial sale will not bring a representative price, the terms of the sale have been varied from those set forth in CPLR 5236 to safeguard the judgment debtor's interest (*see, e.g., Olsen v. Robaey*, 45 Misc. 2d 33, 256 N.Y.S.2d 103).

But while CPLR 5240 grants the courts broad discretionary power to alter the use of the procedures set forth in article 52, it has no application after a Sheriff's sale has been carried out and the deed delivered to the purchaser, at which time the use of the enforcement procedure will have been completed. . . . After the sale has been consummated, the interests of persons other than the judgment debtor and creditor are implicated. Title to property has been transferred, often to a stranger to the judgment who relies on the regularity of the sale and proceeds accordingly. To permit these sales to be set aside merely because a beneficial price has not been obtained especially in view of the "at any time" provision of CPLR 5240, would discourage participation by third parties at judicial sales, for the title acquired at the sale would never be free from the spectre of judicial invalidation. Had the Legislature intended this statute to have such drastic consequences, it surely would have made its intention plain. . . .

This is not to say that a judgment debtor is without remedy once a judicial sale has taken place. CPLR 2003 grants the power to set aside such a Sheriff's sale within one year "for a failure to comply with the requirements of the civil practice law and rules as to the notice, time or manner of such sale, if a substantial right of a party was prejudiced by the defect." . . . And, of course, the court may exercise its inherent equitable power over a sale made pursuant to its judgment or decree to ensure that it is not made the instrument of injustice. . . . Although this power should be exercised sparingly and with great caution, a court of equity may set aside its own judicial sale upon grounds otherwise insufficient to confer an absolute legal right to a resale in order to relieve of oppressive or unfair conduct. . . .

In this case, the sale was conducted in strict conformity with statutory procedure (*see* CPLR 5236), rendering CPLR 2003 inapposite. Nor do general equitable principles furnish respondents any basis for relief. While the sale price was less than respondents' equity in the property, the simple fact is that in most instances the fair market value of the property will exceed the winning bid at an execution sale (*Matter of Superintendent of Banks of State of N.Y.*, 207 N.Y. 11, 16, 100 N.E. 428, 429). For this reason, it is well settled that mere inadequacy of price — the only pertinent showing here — does not furnish sufficient grounds for vacating a sale. . . .

Although respondents' plight is certain to evoke sympathy, here the record is devoid of any showing warranting intervention by a court of equity. Respondents had obtained two postponements of the sale, giving them more than three months after they had received notice that their property was to be sold to satisfy plaintiff's judgment. During that period, they could have avoided the sale by satisfying the judgment. Even on the day of the sale, respondents did not have sufficient funds to meet this obligation. Their delay in arriving at the sale is in no way attributable to appellant or any person connected with the sale and those in attendance had no knowledge of respondents' transportation difficulties. Respondents' rights were protected to the fullest extent that the law provides. . . .

Accordingly, the order of the Appellate Division should be reversed, without costs, and the motion to set aside the Sheriff's sale denied.

NOTES AND QUESTIONS

(1) *Exempt Property.* At the time of the opinion above, New York's homestead exemption reserved to the judgment debtor the first $10,000 realized from the judicial sale of her principal residence. New York's homestead exemption subsequently was increased to $50,000. CPLR 5206(a). Other states have larger homestead exemptions. For example, Texas exempts "urban" homesteads "of not more than 10 acres of land" and "rural" homesteads for single adults "of not more than 100 acres" and for families of "not more than 200 acres." *See* Tex. Prop. C. § 41.002. Because Texas law also exempts substantial amounts of personal property, including current wages for personal services (*see* Tex. Prop. C. § 42.001), much of what most people own or earn is not subject to the satisfaction of judgments obtained by third parties. Is this result appropriate? What explains these policy choices?

(2) *CPLR 5240: The Court's Discretionary Authority to Protect the Judgment Debtor from Unreasonably Disadvantageous Consequences of Otherwise Lawful Enforcement of Judgments.* Equity courts traditionally have had authority to protect the judgment debtor from unreasonable effects of judgment enforcement (and in fact sometimes enjoined execution of judgments at law before the merger of law and equity). In New York, CPLR 5240 contains a broad express grant of discretion to the trial courts. If you represented the judgment debtors in *Guardian Loan Co. v. Early*, how might you have used this provision? [Note: Would execution on chattels, or income execution, have been preferable for them?]

Read Fed. R. Civ. P. 69 (execution and other enforcement mechanisms).

NOTE ON THE APPROACH OF THE FEDERAL RULES IN BORROWING STATE ENFORCEMENT PROCEDURES AND PROVISIONAL REMEDIES

Rules 64 and 69: Federal Courts Borrow State Enforcement Mechanisms and Provisional Remedies. Rules 64 and 69, respectively, adopt the mechanisms available in the state in which the District Court sits for non-injunctive provisional remedies and for enforcement of judgment. Thus, in New York, that state's attachment procedure would be available under the same terms as in state courts, and the judicial sale rules illustrated by *Guardian Loan Co. v. Early* would apply.

Should Federal Courts Have Federal Enforcement Provisions? The borrowing of state law is defensible on the theory that it leads to uniformity in the law that practitioners in a given state must use, and it produces results in conformity with the *Erie* doctrine in diversity cases. But it is open to criticism. Imagine two plaintiffs, one in Texas and one in New York (or California), who had obtained judgments for serious injuries received during the deprivation of their civil rights. The first plaintiff may find enforcement of her judgment impractical because of Texas' exemption of most property and earnings; and the other will find enforcement more readily obtainable. Does the vindication of federal policy call for a uniform federal procedure here?

[B] Judgment Liens

NOTE ON JUDGMENT LIENS

Judgment Liens on Realty. In most states, a judgment can be the basis of a lien upon the judgment debtor's real property. The manner in which the lien is perfected varies significantly from state to state. In New York, for example, the judgment lien attaches automatically to any real property within a given county in which the judgment debtor has or acquires an interest, once the judgment is docketed with the clerk of the county. CPLR 5203(a). Texas follows a roughly similar procedure: The lien attaches to real property in any county in which an abstract of judgment has been filed among the deed records. Tex. Prop. Code Ann. §§ 52.001 *et seq.*

Judgment Liens on Personalty. In some states, judgment liens can be perfected upon personalty, too, usually by delivery of a writ of execution or other appropriate writ to the appropriate officer.

Foreclosure of Judgment Lien; Priorities; Bankruptcy Proceedings. A judgment lien creates a claim against the property as security for the judgment debt. It may create a right of foreclosure against the property — and thus, the judgment debtor may be able to cause its sale not only while it is owned by the judgment debtor, but also while it is owned by most kinds of subsequent purchasers or other transferees. Also, a perfected judgment lien may give the judgment creditor the right to have his debt satisfied from the property in question in higher priority than other creditors (for example, the principle of "first in time, first in right" ordinarily will mean that the earliest judgment creditor prevails over later judgment creditors).

TEXACO INC. v. PENNZOIL COMPANY, 784 F.2d 1133 (2d Cir. 1986).[b] Reconsider this case (which appears in fuller form in § 12.02[B], above, in connection with supersedeas bonds). Pennzoil obtained a judgment for $11.12 billion from Texaco in a Texas state court. In order to stay enforcement of the judgment pending appeal, under Texas law, Texaco was required to post a supersedeas bond "in at least the amount of the judgment, interest, and costs," or more than $12 billion. The Second Circuit affirmed a preliminary injunction allowing Texaco to supersede the judgment by filing a bond for only $1 billion. Part of the court's analysis included a finding that Texaco otherwise

[b] As is indicated in Chapter 12, the Supreme Court reversed on other grounds, but the Second Circuit's analysis of the judgment liens remains useful. *See supra* § 12.02[B].

would suffer irreparable injury, not only from active enforcement of the judgment, but also from the lien on Texaco's real property that would result from the filing of an abstract of the judgment among county deed records:

> It is beyond dispute that absent injunctive relief, enforcement of Texas' lien and supersedeas bond provisions would rapidly produce a catastrophe of major proportions, causing substantial harm to Texaco itself and to thousands of others throughout the United States. . . . Pennzoil concedes that Texaco . . . could not possibly post a bond or security in the sum of the approximately $12 billion that is mandated by [Texas law]. The simultaneous attachment of a lien pursuant to Tex. Prop. Code Ann. §§ 52.001 *et seq.* on Texaco's real property in Texas, valued at $5 billion, would seal the company's fate. Unable to finance its operations or obtain credit lines needed for its continued existence [because of the lien], Texaco, the fifth largest business organization in the United States, would be forced into bankruptcy or liquidation. . . .

NOTES AND QUESTIONS

(1) *Judgment Liens in Bankruptcy Proceedings.* Many of the cases dealing with judgment liens are, in fact, bankruptcy cases. A properly perfected and enforceable lien is an important advantage in a bankruptcy proceeding, since liquidation proceedings generally mean that the debtor's assets will not satisfy all creditors, and "general" or unsecured creditors usually are satisfied out of given property only after other creditors with liens against that property ("secured" creditors). In fact, the bankruptcy trustee (who is appointed by the court to collect and preserve the estate of the bankrupt) is given, by the Bankruptcy Code, the status of a hypothetical judgment lien creditor whose lien is perfected as of the commencement of the bankruptcy case. Thus, the judgment lien concept is fundamental to the structure of the Bankruptcy Code. In *Texaco v. Pennzoil,* notice that the court concludes that judgment liens could force Texaco into bankruptcy. Such a lien may constitute an act of default under some lending agreements, may be a reason for creditors to deem themselves insecure, may discourage suppliers, etc.

(2) *Judgment Liens as Preventing Purchase and Sale of Realty; Title Insurance or Opinions.* Title insurers, or attorneys rendering title opinions, routinely check judgment records; outstanding judgment liens will appear as exceptions to the title insurance policy or to the opinion of marketable title, and purchasers ordinarily will not complete the transaction until these defects are cured, ordinarily by satisfaction of the judgment and filing of a release.

PROBLEM E

RELEASING THE JUDGMENT LIEN. You are sitting in your office when the telephone rings. "Good afternoon, Mr./Ms. Attorney," says a voice. "I'm Lynn Jones, a closer at East America Title Company. You remember that judgment your client took against Dan Debtor seven years ago? Well, Mr. Debtor is here, ready to close the sale of a parcel of real property, and I have a release of judgment for you and your client to sign, and Mr. Debtor has drafted a check to bring to you." You begin to have a warm feeling, based upon the conclusion that justice does exist after all. The closer continues: "Mr. Debtor is on his way over to clear this matter up right now, because we really must close the transaction this afternoon, and it's already four o'clock." What do you say in return?

[C] Post-Judgment Garnishment

RIGGS NATIONAL BANK OF WASHINGTON, D.C. v. SIMPLICIO, 54 U.S.L.W. 2457 (D.C. Super. Ct. Feb. 20, 1986). The judgment debtor made her living as a real estate agent, receiving commissions on sales completed by a broker with whom she worked. The judgment creditor applied for and obtained a post-judgment writ of garnishment, naming the broker as garnishee. Thereafter, the agent complained to the court that the broker remitted to the judgment creditor 100 percent of the commissions due her as they became due, leaving her no income at all. The federal Consumer Credit Protection Act provides that an attachment or garnishment of "wages due or to become due to the judgment debtor" shall not exceed "25 per centum of his disposable wages." This provision prohibits the garnishment of more than one-fourth of a person's disposable wages; the court, as a court of equity, can reduce the percentage further, if appropriate. Disposable wages, in turn, are defined as "that part of the earnings of any individual remaining after the deduction from those earnings of any amounts required by law to be withheld." The question whether this statutory restriction covered commissions paid to an independent contractor was one of first impression.

The court limited payments to the judgment creditor to 25 percent of the agent's commissions, construing the statute to require that result. Although a literal reading of the statute did not resolve the question, the legislative history of the Act revealed that Congress sought to limit reductions of individuals' personal income so that they could continue to support their families and themselves while paying their debts. The court could see no reason why secretaries, clerks, and corporate officers of the broker should have the benefit of the 25 percent limit, while real estate agents, who produced the sales contracts that are the "lifeblood" of the business, should not.

NOTES AND QUESTIONS

(1) *How Post-Judgment Garnishment Works.* The judgment creditor, as garnishor, serves the application on a third person, such as a bank or employer, who has funds payable to the judgment debtor. This third person is called the garnishee. In many states, garnishment proceedings technically are a separate suit, ancillary to the main action, in which the garnishee is the named defendant. The proceeding is *in rem*, but the judgment debtor must be provided with notice. The garnishee may have obligations to the judgment debtor to exercise due care to preserve his property (*e.g.*, by filing an answer) and may be entitled to attorney's fees. The result, in the banking situation, is that the judgment debtor's account effectively is frozen, up to the amount of the garnishment plus the bank's attorney's fees, frequently causing unpaid checks and other losses to the judgment debtor; accordingly, the garnishor may be liable for wrongful garnishment, just as for other wrongful use of provisional remedies or enforcement procedures.

(2) *Putting the Judgment Debtor on "a Budget"; The Employer's Position.* In a sense, wage garnishment "puts the judgment debtor on a budget"; if the 25 percent limit insufficiently protects the debtor, notice that a court of equity can further reduce the percentage. The reaction of employer-garnishors, quite understandably, is that the process is a costly nuisance, creating potential liability for failure to withhold the right amounts, undesired and undeserved relationships with courts and lawyers, and complicated paperwork, all for an employee who didn't pay her debts. Most jurisdictions prohibit the employer from taking any adverse action toward the employee, motivated by the garnishment. Would you expect such a prohibition to be 100 percent effective? [Note that the question is one of motive for the termination or other action, and employees

who neglect their debts to such a point as to suffer wage garnishment may have neglected other duties, too.]

[D] Turnover Orders, Receiverships, and Other Equitable Supplementary Proceedings

[1] Turnover Orders

NOTE ON THE NEED FOR TURNOVER RELIEF

Non-Exempt Property that Cannot Readily Be Levied Upon: In re Dunlap, 27 B.R. 728 (Bkrptcy. N.C. 1983). It often happens that a judgment debtor has valuable property or rights that are not exempt from process but are not subject to execution (or cannot easily be executed upon). For example, in the *Dunlap* bankruptcy, the court held that a judgment debtor who had sold his interest in an insurance agency for monthly payments based on 30% of certain other sums, but who had certain contractual obligations himself in exchange (including the obligation not to compete with the sold business), had only a "contingent" right to payment. In accordance with the general rule, the court held that this contingent interest was not subject to execution. But if a judgment creditor had no systematic way of reaching such assets, the debtor could avoid satisfying the judgment simply by secreting and spending the funds as they were received. The law governing what property is subject to execution varies from state to state and is not completely consistent. *Compare, e.g., First Northwestern Trust Co. v. Internal Revenue Serv.*, 622 F.2d 387 (8th Cir. 1980) (income from discretionary trust is not "property" subject to execution); *George v. Kitchens by Rice Bros., Inc.*, 665 F.2d 7 (1st Cir. 1981) (power to revoke a trust is not "property" and cannot be reached by process), *with Springsteen v. Meadows, Inc.*, 534 F. Supp. 504 (D. Mass. 1982) (Massachusetts liquor license was subject to execution as a transferrable asset even though it could be revoked by issuing authority); *New Jersey Bank, N.A. v. Community Association/Farms, Inc.*, 666 F.2d 813 (3d Cir. 1981) (reserve account retained by bank as security for performance was subject to levy even though subject to possible offset for noncompliance with contract obligations).

The Need for Turnover Relief. In situations such as these, the judgment debtor has valuable rights that are not exempt from process but are difficult to reach by ordinary means. The debtor may be able to continue to enjoy the fruits of these rights without satisfying her judgment creditors unless there is a means of requiring her to cooperate with the court in securing them for payment.

The Nature of Turnover Relief: A Statutory Example. The Texas statute is an example of broad turnover authority. Tex. Civ. Prac. & Rem. Code § 31.002 (Vernon 1986) provides that if a judgment debtor owns "property, including present or future rights to property, that (1) cannot readily be attached or levied upon by ordinary legal process; and (2) is not exempt from attachment, execution, or seizure for the satisfaction of liabilities," the judgment creditor "is entitled to aid from a court of appropriate jurisdiction through injunction or other means to reach property to obtain satisfaction on the judgment. . . ." The debtor may be required, for example, to assemble and turn over records of various kinds, to pay property into the registry of the court as it is received, or to separate nonexempt property from property claimed to be exempt. In addition, the court may order other persons to perform acts facilitating the collection process, since the statute is not limited to relief directly ordered against the debtor.

The Turnover Order as a Modern Creditor's Bill. Historically, courts of equity provided relief to judgment creditors through creditors' bills, by which discovery could be obtained and supplementary relief initiated. Turnover provisions are modern manifestations of this procedure.

IN RE BRECHEISEN, 665 S.W.2d 191 (Tex. App.—Dallas 1984, writ ref'd n.r.e.). Brecheisen's former wife filed a motion under the turnover statute for aid in satisfying a money judgment previously awarded her for child support unpaid by Brecheisen. The trial court ordered Brecheisen to turn over all cash in his possession, the contents of all checking, savings, or money market accounts under his control, and all certificates for securities that he owned or might acquire. The order further required Brecheisen to continue to deposit funds and property, upon receipt, into the registry of the court until the total was sufficient to discharge all sums owed under judgments against him, and it enjoined him from secreting or alienating certain assets. Finally, the order provided that the former wife, as judgment creditor, would be allowed to withdraw property or funds from time to time when approved by order of the court, and the property would be credited to the satisfaction of the judgment. The Court of Appeals declined to reverse on the ground that the continuing nature of this turnover order prevented it from being final and appealable (although presumably the appellant could obtain review by mandamus, prohibition or habeas corpus).

NOTES AND QUESTIONS

(1) *New York's Turnover Provision (CPLR 5225): Clarkson Co. Ltd. v. Shaheen, 533 F. Supp. 905 (S.D.N.Y. 1982).* New York enforcement provisions, including its turnover provision, create a comparably broad authority in the court. In *Clarkson*, for example, the federal District Court, applying New York's turnover provision as a consequence of Fed. R. Civ. P. 69, held that the judgment creditor was entitled to a turnover order requiring the pledgee of stock owned by the debtor to deliver the certificates. The court found that the pledge, although nominally made to secure the debtor's obligations to the pledgee, was a sham because the debtor had control over the pledgee corporation and never relinquished dominion over the stock in question. [Note: For California's comparable procedures, *see Olsan v. Comora*, below.]

(2) *New York's Income Execution and Installment Payment Order: Schwartz v. Goldberg, 58 Misc. 2d 308, 295 N.Y.S.2d 245 (Sup. Ct. 1968).* New York provides for execution on income; it also provides for an installment payment order "where it is shown that the judgment debtor is receiving or will receive money from any source, or is attempting to impede the judgment creditor. . . ." CPLR 5231, 5226; *see* O. Chase, *2 Weinstein, Korn & Miller CPLR Manual* §§ 27.13-27.16 (1997). The income execution does not require a particularized court order and is effective as to only ten percent of income, with certain exemptions; the installment payment order, on the other hand, is an order, similar to a turnover order, not subject to the same limitations. In *Schwartz v. Goldberg*, for example, there were six judgment creditors waiting in line for payment by income executions; a seventh creditor obtained an installment payment order and, by virtue of its nature as a court order, was entitled to receive payment before the other six!

(3) *Enforcement of Decrees in Matrimonial (i.e., Divorce) Cases.* The *Brecheisen* case is interesting as an example of enforcement of a marital dissolution decree, which several

of the authors of this book consider among the most formidable challenges in the enforcement area. Wealthy, determined former spouses who are ill disposed toward each other sometimes fight with primitive energy even after the decree. For a discussion of sophisticated uses of such devices as liens, turnover, and the like in the post-divorce context, see George, *After the Divorce — Securing and Obtaining the Property: Post-Judgment Relief in Texas*, 17 Texas Tech. L. Rev. 1349 (1986).

PROBLEM F

USE OF TURNOVER PROVISIONS TO REACH TRUST PROPERTY IN FIRST NORTHWESTERN TRUST CO. v. IRS AND GEORGE v. KITCHENS BY RICE BROS., INC. You have directed interrogatories to a judgment debtor to locate and identify his property. The answers indicate that he created a trust for the benefit of his 21-year-old son; the trust is revocable at will. Further, he is the beneficiary of a trust that pays income to him in the discretion of the trustee. If you were practicing in a state with a general turnover statute similar to Tex. Civ. Prac. & Rem. Code § 31.002 (Vernon 1986) (discussed in the notes beginning this subsection), what steps might you take with respect to these trust properties? What orders might you request that the court issue to the judgment debtor and to third parties, and would you expect the court to issue them? [Note: In *First Northwestern Trust Co. v. IRS*, 622 F.2d 387 (8th Cir. 1980), and *George v. Kitchens by Rice Bros., Inc.*, 665 F.2d 7 (1st Cir. 1981), the courts held, respectively, that these rights could not be reached through execution.]

[2] Receivership

Read Fed. R. Civ. P. 66 (receivers).

OLSAN v. COMORA

73 Cal. App. 3d 642, 140 Cal. Rptr. 835 (2d Dist. 1977)

HASTINGS, ASSOCIATE JUSTICE.

The presiding judge in department 85 of the Superior Court of Los Angeles County appointed a receiver to take possession and collect all earnings, cash, bank deposits and checks representing amounts received by defendant-appellant Emanuel Comora for services performed by him as a dentist. He appeals from the order appointing such receiver primarily on the ground that a receiver cannot be appointed to collect a simple money judgment.

On July 31, 1972, a money judgment was obtained by Barbara R. Olsan, plaintiff and respondent, against appellant Comora and Cybertronics-Nevada, Inc., a corporation, in Los Angeles Superior Court, for the sum of $382,886 plus costs. The judgment became final after being affirmed on appeal. By means of an execution and garnishment, respondent collected $36,560 from appellant Comora out of a pending escrow.

A receivership proceeding was then instigated . . . . This proceeding was initiated by the issuance of an order *ex parte* to show cause why a receiver should not be appointed to marshal and disburse Comora's assets to satisfy the judgment. Two documents were filed in support of the motion. The first was a declaration of Sherman Shelton, President of Metropolitan Adjustment Bureau, which in substance states that he is President of Metropolitan, the assignee, and that after judgment was entered against Comora, Olsan made demand upon Comora to pay the judgment, but he refused; that Olsan, as the judgment creditor, is unable to levy execution upon Comora's earnings, and that the only process available to enforce payment is by the appointment of a receiver who would collect Comora's earnings and disburse the funds to the judgment creditor toward the satisfaction of the judgment in accordance with section 690.6 of the Code of Civil Procedure (exempting certain earnings for personal services).

The second document was a declaration by Andrew S. Garb, an attorney at law and member of the firm of Loeb & Loeb, the firm that successfully tried the action resulting in the money judgment for Olsan. It stated that the only amount which Olsan had been able to collect from Comora was $36,560 which had been held in Comora's name at a pending escrow. Although Comora had an apartment building in his own name, when garnishment on the rents was sought it was met by a claim by Comora's mother-in-law that she had a trust deed promissory note on the property with an assignment of rents clause. Comora, at the time, was in default on the note; therefore, she had a prior claim to the rents. This issue was litigated in the Los Angeles Municipal Court. Olsan was unable to prove collusion between Comora and his mother-in-law, and therefore could not establish a right to the rents. Garb's declaration also stated that, although Comora is a practicing dentist, he was personally advised by Comora that his accounts receivable were subject to a factoring arrangement and that a judgment creditor of his would have great difficulty in collecting a judgment. He was further advised by Comora that Miss Olsan would have great difficulty locating any of his assets that were subject to levy. Because of these difficulties in locating assets subject to levy, Olsan decided to assign the judgment for collection. The declaration concluded that under these circumstances a receiver would be the only feasible way to enforce respondent's rights under the judgment. . . .

On February 6, 1976, the court made its minute order appointing Gilbert Robinson as receiver. . . .

Comora's first argument is that a receiver cannot be appointed to collect a simple money judgment. The law, both statutory and decisional, does not support this contention. . . .

In *Jackson v. Jackson*, 253 Cal. App. 2d 1026, 1040-1041, 62 Cal. Rptr. 121, 131, the court said: "Generally, because of its drastic nature, receivership should not be resorted to unless other remedies are inadequate. [Citations.] Receivership may not ordinarily be used for the enforcement of a simple money judgment [Citations], *but under proper circumstances a receiver may be appointed in aid of execution. . . .*"

The provision of section 564, subdivision 4 pertinent to this appeal states that a receiver *may* be appointed "in proceedings in aid of execution, when an execution has been returned unsatisfied, or when the judgment debtor refuses to apply his property in satisfaction of the judgment. . . ." These words, clear and unambiguous, do not exclude appointment of a receiver to collect a simple money judgment. The wording only limits the circumstances under which the court *may* use this somewhat harsh remedy. . . .

Comora's second argument assumes *arguendo* that a receiver may be appointed to collect a simple money judgment, but that the appointment can only be made in connection with a section 714 or 715 proceeding (*see* fn. 4 *infra*). [Note: These provisions govern discovery of assets in aid of execution, *i.e.*, the finding or location of executable assets, and they have been replaced by more detailed coverage of the same matters in CCP § 708.010 — Eds.] It is true that most, if not all, cases to date affirming the appointment of a receiver in a money judgment situation have done so in conjunction with a supplementary [*i.e.*, discovery] proceeding under one of the two sections. . . .

The cases and the statute do not, however, exclude the direct appointment of a receiver by a court sans supplementary proceedings. There is no provision in section 564, subdivision 4 requiring supplementary proceedings before the remedies of the section can be invoked, nor is there any such provisional language in sections 714 or 715. The current practice of superior courts in numerous counties is that a petitioning party has procedural alternatives, *i.e.*, a [discovery] proceeding under section 714 or 715 or a direct proceeding by motion to the court [for discovery] under section 564, subdivision 4. . . . There is a logical and expeditious reason for such pragmatic procedure, and our present case is a good example. . . . Statements by Comora to Olsan's attorneys made after the first execution support a conclusion that no assets other than his business income were available to satisfy the judgment or, if there were, he had, or would, take such action as necessary to prevent their seizure to satisfy the judgment. . . . Under such circumstances, the judge was not required to order a supplementary proceeding that would only establish anew the need for a receiver. . . .

The order appointing the receiver is affirmed. . . .

NOTES AND QUESTIONS

(1) *Receivership as a "Drastic" Remedy.* Why does the court refer to the appointment of a receiver as a "drastic" remedy? [The receiver takes charge of the affairs of an ongoing business. Her decisions displace those of the usual management of the business.]

(2) *Receiverships to Enforce Non-Money Judgments: The South Boston School Desegregation Receivership.* In business litigation, a receivership may be ordered when management seriously has breached its obligations to shareholders or in situations of consumer fraud, if the equities so require. Non-business usage of the receiver may be illustrated by Judge Arthur Garrity's ordering of a receiver for the South Boston schools in desegregation litigation. *Morgan v. Kerrigan*, 401 F. Supp. 216 (D. Mass. 1975).

PROBLEM G

MOTION TO APPOINT RECEIVERSHIP TO ENFORCE DECREE SIMILAR TO THAT IN WILLIAMS v. NEW ORLEANS, 729 F.2d 1554 (5th Cir. 1984) (en banc). Imagine that you are a federal district judge who previously has entered a decree similar to that in *Williams*. The decree is designed to remedy longstanding and serious racial discrimination in employment of black police officers; it contains draconian requirements about recruiting, testing, training, probation, termination, and promotion of black and non-black officers, and governs "virtually every phase of an officer's employment by the . . . Police Department." It also requires extensive and frequent reports by the defendants concerning their compliance. Some of the terms (such as racial quotas) are highly specific; others are general and require cooperative effort. Representatives of the plaintiff class are now, a year later, claiming massive and deliberate violations of the decree and falsification of the reports. They urge you to appoint a receiver to implement the decree. The defendants argue that while the goals of the decree have not been fully achieved, they have not engaged in any intentional violations, and they vehemently argue that appointment of a receiver would be unlawful, inappropriate and harmful. What considerations militate in favor of appointment of a receiver, and what considerations against?

[3] Discovery in Aid of Enforcement of Judgment

Use of Discovery Devices to Locate Assets and Enforce Judgment. Rule 69 provides for the use of discovery devices in aid of enforcement. It is permissible, for example, to take the deposition of the judgment debtor (or of other persons) to ask about property, interests, or other rights he has or may have; likewise, the judgment creditor may use interrogatories or requests for production. State rules typically contain similar provisions. This discovery first was developed by courts of equity in the creditor's bill (as was the turnover order).

AN EXAMPLE: MATTER OF SILVERMAN, 6 B.R. 991 (D.N.J. 1980). In this case, the propriety of execution on the judgment debtor's realty depended upon whether the creditor had made a good faith effort first to locate personalty (which in New Jersey must be levied upon first). The creditor, through its attorney, had undertaken an "examination in aid of execution" (equivalent to a deposition) and used "standard form interrogatories prepared by [the creditor's] law firm." This discovery "contain[ed] numerous particular questions about the debtor's ownership of such personalty as motor vehicles, other vehicles or trailers, aircraft, firearms, coin or stamp collections, tools or equipment, sporting goods or equipment, paintings or other art objects, interests in business, bank accounts, securities, patents or copyrights, and insurance policies." However, "[n]otably missing . . . [were] inquiries into the debtor's cash on hand and ownership of furniture, appliances, and other household goods," and there was "no generalized question as to the personal property owned by the debtor." The court concluded that this discovery was sufficiently "thorough and conscientious" to constitute a good faith effort, so that the levy on the debtor's realty was not unlawful even though he owned leviable personalty. But was the discovery skillfully conducted?

[E] Contempt and Arrest

CHARLES MANUFACTURING CO. v. UNITED FURNITURE WORKERS, 361 So. 2d 1033 (Ala. 1978). The trial court enjoined the union and certain of its officers from committing eleven kinds of acts, including violence, mass picketing, threats, coercion, obstruction of public roads, and interference with ingress or egress from Charles Manufacturing's plant. A month later, plaintiff Charles Manufacturing filed a complaint praying that the union and several of the individuals be held in contempt. The complaint contained a single paragraph describing the violations, stating only that the defendants had "willfully failed and refused to obey" the injunction. The complaint and court's order to show cause why the defendants should not be held in contempt were mailed to and received by defendant's attorney of record, who represented all of them, but the papers were not individually served upon each defendant. The defendants moved to dismiss on the ground that the complaint failed to set forth specific facts constituting the violations. The court denied the motion, defendants filed an answer denying contempt, and, after hearing evidence, the trial judge rendered twenty-three judgments of contempt, for such acts as scattering nails on the public road, threats of physical abuse, harassment of nonunion workers, and throwing objects at cars of nonunion workers. The Court of Appeals reversed.

First, the court rejected the union's argument that notice was insufficiently served. Service on the defendants' attorney of record was sufficient. Secondly, the court rejected some of the individuals' argument that they were not specifically named in the injunction. The injunction was directed to the union "and its agents and representatives," who also were named as defendants in the original injunction proceedings, as well as "all persons acting at the direction or in active concert or participation with them . . . and all persons receiving notice of this order." If this designation were insufficient, said the court, "it would be necessary to name each member of the union by name."

However, the court agreed with the contention that adequate notice of the contempt charges was not afforded the defendants:

> Contempts are divided along two lines: first, civil or criminal contempt. Civil contempt sanctions seek to compel or coerce compliance with orders of the court in the future [and typically exempt the respondent from sanctions if he complies], while a criminal contempt is one in which the purpose of the proceeding is to impose punishment for disobedience of orders of the court. . . . The second line divides contempts into those which are either direct or indirect. Direct contempts are those committed in the "presence" of the judge, where all of the essential elements of the misconduct are under the eye of the court, and are actually observed by the court. If some of the essential elements are not personally observed by the judge it is an indirect contempt. . . .
>
> Proceedings charging one with an indirect criminal contempt [require] that the accused be afforded due process of law. . . . Where an individual is accused of indirect or constructive contempt, due process requires that he be given notice of the charges and a reasonable opportunity to meet them. . . .
>
> [The complaint for contempt] must set forth all facts essential to the court's jurisdiction, including facts constituting a contempt, and, the statement must clearly apprise the person charged of the nature and cause of the accusation. . . .
>
> For the stated reasons this cause is due to be reversed and remanded. We do not deem it necessary to address the other errors urged by petitioners.

NOTES AND QUESTIONS

(1) *The Requirement That the Underlying Order Be Specific and Unequivocal: Inmates of Allegheny County Jail v. Wecht, 754 F.2d 120 (3d Cir. 1985).* Faced with an order for limiting the population in the county jail, in circumstances in which the court contemplated preparation and implementation of a plan for alternative housing of the inmates, county officials instead released prisoners in order to "comply." The Court of Appeals held that, however irresponsible that action may have been, since the officials were not subject to any specific order to prepare or implement an alternative plan, they could not be subjected to contempt proceedings, either civil or criminal.

(2) *The Requirement of Willful Disobedience: Vaughn v. City of Flint, 752 F.2d 1160 (6th Cir. 1985).* Criminal contempt, whether enforced by fine or incarceration, is a quasi-criminal proceeding, and it requires proof of willful disobedience. Willfulness, in this context, means a deliberate or intended violation, as distinguished from one that is accidental, inadvertent, or negligent. This element, as well as all other elements, must be proved beyond a reasonable doubt to support criminal contempt. Note, however, that contempt validly lies in some instances of willful disobedience even if the underlying injunction is invalid; *see Walker v. City of Birmingham*, 388 U.S. 307 (1967). The issue is a difficult one; *cf. In re Providence Journal Co.*, 820 F.2d 1342 (1st Cir. 1986) (newspaper may challenge press injunction by violating it, without contempt — but only if injunction is not merely invalid, but "transparently" invalid).

PROBLEM H

HYPOTHETICAL CRIMINAL CONTEMPT PROCEEDINGS BASED UPON GALELLA v. ONASSIS, SUPRA. In this case, which appears in § 14.03[A][2] of this Chapter, above, the court enjoined a "paparazzo" photographer from approaching closer than 25 feet to the widow of former President Kennedy and from doing certain acts such as harassing, annoying, or frightening her. One judge, who supported the broader injunction issued by the trial court, pointed out that abstract prohibitions had proved unworkable. Imagine that Mrs. Onassis goes swimming in the ocean, whereupon Galella, using a speedboat, circles about her (but never comes closer than 25 feet), and that this conduct in fact harasses, annoys and frightens her. (In fact, Galella had engaged in very similar conduct before issuance of the injunction.) If you represented Mrs. Onassis, and you wished to invoke the court's authority to hold Galella in contempt, how would you go about pleading and serving the complaint? What would be the most significant difficulty you would encounter in obtaining an adjudication of contempt? What does this example tell you about the way in which injunctions should be drafted?

[F] Interstate Enforcement of Judgments

Action on the Judgment. From Chapters 1 and 2, you should recall that a judgment by a court of State X cannot directly be enforced by officers of State Y in State Y. The judgment creditor obtains enforcement by bringing an "action on the judgment" in a court of State Y, which will issue its own judgment based upon the State X judgment.

The Federal Procedure for "Registration" of Judgments. For a judgment taken in a federal court, an action on the judgment is unnecessary. In 1948, Congress streamlined the procedure by providing that a federal judgment may be "registered" in any other District, and it then has the same force as if it had been rendered in that District. 28 U.S.C. § 1963.

The Uniform Enforcement of Foreign Judgments Act. The Commissioners on Uniform State Laws have drafted a Uniform Enforcement of Foreign Judgments Act, which allows sister state judgments to be treated in the same manner as federal judgments. The UEFJA now has been adopted in many of the states, eliminating the need for actions upon judgments in most instances. The same process has produced the Uniform Foreign Country Money Judgment Recognition Act (UFCMJRA), which also has been widely adopted.

AN EXAMPLE OF THE OPERATION OF THE UEFJA: L&W AIR CONDITIONING CO., INC. v. VARSITY INN OF ROCHESTER, INC., 82 Misc. 2d 937, 371 N.Y.S.2d 997 (Sup. Ct. Monroe Co. 1975). New York's adoption of the UEFJA allows the judgment creditor simply to file the judgment with the clerk along with an affidavit containing such information as the name and last known address of the judgment debtor and the assertion that the judgment remains unsatisfied. Interestingly, however, New York did not adopt the UEFJA for default judgments, which still require an action on the judgment. In the *L&W Air Conditioning* case, the plaintiff had taken a judgment in Georgia after the defendant had answered but did not appear for trial. When the plaintiff filed the judgment in New York, the defendant moved to stay, on the ground that the judgment was by default; but the court held that the judgment was entitled to enforcement, because New York's exception excluded "only those default judgments where there is no appearance at all in the action." *See also* O. Chase, *2 Weinstein, Korn & Miller CPLR Manual* § 27.28 (1997). Does it make sense to exclude default judgments from the UEFJA? [Note that a defaulting defendant with meritorious grounds could move to stay enforcement even in the absence of such an exception.]

CHAPTER 15

ALTERNATE METHODS OF DISPUTE RESOLUTION

§ 15.01 The Case For and Against, and the Types of, ADR's

[A] The Mechanisms of Alternate Dispute Resolution: An Introduction

Throughout American history, private, community, and religious institutions have furnished forums as alternatives to the courts. See generally Stamato & Jaffee, *Dispute Resolution, New Jersey Style*, National Institute of Justice Reports, March 1986, at 6. During the last century, adjudication has dominated, but the recent expansion of alternatives has emphasized that it is only one model of litigation.

Arbitration is a contractual proceeding by which the parties submit their dispute to a third-party decisionmaker, often one with special expertise in the subject matter of the dispute. Contractual arbitration usually is binding.

Mediation also involves a third party, who acts as a facilitator rather than as a judge or arbiter, in an effort to assist the parties in reaching a voluntary resolution.

Traditional Negotiation, Compromise, and Settlement. Of course, the prevalent method of dispute resolution (at least in terms of frequency of use) is negotiation and compromise. In fact, it might be said that we have a settlement system, in which adjudicatory processes force the issue and resolve only the unusual case.

Private Judging. Some states, such as California, have "rent-a-judge" statutes, which enable the parties to hire a judge for their particular dispute, who then presides over a traditional trial. The parties gain flexibility in the timing of trial.

Neutral Expert Fact Finding. The parties may hire, or the court may appoint, an expert to conduct an investigation of the matter in dispute. The expert's report may be a tool for use in settlement, or (in some instances) may be admissible in evidence.

Mini-Trial. It may be worthwhile for the parties to a large business dispute to present summary versions of their cases to a neutral person as an adjunct of their settlement efforts. The recent invention of the "mini-trial" fulfills this function. The parties usually set time limits upon their presentations, receive suggestions from the neutral advisor (including a predicted outcome), and attempt settlement.

Summary Jury Trials are a variant on the mini-trial, using advisory juries.

Screening Panels. Some states require presentation of the claim to a panel or administrative agency before litigation in court. The most common models are worker's compensation boards and medical malpractice screening panels. The usual pattern is that the result is advisory, but some jurisdictions attach conditions such as requirements that the plaintiff advance costs if the panel has advised against her, admit the result into evidence, or make it binding in the absence of litigation in court.

Settlement Conference. The court may require the parties to appear for a pretrial conference relating specifically to settlement.

Court-Annexed ADR. The court may require the parties to submit to a given ADR mechanism for an advisory ruling (*e.g.*, nonbinding arbitration).

Industry-Wide Claims Settlement. Asbestos producers have entered into what is known as the "Wellington Agreement," which provides for a number of alternatives to adjudication and is designed to provide flexible, yet consistent and low-cost, means of addressing claims.

The "Multiple-Door Courthouse." Some commentators have advocated the emergence of public or private facilities to which disputants may apply for the furnishing of whichever method of resolution seems most appropriate to their individual circumstances.

*A Chart of Some Common ADR'S: Green, A Comprehensive Approach to the Theory and Practice of Dispute Resolution, 34 J. Legal Ed. 245, 257-58 (1984).** Figure 15A below contains a chart prepared by Professor Eric Green, setting out the characteristics of some commonly used mechanisms for dispute resolution. *See also* Goldberg, Green & Sander, *ADR Problems and Prospects: Looking to the Future*, 69 Judicature 291 (1985); Ray, *Emerging Options in Dispute Resolution*, ABA Journal, June 1989, at 66.

PROBLEM A: CHAPTER 15 SUMMARY PROBLEM

WHICH ALTERNATE DISPUTE RESOLUTION DEVICE (IF ANY) — ARBITRATION, MEDIATION, MINI-TRIAL, SUMMARY JURY TRIAL, ETC.? The following are potential disputes. State whether you think a particular alternate dispute resolution device is appropriate — including arbitration, mediation, mini-trial, summary jury trial, etc. — or whether traditional litigation would be most appropriate:

(a) *The Fact-Dispute Price-Fixing Case.* Acme Sales Co., a widget buyer, sues three widget manufacturers under the antitrust laws, accusing them of fixing prices, which is a *per se* antitrust violation. The dispute depends mainly upon whether the fact finder believes the plaintiff's evidence of price fixing (which consists of memoranda of meetings, price similarity, and a few insider witnesses who say the defendants met and verbally agreed on the prices they would charge) or the defendants' (which consists of vehement direct denials by defendants' officers).

(b) *The Interwoven Fact-Law Tying Arrangement Dispute.* Acme Sales Co. sues United States Widget Co. for $50 million, claiming that the defendant refuses to sell widgets to Acme unless Acme also buys a thingummy with each widget (Acme doesn't need any thingummys). Acme claims that this practice constitutes a prohibited "tying arrangement," in violation of the antitrust laws. The facts can be interpreted in various ways to support arguments that the defendant's conduct is, or is not, a tying arrangement. The law also is complex and can be applied to the facts in various ways.

(c) *The Antitrust Dispute Overlapped by a Personality Clash.* Acme Sales Co., one of North America's larger widget buyers, often buys from Consolidated Widget, one of the larger sellers. Acme has a longstanding complaint about the sales policy of

Consolidated, in that it does not discount for large volumes even though it probably has cost savings. Acme has threatened suit under the antitrust laws (although the claim is weak). The two vice presidents who have responsibility for the purchases and sales have talked about the problem, know it must be resolved and yet have difficulty working with each other personally.

(d) *The Recurrent Commercial Dispute.* Acme Sales Co. buys large quantities of widgets on a long-term contract from Hy-Jinks Widget Corporation. It repeatedly has found that the widgets are defective. It could attempt to terminate the entire contract, but that would be risky; it could sue on each delivery that is nonconforming, but that would be expensive and disruptive of the relationship; it could simply accept the goods, but that would hurt its sales. It has attempted negotiation, but has found that Hy-Jinks' personnel, though friendly, revert to bad habits rapidly and continue to send defective shipments occasionally.

FIGURE 15A
Green, *A COMPREHENSIVE APPROACH TO THE THEORY AND PRACTICE OF DISPUTE RESOLUTION*, 34 J. LEGAL ED. 245, 257-58 (1984)

Appendix

"PRIMARY" DISPUTE RESOLUTION PROCESSES

ADJUDICATION	ARBITRATION	MEDIATION/ CONCILIATION	TRADITIONAL NEGOTIATION
Nonvoluntary	Voluntary unless contractual or court centered	Voluntary	Voluntary
Binding, subject to appeal	Binding (usually), no appeal	Nonbinding	Nonbinding (except through use of adjudication to enforce agreement)
Imposed third-party neutral decision maker, with no specialized expertise in dispute subject	Party-selected third-party decision maker, usually with specialized subject expertise	Party-selected outside facilitator, often with specialized subject expertise	No third-party facilitator
Highly procedural; formalized and highly structured by predetermined, rigid rules	Procedurally less formal; procedural rules and substantive law may be set by parties	Usually informal, unstructured	Usually informal, unstructured
Opportunity for each party to present proofs supporting decision in its favor	Opportunity for each party to present proofs supporting decision in its favor	Presentation of proofs less important than attitudes of each party; may include principled argument	Presentation of proofs usually indirect or non-existent; may include principled argument
Win/Lose result	Compromise result possible (probable?)	Mutually acceptable agreement sought	Mutually acceptable agreement sought
Expectation of reasoned statement	Reason for result not usually required	Agreement usually embodied in contract of release	Agreement usually embodied in contract or release

Process emphasizes attaining substantive consistency and predictability of results	Consistency and predictability balanced against concern for disputants' relationship	Emphasis on disputants' relationship, not on adherence to or development of consistent rules	Emphasis on disputants' relationship, not on adherence to or development of consistent rules
Public process: lack of privacy of submissions	Private process unless judicial enforcement sought	Private process	Highly private process

FIGURE 15A (CONTINUED)

Appendix (page 2)

"HYBRID" DISPUTE RESOLUTION PROCESSES

PRIVATE JUDGING	NEUTRAL EXPERT FACT FINDING	MINITRIAL	SETTLEMENT CONFERENCE
Voluntary	Voluntary or nonvoluntary under FRE 706	Voluntary	Voluntary or mandatory
Binding but subject to appeal and possibly review by trial court	Nonbinding but results may be admissible	Nonbinding (except through use of adjudication to enforce agreement)	Binding or nonbinding
Party-selected third-party decision maker; may have to be former judge or lawyer	Third-party neutral with specialized subject matter expertise may be selected by the parties	Third-party neutral advisor with specialized subject expertise	Judge, other judge, or third-party neutral selected by parties
Statutory procedure (*see, e.g.*, Cal. Code Civ. Proc. § 638 et seq.) but highly flexible as to timing, place and procedures	Informal	Less formal than adjudication and arbitration but procedural rules and scope of issues may be set by the parties and implemented by neutral advisor	Informal, off-the-record
Opportunity for each party to present proofs supporting decision in its favor	Investigatory	Opportunity and responsibility to present proofs supporting result in its favor	Presentation of proofs may or may not be allowed
Win/lose result (judgment of court)	Report or testimony	Mutually acceptable agreement sought	Mutually acceptable agreement sought; binding conference is similar to arbitration
Findings of fact and conclusions of law possible but not required	May influence result or settlement	Agreement usually embodied in contract or release	Agreement usually embodied in contract or release

FIGURE 15A (CONTINUED)
Appendix (page 2)
"HYBRID" DISPUTE RESOLUTION PROCESSES

PRIVATE JUDGING	NEUTRAL EXPERT FACT FINDING	MINITRIAL	SETTLEMENT CONFERENCE
Adherence to norms, laws and precedent	Emphasis on reliable fact determination	Emphasis on sound, cost-effective and fair resolution satisfactory to both parties	Emphasis on resolving the dispute
Private process unless judicial enforcement sought	May be highly private or discussed in court	Highly private process	Private process but may be discovered

[B] The Case for ADR'S; The Disadvantages of Traditional Adjudication: Notes and Questions

(1) *The Cost of Traditional Adjudication as an Argument for ADR'S.* Whether they agree upon a mini-trial and settle their dispute, or whether they contract for binding arbitration, the parties to major business litigation are likely to be motivated in part by cost savings. One should not underestimate the costs of traditional litigation. Derek Bok, president of Harvard University, says that the United States has "developed a legal system that is the most expensive in the world." D. Bok, *Annual Report to the Board of Overseers of Harvard College* (1983), *quoted in* Insurance Information Institute, *The Civil Justice Crisis* 5 (1985). Consider the following:

> WASHINGTON — Transaction costs in the American civil justice system consumed almost half the $28 billion to $35 billion spent on tort litigation in 1985, according to a partly released study of civil litigation produced by the Rand Corp.
>
> [T]he report concluded that tort lawsuits last year resulted in an estimated $19 billion to $24 billion in total compensation to plaintiffs — an average of $22,000 to $27,000 per suit.
>
> But plaintiffs lost about 31 percent of their awards in attorney fees and other costs, the study found, meaning the system consumed more than 45 percent of the amount ultimately collected by injured parties.
>
> Looking at both state and federal court systems, the study estimated defense costs in tort litigation at $8 billion to $11 billion, with legal fees accounting for $5 billion to $6 billion of that sum. . . .

Strasser, *Costs Run High in Tort Cases*, Nat. L.J., Aug. 18, 1986, at 38, col. 2. But should we question whether encouragement of ADR is the solution to this problem? Perhaps the solution should include decreasing these costs.

(2) *Access to Justice: Claims Too Small for Efficient Adjudication.* A corollary of the expense of traditional adjudication is that many litigants cannot afford it. In particular, a claim under $1,000 is unlikely to support a reasonable fee for a lawyer; in fact, even a claim as large as $20,000 to $50,000 may not. Consider the following:

> The tradition of seeking redress in small claims court may someday be a thing of the past for many Americans. Big innovations appear on the horizon for handling small claims out of court.

> Conciliatory resolution of disputes has gained great momentum as a result of a highly successful pilot project sponsored by the American Bar Association. In its initial 18-month phase, the pilot project sought to implement in three cities alternatives to courtroom adjudication of small claims. . . .
>
> The pilot project is known as the Multi-Door Dispute Resolution Centers Project. It was developed by Professor Frank Sander of Harvard Law School in 1976 as a means to refer complaints to the most appropriate forum. Funds for Multi-Door were solicited in each of the program's communities. The ABA also funded part of the project.
>
> Chief Justice Warren E. Burger has praised the ABA's program for providing "better, cheaper" alternatives. . . .

Hyman, *Small Claims and the Courts*, Litigation News, Summer 1986, at 5. But this rationale may be questioned, too. It is appropriate for small disputes to be resolved by conciliation if the parties so choose, but should they be forced to adopt that approach by the fact that our litigation system is too costly for them to do otherwise?

(3) *Delay, Uncertainty, and Lost Creative Product.* Imagine a patent dispute delayed for many years in its resolution. The cost attributable to the uncertainty of the outcome may exceed the transaction costs of the litigation itself. All parties may be reluctant to develop needed, valuable products whose commercial viability depends on the outcome of the dispute. Consider the following:

> One of our country's greatest lawyers, Abraham Lincoln, said:
>
> Discourage litigation. Persuade your neighbors to compromise whenever you can. Point out to them how the nominal winner is often a real loser — in fees, expenses, and waste of time. As a peace-maker the lawyer has a superior opportunity of being a good man. . . .
>
> Large commercial litigation takes businessmen and their staffs off the creative paths of production and often produces more wear and tear on them than the most difficult business problems. Consider the costs of lost productivity in the IBM antitrust litigation, with six years of discovery leading to a trial that went on for nearly seven years. . . .
>
> My own experience persuades me that in terms of cost, time, and human wear and tear, arbitration is vastly better than conventional litigation for many kinds of cases. . . .

Burger, Speech to Members of the Minnesota Bar Ass'n and American Arbitration Ass'n, *reprinted in Chief Justice Burger: Reflections on ADR, Alternatives to the High Cost of Litigation*, October 10, 1985, at 5 (Center for Public Resources Publication). Question: How should this ADR approach to court congestion be related to the administrative proposals set forth in Chapter 8 ("Pretrial Conferences and Case Management")?

(4) *Enlarging the Size of the Pie: "Polycentric" Solutions.* It often happens that disputing parties can devise a solution that improves on the result both can expect from litigation. A common example is a will contest between two museums to which the decedent has bequeathed ten paintings; if they litigate to judgment, one wins all ten (including five it may not really want), but if they divide by compromise, the Museum of Western Art can take the five Remingtons while the French Impressionism Museum takes the five Monets. This approach has been described as "polycentric," or many-centered, in that it recognizes multiple centers of interest. Consider the following:

> The case of Israel and Egypt negotiating over who should keep how much of the Sinai Peninsula illustrates both a major problem in negotiation and a key opportunity.
>
> The problem is a common one. There seems to be no way to split the pie that leaves both parties satisfied. Often you are negotiating along a single dimension, such as the amount of territory, the price of a car, the length of a lease on an apartment, or the size of a commission on a sale. At other times you face what appears to be an either/or choice that is either markedly favorable to you or to the other side. [Y]ou may see the choice as one between winning and losing — and neither side will agree to lose. . . .
>
> The Sinai example also makes clear the opportunity. A creative option like a demilitarized Sinai can often make the difference between deadlock and agreement. One lawyer we know attributes his success directly to his ability to invent solutions advantageous to both his client and the other side. He expands the pie before dividing it. Skill at inventing options is one of the most useful assets a negotiator can have.

Fisher & Ury, *Getting to Yes: Negotiating Agreement Without Giving In* 58-59 (1981). In fact, it may be possible in a divorce case to structure the equity division in the house so that one party lives in it but the other shares the benefit of its appreciation, or even to provide for such liberal visitation or joint custody that the custody determination is no longer an "either-or" proposition. But again, one may question these premises. Should a party who would win the entire pie by adjudication be encouraged to give up a part of it so that the sum of pie owned by the two parties will be greater?

(5) *"People's" Solutions, Rather than "Legal" Solutions.* Advocates of ADR sometimes argue that it provides qualitatively better solutions by avoiding the strict mechanisms of the law and substituting solutions chosen by the parties themselves, or by a neutral person less subject to those mechanisms than the traditional judge would be. To some extent, this argument may be a restatement of the "enlarged pie" argument. It also may be the result of suspicion that attorneys will impede actual communication. Finally, it may reflect anomalies in the law that would give unjust results. Is there merit to this argument?

(6) *Avoidance of the Harm to Long-Term Relationships that Results from the Highly Adversary Process of Adjudicatory Litigation.* A homeowner allows his dog to bark throughout the night, and a neighbor can think of no better solution than to sue for an injunction. A customer sues the major supplier with whom she has had a ten-year relationship on the theory that a shipment of goods is nonconforming. Obviously there is something counterproductive about the adjudicatory method of resolving both of these disputes. It maximizes the adversary nature of the dispute and has high potential for injecting unnecessary rancor into the underlying relationship. A less formal method, such as arbitration, might be preferable, and conciliation would be better still. This concern is one reason for the popularity of mediation in the divorce context, since divorce often signals only a change in the nature of the relationship rather than its termination.

(7) *Privacy.* "A privately selected trier can conduct all proceedings in private with only the parties present, and confidentiality can be preserved where there is a valid basis for it — as in the protection of trade secrets." Burger, *supra*, at 16. Opponents of ADR sometimes criticize its "secrecy," alleging that decisionmaking should be done in the open. Is this argument valid?

[C] The Case for Caution in Encouraging ADR's

Fiss, AGAINST SETTLEMENT, 93 Yale L.J. 1073 (1984).* In my view, . . . the case for settlement rest[s] on questionable premises. I do not believe that settlement as a generic practice is preferable to judgment or should be institutionalized on a wholesale and indiscriminate basis. It should be treated instead as a highly problematic technique for streamlining dockets. Settlement is for me the civil analogue of plea bargaining: Consent is often coerced; the bargain may be struck by someone without authority; the absence of a trial and judgment renders subsequent judicial involvement troublesome; and although dockets are trimmed, justice may not be done. Like plea bargaining, settlement is a capitulation to the conditions of mass society and should be neither encouraged nor praised. . . .

[ADR advocates see] adjudication in essentially private terms: The purpose of lawsuits and the civil courts is to resolve disputes, and the amount of litigation we encounter is evidence of the needlessly combative and quarrelsome character of Americans. . . . I, on the other hand, see adjudication in more public terms: Civic litigation is an institutional arrangement for using state power to bring a recalcitrant reality closer to our chosen ideals. . . .

To conceive of the civil lawsuit in public terms as America does might be unique. I am willing to assume that no other country . . . has a case like *Brown v. Board of Education* in which the judicial power is used to eradicate the caste structure. . . . But this should be a source of pride rather than shame. . . . Adjudication American-style is not a reflection of our combativeness but rather a tribute to our inventiveness and perhaps even more to our commitment.

NOTES AND QUESTIONS

(1) For additional reading regarding the impact of alternative dispute resolution, see Perschbacher & Bassett, *The End of Law*, 84 B.U. L. Rev. 1 (2006) (building on Professor Fiss's arguments); *see also* Goldberg, Green & Sander, *Litigation, Arbitration or Mediation: A Dialogue*, ABA Journal, June 1989, at 70 (answering criticisms of ADR in the form of a "dialogue" between a litigator and an ADR specialist).

(2) *The Limits of ADR: Consent, Coercion, Ethics, and the Public Purpose.* If expenses of litigation are to be borne by the parties, it does not seem inappropriate for the costs of the system to influence the choice; nor does it seem improper for the judge to counteract the posturing that goes with negotiation or the lack of education that makes attorneys suspicious of ADR. But doesn't a mediator — including a judge who encourages settlement — have ethical obligations to avoid overreaching? And isn't it necessary to ensure that important cases affecting the public interest (*e.g., Brown v. Board of Education*) are not shunted off to court-annexed arbitration? But if we institutionalize the encouragement of ADR, can we avoid the overreaching judge and the shunting off of future *Brown*-type cases?

(3) *Formal Procedures as Protecting against Prejudice, Unfairness, and Inequality.* One interesting hypothesis is that "formal" adjudication minimizes unfairness, inequality, and prejudice. *Cf.* Delgado, Dunn, Brown, Lee & Hubbert, *Fairness and Formality: Minimizing the Risk of Prejudice in Alternate Dispute Resolution*, 1985 Wis. L. Rev. 1359. Are juries, properly instructed, likely to reflect less prejudice than mediators at

dispute resolution centers? Are arbitrators more likely than courtroom judges to be subtly influenced by better presentations made by more expensive counsel? It may be that, whatever the setting, prejudice can be reduced by formal and repeatable procedures. But if there are too many formal procedures, won't the cost and skill required to participate then reintroduce precisely the inequality that formality was designed to remove?

PROBLEM B

THE CASE OF THE TILTED HOUSE — ADJUDICATION OR ARBITRATION? You represent Don and Kathleen Fuller, who purchased a house built by Super Constructors, Inc. The house has a slab that is not level. The discrepancy is significant enough so that it can be perceived by a person sitting in a chair or lying in bed; in fact, the Fullers have found it necessary to prop up some of their furniture with boards, including the bed. There is little controversy about the existence of this defect. In fact, before consulting you, the Fullers availed themselves of the mediation services offered by the Greater Metropolitan Association of Home Builders in the same city, and that body wrote a short report concluding with the words, "Slab is not level. Warrantable." Promptly after undertaking to represent the Fullers, you filed a diversity suit in federal court asserting a claim under the state Consumer Protection Act, which provides liberal recovery of damages, attorney's fees, and (in some instances) punitive damages for breaches of express or implied warranty, You offer to settle for the current market value of the house and rescission of the contract. The lawyer for Super Constructors refuses this offer and proposes that, instead of proceeding with the suit, both parties submit to binding arbitration according to a program sponsored by the Greater Metropolitan Association of Home Builders. This program involves a three-person panel; one arbiter is chosen by each of the parties, and these two arbiters then jointly choose the third. Neither formal rules of evidence nor formal rules of law are required to be followed, but the award is enforceable in court unless it is without any rational basis. What factors favor your agreement to submit to arbitration? What disadvantages do you see?

[D] The Reality: Our System Vastly Favors Settlement Over Judicial Resolution

PROBLEM C

CAN YOU GUESS WHICH TOTAL IS CLOSEST TO THE NUMBER OF CIVIL JURY TRIALS IN CALIFORNIA SUPERIOR COURTS IN 1990-91? California has fifty-eight (58) superior courts, each with at least one judge (Los Angeles has hundreds). The total in 1991 was 789 judges. Which of the following is closest to the number of California superior court civil jury trials in a typical twelve-month period during 1990-91? The answer is in the margin.*

a. 1,000
b. 10,000
c. 25,000
d. 50,000
e. 100,000

* The answer is (a) (i.e., 1,000). The actual number is 3,644. If you are surprised by how low the number is, so are most people — but then, that's the point! *See* the authority excerpted in the next item for the backup data.

Samuel R. Gross & Kent D. Syverud, DON'T TRY: CIVIL VERDICTS IN A SYSTEM GEARED TO SETTLEMENT

*44 UCLA L. REV. 1, 2-6 (1996)**

If it is true, as we often hear, that we are one of the most litigious societies on earth, it is because of our propensity to sue, not our affinity for trials. Of the hundreds of thousands of civil lawsuits that are filed each year in America, the great majority are settled; of those that are not settled, most are ultimately dismissed by the plaintiffs or by the courts; only a few percent are tried to a jury or a judge. This is no accident. We prefer settlements and have designed a system of civil justice that embodies and expresses that preference in everything from the rules of procedure and evidence, to appellate opinions, to legal scholarship, to the daily work of our trial judges. Our culture portrays trial — especially trial by jury — as the quintessential dramatic instrument of justice. Our judicial system operates on a different premise: Trial is a disease, not generally fatal, but serious enough to be avoided at any reasonable cost. . . .

Trials, of course, are important beyond their numbers. For the public, trials have the advantage of visibility. They are open and dramatic, while settlements are usually boring and private — in fact, invisible. Their openness also makes trials attractive subjects for study by scholars, with the added benefit that cases that are fought to the end are likely to present more of the issues that we like to study and need to teach. But for practitioners, trials are important primarily because they influence the terms of settlement for the mass of cases that are not tried; trials cast a major part of the legal shadow within which private bargaining takes place. Trials have this standard-setting effect despite the fact that they are not typical of the cases in which their results are used as guides for settlement. Scholars are unanimous in recognizing that trials are not representative of the mass of litigated disputes. They seem to be selected because of unusual, rather than common, features such as high stakes, extreme uncertainty about the outcome, and reputational stakes of the parties. . . .

In the first part of the Article we draw a rough portrait of the civil jury trial caseload of the California superior courts, the state courts of general jurisdiction. . . . Briefly, we find that most civil jury trials in California (over 70%) concern personal injury claims of one sort or another; that almost all plaintiffs, in trials of every sort, are individuals; that the overwhelming majority of these plaintiffs (especially in personal injury cases) pay their attorneys on a contingent basis; and that almost all defendants, except some large businesses and most government entities, have insurance that covers the cost of defending the lawsuit and all or some of the potential damages. Thus, the typical civil jury trial is a personal injury claim by an individual against a large company, in which neither party is playing with its own money. . . .

In Part II [of this Article,] we describe the outcomes of these trials. There are three notable patterns:

First, most of the total sum of money awarded in these trials is concentrated in a small number of very large cases.

Second, the pattern of outcomes in personal injury trials is very different from that in commercial trials. Plaintiffs lose most personal injury trials — that is, they do less well at trial than they would have by settling — while defendants are more likely to lose in commercial trials. On average, personal injury verdicts are roughly midway between what the plaintiffs demand and what the defendants offer in settlement; on average, commercial verdicts are considerably larger than the plaintiffs' demands as well as the defendants' offers.

Third, jury verdicts are rarely compromises. Compromise, of course, is the essence of settlement, but compromise judgments are also possible at trial. In fact, they hardly ever happen. When a civil dispute ends in trial there is almost always a clear loser, and usually a clear winner as well. . . .

NOTES AND QUESTIONS

(1) *Why So Few Jury Trials?* Which of the following statements do you think is true, and which are related to the reasons for the small number of jury trials? (a) Our society provides too few judges to try many more cases. (b) Judges are lazy. (c) Even if you desire a certain, early date for trial, you can't get one. (d) Judges' time is disproportionately consumed by other matters, including pretrial issues and non-civil trials. (e) Clients are risk-averse. (f) Attorneys are risk-averse. (g) Attorneys are lazy. (h) The expense of litigation makes settlement rational. (i) Settlement is rational in most cases even apart from the expense of litigation. (j) Both sides typically have more confidence in their own ability to value their cases appropriately than they do in a prospective jury. (k) Jury trial, despite our societal adoration of the concept, is less than attractive in reality if you are a participant. (l) Extrinsic factors, such as the attention drained by unresolved grievances or the desire not to discuss sensitive matters with strangers, favor settlement. (m) There are other important factors.

(2) *Why Does One Side or the Other Decline to Settle and Insist on the (Unusual) Resolution of a Trial in a Given Case?* Which of the following do you think are true and related to the reasons why a given case might succumb to (the unusual) resolution of being tried? (a) One side has a bullheaded lawyer. (b) One side has a bullheaded client. (c) The lawyer or the client on one side remains ignorant of the factors that would lead to an accurate assessment of the value of the case. (d) Our society sends everyone the message that it is ethically superior to try the case than to settle. (e) The parties are paying the expenses with someone else's money. (f) There are structural factors preventing settlement (*e.g.*, only a clean win for plaintiff [or defendant] will result in the payment of enough money to stave off bankruptcy). (g) There are institutional reasons in the form of indecisive or unresponsive management in one client. (h) The judge or lawyers have mismanaged the case. (i) There are institutional reasons why one party refuses to settle a given category of case. (j) One party or another likes risk. (k) One party or another desires to create precedent or public communication of its position. (l) There are other important factors.

(3) *To What Conclusions About Our System Do Your Analyses of the Questions above Lead?* Consider whether your analyses of the above questions might lead to the conclusion that (a) radical or (b) selective reform in our system is warranted or to the conclusion that (c) the system works properly.

(4) *To What Conclusions about Your Role as a Litigation or Trial Lawyer Do Your Analyses of the Questions above Lead?* One possible conclusion is that the typical student in your class who becomes a trial lawyer is actually not going to try very many cases. Consider what other conclusions can be drawn about the meaning of these data to the individual practitioner.

§ 15.02 Negotiation

[A] Methods and Tactics

W. Dorsaneo, D. Crump, E. Carlson & E. Thornburg, HOW DOES LITIGATION GET SETTLED?

*Texas Civil Procedure: Pretrial Litigation § 11.06 (4th ed. 1999)**

Just how do lawsuits get settled? We all are aware that most disputes are settled rather than tried. How does this happen?

It can happen at almost any stage of the proceedings, in almost any kind of case and in almost any way. The case can be settled before suit is filed, or it may be settled after the Supreme Court has denied certiorari. Small claims cases are settled, and so are death penalty criminal cases. Settlement may be precipitated by a telephone call from defendant to plaintiff, to set up a discovery schedule, culminating in the offhand question: "What will it take to settle this case?" Or it may be precipitated by the stern commands of an irascible federal judge to "sit down and settle this case," together with an implied (or explicit) threat to hold the failure to do so against any party appearing recalcitrant. . . .

The description that follows attempts to catalog and explain certain negotiation techniques. [S]ome of the listed techniques are ethically dubious. However, even an ethical negotiator needs to know *all* of the "tricks of the trade," so that he [or she] can [d]eal with improper ones when they are used by others. Also, this catalog includes several techniques that can only be used in very limited situations. Finally, no claim is made of completeness . . . , because the varieties of successful negotiating behaviors are infinite.

1. REFUSAL TO BARGAIN: THE "FIRM, FAIR OFFER." Conceptually, the simplest negotiating technique is to determine a satisfactory point of resolution, communicate it to one's adversary and refuse to bargain about it. There are situations in which this technique is the only reasonable approach. For example, the Charles Manson murder case was not plea-bargained, and it could not have been unless the defendant had been willing to accept liability for the maximum sentence. Historically, the "firm, fair offer" is associated with a General Electric Company labor negotiator named Boulware, who customarily figured an acceptable settlement point and communicated it, along with his refusal to bargain, to the union. [T]he technique was so successful at undermining the union's authority that the refusal to bargain has since become the archetypical unfair labor practice. It is sometimes known as "Boulwareism."

The refusal to bargain is effective only if it is convincing enough so that rational negotiators will capitulate to it. Even then, [o]ne may have to litigate often. And if one deals each time with a different adversary who has no reason to know or be convinced of one's track record, the firm, fair offer will not be an effective technique, because many will interpret it as an invitation to bargain further. An institutional litigator with a large volume of claims may successfully use the technique. . . . The result will be that the litigant will have to try many cases that might more rationally be settled, but it may believe that its "tough" reputation among plaintiff's attorneys has offsetting value.

Frequently, a prosecutor's office may be in a position to use a modified "firm, fair offer" approach. Interestingly, when given descriptions of such a system, law students

---

generally appear to consider it ethically superior for a prosecutor's office, on the theory that variations in sentences owing to negotiating ability should be minimized. But there are situations, too, when the firm, fair offer can be ethically dubious, such as when an insurer engages in the unfair settlement practice of offering unrealistically low amounts upon pain of forcing economically impractical litigation.

2. CONCEALMENT OF ONE'S OWN SETTLEMENT POINT. This is the opposite result from the firm, fair offer, and in a world of strangers negotiating for maximum advantage, it is generally the more successful approach. The technique works because an opponent who does not know the negotiator's true settlement point may have undervalued his own position, or overvalued the resistance of the negotiator, so that the opponent may make greater concessions than are really necessary to settle the dispute to the satisfaction of the negotiator. Conversely, a negotiator who discloses his true settlement point has indicated to his opponent the maximum concession the opponent need make. An opponent may not believe a statement of one's "true" settlement point and may require one to decide between further concessions and litigation.

3. INDUCING THE OPPONENT TO START THE BARGAINING. There is an advantage to having the opponent state his position first. By doing so, a negotiator not only can avoid giving away his own settlement point, but he can also begin to assemble data from which he can infer his opponent's settlement point.

An inexperienced opponent may be induced to make the first offer by being asked the question, "What will it take to settle this case?" One with more experience is likely to respond differently. He will make a first offer that is unrealistically high, concealing his realization that it is unrealistically high, and thus he will avoid disclosing any information about his settlement point. . . . This tactic — that of making an unreasonable offer as the first statement of position and communicating a belief that it is reasonable — is so common that it might be deemed *the* fundamental negotiating technique. The belief in reasonableness (which is frequently deceptive) may be stated explicitly, or it may be implied in non-verbal conduct, but it is an essential part of the technique.

Many people dislike negotiating because of the prevalence and undeniable success of this simple but seemingly dishonest technique. Several ethical theories have been advanced to justify the technique, including the argument that negotiation is a separate endeavor with rules different from that of other human activity [or] the argument that there may be an element of "self-fulfilling prophecy" in the mere statement of one's true position because it sets, instead, the perimeter of the opponent's maximum concession, and similar arguments.

4. THE APPEARANCE OF IRRATIONALITY. Negotiation is a rational process. It depends upon the willingness of both parties to concede something to get something in return. If one of the parties is irrational, no negotiation can take place. . . . [A] person negotiating with another perceived as "crazy" may understand that he will have to make greater concessions than he would against a rational opponent, or will have resort to a test of force.

Anger, cantankerousness, indifference to consequences and even ignorance in some cases enhance a negotiator's bargaining strength. . . . It follows that the *appearance* of anger, cantankerousness, indifference to consequences or ignorance may likewise create a bargaining advantage. Successful negotiators are often good actors.

5. BLAMING THE CLIENT OR SOME OTHER PERSON OVER WHOM ONE HAS NO CONTROL. This technique is really a different form of irrationality. It puts the

opponent in the position of arguing with a rational person, [b]ut with the final result to be determined by another person impervious to rational arguments. "It's entirely up to him, and he refuses your offer," is a typical way of invoking this technique. . . . The "Mutt and Jeff Routine" (in which one of a team of negotiators [u]ses the feigned irrationality of another on the same team to induce concessions) is another example.

It should go without saying that blaming it on the client may be a statement of the true facts. But the point is that it may also be a pure negotiating technique. The client may have already given settlement authority to the lawyer or [w]ould accept the advice of the lawyer, but the lawyer pretends that the client is independent.

6. USING A MEDIATOR. Sometimes, a person confronted with an ostensibly irrational opponent may call in a neutral third person to help dispose of the claim. Not infrequently in lawsuit litigation, the trial judge can be induced to occupy this role (assuming he does not naturally undertake it). A mediator is a useful countervailing tool against most of the preceding techniques, undercutting the effort to avoid stating a realistic position as well as blaming the client.

7. APPEALS TO THE MERITS. Inexperienced negotiators tend to place more stock in statements about the merits of the dispute than do experienced negotiators. However, there is an advantage to having one's opponent know the facts advantageous to one's position. Accordingly, even experienced negotiators often take great pains to ensure that the opposing side is aware of all evidence and law that could possibly be helpful. The difference between the inexperienced and experienced negotiator is the former's belief that the latter will accept such information as dispositive.

Experienced negotiators do, however, do a fair amount of posturing over the merits of the suit. This posturing often takes the form of expressing unshakable conviction in the prediction that one will prevail. This approach is an effort to shore up the appearance of reasonableness that is essential to the unrealistically high offer technique. The experienced negotiator will also take a position more extreme than that of the inexperienced negotiator on the merits, and he will advance it with ironclad certainty. These approaches are part of the strategies of concealment of position.

8. THROWING ONESELF ON THE OPPONENT'S MERCY. A negotiator may say, "We can't possibly dispute your claim. You've got us over a barrel. Please don't take advantage of your superior position and punish us." . . . [T]he technique is reserved to peculiar situations, specifically those in which one has little or no bargaining strength and the opponent does not seem cold blooded enough to take absolute advantage. . . .

What must be borne in mind is that throwing one's self on the mercy of one's opponent is a bargaining technique. . . . For example, it is not unheard of for a person using this gambit, and who is successful in inducing a "merciful" offer, to respond by saying, "Oh! That doesn't seem fair. What I had in mind was the following," and then state an unreasonably high counteroffer, having thus induced his opponent to make the first step in the bargaining.

9. INDUCING THE OPPONENT TO BARGAIN AGAINST HIMSELF. Sometimes, an inexperienced opponent, having made the first offer, can be induced to make the first concession, too. The methodology is familiar: "Your offer is not even in the ballpark. Come up with something more realistic and then we'll talk."

[A] pattern of concessions by one party not matched by the other tends to carry over into later stages of the process.

10. FORCING TWO OPPONENTS TO BARGAIN AGAINST EACH OTHER. This technique is often used by experienced negotiators in sales situations, sometimes with a "phantom" second bidder. In lawsuits, it requires the presence of multiple parties. The "Mary Carter" agreement, named after a case in which the Mary Carter Paint Company was one of the litigants, enables a plaintiff to settle with one of multiple defendants on the condition that the settling defendant will be repaid out of any recovery from others. [E]ach of the defendants is exposed to the implied threat that such an agreement will be made with the others. Plaintiff may make the threat explicit, saying, "If you don't settle the case, [I]'ll make an agreement with the other defendant and that will give me a war chest to go after you."

11. "GANGING UP." The Mary Carter agreement or, the multiple-party situation in general, carries another implied threat. A settling defendant may be retained in the lawsuit and may assist the plaintiff in pinning blame on the other defendant. A third party impleaded by a defendant may threaten, "If you don't release me, I'm going to cooperate with the plaintiff in pinning blame on you."

12. FLATTERY, CLUBBINESS, AND OTHER ATTITUDES. Experienced negotiators sometimes resort to flattery ("You're too good a lawyer to be handling this kind of case"). Or the negotiator may depict himself and the opposing lawyer as having more in common than the opponent and his client ("You have my sympathies in having to deal with a person as crazy as that. [I] know what you must be going through"). Behind these statements lies the psychological truth that it is easier for a person to make concessions if he can do so in an atmosphere of dignity. . . .

13. TIMING. Time is usually on one side or the other in a negotiation. The person who can afford to wait, who can give the appearance of being able to afford to wait, or who forces himself to wait, has an advantage. . . . A litigant who has just been ordered to prepare a pretrial order that will require the assimilation and labeling of 100,000 documents may be more willing to settle at a reasonable figure than one who has done the work and is prepared for trial.

. . . Bargaining terminated with all parties angry may be resumed at a later session with time having erased the rancor from the process. Experienced negotiators . . . know that repeated statement of the same position, made in several separate sessions with intervening periods of waiting, is an effective negotiating technique.

14. ACTIVITY. Vigorous and aggressive activity moving the litigation toward a point of conclusion can have advantageous effects. Many cases settle on the courthouse steps. [T]he initiation of sequential steps before trial, including discovery, a motion for summary judgment and like steps, communicating to the opponent a determination to resolve the case and forcing the opponent, repeatedly, to confront and evaluate the situation, is an effective means of precipitating settlement.

At the same time, however, activity must be undertaken with the realization that it often costs money. A litigant who undertakes vigorous and purposeful activity, only to find that he has expended large amounts of money in discovery and in unsuccessful pretrial motions, may find his opponent's settlement position unaffected. . . .

15. COLLATERAL CONSEQUENCES TO THE OPPONENT. There are many litigants whose initial reaction is to "fight it all the way to the Supreme Court" until educated as to the cost of doing so. Some negotiators, taking this fact one step further, tend to increase expense to the opponent by causing collateral consequences to ensue. The drafting of interrogatories that are expensive to answer, the taking of lengthy depositions

that tie up the time of the opposing lawyer or make a client himself realize how much of his time is being wasted, or the use of discovery to embarrass, threaten trade secrets and the like are all examples. . . . Many of these tactics are ethically dubious, but they are nevertheless common.

16. DEADLINES AND "LOCKING IN." Some negotiators place deadlines upon the acceptance of a given offer in order to avoid the opponent's "riding" the case to get the benefit of future developments. Thus one may say, "If you wait until discovery is finished and I'm ready for trial, my settlement offer is going to go up by $10,000." The effectiveness of this technique is dependent upon its credibility. It is a variant of the "firm, fair offer," and, like that technique, it depends upon the opponent's belief that one is indeed "locked in" to the deadline. . . .

17. FOCAL POINT SOLUTIONS. As differences narrow in the negotiation process, the likelihood of a "splitting of the difference" or adoption of some "standard" solution close to the bargaining position of the parties increases. Round numbers are more likely resolutions. . . . The experienced negotiator . . . attempts to make and elicit offers aiming for the elusive "point in the middle" that is advantageous to him. [I]f the parties' latest positions are $5,000 and $12,000, respectively, the . . . negotiator . . . will try to keep his position a respectable increment over $10,000, so that this figure, rather than, say, $7,500, will be the natural focal point.

18. DRAFTING THE AGREEMENT. In a straight monetary claim situation, the drafting of the agreement may not be highly important. But in litigation involving a multiplicity of issues, such as a divorce or employment discrimination case, it can be a significant advantage to be the drafter. There are frequently minor points that are incompletely negotiated. The drafter, naturally, drafts these so as to resolve them in her favor. There is always the likelihood that the opponent will not notice the difference . . . or that he may consider some objections too small . . . to make.

19. CONTROL OF THE AGENDA. In a litigation matter with many issues to resolve, the person who sets the order of discussion may have an advantage. For some reason, concessions seem to come more easily at the beginning of a negotiation process (or at its end, when agreement is approached). Thus the experienced negotiator attempts to cause those matters most important to him to be considered early. He may even insist that the resolution of a particularly important point is a "precondition" to further negotiation. Conversely, he may suggest with reference to an important, but sticky, point, "Let's put that issue to the side and come back to it later," believing that his opponent will, in the meantime, acquire . . . a stake in preserving agreement. . . .

20. THE "BARGAINING CHIP" OR THE FALSE DEMAND. One may ask for something one does not really want or expect so that one may appear to give it up in exchange for something else. If this happens, one has "given" a concession without really making one. Sometimes, for example, a party to a divorce case who really wants a reasonable property settlement and visitation schedule will demand custody as well. This technique (like the unrealistically high offer) is dependent upon the concealment of one's true position; *i.e.*, it is dependent upon the opponent's belief that the bargaining chip represents a real desire conceded.

21. "REVERSE PSYCHOLOGY." Against a perverse opponent, one expected to take a contrary position simply because it is contrary, one can occasionally get what one wants by appearing to be asking for the opposite. "The last thing we want is custody. My client wants to be free of the responsibility." Obviously, this technique [which sometimes is

called the "Bre'r Rabbit"; can you see why?] is useful in its purest form only in very limited situations.

22. PHYSICAL FACTORS. Negotiating on familiar ground, among familiar people and under familiar conditions gives one a psychological edge. . . .

23. DIRECT INVOLVEMENT OF THE PRINCIPAL. Occasionally, a negotiator may see some advantage in having his opponent and his principal communicate directly. The opponent may have undervalued the determination or persuasiveness of the principal (or vice versa). In some situations, *e.g.* criminal defense or personal injury plaintiff's litigation, exposure of the opponent to the human qualities of the principal may have a moderating influence. Sometimes direct communication facilitates balanced concessions that would be difficult to obtain through an intermediary. In a divorce case, [t]he "four parties meeting" (with both attorneys and both clients present) may be a way of cutting through the posturing [a]nd animosity.

24. MAKING THE OPPONENT FEEL HE HAS NEGOTIATED CAPABLY. An experienced negotiator generally refrains from "crowing" about an attractive result. Knowing that he may have to meet his opponent again, he instead makes the opponent feel that the result was advantageous to him.

25. THE TEST OF STRENGTH, TOTAL OR PARTIAL. It is worth reemphasizing that not every dispute can be settled by negotiation. Some require a total — or partial — test of strength. The willingness to "go to the mat" is part of the arsenal of the skillful negotiator. However, the hallmark of the good negotiator is the settlement, without the delay or expense or trauma of litigation, of that vast majority of disputes that can be settled. . . .

NOTES AND QUESTIONS

(1) *Negotiation Ethics.* Most of the preceding discussion has been done without consideration of the ethical aspects of each technique. Accordingly, it seems appropriate to ask, which of the preceding techniques seem most vulnerable to ethical criticisms? [Actually, the preceding discussion omits some of the most dubious tactics. One team of writers posits the following technique: "After agreement has been reached, have your client reject it and raise his demands." Meltsner & Schrag, *Negotiating Techniques for Legal Services Lawyers*, 7 Clearinghouse Review 262 (1973). The authors acknowledge that "This is the most ethically dubious of the tactics listed, but there will be occasions where a lawyer will have to defend against it or even employ it." [For further discussion of ethical issues, *see* subsection [D], below.]

(2) *How Important Are Negotiation Skills to Practicing Lawyers?* Decotiis and Steele observed a sample of skilled general practitioners and recorded how the practitioners spent their professional time. Decotiis & Steele, *The Skills of the Lawyering Process*, 41 Tex. B.J. 483 (1977). They conclude that negotiation is "the most highly developed skill" employed by the lawyers observed.

(3) *What (if Any) Importance Do Negotiating Lawyers Attach to the Underlying Merits (Are the Merits Irrelevant)?: Alexander, Do the Merits Matter? A Study of Settlements in Securities Class Actions, 43 Stan. L. Rev. 497 (1991).* Professor Alexander studied this question in the context of securities class actions. Her stunning conclusion: These actions settle for relatively consistent percentages of the projected damages, apparently uninfluenced by the relative merits of the plaintiffs' liability cases! In "big" cases, both sides are risk-averse. The "bet the company" (or "bet the plaintiffs' attorney's fee")

approach becomes "unthinkable." In this atmosphere, the lawyers all know that the case will not be tried, and so settlement negotiations tend to be "based on non-merits factors." Question: Has our system reached a point where the merits of litigation are irrelevant?

PROBLEM D

NEGOTIATING TACTICS. Identify the technique that is used in each of the following negotiation statements and explain why the technique may "work," when it would be useful, how it might be defended against and whether it is ethical.

(a) "When we have a case that we don't think there's a good chance of liability on, we always take the position of offering out-of-pocket medical expenses, only."

(b) "This lawsuit's going to cost a lot just to try. Why don't you get with your man and tell me your best shot, and I'll see if I can get my people to take it."

(c) "My client is being totally unreasonable about this case. I'd almost be willing to recommend your last offer, but what it amounts to is that you're really dealing with him. I do think I can get him to take it if you up the offer another $5000, though."

(d) "Well, you keep telling me that we can't win on the merits of the case. Frankly, you're probably correct. But let's talk about what's right. The suit's incidental to the fact that your folks know they owe my man something. Why don't you approach it on that basis? I'm sure my man will take anything that is fair."

(e) "If you guys don't come up with at least a hundred thousand, I'm going to be forced to make a deal with the other defendants and have them testify at the trial."

(f) "My client really doesn't want the corporation to buy her stock back, even though that's what she's suing for, because then she'd miss out on what looks like a really good deal. The last thing she really wants is to be cashed out."

[B] Encouragement by the Court

KOTHE v. SMITH, 771 F.2d 667 (2d Cir. 1985). Read (or re-read) this case, which appears in § 8.02[B] of Chapter 8, above. Judge Sweet recommended that this medical malpractice suit be settled for between $20,000 and $30,000 and warned the parties that if they settled for a comparable amount after trial had begun, he would impose sanctions on the dilatory party. Although the plaintiff's attorney had informed the judge that the plaintiff would settle for $20,000, he had requested confidentiality and had communicated a demand of $50,000 to the defendant. After one day of trial, the case was settled for $20,000, and Judge Sweet imposed sanctions in the form of a requirement that the defendant pay $1,000 each to the plaintiff and the plaintiff's expert witness, plus $480 to the clerk of the court (presumably representing jury fees and other costs to the Government). The Court of Appeals reversed, reasoning that Rule 16(c)(7) was "designed to encourage pretrial settlement discussions" but not to "impose settlement negotiations on unwilling litigants." Further, settlement was a "two-way street," yet the defendant had never received an offer below $20,000; furthermore, the defendant's attorney should not be condemned "for changing his evaluation of the case after listening to [the plaintiff's] testimony." The Court of Appeals closed with a commendation of Judge Sweet, however, for his efforts.

NOTES AND QUESTIONS

(1) *Permissible Sanctions for Failure to Participate in "Good Faith."* Rule 16 permits sanctions in various situations for failing to participate in good faith in pretrial conference

activities. Would sanctions be permissible if the defendant's attorney contemptuously refused even to consider settlement negotiations but then settled after trial had begun for $20,000? [If not, is there any meaning to the provisions of Rule 16 empowering the judge to encourage settlement?]

(2) *Proper "Persuasion" Versus "Coercion."* Might it be difficult to tell the difference between "encouragement" of settlement and "coercion" by the judge?

(3) *A Case to Contrast with Kothe: Newton v. A.C. & S., Inc., 918 F.2d 1121 (3d Cir. 1990).* "In an innovative effort to manage its trial docket, the District Court instituted the practice of 'stacking' asbestos cases. Under this practice, the District Court assigned the asbestos injury cases to a designated time slot. As a scheduled case is disposed of, either by trial or settlement, the District Court moves the next case into the allotted slot. To give the parties of the next case in line sufficient notice of their trial date, the District Court judge sets a deadline for settlement negotiations of two weeks prior to the trial date. If the litigants settle after the deadline, the district court imposes a fine regardless of fault and without a prior hearing." This procedure certainly is innovative. But is it lawful? Yes, said the Court of Appeals: "[I]mposing sanctions for unjustified failure to comply with the Court's schedule for settlement is entirely consistent with the spirit of Rule 16." That Rule is designed "to maximize the efficiency of the court system by insisting that attorneys [c]ooperate with the court and abandon practices which unreasonably interfere with [e]xpeditious management." The Court of Appeals nevertheless reversed because the amount of the fine ($1,000) was not tied to any cost factors, and therefore it implicated the higher due process protections of criminal contempt proceedings; but the court clearly upheld the concept. [Is this holding correct?]

[C] Legal Rules Encouraging Settlement: Pre-Judgment Interest, Attorney's Fee Changes, and Rule 68

NOTES AND QUESTIONS

(1) *The Influence of Pre-Judgment Interest on the Settlement Process.* If a state adopts a rule of substantive law awarding pre-judgment interest to the prevailing plaintiff, what impact would this rule have on the encouragement of settlement? (Would it actually induce settlements more frequently or earlier in litigation — or would it simply shift the balance in favor of plaintiffs to some degree?) Reconsider the materials on pre-judgment interest in § 14.05 of Chapter 14, above.

(2) *The Influence of Attorney's Fees.* Would a rule awarding attorney's fees to a prevailing plaintiff encourage settlement (or would it shift the balance of advantages in favor of plaintiffs, so that litigation would settle for greater amounts)? Might such a rule be more effective if it resulted in an award of attorney's fees to the prevailing party, whether plaintiff or defendant, whichever party prevailed? Reconsider the materials on attorney's fees in § 14.05 of Chapter 14, above. In *City of Riverside v. Rivera*, reproduced in that section, the Court held that recoverable attorney's fees are not required to be proportional to the amount of the recovery; it upheld an award of attorney's fees of roughly $250,000 where the recovery was roughly $33,000. What effect would you expect that this holding would have upon settlements?

(3) *Rule 68: Direct Encouragement of Settlement by Encouragement of Offers of Judgment.* The *City of Riverside* case, however, is only part of the story. Rule 68 provides for a pretrial offer of judgment and cuts off recovery of costs after the offer if the plaintiff recovers less than the offer. Consider the case that follows; together with the *City of*

Riverside case, doesn't it seem likely to exert strong influence on settlements? Is it fair to plaintiffs? Are the two cases, taken together, fair to defendants? *See* Note, *The Impact of Proposed Rule 68 on Civil Rights Litigation*, 34 Colum. L. Rev. 719 (1984).

Read Fed. R. Civ. P. 68 (offer of judgment).

MAREK v. CHESNY

473 U.S. 1 (1985)

CHIEF JUSTICE BURGER delivered the opinion of the Court.

We granted certiorari to decide whether attorney's fees incurred by a plaintiff subsequent to an offer of settlement under Federal Rule of Civil Procedure 68 must be paid by the defendant under 42 U.S.C. § 1988, when the plaintiff recovers a judgment less than the offer.

I

Petitioners, three police officers, in answering a call on a domestic disturbance, shot and killed respondent's adult son. Respondent [f]iled suit against the officers in the United States District Court under 42 U.S.C. § 1983 and state tort law.

Prior to trial, petitioners made a timely offer of settlement "for a sum, including costs now accrued and attorney's fees, of ONE HUNDRED THOUSAND ($100,000) DOLLARS." Respondent did not accept the offer. The case went to trial and respondent was awarded $5,000 on the state law "wrongful death" claim, $52,000 for the § 1983 violation, and $3,000 in punitive damages.

Respondent filed a request for $171,692.47 in costs, including attorney's fees. This amount included costs incurred after the settlement offer. Petitioners opposed the claim for post-offer costs, relying on Federal Rule of Civil Procedure 68, which shifts to the plaintiff all "costs" incurred subsequent to an offer of judgment not exceeded by the ultimate recovery at trial. Petitioners argued that attorney's fees are part of the "costs" covered by Rule 68. The District Court agreed with petitioners and declined to award respondent "costs, including attorney's fees, incurred after the offer of judgment." . . . The parties subsequently agreed that $32,000 fairly represented the allowable costs, including attorney's fees, accrued prior to petitioner's offer of settlement. Respondent appealed the denial of post-offer costs.

The Court of Appeals reversed. . . . The court rejected what it termed the "rather mechanical linking up of Rule 68 and section 1988." . . . Plaintiffs' attorneys, the court reasoned, would be forced to "think very hard" before rejecting even an inadequate offer, and would be deterred from bringing good faith actions because of the prospect of losing the right to attorney's fees if a settlement offer more favorable than the ultimate recovery were rejected. . . . [We reverse.]

II

Rule 68 provides that if a timely pretrial offer of settlement is not accepted and "the judgment finally obtained by the offeree is not more favorable than the offer, the offeree must pay *the costs incurred after the making of the offer.*" Fed. Rule Civ. Proc. 68 (emphasis added). [The 2007 "restyling" amendments changed this language slightly — Eds.] The plain purpose of Rule 68 is to encourage settlement and avoid litigation. . . .

A

The first question we address is whether petitioners' offer was valid under Rule 68. Respondent contends that the offer was invalid because it lumped petitioners' proposal for damages with their proposal for costs. Respondent argues that Rule 68 requires that an offer must separately recite the amount that the defendant is offering in settlement of the substantive claim and the amount he is offering to cover accrued costs. . . .

The critical feature of this portion of the Rule is that the offer be one that *allows judgment to be taken against the defendant for both the damages caused by the challenged conduct and the costs then accrued.* In other words, the drafters' concern was not so much with the particular components of offers, but with the *judgments* to be allowed against defendants. If an offer recites that costs are included or specifies an amount for costs, and the plaintiff accepts the offer, the judgment will necessarily include costs; if the offer does not state that costs are included and an amount for costs if not specified, the court will be obliged by the terms of the Rule to include in its judgment an additional amount which in its discretion, . . . [it] determines to be sufficient to cover the costs. In either case, however, the offer has *allowed* judgment to be entered against the defendant both for damages caused by the challenged conduct and for costs. Accordingly, it is immaterial whether the offer recites that costs are included, whether it specifies the amount the defendant is allowing for costs, or for that matter, whether it refers to costs at all. As long as the offer does not implicitly or explicitly provide that the judgment *not* include costs, a timely offer will be valid.

This construction of the Rule best furthers the objective of the Rule, which is to encourage settlements. . . .

B

The second question we address is whether the term "costs" in Rule 68 includes attorney's fees awardable under 42 U.S.C. § 1988. By the time the Federal Rules of Civil Procedure were adopted in 1938, federal statutes had authorized and defined awards of costs to prevailing parties for more than 85 years. *See* Act of Feb. 26, 1853, 10 Stat. 161; *see generally Alyeska Pipeline Service Co. v. Wilderness Society*, 421 U.S. 240, 95 S. Ct. 1612, 44 L. Ed. 2d 141 (1975). Unlike in England, such "costs" generally had not included attorney's fees; under the "American Rule," each party had been required to bear its own attorney's fees. The "American Rule" as applied in federal courts, however, had become subject to certain exceptions by the late 1930's. [B]ut most of the exceptions were found in federal statutes that directed courts to award attorney's fees as part of costs in particular cases. . . .

Section 407 of the Communications Act of 1934, for example, provided in relevant part that, "[i]f the petitioner shall finally prevail, he shall be allowed a reasonable attorney's fee, to be taxed and collected as a part of the costs of the suit." 47 U.S.C. § 407. There was identical language in Section 3(p) of the Railway Labor Act, 45 U.S.C. § 153(p) (1934 ed.). . . .

The authors of Federal Rule of Civil Procedure 68 were fully aware of these exceptions to the American Rule. . . . In this setting, given the importance of "costs" to the Rule, it is very unlikely that this omission was mere oversight; on the contrary, the most reasonable inference is that the term "costs" in Rule 68 was intended to refer to all costs properly awardable under the relevant substantive statute or other authority. . . . Thus, absent Congressional expressions to the contrary, where the underlying statute defines "costs" to include attorney's fees, we are satisfied such fees are to be included as costs for purposes of Rule 68. . . . Here, respondents sued under 42 U.S.C. § 1983. Pursuant to the Civil Rights Attorney's Fees Awards Act of 1976, 42 U.S.C. § 1988, a prevailing party in a § 1983 action may be awarded attorney's fees "as part of the costs." Since Congress expressly included attorney's fees as "costs" available to a plaintiff in a § 1983 suit, such fees are subject to the cost-shifting provision of Rule 68. This "plain meaning" interpretation of the interplay between Rule 68 and § 1988 is the only construction that gives meaning to each word in both Rule 68 and § 1988.

Unlike the Court of Appeals, we do not believe that this "plain meaning" construction [w]ill frustrate Congress' objective in § 1988 of ensuring that civil rights plaintiffs obtain "effective access to the judicial process." . . .

To be sure, application of Rule 68 will require plaintiffs to "think very hard" about whether continued litigation is worthwhile; that is precisely what Rule 68 contemplates. This effect of Rule 68, however, is in no sense inconsistent with the congressional policies underlying § 1983 and § 1988. [I]n *Hensley v. Eckerhart*, 461 U.S. 424, 103 S. Ct. 1933, 76 L. Ed. 2d 40 (1983), we held that "the most critical factor" in determining a reasonable fee "is the degree of success obtained." . . . In a case where a rejected settlement offer exceeds the ultimate recovery, the plaintiff — although technically the prevailing party — has not received any monetary benefits from the post-offer services of his attorney. This case presents a good example: the $139,692 in post-offer legal services resulted in a recovery $8,000 less than petitioner's settlement offer. Given Congress' focus on the success achieved, we are not persuaded that shifting the post-offer costs to respondent in these circumstances would in any sense thwart its intent under § 1988. . . . [Reversed.]

[The concurring opinions of Justices Powell and Rehnquist are omitted.]

JUSTICE BRENNAN, with whom JUSTICE MARSHALL and JUSTICE BLACKMUN join, dissenting.

The question presented by this case is whether the term "costs" as it is used in Rule 68 [r]efers simply to those taxable costs defined in 28 U.S.C. § 1920 and traditionally understood as "costs" — court's fees, printing expenses, and the like — or instead includes attorney's fees. . . .

Congress has enacted well over 100 attorney's fees statutes, many of which would appear to be affected by today's decision. As the Appendix to this dissent illustrates, Congress has employed a variety of slightly different wordings in these statutes. It sometimes has referred to the awarding of "attorney's fees as *part of* the costs," to "costs *including* attorney's fees," and to "attorney's fees and *other* litigation costs." . . . But Congress frequently has referred in other statutes to the awarding of "costs *and* a reasonable attorney's fee," of "costs *together* with a reasonable attorney's fee," or simply of "attorney's fees" without reference to costs. Under the Court's "plain language" analysis, Rule 68 obviously will *not* include [a]ttorney's fees as a settlement incentive [u]nder these statutes because they do not refer to fees "as" costs. [The Appendix listed over 100 statutes, with roughly equivalent numbers of both kinds of statutes.] . . .

Although the Court's opinion fails to discuss any of the problems reviewed above, it does devote some space to arguing that its interpretation of Rule 68 "is in no sense inconsistent with the Congressional policies underlying § 1983 and § 1988." . . .

The Court is wrong. Congress has instructed that attorney's fee entitlement under § 1988 be governed by a *reasonableness* standard. Until today the Court always has recognized that this standard precludes reliance on any mechanical "bright-line" rules automatically denying a portion of fees, acknowledging that such "mathematical approach[es]" provide "little aid in determining what is a reasonable fee in light of all the relevant factors." . . .

. . . Interpreting Rule 68 in its current version to include attorney's fees will lead to a number of skewed settlement incentives that squarely conflict with Congress' intent. To discuss but one example, Rule 68 [g]ives the plaintiff only 10 days to accept or reject. The Court's decision inevitably will encourage defendants who know they have violated the law to make "lowball" offers immediately after suit is filed and before [d]iscovery. . . . Indeed, because Rule 68 offers may be made recurrently without limitation, defendants will be well advised to make ever-slightly larger offers throughout the discovery process and before plaintiffs have conducted all reasonably necessary discovery. . . .

NOTES AND QUESTIONS

(1) As explained in *Marek v. Chesny*, above, the term "costs" was intended to refer to "all costs properly awardable under the relevant substantive statute or other authority," and thus, when the underlying statute defines "costs" as including attorney fees, such fees are included as costs for Rule 68 purposes. In addition, in *Utility Automation 2000, Inc. v. Choctawhatchee Electric Cooperative, Inc.*, 298 F.3d 1238 (11th Cir. 2002), the Eleventh Circuit held that when a Rule 68 offer is silent as to whether it includes attorney fees, a contract provision authorizing an award of such fees to the prevailing party in any action to enforce the contract may be sufficient to award fees as "costs" under Rule 68. In *Utility Automation 2000*, the plaintiff sued the defendant for breach of contract and misappropriation of trade secrets in violation of the Alabama Trade Secrets Act. The state trade secrets statute did not include attorney fees in its definition of costs. However, the Eleventh Circuit noted that the underlying contract between the plaintiff and the defendant provided that "[i]n the event either party incurs legal expenses to enforce or interpret any provision of this Agreement, the prevailing party shall be entitled to recover such legal expenses, including, without limitation, reasonable attorney's fees, court costs and all related expenses." *Id.* at 1245-46. The circuit court held that this contract provision defined fees as costs, and therefore permitted an award of fees as "costs" under Rule 68.

(2) In a case involving a Rule 68 offer of judgment in a class action, the Third Circuit refused to find that such an offer, made to the named plaintiff before the filing of a class certification motion, mooted the lawsuit. In *Weiss v. Regal Collections*, 385 F.3d 337 (3d Cir. 2004), involving the Fair Debt Collection Practices Act, the court concluded that permitting a defendant to moot the action by picking off the named plaintiff would frustrate the purposes of the class action device generally, and of the Fair Debt Collection Practices Act specifically.

[D] Ethics and Overreaching

STATE NATIONAL BANK OF EL PASO v. FARAH MANUFACTURING CO., 678 S.W.2d 661 (Tex. App.—El Paso 1984, no writ). Farah Manufacturing Company was originally a family-owned apparel manufacturer, which became a large, publicly held corporation under the leadership of William Farah as Chief Executive Officer (CEO). But during several turbulent years in the 1970s, which included a lengthy strike and nationwide boycott, Farah sustained large losses, and William Farah was replaced as CEO. The company's loan agreements had contained "management change" clauses. In the wake of these events, the lenders, in restructuring the company's financing, insisted upon the inclusion of a strengthened management change clause, which provided, "Any change in the office of President and Chief Executive Officer . . . or any other change in the executive management . . . which any two Banks shall consider, for any reason whatsoever, to be adverse to the interest of the Banks" would be an event of default. The evidence showed that this clause was intended, among other things, to prevent the return of William Farah to the position of CEO. The evidence also indicated that the lenders influenced the election of directors and the selection of consultants to the company.

Under its new management, however, the company produced a product line that was not what the market demanded; priced it inappropriately, and merchandised it poorly, producing mounting losses. William Farah attempted to return to active management. The lenders met and discussed their options, reaching no final decision on whether to declare default if William Farah was reelected to management. Nevertheless, Donohoe, an attorney for one of the lenders, wrote a letter to the company's board stating that William Farah's return was "unacceptable to the Banks" and that "the Banks will not grant any waiver of default based thereon." A complex series of negotiations followed, the character of which was hotly contested in the evidence at trial. In one meeting with several directors, Donohoe was quoted as saying that "if Willie Farah was elected president of the company, why, [the banks] would automatically bankrupt the company and padlock it the next day." One of the directors responded that Donohoe "could take his loan agreement and shove it." The director later responded that he was merely "trying to determine how serious they were about bankrupting and closing the company, what was his intent. I intended to push him to the very brink and very edge and find out." Donohoe's response, as quoted by witnesses, was, "We will." The board of directors apparently believed the lenders would declare default and therefore did not re-elect William Farah.

The company continued to sustain losses. William Farah continued to fight to regain his management position, through litigation and through a proxy fight. Ultimately, he was successful. After his return to management, the company was restored to profitability. Farah Manufacturing Company then sued the lenders on the theory that their conduct during negotiations constituted (1) fraud, (2) tortious economic duress, and (3) tortious interference with business relationship. The jury found in favor of Farah Manufacturing Company and further found damages totaling $18,947,348.77, mostly in lost profits due to the exclusion of William Farah from management.

The Court of Appeals affirmed. It upheld each of the three claims under the evidence:

> [Farah's] cause of action for fraud focuses on the . . . letter and the statements made by Donohoe to [William] Farah and other board members . . . of bankruptcy and padlocking if [William] Farah were elected as CEO. The evidence is legally and factually sufficient, albeit conflicting, that . . . the lenders had either decided not to declare a default or reached no decision on the matter. . . .
>
> Fraud may be effected by a misrepresentation. . . . State National . . . maintains that fraud cannot arise from a warning of an intention to enforce legal rights. . . .
>
> State National cites no cases directly supporting this position. It cannot overcome the legal and factual sufficiency of the evidence that the lenders [made representations] which they knew to be false and which, as intended, were relied upon and acted upon by [William] Farah and other board members. . . .

[Farah's] cause of action for duress focuses upon the . . . letter, the statements made by Donohoe . . . , and [other events]. . . .

It has been held that threatening to do that which a party has a legal right to do cannot form the basis of a claim of duress by business compulsion. . . .

[But] [e]ven where an insecurity clause is drafted in the broadest possible terms, the primary question is whether the creditor's attempt to [enforce it] stemmed from a reasonable, good-faith belief that its security was about to be impaired. . . . [Such] clauses . . . do not permit [declaration of default] when the facts make its use unjust or oppressive. . . .

Reformed [as to amount of damages], and as reformed, affirmed.

NOTES AND QUESTIONS

(1) *Does This Case Make It a Tort to Negotiate?* Aren't the lenders here held liable because their attorney overstated the strength of their position and thereby concealed their settlement point (or is this an oversimplification)? To those who find the *Farah* decision disturbing, the answer is Yes. It might be said that the essence of negotiation is the statement of settlement demands in such a way as to assemble information about the opponent's ultimate settlement point while avoiding tipping one's own hand. In fact, a member of the company's board used precisely the same technique against Donohoe, for the stated reason of "push[ing] him to the very brink . . . and find[ing] out." Perhaps *Farah* means that one may never "bluff" during a negotiation. But won't the parties necessarily have to "bluff," at least by what they imply to their opponents, if they are to engage in normal negotiating behavior?

(2) *Are Some "Misrepresentations" Permissible in Negotiations?* To avoid making it a tort to negotiate, one author suggests that prohibited misrepresentations should be confined to "the operative facts of the case" (*e.g.*, "my client denies driving the car," when the attorney knows that the client was driving the car). A misrepresentation of a fact "external to the operative facts of the case calculated to produce a tactical advantage" (*e.g.*, "my client says he will pay no more than $X in this case") would be permissible. Steele, *Ethical Issues in the Negotiation of Civil Matters*, in State Bar of Texas, Litigation Update I-10 through I-11 (1985). This dichotomy has intuitive appeal. But isn't it inconsistent with the reasoning in *Farah*? *See also* Shaffer, *Negotiation Ethics: A Report to Cartaphila*, 7 Litigation 37 (1981).

(3) *Does Farah Require a Return to the "Firm, Fair Offer"?* If this decision is extended to its logical conclusion, doesn't it require that a negotiator state her true "bottom line" in order to avoid "misrepresentation" of her position? If so, it may induce negotiators to avoid trading and to adopt the firm, fair offer approach, which is an unfair method of negotiation in many contexts. Consider the following note.

(4) *Will Farah Induce Lenders to Refuse to Negotiate with Defaulting Debtors, and, Instead, to Insist on Their Legal Rights by Declaring Default and Foreclosing without Discussion?* Farah Manufacturing Company's position in its suit, in fact, was that "the banks had two legitimate options. They could attempt to call the loan or elect not to and live with [William] Farah as CEO." 678 S.W.2d at 688. This all-or-nothing position seems to be furthered by the opinion. If you represented a lender in these banks' position, wouldn't you advise the bank not to try to generate other options through negotiation, but to simply declare default and foreclose without warning? Consider the following advice from a bank attorney: "The *Farah* case [means] . . . a bank should not threaten

a borrower with default in a workout situation unless the bank presently intends and has the legal right to carry out the threat. . . . The bank should not enforce a loan agreement's management clause by lobbying efforts. . . . Rather, the bank should either waive a default under the clause or declare a default. . . ." Keyes, *State National Bank of El Paso v. Farah Manufacturing Co.*, The Texas Bank Lawyer, Dec. 1984, at 9, 10-11. But if a lender deliberately delays warning a troubled debtor about its anticipated declaration of default until the decision has been made, is that result advantageous either to debtors or creditors? The discouragement of exploration for middle ground options would be particularly counterproductive. In fact, Fisher & Ury, *Getting to Yes* ch. 4 (1981), *supra*, suggest that negotiators attempt to generate new options during a "brainstorming" session without judging the ideas initially; that they "broaden the options"; and that they "invent ways of making [the other side's] decisions easy."

(5) *What Reasons or Justifications Underlie the Farah Holding?* If it appears that the *Farah* reasoning cannot be extended to other negotiations in other contexts, what is it about the *Farah* case that explains or justifies the result? Consider the following:

(a) *Donohoe's Status as an Attorney and Spokesperson for the Lender Group.* Do more restrictive ethical norms apply to attorneys than to lay persons? If so, does that difference explain the *Farah* result? *Cf.* Perschbacher, *Regulating Lawyers' Negotiations*, below.

(b) *The Defendants' Status as Banks.* Were the banks held liable, in part, because they were banks? Is it possible that "bluffing" on the part of debtors is proper while the same conduct, if engaged in by creditors, is a tortious "misrepresentation"?

(c) *"Bargaining Power."* Did the result follow because the court saw Farah as a debtor in trouble and the banks as solvent, so that they had more "bargaining power"? If your answer is yes, would a different result follow if the banks were in financial trouble themselves and dependent upon recovery of the funds they had loaned to Farah?

(d) *"Oppression."* The court's holding included the conclusion that the default warning could have been considered "oppressive." But what distinguishes oppressive as versus non-oppressive bargaining by a bank with a troubled debtor?

(e) *Lack of Candor.* The court certainly appears to conclude that the banks' conduct in the negotiation could be considered lacking in candor, or untruthful, or (as the court put it) "misrepresentation" amounting to fraud. Is this consideration a major reason for the outcome? If so, can a party ever bluff during a negotiation?

(f) *Management Control by the Bank under the "Management Change" Clause.* While clauses of the generic type at issue in the *Farah* case are not unusual in loan agreements of this kind, management control is dangerous for the lender. Having undertaken the responsibility for influencing management, perhaps the lender undertakes a greater than normal risk of liability. But this rationale might construe the *Farah* holding too narrowly. The court's statements about liability for misrepresentation are not limited to the management control rationale.

R. Perschbacher, REGULATING LAWYERS' NEGOTIATIONS, 27 Ariz. L. Rev. 75 (1985).* While no express code governs the conduct of negotiations, significant elements of such a code can be extrapolated from other fields of law. This Article derives a "law of lawyers' negotiations" from contract, tort, agency, and malpractice law, as well as rules of professional ethics.

As a preview, the law of lawyers' negotiations that emerges is as follows. Lawyers are subject to most of the same regulatory constraints as other negotiators. Where negotiations are not an adjunct to civil or criminal litigation, lawyers' responsibilities to their clients are subject to control along the lines of traditional agency law. They must ordinarily abide by client instructions and provide adequate information to the client to facilitate informed decisionmaking. Their obligation to use due care and skill in acting for the client is enforceable through malpractice actions. Lawyer-negotiators also have a duty of loyalty enforceable in a malpractice action, or more directly in a suit to recover damages for breach of fiduciary duties. In litigation settlement negotiations, however, lawyers' special obligations to the tribunal require some modification of these rules. The strict application of agency principles is relaxed and lawyers are more free to exercise judgment without being subject to malpractice liability if that judgment is mistaken. The duty of candor, part of lawyers' responsibilities as officers of the court, also limits their otherwise absolute loyalty to their clients.

Tort and contract-based rules restrain lawyer-negotiators in dealing with adversaries and other third parties. At the extreme, these rules require lawyers to limit their tactics to avoid engaging in criminal activities on a client's behalf. A wider variety of tactics may be acceptable, depending upon the circumstances in which they are employed, including the relative sophistication of the adversary and the extent of any dependency relationship between the parties. Thus, threats and economic and litigation pressures may either be acceptable negotiation tactics or may amount to duress or misrepresentation voiding any resulting agreement. Furthermore, the rules of fraud and deceit are generally applicable to lawyers' negotiations. Whether misrepresentations will either undercut agreement or subject lawyers to a potential damage action largely depends upon whether the disadvantaged party reasonably relied on the statements. Even when the misrepresentations do not result in an unenforceable agreement, third party reliance on a lawyer's statements made during negotiations may nevertheless expose lawyers to liability for resulting damages. Finally, there are emerging duties of good faith owed to third parties in negotiations — duties to supply certain necessary information and not to negotiate without the expectation of any agreement. A requirement of good faith negotiations may be judicially enforced directly in litigation negotiation and may also develop independently into a basis for tort liability analogous to the existing abuse of process action. . . .

§ 15.03 Settlement Agreements

[A] Settlement as the Norm in Litigation

"I learned nothing about settlements in law schools, and yet that was the nature of my practice. 90% of all civil lawsuits are settled." — United States District Judge Richard A. Enslen of Kalamazoo, Michigan, at the Conference on Litigation Management at Yale Law School, Oct. 4, 1985, *quoted in Alternatives to the High Cost of Litigation*, Oct. 1985, at 18 (Center for Public Resources publication). *See also* Lee, *Some Comments on Negotiation and Settlement*, 4 Am. J. of Trial Advoc. 277 (1980).

This statement is really about two things. First, it makes the point that settlement is the norm. Second, and less obviously, it makes the point that there are lawyering skills that must be brought to bear on the settlement process. A person unfamiliar with the process might conclude that settled cases involve trivial attorney input, in comparison to those that are tried — but the conclusion would be erroneous. Consider the following.

PROBLEM E

BLAKE v. WILLISTON PHARMACEUTICALS, INC. Andrew Blake's attorney has written a demand letter to your client, Williston Pharmaceuticals, Inc., claiming damages from the ingestion of an over-the-counter medicine by his son, Andrew Jr. After investigating the matter, you have concluded that the claim is possibly subject to defense, but is substantial. You have negotiated with Blake's attorney and have tentatively agreed to pay $40,000 in exchange for a release of all liability. In drafting the papers, you begin with a form containing a general release of all claims and an agreement to the entry of a dismissal with prejudice. (An example appears at the very end of the Appendix to Chapter 2.) You know that this document has been used for the satisfactory resolution of many other claims. In this case, while you would prefer not to pay anything, you have concluded that the ability to buy peace for a little over the "nuisance value" of the suit makes settlement attractive. Are there any other considerations to which you should be alert in settling this case? See the next section.

[B] The Enforcement and Effects of Releases

SPECTOR v. K-MART CORPORATION
99 A.D.2d 605, 471 N.Y.S.2d 711 (1984)

MEMORANDUM DECISION. . . .

Plaintiff allegedly sustained ill effects from the use of Selacryn, a prescription drug manufactured by SmithKline Beckman Corporation, and Colchicine, both of which medications he purchased from K-Mart Corporation between July 2 and November 19, 1979. On January 26, 1982, plaintiff executed a general release to SmithKline in which he settled all of his claims for damages for personal injuries arising out of the ingestion of Selacryn "including, but not limited to, all liability for contribution and/or indemnity." He was paid $40,000 as consideration by SmithKline. By service of a complaint dated October 18, 1982, plaintiff commenced the underlying action against K-Mart, stating causes of action in negligence, strict products liability and breach of warranty. Following joinder of issue, K-Mart served a third-party summons and complaint upon SmithKline seeking contribution or indemnification. Special Term denied SmithKline's CPLR 3211 (subd. [a], par. 5) motion to dismiss both the complaint and third-party complaint. For the reasons which follow, we affirm.

Essentially, SmithKline reasons that since the subject release, by its terms, also released K-Mart, both the principal action and third-party action must fall pursuant to the mandate of section 15-108 (subd. [a]) of the General Obligations Law. We disagree. That section provides that a release given to one of two or more tort-feasors does not extend to the remaining tort-feasors "unless its terms expressly so provide." The statute was designed to eliminate the inequities existent under the common-law rule where a general release given to one wrongdoer discharged all others (*see Williams v. Pitts*, 40 A.D.2d 1057, 1058, 338 N.Y.S.2d 969). Consistent with this purpose, section 15-108 has been construed to require an express designation by name or other specific identification of which parties are intended to be released. . . .

Here, the release stated that SmithKline and "all other persons, firms, or corporations" were released from liability for plaintiff's ingestion of Selacryn. In our view, this broad language fails to satisfy the statutory requirement. When read in context, the quoted language constitutes more of an attempt to insulate the entire corporate structure of SmithKline than to release some outside entity such as K-Mart. It follows that SmithKline may not rely on a purported unspecified release of K-Mart in seeking dismissal of the third-party complaint. Nor would dismissal be appropriate pursuant to subdivision (b) of section 15-108 of the General Obligations Law, which provides, in pertinent part, that a released tort-feasor is relieved "from liability to any other person for contribution as provided in article fourteen of the civil practice law and rules." This provision applies only to claims for contribution under CPLR article 14. . . .

Where, as here, a product claim against a retailer may give rise to an indemnity claim against the manufacturer (*see Guyot v. Al Charyn, Inc.*, 69 A.D.2d 79, 417 N.Y.S.2d 941; 2 Weinberger, New York Products Liability, § 24.03 p. 3; Restatement Torts 2d, § 886[B]), the third-party complaint should not be dismissed. . . .

Order affirmed, with costs to plaintiff.

NOTES AND QUESTIONS

(1) *The Parties Released: Generality.* The *Spector* case represents the nightmare of every settling lawyer: the fear that the release, though drafted in the most all-encompassing language, is ineffective to extinguish all claims, or fails to exonerate all persons or entities identified with the defendant, so that the suit must be defended all over again, with the very real possibility of double liability. In the situation shown in *Spector*, the defendant understandably may wish to make the release as global as possible, because it is difficult to anticipate specifically every particular defendant whom the plaintiff might next sue. However, as *Spector* indicates, that strategy is likely to be ineffective in states that require identification of released parties (a common rule). Consider the language incorporated into the release at the end of the Chapter 2 Appendix, which exonerates "each [litigant's] successors and assigns, and each other's related corporations, partnerships, or business entities, through or with which each, respectively, does business, and also all of each other's present and past officers, directors, employees, representatives, and agents," as well as the primary disputants. Would this language be sufficient to prevent a litigant such as Spector from suing the corporation's president on the same claim the very next week? Would it protect a separate corporation that is a subsidiary of the defendant and that conducts all of the defendant's marketing operations? What about an independent jobber who purchases from the defendant and then sells to retailers? Finally, would this language adequately deal with the situation in *Spector* itself? [Note: One solution might be to include a provision for indemnification of the defendant by the plaintiff. *See* section [C] below.]

(2) *The Claims Released: Generality.* For similar reasons, a defendant does not wish to pay money for the release of a given claim only to be sued the next week in the same court by the same plaintiff on a different theory. Thus the Chapter 2 Appendix release covers all "claims, demands, controversies, contracts, actions or causes of action which either [litigant] has held or may now or in the future own or hold, or which the heirs, executors, assigns, successors, or administrators of either hereafter can, shall, or may have, own or hold, for or by reason of any matter, cause or thing whatsoever occurring or existing prior to the date of this agreement, whether or not now known, including but not limited to all claims [in the present suit] or which could have been asserted therein by amendment, counterclaim or other addition." (Sometimes the efforts at global coverage describe the bases of the released claims by amusing but vivid language, such as anything existing "from the beginning of the world to the present day.") A "specific" release, as opposed to these "general" releases, releases only a particular claim. For an example, see *Marchello v. Lenox Hill Hospital*, 107 A.D.2d 566, 483 N.Y.S.2d 305 (1st Dept.

1985) (plaintiff gave release for leg burns due to medical malpractice, but later sued for "drop-foot" condition that developed as result of burns; held, release also extinguished claim in second suit). Should the defendant in *Marchello* have insisted upon a general release in the first place? When should a plaintiff, although agreeing to settle, resist giving a general release?

(3) *The Persons Whose Claims Are Released: Generality.* In the *Spector* situation, counsel for the defendant should also ask himself whether, under the applicable law, the injured child's father or mother might have their own claims (*e.g.*, for loss of the child's society or companionship), which they might assert in the same court the following week. There may be other potential claimants (*e.g.*, a retailer or other person in the distribution chain with whom the plaintiff has already, previously settled).

(4) *The "Mutual General Release": Should the Plaintiff Demand a Global Release, Too?* In many kinds of litigation, particularly business litigation, the plaintiff should think about future liability, too. If the plaintiff receives payment for goods sold and gives a "unilateral" general release (as opposed to a mutual one), the defendant may bring suit against the plaintiff the following week on a complex antitrust theory that is not within the compulsory counterclaim rule. If this possibility is suspected, the solution may be for the plaintiff to insist that its consideration include not only payment but also a mutual general release. For an example, see *Sawyer v. First City Financial Corporation*, 124 Cal. App. 3d 390, 177 Cal. Rptr. 398 (1981), in which a mutual general release providing that it would "inure to the benefit of the parties and their respective employees" was held effective to protect the officers of a claiming party in a subsequent suit in which they were defendants.

(5) *Enforceability as to Persons under Disability to Settle: The Need for a "Friendly Suit."* Settlements in some situations or with some parties may be legally ineffective. For example, many jurisdictions have rules requiring court approval of settlements with minors. A mere release signed by the minor or her guardian, even after payment, may not prevent the minor and her guardian from suing again on the same claim. The solution, generally, is to file a "friendly suit" even if the parties have agreed upon all the terms of settlement. [How should this consideration affect your analysis of Problem B, above?] For an example of a different kind of claimed disability affecting the validity of settlement, see the following case.

RUNYAN v. NATIONAL CASH REGISTER CORPORATION, 787 F.2d 1039 (6th Cir. 1986). NCR's general counsel informed Runyan, an experienced labor attorney, that the company planned to terminate him for unsatisfactory performance. Runyan, then 59, responded that his termination "was related to age discrimination" in violation of the Age Discrimination in Employment Act (ADEA). After several subsequent discussions, the parties executed a written "Consulting Agreement." NCR later agreed to increase the minimum in exchange for a release of all claims. The release specifically covered all claims "arising out of the course of my employment and/or the termination of any employment," as well as any other claim Runyan might have "by reason of any matter, cause or thing whatsoever from the beginning of the world to the day of the date of these presents." Runyan accepted the increased compensation. After the expiration of the consulting agreement, Runyan promptly filed a complaint of age discrimination against NCR with the Secretary of Labor and later brought an ADEA action in a federal District Court.

Runyan sought to avoid the effect of his release by reliance on cases decided under the Fair Labor Standards Act (FLSA), which provides for a standard minimum wage and requires extra compensation for overtime work. In such cases as *Brooklyn Savings Bank v. O'Neil*, 324 U.S. 697 (1945), and *Schulte, Inc, v. Gangi*, 328 U.S. 108 (1946), the Supreme Court held that "due to the unequal bargaining power as between employer and employee," protected workers were forbidden to waive their rights under the FLSA; "neither wages nor the damages for withholding them are capable of reduction by compromise. . . ." The ADEA expressly incorporates the enforcement provisions of the FLSA, and therefore, Runyan claimed that his release was void and of no effect, although he had received his increased compensation as express consideration for it.

The Sixth Circuit disagreed with Runyan and upheld a dismissal of his ADEA claim. The en banc court reasoned as follows:

> [W]e are satisfied that the present case concerns an issue that the Supreme Court in *Gangi* specifically left undecided. In this case, a bona fide dispute does exist. . . . The dispute is not over legal issues. . . . Rather, the parties contest factual issues concerning the motivation and intent behind NCR's decision to discharge Runyan. . . .
>
> . . . Runyan is not among the "lowest paid segment of the nation's workers," . . . a factor which the Court in *O'Neil* and *Gangi* deemed very important. Rather, Runyan is a well-paid, well-educated labor lawyer with many years of experience in this area. Indeed, evidence in the record suggests Runyan tried to take advantage of NCR by taking the full benefit of a reasonable and understood bargain, while attempting to part with what he thought might be illusory consideration in return. . . .
>
> In determining whether an ADEA settlement and release is valid, a court should apply the principles expressed by Justice Frankfurter [in his dissent in *Gangi*] that encourage "amicable settlement of honest differences . . . where overreaching or exploitation is not inherent in the situation." . . .

NOTES AND QUESTIONS

(1) *The Authority of the Parties to Settle, Free of Interference by the Court: Gardiner v. A.H. Robins Co., 747 F.2d 1180, 1189-90 (8th Cir. 1984).* The policy expressed in *Gangi, O'Neil,* and (for that matter) in *Runyan,* in opposition to settlements unsupervised by a court, is unusual and is a consequence of statutory interpretation of the intent of Congress. Indeed, the more general principle seems to be that the parties are free to settle in most instances without unwarranted intervention by the court — subject, always, to ordinary contract principles such as fraud or duress. In addition to *Gardiner, supra, see United States v. Altman,* 750 F.2d 684 (8th Cir. 1984); *United States v. City of Miami,* 614 F.2d 1322 (5th Cir. 1980). Should these principles be extended to ADEA and FLSA claims?

(2) *Release of § 1983 Claims as a Condition of Discretionary Dismissal of Criminal Charges: Should It Be Effective?* The defendant is charged with assaulting a police officer. As is frequently the case, defendant claims that the officer assaulted her, and as is also frequently the case, the evidence is ambiguous and conflicting — it depends upon whether the officer used a reasonable amount of force in effecting arrest. The defendant's counsel points out that the defendant has since led an exemplary life and wants to go to law school; she requests that the prosecutor move for dismissal in an exercise of prosecutorial discretion. Recognizing that the prosecutor would regard it as unfair for the defendant

to sue the police officer under the civil rights statute promptly after the discretionary dismissal, she suggests that her client execute a release of all claims she may have against the officer, including any claims under § 1983. Should releases of § 1983 claims as a condition of dismissal of criminal charges be void as a matter of public policy? Or should the transaction proposed by this defense attorney be permissible? *See Rumery v. Town of Newton*, 778 F.2d 66 (1st Cir. 1985) (in subsequent § 1983 suit, court held release "void as against public policy," even though procured with participation of accused's attorney).

(3) *Can Governmental Defendants Condition Settlement Advantageous to the Plaintiff on Waiver of Statutory Fees by Plaintiff's Attorneys? Evans v. Jeff D., 743 F.2d 648 (9th Cir. 1984), rev'd, 475 U.S. 717 (1986).* Class counsel in this constitutional institutional reform litigation received an offer he couldn't refuse: the state offered relief that probably exceeded what could be won by the plaintiff in a trial, but on one condition — that all attorney's fees under the civil rights attorney's fee statute be waived. The plaintiff's counsel settled, but pursued the argument that this condition was void. In *Evans v. Jeff D., supra*, the Supreme Court upheld the settlement — including the waiver of attorney's fees that the government defendants had made an express condition of it.

§ 15.03[B] Appendix A Settlement Agreement

Read (or re-read) the Release and Settlement Agreement in *George Miller Co. v. Compudata, Inc.*, which appears at the end of the Appendix to Chapter 2, *supra*.

[C] Other Common Clauses in Settlement Agreements

Indemnity Agreements: A Solution to the Problem of Spector v. K-Mart, supra? It is not uncommon for a settlement agreement to provide that the payee indemnifies the payor for any further claims or expenses that she may incur as a result of the incident made the basis of the suit. After all, the defendant is the one paying money to the plaintiff; therefore, it is sometimes not inappropriate for the defendant to insist that the plaintiff ensure that this payment is all that the defendant will be required to pay on account of the plaintiff's claims. The following clause is an example:

> As further part of the consideration for the payment of the above sum of money by KEYWEST SAVINGS ASSOCIATION, we, for ourselves, our heirs, executors, administrators, legal representatives, successors, and assigns, do hereby agree to indemnify and hold harmless KEYWEST SAVINGS ASSOCIATION from any and all claims, demands, damages, losses, expenses, actions and causes of action of whatsoever nature or character which have been or which may hereafter be asserted by any person, firm, corporation or any other legal entity whatsoever resulting from either or both of (1) a claim through or under either or both of us arising out of, relating to, in connection with or resulting from the above described, including, but expressly not limited to, any claim for contribution in the above described or any subsequent suit, or (2) a breach of either or both of us of any part of this agreement.

W. Dorsaneo & D. Crump, *Texas Civil Procedure: Pretrial Litigation* § 11.05 (2d ed. 1983). Notice that this clause covers "expenses" as well as claims; does it cover the defendant's attorney's fees for the defense of a subsequent suit for contribution or indemnity? (It might or might not, depending upon how it is construed). Would it protect SmithKline in the situation in *Spector v. K-Mart*? (Presumably, after Spector sued K-Mart and K-Mart made its third-party claim against SmithKline, SmithKline would itself file a third-party claim against Spector, completing the circle! And it then would move for summary judgment or judgment on the pleadings.)

Warranties. It is common for the defendant to insist that the plaintiff warrant that she is competent and under no disability to sign the release and has not assigned the claim. This clause may provide some slight protection against the situation in which the plaintiff is prohibited from settling (although a plaintiff disenabled from settling is probably disenabled from giving a warranty that will support an effective claim for damages for its breach).

Attorney's Fees. It is not uncommon for a settlement agreement to provide that a party breaching the agreement is liable for the other party's attorney's fees. The plaintiff should ensure that the provision is mutual (and may wish to insist that the clause provide for payment to the prevailing party in any litigation over the agreement, whether or not it results in a finding of breach).

Prevention of Fraud Claims. One of the ways in which releases can be invalidated is by a showing that they are affected by fraud. The party seeking invalidation is usually the plaintiff, who may claim that suppression of discovery material or statements made during settlement negotiations resulted in misrepresentations that fraudulently induced her to enter into the agreement. To discourage such a claim, the defendant may insist upon a clause to the effect that neither party has relied upon any statement or information provided by the other but instead has made independent investigation of the claim (an example of such a clause is in the release and settlement agreement in the Appendix to Chapter 2, above).

"Keep Them Honest" Clause. On the other hand, the plaintiff may be acutely aware that the settlement value of the claim depends upon information known only to the defendant, and may therefore insist upon a warranty by defendant that she has made full disclosure and knows that the plaintiff has relied on the information provided. This approach is sometimes called a "keep them honest" clause. A common usage of it is in divorce settlement agreements, for the protection of the spouse who is less knowledgeable about the extent of the parties' property and is dependent upon the other's inventory.

Disposition of Suit and Tying Up Loose Ends. At the same time that the release and agreement is signed, the parties should execute documents disposing of the suit (a joint agreed motion and either an order of dismissal with prejudice or a take-nothing judgment). It may be necessary to execute other documents to tie up loose ends (*e.g.*, a release of *lis pendens* in a suit affecting land). The defendant may insist that the check be made out jointly to the plaintiff and her attorney (who, if her fee is contingent, may also be a holder of part of the claim). The defendant commonly sends all of the papers, including the executed check, to the plaintiff's attorney with the (often written) understanding that the check will not be negotiated until the plaintiff and her attorney have executed them and the order disposing of the case has been entered.

[D] Adjudicative Effects of Settlement, Structured Settlements, and "Mary Carter" Agreements

NOTE ON ADJUDICATIVE EFFECTS OF SETTLEMENT

The Basic Notion: Release of One Claim May Extinguish Other Claims against Other Defendants. The plaintiff should be alert to the possibility that, in releasing her claim against one defendant, she may automatically affect claims against others. For example, the common law followed the "unity of release" rule: A release of one joint tortfeasor automatically was a release of all. This inflexible rule discouraged settlement, and it has been replaced in many jurisdictions by the approach shown in *Spector v. K-Mart*, above: A release releases those identified in it, plus other categories of persons identified by statute or decisional law.

Partial Release of Claims against Joint Tortfeasors. In particular, it is common for a given jurisdiction to have a rule that partially extinguishes claims against joint tortfeasors upon the release of any one of them. There are many different patterns followed by different states, and the rules can be extremely complex when applied to litigation with many different kinds of parties. One of the simplest approaches would be to provide that half the claim is released when one of two tortfeasors is released. *E.g., Palestine Contractors, Inc. v. Perkins*, 386 S.W.2d 764 (Tex. 1964) (but this holding has been superseded in the most common situations to which it originally was applied). A more modern approach is to release the percentage of damage found by the jury to have been attributable to the released tortfeasor's negligence or to credit the amount of the settlement to the satisfaction of the judgment. *E.g.*, Tex. Rev. Civ. Stat. Ann. art. 2212a (comparative negligence). *See also Spector v. K-Mart, Inc., supra* (adjudicative effects of settlement would have extinguished claim for contribution but not indemnity).

Structured Settlements; How to Read the Case of Franck v. Polaris E-Z Go Div. of Textron, Inc., Below. The case that follows is complex because it contains two issues: first, the adjudicative effect of a settlement with one tortfeasor and, second, how to treat the settlement if it provides for periodic future payments rather than for a lump sum. California's settlement provision, in general, is simple: It reduces judgments against other tortfeasors by the amount of the settlement. But how is a structured settlement to be treated? The defendant argues that all future payments should be added together, and the sum subtracted from the award. This approach would make for a very large reduction. The plaintiff argues that the present cash value should be subtracted, since after all, that is the "real" value of the settlement. This approach would result in a much smaller reduction of the judgment against the second tortfeasor.

FRANCK v. POLARIS E-Z GO DIV. OF TEXTRON, INC.

157 Cal. App. 3d 1107, 204 Cal. Rptr. 321 (1984)

CARR, ASSOCIATE JUSTICE.

In this appeal we consider an issue of first impression: the proper reduction of a damages award against a nonsettling tortfeasor under Code of Civil Procedure section 877 when plaintiff and other defendants agree to a structured settlement calling for future periodic payments.

Defendant Polaris E-Z Go Division of Textron, Inc. ("Polaris") was found liable for injuries sustained by plaintiff while riding on a snowmobile manufactured by Polaris. Damages were assessed at $300,000.

Prior to trial, plaintiff settled with defendants Todd and Robert Weichers (respectively, the driver and owner of the snowmobile) for a total of $215,000. Under the settlement they agreed to pay $25,000 upon court approval of the settlement and a total of $190,000 in future periodic payments, commencing in 1983 and continuing until the year 2000. The Weichers' insurance had a single accident coverage limit of $100,000. After paying $25,000, the insurance company used the balance of $75,000 to purchase an annuity contract that would finance the future payments of $190,000. Another defendant, the seller of the snowmobile, settled for a lump sum payment of $2,500. The court approved the settlement.

After finding against Polaris and fixing damages at $300,000, the trial court was requested by both parties to determine, in light of the settlement agreement, the amount by which the damages award should be reduced pursuant to Code of Civil Procedure section 877, subdivision (a). Plaintiff contended the award should be reduced only by the amount of cash presently paid under the settlement and the *present cash value or cost* of future payments ($102,500: $2,500 cash from seller; $25,000 cash from Weichers; $75,000 premium for annuity). Polaris contended the award should be reduced by the *total amount to be paid* under the settlement agreement ($217,500: $2,500 cash from seller; $25,000 cash from Weichers; $190,000 in future payments). The trial court decided in favor of Polaris.

Plaintiff appeals from the damages portion of the judgment. Polaris cross-appeals from the portion of the judgment finding it liable for plaintiff's injuries. . . .

On January 23, 1977, plaintiff Jan "Cricket" Franck, then 11 years old, was riding on a snowmobile with her friend, Stephanie Weichers, and Stephanie's brother, Todd. [An accident resulted.] When the snowmobile came to a rest, plaintiff was lying on the ground with her right foot lodged in the moving track portion at the rear of the machine. . . .

The trial court found the sharp metal cleats of the snowmobile were defectively designed or defectively guarded and such defectively designed cleats proximately caused plaintiff's injuries by snagging her foot and pulling it into the snowmobile's suspension system above the track belt. The court found plaintiff sustained damages of $300,000. Subtracting the total amount of the settlement, the court entered judgment against Polaris for $82,500. . . .

Section 877, subdivision (a), of the Code of Civil Procedure provides: "Where a release, dismissal with or without prejudice, or a covenant not to sue or not to enforce judgment is given in good faith before verdict or judgment to one or more of a number of tortfeasors claimed to be liable for the same tort — [¶] (a) It shall not discharge any other such tortfeasor from liability unless its terms so provide, but it shall reduce the claims against the others in the amount stipulated by the release, the dismissal or the covenant, or in the amount of the consideration paid for it whichever is the greater. . . ."

At issue here is the amount of reduction to which a nonsettling tortfeasor is entitled in the case of a structured settlement calling for future periodic payments. Polaris contends we must literally read the words "amount stipulated by the release" and reduce the award by the total amount of future payments stipulated in the settlement agreement. Plaintiff and amicus curiae California Trial Lawyers Association contend the future payments must be discounted to their present cash value to arrive at the amount of reduction to which Polaris is entitled. We agree with plaintiff and amicus curiae.

Our consideration of this issue is guided by two policy interests strongly supported in the law. First is the maximization of recovery to the plaintiff for the amount of her injury to the extent that negligence or fault of others has contributed to it. Second is the encouragement of settlement of claims, a policy reflected in section 877. . . .

Plaintiff has obtained a judgment of $300,000; therefore she *presently* is entitled to recover that amount. It is simple economics that money received by plaintiff in the year 2000 is not worth as much as the same amount of money if she received it today. If we discount the award by the total amount of future payments ($190,000), in the year

2000 plaintiff will have received a total amount of money that is presently worth less than $300,000. Only by discounting the future payments to their present cash value and reducing the award by that amount will plaintiff receive the recovery to which she *presently* is entitled.

The unfairness of Polaris' approach is demonstrated by consideration of the hypothetical situation wherein a plaintiff obtains a structured settlement for future payments in an amount *equal* to the judgment award against a nonsettling tortfeasor. Under Polaris' theory, the nonsettling tortfeasor would be completely relieved of liability and the plaintiff would have only a settlement worth much less than the amount to which he or she is entitled at the time of judgment. . . .

Polaris complains that if the future payments are reduced to their present cash value, plaintiff will receive a tax "windfall" because the future payments will not be subject to federal income taxation (26 U.S.C. § 104, subd. (a)(2)) but if plaintiff received the present value in a lump sum and invested it in an annuity, the income derived therefrom would be taxable.

This consideration is irrelevant. Congress and the Legislature provide many tax benefits, and each instance reflects a policy decision to benefit the recipient of the particular type of income in question. . . .

Moreover, Polaris' position would require speculation of the most amorphous nature. We cannot predict what the tax consequences would be over the next 17 years if plaintiff received a presently valued lump sum rather than future periodic payments. . . .

The second consideration on this issue is the need to encourage settlement of claims. "[I]t is the policy of the law to discourage litigation and to favor compromises of doubtful rights and controversies, made either in or out of court. Settlement agreements 'are highly favored as productive of peace and goodwill in the community, and reducing the expense and persistency of litigation.' Indeed, it has been said that a major goal of section 877 is the 'encouragement of settlements.' " . . .

Structured settlements appeared on the California scene quite recently and are becoming increasingly commonplace. Such settlements have advantages for both plaintiffs and defendants. Plaintiffs receive tax-free periodic income over a period of time, thereby preventing recoveries from being squandered and ensuring that money is received in the future at times when it is actually needed. Defendants, on the other hand, are able to offer plaintiffs large settlements at a relatively small up-front cost by spreading payments out over a period of years through an annuity. These factors work to further encourage settlements.

The interpretation of section 877 urged by Polaris would work diametrically against the purpose of section 877 by discouraging structured settlements in multiple defendant cases. Few plaintiffs would be willing to enter into structured settlements unless they could obtain future payments large enough to cover the possibility of a nonsettling defendant being relieved of paying damages. The large amounts demanded by plaintiffs would in turn discourage defendants from settling. Using tax considerations to reduce a nonsettling defendant's liability would further discourage structured settlements by nullifying their tax advantage. Moreover, Polaris' interpretation of the law would considerably lessen the incentive for nonsettling defendants to settle. If a plaintiff settles with other defendants for large future payments, a nonsettling defendant will be more willing to go to trial on the chance that the court will find damages in an amount equal to or less than the amount of future payments under the settlement. Such a system would effectively reward defendants with liability for not settling.

Accordingly, we hold that [t]he amount by which the judgment award against a nonsettling defendant is reduced under section 877 [s]hall be the present cash value of the future payments. Polaris is entitled to a reduction in the $300,000 award of the amount of cash presently paid to plaintiff under the settlement ($27,500) plus the present cash value of $190,000 in future payments. . . .

. . . The portion of the judgment with respect to net damages against Polaris is reversed and remanded with instructions to the trial court to take evidence on and determine the present cash value of future payments to be made under the settlement agreement, and to render judgment in an amount which represents the difference between $300,000 less the present cash payments plus the present cash value of the future judgments.

NOTES AND QUESTIONS

(1) *The Present Cash Value of a Structured Settlement May Be Much, Much Less than the Sum of Payments; Ensuring Solvency of the Annuity Provider.* Franck's settlement with the Weichers provided for them (or their insurer) to pay $190,000 in eighteen annual future payments. A plaintiff's attorney should be careful to evaluate the present cash value of such a settlement. Valuation consists primarily of the application of an algebraic formula with a selected rate of interest, but there are commercially available services that will perform the calculation for either party. It is important to realize that, since the algebra involves an exponential function, the discount can be very large, particularly if payments are spread over many years and the interest rate selected is high. [Notice that, in this case, the $190,000 annuity was purchased for only $75,000.] Another problem is the need to ensure that the annuity provider will be solvent when the last payments are due, decades from now. Plaintiff's counsel should consult solvency rating services and refuse agreement to "structureds" payable by any but high-rated providers.

(2) *Protecting the Non-Settling Tortfeasor by Assuring that the Reduction Approximates Full Settlement Value: The Problem of the "War Chest" Used Against the Least Liable Defendant.* One problem with multiple-tortfeasor settlements is that there is a tendency for the plaintiff to settle, first, with the "most guilty" defendant. The plaintiff then has a "war chest" with which to pursue the least guilty defendant, and may be able to try the case against this defendant with the hope of getting large damages. The problem is that the least-guilty defendant should have the benefit of reduction that reflects full and fair settlement value of the claim against the other tortfeasor. To address this problem, California's statute provides that the settlement releases contribution or equitable indemnity claims only if made in "good faith." Cal. Code Civ. Pro. §§ 877, 877.6. Application of this doctrine can be surprisingly complex; *see Torres v. Union Pacific Ry. Co.*, 157 Cal. App. 3d 499, 203 Cal. Rptr. 825 (1984) ("sliding scale" settlement, whose amount depended upon recovery against second defendant, was made in good faith); *see generally Tech-Bilt, Inc. v. Woodward-Clyde & Associates,* 38 Cal. 3d 488, 213 Cal. Rptr. 256 (1985) (setting out factors to determine good faith, including the court's own "rough" estimate of plaintiff's total recovery and the settling defendant's proportionate liability). The advent of California's Proposition 51, which eliminates joint and several liability for non-economic damages, has confused this issue further. *See* Klein & Day, *Prop. 51 and the House that Tech Built,* 6 Cal. Lawyer 25 (Nov. 1986). Another way of addressing the problem (perhaps more simply) is to allow the non-settling defendant to obtain a jury finding that fixes the liability the settling defendant would have faced, and to subtract this amount from the award. *See, e.g.*, Tex. Rev. Civ. Stat. Ann. art. 2212a (comparative negligence); *see also* N.Y. Gen. Obligation Law § 15-108.

This latter method is more precise, but it produces uncertainty on the plaintiff's part as to the effect of the settlement at the time, and it may therefore have a tendency to discourage settlement.

(3) *"Mary Carter" Agreements.* Sometimes, in a multiple-defendant case, the plaintiff may settle with one defendant, but agree to pay back portions of the settlement from amounts recovered against other defendants. There are many ways to structure such an arrangement, but the common characteristic of these "Mary Carter" agreements, as they are called, is that they give the settling defendant an interest in the recovery against the other defendants — and, hence, they create an alliance between the settling defendant and the plaintiff. Further, the settling defendant remains in the case as a party. Some jurisdictions have treated Mary Carter agreements as against public policy and unenforceable. California's approach, exemplified in *Torres v. Union Pacific Ry. Co., supra,* is to subject such agreements to "good faith" scrutiny; in addition, California requires disclosure of such agreements, and they are admissible in evidence before the jury, even though settlements generally are not admissible. Consider the following case; *but cf. Mary Carter Agreements: Unfair and Unnecessary,* 32 Sw. L.J. 779 (1978). [*See also Abbott Ford, Inc. v. Superior Court,* 43 Cal. 3d 858, 741 P.2d 124, 239 Cal. Rptr. 626 (1987), in which the California Supreme Court upheld the use of "Mary Carter" agreements if the amount of the settlement "is within the reasonable range of the settling tortfeasor's proportional share of comparative liability for the plaintiff's injuries," to be determined on a case-by-case basis by considering fairness to the non-settling defendants.]

GENERAL MOTORS CORP. v. SIMMONS, 558 S.W.2d 855 (Tex. 1977). Plaintiff Simmons was injured when Johnston, an employee of Feld Truck Leasing Co., failed to stop at a traffic signal and drove into the left front door of Simmons' 1962 Chevrolet. The glass in the car window shattered and flew into Simmons' eyes, blinding him. As a result, Simmons had potential claims against Feld and Johnston (for negligence) and against General Motors, the manufacturer of Simmons' car (for product liability). Prior to trial, however, Simmons entered into a settlement with Feld and Johnston, by which they paid Simmons a sum of money of undisclosed amount. "Simmons . . . agreed also to pay Feld fifty percent of each dollar Simmons recovered against General Motors until Feld received 200,000 dollars." The case then went to trial solely against General Motors and resulted in a verdict and judgment in Simmons' favor for $1 million. General Motors appealed, arguing that the trial court had erred in excluding from the jury's consideration the agreement of Simmons to pay $200,000 back to Feld. The Texas Supreme Court agreed with General Motors and reversed:

> The traditional . . . rule is that settlement agreements between the plaintiff and a co-defendant should be excluded from the jury. A contrary rule would frustrate the policy favoring the settlement of lawsuits. . . . The plaintiff Simmons and also the settling defendants, Feld and Johnston, strongly insist that there was no harm in excluding the evidence or explanation about the agreement since it was made clear to General Motors, the court and the jury that Feld and Johnston were not adverse to Simmons and were adverse to General Motors. In fact the attorneys for Simmons, Feld and Johnston, and General Motors each explained to the jury that Simmons, Feld and Johnston were allies against General Motors. . . .
>
> . . . [This] was not an ordinary settlement agreement. By its terms, Feld acquired a direct financial interest in Simmons' lawsuit. The financial interest of parties and

witnesses in the success of a party is a proper subject of disclosure by direct evidence or cross-examination. While the alignment of the adversaries was disclosed, the jury did not know the extent of Feld's interest or that it was a financial interest which depended upon the amount of the judgment for Simmons. . . .

Agreements with a settling defendant who remains a party and retains a financial stake in the plaintiff's recovery have been called "Mary Carter" agreements since the 1967 Florida decision of *Booth v. Mary Carter Paint Co.*, 202 So. 2d 8 (Fla. App. 1967). Some courts have wholly voided the agreements as against public policy. *Lum v. Stinett*, 87 Nev. 402, 488 P.2d 347 (1971); *Trampe v. Wisconsin Telephone Co.*, 214 Wis. 210, 252 N.W. 675 (1934). . . . Most courts that have addressed the issue, while not declaring these agreements void, have permitted the disclosure of the contracts to the jury when offered by a non-settling defendant. . . .

Feld stood to recover one out of every two dollars from the first 400,000 dollars of a judgment against General Motors. That kind of interest is a proper subject of cross-examination and proof. . . . The exclusion of the evidence was harmful error and the judgment must be reversed for that reason.

NOTE ON REJECTIONS OF MARY CARTER AGREEMENTS

Texas and Florida Declare Mary Carter Agreements Void as Against Public Policy. Elbaor v. Smith, 845 S.W.2d 240 (Tex. 1992). In Elbaor, the Texas Supreme Court went a step further than it did in Simmons, and outlawed these controversial arrangements wherein settling defendants retain a financial stake in the plaintiff's case against non-settling defendants. The plaintiff Smith suffered a compound ankle fracture in a car accident, and after lengthy treatment and several operations, was left permanently disabled. In Smith's subsequent medical malpractice suit, several of the doctor defendants settled in Mary Carter agreements. This left the non-settling Dr. Elbaor to defend not only against the charges of the plaintiff, but also against the settling doctors, whose attorneys sat at Mr. Elbaor's table, but "vigorously assisted Ms. Smith in pointing the finger of culpability at Dr. Elbaor."

While the primary justification for Mary Carter agreements is that they encourage settlement, the Texas Supreme Court held instead that they frequently make litigation inevitable by granting the settling defendant veto power over any proposed settlement between the plaintiff and the remaining defendants. While the lower Texas court had taken extensive precautionary measures to minimize the dangers of Mary Carter agreements, the Supreme Court found that the agreements "skew the trial process, mislead the jury, promote unethical collusion among nominal adversaries, and create the likelihood that a less culpable defendant will be hit with the full judgment." Florida has also reached this result. *Dosdourian v. Carsten,* 624 So. 2d 241 (1993).

§ 15.04 Arbitration and Other Substitutes for Court Adjudication

[A] The Nature of Arbitration

PROBLEM F

THE CASE OF THE TILTED HOUSE, RECONSIDERED. Reconsider Problem B, above, in which Super Constructors, Inc. has proposed to your clients, Don and Kathleen Fuller, an agreement to arbitrate their claim for the tilted slab in the new house they bought from Super. Assume that you have accepted the proposal and have presented your case to the arbiters, who have been named as indicated in Problem B. The arbiters have considered the case entirely on the basis of written submissions, without hearing live witnesses. Their award requires Super to pay the current market value of the house to the Fullers; however, it expressly states that Super need not pay the Fullers' attorney's fees and is not liable for any penalty or exemplary damages. Under the applicable state law, it appears that a prevailing party is entitled to attorney's fees and to a $2,000 penalty provided for by state consumer protection litigation. Worst of all, you have since discovered that two of the three arbiters are members of the Greater Metropolitan Association of Home Builders, of which the president of Super is a past president. Was it wise for you to have entered into the agreement to arbitrate? If you are dissatisfied with the award, do you have grounds that will suffice for setting it aside and recovering other relief in court? Consider the following materials.

SPRINZEN v. NOMBERG

46 N.Y.2d 623, 389 N.E.2d 456, 415 N.Y.S.2d 974 (1979)

JASEN, JUDGE.

This appeal requires us to determine whether an arbitrator's award which enforces the terms of a restrictive covenant of employment is unenforceable as being contrary to public policy.

Respondent Murray Nomberg was employed by the petitioner Local 1115 Joint Board in April, 1973 as a business agent in its health-care division. . . .

Upon commencement of his employment with Local 1115 in April 1973, Nomberg signed an agreement which contained a restrictive covenant. . . . Nomberg agreed that "[u]pon the termination of his employment . . . he shall not directly or indirectly, within the States of New York, Pennsylvania, New Jersey and Connecticut . . . enter into or engage in organizing workers, either as an individual or as a part of a labor organization, for a period of five (5) years after the date of termination of his employment hereunder." The agreement also contained a sweeping arbitration clause which prescribed that "[a]ll complaints, disputes whatsoever of whatever kind or nature . . . concerning any provision of this contract . . . or otherwise . . . shall be submitted for arbitration" pursuant to a clearly delineated process.

In February, 1976, Nomberg left Local 1115 and began employment as a business representative for Local 144 of the Hotel, Hospital, Nursing Home and Allied Services Union, a union also involved in organizing and representing employees in the health-care field. With Local 144, Nomberg's geographical responsibilities included only Manhattan and Staten Island, areas with which he had no previous dealings.

Petitioner Local 1115 demanded arbitration to compel compliance with the terms of the restrictive covenant and to enjoin Nomberg from employment as a business representative for Local 144. The parties proceeded to arbitration, where Nomberg, after unsuccessfully contesting the partiality of the arbitrator named in the April, 1973 agreement, walked out of the hearing, refusing to participate further. After petitioner presented its case, the arbitrator ruled that Local 1115 was entitled to the relief sought and issued an award enjoining Nomberg from working for Local 144 until February 6, 1981, five years after his employment ceased with Local 1115, and further restrained Nomberg from engaging in any of the other practices and acts specifically prohibited by the restrictive covenant.

Petitioner moved to confirm the arbitrator's award, and Nomberg cross-moved to vacate the same, contending that his rights were prejudiced by the arbitrator's partiality and that the award itself was unjust. Special Term [i.e., the trial-level court] confirmed the award [i.e., upheld the results of the arbitration] and denied Nomberg's cross motion in all respects. On appeal, the Appellate Division, with two Justices dissenting, reversed and vacated the award, holding that "the arbitration award under the circumstances of this case [is] in contravention of public policy." [This court, however, now orders] a reversal and the judgment of Special Term confirming the award of the arbitrator reinstated. . . .

Over the years, courts have had not infrequent occasion to test restrictive covenants against the fabric of prevailing public policy. While it has been consistently asserted that the policy considerations against depriving the public of a person's industry and precluding an individual from pursuing his occupation [m]ust be weighed against the enforcement of such covenants . . . no hard-and-fast rules have yet been formulated. . . .

[A]n agreement to submit to arbitration disputes arising out of a contract . . . is now favorably recognized as an efficacious procedure whereby parties can select their own nonjudicial forum for the "private and practical" resolution of their disputes "with maximum dispatch and at minimum expense." (*Matter of Siegel [Lewis]*, 40 N.Y.2d 687, 689, 389 N.Y.S.2d 800, 801, 358 N.E.2d 484, 485, *mot. for rearg. den.* 41 N.Y.2d 901, 393 N.Y.S.2d 1028, 362 N.E.2d 640; *see, generally*, Siegel, *New York Practice* § 586).

In furtherance of the laudable purposes served by permitting consenting parties to submit controversies to arbitration, the law has adopted a policy of noninterference, with few exceptions, in this mode of dispute resolution. Quite simply, it can be said that the arbitrator is not bound to abide by, absent a contrary provision in the arbitration agreement, those principles of substantive law or rules of procedure which govern the traditional litigation process. (*E.g., Matter of Associated Teachers of Huntington v. Board of Educ.*, 33 N.Y.2d 229, 235, 351 N.Y.S.2d 670, 674, 306 N.E.2d 791, 794; *Lentine v. Fundaro*, 29 N.Y.2d 382, 385, 328 N.Y.S.2d 418, 421, 278 N.E.2d 633, 635.) An arbitrator's paramount responsibility is to reach an equitable result, and the courts will not assume the role of overseers to mold the award to conform to their sense of justice. Thus, an arbitrator's award will not be vacated for errors of law and fact committed by the arbitrator . . . and "[e]ven where the arbitrator states an intention to apply a law, and then misapplies it, the award will not be set aside (*Matter of Schine Enterprises [Real Estate Portfolio of N.Y.]*, 26 N.Y.2d 799, 801, 309 N.Y.S.2d 222, 223, 257 N.E.2d 665, 666)." . . .

Despite this policy of according an arbitrator seemingly unfettered discretion in matters submitted to him by the consent of the parties, it is the established law in this State that an award which is violative of public policy will not be permitted to stand. . . . The courts, however, must exercise due restraint in this regard, for the preservation of the arbitration process and the policy of allowing parties to choose a nonjudicial forum, embedded in freedom to contract principles, must not be disturbed by courts, acting under the guise of public policy, wishing to decide the dispute on its merits, for arguably every controversy has at its core some issue requiring the application, or weighing, of policy considerations. Thus, there are now but a few matters of concern which have been recognized as so intertwined with overriding public policy considerations as to either place them beyond the bounds of the arbitration process itself or mandate the vacatur of awards which do violence to the principles upon which such matters rest.

Some examples would be instructive. It has been held that [in New York] an arbitrator is without power to award punitive damages, a sanction reserved solely to the State

(*Garrity v. Lyle Stuart, Inc.*, 40 N.Y.2d 354, 386 N.Y.S.2d 831, 353 N.E.2d 793, *supra; Matter of Publishers' Assn. of N.Y. City [Newspaper Union]*, 280 App. Div. 500, 114 N.Y.S.2d 401), and that an agreement to arbitrate, when sought to be enforced by a lender, cannot divest the courts of their responsibility to determine whether a purported sales agreement is in fact a usurious loan, and thus illegal. [Note that these limits in New York might not be followed in other jurisdictions and would be preempted by the Federal Arbitration Act today when it applies. *See* Notes 1–3 below — Eds.]

[The court cites several additional matters that an arbitrator cannot order under New York law as a matter of public policy, including liquidations of insolvent insurers, access to confidential teacher personnel files, or the granting of teacher tenure. Again, these nonarbitrable matters might be dealt with differently by other jurisdictions and might be altered by the Federal Act when it applies.]

These illustrations of instances where courts will intervene in the arbitration process are, without apparent exception, cases in which public policy considerations, embodied in statute or decisional law, prohibit, in an absolute sense, particular matters being decided or certain relief being granted by an arbitrator. Stated another way, the courts must be able to examine an arbitration agreement or an award on its face, without engaging in extended factfinding or legal analysis, and conclude that public policy precludes its enforcement. This is so because, as has been previously noted, an arbitrator is free to apply his own sense of law and equity to the facts as he has found them to be in resolving a controversy.

Applying these principles to this case, we now hold that disputes involving restrictive covenants of employment can be, by mutual consent of the parties, submitted to arbitration, and an arbitrator's award which specifically enforces such covenants, even to the extent of enjoining an individual from engaging in like employment for a reasonable period of years in the future, will not be vacated on public policy grounds. . . .

[W]hile there may be some doubt whether we would have enforced the restrictive covenant now before us had this dispute been adjudicated in the courts, such consideration is irrelevant to the disposition of this case, for courts will not second-guess the factual findings or the legal conclusions of the arbitrator. The utility of the arbitration process itself is derived from its autonomy, and courts must honor the choice of the parties to have their controversy decided within this framework. . . .

In passing, we reject respondent's contention that the award must be vacated on the ground of the arbitrator's alleged bias. (CPLR 7511, subd. [b], para. 1, cl. [ii].) The arbitrator, known to respondent to have been designated by petitioner as an impartial arbitrator in various collective bargaining agreements between the union and certain employers, was expressly named in the April, 1973 agreement signed by the parties. The receipt of compensation from the union for his services is not sufficient to constitute bias. (*See Matter of Siegel [Lewis]*, 40 N.Y.2d 687, 689-690, 389 N.Y.S.2d 800, 802, 358 N.E.2d 484, 487, *supra*.) [Note that the Federal Arbitration Act has a somewhat different approach to this issue. *See* Note 3 below — Eds.]

Accordingly, the order of the Appellate Division should be reversed, with costs, and the judgment of Supreme Court, New York County, confirming the arbitrator's award reinstated.

NOTES AND QUESTIONS

(1) *The Arbiter's Authority: Lentine v. Fundaro, 29 N.Y.2d 382, 328 N.Y.S.2d 418, 278 N.E.2d 633 (1972).* In this case, the New York high court said that an arbiter exceeds

his authority if he makes a "completely irrational" award. For example, what if a contract contains an express damage limit, and the arbiter simply ignores the limit without finding it to be unenforceable or unconscionable? *See Granite Worsted Mills, Inc. v. Aaronson Cowen, Ltd.*, 25 N.Y.2d 451, 306 N.Y.S.2d 934, 255 N.E.2d 168 (1969) (award vacated). The arbiter's inability under New York law to award punitive damages apparently stems from the lack of clear standards for these awards, so that a party agreeing to arbitration might be surprised by the outcome. *See Garrity v. Lyle Stuart, Inc.*, cited in *Sprinzen.* Additionally, New York denies the arbiter the authority to award attorney's fees unless the agreement for arbitration so provides (although his award may cover the arbitrator's own fees and expenses). CPLR 7513. But these limits would not apply if the arbitration were conducted under the Federal Arbitration Act. *Mastrobuono v. Shearson Lehman Hutton, Inc.,* 514 U.S. 52 (1995). The Federal Act today is broad in coverage — see the subsection [C].

(2) *Does the Arbiter Have to Be "Neutral" or Disinterested? J.P. Stevens & Co. v. Rytex Corp., 34 N.Y.2d 123, 356 N.Y.S.2d 278, 312 N.E.2d 466 (1974).* In the *J.P. Stevens* case, the court vacated the award because the arbiter had been appointed "as a neutral," whereas in fact his firm had done undisclosed business worth millions of dollars with the prevailing party. But if the arbiter is not appointed as a "neutral," it will be very difficult to vacate her award on grounds of partiality falling short of actual fraud or corruption. For example, in *Matter of Siegel [Lewis]*, cited in *Sprinzen*, the court refused to vacate the appointment of two arbiters who were, respectively, the opposing party's attorney and accountant, who had extensive knowledge of the transaction because of their service to the opposing party. The court said: "Strange as it may seem to those steeped in the proscriptions of legal and judicial ethics, a fully known relationship between an arbitrator and a party, including one as close as employer and employee . . . or attorney and client . . . will not in itself disqualify the designee. Of course, if there has been a failure to disclose such an existing or past financial, business, family or social relationship, . . . the situation would be different. The consensual basis for the choice then would be lacking." The arbiter is required to take an oath to decide "faithfully and fairly," CPLR 7506(a), and cannot serve if unable to do so. Do these principles make sense? If both parties know about it, shouldn't they be allowed to agree to an arbiter who has prior knowledge of the events or a relationship to one (or both) of the parties?

(3) *The Federal Arbitration Act — Vacating the Award for Corruption, Partiality, Misconduct, or Manifest Disregard of Law: Greenberg v. Bear, Stearns & Co., 220 F.3d 22 (2d Cir. 2000).* The Federal Arbitration Act requires analogous but different (and perhaps slightly less broad) deference to the arbiter. An award can be vacated upon a showing of corruption, partiality, or misconduct. This standard cannot be met merely by proof of some relationship to the parties or issues; the evidence must contain some reason for inferring partiality (or corruption or misconduct). The circumstances of *Sprinzen v. Nomberg*, for example, might not have produced any difference on this issue if the FAA had been applicable.

The FAA also allows the award to be vacated if it is based upon "manifest disregard" of the law, as well as if its enforcement would violate public policy. Nevertheless, as the *Greenberg* case shows in upholding an award, the federal standard also is deferential to arbitration. The award is not subject to being vacated as readily as a court of appeals can reverse a district court, because the Act requires not merely an error of law, but "manifest" or obvious disregard of the law.

(4) *Breadth of the Federal Act: Any "Transaction Involving [Interstate] Commerce" That Includes a Written Agreement to Arbitrate.* The FAA enforces written agreements

to arbitrate whenever they involve a transaction in interstate commerce. As is indicated by the cases and notes that follow, the scope of the Act is broad, and it displaces state laws that restrict arbitration and that conflict with it.

[B] Procedure, Evidence, Precedent, and Enforcement

Procedure. Arbitration is not rigidly governed by procedural rules such as the federal or state rules of civil procedure, although there may be a statutory framework (particularly for enforcement). Such matters as scheduling, discovery, pleadings, and order of presentation at hearings may be governed by the agreement upon which arbitration is based, by agreement of the parties during the arbitration process, or by decision of the arbiter, tailored to the case. For example, the arbiter may allow depositions or document production on a more streamlined schedule than would be recognized in court.

Evidence. As *Sprinzen v. Nomberg* hints, the arbiter is not bound by the rules of evidence applicable to litigation in court, but may accept reasonable substitutes for that kind of evidence. Ironically, it sometimes happens that arbiters refuse to receive evidence that would be admissible in court under the rules of evidence.

Precedent. As *Sprinzen v. Nomberg* also indicates, the arbiter is not bound rigidly by most decisional law. This principle does not mean, however, that the application of precedent is irrelevant to arbitration. The arbiter normally will be persuaded by judicial or statutory precedent (and indeed her award is subject to vacatur if it is an "irrational" error of law or, under the FAA, if it is a "manifest disregard" of the law). In addition, certain arbitration reports exist, which give the results of arbitrations by reproducing opinions similar to judicial opinions; and the arbiter very well may regard these precedents as persuasive. Thus, briefing the case for the arbiter may closely resemble briefing the law for judicial adjudication in some cases.

Opinion; Statement of Reasons. The arbiter may not be bound to provide an opinion or statement of reasons; however, since confirmation or vacatur of the award may in some instances depend upon the basis of the award, it may be advisable for the arbiter to provide an opinion or statement of reasons.

Confirmation, Vacatur, and Enforcement. A prevailing party may apply for "confirmation" of the award in a court of proper jurisdiction. The confirmation entitles this party to a judgment carrying out the award, which can be enforced by the available judicial mechanisms. In New York, these matters are governed by CPLR 7510-7514, and are subject to a time limit of one year (after which the award becomes judicially nonenforceable, CPLR 215(5)). The opposing party may seek to vacate the award or may challenge it in response to an application for confirmation by asserting any of the available (but limited) defenses. *See* CPLR 7510-11. There is a split of authority regarding the time limit for confirming an arbitration award under the Federal Arbitration Act. In *Photopaint Technologies LLC v. Smartlens Corp.*, 335 F.3d 152 (2d Cir. 2003), the Second Circuit held that Section 9 of the Federal Arbitration Act imposes a one-year statute of limitations for motions to confirm an arbitration award. The court noted that the Fourth and Sixth Circuits previously had held that the time limit was permissive rather than mandatory. However, the Second Circuit noted, section 9 expressly refers to "any time within one year after the award is made," and therefore concluded that the one-year window was mandatory.

[C] Compelling Arbitration: The Arbitration Agreement

SOUTHLAND CORPORATION v. KEATING, 465 U.S. 1 (1984). Keating was a franchisee of the Southland Corporation, which was the owner and franchisor of Seven-Eleven convenience stores. Southland's franchise agreements, including the one with Keating, contained a provision requiring arbitration, as follows:

> Any controversy or claim arising out of or relating to this agreement shall be settled by arbitration in accordance with the Rules of the American Arbitration Association . . . and judgment upon any award rendered by the arbitrator may be entered in any court having jurisdiction thereof.

Keating and other franchisees in California brought a class action in a California state court, alleging fraud, misrepresentation, breach of contract, breach of fiduciary duty, and violation of the disclosure requirements of the California Franchise Investment Law, Cal. Corp. Code § 31000 *et seq.* (1977). Southland, the defendant, responded by petitioning the court to compel arbitration, relying on the arbitration clause of the franchise agreement and on the Federal Arbitration Act ("FAA"), which provides:

> A written provision in any maritime transaction or a contract evidencing a transaction involving [interstate] commerce to settle by arbitration a controversy thereafter arising out of such contract or transaction, or an agreement in writing to submit to arbitration an existing controversy arising out of such a contract [or] transaction . . . , shall be valid, irrevocable, and enforceable, save upon such grounds as exist at law or in equity for the revocation of any contract.

The California courts' order compelled arbitration of all the claims except the one arising under the California Franchise Investment Law. This Law, by its terms, provided for judicial consideration of claims, and it further provided that any agreement waiving compliance with the provisions of the Law "is void." The California Supreme Court concluded that, in this proceeding in the California state courts, the non-waiver provision was controlling. [The California court also held that there was nothing "to preclude a court from ordering classwide arbitration in an appropriate [class action] case," but this holding was not reviewed on certiorari].

After granting certiorari, the United States Supreme Court reversed and ordered arbitration, reasoning as follows:

> In enacting § 2 of the federal [Arbitration] Act, Congress declared a national policy favoring arbitration and withdrew the power of the states to require a judicial resolution of claims which the contracting parties agreed to resolve by arbitration. . . . Congress thus mandated the enforcement of arbitration agreements.
>
> . . . We see nothing in the Act indicating that the broad principle of enforceability is subject to . . . limitations under State law.
>
> The Federal Arbitration Act rests on the authority of the Congress to enact substantive rules under the Commerce Clause. . . .
>
> Although the legislative history is not without ambiguities, there are strong indications that Congress had in mind something more than making arbitration agreements enforceable only in the federal courts. . . .
>
> . . . The Arbitration Act sought to "overcome the rule of equity, that equity will not specifically enforce any arbitration agreement." . . .
>
> . . . Congress also showed its awareness of the widespread unwillingness of state courts to enforce arbitration agreements. . . . The problems Congress faced were

therefore twofold: the old common law hostility toward arbitration, and the failure of state arbitration statutes to mandate enforcement of arbitration agreements. To confine the scope of the Act to . . . federal courts would frustrate what we believe Congress intended to be a broad enactment. . . .

. . . Congress would need to call on the Commerce Clause if it intended the Act to apply to state courts. Yet at the same time, its reach would be limited to transactions involving interstate commerce. . . .

. . . [S]ince the overwhelming proportion of all civil litigation in this country is in the state courts, we cannot believe Congress intended to limit the Arbitration Act to disputes subject only to federal court jurisdiction. [Congress declared its intention] to place "[a]n arbitration agreement . . . upon the same footing as other contracts, where it belongs." . . .

. . . We hold that § 31512 of the California Franchise Investment Law violates the Supremacy Clause. . . .

NOTES AND QUESTIONS

(1) *What Questions Are Arbitrable If There Is an Arbitration Agreement? Prima Paint Corp. v. Flood & Conklin Mfg. Corp., 388 U.S. 395 (1967).* In general, the question whether a dispute should be compelled to be submitted to arbitration is a question for the courts; the Arbitration Act provides that an agreement to arbitrate may be attacked "upon such grounds as exist at law or in equity for the revocation of any contract." Thus, if it is unclear whether there really is an agreement to arbitrate, or if the arbitration clause itself allegedly was obtained by fraud, the question is one for the courts. *See AT & T Technologies, Inc. v. Communications Workers*, 475 U.S. 643 (1986) (where arbitration clause was ambiguous as to whether right to lay off workers was arbitrable, court should decide arbitrability). But the courts have been careful to avoid reading this authority too broadly, so as to defeat the scope of the Arbitration Act. For example, in the *Prima Paint* case, one party alleged that the other had committed fraud in the inducement of the contract, although not of the arbitration clause in particular, and sought to have the claim of fraud adjudicated in federal court. The Court held that consideration of a claim of fraud in the inducement of a contract "is for the arbitrators and not for the courts." [But since all the terms of a contract are in some sense interrelated, does this holding make sense?] In *Glazer v. Lehman Brothers, Inc.*, 394 F.3d 444 (6th Cir. 2005), the Sixth Circuit cited *Prima Paint* in holding that an arbitration clause must be viewed separately from the entire contract in deciding whether fraud in its inducement bars arbitrability under the Federal Arbitration Act. However, the Sixth Circuit also held that an arbitration clause is not severable from the integrated contract for purposes of applying the parol evidence rule to the alleged fraudulent inducement. Rather, the court noted that if arbitration clauses are not separate contracts for purposes of contract formation purposes, neither are they for purposes of applying the parol evidence rule.

(2) *Arbitration Clause and Adhesion Contracts.* In *Nagrampa v. MailCoups, Inc.*, 413 F.3d 1024 (9th Cir. 2005), the Ninth Circuit held that an arbitrator must decide whether an agreement containing an arbitration clause is a contract of adhesion, but the court may determine whether an arbitration clause buried within the agreement is procedurally unconscionable and therefore invalid.

(3) *Arbitrator Makes Initial Determination Regarding Availability of Class Arbitration.* In *Green Tree Financial Corp. v. Bazzle*, 539 U.S. 444 (2003), the Supreme Court held

that the arbitrator must make the initial determination as to whether a contract's arbitration clause forbids class arbitration of a dispute.

(4) *The Supreme Court Construes the Federal Arbitration Act and Broadens Its Effect: What Involvement With Interstate Commerce Is Needed? Allied–Bruce Terminix Companies, Inc. v. Dobson,* 513 U.S. 265 (1995). The parties had agreed to arbitrate "any controversy or claim" under a home termite protection plan. When a controversy arose, the Alabama court refused to enforce the agreement, finding the Alabama statute treating such agreements as unenforceable was not pre-empted by the federal Arbitration Act because the connection between the contract and interstate commerce was too slight. The Supreme Court reversed. It held the Act's language that applied to "a contract evidencing a transaction involving interstate commerce" should be read broadly to reach the limits of Congress' Interstate Commerce power. The Court referred to the Act's purpose, which was to overcome judicial hostility to arbitration agreements, and ruled that this purpose made appropriate application of the Act to both federal diversity cases and state court cases in which it would pre-empt state statutes. The parties did not contest that the transaction involved interstate commerce. Did they miss their best argument? *See United States v. Lopez,* 514 U.S. 549 (1995) (Gun-Free School Zones Act of 1990, which forbid possession of firearm in school zone, exceeded Congress' Commerce Clause authority).

(5) *The Federal Act Further Broadens Arbitrability by Nullifying State Laws Restricting Arbitration.* In the next year after *Allied-Bruce,* in a case remanded for further consideration in light of *Allied-Bruce,* the Court signaled the breadth of federal preemption in this area. *Doctor's Associates, Inc. v. Casarotto,* 517 U.S. 681 (1996). In *Doctor's Associates,* the Court struck down a Montana law requiring that any contract subject to arbitration contain a notice "typed in underlined capital letters on the first page of the contract" on the grounds that this law was in conflict with the FAA and thus was preempted by federal law. The Court emphasized that the Montana law ran afoul of section 2 of the FAA "because the State's law conditions the enforceability of arbitration agreements on compliance with a special notice requirement not applicable to contracts generally." 517 U.S. at 687.

(6) *The Supreme Court Again Construes the Federal Arbitration Act in a Way That Broadens Its Effect by Limiting an Exemption.* In *Circuit City Stores, Inc. v. Adams*, 532 U.S. 105 (2001), the Supreme Court held that the FAA's exclusion of "contracts of employment of seamen, railroad employees, or any other class of workers engaged in foreign or interstate commerce" from its coverage is confined to transportation workers, and not all contracts of employment. Accordingly, it required Adams to submit his state-law employment discrimination claim against Circuit City to binding arbitration as provided in his employment application.

[D] Other Streamlined Quasi-Adjudicatory Procedures: "Rent-a-Judge" Statutes, New York's "Simplified Procedure," and "Court-Annexed Arbitration"

(1) *New York's "Simplified Procedure for Court Determination of Disputes," CPLR 3031-3037.* This procedure obtains the speed and flexibility of arbitration without sacrificing the right to judicial resolution. All that is necessary to commence a proceeding under the "Simplified Procedure" is for the parties to execute and submit to the court a statement specifying the claims and defenses and the relief requested. The statement has the effect of waiving the right to trial by jury and vesting the court with great discretion to adapt the proceedings to the goal of simplicity. Pretrial discovery is available

only by court order; the court may waive preliminary calendaring steps and should order trial as promptly as "may be practicable"; the court may limit the use of expert witnesses and, perhaps most importantly, is empowered to dispense with the usual rules regarding admissibility of evidence (except those protecting privileged communications). Appeal is authorized, but it is restricted to final judgments unless the court directs otherwise, and the decision of the trial judge is final if it is supported by any "substantial evidence." *See generally* Chase, *2 Weinstein, Korn & Miller CPLR Manual* § 31.16 (1997). This mechanism is rarely used. Why do you think this is so?

(2) *Private Judging (or "Rent-a-Judge" Statutes).* Some states permit the parties to agree to the appointment of an attorney or judge (usually retired) as the presiding judge in their case. The proceedings closely resemble the trial and (if allowed by governing law) the appeal of any other judicially determined dispute, except with respect to the identity of the judge. By this means, the parties may gain the advantages of speedy disposition, certainty of trial date, and a judge of their choice. The pioneering legislation in this field is that of California. *See* Cal. Code Civ. Pro. § 638; *see also* Note, *The California Rent-A-Judge Experiment: Constitutional and Policy Considerations of Pay-as-You-Go Courts*, 94 Harv. L. Rev. 1592 (1981).

(3) *"Court Annexed Arbitration."* Governing law may authorize or require the court to refer the parties to an arbiter as a preliminary step prior to presentation of the dispute in court. This procedure generally differs sharply from ordinary arbitration in that it is not binding, but is advisory only. It therefore is somewhat related to mediation or to advisory simulations and is treated together with those procedures in § 15.05, below.

[E] Administrative and Industry Adjudication

CHRYSLER CORP. v. TEXAS MOTOR VEHICLE COMM'N, 755 F.2d 1192 (5th Cir. 1985). Section 6.07 of the Texas Motor Vehicle Code creates new warranty remedies for automobile purchasers and offers them an administrative forum — an adjudicative proceeding before the Texas Motor Vehicle Commission — in which to assert those remedies. Chrysler challenged this "Lemon Law," as it was informally known, as unconstitutional. First, Chrysler argued that five of the nine members of the Commission were by statute required to be automobile dealers, and these dealers would be biased toward blaming manufacturers rather than dealers for warranty defects. Second, Chrysler argued that the administrative proceeding, in effect, was binding against car manufacturers but not against consumers, who could sue in court on other theories after losing their lemon law claims. Further, the consumer could obtain review of the lemon law decision simply by appealing to a court, while car manufacturers would have to obtain temporary injunctive relief first, to postpone the effect of an adverse decision.

The trial court agreed with Chrysler and held the Texas Lemon Law unconstitutional under the Due Process Clause of the Fourteenth Amendment. The Court of Appeals, in this opinion, reversed. First, it held that the composition of the Commission did not violate due process. Chrysler argued that dealers, who are also targets of warranty suits, would prefer to find manufacturers liable. "Yet, we can equally speculate, if we are to speculate, that a dealer will be quick to find fault with his direct competitor — the dealer. Moreover, it is also possible that a dealer member of the Commission would tend to be biased in favor of manufacturers of his own make of car so that the brand he sells will not develop a reputation as a 'lemon.' " The suggestion of bias, said the Court, "is . . . overdrawn."

The Court of Appeals then considered Chrysler's argument that lemon law decisions were unfairly binding on manufacturers but not on consumers. Although it was true that a consumer could sue in court on another theory after losing his lemon law claim before the Commission, this result was no different from any situation in which a person may have several claims, one of which is subject to the exclusive jurisdiction of a special tribunal. Chrysler further argued that the consumer could petition for review directly, but the manufacturer could stay the effect of an adverse Commission decision during review only if it first obtained a temporary injunction from the court against enforcement of the Commission order. The court agreed with Chrysler that the law must treat equally situated parties equally — but it accepted the state's argument that the parties were not in equal positions. A consumer who has won a lemon law claim only to have it stayed during court review is under economic pressure, whereas a manufacturer who has lost such a claim is not under that pressure during court review. The procedural system, said the court, uses asymmetrical procedural rules to adjust burdens or advantages throughout the procedural system. The court reasoned as follows:

> [T]he Texas lemon law reflects a determination by the legislature that automobile manufacturers and purchasers are not similarly situated in warranty-related disputes. . . . Supreme Court cases recognize a duty of government to equalize access to the courts by assisting the poor, . . . and Texas has here attempted to balance the economic interests of litigants who otherwise might be unevenly matched.
>
> Chrysler argues that its advantages are no greater than in all cases where litigants have widely different financial resources and that procedures ought not be adjusted to even that score. . . . [But] the legislature was here responding to more than the relative length of the parties' purses. It was also, as it was entitled to do, recognizing the distinct economic stakes of the parties. The legislature could permissibly assume that a car purchaser has little economic incentive to risk more than the value of his purchase to protect it. A manufacturer, on the other hand, has distinct economic concerns, including product image and reputation for toughness in its litigation posture, and accordingly its interests in warranty suits are plainly greater than its immediate exposure, or at least the legislature was entitled to conclude. Indeed, much of tort law rests on such economic adjustments and legislative assumptions about economic incentives and allocative efficiencies. If a state can create liability without fault as an exercise of its power to regulate matters of economic interests, that it can increase the chances of a claimant in a fault-based system necessarily follows.

NOTES AND QUESTIONS

(1) *Are Decisionmakers with Expertise Better — Or Will They Have an Axe to Grind?* Presumably, one advantage of car dealers as Commission members is that they immediately will understand what a PCV valve is and know the likelihood of its becoming defective. But this very expertise creates potential problems of prejudgment or bias. Individuals chosen from a cross-section of the community would be less biased. Should we therefore avoid experienced decisionmakers?

(2) *Adjusting Procedures to Favor One Side or Another in ADR.* The court attributes to the state legislature a decision that, if ADR is to work in the automobile warranty setting, the scales must be adjusted so that they favor the consumer in ways that traditional adjudication would not. The automobile industry trade associations vigorously disagreed with this approach. They filed an amicus curiae brief supporting Chrysler, in which they argued that asymmetrical procedural rules were "dangerous" and "totalitarian." Is this view persuasive? Or can the state take into account the situation of a lemon law claim

winner who is without her car during an appeal or the possible motive of a manufacturer to defend by expending resources exceeding the claim?

(3) *Constitutional Problems.* This case is useful in pointing out that, at some point, ADR might violate due process or other constitutional provisions. At the same time, it is important for courts considering the constitutionality of ADR to give the deference to legislatures that the Constitution requires — and to avoid disfavoring a procedure merely because it differs from traditional judicial litigation.

(4) *Industry-Created Alternatives: The Example of the Ford Motor Company Consumer Appeals Board.* Ford receives hundreds of written and telephone communications daily. Many are warranty complaints. At one time, Ford handled these complaints only by dealer and regional office investigation, to which the disgruntled consumer's only alternative was litigation. Now, Ford's Consumer Appeals Board supplies a third-party dispute resolution mechanism, which Ford has found to be superior in many respects. Each FCAB consists of five members: three consumer representatives, a Ford dealer, and a Lincoln-Mercury dealer. Presentations are entirely in writing unless the FCAB invites an oral argument by a consumer, dealer, or company representative. Importantly, Ford and its dealers are bound by the FCAB decision, but consumers are not bound, and they can go to the courts if dissatisfied with the FCAB decisions. Dealer support of this program is surprisingly strong; only three of 1,195 dealers in initial test areas refused to participate. Ford came to conclude that the program was a positive marketing tool. *See* Smith, *The Ford Motor Company Appeals Board, in* Center for Public Resources, *Dispute Resolution: A Manual of Innovative Corporate Strategies for the Avoidance and Resolution of Legal Disputes* III-B.1 (1980).

(5) *The Wellington Agreement: An Industry-Wide Claims Settlement Facility Employing the Multi-Door Courthouse Approach.* A number of manufacturers of asbestos products are signatories of the Wellington agreement, which establishes various modalities for the resolution of claims for asbestos-related injuries. Its purpose is to reduce transaction costs so as to conserve the resources of asbestos manufacturers while satisfying the claims of the largest possible number of meritorious claimants with the largest possible percentage of monies actually allocated to payment of claims. Depending upon the claimant's choices and the nature of the injury, various different ADR's may be used.

§ 15.05 Mediation and Other Advisory Processes

[A] Voluntary Mediation or Conciliation

Kusnetz, DIVORCE MEDIATION

*24 Hous. Law. 33 (1986)**

The national movement toward alternative methods of dispute resolution now features divorce mediation as one of its components. In an era that has seen major changes in family law, such as no-fault divorce and joint custody, it makes little sense to believe that adversary divorce is the only way to satisfy the legal process. [F]urther impetus comes from new research on the devastating effects of divorce on children. Mediation is one way to reduce the hazards of divorce while helping families to learn constructive problem-solving skills. . . .

Definition

Mediation is a voluntary process in which parties to a dispute, with the help of a neutral third party, explore ways to negotiate their differences and reach a satisfactory resolution. This resolution is incorporated into a memorandum of agreement which is taken to the couple's attorneys and becomes the basis of a court order.

Mediation is not arbitration. In arbitration, a neutral third-party is empowered to decide the issues. In mediation, a neutral third party facilitates negotiations between the parties, but is not empowered to make decisions. All decision-making power stays with the parties.

Mediation is neither traditional legal negotiation nor representation. In the traditional adversarial process, lawyers negotiate for their clients. [I]n mediation, the parties negotiate for themselves, most often face-to-face, with the mediator present. The mediator does not represent either party. . . .

Where Does Mediation Fit?

Divorce mediation is not meant to supplant the adversarial system. For many couples, the traditional adversary system is clearly necessary and desirable; for example, when one party needs physical protection from the other; when there is dependency on drugs or alcohol; or when couples are simply committed to fighting each other. . . .

The Mediation Process

The goal of divorce mediation is an agreement by both parties covering all those issues the parties want to deal with: property, custody, child support, visitation and contractual alimony. . . .

The mediator will usually see the couple together. If this does not work for a particular couple or a particular session, the mediator may separate them and shuttle back and forth. The mediator may try to see each party alone at least once in order to get a clear idea of one's goals and needs, and to gauge where each person is in the emotional process of divorce.

In a private mediation setting the process may proceed as follows:

1. The couple meets with the mediator at an orientation session, usually one hour. The process is explained, including rules for the couple's conduct during mediation, full disclosure of assets, confidentiality, the use of outside experts, and the costs anticipated. It is stressed that the mediation process expects and encourages cooperation, respect for each other's problems and protection of children.

2. The parties explain their situation and the problems they need to resolve.

3. If the parties and the mediator agree that mediation is appropriate for them, all sign an agreement to mediate. This agreement is an acceptance of the mediator's rules, a waiver of the parties' right to call the mediator as a witness, and the mediator's guarantee not to represent either party in any future legal action.

4. A schedule of meetings is outlined and the parties are asked to fill out budget forms, to prepare lists of assets and liabilities, and to produce documents that show the present value of each item. For some this task is sobering as they learn the realistic parameters within which they will negotiate.

5. When information gathering is complete, the parties start to define the issues and formulate agreements. Often the mediator will address an easy issue first to bolster

the parties' confidence in their ability to negotiate. The mediator builds on that success for the more difficult issues.

6. Experts are brought in as necessary and may include an accountant, an appraiser, or a child psychiatrist. Children are sometimes brought into the process if a particular issue warrants it. Therapists and attorneys are consulted as needed throughout the process. Mediation may be suspended temporarily while one arrangement or another is tested before a final decision is reached.

7. When an agreement is reached, a memorandum of agreement is prepared by the mediator. The parties take it to their respective attorneys for review. [T]he document is then signed and given to the attorney who will prepare the court order. Many mediators reserve the right to review the order before it is signed to ensure it reflects the agreements reached by the parties. The attorney for a party in mediation plays an important role — giving advice, protecting legal rights, suggesting possible resolutions, and helping to ensure that the mediation process is fair. . . .

NOTES AND QUESTIONS

(1) *Legal, Ethical, and Practical Problems.* There are great advantages to mediation, but there also are many pitfalls to avoid.

(2) *Problems of Inequality of Information, Determination, or Negotiating Ability.* One spouse may have access to much more information about the extent and nature of property than the other. An even more frequent problem is the situation in which one spouse simply is more used to techniques of negotiation than the other — or is more determined. What should be done if the spouses, for example, produce an agreement that is skewed toward one or the other so severely that no person familiar with the court would expect it to be produced in that system? "If an imbalance cannot be rectified to the point where each party can negotiate in his or her interest, serious thought should be given to terminating the mediation." Kusnetz, *supra*, at 34.

(3) *Are Efforts by the Mediator to Redress Imbalances Appropriate?* The tempting answer to these problems of inequality is for the mediator to redress the imbalance by advocating the rights of one party or the other, invoking "what is customary in this situation," or like behaviors. To some extent, this behavior is unavoidable, but it should be carefully confined.

(4) *Dual Representation.* For an attorney-mediator, professional responsibility rules regarding conflict of interest can be a serious concern. The prevailing opinion appears to be that, in acting solely as a mediator, the attorney represents neither party. *E.g.*, Silberman, *Professional Responsibility Problems in Divorce Mediation*, 16 Fam. L.Q. 107, 111 (1982). But what if the attorney files the divorce complaint, advises either or both parties on their legal rights, comments on the meaning of the settlement agreement or the judgment, appears in court to obtain an uncontested divorce, or advocates one solution or another to the advantage of one spouse or another? It's probably quite difficult to avoid all of these actions in mediating between spouses who are not wealthy. The rules do, generally, allow dual representation if each party consents to it after full disclosure of the conflict of interest, but if this route is chosen, the mediator should establish and document the disclosure and the consent. *See generally* Comment, *The Attorney as Mediator — Inherent Conflict of Interest?*, 32 UCLA L. Rev. 986 (1985).

(5) *Personal Liability on the Part of the Mediator; "Shield" Laws.* As the preceding comments should suggest, mediators have become concerned that they might be sued

successfully on numerous theories — breach of contract ("you were supposed to be impartial but weren't"), negligence ("you failed to keep informed of developments and didn't explain the solution that happened to be best"), implied claims arising from codes of professional responsibility, consumer protection legislation, etc. In response to this concern, mediators in many states have sought "shield" laws providing a defense to liability for other than gross misconduct — but the difficulty lies in defining a meaningful kind of immunity that does not also protect the seriously deficient mediator.

(6) *Confidentiality.* Mediation probably works best when both parties feel free to express themselves. Accordingly, there is a need for confidentiality, and mediators seek to provide it by agreement between the parties. In many jurisdictions, statements during settlement negotiations are excluded from evidence. The difficulty is, if a person makes a statement of fact during mediated negotiations, and then makes precisely the opposite statement during a later trial after mediation has failed, excluding the contrary statement may amount to condoning perjury.

(7) *Non-Lawyer Mediators; Inexperienced Mediators.* A mediator who lacks knowledge of typical legal solutions to divorce problems — *e.g.*, one who is not fully cognizant of ways in which occupation and ownership of the home may be structured or how child support, alimony and tax issues relate — is unable to mediate meaningfully. There may arise issues of unauthorized practice of law in such a context. Furthermore, an inexperienced mediator, whether lawyer or not, may assist the parties in reaching solutions that will not work in practice — *e.g.*, unsecured alimony from a spouse who is unlikely to make payments regularly, or changes of custody so frequent that the children will be disoriented.

(8) *Representation of Both Parties by Lawyers.* For all of the reasons given above, there is widespread agreement that divorce mediation works best if both parties are represented by counsel of their own choosing, separate and apart from the mediator.

(9) *The Success of Mediation: Expressed Satisfaction of Participants.* Studies show higher rates of satisfaction in mediated settlement agreements than in settlement agreements reached through litigation without mediation. *See generally* Bahr, *Mediation is the Answer*, 3 Family Advocate 32 (1981). In addition, Bahr found that the average couple using mediation paid about $550 less for their divorce than the average non-mediated couple, and effects on children presumably were ameliorated by significantly higher perceptions of fairness as to custody and visitation issues. A study of dispute resolution centers using the multi-door courthouse approach showed that 92 percent of disputants would use the program again, and in the LEAA funded project with the highest rate (Houston), 97 percent reported that they were fully or partially satisfied with the service. Roehl & Cook, *The Multi-Door Dispute Resolution Program: Phase I Assessment, Final Report* (Institute of Social Analysis ed. 1985).

(10) *Other Uses of Mediation: Inter-Corporate Disputes.* "Everyone is familiar with mediation in connection with labor and family disputes, but the use of mediators to help resolve significant business disputes is less well known. [S]triking results have been achieved in resolving corporate disputes through mediation." Wilson, *ADR and Resolving Corporate Disputes*, 24 Hous. Law. 18, 20 (1986).

Ehrman, WHY BUSINESS LAWYERS SHOULD USE MEDIATION

*ABA Journal, June 1989, at 73**

"I'll talk to my client and get back to you — but frankly, I don't think I want to give you a free ride with all my facts and lose my right to appeal some guy's decision."

Chris, the plaintiff's lawyer, was gently refusing a suggestion by the defendant's lawyer that they hire a mediator to help resolve a bitter fight between business partners that had gone on way too long and cost entirely too much.

Clearly, Chris didn't understand mediation.

[He] confused mediation with arbitration — and he isn't alone. . . .

The success rate of mediation in resolving business disputes, according to those in the field, is about 80 percent.

Why, then, is mediation so little used by business lawyers?

The ignorance displayed by Chris is a principal reason. [B]ut let's face it — the most potent enemy of mediation is that good old adversarial mindset. . . .

In fact, neither side has anything to lose in mediation. The parties make their own rules. They can reveal as much or as little as they like. Separate meetings with the mediator (caucuses) are absolutely confidential. In most states nothing said or produced in mediation can be used in a later civil proceeding. . . .

But there sometimes are other fears. Like the unspoken: "Will it cost me fees if we settle too soon?"

Yes, mediation may result in fewer billable hours in a particular case. [N]evertheless, lawyers who help their clients to fast, economical, and above all, satisfactory results will profit in the long run from their reputations as problem solvers. . . .

Lawyers also may fear losing control of the client. [B]ut it is an arrogant presumption on the attorney's part that he always knows best.

Some lawyers are afraid mediation will uncover confidential information, exposing the weakest elements of their cases. . . .

[But] in the confidential caucus the party can lay out all his facts safely, including the vulnerable aspects of his case. The mediator, who is sworn to secrecy, is able to use the information to help the lawyer test the strength of his client's position, learn the needs of the parties, bring objectivity to the case and suggest options for settlement. . . .

The adversary attitude sometimes is encouraged or even demanded by the client. Some corporate executives don't want to look wimpy to their superiors. Others like the idea of putting a lawyer between themselves and the problem. . . .

[A]nd on occasion the executive may know he made a mistake, and a long proceeding whose ultimate bad result can be blamed on the lawyer is the perfect solution. . . .

But cases where mediation is completely useless are rare. Even mediation that fails to settle all the issues is useful, since it can limit the issues to be tried and narrow discovery, as well as defuse anger. And, wider use of the process might improve the public image of lawyers, which could use a little polishing.

[B] The Mini-Trial (and Neutral Experts)

Eric Green, THE MINI-TRIAL APPROACH TO COMPLEX LITIGATION

*in Center for Public Resources, Dispute Management: Corporate Strategies for the Avoidance and Resolution of Legal Disputes I-A.1 (1980)**

The dispute resolution model described here has come to be known as a "Mini-Trial," thanks to a creative headline writer for the *New York Times*. It has also been described at various times as an Information Exchange, a Mock Trial, an Advisory Proceeding, and non-binding arbitration. Without getting bogged down in semantics, this model is a dispute-resolution hybrid that merges certain characteristics of adjudicative, arbitral, mediational and negotiational processes into a unique creation.

The goal of the mini-trial is to effect speedy cost-effective resolution of the dispute by

- narrowing the dispute;
- promoting a dialogue on the merits of the case rather than just the dollars;
- reconverting what has become a typical lawyers' dispute back into a businessman's problem by removing many of the legalistic, collateral issues in the case.

Properly applied to the right case, at the right time, by parties who genuinely want to resolve their dispute, the mini-trial can produce spectacular results. Experience to date indicates that best results are obtained in mini-trials of cases involving complex questions, of mixed law and fact (for example, patent, products liability, antitrust, unfair competition) — just the kinds of cases in which litigation is often intractable and costly. . . .

Key Ingredients

The key elements of a mini-trial are:

- A voluntary, confidential and non-binding procedure, consisting of
- informal, summary presentations by the lawyers and experts for each party to the dispute of its best case, followed by rebuttal and questions concerning those presentations,
- before top management representatives (with settling authority) of each party,
- presided over a jointly selected "neutral advisor" or moderator who, if necessary, after the mini-trial will advise the parties as to the strengths and weaknesses of their respective cases.

Case History

An actual example will give some life to these concepts. The first widely publicized application of the mini-trial concept involved a legally and technically complex patent infringement case between Telecredit, Inc., the owner of a number of patents relating to computerized check verification and charge authorization systems, and TRW Inc., the manufacturer of a number of such systems for banks and retail outlets. Like many cases, this one had been stalled in a federal court traffic jam. In nearly three years of litigation the case had consumed several hundred thousand dollars in legal fees on both sides, with no trial date yet in sight. The standard alternative — binding arbitration — was unacceptable for several reasons and traditional dollar negotiations were unproductive, so counsel and management of the parties involved developed the mini-trial concept.

The procedure developed by the retained attorneys and house counsel consisted in essence of a non-binding *mini-trial* before top corporate management and a privately hired, neutral advisor, James Davis, who formerly had served as a United States Court of Claims trial judge, but was then privately practicing law. The entire procedure, which took several months to organize but *only two days of presentation time*, was conducted completely outside the judicial system and contained no coercive characteristics. Yet within one-half hour of the close of the procedure, the parties reached a settlement in principle of what had been a long and bitterly fought lawsuit. And both sides walked away believers in the process they had been through.

In greater detail, the procedure consisted of a six-week pre-trial schedule that provided for expedited, limited exchange of documents, short depositions of key witnesses and the exchange of position papers and exhibits. The procedure then culminated in the two-day *Information Exchange*, or *mini-trial*. . . . At the Information Exchange each side had the opportunity and responsibility to present orally to top management representatives of both companies its *best case* on the issues in dispute. Management then assessed the theories, strengths and weaknesses of the respective positions and met together, without counsel, to attempt to resolve the dispute from the new perspective obtained at the Information Exchange. . . .

Surprisingly, considering the amount of time and money that had already been invested in the dispute, each side gained significant new insights into the opposing parties' claims during the Information Exchange. . . . Where difficulties arose, Judge Davis facilitated the discussion with his questions. Occasionally, his comments indicated where he felt serious problems existed for each side. . . .

Immediately after the Information Exchange ended, top management for each side met privately without lawyers. Within one-half hour, they resolved the dispute. Although the details took several weeks to tie up, the drain on both corporations' treasuries was plugged and a case which had threatened to occupy the time and energy of a federal court for months was terminated without an additional day of court time. This was a success by any standard for the parties involved in the case. . . .

Custom-Made Contours

Others who may be interested in similar experimentation should recognize that every case is different, and what worked in this case might not work at all in another situation. Counsel considering some form of mini-trial must be flexible enough to adopt a wide variety of procedures to the particular dispute.

In the case described, enough pre-trial discovery and sparring already had been conducted to educate the parties somewhat in the disputed issues of the case and also to bring home to them the cost of continuing litigative combat. Further, . . . each party was still capable of acting with a degree of rationality — desiring to resolve the case as favorably as possible, with the least expense and risk, and the least delay. . . .

Perhaps even more important, the issues in the patent case were of the type most susceptible to resolution through this procedure. That is, they tended to involve mixed questions of law and fact — questions dealing with the legal consequences of a variety of factual circumstances — rather than questions solely, or primarily, of law or credibility.

Thus, for example, the Information Exchange procedure seems well-suited to resolving an antitrust case where the sticking point to settlement is the scope and definition of the relevant market, an unfair competition case where the crucial issue is the propriety of certain disputed business practices, or a products liability case where the issue is whether a specially built component part met the required standard of quality.

By contrast, where a case turns solely on legal issues, traditional summary judgment procedures are likely to provide a means to resolve it. And where a case primarily turns on factual disputes involving credibility, the kind of Information Exchange procedure described above is not likely to be any more effective in resolving the case than traditional settlement negotiations or arbitration. . . .

The point that management and counsel must keep in mind is that the variety of dispute resolution procedures is unlimited.

[C] "Screening" Panels and Related Procedures

JOHNSON v. ST. VINCENT HOSPITAL, INC., 404 N.E.2d 585 (Ind. 1980). The Indiana Medical Malpractice Act resulted from conditions in which seven of ten malpractice insurance carriers withdrew from the state, premiums increased as much as 1200 percent over a period of fifteen years, high-risk specialists such as anesthesiologists were hard-pressed or totally unable to obtain insurance, emergency services were cancelled in some hospitals, and surgery generally was cancelled in some rural areas. The Act, codified in Ind. Code §§ 16-9.5-1-1 through 16-9.5-10-5, provided (among other provisions) that before filing suit, plaintiffs must submit their complaints to a medical review panel. The panel renders an opinion which is admissible at trial and is disclosed to the jury. The Johnsons, whose minor child had died in the aftermath of a tonsillectomy, brought suit against the hospital without first submitting their claim to a medical review panel as the Act required. Their complaint included a separate paragraph seeking a declaration that the Act was unconstitutional because it violated (A) the right to trial by jury guaranteed by the Indiana Constitution; (B) the Due Process Clauses and (C) Equal Protection Clauses of both the federal and Indiana Constitutions; and (D) the separation of powers doctrine of the Indiana Constitution. The Indiana Supreme Court upheld the constitutionality of the Act and affirmed a dismissal of the Johnsons' complaint.

The court rejected the argument that additional delay and expense before the filing of suit denied plaintiffs the right to jury trial, saying, "Delay in the commencement of a trial and the expense of investigating and marshaling evidence are part and parcel of the preparation of any piece of civil litigation." The plaintiffs also argued that the effect of placing an unfavorable review panel opinion before the jury would be to deny plaintiff a trial by jury by increasing the plaintiff's burden of persuasion. "For our purposes here," said the Court, "we do not find this situation significantly different from the situation in which a plaintiff presents but a lone general practitioner witness and the defendant then fields three distinguished specialists." The plaintiffs also argued that they were denied the right to trial by jury because the opinion would be biased, in that the panel consisted of an attorney as chair and three health-care providers as members. But since each side selected one of the health-care providers, the "structural features will tend to ameliorate any tendency toward bias." The court also rejected the due process, equal protection, and separation of powers challenges by concluding that the classification was reasonable and that the Act was a proper subject for legislation.

NOTES AND QUESTIONS

(1) *An Unconstitutional Screening Mechanism in Illinois: Bernier v. Burris, 113 Ill. 2d 219, 497 N.E.2d 763 (1986).* The parallel Illinois legislation provided for a screening panel composed of the judge, plus a practicing attorney and a health care professional. The Illinois law did not allow the panel's opinion to be heard by the jury, but a party who rejected a unanimous panel decision and lost at trial would be liable for the "costs, reasonable attorney's fees and expenses" of the prevailing party. The court rejected due process and similar attacks, but it held the provision unconstitutional, nevertheless, because of the judge's role on the panel. This role meant that the judge either must serve in his judicial capacity while being forced to share his judicial authority with two non-members of the judiciary, or he must be denied his judicial authority; neither alternative was acceptable, said the court.

(2) *Should an Opinion of a Statutory Panel of Experts Be Heard by the Jury?* While many provisions for malpractice screening have some "bite" (such as Illinois' shifting of attorney's fees), the vast majority do not allow the panel's opinion to go to the jury, as Indiana's law does. It is possible to characterize this approach as invading the function of the jury. But is it? The rules of evidence allow the trial judge to appoint an expert witness, who may investigate the subject of the action and can be permitted to testify before the jury. Perhaps this longstanding authority doesn't differ in principle from the Indiana provision.

[D] Court-Annexed Arbitration and Summary Jury Trials

LOCAL ARBITRATION RULE FOR THE EASTERN DISTRICT OF NEW YORK (1999)

Section 1. Certification of Arbitrators

(a) The Chief Judge or a judge or judges authorized by the Chief Judge to act (hereafter referred to as the certifying judge) shall certify as many arbitrators as may be determined to be necessary under this rule. . . .

Section 3. Civil Cases Eligible for Compulsory Arbitration

(a) The Clerk of Court shall [d]esignate and process for compulsory arbitration all civil cases (excluding [certain kinds of cases such as Social Security cases and prisoners' civil rights cases]) wherein money damages only are being sought in an amount not in excess of $100,000.00, exclusive of interest and costs.

[The Rule contains further provisions allowing parties to stipulate to arbitration and creating a presumption that damages are less than $100,000.00 unless a party files a certification to the contrary.]

Section 4. Referral to Arbitration

(a) After an answer is filed in a case determined eligible for arbitration, the arbitration clerk shall send a notice to counsel setting forth the date and time for the arbitration hearing. . . . The notice shall also advise counsel that they have 90 days to complete discovery unless the judge to whom the case has been assigned orders a shorter or longer period for discovery. . . .

(b) Cases not originally designated as eligible for compulsory arbitration, but which in the discretion of the assigned judge, are later found to qualify, may be referred to arbitration. . . .

(c) The arbitration shall be held before one arbitrator, unless a panel of three arbitrators is requested by a party, in which case one of whom shall be designated as chairperson of the panel. . . . The arbitration panel shall be chosen at random by the Clerk of the Court . . . .

Section 5. Arbitration Hearing

[The Rule provides for continuances and scheduling, for subpoenas, and for use of the Rules of Evidence as guides to admissibility. Exhibits, however, usually are to be received without formal predicate proof. If a noticed party fails to participate "in a meaningful manner," the arbitration nevertheless may proceed, and the court may impose sanctions — which may include denial of trial *de novo*.]

Section 6. Arbitration Award and Judgment

(a) The arbitration award shall be filed with the court promptly after the hearing is concluded and shall be entered as the judgment of the court after the 30 day period for requesting a trial *de novo* pursuant to Section 7 has expired, unless a party has demanded a trial *de novo*. The judgment so entered [s]hall have the same force and effect as a judgment of the court in a civil action, except that it shall not be appealable. . . .

(b) The contents of any arbitration award shall not be made known to any judge who might be assigned the case [except for the purposes of assessing fees or costs or filing required reports, or when the judgment has become final].

Section 7. Trial De Novo

(a) Within 30 days after the arbitration award is entered on the docket, any party may demand in writing a trial *de novo* in the district court. . . .

(b) Upon demand for a trial *de novo* and the payment to the clerk required by paragraph (d) of this section, the action shall be placed on the calendar of the court and treated for all purposes as if it had not been referred to arbitration . . . .

(c) At the trial *de novo*, the court shall not admit evidence that there had been an arbitration proceeding, the nature or amount of the award, or any other matter concerning the conduct of the arbitration proceeding.

(d) Upon making a demand for trial *de novo*, the moving party shall, unless permitted to proceed *in forma pauperis*, deposit with the clerk of court an amount equal to the arbitration fees of the arbitrators as provided in Section 2 [usually $100 or $250]. The sum so deposited shall be returned to the party demanding a trial *de novo* in the event that party obtains a final judgment [m]ore favorable than the arbitration award. If the party demanding a trial *de novo* does not obtain a more favorable result after trial, or if the court determines that the party's conduct in seeking a trial *de novo* was in bad faith, the sum so deposited shall be paid by the Clerk to the Treasury of the United States.

NOTES AND QUESTIONS

(1) *Is Non-Binding Court-Annexed Arbitration Really "Mediation" or "Arbitration"?* After the arbitration award, there is a 30-day period under these rules during which either

party may wipe the slate clean and proceed to trial. What will be happening during those 30 days, and what effect will the award have on the parties?

(2) *Criticisms.* For parties who proceed to trial, this local rule arguably imposes an additional layer of bureaucracy. It might even impose costs that would deter a litigant who would otherwise go to trial and win. It forces on the parties an advisory decision-maker different from the jury that would decide at trial. Some critics would see disadvantages in the "privatizing" of disputes that ought to be aired in public. Finally, this local rule might induce undesirable kinds of behavior from litigants. Plaintiffs wishing to avoid arbitration may claim artificially inflated damages, and defendants may remove or not remove depending upon their view of this process. Judges can exercise their discretion to refer disputes much larger than $100,000.00, simply by recharacterizing the amounts really at stake.

(3) *Advantages.* According to Judge Weinstein, "The court-annexed arbitration program [a]ppears to have worked well. . . . Similar programs in other federal district courts — particularly the Eastern District of Pennsylvania — have reduced the number of cases going to trial by as much as 50%." Some districts have higher thresholds than $100,000.00; and while the above Rules provide for shifting of the costs of arbitration (which are small), some districts provide for shifting of all attorneys' fees after trial. *See Ten Courts Try Arbitration, in Alternatives to the High Cost of Litigation*, Oct. 1985, at 1 (Center for Public Resources); *but cf. Tiedel v. Northwestern Michigan College*, 865 F.2d 88 (6th Cir. 1988) (invalidating shifting of attorneys' fees under District Court rule governing arbitration).

NOTE ON SUMMARY JURY TRIALS

The development of summary jury trials is widely credited to Judge Thomas D. Lambros of the Northern District of Ohio. This procedure is roughly analogous to the substitution of a jury for court-annexed arbitration, with severely limited presentation time. Consider the following excerpts from Harlan, *Asbestos Backlog Moving: Controversial System Clears Cases*, Texas Lawyer, Sept. 29, 1986, at 1, col. 1.*

> Nine months after the federal courts in Houston began an experimental program for handling the docket of asbestos injury cases, plaintiffs' and defense lawyers can agree on one thing: the cases are moving.
>
> Otherwise, the lawyers disagree about the benefits of the experiment's key component, the "summary jury trial," in which live testimony is *verboten*, and evidence is compacted into 90-minute statements from the lawyers to a six-member jury.
>
> The jurors [a]re not told that their verdict is non-binding on the parties, who will simply use the damage "award" as a guide for settling the case.
>
> The parties have the option of rejecting the jury's verdict . . . but no one has opted for that since the summary jury trials began in late January. Instead, settlements have been reached in all of the 20-30 cases that have been set for summary jury trials. . . .
>
> "Typically, an asbestos case can take anywhere from 10 days to two weeks to three weeks to try," [Special Master Ronald J.] Blask said. "This whole procedure [a summary jury trial] usually can be done in one day. . . . It's been very effective." . . .
>
> "I'm totally against it," said plaintiffs' attorney Robert E. Ballard, a partner in Houston's Abraham, Watkins, Nichols, Ballard, Onstad & Friend. The summary jury

> trials, he said, "are meaningless. I get no judgments. I get no verdicts I can enforce. . . . You've got a jury evaluating your case in a vacuum.". . . .
>
> [D]efense lawyer, Sam Stubbs, a partner at Fulbright & Jaworski, said he has seen most summary jury verdicts come in at less than the defendant's original settlement offer and well below the plaintiff's demand.
>
> But the defendants usually end up settling for their higher, original offer because "Judge Blask has instilled in us the feeling that it would be unfair to withdraw what we previously offered," Stubbs said. "It's not fair [to the defendants], but you ought to see what we're up against in the regular court."
>
> "If we lose, we lose big," he said. "If we win, we lose." . . .
>
> Each side is given 10-15 minutes for voir dire and 30 minutes for opening remarks, Blask said. For the presentation of "evidence" — summaries of medical evidence, experts' qualifications, diagnoses, deposition excerpts — each side is allowed an hour to 90 minutes, he said.
>
> Defense attorney Robert Ballard said lawyers preparing for the summary jury trials "work at least as hard" as they do in preparing for full jury trials. . . .
>
> In the 13 months since Blask took charge of the asbestos docket, about 80 cases have been disposed of. . . .
>
> "Judge Blask is doing everything he can to see that the cases are efficiently and effectively moving," Stubbs said. "In the previous year, none [of the asbestos cases] moved. In the year before that, one moved. And in the year before that, maybe 10 moved." . . .

Is this procedure superior to court-annexed arbitration — and, perhaps more importantly, is it superior to judicial adjudication? *See also* Lambros, *The Summary Jury Trial and Other Alternative Methods of Dispute Resolution: A Report to the Judicial Conference of the United States Committee on the Operation of the Jury System*, 103 F.R.D. 461 (1985).

NOTES AND QUESTIONS

(1) *The Court's Authority to Summon Citizens for Summary Jury Trials: The Civil Justice Reform Act and United States v. Exum, 748 F. Supp. 512 (N.D. Ohio 1990).* In this case, the district judge rejected his Chief Judge's (Judge Lambros') approach, holding that the federal law governing jury service did not authorize summonses for service in summary jury trials. He reasoned that the court had no more power to force citizens to serve as settlement advisors than it did to "summon [them] to serve as hand servants." But that was not the extent of his disagreement with Judge Lambros: He also took the extraordinary step of suspending all jury trials on the theory that use of part of the jury pool for summary jury trials would "impermissibly alter" the jury selection process! This approach virtually would have eliminated summary jury trials if upheld. The Civil Justice Reform Act of 1990, however, explicitly encouraged the use of summary jury trials — and after the adoption of this Act, the district judge rescinded his orders.

(2) *What Kinds of Cases Benefit From Summary Jury Trials?: Ray, Emerging Options in Dispute Resolution, ABA Journal, June 1989, at 66, 68.* Mr. Ray reports that Judge Lambros refers a case to summary jury trial by considering the following factors: (1) there is low chance of a liability finding, but damages are potentially high; (2) emotions

run high over the issue; and (3) the amount of damages is subject to great uncertainty. Asbestos injury claims seem to fit these criteria. What other kinds of cases would fit?

CHAPTER 16

APPENDIX: THE PERSONAL DIMENSION OF LITIGATION — OR, "CAN A LITIGATOR BE COMPETENT, ADVERSARIAL, PROFESSIONAL, SUCCESSFUL, AND ALTRUISTIC . . . AND ALSO LIVE A FULL LIFE?"

SYNOPSIS

---

§ 16.01 Why We Have Included This (Unusual) Appendix

[A] A Disclaimer

This Appendix is Subject to Disagreement, Contains Controversial Opinions, and Requires Individualized Adaptation to Your Personal Circumstances. It is inherently difficult to describe the job satisfactions and dissatisfactions of litigators. To say what clients are "like," or to identify what to watch out for in your dealings with judges, obstreperous opponents, or (for that matter) alcohol, obviously will result in some ill-fitting advice. Nevertheless, the effort may be worthwhile. Today, for example, the State of California has decided to require — not to suggest, but to *require* — every single practicing lawyer to undertake regular instruction in substance abuse avoidance, stress reduction, and office management. In fact, litigators' complaints in many respects are surprisingly uniform. The life of a litigator can be very hard if one does it the wrong way, and our modest goal in this Appendix is to help you confront the consequences of the choices you must make.

[B] The Depth of Lawyer Dissatisfaction — and, the Good News

(1) *Lawyer Dissatisfaction Is Surprisingly Prevalent: An ABA Survey Showed That Only About Half Were Satisfied With Their Career.* An ABA survey revealed that about half (55%) of the 800 lawyers surveyed were satisfied with their career; the least satisfied were in large firms, while two-thirds (68%) of lawyers in the public sector reported career satisfaction. Stephanie Francis Ward, *Pulse of the Legal Profession*, ABA Journal, Oct. 2007, at 30. Of the lawyers surveyed, less than half (44%) "would recommend a legal career to young people." *Id.* Other surveys, too, have shown surprisingly large percentages of lawyer discontent. *See, e.g.*, Grimes, *Are There Too Many Lawyers (And Are They Happy?)*, Houston Lawyer, Sept.-Oct. 1990, at 6 (43% of lawyers wouldn't enter the legal profession if they had to make the choice again); Robert A. Stein, *Help Is Available*, ABA Journal, June 2005, at 64 (one in four "lawyers suffers from stress," lawyers rank highest in depression among 105 occupations, and have disproportionately high suicide rates).

(2) *The Good News.* The same surveys also showed, however, that most lawyers were basically content with the profession they had chosen. Eighty percent of respondents in the ABA survey stated they were proud to be lawyers and eighty-one percent believe the practice of law is intellectually stimulating. Stephanie Francis Ward, *Pulse of the*

Legal Profession, ABA Journal, Oct. 2007, at 30. Again, these lawyers clearly share many of the same problems. What distinguishes the malcontents?

(3) *A Variety of Causes That, Unfortunately, Are Built Into the System.* Lawyers complain bitterly about opposing counsel, whom they see as "dumb," or "pushy," or "sneaky." (See below.) They also are disappointed in judges, possibly because the societal image of judges is inflated. Clients are unappreciative, uncooperative, and enthralled with unrealistic expectations; partners or employers are exploitative; and the adversary system produces constant stress, injustice and oppression. There is no time for the lawyer's own concerns — not for hobbies, not even for errands. *Cf.* ABA Journal, Sept. 1986, at 44; ABA Journal, Oct. 1991, at 42-43.

[C] Life, Litigation and Law School: How Much Correlation Between Your Preparation and the Real World?

(1) *Decotiis & Steele, The Skills of the Lawyering Process*, 40 Tex. B.J. 483 (1977). These two researchers observed five general practitioners of high reputation to find how they spent their time on a day-to-day basis. The results were surprising. The lawyers did very little reading, "except proofreading." They also did very little expository writing, except for short letters, although they did exercise a different kind of skill that the researchers called "document preparation" (which differed from writing because it normally involved the "cannibalizing" of clauses from existing documents, although it sometimes required a high degree of experience, knowledge and judgment). As for legal research (the only skill other than appellate opinion analysis that universally is taught to all law students), these practitioners eschewed it as a low-level endeavor. They hired others, such as law clerks, to do their research. The most highly developed skill, according to Decotiis and Steele: negotiation. The lawyers also were adept at interviewing and at explaining the legal system and legal choices to others (such as clients).

(2) *The Implications: Practice Requires a Greater Adjustment than You Might Expect, and Career Choices Are More Difficult — Cf. Biehl, Things They Didn't Teach You in Law School*, ABA Journal, Jan. 1989, at 52. Thus, law school may provide an idealized view of the profession — one in which the more prosaic and the more seamy side is underexplored. New lawyers also sometimes are surprised about the depth and persistence of their skill deficiencies (especially in litigation). Finally, because law school course content does not correspond to the daily tasks of lawyering, new lawyers lack a basis for career choices (or for daily choices that a career presents, such as whether to accept a given contingent fee case). The point, however, is not that there is something "wrong" with the material selected for teaching in law school. The ability to analyze an appellate decision, for example, is essential, because one must appreciate legal analysis before knowing how to go about "fact gathering." Rather, the point is that there are aspects of the legal profession that law school does not aspire to teach.

[D] Coping with a Changing Litigation Marketplace

(1) *Are There Really "Too Many" Litigators?* The legal market is projected to grow at about the same rate as all occupations until at least 2014, primarily due to population and business growth. U.S. Dep't of Labor, Bureau of Labor Statistics, *Occupational Outlook Handbook* (2006). Much of the growth will be in services for the middle class, as a result of "wider availability and affordability of legal clinics." *Id.* Businesses, however, are reducing their legal costs by using accounting firms and even paralegals to accomplish some of the tasks historically left to lawyers. *Id.* Increased reliance on

ADR, such as mediation and arbitration, is also decreasing the amount of traditional litigation word. *Id.* As a result of the increases prevalence of large law firms, the number of solo practitioners is expected to slowly decline and solo practitioners will be more successful in smaller communities. *Id.* As the number of law school graduates continues to rise, there has been rigorous competition for available jobs, suppressing wages and forcing some to accept jobs for which they may be overqualified and even filling legal positions through temporary staffing agencies. *Id.*

(2) *The Solutions: Flexibility about Professional Prospects and Careful Study of New Market Conditions in Litigation.* The legal market is cyclical and when discretionary demand decreases during recessionary periods, demand will increase in other areas as disputes arise in areas "such as bankruptcies, foreclosure, and divorces requiring legal action" *Id.* The practice areas that have seen declines in recent years include personal injury and medical malpractice claims, which have been affected by tort reform movements. Amir Efrati, *Hard Case: Job Market Wanes for U.S. Lawyers*, Wall St. J., September 24, 2007, at A1. Other practice areas are either currently booming or expected to be hot in the future. These include complex litigation, asbestos, antitrust, immigration, family law, nursing home litigation, and employment law. Robert W. Denney, *What's Hot and What's Not in the Legal Profession*, No. 1 ABA Law Practice 10 (Jan./Feb. 2007). Environmental law has been declining in importance, but with growing global warming concerns, this practice may also be on an uptrend in the near future. *Id.* Other trends to keep in mind are technological development, globalization, and upcoming retirement of baby boomers. *See id.* In addition to varying demand among practice groups, demand for lawyers varies depending on geographic location, so the ability to relocate can be beneficial to one's job search. *See* U.S. Dep't of Labor, Bureau of Labor Statistics, *Occupational Outlook Handbook* (2006). In summary, you will need to be flexible and maximize opportunities by studying market conditions carefully. But if you do so, and if you have the makeup of a litigator, you can develop sound prospects of finding job satisfaction in the field.

§ 16.02 Litigation In Human Terms: The "Down Side"

This Section Gives You the Bad News First, Then the Good News. The materials that follow may appear unrelentingly gloomy. For three reasons, they are not. First, if you anticipate these problems, you will have a better chance of avoiding them. Second, we plan to offer solutions when they are available (and often, even for the most serious problems, they are). Third, remember the disclaimer, above: There are two sides to this picture, and we plan to give you the "up" side, also, after we finish with the "down" side.

PROBLEM A

A CAUTIONARY TALE ABOUT A FAST-LANE DIVORCE, adapted from Houston Chronicle, Sept. 20, 1994, at 4A (New York Times report).

"When [wife] surrendered her two sons to her former husband's custody 11 days ago, it was the climactic act in a cautionary tale of two-career couples in the 1990's.

"To [wife], 43, a counsel to [the United States Senator who chairs the Senate Judiciary Committee], and [to] the feminist legal groups rallying around her, the decision by a Washington judge to award custody to the father is chilling evidence of a judicial backlash against professional women.

". . . [But] her former husband, . . . 48, the assistant executive director of the American Federation of Television and Radio Artists, [sees the matter differently]. . . .

"The battle lines were drawn after a July decision by Judge Harriet Taylor of the District of Columbia Superior Court.

"In a sharply worded opinion, . . . [Judge] Taylor painted [the wife] as a driven workaholic who seldom arrived home before dinner and [the husband] as a doting father who put his children first.

"In her opinion [Judge] Taylor quotes friends and relatives of [the husband's], as well as a baby-sitter who said [the wife] often ate dinner alone and very late at night, 'while sitting on the kitchen floor, with her plate on the floor, talking on the telephone or writing while she was eating.' Friends of [the husband] described [the wife] as working even during her children's birthday parties, of 'barking orders,' and of being 'very tightly wound.'

". . . Taylor said [the wife] was 'more devoted and absorbed by her work and her career than anything else in her life, including her health, her children, and her family.' "

(1) *First Question: Why Did This Sad Divorce Decision Occur?* Consider the following hypotheses as reasons for this result. (a) Has the wife's training made her take on counterproductive behaviors? [Before you reject this hypothesis, wait to read Problem B, below, which considers whether law school "teaches" obsessive-compulsive personality characteristics.] (b) Is the wife the victim of gender bias? (c) Did the wife's decision to combine a legal career with a family create the problem? (d) Was the wife's decision to take on a particularly all-consuming position inconsistent with being a good custodial mother (or for that matter, for a man, a good custodial father)? (e) Could the wife have handled the balance by changing some of her behaviors or circumstances? (f) Are all of the above possibly true (or partially true)? (g) Are there other possibilities that you can think of?

(2) *Second Question: Can a Lawyer Avoid This Sort of Outcome?* Consider the following possibilities as a means of avoiding a similarly unfortunate result in your own life and career. (a) Good time management (as you will see below, some people consider this the single biggest factor within a lawyer's control). (b) Stress management. (c) Business management. (d) Effective dealings with adversaries, with the adversary system, and with the people on your side. (e) Finding a position that fits your life and personality. (f) Avoiding dysfunctional dependencies (on drugs or on work). (g) Recognizing what the problems are. (h) Other possibilities that you may recognize.

[A] Institutional Causes of Lawyer Dissatisfaction (and Solutions)

[1] Time: How Lawyers Measure, Manage and Use It

(1) *Time, and Keeping "Time Records": The Negative Psychological Effects* — Hecht, *Lawyer's Life Governed by the Tick of the Clock*, Nat'l L.J., April 21, 1986, at 17, col. 1. The evidence strongly indicates that lawyers who keep time records are more effective than lawyers who do not. (Time records are the only accepted billing method for major areas of practice.) Even contingent-fee lawyers need to record time regularly because "reasonable" attorney's fees so frequently are part of the remedy, and government or corporate employers often require time keeping by their in-house lawyers as a means of efficient resource allocation. But a new lawyer who never has experienced the negative personal effects of dividing her professional life into tenths of an hour is in for a shock.

For example, one lawyer who left the practice says she felt "worn away in six-minute increments." Jefferson, above, ABA Journal, Dec. 1991, at 60. Interruptions become intolerable because they sidetrack the lawyer's record keeping; the learning curve with unfamiliar law becomes a source of frustration (and so does the series of short telephone calls that the lawyer did not immediately memorialize); and at the end of the day, the lawyer faces major gaps that are impossible to reconstruct. The temptation toward "padding" is enormous. But perhaps the worst effect surfaces when the lawyer's spouse or friend calls to discuss this evening's social engagement, or just to talk. At that point, the lawyer's values turn upside down. Glancing continuously at her watch, the lawyer struggles with the question: "How am I going to bill this time?," while attempting in frustration to end the conversation!

(2) *Time as "Stock in Trade": Not Enough Time for Avocations, People, or Even Personal Errands — see id.; see also* Blodgett, *Time and Money: A Look at Today's Lawyer*, ABA Journal, Sept. 1986, at 47. Time keeping leads to yet another problem. The focus is not how valuable is the time the lawyer has spent, or even whether it was effective; and it certainly is not whether the lawyer has enough time left for personal pursuits. In recent years, it appears that lawyer billable hours have increased. *See* Jefferson, above, ABA Journal, Dec. 1991, at 60 ("As overhead went up through the Eighties, firms kept upping the number of hours people were required to bill . . . . That's how we ended up with this 2500–hour-a-year rat race"). Many lawyers who once were avid pleasure-readers virtually stop reading non-law books, and many have little time for hobbies, avocations, or personal (non-business) friends. Not only is it difficult to find time to take an art class (for example); the lawyer cannot even find time for car repairs, exercise, or necessary personal errands. And this problem may be getting worse instead of better. *See Look at the Time*, ABA Journal, December 1989, at 88 (reporting that many firms now insist on posting all lawyers' time daily, rather than weekly); Jefferson, above, at 64 (to bill 1,900 or 2,000 hours a year, "[Y]ou're probably going to be in the office at least 10 hours a day." [What about to bill 2,500?]).

(3) *Deadlines and the Court Management Revolution: See Chapter 8, Above.* Statutes of limitation and time limits for post-trial motions have long existed, and pretrial cutoffs have existed for some time. These deadlines have always meant that a lawyer with (say) 200 active matters needs to be alert to the calendar, and many lawyers have suffered the experience of time-barring a client's rights by inadvertence. But today, the consequences of inadvertent noncompliance have increased exponentially with the court management revolution, which includes such innovations as differential case management, staging and fast-tracking. The ultimate result: The lawyer must spend much more time managing calendar systems. And worst of all, the lawyer inevitably feels a twinge in his stomach while locking the office door to leave for the night. He fears that a glitch in his time management system will cause one of his clients' rights to be "adjudicated" by deadline when the clock strikes midnight.

(4) *The Solution: Short-Term Time Management, Long-Term Time Management, and Vigorous Self-Discipline* — Hanson, *Laughing All the Way Home: A "Tickler" System That Works*, 29 Tex. B.J. 568 (1966). Numerous systems are on the market for time keeping. Initial negotiation with the client of how time billing should be submitted is essential. When the client's demands for billing detail become excessive, the lawyer should consider declining the representation or altering the fee arrangement to reflect increased *de facto* costs. As for deadline management, in Chapter 8 we considered the "double entry tickler system," and the lawyer should also set up a device called a

"perpetual calendar" because some deadlines may span as much as ten years (*e.g.*, execution on an existing judgment). [These are paper-and-pencil systems for low-tech lawyers. Recall that increased technology may not be the trend.] Finally, the lawyer must use rigorous self-discipline about time. *See also* Brill, *How Planning Your Priorities Will Improve Your Pleasure and Profitability*, 44 Tex. B.J. 1360 (1981). Careful attention to selection and refusal of representation, attention to the quality of results from different kinds of efforts, reservation of time for non-billable matters, and (perhaps most importantly) insistence upon time for exercise, family, friends and avocations, are all important.

(5) *But Time also Involves Cancellations, Washouts, Unexpected Events, and Chaos: The Paradox of Time Management.* Yet efficient time management is not enough. You must have patience, too. A deposition that you had scheduled for this morning washes out because the "Rambo" litigator on the other side instructed his client not to appear, and the two conflicting meetings that you had scheduled for two o'clock this afternoon both cancelled. You must adjust quickly if you are to avoid wasting your "stock in trade." Here is the paradox: You must be rigorous in insisting on time management, but at the same time you must be flexible. You must be able to tolerate the frustration of your time plans. Again, self-discipline is a key attribute.

[2] The Dark Side of the Adversary System

(1) *Failure and Loss — It Occurs Frequently: Can You Deal With It?* A trial is a zero-sum game. Logically, one side has to lose what the other side wins. And it is difficult to overstate how bad it feels to some lawyers to lose a jury trial. Almost always, the losing lawyer perceives the loss as an injustice; the defeat is public; it may be published in trial reports in many jurisdictions; the fact that it actually is the loss of the client, who trusted the lawyer, makes matters worse; all too often, the lawyer identifies something he "could have done" to avoid disaster; and sometimes, the opposing (winning) lawyer has seemed to be obstreperous, condescending, and (occasionally) sleazy. The good lawyer's personal commitment works against him, here: It elevates the defeat to a personal rejection. In fact, some lawyers, after losing a jury trial, actually experience the stages of grief that are associated with much more serious losses: denial ("the judge will give me a new trial"); anger ("the other side's witnesses didn't tell the truth and the judge didn't let me show that"); self-abnegation ("I could have hired a metallurgy expert — but then, maybe that wouldn't have made any difference either"); and finally, acceptance ("well, I'll take it as a learning experience").

(2) *The Vince Lombardi Approach: "Winning [Is] the Only Thing."* "Winning isn't everything; it's the only thing," said legendary Green Bay Packer Coach Vince Lombardi. (From Lombardi's standpoint, that astounding statement probably made sense: Instilling into young professional football players an instinctive rejection of anything associated with failure probably motivated them to win, but it did so at a high cost, because of the inevitability of some losses).

(3) *How Effective Will You Be After Law School in Dealing With Losses or Failures?* Imagine that your professor asks, "Now, this lawyer lost the case. What could he have done to win it?" This is a useful question to expose the impact of substantive law or litigation choices. But you should not misunderstand the professor's question as an indication that all trial losses are the fault of lawyers. You should not, for example, infer that favorable verdicts result from sheer lawyer cleverness uninfluenced by the case facts. Furthermore, you should not assume that the trial result was completely predictable,

because litigation often is unavoidably chaotic. (Thus, chances are good that any given "solution" was foreclosed by events not contained in the casebook — which, after all, reflects only a tiny fraction of the lawyering by the parties.) Above all, you should avoid assuming that the lawyer "lost" the case through misfeasance. Quite possibly, two skillful lawyers battled vigorously to a close victory for one of them, and there are many choices that "could" have made a difference — just as Lombardi's Packers could have lost to any other professional team on a given Sunday.

(4) *Dealing with Frequent Losses: Do a Good Job Anyway.* In fact, in some areas of practice, lawyers lose trials much more often than they win them. "We lose 90 percent of the time, so if you're a person who hates to lose, you're going to have a lot of dissatisfaction," says one public defender who nevertheless is happy with her job. Jefferson, above, at 64. The point is that frequent failures and losses are inherent in litigation, and law school may not prepare you for them. Living a satisfying life as a litigator requires learning to deal with them on your own. Lawyers, like other people, can and should get satisfaction from doing the job well: We guarantee effort, but not results.

(5) *The Opposite Problem — Oppression of Innocent People:* Benson, *Why I Quit Practicing Law*, Newsweek, Nov. 4, 1991, at 10. In this remarkable essay, former Colorado lawyer Sam Benson describes the instant when he realized he was going to quit. He was weary of what he saw as trickery and deception; he did not like pushy lawyers and clients; but his most significant source of discontent was the oppression that was inevitable in the adversary system. "Most of all," he writes, "I was tired of the misery my job caused other people." The problem is that most professional codes require lawyers to represent their clients "zealously" within the bounds of the law. Many if not most litigators interpret this command as requiring them to stretch both facts and law just short of ethical limits, and unfortunately, says Benson, "they may be right." The result is the litigator as a "hired gun" who thinks only about winning cases without actually breaking enforceable rules, not about avoiding oppression of innocent people or solving problems cooperatively. Benson adds: "A nice guy does not usually make a good attorney in the adversarial system." [Do you think Benson's description is too starkly pessimistic? (We do, at least in some respects — Eds.) Even if so, isn't it clear that a person who makes his living as a litigator in the real world regularly will be subject to a perceived "duty to oppress"?]

(6) *Truthtelling, Falsification, and "Zealous" Advocacy — Do the Difficulty of Line-Drawing and the Infrequency of Detection Lead to Cynical Toleration?* In one (real) case, an interrogatory asked, "Identify all photographs of the relevant event." The responding lawyer (who later became president of a major bar association) had a professionally-produced videotape of the entire event — but he answered, with technical correctness, "I know of none." Under applicable discovery rules, it is difficult to argue that this response was anything other than proper. In another case, the interrogatory asked, "Identify all depictions of the product's packaging," and the responding lawyer attempted to justify a similar "no" answer by the argument that the photographs in his possession were not technically "depictions." [One of the authors of this book, as co-counsel, insisted on a "yes" answer, which actually is the answer that the other co-counsel would have arrived at anyway.] The trouble is that the difference between these two definitional problems turns on matters of degree, about which argument is possible in both cases. And often, even looser standards of "reasonableness" or the like govern the propriety of an argument.

(7) *The Mushiness of Standards — and the Result:* Burke, *"Truth in Lawyering": An Essay on Lying and Deceit in the Practice of Law*, 38 Ark. L. Rev. 1 (1984). These circumstances breed cynicism as lawyers see adversaries define terms aggressively and succeed at it. Their own experience calls for similar kinds of self-serving interpretation — with only a blurred line, representing vague matters of degree, demarcating what is forbidden. The result? "For years we have 'winked, blinked, and nodded' at blatant if not outrageous lying and deception in pleading, negotiating, investigating, testifying and bargaining. [W]e have come to accept, in fact, to expect, a certain amount of lying and deception . . . ," according to Professor Burke, above. But perhaps the worst news is that Professor Burke sees lawyers' codes of ethics, as well as the rules of evidence and procedure, as "largely responsible" for this ethical confusion! [Are these conclusions justified? Probably, many lawyers would disagree with some of what Professor Burke says, but his essay is valuable even if only to demonstrate the moral conflict. And, consider: "[I]t is easy to tell a lie, but harder to tell only one . . . . [A]fter the first lies, [o]thers come more easily." S. Bok, *Lying: Moral Choice in Public and Private Life* 25 (1978); *see also* Tuohy & Warden, *The Fall from Grace of a Greylord Judge*, ABA Journal, Feb. 1989, at 60.]

(8) *Injustice: Its Incidence and Its Effects.* Injustice, or at least perceived injustice, is a frequent condition of litigation. The object, after all, is resolving disputes, and that is a messy business. To avoid becoming consumed by stress, the litigator must prevent himself from feeling responsible for every injustice that happens to occur. But the trouble is, he also must prevent this attitude from subtly developing into toleration of (or willing participation in) those injustices. And that is not as easy as it sounds.

(9) *The Spectre of Malpractice — and the Situations in Which You are "Damned If You Do and Damned If You Don't."* A young litigator perceives the testimony of an opposing party as willful perjury and believes that his duty is to expose it. After several months of vigorous effort, he is sanctioned under Rule 11 for an amount in the hundreds of thousands of dollars because the court found the allegation unreasonable. [This example is taken from a real case, or at least is taken from the "real" version given by the young lawyer.] Situations like this one, in which you are "damned if you do and damned if you don't," occur sometimes in litigation. (Consider, for another example, Alice Delagroi's medical malpractice claim, which is the focus of the Chapter 5 summary problem, above. *See also Costly Errors*, ABA Journal, June 1989, at 28.)

(10) *Solutions ("Am I Insured for This?")* — Cross, *The Spectre of the Malpractice Suit: Increasingly Visible*, Legal Advocate, Mar. 1979, at 3, col. 1. How can the lawyer avoid disaster in these problem situations? Experience is helpful, as is hard work; the humility of a lawyer who recognizes that she is not omniscient may be even more important, because it helps her to recognize the impending disaster. But even competent, ethical lawyers make mistakes, especially in today's climate, with occasionally disastrous losses to their clients, and with the spectre of malpractice liability more real today than ever. As for malpractice insurance, it is only a partial solution. It is sufficiently expensive so that lawyers in less lucrative practices may determine that they cannot afford it. Increasingly, too, malpractice insurers are insisting on "claims made" policies, covering only claims that are asserted against the insured during the policy period. *See Bar Plan v. Campbell*, Chapter 5, above. If the act of malpractice or the loss occurred in an earlier year and the lawyer no longer is insured, there is no coverage under such a policy. And since the annual application requires disclosure of prior conduct that might give rise to claims, the insurer may be in a position to refuse the coverage. *See also* Mary Kathleen Hartley, *Top Trends in Malpractice*, GP Solo, April/May 2003, at 22.

[3] People Problems, Part I: The People On Your Side

(1) *Clients Who Are Difficult or Uncooperative:* Hecht, Nat'l L.J., Mar. 9, 1987, at 11, col. 2. "The case may be good. The issues may be interesting and important. The pot of gold at the end of the rainbow may be attractive. But what can you do when the client doesn't help you represent him?" Hecht identifies "four categories" of uncooperative clients: (1) the "Never-in Nellie," who is never in and who "never returns your phone calls" (send the client a "please call me" letter after three attempts), (2) "the great Houdini," who is reachable on the telephone but "never appears for depositions, contract signings, court dates and the like," (3) "Mal Content," who "disagrees with everything you do and, if that isn't enough, despises you," (solution: "don't even try" to please this client), and (4) "Double-Dealing Debbie," who generates second opinions herself (or obtains them from dubious sources) and asks questions like "Why didn't you raise the defense of collateral estoppel?" The result may be that "your Rolaids bill" may exceed the fee you earn. Hecht suggests: first, transferring these clients to a colleague; second, telling the client that the case is "flawed (even if it isn't)" to make the client feel a degree of responsibility; and third, making the client "an adversary." This last solution is accomplished by a lengthy series of letters warning the client that "unless X is provided, the case may be dismissed." Hecht's conclusion: "At least estate attorneys do not have these problems since their clients [n]ever utter a complaint, since they are dead. Lucky guys." [What do you think of this advice — is it ethical? And if so, is it unduly cynical?]

(2) *"Cases and Clients That Should Be Turned Down,"* in J. Foonberg, *How to Start and Build a Law Practice*, 51-54 (1976). Foonberg's ostensibly cynical (but more often sensible) advice is that the beginning lawyer should refuse employment in certain situations, including: (1) "When you are the second or third lawyer on the case" (earlier lawyers may have had honest differences with the client but often they indicate "a. a nonmeritorious case[;] b. an uncooperative client[; or] c. a nonpaying client"); (2) " 'hurt feeling' cases" such as cases of libel, brawls, or assault and battery (which have arguably wrongful conduct, but "nominal damages at best"); (3) "landlord-tenant cases (unless you are paid in full in advance)," in which representing either party is equally undesirable ("each side wants to use the lawyer for revenge if he can use the lawyer for free"). In addition, Foonberg recommends against acceptance of bankruptcy cases unless the lawyer is prepaid in full ("It was embarrassing when my client amended his bankruptcy schedules to include the unpaid balance of the fee due me"), clients who "use your telephones, secretary and offices to do their business" (this client, he says, somehow always ends up being "trouble"), and the like. For cases totally without merit, Foonberg's solution is, "Tell your client the truth."

(3) *"Firing the Client": The Solution of Withdrawal.* Some commentators recommend liberal use of the withdrawal option for serious problem clients, unless withdrawal is impractical or unethical (*e.g.*, it would prejudice the client's case). *See* Foonberg, above, at 102; *cf.* Hecht, above, at 14. Often, conflict or nonpayment makes the client avoid the lawyer; in that situation, a "due process trail" of letters may be necessary to avoid prejudicing the client and to protect the lawyer.

(4) *"The Client's Curve of Gratitude."* Foonberg reproduces this "curve," which is similar to the Bell curve familiar to statisticians. The curve begins with the day the complaint is served on the client, who recognizes that he is in trouble: "I didn't know [those pulleys I sold and didn't check] were defective and would be used in a jet airplane which crashed." The curve reaches its topmost point on the day when the lawyer's hard work produces a favorable settlement on the courthouse steps: "No other lawyer could

have done what he did. I owe him my business, my career, everything." Mysteriously, the curve turns downward, until, ten weeks later, the client considers the lawyer "crazy if he thinks I'm going to pay" and, eventually, decides to complain to the bar association and sue the lawyer "for malpractice." Foonberg's message is simple: the lawyer should insist on payment in advance (or bill monthly and take steps to collect). For reasons that involve the client's welfare as well as his own, Foonberg implies that the sensible lawyer never lets the client get "too far ahead" of him.

(5) *Fee Disputes.* A large percentage of complaints or grievances presented by clients to disciplinary boards originate in fee disputes. A partial solution lies in the nearly universal advice that the attorney insist upon a written fee agreement in every case (which is more difficult that it might appear). Another partial solution is the practice of regular billing and collection, which tends to insure that disputes are confronted early.

(6) *Clients in Divorce, Personal Injury and Criminal Cases: A Special Problem* — Buchmeyer, *How to Avoid Grievance Complaints*, 47 Tex. B.J. 162 (1983). Consider the following client dilemma. The only sensible course is for your client to accept insurance policy limits of $20,000, even though he is horribly disfigured, because his case is weak on liability and there is no defendant who even approaches solvency. Naturally, the client objects to the proposed settlement. But assuming that trial absolutely cannot produce more money and that a zero verdict is a real possibility, your duty is to persist in your advice. Here is the point: If you must overcome strong client resistance, watch out, even though there clearly is no other alternative. In this area of practice (personal injury) — and in divorce and criminal law — clients make disciplinary complaints at a much higher rate than in other areas, even where monetary losses are larger. In these areas, lawyers deal almost invariably with unsophisticated clients who are unfamiliar with the litigation system and have unrealistic expectations. (Incidentally, Buchmeyer convincingly refutes the hypothesis that there is a lesser standard among these practitioners.) The solutions: consider declining representation; don't promise the moon; help your client to confront the weaknesses in the case; don't coerce settlement; seek another lawyer's assistance in explaining the problems to the client when necessary; and treat the client with respect. *See also* Mary Kathleen Hartley, *Top Trends in Malpractice*, GP Solo, April/May 2003, at 22.

(7) *Pick Your Mentor Carefully for Courage, Time Availability, and Willingness to Give Support: The Problems of Co-Counsel, Employers and Supervisors.* In addition to trouble with opposing counsel, lawyers often have trouble with counsel who ostensibly are on the same side. To take a situation that (we hope) is infrequent: If a superior is untrustworthy or mendacious, it can be surprisingly difficult for a beginning lawyer to avoid entanglement in ethical violations or sanctionable conduct. The beginner's inexperience makes and subordinate position makes the subordinate eager to please. Sometimes, the problem is even worse: The superior who lacks integrity also lacks courage, and may take steps to insure that his subordinate is the one in the compromised position. The solution: Pick your mentors with care. Look for the time availability that will let you obtain guidance (although this quality is not as abundant as one might hope in experienced attorneys). Look to see whether she takes the responsibility herself rather than placing it on subordinates. And, finally, look for integrity.

PROBLEM B

MILGRAM'S EXPERIMENTS WITH AUTHORITY AND OBEDIENCE. The social psychology of authority and obedience has produced some disturbing results. For example, Stanley Milgram's authority experiment is a classic. Milgram set up a phony "experimenter" in an official-looking white lab coat, who actually was a stooge, and who instructed subjects to administer electrical "shocks" to a strapped-down "learner" whenever the learner made errors. The scale for the "shocks" began at "15 Volts-'Slight' Shock" and went through 150 Volts (" 'Strong' Shock"), all the way to 450 Volts.

But in reality there were no shocks, and the learner was a stooge, who both erred intentionally and grunted or gasped in pain at the lower settings. At 120 volts, the stooge playing the part of the learner protested that the shocks were painful; at 150, the stooge (through a voice recorder) shouted "Get me out of here! . . . I refuse!" But if the subject faltered, the experimenter responded firmly that "the experiment requires that you go on." At "180 volts," the learner shouted that he "couldn't stand" the pain; at 300, responses stopped, and the experimenter told the subject to treat a non-response as a wrong answer. Most subjects who "prematurely" terminated this charade were highly agitated, and so were those who continued, protesting all the way, to 450 volts. The white-jacketed "experimenter" used a simple technique, simply telling the subject that "the experiment requires you to continue," or words to that effect.

But astonishingly, more than 60 percent of the subjects continued to the end of the scale, hearing increasingly agonized cries from the stooge. Milgram's conclusion was that "ordinary people" were sufficiently obedient to purported authority that they could be readily engaged in a "terribly destructive process."

(1) *First Question: What Significance Does This Have for Lawyers?* A new lawyer will encounter many authority figures, ranging from clients to judges to employers to partners. Does Milgram's experiment demonstrate that these authoritative people might succeed to a surprising degree in inducing the new lawyer to behave dysfunctionally?

(2) *Second Question: What Factors or Behaviors Increase or Decrease the Likelihood That an Authority Can Induce Bad Behavior in You?* Milgram's experiments also showed some of the factors that affected obedience to commands to shock. Obedience increased (a) when the authority (the white-coated "experimenter") had high status, (b) when there was no disobeying role model, (c) when the experimenter was physically close, (d) when the victim was distant, and (e) when the subject was depersonalized (*e.g.*, when the subject wore a mask). Other experiments have shown that conformity increases (f) when the subject has no clear commitment against the suggestion, (g) when the subject belongs to a culture that values conformity, (h) when a sizable group is the authority, and (i) when the correctness or wrongness of the suggested behavior is ambiguous. What do these factors suggest about how you can avoid being led into destructive behavior by the people on your side?

[4] People Problems, Part II: The Other Participants

(1) *Disappointments With Judges and Courts: Report of the Texas Judicial Qualification Commission*, 58 Tex. B.J. 1095 (1991). The public impression of judges is that they are selfless and scholarly. Courtroom etiquette reinforces the natural tendency to hold judges in esteem. Perhaps for that reason, judges often are sources of attorney disappointment. First, in today's disposition-oriented climate, docket pressures often motivate judges to become abusive, to cut off arguments, to refuse relief, and to treat disputants like feuding children even when they have honest differences requiring adjudication. (Thus, the above report notes one judge who "used profanity and became personally abusive toward a defendant when the judge lost his temper in the course of a judicial proceeding." *See also Kothe v. Smith*, above.) Second, sometimes the judge acts

energetically and with good motives, but with an unfortunate disassociation from rules and consequences: "In an effort to avoid further conflict between the parties, a judge heard evidence from each party outside the presence of the other party, thereby failing to allow cross-examination." Another judge "personally conducted a field investigation concerning a case pending in his court, which included surveillance of the defendant's home and interviewing the defendant's neighbors." *Id.* (If that last report troubles you, consider the *Business Guides* case, Chapter 5, above, in which the Supreme Court apparently condoned extensive telephone detective work by the trial court.) Third, judges sometimes abuse their positions: "A judge telephoned a member of a law firm, which had other cases pending in the judge's court, to inquire into the progress of a civil matter, on behalf of a friend who had an interest in that civil matter." *Id.* Fourth, judges sometimes have garden-variety prejudices. These kinds of disappointing conduct occur in every state and are especially troublesome when the judge cannot be removed. Often, the inexperienced lawyer is helpless to counteract judicial misbehavior. *See also, e.g.*, Gilbert, *Difficult Judges: How to Survive Them*, California Litigation, Winter 1991, at 3 (even if the judge acts in a blatantly sexist manner toward you or your client in front of the jury, "a quick lesson on the evils of sexism may hurt rather than help your client"); Smolin, *Thirteen Deadly Sins: How Lawyers Irritate Judges*, California Litigation, Winter 1991 at 11 (the "greatest" deadly sin, according to this article: "boring the judge"(!)).

(2) *Opposing Counsel Who Are Uncooperative, Unresponsive or Incompetent: Cf. Documents in Bayne v. The Proctor Corporation, Chapter 5, Above.* These Chapter 5 materials show the efforts of a competent lawyer dealing with an adversary who simply did not understand the concept of summary judgment. Unless the trial judge has the time, the experience, and the fortitude to impose sanctions, dealing with such an adversary can be maddeningly frustrating. Often, the judge chooses forbearance, rather than visitation of the sins from the opposing lawyer's ignorance on his client — although the judge perhaps should be aware that this forbearance visits them instead on the competent lawyer's client. The only solution, then, is patience.

(3) *The Difficult Problem of the "Rambo" Litigator.* Imagine the following scenario. Your client has cancelled a potentially profitable meeting to be present for his deposition, and you have taken several hours to prepare him. The Rambo litigator on the other side, of course, set it up by notice without calling you beforehand. Together with your client, you wait . . . and you wait. After almost an hour, you call Rambo's office, only to hear an unconcerned receptionist explain that Rambo is vacationing in Steamboat Springs! Surprise: You have just experienced one of Rambo's favorite tactics, which is to notice depositions and not show up. (You can file a motion for sanctions, but don't place inordinate faith in it: Rambo knows how to stop just short of conduct that will truly invoke sanctions. He will have an excuse, which perhaps will involve a telephone call in which he left a message with "someone" in your office cancelling the deposition.)

(4) *The Varieties of Rambo Tactics:* Lynn, *Handling the Obstructionist Litigator*, in University of Houston, *Advanced Civil Discovery* (D. Crump ed. 1990). Rambo's client declines to answer deposition questions about documents, because he "doesn't know what the word 'document' means." When you define it as any paper he uses in his business, he again will demur, feigning ignorance of what the word "business" means to a lawyer. This conduct is not accidental but results from Rambo's tutelage. When it comes to pushing, Rambo knows how to draft an interrogatory that will require you to assemble information from every one of your client's 10,000 installations. He knows how to set depositions on five days' notice, to force your hand in attending them, and to threaten

his own motion for sanctions if you insist on terminating at 3:00 p.m. for a previous engagement. He is abusive to your client, repeatedly calling him (or you) a "liar" during the deposition.

(5) *What Can You Do, In the Real World, About the Rambo Lawyer?:* Cardwell, *Dealing With Rambo Lawyers*, in University of Houston, *Advanced Civil Discovery* (D. Crump ed. 1991). First, slow down. Painstaking care and patience pay off. There may be no way to avoid the additional dollars that Rambo will cost your client, in that all other alternatives may cost even more. Second, avoid trying to out-Rambo Rambo. Most of us are not as good at it as he is, and your inept imitations will give Rambo his best arguments for avoiding sanctions (or for imposing sanctions on you; remember, motions for sanctions are another favorite arrow in Rambo's quiver). Third, proceed methodically but relentlessly. Fourth, advise your client of the reasons you have chosen this course and of the need for perseverance. Fifth, do not file a motion for sanctions at the first slight opportunity. You invite the judge (who, after all, does not assume that Rambo is Rambo) to treat your complaints as the initiation of a childish squabble, diminishing the credibility of later, more serious motions. Ted Allen, *Your First Deposition*, 224 N.Y.L.J. 24, Sept. 15, 2000, col. 1 (calling the judge to whine about opposing counsel being mean at a deposition will irritate the judge). Finally, document the offending behavior carefully, and seek sanctions only when the conduct is egregious, persistent, and indisputably provable to the neutral observer. Lawrence D. Rosenberg, *Aristotle's Methods for Outstanding Oral Arguments*, 33 No. 4 Litigation 33 (2007) (failing to answer or providing evasive answers may irritate the judge and influence his opinion). Set the motion far enough in the future so that you can invite compliance by Rambo in the meantime. If you must present the motion, handle it with professional restraint. Remember, as far as this motion is concerned, you're the prosecutor, the "heavy," and you must avoid overstatement. *See Abraham v. Super Buy Tires, Inc.*, No. 05CV1296-B(NLS), 2007 U.S. Dist. LEXIS 2229, at *13–14 (S.D. Cal. 2007) (court denied sanctions even where attorney's conduct violated the rules of professionalism through "gratuitous, rude, unsubstantiated, and impertinent remarks"); *Ofoedu v. St. Francis Hosp.*, 234 F.R.D. 26, 34–35 (D. Conn. 2006) (court declined to award sanctions despite abusive conduct of opposing counsel and failure of production during discovery, although the court noted that such sanctions could be properly awarded).

(6) *Avoid Confusing "Negotiating Behavior" with Malfeasance or Rambo Tactics.* Consider these scenarios: Your opponent identifies internal investigative documents but declines to produce them on a marginal claim of work product. Or: In an antitrust case, your opponent seeks documents relevant to "every meeting" participated in by your client's bidding agent over a ten-year period. Or: Your opponent communicates the insurance adjuster's settlement offer of $5,000 for your client's paraplegic injuries. Pause before you react to this conduct; in each instance, it may be the opening of a normal course of negotiation. If the work product claim is "marginal," that still means it is subject to reasonable argument, and your adversary may be able to make reciprocal concessions with you during discovery. The $5,000 offer represents the opening of a channel of communication, and you are perfectly at liberty to respond with your demand of $10 million. The distinction between negotiation and Rambo tactics is important, but it often eludes beginning lawyers. *See also, e.g., In re Snyder*, 472 U.S. 634 (1985) (even if opponent is rude or lacks professional courtesy, a single incident may not invoke sanctions).

[5] Business Management in the Law Practice

(1) *Litigation Management (and the Impact of Money Concerns).* Imagine that your client has suffered an adverse jury verdict in a case with clear error. But the difficulty of showing harm reduces the likelihood of reversal to less than 25%. The posting of a supersedeas bond (at a premium of 10% of the judgment), plus the costs of preparing the record, printing briefs, and attorney's fees for the appeal, exceed the mathematical expectancy of the gain that might result from reversal. In another case, the judge indicates that he will grant your client's request for a temporary restraining order, but he sets a bond that your client cannot afford. Many lawyers suffer severe frustration with these kinds of money-driven dispositions. But don't let it get to you: Like these examples, much of the decisionmaking in litigation is economically determined, and the only solutions are anticipation of these bottlenecks — and acceptance. (After all, if litigation were cost-free it would inundate us all.)

(2) *The Cost of Accomplishing Even Small Steps Seems Inordinately Large.* Filing and serving a complaint may seem easy, but the number of steps required in some instances to serve even a non-evasive out-of-state defendant can be formidable. And one of the authors had the experience of having a complaint rejected for filing three times for noncompliance with local rules, each time producing wasted (and expensive, non-billable) effort. The costs of taking depositions in another city for two days readily can exceed $5,000, and experts in a serious personal injury case may well exceed $50,000 (which the lawyer, as a practical matter, must advance). The solution is not to take these steps for granted and to deal with clients and opponents accordingly.

(3) *Money in the Law Practice.* One partner practices law diligently, billing thousands of hours over the year. Another partner has frequent 3-hour lunches and bills a fraction of the first partner's production — but this partner is the "rainmaker," the one who has the clients. How should these two partners divide the pie? This question, and others like it, are what bitter partnership dissolutions are made of. The truth may well be that both partners work hard, both have something valuable to offer, and each needs the other. [In declining economic times, the calculus becomes even more difficult, because there is no attractive way to allocate the losses attributable to a shrinking pie.] The best solution is to recognize the problem, to avoid egocentricism when recognizing the other partner's worth, and to negotiate without attributing motives.

(4) *Management Systems (and Lawyers' Aversion to Them): See Special Bar Journal Section [on Professional Management]: An Introduction*, 53 Tex. B.J. 204 *et seq.* (1990). The values of efficient timekeeping, standardized office procedures, personnel management, and other organizational devices are clear. They become obscured, however, by deadlines and daily production needs. Furthermore, legal education contains little that concerns office management — and, indeed, the every-case-is-unique approach of the Socratic dialogue tends to depreciate the value of management, which is concerned with efficient handling of repetitive problems. The solution to this problem is to have the self-discipline to investigate and implement office systems — by setting aside the time to do so.

[B] The Personal Costs of the Litigator's Life — and Solutions

[1] Stress

(1) *What Stress Is and What It Does:* Finney, *The Stressful Workplace*, Management Digest, in Newsweek, Nov. 4, 1991, at A-6. Stress is caused partly by external stimuli,

such as conflicting demands, unreasonable expectations, unclear directions, and frequent frustrations or "hassles." Lawyers are more susceptible to stress than most other professions, likely due to "the unique interplay of the legal profession and lawyer personality." Jennifer Pirtle, *Stressing Yourself Sick*, ABA Journal, Sept. 2006, at 34. The adversarial nature of the legal profession is likely to cause stressful situations, and lawyers are generally "thinkers" instead of "feelers," and therefore, do not tend to recognize or understand stress-related emotions when they occur. *Id.* When faced with a stressful situation, the brain releases adrenaline, which increases one's heart rate, and cortisol, which provides an energy boost. *Id.* After the stress subsides, the body relaxes and normalizes hormone levels; but since lawyers experience frequent stressors, their hormone levels often remain elevated, resulting in symptoms of chronic stress. Such symptoms include an accelerated aging process, a weakened immune system, sleep disorders, gastrointestinal disorders, hypertension, and heart disease. *Id.* Stress also affects one's mood, with short term effects "such as low self-esteem, irritability, guilt, pessimism, procrastination and general grouchiness"; whereas chronic stress can lead to "depression and anxiety." *Id.*

Additional causes of stress, ironically, are self-imposed: They include poor self-image, anger, impatience and intolerance. Finally, there are life change stressors, which the Holmes-Rahe "Social Readjustment Rating Scale" measures (in this scale, the death of a spouse is the highest stressor, at 100 points, with divorce, promotion, intercity moves, and other life events occupying lower ratings; the cumulative total over a period of time is what indicates disadvantageous stress). Dysfunctional stress interferes with relationships as well as job performance.

(2) *What Conditions are Correlated With Dysfunctional Stress?: A Multiple-Choice Test.* Which of the following is most likely to produce conditions of dysfunctional stress?

(a) Learning that a friend who lives in a distant city has died.

(b) Hearing from a lawyer who recently opposed you in a case that he has referred a client to you.

(c) Receiving an adverse jury verdict in a case in which you expended a large effort and which represents a major loss to the client.

(d) After running behind and missing meetings all day because you are trying to prepare for a hearing early tomorrow morning, having the temporary secretary tell you that the computer lost the only copy of the brief you must file tomorrow.

(e) Learning that you did not make partner this year.

[Note: The above source suggests that the correct answer is (d). Repetitive, cumulative assaults by life's smaller hassles, according to consistent research, often creates more dysfunctional stress than a single (even very serious) event. *See* Management Digest, above.]

(3) *"But Wait — Those 'Stress-Producing Conditions' Are Exactly What Litigation Itself Inevitably Produces!"* Exactly. That's the point. Litigators are particularly prone to stress because they are constantly in ambiguous, conflicted, acrimonious, irritating, unjust and often humiliating situations. It is for this reason that California now requires every practicing lawyer to take regular instruction in stress reduction (see above) — and it also is why this section is in this book.

(4) *But Some Stress is "Good," Some People Thrive on It, and Even Dysfunctional Stress Has Its Uses.* Exciting, interesting experiences often are stressful. Most people

would find a stress-free existence to be intolerably boring. (*See* below.) And even dysfunctional stress has its uses; without the stress of confronting a jury trial together with you, your client might never evaluate the settlement offer that is his best alternative. [Incidentally, the Rambo litigator is unethical and unpleasant, but he's no fool; he knows about stress, and he uses it.]

(5) *A Multiple-Choice Test About Stressor Effects.* Lawyer Brown and Lawyer Green both are handling large dockets of difficult cases. Brown seems to thrive on it, while Green is becoming depressed and frustrated. Why?

(a) Brown went to a better law school.

(b) Brown is older.

(c) Brown functions happily under stress while Green does not.

(d) Brown is more motivated by prestige and money.

(e) Brown took a trial practice course in law school.

[Undoubtedly, you have guessed that the answer is (c). Some individuals enjoy a work environment that others would find dysfunctionally stressful. If Brown were deprived of the excitement he gets at work, he might seek his stress by skydiving or gaming in Las Vegas.]

(6) *Dealing With Stress: Some Solutions.* Effective time management can help reduce stress by making the individual "feel more in control" and helping him realize when to decline a task that would leave him overextended. *See* Jennifer Pirtle, *Stressing Yourself Sick*, ABA Journal, Sept. 2006, at 34. Learning to recognize stressors and stress signals allows an individual to learn to avoid or better respond to stressful situations. *Id.* Other stress management techniques include keeping a positive outlook, taking short breaks to relax during the day, diet, and exercise. *Id.* Social relationships can also relieve stress by boosting the body's oxytocin levels. *Id.*

PROBLEM C

THE EXECUTIVE MONKEY EXPERIMENT. The famous "executive monkey" experiment paired two monkeys, both of which were subject to a series of electric shocks, but one of which, the executive monkey, controlled the timing of each shock. The difference in manifestations of stress between the two monkeys was dramatic. This was so even though there was no difference in the number or intensity of the shocks. Photographs clearly show the executive monkey, which differed only in having the ability to determine when the shocks occurred, as relatively relaxed. The other monkey, which was unable to control the shocks, remained rigidly anxious.

Question: Given that a litigator often is subject to unpleasant stimuli delivered unpredictably by judges, juries, adversaries, clients, and employers and cannot very well control his or her schedule, what does the executive monkey experiment suggest about the resultant stress on a litigator?

[2] Secondary Effects: Substance Abuse and Dysfunctional Personal Relationships

(1) *Substance Abuse: Alcohol and Beyond.* Whereas studies indicate that "10 percent of the general population" suffers from alcohol or substance abuse, it is estimated that the percentage of lawyers is nearly double that of the general population. Michael J.

Flaherty & Richard J. Jacobson, *Smart Practices: Confronting Alcoholism in the Legal Profession*, Law Practice Mgmt., Oct. 2001, at 39. Of 105 occupations surveyed, lawyers ranked at the top of the list for depression and have disproportionately high suicide rates. Robert A. Stein, *Help Is Available*, ABA Journal, June 2005, at 64. A lawyer assistance program now exists in every state to help lawyers fight not only their addiction problems but also to cope with stress and depression. *Id.*

(2) *Effects of Stress, Time Management and the Adversary System on the Lawyer's Personal Relationships: Divorce, Children and Friends.* Litigators often have days that they feel have been consumed entirely in fighting with other people. (After all, one of the main things a lawyer has to offer to a client is the ability to induce a third person or entity to do something that that person otherwise would not do.) It is difficult for human beings to "turn off" this kind of behavior immediately upon leaving the job, and therefore, lawyers tend to extend their argumentation to spouses, children, and friends. Thus, "battles in the courtroom" become "battles in the bedroom." Likewise, the difficulties that lawyers have in reserving time for personal obligations lead to neglect of spouses, children and friends. Among the results: a high divorce rate for the legal profession. The solution? Again, it is self-discipline, good time management, stress control, professional counseling when one can benefit from it — and an awareness of the problem in the first place. *See generally* Steven Keeva, *Why Lawyers Lose in Love*, ABA Journal, May 2005, at 76.

PROBLEM D

DSM-IV AND THE OBSESSIVE-COMPULSIVE PERSONALITY DISORDER: CAN LAW SCHOOL INDUCE SOME DYSFUNCTIONAL CHARACTERISTICS?

The American Psychiatric Association's Diagnostic and Statistical Manual of Mental Disorders is knowns as "DSM" for short. The fourth edition, DSM-IV, is the current Bible for diagnosticians of clinical psychological disorders. Under the heading, "Obsessive-Compulsive Disorder," DSM sets forth the following diagnostic criteria:

301.4 Obsessive-Compulsive Personality Disorder

A pervasive pattern of preoccupation with orderliness, perfectionism, and mental and interpersonal control, at the expense of flexibility, openness, and efficiency, beginning by early adulthood and present in a variety of contexts, as indicated by four (or more) of the following:

(1) is preoccupied with details, rules, lists, order, organization, or schedules to the extent that the major point of the activity is lost

(2) shows perfectionism that interferes with task completion (e.g., is unable to complete a project because his or her own overly strict standards are not met)

(3) is excessively devoted to work and productivity to the exclusion of leisure activities and friendships (not accounted for by obvious economic necessity)

(4) is overconscientious, scrupulous, and inflexible about matters of morality, ethics, or values (not accounted for by cultural or religious identification)

(5) is unable to discard worn-out or worthless objects even when they have no sentimental value

(6) is reluctant to delegate tasks or to work with others unless they submit to exactly his or her way of doing things

(7) adopts a miserly spending style toward both self and others; money is viewed as something to be hoarded for future catastrophes

(8) shows rigidity and stubbornness

Other sources suggest that, in moderation, some measure of these characteristics may be functional (perhaps in a lawyer, for example). Excessive manifestation of these behaviors, however, has a number of unpleasant results, not the least of which is that it drives to distraction anyone close to such a person.

(1) *Can Law School "Teach" You These Characteristics in a Dysfunctional Way?* No one is suggesting that everyone who emerges from law school is clinically obsessive-compulsive (or even a significant percentage) or that your professors are setting out to "teach" you how to be dysfunctional. But doesn't DSM's list display a striking coincidence with some of what law school seems to inculcate, such as "preoccup[ation] with details, rules, lists, order," etc. that often departs from the "major point" (the just outcome), or "excessive devot[ion] to work and productivity"?

(2) *How Can You Maintain "Good" Compulsiveness (Meticulous Professionalism) but Keep It in Balance?* No one is saying that a law school education is a bad thing, either. In context, concentration on rules and devotion to work are good things. Maybe the meticulous professional simply is bound to appear a little obsessive at times. But how can you ensure that your compulsivity won't get out of balance?

[3] Lack of Significance in One's Work

(1) *There are Boring Jobs In Litigation, and Boring Parts of Any Job.* Civil procedure courses often treat discovery as though beginning lawyers spent the bulk of their time drafting interrogatories or motions to produce. On the contrary, they spend a great deal more time *responding* to interrogatories or motions to produce (or sifting through the results) — which is a much less exciting task. Indeed, like any endeavor, litigation is composed in large percentage of tasks that are neither interesting nor inherently valuable in isolation.

(2) *The Deeper Problem of Lack of Significance.* Benson's explanation, cited above, of his reasons for quitting the practice of law indicates a deeper kind of dissatisfaction than intermittent boredom. Benson, *Why I Quit Practicing Law*, Newsweek, Nov. 4, 1991, at 10. Many lawyers are not only bored and stressed, but convinced that their efforts do not matter. Sometimes, this perception results from the enormous costs of discovery in proportion to the perceived gains. Because many cases take years to resolve, our system creates the impression that litigation is ineffective to resolve real disputes.

(3) *The Solutions: Information, Flexibility, Persistence.* The solution to this problem is to learn as much as possible about the job, including what lawyers who do it really do on a daily basis, *before* accepting the position. A second solution is to avoid prejudice about what you really would like to do. Sometimes, a law student who seems to have the soul of a poet thrives in a large competitive law firm, where he finds that the interests he serves ultimately benefit society, and that his own abilities are well used. Sometimes such a lawyer even finds caring mentors in that "impersonal" law firm. On the other hand, it is surprising how often a law student who seems drawn to prestige and financial rewards is happier in the district attorney's office — or in a solo practice, or in a setting that more explicitly claims to serve the public interest. Likewise, another attorney may be astounded to find that, for him, a corporate legal department offers a better combination of lifestyle and professional interest. *Cf.* Machlovitz, *Lawyers Move In-House*, ABA

Journal, May 1989, at 66 (reporting, counterintuitively, that the buildup of corporate legal departments may mean not only that that is where jobs are, but also a better quality of life for many lawyers). Thus, a full exploration of the alternatives, without prejudice, pays enormous dividends later in life. Third, it is inadvisable to forsake a chosen path at the first sign of boredom or conflict, because those conditions are unavoidable in any legal career. Finally, persistent conviction that one's work lacks significance should lead, as it did in Benson's case, to a decision to forsake litigation. After all, there are many other worthwhile things to do.

§ 16.03 Updating the Personal Dimension: Justice O'Connor's View

(1) *Justice O'Connor's View, Expressed in 1999: Reports Say That "More than Half" of Lawyers Call Themselves Dissatisfied*, Houston Chronicle, May 24, 1999, at 8A. In a speech at American University's Washington College of Law on May 23, 1999, Justice Sandra Day O'Connor reportedly cited surveys concluding that "more than half" the country's lawyers say that they are dissatisfied at work. The Justice mentioned such irritants as money, public perceptions of lawyers, and frustration at lack of social worth in lawyers' work. Her reported solution: civility, and devoting more time to pro bono work. Justice O'Connor particularly emphasized providing more legal services to the poor as a means of reducing frustration. *See also* Sandra Day O'Connor, *Professionalism*, 78 Ore. L. Rev. 385, 386, 390–91 (1999) (speech at University of Oregon Law School, citing a RAND study concluding that "only half would choose to become lawyers if they had to do it over," and repeating the call for pro bono services as part of a solution).

(2) *Skepticism About Justice O'Connor's Proposed Solution.* Some authors of this book, having been involved extensively in pro bono work, are skeptical of Justice O'Connor's proposed solution. These authors advocate pro bono work for its own sake, but the source of the skepticism is doubt that doing more pro bono will decrease dissatisfaction. Representing the poor, unfortunately, is itself frustrating, difficult, stressful, and disappointing. Therefore, while endorsing the idea of performing pro bono, these authors caution that the work should not be viewed as a ready means of decreasing frustration or stress, because it may have the opposite effect.

§ 16.04 The "Up" Side: Positive Reasons For Practicing Law

[A] "Good" Stress: Challenge and Adventure

(1) *Practicing Law Can Involve "Good" Stress — Or, Work That Is Interesting and Exciting.* In explaining the significance of his work, a personal injury lawyer asks: "Where else could I depose a safety expert from [a major automobile manufacturer], and make him answer my questions about defects in the way his company designs cars?" Short of election to Congress (and perhaps not even then), he is right. There are few other positions offering such an opportunity to make a difference, to deal with issues of significance, and, indeed, to have such interesting experiences. Even in cases that themselves seem to be devoid of social significance, issues about an obscure security interest provision in the UCC can be fantastically interesting, when coupled with the stimulus provided by the adversary system.

(2) *Interest and Excitement as the Number One Reason Given by Lawyers for Entering the Profession*, ABA Journal, Sept. 1986, at 44. People go to law school because they think it will be interesting. "Roughly three in five lawyers (58.4%) said they studied law because the subject interested them, and more than half (58.1%) did so in the expectation

that their work as lawyers would be interesting." This reason — interest and excitement — was mentioned by more lawyers in this survey than income potential (46.3%), prestige (43.1%), or the desire to improve society (23.4%). In fact, the "interesting subject matter" motivation prevailed over wanting to "see justice done" (21.6%) by more than 2 to 1. Therefore, you should seek work that interests you, whether it is bankruptcy, environmental litigation (where lawyers go to court infrequently), personal injury defense in a small-to-medium sized firm (where trial work is much more frequent) or something else.

[B] Service

(1) *A High Proportion of Civic Activities:* Blodgett, *Time and Money: A Look At Today's Lawyer*, ABA Journal, Sept. 1, 1986, at 47. Today's lawyer "would like to spend more time with his family yet willingly assumes a host of duties and civic activities." These activities included not only *pro bono* litigation, but serving upon local boards of directors of hospitals and other nonprofit organizations. It appears that these kinds of organizations value lawyers because of their organizational ability, practical approach to getting things done and dedication to service. Consider, also, the following:

> Lawyers make things work. They may do it in a variety of ways. They may do it by sabbaticals and periodic service in government. They may do it by commissions and boards and special roles. They may do it solely in their community or in their church, or in fund-raising or legislative activities, reforms or programs within the system. They certainly serve the public interest day in and day out by guaranteeing due process and protecting the rights and liberties of our citizens.

Civiletti, *Projecting Law Practice in the 1990's*, Nat'l L.J., Aug. 10, 1987, at 22.

(2) *Public Service Through Service to Clients.* Furthermore, *pro bono* efforts are not the only way in which lawyers are of service. The plaintiff's attorney who deposed the safety expert, referred to above, provided a service to his client, and in the traditional manner, thereby indirectly served the larger public by advocating safer products — as did his counterpart on the defense side, who advocated products that were functional and affordable. As Civiletti says, lawyers "make things work" as well as preserving values such as due process — and they do it by doing their jobs.

(3) *Service to a Legal System That "Works" Overall and That Is a Part of Democratic Government, Even Though It Miscarries in Some Cases.* Every society must have a system of dispute resolution that has public confidence. It is an essential part of the "glue" that allows the society to function. Our own legal system reflects such deeply held values as the individual's right to be heard before an impartial decision-maker subject to a neutral body of norms applicable to all. The lawyer, as advocate, plays an indispensable role in that system. Thus, the work of the litigator contributes to the function of our democracy and to a system that "works," at least in the overall sense — even when the particular case is only of routine importance and even though the system has imperfections.

[C] Financial Rewards (or, How Real Is "L.A. Law"?)

(1) *Personal Wealth.* According to the Occupational Outlook Handbook of the Department of Labor, Bureau of Labor Statistics, the median salary of all lawyers was $94,930 in 2004, with the middle fifty percent earning between $64,620 and $143,620. The median salary for new attorneys nine months after graduation was $55,000, including great disparity between the median salary in private practice ($80,000) and the median salary in government positions ($44,700). *Id.* In 2007, large firms increased starting

salaries for new associates to $160,000, but those positions are generally filled with the top graduates of the top law schools. Amir Efrati, *Hard Case: Job Market Wanes for U.S. Lawyers*, Wall St. J., Sept. 24, 2007, A1. A national oversupply of lawyers, in conjunction with weakened demand, is keeping wages suppressed for all but the top paying jobs, leaving many new graduates struggling to repay law school debt that can often exceed $100,000. *Id.*

(2) *Independence and Self-Development.* But these financial factors understate a distinct advantage: The lawyer has greater independence than many other workers. He can choose to establish his own practice, but this is generally "easiest in small towns and expanding suburban areas" where there is likely to be less competition from large, established firms, which dominate the legal market in big cities. Bureau of Labor Statistics, *Occupational Outlook Handbook: Lawyers* (2006). A law degree is also an attractive asset, although not a necessity, for positions in "nontraditional areas" such as "administrative, managerial, and business positions in banks, insurance firms, real estate companies, government agencies, and other organizations." *Id.* The dues that lawyers pay as they struggle with time pressures, adversaries and stress give them a freedom that is unusual.

[D] The Profession — And the Fellowship of Other Lawyers

(1) *A Profession With a History:* Trevathan, *No More Lawyer-Bashing*, Hous. Lawyer, Nov. 1991, at 11. "Our 'ancestors' include Cicero, Patrick Henry, Justice Louis D. Brandeis, and Oliver Wendell Holmes" — to which we could add Sir Thomas More and Abraham Lincoln.

(2) *The Fellowship of Other Lawyers.* As one California lawyer put it: "If I scored big in the lottery, I'd still keep practicing law." Blodgett, above, ABA Journal at 48. Lawyers make wonderful company to work with or to know socially. Even the less professional and altruistic members of the profession tend, at least, to be interesting.

[E] It's Up to You

The Point of This Appendix. The point is that the choices you make in how you select your career, the organization in which you undertake it, the way you manage it, and the ways you balance it with your personal life, all will make a difference in whether you can find the elusive path to combining competence, adversary practice, ethics, altruism and success with a full life as a lawyer. And you can enhance the quality of your choices by careful examination and self-discipline. You will have to live with the consequences, but you can make them turn out positively. It's up to you.

TABLE OF CASES

[References are to pages and footnotes.]

A

[References are to pages and footnotes.]

B

[References are to pages and footnotes.]

[References are to pages and footnotes.]

[References are to pages and footnotes.]

C

[References are to pages and footnotes.]

[References are to pages and footnotes.]

D

[References are to pages and footnotes.]

E

F

[References are to pages and footnotes.]

[References are to pages and footnotes.]

[References are to pages and footnotes.]

H

[References are to pages and footnotes.]

[References are to pages and footnotes.]

I

J

[References are to pages and footnotes.]

[References are to pages and footnotes.]

M

[References are to pages and footnotes.]

[References are to pages and footnotes.]

[References are to pages and footnotes.]

N

O

[References are to pages and footnotes.]

P

[References are to pages and footnotes.]

Q

[References are to pages and footnotes.]

R

[References are to pages and footnotes.]

S

[References are to pages and footnotes.]

[References are to pages and footnotes.]

T

[References are to pages and footnotes.]

U

[References are to pages and footnotes.]

V

W

[References are to pages and footnotes.]

[References are to pages and footnotes.]

X

Y

Z

INDEX

[References are to pages.]

A

[References are to pages.]

[References are to pages.]

[References are to pages.]

[References are to pages.]

[References are to pages.]

[References are to pages.]

V

ISBN: 978-1-4224-2564-0
90000
9 781422 425640